THE COLLINS
POCKET REFERENCE
FRENCH
DICTIONARY

FRENCH·ENGLISH   ENGLISH·FRENCH

HarperCollins*Publishers*

First published 1989

© William Collins Sons & Co. Ltd. 1989

Latest reprint 1991

ISBN 0 00 433255 5

Printed in Great Britain by
HarperCollins Manufacturing, Glasgow

INTRODUCTION

This dictionary of French and English is designed to provide the user with wide-ranging and up-to-date coverage of the two languages, and is ideal for both school and reference use.

A special feature of Collins dictionaries is the comprehensive 'sign-posting' of meanings on both sides of the dictionary, guiding the user to the most appropriate translation for a given context. We hope you will find this dictionary easy and pleasant to consult for all your study and reference needs.

ABRÉVIATIONS

		ABBREVIATIONS
adjectif, locution adjective	a	adjective, adjectival phrase
abréviation	ab(b)r	abbreviation
adverbe, locution adverbiale	ad	adverb, adverbial phrase
administration	ADMIN	administration
agriculture	AGR	agriculture
anatomie	ANAT	anatomy
architecture	ARCHIT	architecture
l'automobile	AUT(O)	the motor car and motoring
aviation, voyages aériens	AVIAT	flying, air travel
biologie	BIO(L)	biology
botanique	BOT	botany
anglais de Grande-Bretagne	Brit	British English
conjonction	cj	conjunction
langue familière (! emploi vulgaire)	col (!)	colloquial usage (! particularly offensive)
commerce, finance, banque	COMM	commerce, finance, banking
informatique	COMPUT	computing
construction	CONSTR	building
nom utilisé comme adjectif, ne peut s'employer ni comme attribut, ni après le nom qualifié	cpd	compound element: noun used as an adjective and which cannot follow the noun it qualifies
cuisine, art culinaire	CULIN	cookery
déterminant: article, adjectif démonstratif ou indéfini etc	dét	determiner: article, demonstrative etc.
économie	ECON	economics
électricité, électronique	ELEC	electricity, electronics
exclamation, interjection	excl	exclamation, interjection
féminin	f	feminine
langue familière (! emploi vulgaire)	fam (!)	colloquial usage (! particularly offensive)
emploi figuré	fig	figurative use
(verbe anglais) dont la particule est inséparable du verbe	fus	(phrasal verb) where the particle cannot be separated from main verb
dans la plupart des sens; généralement	gén, gen	in most or all senses; generally
géographie, géologie	GEO	geography, geology
géométrie	GEOM	geometry
informatique	INFORM	computing
invariable	inv	invariable
irrégulier	irg	irregular
domaine juridique	JUR	law
grammaire, linguistique	LING	grammar, linguistics
masculin	m	masculine
mathématiques, algèbre	MATH	mathematics, calculus
médecine	MED	medical term, medicine
masculin ou féminin, suivant le sexe	m/f	either masculine or feminine depending on sex
domaine militaire, armée	MIL	military matters
musique	MUS	music
nom	n	noun

iv

ABRÉVIATIONS

ABBREVIATIONS

navigation, nautisme	**NAVIG, NAUT**	sailing, navigation
adjectif ou nom numérique	**num**	numeral adjective or noun
	o.s.	oneself
péjoratif	**péj, pej**	derogatory, pejorative
photographie	**PHOT(O)**	photography
physiologie	**PHYSIOL**	physiology
pluriel	**pl**	plural
politique	**POL**	politics
participe passé	**pp**	past participle
préposition	**prép, prep**	preposition
psychologie, psychiatrie	**PSYCH**	psychology, psychiatry
temps du passé	**pt**	past tense
nom non comptable: ne peut s'utiliser au pluriel	**q**	collective (uncountable) noun: is not used in the plural
quelque chose	**qch**	
quelqu'un	**qn**	
religions, domaine ecclésiastique	**REL**	religions, church service
	sb	somebody
enseignement, système scolaire et universitaire	**SCOL**	schooling, schools and universities
singulier	**sg**	singular
	sth	something
subjonctif	**sub**	subjunctive
sujet (grammatical)	**su(b)j**	(grammatical) subject
techniques, technologie	**TECH**	technical term, technology
télécommunications	**TEL**	telecommunications
télévision	**TV**	television
typographie	**TYP(O)**	typography, printing
anglais des USA	**US**	American English
verbe	**vb**	verb
verbe ou groupe verbal à fonction intransitive	**vi**	verb or phrasal verb used intransitively
verbe ou groupe verbal à fonction transitive	**vt**	verb or phrasal verb used transitively
zoologie	**ZOOL**	zoology
marque déposée	**®**	registered trademark
indique une équivalence culturelle	**≈**	introduces a cultural equivalent

TRANSCRIPTION PHONÉTIQUE

CONSONNES

CONSONANTS

NB. p, b, t, d, k, g sont suivis d'une aspiration en anglais.

NB. p, b, t, d, k, g are not aspirated in French.

poupée	p	puppy
bombe	b	baby
tente thermal	t	tent
dinde	d	daddy
coq qui képi	k	cork kiss chord
gag bague	g	gag guess
sale ce nation	s	so rice kiss
zéro rose	z	cousin buzz
tache chat	ʃ	sheep sugar
gilet juge	ʒ	pleasure beige
	tʃ	church
	dʒ	judge general
fer phare	f	farm raffle
valve	v	very rev
	θ	thin maths
	ð	that other
lent salle	l	little ball
rare rentrer	ʀ	
	r	rat rare
maman femme	m	mummy comb
non nonne	n	no ran
agneau vigne	ɲ	
	ŋ	singing bank
hop!	h	hat reheat
yeux paille pied	j	yet
nouer oui	w	wall bewail
huile lui	ɥ	
	x	loch

DIVERS

MISCELLANEOUS

pour l'anglais: précède la syllabe accentuée

'

in French wordlist and transcription: no liaison

pour l'anglais: le r final se prononce en liaison devant une voyelle

★

PHONETIC TRANSCRIPTION

VOYELLES

NB. La mise en équivalence de certains sons n'indique qu'une ressemblance approximative.

VOWELS

NB. The pairing of some vowel sounds only indicates approximate equivalence.

ici vie lyre	i i:	heel bead
	ɪ	hit pity
jouer été	e	
lait jouet merci	ɛ	set tent
plat amour	a æ	bat apple
bas pâte	ɑ ɑ:	after car calm
	ʌ	fun cousin
le premier	ə	over above
beurre peur	œ	
peu deux	ø ə:	urn fern work
or homme	ɔ	wash pot
mot eau gauche	o ɔ:	born cork
genou roue	u	full soot
	u:	boon lewd
rue urne	y	

DIPHTONGUES

DIPHTHONGS

	ɪə	beer tier
	ɛə	tear fair there
	eɪ	date plaice day
	aɪ	life buy cry
	au	owl foul now
	əu	low no
	ɔɪ	boil boy oily
	uə	poor tour

NASALES

NASAL VOWELS

matin plein	ɛ̃
brun	œ̃
sang an dans	ɑ̃
non pont	ɔ̃

FRANÇAIS - ANGLAIS
FRENCH - ENGLISH

A

A *abr de* **autoroute**.

a *vb voir* **avoir**.

à (*à + le* = **au**, *à + les* = **aux**) [a, o] *prép* **1** (*endroit, situation*) at, in; **être à Paris/au Portugal** to be in Paris/Portugal; **être à la maison/à l'école** to be at home/at school; **à la campagne** in the country; **c'est à 10 km/à 20 minutes (d'ici)** it's 10 km/20 minutes away

2 (*direction*) to; **aller à Paris/au Portugal** to go to Paris/Portugal; **aller à la maison/à l'école** to go home/to school; **à la campagne** to the country

3 (*temps*): **à 3 heures/minuit** at 3 o'clock/midnight; **au printemps/mois de juin** in the spring/the month of June

4 (*attribution, appartenance*) to; **le livre est à Paul/à lui/à nous** this book is Paul's/his/ours; **donner qch à qn** to give sth to sb

5 (*moyen*) with; **se chauffer au gaz** to have gas heating; **à bicyclette** on a *ou* by bicycle; **à la main/machine** by hand/machine

6 (*provenance*) from; **boire à la bouteille** to drink from the bottle

7 (*caractérisation, manière*): **l'homme aux yeux bleus** the man with the blue eyes; **à la russe** the Russian way

8 (*but, destination*): **tasse à café** coffee cup; **maison à vendre** house for sale

9 (*rapport, évaluation, distribution*): **100 km/unités à l'heure** 100 km/units per *ou* an hour; **payé à l'heure** paid by the hour; **cinq à six** five to six.

abaisser [abese] *vt* to lower, bring down; (*manette*) to pull down; (*fig*) to debase; to humiliate; **s'~** *vi* to go down; (*fig*) to demean o.s.

abandon [abɑ̃dɔ̃] *nm* abandoning; giving up; withdrawal; **être à l'~** to be in a state of neglect.

abandonner [abɑ̃dɔne] *vt* (*personne*) to abandon; (*projet, activité*) to abandon, give up; (*SPORT*) to retire *ou* withdraw from; (*céder*) to surrender; **s'~** *vi* to let o.s. go; **s'~ à** (*paresse, plaisirs*) to give o.s. up to.

abasourdir [abazurdir] *vt* to stun, stagger.

abat-jour [abaʒur] *nm inv* lampshade.

abats [aba] *nmpl* (*de bœuf, porc*) offal *sg*; (*de volaille*) giblets.

abattement [abatmɑ̃] *nm* (*déduction*) reduction; **~ fiscal** ≈ tax allowance.

abattis [abati] *nmpl* giblets.

abattoir [abatwaʀ] *nm* slaughterhouse.

abattre [abatʀ(ə)] *vt* (*arbre*) to cut down, fell; (*mur, maison*) to pull down; (*avion, personne*) to shoot down; (*animal*) to shoot, kill; (*fig*) to wear out, tire out; to demoralize; **s'~** *vi* to crash down; **s'~ sur** to beat down on; to rain down on.

abbaye [abei] *nf* abbey.

abbé [abe] *nm* priest; (*d'une abbaye*) abbot.

abcès [apsɛ] *nm* abscess.

abdiquer [abdike] *vi* to abdicate // *vt* to renounce, give up.

abeille [abɛj] *nf* bee.

aberrant, e [abɛrɑ̃, -ɑ̃t] *a* absurd.

abêtir [abetir] *vt* to make morons of (*ou* a moron of).

abîme [abim] *nm* abyss, gulf.

abîmer [abime] *vt* to spoil, damage; **s'~** *vi* to get spoilt *ou* damaged.

ablation [ablɑsjɔ̃] *nf* removal.

aboiement [abwamɑ̃] *nm* bark, barking *q*.

abois [abwa] *nmpl*: **aux ~** at bay.

abolir [abɔlir] *vt* to abolish.

abondance [abɔ̃dɑ̃s] *nf* abundance; (*richesse*) affluence.

abondant, e [abɔ̃dɑ̃, -ɑ̃t] *a* plentiful, abundant, copious.

abonder [abɔ̃de] *vi* to abound, be plentiful; **~ dans le sens de qn** to concur with sb.

abonné, e [abɔne] *nm/f* subscriber; season ticket holder.

abonnement [abɔnmɑ̃] *nm* subscription; (*transports, concerts*) season ticket.

abonner [abɔne] *vt*: **s'~ à** to subscribe to, take out a subscription to.

abord [abɔr] *nm*: **être d'un ~ facile** to be approachable; **~s** *nmpl* surroundings; **au premier ~** at first sight, initially; **d'~** *ad* first.

abordable [abɔrdabl(ə)] *a* approachable; reasonably priced.

aborder [abɔrde] *vi* to land // *vt* (*sujet, difficulté*) to tackle; (*personne*) to approach; (*rivage etc*) to reach; (*NAVIG: attaquer*) to board.

aboutir [abutir] *vi* (*négociations etc*) to succeed; **~ à/dans/sur** to end up at/in/on.

aboyer [abwaje] *vi* to bark.

abrégé [abreʒe] *nm* summary.

abréger [abreʒe] *vt* to shorten.

abreuver [abrœve] *vt* (*fig*): **~ qn de** to

shower *ou* swamp sb with; **s'~** *vi* to drink; **abreuvoir** *nm* watering place.

abréviation [abʀevjɑsjɔ̃] *nf* abbreviation.

abri [abʀi] *nm* shelter; **à l'~** under cover; **à l'~** de sheltered from; *(fig)* safe from.

abricot [abʀiko] *nm* apricot; **abricotier** *nm* apricot tree.

abriter [abʀite] *vt* to shelter; *(loger)* to accommodate; **s'~** to shelter, take cover.

abroger [abʀɔʒe] *vt* to repeal.

abrupt, e [abʀypt] *a* sheer, steep; *(ton)* abrupt.

abrutir [abʀytiʀ] *vt* to daze; to exhaust; to stupefy.

absence [apsɑ̃s] *nf* absence; *(MÉD)* blackout; mental blank.

absent, e [apsɑ̃, -ɑ̃t] *a* absent; *(distrait: air)* vacant, faraway // *nm/f* absentee; **s'absenter** *vi* to take time off work; *(sortir)* to leave, go out.

absolu, e [apsɔly] *a* absolute; *(caractère)* rigid, uncompromising; **~ment** *ad* absolutely.

absolve *etc vb voir* **absoudre**.

absorber [apsɔʀbe] *vt* to absorb; *(gén MÉD: manger, boire)* to take.

absoudre [apsudʀ(ə)] *vt* to absolve.

abstenir [apstəniʀ]: **s'~** *vi (POL)* to abstain; **s'~** de qch/de faire to refrain from sth/from doing.

abstraction [apstʀaksjɔ̃] *nf* abstraction; faire ~ de to set *ou* leave aside.

abstrait, e [apstʀɛ, -ɛt] *a* abstract.

absurde [apsyʀd(ə)] *a* absurd.

abus [aby] *nm* abuse; ~ de confiance breach of trust.

abuser [abyze] *vi* to go too far, overstep the mark // *vt* to deceive, mislead; ~ de *vt* to misuse; *(violer, duper)* to take advantage of; **s'~** *vi* to be mistaken; **abusif, ive** *a* exorbitant; excessive; improper.

acabit [akabi] *nm*: de cet ~ of that type.

académie [akademi] *nf* academy; *(ART: nu)* nude; *(SCOL: circonscription)* ≈ regional education authority.

acajou [akaʒu] *nm* mahogany.

acariâtre [akaʀjɑtʀ(ə)] *a* cantankerous.

accablement [akabləmɑ̃] *nm* despondency.

accabler [akable] *vt* to overwhelm, overcome; *(suj: témoignage)* to condemn, damn; ~ qn d'injures to heap *ou* shower abuse on sb.

accalmie [akalmi] *nf* lull.

accaparer [akapaʀe] *vt* to monopolize; *(suj: travail etc)* to take up (all) the time *ou* attention of.

accéder [aksede]: ~ à *vt (lieu)* to reach; *(fig)* to accede to, attain; *(accorder: requête)* to grant, accede to.

accélérateur [akseleʀatœʀ] *nm* accelerator.

accélération [akseleʀɑsjɔ̃] *nf* acceleration.

accélérer [akseleʀe] *vt* to speed up // *vi* to accelerate.

accent [aksɑ̃] *nm* accent; *(inflexions expressives)* tone (of voice); *(PHONÉTIQUE, fig)* stress; mettre l'~ sur *(fig)* to stress; ~ aigu/grave acute/grave accent.

accentuer [aksɑ̃tɥe] *vt (LING)* to accent; *(fig)* to accentuate, emphasize; **s'~** *vi* to become more marked *ou* pronounced.

acceptation [akseptɑsjɔ̃] *nf* acceptance.

accepter [aksepte] *vt* to accept; *(tolérer)*: ~ que qn fasse to agree to sb doing; ~ de faire to agree to do.

acception [aksepsjɔ̃] *nf* meaning, sense.

accès [aksɛ] *nm (à un lieu)* access; *(MÉD)* attack; fit, bout; outbreak // *nmpl (routes etc)* means of access, approaches; d'~ facile easily accessible; ~ de colère fit of anger.

accessible [aksesibl(ə)] *a* accessible; *(livre, sujet)*: ~ à qn within the reach of sb; *(sensible)*: ~ à open to.

accessoire [akseswaʀ] *a* secondary; incidental // *nm* accessory; *(THÉÂTRE)* prop.

accident [aksidɑ̃] *nm* accident; par ~ by chance; ~ de la route road accident; ~ du travail industrial injury *ou* accident; **accidenté, e** *a* damaged; injured; *(relief, terrain)* uneven; hilly.

acclamer [aklame] *vt* to cheer, acclaim.

accointances [akwɛ̃tɑ̃s] *nfpl*: avoir des ~ avec to have contacts with.

accolade [akɔlad] *nf (amicale)* embrace; *(signe)* brace.

accoler [akɔle] *vt* to place side by side.

accommodant, e [akɔmɔdɑ̃, -ɑ̃t] *a* accommodating; easy-going.

accommoder [akɔmɔde] *vt (CULIN)* to prepare; *(points de vue)* to reconcile; **s'~** de to put up with; to make do with.

accompagnateur, trice [akɔ̃paɲatœʀ, -tʀis] *nm/f (MUS)* accompanist; *(de voyage: guide)* guide; *(: d'enfants)* accompanying adult; *(de voyage organisé)* courier.

accompagner [akɔ̃paɲe] *vt* to accompany, be *ou* go *ou* come with; *(MUS)* to accompany.

accompli, e [akɔ̃pli] *a* accomplished.

accomplir [akɔ̃pliʀ] *vt (tâche, projet)* to carry out; *(souhait)* to fulfil; **s'~** *vi* to be fulfilled.

accord [akɔʀ] *nm* agreement; *(entre des styles, tons etc)* harmony; *(MUS)* chord; d'~! OK!; se mettre d'~ to come to an agreement; être d'~ to agree.

accordéon [akɔʀdeɔ̃] *nm (MUS)* accordion.

accorder [akɔʀde] *vt (faveur, délai)* to grant; *(harmoniser)* to match; *(MUS)* to tune; s'~ to get on together; to agree.

accoster [akɔste] (NAVIG) vt to draw alongside // vi to berth.

accotement [akɔtmɑ̃] nm verge (Brit), shoulder.

accouchement [akuʃmɑ̃] nm delivery, (child)birth; labour.

accoucher [akuʃe] vi to give birth, have a baby; (être en travail) to be in labour // vt to deliver; ~ d'un garçon to give birth to a boy.

accouder [akude]: s'~ vi: s'~ à/contre to rest one's elbows on/against; **accoudoir** nm armrest.

accoupler [akuple] vt to couple; (pour la reproduction) to mate; s'~ to mate.

accourir [akuRiR] vi to rush ou run up.

accoutrement [akutrəmɑ̃] nm (péj: tenue) outfit.

accoutumance [akutymɑ̃s] nf (gén) adaptation; (MÉD) addiction.

accoutumé, e [akutyme] a (habituel) customary, usual.

accoutumer [akutyme] vt: s'~ à to get accustomed ou used to.

accréditer [akredite] vt (nouvelle) to substantiate.

accroc [akro] nm (déchirure) tear; (fig) hitch, snag.

accrochage [akrɔʃaʒ] nm (AUTO) collision.

accrocher [akrɔʃe] vt (suspendre): ~ qch à to hang sth (up) on; (attacher: remorque): ~ qch à to hitch sth (up) to; (heurter) to catch; to catch on; to hit; (déchirer): ~ qch (à) to catch sth (on); (MIL) to engage; (fig) to catch, attract; s'~ (se disputer) to have a clash ou brush; s'~ à (rester pris à) to catch on; (agripper, fig) to hang on ou cling to.

accroître [akrwatr(ə)] vt to increase; s'~ vi to increase.

accroupir [akrupiR]: s'~ vi to squat, crouch (down).

accru, e [akry] pp de accroître.

accueil [akœj] nm welcome; comité d'~ reception committee.

accueillir [akœjiR] vt to welcome; (loger) to accommodate.

acculer [akyle] vt: ~ qn à ou contre to drive sb back against.

accumuler [akymyle] vt to accumulate, amass; s'~ vi to accumulate; to pile up.

accusation [akyzasjɔ̃] nf (gén) accusation; (JUR) charge; (partie): l'~ the prosecution; mettre en ~ to indict.

accusé, e [akyze] nm/f accused; defendant; ~ de réception acknowledgement of receipt.

accuser [akyze] vt to accuse; (fig) to emphasize, bring out; to show; ~ qn de to accuse sb of; (JUR) to charge sb with; ~ qch de (rendre responsable) to blame sth for; ~ réception de to acknowledge receipt of.

acerbe [asɛrb(ə)] a caustic, acid.

acéré, e [asere] a sharp.

achalandé, e [aʃalɑ̃de] a: bien ~ well-stocked; well-patronized.

acharné, e [aʃarne] a (lutte, adversaire) fierce, bitter; (travail) relentless, unremitting.

acharner [aʃarne]: s'~ vi: s'~ sur to go at fiercely; s'~ contre to set o.s. against; to dog; s'~ à faire to try doggedly to do; to persist in doing.

achat [aʃa] nm buying q; purchase; faire des ~s to do some shopping.

acheminer [aʃmine] vt (courrier) to forward, dispatch; (troupes) to convey, transport; (train) to route; s'~ vers to head for.

acheter [aʃte] vt to buy, purchase; (soudoyer) to buy; ~ qch à (marchand) to buy ou purchase sth from; (ami etc: offrir) to buy sth for; **acheteur, euse** nm/f buyer; shopper; (COMM) buyer.

achever [aʃve] vt to complete, finish; (blessé) to finish off; s'~ vi to end.

achoppement [aʃɔpmɑ̃] nm: pierre d'~ stumbling block.

acide [asid] a sour, sharp; (CHIMIE) acid(ic) // nm (CHIMIE) acid.

acier [asje] nm steel; **aciérie** nf steelworks sg.

acné [akne] nf acne.

acolyte [akɔlit] nm (péj) associate.

acompte [akɔ̃t] nm deposit; (versement régulier) instalment; (sur somme due) payment on account.

à-côté [akote] nm side-issue; (argent) extra.

à-coup [aku] nm (du moteur) (hic)cough; (fig) jolt; par ~s by fits and starts.

acoustique [akustik] nf (d'une salle) acoustics pl.

acquéreur [akerœr] nm buyer, purchaser.

acquérir [akeriR] vt to acquire.

acquis, e [aki, -iz] pp de acquérir // nm (accumulated) experience; être ~ à (plan, idée) to fully agree with; son aide nous est ~e we can count on her help.

acquit [aki] vb voir acquérir // nm (quittance) receipt; par ~ de conscience to set one's mind at rest.

acquitter [akite] vt (JUR) to acquit; (facture) to pay, settle; s'~ de to discharge, fulfil.

âcre [akr(ə)] a acrid, pungent.

acrobate [akrɔbat] nm/f acrobat.

acte [akt(ə)] nm act, action; (THÉÂTRE) act; ~s nmpl (compte-rendu) proceedings; prendre ~ de to note, take note of; faire ~ de candidature to apply; faire ~ de présence to put in an appearance; ~ de naissance birth certificate.

acteur [aktœr] nm actor.

actif, ive [aktif, -iv] a active // nm

(*COMM*) assets *pl*; (*fig*): **avoir à son ~** to have to one's credit; **population active** working population.

action [aksjɔ̃] *nf* (*gén*) action; (*COMM*) share; **une bonne ~** a good deed; **actionnaire** *nm/f* shareholder; **actionner** *vt* to work; to activate; to operate.

activer [aktive] *vt* to speed up; **s'~** *vi* to bustle about; to hurry up.

activité [aktivite] *nf* activity.

actrice [aktRis] *nf* actress.

actualiser [aktɥalize] *vt* to actualize; to bring up to date.

actualité [aktɥalite] *nf* (*d'un problème*) topicality; (*événements*): **l'~** current events; **les ~s** (*CINÉMA, TV*) the news.

actuel, le [aktɥɛl] *a* (*présent*) present; (*d'actualité*) topical; **~lement** *ad* at present; at the present time.

acuité [akɥite] *nf* acuteness.

adaptateur [adaptatœR] *nm* (*ÉLEC*) adapter.

adapter [adapte] *vt* to adapt; **~ qch à** (*approprier*) to adapt sth to (fit); **~ qch sur/dans/à** (*fixer*) to fit sth on/into/to; **s'~** (**à**) (*suj: personne*) to adapt (to).

addition [adisjɔ̃] *nf* addition; (*au café*) bill.

additionner [adisjɔne] *vt* to add (up).

adepte [adɛpt(ə)] *nm/f* follower.

adéquat, e [adekwa, -at] *a* appropriate, suitable.

adhérent, e [adeRã, -ãt] *nm/f* (*de club*) member.

adhérer [adeRe] **~ à** *vi* (*coller*) to adhere *ou* stick to; (*se rallier à*) to join; to support; (*s'associer à*) **adhésif, ive** *a* adhesive, sticky // *nm* adhesive; **adhésion** *nf* joining; membership; support.

adieu, x [adjø] *excl* goodbye // *nm* farewell; **dire ~ à qn** to say goodbye *ou* farewell to sb.

adjectif [adʒɛktif] *nm* adjective.

adjoindre [adʒwɛ̃dR(ə)] *vt*: **~ qch à** to attach sth to; to add sth to; **s'~** (*collaborateur etc*) to take on, appoint; **adjoint, e** *nm/f* assistant; **adjoint au maire** deputy mayor; **directeur adjoint** assistant manager.

adjudant [adʒydã] *nm* (*MIL*) warrant officer.

adjudication [adʒydikɑsjɔ̃] *nf* sale by auction; (*pour travaux*) invitation to tender (*Brit*) ou bid (*US*).

adjuger [adʒyʒe] *vt* (*prix, récompense*) to award; (*lors d'une vente*) to auction (off); **s'~** *vt* to take for o.s.

adjurer [adʒyRe] *vt*: **~ qn de faire** to implore *ou* beg sb to do.

admettre [admɛtR(ə)] *vt* (*laisser entrer*) to admit; (*candidat: SCOL*) to pass; (*tolérer*) to allow, accept; (*reconnaître*) to admit, acknowledge.

administrateur, trice [administratœR, -tRis] *nm/f* (*COMM*) director; (*ADMIN*) administrator; **~ judiciaire** receiver; **~ délégué** managing director.

administration [administRasjɔ̃] *nf* administration; **l'A~** ≈ the Civil Service.

administrer [administRe] *vt* (*firme*) to manage, run; (*biens, remède, sacrement etc*) to administer.

admirable [admiRabl(ə)] *a* admirable, wonderful.

admirateur, trice [admiRatœR, -tRis] *nm/f* admirer.

admiration [admiRɑsjɔ̃] *nf* admiration.

admirer [admiRe] *vt* to admire.

admis, e *pp de* **admettre**.

admissible [admisibl(ə)] *a* (*candidat*) eligible; (*comportement*) admissible, acceptable.

admission [admisjɔ̃] *nf* admission; acknowledgement; **demande d'~** application for membership.

adolescence [adɔlesɑ̃s] *nf* adolescence.

adolescent, e [adɔlesɑ̃, -ɑ̃t] *nm/f* adolescent, teenager.

adonner [adɔne]: **s'~ à** *vt* (*sport*) to devote o.s. to; (*boisson*) to give o.s. over to.

adopter [adɔpte] *vt* to adopt; (*projet de loi etc*) to pass; **adoptif, ive** *a* (*parents*) adoptive; (*fils, patrie*) adopted.

adorer [adɔRe] *vt* to adore; (*REL*) to worship.

adosser [adose] *vt*: **~ qch à ou contre** to stand sth against; **s'~ à ou contre** to lean with one's back against.

adoucir [adusiR] *vt* (*goût, température*) to make milder; (*avec du sucre*) to sweeten; (*peau, voix*) to soften; (*caractère*) to mellow.

adresse [adRɛs] *nf* (*voir adroit*) skill, dexterity; (*domicile*) address; **à l'~ de** (*pour*) for the benefit of.

adresser [adRese] *vt* (*lettre: expédier*) to send; (: *écrire l'adresse sur*) to address; (*injure, compliments*) to address; **~ la parole à** to speak to, address; **s'~ à** (*parler à*) to speak to, address; (*s'informer auprès de*) to go and see; (: *bureau*) to enquire at; (*suj: livre, conseil*) to be aimed at.

adroit, e [adRwa, -wat] *a* skilful, skilled.

adulte [adylt(ə)] *nm/f* adult, grown-up // *a* (*chien, arbre*) fully-grown, mature; (*attitude*) adult, grown-up.

adultère [adyltɛR] *nm* (*acte*) adultery.

advenir [advəniR] *vi* to happen.

adverbe [advɛRb(ə)] *nm* adverb.

adversaire [advɛRsɛR] *nm/f* (*SPORT, gén*) opponent, adversary; (*MIL*) adversary, enemy.

adverse [advɛRs(ə)] *a* opposing.

aération [aeRɑsjɔ̃] *nf* airing; ventilation.

aérer [aeRe] *vt* to air; (*fig*) to lighten; **s'~** *vi* to get some (fresh) air.

aérien, ne [aeRjɛ̃, -jɛn] *a* (*AVIAT*) air

cpd, aerial; (*câble, métro*) overhead; (*fig*) light.

aéro... [aeʀɔ] *préfixe*: ~**bic** *nm* aerobics *sg*; ~**gare** *nf* airport (buildings); (*en ville*) air terminal; ~**glisseur** *nm* hovercraft; ~**naval, e** *a* air and sea *cpd*; ~**port** *nm* airport; ~**porté, e** *a* airborne, airlifted; ~**sol** *nm* aerosol.

affaiblir [afeblir] *vt*, **s'**~ *vi* to weaken.

affaire [afɛʀ] *nf* (*problème, question*) matter; (*criminelle, judiciaire*) case; (*scandaleuse -etc*) affair; (*entreprise*) business; (*marché, transaction*) deal; business *q*; (*occasion intéressante*) bargain; ~**s** *nfpl* affairs; (*activité commerciale*) business *sg*; (*effets personnels*) things, belongings; **ce sont mes** ~**s** (*cela me concerne*) that's my business; **ceci fera l'**~ this will do (nicely); **avoir** ~ **à** to be faced with; to be dealing with; **les A~s étrangères** Foreign Affairs; **s'affairer** *vi* to busy o.s., bustle about.

affaisser [afese]: **s'**~ *vi* (*terrain, immeuble*) to subside, sink; (*personne*) to collapse.

affaler [afale]: **s'**~ *vi*: **s'**~ **dans/sur** to collapse ou slump into/onto.

affamé, e [afame] *a* starving.

affecter [afɛkte] *vt* to affect; (*telle ou telle forme etc*) to take on; ~ **qch à** to allocate ou allot sth to; ~ **qn à** to appoint sb to; (*diplomate*) to post sb to.

affectif, ive [afɛktif, -iv] *a* emotional.

affection [afɛksjɔ̃] *nf* affection; (*mal*) ailment; **affectionner** *vt* to be fond of.

affectueux, euse [afɛktɥø, -øz] *a* affectionate.

afférent, e [aferɑ̃, -ɑ̃t] *a*: ~ **à** pertaining ou relating to.

affermir [afɛʀmiʀ] *vt* to consolidate, strengthen.

affichage [afiʃaʒ] *nm* billposting; (*électronique*) display.

affiche [afiʃ] *nf* poster; (*officielle*) notice; (*THÉÂTRE*) bill; **tenir l'**~ to run.

afficher [afiʃe] *vt* (*affiche*) to put up; (*réunion*) to put up a notice about; (*électroniquement*) to display; (*fig*) to exhibit, display.

affilée [afile]: **d'**~ *ad* at a stretch.

affiler [afile] *vt* to sharpen.

affiner [afine] *vt* to refine.

affirmatif, ive [afiʀmatif, -iv] *a* affirmative.

affirmation [afiʀmasjɔ̃] *nf* assertion.

affirmer [afiʀme] *vt* (*prétendre*) to maintain, assert; (*autorité etc*) to assert.

affligé, e [afliʒe] *a* distressed, grieved; ~ **de** (*maladie, tare*) afflicted with.

affliger [afliʒe] *vt* (*peiner*) to distress, grieve.

affluence [aflyɑ̃s] *nf* crowds *pl*; **heures d'**~ rush hours; **jours d'**~ busiest days.

affluent [aflyɑ̃] *nm* tributary.

affluer [aflye] *vi* (*secours, biens*) to flood in, pour in; (*sang*) to rush, flow.

affolement [afɔlmɑ̃] *nm* panic.

affoler [afɔle] *vt* to throw into a panic; **s'**~ *vi* to panic.

affranchir [afʀɑ̃ʃiʀ] *vt* to put a stamp ou stamps on; (*à la machine*) to frank (*Brit*), meter (*US*); (*fig*) to free, liberate; **affranchissement** *nm* postage.

affréter [afʀete] *vt* to charter.

affreux, euse [afʀø, -øz] *a* dreadful, awful.

affrontement [afʀɔ̃tmɑ̃] *nm* clash, confrontation.

affronter [afʀɔ̃te] *vt* to confront, face.

affubler [afyble] *vt* (*péj*): ~ **qn de** to rig ou deck sb out in; (*surnom*) to attach to sb.

affût [afy] *nm*: **à l'**~ **(de)** (*gibier*) lying in wait (for); (*fig*) on the look-out (for).

affûter [afyte] *vt* to sharpen, grind.

afin [afɛ̃]: ~ **que** *cj* so that, in order that; ~ **de faire** in order to do, so as to do.

africain, e [afʀikɛ̃, -ɛn] *a, nm/f* African.

Afrique [afʀik] *nf*: **l'**~ Africa; **l'**~ **du Sud** South Africa.

agacer [agase] *vt* to pester, tease; (*involontairement*) to irritate.

âge [ɑʒ] *nm* age; **quel** ~ **as-tu?** how old are you?; **prendre de l'**~ to be getting on (in years); **l'**~ **ingrat** the awkward age; **l'**~ **mûr** maturity; **âgé, e** *a* old, elderly; **âgé de 10 ans** 10 years old.

agence [aʒɑ̃s] *nf* agency, office; (*succursale*) branch; ~ **immobilière** estate (*Brit*) ou real estate (*US*) agent's (office); ~ **matrimoniale** marriage bureau; ~ **de voyages** travel agency.

agencer [aʒɑ̃se] *vt* to put together; to arrange, lay out.

agenda [aʒɛ̃da] *nm* diary.

agenouiller [aʒnuje]: **s'**~ *vi* to kneel (down).

agent [aʒɑ̃] *nm* (*aussi:* ~ **de police**) policeman; (*ADMIN*) official, officer; (*fig: élément, facteur*) agent; ~ **d'assurances** insurance broker; ~ **de change** stockbroker; ~ **(secret)** (secret) agent.

agglomération [aglɔmeʀasjɔ̃] *nf* town; built-up area; **l'**~ **parisienne** the urban area of Paris.

aggloméré [aglɔmeʀe] *nm* (*bois*) chipboard; (*pierre*) conglomerate.

agglomérer [aglɔmeʀe] *vt* to pile up; (*TECH: bois, pierre*) to compress.

aggraver [agʀave] *vt* to worsen, aggravate; (*JUR: peine*) to increase; **s'**~ *vi* to worsen.

agile [aʒil] *a* agile, nimble.

agir [aʒiʀ] *vi* to act; **il s'agit de** it's a matter ou question of; it is about; (*il importe que*): **il s'agit de faire** we (ou you etc) must do.

agitation [aʒitɑsjɔ̃] nf (hustle and) bustle; agitation, excitement; (politique) unrest, agitation.

agité, e [aʒite] a fidgety, restless; agitated, perturbed; (mer) rough.

agiter [aʒite] vt (bouteille, chiffon) to shake; (bras, mains) to wave; (préoccuper, exciter) to perturb.

agneau, x [aɲo] nm lamb.

agonie [agɔni] nf mortal agony, death pangs pl; (fig) death throes pl.

agrafe [agʀaf] nf (de vêtement) hook, fastener; (de bureau) staple; **agrafer** vt to fasten; to staple; **agrafeuse** nf stapler.

agraire [agʀɛʀ] a land cpd.

agrandir [agʀɑ̃diʀ] vt to enlarge; (magasin, domaine) to extend, enlarge; s'~ vi to be extended; to be enlarged; **agrandissement** nm (PHOTO) enlargement.

agréable [agʀeabl(ə)] a pleasant, nice.

agréé, e [agʀee] a: concessionnaire ~ registered dealer.

agréer [agʀee] vt (requête) to accept; ~ à vt to please, suit; veuillez ~ ... (formule épistolaire) yours faithfully.

agrégation [agʀegɑsjɔ̃] nf highest teaching diploma in France; **agrégé, e** nm/f holder of the agrégation.

agrément [agʀemɑ̃] nm (accord) consent, approval; (attraits) charm, attractiveness; (plaisir) pleasure.

agrémenter [agʀemɑ̃te] vt to embellish, adorn.

agresser [agʀese] vt to attack.

agresseur [agʀesœʀ] nm aggressor, attacker; (POL, MIL) aggressor.

agressif, ive [agʀesif, -iv] a aggressive.

agricole [agʀikɔl] a agricultural.

agriculteur [agʀikyltœʀ] nm farmer.

agriculture [agʀikyltyʀ] nf agriculture; farming.

agripper [agʀipe] vt to grab, clutch; (pour arracher) to snatch, grab; s'~ à to cling (on) to, clutch, grip.

agrumes [agʀym] nmpl citrus fruit(s).

aguerrir [agɛʀiʀ] vt to harden.

aguets [agɛ]: aux ~ ad: être aux ~ to be on the look-out.

aguicher [agiʃe] vt to entice.

ahuri, e [ayʀi] a (stupéfait) flabbergasted; (idiot) dim-witted.

ai vb voir **avoir.**

aide [ɛd] nm/f assistant // nf assistance, help; (secours financier) aid; à l'~ de (avec) with the help ou aid of; appeler (qn) à l'~ to call for help (from sb); ~ judiciaire nf legal aid; ~ sociale nf (assistance) state aid; ~ soignant, e nm/f auxiliary nurse; ~-mémoire nm inv memoranda pages pl; (key facts) handbook.

aider [ede] vt to help; ~ à qch (faciliter) to help (towards) sth; s'~ de (se servir

de) to use, make use of.

aie etc vb voir **avoir.**

aïe [aj] excl ouch.

aïeul, e [ajœl] nm/f grandparent, grandfather/grandmother; forebear.

aïeux [ajø] nmpl grandparents; forebears, forefathers.

aigle [ɛgl(ə)] nm eagle.

aigre [ɛgʀ(ə)] a sour, sharp; (fig) sharp, cutting; **aigreur** nf sourness; sharpness; aigreurs d'estomac heartburn sg; **aigrir** vt (personne) to embitter; (caractère) to sour.

aigu, ë [egy] a (objet, arête, douleur, intelligence) sharp; (son, voix) high-pitched, shrill; (note) high(-pitched).

aiguille [eguij] nf needle; (de montre) hand; ~ à tricoter knitting needle.

aiguiller [eguije] vt (orienter) to direct.

aiguillon [eguijɔ̃] nm (d'abeille) sting; **aiguillonner** vt to spur ou goad on.

aiguiser [egize] vt to sharpen; (fig) to stimulate; to excite.

ail [aj] nm garlic.

aile [ɛl] nf wing; **aileron** nm (de requin) fin; **ailier** nm winger.

aille etc vb voir **aller.**

ailleurs [ajœʀ] ad elsewhere, somewhere else; partout/nulle part ~ everywhere/ nowhere else; d'~ ad (du reste) moreover, besides; par ~ ad (d'autre part) moreover, furthermore.

ailloli [ajɔli] nm garlic mayonnaise.

aimable [ɛmabl(ə)] a kind, nice.

aimant [ɛmɑ̃] nm magnet.

aimer [eme] vt to love; (d'amitié, affection, par goût) to like; (souhait): j'aimerais... I would like...; bien ~ qn/ qch to like sb/sth; j'aime mieux ou autant vous dire que I may as well tell you that; j'aimerais autant y aller maintenant I'd rather go now; j'aimerais mieux faire I'd much rather do.

aine [ɛn] nf groin.

aîné, e [ene] a elder, older; (le plus âgé) eldest, oldest // nm/f oldest child ou one, oldest boy ou son/girl ou daughter; **aînesse** nf: droit d'aînesse birthright.

ainsi [ɛ̃si] ad (de cette façon) like this, in this way, thus; (ce faisant) thus // cj thus, so; ~ que (comme) (just) as; (et aussi) as well as; pour ~ dire so to speak; et ~ de suite and so on.

air [ɛʀ] nm air; (mélodie) tune; (expression) look, air; prendre l'~ to get some (fresh) air; (avion) to take off; avoir l'~ (sembler) to look, appear; avoir l'~ de to look like; avoir l'~ de faire to look as though one is doing, appear to be doing.

aire [ɛʀ] nf (zone, fig, MATH) area.

aisance [ɛzɑ̃s] nf ease; (richesse) affluence.

aise [ɛz] nf comfort // a: être bien ~ que to be delighted that; être à l'~ ou à son ~ to be comfortable; (pas embarrassé) to be at ease; (*financièrement*) to be comfortably off; **se mettre à l'~** to make o.s. comfortable; **être mal à l'~** *ou* **à son ~** to be uncomfortable; to be ill at ease; **en faire à son ~** to do as one likes; **aisé, e** *a* easy; (*assez riche*) well-to-do, well-off.

aisselle [εsεl] *nf* armpit.

ait *vb voir* **avoir**.

ajonc [aʒɔ̃] *nm* gorse *q*.

ajourner [aʒuʀne] *vt* (*réunion*) to adjourn; (*décision*) to defer, postpone.

ajouter [aʒute] *vt* to add; **~ foi à** to lend *ou* give credence to.

ajusté, e [aʒyste] *a*: **bien ~** (*robe etc*) close-fitting.

ajuster [aʒyste] *vt* (*régler*) to adjust; (*vêtement*) to alter; (*coup de fusil*) to aim; (*cible*) to aim at; (*TECH, gén: adapter*): **~ qch à** to fit sth to.

alambic [alɑ̃bik] *nm* still.

alarme [alaʀm(ə)] *nf* alarm; **donner l'~** to give *ou* raise the alarm; **alarmer** *vt* to alarm; **s'alarmer** *vi* to become alarmed.

album [albɔm] *nm* album.

albumine [albymin] *nf* albumin; **avoir** *ou* **faire de l'~** to suffer from albuminuria.

alcool [alkɔl] *nm*: **l'~** alcohol; **un ~** a spirit, a brandy; **~ à brûler** methylated spirits (*Brit*), wood alcohol (*US*); **~ à 90°** surgical spirit; **~ique** *a, nm/f* alcoholic; **~isé, e** *a* alcoholic; **~isme** *nm* alcoholism; **alco(o)test** ® *nm* Breathalyser ®; (*test*) breath-test.

aléas [alea] *nmpl* hazards; **aléatoire** *a* uncertain; (*INFORM*) random.

alentour [alɑ̃tuʀ] *ad* around (about); **~s** *nmpl* surroundings; **aux ~s de** in the vicinity *ou* neighbourhood of, around about; (*temps*) around about.

alerte [alεʀt(ə)] *a* agile, nimble; brisk, lively // *nf* alert; warning; **alerter** *vt* to alert.

algèbre [alʒεbʀ(ə)] *nf* algebra.

Alger [alʒe] *n* Algiers.

Algérie [alʒeʀi] *nf*: **l'~** Algeria; **algérien, ne** *a, nm/f* Algerian.

algue [alg(ə)] *nf* (*gén*) seaweed *q*; (*BOT*) alga (*pl* algae).

alibi [alibi] *nm* alibi.

aliéné, e [aljene] *nm/f* insane person, lunatic (*péj*).

aligner [aliɲe] *vt* to align, line up; (*idées, chiffres*) to string together; (*adapter*): **~ qch sur** to bring sth into alignment with; **s'~** (*soldats etc*) to line up; **s'~ sur** (*POL*) to align o.s. on.

aliment [alimɑ̃] *nm* food.

alimentation [alimɑ̃tasjɔ̃] *nf* feeding; supplying; (*commerce*) food trade; (*produits*) groceries *pl*; (*régime*) diet; (*INFORM*) feed.

alimenter [alimɑ̃te] *vt* to feed; (*TECH*):

~ (en) to supply (with); to feed (with); (*fig*) to sustain, keep going.

alinéa [alinea] *nm* paragraph.

aliter [alite]: **s'~** *vi* to take to one's bed.

allaiter [alεte] *vt* to (breast-)feed, nurse; (*suj: animal*) to suckle.

allant [alɑ̃] *nm* drive, go.

allécher [aleʃe] *vt*: **~ qn** to make sb's mouth water; to tempt *ou* entice sb.

allée [ale] *nf* (*de jardin*) path; (*en ville*) avenue, drive; **~s et venues** *nfpl* comings and goings.

alléger [aleʒe] *vt* (*voiture*) to make lighter; (*chargement*) to lighten; (*souffrance*) to alleviate, soothe.

allègre [alεgʀ(ə)] *a* lively, cheerful.

alléguer [alege] *vt* to put forward (as proof *ou* an excuse).

Allemagne [aləmaɲ] *nf*: **l'~** Germany; **l'~ de l'Est/Ouest** East/West Germany; **allemand. e** *a, nm, nf* German.

aller [ale] *nm* (*trajet*) outward journey; (*billet: aussi*: **~ simple**) single (*Brit*) *ou* one-way (*US*) ticket // *vi* (*gén*) to go; **~ à** (*convenir*) to suit; (*suj: forme, pointure etc*) to fit; **~ avec** (*couleurs, style etc*) to go (well) with; **je vais y aller/me fâcher** I'm going to go/to get angry; **~ voir** to go and see, go to see; **allez!** come on!; **allons!** come now!; **comment allez-vous?** how are you?; **comment ça va?** how are you?; (*affaires etc*) how are things?; **il va bien/mal** he's well/not well, he's fine/ill; **ça va bien/mal** (*affaires etc*) it's going well/not going well; **~ mieux** to be better; **cela va sans dire** that goes without saying; **il y va de leur vie** their lives are at stake; **s'en ~** *vi* (*partir*) to be off, go, leave; (*disparaître*) to go away; **~ (et) retour** *nm* (*trajet*) return journey (*Brit*), round trip; (*billet*) return (ticket) (*Brit*), round trip ticket (*US*).

allergique [alεʀʒik] *a*: **~ à** allergic to.

alliage [aljaʒ] *nm* alloy.

alliance [aljɑ̃s] *nf* (*MIL, POL*) alliance; (*mariage*) marriage; (*bague*) wedding ring.

allier [alje] *vt* (*métaux*) to alloy; (*POL, gén*) to ally; (*fig*) to combine; **s'~** to become allies; to combine.

allô [alo] *excl* hullo, hallo.

allocation [alɔkasjɔ̃] *nf* allowance; **~ (de) chômage** unemployment benefit; **~ (de) logement** rent allowance; **~s familiales** ≈ child benefit.

allocution [alɔkysjɔ̃] *nf* short speech.

allonger [alɔ̃ʒe] *vt* to lengthen, make longer; (*étendre: bras, jambe*) to stretch (out); **~** *vi* to get longer; **s'~** *vi* (*se coucher*) to lie down, stretch out; **~ le pas** to hasten one's step(s).

allouer [alwe] *vt* to allocate, allot.

allumage [alymaʒ] *nm* (*AUTO*) ignition.

allume... [alym] *préfixe*: **~-cigare** *nm*

inv cigar lighter; **~-gaz** *nm inv* gas lighter.

allumer [alyme] *vt* (*lampe, phare, radio*) to put *ou* switch on; (*pièce*) to put *ou* switch the light(s) on in; (*feu*) to light; **s'~** *vi* (*lumière, lampe*) to come *ou* go on.

allumette [alymɛt] *nf* match.

allure [alyʀ] *nf* (*vitesse*) speed, pace; (*démarche*) walk; (*maintien*) bearing; (*aspect, air*) look; **avoir de l'~** to have style; **à toute ~** at top speed.

allusion [alyzjɔ̃] *nf* allusion; (*sous-entendu*) hint; **faire ~ à** to allude *ou* refer to; to hint at.

aloi [alwa] *nm*: **de bon ~** of genuine worth *ou* quality.

alors [alɔʀ] *ad* **1** (*à ce moment-là*) then, at that time; **il habitait ~ à Paris** he lived in Paris at that time

2 (*par conséquent*) then; **tu as fini? ~ je m'en vais** have you finished? I'm going then; **et ~?** so what?

alors que *cj* **1** (*au moment où*) when, as; **il est arrivé ~ que je partais** he arrived as I was leaving

2 (*pendant que*) while, when; **~ qu'il était à Paris, il a visité ...** while *ou* when he was in Paris, he visited ...

3 (*tandis que*) whereas, while; **~ que son frère travaillait dur, lui se reposait** whereas *ou* while his brother was working hard, HE would rest.

alouette [alwɛt] *nf* (sky)lark.

alourdir [aluʀdiʀ] *vt* to weigh down, make heavy.

aloyau [alwajo] *nm* sirloin.

alpage [alpaʒ] *nm* pasture.

Alpes [alp(ə)] *nfpl*: **les ~ the** Alps.

alphabet [alfabɛ] *nm* alphabet; (*livre*) ABC (book); **alphabétiser** *vt* to teach to read and write; to eliminate illiteracy in.

alpinisme [alpinism(ə)] *nm* mountaineering, climbing; **alpiniste** *nm/f* mountaineer, climber.

Alsace [alzas] *nf* Alsace; **alsacien, ne** *a, nm/f* Alsatian.

altérer [alteʀe] *vt* to falsify; to distort; to debase; to impair.

alternateur [altɛʀnatœʀ] *nm* alternator.

alternatif, ive [altɛʀnatif, -iv] *a* alternating // *nf* (*choix*) alternative; **alternativement** *ad* alternately.

Altesse [altɛs] *nf* Highness.

altitude [altityd] *nf* altitude, height.

alto [alto] *nm* (*instrument*) viola.

altruisme [altʀɥism(ə)] *nm* altruism.

aluminium [alyminjɔm] *nm* aluminium (*Brit*), aluminum (*US*).

alunir [alyniʀ] *vi* to land on the moon.

amabilité [amabilite] *nf* kindness, amiability.

amadouer [amadwe] *vt* to coax, cajole; to mollify, soothe.

amaigrir [amegʀiʀ] *vt* to make thin(ner).

amande [amɑ̃d] *nf* (*de l'amandier*) almond; (*de noyau de fruit*) kernel; **amandier** *nm* almond (tree).

amant [amɑ̃] *nm* lover.

amarrer [amaʀe] *vt* (*NAVIG*) to moor; (*gén*) to make fast.

amas [ama] *nm* heap, pile.

amasser [amase] *vt* to amass.

amateur [amatœʀ] *nm* amateur; **en ~** (*péj*) amateurishly; **~ de musique/sport** *etc* music/sport *etc* lover.

amazone [amazon] *nf*: **en ~** sidesaddle.

ambages [ɑ̃baʒ]: **sans ~** *ad* plainly.

ambassade [ɑ̃basad] *nf* embassy; (*mission*): **en ~** on a mission; **ambassadeur, drice** *nm/f* ambassador/ambassadress.

ambiance [ɑ̃bjɑ̃s] *nf* atmosphere.

ambiant, e [ɑ̃bjɑ̃, -ɑ̃t] *a* (*air, milieu*) surrounding; (*température*) ambient.

ambigu, ë [ɑ̃bigy] *a* ambiguous.

ambitieux, euse [ɑ̃bisjø, -øz] *a* ambitious.

ambition [ɑ̃bisjɔ̃] *nf* ambition.

ambulance [ɑ̃bylɑ̃s] *nf* ambulance; **ambulancier, ière** *nm/f* ambulance man/woman (*Brit*), paramedic (*US*).

ambulant, e [ɑ̃bylɑ̃, -ɑ̃t] *a* travelling, itinerant.

âme [ɑm] *nf* soul; **~ sœur** kindred spirit.

améliorer [ameljɔʀe] *vt* to improve; **s'~** *vi* to improve, get better.

aménagements [amenaʒmɑ̃] *nmpl* developments; **~ fiscaux** tax adjustments.

aménager [amenaʒe] *vt* (*agencer, transformer*) to fit out; to lay out; (*: quartier, territoire*) to develop; (*installer*) to fix up, put in; **ferme aménagée** converted farmhouse.

amende [amɑ̃d] *nf* fine; **mettre à l'~** to penalize; **faire ~ honorable** to make amends.

amender [amɑ̃de] *vt* (*loi*) to amend; **s'~** *vi* to mend one's ways.

amène [amɛn] *a* affable; **peu ~** unkind.

amener [amne] *vt* to bring; (*causer*) to bring about; (*baisser: drapeau, voiles*) to strike; **s'~** *vi* (*fam*) to show up, turn up.

amenuiser [amənɥize]: **s'~** *vi* to grow slimmer, lessen; to dwindle.

amer, amère [amɛʀ] *a* bitter.

américain, e [ameʀikɛ̃, -ɛn] *a, nm/f* American.

Amérique [ameʀik] *nf* America; **l'~ centrale/latine** Central/Latin America; **l'~ du Nord/du Sud** North/South America.

amerrir [ameʀiʀ] *vi* to land (on the sea).

amertume [amɛʀtym] *nf* bitterness.

ameublement [amœblamɑ̃] *nm* furnishing; (*meubles*) furniture.

ameuter [amøte] *vt* (*badauds*) to draw a crowd of; (*peuple*) to rouse.

ami, e [ami] *nm/f* friend; *(amant/maîtresse)* boyfriend/girlfriend // *a:* **pays/groupe** ~ friendly country/group; **être** ~ **de l'ordre** to be a lover of order; **un** ~ **des arts** a patron of the arts.

amiable [amjabl(ə)]: **à l'**~ *ad (JUR)* out of court; *(gén)* amicably.

amiante [amjɑ̃t] *nm* asbestos.

amical, e, aux [amikal, -o] *a* friendly // *nf (club)* association; **amicalement** *ad* in a friendly way; *(formule épistolaire)* regards.

amidon [amidɔ̃] *nm* starch.

amincir [amɛ̃siʀ] *vt (objet)* to thin (down); ~ **qn** to make sb thinner *ou* slimmer; **s'**~ *vi* to get thinner *ou* slimmer.

amiral, aux [amiʀal, -o] *nm* admiral.

amitié [amitje] *nf* friendship; **prendre en** ~ to befriend; **faire** *ou* **présenter ses** ~**s à qn** to send sb one's best wishes.

ammoniac [amɔnjak] *nm*: **(gaz)** ~ ammonia.

ammoniaque [amɔnjak] *nf* ammonia (water).

amoindrir [amwɛ̃dʀiʀ] *vt* to reduce.

amollir [amɔliʀ] *vt* to soften.

amonceler [amɔ̃sle] *vt*, **s'**~ *vi* to pile *ou* heap up; *(fig)* to accumulate.

amont [amɔ̃]: **en** ~ *ad* upstream; *(sur une pente)* uphill.

amorce [amɔʀs(ə)] *nf (sur un hameçon)* bait; *(explosif)* cap; primer; priming; *(fig: début)* beginning(s), start.

amorphe [amɔʀf(ə)] *a* passive, lifeless.

amortir [amɔʀtiʀ] *vt (atténuer: choc)* to absorb, cushion; *(bruit, douleur)* to deaden; *(COMM: dette)* to pay off; *(: mise de fonds, matériel)* to write off; ~ **un abonnement** to make a season ticket pay (for itself); **amortisseur** *nm* shock absorber.

amour [amuʀ] *nm* love; *(liaison)* love affair, love; **faire l'**~ to make love; **s'**~**-acher de** *(péj)* to become infatuated with; ~**eux, euse** *a (regard, tempérament)* amorous; *(vie, problèmes)* love *cpd*; *(personne)*: ~**eux (de qn)** in love (with sb) // *nmpl* courting couple(s); ~**-propre** *nm* self-esteem, pride.

amovible [amɔvibl(ə)] *a* removable, detachable.

ampère [ɑ̃pɛʀ] *nm* amp(ere).

amphithéâtre [ɑ̃fiteɑtʀ(ə)] *nm* amphitheatre; *(d'université)* lecture hall *ou* theatre.

ample [ɑ̃pl(ə)] *a (vêtement)* roomy, ample; *(gestes, mouvement)* broad; *(ressources)* ample; **ampleur** *nf (importance)* scale, size; extent.

amplificateur [ɑ̃plifikatœʀ] *nm* amplifier.

amplifier [ɑ̃plifje] *vt (son, oscillation)* to amplify; *(fig)* to expand, increase.

ampoule [ɑ̃pul] *nf (électrique)* bulb; *(de médicament)* phial; *(aux mains, pieds)* blister.

ampoulé, e [ɑ̃pule] *a (péj)* pompous, bombastic.

amputer [ɑ̃pyte] *vt (MÉD)* to amputate; *(fig)* to cut *ou* reduce drastically.

amusant, e [amyzɑ̃, -ɑ̃t] *a (divertissant, spirituel)* entertaining, amusing; *(comique)* funny, amusing.

amuse-gueule [amyzgœl] *nm inv* appetizer, snack.

amusement [amyzmɑ̃] *nm* amusement; *(jeu etc)* pastime, diversion.

amuser [amyze] *vt (divertir)* to entertain, amuse; *(égayer, faire rire)* to amuse; *(détourner l'attention de)* to distract; **s'**~ *vi (jouer)* to amuse o.s., play; *(se divertir)* to enjoy o.s., have fun; *(fig)* to mess around.

amygdale [amidal] *nf* tonsil.

amygdalite [amidalit] *nf* tonsilitis.

an [ɑ̃] *nm* year; **le jour de l'**~, **le premier de l'**~, **le nouvel** ~ New Year's Day.

analogique [analɔʒik] *a* analogical; *(IN-FORM, montre)* analog.

analogue [analɔg] *a:* ~ **(à)** analogous (to), similar (to).

analphabète [analfabɛt] *nm/f* illiterate.

analyse [analiz] *nf* analysis; *(MÉD)* test; **analyser** *vt* to analyse; to test.

ananas [anana] *nm* pineapple.

anarchie [anaʀʃi] *nf* anarchy.

anathème [anatɛm] *nm*: **jeter l'**~ **sur** to curse.

anatomie [anatɔmi] *nf* anatomy.

ancêtre [ɑ̃sɛtʀ(ə)] *nm/f* ancestor.

anchois [ɑ̃ʃwa] *nm* anchovy.

ancien, ne [ɑ̃sjɛ̃, -jɛn] *a* old; *(de jadis, de l'antiquité)* ancient; *(précédent, ex-)* former, old // *nm/f (dans une tribu)* elder; **anciennement** *ad* formerly; **ancienneté** *nf* oldness; antiquity; *(AD-MIN)* (length of) service; seniority.

ancre [ɑ̃kʀ(ə)] *nf* anchor; **jeter/lever l'**~ to cast/weigh anchor; **à l'**~ at anchor.

ancrer [ɑ̃kʀe] *vt (CONSTR: câble etc)* to anchor; *(fig)* to fix firmly; **s'**~ *vi (NA-VIG)* to (cast) anchor.

Andorre [ɑ̃dɔʀ] *nf* Andorra.

andouille [ɑ̃duj] *nf (CULIN)* sausage made of chitterlings; *(fam)* clot, nit.

âne [ɑn] *nm* donkey, ass; *(péj)* dunce.

anéantir [aneɑ̃tiʀ] *vt* to annihilate, wipe out; *(fig)* to obliterate, destroy; to overwhelm.

anémie [anemi] *nf* anaemia; **anémique** *a* anaemic.

ânerie [ɑnʀi] *nf* stupidity; stupid *ou* idiotic comment *etc*.

anesthésie [anɛstezi] *nf* anaesthesia; **faire une** ~ **locale/générale à qn** to give sb a local/general anaesthetic.

ange [ɑ̃ʒ] *nm* angel; **être aux** ~**s** to be over the moon.

angélus [ɑ̃ʒelys] *nm* angelus; evening

bells *pl*.

angine [ãʒin] *nf* throat infection; ~ de poitrine angina.

anglais, e [ãglɛ, -ɛz] *a* English // *nm/f*: A~, e Englishman/woman // *nm* (*LING*) English; les A~ the English; filer à l'~e to take French leave.

angle [ãgl(ə)] *nm* angle; (*coin*) corner; ~ droit right angle.

Angleterre [ãglətɛr] *nf*: l'~ England.

anglo... [ãglɔ] *préfixe* Anglo-, anglo(-); ~phone *a* English-speaking.

angoissé, e [ãgwase] *a* (*personne*) full of anxieties *ou* hang-ups (*fam*).

angoisser [ãgwase] *vt* to harrow, cause anguish to // *vi* to worry, fret.

anguille [ãgij] *nf* eel.

anicroche [anikrɔʃ] *nf* hitch, snag.

animal, e, aux [animal, -o] *a*, *nm* animal.

animateur, trice [animatœr, -tris] *nm/f* (*de télévision*) host; (*de groupe*) leader, organizer.

animation [animɑsjɔ̃] *nf* (*voir animé*) busyness; liveliness; (*CINÉMA*: *technique*) animation.

animé, e [anime] *a* (*lieu*) busy, lively; (*conversation, réunion*) lively, animated; (*opposé à inanimé*) animate.

animer [anime] *vt* (*ville, soirée*) to liven up; (*mettre en mouvement*) to drive.

anis [ani] *nm* (*CULIN*) aniseed; (*BOT*) anise.

ankyloser [ãkiloze]: s'~ *vi* to get stiff.

anneau, x [ano] *nm* (*de rideau, bague*) ring; (*de chaîne*) link.

année [ane] *nf* year.

annexe [anɛks(ə)] *a* (*problème*) related; (*document*) appended; (*salle*) adjoining // *nf* (*bâtiment*) annex(e); (*de document, ouvrage*) annex, appendix; (*jointe à une lettre*) enclosure.

anniversaire [anivɛrsɛr] *nm* birthday; (*d'un événement, bâtiment*) anniversary.

annonce [anɔ̃s] *nf* announcement; (*signe, indice*) sign; (*aussi:* ~ *publicitaire*) advertisement; les petites ~s the classified advertisements, the small ads.

annoncer [anɔ̃se] *vt* to announce; (*être le signe de*) to herald; s'~ bien/difficile to look promising/difficult; **annonceur, euse** *nm/f* (*TV, RADIO*: *speaker*) announcer; (*publicitaire*) advertiser.

annuaire [anɥɛr] *nm* yearbook, annual; ~ téléphonique (telephone) directory, phone book.

annuel, le [anɥɛl] *a* annual, yearly.

annuité [anɥite] *nf* annual instalment.

annulaire [anɥlɛr] *nm* third finger.

annuler [anɥle] *vt* (*rendez-vous, voyage*) to cancel, call off; (*mariage*) to annul; (*jugement*) to quash (*Brit*), repeal (*US*); (*résultats*) to declare void; (*MATH, PHYSIQUE*) to cancel out.

anodin, e [anɔdɛ̃, -in] *a* harmless; in-

significant, trivial.

anonyme [anɔnim] *a* anonymous; (*fig*) impersonal.

anorak [anɔrak] *nm* anorak.

ANPE *sigle f* (= *Agence nationale pour l'emploi*) national employment agency.

anse [ãs] *nf* (*de panier, tasse*) handle; (*GÉO*) cove.

antan [ãtã]: d'~ *a* of long ago.

antarctique [ãtarktik] *a* Antarctic // *nm*: l'A~ the Antarctic.

antécédents [ãtesedã] *nmpl* (*MÉD etc*) past history *sg*.

antenne [ãtɛn] *nf* (*de radio*) aerial; (*d'insecte*) antenna (*pl* ae), feeler; (*poste avancé*) outpost; (*petite succursale*) sub-branch; passer à l'~ to go on the air; prendre l'~ to tune in; 2 heures d'~ 2 hours' broadcasting time.

antérieur, e [ãterjœr] *a* (*d'avant*) previous, earlier; (*de devant*) front.

anti... [ãti] *préfixe* anti..; ~aérien, ne *a* anti-aircraft; abri ~aérien air-raid shelter; ~alcoolique *a* anti-alcohol; ~atomique *a*: abri ~atomique fallout shelter; ~biotique *nm* antibiotic; ~brouillard *a*: phare ~brouillard fog lamp.

anticipation [ãtisipɑsjɔ̃] *nf*: livre/film d'~ science fiction book/film.

anticipé, e [ãtisipe] *a*: avec mes remerciements ~s thanking you in advance *ou* anticipation.

anticiper [ãtisipe] *vt* (*événement, coup*) to anticipate, foresee.

anticonceptionnel, le [ãtikɔ̃sɛpsjɔnɛl] *a* contraceptive.

antidote [ãtidɔt] *nm* antidote.

antienne [ãtjɛn] *nf* (*fig*) chant, refrain.

antigel [ãtiʒɛl] *nm* antifreeze.

antihistaminique [ãtiistaminik] *nm* antihistamine.

Antilles [ãtij] *nfpl*: les ~ the West Indies.

antilope [ãtilɔp] *nf* antelope.

antimite(s) [ãtimit] *a, nm*: (*produit*) ~ mothproofer; moth repellent.

antiparasite [ãtiparazit] *a* (*RADIO, TV*): dispositif ~ suppressor.

antipathique [ãtipatik] *a* unpleasant, disagreeable.

antiphrase [ãtifraz] *nf*: par ~ ironically.

antipodes [ãtipɔd] *nmpl* (*GÉO*): les ~ the antipodes; (*fig*): être aux ~ de to be the opposite extreme of.

antiquaire [ãtikɛr] *nm/f* antique dealer.

antique [ãtik] *a* antique; (*très vieux*) ancient, antiquated.

antiquité [ãtikite] *nf* (*objet*) antique; l'A~ Antiquity; magasin d'~s antique shop.

antirabique [ãtirabik] *a* rabies *cpd*.

antirouille [ãtiruj] *a inv* anti-rust *cpd*; traitement ~ rustproofing.

antisémite [ɑ̃tisemit] *a* anti-semitic.

antiseptique [ɑ̃tisɛptik] *a, nm* antiseptic.

antivol [ɑ̃tivɔl] *a, nm*: (dispositif) ~ anti-theft device.

antre [ɑ̃tʀ(ə)] *nm* den, lair.

anxieux, euse [ɑ̃ksjø, -øz] *a* anxious, worried.

AOC *sigle f* (= *appellation d'origine contrôlée*) label guaranteeing the quality of wine.

août [u] *nm* August.

apaiser [apeze] *vt* (colère, douleur) to soothe; (faim) to appease; (personne) to calm (down), pacify; **s'~** *vi* (tempête, bruit) to die down, subside.

apanage [apanaʒ] *nm*: être l'~ de to be the privilege ou prerogative of.

aparté [aparte] *nm* (THÉÂTRE) aside; (entretien) private conversation.

apatride [apatrid] *nm/f* stateless person.

apercevoir [apɛʀsəvwaʀ] *vt* to see; **s'~ de** *vt* to notice; **s'~ que** to notice that.

aperçu [apɛʀsy] *nm* (vue d'ensemble) general survey; (intuition) insight.

apéritif [apeʀitif] *nm* (boisson) aperitif; (réunion) drinks *pl*.

à-peu-près [apøpʀɛ] *nm inv* (péj) vague approximation.

apeuré, e [apœʀe] *a* frightened, scared.

aphone [afɔn] *a* voiceless.

aphte [aft(ə)] *nm* mouth ulcer.

aphteuse [aftøz] *af*: fièvre ~ foot-and-mouth disease.

apiculture [apikyltyʀ] *nf* beekeeping, apiculture.

apitoyer [apitwaje] *vt* to move to pity; **s'~ (sur)** to feel pity (for).

aplanir [aplaniʀ] *vt* to level; (fig) to smooth away, iron out.

aplatir [aplatiʀ] *vt* to flatten; **s'~** *vi* to become flatter; to be flattened; (fig) to lie flat on the ground.

aplomb [aplɔ̃] *nm* (équilibre) balance, equilibrium; (fig) self-assurance; nerve; **d'~** *ad* steady; (CONSTR) plumb.

apogée [apɔʒe] *nm* (fig) peak, apogee.

apologie [apɔlɔʒi] *nf* vindication, praise.

apostolat [apɔstɔla] *nm* (REL) apostolate; (gén) evangelism.

apostrophe [apɔstʀɔf] *nf* (signe) apostrophe.

apostropher [apɔstʀɔfe] *vt* (interpeller) to shout at, address sharply.

apothéose [apɔteoz] *nf* pinnacle (of achievement); (MUS) grand finale.

apôtre [apoʀ(ə)] *nm* apostle.

apparaître [apaʀɛtʀ(ə)] *vi* to appear // *vb avec attribut* to appear, seem.

apparat [apaʀa] *nm*: tenue/dîner d'~ ceremonial dress/dinner.

appareil [apaʀɛj] *nm* (outil, machine) piece of apparatus, device; appliance; (politique, syndical) machinery; (avion) (aero)plane, aircraft *inv*; (téléphonique)

phone; (dentier) brace (Brit), braces (US); qui est à l'~? who's speaking?; dans le plus simple ~ in one's birthday suit; ~ photographique, ~(-photo) *nm* camera; ~ 24 x 36 *ou* petit format 35mm camera.

appareiller [apaʀeje] *vi* (NAVIG) to cast off, get under way // *vt* (assortir) to match up.

apparemment [apaʀamɑ̃] *ad* apparently.

apparence [apaʀɑ̃s] *nf* appearance.

apparent, e [apaʀɑ̃, -ɑ̃t] *a* visible; obvious; (superficiel) apparent.

apparenté, e [apaʀɑ̃te] *a*: ~ à related to; (fig) similar to.

appariteur [apaʀitœʀ] *nm* attendant, porter (in French universities).

apparition [apaʀisjɔ̃] *nf* appearance; (surnaturelle) apparition.

appartement [apaʀtəmɑ̃] *nm* flat (Brit), apartment (US).

appartenir [apaʀtəniʀ]: ~ à *vt* to belong to; il lui appartient de it is up to him to, it is his duty to.

apparu, e *pp* de **apparaître**.

appât [apɑ] *nm* (PÊCHE) bait; (fig) lure, bait.

appauvrir [apovʀiʀ] *vt* to impoverish.

appel [apɛl] *nm* call; (nominal) roll call; (: SCOL) register; (MIL: recrutement) call-up; faire ~ à (invoquer) to appeal to; (avoir recours à) to call on; (nécessiter) to call for, require; faire ~ (JUR) to appeal; faire l'~ to call the roll; to call the register; sans ~ (fig) final, irrevocable; ~ d'offres (COMM) invitation to tender; faire un ~ de phares to flash one's headlights; ~ (téléphonique) (tele)phone call.

appelé [aple] *nm* (MIL) conscript.

appeler [aple] *vt* to call; (faire venir: médecin etc) to call, send for; (fig: nécessiter) to call for, demand; être appelé à (fig) to be destined to; ~ qn à comparaître (JUR) to summon sb to appear; en ~ à to appeal to; **s'~**: elle s'appelle Gabrielle her name is Gabrielle, she's called Gabrielle; comment ça s'appelle? what is it called?

appendice [apɛ̃dis] *nm* appendix; **appendicite** *nf* appendicitis.

appentis [apɑ̃ti] *nm* lean-to.

appesantir [apzɑ̃tiʀ]: **s'~** *vi* to grow heavier; **s'~ sur** (fig) to dwell on.

appétissant, e [apetisɑ̃, -ɑ̃t] *a* appetizing, mouth-watering.

appétit [apeti] *nm* appetite; bon ~! enjoy your meal!

applaudir [aplodiʀ] *vt* to applaud // *vi* to applaud, clap; **applaudissements** *nmpl* applause *sg*, clapping *sg*.

application [aplikasjɔ̃] *nf* application.

applique [aplik] *nf* wall lamp.

appliquer [aplike] *vt* to apply; (loi) to

enforce; **s'~** *vi (élève etc)* to apply o.s.

appoint [apwɛ̃] *nm* (extra) contribution *ou* help; **avoir/faire l'~** *(en payant)* to have/give the right change *ou* money; **chauffage d'~** extra heating.

appointements [apwɛ̃tmɑ̃] *nmpl* salary *sg.*

appontement [apɔ̃tmɑ̃] *nm* landing stage, wharf.

apport [apɔʀ] *nm* supply; contribution.

apporter [apɔʀte] *vt* to bring.

apposer [apoze] *vt* to append; to affix.

apprécier [apʀesje] *vt* to appreciate; *(évaluer)* to estimate, assess.

appréhender [apʀeɑ̃de] *vt (craindre)* to dread; *(arrêter)* to apprehend.

apprendre [apʀɑ̃dʀ(ə)] *vt* to learn; *(événement, résultats)* to learn of, hear of; **~ qch à qn** *(informer)* to tell sb (of) sth; *(enseigner)* to teach sb sth; **~ à faire qch** to learn to do sth; **~ à qn à faire qch** to teach sb to do sth; **appren- ti, e** *nm/f* apprentice; *(fig)* novice, beginner; **apprentissage** *nm* learning; *(COMM, SCOL: période)* apprenticeship.

apprêté, e [apʀete] *a (fig)* affected.

apprêter [apʀete] *vt* to dress, finish.

appris, e *pp* de **apprendre.**

apprivoiser [apʀivwaze] *vt* to tame.

approbation [apʀɔbasjɔ̃] *nf* approval.

approche [apʀɔʃ] *nf* approaching; approach.

approcher [apʀɔʃe] *vi* to approach, come near // *vt* to approach; *(rapprocher):* **~ qch (de qch)** to bring *ou* put sth near (to sth); **~ de** *vt* to draw near to; *(quantité, moment)* to approach; **s'~ de** *vt* to approach, go *ou* come near to.

approfondir [apʀɔfɔ̃diʀ] *vt* to deepen; *(question)* to go further into.

approprié, e [apʀɔpʀije] *a:* **~ (à)** appropriate (to), suited to.

approprier [apʀɔpʀije]: **s'~** *vt* to appropriate, take over.

approuver [apʀuve] *vt* to agree with; *(autoriser: loi, projet)* to approve, pass; *(trouver louable)* to approve of.

approvisionner [apʀɔvizjɔne] *vt* to supply; *(compte bancaire)* to pay funds into; **s'~ en** to stock up with.

approximatif, ive [apʀɔksimatif, -iv] *a* approximate, rough; vague.

appt *abr de* **appartement.**

appui [apɥi] *nm* support; **prendre ~ sur** to lean on; to rest on; **l'~ de la fenêtre** the windowsill, the window ledge; **appui-tête, appuie-tête** *nm inv* headrest.

appuyer [apɥije] *vt (poser):* **~ qch sur/ contre** to lean *ou* rest sth on/against; *(soutenir: personne, demande)* to support, back (up) // *vi:* **~ sur** *(bouton,*

frein) to press, push; *(mot, détail)* to stress, emphasize; *(suj: chose: peser sur)* to rest (heavily) on, press against; **s'~ sur** *vt* to lean on; to rely on; **~ à droite** to bear (to the) right.

âpre [ɑpʀ(ə)] *a* acrid, pungent; *(fig)* harsh; bitter; **~ au gain** grasping.

après [apʀe] *prép* after // *ad* afterwards; **2 heures ~** 2 hours later; **~ qu'il est** *ou* **soit parti/avoir fait** after he left/having done; **d'~** *prép (selon)* according to; **~ coup** *ad* after the event, afterwards; **~ tout** *ad (au fond)* after all; **et (puis) ~?** so what?; **~-demain** *ad* the day after tomorrow; **~-guerre** *nm* post-war years *pl;* **~-midi** *nm ou nf inv* afternoon.

à-propos [apʀopo] *nm (d'une remar- que)* aptness; **faire preuve d'~** to show presence of mind.

apte [apt(ə)] *a* capable; *(MIL)* fit.

aquarelle [akwaʀɛl] *nf (tableau)* water-colour; *(genre)* watercolours *pl.*

aquarium [akwaʀjɔm] *nm* aquarium.

arabe [aʀab] *a* Arabic; *(désert, cheval)* Arabian; *(nation, peuple)* Arab // *nm/f:* **A~** Arab // *nm (LING)* Arabic.

Arabie [aʀabi] *nf:* **l'~ (Saoudite)** Saudi Arabia.

arachide [aʀaʃid] *nf (plante)* groundnut (plant); *(graine)* peanut, groundnut.

araignée [aʀeɲe] *nf* spider.

arbitraire [aʀbitʀɛʀ] *a* arbitrary.

arbitre [aʀbitʀ(ə)] *nm (SPORT)* referee; *(: TENNIS, CRICKET)* umpire; *(fig)* arbiter, judge; *(JUR)* arbitrator; **arbitrer** *vt* to referee; to umpire; to arbitrate.

arborer [aʀbɔʀe] *vt* to bear, display.

arbre [aʀbʀ(ə)] *nm* tree; *(TECH)* shaft; **~ généalogique** family tree; **~ de transmission** *(AUTO)* driveshaft.

arbuste [aʀbyst(ə)] *nm* small shrub.

arc [aʀk] *nm (arme)* bow; *(GÉOM)* arc; *(ARCHIT)* arch; **en ~ de cercle** *a* semi-circular.

arcade [aʀkad] *nf* arch(way); **~s** arcade *sg,* arches.

arcanes [aʀkan] *nmpl* mysteries.

arc-boutant [aʀkbutɑ̃] *nm* flying buttress.

arc-bouter [aʀkbute]: **s'~** *vi:* **s'~ contre** to lean *ou* press against.

arceau, x [aʀso] *nm (métallique etc)* hoop.

arc-en-ciel [aʀkɑ̃sjɛl] *nm* rainbow.

arche [aʀʃ(ə)] *nf* arch; **~ de Noé** Noah's Ark.

archéologie [aʀkeɔlɔʒi] *nf* archeology; **archéologue** *nm/f* archeologist.

archet [aʀʃɛ] *nm* bow.

archevêque [aʀʃəvɛk] *nm* archbishop.

archipel [aʀʃipɛl] *nm* archipelago.

architecte [aʀʃitɛkt(ə)] *nm* architect.

architecture [aʀʃitɛktyʀ] *nf* architecture.

archive [aʁʃiv] *nf* file; ~s *nfpl* archives.

arctique [aaktik] *a* Arctic // *nm*: **l'A~** the Arctic.

ardemment [aʁdamɑ̃] *ad* ardently, fervently.

ardent, e [aʁdɑ̃, -ɑ̃t] *a* (*soleil*) blazing; (*fièvre*) raging; (*amour*) ardent, passionate; (*prière*) fervent.

ardoise [aʁdwaz] *nf* slate.

ardt *abr de* **arrondissement**.

arène [aʁɛn] *nf* arena; ~s *nfpl* bull-ring *sg*.

arête [aʁɛt] *nf* (*de poisson*) bone; (*d'une montagne*) ridge; (*GÉOM etc*) edge.

argent [aʁʒɑ̃] *nm* (*métal*) silver; (*monnaie*) money; ~ **liquide** ready money, (ready) cash; ~ **de poche** pocket money; **argenterie** *nf* silverware; silver plate.

argentin, e [aʁʒɑ̃tɛ̃, -in] *a* (*son*) silvery; (*d'Argentine*) Argentinian, Argentine.

Argentine [aʁʒɑ̃tin] *nf*: **l'~** Argentina, the Argentine.

argile [aʁʒil] *nf* clay.

argot [aʁgo] *nm* slang; **argotique** *a* slang *cpd*; slangy.

arguer [aʁgɥe]: ~ **de** *vt* to put forward as a pretext *ou* reason.

argument [aʁgymɑ̃] *nm* argument.

argumentaire [aʁgymɑ̃tɛʁ] *nm* sales leaflet.

argumenter [aʁgymɑ̃te] *vi* to argue.

argus [aʁgys] *nm* guide to second-hand car etc prices.

arguties [aʁgysi] *nfpl* quibbles.

aristocratique [aʁistɔkʁatik] *a* aristocratic.

arithmétique [aʁitmetik] *a* arithmetic(al) // *nf* arithmetic.

armateur [aʁmatœʁ] *nm* shipowner.

armature [aʁmatyʁ] *nf* framework; (*de tente etc*) frame.

arme [aʁm(ə)] *nf* weapon; (*section de l'armée*) arm; ~s *nfpl* weapons, arms; (*blason*) (coat of) arms; ~ **à feu** firearm.

armée [aʁme] *nf* army; ~ **de l'air** Air Force; **l'~ du Salut** the Salvation Army; ~ **de terre** Army.

armement [aʁməmɑ̃] *nm* (*matériel*) arms *pl*, weapons *pl*; (: *d'un pays*) arms *pl*, armament.

armer [aʁme] *vt* to arm; (*arme à feu*) to cock; (*appareil-photo*) to wind on; ~ **qch de** to fit sth with; to reinforce sth with.

armistice [aʁmistis] *nm* armistice; **l'A~** ≈ Remembrance (*Brit*) *ou* Veterans (*US*) Day.

armoire [aʁmwaʁ] *nf* (tall) cupboard; (*penderie*) wardrobe (*Brit*), closet (*US*).

armoiries [aʁmwaʁi] *nfpl* coat *sg* of arms.

armure [aʁmyʁ] *nf* armour *q*, suit of armour.

armurier [aʁmyʁje] *nm* gunsmith;

armourer.

arnaquer [aʁnake] *vt* to swindle.

aromates [aʁɔmat] *nmpl* seasoning *sg*, herbs (and spices).

aromatisé, e [aʁɔmatize] *a* flavoured.

arôme [aʁom] *nm* aroma; fragrance.

arpenter [aʁpɑ̃te] *vt* (*salle, couloir*) to pace up and down.

arpenteur [aʁpɑ̃tœʁ] *nm* surveyor.

arqué, e [aʁke] *a* bandy; arched.

arrache-pied [aʁaʃpje]: **d'~** *ad* relentlessly.

arracher [aʁaʃe] *vt* to pull out; (*page etc*) to tear off, tear out; (*légumes, herbe*) to pull up; (*bras etc*) to tear off; ~ **qch à qn** to snatch sth from sb; (*fig*) to wring sth out of sb; **s'~** *vt* (*article recherché*) to fight over.

arraisonner [aʁɛzɔne] *vt* (*bateau*) to board and search.

arrangeant, e [aʁɑ̃ʒɑ̃, -ɑ̃t] *a* accommodating, obliging.

arranger [aʁɑ̃ʒe] *vt* (*gén*) to arrange; (*réparer*) to fix, put right; (*régler*) to settle, sort out; (*convenir à*) to suit, be convenient for; **s'~** (*se mettre d'accord*) to come to an agreement; **je vais m'~** I'll manage; **ça va s'~** it'll sort itself out.

arrestation [aʁɛstasjɔ̃] *nf* arrest.

arrêt [aʁɛ] *nm* stopping; (*de bus etc*) stop; (*JUR*) judgment, decision; **rester** *ou* **tomber en** ~ **devant** to stop short in front of; **sans** ~ non-stop; continually; ~ **de mort** capital sentence; ~ **de travail** stoppage (of work).

arrêté [aʁete] *nm* order, decree.

arrêter [aʁete] *vt* to stop; (*chauffage etc*) to turn off, switch off; (*fixer: date etc*) to appoint, decide on; (*criminel, suspect*) to arrest; ~ **de faire** to stop doing; **s'~** *vi* to stop.

arrhes [aʁ] *nfpl* deposit *sg*.

arrière [aʁjɛʁ] *nm* back; (*SPORT*) fullback // *a inv*: **siège/roue** ~ back *ou* rear seat/wheel; **à l'~** *ad* behind, at the back; **en** ~ *ad* behind; (*regarder*) back, behind; (*tomber, aller*) backwards; **arriéré, e** *a* (*péj*) backward // *nm* (*d'argent*) arrears *pl*; ~**-goût** *nm* aftertaste; ~**-grand-mère** *nf* greatgrandmother; ~**-grand-père** *nm* greatgrandfather; ~**-pays** *nm inv* hinterland; ~**-pensée** *nf* ulterior motive; mental reservation; ~**-plan** *nm* background; ~**-saison** *nf* late autumn; ~**-train** *nm* hindquarters *pl*.

arrimer [aʁime] *vt* to stow; to secure.

arrivage [aʁivaʒ] *nm* arrival.

arrivée [aʁive] *nf* arrival; (*ligne d'arrivée*) finish; ~ **d'air/de gaz** air/gas inlet.

arriver [aʁive] *vi* to arrive; (*survenir*) to happen, occur; **il arrive à Paris à 8h** he gets to *ou* arrives in Paris at 8; ~ **à** (*at-*

teindre) to reach; ~ **à faire qch** to succeed in doing sth; **il arrive que** it happens that; **il lui arrive de faire** he sometimes does; **arriviste** *nm/f* go-getter.

arrogant, e [aʀɔgɑ̃, -ɑ̃t] *a* arrogant.

arroger [aʀɔʒe]: **s'~** *vt* to assume (without right).

arrondir [aʀɔ̃diʀ] *vt* (*forme, objet*) to round; (*somme*) to round off; **s'~** *vi* to become round(ed).

arrondissement [aʀɔ̃dismɑ̃] *nm* (*ADMIN*) ≈ district.

arroser [aʀoze] *vt* to water; (*victoire*) to celebrate (over a drink); (*CULIN*) to baste; **arrosoir** *nm* watering can.

arsenal, aux [aʀsənal, -o] *nm* (*NAVIG*) naval dockyard; (*MIL*) arsenal; (*fig*) gear, paraphernalia.

art [aʀ] *nm* art; ~**s ménagers** home economics *sg*.

artère [aʀtɛʀ] *nf* (*ANAT*) artery; (*rue*) main road.

arthrite [aʀtʀit] *nf* arthritis.

artichaut [aʀtiʃo] *nm* artichoke.

article [aʀtikl(ə)] *nm* article; (*COMM*) item, article; **à l'~ de la mort** at the point of death; ~ **de fond** (*PRESSE*) feature article.

articulation [aʀtikylasjɔ̃] *nf* articulation; (*ANAT*) joint.

articuler [aʀtikyle] *vt* to articulate.

artifice [aʀtifis] *nm* device, trick.

artificiel, le [aʀtifisjɛl] *a* artificial.

artificieux, euse [aʀtifisjø, -øz] *a* guileful, deceitful.

artisan [aʀtizɑ̃] *nm* artisan, (*self-employed*) craftsman; **artisanal, e, aux** *a* of *ou* made by craftsmen; (*péj*) cottage industry *cpd*, unsophisticated; **artisanat** *nm* arts and crafts *pl*.

artiste [aʀtist(ə)] *nm/f* artist; (*de variétés*) entertainer; performer; **artistique** *a* artistic.

as [a] *vb voir* **avoir** // *nm* [ɑs] ace.

ascendance [asɑ̃dɑ̃s] *nf* (*origine*) ancestry.

ascendant, e [asɑ̃dɑ̃, -ɑ̃t] *a* upward // *nm* influence.

ascenseur [asɑ̃sœʀ] *nm* lift (*Brit*), elevator (*US*).

ascension [asɑ̃sjɔ̃] *nf* ascent; climb; **l'A~** (*REL*) the Ascension.

aseptiser [asɛptize] *vt* to sterilize; to disinfect.

asiatique [azjatik] *a, nm/f* Asiatic, Asian.

Asie [azi] *nf*: **l'~** Asia.

asile [azil] *nm* (*refuge*) refuge, sanctuary; (*POL*): **droit d'~** (*political*) asylum; (*pour malades etc*) home.

aspect [aspɛ] *nm* appearance, look; (*fig*) aspect, side; **à l'~ de** at the sight of.

asperge [aspɛʀʒ(ə)] *nf* asparagus *q*.

asperger [aspɛʀʒe] *vt* to spray, sprinkle.

aspérité [aspeʀite] *nf* excrescence, protruding bit (of rock *etc*).

asphalte [asfalt(ə)] *nm* asphalt.

asphyxier [asfiksje] *vt* to suffocate, asphyxiate; (*fig*) to stifle.

aspirateur [aspiʀatœʀ] *nm* vacuum cleaner.

aspirer [aspiʀe] *vt* (*air*) to inhale; (*liquide*) to suck (up); (*suj: appareil*) to suck up; ~ **à** *vt* to aspire to.

aspirine [aspiʀin] *nf* aspirin.

assagir [asaʒiʀ] *vt*, **s'~** *vi* to quieten down, sober down.

assaillir [asajiʀ] *vt* to assail, attack.

assainir [aseniʀ] *vt* to clean up; to purify.

assaisonner [asɛzɔne] *vt* to season.

assassin [asasɛ̃] *nm* murderer; assassin.

assassiner [asasine] *vt* to murder; (*esp POL*) to assassinate.

assaut [aso] *nm* assault, attack; **prendre d'~** to storm, assault; **donner l'~** to attack; **faire ~ de** (*rivaliser*) to vie with each other in.

assécher [aseʃe] *vt* to drain.

assemblée [asɑ̃ble] *nf* (*réunion*) meeting; (*public, assistance*) gathering; assembled people; (*POL*) assembly.

assembler [asɑ̃ble] *vt* (*joindre, monter*) to assemble, put together; (*amasser*) to gather (together), collect (together); **s'~** *vi* to gather.

assener, asséner [asene] *vt*: ~ **un coup à qn** to deal sb a blow.

assentiment [asɑ̃timɑ̃] *nm* assent, consent; approval.

asseoir [aswaʀ] *vt* (*malade, bébé*) to sit up; to sit down; (*autorité, réputation*) to establish; **s'~** *vi* to sit (o.s.) down.

assermenté, e [asɛʀmɑ̃te] *a* sworn, on oath.

asservir [asɛʀviʀ] *vt* to subjugate, enslave.

asseye *etc vb voir* **asseoir**.

assez [ase] *ad* (*suffisamment*) enough, sufficiently; (*passablement*) rather, quite, fairly; ~ **de pain/livres** enough *ou* sufficient bread/books; **vous en avez ~?** have you got enough?

assidu, e [asidy] *a* assiduous, painstaking; regular; **assiduités** *nfpl* assiduous attentions.

assied *etc vb voir* **asseoir**.

assiéger [asjeʒe] *vt* to besiege.

assiérai *etc vb voir* **asseoir**.

assiette [asjɛt] *nf* plate; (*contenu*) plate(ful); ~ **anglaise** assorted cold meats; ~ **creuse** (soup) dish, soup plate; ~ **à dessert** dessert plate; ~ **de l'impôt** basis of (tax) assessment; ~ **plate** (dinner) plate.

assigner [asiɲe] *vt*: ~ **qch à** (*poste, part, travail*) to assign sth to; (*limites*) to set sth to; (*cause, effet*) to ascribe sth to; ~ **qn à** to assign sb to.

assimiler [asimile] *vt* to assimilate, absorb; (*comparer*): ~ qch/qn à to liken *ou* compare sth/sb to; s'~ *vi* (*s'intégrer*) to be assimilated *ou* absorbed.

assis, e [asi, -iz] *pp de* asseoir // *a* sitting (down), seated // *nf* (*fig*) basis (*pl* bases), foundation; ~es *nfpl* (*JUR*) assizes; (*congrès*) (annual) conference.

assistance [asistãs] *nf* (*public*) audience; (*aide*) assistance.

assistant, e [asistã, -ãt] *nm/f* assistant; (*d'université*) probationary lecturer; les ~s *nmpl* (*auditeurs etc*) those present; ~e sociale social worker.

assisté, e [asiste] *a* (*AUTO*) power assisted.

assister [asiste] *vt* to assist; ~ à *vt* (*scène, événement*) to witness; (*conférence, séminaire*) to attend, be at; (*spectacle, match*) to be at, see.

association [asɔsjasjɔ̃] *nf* association.

associé, e [asɔsje] *nm/f* associate; partner.

associer [asɔsje] *vt* to associate; ~ qn à (*profits*) to give sb a share of; (*affaire*) to make sb a partner in; (*joie, triomphe*) to include sb in; ~ qch à (*joindre, allier*) to combine sth with; s'~ (*suj pl*) to join together; (*COMM*) to form a partnership; s'~ *vt* (*collaborateur*) to take on (as a partner); s'~ à qn pour faire to join (forces) with sb to do; s'~ à to be combined with; (*opinions, joie de qn*) to share in.

assoiffé, e [aswafe] *a* thirsty.

assombrir [asɔ̃bʀiʀ] *vt* to darken; (*fig*) to fill with gloom.

assommer [asɔme] *vt* to batter to death; (*étourdir, abrutir*) to knock out; to stun.

Assomption [asɔ̃psjɔ̃] *nf*: l'~ the Assumption.

assorti, e [asɔʀti] *a* matched, matching; (*varié*) assorted; ~ à matching.

assortiment [asɔʀtimã] *nm* assortment, selection.

assortir [asɔʀtiʀ] *vt* to match; ~ qch à to match sth with; ~ qch de to accompany sth with; s'~ de to be accompanied by.

assoupi, e [asupi] *a* dozing, sleeping; (*fig*) (be)numbed; dulled; stilled.

assouplir [asupliʀ] *vt* to make supple; (*fig*) to relax.

assourdir [asuʀdiʀ] *vt* (*bruit*) to deaden, muffle; (*suj: bruit*) to deafen.

assouvir [asuviʀ] *vt* to satisfy, appease.

assujettir [asyʒetiʀ] *vt* to subject.

assumer [asyme] *vt* (*fonction, emploi*) to assume, take on.

assurance [asyʀãs] *nf* (*certitude*) assurance; (*confiance en soi*) (self-)confidence; (*contrat*) insurance (policy); (*secteur commercial*) insurance; ~ maladie health insurance; ~ tous risques (*AUTO*) comprehensive insurance; ~s

sociales ≈ National Insurance (*Brit*), ≈ Social Security (*US*); ~-vie *nf* life assurance *ou* insurance.

assuré, e [asyʀe] *a* (*certain*): ~ de confident of // *nm/f* insured (person); ~ment *ad* assuredly, most certainly.

assurer [asyʀe] *vt* to insure; (*stabiliser*) to steady; to stabilize; (*victoire etc*) to ensure; (*frontières, pouvoir*) to make secure; (*service, garde*) to provide; to operate; ~ qch à qn (*garantir*) to secure sth for sb; (*certifier*) to assure sb of sth; ~ à qn que to assure sb that; ~ qn de to assure sb of; s'~ (*contre*) (*COMM*) to insure o.s. (against); s'~ de/que (*vérifier*) to make sure of/that; s'~ (de) (*aide de qn*) to secure.

asthme [asm(ə)] *nm* asthma.

asticot [astiko] *nm* maggot.

astiquer [astike] *vt* to polish, shine.

astre [astʀ(ə)] *nm* star.

astreignant, e [astʀeɲã, -ãt] *a* demanding.

astreindre [astʀɛ̃dʀ(ə)] *vt*: ~ qn à qch to force sth upon sb; ~ qn à faire to compel *ou* force sb to do.

astrologie [astʀɔlɔʒi] *nf* astrology.

astronaute [astʀɔnot] *nm/f* astronaut.

astronomie [astʀɔnɔmi] *nf* astronomy.

astuce [astys] *nf* shrewdness, astuteness; (*truc*) trick, clever way; (*plaisanterie*) wisecrack; **astucieux, euse** *a* clever.

atelier [atəlje] *nm* workshop; (*de peintre*) studio.

athée [ate] *a* atheistic // *nm/f* atheist.

Athènes [atɛn] *n* Athens.

athlète [atlɛt] *nm/f* (*SPORT*) athlete; **athlétisme** *nm* athletics sg.

atlantique [atlɑ̃tik] *a* Atlantic // *nm*: l'(océan) A~ the Atlantic (Ocean).

atlas [atlɑs] *nm* atlas.

atmosphère [atmɔsfɛʀ] *nf* atmosphere.

atome [atom] *nm* atom; **atomique** *a* atomic, nuclear; (*nombre, masse*) atomic.

atomiseur [atomizœʀ] *nm* atomizer.

atone [atɔn] *a* lifeless.

atours [atuʀ] *nmpl* attire *sg*, finery *sg*.

atout [atu] *nm* trump; (*fig*) asset; trump card.

âtre [ɑtʀ(ə)] *nm* hearth.

atroce [atʀɔs] *a* atrocious.

attabler [atable]: s'~ *vi* to sit down at (the) table.

attachant, e [ataʃã, -ãt] *a* engaging, lovable, likeable.

attache [ataʃ] *nf* clip, fastener; (*fig*) tie.

attacher [ataʃe] *vt* to tie up; (*étiquette*) to attach, tie on; (*souliers*) to do up // *vi* (*poêle, riz*) to stick; s'~ à (*par affection*) to become attached to; s'~ à faire to endeavour to do; ~ qch à to tie *ou* attach sth to.

attaque [atak] *nf* attack; (*cérébrale*) stroke; (*d'épilepsie*) fit.

attaquer [atake] vt to attack; (en justice) to bring an action against, sue; (travail) to tackle, set about // vi to attack.

attardé, e [atarde] a (passants) late; (enfant) backward; (conceptions) old-fashioned.

attarder [atarde]: s'~ vi to linger; to stay on.

atteindre [atɛ̃dʀ(ə)] vt to reach; (blesser) to hit; (émouvoir) to affect.

atteint, e [atɛ̃, -ɛ̃t] a (MÉD): être ~ de to be suffering from // nf attack; hors d'~e out of reach; porter ~e à to strike a blow at; to undermine.

atteler [atle] vt (cheval, bœufs) to hitch up; (wagons) to couple; s'~ à (travail) to buckle down to.

attelle [atɛl] nf splint.

attenant, e [atnã, -ãt] a: ~ (à) adjoining.

attendre [atãdʀ(ə)] vt (gén) to wait for; (être destiné ou réservé à) to await, be in store for // vi to wait; s'~ à (ce que) to expect (that); ~ un enfant to be expecting a baby; ~ de faire/d'être to wait until one does/is; ~ que to wait until; ~ qch de to expect sth of; en attendant ad meanwhile, in the meantime; be that as it may.

attendrir [atãdʀiʀ] vt to move (to pity); (viande) to tenderize.

attendu, e [atãdy] a (visiteur) expected; ~ que cj considering that, since.

attentat [atãta] nm assassination attempt; ~ à la bombe bomb attack; ~ à la pudeur indecent exposure q; indecent assault q.

attente [atãt] nf wait; (espérance) expectation.

attenter [atãte]: ~ à vt (liberté) to violate; ~ à la vie de qn to make an attempt on sb's life.

attentif, ive [atãtif, -iv] a (auditeur) attentive; (travail) scrupulous; careful; ~ à mindful of; careful to.

attention [atãsjɔ̃] nf attention; (prévenance) attention, thoughtfulness q; à l'~ de for the attention of; faire ~ (à) to be careful (of); faire ~ (à ce) que to be ou make sure that; ~! careful!, watch out!; **attentionné, e** a thoughtful, considerate.

atténuer [atenɥe] vt to alleviate, ease; to lessen.

atterrer [atere] vt to dismay, appal.

atterrir [ateriʀ] vt to land; **atterrissage** nm landing.

attestation [atɛstasjɔ̃] nf certificate.

attester [atɛste] vt to testify to.

attirail [atiraj] nm gear; (péj) paraphernalia.

attirant, e [atirã, -ãt] a attractive, appealing.

attirer [atiʀe] vt to attract; (appâter) to

lure, entice; ~ qn dans un coin/vers soi to draw sb into a corner/towards one; ~ l'attention de qn (sur) to attract sb's attention (to); to draw sb's attention (to); s'~ des ennuis to bring trouble upon o.s., get into trouble.

attiser [atize] vt (feu) to poke (up).

attitré, e [atitre] a qualified; accredited; appointed.

attitude [atityd] nf attitude; (position du corps) bearing.

attouchements [atuʃmã] nmpl touching sg; (sexuels) fondling sg.

attraction [atraksjɔ̃] nf (gén) attraction; (de cabaret, cirque) number.

attrait [atrɛ] nm appeal, attraction; lure.

attrape-nigaud [atrapnigo] nm con.

attraper [atrape] vt (gén) to catch; (habitude, amende) to get, pick up; (fam: duper) to con.

attrayant, e [atrɛjã, -ãt] a attractive.

attribuer [atribɥe] vt (prix) to award; (rôle, tâche) to allocate, assign; (imputer): ~ qch à to attribute sth to; s'~ vt (s'approprier) to claim for o.s.

attribut [atriby] nm attribute; (LING) complement.

attrister [atriste] vt to sadden.

attroupement [atrupmã] nm crowd, mob.

attrouper [atrupe]: s'~ vi to gather.

au [o] prép + dét voir à.

aubade [obad] nf dawn serenade.

aubaine [obɛn] nf godsend; (financière) windfall.

aube [ob] nf dawn, daybreak; à l'~ at dawn ou daybreak.

aubépine [obepin] nf hawthorn.

auberge [obɛʀʒ(ə)] nf inn; ~ de jeunesse youth hostel.

aubergine [obɛʀʒin] nf aubergine.

aubergiste [obɛʀʒist(ə)] nm/f innkeeper, hotel-keeper.

aucun, e [okœ̃, -yn] dét no, tournure négative + any; (positif) any // pronom none, tournure négative + any; any(one); sans ~ doute without any doubt; plus qu'~ autre more than any other; ~ des deux neither of the two; ~ d'entre eux none of them; d'~s (certains) some; **aucunement** ad in no way, not in the least.

audace [odas] nf daring, boldness; (péj) audacity; **audacieux, euse** a daring, bold.

au-delà [odla] ad beyond // nm: l'~ the hereafter; ~ de prép beyond.

au-dessous [odsu] ad underneath; below; ~ de prép under(neath); below; (limite, somme etc) below, under; (dignité, condition) below.

au-dessus [odsy] ad above; ~ de prép above.

au-devant [odvã]: ~ de prép: aller ~

de (*personne, danger*) to go (out) and meet; (*souhaits de qn*) to anticipate.
audience [odjɑ̃s] *nf* audience; (*JUR: séance*) hearing.
audio-visuel, le [odjovizɥɛl] *a* audio-visual.
auditeur, trice [oditœʀ, -tʀis] *nm/f* listener.
audition [odisjɔ̃] *nf* (*ouïe, écoute*) hearing; (*JUR: de témoins*) examination; (*MUS, THÉÂTRE: épreuve*) audition.
auditoire [oditwaʀ] *nm* audience.
auge [oʒ] *nf* trough.
augmentation [ɔgmɑ̃tɑsjɔ̃] *nf*: ~ (de salaire) rise (in salary) (*Brit*), (pay) raise (*US*).
augmenter [ɔgmɑ̃te] *vt* (*gén*) to increase; (*salaire, prix*) to increase, raise, put up; (*employé*) to increase the salary of // *vi* to increase.
augure [ɔgyʀ] *nm* soothsayer, oracle; de bon/mauvais ~ of good/ill omen.
augurer [ɔgyʀe] *vt*: ~ bien de to augur well for.
aujourd'hui [oʒuʀdɥi] *ad* today.
aumône [omon] *nf* alms *sg* (*pl inv*); faire l'~ (à qn) to give alms (to sb).
aumônier [omonje] *nm* chaplain.
auparavant [opaʀavɑ̃] *ad* before(hand).
auprès [opʀɛ]: ~ de *prép* next to, close to; (*recourir, s'adresser*) to; (*en comparaison de*) compared with.
auquel [okɛl] *prép* + *pronom voir* **lequel**.
aurai *etc vb voir* **avoir**.
auréole [ɔʀeɔl] *nf* halo; (*tache*) ring.
auriculaire [ɔʀikylɛʀ] *nm* little finger.
aurons *etc vb voir* **avoir**.
aurore [ɔʀɔʀ] *nf* dawn, daybreak.
ausculter [oskylte] *vt* to sound.
aussi [osi] *ad* (*également*) also, too; (*de comparaison*) as // *cj* therefore, consequently; ~ **fort que** as strong as; **moi** ~ me too; ~ **bien que** (*de même que*) as well as.
aussitôt [osito] *ad* straight away, immediately; ~ **que** as soon as.
austère [ostɛʀ] *a* austere; stern.
austral, e [ostʀal] *a* southern.
Australie [ostʀali] *nf*: l'~ Australia; **australien, ne** *a*, *nm/f* Australian.
autant [otɑ̃] *ad* so much; (*comparatif*): ~ (**que**) as much (as); (*nombre*) as many (as); ~ (**de**) so much (*ou* many); as much (*ou* many); ~ **partir** we (*ou* you *etc*) may as well leave; ~ **dire que...** one might as well say that...; **pour** ~ for all that; **pour** ~ **que** *cj* assuming, as long as; **d'**~ **plus/mieux (que)** all the more/ the better (since).
autel [otɛl] *nm* altar.
auteur [otœʀ] *nm* author.
authentique [otɑ̃tik] *a* authentic, genuine.
auto [oto] *nf* car.

auto... [oto] *préfixe* auto..., self-; ~**biographie** *nf* autobiography.
autobus [otobys] *nm* bus.
autocar [otokaʀ] *nm* coach.
autochtone [otoktɔn] *nm/f* native.
auto-collant, e [otokɔlɑ̃, -ɑ̃t] *a* self-adhesive; (*enveloppe*) self-seal // *nm* sticker.
auto-couchettes [otokuʃɛt] *a*: **train** ~ car sleeper train.
autocuiseur [otokɥizœʀ] *nm* pressure cooker.
autodéfense [otodefɑ̃s] *nf* self-defence; **groupe d'**~ vigilante committee.
autodidacte [otodidakt(ə)] *nm/f* self-taught person.
auto-école [otoekɔl] *nf* driving school.
autogestion [otoʒɛstjɔ̃] *nf* self-management.
autographe [otogʀaf] *nm* autograph.
auto- mate [otomat] *nm* (*machine*) (automatic) machine.
automatique [otomatik] *a* automatic // *nm*: l'~ direct dialling; ~**ment** *ad* automatically; **automatiser** *vt* to automate.
automne [otɔn] *nm* autumn (*Brit*), fall (*US*).
automobile [otomɔbil] *a* motor *cpd* // *nf* (motor) car; l'~ motoring; the car industry; **automobiliste** *nm/f* motorist.
autonome [otonɔm] *a* autonomous; **autonomie** *nf* autonomy; (*POL*) self-government, autonomy.
autopsie [otopsi] *nf* post-mortem (examination), autopsy.
autoradio [otoʀadjo] *nm* car radio.
autorisation [otoʀizasjɔ̃] *nf* permission, authorization; (*papiers*) permit.
autorisé, e [otoʀize] *a* (*opinion, sources*) authoritative.
autoriser [otoʀize] *vt* to give permission for, authorize; (*fig*) to allow (of), sanction.
autoritaire [otoʀitɛʀ] *a* authoritarian.
autorité [otoʀite] *nf* authority; **faire** ~ to be authoritative.
autoroute [otoʀut] *nf* motorway (*Brit*), highway (*US*).
auto-stop [otostɔp] *nm*: **faire de l'**~ to hitch-hike; ~**peur, euse** *nm/f* hitch-hiker.
autour [otuʀ] *ad* around; ~ **de** *prép* around; **tout** ~ *ad* all around.
autre [otʀ(ə)] ♦ *a* **1** (*différent*) other, different; **je préférerais un** ~ **verre** I'd prefer another *ou* a different glass
2 (*supplémentaire*) other; **je voudrais un** ~ **verre d'eau** I'd like another glass of water
3: ~ **chose** something else; ~ **part** *ad* somewhere else; **d'**~ **part** *ad* on the other hand
♦ *pronom*: **un** ~ another (one); **nous/vous** ~**s** us/you; **d'**~**s** others; l'~ the

other (one); **les ~s** the others; (*autrui*) others; **l'un et l'~** both of them; **se détester l'un l'~/les uns les ~s** to hate each other *ou* one another; **d'une semaine à l'~** from one week to the next; (*incessamment*) any week now; **entre ~s** among other things.

autrefois [otʀəfwa] *ad* in the past.

autrement [otʀəmã] *ad* differently; in another way; (*sinon*) otherwise; **~ dit** in other words.

Autriche [otʀiʃ] *nf*: **l'~** Austria; **autrichien, ne** *a*, *nm/f* Austrian.

autruche [otʀyʃ] *nf* ostrich.

autrui [otʀɥi] *pronom* others.

auvent [ovã] *nm* canopy.

aux [o] *prép* + *dét voir* **à**.

auxiliaire [ɔksiljɛʀ] *a*, *nm/f* auxiliary.

auxquels, auxquelles [okɛl] *prép* + *pronom voir* **lequel**.

av. *abr de* **avenue**.

avachi, e [avaʃi] *a* limp, flabby.

aval [aval] *nm* (*accord*) endorsement, backing; (*GÉO*) **en ~** downstream, downriver; (*sur une pente*) downhill.

avalanche [avalãʃ] *nf* avalanche.

avaler [avale] *vt* to swallow.

avance [avãs] *nf* (*de troupes etc*) advance; progress; (*d'argent*) advance; (*opposé à retard*) lead; being ahead of schedule; **~s** *nfpl* overtures; (*amoureuses*) advances; (**être**) **en ~** (to be) early; (*sur un programme*) (to be) ahead of schedule; **à l'~, d'~** in advance.

avancé, e [avãse] *a* advanced; well on *ou* under way.

avancement [avãsmã] *nm* (*professionnel*) promotion.

avancer [avãse] *vi* to move forward, advance; (*projet, travail*) to make progress; (*être en saillie*) to overhang; to jut out; (*montre, réveil*) to be fast; to gain // *vt* to move forward, advance; (*argent*) to advance; (*montre, pendule*) to put forward; **s'~** *vi* to move forward, advance; (*fig*) to commit o.s.; to overhang; to jut out.

avant [avã] *prép* before // *ad*: **trop/plus ~** too far/further forward // *a inv*: **siège/roue ~** front seat/wheel // *nm* (*d'un véhicule, bâtiment*) front; (*SPORT: joueur*) forward; **~ qu'il parte/de faire** before he leaves/doing; **~ tout** (*surtout*) above all; **à l'~** (*dans un véhicule*) in (the) front; **en ~** *ad* forward(s); **en ~ de** *prép* in front of.

avantage [avãtaʒ] *nm* advantage; **~s sociaux** fringe benefits; **avantager** *vt* (*favoriser*) to favour; (*embellir*) to flatter; **avantageux, euse** *a* attractive; attractively priced.

avant-bras [avãbʀa] *nm inv* forearm.

avant-dernier, ère [avãdɛʀnje, -ɛʀ] *a*, *nm/f* next to last, last but one.

avant-goût [avãgu] *nm* foretaste.

avant-hier [avãtjɛʀ] *ad* the day before yesterday.

avant-première [avãpʀəmjɛʀ] *nf* (*de film*) preview.

avant-projet [avãpʀɔʒɛ] *nm* (preliminary) draft.

avant-propos [avãpʀopo] *nm* foreword.

avant-veille [avãvɛj] *nf*: **l'~** two days before.

avare [avaʀ] *a* miserly, avaricious // *nm/f* miser; **~ de** (*compliments etc*) sparing of.

avarié, e [avaʀje] *a* rotting.

avaries [avaʀi] *nfpl* (*NAVIG*) damage *sg*.

avatar [avataʀ] *nm* misadventure.

avec [avɛk] *prép* with; (*à l'égard de*) to(wards), with.

avenant, e [avnã, -ãt] *a* pleasant; **à l'~** *ad* in keeping.

avènement [avɛnmã] *nm* (*d'un roi*) accession, succession; (*d'un changement*) advent, coming.

avenir [avniʀ] *nm* future; **à l'~** in future; **politicien d'~** politician with prospects *ou* a future.

Avent [avã] *nm*: **l'~** Advent.

aventure [avãtyʀ] *nf* adventure; (*amoureuse*) affair; **s'aventurer** *vi* to venture; **aventureux, euse** *a* adventurous, venturesome; (*projet*) risky, chancy.

avenue [avny] *nf* avenue.

avérer [aveʀe]: **s'~** *vb avec attribut* to prove (to be).

averse [avɛʀs(ə)] *nf* shower.

averti, e [avɛʀti] *a* (well-)informed.

avertir [avɛʀtiʀ] *vt*: **~ qn (de qch/que)** to warn sb (of sth/that); (*renseigner*) to inform sb (of sth/that); **avertissement** *nm* warning; **avertisseur** *nm* horn, siren.

aveu, x [avø] *nm* confession.

aveugle [avœgl(ə)] *a* blind; **aveuglément** *ad* blindly; **aveugler** *vt* to blind.

aviateur, trice [avjatœʀ, -tʀis] *nm/f* aviator, pilot.

aviation [avjasjɔ̃] *nf* aviation; (*sport*) flying; (*MIL*) air force.

avide [avid] *a* eager; (*péj*) greedy, grasping.

avilir [aviliʀ] *vt* to debase.

avion [avjɔ̃] *nm* (aero)plane (*Brit*), (air)plane (*US*); **aller (quelque part) en ~** to go (somewhere) by plane, fly (somewhere); **par ~** by airmail; **~ à réaction** jet (plane).

aviron [aviʀɔ̃] *nm* oar; (*sport*): **l'~** rowing.

avis [avi] *nm* opinion; (*notification*) notice; **changer d'~** to change one's mind; **jusqu'à nouvel ~** until further notice.

avisé, e [avize] *a* sensible, wise.

aviser [avize] *vt* (*voir*) to notice, catch sight of; (*informer*): ~ qn de/que to advise *ou* inform sb of/that // *vi* to think about things, assess the situation; s'~ de qch/que to become suddenly aware of sth/that; s'~ de faire to take it into one's head to do.

avocat, e [avɔka, -at] *nm/f* (*JUR*) barrister (*Brit*), lawyer // *nm* (*CULIN*) avocado (pear); ~ **général** assistant public prosecutor.

avoine [avwan] *nf* oats *pl*.

avoir [avwar] ♦ *nm* assets *pl*, resources *pl*; (*COMM*) credit

♦ *vt* **1** (*posséder*) to have; elle a 2 enfants/une belle maison she has (got) 2 children/a lovely house; il a les yeux bleus he has (got) blue eyes

2 (*âge, dimensions*) to be; il a 3 ans he is 3 (years old); le mur a 3 mètres de haut the wall is 3 metres high; *voir* faim, peur *etc*

3 (*fam: duper*) to do, have; on vous a eu! you've been done *ou* had!

4: en ~ contre qn to have a grudge against sb; en ~ assez to be fed up; j'en ai pour une demi-heure it'll take me half an hour

♦ *vb auxiliaire* **1** to have; ~ mangé/ dormi to have eaten/slept

2 (*avoir + à + inf*): ~ à faire qch to have to do sth; vous n'avez qu'à lui demander you only have to ask him

♦ *vb impersonnel* **1**: il y a (+ *sing*) there is; (+ *pl*) there are; qu'y-a-t-il?, qu'est-ce qu'il y a? what's the matter?, what is it?; il doit y ~ une explication there must be an explanation; il n'y a qu'à ... we (*ou* you *etc*) will just have to ...

2 (*temporel*): il y a 10 ans 10 years ago; il y a 10 ans/longtemps que je l'ai ... I've known it for 10 years/a long time; il y a 10 ans qu'il est arrivé it's 10 years since he arrived.

avoisiner [avwazine] *vt* to be near *ou* close to; (*fig*) to border *ou* verge on.

avortement [avɔrtəmɑ̃] *nm* abortion.

avorter [avɔrte] *vi* (*MÉD*) to have an abortion; (*fig*) to fail.

avoué, e [avwe] *a* avowed // *nm* (*JUR*) ≈ solicitor.

avouer [avwe] *vt* (*crime, défaut*) to confess (to); ~ avoir fait/que to admit *ou* confess to having done/that.

avril [avril] *nm* April.

axe [aks(ə)] *nm* axis (*pl* axes); (*de roue etc*) axle; (*fig*) main line; ~ **routier** trunk road, main road; **axer** *vt*: axer qch sur to centre sth on.

ayons *etc vb voir* avoir.

azote [azɔt] *nm* nitrogen.

B

babines [babin] *nfpl* chops.

babiole [babjɔl] *nf* (*bibelot*) trinket; (*vétille*) trifle.

bâbord [babɔr] *nm*: à *ou* par ~ to port, on the port side.

baby-foot [babifut] *nm* table football.

bac [bak] *abr m de* baccalauréat // *nm* (*bateau*) ferry; (*récipient*) tub; tray; tank.

baccalauréat [bakalɔrea] *nm* high school diploma.

bachelier, ière [baʃəlje, -jɛr] *nm/f* holder of the baccalauréat.

bâcher [baʃe] *vt* to cover (with a canvas sheet *ou* a tarpaulin).

bachot [baʃo] *abr m de* baccalauréat.

bachoter [baʃɔte] *vi* (*fam*) to cram (for an exam).

bâcler [bakle] *vt* to botch (up).

badaud, e [bado, -od] *nm/f* idle onlooker, stroller.

badigeonner [badiʒɔne] *vt* to distemper; to colourwash; (*barbouiller*) to daub.

badin, e [badɛ̃, -in] *a* playful.

badiner [badine] *vi*: ~ avec qch to treat sth lightly.

badminton [badmintɔn] *nm* badminton.

baffe [baf] *nf* (*fam*) slap, clout.

bafouer [bafwe] *vt* to deride, ridicule.

bafouiller [bafuje] *vi, vt* to stammer.

bagage [bagaʒ] *nm*: ~s luggage *sg*; ~s à main hand-luggage.

bagarre [bagar] *nf* fight, brawl; **se bagarrer** *vi* to have a fight *ou* scuffle, fight.

bagatelle [bagatɛl] *nf* trifle.

bagne [baɲ] *nm* penal colony.

bagnole [baɲɔl] *nf* (*fam*) car.

bagout [bagu] *nm*: avoir du ~ to have the gift of the gab.

bague [bag] *nf* ring; ~ de fiançailles engagement ring; ~ de serrage clip.

baguette [bagɛt] *nf* stick; (*cuisine chinoise*) chopstick; (*de chef d'orchestre*) baton; (*pain*) stick of (French) bread; ~ magique magic wand.

bahut [bay] *nm* chest.

baie [bɛ] *nf* (*GÉO*) bay; (*fruit*) berry; ~ (vitrée) picture window.

baignade [bɛɲad] *nf* bathing.

baigner [beɲe] *vt* (*bébé*) to bath; se ~ *vi* to have a swim, go swimming *ou* bathing; **baignoire** *nf* bath(tub).

bail, baux [baj, bo] *nm* lease.

bâiller [baje] *vi* to yawn; (*être ouvert*) to gape.

bailleur [bajœr] *nm*: ~ de fonds sponsor, backer.

bâillon [bajɔ̃] *nm* gag; **bâillonner** *vt* to gag.

bain [bɛ̃] *nm* bath; **prendre un ~** to have a bath; **se mettre dans le ~** (*fig*) to get into it *ou* things; **~ de foule** walkabout; **prendre un ~ de soleil** to sunbathe; **~s de mer** sea bathing *sg*; **faire chauffer au ~-marie** (*boîte etc*) to immerse in boiling water.

baiser [beze] *nm* kiss // *vt* (*main, front*) to kiss; (*fam!*) to screw (*!*).

baisse [bɛs] *nf* fall, drop; **'~ sur la viande'** 'meat prices down'.

baisser [bese] *vt* lower; (*radio, chauffage*) to turn down; (*AUTO: phares*) to dip (*Brit*), to lower (*US*) // *vi* to fall, drop, go down; **se ~** *vi* to bend down.

bal [bal] *nm* dance; (*grande soirée*) ball; **~ costumé** fancy-dress ball.

balader [balade] *vt* (*traîner*) to trail round; **se ~** *vi* to go for a walk *ou* stroll; to go for a drive.

balafre [balafʀ(ə)] *nf* gash, slash; (*cicatrice*) scar.

balai [balɛ] *nm* broom, brush; **~-brosse** *nm* (long-handled) scrubbing brush.

balance [balɑ̃s] *nf* scales *pl*; (*de précision*) balance; (*signe*): **la B~** Libra.

balancer [balɑ̃se] *vt* to swing; (*lancer*) to fling, chuck; (*renvoyer, jeter*) to chuck out // *vi* to swing; **se ~** *vi* to swing; to rock; to sway; **se ~ de** not to care about; **balancier** *nm* (*de pendule*) pendulum; (*perche*) (balancing) pole; **balançoire** *nf* swing; (*sur pivot*) seesaw.

balayer [balɛje] *vt* (*feuilles etc*) to sweep up, brush up; (*pièce*) to sweep; (*chasser*) to sweep away; to sweep aside; (*suj: radar*) to scan; **balayeur, euse** *nm/f*, *nf* roadsweeper.

balbutier [balbysje] *vi*, *vt* to stammer.

balcon [balkɔ̃] *nm* balcony; (*THÉÂTRE*) dress circle.

baleine [balɛn] *nf* whale; (*de parapluie, corset*) rib; **baleinière** *nf* whaleboat.

balise [baliz] *nf* (*NAVIG*) beacon; (marker) buoy; (*AVIAT*) runway light, beacon; (*AUTO, SKI*) sign, marker; **baliser** *vt* to mark out (with lights *etc*).

balivernes [balivɛʀn(ə)] *nfpl* nonsense *sg*.

ballant, e [balɑ̃, -ɑ̃t] *a* dangling.

balle [bal] *nf* (*de fusil*) bullet; (*de sport*) ball; (*paquet*) bale; (*fam: franc*) franc; **~ perdue** stray bullet.

ballerine [balʀin] *nf* ballet dancer.

ballet [balɛ] *nm* ballet.

ballon [balɔ̃] *nm* (*de sport*) ball; (*jouet, AVIAT*) balloon; (*de vin*) glass; **~ de football** football.

ballot [balo] *nm* bundle; (*péj*) nitwit.

ballottage [balɔtaʒ] *nm* (*POL*) second ballot.

ballotter [balɔte] *vi* to roll around; to toss // *vt* to shake about; to toss.

balnéaire [balneɛʀ] *a* seaside *cpd*.

balourd, e [balur, -urd(ə)] *a* clumsy // *nm/f* clodhopper.

balustrade [balystʀad] *nf* railings *pl*, handrail.

bambin [bɑ̃bɛ̃] *nm* little child.

ban [bɑ̃] *nm* round of applause, cheer; **~s** *nmpl* (*de mariage*) banns; **mettre au ~ de** to outlaw from.

banal, e [banal] *a* banal, commonplace; (*péj*) trite.

banane [banan] *nf* banana.

banc [bɑ̃] *nm* seat, bench; (*de poissons*) shoal; **~ d'essai** (*fig*) testing ground; **~ de sable** sandbank.

bancaire [bɑ̃kɛʀ] *a* banking, bank *cpd*.

bancal, e [bɑ̃kal] *a* a wobbly; bow-legged.

bandage [bɑ̃daʒ] *nm* bandage.

bande [bɑ̃d] *nf* (*de tissu etc*) strip; (*MÉD*) bandage; (*motif*) stripe; (*magnétique etc*) tape; (*groupe*) band; (: *péj*) bunch; **par la ~** in a roundabout way; **donner de la ~** to list; **faire ~ à part** to keep to o.s.; **~ dessinée** comic strip; **~ sonore** sound track.

bandeau, x [bɑ̃do] *nm* headband; (*sur les yeux*) blindfold; (*MÉD*) head bandage.

bander [bɑ̃de] *vt* (*blessure*) to bandage; (*muscle*) to tense; **~ les yeux à qn** to blindfold sb.

banderole [bɑ̃dʀɔl] *nf* banner, streamer.

bandit [bɑ̃di] *nm* bandit; **banditisme** *nm* violent crime, armed robberies *pl*.

bandoulière [bɑ̃duljɛʀ] *nf*: **en ~** (slung *ou* worn) across the shoulder.

banlieue [bɑ̃ljø] *nf* suburbs *pl*; **lignes/quartiers de ~** suburban lines/areas; **trains de ~** commuter trains.

bannière [banjɛʀ] *nf* banner.

bannir [baniʀ] *vt* to banish.

banque [bɑ̃k] *nf* bank; (*activités*) banking; **~ d'affaires** merchant bank.

banqueroute [bɑ̃kʀut] *nf* bankruptcy.

banquet [bɑ̃kɛ] *nm* dinner; (*d'apparat*) banquet.

banquette [bɑ̃kɛt] *nf* seat.

banquier [bɑ̃kje] *nm* banker.

banquise [bɑ̃kiz] *nf* ice field.

baptême [batɛm] *nm* christening; baptism; **~ de l'air** first flight.

baquet [bakɛ] *nm* tub, bucket.

bar [baʀ] *nm* bar.

baraque [baʀak] *nf* shed; (*fam*) house; **~ foraine** fairground stand.

baraqué, e [baʀake] *a* well-built, hefty.

baraquements [baʀakmɑ̃] *nmpl* huts (for refugees, workers etc).

baratin [baʀatɛ̃] *nm* (*fam*) smooth talk, patter; **baratiner** *vt* to chat up.

barbare [baʀbaʀ] *a* barbaric.

barbe [baʀb(ə)] *nf* beard; **quelle ~!** (*fam*) what a drag *ou* bore!; **à la ~ de qn** under sb's nose; **~ à papa** candy-floss (*Brit*), cotton candy (*US*).

barbelé [baʀbəle] *nm* barbed wire *q*.

barboter [baʀbɔte] *vi* to paddle, dabble.

barboteuse [baʀbɔtøz] *nf* rompers *pl*.

barbouiller [baʀbuje] *vt* to daub; **avoir l'estomac barbouillé** to feel queasy.

barbu, e [baʀby] *a* bearded.

barda [baʀda] *nm* (*fam*) kit, gear.

barde [baʀd(ə)] *nf* piece of fat bacon.

barder [baʀde] *vi* (*fam*): **ça va ~** sparks will fly, things are going to get hot.

barème [baʀɛm] *nm* scale; table.

baril [baʀil] *nm* barrel; keg.

baromètre [baʀɔmɛtʀ(ə)] *nm* barometer.

baron [baʀɔ̃] *nm* baron; **baronne** *nf* baroness.

baroque [baʀɔk] *a* (*ART*) baroque; (*fig*) weird.

barque [baʀk(ə)] *nf* small boat.

barrage [baʀaʒ] *nm* dam; (*sur route*) roadblock, barricade.

barre [baʀ] *nf* bar; (*NAVIG*) helm; (*écrite*) line, stroke.

barreau, x [baʀo] *nm* bar; (*JUR*): **le ~** the Bar.

barrer [baʀe] *vt* (*route etc*) to block; (*mot*) to cross out; (*chèque*) to cross (*Brit*); (*NAVIG*) to steer; **se ~** *vi* (*fam*) to clear off.

barrette [baʀɛt] *nf* (*pour cheveux*) (hair) slide (*Brit*) *ou* clip (*US*).

barricader [baʀikade] *vt* to barricade.

barrière [baʀjɛʀ] *nf* fence; (*obstacle*) barrier; (*porte*) gate.

barrique [baʀik] *nf* barrel, cask.

bas, basse [ba, bas] *a* low // *nm* bottom, lower part; (*vêtement*) stocking // *nf* (*MUS*) bass // *ad* low; (*parler*) softly; **avoir la vue basse** to be short-sighted; **au ~ mot** at the lowest estimate; **en ~** down below; **at** (*ou* **to**) **the bottom**; (*dans une maison*) downstairs; **en ~ de** at the bottom of; **mettre ~** *vi* to give birth; **à ~ ...!** 'down with ...!'; **~ morceaux** *nmpl* (*viande*) cheap cuts.

basané, e [bazane] *a* tanned, bronzed.

bas-côté [bakote] *nm* (*de route*) verge (*Brit*), shoulder (*US*).

bascule [baskyl] *nf*: (**jeu de**) **~** seesaw; (**balance à**) **~** scales *pl*; **fauteuil à ~** rocking chair.

basculer [baskyle] *vi* to fall over, topple (over); (*benne*) to tip up // *vt* to topple over; to tip out, tip up.

base [baz] *nf* base; (*POL*) rank and file; (*fondement, principe*) basis (*pl* bases); **de ~** basic; **à ~ de café** *etc* coffee *etc* -based; **~ de données** database; **baser** *vt* to base; **se baser sur** (*preuves*) to base one's argument on.

bas-fond [bafɔ̃] *nm* (*NAVIG*) shallow; **~s** (*fig*) dregs.

basilic [bazilik] *nm* (*CULIN*) basil.

basket [baskɛt] *nm* trainer (*Brit*), sneaker (*US*); (*aussi*: **~-ball**) basketball.

basque [bask(ə)] *a*, *nm/f* Basque.

basse [bas] *a*, *nf voir* **bas**; **~-cour** *nf* farmyard.

bassin [basɛ̃] *nm* (*cuvette*) bowl; (*pièce d'eau*) pond, pool; (*de fontaine*, *GÉO*) basin; (*ANAT*) pelvis; (*portuaire*) dock.

basson [basɔ̃] *nm* bassoon.

bastingage [bastɛ̃gaʒ] *nm* (ship's) rail.

bas-ventre [bavɑ̃tʀ(ə)] *nm* (lower part of the) stomach.

bat *vb voir* **battre**.

bât [ba] *nm* packsaddle.

bataille [bataj] *nf* battle; fight.

bâtard, e [batɑʀ, -aʀd(ə)] *nm/f* illegitimate child, bastard (*péj*).

bateau, x [bato] *nm* boat, ship; **~-mouche** *nm* (passenger) pleasure boat (*on the Seine*).

bateleur, euse [batlœʀ, -øz] *nm/f* street performer.

batelier, ière [batəlje, -jɛʀ] *nm/f* (*de bac*) ferryman/woman.

bâti, e [bati] *a*: **bien ~** well-built.

batifoler [batifɔle] *vi* to frolic about.

bâtiment [batimɑ̃] *nm* building; (*NAVIG*) ship, vessel; (*industrie*) building trade.

bâtir [batiʀ] *vt* to build.

bâtisse [batis] *nf* building.

bâton [batɔ̃] *nm* stick; **à ~s rompus** informally.

bâtonnier [batɔnje] *nm* ≈ president of the Bar.

bats *vb voir* **battre**.

battage [bataʒ] *nm* (*publicité*) (hard) plugging.

battant [batɑ̃] *nm* (*de cloche*) clapper; (*de volets*) shutter, flap; (*de porte*) side; (*fig: personne*) fighter; **porte à double ~** double door.

battement [batmɑ̃] *nm* (*de cœur*) beat; (*intervalle*) interval (*between classes, trains etc*); **~ de paupières** blinking *q* (of eyelids); **10 minutes de ~** 10 minutes to spare.

batterie [batʀi] *nf* (*MIL*, *ÉLEC*) battery; (*MUS*) drums *pl*, drum kit; **~ de cuisine** pots and pans *pl*; kitchen utensils *pl*.

batteur [batœʀ] *nm* (*MUS*) drummer; (*appareil*) whisk.

battre [batʀ(ə)] *vt* to beat; (*suj: pluie, vagues*) to beat *ou* lash against; (*blé*) to thresh; (*passer au peigne fin*) to scour // *vi* (*cœur*) to beat; (*volets etc*) to bang, rattle; **se ~** *vi* to fight; **~ la mesure** to beat time; **~ en brèche** to demolish; **~ son plein** to be at its height, be going full swing; **~ des mains** to clap one's hands.

battue [baty] *nf* (*chasse*) beat; (*policière*) search, hunt.

baume [bom] *nm* balm.

bavard, e [bavaʀ, -aʀd(ə)] *a* (very) talkative; gossipy; **bavarder** *vi* to chatter; (*indiscrètement*) to gossip; to blab.

bave [bav] *nf* dribble; (*de chien etc*) slobber; (*d'escargot*) slime; **baver** *vi* to dribble; to slobber; **en baver** (*fam*) to have a hard time (of it); **bavette** *nf* bib; **baveux, euse** *a* (*omelette*) runny.

bavure [bavyʀ] *nf* smudge; (*fig*) hitch; blunder.

bayer [baje] *vi*: ~ aux corneilles to stand gaping.

bazar [bazaʀ] *nm* general store; (*fam*) jumble; **bazarder** *vt* (*fam*) to chuck out.

B.C.B.G. *sigle a* (= *bon chic bon genre*) preppy, smart and trendy.

B.C.G. *sigle m* (= *bacille Calmette-Guérin*) BCG.

bd. *abr de* boulevard.

B.D. *sigle f de* bande dessinée.

béant, e [beã, -ãt] *a* gaping.

béat, e [bea, -at] *a* showing open-eyed wonder; blissful; **béatitude** *nf* bliss.

beau(bel), belle, beaux [bo, bɛl] *a* beautiful, lovely; (*homme*) handsome // *nf* (*SPORT*) decider // *ad*: **il fait ~ the** weather's fine; **un ~ jour** one (fine) day; **de plus belle** more than ever, even more; **on a ~ essayer** however hard we try; **bel et bien** well and truly; **faire le ~** (*chien*) to sit up and beg.

beaucoup [boku] *ad* **1** a lot; **il boit ~** he drinks a lot; **il ne boit pas ~** he doesn't drink much *ou* a lot

2 (*suivi de plus, trop etc*) much, a lot, far; **il est ~ plus grand** he is much *ou* a lot *ou* far taller

3: ~ **de** (*nombre*) many, a lot of; (*quantité*) a lot of; ~ **d'étudiants/de touristes** a lot of *ou* many students/tourists; ~ **de courage** a lot of courage; **il n'a pas ~ d'argent** he hasn't got much *ou* a lot of money

4: **de ~** *ad* by far.

beau-fils [bofis] *nm* son-in-law; (*remariage*) stepson.

beau-frère [bofʀɛʀ] *nm* brother-in-law.

beau-père [bopɛʀ] *nm* father-in-law; (*remariage*) stepfather.

beauté [bote] *nf* beauty; **de toute ~** beautiful; **en ~** *ad* brilliantly.

beaux-arts [bozaʀ] *nmpl* fine arts.

beaux-parents [bopaʀã] *nmpl* wife's/ husband's family *sg ou pl*, in-laws.

bébé [bebe] *nm* baby.

bec [bɛk] *nm* beak, bill; (*de récipient*) spout; lip; (*fam*) mouth; ~ **de gaz** (street) gaslamp; ~ **verseur** pouring lip.

bécane [bekan] *nf* (*fam*: vélo) bike.

bec-de-lièvre [bɛkdəljɛvʀ(ə)] *nm* harelip.

bêche [bɛʃ] *nf* spade; **bêcher** *vt* to dig.

bécoter [bekɔte]: **se ~** *vi* to smooch.

becqueter [bɛkte] *vt* (*fam*) to eat.

bedaine [bədɛn] *nf* paunch.

bedonnant, e [bədɔnã, -ãt] *a* potbellied.

bée [be] *a*: **bouche ~** gaping.

beffroi [befʀwa] *nm* belfry.

bégayer [begeje] *vt, vi* to stammer.

bègue [bɛg] *nm/f*: **être ~** to have a stammer.

béguin [begɛ̃] *nm*: **avoir le ~ de** *ou* **pour** to have a crush on.

beige [bɛʒ] *a* beige.

beignet [bɛɲɛ] *nm* fritter.

bel [bɛl] *a voir* beau.

bêler [bele] *vi* to bleat.

belette [bəlɛt] *nf* weasel.

belge [bɛlʒ(ə)] *a, nm/f* Belgian.

Belgique [bɛlʒik] *nf*: **la ~** Belgium.

bélier [belje] *nm* ram; (*signe*): **le B~** Aries.

belle [bɛl] *af, nf voir* beau; **~-fille** *nf* daughter-in-law; (*remariage*) step-daughter; **~-mère** *nf* mother-in-law; stepmother; **~-sœur** *nf* sister-in-law.

belliqueux, euse [belikø, -øz] *a* aggressive, warlike.

belvédère [belvedɛʀ] *nm* panoramic viewpoint (*or small building there*).

bémol [bemɔl] *nm* (*MUS*) flat.

bénédiction [benediksjɔ̃] *nf* blessing.

bénéfice [benefis] *nm* (*COMM*) profit; (*avantage*) benefit; **bénéficier de** *vt* to enjoy; to benefit by *ou* from; to get, be given; **bénéfique** *a* beneficial.

benêt [bənɛ] *nm* simpleton.

bénévole [benevɔl] *a* voluntary, unpaid.

bénin, igne [benɛ̃, -iɲ] *a* minor, mild; (*tumeur*) benign.

bénir [beniʀ] *vt* to bless; **bénit, e** *a* consecrated; **eau bénite** holy water; **bénitier** *nm* font.

benjamin, e [bɛ̃ʒamɛ̃, -in] *nm/f* youngest child.

benne [bɛn] *nf* skip; (*de téléphérique*) (cable) car; ~ **basculante** tipper (*Brit*), dump truck (*US*).

béotien, ne [beɔsjɛ̃, -jɛn] *nm/f* philistine.

B.E.P.C. *sigle m voir* brevet.

béquille [bekij] *nf* crutch; (*de bicyclette*) stand.

bercail [bɛʀkaj] *nm* fold.

berceau, x [bɛʀso] *nm* cradle, crib.

bercer [bɛʀse] *vt* to rock, cradle; (*suj: musique etc*) to lull; ~ **qn de** (*promesses etc*) to delude sb with; **berceuse** *nf* lullaby.

béret (basque) [beʀɛ(bask(ə))] *nm* beret.

berge [bɛʀʒ(ə)] *nf* bank.

berger, ère [bɛʀʒe, -ɛʀ] *nm/f* shepherd/ shepherdess.

berlingot [bɛʀlɛ̃go] *nm* (*emballage*) carton (*pyramid shaped*).

berlue [bɛʀly] *nf*: **j'ai la ~** I must be seeing things.

berne [bɛʀn(ə)] *nf*: **en ~** at half-mast.

berner [bɛʀne] *vt* to fool.

besogne [bəzɔɲ] *nf* work *q*, job; **beso-**

gneux, euse *a* hard-working.

besoin [bəzwɛ̃] *nm* need; (*pauvreté*): le ~ need, want; **faire ses** ~**s** to relieve o.s.; **avoir** ~ **de qch/faire qch** to need sth/to do sth; **au** ~ if need be.

bestiaux [bɛstjo] *nmpl* cattle.

bestiole [bɛstjɔl] *nf* (tiny) creature.

bétail [betaj] *nm* livestock, cattle *pl*.

bête [bɛt] *nf* animal; (*bestiole*) insect, creature // *a* stupid, silly; **il cherche la petite** ~ he's being pernickety *ou* overfussy; ~ **noire** pet hate.

bêtise [betiz] *nf* stupidity; stupid thing (to say *ou* do).

béton [betɔ̃] *nm* concrete; **(en)** ~ (*alibi, argument*) cast iron; ~ **armé** reinforced concrete; **bétonnière** *nf* cement mixer.

betterave [bɛtrav] *nf* beetroot (*Brit*), beet (*US*); ~ **sucrière** sugar beet.

beugler [bøgle] *vi* to low; (*radio etc*) to blare // *vt* (*chanson*) to bawl out.

beurre [bœr] *nm* butter; **beurrer** *vt* to butter; **beurrier** *nm* butter dish.

beuverie [bœvri] *nf* drinking session.

bévue [bevy] *nf* blunder.

Beyrouth [berut] *n* Beirut.

bi... [bi] *préfixe* bi..., two-.

biais [bjɛ] *nm* (*moyen*) device, expedient; (*aspect*) angle; **en** ~, **de** ~ (*obliquement*) at an angle; (*fig*) indirectly; **biaiser** *vi* (*fig*) to sidestep the issue.

bibelot [biblo] *nm* trinket, curio.

biberon [bibrɔ̃] *nm* (feeding) bottle; **nourrir au** ~ to bottle-feed.

bible [bibl(ə)] *nf* bible.

biblio... [biblijo] *préfixe*: ~**bus** *nm* mobile library van; ~**phile** *nm/f* booklover; ~**thécaire** *nm/f* librarian; ~**thèque** *nf* library; (*meuble*) bookcase.

bicarbonate [bikarbɔnat] *nm*: ~ (**de soude**) bicarbonate of soda.

biceps [bisɛps] *nm* biceps.

biche [biʃ] *nf* doe.

bichonner [biʃɔne] *vt* to groom.

bicolore [bikɔlɔr] *a* two-coloured.

bicoque [bikɔk] *nf* (*péj*) shack.

bicyclette [bisiklɛt] *nf* bicycle.

bide [bid] *nm* (*fam*: *ventre*) belly; (*THÉÂTRE*) flop.

bidet [bidɛ] *nm* bidet.

bidon [bidɔ̃] *nm* can // *a inv* (*fam*) phoney.

bidonville [bidɔ̃vil] *nm* shanty town.

bidule [bidyl] *nm* (*fam*) thingumajig.

bielle [bjɛl] *nf* connecting rod.

bien [bjɛ̃] ♦ *nm* **1** (*avantage, profit*): **faire du** ~ **à qn** to do sb good; **dire du** ~ **de** to speak well of; **c'est pour son** ~ it's for his own good

2 (*possession, patrimoine*) possession, property; **son** ~ **le plus précieux** his most treasured possession; **avoir du** ~ to have property; ~**s** (*de consommation etc*) (consumer *etc*) goods

3 (*moral*): **le** ~ good; **distinguer le** ~ **du mal** to tell good from evil

♦ *ad* **1** (*de façon satisfaisante*) well; **elle travaille/mange** ~ she works/eats well; **croyant** ~ **faire, je/il ...** thinking I/he was doing the right thing, I/he ...; **c'est** ~ **fait!** it serves him (*ou* her *etc*) right!

2 (*valeur intensive*) quite; ~ **jeune** quite young; ~ **assez** quite enough; ~ **mieux** (very) much better; **j'espère** ~ **y aller** I do hope to go; **je veux** ~ **le faire** (*concession*) I'm quite willing to do it; **il faut** ~ **le faire** it has to be done

3: ~ **du temps/des gens** quite a time/a number of people

♦ *a inv* **1** (*en bonne forme, à l'aise*): **je me sens** ~. I feel fine; **je ne me sens pas** ~ I don't feel well; **on est** ~ **dans ce fauteuil** this chair is very comfortable

2 (*joli, beau*) good-looking; **tu es** ~ **dans cette robe** you look good in that dress

3 (*satisfaisant*) good; **elle est** ~, **cette maison/secrétaire** it's a good house/she's a good secretary

4 (*moralement*) right; (: *personne*) good, nice; (*respectable*) respectable; **ce n'est pas** ~ **de ...** it's not right to ...; **elle est** ~, **cette femme** she's a nice woman, she's a good sort; **des gens** ~ respectable people

5 (*en bons termes*): **être** ~ **avec qn** to be on good terms with sb

♦ *préfixe*: ~**-aimé, e** *a*, *nm/f* beloved; ~**-être** *nm* well-being; ~**faisance** *nf* charity; ~**faisant, e** *a* (*chose*) beneficial; ~**fait** *nm* act of generosity, benefaction; (*de la science etc*) benefit; ~**faiteur, trice** *nm/f* benefactor/benefactress; ~**-fondé** *nm* soundness; ~**-fonds** *nm* property; ~**heureux, euse** *a* happy; (*REL*) blessed, blest

bien que *cj* (al)though

bien sûr *ad* certainly.

bienséant, e [bjɛ̃seã, -ãt] *a* seemly.

bientôt [bjɛ̃to] *ad* soon; **à** ~ see you soon.

bienveillant, e [bjɛ̃vɛjã, -ãt] *a* kindly.

bienvenu, e [bjɛ̃vny] *a* welcome // *nf*: **souhaiter la** ~**e à** to welcome; ~**e à** welcome to.

bière [bjɛr] *nf* (*boisson*) beer; (*cercueil*) bier; ~ **blonde** lager; ~ **brune** brown ale; ~ (**à la**) **pression** draught beer.

biffer [bife] *vt* to cross out.

bifteck [biftɛk] *nm* steak.

bifurquer [bifyrke] *vi* (*route*) to fork; (*véhicule*) to turn off.

bigarré, e [bigare] *a* multicoloured; (*disparate*) motley.

bigarreau, x [bigaro] *nm* type of cherry.

bigorneau, x [bigɔrno] *nm* winkle.

bigot, e [bigo, -ɔt] (*péj*) *a* bigoted.

bigoudi [bigudi] *nm* curler.

bijou, x [biʒu] *nm* jewel; ~**terie** *nf*

jeweller's (shop); jewellery; **~tier, ière** *nm/f* jeweller.

bikini [bikini] *nm* bikini.

bilan [bilɑ̃] *nm* (*COMM*) balance sheet(s); end of year statement; (*fig*) (net) outcome; (: *de victimes*) toll; **faire le ~ de** to assess; to review; **déposer son ~** to file a bankruptcy statement.

bile [bil] *nf* bile; **se faire de la ~** (*fam*) to worry o.s. sick.

bilieux, euse [biljø, -jøz] *a* bilious; (*fig: colérique*) testy.

bilingue [bilɛ̃g] *a* bilingual.

billard [bijaʀ] *nm* billiards *sg*; billiard table; **c'est du ~** (*fam*) it's a cinch.

bille [bij] *nf* (*gén*) ball; (*du jeu de billes*) marble; (*de bois*) log.

billet [bijɛ] *nm* (*aussi:* ~ **de banque**) (bank)note; (*de cinéma, de bus etc*) ticket; (*courte lettre*) note; ~ **circulaire** round-trip ticket; ~ **de faveur** complimentary ticket.

billion [biljɔ̃] *nm* billion (*Brit*), trillion (*US*).

billot [bijo] *nm* block.

bimensuel, le [bimɑ̃sɥɛl] *a* bimonthly.

binette [binɛt] *nf* hoe.

binocle [binɔkl(ə)] *nm* pince-nez.

bio... [bjɔ] *préfixe* bio...; **~graphie** *nf* biography; **~logie** *nf* biology; **~logique** *a* biological.

Birmanie [biʀmani] *nf* Burma.

bis, e [bi, biz] *a* (*couleur*) greyish brown // *ad* [bis]: 12 ~ 12a *ou* A // *excl*, *nm* [bis] encore // *nf* (*baiser*) kiss; (*vent*) North wind.

bisannuel, le [bizanɥɛl] *a* biennial.

biscornu, e [biskɔʀny] *a* twisted.

biscotte [biskɔt] *nf* (breakfast) rusk.

biscuit [biskɥi] *nm* biscuit; sponge cake.

bise [biz] *a, nf voir* **bis**.

bissextile [bisɛkstil] *a*: **année ~** leap year.

bistouri [bisturi] *nm* lancet.

bistro(t) [bistro] *nm* bistro, café.

bitume [bitym] *nm* asphalt.

bizarre [bizaʀ] *a* strange, odd.

blafard, e [blafaʀ, -aʀd(ə)] *a* wan.

blague [blag] *nf* (*propos*) joke; (*farce*) trick; **sans ~!** no kidding!; ~ **à tabac** tobacco pouch.

blaguer [blage] *vi* to joke // *vt* to tease.

blaireau, x [blɛʀo] *nm* (*ZOOL*) badger; (*brosse*) shaving brush.

blairer [blere] *vt* (*fam*): **je ne peux pas le ~** I can't bear *ou* stand him.

blâme [blɑm] *nm* blame; (*sanction*) reprimand.

blâmer [blɑme] *vt* to blame.

blanc, blanche [blɑ̃, blɑ̃ʃ] *a* white; (*non imprimé*) blank; (*innocent*) pure // *nm/f* white, white man/woman // *nm* (*couleur*) white; (*espace non écrit*) blank; (*aussi:* ~ **d'œuf**) (egg-)white; (*aussi:* ~ **de poulet**) breast, white meat;

(*aussi:* **vin ~**) white wine // *nf* (*MUS*) minim (*Brit*), half-note (*US*); ~ **cassé** off-white; **chèque en ~** blank cheque; **à ~** *ad* (*chauffer*) white-hot; (*tirer, charger*) with blanks; **~-bec** *nm* greenhorn; **blancheur** *nf* whiteness.

blanchir [blɑ̃ʃiʀ] *vt* (*gén*) to whiten; (*linge*) to launder; (*CULIN*) to blanch; (*fig: disculper*) to clear // *vi* to grow white; (*cheveux*) to go white; **blanchisserie** *nf* laundry.

blaser [blaze] *vt* to make blasé.

blason [blazɔ̃] *nm* coat of arms.

blatte [blat] *nf* cockroach.

blazer [blazɛʀ] *nm* blazer.

blé [ble] *nm* wheat.

bled [blɛd] *nm* (*péj*) hole.

blême [blɛm] *a* pale.

blessé, e [blese] *a* injured // *nm/f* injured person; casualty.

blesser [blese] *vt* to injure; (*délibérément: MIL etc*) to wound; (*suj: souliers etc, offenser*) to hurt; **se ~** to injure o.s.; **se ~ au pied** *etc* to injure one's foot *etc*.

blessure [blesyʀ] *nf* injury; wound.

bleu, e [blø] *a* blue; (*bifteck*) very rare // *nm* (*couleur*) blue; (*novice*) greenhorn; (*contusion*) bruise; (*vêtement: aussi:* ~**s**) overalls *pl*; ~ **marine** navy blue.

bleuet [bløɛ] *nm* cornflower.

bleuté, e [bløte] *a* blue-shaded.

blinder [blɛ̃de] *vt* to armour; (*fig*) to harden.

bloc [blɔk] *nm* (*de pierre etc*) block; (*de papier à lettres*) pad; (*ensemble*) group, block; **serré à ~** tightened right down; **en ~** as a whole; wholesale; ~ **opératoire** operating *ou* theatre block; ~ **sanitaire** toilet block.

blocage [blɔkaʒ] *nm* blocking; jamming; freezing; (*PSYCH*) hang-up.

bloc-notes [blɔknɔt] *nm* note pad.

blocus [blɔkys] *nm* blockade.

blond, e [blɔ̃, -ɔ̃d] *a* fair; blond; (*sable, blés*) golden; ~ **cendré** ash blond.

bloquer [blɔke] *vt* (*passage*) to block; (*pièce mobile*) to jam; (*crédits, compte*) to freeze.

blottir [blɔtiʀ]: **se ~** *vi* to huddle up.

blouse [bluz] *nf* overall.

blouson [bluzɔ̃] *nm* blouson jacket; ~ **noir** (*fig*) ≈ rocker.

bluffer [blœfe] *vi* to bluff.

bobard [bɔbaʀ] *nm* (*fam*) tall story.

bobine [bɔbin] *nf* reel; (*ÉLEC*) coil.

bocage [bɔkaʒ] *nm* grove.

bocal, aux [bɔkal, -o] *nm* jar.

bock [bɔk] *nm* glass of beer.

bœuf [bœf, *pl* bø] *nm* ox (*pl* oxen), steer; (*CULIN*) beef.

bof! [bɔf] *excl* (*fam*) don't care!; (: *pas terrible*) nothing special.

bohème [bɔɛm] *a* happy-go-lucky, unconventional.

bohémien, ne [bɔemjẽ, -jɛn] *nm/f* gipsy.

boire [bwaʀ] *vt* to drink; (*s'imprégner de*) to soak up; ~ **un coup** to have a drink.

bois [bwa] *nm* wood; **de ~, en ~** wooden.

boisé, e [bwaze] *a* woody, wooded.

boisson [bwasɔ̃] *nf* drink; **pris de ~** drunk, intoxicated.

boîte [bwat] *nf* box; (*entreprise*) place, firm; **aliments en ~** canned *ou* tinned (*Brit*) foods; **~ d'allumettes** box of matches; (*vide*) matchbox; **~** (**de conserves**) can *ou* tin (*Brit*) (of food); **~ à gants** glove compartment; **~ aux lettres** letter box; **~ de nuit** night club; **~ postale** (**B.P.**) PO Box; **~ de vitesses** gear box.

boiter [bwate] *vi* to limp; (*fig*) to wobble; to be shaky.

boîtier [bwatje] *nm* case.

boive *etc vb voir* **boire.**

bol [bɔl] *nm* bowl; **un ~ d'air** a breath of fresh air.

bolide [bɔlid] *nm* racing car; **comme un ~** at top speed, like a rocket.

bombance [bɔ̃bɑ̃s] *nf:* **faire ~** to have a feast, revel.

bombarder [bɔ̃baʀde] *vt* to bomb; **~ qn de** (*cailloux, lettres*) to bombard sb with; **bombardier** *nm* bomber.

bombe [bɔ̃b] *nf* bomb; (*atomiseur*) (aerosol) spray.

bomber [bɔ̃be] *vi* to bulge; to camber // *vt:* **~ le torse** to swell out one's chest.

bon, bonne [bɔ̃, bɔn] ♦ *a* **1** (*agréable, satisfaisant*) good; **un ~ repas/restaurant** a good meal/restaurant; **être ~ en maths** to be good at maths **2** (*charitable*): **être ~ (envers)** to be good (to) **3** (*correct*) right; **le ~ numéro/moment** the right number/moment **4** (*souhaits*): **~ anniversaire** happy birthday; **~ voyage** have a good trip; **bonne chance** good luck; **bonne année** happy New Year; **bonne nuit** good night **5** (*approprié, apte*): **~ à/pour** fit to/for **6:** **~ enfant** *a inv* accommodating, easygoing; **bonne femme** *nf* (*péj*) woman; **de bonne heure** *ad* early; **~ marché** *a inv, ad* cheap; **~ mot** *nm* witticism; **~ sens** *nm* common sense; **~ vivant** *nm* jovial chap; **bonnes œuvres** *nfpl* charitable works, charities ♦ *nm* **1** (*billet*) voucher; (*aussi:* **~ cadeau**) gift voucher; **~ d'essence** petrol coupon; **~ du Trésor** Treasury bond **2:** **avoir du ~** to have its good points; **pour de ~** for good ♦ *nf* (*domestique*) maid; **bonne d'enfant** nanny; **bonne à tout faire** general help ♦ *ad:* **il fait ~** it's *ou* the weather is fine;

sentir ~ to smell good; **tenir ~** to stand firm

♦ *excl* good!; **ah ~?** really?

bonbon [bɔ̃bɔ̃] *nm* (boiled) sweet.

bonbonne [bɔ̃bɔn] *nf* demijohn.

bond [bɔ̃] *nm* leap; **faire un ~** to leap in the air.

bonde [bɔ̃d] *nf* (*d'évier etc*) plug; (: *trou*) plughole; (*de tonneau*) bung; bunghole.

bondé, e [bɔ̃de] *a* packed (full).

bondir [bɔ̃diʀ] *vi* to leap.

bonheur [bɔnœʀ] *nm* happiness; **porter ~ (à qn)** to bring (sb) luck; **au petit ~** haphazardly; **par ~** fortunately.

bonhomie [bɔnɔmi] *nf* goodnaturedness.

bonhomme [bɔnɔm] *nm* (*pl* **bonshommes** [bɔ̃zɔm]) fellow; **~ de neige** snowman.

bonification [bɔnifikasjɔ̃] *nf* bonus.

bonifier [bɔnifje] *vt* to improve.

boniment [bɔnimɑ̃] *nm* patter *q*.

bonjour [bɔ̃ʒuʀ] *excl, nm* hello; good morning (*ou* afternoon).

bonne [bɔn] *a, nf voir* **bon; ~ment** *ad:* **tout ~ment** quite simply.

bonnet [bɔnɛ] *nm* bonnet, hat; (*de soutien-gorge*) cup; **~ d'âne** dunce's cap; **~ de bain** bathing cap.

bonneterie [bɔnɛtʀi] *nf* hosiery.

bonsoir [bɔ̃swaʀ] *excl* good evening.

bonté [bɔ̃te] *nf* kindness *q*.

bonus [bɔnys] *nm* no-claims bonus.

bord [bɔʀ] *nm* (*de table, verre, falaise*) edge; (*de rivière, lac*) bank; (*de route*) side; (*monter*) **à ~** (to go) on board; **jeter par-dessus ~** to throw overboard; **le commandant/les hommes du ~** the ship's master/crew; **au ~ de la mer** at the seaside; **être au ~ des larmes** to be on the verge of tears.

bordeaux [bɔʀdo] *nm* Bordeaux (wine) // *a inv* maroon.

bordel [bɔʀdɛl] *nm* brothel; (*fam!*) bloody mess (!).

border [bɔʀde] *vt* (*être le long de*) to border; to line; (*garnir*): **~ qch de** to line sth with; to trim sth with; (*qn dans son lit*) to tuck up.

bordereau, x [bɔʀdəʀo] *nm* slip; statement.

bordure [bɔʀdyʀ] *nf* border; **en ~ de** on the edge of.

borgne [bɔʀɲ(ə)] *a* one-eyed.

borne [bɔʀn(ə)] *nf* boundary stone; (*aussi:* **~ kilométrique**) kilometremarker, ≈ milestone; **~s** *nfpl* (*fig*) limits; **dépasser les ~s** to go too far.

borné, e [bɔʀne] *a* narrow; narrow-minded.

borner [bɔʀne] *vt* to limit; to confine; **se ~ à faire** to content o.s. with doing; to limit o.s. to doing.

bosquet [bɔskɛ] *nm* grove.

bosse [bɔs] *nf* (*de terrain etc*) bump; (*enflure*) lump; (*du bossu, du chameau*) hump; avoir la ~ des maths *etc* to have a gift for maths *etc*; il a roulé sa ~ he's been around.

bosser [bɔse] *vi* (*fam*) to work; to slave (away).

bossu, e [bɔsy] *nm/f* hunchback.

bot [bo] *am*: pied ~ club foot.

botanique [bɔtanik] *nf* botany // *a* botanic(al).

botte [bɔt] *nf* (*soulier*) (high) boot; (*gerbe*): ~ de paille bundle of straw; ~ de radis bunch of radishes; ~s de caoutchouc wellington boots.

botter [bɔte] *vt* to put boots on; to kick; (*fam*): ça me botte I fancy that.

bottin [bɔtɛ̃] *nm* directory.

bottine [bɔtin] *nf* ankle boot.

bouc [buk] *nm* goat; (*barbe*) goatee; ~ émissaire scapegoat.

boucan [bukɑ̃] *nm* din, racket.

bouche [buʃ] *nf* mouth; le ~ à ~ the kiss of life; ~ d'égout manhole; ~ d'incendie fire hydrant; ~ de métro métro entrance.

bouché, e [buʃe] *a* (*temps, ciel*) overcast; (*péj: personne*) thick.

bouchée [buʃe] *nf* mouthful; ~s à la reine chicken vol-au-vents.

boucher, ère [buʃe, -ɛʀ] *nm/f* butcher // *vt* (*pour colmater*) to stop up; to fill up; (*obstruer*) to block (up); se ~ le nez to hold one's nose; se ~ *vi* (*tuyau etc*) to block up, get blocked up.

boucherie [buʃʀi] *nf* butcher's (shop); (*fig*) slaughter.

bouche-trou [buʃtʀu] *nm* (*fig*) stopgap.

bouchon [buʃɔ̃] *nm* stopper; (*en liège*) cork; (*fig: embouteillage*) holdup; (*PÊCHE*) float; ~ doseur measuring cap.

boucle [bukl(ə)] *nf* (*forme, figure*) loop; (*objet*) buckle; ~ (de cheveux) curl; ~ d'oreilles earring.

bouclé, e [bukle] *a* curly.

boucler [bukle] *vt* (*fermer: ceinture etc*) to fasten; (: *magasin*) to shut; (*terminer*) to finish off; (: *budget*) to balance; (*enfermer*) to shut away; (: *quartier*) to seal off // *vi* to curl.

bouclier [buklije] *nm* shield.

bouddhiste [budist(ə)] *nm/f* Buddhist.

bouder [bude] *vi* to sulk // *vt* to turn one's nose up at; to refuse to have anything to do with.

boudin [budɛ̃] *nm* (*CULIN*) black pudding.

boue [bu] *nf* mud.

bouée [bwe] *nf* buoy; ~ (de sauvetage) lifebuoy.

boueux, euse [bwø, -øz] *a* muddy // *nm* refuse collector.

bouffe [buf] *nf* (*fam*) grub, food.

bouffée [bufe] *nf* puff; ~ de fièvre/de honte flush of fever/shame.

bouffer [bufe] *vi* (*fam*) to eat.

bouffi, e [bufi] *a* swollen.

bouge [buʒ] *nm* (low) dive; hovel.

bougeoir [buʒwaʀ] *nm* candlestick.

bougeotte [buʒɔt] *nf*: avoir la ~ to have the fidgets.

bouger [buʒe] *vi* to move; (*dent etc*) to be loose; (*changer*) to alter; (*agir*) to stir // *vt* to move.

bougie [buʒi] *nf* candle; (*AUTO*) sparking plug.

bougonner [bugɔne] *vi, vt* to grumble.

bouillabaisse [bujabɛs] *nf* type of fish soup.

bouillant, e [bujɑ̃, -ɑ̃t] *a* (*qui bout*) boiling; (*très chaud*) boiling (hot).

bouillie [buji] *nf* gruel; (*de bébé*) cereal; en ~ (*fig*) crushed.

bouillir [bujiʀ] *vi, vt* to boil.

bouilloire [bujwaʀ] *nf* kettle.

bouillon [bujɔ̃] *nm* (*CULIN*) stock *q*.

bouillonner [bujɔne] *vi* to bubble; (*fig*) to bubble up; to foam.

bouillotte [bujɔt] *nf* hot-water bottle.

boulanger, ère [bulɑ̃ʒe, -ɛʀ] *nm/f* baker.

boulangerie [bulɑ̃ʒʀi] *nf* bakery.

boule [bul] *nf* (*gén*) ball; (*pour jouer*) bowl; (*de machine à écrire*) golf-ball; ~ de neige snowball.

bouleau, x [bulo] *nm* (silver) birch.

boulet [bulɛ] *nm* (*aussi*: ~ de canon) cannonball.

boulette [bulɛt] *nf* ball.

boulevard [bulvaʀ] *nm* boulevard.

bouleversement [bulvɛʀsəmɑ̃] *nm* upheaval.

bouleverser [bulvɛʀse] *vt* (*émouvoir*) to overwhelm; (*causer du chagrin*) to distress; (*pays, vie*) to disrupt; (*papiers, objets*) to turn upside down.

boulier [bulje] *nm* abacus.

boulon [bulɔ̃] *nm* bolt.

boulot [bulo] *nm* (*fam: travail*) work.

boulot, te [bulo, -ɔt] *a* plump, tubby.

boum [bum] *nm* bang // *nf* party.

bouquet [bukɛ] *nm* (*de fleurs*) bunch (of flowers), bouquet; (*de persil etc*) bunch; (*parfum*) bouquet.

bouquin [bukɛ̃] *nm* (*fam*) book; **bouquiner** *vi* to read; to browse around (in a bookshop); **bouquiniste** *nm/f* bookseller.

bourbeux, euse [buʀbø, -øz] *a* muddy.

bourbier [buʀbje] *nm* (quag)mire.

bourde [buʀd(ə)] *nf* (*erreur*) howler; (*gaffe*) blunder.

bourdon [buʀdɔ̃] *nm* bumblebee.

bourdonner [buʀdɔne] *vi* to buzz.

bourg [buʀ] *nm* small market town.

bourgeois, e [buʀʒwa, -waz] *a* (*péj*) ≈ (upper) middle class; bourgeois.

bourgeoisie [buʀʒwazi] *nf* ≈ upper

middle classes *pl*; bourgeoisie.
bourgeon [buʀʒɔ̃] *nm* bud.
Bourgogne [buʀgɔɲ] *nf*: la ~ Burgundy // *nm*: b~ burgundy (wine).
bourguignon, ne [buʀgiɲɔ̃, -ɔn] *a* of *ou* from Burgundy, Burgundian.
bourlinguer [buʀlɛ̃ge] *vi* to knock about a lot, get around a lot.
bourrade [buʀad] *nf* shove, thump.
bourrage [buʀaʒ] *nm*: ~ de crâne brainwashing; (*SCOL*) cramming.
bourrasque [buʀask(ə)] *nf* squall.
bourreau, x [buʀo] *nm* executioner; (*fig*) torturer; ~ de travail workaholic.
bourrelet [buʀlɛ] *nm* draught excluder; (*de peau*) fold *ou* roll (of flesh).
bourrer [buʀe] *vt* (*pipe*) to fill; (*poêle*) to pack; (*valise*) to cram (full); ~ de coups to hammer blows on, pummel.
bourrique [buʀik] *nf* (*âne*) ass.
bourru, e [buʀy] *a* surly, gruff.
bourse [buʀs(ə)] *nf* (*subvention*) grant; (*porte-monnaie*) purse; la B~ the Stock Exchange.
boursoufler [buʀsufle] *vt* to puff up, bloat.
bous *vb voir* **bouillir.**
bousculade [buskylad] *nf* rush; crush.
bousculer [buskyle] *vt* to knock over; to knock into; (*fig*) to push, rush.
bouse [buz] *nf* dung *q.*
boussole [busɔl] *nf* compass.
bout [bu] *vb voir* **bouillir** // *nm* bit; (*extrémité: d'un bâton etc*) tip; (: *d'une ficelle, table, rue, période*) end; **au** ~ **de** at the end of, after; **pousser qn à** ~ to push sb to the limit; **venir à** ~ **de** to manage to finish; **à** ~ **portant** at point-blank range; ~ **filtre** filter tip.
boutade [butad] *nf* quip, sally.
boute-en-train [butɑ̃tʀɛ̃] *nm inv* live wire (*fig*).
bouteille [butɛj] *nf* bottle; (*de gaz butane*) cylinder.
boutique [butik] *nf* shop; **boutiquier, ière** *nm/f* shopkeeper.
bouton [butɔ̃] *nm* button; (*BOT*) bud; (*sur la peau*) spot; (*de porte*) knob; ~ de manchette cuff-link; ~ d'or buttercup; **boutonner** *vt* to button up; **boutonnière** *nf* buttonhole; ~-**pression** *nm* press stud.
bouture [butyʀ] *nf* cutting.
bovins [bɔvɛ̃] *nmpl* cattle.
bowling [bɔliaj] *nm* (tenpin) bowling; (*salle*) bowling alley.
box [bɔks] *nm* lock-up (garage); (*d'écurie*) loose-box.
boxe [bɔks(ə)] *nf* boxing.
boyau, x [bwajo] *nm* (*galerie*) passage(way); (narrow) gallery // *nmpl* (*viscères*) entrails, guts.
B.P. *abr de* **boîte postale.**
bracelet [bʀaslɛ] *nm* bracelet; ~-**montre** *nm* wristwatch.

braconnier [bʀakɔnje] *nm* poacher.
brader [bʀade] *vt* to sell off.
braderie [bʀadʀi] *nf* cut-price shop *ou* stall.
braguette [bʀagɛt] *nf* fly *ou* flies *pl* (*Brit*), zipper (*US*).
brailler [bʀaje] *vi* to bawl, yell.
braire [bʀɛʀ] *vi* to bray.
braise [bʀɛz] *nf* embers *pl.*
brancard [bʀɑ̃kaʀ] *nm* (*civière*) stretcher; (*bras, perche*) shaft; **brancardier** *nm* stretcher-bearer.
branchages [bʀɑ̃ʃaʒ] *nmpl* boughs.
branche [bʀɑ̃ʃ] *nf* branch.
branché, e [bʀɑ̃ʃe] *a* (*fam*) trendy.
brancher [bʀɑ̃ʃe] *vt* to connect (up); (*en mettant la prise*) to plug in.
branle [bʀɑ̃l] *nm*: **donner le** ~ à, **mettre en** ~ to set in motion.
branle-bas [bʀɑ̃lba] *nm inv* commotion.
branler [bʀɑ̃le] *vi* to be shaky // *vt*: ~ **la tête** to shake one's head.
braquer [bʀake] *vi* (*AUTO*) to turn (the wheel) // *vt* (*revolver etc*): ~ qch sur to point sth at, point sth at; (*mettre en colère*): ~ qn to put sb's back up.
bras [bʀa] *nm* arm // *nmpl* (*fig: travailleurs*) labour *sg*, hands; **saisir qn à** ~-**le-corps** to take hold of sb (a)round the waist; **à** ~ **raccourcis** with fists flying; ~ **droit** (*fig*) right hand man.
brasier [bʀazje] *nm* blaze, inferno.
brassard [bʀasaʀ] *nm* armband.
brasse [bʀas] *nf* (*nage*) breast-stroke; ~ **papillon** butterfly.
brassée [bʀase] *nf* armful.
brasser [bʀase] *vt* to mix; ~ **l'argent**/ **les affaires** to handle a lot of money/ business.
brasserie [bʀasʀi] *nf* (*restaurant*) café-restaurant; (*usine*) brewery.
bravache [bʀavaʃ] *nm* blusterer, braggart.
brave [bʀav] *a* (*courageux*) brave; (*bon, gentil*) good, kind.
braver [bʀave] *vt* to defy.
bravo [bʀavo] *excl* bravo // *nm* cheer.
bravoure [bʀavuʀ] *nf* bravery.
break [bʀɛk] *nm* (*AUTO*) estate car.
brebis [bʀəbi] *nf* ewe; ~ **galeuse** black sheep.
brèche [bʀɛʃ] *nf* breach, gap; **être sur la** ~ (*fig*) to be on the go.
bredouille [bʀəduj] *a* empty-handed.
bredouiller [bʀəduje] *vi, vt* to mumble, stammer.
bref, brève [bʀɛf, bʀɛv] *a* short, brief // *ad* in short; **d'un ton** ~ sharply, curtly; **en** ~ in short, in brief.
Brésil [bʀezil] *nm* Brazil.
Bretagne [bʀətaɲ] *nf* Brittany.
bretelle [bʀətɛl] *nf* (*de fusil etc*) sling; (*de vêtement*) strap; (*d'autoroute*) slip road (*Brit*), entrance/exit ramp (*US*); ~**s** *nfpl* (*pour pantalon*) braces (*Brit*),

suspenders (US).

breton, ne [brətɔ̃, -ɔn] a, nm/f Breton.

breuvage [brœvaʒ] nm beverage, drink.

brève [brɛv] a, nf voir **bref**.

brevet [brəvɛ] nm diploma, certificate; **~ (d'invention)** patent; **~ d'études du premier cycle (B.E.P.C.)** school certificate (taken at age 16); **breveté, e** a patented; (diplômé) qualified.

bribes [brib] nfpl bits, scraps; snatches; **par ~** piecemeal.

bricolage [brikɔlaʒ] nm: **le ~** do-it-yourself.

bricole [brikɔl] nf trifle; small job.

bricoler [brikɔle] vi to do DIY jobs; to potter about // vt to fix up; to tinker with; **bricoleur, euse** nm/f handyman/woman, DIY enthusiast.

bride [brid] nf bridle; (d'un bonnet) string, tie; **à ~ abattue** flat out, hell for leather; **laisser la ~ sur le cou à** to give free rein to.

bridé, e [bride] a: **yeux ~s** slit eyes.

brider [bride] vt (réprimer) to keep in check; (cheval) to bridle; (CULIN: volaille) to truss.

bridge [bridʒ(ə)] nm bridge.

brièvement [brijɛvmɑ̃] ad briefly.

brigade [brigad] nf (POLICE) squad; (MIL) brigade; (gén) team.

brigadier [brigadje] nm sergeant.

brigandage [brigɑ̃daʒ] nm robbery.

briguer [brige] vt to aspire to.

brillamment [brijamɑ̃] ad brilliantly.

brillant, e [brijɑ̃, -ɑ̃t] a brilliant; bright; (luisant) shiny, shining // nm (diamant) brilliant.

briller [brije] vi to shine.

brimer [brime] vt to harass; to bully.

brin [brɛ̃] nm (de laine, ficelle etc) strand; (fig): **un ~ de** a bit of; **~ d'herbe** blade of grass; **~ de muguet** sprig of lily of the valley.

brindille [brɛ̃dij] nf twig.

brio [brijo] nm: **avec ~** with panache.

brioche [brijɔʃ] nf brioche (bun); (fam: ventre) paunch.

brique [brik] nf brick // a inv brick red.

briquer [brike] vt to polish up.

briquet [brikɛ] nm (cigarette) lighter.

brise [briz] nf breeze.

briser [brize] vt, se **~** vi to break.

britannique [britanik] a British // nm/f British person, Briton; **les B~s** the British.

broc [bro] nm pitcher.

brocante [brɔkɑ̃t] nf junk, second-hand goods pl.

brocanteur, euse [brɔkɑ̃tœr, -øz] nm/f junkshop owner; junk dealer.

broche [brɔʃ] nf brooch; (CULIN) spit; (MÉD) pin; **à la ~** spit-roasted.

broché, e [brɔʃe] a (livre) paperbacked.

brochet [brɔʃɛ] nm pike inv.

brochette [brɔʃɛt] nf skewer.

brochure [brɔʃyr] nf pamphlet, brochure, booklet.

broder [brɔde] vt to embroider // vi to embroider the facts; **broderie** nf embroidery.

broncher [brɔ̃ʃe] vi: **sans ~** without flinching; without turning a hair.

bronches [brɔ̃ʃ] nfpl bronchial tubes; **bronchite** nf bronchitis.

bronze [brɔ̃z] nm bronze.

bronzer [brɔ̃ze] vt to tan // vi to get a tan; se **~** to sunbathe.

brosse [brɔs] nf brush; **coiffé en ~** with a crewcut; **~ à cheveux** hairbrush; **~ à dents** toothbrush; **~ à habits** clothesbrush; **brosser** vt (nettoyer) to brush; (fig: tableau etc) to paint; to draw; **brosser les dents** to brush one's teeth.

brouette [bruɛt] nf wheelbarrow.

brouhaha [bruaa] nm hubbub.

brouillard [brujar] nm fog.

brouille [bruj] nf quarrel.

brouiller [bruje] vt to mix up; to confuse; (rendre trouble) to cloud; (désunir: amis) to set at odds; se **~** vi (vue) to cloud over; (détails) to become confused; (gens) to fall out.

brouillon, ne [brujɔ̃, -ɔn] a disorganised; unmethodical // nm draft.

broussailles [brusaj] nfpl undergrowth sg; **broussailleux, euse** a bushy.

brousse [brus] nf: **la ~** the bush.

brouter [brute] vi to graze.

broutille [brutij] nf trifle.

broyer [brwaje] vt to crush; **~ du noir** to be down in the dumps.

bru [bry] nf daughter-in-law.

bruiner [brɥine] vb impersonnel: **il bruine** it's drizzling, there's a drizzle.

bruire [brɥir] vi to murmur; to rustle.

bruit [brɥi] nm: **un ~** a noise, a sound; (fig: rumeur) a rumour; **le ~** noise; **sans ~** without a sound, noiselessly; **~ de fond** background noise.

bruitage [brɥitaʒ] nm sound effects pl.

brûlant, e [brylɑ̃, -ɑ̃t] a burning; (liquide) boiling (hot); (regard) fiery.

brûlé, e [bryle] a (fig: démasqué) blown // nm: **odeur de ~** smell of burning.

brûle-pourpoint [brylpurpwɛ̃]: **à ~** ad point-blank.

brûler [bryle] vt to burn; (suj: eau bouillante) to scald; (consommer: électricité, essence) to use; (feu rouge, signal) to go through // vi to burn; (jeu) to be warm; se **~** to burn o.s.; to scald o.s.; se **~ la cervelle** to blow one's brains out.

brûlure [brylyr] nf (lésion) burn; (sensation) burning (sensation); **~s d'estomac** heartburn sg.

brume [brym] nf mist.

brun, e [brœ̃, -yn] a brown; (cheveux, personne) dark; **brunir** vi to get a tan.

brusque [bʀysk(ə)] a abrupt; ~**ment** ad abruptly; **brusquer** vt to rush.

brut, e [bʀyt] a raw, crude, rough; (COMM) gross; (données) raw // nf brute; (pétrole) ~ crude (oil).

brutal, e, aux [bʀytal, -o] a brutal; ~**iser** vt to handle roughly, manhandle.

brute [bʀyt] a, nf voir **brut**.

Bruxelles [bʀysɛl] n Brussels.

bruyamment [bʀɥijamɑ̃] ad noisily.

bruyant, e [bʀɥijɑ̃, -ɑ̃t] a noisy.

bruyère [bʀɥijɛʀ] nf heather.

bu, e pp de **boire**.

buccal, e, aux [bykal, -o] a: par voie ~e orally.

bûche [byʃ] nf log; prendre une ~ (fig) to come a cropper; ~ de Noël Yule log.

bûcher [byʃe] nm pyre; bonfire // vb (fam) vi to swot (Brit), slave (away) // vt to swot up (Brit), slave away at.

bûcheron [byʃʀɔ̃] nm woodcutter.

budget [bydʒɛ] nm budget.

buée [bɥe] nf (sur une vitre) mist; (de l'haleine) steam.

buffet [byfɛ] nm (meuble) sideboard; (de réception) buffet; ~ (de gare) (station) buffet, snack bar.

buffle [byfl(ə)] nm buffalo.

buis [bɥi] nm box tree; (bois) box(wood).

buisson [bɥisɔ̃] nm bush.

buissonnière [bɥisɔnjɛʀ] af: faire l'école ~ to skip school.

bulbe [bylb(ə)] nm (BOT, ANAT) bulb; (coupole) onion-shaped dome.

Bulgarie [bylgaʀi] nf Bulgaria.

bulle [byl] nf bubble; (papale) bull.

bulletin [byltɛ̃] nm (communiqué, journal) bulletin; (papier) form; (SCOL) report; ~ **d'informations** news bulletin; ~ **météorologique** weather report; ~ **de salaire** pay-slip; ~ **de santé** medical bulletin; ~ (**de vote**) ballot paper.

bureau, x [byʀo] nm (meuble) desk; (pièce, service) office; ~ **de change** (foreign) exchange office ou bureau; ~ **d'embauche** employment office; ~ **de location** box office; ~ **de poste** post office; ~ **de tabac** tobacconist's (shop); ~ **de vote** polling station; ~**cratie** [-kʀasi] nf bureaucracy.

burin [byʀɛ̃] nm cold chisel; (ART) burin.

burlesque [byʀlɛsk(ə)] a ridiculous; (LITTÉRATURE) burlesque.

bus vb [by] voir **boire** // nm [bys] bus.

busqué, e [byske] a (nez) hook(ed).

buste [byst(ə)] nm (ANAT) chest; bust.

but [by] vb voir **boire** // nm (cible) target; (fig) goal; aim; (FOOTBALL etc) goal; de ~ en blanc point-blank; avoir pour ~ de faire to aim to do; dans le ~ de with the intention of.

butane [bytan] nm butane; Calor gas ®.

buter [byte] vi: ~ **contre/sur** to bump

into; to stumble against // vt to antagonize; se ~ vi to get obstinate; to dig in one's heels.

butin [bytɛ̃] nm booty, spoils pl; (d'un vol) loot.

butte [byt] nf mound, hillock; être en ~ à to be exposed to.

buvais etc vb voir **boire**.

buvard [byvaʀ] nm blotter.

buvette [byvɛt] nf bar.

buveur, euse [byvœʀ, -øz] nm/f drinker.

C

c' [s] dét voir **ce**.

CA sigle m de **chiffre d'affaires**.

ça [sa] pronom (pour désigner) this; (: plus loin) that; (comme sujet indéfini) it; ~ **va?** how are you?; how are things?; (d'accord?) OK?, all right?; ~ **alors!** well really!; ~ **fait 10 ans (que)** it's 10 years (since); **c'est** ~ that's right.

çà [sa] ad: ~ **et là** here and there.

cabane [kaban] nf hut, cabin.

cabaret [kabaʀɛ] nm night club.

cabas [kaba] nm shopping bag.

cabillaud [kabijo] nm cod inv.

cabine [kabin] nf (de bateau) cabin; (de plage) (beach) hut; (de piscine etc) cubicle; (de camion, train) cab; (d'avion) cockpit; ~ **d'essayage** fitting room; ~ **spatiale** space capsule; ~ (**téléphonique**) call ou (tele)phone box.

cabinet [kabinɛ] nm (petite pièce) closet; (de médecin) surgery (Brit), office (US); (de notaire etc) office; (: clientèle) practice; (POL) Cabinet; ~s nmpl (w.-c.) toilet sg; ~ **d'affaires** business consultants' (bureau), business partnership; ~ **de toilette** toilet; ~ **de travail** study.

câble [kɑbl(ə)] nm cable.

cabrer [kabʀe]: se ~ vi (cheval) to rear up; (avion) to nose up; (fig) to revolt, rebel.

cabriole [kabʀijɔl] nf caper; somersault.

cacahuète [kakaɥɛt] nf peanut.

cacao [kakao] nm cocoa (powder); (boisson) cocoa.

cache [kaʃ] nm mask, card (for masking) // nf hiding place.

cache-cache [kaʃkaʃ] nm: jouer à ~ to play hide-and-seek.

cachemire [kaʃmir] nm cashmere.

cache-nez [kaʃne] nm inv scarf, muffler.

cacher [kaʃe] vt to hide, conceal; ~ **qch à qn** to hide ou conceal sth from sb; se ~ vi to hide; to be hidden ou concealed; **il ne s'en cache pas** he makes no secret of it.

cachet [kaʃɛ] nm (comprimé) tablet; (sceau: du roi) seal; (: de la poste) postmark; (*rétribution*) fee; (*fig*) style, character; **cacheter** *vt* to seal.

cachette [kaʃɛt] *nf* hiding place; **en ~** on the sly, secretly.

cachot [kaʃo] *nm* dungeon.

cactus [kaktys] *nm* cactus.

cadavre [kadavʀ(ə)] *nm* corpse, (dead) body.

caddie [kadi] *nm* (supermarket) trolley.

cadeau, x [kado] *nm* present, gift; **faire un ~ à qn** to give sb a present *ou* gift; **faire ~ de qch à qn** to make a present of sth to sb, give sb sth as a present.

cadenas [kadna] *nm* padlock.

cadence [kadɑ̃s] *nf* (*MUS*) cadence; (*: tempo*) rhythm; (*de travail etc*) rate; **en ~** rhythmically; in time.

cadet, te [kadɛ, -ɛt] *a* younger; (*le plus jeune*) youngest // *nm/f* youngest child *ou* one, youngest boy *ou* son/girl *ou* daughter.

cadran [kadʀɑ̃] *nm* dial; **~ solaire** sundial.

cadre [kadʀ(ə)] *nm* frame; (*environnement*) surroundings *pl*; (*limites*) scope // *nm/f* (*ADMIN*) managerial employee, executive; **rayer qn des ~s** to dismiss sb; **dans le ~ de** (*fig*) within the framework *ou* context of.

cadrer [kadʀe] *vi*: **~ avec** to tally *ou* correspond with // *vt* to centre.

caduc, uque [kadyk] *a* obsolete; (*BOT*) deciduous.

cafard [kafaʀ] *nm* cockroach; **avoir le ~** to be down in the dumps.

café [kafe] *nm* coffee; (*bistro*) café // *a inv* coffee(-coloured); **~ au lait** white coffee; **~ noir** black coffee; **~ tabac** tobacconist's or newsagent's also serving coffee and spirits; **cafetier, ière** *nm/f* café-owner // *nf* (*pot*) coffee-pot.

cafouillage [kafujaʒ] *nm* shambles *sg*.

cage [kaʒ] *nf* cage; **~ (des buts)** goal; **~ d'escalier** (stair)well; **~ thoracique** rib cage.

cageot [kaʒo] *nm* crate.

cagibi [kaʒibi] *nm* shed.

cagneux, euse [kaɲø, -øz] *a* knock-kneed.

cagnotte [kaɲɔt] *nf* kitty.

cagoule [kagul] *nf* cowl; hood; (*SKI etc*) cagoule.

cahier [kaje] *nm* notebook; **~ de brouillons** roughbook, jotter; **~ d'exercices** exercise book.

cahot [kao] *nm* jolt, bump.

caïd [kaid] *nm* big chief, boss.

caille [kaj] *nf* quail.

cailler [kaje] *vi* (*lait*) to curdle; (*sang*) to clot.

caillot [kajo] *nm* (blood) clot.

caillou, x [kaju] *nm* (little) stone; **~teux, euse** *a* stony; pebbly.

Caire [kɛʀ] *nm*: **le ~** Cairo.

caisse [kɛs] *nf* box; (*où l'on met la re-*

cette) cashbox; till; (*où l'on paye*) cash desk (*Brit*), check-out; (*de banque*) cashier's desk; (*TECH*) case, casing; **~ enregistreuse** cash register; **~ d'épargne** savings bank; **~ de retraite** pension fund; **caissier, ière** *nm/f* cashier.

cajoler [kaʒɔle] *vt* to wheedle, coax; to surround with love.

cake [kɛk] *nm* fruit cake.

calandre [kalɑ̃dʀ(ə)] *nf* radiator grill.

calanque [kalɑ̃k] *nf* rocky inlet.

calcaire [kalkɛʀ] *nm* limestone // *a* (*eau*) hard; (*GÉO*) limestone *cpd*.

calciné, e [kalsine] *a* burnt to ashes.

calcul [kalkyl] *nm* calculation; **le ~** (*SCOL*) arithmetic; **~ (biliaire)** (gall)stone; **~ (rénal)** (kidney) stone; **~ateur** *nm*, **~atrice** *nf* calculator.

calculer [kalkyle] *vt* to calculate, work out; (*combiner*) to calculate.

calculette [kalkylɛt] *nf* pocket calculator.

cale [kal] *nf* (*de bateau*) hold; (*en bois*) wedge; **~ sèche** dry dock.

calé, e [kale] *a* (*fam*) clever, bright.

caleçon [kalsɔ̃] *nm* pair of underpants, trunks *pl*; **~ de bain** bathing trunks *pl*.

calembour [kalɑ̃buʀ] *nm* pun.

calendes [kalɑ̃d] *nfpl*: **renvoyer aux ~ grecques** to postpone indefinitely.

calendrier [kalɑ̃dʀije] *nm* calendar; (*fig*) timetable.

calepin [kalpɛ̃] *nm* notebook.

caler [kale] *vt* to wedge; **~ (son moteur/véhicule)** to stall (one's engine/vehicle).

calfeutrer [kalføtʀe] *vt* to (make) draughtproof; **se ~** *vi* to make o.s. snug and comfortable.

calibre [kalibʀ(ə)] *nm* (*d'un fruit*) grade; (*d'une arme*) bore, calibre; (*fig*) calibre.

califourchon [kalifuʀʃɔ̃]: **à ~** *ad* astride.

câlin, e [kalɛ̃, -in] *a* cuddly, cuddlesome; tender.

câliner [kaline] *vt* to fondle, cuddle.

calmant [kalmɑ̃] *nm* tranquillizer, sedative; (*pour la douleur*) painkiller.

calme [kalm(ə)] *a* calm, quiet // *nm* calm(ness), quietness.

calmer [kalme] *vt* to calm (down); (*douleur, inquiétude*) to ease, soothe; **se ~** *vi* to calm down.

calomnie [kalɔmni] *nf* slander; (*écrite*) libel; **calomnier** *vt* to slander; to libel.

calorie [kalɔʀi] *nf* calorie.

calorifuge [kalɔʀifyʒ] *a* (heat-)insulating, heat-retaining.

calotte [kalɔt] *nf* (*coiffure*) skullcap; (*gifle*) slap.

calquer [kalke] *vt* to trace; (*fig*) to copy exactly.

calvaire [kalvɛʀ] *nm* (*croix*) wayside cross, calvary; (*souffrances*) suffering.

calvitie [kalvisi] *nf* baldness.

camarade [kamaʀad] *nm/f* friend, pal; (*POL*) comrade; **~rie** *nf* friendship.

cambiste [kãbist(ə)] *nm* (*COMM*) foreign exchange dealer, exchange agent.

cambouis [kãbwi] *nm* dirty oil *ou* grease.

cambrer [kãbʀe] *vt* to arch.

cambriolage [kãbʀijɔlaʒ] *nm* burglary.

cambrioler [kãbʀijɔle] *vt* to burgle (*Brit*), burglarize (*US*); **cambrioleur, euse** *nm/f* burglar.

came [kam] *nf*: arbre à ~s camshaft.

camelot [kamlo] *nm* street pedlar.

camelote [kamlɔt] *nf* rubbish, trash, junk.

caméra [kameʀa] *nf* (*CINÉMA*, *TV*) camera; (*d'amateur*) cine-camera.

camion [kamjɔ̃] *nm* lorry (*Brit*), truck; (*plus petit, fermé*) van; ~ de dépannage breakdown (*Brit*) *ou* tow (*US*) truck; **~-citerne** *nm* tanker; **camionnage** *nm* haulage (*Brit*), trucking (*US*); **camionnette** *nf* (small) van; **camionneur** *nm* (*entrepreneur*) haulage contractor (*Brit*), trucker (*US*); (*chauffeur*) lorry (*Brit*) *ou* truck driver; van driver.

camisole [kamizɔl] *nf*: ~ (de force) straitjacket.

camomille [kamɔmij] *nf* camomile; (*boisson*) camomile tea.

camoufler [kamufle] *vt* to camouflage; (*fig*) to conceal, cover up.

camp [kã] *nm* camp; (*fig*) side.

campagnard, e [kãpaɲaʀ, -aʀd(ə)] *a* country *cpd*.

campagne [kãpaɲ] *nf* country, countryside; (*MIL, POL, COMM*) campaign; à la ~ in the country.

camper [kãpe] *vi* to camp // *vt* to sketch; se ~ devant to plant o.s. in front of; **campeur, euse** *nm/f* camper.

camphre [kãfʀ(ə)] *nm* camphor.

camping [kãpiaʒ] *nm* camping; (*terrain de*) ~ campsite, camping site; faire du ~ to go camping.

Canada [kanada] *nm*: le ~ Canada; **canadien, ne** *a*, *nm/f* Canadian // *nf* (*veste*) fur-lined jacket.

canaille [kanaj] *nf* (*péj*) scoundrel.

canal, aux [kanal, -o] *nm* canal; (*naturel*) channel.

canalisation [kanalizasjɔ̃] *nf* (*tuyau*) pipe.

canaliser [kanalize] *vt* to canalize; (*fig*) to channel.

canapé [kanape] *nm* settee, sofa.

canard [kanaʀ] *nm* duck.

canari [kanaʀi] *nm* canary.

cancans [kãkã] *nmpl* (malicious) gossip *sg*.

cancer [kãsɛʀ] *nm* cancer; (*signe*): le C~ Cancer.

cancre [kãkʀ(ə)] *nm* dunce.

candeur [kãdœʀ] *nf* ingenuousness,

guilelessness.

candi [kãdi] *a inv*: sucre ~ (sugar-)candy.

candidat, e [kãdida, -at] *nm/f* candidate; (*à un poste*) applicant, candidate; **candidature** *nf* candidature; application; **poser sa candidature** to submit an application, apply.

candide [kãdid] *a* ingenuous, guileless.

cane [kan] *nf* (female) duck.

caneton [kantɔ̃] *nm* duckling.

canette [kanɛt] *nf* (*de bière*) (flip-top) bottle.

canevas [kanva] *nm* (*COUTURE*) canvas.

caniche [kaniʃ] *nm* poodle.

canicule [kanikyl] *nf* scorching heat.

canif [kanif] *nm* penknife, pocket knife.

canine [kanin] *nf* canine (tooth).

caniveau, x [kanivo] *nm* gutter.

canne [kan] *nf* (walking) stick; ~ à pêche fishing rod; ~ à sucre sugar cane.

cannelle [kanɛl] *nf* cinnamon.

canoë [kanɔe] *nm* canoe; (*sport*) canoeing.

canon [kanɔ̃] *nm* (*arme*) gun; (*HISTOIRE*) cannon; (*d'une arme: tube*) barrel; (*fig*) model; (*MUS*) canon; ~ rayé rifled barrel.

canot [kano] *nm* ding(h)y; ~ pneumatique inflatable ding(h)y; ~ de sauvetage lifeboat; **canotage** *nm* rowing.

canotier [kanɔtje] *nm* boater.

cantatrice [kãtatʀis] *nf* (opera) singer.

cantine [kãtin] *nf* canteen.

cantique [kãtik] *nm* hymn.

canton [kãtɔ̃] *nm* district consisting of several communes; (*en Suisse*) canton.

cantonade [kãtɔnad]: à la ~ *ad* to everyone in general; from the rooftops.

cantonner [kãtɔne] *vt* (*MIL*) to quarter, station; se ~ dans to confine o.s. to.

cantonnier [kãtɔnje] *nm* roadmender.

canular [kanylaʀ] *nm* hoax.

caoutchouc [kautʃu] *nm* rubber; ~ mousse foam rubber.

cap [kap] *nm* (*GÉO*) cape; headland; (*fig*) hurdle; watershed; (*NAVIG*): changer de ~ to change course; mettre le ~ sur to head *ou* steer for.

C.A.P. *sigle m* (= *Certificat d'aptitude professionnelle*) *vocational training certificate taken at secondary school*.

capable [kapabl(ə)] *a* able, capable; ~ de qch/faire capable of sth/doing.

capacité [kapasite] *nf* (*compétence*) ability; (*JUR, contenance*) capacity; ~ (*en droit*) basic legal qualification.

cape [kap] *nf* cape, cloak; **rire sous ~** to laugh up one's sleeve.

C.A.P.E.S. [kapɛs] *sigle m* (= *Certificat d'aptitude pédagogique à l'enseignement secondaire*) *teaching diploma*.

capillaire [kapilɛʀ] *a* (*soins, lotion*) hair

cpd; (*vaisseau etc*) capillary.

capitaine [kapitɛn] *nm* captain; ~ des pompiers fire chief, firemaster.

capital, e, aux [kapital, -o] *a* major; of paramount importance; fundamental // *nm* capital; (*fig*) stock; asset // *nf* (*ville*) capital; (*lettre*) capital (letter); // *nmpl* (*fonds*) capital *sg*; ~ (**social**) authorized capital; **~iser** *vt* to amass, build up; **~isme** *nm* capitalism; **~iste** *a, nm/f* capitalist.

capiteux, euse [kapitø, -øz] *a* heady.

capitonné, e [kapitɔne] *a* padded.

caporal, aux [kapɔral, -o] *nm* lance corporal.

capot [kapo] *nm* (*AUTO*) bonnet (*Brit*), hood (*US*).

capote [kapɔt] *nf* (*de voiture*) hood (*Brit*), top (*US*); (*fam*) condom.

capoter [kapɔte] *vi* to overturn.

câpre [kɑpʀ(ə)] *nf* caper.

caprice [kapʀis] *nm* whim, caprice; passing fancy; **capricieux, euse** *a* capricious; whimsical; temperamental.

Capricorne [kapʀikɔʀn] *nm:* le ~ Capricorn.

capsule [kapsyl] *nf* (*de bouteille*) cap; (*BOT etc, spatiale*) capsule.

capter [kapte] *vt* (*ondes radio*) to pick up; (*eau*) to harness; (*fig*) to win, capture.

captieux, euse [kapsjø, -øz] *a* specious.

captivité [kaptivite] *nf* captivity.

capturer [kaptyʀe] *vt* to capture.

capuche [kapyʃ] *nf* hood.

capuchon [kapyʃɔ̃] *nm* hood; (*de stylo*) cap, top.

capucine [kapysin] *nf* (*BOT*) nasturtium.

caquet [kakɛ] *nm:* rabattre le ~ à qn to bring sb down a peg or two.

caqueter [kakte] *vi* to cackle.

car [kaʀ] *nm* coach // *cj* because, for.

carabine [kaʀabin] *nf* carbine, rifle.

caractère [kaʀaktɛʀ] *nm* (*gén*) character; **en ~s gras** in bold type; **en petits ~s** in small print; **~s d'imprimerie** (block) capitals; **avoir bon/mauvais ~** to be good-/ill-natured; **caractériel, le** *a* (of) character // *nm/f* emotionally disturbed child.

caractérisé, e [kaʀakteʀize] *a:* c'est une grippe ~e it is a clear(-cut) case of flu.

caractéristique [kaʀakteʀistik] *a, nf* characteristic.

carafe [kaʀaf] *nf* decanter; carafe.

caraïbe [kaʀaib] *a* Caribbean // *n:* les C~s the Caribbean (Islands); **la mer des** C~s the Caribbean Sea.

carambolage [kaʀɑ̃bɔlaʒ] *nm* multiple crash, pileup.

caramel [kaʀamɛl] *nm* (*bonbon*) caramel, toffee; (*substance*) caramel.

carapace [kaʀapas] *nf* shell.

caravane [kaʀavan] *nf* caravan; **caravaning** *nm* caravanning; (*emplacement*) caravan site.

carbone [kaʀbɔn] *nm* carbon; (*feuille*) carbon, sheet of carbon paper; (*double*) carbon (copy).

carbonique [kaʀbɔnik] *a:* **neige ~** dry ice.

carbonisé, e [kaʀbɔnize] *a* charred.

carboniser [kaʀbɔnize] *vt* to carbonize; to burn down, reduce to ashes.

carburant [kaʀbyʀɑ̃] *nm* (motor) fuel.

carburateur [kaʀbyʀatœʀ] *nm* carburettor.

carcan [kaʀkɑ̃] *nm* (*fig*) yoke, shackles *pl*.

carcasse [kaʀkas] *nf* carcass; (*de véhicule etc*) shell.

cardiaque [kaʀdjak] *a* cardiac, heart *cpd* // *nm/f* heart patient.

cardigan [kaʀdigɑ̃] *nm* cardigan.

cardiologue [kaʀdjɔlɔg] *nm/f* cardiologist, heart specialist.

carême [kaʀɛm] *nm:* le C~ Lent.

carence [kaʀɑ̃s] *nf* incompetence, inadequacy; (*manque*) deficiency.

caresse [kaʀɛs] *nf* caress.

caresser [kaʀɛse] *vt* to caress, fondle; (*fig: projet*) to toy with.

cargaison [kaʀgɛzɔ̃] *nf* cargo, freight.

cargo [kaʀgo] *nm* cargo boat, freighter.

carie [kaʀi] *nf:* la ~ (**dentaire**) tooth decay; **une ~** a bad tooth.

carillon [kaʀijɔ̃] *nm* (*d'église*) bells *pl*; (*de pendule*) chimes *pl*; (*de porte*) door chime *ou* bell.

carlingue [kaʀlɛ̃g] *nf* cabin.

carnassier, ière [kaʀnasje, -jɛʀ] *a* carnivorous.

carnaval [kaʀnaval] *nm* carnival.

carnet [kaʀnɛ] *nm* (*calepin*) notebook; (*de tickets, timbres etc*) book; (*d'école*) school report; (*journal intime*) diary; **~ de chèques** cheque book.

carotte [kaʀɔt] *nf* carrot.

carpette [kaʀpɛt] *nf* rug.

carré, e [kaʀe] *a* square; (*fig: franc*) straightforward // *nm* (*de terrain, jardin*) patch, plot; (*MATH*) square; **mètre/ kilomètre ~** square metre/kilometre.

carreau, x [kaʀo] *nm* (*en faïence etc*) (floor) tile; (*wall*) tile; (*de fenêtre*) (window) pane; (*motif*) check, square; (*CARTES: couleur*) diamonds *pl*; (*: carte*) diamond; **tissu à ~x** checked fabric.

carrefour [kaʀfuʀ] *nm* crossroads *sg*.

carrelage [kaʀlaʒ] *nm* tiling; (tiled) floor.

carrelet [kaʀlɛ] *nm* (*poisson*) plaice.

carrément [kaʀemɑ̃] *ad* straight out, bluntly; completely, altogether.

carrer [kaʀe]: se ~ *vi:* se ~ dans to settle o.s. comfortably in.

carrière [kaʀjɛʀ] *nf* (*de roches*) quarry;

(*métier*) career; **militaire de ~** professional soldier.

carriole [kaʀjɔl] *nf* (*péj*) old cart.

carrossable [kaʀɔsabl(ə)] *a* suitable for (motor) vehicles.

carrosse [kaʀɔs] *nm* (horse-drawn) coach.

carrosserie [kaʀɔsʀi] *nf* body, coachwork *q*; (*activité, commerce*) coachbuilding.

carrousel [kaʀuzɛl] *nm* (*ÉQUITATION*) carousel; (*fig*) merry-go-round.

carrure [kaʀyʀ] *nf* build; (*fig*) stature, calibre.

cartable [kaʀtabl(ə)] *nm* (*d'écolier*) satchel, (school)bag.

carte [kaʀt(ə)] *nf* (*de géographie*) map; (*marine, du ciel*) chart; (*de fichier, d'abonnement etc, à jouer*) card; (*au restaurant*) menu; (*aussi*: ~ **postale**) (post)card; (*aussi*: ~ **de visite**) (visiting) card; **à la ~** (*au restaurant*) à la carte; ~ **bancaire** cash card; ~ **de crédit** credit card; **la ~ grise** (*AUTO*) ≈ the (car) registration book, the logbook; ~ **d'identité** identity card; ~ **routière** road map; ~ **de séjour** residence permit.

carter [kaʀtɛʀ] *nm* sump.

carton [kaʀtɔ̃] *nm* (*matériau*) cardboard; (*boîte*) (cardboard) box; (*d'invitation*) invitation card; **faire un ~** (*au tir*) to have a go at the rifle range; to score a hit; ~ (**à dessin**) portfolio; **cartonné, e** *a* (*livre*) hardback, cased; **~-pâte** *nm* pasteboard.

cartouche [kaʀtuʃ] *nf* cartridge; (*de cigarettes*) carton.

cas [kɑ] *nm* case; **faire peu de ~/grand ~ de** to attach little/great importance to; **en aucun ~** no account; **au ~ où** in case; **en ~ de** in case of, in the event of; **en ~ de besoin** if need be; **en tout ~** in any case, at any rate; ~ **de conscience** matter of conscience.

casanier, ière [kazanje, -jɛʀ] *a* stay-at-home.

casaque [kazak] *nf* (*de jockey*) blouse.

cascade [kaskad] *nf* waterfall, cascade; (*fig*) stream, torrent.

cascadeur, euse [kaskadœʀ, -øz] *nm/f* stuntman/girl.

case [kɑz] *nf* (*hutte*) hut; (*compartiment*) compartment; (*pour le courrier*) pigeonhole; (*sur un formulaire, de mots croisés, d'échiquier*) box.

caser [kɑze] *vt* (*trouver de la place pour*) to put in *ou* away; to put up; (*fig*) to find a job for; to marry off.

caserne [kazɛʀn(ə)] *nf* barracks.

cash [kaʃ] *ad*: **payer ~** to pay cash down.

casier [kɑzje] *nm* (*à journaux etc*) rack; (*de bureau*) filing cabinet; (*: à cases*) set of pigeonholes; (*case*) compartment; pigeonhole; (*: à clef*) locker; ~

judiciaire police record.

casino [kazino] *nm* casino.

casque [kask(ə)] *nm* helmet; (*chez le coiffeur*) (hair-)drier; (*pour audition*) (head-)phones *pl*, headset.

casquette [kaskɛt] *nf* cap.

cassant, e [kasɑ̃, -ɑ̃t] *a* brittle; (*fig*) brusque, abrupt.

cassation [kasɑsjɔ̃] *nf*: **cour de ~** final court of appeal.

casse [kɑs] *nf* (*pour voitures*): **mettre à la ~** to scrap; (*dégâts*): **il y a eu de la ~** there were a lot of breakages.

casse... [kɑs] *préfixe*: **~-cou** *a inv* daredevil, reckless; **~-croûte** *nm inv* snack; **~-noisette(s), ~-noix** *nm inv* nutcrackers *pl*; **~-pieds** (*fam*): **il est ~-pieds** he's a pain (in the neck).

casser [kɑse] *vt* to break; (*ADMIN: gradé*) to demote; (*JUR*) to quash; **se ~** *vi* to break.

casserole [kasʀɔl] *nf* saucepan.

casse-tête [kɑstɛt] *nm inv* (*jeu*) brain teaser; (*difficultés*) headache (*fig*).

cassette [kasɛt] *nf* (*bande magnétique*) cassette; (*coffret*) casket.

casseur [kɑsœʀ] *nm* hooligan.

cassis [kasis] *nm* blackcurrant; (*de la route*) dip, bump.

cassoulet [kasulɛ] *nm* bean and sausage hot-pot.

cassure [kɑsyʀ] *nf* break, crack.

castor [kastɔʀ] *nm* beaver.

castrer [kastʀe] *vt* (*mâle*) to castrate; (*: cheval*) to geld; (*femelle*) to spay.

catalogue [katalɔg] *nm* catalogue.

cataloguer [katalɔge] *vt* to catalogue, to list; (*péj*) to put a label on.

catalyseur [katalizœʀ] *nm* catalyst.

cataplasme [kataplasm(ə)] *nm* poultice.

cataracte [kataʀakt(ə)] *nf* cataract.

catastrophe [katastʀɔf] *nf* catastrophe, disaster.

catastrophé [katastʀɔfe] *a* (*fam*) deeply saddened.

catch [katʃ] *nm* (all-in) wrestling; **~eur, euse** *nm/f* (all-in) wrestler.

catéchisme [kateʃism(ə)] *nm* catechism.

catégorie [kategɔʀi] *nf* category.

cathédrale [katedʀal] *nf* cathedral.

catholique [katɔlik] *a, nm/f* (Roman) Catholic; **pas très ~** a bit shady *ou* fishy.

catimini [katimini] : **en ~** *ad* on the sly.

cauchemar [koʃmaʀ] *nm* nightmare.

cause [koz] *nf* cause; (*JUR*) lawsuit, case; **à ~ de** because of, owing to; **pour ~ de** on account of; owing to; **(et) pour ~** and for (a very) good reason; **être en ~** to be at stake; to be involved; to be in question; **mettre en ~** to implicate; to call into question; **remettre en ~** to challenge.

causer [koze] *vt* to cause // *vi* to chat,

talk.

causerie [kozʀi] *nf* talk.

caution [kosjɔ̃] *nf* guarantee, security; deposit; (*JUR*) bail (bond); (*fig*) backing, support; **payer la ~ de qn** to stand bail for sb; **libéré sous ~** released on bail.

cautionner [kosjɔne] *vt* to guarantee; (*soutenir*) to support.

cavalcade [kavalkad] *nf* (*fig*) stampede.

cavalier, ière [kavalje, -jɛʀ] *a* (*désinvolte*) offhand // *nm/f* rider; (*au bal*) partner // *nm* (*ÉCHECS*) knight; **faire ~ seul** to go it alone.

cave [kav] *nf* cellar // *a*: **yeux ~s** sunken eyes.

caveau, x [kavo] *nm* vault.

caverne [kavɛʀn(ə)] *nf* cave.

caviar [kavjaʀ] *nm* caviar(e).

C.C.P. *sigle m voir* **compte.**

CD *sigle m* = **compact disc.**

ce(c'), cet, cette, ces [sə, sɛt, se] ♦ *dét* (*proximité*) this; these *pl*; (*non-proximité*) that; those *pl*; **cette maison(-ci/-là)** this/that house; **cette nuit** (*qui vient*) tonight; (*passée*) last night ♦ *pronom* **1**: **c'est it's** *ou* it is; **c'est un peintre** he's *ou* he is a painter; **ce sont des peintres** they're *ou* they are painters; **c'est le facteur etc** (*pour identifier*) it's the postman; **qui est-ce?** who is it?; (*en désignant*) who is he/she?; **qu'est-ce?** what is it? **2**: **~ qui, ~ que** what; (*chose qui*): **il est bête, ~ qui me chagrine** he's stupid, which saddens me; **tout ~ qui bouge** everything *ou* which moves; **tout ~ que je sais** all I know; **~ dont j'ai parlé** what I talked about; **~ que c'est grand!** it's so big!; *voir aussi* **-ci, est-ce que, n'est-ce pas, c'est-à-dire.**

ceci [səsi] *pronom* this.

cécité [sesite] *nf* blindness.

céder [sede] *vt* to give up // *vi* (*pont, barrage*) to give way; (*personne*) to give in; **~ à** to yield to, give in to.

CEDEX [sedɛks] *sigle m* (= *courrier d'entreprise à distribution exceptionnelle*) postal service for bulk users.

cédille [sedij] *nf* cedilla.

cèdre [sɛdʀ(ə)] *nm* cedar.

C.E.E. *sigle f* (= *Communauté économique européenne*) EEC.

ceinture [sɛ̃tyʀ] *nf* belt; (*taille*) waist; (*fig*) ring; belt; circle; **~ de sécurité** safety *ou* seat belt; **ceinturer** *vt* (*saisir*) to grasp (round the waist).

cela [səla] *pronom* that; (*comme sujet indéfini*) it; **quand/où ~?** when/where (was that)?

célèbre [selɛbʀ(ə)] *a* famous.

célébrer [selebʀe] *vt* to celebrate; (*louer*) to extol.

céleri [sɛlʀi] *nm*: **~(-rave)** celeriac; **~ (en branche)** celery.

célérité [seleʀite] *nf* speed, swiftness.

célibat [seliba] *nm* celibacy; bachelor/ spinsterhood.

célibataire [selibatɛʀ] *a* single, unmarried.

celle, celles [sɛl] *pronom voir* **celui.**

cellier [selje] *nm* storeroom.

cellulaire [selylɛʀ] *a*: **voiture** *ou* **fourgon ~** prison *ou* police van.

cellule [selyl] *nf* (*gén*) cell.

cellulite [selylit] *nf* excess fat, cellulite.

celui, celle, ceux, celles [səlɥi, sɛl, sø] *pronom* **1**: **~-ci/-là, celle-ci/-là** this one/that one; **ceux-ci, celles-ci** these (ones); **ceux-là, celles-là** those (ones); **~ de mon frère** my brother's; **~ du salon/du dessous** the one in (*ou* from) the lounge/below **2**: **~ qui bouge** the one which *ou* that moves; (*personne*) the one who moves; **~ que je vois** the one (which *ou* that) I see; **~ dont je parle** the one I'm talking about **3** (*valeur indéfinie*): **~ qui veut** whoever wants.

cendre [sɑ̃dʀ(ə)] *nf* ash; **~s** (*d'un foyer*) ash(es), cinders; (*volcaniques*) ash *pl*; (*d'un défunt*) ashes; **sous la ~** (*CULIN*) in (the) embers; **cendrier** *nm* ashtray.

cène [sɛn] *nf*: **la ~** (*Holy*) Communion.

censé, e [sɑ̃se] *a*: **être ~ faire** to be supposed to do.

censeur [sɑ̃sœʀ] *nm* (*SCOL*) deputy-head (*Brit*), vice-principal (*US*); (*CINÉMA, POL*) censor.

censure [sɑ̃syʀ] *nf* censorship.

censurer [sɑ̃syʀe] *vt* (*CINÉMA, PRESSE*) to censor; (*POL*) to censure.

cent [sɑ̃] *num* a hundred, one hundred; **centaine** *nf*: **une centaine (de)** about a hundred, a hundred or so; **plusieurs centaines (de)** several hundred; **des centaines (de)** hundreds (of); **centenaire** *a* hundred-year-old // *nm* (*anniversaire*) centenary; **centième** *num* hundredth; **centigrade** *nm* centigrade; **centilitre** *nm* centilitre; **centime** *nm* centime; **centimètre** *nm* centimetre; (*ruban*) tape measure, measuring tape.

central, e, aux [sɑ̃tʀal, -o] *a* central // *nm*: **~ (téléphonique)** (telephone) exchange // *nf* power station.

centre [sɑ̃tʀ(ə)] *nm* centre; **~ d'apprentissage** training college; **~ commercial** shopping centre; **le ~-ville** the town centre, downtown (*area*) (*US*).

centuple [sɑ̃typl(ə)] *nm*: **le ~ de qch** a hundred times sth; **au ~** a hundredfold.

cep [sɛp] *nm* (vine) stock.

cèpe [sɛp] *nm* (edible) boletus.

cependant [səpɑ̃dɑ̃] *ad* however.

céramique [seʀamik] *nf* ceramics *sg*.

cercle [sɛʀkl(ə)] *nm* circle; (*objet*) band, hoop; **~ vicieux** vicious circle.

cercueil [sɛʀkœj] *nm* coffin.

céréale [seʀeal] *nf* cereal.
cérémonie [seʀemɔni] *nf* ceremony; ~s (*péj*) fuss *sg*, to-do *sg*.
cerf [seʀ] *nm* stag.
cerfeuil [seʀfœj] *nm* chervil.
cerf-volant [seʀvɔlɑ̃] *nm* kite.
cerise [sɔʀiz] *nf* cherry; **cerisier** *nm* cherry (tree).
cerné, e [seʀne] *a*: **les yeux** ~s with dark rings *ou* shadows under the eyes.
cerner [seʀne] *vt* (MIL etc) to surround; (*fig: problème*) to delimit, define.
certain, e [seʀtɛ̃, -ɛn] *a* certain // **dét** certain; **d'un** ~ **âge** past one's prime, not so young; **un** ~ **temps** (quite) some time; ~s *pronom* some; **certainement** *ad* (*probablement*) most probably *ou* likely; (*bien sûr*) certainly, of course.
certes [seʀt(ə)] *ad* admittedly; of course; indeed (yes).
certificat [seʀtifika] *nm* certificate.
certitude [seʀtityd] *nf* certainty.
cerveau, x [seʀvo] *nm* brain.
cervelas [seʀvəla] *nm* saveloy.
cervelle [seʀvɛl] *nf* (ANAT) brain.
ces [se] *dét voir* **ce.**
C.E.S. *sigle m* (= *Collège d'Enseignement Secondaire*) ≈ (junior) secondary school (*Brit*), ≈ junior high school (*US*).
cesse [sɛs]: **sans** ~ *ad* continually, constantly; continuously; **il n'avait de** ~ **que** he would not rest until.
cesser [sese] *vt* to stop // *vi* to stop, cease; ~ **de faire** to stop doing.
cessez-le-feu [seselfø] *nm inv* ceasefire.
c'est-à-dire [sɛtadiʀ] *ad* that is (to say).
cet [sɛt] *dét voir* **ce.**
cette [sɛt] *dét voir* **ce.**
ceux [sø] *pronom voir* **celui.**
C.F.D.T. *sigle f* = *Confédération française et démocratique du travail.*
C.G.C. *sigle f* = *Confédération générale des cadres.*
C.G.T. *sigle f* = *Confédération générale du travail.*
chacun, e [ʃakœ̃, -yn] *pronom* each; (*indéfini*) everyone, everybody.
chagrin [ʃagʀɛ̃] *nm* grief, sorrow; **chagriner** *vt* to grieve; to bother.
chahut [ʃay] *nm* uproar; **chahuter** *vt* to rag, bait // *vi* to make an uproar.
chai [ʃɛ] *nm* wine store.
chaîne [ʃɛn] *nf* chain; (RADIO, TV: *stations*) channel; **travail à la** ~ production line work; ~ **(haute-fidélité** *ou* **hi-fi)** hi-fi system; ~ **(de montage** *ou* **de fabrication)** production *ou* assembly line; ~ **(de montagnes)** (mountain) range; ~ **(stéréo)** stereo (system).
chair [ʃɛʀ] *nf* flesh // *a*: **(couleur)** ~ flesh-coloured; **avoir la** ~ **de poule** to have goosepimples *ou* gooseflesh; **bien en** ~ plump, well-padded; **en** ~ **et en os** in the flesh.

chaire [ʃɛʀ] *nf* (*d'église*) pulpit; (*d'université*) chair.
chaise [ʃɛz] *nf* chair; ~ **longue** deck-chair.
chaland [ʃalɑ̃] *nm* (*bateau*) barge.
châle [ʃɑl] *nm* shawl.
chaleur [ʃalœʀ] *nf* heat; (*fig*) warmth; fire, fervour; heat.
chaleureux, euse [ʃalœʀø, -øz] *a* warm.
chaloupe [ʃalup] *nf* launch; (*de sauvetage*) lifeboat.
chalumeau, x [ʃalymo] *nm* blowlamp, blowtorch.
chalutier [ʃalytje] *nm* trawler.
chamailler [ʃamaje]: **se** ~ *vi* to squabble, bicker.
chambard [ʃɑ̃baʀ] *nm* rumpus.
chambouler [ʃɑ̃bule] *vt* to disrupt, turn upside down.
chambranle [ʃɑ̃bʀɑ̃l] *nm* (door) frame.
chambre [ʃɑ̃bʀ(ə)] *nf* bedroom; (TECH) chamber; (POL) chamber, house; (JUR) court; (COMM) chamber; federation; **faire** ~ **à part** to sleep in separate rooms; ~ **à un lit/deux lits** (*à l'hôtel*) single-/twin-bedded room; ~ **à air** (*de pneu*) (inner) tube; ~ **d'amis** spare *ou* guest room; ~ **à coucher** bedroom; ~ **noire** (PHOTO) dark room.
chambrer [ʃɑ̃bʀe] *vt* (*vin*) to bring to room temperature.
chameau, x [ʃamo] *nm* camel.
champ [ʃɑ̃] *nm* field; **prendre du** ~ to draw back; ~ **de bataille** battlefield; ~ **de courses** racecourse; ~ **de tir** rifle range.
champagne [ʃɑ̃paɲ] *nm* champagne.
champêtre [ʃɑ̃pɛtʀ(ə)] *a* country *cpd*, rural.
champignon [ʃɑ̃piɲɔ̃] *nm* mushroom; (*terme générique*) fungus (*pl* i); ~ **de Paris** button mushroom.
champion, ne [ʃɑ̃pjɔ̃, -jɔn] *a, nm/f* champion; **championnat** *nm* championship.
chance [ʃɑ̃s] *nf*: **la** ~ luck; **une** ~ a stroke *ou* piece of luck *ou* good fortune; (*occasion*) a lucky break; ~s *nfpl* (*probabilités*) chances; **avoir de la** ~ to be lucky.
chanceler [ʃɑ̃sle] *vi* to totter.
chancelier [ʃɑ̃səlje] *nm* (*allemand*) chancellor.
chanceux, euse [ʃɑ̃sø, -øz] *a* lucky.
chandail [ʃɑ̃daj] *nm* (thick) sweater.
chandelier [ʃɑ̃dəlje] *nm* candlestick.
chandelle [ʃɑ̃dɛl] *nf* (*tallow*) candle; **dîner aux** ~s candlelight dinner.
change [ʃɑ̃ʒ] *nm* (COMM) exchange.
changement [ʃɑ̃ʒmɑ̃] *nm* change; ~ **de vitesses** gears; gear change.
changer [ʃɑ̃ʒe] *vt* (*modifier*) to change, alter; (*remplacer, COMM, rhabiller*) to change // *vi* to change, alter; **se** ~ *vi* to

change (o.s.); ~ **de** (remplacer: adresse, nom, voiture etc) to change one's; (échanger, alterner: côté, place, train etc) to change + npl; ~ **de couleur/ direction** to change colour/direction; ~ **d'idée** to change one's mind; ~ **de vitesse** to change gear.

chanson [ʃɑ̃sɔ̃] nf song.

chant [ʃɑ̃] nm song; (art vocal) singing; (d'église) hymn.

chantage [ʃɑ̃taʒ] nm blackmail; **faire du** ~ to use blackmail.

chanter [ʃɑ̃te] vt, vi to sing; **si cela lui chante** (fam) if he feels like it.

chanteur, euse [ʃɑ̃tœr, -øz] nm/f singer.

chantier [ʃɑ̃tje] nm (building) site; (sur une route) roadworks pl; **mettre en** ~ to put in hand; ~ **naval** shipyard.

chantilly [ʃɑ̃tiji] nf voir **crème**.

chantonner [ʃɑ̃tɔne] vi, vt to sing to oneself, hum.

chanvre [ʃɑ̃vr(ə)] nm hemp.

chaparder [ʃaparde] vt to pinch.

chapeau, x [ʃapo] nm hat; ~ **mou** trilby.

chapelet [ʃaplɛ] nm (REL) rosary.

chapelle [ʃapɛl] nf chapel; ~ **ardente** chapel of rest.

chapelure [ʃaplyr] nf (dried) breadcrumbs pl.

chapiteau, x [ʃapito] nm (de cirque) marquee, big top.

chapitre [ʃapitr(ə)] nm chapter; (fig) subject, matter.

chapitrer [ʃapitre] vt to lecture.

chaque [ʃak] dét each, every; (indéfini) every.

char [ʃar] nm (à foin etc) cart, waggon; (de carnaval) float; ~ **(d'assaut)** tank.

charabia [ʃarabja] nm (péj) gibberish.

charade [ʃarad] nf riddle; (mimée) charade.

charbon [ʃarbɔ̃] nm coal; ~ **de bois** charcoal.

charcuterie [ʃarkytri] nf (magasin) pork butcher's shop and delicatessen; (produits) cooked pork meats pl; **charcutier, ère** nm/f pork butcher.

chardon [ʃardɔ̃] nm thistle.

charge [ʃarʒ(ə)] nf (fardeau) load, burden; (explosif, ÉLEC, MIL, JUR) charge; (rôle, mission) responsibility; ~s nfpl (du loyer) service charges; **à la** ~ **de** (dépendant de) dependent upon; (aux frais de) chargeable to; **j'accepte, à** ~ **de revanche** I accept, provided I can do the same for you one day; **prendre en** ~ to take charge of; (suj: véhicule) to take on; (dépenses) to take care of; ~s **sociales** social security contributions.

chargement [ʃarʒəmɑ̃] nm (objets) load.

charger [ʃarʒe] vt (voiture, fusil, caméra) to load; (batterie) to charge // vi

(MIL etc) to charge; **se** ~ **de** vt to see to; ~ **qn de (faire) qch** to put sb in charge of (doing) sth.

chariot [ʃarjo] nm trolley; (charrette) waggon; (de machine à écrire) carriage.

charité [ʃarite] nf charity; **faire la** ~ **à** to give (something) to.

charmant, e [ʃarmɑ̃, -ɑ̃t] a charming.

charme [ʃarm(ə)] nm charm; **charmer** vt to charm.

charnel, le [ʃarnɛl] a carnal.

charnière [ʃarnjɛr] nf hinge; (fig) turning-point.

charnu, e [ʃarny] a fleshy.

charpente [ʃarpɑ̃t] nf frame(work); **charpentier** nm carpenter.

charpie [ʃarpi] nf: **en** ~ (fig) in shreds ou ribbons.

charrette [ʃarɛt] nf cart.

charrier [ʃarje] vt to carry (along); to cart, carry.

charrue [ʃary] nf plough (Brit), plow (US).

chasse [ʃas] nf hunting; (au fusil) shooting; (poursuite) chase; (aussi: ~ **d'eau**) flush; **la** ~ **est ouverte** the hunting season is open; **gardée** private hunting grounds pl; **prendre en** ~ to give chase to; **tirer la** ~ **(d'eau)** to flush the toilet, pull the chain; ~ **à courre** hunting.

chassé-croisé [ʃasekrwaze] nm (fig) mix-up where people miss each other in turn.

chasse-neige [ʃasnɛʒ] nm inv snowplough.

chasser [ʃase] vt to hunt; (expulser) to chase away ou out, drive away ou out; **chasseur, euse** nm/f hunter // nm (avion) fighter.

châssis [ʃasi] nm (AUTO) chassis; (cadre) frame; (de jardin) cold frame.

chat [ʃa] nm cat; ~ **sauvage** wildcat.

châtaigne [ʃatɛɲ] nf chestnut; **châtaignier** nm chestnut (tree).

châtain [ʃatɛ̃] a inv chestnut (brown); chestnut-haired.

château, x [ʃato] nm castle; ~ **d'eau** water tower; ~ **fort** stronghold, fortified castle.

châtier [ʃatje] vt to punish; (fig: style) to polish; **châtiment** nm punishment.

chaton [ʃatɔ̃] nm (ZOOL) kitten.

chatouiller [ʃatuje] vt to tickle; (l'odorat, le palais) to titillate; **chatouilleux, euse** a ticklish; (fig) touchy, over-sensitive.

chatoyer [ʃatwaje] vi to shimmer.

châtrer [ʃatre] vt (mâle) to castrate; (: cheval) to geld; (femelle) to spay.

chatte [ʃat] nf (she-)cat.

chaud, e [ʃo, -od] a (gén) warm; (très chaud) hot; (fig) hearty; heated; **il fait** ~ it's warm; it's hot; **avoir** ~ to be warm; to be hot; **ça me tient** ~ it keeps me warm; **rester au ~** to stay in the warm.

chaudière [ʃodjɛʀ] *nf* boiler.

chaudron [ʃodʀɔ̃] *nm* cauldron.

chauffage [ʃofaʒ] *nm* heating; **~ central** central heating.

chauffard [ʃofaʀ] *nm* (*péj*) reckless driver; hit-and-run driver.

chauffe-eau [ʃofo] *nm inv* water-heater.

chauffer [ʃofe] *vt* to heat // *vi* to heat up, warm up; (*trop chauffer: moteur*) to overheat; **se ~** *vi* (*se mettre en train*) to warm up; (*au soleil*) to warm o.s.

chauffeur [ʃofœʀ] *nm* driver; (*privé*) chauffeur.

chaume [ʃom] *nm* (*du toit*) thatch.

chaumière [ʃomjɛʀ] *nf* (thatched) cottage.

chaussée [ʃose] *nf* road(way).

chausse-pied [ʃospje] *nm* shoe-horn.

chausser [ʃose] *vt* (*bottes, skis*) to put on; (*enfant*) to put shoes on; **~ du 38/42** to take size 38/42.

chaussette [ʃosɛt] *nf* sock.

chausson [ʃosɔ̃] *nm* slipper; (*de bébé*) bootee; **~ (aux pommes)** (apple) turn-over.

chaussure [ʃosyʀ] *nf* shoe; **~s basses** flat shoes; **~s de ski** ski boots.

chauve [ʃov] *a* bald.

chauve-souris [ʃovsuʀi] *nf* bat.

chauvin, e [ʃovɛ̃, -in] *a* chauvinistic.

chaux [ʃo] *nf* lime; **blanchi à la ~** white-washed.

chavirer [ʃaviʀe] *vi* to capsize.

chef [ʃɛf] *nm* head, leader; (*de cuisine*) chef; **en ~** (*MIL etc*) in chief; **~ d'accusation** charge; **~ d'entreprise** company head; **~ d'état** head of state; **~ de file** (*de parti etc*) leader; **~ de gare** station master; **~ d'orchestre** conductor.

chef-d'œuvre [ʃɛdœvʀ(ə)] *nm* masterpiece.

chef-lieu [ʃɛfljø] *nm* county town.

chemin [ʃəmɛ̃] *nm* path; (*itinéraire, direction, trajet*) way; **en ~** on the way; **~ de fer** railway (*Brit*), railroad (*US*); **par ~ de fer** by rail.

cheminée [ʃəmine] *nf* chimney; (*à l'intérieur*) chimney piece, fireplace; (*de bateau*) funnel.

cheminement [ʃəminmɑ̃] *nm* progress, course.

cheminer [ʃəmine] *vi* to walk (along).

cheminot [ʃəmino] *nm* railwayman.

chemise [ʃəmiz] *nf* shirt; (*dossier*)-folder; **~ de nuit** nightdress.

chemisier [ʃəmizje] *nm* blouse.

chenal, aux [ʃənal, -o] *nm* channel.

chêne [ʃɛn] *nm* oak (tree); (*bois*) oak.

chenil [ʃənil] *nm* kennels *pl*.

chenille [ʃənij] *nf* (*ZOOL*) caterpillar; (*AUTO*) caterpillar track.

chèque [ʃɛk] *nm* cheque (*Brit*), check (*US*); **~ sans provision** bad cheque; **~ de voyage** traveller's cheque; **chéquier** *nm* cheque book.

cher, ère [ʃɛʀ] *a* (*aimé*) dear; (*coûteux*) expensive, dear // *ad*: **cela coûte ~** it's expensive // *nf*: **la bonne chère** good food.

chercher [ʃɛʀʃe] *vt* to look for; (*gloire etc*) to seek; **aller ~** to go for, go and fetch; **~ à faire** to try to do.

chercheur, euse [ʃɛʀʃœʀ, -øz] *nm/f* researcher, research worker.

chère [ʃɛʀ] *a*, *nf voir* **cher**.

chéri, e [ʃeʀi] *a* beloved, dear; **(mon) ~** darling.

chérir [ʃeʀiʀ] *vt* to cherish.

cherté [ʃɛʀte] *nf*: **la ~ de la vie** the high cost of living.

chétif, ive [ʃetif, -iv] *a* puny, stunted.

cheval, aux [ʃəval, -o] *nm* horse; (*AUTO*): **~ (vapeur)** (C.V.) horsepower *q*; **faire du ~** to ride; **à ~** on horseback; **à ~ sur** astride; (*fig*) overlapping; **~ de course** race horse.

chevalet [ʃəvalɛ] *nm* easel.

chevalier [ʃəvalje] *nm* knight.

chevalière [ʃəvaljɛʀ] *nf* signet ring.

chevalin, e [ʃəvalɛ̃, -in] *a*: **boucherie ~e** horse-meat butcher's.

chevaucher [ʃəvoʃe] *vi* (*aussi*: **se ~**) to overlap (each other) // *vt* to be astride, straddle.

chevaux [ʃəvo] *nmpl voir* **cheval**.

chevelu, e [ʃəvly] *a* with a good head of hair, hairy (*péj*).

chevelure [ʃəvlyʀ] *nf* hair *q*.

chevet [ʃəvɛ] *nm*: **au ~ de qn** at sb's bedside; **lampe de ~** bedside lamp.

cheveu, x [ʃəvø] *nm* hair // *nmpl* (*chevelure*) hair *sg*; **avoir les ~x courts** to have short hair.

cheville [ʃəvij] *nf* (*ANAT*) ankle; (*de bois*) peg; (*pour une vis*) plug.

chèvre [ʃɛvʀ(ə)] *nf* (she-)goat.

chevreau, x [ʃəvʀo] *nm* kid.

chèvrefeuille [ʃɛvʀəfœj] *nm* honey-suckle.

chevreuil [ʃəvʀœj] *nm* roe deer *inv*; (*CULIN*) venison.

chevronné, e [ʃəvʀɔne] *a* seasoned.

chevrotant, e [ʃəvʀɔtɑ̃, -ɑ̃t] *a* quavering.

chez [ʃe] *prép* **1** (*à la demeure de*) at; (*: direction*) to; **~ qn** at/to sb's house *ou* place; **~ moi** at home; (*direction*) home **2** (*+ profession*) at; (*: direction*) to; **~ le boulanger/dentiste** at the baker's/dentist's; to the baker's/dentist's **3** (*dans le caractère, l'œuvre de*) in; **les renards/Racine** in foxes/Racine.

chez-soi [ʃeswa] *nm inv* home.

chic [ʃik] *a inv* chic, smart; (*généreux*) nice, decent // *nm* stylishness; **avoir le ~ de** to have the knack of; **~!** great!

chicane [ʃikan] *nf* (*obstacle*) zigzag;

(*querelle*) squabble.

chiche [ʃiʃ] *a* niggardly, mean // *excl* (*à un défi*) you're on!

chichi [ʃiʃi] *nm* (*fam*) fuss.

chicorée [ʃikɔʀe] *nf* (*café*) chicory; (*salade*) endive.

chien [ʃjɛ̃] *nm* dog; **en ~ de fusil** curled up; **~ de garde** guard dog.

chiendent [ʃjɛ̃dɑ̃] *nm* couch grass.

chienne [ʃjɛn] *nf* dog, bitch.

chier [ʃje] *vi* (*fam!*) to crap (*!*).

chiffon [ʃifɔ̃] *nm* (piece of) rag.

chiffonner [ʃifɔne] *vt* to crumple; (*tracasser*) to concern.

chiffonnier [ʃifɔnje] *nm* rag-and-bone man.

chiffre [ʃifʀ(ə)] *nm* (*représentant un nombre*) figure; numeral; (*montant, total*) total, sum; **en ~s ronds** in round figures; **~ d'affaires** turnover; **chiffrer** *vt* (*dépense*) to put a figure to, assess; (*message*) to (en)code, cipher.

chignon [ʃiɲɔ̃] *nm* chignon, bun.

Chili [ʃili] *nm*: **le ~** Chile.

chimie [ʃimi] *nf* chemistry; **chimique** *a* chemical; **produits chimiques** chemicals.

Chine [ʃin] *nf*: **la ~** China.

chinois, e [ʃinwa, -waz] *a* Chinese // *nm/f* Chinese.

chiot [ʃjo] *nm* pup(py).

chips [ʃips] *nfpl* crisps.

chiquenaude [ʃiknod] *nf* flick, flip.

chiromancien, ne [kiʀɔmɑ̃sjɛ̃, -ɛn] *nm/f* palmist.

chirurgical, e, aux [ʃiʀyʀʒikal, -o] *a* surgical.

chirurgie [ʃiʀyʀʒi] *nf* surgery; **~ esthétique** plastic surgery; **chirurgien, ne** *nm/f* surgeon.

choc [ʃɔk] *nm* impact; shock; crash; (*moral*) shock; (*affrontement*) clash.

chocolat [ʃɔkɔla] *nm* chocolate; (*boisson*) (hot) chocolate; **~ au lait** milk chocolate.

chœur [kœʀ] *nm* (*chorale*) choir; (*OPÉRA, THÉÂTRE*) chorus; **en ~** in chorus.

choisir [ʃwaziʀ] *vt* to choose, select.

choix [ʃwa] *nm* choice, selection; **avoir le ~** to have the choice; **premier ~** (*COMM*) class one; **de ~** choice, selected; **au ~** as you wish.

chômage [ʃomaʒ] *nm* unemployment; **mettre au ~** to make redundant, put out of work; **être au ~** to be unemployed *ou* out of work; **chômeur, euse** *nm/f* unemployed person.

chope [ʃɔp] *nf* tankard.

choquer [ʃɔke] *vt* (*offenser*) to shock; (*commotionner*) to shake (up).

choriste [kɔʀist(ə)] *nm/f* choir member; (*OPÉRA*) chorus member.

chorus [kɔʀys] *nm*: **faire ~** (**avec**) to voice one's agreement (with).

chose [ʃoz] *nf* thing; **c'est peu de ~** it's

nothing (really); it's not much.

chou, x [ʃu] *nm* cabbage; **mon petit ~** (my) sweetheart; **~ à la crème** cream bun (*made of choux pastry*).

chouchou, te [ʃuʃu, -ut] *nm/f* (*SCOL*) teacher's pet.

choucroute [ʃukʀut] *nf* sauerkraut.

chouette [ʃwɛt] *nf* owl // *a* (*fam*) great, smashing.

chou-fleur [ʃuflœʀ] *nm* cauliflower.

choyer [ʃwaje] *vt* to cherish; to pamper.

chrétien, ne [kʀetjɛ̃, -ɛn] *a*, *nm/f* Christian.

Christ [kʀist] *nm*: **le ~** Christ; **christianisme** *nm* Christianity.

chrome [kʀom] *nm* chromium; **chromé, e** *a* chromium-plated.

chronique [kʀɔnik] *a* chronic // *nf* (*de journal*) column, page; (*historique*) chronicle; (*RADIO, TV*): **la ~ sportive/théâtrale** the sports/theatre review; **la ~ locale** local news and gossip.

chronologique [kʀɔnɔlɔʒik] *a* chronological.

chronomètre [kʀɔnɔmɛtʀ(ə)] *nm* stopwatch; **chronométrer** *vt* to time.

chrysanthème [kʀizɑ̃tɛm] *nm* chrysanthemum.

C.H.U. *sigle m* (= *centre hospitalier universitaire*) ≈ (teaching) hospital.

chuchoter [ʃyʃɔte] *vt*, *vi* to whisper.

chuinter [ʃɥɛ̃te] *vi* to hiss.

chut [ʃyt] *excl* sh!

chute [ʃyt] *nf* fall; (*de bois, papier: déchet*) scrap; **la ~ des cheveux** hair loss; **faire une ~ (de 10 m)** to fall (10 m); **~s de pluie/neige** rain/snowfalls; **~ (d'eau)** waterfall; **~ libre** free fall.

Chypre [ʃipʀ] Cyprus.

-ci, ci- [si] *ad voir* **par, ci-contre, ci-joint** etc // *dét*: **ce garçon-ci/-là** this/that boy; **ces femmes-ci/-là** these/those women.

ci-après [siapʀɛ] *ad* hereafter.

cible [sibl(ə)] *nf* target.

ciboulette [sibulɛt] *nf* (smaller) chive.

cicatrice [sikatʀis] *nf* scar.

cicatriser [sikatʀize] *vt* to heal.

ci-contre [sikɔ̃tʀ(ə)] *ad* opposite.

ci-dessous [sidəsu] *ad* below.

ci-dessus [sidəsy] *ad* above.

cidre [sidʀ(ə)] *nm* cider.

Cie *abr* (= *compagnie*) Co.

ciel [sjɛl] *nm* sky; (*REL*) heaven; **cieux** *nmpl* sky *sg*, skies; **à ~ ouvert** open-air; (*mine*) opencast.

cierge [sjɛʀʒ(ə)] *nm* candle.

cieux [sjø] *nmpl voir* **ciel**.

cigale [sigal] *nf* cicada.

cigare [sigaʀ] *nm* cigar.

cigarette [sigaʀɛt] *nf* cigarette.

ci-gît [siʒi] *ad* + *vb* here lies.

cigogne [sigɔɲ] *nf* stork.

ci-inclus, e [siɛ̃kly, -yz] *a*, *ad* enclosed.

ci-joint, e [siʒwɛ̃, -ɛ̃t] *a*, *ad* enclosed.

cil [sil] *nm* (eye)lash.

ciller [sije] *vi* to blink.

cime [sim] *nf* top; (*montagne*) peak.

ciment [simɑ̃] *nm* cement; ~ **armé** reinforced concrete.

cimetière [simtjɛʀ] *nm* cemetery; (*d'église*) churchyard.

cinéaste [sineast(ə)] *nm/f* film-maker.

cinéma [sinema] *nm* cinema; ~**tographique** *a* film *cpd*, cinema *cpd*.

cinéphile [sinefil] *nm/f* cinema-goer.

cinglant, e [sɛ̃glɑ̃, -ɑ̃t] *a* (*échec*) crushing.

cinglé, e [sɛ̃gle] *a* (*fam*) crazy.

cingler [sɛ̃gle] *vt* to lash; (*fig*) to sting.

cinq [sɛ̃k] *num* five.

cinquantaine [sɛ̃kɑ̃tɛn] *nf*: **une** ~ **(de)** about fifty; **avoir la** ~ (*âge*) to be around fifty.

cinquante [sɛ̃kɑ̃t] *num* fifty; ~**naire** *a*, *nm/f* fifty-year-old.

cinquième [sɛ̃kjɛm] *num* fifth.

cintre [sɛ̃tʀ(ə)] *nm* coat-hanger.

cintré, e [sɛ̃tʀe] *a* (*chemise*) fitted.

cirage [siʀaʒ] *nm* (shoe) polish.

circonflexe [siʀkɔ̃flɛks(ə)] *a*: **accent** ~ circumflex accent.

circonscription [siʀkɔ̃skʀipsjɔ̃] *nf* district; ~ **électorale** (*d'un député*) constituency.

circonscrire [siʀkɔ̃skʀiʀ] *vt* to define, delimit; (*incendie*) to contain.

circonstance [siʀkɔ̃stɑ̃s] *nf* circumstance; (*occasion*) occasion.

circonstancié, e [siʀkɔ̃stɑ̃sje] *a* detailed.

circonvenir [siʀkɔ̃vniʀ] *vt* to circumvent.

circuit [siʀkɥi] *nm* (*trajet*) tour, (round) trip; (*ÉLEC, TECH*) circuit.

circulaire [siʀkylɛʀ] *a*, *nf* circular.

circulation [siʀkylasjɔ̃] *nf* circulation; (*AUTO*): **la** ~ (the) traffic.

circuler [siʀkyle] *vi* to drive (along); to walk along; (*train etc*) to run; (*sang, devises*) to circulate; **faire** ~ (*nouvelle*) to spread (about), circulate; (*badauds*) to move on.

cire [siʀ] *nf* wax.

ciré [siʀe] *nm* oilskin.

cirer [siʀe] *vt* to wax, polish.

cirque [siʀk(ə)] *nm* circus; (*GÉO*) cirque; (*fig*) chaos, bedlam; carry-on.

cisaille(s) [sizaj] *nf(pl)* (gardening) shears *pl*.

ciseau, x [sizo] *nm*: ~ **(à bois)** chisel // *nmpl* (pair of) scissors.

ciseler [sizle] *vt* to chisel, carve.

citadin, e [sitadɛ̃, -in] *nm/f* city dweller.

citation [sitasjɔ̃] *nf* (*d'auteur*) quotation; (*JUR*) summons *sg*.

cité [site] *nf* town; (*plus grande*) city; ~ **universitaire** students' residences *pl*.

citer [site] *vt* (*un auteur*) to quote (from); (*nommer*) to name; (*JUR*) to summon.

citerne [sitɛʀn(ə)] *nf* tank.

citoyen, ne [sitwajɛ̃, -ɛn] *nm/f* citizen.

citron [sitʀɔ̃] *nm* lemon; ~ **vert** lime; **citronnade** *nf* lemonade; **citronnier** *nm* lemon tree.

citrouille [sitʀuj] *nf* pumpkin.

civet [sivɛ] *nm* stew.

civière [sivjɛʀ] *nf* stretcher.

civil, e [sivil] *a* (*JUR, ADMIN, poli*) civil; (*non militaire*) civilian; **en** ~ in civilian clothes; **dans le** ~ in civilian life.

civilisation [sivilizasjɔ̃] *nf* civilization.

civisme [sivism(ə)] *nm* public-spiritedness.

clair, e [klɛʀ] *a* (*chambre*) light, bright; (*eau, son, fig*) clear // *ad*: **voir** ~ to see clearly; **tirer qch au** ~ to clear sth up, clarify sth; **mettre au** ~ (*notes etc*) to tidy up; **le plus** ~ **de son temps** the better part of his time; ~ **de lune** *nm* moonlight; ~**ement** *ad* clearly.

clairière [klɛʀjɛʀ] *nf* clearing.

clairon [klɛʀɔ̃] *nm* bugle.

clairsemé, e [klɛʀsəme] *a* sparse.

clairvoyant, e [klɛʀvwajɑ̃, -ɑ̃t] *a* perceptive, clear-sighted.

clandestin, e [klɑ̃dɛstɛ̃, -in] *a* clandestine, covert; **passager** ~ stowaway.

clapier [klapje] *nm* (rabbit) hutch.

clapoter [klapɔte] *vi* to lap.

claque [klak] *nf* (*gifle*) slap.

claquer [klake] *vi* (*drapeau*) to flap; (*porte*) to bang, slam; (*coup de feu*) to ring out // *vt* (*porte*) to slam, bang; (*doigts*) to snap; **se** ~ **un muscle** to pull *ou* strain a muscle.

claquettes [klakɛt] *nfpl* tap-dancing *sg*.

clarinette [klaʀinɛt] *nf* clarinet.

clarté [klaʀte] *nf* lightness; brightness; (*d'un son, de l'eau*) clearness; (*d'une explication*) clarity.

classe [klɑs] *nf* class; (*SCOL: local*) class(room); (: *leçon, élèves*) class; **faire la** ~ (*SCOL*) to be a *ou* the teacher; to teach.

classement [klɑsmɑ̃] *nm* (*rang: SCOL*) place; (: *SPORT*) placing; (*liste: SCOL*) class list (in order of merit); (: *SPORT*) placings *pl*.

classer [klɑse] *vt* (*idées, livres*) to classify; (*papiers*) to file; (*candidat, concurrent*) to grade; (*JUR: affaire*) to close; **se** ~ **premier/dernier** to come first/last; (*SPORT*) to finish first/last.

classeur [klɑsœʀ] *nm* (*cahier*) file; (*meuble*) filing cabinet.

classique [klasik] *a* classical; (*sobre: coupe etc*) classic(al); (*habituel*) standard, classic.

claudication [klodikasjɔ̃] *nf* limp.

clause [kloz] *nf* clause.

claustrer [klostʀe] *vt* to confine.

clavecin [klavsɛ̃] *nm* harpsichord.

clavicule [klavikyl] *nf* collarbone.

clavier [klavje] *nm* keyboard.

clé *ou* **clef** |kle| *nf* key; (*MUS*) clef; (*de mécanicien*) spanner (*Brit*), wrench (*US*); **prix ~s en main** (*d'une voiture*) on-the-road price; **~ anglaise** (*monkey*) wrench; **~ de contact** ignition key.

clément, e |klemɑ̃, -ɑ̃t| *a* (*temps*) mild; (*LING*) cliché.

clerc |klɛR| *nm*: **~ de notaire** solicitor's clerk.

clergé |klɛRʒe| *nm* clergy.

cliché |kliʃe| *nm* (*PHOTO*) negative; print; (*LING*) cliché.

client, e |klijɑ̃, -ɑ̃t| *nm/f* (*acheteur*) customer, client; (*d'hôtel*) guest, patron; (*du docteur*) patient; (*de l'avocat*) client; **clientèle** *nf* (*du magasin*) customers *pl*, clientèle; (*du docteur, de l'avocat*) practice.

cligner |kliɲe| *vi*: **~ des yeux** to blink (one's eyes); **~ de l'œil** to wink.

clignotant |kliɲɔtɑ̃| *nm* (*AUTO*) indicator.

clignoter |kliɲɔte| *vi* (*étoiles etc*) to twinkle; (*lumière*) to flash; (*: vaciller*) to flicker.

climat |klima| *nm* climate.

climatisation |klimatizɑsjɔ̃| *nf* air conditioning; **climatisé, e** *a* air-conditioned.

clin d'œil |klɛ̃dœj| *nm* wink; **en un ~ in a flash**.

clinique |klinik| *nf* nursing home.

clinquant, e |klɛ̃kɑ̃, -ɑ̃t| *a* flashy.

cliqueter |klikte| *vi* to clash; to jangle; jingle; to chink.

clochard, e |klɔʃaR, -aRd(ə)| *nm/f* tramp.

cloche |klɔʃ| *nf* (*d'église*) bell; (*fam*) clot; **~ à fromage** cheese-cover.

cloche-pied |klɔʃpje|: **à ~** *ad* on one leg, hopping (along).

clocher |klɔʃe| *nm* church tower; (*en pointe*) steeple // *vi* (*fam*) to be *ou* go wrong; **de ~** (*péj*) parochial.

cloison |klwazɔ̃| *nf* partition (wall).

cloître |klwatR(ə)| *nm* cloister.

cloîtrer |klwatRe| *vt*: **se ~** to shut o.s. up *ou* away.

cloque |klɔk| *nf* blister.

clore |klɔR| *vt* to close; **clos, e** *a voir* **maison, huis** // *nm* (enclosed) field.

clôture |klotyR| *nf* closure; (*barrière*) enclosure; **clôturer** *vt* (*terrain*) to enclose; (*débats*) to close.

clou |klu| *nm* nail; (*MÉD*) boil; **~s** *nmpl* = **passage clouté**; **pneus à ~s** studded tyres; **le ~ du spectacle** the highlight of the show; **~ de girofle** clove; **~er** *vt* to nail down *ou* up.

clown |klun| *nm* clown.

club |klœb| *nm* club.

C.N.R.S. *sigle m* = *centre national de la recherche scientifique*.

coasser |kɔase| *vi* to croak.

cobaye |kɔbaj| *nm* guinea-pig.

coca |kɔka| *nm* Coke ®.

cocagne |kɔkaɲ| *nf*: **pays de ~** land of plenty.

cocaïne |kɔkain| *nf* cocaine.

cocasse |kɔkas| *a* comical, funny.

coccinelle |kɔksinɛl| *nf* ladybird (*Brit*), ladybug (*US*).

cocher |kɔʃe| *nm* coachman // *vt* to tick off; (*entailler*) to notch.

cochère |kɔʃɛR| *af*: **porte ~** carriage entrance.

cochon, ne |kɔʃɔ̃, -ɔn| *nm* pig // *a* (*fam*) dirty, smutty; **cochonnerie** *nf* (*fam*) filth; rubbish, trash.

cocktail |kɔktɛl| *nm* cocktail; (*réception*) cocktail party.

coco |kɔko| *nm voir* **noix**; (*fam*) bloke.

cocorico |kɔkɔRiko| *excl, nm* cock-a-doodle-do.

cocotier |kɔkɔtje| *nm* coconut palm.

cocotte |kɔkɔt| *nf* (*en fonte*) casserole; **~ (minute)** pressure cooker; **ma ~** (*fam*) sweetie (pie).

cocu |kɔky| *nm* cuckold.

code |kɔd| *nm* code // *a*: **phares ~s** dipped lights; **se mettre en ~(s)** to dip one's (head)lights; **~ à barres** bar code; **~ civil** Common Law; **~ pénal** penal code; **~ postal** (*numéro*) post (*Brit*) *ou* zip (*US*) code; **~ de la route** highway code.

cœur |kœR| *nm* heart; (*CARTES*: *couleur*) hearts *pl*; (*: carte*) heart; **avoir bon ~** to be kind-hearted; **avoir mal au ~** to feel sick; **en avoir le ~ net** to be clear in one's own mind (about it); **par ~** by heart; **de bon ~** willingly; **cela lui tient à ~** that's (very) close to his heart.

coffre |kɔfR(ə)| *nm* (*meuble*) chest; (*d'auto*) boot (*Brit*), trunk (*US*); **~(-fort)** *nm* safe.

coffret |kɔfRɛ| *nm* casket.

cognac |kɔɲak| *nm* brandy, cognac.

cogner |kɔɲe| *vi* to knock.

cohérent, e |kɔeRɑ̃, -ɑ̃t| *a* coherent, consistent.

cohorte |kɔɔRt(ə)| *nf* troop.

cohue |kɔy| *nf* crowd.

coi, coite |kwa, kwat| *a*: **rester ~** to remain silent.

coiffe |kwaf| *nf* headdress.

coiffé, e |kwafe| *a*: **bien/mal ~** with tidy/untidy hair; **~ en arrière** with one's hair brushed *ou* combed back.

coiffer |kwafe| *vt* (*fig*) to cover, top; **~ qn** to do sb's hair; **se ~** *vi* to do one's hair; to put on one's hat.

coiffeur, euse |kwafœR, -øz| *nm/f* hairdresser // *nf* (*table*) dressing table.

coiffure |kwafyR| *nf* (*cheveux*) hairstyle, hairdo; (*chapeau*) hat, headgear *q*; (*art*): **la ~** hairdressing.

coin |kwɛ̃| *nm* corner; (*pour coincer*) wedge; (*poinçon*) stamp; **l'épicerie du ~** the local grocer; **dans le ~** (*aux alentours*) in the area, around about; locally; **au ~ du feu** by the fireside; **regard en** ~ sideways glance.

coincer [kwɛ̃se] vt to jam.

coïncidence [kɔɛ̃sidɑ̃s] nf coincidence.

coïncider [kɔɛ̃side] vi to coincide.

coite [kwat] af voir **coi**.

col [kɔl] nm (de chemise) collar; (encolure, cou) neck; (de montagne) pass; ~ **roulé** polo-neck; ~ **de l'utérus** cervix.

colère [kɔlɛʀ] nf anger; **une** ~ **a** fit of anger; **(se mettre) en** ~ (to get) angry; **coléreux, euse a, colérique a** quick-tempered, irascible.

colifichet [kɔlifiʃɛ] nm trinket.

colimaçon [kɔlimasɔ̃] nm: **escalier en** ~ spiral staircase.

colin [kɔlɛ̃] nm hake.

colique [kɔlik] nf diarrhoea; colic (pains).

colis [kɔli] nm parcel.

collaborateur, trice [kɔlabɔʀatœʀ, -tʀis] nm/f (aussi POL) collaborator; (d'une revue) contributor.

collaborer [kɔlabɔʀe] vi to collaborate; ~ **à** to collaborate on; (revue) to contribute to.

collant, e [kɔlɑ̃, -ɑ̃t] a sticky; (robe etc) clinging, skintight; (péj) clinging // nm (bas) tights pl.

collation [kɔlasjɔ̃] nf light meal.

colle [kɔl] nf glue; (à papiers peints) (wallpaper) paste; (devinette) teaser, riddle; (SCOL fam) detention.

collecte [kɔlɛkt(ə)] nf collection.

collectif, ive [kɔlɛktif, -iv] a collective; (visite, billet) group cpd.

collection [kɔlɛksjɔ̃] nf collection; (ÉDITION) series; **collectionner** vt (tableaux, timbres) to collect; **collectionneur, euse** nm/f collector.

collectivité [kɔlɛktivite] nf group.

collège [kɔlɛʒ] nm (école) (secondary) school; (assemblée) body; **collégien, ne** nm/f schoolboy/girl.

collègue [kɔlɛg] nm/f colleague.

coller [kɔle] vt (papier, timbre) to stick (on); (affiche) to stick up; (enveloppe) to stick down; (morceaux) to stick ou glue together; (fam: mettre, fourrer) to stick, shove; (SCOL fam) to keep in // vi (être collant) to be sticky; (adhérer) to stick; ~ **à** to stick to.

collet [kɔlɛ] nm (piège) snare, noose; (cou): **prendre qn au** ~ to grab sb by the throat; ~ **monté** a inv straight-laced.

collier [kɔlje] nm (bijou) necklace; (de chien, TECH) collar; ~ (**de barbe**) narrow beard along the line of the jaw.

collimateur [kɔlimatœʀ] nm: **avoir qn/qch dans le** ~ (fig) to have sb/sth in one's sights.

colline [kɔlin] nf hill.

collision [kɔlizjɔ̃] nf collision, crash; en-

trer en ~ (avec) to collide (with).

colmater [kɔlmate] vt (fuite) to seal off; (brèche) to plug, fill in.

colombe [kɔlɔ̃b] nf dove.

colon [kɔlɔ̃] nm settler.

colonel [kɔlɔnɛl] nm colonel.

colonie [kɔlɔni] nf colony; ~ (**de vacances**) holiday camp (for children).

colonne [kɔlɔn] nf column; **se mettre en** ~ **par deux** to get into twos; ~ (**vertébrale**) spine, spinal column.

colorant [kɔlɔʀɑ̃] nm colouring.

colorer [kɔlɔʀe] vt to colour.

colorier [kɔlɔʀje] vt to colour (in).

coloris [kɔlɔʀi] nm colour, shade.

colporter [kɔlpɔʀte] vt to hawk, peddle.

colza [kɔlza] nm rape.

coma [kɔma] nm coma.

combat [kɔ̃ba] nm fight; fighting q; ~ **de boxe** boxing match.

combattant [kɔ̃batɑ̃] nm: **ancien** ~ war veteran.

combattre [kɔ̃batʀ(ə)] vt to fight; (épidémie, ignorance) to combat, fight against.

combien [kɔ̃bjɛ̃] ad (quantité) how much; (nombre) how many; (exclamatif) how; ~ **de** how much; how many; ~ **de temps** how long; ~ **coûte/pèse ceci?** how much does this cost/weigh?

combinaison [kɔ̃binɛzɔ̃] nf combination; (astuce) device, scheme; (de femme) slip; (d'aviateur) flying suit; (d'homme-grenouille) wetsuit; (bleu de travail) boiler suit (Brit), coveralls pl (US).

combine [kɔ̃bin] nf trick; (péj) scheme, fiddle (Brit).

combiné [kɔ̃bine] nm (aussi: ~ **téléphonique**) receiver.

combiner [kɔ̃bine] vt to combine; (plan, horaire) to work out, devise.

comble [kɔ̃bl(ə)] a (salle) packed (full) // nm (du bonheur, plaisir) height; ~**s** nmpl (CONSTR) attic sg, loft sg; **c'est le** ~! that beats everything!

combler [kɔ̃ble] vt (trou) to fill in; (besoin, lacune) to fill; (déficit) to make good; (satisfaire) to fulfil.

combustible [kɔ̃bystibl(ə)] nm fuel.

comédie [kɔmedi] nf comedy; (fig) playacting q; ~ **musicale** musical; **comédien, ne** nm/f actor/actress.

comestible [kɔmɛstibl(ə)] a edible.

comique [kɔmik] a (drôle) comical; (THÉÂTRE) comic // nm (artiste) comic, comedian.

comité [kɔmite] nm committee; ~ **d'entreprise** works council.

commandant [kɔmɑ̃dɑ̃] nm (gén) commander, commandant; (NAVIG, AVIAT) captain.

commande [kɔmɑ̃d] nf (COMM) order; ~**s** nfpl (AVIAT etc) controls; **sur** ~ to order; ~ à distance remote control.

commandement [kɔmãdmã] *nm* command; (*REL*) commandment.

commander [kɔmãde] *vt* (*COMM*) to order; (*diriger, ordonner*) to command; ~ à qn de faire to command *ou* order sb to do.

commando [kɔmãdo] *nm* commando (squad).

comme [kɔm] ♦ *prép* **1** (*comparaison*) like; **tout ~ son père** just like his father; **fort ~ un bœuf** as strong as an ox; **joli ~ tout** ever so pretty **2** (*manière*) like; **faites-le ~ ça** do it like this, do it this way; **~ ci, ~ ça** so-so, middling **3** (*en tant que*) as a; **donner ~ prix** to give as a prize; **travailler ~ secrétaire** to work as a secretary ♦ *cj* **1** (*ainsi que*) as; **elle écrit ~ elle parle** she writes as she talks; **~ si** as if **2** (*au moment où, alors que*) as; **il est parti ~ j'arrivais** he left as I arrived **3** (*parce que, puisque*) as; **~ il était en retard, il ...** as he was late, he ... ♦ *ad*: **~ il est fort/c'est bon!** he's so strong/it's so good!

commémorer [kɔmemɔre] *vt* to commemorate.

commencement [kɔmãsmã] *nm* beginning, start, commencement.

commencer [kɔmãse] *vt, vi* to begin, start, commence; **~ à ou de faire** to begin *ou* start doing.

comment [kɔmã] *ad* how; **~?** (*que dites-vous*) pardon? // *nm*: **le ~ et le pourquoi** the whys and wherefores.

commentaire [kɔmãtɛr] *nm* comment; remark.

commenter [kɔmãte] *vt* (*jugement, événement*) to comment (up)on; (*RADIO, TV: match, manifestation*) to cover.

commérages [kɔmeraʒ] *nmpl* gossip *sg*.

commerçant, e [kɔmɛrsã, -ãt] *nm/f* shopkeeper, trader.

commerce [kɔmɛrs(ə)] *nm* (*activité*) trade, commerce; (*boutique*) business; **vendu dans le ~** sold in the shops; **commercial, e, aux** *a* commercial, trading; (*péj*) commercial; **commercialiser** *vt* to market.

commère [kɔmɛr] *nf* gossip.

commettre [kɔmɛtr(ə)] *vt* to commit.

commis [kɔmi] *nm* (*de magasin*) (shop) assistant; (*de banque*) clerk; **~ voyageur** commercial traveller.

commissaire [kɔmisɛr] *nm* (*de police*) ≈ (police) superintendent; **~-priseur** *nm* auctioneer.

commissariat [kɔmisarja] *nm* police station.

commission [kɔmisjɔ̃] *nf* (*comité, pourcentage*) commission; (*message*) message; (*course*) errand; **~s** *nfpl* (*achats*)

shopping *sg*.

commissure [kɔmisyr] *nf*: **les ~s des lèvres** the corners of the mouth.

commode [kɔmɔd] *a* (*pratique*) convenient, handy; (*facile*) easy; (*air, personne*) easy-going; (*personne*): **pas ~** awkward (to deal with) // *nf* chest of drawers; **commodité** *nf* convenience.

commotion [kɔmosjɔ̃] *nf*: **~ (cérébrale)** concussion; **commotionné, e** *a* shocked, shaken.

commun, e [kɔmœ̃, -yn] *a* common; (*pièce*) communal, shared; (*réunion, effort*) joint // *nf* (*ADMIN*) commune, ≈ district; (: *urbaine*) ≈ borough; **~s** *nmpl* (*bâtiments*) outbuildings; **cela sort du ~** it's out of the ordinary; **le ~ des mortels** the common run of people; **en ~** (*faire*) jointly; **mettre en ~** to pool, share.

communauté [kɔmynote] *nf* community; (*JUR*): **régime de la ~** communal estate settlement.

communication [kɔmynikasjɔ̃] *nf* communication; **~ (téléphonique)** (telephone) call; **~ interurbaine** long distance call.

communier [kɔmynje] *vi* (*REL*) to receive communion; (*fig*) to be united.

communion [kɔmynjɔ̃] *nf* communion.

communiquer [kɔmynike] *vt* (*nouvelle, dossier*) to pass on, convey; (*maladie*) to pass on; (*peur etc*) to communicate; (*chaleur, mouvement*) to transmit // *vi* to communicate; **se ~ à** (*se propager*) to spread to.

communisme [kɔmynism(ə)] *nm* communism; **communiste** *a, nm/f* communist.

commutateur [kɔmytatœr] *nm* (*ÉLEC*) (change-over) switch, commutator.

compact, e [kɔ̃pakt] *a* dense; compact.

compagne [kɔ̃paɲ] *nf* companion.

compagnie [kɔ̃paɲi] *nf* (*firme, MIL*) company; (*groupe*) gathering; **tenir ~ à qn** to keep sb company; **fausser ~ à qn** to give sb the slip, slip *ou* sneak away from sb; **~ aérienne** airline (company).

compagnon [kɔ̃paɲɔ̃] *nm* companion.

comparable [kɔ̃parabl(ə)] *a*: **~ (à)** comparable (to).

comparaison [kɔ̃parɛzɔ̃] *nf* comparison.

comparaître [kɔ̃parɛtr(ə)] *vi*: **~ (devant)** to appear (before).

comparer [kɔ̃pare] *vt* to compare; **~ qch/qn à ou et** (*pour choisir*) to compare sth/sb with ou and; (*pour établir une similitude*) to compare sth/sb to.

comparse [kɔ̃pars(ə)] *nm/f* (*péj*) associate, stooge.

compartiment [kɔ̃partimã] *nm* compartment.

comparution [kɔ̃parysjɔ̃] *nf* appearance.

compas [kɔ̃pa] *nm* (*GÉOM*) (pair of)

compasses *pl*; (*NAVIG*) compass.
compassé, e [kɔ̃pɑse] *a* starchy.
compatible [kɔ̃patibl(ə)] *a* compatible.
compatir [kɔ̃patiʀ] *vi*: ~ (à) to sympathize (with).
compatriote [kɔ̃patʀijɔt] *nm/f* compatriot.
compenser [kɔ̃pɑ̃se] *vt* to compensate for, make up for.
compère [kɔ̃pɛʀ] *nm* accomplice.
compétence [kɔ̃petɑ̃s] *nf* competence.
compétent, e [kɔ̃petɑ̃, -ɑ̃t] *a* (*apte*) competent, capable.
compétition [kɔ̃petisjɔ̃] *nf* (*gén*) competition; (*SPORT*: *épreuve*) event; **la** ~ competitive sport; **la** ~ **automobile** motor racing.
complainte [kɔ̃plɛ̃t] *nf* lament.
complaire [kɔ̃plɛʀ]: se ~ *vi*: **se** ~ **dans/ parmi** to take pleasure in/in being among.
complaisance [kɔ̃plɛzɑ̃s] *nf* kindness; **pavillon de** ~ flag of convenience.
complaisant, e [kɔ̃plɛzɑ̃, -ɑ̃t] *a* (*aimable*) kind, obliging.
complément [kɔ̃plemɑ̃] *nm* complement; remainder; ~ **d'information** (*ADMIN*) supplementary *ou* further information; **complémentaire** *a* complementary; (*additionnel*) supplementary.
complet, ète [kɔ̃plɛ, -ɛt] *a* complete; (*plein*: *hôtel etc*) full // *nm* (*aussi*: ~-**veston**) suit; **complètement** *ad* completely; **compléter** *vt* (*porter à la quantité voulue*) to complete; (*augmenter*) to complement, supplement; to add to.
complexe [kɔ̃plɛks(ə)] *a*, *nm* complex; **complexé, e** *a* mixed-up, hung-up.
complication [kɔ̃plikasjɔ̃] *nf* complexity, intricacy; (*difficulté, ennui*) complication.
complice [kɔ̃plis] *nm* accomplice.
compliment [kɔ̃plimɑ̃] *nm* (*louange*) compliment; ~**s** *nmpl* (*félicitations*) congratulations.
compliqué, e [kɔ̃plike] *a* complicated, complex; (*personne*) complicated.
complot [kɔ̃plo] *nm* plot.
comportement [kɔ̃pɔʀtəmɑ̃] *nm* behaviour.
comporter [kɔ̃pɔʀte] *vt* to consist of, comprise; (*être équipé de*) to have; (*impliquer*) to entail; **se** ~ *vi* to behave.
composante [kɔ̃pozɑ̃t] *nf* component.
composé [kɔ̃poze] *nm* compound.
composer [kɔ̃poze] *vt* (*musique, texte*) to compose; (*mélange, équipe*) to make up; (*faire partie de*) to make up, form // *vi* (*transiger*) to come to terms; **se** ~ **de** to be composed of, be made up of; ~ **un numéro** to dial a number.
compositeur, trice [kɔ̃pozitœʀ, -tʀis] *nm/f* (*MUS*) composer.
composition [kɔ̃pozisjɔ̃] *nf* composi-

tion; (*SCOL*) test; **de bonne** ~ (*accommodant*) easy to deal with.
composter [kɔ̃pɔste] *vt* to date stamp; to punch.
compote [kɔ̃pɔt] *nf* stewed fruit *q*; ~ **de pommes** stewed apples; **compotier** *nm* fruit dish *ou* bowl.
compréhensible [kɔ̃pʀeɑ̃sibl(ə)] *a* comprehensible; (*attitude*) understandable.
compréhensif, ive [kɔ̃pʀeɑ̃sif, -iv] *a* understanding.
comprendre [kɔ̃pʀɑ̃dʀ(ə)] *vt* to understand; (*se composer de*) to comprise, consist of.
compresse [kɔ̃pʀɛs] *nf* compress.
compression [kɔ̃pʀesjɔ̃] *nf* compression; reduction.
comprimé [kɔ̃pʀime] *nm* tablet.
comprimer [kɔ̃pʀime] *vt* to compress; (*fig*: *crédit etc*) to reduce, cut down.
compris, e [kɔ̃pʀi, -iz] *pp de* **comprendre** // *a* (*inclus*) included; ~ **entre** (*situé*) contained between; **la maison** ~**e/ non** ~**e, y/non** ~ **la maison** including/ excluding the house; **100 F tout** ~ 100 F all inclusive *ou* all-in.
compromettre [kɔ̃pʀɔmɛtʀ(ə)] *vt* to compromise.
compromis [kɔ̃pʀɔmi] *nm* compromise.
comptabilité [kɔ̃tabilite] *nf* (*activité, technique*) accounting, accountancy; (*d'une société*: *comptes*) accounts *pl*, books *pl*; (: *service*) accounts office.
comptable [kɔ̃tabl(ə)] *nm/f* accountant.
comptant [kɔ̃tɑ̃] *ad*: **payer** ~ to pay cash; **acheter** ~ to buy for cash.
compte [kɔ̃t] *nm* count, counting; (*total, montant*) count, (*right*) number; (*bancaire, facture*) account; ~**s** *nmpl* accounts, books; (*fig*) explanation *sg*; **en fin de** ~ (*fig*) all things considered; **à bon** ~ at a favourable price; (*fig*) lightly; **avoir son** ~ (*fig*: *fam*) to have had it; **pour le** ~ **de** on behalf of; **pour son propre** ~ for one's own benefit; **tenir** ~ **de** to take account of; **travailler à son** ~ to work for oneself; **rendre** ~ (à qn) **de** qch to give (sb) an account of sth; ~ **chèques postaux** (C.C.P.) Post Office account; ~ **courant** current account; ~ **à rebours** countdown; *voir aussi* **rendre**.
compte-gouttes [kɔ̃tgut] *nm inv* dropper.
compter [kɔ̃te] *vt* to count; (*facturer*) to charge for; (*avoir à son actif, comporter*) to have; (*prévoir*) to allow, reckon; (*penser, espérer*) ~ **réussir** to expect to succeed // *vi* to count; (*être économe*) to economize; (*figurer*) ~ **parmi** to be *ou* rank among; ~ **sur** to count (up)on; ~ **avec qch/qn** to reckon with *ou* take account of sth/sb; **sans** ~ **que** besides which.
compte rendu [kɔ̃tʀɑ̃dy] *nm* account,

report; (de film, livre) review.

compte-tours [kɔ̃ttuʀ] nm inv rev(olution) counter.

compteur [kɔ̃tœʀ] nm meter; ~ de vitesse speedometer.

comptine [kɔ̃tin] nf nursery rhyme.

comptoir [kɔ̃twaʀ] nm (de magasin) counter.

compulser [kɔ̃pylse] vt to consult.

comte, comtesse [kɔ̃t, kɔ̃tɛs] nm/f count/countess.

con, ne [kɔ̃, kɔn] a (fam!) damned ou bloody (Brit) stupid (!).

concéder [kɔ̃sede] vt to grant; (défaite, point) to concede.

concentrer [kɔ̃sɑ̃tʀe] vt to concentrate; se ~ vi to concentrate.

concept [kɔ̃sɛpt] nm concept.

conception [kɔ̃sɛpsjɔ̃] nf conception; (d'une machine etc) design.

concerner [kɔ̃sɛʀne] vt to concern; en ce qui me concerne as far as I am concerned.

concert [kɔ̃sɛʀ] nm concert; de ~ ad in unison; together.

concerter [kɔ̃sɛʀte] vt to devise; se ~ vi (collaborateurs etc) to put our ou their etc heads together.

concessionnaire [kɔ̃sesjɔnɛʀ] nm/f agent, dealer.

concevoir [kɔ̃svwaʀ] vt (idée, projet) to conceive (of); (méthode, plan d'appartement, décoration etc) to plan, design; (enfant) to conceive; bien/mal conçu well-/badly- designed.

concierge [kɔ̃sjɛʀʒ(ə)] nm/f caretaker; (d'hôtel) head porter.

concile [kɔ̃sil] nm council.

conciliabules [kɔ̃siljabyl] nmpl (private) discussions, confabulations.

concilier [kɔ̃silje] vt to reconcile; se ~ qn to win sb over.

concitoyen, ne [kɔ̃sitwajɛ̃, -jɛn] nm/f fellow citizen.

concluant, e [kɔ̃klyɑ̃, -ɑ̃t] a conclusive.

conclure [kɔ̃klyʀ] vt to conclude.

conclusion [kɔ̃klyzjɔ̃] nf conclusion.

conçois etc vb voir **concevoir**.

concombre [kɔ̃kɔ̃bʀ(ə)] nm cucumber.

concorder [kɔ̃kɔʀde] vi to tally, agree.

concourir [kɔ̃kuʀiʀ] vi (SPORT) to compete; ~ à vt (effet etc) to work towards.

concours [kɔ̃kuʀ] nm competition; (SCOL) competitive examination; (assistance) aid, help; ~ de circonstances combination of circumstances; ~ hippique horse show.

concret, ète [kɔ̃kʀɛ, -ɛt] a concrete.

concrétiser [kɔ̃kʀetize] vt (plan, projet) to put into concrete form; se ~ vi to materialize.

conçu, e [kɔ̃sy] pp de **concevoir**.

concubinage [kɔ̃kybinaʒ] nm (JUR) cohabitation.

concurrence [kɔ̃kyʀɑ̃s] nf competition;

jusqu'à ~ de up to.

concurrent, e [kɔ̃kyʀɑ̃, -ɑ̃t] nm/f (SPORT, ÉCON etc) competitor; (SCOL) candidate.

condamner [kɔ̃dane] vt (blâmer) to condemn; (JUR) to sentence; (porte, ouverture) to fill in, block up; (malade) to give up (hope for); ~ qn à 2 ans de prison to sentence sb to 2 years' imprisonment.

condensation [kɔ̃dɑ̃sasjɔ̃] nf condensation.

condenser [kɔ̃dɑ̃se] vt, se ~ vi to condense.

condisciple [kɔ̃disipl(ə)] nm/f school fellow, fellow student.

condition [kɔ̃disjɔ̃] nf condition; ~s nfpl (tarif, prix) terms; (circonstances) conditions; sans ~ a unconditional // ad unconditionally; à ~ de/que provided that; **conditionnel, le** a conditional // nm conditional (tense); **conditionner** vt (déterminer) to determine; (COMM: produit) to package; (fig: personne) to condition; air conditionné air conditioning.

condoléances [kɔ̃dɔleɑ̃s] nfpl condolences.

conducteur, trice [kɔ̃dyktœʀ, -tʀis] nm/f driver // nm (ÉLEC etc) conductor.

conduire [kɔ̃dɥiʀ] vt to drive; (délégation, troupeau) to lead; se ~ vi to behave; ~ vers/à to lead towards/to; ~ qn quelque part to take sb somewhere; to drive sb somewhere.

conduite [kɔ̃dɥit] nf (comportement) behaviour; (d'eau, de gaz) pipe; sous la ~ de led by; ~ à gauche left-hand drive; ~ intérieure saloon (car).

cône [kon] nm cone.

confection [kɔ̃fɛksjɔ̃] nf (fabrication) making; (COUTURE): la ~ the clothing industry; vêtement de ~ ready-to-wear ou off-the-peg garment.

confectionner [kɔ̃fɛksjɔne] vt to make.

conférence [kɔ̃feʀɑ̃s] nf (exposé) lecture; (pourparlers) conference; ~ de presse press conference.

confesser [kɔ̃fese] vt to confess; se ~ vi (REL) to go to confession.

confession [kɔ̃fɛsjɔ̃] nf confession; (culte: catholique etc) denomination.

confetti [kɔ̃feti] nm confetti q.

confiance [kɔ̃fjɑ̃s] nf confidence, trust; faith; avoir ~ en to have confidence ou faith in, trust; mettre qn en ~ to win sb's trust; ~ en soi self-confidence.

confiant, e [kɔ̃fjɑ̃, -ɑ̃t] a confident; trusting.

confidence [kɔ̃fidɑ̃s] nf confidence.

confidentiel, le [kɔ̃fidɑ̃sjɛl] a confidential.

confier [kɔ̃fje] vt: ~ à qn (objet en dépôt, travail etc) to entrust to sb; (secret, pensée) to confide to sb; se ~ à qn to confide in sb.

confiné, e |kɔ̃fine| *a* enclosed; stale.
confins |kɔ̃fɛ̃| *nmpl*: aux ~ de on the borders of.
confirmation |kɔ̃firmasjɔ̃| *nf* confirmation.
confirmer |kɔ̃firme| *vt* to confirm.
confiserie |kɔ̃fizri| *nf* (*magasin*) confectioner's *ou* sweet shop; ~s *nfpl* (*bonbons*) confectionery *sg*; **confiseur, euse** *nm/f* confectioner.
confisquer |kɔ̃fiske| *vt* to confiscate.
confit, e |kɔ̃fi, -it| *a*: fruits ~s crystallized fruits // *nm*: ~ d'oie conserve of goose.
confiture |kɔ̃fityr| *nf* jam; ~ d'oranges (orange) marmalade.
conflit |kɔ̃fli| *nm* conflict.
confondre |kɔ̃fɔ̃dr(ə)| *vt* (*jumeaux, faits*) to confuse, mix up; (*témoin, menteur*) to confound; se ~ *vi* to merge; se ~ en excuses to apologize profusely.
confondu, e |kɔ̃fɔ̃dy| *a* (*stupéfait*) speechless, overcome.
conforme |kɔ̃fɔrm(ə)| *a*: ~ à in accordance with, in keeping with; true to.
conformément |kɔ̃fɔrmemã| *ad*: ~ à in accordance with.
conformer |kɔ̃fɔrme| *vt*: se ~ à to conform to.
conformité |kɔ̃fɔrmite| *nf*: en ~ avec in accordance with, in keeping with.
confort |kɔ̃fɔr| *nm* comfort; tout ~ (*comm*) with all modern conveniences; **confortable** *a* comfortable.
confrère |kɔ̃frɛr| *nm* colleague; fellow member; **confrérie** *nf* brotherhood.
confronter |kɔ̃frɔ̃te| *vt* to confront; (*textes*) to compare, collate.
confus, e |kɔ̃fy, -yz| *a* (*vague*) confused; (*embarrassé*) embarrassed.
confusion |kɔ̃fyzjɔ̃| *nf* (*voir confus*) confusion; embarrassement; (*voir confondre*) confusion, mixing up.
congé |kɔ̃ʒe| *nm* (*vacances*) holiday; en ~ on holiday; off (*work*); semaine de ~ week off; prendre ~ de qn to take one's leave of sb; donner son ~ à to give in one's notice to; ~ de maladie sick leave; ~s payés paid holiday.
congédier |kɔ̃ʒedje| *vt* to dismiss.
congélateur |kɔ̃ʒelatœr| *nm* freezer, deep freeze.
congeler |kɔ̃ʒle| *vt* to freeze.
congère |kɔ̃ʒɛr| *nf* snowdrift.
congestion |kɔ̃ʒɛstjɔ̃| *nf* congestion; ~ cérébrale stroke.
congestionner |kɔ̃ʒɛstjɔne| *vt* to congest; (*méd*) to flush.
congrès |kɔ̃grɛ| *nm* congress.
congru, e |kɔ̃gry| *a*: la portion ~e the smallest *ou* meanest book.
conifère |kɔnifɛr| *nm* conifer.
conjoint, e |kɔ̃ʒwɛ̃, -wɛ̃t| *a* joint // *nm/f* spouse.
conjonction |kɔ̃ʒɔ̃ksjɔ̃| *nf* (*LING*) conjunction.

conjonctivite |kɔ̃ʒɔ̃ktivit| *nf* conjunctivitis.
conjoncture |kɔ̃ʒɔ̃ktyr| *nf* circumstances *pl*; climate.
conjugaison |kɔ̃ʒygɛzɔ̃| *nf* (*LING*) conjugation.
conjuguer |kɔ̃ʒyge| *vt* (*LING*) to conjugate; (*efforts etc*) to combine.
conjuration |kɔ̃ʒyrasjɔ̃| *nf* conspiracy.
conjurer |kɔ̃ʒyre| *vt* (*sort, maladie*) to avert; (*implorer*) to beseech, entreat.
connaissance |kɔnɛsãs| *nf* (*savoir*) knowledge *q*; (*personne connue*) acquaintance; être sans ~ to be unconscious; perdre/reprendre ~ to lose/regain consciousness; à ma/sa ~ to (the best of) my/his knowledge; avoir ~ de to be aware of; prendre ~ de (*document etc*) to peruse; en ~ de cause with full knowledge of the facts.
connaître |kɔnɛtr(ə)| *vt* to know; (*éprouver*) to experience; (*avoir*) to have; to enjoy; ~ de nom/vue to know by name/sight; ils se sont connus à Genève they (first) met in Geneva.
connecté, e |kɔnɛkte| *a* on line.
connecter |kɔnɛkte| *vt* to connect.
connerie |kɔnri| *nf* (*fam!*) stupid thing (to do *ou* say).
connu, e |kɔny| *a* (*célèbre*) well-known.
conquérir |kɔ̃kerir| *vt* to conquer, win; **conquête** *nf* conquest.
consacrer |kɔ̃sakre| *vt* (*REL*) to consecrate; (*fig: usage etc*) to sanction, establish; (*employer*) to devote, dedicate.
conscience |kɔ̃sjãs| *nf* conscience; avoir/prendre ~ de to be/become aware of; perdre ~ to lose consciousness; avoir bonne/mauvaise ~ to have a clear/guilty conscience; **consciencieux, euse** *a* conscientious; **conscient, e** *a* conscious.
conscrit |kɔ̃skri| *nm* conscript.
consécutif, ive |kɔ̃sekytif, -iv| *a* consecutive; ~ à following upon.
conseil |kɔ̃sɛj| *nm* (*avis*) piece of advice, advice *q*; (*assemblée*) council; prendre ~ (auprès de qn) to take advice (from sb); ~ d'administration board (of directors); le ~ des ministres ≈ the Cabinet.
conseiller |kɔ̃seje| *vt* (*personne*) to advise; (*méthode, action*) to recommend, advise; ~ à qn de to advise sb to.
conseiller, ère |kɔ̃seje, kɔ̃sejɛr| *nm/f* adviser.
consentement |kɔ̃sãtmã| *nm* consent.
consentir |kɔ̃sãtir| *vt* to agree, consent.
conséquence |kɔ̃sekãs| *nf* consequence; en ~ (*donc*) consequently; (*de façon appropriée*) accordingly; ne pas tirer à ~ to be unlikely to have any repercussions.
conséquent, e |kɔ̃sekã, -ãt| *a* logical, rational; (*fam: important*) substantial;

par ~ consequently.

conservateur, trice |kɔ̃sɛrvatœr, -tris| nm/f (POL.) conservative; (de musée) curator.

conservatoire |kɔ̃sɛrvatwar| nm academy; (ÉCOLOGIE) conservation area.

conserve |kɔ̃sɛrv(ə)| nf (gén pl) canned ou tinned (Brit) food; **en ~** canned, tinned (Brit).

conserver |kɔ̃sɛrve| vt (faculté) to retain, keep; (amis, livres) to keep; (préserver, aussi CULIN) to preserve.

considérable |kɔ̃sideRabl(ə)| a considerable, significant, extensive.

considération |kɔ̃siderasjɔ̃| nf consideration; (estime) esteem.

considérer |kɔ̃sidere| vt to consider; ~ qch comme to regard sth as.

consigne |kɔ̃siɲ| nf (de gare) left luggage (office) (Brit), checkroom (US); (ordre, instruction) instructions pl; ~ (automatique) left-luggage locker.

consigner |kɔ̃siɲe| vt (note, pensée) to record; (punir) to confine to barracks; to put in detention; (COMM) to put a deposit on.

consistant, e |kɔ̃sistɑ̃, -ɑ̃t| a thick; solid.

consister |kɔ̃siste| vi: ~ en/dans/à faire to consist of/in/in doing.

consœur |kɔ̃sœr| nf (lady) colleague; fellow member.

consoler |kɔ̃sɔle| vt to console.

consolider |kɔ̃sɔlide| vt to strengthen; (fig) to consolidate.

consommateur, trice |kɔ̃sɔmatœr, -tris| nm/f (ÉCON) consumer; (dans un café) customer.

consommation |kɔ̃sɔmasjɔ̃| nf (boisson) drink; ~ **aux 100 km** (AUTO) (fuel) consumption per 100 km.

consommer |kɔ̃sɔme| vt (suj: personne) to eat ou drink, consume; (suj: voiture, usine, poêle) to use, consume // vi (dans un café) to (have a) drink.

consonne |kɔ̃sɔn| nf consonant.

conspirer |kɔ̃spire| vi to conspire.

conspuer |kɔ̃spɥe| vt to boo, shout down.

constamment |kɔ̃stamɑ̃| ad constantly.

constant, e |kɔ̃stɑ̃, -ɑ̃t| a constant; (personne) steadfast.

constat |kɔ̃sta| nm (d'huissier) certified report; (de police) report; (affirmation) statement.

constatation |kɔ̃statasjɔ̃| nf (observation) (observed) fact, observation; (affirmation) statement.

constater |kɔ̃state| vt (remarquer) to note; (ADMIN, JUR: attester) to certify; (dire) to state.

consterner |kɔ̃stɛrne| vt to dismay.

constipé, e |kɔ̃stipe| a constipated.

constitué, e |kɔ̃stiɥe| a: ~ de made up ou composed of.

constituer |kɔ̃stiɥe| vt (comité, équipe) to set up; (dossier, collection) to put together; (suj: éléments: composer) to make up, constitute; (représenter, être) to constitute; **se ~ prisonnier** to give o.s. up.

constitution |kɔ̃stitysjɔ̃| nf (composition) composition, make-up; (santé, POL.) constitution.

constructeur |kɔ̃stryktœr| nm manufacturer, builder.

construction |kɔ̃stryksjɔ̃| nf construction, building.

construire |kɔ̃strɥir| vt to build, construct.

consul |kɔ̃syl| nm consul; **~at** nm consulate.

consultation |kɔ̃syltasjɔ̃| nf consultation; **~s** nfpl (POL) talks; **heures de ~** (MÉD) surgery (Brit) ou office (US) hours.

consulter |kɔ̃sylte| vt to consult // vi (médecin) to hold surgery (Brit), be in (the office) (US).

consumer |kɔ̃syme| vt to consume; **se ~** vi to burn.

contact |kɔ̃takt| nm contact; **au ~ de** (air, peau) on contact with; (gens) through contact with; **mettre/couper le ~** (AUTO) to switch on/off the ignition; **entrer en ou prendre ~ avec** to get in touch ou contact with; **~er** vt to contact, get in touch with.

contagieux, euse |kɔ̃taʒjø, -øz| a contagious; infectious.

contaminer |kɔ̃tamine| vt to contaminate.

conte |kɔ̃t| nm tale; ~ **de fées** fairy tale.

contempler |kɔ̃tɑ̃ple| vt to contemplate, gaze at.

contemporain, e |kɔ̃tɑ̃pɔrɛ̃, -ɛn| a, nm/f contemporary.

contenance |kɔ̃tnɑ̃s| nf (d'un récipient) capacity; (attitude) bearing, attitude; **perdre ~** to lose one's composure.

conteneur |kɔ̃tnœr| nm container.

contenir |kɔ̃tnir| vt to contain; (avoir une capacité de) to hold.

content, e |kɔ̃tɑ̃, -ɑ̃t| a pleased, glad; ~ **de** pleased with; **contenter** vt to satisfy, please; **se contenter de** to content o.s. with.

contentieux |kɔ̃tɑ̃sjø| nm (COMM) litigation; litigation department.

contenu |kɔ̃tny| nm (d'un bol) contents pl; (d'un texte) content.

conter |kɔ̃te| vt to recount, relate.

contestable |kɔ̃tɛstabl(ə)| a questionable.

contestation |kɔ̃tɛstasjɔ̃| nf (POL) protest.

conteste |kɔ̃tɛst(ə)|: **sans ~** ad unquestionably, indisputably.

contester |kɔ̃tɛste| vt to question, contest // vi (POL, gén) to protest, rebel (against established authority).

contexte [kɔ̃tɛkst(ə)] *nm* context.

contigu, ë [kɔ̃tigy] *a*: ~ (à) adjacent (to).

continent [kɔ̃tinɑ̃] *nm* continent.

continu, e [kɔ̃tiny] *a* continuous; (*courant*) ~ direct current, DC.

continuel, le [kɔ̃tinɥɛl] *a* (*qui se répète*) constant, continual; (*continu*) continuous.

continuer [kɔ̃tinɥe] *vt* (*travail, voyage etc*) to continue (with), carry on (with), go on (with); (*prolonger: alignement, rue*) to continue // *vi* (*pluie, vie, bruit*) to continue, go on; (*voyageur*) to go on; ~ à *ou* de faire to go on *ou* continue doing.

contorsionner [kɔ̃tɔʀsjɔne]: se ~ *vi* to contort o.s., writhe about.

contour [kɔ̃tuʀ] *nm* outline, contour.

contourner [kɔ̃tuʀne] *vt* to go round.

contraceptif, ive [kɔ̃tʀasɛptif, -iv] *a*, *nm* contraceptive.

contraception [kɔ̃tʀasɛpsjɔ̃] *nf* contraception.

contracté, e [kɔ̃tʀakte] *a* tense.

contracter [kɔ̃tʀakte] *vt* (*muscle etc*) to tense, contract; (*maladie, dette, obligation*) to contract; (*assurance*) to take out; se ~ *vi* (*métal, muscles*) to contract.

contractuel, le [kɔ̃tʀaktɥɛl] *nm/f* (*agent*) traffic warden.

contradiction [kɔ̃tʀadiksjɔ̃] *nf* contradiction; **contradictoire** *a* contradictory, conflicting.

contraindre [kɔ̃tʀɛ̃dʀ(ə)] *vt*: ~ qn à faire to compel sb to do.

contraint, e [kɔ̃tʀɛ̃, -ɛ̃t] *a* (*mine, air*) constrained, forced // *nf* constraint.

contraire [kɔ̃tʀɛʀ] *a, nm* opposite; ~ à contrary to; au ~ *ad* on the contrary.

contrarier [kɔ̃tʀaʀje] *vt* (*personne*) to annoy, bother; (*fig*) to impede; to thwart, frustrate.

contraste [kɔ̃tʀast(ə)] *nm* contrast.

contrat [kɔ̃tʀa] *nm* contract; ~ de travail employment contract.

contravention [kɔ̃tʀavɑ̃sjɔ̃] *nf* (*amende*) fine; (*P.V. pour stationnement interdit*) parking ticket.

contre [kɔ̃tʀ(ə)] *prép* against; (*en échange*) (in exchange) for; **par** ~ on the other hand.

contrebande [kɔ̃tʀəbɑ̃d] *nf* (*trafic*) contraband, smuggling; (*marchandise*) contraband, smuggled goods *pl*; faire la ~ de to smuggle.

contrebas [kɔ̃tʀəbɑ]: **en** ~ *ad* (down) below.

contrebasse [kɔ̃tʀəbas] *nf* (double) bass.

contrecarrer [kɔ̃tʀəkaʀe] *vt* to thwart.

contrecœur [kɔ̃tʀəkœʀ]: **à** ~ *ad* (be)grudgingly, reluctantly.

contrecoup [kɔ̃tʀəku] *nm* repercussions

pl; **par** ~ as an indirect consequence.

contredire [kɔ̃tʀədiʀ] *vt* (*personne*) to contradict; (*témoignage, assertion, faits*) to refute.

contrée [kɔ̃tʀe] *nf* region; land.

contrefaçon [kɔ̃tʀəfasɔ̃] *nf* forgery.

contrefaire [kɔ̃tʀəfɛʀ] *vt* (*document, signature*) to forge, counterfeit; (*personne, démarche*) to mimic; (*dénaturer: sa voix etc*) to disguise.

contre-jour [kɔ̃tʀəʒuʀ]: **à** ~ *ad* against the sunlight.

contremaître [kɔ̃tʀəmɛtʀ(ə)] *nm* foreman.

contrepartie [kɔ̃tʀəpaʀti] *nf* compensation; **en** ~ in return.

contre-performance [kɔ̃tʀəpɛʀfɔʀmɑ̃s] *nf* below-average performance.

contre-pied [kɔ̃tʀəpje] *nm*: **prendre le** ~ **de** to take the opposing view of; to take the opposite course to.

contre-plaqué [kɔ̃tʀəplake] *nm* plywood.

contrepoids [kɔ̃tʀəpwa] *nm* counterweight, counterbalance.

contrer [kɔ̃tʀe] *vt* to counter.

contresens [kɔ̃tʀəsɑ̃s] *nm* misinterpretation; mistranslation; nonsense *q*; **à** ~ *ad* the wrong way.

contretemps [kɔ̃tʀətɑ̃] *nm* hitch; **à** ~ *ad* (*MUS*) out of time; (*fig*) at an inopportune moment.

contrevenir [kɔ̃tʀəvniʀ]: ~ **à** *vt* to contravene.

contribuable [kɔ̃tʀibɥabl(ə)] *nm/f* taxpayer.

contribuer [kɔ̃tʀibɥe]: ~ **à** *vt* to contribute towards; **contribution** *nf* contribution; **contributions directes/indirectes** direct/indirect taxation; **mettre à contribution** to call upon.

contrôle [kɔ̃tʀol] *nm* checking *q*, check; supervision; monitoring; (*test*) test, examination; **perdre le** ~ **de** (*véhicule*) to lose control of; ~ **continu** (*SCOL*) continuous assessment; ~ **d'identité** identity check; ~ **des naissances** birth control.

contrôler [kɔ̃tʀole] *vt* (*vérifier*) to check; (*surveiller*) to supervise; to monitor, control; (*maitriser, COMM: firme*) to control; **contrôleur, euse** *nm/f* (*de train*) (ticket) inspector; (*de bus*) (bus) conductor/tress.

contrordre [kɔ̃tʀɔʀdʀ(ə)] *nm*: **sauf** ~ unless otherwise directed.

controversé, e [kɔ̃tʀɔvɛʀse] *a* (*personnage, question*) controversial.

contusion [kɔ̃tyzjɔ̃] *nf* bruise, contusion.

convaincre [kɔ̃vɛ̃kʀ(ə)] *vt*: ~ qn (de qch) to convince sb (of sth); ~ qn (de faire) to persuade sb (to do); ~ qn de (*JUR: délit*) to convict sb of.

convalescence [kɔ̃valesɑ̃s] *nf* convalescence.

convenable [kɔ̃vnabl(ə)] a suitable; (assez bon, respectable) decent.

convenance [kɔ̃vnɑ̃s] nf: à ma/votre ~ to my/your liking; ~s nfpl proprieties.

convenir [kɔ̃vniʀ] vi to be suitable; ~ à to suit; **il convient de** it is advisable to; (bienséant) it is right ou proper to; ~ de (bien-fondé de qch) to admit (to), acknowledge; (date, somme etc) to agree upon; ~ que (admettre) to admit that; ~ de faire to agree to do.

convention [kɔ̃vɑ̃sjɔ̃] nf convention; ~s nfpl (convenances) convention sg; ~ collective (ÉCON) collective agreement; **conventionnel, e** a (ADMIN) applying charges laid down by the state.

convenu, e [kɔ̃vny] pp de **convenir** // a agreed.

conversation [kɔ̃vɛʀsasjɔ̃] nf conversation.

convertir [kɔ̃vɛʀtiʀ] vt: ~ qn (à) to convert sb (to); ~ qch en to convert sth into; **se** ~ (à) to be converted (to).

conviction [kɔ̃viksjɔ̃] nf conviction.

convienne etc vb voir **convenir**.

convier [kɔ̃vje] vt: ~ qn à (dîner etc) to (cordially) invite sb to.

convive [kɔ̃viv] nm/f guest (at table).

convivial, e [kɔ̃vivjal] a (INFORM) user-friendly.

convocation [kɔ̃vɔkasjɔ̃] nf (document) notification to attend; summons sg.

convoi [kɔ̃vwa] nm (de voitures, prisonniers) convoy; (train) train; ~ (funèbre) funeral procession.

convoiter [kɔ̃vwate] vt to covet.

convoquer [kɔ̃vɔke] vt (assemblée) to convene; (subordonné) to summon; (candidat) to ask to attend; ~ qn (à) (réunion) to invite sb (to attend).

convoyeur [kɔ̃vwajœʀ] nm (NAVIG) escort ship; ~ **de fonds** security guard.

coopération [kɔɔpeʀasjɔ̃] nf co-operation; (ADMIN): **la C~** ≈ Voluntary Service Overseas (Brit), ≈ Peace Corps (US alternative to military service).

coopérer [kɔɔpeʀe] vi: ~ (à) to co-operate (in).

coordonner [kɔɔʀdɔne] vt to coordinate.

copain, copine [kɔpɛ̃, kɔpin] nm/f mate, pal.

copeau, x [kɔpo] nm shaving.

copie [kɔpi] nf copy; (SCOL) script, paper; exercise.

copier [kɔpje] vt, vi to copy; ~ **sur** to copy from.

copieur [kɔpjœʀ] nm (photo)copier.

copieux, euse [kɔpjø, -øz] a copious.

copine [kɔpin] nf voir **copain**.

copropriété [kɔpʀɔpʀijete] nf co-ownership, joint ownership.

coq [kɔk] nm cock, rooster.

coq-à-l'âne [kɔkalan] nm inv abrupt change of subject.

coque [kɔk] nf (de noix, mollusque) shell; (de bateau) hull; **à la** ~ (CULIN) (soft-)boiled.

coquelicot [kɔkliko] nm poppy.

coqueluche [kɔklyʃ] nf whooping-cough.

coquet, te [kɔkɛ, -ɛt] a flirtatious; appearance-conscious; pretty.

coquetier [kɔktje] nm egg-cup.

coquillage [kɔkijaʒ] nm (mollusque) shellfish; (coquille) shell.

coquille [kɔkij] nf shell; (TYPO) misprint; ~ **St Jacques** scallop.

coquin, e [kɔkɛ̃, -in] a mischievous, roguish; (polisson) naughty.

cor [kɔʀ] nm (MUS) horn; (MÉD): ~ (au pied) corn; **réclamer à** ~ **et à cri** to clamour for.

corail, aux [kɔʀaj, -o] nm coral q.

Coran [kɔʀɑ̃] nm: **le** ~ the Koran.

corbeau, x [kɔʀbo] nm crow.

corbeille [kɔʀbɛj] nf basket; ~ **à papier** waste paper basket ou bin.

corbillard [kɔʀbijaʀ] nm hearse.

corde [kɔʀd(ə)] nf rope; (de violon, raquette, d'arc) string; (ATHLÉTISME, AUTO): **la** ~ the rails pl; ~ **à linge** washing ou clothes line; ~ **raide** tight-rope; ~ **à sauter** skipping rope; ~s **vocales** vocal cords; **usé jusqu'à la** ~ threadbare.

cordée [kɔʀde] nf (d'alpinistes) rope, roped party.

cordialement [kɔʀdjalmɑ̃] ad (formule épistolaire) (kind) regards.

cordon [kɔʀdɔ̃] nm cord, string; ~ **sanitaire/de police** sanitary/police cordon; ~ **ombilical** umbilical cord.

cordonnerie [kɔʀdɔnʀi] nf shoe repairer's (shop).

cordonnier [kɔʀdɔnje] nm shoe repairer.

coriace [kɔʀjas] a tough.

corne [kɔʀn(ə)] nf horn; (de cerf) antler.

corneille [kɔʀnɛj] nf crow.

cornemuse [kɔʀnəmyz] nf bagpipes pl.

corner [kɔʀneʀ] nm (FOOTBALL) corner (kick).

cornet [kɔʀnɛ] nm (paper) cone; (de glace) cornet, cone; ~ **à piston** cornet.

corniaud [kɔʀnjo] nm (chien) mongrel; (péj) twit, clot.

corniche [kɔʀniʃ] nf (de meuble, neigeuse) cornice; (route) coast road.

cornichon [kɔʀniʃɔ̃] nm gherkin.

Cornouailles [kɔʀnwaj] nf Cornwall.

corporation [kɔʀpɔʀasjɔ̃] nf corporate body.

corporel, le [kɔʀpɔʀɛl] a bodily; (punition) corporal.

corps [kɔʀ] nm body; **à son** ~ **défendant** against one's will; **à** ~ **perdu** headlong; **perdu** ~ **et biens** lost with all hands; **prendre** ~ to take shape; ~ **à** ~ ad hand-to-hand // nm clinch; **le** ~ **électoral** the electorate; **le** ~ **enseignant** the teach-

ing profession; ~ **de garde** guardroom.
corpulent, e [kɔʀpylɑ̃, -ɑ̃t] *a* stout.
correct, e [kɔʀɛkt] *a* correct; (*passable*) adequate.
correction [kɔʀɛksjɔ̃] *nf* (*voir corriger*) correction; (*voir correct*) correctness; (*rature, surcharge*) correction, emendation; (*coups*) thrashing.
correctionnel, le [kɔʀɛksjɔnɛl] *a* (*JUR*): **tribunal** ~ ≈ criminal court.
correspondance [kɔʀɛspɔ̃dɑ̃s] *nf* correspondence; (*de train, d'avion*) connection; **cours par** ~ correspondence course; **vente par** ~ mail-order business.
correspondant, e [kɔʀɛspɔ̃dɑ̃, -ɑ̃t] *nm/f* correspondent; (*TÉL*) person phoning (*où being phoned*).
correspondre [kɔʀɛspɔ̃dʀ(ə)] *vi* to correspond, tally; ~ **à** to correspond to; ~ **avec qn** to correspond with sb.
corrida [kɔʀida] *nf* bullfight.
corridor [kɔʀidɔʀ] *nm* corridor.
corriger [kɔʀiʒe] *vt* (*devoir*) to correct; (*punir*) to thrash; ~ **qn de** (*défaut*) to cure sb of.
corrompre [kɔʀɔ̃pʀ(ə)] *vt* to corrupt; (*acheter: témoin etc*) to bribe.
corruption [kɔʀypsjɔ̃] *nf* corruption; bribery.
corsage [kɔʀsaʒ] *nm* bodice; blouse.
corse [kɔʀs(ə)] *a, nm/f* Corsican // *nf*: **la C~** Corsica.
corsé, e [kɔʀse] *a* vigorous; (*vin, goût*) full-flavoured; (*fig*) spicy; tricky.
corset [kɔʀsɛ] *nm* corset; bodice.
cortège [kɔʀtɛʒ] *nm* procession.
corvée [kɔʀve] *nf* chore, drudgery *q*.
cosmétique [kɔsmetik] *nm* beauty care product.
cossu, e [kɔsy] *a* well-to-do.
costaud, e [kɔsto, -od] *a* strong, sturdy.
costume [kɔstym] *nm* (*d'homme*) suit; (*de théâtre*) costume; **costumé, e** *a* dressed up.
cote [kɔt] *nf* (*en Bourse etc*) quotation; quoted value; (*d'un cheval*): **la** ~ **de** the odds *pl* on; (*d'un candidat etc*) rating; (*sur un croquis*) dimension; ~ **d'alerte** danger *ou* flood level.
côte [kot] *nf* (*rivage*) coast(line); (*pente*) slope; (*: sur une route*) hill; (*ANAT*) rib; (*d'un tricot, tissu*) rib, ribbing *q*; ~ **à** ~ *ad* side by side; **la C~** (**d'Azur**) the (French) Riviera.
côté [kote] *nm* (*gén*) side; (*direction*) way, direction; **de chaque** ~ (**de**) on each side (of); **de tous les** ~**s** from all directions; **de quel** ~ **est-il parti?** which way did he go?; **de ce/de l'autre** ~ this/the other way; **du** ~ **de** (*provenance*) from; (*direction*) towards; (*proximité*) near; **de** ~ **ad** sideways; on one side; to one side; aside; **laisser/mettre de** ~ **to** leave/put to one side; **à** ~ *ad* (right)

nearby; beside; next door; (*d'autre part*) besides; **à** ~ **de** beside; next to; **être aux** ~**s de** to be by the side of.
coteau, x [kɔto] *nm* hill.
côtelette [kotlɛt] *nf* chop.
coter [kɔte] *vt* (*en Bourse*) to quote.
côtier, ière [kotje, -jɛʀ] *a* coastal.
cotisation [kɔtizasjɔ̃] *nf* subscription, dues *pl*; (*pour une pension*) contributions *pl*.
cotiser [kɔtize] *vi*: ~ (**à**) to pay contributions (to); **se** ~ *vi* to club together.
coton [kɔtɔ̃] *nm* cotton; ~ **hydrophile** cotton wool (*Brit*), absorbent cotton (*US*).
côtoyer [kotwaje] *vt* to be close to; to rub shoulders with; to run alongside.
cou [ku] *nm* neck.
couchant [kuʃɑ̃] *a*: **soleil** ~ setting sun.
couche [kuʃ] *nf* (*strate: gén, GÉO*) layer; (*de peinture, vernis*) coat; (*de bébé*) nappy (*Brit*), diaper (*US*); ~**s** *nfpl* (*MÉD*) confinement *sg*; ~**s sociales** social levels *ou* strata; ~**-culotte** *nf* disposable nappy (*Brit*) *ou* diaper (*US*) and waterproof pants in one.
couché, e [kuʃe] *a* lying down; (*au lit*) in bed.
coucher [kuʃe] *nm* (*du soleil*) setting // *vt* (*personne*) to put to bed; (*: loger*) to put up; (*objet*) to lay on its side // *vi* to sleep; **se** ~ *vi* (*pour dormir*) to go to bed; (*pour se reposer*) to lie down; (*soleil*) to set; ~ **de soleil** sunset.
couchette [kuʃɛt] *nf* couchette; (*de marin*) bunk.
coucou [kuku] *nm* cuckoo.
coude [kud] *nm* (*ANAT*) elbow; (*de tuyau, de la route*) bend; ~ **à** ~ *ad* shoulder to shoulder, side by side.
coudre [kudʀ(ə)] *vt* (*bouton*) to sew on; (*robe*) to sew (up) // *vi* to sew.
couenne [kwan] *nf* (*de lard*) rind.
couette [kwɛt] *nfpl* duvet, quilt.
couffin [kufɛ̃] *nm* Moses basket.
couiner [kwine] *vi* to squeal.
couler [kule] *vi* to flow, run; (*fuir: stylo, récipient*) to leak; (*sombrer: bateau*) to sink // *vt* (*cloche, sculpture*) to cast; (*bateau*) to sink; (*fig*) to ruin, bring down.
couleur [kulœʀ] *nf* colour; (*CARTES*) suit; **film/télévision en** ~**s** colour film/television.
couleuvre [kulœvʀ(ə)] *nf* grass snake.
coulisse [kulis] *nf*: ~**s** *nfpl* (*THÉÂTRE*) wings; (*fig*): **dans les** ~**s** behind the scenes; **coulisser** *vi* to slide, run.
couloir [kulwaʀ] *nm* corridor, passage; (*de bus*) gangway; (*sur la route*) bus lane; (*SPORT: de piste*) lane; (*GÉO*) gully; ~ **aérien/de navigation** air/shipping lane.
coup [ku] *nm* (*heurt, choc*) knock; (*affectif*) blow, shock; (*agressif*) blow;

(*avec arme à feu*) shot; (*de l'horloge*) chime; (*de la cloche, SPORT*) stroke; shot; blow; (*fam: fois*) time; ~ **de coude** nudge (with the elbow); ~ **de tonnerre** clap of thunder; ~ **de sonnette** ring of the bell; ~ **de crayon** stroke of the pencil; **donner un** ~ **de balai** to give the floor a sweep; **avoir le** ~ (*fig*) to have the knack; **boire un** ~ to have a drink; **être dans le** ~ to be in on it; **du** ~... **so** (you see)...; **d'un seul** ~ (*subitement*) suddenly; (*à la fois*) at one go; in one blow; **du premier** ~ first time; **du même** ~ at the same time; **à** ~ **sûr** definitely, without fail; ~ **sur** ~ in quick succession; **sur le** ~ outright; **sous le** ~ **de** (*surprise etc*) under the influence of; ~ **de chance** stroke of luck; ~ **de couteau** stab (of a knife); ~ **d'envoi** kick-off; ~ **d'essai** first attempt; ~ **de feu** shot; ~ **de filet** (*POLICE*) haul; ~ **franc** free kick; ~ **de frein** (sharp) braking *q*; ~ **de main:** **donner un** ~ **de main à qn** to give sb a (helping) hand; ~ **d'œil** glance; ~ **de pied** kick; ~ **de poing** punch; ~ **de soleil** sunburn *q*; ~ **de téléphone** phone call; ~ **de tête** (*fig*) (sudden) impulse; ~ **de théâtre** (*fig*) dramatic turn of events; ~ **de vent** gust of wind; **en** ~ **de vent** in a tearing hurry.

coupable [kupabl(ə)] *a* guilty // *nm/f* (*gén*) culprit; (*JUR*) guilty party.

coupe [kup] *nf* (*verre*) goblet; (*à fruits*) dish; (*SPORT*) cup; (*de cheveux, de vêtement*) cut; (*graphique, plan*) (cross) section; **être sous la** ~ **de** to be under the control of.

coupe-papier [kuppapje] *nm inv* paper knife.

couper [kupe] *vt* to cut; (*retrancher*) to cut (out); (*route, courant*) to cut off; (*appétit*) to take away; (*vin, cidre*) to blend; (: *à table*) to dilute // *vi* to cut; (*prendre un raccourci*) to take a short-cut; **se** ~ *vi* (*se blesser*) to cut o.s.; ~ **la parole à qn** to cut sb short.

couperosé, e [kuproze] *a* blotchy.

couple [kupl(ə)] *nm* couple.

couplet [kuplɛ] *nm* verse.

coupole [kupɔl] *nf* dome; cupola.

coupon [kupɔ̃] *nm* (*ticket*) coupon; (*de tissu*) remnant; roll; ~**-réponse** *nm* reply coupon.

coupure [kupyʀ] *nf* cut; (*billet de banque*) note; (*de journal*) cutting; ~ **de courant** power cut.

cour [kuʀ] *nf* (*de\ ferme, jardin*) (court)yard; (*d'immeuble*) back yard; (*JUR, royale*) court; **faire la** ~ **à qn** to court sb; ~ **d'assises** court of assizes; ~ **martiale** court-martial.

courage [kuʀaʒ] *nm* courage, bravery; **courageux, euse** *a* brave, courageous.

couramment [kuʀamɑ̃] *ad* commonly; (*parler*) fluently.

courant, e [kuʀɑ̃, -ɑ̃t] *a* (*fréquent*) common; (*COMM, gén: normal*) standard; (*en cours*) current // *nm* current; (*fig*) movement; trend; **être au** ~ (**de**) (*fait, nouvelle*) to know (about); **mettre qn au** ~ (**de**) (*fait, nouvelle*) to tell sb (about); (*nouveau travail etc*) to teach sb the basics (of); **se tenir au** ~ (**de**) (*techniques etc*) to keep o.s. up-to-date (on); **dans le** ~ **de** (*pendant*) in the course of; **le 10** ~ (*COMM*) the 10th inst; ~ **d'air** draught; ~ **électrique** (electric) current, power.

courbature [kuʀbatyʀ] *nf* ache.

courbe [kuʀb(ə)] *a* curved // *nf* curve.

courber [kuʀbe] *vt* to bend.

coureur, euse [kuʀœʀ, -øz] *nm/f* (*SPORT*) runner (*ou* driver); (*péj*) womanizer/manhunter; ~ **automobile** racing driver.

courge [kuʀʒ(ə)] *nf* (*CULIN*) marrow.

courgette [kuʀʒɛt] *nf* courgette (*Brit*), zucchini (*US*).

courir [kuʀiʀ] *vi* to run // *vt* (*SPORT: épreuve*) to compete in; (*risque*) to run; (*danger*) to face; ~ **les magasins** to go round the shops; **le bruit court que** the rumour is going round that.

couronne [kuʀɔn] *nf* crown; (*de fleurs*) wreath, circlet.

courons *etc vb voir* **courir.**

courrier [kuʀje] *nm* mail, post; (*lettres à écrire*) letters *pl*; **long/moyen** ~ *a* (*AVIAT*) long-/medium-haul.

courroie [kuʀwa] *nf* strap; (*TECH*) belt.

courrons *etc vb voir* **courir.**

cours [kuʀ] *nm* (*leçon*) lesson; class; (*série de leçons*) course; (*cheminement*) course; (*écoulement*) flow; (*COMM*) rate; price; **donner libre** ~ **à** to give free expression to; **avoir** ~ (*monnaie*) to be legal tender; (*fig*) to be current; (*SCOL*) to have a class *ou* lecture; **en** ~ (*année*) current; (*travaux*) in progress; **en** ~ **de route** on the way; **au** ~ **de** in the course of, during; ~ **d'eau** waterway; ~ **du soir** night school.

course [kuʀs(ə)] *nf* running; (*SPORT: épreuve*) race; (*d'un taxi, autocar*) journey, trip; (*petite mission*) errand; ~**s** *nfpl* (*achats*) shopping *sg*; **faire des** ~**s** to do some shopping.

court, e [kuʀ, kuʀt(ə)] *a* short // *ad* short // *nm:* ~ (**de tennis**) (tennis) court; **tourner** ~ to come to a sudden end; **ça fait** ~ that's not very long; **à** ~ **de** short of; **prendre qn de** ~ to catch sb unawares; **tirer à la** ~**e paille** to draw lots; ~**-circuit** *nm* short-circuit.

courtier, ère [kuʀtje, -jɛʀ] *nm/f* broker.

courtiser [kuʀtize] *vt* to court, woo.

courtois, e [kuʀtwa, -waz] *a* courteous.

couru, e [kuʀy] *pp de* **courir** // *a:* **c'est** ~ it's a safe bet.

cousais *etc vb voir* **coudre.**

couscous [kuskus] *nm* couscous.

cousin, e [kuzɛ̃, -in] *nm/f* cousin.

coussin [kusɛ̃] *nm* cushion.

cousu, e [kuzy] *pp de* **coudre.**

coût [ku] *nm* cost; **le ~ de la vie** the cost of living.

coûtant [kutɑ̃] *am*: **au prix ~** at cost price.

couteau, x [kuto] *nm* knife; **~ à cran d'arrêt** flick-knife.

coûter [kute] *vt, vi* to cost; **combien ça coûte?** how much is it?, what does it cost?; **coûte que coûte** at all costs; **coûteux, euse** *a* costly, expensive.

coutume [kutym] *nf* custom.

couture [kutyʀ] *nf* sewing; dress-making; (*points*) seam.

couturier [kutyʀje] *nm* fashion designer.

couturière [kutyʀjɛʀ] *nf* dressmaker.

couvée [kuve] *nf* brood, clutch.

couvent [kuvɑ̃] *nm* (*de sœurs*) convent; (*de frères*) monastery.

couver [kuve] *vt* to hatch; (*maladie*) to be sickening for // *vi* (*feu*) to smoulder; (*révolte*) to be brewing.

couvercle [kuvɛʀkl(ə)] *nm* lid; (*de bombe aérosol etc, qui se visse*) cap, top.

couvert, e [kuvɛʀ, -ɛʀt(ə)] *pp de* **couvrir** // *a* (*ciel*) overcast // *nm* place setting; (*place à table*) place; (*au restaurant*) cover charge; **~s** *nmpl* cutlery *sg*; **~ de** covered with *ou* in; **mettre le ~ to** lay the table.

couverture [kuvɛʀtyʀ] *nf* blanket; (*de bâtiment*) roofing; (*de livre, assurance, fig*) cover; (*presse*) coverage; **~ chauffante** electric blanket.

couveuse [kuvøz] *nf* (*de maternité*) incubator.

couvre... [kuvʀ(ə)] *préfixe*: **~-chef** *nm* hat; **~-feu** *nm* curfew; **~-lit** *nm* bedspread.

couvrir [kuvʀiʀ] *vt* to cover; **se ~** *vi* (*ciel*) to cloud over; (*s'habiller*) to cover up; (*se coiffer*) to put on one's hat.

crabe [kʀab] *nm* crab.

cracher [kʀaʃe] *vi, vt* to spit.

crachin [kʀaʃɛ̃] *nm* drizzle.

craie [kʀɛ] *nf* chalk.

craindre [kʀɛ̃dʀ(ə)] *vt* to fear, be afraid of; (*être sensible à: chaleur, froid*) to be easily damaged by.

crainte [kʀɛ̃t] *nf* fear; **de ~ de/que** for fear of/that; **craintif, ive** *a* timid.

cramoisi, e [kʀamwazi] *a* crimson.

crampe [kʀɑ̃p] *nf* cramp.

cramponner [kʀɑ̃pɔne]: **se ~** *vi*: **se ~ (à) to** hang *ou* cling on (to).

cran [kʀɑ̃] *nm* (*entaille*) notch; (*de courroie*) hole; (*courage*) guts *pl*; **~ d'arrêt** safety catch.

crâne [kʀɑn] *nm* skull.

crâner [kʀɑne] *vi* (*fam*) to show off.

crapaud [kʀapo] *nm* toad.

crapule [kʀapyl] *nf* villain.

craquement [kʀakmɑ̃] *nm* crack, snap; (*du plancher*) creak, creaking *q*.

craquer [kʀake] *vi* (*bois, plancher*) to creak; (*fil, branche*) to snap; (*couture*) to come apart; (*fig*) to break down // *vt* (*allumette*) to strike.

crasse [kʀas] *nf* grime, filth.

cravache [kʀavaʃ] *nf* (riding) crop.

cravate [kʀavat] *nf* tie.

crawl [kʀol] *nm* crawl; **dos crawlé** backstroke.

crayeux, euse [kʀɛjø, -øz] *a* chalky.

crayon [kʀɛjɔ̃] *nm* pencil; **~ à bille** ballpoint pen; **~ de couleur** crayon, colouring pencil; **~ optique** light pen.

créancier, ière [kʀeɑ̃sje, -jɛʀ] *nm/f* creditor.

création [kʀeasjɔ̃] *nf* creation.

créature [kʀeatyʀ] *nf* creature.

crécelle [kʀesɛl] *nf* rattle.

crèche [kʀɛʃ] *nf* (*de Noël*) crib; (*garderie*) crèche, day nursery.

crédit [kʀedi] *nm* (*gén*) credit; **~s** *nmpl* funds; **payer/acheter à ~** to pay/buy on credit *ou* on easy terms; **faire ~ à qn to** give sb credit; **créditer** *vt*: **créditer un compte (de)** to credit an account (with).

crédule [kʀedyl] *a* credulous, gullible.

créer [kʀee] *vt* to create; (*THÉÂTRE*) to produce (for the first time).

crémaillère [kʀemajɛʀ] *nf* (*RAIL*) rack; **pendre la ~ to** have a house-warming party.

crématoire [kʀematwaʀ] *a*: **four ~** crematorium.

crème [kʀɛm] *nf* cream; (*entremets*) cream dessert // *a inv* cream(-coloured); **un (café) ~** ≈ a white coffee; **~ chantilly, ~ fouettée** whipped cream; **~ à raser** shaving cream; **crémerie** *nf* dairy; **crémeux, euse** *a* creamy.

créneau, x [kʀeno] *nm* (*de fortification*) crenel(le); (*fig*) gap, slot; (*AUTO*): **faire un ~** to reverse into a parking space (*between cars alongside the kerb*).

crêpe [kʀɛp] *nf* (*galette*) pancake // *nm* (*tissu*) crêpe; **crêpé, e** *a* (*cheveux*) backcombed; **~rie** *nf* pancake shop *ou* restaurant.

crépir [kʀepiʀ] *vt* to roughcast.

crépiter [kʀepite] *vi* to sputter, splutter; to crackle.

crépon [kʀepɔ̃] *nm* seersucker.

crépu, e [kʀepy] *a* frizzy, fuzzy.

crépuscule [kʀepyskyl] *nm* twilight, dusk.

cresson [kʀesɔ̃] *nm* watercress.

crête [kʀɛt] *nf* (*de coq*) comb; (*de vague, montagne*) crest.

creuser [kʀøze] *vt* (*trou, tunnel*) to dig; (*sol*) to dig a hole in; (*bois*) to hollow out; (*fig*) to go (deeply) into; **ça creuse** that gives you a real appetite; **se ~ (la cervelle)** to rack one's brains.

creux, euse [kʀø, -øz] a hollow // nm hollow; (fig: sur graphique etc) trough; **heures creuses** slack periods; off-peak periods.

crevaison [kʀəvɛzɔ̃] nf puncture.

crevasse [kʀəvas] nf (dans le sol) crack, fissure; (de glacier) crevasse.

crevé, e [kʀəve] a (fatigué) all in, exhausted.

crever [kʀəve] vt (papier) to tear, break; (tambour, ballon) to burst // vi (pneu) to burst; (automobiliste) to have a puncture (Brit) ou a flat (tire) (US); (fam) to die; **cela lui a crevé un œil** it blinded him in one eye.

crevette [kʀəvɛt] nf: ~ **(rose)** prawn; ~ **grise** shrimp.

cri [kʀi] nm cry, shout; (d'animal: spécifique) cry, call; **c'est le dernier** ~ (fig) it's the latest fashion.

criant, e [kʀijɑ̃, -ɑ̃t] a (injustice) glaring.

criard, e [kʀijaʀ, -aʀd(ə)] a (couleur) garish, loud; yelling.

crible [kʀibl(ə)] nm riddle; **passer qch au** ~ (fig) to go over sth with a fine-tooth comb.

cric [kʀik] nm (AUTO) jack.

crier [kʀije] vi (pour appeler) to shout, cry (out); (de peur, de douleur etc) to scream, yell // vt (ordre, injure) to shout (out), yell (out).

crime [kʀim] nm crime; (meurtre) murder; **criminel, le** nm/f criminal; murderer.

crin [kʀɛ̃] nm hair q; (fibre) horsehair.

crinière [kʀinjɛʀ] nf mane.

crique [kʀik] nf creek, inlet.

criquet [kʀikɛ] nm locust; grasshopper.

crise [kʀiz] nf crisis (pl crises); (MÉD) attack; fit; ~ **cardiaque** heart attack; ~ **de foie** bilious attack; ~ **de nerfs** attack of nerves.

crisper [kʀispe] vt to tense; (poings) to clench; **se** ~ vi to tense; to clench; (personne) to get tense.

crisser [kʀise] vi (neige) to crunch; (pneu) to screech.

cristal, aux [kʀistal, -o] nm crystal.

cristallin, e [kʀistalɛ̃, -in] a crystal-clear.

critère [kʀitɛʀ] nm criterion (pl ia).

critiquable [kʀitikabl(ə)] a open to criticism.

critique [kʀitik] a critical // nm/f (de théâtre, musique) critic // nf criticism; (THÉÂTRE etc: article) review.

critiquer [kʀitike] vt (dénigrer) to criticize; (évaluer, juger) to assess, examine (critically).

croasser [kʀɔase] vi to caw.

croc [kʀo] nm (dent) fang; (de boucher) hook.

croc-en-jambe [kʀɔkɑ̃ʒɑ̃b] nm: **faire un** ~ **à qn** to trip sb up.

croche [kʀɔʃ] nf (MUS) quaver (Brit), eighth note (US).

croche-pied [kʀɔʃpje] nm = **croc-en-jambe**.

crochet [kʀɔʃɛ] nm hook; (détour) detour; (TRICOT: aiguille) crochet hook; (: technique) crochet; ~s nmpl (TYPO) square brackets; **vivre aux** ~**s de qn** to live ou sponge off sb; **crocheter** vt (serrure) to pick.

crochu, e [kʀɔʃy] a hooked; claw-like.

crocodile [kʀɔkɔdil] nm crocodile.

crocus [kʀɔkys] nm crocus.

croire [kʀwaʀ] vt to believe; **se** ~ **fort** to think one is strong; ~ **que** to believe ou think that; ~ **à**, ~ **en** to believe in.

crois vb voir **croître**.

croisade [kʀwazad] nf crusade.

croisé, e [kʀwaze] a (veston) double-breasted.

croisement [kʀwazmɑ̃] nm (carrefour) crossroads sg; (BIO) crossing; cross-breed.

croiser [kʀwaze] vt (personne, voiture) to pass; (route) to cross, cut across; (BIO) to cross // vi (NAVIG) to cruise; ~ **les jambes/bras** to cross one's legs/fold one's arms; **se** ~ vi (personnes, véhicules) to pass each other; (routes, lettres) to cross; (regards) to meet.

croiseur [kʀwazœʀ] nm cruiser (warship).

croisière [kʀwazjɛʀ] nf cruise; **vitesse de** ~ (AUTO etc) cruising speed.

croisillon [kʀwazijɔ̃] nm lattice.

croissance [kʀwasɑ̃s] nf growth.

croissant [kʀwasɑ̃] nm (à manger) croissant; (motif) crescent.

croître [kʀwatʀ(ə)] vi to grow.

croix [kʀwa] nf cross; **en** ~ a, ad in the form of a cross; **la C**~ **Rouge** the Red Cross.

croque... [kʀɔk] préfixe: ~-**monsieur** nm inv toasted ham and cheese sandwich.

croquer [kʀɔke] vt (manger) to crunch; to munch; (dessiner) to sketch // vi to be crisp ou crunchy; **chocolat à** ~ plain dessert chocolate.

croquis [kʀɔki] nm sketch.

crosse [kʀɔs] nf (de fusil) butt; (de revolver) grip.

crotte [kʀɔt] nf droppings pl.

crotté, e [kʀɔte] a muddy, mucky.

crottin [kʀɔtɛ̃] nm dung, manure.

crouler [kʀule] vi (s'effondrer) to collapse; (être délabré) to be crumbling.

croupe [kʀup] nf rump; **en** ~ pillion.

croupir [kʀupiʀ] vi to stagnate.

croustillant, e [kʀustijɑ̃, -ɑ̃t] a crisp; (fig) spicy.

croûte [kʀut] nf crust; (du fromage) rind; (MÉD) scab; **en** ~ (CULIN) in pastry.

croûton [kʀutɔ̃] nm (CULIN) crouton;

(*bout du pain*) crust, heel.
croyable [krwajabl(ə)] *a* credible.
croyant, e [krwajã, -ãt] *nm/f* believer.
C.R.S. *sigle fpl* (= *Compagnies républicaines de sécurité*) *a* state security police force // *sigle m* member of the C.R.S.
cru, e [kry] *pp de* **croire** // *a* (*non cuit*) raw; (*lumière, couleur*) harsh; (*paroles, description*) crude // *nm* (*vignoble*) vineyard; (*vin*) wine.
crû *pp de* **croître**.
cruauté [kryote] *nf* cruelty.
cruche [kryʃ] *nf* pitcher, jug.
crucifix [krysifi] *nm* crucifix.
crucifixion [krysifiksjɔ̃] *nf* crucifixion.
crudités [krydite] *nfpl* (*CULIN*) salads.
crue [kry] *nf voir* **cru**.
cruel, le [kryɛl] *a* cruel.
crus *etc* **crûs** *etc, vb voir* **croire, croître**.
crustacés [krystase] *nmpl* shellfish.
Cuba [kyba] *nf* Cuba.
cube [kyb] *nm* cube; (*jouet*) brick; mètre ~ cubic metre; 2 au ~ 2 cubed.
cueillir [kœjir] *vt* (*fruits, fleurs*) to pick, gather; (*fig*) to catch.
cuiller *ou* **cuillère** [kɥijɛr] *nf* spoon; ~ à café coffee spoon; (*CULIN*) ≈ teaspoonful; ~ à soupe soup-spoon; (*CULIN*) ≈ tablespoonful; **cuillerée** *nf* spoonful.
cuir [kɥir] *nm* leather; ~ chevelu scalp.
cuirassé [kɥirase] *nm* (*NAVIG*) battleship.
cuire [kɥir] *vt* (*aliments*) to cook; (*au four*) to bake; (*poterie*) to fire // *vi* to cook; **bien cuit** (*viande*) well done; **trop cuit** overdone.
cuisant, e [kɥizã, -ãt] *a* (*douleur*) stinging; (*fig: souvenir, échec*) bitter.
cuisine [kɥizin] *nf* (*pièce*) kitchen; (*art culinaire*) cookery, cooking; (*nourriture*) cooking, food; **faire la** ~ to cook; **cuisiner** *vt* to cook; (*fam*) to grill // *vi* to cook; **cuisinier, ière** *nm/f* cook // *nf* (*poêle*) cooker.
cuisse [kɥis] *nf* thigh; (*CULIN*) leg.
cuisson [kɥisɔ̃] *nf* cooking; firing.
cuit, e *pp de* **cuire**.
cuivre [kɥivr(ə)] *nm* copper; **les** ~s (*MUS*) the brass.
cul [ky] *nm* (*fam!*) arse (!).
culasse [kylas] *nf* (*AUTO*) cylinder-head; (*de fusil*) breech.
culbute [kylbyt] *nf* somersault; (*accidentelle*) tumble, fall.
culminant, e [kylminã, -ãt] *a*: **point** ~ highest point.
culminer [kylmine] *vi* to reach its highest point; to tower.
culot [kylo] *nm* (*effronterie*) cheek.
culotte [kylɔt] *nf* (*pantalon*) trousers *pl* (*Brit*), pants *pl* (*US*); (*de femme*) knickers *pl* (*Brit*), panties *pl*; ~ **de cheval** riding breeches *pl*.

culpabilité [kylpabilite] *nf* guilt.
culte [kylt(ə)] *nm* (*religion*) religion; (*hommage, vénération*) worship; (*protestant*) service.
cultivateur, trice [kyltivatœr, -tris] *nm/f* farmer.
cultivé, e [kyltive] *a* (*personne*) cultured, cultivated.
cultiver [kyltive] *vt* to cultivate; (*légumes*) to grow, cultivate.
culture [kyltyr] *nf* cultivation; growing; (*connaissances etc*) culture; ~ **physique** physical training; **culturisme** *nm* bodybuilding.
cumin [kymɛ̃] *nm* (*CULIN*) caraway seeds *pl*; cumin.
cumuler [kymyle] *vt* (*emplois, honneurs*) to hold concurrently; (*salaires*) to draw concurrently; (*JUR: droits*) to accumulate.
cupide [kypid] *a* greedy, grasping.
cure [kyr] *nf* (*MÉD*) course of treatment; **n'avoir** ~ **de** to pay no attention to.
curé [kyre] *nm* parish priest.
cure-dent [kyrdã] *nm* toothpick.
cure-pipe [kyrpip] *nm* pipe cleaner.
curer [kyre] *vt* to clean out.
curieux, euse [kyrjø, -øz] *a* (*étrange*) strange, curious; (*indiscret*) curious, inquisitive // *nmpl* (*badauds*) onlookers; **curiosité** *nf* curiosity; (*site*) unusual feature.
curriculum vitae [kyrikylɔmvite] *nm inv* (*abr* **C.V.**) curriculum vitae (C.V.).
curseur [kyrsœr] *nm* (*INFORM*) cursor.
cuti-réaction [kytireaksjɔ̃] *nf* (*MÉD*) skin-test.
cuve [kyv] *nf* vat; (*à mazout etc*) tank.
cuvée [kyve] *nf* vintage.
cuvette [kyvɛt] *nf* (*récipient*) bowl, basin; (*GÉO*) basin.
C.V. *sigle m* (*AUTO*) *voir* **cheval**; (*COMM*) = **curriculum vitae**.
cyanure [sjanyr] *nm* cyanide.
cyclable [siklabl(ə)] *a*: **piste** ~ cycle track.
cycle [sikl(ə)] *nm* cycle.
cyclisme [siklism(ə)] *nm* cycling.
cycliste [siklist(ə)] *nm/f* cyclist // *a* cycle *cpd*; **coureur** ~ racing cyclist.
cyclomoteur [siklɔmɔtœr] *nm* moped.
cyclone [siklon] *nm* hurricane.
cygne [siɲ] *nm* swan.
cylindre [silɛ̃dr(ə)] *nm* cylinder; **cylindrée** *nf* (*AUTO*) (cubic) capacity.
cymbale [sɛ̃bal] *nf* cymbal.
cynique [sinik] *a* cynical.
cystite [sistit] *nf* cystitis.

D

d' *prép de* **de**.
dactylo [daktilo] *nf* (*aussi*: ~**graphe**) typist; (*aussi*: ~**graphie**) typing;

~**graphier** vt to type (out).
dada [dada] nm hobby-horse.
daigner [deɲe] vt to deign.
daim [dɛ̃] nm (fallow) deer inv; (peau) buckskin; (imitation) suede.
dalle [dal] nf paving stone; slab.
daltonien, ne [daltɔnjɛ̃, -jɛn] a colour-blind.
dam [dam] nm: au grand ~ de much to the detriment (ou disadvantage) of.
dame [dam] nf lady; (CARTES, ÉCHECS) queen; ~s nfpl (jeu) draughts sg (Brit), checkers (US).
damner [dane] vt to damn.
dancing [dɑ̃siŋ] nm dance hall.
Danemark [danmark] nm Denmark.
danger [dɑ̃ʒe] nm danger; **dangereux, euse** a dangerous.
danois, e [danwa, -waz] a Danish // nm/f: D~, e Dane // nm (LING) Danish.
dans [dɑ̃] prép
1 (position) in; (à l'intérieur de) inside; c'est ~ le tiroir/le salon it's in the drawer/lounge; ~ la boîte in ou inside the box; marcher ~ la ville to walk about the town
2 (direction) into; elle a couru ~ le salon she ran into the lounge
3 (provenance) out of, from; je l'ai pris ~ le tiroir/salon I took it out of ou from the drawer/lounge; boire ~ un verre to drink out of ou from a glass
4 (temps) in; ~ 2 mois in 2 months, in 2 months' time
5 (approximation) about; ~ les 20 F about 20 F.
danse [dɑ̃s] nf: la ~ dancing; une ~ a dance; **danser** vi, vt to dance; **danseur, euse** nm/f ballet dancer/ballerina; (au bal etc) dancer; partner.
dard [dar] nm sting (organ).
date [dat] nf date; de longue ~ a long-standing; ~ de naissance date of birth; **dater** vt, vi to date; **dater de** to date from; à dater de (as) from.
datte [dat] nf date; **dattier** nm date palm.
dauphin [dofɛ̃] nm (ZOOL) dolphin.
davantage [davɑ̃taʒ] ad more; (plus longtemps) longer; ~ de more.
de (de + le = du, de + les = des) [də, dy, de] ♦ prép **1** (appartenance) of; le toit de la maison the roof of the house; la voiture d'Élisabeth/de mes parents Elizabeth's/my parents' car
2 (provenance) from; il vient de Londres he comes from London; elle est sortie du cinéma she came out of the cinema
3 (caractérisation, mesure): un mur de brique/bureau d'acajou a brick wall/mahogany desk; un billet de 50 F a 50 franc note; une pièce de 2m de large ou large de 2m a room 2m wide, a 2m-wide room; un bébé de 10 mois a 10-month-old

baby; 12 mois de crédit/travail 12 months' credit/work; augmenter de 10 F to increase by 10 F; de 14 à 18 from 14 to 18
♦ dét **1** (phrases affirmatives) some (souvent omis); du vin, de l'eau, des pommes (some) wine, (some) water, (some) apples; des enfants sont venus some children came; pendant des mois for months
2 (phrases interrogatives et négatives) any; a-t-il du vin? has he got any wine?; il n'a pas de pommes/d'enfants he hasn't (got) any apples/children, he has no apples/children.
dé [de] nm (à jouer) die ou dice (pl dice); (aussi: ~ à coudre) thimble.
déambuler [deɑ̃byle] vi to stroll about.
débâcle [debɑkl(ə)] nf rout.
déballer [debale] vt to unpack.
débandade [debɑ̃dad] nf rout; scattering.
débarbouiller [debarbuje] vt to wash; se ~ vi to wash (one's face).
débarcadère [debarkader] nm wharf.
débardeur [debardœr] nm docker, stevedore; (maillot) tank top.
débarquer [debarke] vt to unload, land // vi to disembark; (fig) to turn up.
débarras [debara] nm lumber room; junk cupboard; bon ~! good riddance!
débarrasser [debarase] vt to clear; ~ qn de (vêtements, paquets) to relieve sb of; se ~ de vt to get rid of.
débat [deba] nm discussion, debate.
débattre [debatr(ə)] vt to discuss, debate; se ~ vi to struggle.
débaucher [deboʃe] vt (licencier) to lay off, dismiss; (entraîner) to lead astray, debauch.
débile [debil] a weak, feeble; (fam: idiot) dim-witted; ~ mental, e nm/f mental defective.
débit [debi] nm (d'un liquide, fleuve) flow; (d'un magasin) turnover (of goods); (élocution) delivery; (bancaire) debit; ~ de boissons drinking establishment; ~ de tabac tobacconist's; **débiter** vt (compte) to debit; (liquide, gaz) to give out; (couper: bois, viande) to cut up; (péj: paroles etc) to churn out; **débiteur, trice** nm/f debtor // a in debit; (compte) debit cpd.
déblayer [debleje] vt to clear.
débloquer [deblɔke] vt (frein) to release; (prix, crédits) to free.
déboires [debwar] nmpl setbacks.
déboiser [debwaze] vt to deforest.
déboîter [debwate] vt (AUTO) to pull out; se ~ le genou etc to dislocate one's knee etc.
débonnaire [debɔnɛr] a easy-going, good-natured.
débordé, e [debɔrde] a: être ~ (de) (travail, demandes) to be snowed under

(with).

déborder [debɔʀde] *vi* to overflow; (*lait etc*) to boil over; ~ (**de**) qch (*dépasser*) to extend beyond sth.

débouché [debuʃe] *nm* (*pour vendre*) outlet; (*perspective d'emploi*) opening.

déboucher [debuʃe] *vt* (*évier, tuyau etc*) to unblock; (*bouteille*) to uncork // *vi*: ~ **de** to emerge from; ~ **sur** to come out onto; to open out onto.

débourser [debuʀse] *vt* to pay out.

debout [dəbu] *ad*: être ~ (*personne*) to be standing, stand; (*: levé, éveillé*) to be up; (*chose*) to be upright; être encore ~ (*fig: en état*) to be still going; se mettre ~ to stand up; se tenir ~ to stand; ~! stand up!; (*du lit*) get up!; cette histoire ne tient pas ~ this story doesn't hold water.

déboutonner [debutɔne] *vt* to undo, unbutton.

débraillé, e [debʀaje] *a* slovenly, untidy.

débrancher [debʀɑ̃ʃe] *vt* to disconnect; (*appareil électrique*) to unplug.

débrayage [debʀɛjaʒ] *nm* (AUTO) clutch.

débrayer [debʀeje] *vi* (AUTO) to declutch; (*cesser le travail*) to stop work.

débris [debʀi] *nm* (*fragment*) fragment // *nmpl* rubbish *sg*; debris *sg*.

débrouillard, e [debʀujaʀ, -aʀd(ə)] *a* smart, resourceful.

débrouiller [debʀuje] *vt* to disentangle, untangle; se ~ *vi* to manage.

débusquer [debyske] *vt* to drive out (from cover).

début [deby] *nm* beginning, start; ~s beginnings; début *sg*.

débutant, e [debytɑ̃, -ɑ̃t] *nm/f* beginner, novice.

débuter [debyte] *vi* to begin, start; (*faire ses débuts*) to start out.

deçà [dəsa]: en ~ **de** *prép* this side of.

décacheter [dekaʃte] *vt* to unseal.

décadence [dekadɑ̃s] *nf* decadence; decline.

décaféiné, e [dekafeine] *a* decaffeinated.

décalage [dekalaʒ] *nm* gap; discrepancy; ~ **horaire** time difference (between time zones); time-lag.

décaler [dekale] *vt* (*dans le temps: avancer*) to bring forward; (*: retarder*) to put back; (*changer de position*) to shift forward *ou* back.

décalquer [dekalke] *vt* to trace; (*par pression*) to transfer.

décamper [dekɑ̃pe] *vi* to clear out *ou* off.

décanter [dekɑ̃te] *vt* to allow to settle (and decant).

décaper [dekape] *vt* to strip; (*avec abrasif*) to scour; (*avec papier de verre*) to sand.

décapiter [dekapite] *vt* to behead; (*par accident*) to decapitate.

décapotable [dekapɔtabl(ə)] *a* convertible.

décapsuler [dekapsyle] *vt* to take the cap *ou* top off; **décapsuleur** *nm* bottle-opener.

décédé, e [desede] *a* deceased.

décéder [desede] *vi* to die.

déceler [desle] *vt* to discover, detect; to indicate, reveal.

décembre [desɑ̃bʀ(ə)] *nm* December.

décemment [desamɑ̃] *ad* decently.

décennie [deseni] *nf* decade.

décent, e [desɑ̃, -ɑ̃t] *a* decent.

déception [desɛpsjɔ̃] *nf* disappointment.

décerner [desɛʀne] *vt* to award.

décès [desɛ] *nm* death, decease.

décevoir [desvwaʀ] *vt* to disappoint.

déchaîner [deʃene] *vt* to unleash, arouse; se ~ to be unleashed.

déchanter [deʃɑ̃te] *vi* to become disillusioned.

décharge [deʃaʀʒ(ə)] *nf* (*dépôt d'ordures*) rubbish tip *ou* dump; (*électrique*) electrical discharge; **à la** ~ **de** in defence of.

décharger [deʃaʀʒe] *vt* (*marchandise, véhicule*) to unload; (*ÉLEC, faire feu*) to discharge; ~ **qn de** (*responsabilité*) to release sb from.

décharné, e [deʃaʀne] *a* emaciated.

déchausser [deʃose] *vt* (*skis*) to take off; se ~ *vi* to take off one's shoes; (*dent*) to come *ou* work loose.

déchéance [deʃeɑ̃s] *nf* degeneration; decay, decline; fall.

déchet [deʃɛ] *nm* (*de bois, tissu etc*) scrap; (*perte: gén COMM*) wastage, waste; ~s *nmpl* (*ordures*) refuse *sg*, rubbish *sg*.

déchiffrer [deʃifʀe] *vt* to decipher.

déchiqueter [deʃikte] *vt* to tear *ou* pull to pieces.

déchirement [deʃiʀmɑ̃] *nm* (*chagrin*) wrench, heartbreak; (*gén pl: conflit*) rift, split.

déchirer [deʃiʀe] *vt* to tear; (*en morceaux*) to tear up; (*pour ouvrir*) to tear off; (*arracher*) to tear out; (*fig*) to rack; to tear (apart); se ~ *vi* to tear, rip; se ~ **un muscle** to tear a muscle.

déchirure [deʃiʀyʀ] *nf* (*accroc*) tear, rip; ~ **musculaire** torn muscle.

déchoir [deʃwaʀ] *vi* (*personne*) to lower o.s., demean o.s.

déchu, e [deʃy] *a* fallen; deposed.

décidé, e [deside] *a* (*personne, air*) determined; c'est ~ it's decided.

décidément [desidemɑ̃] *ad* undoubtedly; really.

décider [deside] *vt*: ~ **qch** to decide on sth; ~ **de faire/que** to decide to do/that; ~ **qn (à faire qch)** to persuade sb (to do sth); ~ **de qch** to decide upon sth; (*suj:*

chose) to determine sth; se ~ (**à faire**) to decide (to do), make up one's mind (to do); se ~ **pour** to decide on *ou* in favour of.

décilitre [desilitʀ(ə)] *nm* decilitre.

décimal, e, aux [desimal, -o] *a, nf* decimal.

décimètre [desimɛtʀ(ə)] *nm* decimetre; **double** ~ (20 cm) ruler.

décisif, ive [desizif, -iv] *a* decisive.

décision [desiʒjɔ̃] *nf* decision; (*fermeté*) decisiveness, decision.

déclaration [deklaʀasjɔ̃] *nf* declaration; registration; (*discours: POL etc*) statement; ~ (**d'impôts**) ≈ tax return; ~ (**de sinistre**) (insurance) claim.

déclarer [deklaʀe] *vt* to declare; (*décès, naissance*) to register; se ~ *vi* (*feu, maladie*) to break out.

déclasser [deklɑse] *vt* to relegate; to downgrade; to lower in status.

déclencher [deklɑ̃ʃe] *vt* (*mécanisme etc*) to release; (*sonnerie*) to set off, activate; (*attaque, grève*) to launch; (*provoquer*) to trigger off; se ~ *vi* to release itself; to go off.

déclic [deklik] *nm* trigger mechanism; (*bruit*) click.

décliner [dekline] *vi* to decline // *vt* (*invitation*) to decline; (*responsabilité*) to refuse to accept; (*nom, adresse*) to state.

déclivité [deklivite] *nf* slope, incline.

décocher [dekɔʃe] *vt* to throw; to shoot.

décoiffer [dekwafe] *vt*: ~ **qn** to mess up sb's hair; to take sb's hat off; se ~ *vi* to take off one's hat.

déçois *etc vb voir* **décevoir**.

décollage [dekɔlaʒ] *nm* (*AVIAT*) takeoff.

décoller [dekɔle] *vt* to unstick // *vi* (*avion*) to take off; se ~ *vi* to come unstuck.

décolleté, e [dekɔlte] *a* low-cut; wearing a low-cut dress // *nm* low neck(line); (*bare*) neck and shoulders; (*plongeant*) cleavage.

décolorer [dekɔlɔʀe] *vt* (*tissu*) to fade; (*cheveux*) to bleach, lighten; se ~ *vi* to fade.

décombres [dekɔ̃bʀ(ə)] *nmpl* rubble *sg*, debris *sg*.

décommander [dekɔmɑ̃de] *vt* to cancel; (*invités*) to put off; se ~ *vi* to cancel one's appointment *etc*, cry off.

décomposé, e [dekɔ̃poze] *a* (*pourri*) decomposed; (*visage*) haggard, distorted.

décompte [dekɔ̃t] *nm* deduction; (*facture*) detailed account.

déconcerter [dekɔ̃sɛʀte] *vt* to disconcert, confound.

déconfit, e [dekɔ̃fi, -it] *a* crestfallen.

déconfiture [dekɔ̃fityʀ] *nf* failure, defeat; collapse, ruin.

décongeler [dekɔ̃ʒle] *vt* to thaw.

déconner [dekɔne] *vi* (*fam*) to talk rubbish.

déconseiller [dekɔ̃seje] *vt*: ~ **qch** (**à qn**) to advise (sb) against sth.

déconsidérer [dekɔ̃sideʀe] *vt* to discredit.

décontracter [dekɔ̃tʀakte] *vt*, se ~ *vi* to relax.

déconvenue [dekɔ̃vny] *nf* disappointment.

décor [dekɔʀ] *nm* décor; (*paysage*) scenery; ~**s** *nmpl* (*THÉÂTRE*) scenery *sg*, décor *sg*; (*CINÉMA*) set *sg*.

décorateur [dekɔʀatœʀ] *nm* (interior) decorator; (*CINÉMA*) set designer.

décoration [dekɔʀasjɔ̃] *nf* decoration.

décorer [dekɔʀe] *vt* to decorate.

décortiquer [dekɔʀtike] *vt* to shell; (*riz*) to hull; (*fig*) to dissect.

découcher [dekuʃe] *vi* to spend the night away from home.

découdre [dekudʀ(ə)] *vt* to unpick; se ~ *vi* to come unstitched; **en** ~ (*fig*) to fight, do battle.

découler [dekule] *vi*: ~ **de** to ensue *ou* follow from.

découper [dekupe] *vt* (*papier, tissu etc*) to cut up; (*volaille, viande*) to carve; (*détacher: manche, article*) to cut out; se ~ **sur** (*ciel, fond*) to stand out against.

décourager [dekuʀaʒe] *vt* to discourage; se ~ *vi* to lose heart, become discouraged.

décousu, e [dekuzy] *a* unstitched; (*fig*) disjointed, disconnected.

découvert, e [dekuvɛʀ, -ɛʀt(ə)] *a* (*tête*) bare, uncovered; (*lieu*) open, exposed // *nm* (*bancaire*) overdraft // *nf* discovery.

découvrir [dekuvʀiʀ] *vt* to discover; (*apercevoir*) to see; (*enlever ce qui couvre ou protège*) to uncover; (*montrer, dévoiler*) to reveal; se ~ *vi* to take off one's hat; to take something off; (*au lit*) to uncover o.s.; (*ciel*) to clear.

décret [dekʀɛ] *nm* decree; **décréter** *vt* to decree; to order; to declare.

décrié, e [dekʀije] *a* disparaged.

décrire [dekʀiʀ] *vt* to describe.

décrocher [dekʀɔʃe] *vt* (*dépendre*) to take down; (*téléphone*) to take off the hook; (: *pour répondre*): ~ (**le téléphone**) to lift the receiver; (*fig: contrat etc*) to get, land // *vi* to drop out; to switch off.

décroître [dekʀwatʀ(ə)] *vi* to decrease, decline.

décrypter [dekʀipte] *vt* to decipher.

déçu, e [desy] *pp de* **décevoir**.

décupler [dekyple] *vt*, *vi* to increase tenfold.

dédaigner [dedeɲe] *vt* to despise, scorn; (*négliger*) to disregard, spurn.

dédain [dedɛ̃] *nm* scorn, disdain.

dédale [dedal] *nm* maze.

dedans [dədɑ̃] ad inside; (pas en plein air) indoors, inside // nm inside; **au ~ on** the inside; inside; **en ~** (vers l'intérieur) inwards; voir aussi **là**.

dédicacer [dedikase] vt: **~ (à qn)** to sign (for sb), autograph (for sb).

dédier [dedje] vt to dedicate.

dédire [dediʀ]: **se ~** vi to go back on one's word; to retract, recant.

dédommager [dedɔmaʒe] vt: **~ qn (de)** to compensate sb (for); (fig) to repay sb (for).

dédouaner [dedwane] vt to clear through customs.

dédoubler [deduble] vt (classe, effectifs) to split (into two); **~ les trains** to run additional trains.

déduire [deduiʀ] vt: **~ qch (de)** (ôter) to deduct sth (from); (conclure) to deduce ou infer sth (from).

déesse [deɛs] nf goddess.

défaillance [defajɑ̃s] nf (syncope) blackout; (fatigue) (sudden) weakness q; (technique) fault, failure; (morale etc) weakness; **~ cardiaque** heart failure.

défaillir [defajiʀ] vi to faint; to feel faint; (mémoire etc) to fail.

défaire [defɛʀ] vt (installation) to take down, dismantle; (paquet etc, nœud, vêtement) to undo; **se ~** vi to come undone; **se ~ de** vt (se débarrasser de) to get rid of; (se séparer de) to part with.

défait, e [defɛ, -ɛt] a (visage) haggard, ravaged // nf defeat.

défalquer [defalke] vt to deduct.

défaut [defo] nm (moral) fault, failing, defect; (d'étoffe, métal) fault, flaw, defect; (manque, carence): **~ de** lack of; shortage of; **en ~** at fault; in the wrong; **faire ~** (manquer) to be lacking; **à ~** ad failing that; **à ~ de** for lack ou want of; **par ~** (JUR) in his (ou her etc) absence.

défavoriser [defavɔʀize] vt to put at a disadvantage.

défection [defɛksjɔ̃] nf defection, failure to give support ou assistance; failure to appear; **faire ~** (d'un parti etc) to withdraw one's support, leave.

défectueux, euse [defɛktyø, -øz] a faulty, defective.

défendre [defɑ̃dʀ(ə)] vt to defend; (interdire) to forbid; **~ à qn qch/de faire** to forbid sb sth/to do; **se ~** vi to defend o.s.; **il se défend** (fig) he can hold his own; **se ~ de/contre** (se protéger) to protect o.s. from/against; **se ~ de** (se garder de) to refrain from; (nier): **se ~ de vouloir** to deny wanting.

défense [defɑ̃s] nf defence; (d'éléphant etc) tusk; **'~ de fumer/cracher'** 'no smoking/spitting'.

déférer [defeʀe] vt (JUR) to refer; **~ à** vt (requête, décision) to defer to.

déferler [defɛʀle] vi (vagues) to break; (fig) to surge.

défi [defi] nm (provocation) challenge; (bravade) defiance.

défiance [defjɑ̃s] nf mistrust, distrust.

déficit [defisit] nm (COMM) deficit.

défier [defje] vt (provoquer) to challenge; (fig) to defy, brave; **se ~ de** vi (se méfier de) to distrust.

défigurer [defigyʀe] vt to disfigure.

défilé [defile] nm (GÉO) (narrow) gorge ou pass; (soldats) parade; (manifestants) procession, march.

défiler [defile] vi (troupes) to march past; (sportifs) to parade; (manifestants) to march; (visiteurs) to pour, stream; **se ~** vi (se dérober) to slip away, sneak off.

définir [definiʀ] vt to define.

définitif, ive [definitif, -iv] a (final) final, definitive; (pour longtemps) permanent, definitive; (sans appel) final, definite // nf: **en définitive** eventually; (somme toute) when all is said and done.

définitivement [definitivmɑ̃] ad definitively; permanently; definitely.

déflagration [deflagʀasjɔ̃] nf explosion.

défoncer [defɔ̃se] vt (caisse) to stave in; (porte) to smash in ou down; (lit, fauteuil) to burst (the springs of); (terrain, route) to rip ou plough up.

déformation [defɔʀmasjɔ̃] nf: **~ professionnelle** conditioning by one's job.

déformer [defɔʀme] vt to put out of shape; (corps) to deform; (pensée, fait) to distort; **se ~** vi to lose its shape.

défouler [defule]: **se ~** vi to unwind, let off steam.

défraîchir [defʀeʃiʀ]: **se ~** vi to fade; to become worn.

défrayer [defʀeje] vt: **~ qn** to pay sb's expenses; **~ la chronique** to be in the news.

défricher [defʀiʃe] vt to clear (for cultivation).

défroquer [defʀɔke] vi (aussi: **se ~**) to give up the cloth.

défunt, e [defœ̃, -œ̃t] a: **son ~ père** his late father // nm/f deceased.

dégagé, e [degaʒe] a clear; (ton, air) casual, jaunty.

dégagement [degaʒmɑ̃] nm: **voie de ~** slip road; **itinéraire de ~** alternative route (to relieve traffic congestion).

dégager [degaʒe] vt (exhaler) to give off; (délivrer) to free, extricate; (désencombrer) to clear; (isoler: idée, aspect) to bring out; **se ~** vi (odeur) to be given off; (passage, ciel) to clear.

dégainer [degene] vt to draw.

dégarnir [degaʀniʀ] vt (vider) to empty, clear; **se ~** vi (tempes, crâne) to go bald.

dégâts [dega] nmpl damage sg.

dégel [deʒɛl] nm thaw.

dégeler [deʒle] *vt* to thaw (out); (*fig*) to unfreeze // *vi* to thaw (out).

dégénérer [deʒenere] *vi* to degenerate; (*empirer*) to go from bad to worse.

dégingandé, e [deʒɛ̃gɑ̃de] *a* gangling.

dégivrer [deʒivre] *vt* (*frigo*) to defrost; (*vitres*) to de-ice.

déglutir [deglytir] *vt, vi* to swallow.

dégonflé, e [degɔ̃fle] *a* (*pneu*) flat.

dégonfler [degɔ̃fle] *vt* (*pneu, ballon*) to let down, deflate; **se ~** *vi* (*fam*) to chicken out.

dégouliner [deguline] *vi* to trickle, drip.

dégourdi, e [degurdi] *a* smart, resourceful.

dégourdir [degurdir] *vt*: **se ~** (**les jambes**) to stretch one's legs (*fig*).

dégoût [degu] *nm* disgust, distaste.

dégoûtant, e [degutɑ̃, -ɑ̃t] *a* disgusting.

dégoûté, e [degute] *a* disgusted; **~ de** sick of.

dégoûter [degute] *vt* to disgust; **~ qn de qch** to put sb off sth.

dégoutter [degute] *vi* to drip.

dégradé [degrade] *nm* (*PEINTURE*) gradation.

dégrader [degrade] *vt* (*MIL: officier*) to degrade; (*abîmer*) to damage, deface; **se ~** *vi* (*relations, situation*) to deteriorate.

dégrafer [degrafe] *vt* to unclip, unhook.

degré [dəgre] *nm* degree; (*d'escalier*) step; **alcool à 90 ~s** surgical spirit.

dégressif, ive [degresif, -iv] *a* on a decreasing scale.

dégrèvement [degrɛvmɑ̃] *nm* tax relief.

dégringoler [degrɛ̃gɔle] *vi* to tumble (down).

dégrossir [degrosir] *vt* (*fig*) to work out roughly; to knock the rough edges off.

déguenillé, e [dɛgnije] *a* ragged, tattered.

déguerpir [degɛrpir] *vi* to clear off.

dégueulasse [degølas] *a* (*fam*) disgusting.

déguisement [degizmɑ̃] *nm* disguise.

déguiser [degize] *vt* to disguise; **se ~** *vi* (*se costumer*) to dress up; (*pour tromper*) to disguise o.s.

déguster [degyste] *vt* (*vins*) to taste; (*fromages etc*) to sample; (*savourer*) to enjoy, savour.

dehors [dəɔr] *ad* outside; (*en plein air*) outdoors // *nm* outside // *nmpl* (*apparences*) appearances; **mettre** *ou* **jeter ~** (*expulser*) to throw out; **au ~** outside; outwardly; **au ~ de** outside; **en ~** (*vers l'extérieur*) outside; outwards; **en ~ de** (*hormis*) apart from.

déjà [deʒa] *ad* already; (*auparavant*) before, already.

déjeuner [deʒœne] *vi* to (have) lunch; (*le matin*) to have breakfast // *nm* lunch;

breakfast.

déjouer [deʒwe] *vt* to elude; to foil.

delà [dəla] *ad*: **par ~, en ~ (de), au ~ (de)** beyond.

délabrer [delabre]: **se ~** *vi* to fall into decay, become dilapidated.

délacer [delase] *vt* to unlace.

délai [dele] *nm* (*attente*) waiting period; (*sursis*) extension (of time); (*temps accordé*) time limit; **à bref ~** shortly, very soon; at short notice; **dans les ~s** within the time limit.

délaisser [delese] *vt* to abandon, desert.

délasser [delase] *vt* (*reposer*) to relax; (*divertir*) to divert, entertain; **se ~** *vi* to relax.

délateur, trice [delatœr, -tris] *nm/f* informer.

délavé, e [delave] *a* faded.

délayer [deleje] *vt* (*CULIN*) to mix (with water *etc*); (*peinture*) to thin down.

delco [dɛlko] *nm* (*AUTO*) distributor.

délecter [delɛkte]: **se ~** *vi*: **se ~ de** to revel *ou* delight in.

délégué, e [delege] *nm/f* delegate; representative.

déléguer [delege] *vt* to delegate.

délibéré, e [delibere] *a* (*conscient*) deliberate; (*déterminé*) determined.

délibérer [delibere] *vi* to deliberate.

délicat, e [delika, -at] *a* delicate; (*plein de tact*) tactful; (*attentionné*) thoughtful; (*exigeant*) fussy, particular; **procédés peu ~s** unscrupulous methods; **délicatement** *ad* delicately; (*avec douceur*) gently.

délice [delis] *nm* delight.

délicieux, euse [delisjø, -jøz] *a* (*au goût*) delicious; (*sensation, impression*) delightful.

délier [delje] *vt* to untie; **~ qn de** (*serment etc*) to release sb from.

délimiter [delimite] *vt* to delimit, demarcate; to determine; to define.

délinquance [delɛ̃kɑ̃s] *nf* criminality.

délinquant, e [delɛ̃kɑ̃, -ɑ̃t] *a, nm/f* delinquent.

délirer [delire] *vi* to be delirious; (*fig*) to be raving, be going wild.

délit [deli] *nm* (criminal) offence.

délivrer [delivre] *vt* (*prisonnier*) to (set) free, release; (*passeport, certificat*) to issue; **~ qn de** (*ennemis*) to deliver *ou* free sb from; (*fig*) to relieve sb of; to rid sb of.

déloger [delɔʒe] *vt* (*locataire*) to turn out; (*objet coincé, ennemi*) to dislodge.

deltaplane [dɛltaplan] *nm* hang-glider.

déluge [delyʒ] *nm* (*biblique*) Flood.

déluré, e [delyre] *a* smart, resourceful; (*péj*) forward, pert.

demain [dəmɛ̃] *ad* tomorrow.

demande [dəmɑ̃d] *nf* (*requête*) request; (*revendication*) demand; (*ADMIN, formulaire*) application; (*ÉCON*): **la ~ de-**

mand; '~s d'emploi' 'situations wanted'; ~ en mariage (marriage) proposal; ~ de poste job application.

demandé, e [dəmɑ̃de] a (article etc): très ~ (very) much in demand.

demander [dəmɑ̃de] vt to ask for; (date, heure etc) to ask; (nécessiter) to require, demand; ~ qch à qn to ask sb for sth; to ask sb sth; ~ à qn de faire to ask sb to do; se ~ si/pourquoi etc to wonder if/why etc; (sens purement réfléchi) to ask o.s. if/why etc; **on vous demande au téléphone** you're wanted on the phone.

demandeur, euse [dəmɑ̃dœr, -øz] nm/f: ~ d'emploi job-seeker; (job) applicant.

démangeaison [demɑ̃ʒɛzɔ̃] nf itching.

démanger [demɑ̃ʒe] vi to itch.

démanteler [demɑ̃tle] vt to break up; to demolish.

démaquillant [demakijɑ̃] nm make-up remover.

démaquiller [demakije] vt: se ~ to remove one's make-up.

démarche [demarʃ(ə)] nf (allure) gait, walk; (intervention) step; approach; (fig: intellectuelle) thought processes pl; approach; **faire des ~s auprès de qn to** approach sb.

démarcheur, euse [demarʃœr, -øz] nm/f (COMM) door-to-door salesman/woman.

démarquer [demarke] vt (prix) to mark down; (joueur) to stop marking.

démarrage [demaraʒ] nm start.

démarrer [demare] vi (conducteur) to start (up); (véhicule) to move off; (travaux) to get moving; **démarreur** nm (AUTO) starter.

démêler [demele] vt to untangle.

démêlés [demele] nmpl problems.

déménagement [demenaʒmɑ̃] nm move, removal; **camion de ~** removal van.

déménager [demenaʒe] vt (meubles) to (re)move // vi to move (house); **déménageur** nm removal man; (entrepreneur) furniture remover.

démener [demne]: se ~ vi to thrash about; (fig) to exert o.s.

dément, e [demɑ̃, -ɑ̃t] a (fou) mad, crazy; (fam) brilliant, fantastic.

démentiel, le [demɑ̃sjɛl] a insane.

démentir [demɑ̃tir] vt to refute; ~ que to deny that.

démerder [demɛrde] (fam): se ~ vi to sort things out for o.s.

démesuré, e [deməzyre] a immoderate.

démettre [demɛtr(ə)] vt: ~ qn de (fonction, poste) to dismiss sb from; se ~ (de ses fonctions) to resign (from) one's duties; se ~ l'épaule etc to dislocate one's shoulder etc.

demeurant [dəmœrɑ̃]: au ~ ad for all that.

demeure [dəmœr] nf residence; **mettre qn en ~ de faire** to enjoin ou order sb to do; à ~ ad permanently.

demeurer [dəmœre] vi (habiter) to live; (séjourner) to stay; (rester) to remain.

demi, e [dəmi] a: et ~: trois heures/bouteilles et ~es three and a half hours/bottles, three hours/bottles and a half; il est 2 heures/midi et ~e it's half past 2/12 // nm (bière) ≈ half-pint (.25 litre); à ~ ad half-; à la ~e (heure) on the half-hour.

demi... [dəmi] préfixe half-, semi..., demi-; **~-cercle** nm semicircle; **en ~ cercle** a semicircular // ad in a half circle; **~-douzaine** nf half-dozen, half a dozen; **~-finale** nf semifinal; **~-frère** nm half-brother; **~-heure** nf half-hour, half an hour; **~-jour** nm half-light; **~-journée** nf half-day, half a day; **~-litre** nm half-litre, half a litre; **~-livre** nf half-pound, half a pound; **~-mot**: à ~-mot ad without having to spell things out; **~-pension** nf (à l'hôtel) half-board; **~-place** nf half-fare.

démis, e [demi, -iz] a (épaule etc) dislocated.

demi-saison [dəmisɛzɔ̃] nf: vêtements de ~ spring ou autumn clothing.

demi-sel [dəmisɛl] a inv (beurre, fromage) slightly salted.

demi-sœur [dəmisœr] nf half-sister.

démission [demisjɔ̃] nf resignation; **donner sa ~** to give ou hand in one's notice; **démissionner** vi (de son poste) to resign.

demi-tarif [dəmitarif] nm half-price; (TRANSPORTS) half-fare.

demi-tour [dəmitur] nm about-turn; **faire ~** to turn (and go) back; (AUTO) to do a U-turn.

démocratie [demokrasi] nf democracy.

démocratique [demokratik] a democratic.

démodé, e [demode] a old-fashioned.

démographique [demografik] a demographic, population cpd.

demoiselle [dəmwazɛl] nf (jeune fille) young lady; (célibataire) single lady, maiden lady; ~ d'honneur bridesmaid.

démolir [demolir] vt to demolish.

démon [demɔ̃] nm (enfant turbulent) devil, demon; le D~ the Devil.

démonstration [demɔ̃strasjɔ̃] nf demonstration; (aérienne, navale) display.

démonté, e [demɔ̃te] a (fig) raging, wild.

démonter [demɔ̃te] vt (machine etc) to take down, dismantle; se ~ vi (personne) to lose countenance.

démontrer [demɔ̃tre] vt to demonstrate.

démordre [demɔʀdʀ(ə)] *vi*: ne pas ~ de to refuse to give up, stick to.

démouler [demule] *vt* (*gâteau*) to turn out.

démuni, e [demyni] *a* (*sans argent*) impoverished.

démunir [demyniʀ] *vt*: ~ qn de to deprive sb of; se ~ de to part with, give up.

dénatalité [denatalite] *nf* fall in the birth rate.

dénaturer [denatyʀe] *vt* (*goût*) to alter; (*pensée, fait*) to distort.

dénégations [denegasjɔ̃] *nfpl* denials.

déniaiser [denjeze] *vt*: ~ qn to teach sb about life.

dénicher [deniʃe] *vt* to unearth; to track ou hunt down.

dénier [denje] *vt* to deny.

dénigrer [denigʀe] *vt* to denigrate, run down.

dénivellation [denivɛlasjɔ̃] *nf*, **dénivellement** [denivɛlmɑ̃] *nm* ramp; dip; difference in level.

dénombrer [denɔ̃bʀe] *vt* (*compter*) to count; (*énumérer*) to enumerate, list.

dénomination [denɔminasjɔ̃] *nf* designation, appellation.

dénommer [denɔme] *vt* to name.

dénoncer [denɔ̃se] *vt* to denounce; se ~ *vi* to give o.s. up, come forward.

dénouement [denumɑ̃] *nm* outcome.

dénouer [denwe] *vt* to unknot, undo.

dénoyauter [denwajɔte] *vt* to stone.

denrée [dɑ̃ʀe] *nf*: ~s (*alimentaires*) foodstuffs.

dense [dɑ̃s] *a* dense.

densité [dɑ̃site] *nf* density.

dent [dɑ̃] *nf* tooth (*pl* teeth); en ~s de scie serrated; jagged; ~ de lait/sagesse milk/wisdom tooth; **dentaire** *a* dental.

dentelé, e [dɑ̃tle] *a* jagged, indented.

dentelle [dɑ̃tɛl] *nf* lace *q*.

dentier [dɑ̃tje] *nm* denture.

dentifrice [dɑ̃tifʀis] *nm* toothpaste.

dentiste [dɑ̃tist(ə)] *nm/f* dentist.

dénuder [denyde] *vt* to bare.

dénué, e [denɥe] *a*: ~ de devoid of; lacking in.

dénuement [denymɑ̃] *nm* destitution.

déodorant [deɔdɔʀɑ̃] *nm* deodorant.

dépannage [depanaʒ] *nm*: service de ~ (*AUTO*) breakdown service.

dépanner [depane] *vt* (*voiture, télévision*) to fix, repair; (*fig*) to bail out, help out; **dépanneuse** *nf* breakdown lorry (*Brit*), tow truck (*US*).

dépareillé, e [depaʀeje] *a* (*collection, service*) incomplete; (*objet*) odd.

déparer [depaʀe] *vt* to spoil, mar.

départ [depaʀ] *nm* leaving *q*, departure; (*SPORT*) start; (*sur un horaire*) departure; **au** ~ at the start; **à son** ~ when he left.

départager [depaʀtaʒe] *vt* to decide between.

département [depaʀtəmɑ̃] *nm* department.

départir [depaʀtiʀ]: se ~ de *vt* to abandon, depart from.

dépassé, e [depɑse] *a* superseded, outmoded; (*affolé*) panic-stricken.

dépasser [depɑse] *vt* (*véhicule, concurrent*) to overtake; (*endroit*) to pass, go past; (*somme, limite*) to exceed; (*fig: en beauté etc*) to surpass, outshine; (*être en saillie sur*) to jut out above (ou in front of) // *vi* (*jupon*) to show.

dépaysé, e [depeize] *a* disoriented.

dépecer [depəse] *vt* to joint, cut up.

dépêche [depɛʃ] *nf* dispatch.

dépêcher [depeʃe] *vt* to dispatch; se ~ *vi* to hurry.

dépeindre [depɛ̃dʀ(ə)] *vt* to depict.

dépendre [depɑ̃dʀ(ə)]: ~ de *vt* to depend on; (*financièrement etc*) to be dependent on.

dépens [depɑ̃] *nmpl*: aux ~ de at the expense of.

dépense [depɑ̃s] *nf* spending *q*, expense, expenditure *q*; (*fig*) consumption; expenditure.

dépenser [depɑ̃se] *vt* to spend; (*gaz, eau*) to use; (*fig*) to expend, use up; se ~ *vi* (*se fatiguer*) to exert o.s.

dépensier, ière [depɑ̃sje, -jɛʀ] *a*: il est ~ he's a spendthrift.

déperdition [depɛʀdisjɔ̃] *nf* loss.

dépérir [depeʀiʀ] *vi* to waste away; to wither.

dépêtrer [depetʀe] *vt*: se ~ de to extricate o.s. from.

dépeupler [depœple] *vt* to depopulate; se ~ *vi* to be depopulated.

déphasé, e [defaze] *a* (*fig*) out of touch.

dépilatoire [depilatwaʀ] *a* depilatory, hair removing.

dépister [depiste] *vt* to detect; (*voleur*) to track down; (*poursuivants*) to throw off the scent.

dépit [depi] *nm* vexation, frustration; en ~ de *prép* in spite of; en ~ du bon sens contrary to all good sense; **dépité, e** *a* vexed, frustrated.

déplacé, e [deplase] *a* (*propos*) out of place, uncalled-for.

déplacement [deplasmɑ̃] *nm* (*voyage*) trip, travelling *q*.

déplacer [deplase] *vt* (*table, voiture*) to move, shift; (*employé*) to transfer, move; se ~ *vi* to move; (*voyager*) to travel // *vt* (*vertèbre etc*) to displace.

déplaire [deplɛʀ] *vi*: ceci me déplaît I don't like this, I dislike this; **déplaisant, e** *a* disagreeable.

dépliant [deplijɑ̃] *nm* leaflet.

déplier [deplije] *vt* to unfold.

déployer [deplwaje] *vt* to open out, spread; to deploy; to display, exhibit.

dépoli, e [depɔli] a: verre ~ frosted glass.

déporter [depɔrte] vt (POL) to deport; (dévier) to carry off course.

déposer [depoze] vt (gén: mettre, poser) to lay ou put down; (à la banque, à la consigne) to deposit; (passager) to drop (off), set down; (roi) to depose; (ADMIN: faire enregistrer) to file; to register; (JUR): ~ (contre) to testify ou give evidence (against); se ~ vi to settle; **dépositaire** nm/f (COMM) agent.

dépôt [depo] nm (à la banque, sédiment) deposit; (entrepôt, réserve) warehouse, store; (gare) depot; (prison) cells pl.

dépotoir [depotwar] nm dumping ground, rubbish dump.

dépouille [depuj] nf (d'animal) skin, hide; (humaine): ~ (mortelle) mortal remains pl.

dépouillé, e [depuje] a (fig) bare, bald.

dépouiller [depuje] vt (animal) to skin; (spolier) to deprive of one's possessions; (documents) to go through, peruse; ~ qn/qch de to strip sb/sth of; ~ le scrutin to count the votes.

dépourvu, e [depurvy] a: ~ de lacking in, without; au ~ ad unprepared.

déprécier [depresje] vt, se ~ vi to depreciate.

déprédations [depredasjɔ̃] nfpl damage sg.

dépression [depresjɔ̃] nf depression; ~ (nerveuse) (nervous) breakdown.

déprimer [deprime] vt to depress.

depuis [dəpɥi] ♦ prép 1 (point de départ dans le temps) since; il habite Paris ~ 1983/l'an dernier he has been living in Paris since 1983/last year; ~ quand le connaissez-vous? how long have you known him?

2 (temps écoulé) for; il habite Paris ~ 5 ans he has been living in Paris for 5 years; je le connais ~ 3 ans I've known him for 3 years

3 (lieu): il a plu ~ Metz it's been raining since Metz; elle a téléphoné ~ Valence she rang from Valence

4 (quantité, rang) from; ~ les plus petits jusqu'aux plus grands from the youngest to the oldest

♦ ad (temps) since (then); je ne lui ai pas parlé ~ I haven't spoken to him since (then)

depuis que cj (ever) since; ~ qu'il m'a dit ça (ever) since he said that to me.

député, e [depyte] nm/f (POL) ≈ Member of Parliament (Brit), ≈ Member of Congress (US).

députer [depyte] vt to delegate.

déraciner [derasine] vt to uproot.

dérailler [deraje] vi (train) to be derailed; faire ~ to derail.

déraisonner [derezɔne] vi to talk non-

sense, rave.

dérangement [derɑ̃ʒmɑ̃] nm (gêne) trouble; (gastrique etc) disorder; (mécanique) breakdown; en ~ (téléphone) out of order.

déranger [derɑ̃ʒe] vt (personne) to trouble, bother; to disturb; (projets) to disrupt, upset; (objets, vêtements) to disarrange; se ~ vi to put o.s. out; to (take the trouble to) come ou go out; est-ce que cela vous dérange si...? do you mind if...?

déraper [derape] vi (voiture) to skid; (personne, semelles, couteau) to slip.

déréglé, e [deregle] a (mœurs) dissolute.

dérégler [deregle] vt (mécanisme) to put out of order; (estomac) to upset.

dérider [deride] vt, se ~ vi to brighten up.

dérision [derizjɔ̃] nf: tourner en ~ to deride.

dérivatif [derivatif] nm distraction.

dérive [deriv] nf (de dériveur) centreboard; aller à la ~ (NAVIG, fig) to drift.

dérivé, e [derive] nm (TECH) byproduct // nf (MATH) derivative.

dériver [derive] vt (MATH) to derive; (cours d'eau etc) to divert // vi (bateau) to drift; ~ de to derive from.

dermatologue [dermatɔlɔg] nm/f dermatologist.

dernier, ière [dernje, -jɛr] a last; (le plus récent) latest, last; lundi/le mois ~ last Monday/month; du ~ chic extremely smart; les ~s honneurs the last tribute; en ~ ad last; ce ~ the latter; **dernièrement** ad recently.

dérobé, e [derɔbe] a (porte) secret, hidden; à la ~e surreptitiously.

dérober [derɔbe] vt to steal; ~ qch à (la vue de) qn to conceal ou hide sth from sb('s view); se ~ vi (s'esquiver) to slip away; to shy away; se ~ sous (s'effondrer) to give way beneath; se ~ à (justice, regards) to hide from; (obligation) to shirk.

dérogation [derɔgasjɔ̃] nf (special) dispensation.

déroger [derɔʒe]: ~ à vt to go against, depart from.

dérouiller [deruje] vt: se ~ les jambes to stretch one's legs (fig).

déroulement [derulmɑ̃] nm (d'une opération etc) progress.

dérouler [derule] vt (ficelle) to unwind; (papier) to unroll; se ~ vi (avoir lieu) to take place; (se passer) to go on; to go (off); to unfold.

déroute [derut] nf rout; total collapse.

dérouter [derute] vt (avion, train) to reroute, divert; (étonner) to disconcert, throw (out).

derrière [derjɛr] ad, prép behind // nm (d'une maison) back; (postérieur) behind, bottom; **les pattes de** ~ the back *ou* hind legs; **par** ~ from behind; *(fig)* behind one's back.

des [de] *dét, prép + dét voir* **de**.

dès [dɛ] *prép* from; ~ **que** *cj* as soon as; ~ **son retour** as soon as he was (*ou* is) back; ~ **lors** *ad* from then on; ~ **lors que** *cj* from the moment (that).

désabusé, e [dezabyze] *a* disillusioned.

désaccord [dezakɔR] *nm* disagreement.

désaccordé, e [dezakɔRde] *a* (*MUS*) out of tune.

désaffecté, e [dezafɛkte] *a* disused.

désaffection [dezafɛksjɔ̃] *nf*: ~ **pour** estrangement from.

désagréable [dezagReable(ə)] *a* unpleasant.

désagréger [dezagReʒe]: **se** ~ *vi* to disintegrate, break up.

désagrément [dezagRemɑ̃] *nm* annoyance, trouble *q*.

désaltérer [dezalteRe] *vt*: **se** ~ to quench one's thirst.

désamorcer [dezamɔRse] *vt* to defuse; to forestall.

désapprouver [dezapRuve] *vt* to disapprove of.

désarçonner [dezaRsɔne] *vt* to unseat, throw; *(fig)* to throw, puzzle.

désarroi [dezaRwa] *nm* disarray.

désarticulé, e [dezaRtikyle] *a* (*pantin, corps*) dislocated.

désastre [dezastR(ə)] *nm* disaster.

désavantage [dezavɑ̃taʒ] *nm* disadvantage; *(inconvénient)* drawback, disadvantage; **désavantager** *vt* to put at a disadvantage.

désavouer [dezavwe] *vt* to disown.

désaxé, e [dezakse] *a (fig)* unbalanced.

descendre [desɑ̃dR(ə)] *vt* (*escalier, montagne*) to go (*ou* come) down; (*valise, paquet*) to take *ou* get down; (*étagère etc*) to lower; (*fam: abattre*) to shoot down // *vi* to go (*ou* come) down; (*passager: s'arrêter*) to get out, alight; ~ **à pied/en voiture** to walk/drive down; ~ **de** (*famille*) to be descended from; ~ **du train** to get out of *ou* get off the train; ~ **d'un arbre** to climb down from a tree; ~ **de cheval** to dismount; ~ **à l'hôtel** to stay at a hotel.

descente [desɑ̃t] *nf* descent, going down; (*chemin*) way down; (*SKI*) downhill (race); **au milieu de la** ~ halfway down; ~ **de lit** bedside rug; ~ (**de police**) (police) raid.

description [dɛskRipsjɔ̃] *nf* description.

désemparé, e [dezɑ̃paRe] *a* bewildered, distraught.

désemparer [dezɑ̃paRe] *vi*: **sans** ~ without stopping.

désemplir [dezɑ̃pliR] *vi*: **ne pas** ~ to be always full.

déséquilibre [dezekilibR(ə)] *nm* (*position*): **en** ~ unsteady; *(fig: des forces,*

du budget) imbalance.

déséquilibré, e [dezekilibRe] *nm/f* (*PSYCH*) unbalanced person.

déséquilibrer [dezekilibRe] *vt* to throw off balance.

désert, e [dezɛR, -ɛRt(ə)] *a* deserted // *nm* desert.

déserter [dezɛRte] *vi, vt* to desert.

désertique [dezɛRtik] *a* desert *cpd*; barren, empty.

désespéré, e [dezɛspeRe] *a* desperate.

désespérer [dezɛspeRe] *vt* to drive to despair // *vi*: ~ **de** to despair of.

désespoir [dezɛspwaR] *nm* despair; **en** ~ **de cause** in desperation.

déshabillé [dezabije] *nm* négligée.

déshabiller [dezabije] *vt* to undress; **se** ~ *vi* to undress (o.s.).

désherbant [dezɛRbɑ̃] *nm* weed-killer.

déshériter [dezeRite] *vt* to disinherit.

déshérités [dezeRite] *nmpl*: **les** ~ the underprivileged.

déshonneur [dezɔnœR] *nm* dishonour.

déshydraté, e [dezidRate] *a* dehydrated.

desiderata [dezideRata] *nmpl* requirements.

désigner [dezipe] *vt* (*montrer*) to point out, indicate; (*dénommer*) to denote; (*candidat etc*) to name.

désinfectant, e [dezɛ̃fɛktɑ̃, -ɑ̃t] *a, nm* disinfectant.

désinfecter [dezɛ̃fɛkte] *vt* to disinfect.

désintégrer [dezɛ̃tegRe] *vt*, **se** ~ *vi* to disintegrate.

désintéressé, e [dezɛ̃teRese] *a* disinterested, unselfish.

désintéresser [dezɛ̃teRese] *vt*: **se** ~ (**de**) to lose interest (in).

désintoxication [dezɛ̃tɔksikasjɔ̃] *nf*: **faire une cure de** ~ to undergo treatment for alcoholism (*ou* drug addiction).

désinvolte [dezɛ̃vɔlt(ə)] *a* casual, offhand; **désinvolture** *nf* casualness.

désir [deziR] *nm* wish; (*fort, sensuel*) desire.

désirer [deziRe] *vt* to want, wish for; (*sexuellement*) to desire; **je désire** ... (*formule de politesse*) I would like ...

désister [deziste]: **se** ~ *vi* to stand down, withdraw.

désobéir [dezɔbeiR] *vi*: ~ (**à qn/qch**) to disobey (sb/sth); **désobéissant, e** *a* disobedient.

désobligeant, e [dezɔbliʒɑ̃, -ɑ̃t] *a* disagreeable.

désodorisant [dezɔdɔRizɑ̃] *nm* air freshener, deodorizer.

désœuvré, e [dezœvRe] *a* idle.

désolé, e [dezɔle] *a* (*paysage*) desolate; **je suis** ~ I'm sorry.

désoler [dezɔle] *vt* to distress, grieve.

désolidariser [desɔlidaRize] *vt*: **se** ~ **de** *ou* **d'avec** to dissociate o.s. from.

désopilant, e [dezɔpilɑ̃, -ɑ̃t] *a* hilarious.

désordonné, e [dezɔrdɔne] a untidy.

désordre [dezɔrdʀ(ə)] nm disorder(liness), untidiness; (anarchie) disorder; ~s nmpl (POL) disturbances, disorder sg; en ~ in a mess, untidy.

désorienté, e [dezɔrjɑ̃te] a disorientated.

désormais [dezɔrmɛ] ad from now on.

désosser [dezɔse] vt to bone.

desquels, desquelles [dekɛl] prép + pronom voir **lequel**.

dessaisir [desɛziʀ]: se ~ de vt to give up, part with.

dessaler [desale] vt (eau de mer) to desalinate; (CULIN) to soak.

desséché, e [deseʃe] a dried up.

dessécher [deseʃe] vt to dry out, parch; se ~ vi to dry out.

dessein [desɛ̃] nm design; à ~ intentionally, deliberately.

desserrer [desɛʀe] vt to loosen; (frein) to release.

dessert [desɛʀ] nm dessert, pudding.

desserte [desɛʀt(ə)] nf (table) side table; (transport): la ~ du village est assurée par autocar there is a coach service to the village.

desservir [desɛʀviʀ] vt (ville, quartier) to serve; (nuire à) to go against, put at a disadvantage; (débarrasser): ~ (la table) to clear the table.

dessin [desɛ̃] nm (œuvre, art) drawing; (motif) pattern, design; (contour) (out)line; ~ animé cartoon (film); ~ humoristique cartoon.

dessinateur, trice [desinatœʀ, -tʀis] nm/f drawer; (de bandes dessinées) cartoonist; (industriel) draughtsman (Brit), draftsman (US).

dessiner [desine] vt to draw; (concevoir) to design.

dessoûler [desule] vt, vi to sober up.

dessous [dəsu] ad underneath, beneath // nm underside // nmpl (sousvêtements) underwear sg; en ~, par ~ underneath; below; au-~ (de) below; (peu digne de) beneath; avoir le ~ to get the worst of it; ~-de-plat nm inv tablemat.

dessus [dəsy] ad on top; (collé, écrit) on it // nm top; en ~ above; par ~ ad over it // prép over; au-~ (de) above; avoir le ~ to get the upper hand; ~-de-lit nm inv bedspread.

destin [dɛstɛ̃] nm fate; (avenir) destiny.

destinataire [dɛstinatɛʀ] nm/f (POSTES) addressee; (d'un colis) consignee.

destination [dɛstinasjɔ̃] nf (lieu) destination; (usage) purpose; à ~ de bound for, travelling to.

destinée [dɛstine] nf fate; (existence, avenir) destiny.

destiner [dɛstine] vt: ~ qn à (poste, sort) to destine sb for; ~ qn/qch à (pré-

destiner) to destine sb/sth to + verbe; ~ qch à qn (envisager de donner) to intend sb to have sth; (adresser) to intend sth for sb; to aim sth at sb; être destiné à (sort) to be destined to + verbe; (usage) to be meant for; (suj: sort) to be in store for.

destituer [dɛstitɥe] vt to depose.

désuet, ète [desɥɛ, -ɛt] a outdated, outmoded; **désuétude** nf: tomber en désuétude to fall into disuse.

détachant [detaʃɑ̃] nm stain remover.

détacher [detaʃe] vt (enlever) to detach, remove; (délier) to untie; (ADMIN): ~ qn (auprès de/à) to post sb (to); se ~ vi (tomber) to come off; to come out; (se défaire) to come undone; se ~ sur to stand out against; se ~ de (se désintéresser) to grow away from.

détail [detaj] nm detail; (COMM): le ~ retail; au ~ ad (COMM) retail; separately; en ~ in detail.

détaillant [detajɑ̃] nm retailer.

détailler [detaje] vt (expliquer) to explain in detail; to detail; (examiner) to look over, examine.

détartrant [detaʀtʀɑ̃] nm scale remover.

détecter [detɛkte] vt to detect.

détective [detɛktiv] nm (Brit: policier) detective; ~ (privé) private detective.

déteindre [detɛ̃dʀ(ə)] vi (tissu) to fade; (fig): ~ sur to rub off on.

dételer [detle] vt to unharness.

détendre [detɑ̃dʀ(ə)] vt: se ~ to lose its tension; to relax.

détenir [detniʀ] vt (fortune, objet, secret) to be in possession of; (prisonnier) to detain, hold; (record, pouvoir) to hold.

détente [detɑ̃t] nf relaxation; (d'une arme) trigger.

détention [detɑ̃sjɔ̃] nf possession; detention; holding; ~ préventive (pre-trial) custody.

détenu, e [detny] nm/f prisoner.

détergent [detɛʀʒɑ̃] nm detergent.

détériorer [deteʀjɔʀe] vt to damage; se ~ vi to deteriorate.

déterminé, e [detɛʀmine] a (résolu) determined; (précis) specific, definite.

déterminer [detɛʀmine] vt (fixer) to determine; (décider): ~ qn à faire qch to decide sb to do.

déterrer [detɛʀe] vt to dig up.

détersif [detɛʀsif] nm detergent.

détestable [detɛstabl(ə)] a foul, ghastly; detestable, odious.

détester [detɛste] vt to hate, detest.

détonation [detɔnasjɔ̃] nf detonation, bang, report (of a gun).

détonner [detɔne] vi (MUS) to go out of tune; (fig) to clash.

détour [detuʀ] nm detour; (tournant) bend, curve; sans ~ (fig) plainly.

détourné, e [detuʀne] a (moyen)

roundabout.

détournement [deturnəmã] *nm*: ~ d'avion hijacking; ~ **de mineur** corruption of a minor.

détourner [deturne] *vt* to divert; (*par la force*) to hijack; (*yeux, tête*) to turn away; (*de l'argent*) to embezzle; se ~ *vi* to turn away.

détracteur, trice [detraktœr, -tris] *nm/f* disparager, critic.

détraquer [detrake] *vt* to put out of order; (*estomac*) to upset; se ~ *vi* to go wrong.

détrempé, e [detrãpe] *a* (*sol*) sodden, waterlogged.

détresse [detres] *nf* distress.

détriment [detrimã] *nm*: **au** ~ **de** to the detriment of.

détritus [detritys] *nmpl* rubbish *sg*, refuse *sg*.

détroit [detrwa] *nm* strait.

détromper [detrõpe] *vt* to disabuse.

détrôner [detrone] *vt* to dethrone.

détrousser [detruse] *vt* to rob.

détruire [detrɥir] *vt* to destroy.

dette [det] *nf* debt.

D.E.U.G. [dœg] *sigle m* = *diplôme d'études universitaires générales.*

deuil [dœj] *nm* (*perte*) bereavement; (*période*) mourning; (*chagrin*) grief; **être en** ~ to be in mourning.

deux [dø] *num* two; **les** ~ both; **ses** ~ **mains** both his hands, his two hands; ~ **points** colon *sg*; **deuxième** *num* second; **deuxièmement** *ad* secondly, in the second place; ~**-pièces** *nm inv* (*tailleur*) two-piece suit; (*de bain*) two-piece (swimsuit); (*appartement*) two-roomed flat (*Brit*) *ou* apartment (*US*); ~**-roues** *nm inv* two-wheeled vehicle.

devais *etc vb voir* **devoir**.

dévaler [devale] *vt* to hurtle down.

dévaliser [devalize] *vt* to rob, burgle.

dévaloriser [devalɔrize] *vt*, se ~ *vi* to depreciate.

dévaluation [devalɥasjõ] *nf* depreciation; (*ÉCON: mesure*) devaluation.

devancer [dəvãse] *vt* to be ahead of; to get ahead of; to arrive before; (*prévenir*) to anticipate.

devant [dəvã] *ad* in front; (*à distance: en avant*) ahead // *prép* in front; ahead of; (*avec mouvement: passer*) past; (*fig*) before, in front of; faced with; in view of // *nm* front; **prendre les** ~**s** to make the first move; **les pattes de** ~ the front legs, the forelegs; **par** ~ (*boutonner*) at the front; (*entrer*) the front way; **aller au-** ~ **de qn** to go out to meet sb; **aller au-** ~ **de** (*désirs de qn*) to anticipate.

devanture [dəvãtyr] *nf* (*façade*) (shop) front; (*étalage*) display; (shop) window.

déveine [deven] *nf* rotten luck *q*.

développement [devlɔpmã] *nm* development.

développer [devlɔpe] *vt* to develop; se ~ *vi* to develop.

devenir [dəvnir] *vb avec attribut* to become; ~ **instituteur** to become a teacher; **que sont-ils devenus?** what has become of them?

dévergondé, e [devergõde] *a* wild, shameless.

déverser [deverse] *vt* (*liquide*) to pour (out); (*ordures*) to tip (out); se ~ **dans** (*fleuve, mer*) to flow into.

dévêtir [devetir] *vt*, se ~ to undress.

devez *etc vb voir* **devoir**.

déviation [devjasjõ] *nf* deviation; (*AUTO*) diversion (*Brit*), detour (*US*).

dévider [devide] *vt* to unwind.

devienne *etc vb voir* **devenir**.

dévier [devje] *vt* (*fleuve, circulation*) to divert; (*coup*) to deflect // *vi* to veer (off course).

devin [dəvẽ] *nm* soothsayer, seer.

deviner [dəvine] *vt* to guess; (*prévoir*) to foresee; (*apercevoir*) to distinguish.

devinette [dəvinet] *nf* riddle.

devins *etc vb voir* **devenir**.

devis [dəvi] *nm* estimate, quotation.

dévisager [devizaʒe] *vt* to stare at.

devise [dəviz] *nf* (*formule*) motto, watchword; (*ÉCON: monnaie*) currency; ~**s** *nfpl* (*argent*) currency *sg*.

deviser [dəvize] *vi* to converse.

dévisser [devise] *vt* to unscrew, undo; se ~ *vi* to come unscrewed.

dévoiler [devwale] *vt* to unveil.

devoir [dəvwar] *nm* duty; (*SCOL*) homework *q*; (: **en classe**) exercise // *vt* (*argent, respect*): ~ **qch (à qn)** to owe (sb) sth; (*suivi de l'infinitif: obligation*): **il doit le faire** he has to do it, he must do it; (: *intention*): **il doit partir demain** he is (due) to leave tomorrow; (: *probabilité*): **il doit être tard** it must be late.

dévolu, e [devɔly] *a*: ~ **à** allotted to // *nm*: **jeter son** ~ **sur** to fix one's choice on.

dévorer [devɔre] *vt* to devour; (*suj: feu, soucis*) to consume.

dévot, e [devo, -ɔt] *a* devout, pious.

dévotion [devosjõ] *nf* devoutness; **être à la** ~ **de qn** to be totally devoted to sb.

dévoué, e [devwe] *a* devoted.

dévouer [devwe]: se ~ *vi* (*se sacrifier*) se ~ (**pour**) to sacrifice o.s. (for); (*se consacrer*): se ~ **à** to devote *ou* dedicate o.s. to.

dévoyé, e [devwaje] *a* delinquent.

devrai *etc vb voir* **devoir**.

diabète [djabet] *nm* diabetes *sg*; **diabétique** *nm/f* diabetic.

diable [djabl(ə)] *nm* devil.

diacre [djakr(ə)] *nm* deacon.

diagnostic [djagnɔstik] *nm* diagnosis *sg*.

diagonal, e, aux [djagɔnal, -o] *a, nf* diagonal; **en** ~**e** diagonally; **lire en** ~**e** to skim through.

diagramme [djagram] nm chart, graph.

dialecte [djalɛkt(ə)] nm dialect.

dialogue [djalɔg] nm dialogue.

diamant [djamɑ̃] nm diamond; **diamantaire** nm diamond dealer.

diamètre [djamɛtʀ(ə)] nm diameter.

diapason [djapazɔ̃] nm tuning fork.

diaphragme [djafʀagm] nm diaphragm.

diaporama [djapoʀama] nm slide show.

diapositive [djapozitiv] nf transparency, slide.

diarrhée [djaʀe] nf diarrhoea.

dictateur [diktatœʀ] nm dictator; **dictature** nf dictatorship.

dictée [dikte] nf dictation.

dicter [dikte] vt to dictate.

dictionnaire [diksjɔnɛʀ] nm dictionary.

dicton [diktɔ̃] nm saying, dictum.

dièse [djez] nm sharp.

diesel [djezɛl] nm, a inv diesel.

diète [djet] nf (jeûne) starvation diet; (régime) diet.

diététique [djetetik] a: magasin ~ health food shop.

dieu, x [djø] nm god; D~ God; mon D~! good heavens!

diffamation [difamasjɔ̃] nf slander; (écrite) libel.

différé [difeʀe] nm (TV): en ~ (pre-)recorded.

différence [difeʀɑ̃s] nf difference; à la ~ de unlike.

différencier [difeʀɑ̃sje] vt to differentiate.

différend [difeʀɑ̃] nm difference (of opinion), disagreement.

différent, e [difeʀɑ̃, -ɑ̃t] a: ~ (de) different (from); ~s objets different ou various objects.

différer [difeʀe] vt to postpone, put off // vi: ~ (de) to differ (from).

difficile [difisil] a difficult; (exigeant) hard to please; ~ment ad with difficulty.

difficulté [difikylte] nf difficulty; en ~ (bateau, alpiniste) in difficulties.

difforme [difɔʀm(ə)] a deformed, misshapen.

diffuser [difyze] vt (chaleur, bruit) to diffuse; (émission, musique) to broadcast; (nouvelle, idée) to circulate; (COMM) to distribute.

digérer [diʒeʀe] vt to digest; (fig: accepter) to stomach, put up with; **digestif** nm (after-dinner) liqueur.

digne [diɲ] a dignified; ~ de worthy of; ~ de foi trustworthy.

dignité [diɲite] nf dignity.

digression [digʀesjɔ̃] nf digression.

digue [dig] nf dike, dyke.

dilapider [dilapide] vt to squander.

dilemme [dilɛm] nm dilemma.

diligence [diliʒɑ̃s] nf stagecoach; (empressement) despatch.

diluer [dilɥe] vt to dilute.

diluvien, ne [dilyvjɛ̃, -jɛn] a: pluie ~ne torrential rain.

dimanche [dimɑ̃ʃ] nm Sunday.

dimension [dimɑ̃sjɔ̃] nf (grandeur) size; (cote, de l'espace) dimension.

diminuer [diminɥe] vt to reduce, decrease; (ardeur etc) to lessen; (personne: physiquement) to undermine; (dénigrer) to belittle // vi to decrease, diminish; **diminutif** nm (surnom) pet name; **diminution** nf decreasing, diminishing.

dinde [dɛ̃d] nf turkey.

dindon [dɛ̃dɔ̃] nm turkey.

dîner [dine] nm dinner // vi to have dinner.

dingue [dɛ̃g] a (fam) crazy.

diplomate [diplomat] a diplomatic // nm diplomat; (fig) diplomatist.

diplomatie [diplomasi] nf diplomacy.

diplôme [diplom] nm diploma; **diplômé, e** a qualified.

dire [diʀ] nm: au ~ de according to; leur ~s what they say // vt to say; (secret, mensonge) to tell; ~ l'heure/la vérité to tell the time/the truth; ~ qch à qn to tell sb sth; ~ à qn qu'il fasse ou de faire to tell sb to do; on dit que they say that; ceci dit that being said; (à ces mots) whereupon; si cela lui dit (plaire) if he fancies it; que dites-vous de (penser) what do you think of; on dirait que it looks (ou sounds etc) as if; dis/dites (donc) I say; (à propos) by the way.

direct, e [diʀɛkt] a direct // nm (TV): en ~ live; ~ement ad directly.

directeur, trice [diʀɛktœʀ, -tʀis] nm/f (d'entreprise) director; (de service) manager/eress; (d'école) head(teacher) (Brit), principal (US).

direction [diʀɛksjɔ̃] nf management; conducting; supervision; steering; (sens) direction; 'toutes ~s' 'all routes'.

dirent vb voir **dire**.

dirigeant, e [diʀiʒɑ̃, -ɑ̃t] a managerial; ruling // nm/f (d'un parti etc) leader; (d'entreprise) manager.

diriger [diʀiʒe] vt (entreprise) to manage, run; (véhicule) to steer; (orchestre) to conduct; (recherches, travaux) to supervise; (braquer: regard, arme): ~ sur to point ou level at; se ~ (s'orienter) to find one's way; se ~ vers ou sur to make ou head for.

dirigisme [diʀiʒism(ə)] nm (ÉCON) state intervention, interventionism.

dis etc vb voir **dire**.

discerner [disɛʀne] vt to discern, make out.

discipline [disiplin] nf discipline; **discipliner** vt to discipline; to control.

discontinu, e [diskɔ̃tiny] a intermittent.

discontinuer [diskɔ̃tinɥe] vi: sans ~

without stopping, without a break.

disconvenir [diskɔ̃vniʀ] *vi*: **ne pas ~ de qch/que** not to deny sth/that.

discordant, e [diskɔʀdɑ̃, -ɑ̃t] *a* discordant; conflicting.

discothèque [diskɔtek] *nf* (*disques*) record collection; (*: dans une bibliothèque*) record library; (*boîte de nuit*) disco(thèque).

discourir [diskuʀiʀ] *vi* to discourse, hold forth.

discours [diskuʀ] *nm* speech.

discret, ète [diskʀɛ, -ɛt] *a* discreet; (*fig*) unobtrusive; quiet.

discrétion [diskʀesjɔ̃] *nf* discretion; **être à la ~ de qn** to be in sb's hands; **à ~** unlimited; as much as one wants.

discrimination [diskʀiminasjɔ̃] *nf* discrimination; **sans ~** indiscriminately.

disculper [diskylpe] *vt* to exonerate.

discussion [diskysjɔ̃] *nf* discussion.

discutable [diskytabl(ə)] *a* debatable.

discuté, e [diskyte] *a* controversial.

discuter [diskyte] *vt* (*contester*) to question, dispute; (*débattre: prix*) to discuss // *vi* to talk; (*ergoter*) to argue; **~ de** to discuss.

dise *etc vb voir* **dire**.

disette [dizet] *nf* food shortage.

diseuse [dizøz] *nf*: **~ de bonne aventure** fortuneteller.

disgracieux, euse [disgʀasjø, -jøz] *a* ungainly, awkward.

disjoindre [disʒwɛ̃dʀ(ə)] *vt* to take apart; **se ~** *vi* to come apart.

disjoncteur [disʒɔ̃ktœʀ] *nm* (*ÉLEC*) circuit breaker.

disloquer [dislɔke] *vt* (*chaise*) to dismantle; **se ~** *vi* (*parti, empire*) to break up; **se ~ l'épaule** to dislocate one's shoulder.

disons *vb voir* **dire**.

disparaître [dispaʀɛtʀ(ə)] *vi* to disappear; (*à la vue*) to vanish, disappear; to be hidden *ou* concealed; (*se perdre: traditions etc*) to die out; **faire ~** to remove; to get rid of.

disparition [dispaʀisjɔ̃] *nf* disappearance.

disparu, e [dispaʀy] *nm/f* missing person; (*défunt*) departed.

dispensaire [dispɑ̃sɛʀ] *nm* community clinic.

dispenser [dispɑ̃se] *vt* (*donner*) to lavish, bestow; (*exempter*): **~ qn de** to exempt sb from; **se ~ de** *vt* to avoid; to get out of.

disperser [dispɛʀse] *vt* to scatter; (*fig: son attention*) to dissipate.

disponibilité [dispɔnibilite] *nf* (*ADMIN*): **être en ~** to be on leave of absence.

disponible [dispɔnibl(ə)] *a* available.

dispos [dispo] *am*: (**frais et**) **~** fresh (as a daisy).

disposé, e [dispoze] *a*: **bien/mal ~** (*hu-*

meur) in a good/bad mood; **~ à** (*prêt à*) willing *ou* prepared to.

disposer [dispoze] *vt* (*arranger, placer*) to arrange // *vi*: **vous pouvez ~** you may leave; **~ de** *vt* to have (at one's disposal); to use; **se ~ à faire** to prepare to do, be about to do.

dispositif [dispozitif] *nm* device; (*fig*) system, plan of action; set-up.

disposition [dispozisjɔ̃] *nf* (*arrangement*) arrangement, layout; (*humeur*) mood; (*tendance*) tendency; **~s** *nfpl* (*mesures*) steps, measures; (*préparatifs*) arrangements; (*loi, testament*) provisions; (*aptitudes*) bent *sg*, aptitude *sg*; **à la ~ de qn** at sb's disposal.

disproportionné, e [dispʀɔpɔʀsjɔne] *a* disproportionate, out of all proportion.

dispute [dispyt] *nf* quarrel, argument.

disputer [dispyte] *vt* (*match*) to play; (*combat*) to fight; (*course*) to run, fight; **se ~** *vi* to quarrel; **~ qch à qn** to fight with sb over sth.

disquaire [diskɛʀ] *nm/f* record dealer.

disqualifier [diskalifje] *vt* to disqualify.

disque [disk(ə)] *nm* (*MUS*) record; (*forme, pièce*) disc; (*SPORT*) discus; **~ compact** compact disc; **~ d'embrayage** (*AUTO*) clutch plate.

disquette [diskɛt] *nf* floppy disk, diskette.

disséminer [disemine] *vt* to scatter.

disséquer [diseke] *vt* to dissect.

dissertation [disɛʀtasjɔ̃] *nf* (*SCOL*) essay.

disserter [disɛʀte] *vi*: **~ sur** to discourse upon.

dissimuler [disimyle] *vt* to conceal.

dissiper [disipe] *vt* to dissipate; (*fortune*) to squander; **se ~** *vi* (*brouillard*) to clear, disperse; (*doutes*) to melt away; (*élève*) to become unruly.

dissolu, e [disɔly] *a* dissolute.

dissolvant, e [disɔlvɑ̃, -ɑ̃t] *nm* solvent; **~ (gras)** nail polish remover.

dissonant, e [disɔnɑ̃, -ɑ̃t] *a* discordant.

dissoudre [disudʀ(ə)] *vt* to dissolve; **se ~** *vi* to dissolve.

dissuader [disɥade] *vt*: **~ qn de faire/ de qch** to dissuade sb from doing/from sth.

dissuasion [disɥazjɔ̃] *nf*: **force de ~** deterrent power.

distance [distɑ̃s] *nf* distance; (*fig: écart*) gap; **à ~** at *ou* from a distance; **distancer** *vt* to outdistance.

distant, e [distɑ̃, -ɑ̃t] *a* (*réservé*) distant; **~ de** (*lieu*) far away from.

distendre [distɑ̃dʀ(ə)] *vt*, **se ~** *vi* to distend.

distiller [distile] *vt* to distil; **distillerie** *nf* distillery.

distinct, e [distɛ̃(kt), distɛ̃kt(ə)] *a* distinct; **distinctif, ive** *a* distinctive.

distingué, e [distɛ̃ge] *a* distinguished.

distinguer [distɛ̃ge] *vt* to distinguish.
distraction [distraksjɔ̃] *nf* (*manque d'attention*) absent-mindedness; (*oubli*) lapse (in concentration); (*détente*) diversion, recreation; (*passe-temps*) distraction, entertainment.
distraire [distrɛr] *vt* (*déranger*) to distract; (*divertir*) to entertain, divert; se ~ *vi* to amuse *ou* enjoy o.s.
distrait, e [distrɛ, -ɛt] *a* absent-minded.
distribuer [distribɥe] *vt* to distribute; to hand out; (*CARTES*) to deal (out); (*courrier*) to deliver; **distributeur** *nm* (*COMM*) distributor; (*automatique*) (vending) machine; (*: de billets*) (cash) dispenser; **distribution** *nf* distribution; (*postale*) delivery; (*choix d'acteurs*) casting, cast.
dit, e [di, dit] *pp de* **dire** // *a* (*fixé*): **le jour** ~ the arranged day; (*surnommé*): **X, ~ Pierrot** X, known as Pierrot.
dites *vb voir* **dire**.
divaguer [divage] *vi* to ramble; to rave.
divan [divɑ̃] *nm* divan.
divers, e [divɛr, -ɛrs(ə)] *a* (*varié*) diverse, varied; (*différent*) different, various // *dét* (*plusieurs*) various, several; (*frais*) ~ **sundries**, miscellaneous (expenses).
divertir [divɛrtir] *vt* to amuse, entertain; se ~ *vi* to amuse *ou* enjoy o.s.
divin, e [divɛ̃, -in] *a* divine.
diviser [divize] *vt* (*gén, MATH*) to divide; (*morceler, subdiviser*) to divide (up), split (up); **division** *nf* division.
divorce [divɔrs(ə)] *nm* divorce; **divorcé, e** *nm/f* divorcee; **divorcer** *vi* to get a divorce, get divorced; **divorcer de** *ou* **d'avec qn** to divorce sb.
divulguer [divylge] *vt* to divulge, disclose.
dix [dis] *num* ten; **dixième** *num* tenth.
dizaine [dizɛn] *nf* (*10*) ten; (*environ 10*): **une** ~ (**de**) about ten, ten or so.
do [do] *nm* (*note*) C; (*en chantant la gamme*) do(h).
dock [dɔk] *nm* dock.
docker [dɔkɛr] *nm* docker.
docte [dɔkt(ə)] *a* learned.
docteur [dɔktœr] *nm* doctor.
doctorat [dɔktɔra] *nm*: ~ (**d'Université**) doctorate; ~ **d'état** ≈ Ph.D.
doctrine [dɔktrin] *nf* doctrine.
document [dɔkymɑ̃] *nm* document.
documentaire [dɔkymɑ̃tɛr] *a, nm* documentary.
documentaliste [dɔkymɑ̃talist(ə)] *nm/f* archivist; researcher.
documentation [dɔkymɑ̃tasjɔ̃] *nf* documentation, literature; (*PRESSE, TV*: service) research.
documenter [dɔkymɑ̃te] *vt*: se ~ (**sur**) to gather information (on).
dodeliner [dɔdline] *vi*: ~ **de la tête** to

nod one's head gently.
dodo [dodo] *nm*: **aller faire** ~ to go to beddy-byes.
dodu, e [dody] *a* plump.
dogue [dɔg] *nm* mastiff.
doigt [dwa] *nm* finger; **à deux** ~**s de** within an inch of; **un** ~ **de lait** a drop of milk; ~ **de pied** toe.
doigté [dwate] *nm* (*MUS*) fingering; (*fig: habileté*) diplomacy, tact.
doit *etc vb voir* **devoir**.
doléances [dɔleɑ̃s] *nfpl* complaints; grievances.
dolent, e [dɔlɑ̃, -ɑ̃t] *a* doleful.
dollar [dɔlar] *nm* dollar.
D.O.M. [deɔɛm, dɔm] *sigle m ou mpl* = **département(s) d'outre-mer.**
domaine [dɔmɛn] *nm* estate, property; (*fig*) domain, field.
domanial, e, aux [dɔmanjal, -o] *a* (*forêt, biens*) national, state *cpd*.
domestique [dɔmɛstik] *a* domestic // *nm/f* servant, domestic.
domicile [dɔmisil] *nm* home, place of residence; **à** ~ at home; **domicilié, e** *a*: **être domicilié à** to have one's home in *ou* at.
dominant, e [dɔminɑ̃, -ɑ̃t] *a* dominant; predominant.
dominateur, trice [dɔminatœr, -tris] *a* dominating; domineering.
dominer [dɔmine] *vt* to dominate; (*passions etc*) to control, master; (*surpasser*) to outclass, surpass // *vi* to be in the dominant position; se ~ *vi* to control o.s.
domino [dɔmino] *nm* domino.
dommage [dɔmaʒ] *nm* (*préjudice*) harm, injury; (*dégâts, pertes*) damage *q*; **c'est** ~ **de faire/que** it's a shame *ou* pity to do/that; ~**s-intérêts** *nmpl* damages.
dompter [dɔ̃te] *vt* to tame; **dompteur, euse** *nm/f* trainer; liontamer.
don [dɔ̃] *nm* (*cadeau*) gift; (*charité*) donation; (*aptitude*) gift, talent; **avoir des** ~**s pour** to have a gift *ou* talent for.
donc [dɔ̃k] *cj* therefore, so; (*après une digression*) so, then.
donjon [dɔ̃ʒɔ̃] *nm* keep.
donné, e [dɔne] *a* (*convenu*) given; (*pas cher*): **c'est** ~ it's a gift // *nf* (*MATH, gén*) datum (*pl* data); **étant** ~ ... given ....
donner [dɔne] *vt* to give; (*vieux habits etc*) to give away; (*spectacle*) to put on; (*film*) to show; ~ **qch à qn** to give sb sth, give sth to sb; ~ **sur** (*suj: fenêtre, chambre*) to look (out) onto; ~ **dans** (*piège etc*) to fall into; se ~ **à fond** to give one's all; **s'en** ~ **à cœur joie** (*fam*) to have a great time.
dont [dɔ̃] *pronom relatif* **1** (*appartenance: objets*) whose, of which; (*: êtres animés*) whose; **la maison** ~ **le toit est**

rouge the house the roof of which is red, the house whose roof is red; **l'homme ~ je connais la sœur** the man whose sister I know

2 *(parmi lesquel(le)s)*: 2 **livres, ~ l'un est ... 2 books, one of which is ...; il y avait plusieurs personnes, ~ Gabrielle** there were several people, among them Gabrielle; **10 blessés, ~ 2 grièvement 10** injured, 2 of them seriously

3 *(complément d'adjectif, de verbe)*: **le fils ~ il est si fier** the son he's so proud of; **ce ~ je parle** what I'm talking about; *voir adjectifs et verbes à complément prépositionnel*: **responsable de, souffrir de** *etc.*

doré, e [dɔʀe] *a* golden; *(avec dorure)* gilt, gilded.

dorénavant [dɔʀenavɑ̃] *ad* henceforth.

dorer [dɔʀe] *vt (cadre)* to gild; **(faire) ~** *(CULIN)* to brown.

dorloter [dɔʀlɔte] *vt* to pamper.

dormir [dɔʀmiʀ] *vi* to sleep; *(être endormi)* to be asleep.

dortoir [dɔʀtwaʀ] *nm* dormitory.

dorure [dɔʀyʀ] *nf* gilding.

dos [do] *nm* back; *(de livre)* spine; **'voir au ~'** 'see over'; **de ~** from the back.

dosage [dozaʒ] *nm* mixture.

dose [doz] *nf* dose.

doser [doze] *vt* to measure out; to mix in the correct proportions; *(fig)* to expend in the right amounts; to strike a balance between.

dossard [dɔsaʀ] *nm* number *(worn by competitor)*.

dossier [dɔsje] *nm (renseignements, fichier)* file; *(de chaise)* back; *(PRESSE)* feature.

dot [dɔt] *nf* dowry.

doter [dɔte] *vt* to equip.

douane [dwan] *nf (poste, bureau)* customs *pl*; *(taxes)* (customs) duty; **douanier, ière** *a* customs *cpd* // *nm* customs officer.

double [dubl(ə)] *a, ad* double // *nm (2 fois plus)*: **le ~ (de)** twice as much *(ou* many*)* (as); *(autre exemplaire)* duplicate, copy; *(sosie)* double; *(TENNIS)* doubles *sg*; **en ~ (exemplaire)** in duplicate; **faire ~ emploi** to be redundant.

doubler [duble] *vt (multiplier par 2)* to double; *(vêtement)* to line; *(dépasser)* to overtake, pass; *(film)* to dub; *(acteur)* to stand in for // *vi* to double.

doublure [dublyʀ] *nf* lining; *(CINÉMA)* stand-in.

douce [dus] *a voir* **doux**; **~âtre** a sickly sweet; **~ment** *ad* gently; slowly; **~reux, euse** *a (péj)* sugary; **douceur** *nf* softness; sweetness; mildness; gentleness; **douceurs** *nfpl (friandises)* sweets.

douche [duʃ] *nf* shower; **~s** *nfpl (salle)* shower room *sg*; **se doucher** *vi* to have

 ou take a shower.

doué, e [dwe] *a* gifted, talented; **~ de** endowed with.

douille [duj] *nf (ÉLEC)* socket; *(de projectile)* case.

douillet, te [dujɛ, -ɛt] *a* cosy; *(péj)* soft.

douleur [dulœʀ] *nf* pain; *(chagrin)* grief, distress; **douloureux, euse** *a* painful.

doute [dut] *nm* doubt; **sans ~** *ad* no doubt; *(probablement)* probably.

douter [dute] *vt* to doubt; **~ de** *vt (allié)* to doubt, have (one's) doubts about; *(résultat)* to be doubtful of; **se ~ de qch/que** to suspect sth/that; **je m'en doutais** I suspected as much.

douteux, euse [dutø, -øz] *a (incertain)* doubtful; *(discutable)* dubious, questionable; *(péj)* dubious-looking.

Douvres [duvʀ(ə)] *n* Dover.

doux, douce [du, dus] *a (gén)* soft; *(sucré, agréable)* sweet; *(peu fort: moutarde, clément: climat)* mild; *(pas brusque)* gentle.

douzaine [duzɛn] *nf (12)* dozen; *(environ 12)*: **une ~ (de)** a dozen or so, twelve or so.

douze [duz] *num* twelve; **douzième** *num* twelfth.

doyen, ne [dwajɛ̃, -ɛn] *nm/f (en âge, ancienneté)* most senior member; *(de faculté)* dean.

dragée [dʀaʒe] *nf* sugared almond; *(MÉD)* (sugar-coated) pill.

dragon [dʀagɔ̃] *nm* dragon.

draguer [dʀage] *vt (rivière)* to dredge; to drag; *(fam)* to try to pick up.

dramatique [dʀamatik] *a* dramatic; *(tragique)* tragic // *nf (TV)* (television) drama.

dramaturge [dʀamatyʀʒ(ə)] *nm* dramatist, playwright.

drame [dʀam] *nm (THÉÂTRE)* drama.

drap [dʀa] *nm (de lit)* sheet; *(tissu)* woollen fabric.

drapeau, x [dʀapo] *nm* flag; **sous les ~x** with the colours, in the army.

dresser [dʀese] *vt (mettre vertical, monter)* to put up, erect; *(fig: liste, bilan, contrat)* to draw up; *(animal)* to train; **se ~** *vi (falaise, obstacle)* to stand; to tower (up); *(personne)* to draw o.s. up; **~ qn contre qn** to set sb against sb; **~ l'oreille** to prick up one's ears.

drogue [dʀɔg] *nf* drug; **la ~** drugs *pl*.

drogué, e [dʀɔge] *nm/f* drug addict.

droguer [dʀɔge] *vt (victime)* to drug; *(malade)* to give drugs to; **se ~** *vi (aux stupéfiants)* to take drugs; *(péj: de médicaments)* to dose o.s. up.

droguerie [dʀɔgʀi] *nf* hardware shop.

droguiste [dʀɔgist(ə)] *nm* keeper *(ou* owner*)* of a hardware shop.

droit, e [dʀwa, dʀwat] *a (non courbe)*

straight; (*vertical*) upright, straight; (*fig: loyal*) upright, straight(forward); (*opposé à gauche*) right, right-hand // *ad* straight // *nm* (*prérogative*) right; (*taxe*) duty, tax; (: *d'inscription*) fee; (*JUR*): le ~ law // *nf* (*POL*): la ~e the right (wing); avoir le ~ de to be allowed to; avoir ~ à to be entitled to; être en ~ de to have a *ou* the right to; être dans son ~ to be within one's rights; à ~e on the right; (*direction*) (to the) right; ~s d'auteur royalties.

droitier, ière [dʀwatje, -jɛʀ] *nm/f* right-handed person.

droiture [dʀwatyʀ] *nf* uprightness, straightness.

drôle [dʀol] *a* funny; ~**ment** *ad* (*très*) terribly, awfully; une ~ d'idée a funny idea.

dromadaire [dʀɔmadɛʀ] *nm* dromedary.

dru, e [dʀy] *a* (*cheveux*) thick, bushy; (*pluie*) heavy.

du [dy] *prép* + *dét, dét voir* **de**.

dû, due [dy] *vb voir* **devoir** // *a* (*somme*) owing, owed; (: *venant à échéance*) due; (*causé par*): ~ à due to // *nm* due; (*somme*) dues *pl*.

dubitatif, ive [dybitatif, -iv] *a* doubtful, dubious.

duc [dyk] *nm* duke; **duchesse** *nf* duchess.

dûment [dymɑ̃] *ad* duly.

Dunkerque [dœ̃kɛʀk] *n* Dunkirk.

duo [dyo] *nm* (*MUS*) duet.

dupe [dyp] *nf* dupe // *a*: (ne pas) être ~ de (not) to be taken in by.

duplex [dyplɛks] *nm* (*appartement*) split-level apartment, duplex.

duplicata [dyplikata] *nm* duplicate.

duquel [dykɛl] *prép* + *pronom voir* **lequel**.

dur, e [dyʀ] *a* (*pierre, siège, travail, problème*) hard; (*lumière, voix, climat*) harsh; (*sévère*) hard, harsh; (*cruel*) hard(-hearted); (*porte, col*) stiff; (*viande*) tough // *ad* hard; ~ d'oreille hard of hearing.

durant [dyʀɑ̃] *prép* (*au cours de*) during; (*pendant*) for; des mois ~ for months.

durcir [dyʀsiʀ] *vt, vi, se* ~ *vi* to harden.

durée [dyʀe] *nf* length; (*d'une pile etc*) life; (*déroulement: des opérations etc*) duration.

durement [dyʀmɑ̃] *ad* harshly.

durer [dyʀe] *vi* to last.

dureté [dyʀte] *nf* hardness; harshness; stiffness; toughness.

durit [dyʀit] *nf* ® (car radiator) hose.

dus *etc vb voir* **devoir**.

duvet [dyvɛ] *nm* down; (*sac de couchage*) down-filled sleeping bag.

dynamique [dinamik] *a* dynamic.

dynamite [dinamit] *nf* dynamite.

dynamiter [dinamite] *vt* to (blow up with) dynamite.

dynamo [dinamo] *nf* dynamo.

dysenterie [disɑ̃tʀi] *nf* dysentery.

dyslexie [dislɛksi] *nf* dyslexia, word-blindness.

E

eau, x [o] *nf* water // *nfpl* waters; prendre l'~ to leak, let in water; tomber à l'~ (*fig*) to fall through; ~ de Cologne Eau de Cologne; ~ **courante** running water; ~ douce fresh water; ~ de Javel bleach; ~ **minérale** mineral water; ~ plate still water; ~ **salée** salt water; ~ de toilette toilet water; ~**-de-vie** *nf* brandy; ~**-forte** *nf* etching.

ébahi, e [ebai] *a* dumbfounded.

ébattre [ebatʀ(ə)]: s'~ *vi* to frolic.

ébaucher [eboʃe] *vt* to sketch out, outline; s'~ *vi* to take shape.

ébène [ebɛn] *nf* ebony.

ébéniste [ebenist(ə)] *nm* cabinetmaker.

éberlué, e [ebɛʀlɥe] *a* astounded.

éblouir [ebluiʀ] *vt* to dazzle.

éblouissement [ebluismɑ̃] *nm* (*faiblesse*) dizzy turn.

éborgner [ebɔʀɲe] *vt*: ~ qn to blind sb in one eye.

éboueur [ebwœʀ] *nm* dustman (*Brit*), garbageman (*US*).

ébouillanter [ebujɑ̃te] *vt* to scald; (*CULIN*) to blanch.

éboulement [ebulmɑ̃] *nm* rock fall.

ébouler [ebule]: s'~ *vi* to crumble, collapse.

éboulis [ebuli] *nmpl* fallen rocks.

ébouriffé, e [eburife] *a* tousled.

ébranler [ebʀɑ̃le] *vt* to shake; (*rendre instable: mur*) to weaken; s'~ *vi* (*partir*) to move off.

ébrécher [ebʀeʃe] *vt* to chip.

ébriété [ebʀijete] *nf*: en état d'~ in a state of intoxication.

ébrouer [ebʀue]: s'~ *vi* to shake o.s.; (*souffler*) to snort.

ébruiter [ebʀɥite] *vt* to spread, disclose.

ébullition [ebylisjɔ̃] *nf* boiling point; en ~ boiling; (*fig*) in an uproar.

écaille [ekaj] *nf* (*de poisson*) scale; (*de coquillage*) shell; (*matière*) tortoiseshell.

écailler [ekaje] *vt* (*poisson*) to scale; (*huître*) to open; s'~ *vi* to flake *ou* peel (off).

écarlate [ekaʀlat] *a* scarlet.

écarquiller [ekaʀkije] *vt*: ~ les yeux to stare wide-eyed.

écart [ekaʀ] *nm* gap; (*embardée*) swerve; sideways leap; (*fig*) departure, deviation; à l'~ *ad* out of the way; à l'~ de *prép* away from.

écarté, e [ekaʀte] *a* (*lieu*) out-of-the-way, remote; (*ouvert*): les jambes ~es legs apart; les bras ~s arms out-stretched.

écarteler [ekaʀtəle] *vt* to quarter; (*fig*) to tear.

écarter [ekaʀte] *vt* (*séparer*) to move apart, separate; (*éloigner*) to push back, move away; (*ouvrir: bras, jambes*) to spread, open; (: *rideau*) to draw (back); (*éliminer: candidat, possibilité*) to dismiss; s'~ *vi* to part; to move away; s'~ de to wander from.

écervelé, e [esɛʀvəle] *a* scatterbrained, featherbrained.

échafaud [eʃafo] *nm* scaffold.

échafaudage [eʃafodaʒ] *nm* scaffolding.

échafauder [eʃafode] *vt* (*plan*) to construct.

échalote [eʃalɔt] *nf* shallot.

échancrure [eʃãkʀyʀ] *nf* (*de robe*) scoop neckline; (*de côte, arête rocheuse*) indentation.

échange [eʃãʒ] *nm* exchange; en ~ de in exchange ou return for.

échanger [eʃãʒe] *vt*: ~ qch (contre) to exchange sth (for); **échangeur** *nm* (*AUTO*) interchange.

échantillon [eʃãtijɔ̃] *nm* sample.

échappée [eʃape] *nf* (*vue*) vista.

échappement [eʃapmã] *nm* (*AUTO*) exhaust.

échapper [eʃape]: ~ à *vt* (*gardien*) to escape (from); (*punition, péril*) to escape; ~ à qn (*détail, sens*) to escape sb; (*objet qu'on tient*) to slip out of sb's hands; s'~ *vi* to escape; laisser ~ (*cri etc*) to let out; l'~ belle to have a narrow escape.

écharde [eʃaʀd(ə)] *nf* splinter (of wood).

écharpe [eʃaʀp(ə)] *nf* scarf (*pl* scarves); (*de maire*) sash; (*MÉD*) sling.

échasse [eʃas] *nf* stilt.

échauffer [eʃofe] *vt* (*métal, moteur*) to overheat; (*fig: exciter*) to fire, excite; s'~ *vi* (*SPORT*) to warm up; (*dans la discussion*) to become heated.

échauffourée [eʃofuʀe] *nf* clash, brawl.

échéance [eʃeãs] *nf* (*d'un paiement: date*) settlement date; (: *somme due*) financial commitment(s); (*fig*) deadline; à brève/longue ~ *sg*; tenir en ~ to hold in the short/long run.

échéant [eʃeã]: le cas ~ *ad* if the case arises.

échec [eʃɛk] *nm* failure; (*ÉCHECS*): ~ et mat/au roi checkmate/check; ~s *nmpl* (*jeu*) chess *sg*; tenir en ~ to hold in check; faire ~ à to foil *ou* thwart.

échelle [eʃɛl] *nf* ladder; (*fig, d'une carte*) scale.

échelon [eʃlɔ̃] *nm* (*d'échelle*) rung; (*ADMIN*) grade.

échelonner [eʃlɔne] *vt* to space out.

échevelé, e [eʃəvle] *a* tousled, di-shevelled; wild, frenzied.

échine [eʃin] *nf* backbone, spine.

échiquier [eʃikje] *nm* chessboard.

écho [eko] *nm* echo; ~s *nmpl* (*potins*) gossip *sg*, rumours.

échoir [eʃwaʀ] *vi* (*dette*) to fall due; (*délais*) to expire; ~ à *vt* to fall to.

échoppe [eʃɔp] *nf* stall, booth.

échouer [eʃwe] *vi* to fail; s'~ *vi* to run aground.

échu, e [eʃy] *pp* de **échoir**.

éclabousser [eklabuse] *vt* to splash.

éclair [eklɛʀ] *nm* (*d'orage*) flash of lightning, lightning *q*; (*gâteau*) éclair.

éclairage [eklɛʀaʒ] *nm* lighting.

éclaircie [eklɛʀsi] *nf* bright interval.

éclaircir [eklɛʀsiʀ] *vt* to lighten; (*fig*) to clear up; to clarify; (*CULIN*) to thin (down); s'~ (*ciel*) to clear; s'~ la voix to clear one's throat; **éclaircissement** *nm* clearing up; clarification.

éclairer [eklɛʀe] *vt* (*lieu*) to light (up); (*personne: avec une lampe etc*) to light the way for; (*fig*) to enlighten; to shed light on // *vi*: ~ mal/bien to give a poor/good light; s'~ à l'électricité to have electric lighting.

éclaireur, euse [eklɛʀœʀ, -øz] *nm/f* (*scout*) (boy) scout/(girl) guide // *nm* (*MIL*) scout.

éclat [ekla] *nm* (*de bombe, de verre*) fragment; (*du soleil, d'une couleur etc*) brightness, brilliance; (*d'une cérémonie*) splendour; (*scandale*): faire un ~ to cause a commotion; ~s de voix shouts.

éclatant, e [eklatã, -ãt] *a* brilliant.

éclater [eklate] *vi* (*pneu*) to burst; (*bombe*) to explode; (*guerre, épidémie*) to break out; (*groupe, parti*) to break up; ~ en sanglots/de rire to burst out sobbing/laughing.

éclipse [eklips(ə)] *nf* eclipse.

éclipser [eklipse]: s'~ *vi* to slip away.

éclopé, e [eklɔpe] *a* lame.

éclore [eklɔʀ] *vi* (*œuf*) to hatch; (*fleur*) to open (out).

écluse [eklyz] *nf* lock.

écœurant, e [ekœʀã, -ãt] *a* (*gâteau etc*) sickly.

écœurer [ekœʀe] *vt*: ~ qn to make sb feel sick.

école [ekɔl] *nf* school; aller à l'~ to go to school; ~ normale teachers' training college; **écolier, ière** *nm/f* schoolboy/girl.

écologie [ekɔlɔʒi] *nf* ecology; environmental studies *pl*.

éconduire [ekɔ̃dɥiʀ] *vt* to dismiss.

économe [ekɔnɔm] *a* thrifty // *nm/f* (*de lycée etc*) bursar (*Brit*), treasurer (*US*).

économie [ekɔnɔmi] *nf* economy; (*gain: d'argent, de temps etc*) saving; (*science*) economics *sg*; ~s *nfpl* (*pécule*) savings; **économique** *a* (*avantageux*) economical; (*ÉCON*) economic.

économiser [ekɔnɔmize] vt, vi to save.

écoper [ekɔpe] vi to bale out; (fig) to cop it; ~ (de) vt to get.

écorce [ekɔʀs(ə)] nf bark; (de fruit) peel.

écorcher [ekɔʀʃe] vt (animal) to skin; (égratigner) to graze; **écorchure** nf graze.

écossais, e [ekɔsɛ, -ɛz] a Scottish // nm/f: É~, e Scot.

Écosse [ekɔs] nf: l'~ Scotland.

écosser [ekɔse] vt to shell.

écouler [ekule] vt to sell; to dispose of; s'~ vi (eau) to flow (out); (jours, temps) to pass (by).

écourter [ekuʀte] vt to curtail, cut short.

écoute [ekut] nf (RADIO, TV): temps/ heure d'~ (listening ou viewing) time/ hour; prendre l'~ to tune in; rester à l'~ (de) to stay tuned in (to); ~s télé-phoniques phone tapping sg.

écouter [ekute] vt to listen to; **écouteur** nm (TÉL) receiver; (RADIO) headphones pl, headset.

écoutille [ekutij] nf hatch.

écran [ekʀɑ̃] nm screen.

écrasant, e [ekʀɑzɑ̃, -ɑ̃t] a overwhelm-ing.

écraser [ekʀaze] vt to crush; (piéton) to run over; s'~ vi (fam) to pipe down; s'~ (au sol) to crash; s'~ contre to crash into.

écrémer [ekʀeme] vt to skim.

écrevisse [ekʀəvis] nf crayfish inv.

écrier [ekʀije]: s'~ vi to exclaim.

écrin [ekʀɛ̃] nm case, box.

écrire [ekʀiʀ] vt to write; s'~ to write to each other; ça s'écrit comment? how is it spelt?; **écrit** nm document; (examen) written paper; par écrit in writing.

écriteau, x [ekʀito] nm notice, sign.

écriture [ekʀityʀ] nf writing; (COMM) entry; ~s nfpl (COMM) accounts, books; l'É~, les É~s the Scriptures.

écrivain [ekʀivɛ̃] nm writer.

écrou [ekʀu] nm nut.

écrouer [ekʀue] vt to imprison; to re-mand in custody.

écrouler [ekʀule]: s'~ vi to collapse.

écru, e [ekʀy] a (toile) raw, unbleached; (couleur) off-white, écru.

écueil [ekœj] nm reef; (fig) pitfall; stumbling block.

écuelle [ekɥɛl] nf bowl.

éculé, e [ekyle] a (chaussure) down-at-heel; (fig: péj) hackneyed.

écume [ekym] nf foam; (CULIN) scum; **écumer** vt (CULIN) to skim; (fig) to plunder.

écureuil [ekyʀœj] nm squirrel.

écurie [ekyʀi] nf stable.

écusson [ekysɔ̃] nm badge.

écuyer, ère [ekɥije, -ɛʀ] nm/f rider.

eczéma [ɛgzema] nm eczema.

édenté, e [edɑ̃te] a toothless.

E.D.F. sigle f (= Électricité de France) national electricity company.

édifier [edifje] vt to build, erect; (fig) to edify.

édiles [edil] nmpl city fathers.

édit [edi] nm edict.

éditer [edite] vt (publier) to publish; (: disque) to produce; **éditeur, trice** nm/f editor; publisher; **édition** nf editing q; edition; (industrie du livre) publishing.

édredon [edʀədɔ̃] nm eiderdown.

éducatif, ive [edykatif, -iv] a educa-tional.

éducation [edykasjɔ̃] nf education; (fa-miliale) upbringing; (manières) (good) manners pl; ~ **physique** physical education.

édulcorer [edylkɔʀe] vt to sweeten; (fig) to tone down.

éduquer [edyke] vt to educate; (élever) to bring up; (faculté) to train.

effacé, e [efase] a unassuming.

effacer [efase] vt to erase, rub out; s'~ vi (inscription etc) to wear off; (pour laisser passer) to step aside.

effarer [efaʀe] vt to alarm.

effaroucher [efaʀuʃe] vt to frighten ou scare away; to alarm.

effectif, ive [efɛktif, -iv] a real; effec-tive // nm (MIL) strength; (SCOL) (pu-pil) numbers pl; **effectivement** ad ef-fectively; (réellement) actually, really; (en effet) indeed.

effectuer [efɛktɥe] vt (opération) to car-ry out; (déplacement, trajet) to make; (mouvement) to execute.

efféminé, e [efemine] a effeminate.

effervescent, e [efɛʀvesɑ̃, -ɑ̃t] a effer-vescent; (fig) agitated.

effet [efɛ] nm (résultat, artifice) effect; (impression) impression; ~s nmpl (vêtements etc) things; faire de l'~ (médicament, menace) to have an ef-fect; en ~ ad indeed.

efficace [efikas] a (personne) efficient; (action, médicament) effective.

effilé, e [efile] a slender; sharp; stream-lined.

effiler [efile] vt (tissu) to fray.

effilocher [efilɔʃe]: s'~ vi to fray.

efflanqué, e [eflɑ̃ke] a emaciated.

effleurer [eflœʀe] vt to brush (against); (sujet) to touch upon; (suj: idée, pen-sée): ~ qn to cross sb's mind.

effluves [eflyv] nmpl exhalation(s).

effondrer [efɔ̃dʀe]: s'~ vi to collapse.

efforcer [efɔʀse]: s'~ de vt: s'~ de faire to try hard to do, try hard to.

effort [efɔʀ] nm effort.

effraction [efʀaksjɔ̃] nf: s'introduire par ~ dans to break into.

effrayant, e [efʀɛjɑ̃, -ɑ̃t] a frightening.

effrayer [efʀeje] vt to frighten, scare.

effréné, e [efʀene] a wild.

effriter [efʀite]: s'~ *vi* to crumble.
effroi [efʀwa] *nm* terror, dread *q*.
effronté, e [efʀɔte] *a* insolent, brazen.
effroyable [efʀwajabl(ə)] *a* horrifying, appalling.
effusion [efyzjɔ̃] *nf* effusion; **sans ~ de sang** without bloodshed.
égal, e, aux [egal, -o] *a* equal; (*plan: surface*) even, level; (*constant: vitesse*) steady; (*équitable*) even // *nm/f* equal; **être ~ à** (*prix, nombre*) to be equal to; **ça lui est ~** it's all the same to him; he doesn't mind; **sans ~** matchless, unequalled; **à l'~ de** (*comme*) just like; **d'~ à ~** as equals; **~ement** *ad* equally; evenly; steadily; (*aussi*) too, as well; **~er** *vt* to equal; **~iser** *vt* (*sol, salaires*) to level (out); (*chances*) to equalize // *vi* (*SPORT*) to equalize; **~ité** *nf* equality; evenness; steadiness; (*MATH*) identity; **être à ~ité (de points)** to be level.
égard [egaʀ] *nm:* **~s** *nmpl* consideration *sg*; **à cet ~** in this respect; **eu ~ à** in view of; **par ~ pour** out of consideration for; **sans ~ pour** without regard for; **à l'~ de** *prép* towards; concerning.
égarement [egaʀmɑ̃] *nm* distraction; aberration.
égarer [egaʀe] *vt* to mislay; (*moralement*) to lead astray; s'~ *vi* to get lost, lose one's way; (*objet*) to go astray; (*dans une discussion*) to wander.
égayer [egeje] *vt* (*personne*) to amuse; to cheer up; (*récit, endroit*) to brighten up, liven up.
églantine [eglɑ̃tin] *nf* wild *ou* dog rose.
églefin [egləfɛ̃] *nm* haddock.
église [egliz] *nf* church; **aller à l'~** to go to church.
égoïsme [egɔism(ə)] *nm* selfishness; **égoïste** *a* selfish.
égorger [egɔʀʒe] *vt* to cut the throat of.
égosiller [egozije]: s'~ *vi* to shout o.s. hoarse.
égout [egu] *nm* sewer.
égoutter [egute] *vt* (*linge*) to wring out; (*vaisselle*) to drain // *vi*, s'~ *vi* to drip; **égouttoir** *nm* draining board; (*mobile*) draining rack.
égratigner [egʀatiɲe] *vt* to scratch; **égratignure** *nf* scratch.
égrillard, e [egʀijaʀ, -aʀd(ə)] *a* ribald.
Egypte [eʒipt(ə)] *nf:* **l'~** Egypt; **égyptien, ne** *a, nm/f* Egyptian.
eh [e] *excl* hey!; **~ bien** well.
éhonté, e [eɔ̃te] *a* shameless, brazen.
éjecter [eʒɛkte] *vt* (*TECH*) to eject; (*fam*) to kick *ou* chuck out.
élaborer [elabɔʀe] *vt* to elaborate; (*projet, stratégie*) to work out; (*rapport*) to draft.
élaguer [elage] *vt* to prune.
élan [elɑ̃] *nm* (*ZOOL*) elk, moose; (*SPORT: avant le saut*) run up; (*d'objet en mouvement*) momentum; (*fig: de ten-* *dresse etc*) surge; **prendre de l'~** to gather speed.
élancé, e [elɑ̃se] *a* slender.
élancement [elɑ̃smɑ̃] *nm* shooting pain.
élancer [elɑ̃se]: s'~ *vi* to dash, hurl o.s.; (*fig: arbre, clocher*) to soar (upwards).
élargir [elaʀʒiʀ] *vt* to widen; (*vêtement*) to let out; (*JUR*) to release; s'~ *vi* to widen; (*vêtement*) to stretch.
élastique [elastik] *a* elastic // *nm* (*de bureau*) rubber band; (*pour la couture*) elastic *q*.
électeur, trice [elɛktœʀ, -tʀis] *nm/f* elector, voter.
élection [elɛksjɔ̃] *nf* election.
électorat [elɛktɔʀa] *nm* electorate.
électricien, ne [elɛktʀisjɛ̃, -jɛn] *nm/f* electrician.
électricité [elɛktʀisite] *nf* electricity; **allumer/éteindre l'~** to put on/off the light.
électrique [elɛktʀik] *a* electric(al).
électro... [elɛktʀo] *préfixe:* **~choc** *nm* electric shock treatment; **~ménager** *a, nm:* **appareils ~ménagers, l'~ménager** domestic (electrical) appliances.
électronique [elɛktʀɔnik] *a* electronic // *nf* electronics *sg*.
électrophone [elɛktʀɔfɔn] *nm* record player.
élégant, e [elegɑ̃, -ɑ̃t] *a* elegant; (*solution*) neat, elegant; (*attitude, procédé*) courteous, civilized.
élément [elemɑ̃] *nm* element; (*pièce*) component, part; **élémentaire** *a* elementary.
éléphant [elefɑ̃] *nm* elephant.
élevage [elvaʒ] *nm* breeding; (*de bovins*) cattle rearing.
élévation [elevasjɔ̃] *nf* (*gén*) elevation; (*voir élever*) raising; (*voir s'elever*) rise.
élevé, e [elve] *a* (*prix, sommet*) high; (*fig: noble*) elevated; **bien/mal ~** well-/ill-mannered.
élève [elɛv] *nm/f* pupil.
élever [elve] *vt* (*enfant*) to bring up, raise; (*bétail, volaille*) to breed; (*abeilles*) to keep; (*hausser: taux, niveau*) to raise; (*fig: âme, esprit*) to elevate; (*édifier: monument*) to put up, erect; s'~ *vi* (*avion, alpiniste*) to go up; (*niveau, température, aussi: cri etc*) to rise; (*survenir: difficultés*) to arise; s'~ **à** (*suj: frais, dégâts*) to amount to, add up to; s'~ **contre qch** to rise up against sth; **~ la voix** to raise one's voice; **éleveur, euse** *nm/f* breeder.
élimé, e [elime] *a* threadbare.
éliminatoire [eliminatwaʀ] *nf* (*SPORT*) heat.
éliminer [elimine] *vt* to eliminate.
élire [eliʀ] *vt* to elect.
elle [ɛl] *pronom* (*sujet*) she; (*: chose*) it; (*complément*) her; it; **~s** they; them;

~-**même** herself; itself; ~**s-mêmes** themselves; *voir* il.

élocution [elɔkysjɔ̃] *nf* delivery; **défaut d'**~ speech impediment.

éloge [elɔʒ] *nm* praise (*gén q*); **élogieux, euse** *a* laudatory, full of praise.

éloigné, e [elwaɲe] *a* distant, far-off.

éloignement [elwaɲmɑ̃] *nm* removal; putting off; estrangement; (*fig*) distance.

éloigner [elwaɲe] *vt* (*objet*): ~ **qch** (**de**) to move *ou* take sth away (from); (*personne*): ~ **qn** (**de**) to take sb away *ou* remove sb (from); (*échéance*) to put off, postpone; (*soupçons, danger*) to ward off; **s'**~ (**de**) (*personne*) to go away (from); (*véhicule*) to move away (from); (*affectivement*) to become estranged (from).

élongation [elɔ̃gasjɔ̃] *nf* strained muscle.

éloquent, e [elɔkɑ̃, -ɑ̃t] *a* eloquent.

élu, e [ely] *pp de* **élire** // *nm/f* (*POL*) elected representative.

élucubrations [elykybrɑsjɔ̃] *nfpl* wild imaginings.

éluder [elyde] *vt* to evade.

émacié, e [emasje] *a* emaciated.

émail, aux [emaj, -o] *nm* enamel.

émaillé, e [emaje] *a* (*fig*): ~ **de** dotted with.

émanciper [emɑ̃sipe] *vt* to emancipate; **s'**~ *vi* (*fig*) to become emancipated *ou* liberated.

émaner [emane]: ~ **de** *vt* to come from; (*ADMIN*) to proceed from.

emballage [ɑ̃balaʒ] *nm* wrapping; packaging.

emballer [ɑ̃bale] *vt* to wrap (up); (*dans un carton*) to pack (up); (*fig: fam*) to thrill (to bits); **s'**~ *vi* (*moteur*) to race; (*cheval*) to bolt; (*fig: personne*) to get carried away.

embarcadère [ɑ̃barkadɛr] *nm* wharf, pier.

embarcation [ɑ̃barkɑsjɔ̃] *nf* (*small*) boat, (*small*) craft *inv*.

embardée [ɑ̃barde] *nf*: **faire une** ~ to swerve.

embarquement [ɑ̃barkəmɑ̃] *nm* embarkation; loading; boarding.

embarquer [ɑ̃barke] *vt* (*personne*) to embark; (*marchandise*) to load; (*fam*) to cart off; to nick // *vi* (*passager*) to board; **s'**~ *vi* to board; **s'**~ **dans** (*affaire, aventure*) to embark upon.

embarras [ɑ̃bara] *nm* (*obstacle*) hindrance; (*confusion*) embarrassment.

embarrassant, e [ɑ̃barasɑ̃, -ɑ̃t] *a* embarrassing.

embarrasser [ɑ̃barase] *vt* (*encombrer*) to clutter (up); (*gêner*) to hinder, hamper; (*fig*) to cause embarrassment to; to put in an awkward position.

embauche [ɑ̃boʃ] *nf* hiring; **bureau d'**~ labour office.

embaucher [ɑ̃boʃe] *vt* to take on, hire.

embaumer [ɑ̃bome] *vt* to embalm; to fill with its fragrance; ~ **la lavande** to be fragrant with (the scent of) lavender.

embellie [ɑ̃beli] *nf* brighter period.

embellir [ɑ̃belir] *vt* to make more attractive; (*une histoire*) to embellish // *vi* to grow lovelier *ou* more attractive.

embêtements [ɑ̃bɛtmɑ̃] *nmpl* trouble *sg*.

embêter [ɑ̃bete] *vt* to bother; **s'**~ *vi* (*s'ennuyer*) to be bored.

emblée [ɑ̃ble]: **d'**~ *ad* straightaway.

emboîter [ɑ̃bwate] *vt* to fit together; **s'**~ (**dans**) to fit (into); ~ **le pas à qn** to follow in sb's footsteps.

embonpoint [ɑ̃bɔ̃pwɛ̃] *nm* stoutness.

embouchure [ɑ̃buʃyr] *nf* (*GÉO*) mouth.

embourber [ɑ̃burbe]: **s'**~ *vi* to get stuck in the mud.

embourgeoiser [ɑ̃burʒwaze]: **s'**~ *vi* to adopt a middle-class outlook.

embouteillage [ɑ̃butɛjaʒ] *nm* traffic jam.

emboutir [ɑ̃butir] *vt* (*heurter*) to crash into, ram.

embranchement [ɑ̃brɑ̃ʃmɑ̃] *nm* (*routier*) junction; (*classification*) branch.

embraser [ɑ̃brɑze]: **s'**~ *vi* to flare up.

embrasser [ɑ̃brɑse] *vt* to kiss; (*sujet, période*) to embrace, encompass; (*carrière, métier*) to enter upon.

embrasure [ɑ̃brɑzyr] *nf*: **dans l'**~ **de la porte** in the door(way).

embrayage [ɑ̃brɛjaʒ] *nm* clutch.

embrayer [ɑ̃brɛje] *vi* (*AUTO*) to let in the clutch.

embrigader [ɑ̃brigade] *vt* to recruit.

embrocher [ɑ̃brɔʃe] *vt* to put on a spit.

embrouiller [ɑ̃bruje] *vt* (*fils*) to tangle (up); (*fiches, idées, personne*) to muddle up; **s'**~ *vi* (*personne*) to get in a muddle.

embruns [ɑ̃brœ̃] *nmpl* sea spray *sg*.

embûches [ɑ̃byʃ] *nfpl* pitfalls, traps.

embué, e [ɑ̃bɥe] *a* misted up.

embuscade [ɑ̃byskad] *nf* ambush.

éméché, e [emeʃe] *a* tipsy, merry.

émeraude [ɛmrod] *nf* emerald.

émerger [emɛrʒe] *vi* to emerge; (*faire saillie, aussi fig*) to stand out.

émeri [ɛmri] *nm*: **toile** *ou* **papier** ~ emery paper.

émérite [emerit] *a* highly skilled.

émerveiller [emɛrveje] *vt* to fill with wonder; **s'**~ **de** to marvel at.

émetteur, trice [emetœr, -tris] *a* transmitting; (*poste*) ~ transmitter.

émettre [emɛtr(ə)] *vt* (*son, lumière*) to give out, emit; (*message etc*: *RADIO*) to transmit; (*billet, timbre, emprunt*) to issue; (*hypothèse, avis*) to voice, put forward // *vi* to broadcast.

émeus *etc vb voir* **émouvoir**.

émeute [emøt] *nf* riot.

émietter [emjete] *vt* to crumble.

émigrer [emigʀe] *vi* to emigrate.

eminence [eminɑ̃s] *nf* distinction; *(colline)* knoll, hill; **Son É~** his *(ou her)* Eminence.

éminent, e [eminɑ̃, -ɑ̃t] *a* distinguished.

émission [emisjɔ̃] *nf* emission; transmission; issue; *(RADIO, TV)* programme, broadcast.

emmagasiner [ɑ̃magazine] *vt* to (put into) store; *(fig)* to store up.

emmailloter [ɑ̃majɔte] *vt* to wrap up.

emmanchure [ɑ̃mɑ̃ʃyʀ] *nf* armhole.

emmêler [ɑ̃mele] *vt* to tangle (up); *(fig)* to muddle up; **s'~** *vi* to get into a tangle.

emménager [ɑ̃menaʒe] *vi* to move in; **~ dans** to move into.

emmener [ɑ̃mne] *vt* to take (with one); *(comme otage, capture)* to take away; **~ qn au cinéma** to take sb to the cinema.

emmerder [ɑ̃mɛʀde] *(fam!)* *vt* to bug, bother; **s'~** *vi* to be bored stiff.

emmitoufler [ɑ̃mitufle] *vt* to wrap up (warmly).

émoi [emwa] *nm* commotion; *(trouble)* agitation.

émoluments [emɔlymɑ̃] *nmpl* remuneration *sg*, fee *sg*.

émonder [emɔ̃de] *vt* to prune.

émotif, ive [emɔtif, -iv] *a* emotional.

émotion [emɔsjɔ̃] *nf* emotion.

émousser [emuse] *vt* to blunt; *(fig)* to dull.

émouvoir [emuvwaʀ] *vt* *(troubler)* to stir, affect; *(toucher, attendrir)* to move; *(indigner)* to rouse; **s'~** *vi* to be affected; to be moved; to be roused.

empailler [ɑ̃paje] *vt* to stuff.

empaler [ɑ̃pale] *vt* to impale.

emparer [ɑ̃paʀe] **s'~ de** *vt* *(objet)* to seize, grab; *(comme otage, MIL)* to seize; *(suj: peur etc)* to take hold of.

empâter [ɑ̃pɑte] **s'~** *vi* to thicken out.

empêchement [ɑ̃pɛʃmɑ̃] *nm* (unexpected) obstacle, hitch.

empêcher [ɑ̃peʃe] *vt* to prevent; **~ qn de faire** to prevent *ou* stop sb (from) doing; **il n'empêche que** nevertheless; **il n'a pas pu s'~ de rire** he couldn't help laughing.

empereur [ɑ̃pʀœʀ] *nm* emperor.

empeser [ɑ̃pəze] *vt* to starch.

empester [ɑ̃pɛste] *vi* to stink, reek.

empêtrer [ɑ̃pɛtʀe] *vt*: **s'~ dans** *(fils etc)* to get tangled up in.

emphase [ɑ̃faz] *nf* pomposity, bombast.

empiéter [ɑ̃pjete] *vi*: **~ sur** to encroach upon.

empiffrer [ɑ̃pifʀe] **s'~** *vi* *(péj)* to stuff o.s.

empiler [ɑ̃pile] *vt* to pile (up).

empire [ɑ̃piʀ] *nm* empire; *(fig)* influence.

empirer [ɑ̃piʀe] *vi* to worsen, deteriorate.

emplacement [ɑ̃plasmɑ̃] *nm* site.

emplettes [ɑ̃plɛt] *nfpl* shopping *sg*.

emplir [ɑ̃pliʀ] *vt* to fill; **s'~ (de)** to fill (with).

emploi [ɑ̃plwa] *nm* use; *(COMM, ÉCON)* employment; *(poste)* job, situation; **~ du temps** timetable, schedule.

employé, e [ɑ̃plwaje] *nm/f* employee; **~ de bureau** office employee *ou* clerk.

employer [ɑ̃plwaje] *vt* *(outil, moyen, méthode, mot)* to use; *(ouvrier, main-d'œuvre)* to employ; **s'~ à faire** to apply *ou* devote o.s. to doing; **employeur, euse** *nm/f* employer.

empocher [ɑ̃pɔʃe] *vt* to pocket.

empoignade [ɑ̃pwaɲad] *nf* row, set-to.

empoigner [ɑ̃pwaɲe] *vt* to grab.

empoisonner [ɑ̃pwazɔne] *vt* to poison; *(empester: air, pièce)* to stink out; *(fam)*: **~ qn** to drive sb mad.

emporter [ɑ̃pɔʀte] *vt* to take (with one); *(en dérobant ou enlevant, emmener: blessés, voyageurs)* to take away; *(entraîner)* to carry away; *(arracher)* to tear off; *(avantage, approbation)* to win; **s'~** *vi* *(de colère)* to lose one's temper; **l'~ (sur)** to get the upper hand (of); *(méthode etc)* to prevail (over); **boissons à ~** take-away drinks.

empreint, e [ɑ̃pʀɛ̃, -ɛ̃t] *a*: **~ de** marked with; tinged with; **~** *nf* *(de pied, main)* print; *(fig)* stamp, mark; **~e (digitale)** fingerprint.

empressé, e [ɑ̃pʀese] *a* attentive.

empressement [ɑ̃pʀɛsmɑ̃] *nm* *(hâte)* eagerness.

empresser [ɑ̃pʀese] **s'~** *vi*: **s'~ auprès de qn** to surround sb with attentions; **s'~ de faire** *(se hâter)* to hasten to do.

emprise [ɑ̃pʀiz] *nf* hold, ascendancy.

emprisonner [ɑ̃pʀizɔne] *vt* to imprison.

emprunt [ɑ̃pʀœ̃] *nm* borrowing *q*, loan.

emprunté, e [ɑ̃pʀœ̃te] *a* *(fig)* ill-at-ease, awkward.

emprunter [ɑ̃pʀœ̃te] *vt* to borrow; *(itinéraire)* to take, follow; *(style, manière)* to adopt, assume.

ému, e [emy] *pp de* **émouvoir** // *a* excited; touched; moved.

émulsion [emylsjɔ̃] *nf* *(cosmetic)* (water-based) lotion.

en [ɑ̃] ♦ *prép* **1** *(endroit, pays)* in; *(direction)* to; **habiter ~ France/ville** to live in France/town; **aller ~ France/ville** to go to France/town

2 *(moment, temps)* in; **~ été/juin** in summer/June

3 *(moyen)* by; **~ avion/taxi** by plane/taxi

4 *(composition)* made of; **c'est ~ verre** it's (made of) glass; **un collier ~ argent** a silver necklace

5 *(description, état)*: **une femme (habillée) ~ rouge** a woman (dressed) in red; **peindre qch ~ rouge** to paint sth red; **~ T/étoile** T-/star-shaped; **~**

chemise/chaussettes in one's shirt-sleeves/socks; ~ soldat as a soldier; cassé ~ plusieurs morceaux broken into several pieces; ~ réparation being repaired, under repair; ~ vacances on holiday; ~ deuil in mourning; le même ~ plus grand the same but ou only bigger

6 (avec gérondif) while; · on; by; ~ dormant while sleeping, as one sleeps; ~ sortant on going out, as he etc went out; sortir ~ courant to run out

♦ pronom **1** (indéfini): j'~ ai/veux I have/want some; ~ as-tu? have you got any?; je n'~ veux pas I don't want any; j'~ ai 2 I've got 2; combien y ~ a-t-il? how many (of them) are there?; j'~ ai assez I've got enough (of it ou them); (j'en ai marre) I've had enough **2** (provenance) from there; j'~ viens I've come from there **3** (cause): il ~ est malade/perd le sommeil he is ill/can't sleep because of it **4** (complément de nom, d'adjectif, de verbe): j'~ connais les dangers I know its ou the dangers; j'~ suis fier/ai besoin I am proud of it/need it; voir le verbe ou l'adjectif lorsque 'en' correspond à 'de' introduisant un complément prépositionnel.

E.N.A. [ena] sigle f (= École Nationale d'Administration) one of the Grandes Écoles.

encadrer [ɑ̃kadʀe] vt (tableau, image) to frame; (fig: entourer) to surround; (personnel, soldats etc) to train.

encaisse [ɑ̃kɛs] nf cash in hand; ~ or/métallique gold/gold and silver reserves.

encaissé, e [ɑ̃kese] a steep-sided; with steep banks.

encaisser [ɑ̃kese] vt (chèque) to cash; (argent) to collect; (fig: coup, défaite) to take.

encan [ɑ̃kɑ̃]: à l'~ ad by auction.

encart [ɑ̃kaʀ] nm insert.

encastrer [ɑ̃kastʀe] vt: ~ qch dans (mur) to embed sth in(to); (boîtier) to fit sth into.

encaustique [ɑ̃kostik] nf polish, wax.

enceinte [ɑ̃sɛ̃t] af: ~ (de 6 mois) (6 months) pregnant // nf (mur) wall; (espace) enclosure.

encens [ɑ̃sɑ̃] nm incense.

encercler [ɑ̃sɛʀkle] vt to surround.

enchaîner [ɑ̃ʃene] vt to chain up; (mouvements, séquences) to link (together) // vi to carry on.

enchanté, e [ɑ̃ʃɑ̃te] a delighted; enchanted; ~ (de faire votre connaissance) pleased to meet you.

enchantement [ɑ̃ʃɑ̃tmɑ̃] nm delight; (magie) enchantment.

enchâsser [ɑ̃ʃɑse] vt to set.

enchère [ɑ̃ʃɛʀ] nf bid; mettre/vendre aux ~s to put up for (sale by)/sell by auction.

enchevêtrer [ɑ̃ʃvetʀe] vt to tangle (up).

enclencher [ɑ̃klɑ̃ʃe] vt (mécanisme) to engage; s'~ vi to engage.

enclin, e [ɑ̃klɛ̃, -in] a: ~ à inclined ou prone to.

enclos [ɑ̃klo] nm enclosure.

enclume [ɑ̃klym] nf anvil.

encoche [ɑ̃kɔʃ] nf notch.

encoignure [ɑ̃kɔɲyʀ] nf corner.

encolure [ɑ̃kɔlyʀ] nf (tour de cou) collar size; (col, cou) neck.

encombrant, e [ɑ̃kɔ̃bʀɑ̃, -ɑ̃t] a cumbersome, bulky.

encombre [ɑ̃kɔ̃bʀ(ə)]: sans ~ ad without mishap ou incident.

encombrer [ɑ̃kɔ̃bʀe] vt to clutter (up); (gêner) to hamper; s'~ de (bagages etc) to load ou burden o.s. with.

encontre [ɑ̃kɔ̃tʀ(ə)]: à l'~ de prép against, counter to.

encore [ɑ̃kɔʀ] ad **1** (continuation) still; il y travaille ~ he's still working on it; pas ~ not yet **2** (de nouveau) again; j'irai ~ demain I'll go again tomorrow; ~ une fois (once) again; ~ deux jours two more days **3** (intensif) even, still; ~ plus fort/mieux even louder/better, louder/better still **4** (restriction) even so ou then, only; ~ pourrais-je le faire si ... even so, I might be able to do it if ...; si ~ if only

encore que cj although.

encourager [ɑ̃kuʀaʒe] vt to encourage.

encourir [ɑ̃kuʀiʀ] vt to incur.

encre [ɑ̃kʀ(ə)] nf ink; ~ de Chine Indian ink; **encrier** nm inkwell.

encroûter [ɑ̃kʀute]: s'~ vi (fig) to get into a rut, get set in one's ways.

encyclopédie [ɑ̃siklɔpedi] nf encyclopaedia.

endetter [ɑ̃dete] vt, s'~ vi to get into debt.

endiablé, e [ɑ̃djable] a furious; boisterous.

endiguer [ɑ̃dige] vt to dyke (up); (fig) to check, hold back.

endimancher [ɑ̃dimɑ̃ʃe] vt: s'~ to put on one's Sunday best.

endive [ɑ̃div] nf chicory q.

endoctriner [ɑ̃dɔktʀine] vt to indoctrinate.

endommager [ɑ̃dɔmaʒe] vt to damage.

endormi, e [ɑ̃dɔʀmi] a asleep.

endormir [ɑ̃dɔʀmiʀ] vt to put to sleep; (suj: chaleur etc) to send to sleep; (MÉD: dent, nerf) to anaesthetize; (fig: soupçons) to allay; s'~ vi to fall asleep, go to sleep.

endosser [ɑ̃dose] vt (responsabilité) to take, shoulder; (chèque) to endorse; (uniforme, tenue) to put on, don.

endroit [ɑ̃dʀwa] nm place; (opposé à

l'envers) right side; **à l'~** the right way out; the right way up; **à l'~ de** *prép* regarding.

enduire [ɑ̃dɥiʀ] *vt* to coat.

endurant, e [ɑ̃dyʀɑ̃, -ɑ̃t] *a* tough, hardy.

endurcir [ɑ̃dyʀsiʀ] *vt* (*physiquement*) to toughen; (*moralement*) to harden; **s'~** *vi* to become tougher; to become hardened.

endurer [ɑ̃dyʀe] *vt* to endure, bear.

énergie [enɛʀʒi] *nf* (*PHYSIQUE*) energy; (*TECH*) power; (*morale*) vigour, spirit; **énergique** *a* energetic; vigorous; (*mesures*) drastic, stringent.

énergumène [enɛʀgymɛn] *nm* rowdy character *ou* customer.

énerver [enɛʀve] *vt* to irritate, annoy; **s'~** *vi* to get excited, get worked up.

enfance [ɑ̃fɑ̃s] *nf* (*âge*) childhood; (*fig*) infancy; (*enfants*) children *pl*.

enfant [ɑ̃fɑ̃] *nm/f* child (*pl* children); **~ de chœur** *nm* (*REL*) altar boy; **enfanter** *vi* to give birth // *vt* to give birth to; **enfantillage** *nm* (*péj*) childish behaviour *q*; **enfantin, e** *a* childlike; child *cpd*.

enfer [ɑ̃fɛʀ] *nm* hell.

enfermer [ɑ̃fɛʀme] *vt* to shut up; (*à clef, interner*) to lock up.

enfiévré, e [ɑ̃fjevʀe] *a* (*fig*) feverish.

enfiler [ɑ̃file] *vt* (*vêtement*) to slip on, slip into; (*insérer*): **~ qch dans** to stick sth into; (*rue, couloir*) to take; (*perles*) to string; (*aiguille*) to thread.

enfin [ɑ̃fɛ̃] *ad* at last; (*en énumérant*) lastly; (*de restriction, résignation*) still; well; (*pour conclure*) in a word.

enflammer [ɑ̃flame] *vt* to set fire to; (*MÉD*) to inflame; **s'~** *vi* to catch fire; to become inflamed.

enflé, e [ɑ̃fle] *a* swollen.

enfler [ɑ̃fle] *vi* to swell (up).

enfoncer [ɑ̃fɔ̃se] *vt* (*clou*) to drive in; (*faire pénétrer*): **~ qch dans** to push (*ou* drive) sth into; (*forcer: porte*) to break open; (: *plancher*) to cause to cave in // *vi* (*dans la vase etc*) to sink in; (*sol, surface*) to give way; **s'~** *vi* to sink; **s'~ dans** to sink into; (*forêt, ville*) to disappear into.

enfouir [ɑ̃fwiʀ] *vt* (*dans le sol*) to bury; (*dans un tiroir etc*) to tuck away.

enfourcher [ɑ̃fuʀʃe] *vt* to mount.

enfourner [ɑ̃fuʀne] *vt* to put in the oven.

enfreindre [ɑ̃fʀɛ̃dʀ(ə)] *vt* to infringe, break.

enfuir [ɑ̃fɥiʀ]: **s'~** *vi* to run away *ou* off.

enfumer [ɑ̃fyme] *vt* to smoke out.

engageant, e [ɑ̃gaʒɑ̃, -ɑ̃t] *a* attractive, appealing.

engagement [ɑ̃gaʒmɑ̃] *nm* (*promesse, contrat, POL*) commitment; (*MIL: combat*) engagement.

engager [ɑ̃gaʒe] *vt* (*embaucher*) to take

on, engage; (*commencer*) to start; (*lier*) to bind, commit; (*impliquer, entraîner*) to involve; (*investir*) to invest, lay out; (*faire intervenir*) to engage; (*inciter*) to urge; (*faire pénétrer*) to insert; **s'~** *vi* to hire o.s., get taken on; (*MIL*) to enlist; (*promettre, politiquement*) to commit o.s.; (*débuter*) to start (up); **s'~ à faire** to undertake to do; **s'~ dans** (*rue, passage*) to turn into; (*s'emboîter*) to engage into; (*fig: affaire, discussion*) to enter into, embark on.

engelures [ɑ̃ʒlyʀ] *nfpl* chilblains.

engendrer [ɑ̃ʒɑ̃dʀe] *vt* to father.

engin [ɑ̃ʒɛ̃] *nm* machine; instrument; vehicle; (*AVIAT*) aircraft *inv*; missile.

englober [ɑ̃glɔbe] *vt* to include.

engloutir [ɑ̃glutiʀ] *vt* to swallow up.

engoncé, e [ɑ̃gɔ̃se] *a*: **~ dans** cramped in.

engorger [ɑ̃gɔʀʒe] *vt* to obstruct, block.

engouement [ɑ̃gumɑ̃] *nm* (sudden) passion.

engouffrer [ɑ̃gufʀe] *vt* to swallow up, devour; **s'~ dans** to rush into.

engourdir [ɑ̃guʀdiʀ] *vt* to numb; (*fig*) to dull, blunt; **s'~** *vi* to go numb.

engrais [ɑ̃gʀɛ] *nm* manure; **~ (chimique)** (chemical) fertilizer.

engraisser [ɑ̃gʀese] *vt* to fatten (up).

engrenage [ɑ̃gʀənaʒ] *nm* gears *pl*, gearing; (*fig*) chain.

engueuler [ɑ̃gœle] *vt* (*fam*) to bawl at.

enhardir [ɑ̃aʀdiʀ]: **s'~** *vi* to grow bolder.

énigme [enigm(ə)] *nf* riddle.

enivrer [ɑ̃nivʀe] *vt*: **s'~** to get drunk; **s'~ de** (*fig*) to become intoxicated with.

enjambée [ɑ̃ʒɑ̃be] *nf* stride.

enjamber [ɑ̃ʒɑ̃be] *vt* to stride over; (*suj: pont etc*) to span, straddle.

enjeu, x [ɑ̃ʒø] *nm* stakes *pl*.

enjoindre [ɑ̃ʒwɛ̃dʀ(ə)] *vt* to enjoin, order.

enjôler [ɑ̃ʒole] *vt* to coax, wheedle.

enjoliver [ɑ̃ʒɔlive] *vt* to embellish; **enjoliveur** *nm* (*AUTO*) hub cap.

enjoué, e [ɑ̃ʒwe] *a* playful.

enlacer [ɑ̃lase] *vt* (*étreindre*) to embrace, hug.

enlaidir [ɑ̃lediʀ] *vt* to make ugly // *vi* to become ugly.

enlèvement [ɑ̃lɛvmɑ̃] *nm* (*rapt*) abduction, kidnapping.

enlever [ɑ̃lve] *vt* (*ôter: gén*) to remove; (: *vêtement, lunettes*) to take off; (*emporter: ordures etc*) to take away; (*prendre*): **~ qch à qn** to take sth (away) from sb; (*kidnapper*) to abduct, kidnap; (*obtenir: prix, contrat*) to win.

enliser [ɑ̃lize]: **s'~** *vi* to sink, get stuck.

enluminure [ɑ̃lyminyʀ] *nf* illumination.

enneigé, e [ɑ̃neʒe] *a* snowy; snowed-up.

ennemi, e [ɛnmi] *a* hostile; (*MIL*) enemy *cpd* // *nm/f* enemy.

ennui [ɑ̃nɥi] *nm* (*lassitude*) boredom; (*difficulté*) trouble *q*; avoir des ~s to have problems; **ennuyer** *vt* to bother; (*lasser*) to bore; **s'ennuyer** *vi* to be bored; **s'ennuyer de** (*regretter*) to miss; **ennuyeux, euse** *a* boring, tedious; annoying.

énoncé [enɔ̃se] *nm* terms *pl*; wording.

énoncer [enɔ̃se] *vt* to say, express; (*conditions*) to set out, state.

enorgueillir [ɑ̃nɔʀgœjiʀ]: **s'~ de** *vt* to pride o.s. on; to boast.

énorme [enɔʀm(ə)] *a* enormous, huge; **énormément** *ad* enormously; **énormément de neige/gens** an enormous amount of snow/number of people.

enquérir [ɑ̃keʀiʀ]: **s'~ de** *vt* to inquire about.

enquête [ɑ̃kɛt] *nf* (*de journaliste, de police*) investigation; (*judiciaire, administrative*) inquiry; (*sondage d'opinion*) survey; **enquêter** *vi* to investigate; to hold an inquiry; to conduct a survey.

enquiers *etc vb voir* **enquérir**.

enraciné, e [ɑ̃ʀasine] *a* deep-rooted.

enragé, e [ɑ̃ʀaʒe] *a* (*MÉD*) rabid, with rabies; (*fig*) fanatical.

enrageant, e [ɑ̃ʀaʒɑ̃, -ɑ̃t] *a* infuriating.

enrager [ɑ̃ʀaʒe] *vi* to be in a rage.

enrayer [ɑ̃ʀeje] *vt* to check, stop; **s'~** *vi* (*arme à feu*) to jam.

enregistrement [ɑ̃ʀʒistʀəmɑ̃] *nm* recording; (*ADMIN*) registration; ~ **des bagages** (*à l'aéroport*) baggage check-in.

enregistrer [ɑ̃ʀʒistʀe] *vt* (*MUS etc, remarquer, noter*) to record; (*fig: mémoriser*) to make a mental note of; (*ADMIN*) to register; (*bagages: par train*) to register; (: *à l'aéroport*) to check in.

enrhumer [ɑ̃ʀyme]: **s'~** *vi* to catch a cold.

enrichir [ɑ̃ʀiʃiʀ] *vt* to make rich(er); (*fig*) to enrich; **s'~** *vi* to get rich(er).

enrober [ɑ̃ʀɔbe] *vt*: ~ **qch de** to coat sth with; (*fig*) to wrap sth up in.

enrôler [ɑ̃ʀole] *vt* to enlist; **s'~** (**dans**) to enlist (in).

enrouer [ɑ̃ʀwe]: **s'~** *vi* to go hoarse.

enrouler [ɑ̃ʀule] *vt* (*fil, corde*) to wind (up); ~ **qch autour de** to wind sth (a)round; **s'~** *vi* to coil up; to wind.

ensanglanté, e [ɑ̃sɑ̃glɑ̃te] *a* covered with blood.

enseignant, e [ɑ̃sɛɲɑ̃, -ɑ̃t] *nm/f* teacher.

enseigne [ɑ̃sɛɲ] *nf* sign; **à telle ~ que** so much so that; ~ **lumineuse** neon sign.

enseignement [ɑ̃sɛɲmɑ̃] *nm* teaching; (*ADMIN*) education.

enseigner [ɑ̃seɲe] *vt, vi* to teach; ~ **qch à qn/à qn que** to teach sb sth/sb that.

ensemble [ɑ̃sɑ̃bl(ə)] *ad* together // *nm* (*assemblage, MATH*) set; (*totalité*): **l'~ du/de la** the whole *ou* entire; (*unité, harmonie*) unity; **impression/idée d'~** over-

all *ou* general impression/idea; **dans l'~** (*en gros*) on the whole.

ensemencer [ɑ̃smɑ̃se] *vt* to sow.

ensevelir [ɑ̃səvliʀ] *vt* to bury.

ensoleillé, e [ɑ̃sɔleje] *a* sunny.

ensommeillé, e [ɑ̃sɔmeje] *a* drowsy.

ensorceler [ɑ̃sɔʀsəle] *vt* to enchant, bewitch.

ensuite [ɑ̃sɥit] *ad* then, next; (*plus tard*) afterwards, later; ~ **de quoi** after which.

ensuivre [ɑ̃sɥivʀ(ə)]: **s'~** *vi* to follow, ensue.

entailler [ɑ̃taje] *vt* to notch; to cut.

entamer [ɑ̃tame] *vt* (*pain, bouteille*) to start; (*hostilités, pourparlers*) to open; (*fig: altérer*) to make a dent in; to shake; to damage.

entasser [ɑ̃tase] *vt* (*empiler*) to pile up, heap up; (*tenir à l'étroit*) to cram together; **s'~** *vi* to pile up; to cram.

entendre [ɑ̃tɑ̃dʀ(ə)] *vt* to hear; (*comprendre*) to understand; (*vouloir dire*) to mean; (*vouloir*): ~ **être obéi/que** to mean to be obeyed/that; **j'ai entendu dire que** I've heard (it) said that; **s'~** *vi* (*sympathiser*) to get on; (*se mettre d'accord*) to agree; **s'~ à qch/à faire** (*être compétent*) to be good at sth/doing.

entendu, e [ɑ̃tɑ̃dy] *a* (*réglé*) agreed; (*au courant: air*) knowing; (**c'est**) ~ all right, agreed; **c'est** ~ (*concession*) all right, granted; **bien** ~ of course.

entente [ɑ̃tɑ̃t] *nf* understanding; (*accord, traité*) agreement; **à double** ~ (*sens*) with a double meaning.

entériner [ɑ̃teʀine] *vt* to ratify, confirm.

enterrement [ɑ̃tɛʀmɑ̃] *nm* (*cérémonie*) funeral, burial.

enterrer [ɑ̃teʀe] *vt* to bury.

entêtant, e [ɑ̃tɛtɑ̃, -ɑ̃t] *a* heady.

entêté, e [ɑ̃tɛte] *a* stubborn.

en-tête [ɑ̃tɛt] *nm* heading; **papier à** ~ headed notepaper.

entêter [ɑ̃tete]: **s'~** *vi*: **s'~** (**à faire**) to persist (in doing).

enthousiasme [ɑ̃tuzjasm(ə)] *nm* enthusiasm; **s'enthousiasmer** *vt* to fill with enthusiasm; **s'enthousiasmer** (**pour qch**) to get enthusiastic (about sth).

enticher [ɑ̃tiʃe]: **s'~ de** *vt* to become infatuated with.

entier, ère [ɑ̃tje, -jɛʀ] *a* (*non entamé, en totalité*) whole; (*total, complet*) complete; (*fig: caractère*) unbending // *nm* (*MATH*) whole; **en** ~ totally; in its entirety; **lait** ~ full-cream milk; **entièrement** *ad* entirely, wholly.

entonner [ɑ̃tɔne] *vt* (*chanson*) to strike up.

entonnoir [ɑ̃tɔnwaʀ] *nm* funnel.

entorse [ɑ̃tɔʀs(ə)] *nf* (*MÉD*) sprain; (*fig*): ~ **au reglement** infringement of the rule.

entortiller [ɑ̃tɔʀtije] *vt* (*envelopper*) to wrap; (*enrouler*) to twist, wind; (*duper*) to deceive.

entourage [ɑ̃turaʒ] *nm* circle; family (circle); entourage; (*ce qui enclôt*) surround.

entourer [ɑ̃ture] *vt* to surround; (*apporter son soutien à*) to rally round; ~ **de** to surround with; (*trait*) to encircle with.

entourloupettes [ɑ̃turlupɛt] *nfpl* mean tricks.

entracte [ɑ̃trakt(ə)] *nm* interval.

entraide [ɑ̃trɛd] *nf* mutual aid; **s'entraider** *vi* to help each other.

entrain [ɑ̃trɛ̃] *nm* spirit; **avec/sans** ~ spiritedly/half-heartedly.

entraînement [ɑ̃trɛnmɑ̃] *nm* training; (*TECH*) drive.

entraîner [ɑ̃trene] *vt* (*tirer: wagons*) to pull; (*charrier*) to carry ou drag along; (*TECH*) to drive; (*emmener: personne*) to take (off); (*mener à l'assaut, influencer*) to lead; (*SPORT*) to train; (*impliquer*) to entail; (*causer*) to lead to, bring about; ~ **qn à faire** (*inciter*) to lead sb to do; **s'**~ *vi* (*SPORT*) to train; **s'**~ **à qch/à faire** to train o.s. for sth/to do; **entraîneur, euse** *nm/f* (*SPORT*) coach, trainer // *nm* (*HIPPISME*) trainer // *nf* (*de bar*) hostess.

entraver [ɑ̃trave] *vt* (*circulation*) to hold up; (*action, progrès*) to hinder.

entre [ɑ̃tr(ə)] *prép* between; (*parmi*) among(st); **l'un d'**~ **eux/nous** one of them/us; ~ **eux** among(st) themselves.

entrebâillé, e [ɑ̃trəbaje] *a* half-open, ajar.

entrechoquer [ɑ̃trəʃɔke]: **s'**~ *vi* to knock ou bang together.

entrecôte [ɑ̃trəkot] *nf* entrecôte ou rib steak.

entrecouper [ɑ̃trəkupe] *vt*: ~ **qch de** to intersperse sth with.

entrecroiser [ɑ̃trəkrwaze]: **s'**~ *vi* intertwine.

entrée [ɑ̃tre] *nf* entrance; (*accès: au cinéma etc*) admission; (*billet*) (admission) ticket; (*CULIN*) first course; **d'**~ *ad* from the outset; ~ **en matière** introduction.

entrefaites [ɑ̃trəfɛt]: **sur ces** ~ *ad* at this juncture.

entrefilet [ɑ̃trəfile] *nm* paragraph (*short article*).

entrejambes [ɑ̃trəʒɑ̃b] *nm* crotch.

entrelacer [ɑ̃trəlase] *vt* to intertwine.

entrelarder [ɑ̃trəlarde] *vt* to lard.

entremêler [ɑ̃trəmele] *vt*: ~ **qch de** to (inter)mingle sth with.

entremets [ɑ̃trəmɛ] *nm* (cream) dessert.

entremetteur, euse [ɑ̃trəmɛtœr, -øz] *nm/f* go-between.

entremise [ɑ̃trəmiz] *nf* intervention; **par l'**~ **de** through.

entreposer [ɑ̃trəpoze] *vt* to store, put

into storage.

entrepôt [ɑ̃trəpo] *nm* warehouse.

entreprenant, e [ɑ̃trəprənɑ̃, -ɑ̃t] *a* (*actif*) enterprising; (*trop galant*) forward.

entreprendre [ɑ̃trəprɑ̃dr(ə)] *vt* (*se lancer dans*) to undertake; (*commencer*) to begin ou start (upon); (*personne*) to buttonhole; to tackle.

entrepreneur [ɑ̃trəprənœr] *nm*: ~ **(en bâtiment)** (building) contractor.

entreprise [ɑ̃trəpriz] *nf* (*société*) firm, concern; (*action*) undertaking, venture.

entrer [ɑ̃tre] *vi* to go (ou come) in, enter // *vt* (*INFORM*) to enter, input; **(faire)** ~ **qch dans** to get sth into; ~ **dans** (*gén*) to enter; (*pièce*) to go (ou come) into, enter; (*club*) to join; (*heurter*) to run into; (*être une composante de*) to go into; to form part of; ~ **à l'hôpital** to go into hospital; **faire** ~ (*visiteur*) to show in.

entresol [ɑ̃trəsɔl] *nm* mezzanine.

entre-temps [ɑ̃trətɑ̃] *ad* meanwhile.

entretenir [ɑ̃trətnir] *vt* to maintain; (*famille, maîtresse*) to support, keep; ~ **qn (de)** to speak to sb (about); **s'**~ (**de**) to converse (about).

entretien [ɑ̃trətjɛ̃] *nm* maintenance; (*discussion*) discussion, talk; (*audience*) interview.

entrevoir [ɑ̃trəvwar] *vt* (*à peine*) to make out; (*brièvement*) to catch a glimpse of.

entrevue [ɑ̃trəvy] *nf* meeting; (*audience*) interview.

entrouvert, e [ɑ̃truvɛr, -ɛrt(ə)] *a* half-open.

énumérer [enymere] *vt* to list, enumerate.

envahir [ɑ̃vair] *vt* to invade; (*suj: inquiétude, peur*) to come over; **envahissant, e** *a* (*péj: personne*) interfering, intrusive.

enveloppe [ɑ̃vlɔp] *nf* (*de lettre*) envelope; (*TECH*) casing; outer layer.

envelopper [ɑ̃vlɔpe] *vt* to wrap; (*fig*) to envelop, shroud.

envenimer [ɑ̃vnime] *vt* to aggravate.

envergure [ɑ̃vɛrgyr] *nf* (*fig*) scope; calibre.

enverrai *etc vb voir* **envoyer**.

envers [ɑ̃vɛr] *prép* towards, to // *nm* other side; (*d'une étoffe*) wrong side; **à l'**~ upside down; back to front; (*vêtement*) inside out.

envie [ɑ̃vi] *nf* (*sentiment*) envy; (*souhait*) desire, wish; **avoir** ~ **de (faire)** to feel like (doing); (*plus fort*) to want (to do); **avoir** ~ **que** to wish that; **ça lui fait** ~ he would like that; **envier** *vt* to envy; **envieux, euse** *a* envious.

environ [ɑ̃virɔ̃] *ad*: ~ **3 h/2 km** (around) about 3 o'clock/2 km; ~**s** *nmpl* surroundings.

environnement [ɑ̃virɔnmɑ̃] *nm* environment.

environner [ãvirɔne] *vt* to surround.

envisager [ãvizaʒe] *vt* (*examiner, considérer*) to view, contemplate; (*avoir en vue*) to envisage.

envoi [ãvwa] *nm* (*paquet*) parcel, consignment.

envoler [ãvɔle]: **s'~** *vi* (*oiseau*) to fly away *ou* off; (*avion*) to take off; (*papier, feuille*) to blow away; (*fig*) to vanish (into thin air).

envoûter [ãvute] *vt* to bewitch.

envoyé, e [ãvwaje] *nm/f* (*POL*) envoy; (*PRESSE*) correspondent.

envoyer [ãvwaje] *vt* to send; (*lancer*) to hurl, throw; **~ chercher** to send for.

épagneul, e [epaɲœl] *nm/f* spaniel.

épais, se [epɛ, -ɛs] *a* thick; **épaisseur** *nf* thickness.

épancher [epãʃe]: **s'~** *vi* to open one's heart.

épanouir [epanwir]: **s'~** *vi* (*fleur*) to bloom, open out; (*visage*) to light up; (*fig*) to blossom; to open up.

épargne [eparɲ(ə)] *nf* saving.

épargner [eparɲe] *vt* to save; (*ne pas tuer ou endommager*) to spare // *vi* to save; **~ qch à qn** to spare sb sth.

éparpiller [eparpije] *vt* to scatter; (*pour répartir*) to disperse; **s'~** *vi* to scatter; (*fig*) to dissipate one's efforts.

épars, e [epar, -ars(ə)] *a* scattered.

épatant, e [epatã, -ãt] *a* (*fam*) super.

épater [epate] *vt* to amaze; to impress.

épaule [epol] *nf* shoulder.

épauler [epole] *vt* (*aider*) to back up, support; (*arme*) to raise (to one's shoulder) // *vi* to (take) aim.

épave [epav] *nf* wreck.

épée [epe] *nf* sword.

épeler [ep(ə)le] *vt* to spell.

éperdu, e [eperdy] *a* distraught, overcome; passionate; frantic.

éperon [eprɔ̃] *nm* spur.

épi [epi] *nm* (*de blé, d'orge*) ear.

épice [epis] *nf* spice.

épicer [epise] *vt* to spice.

épicerie [episri] *nf* grocer's shop; (*denrées*) groceries *pl*; **~ fine** delicatessen; **épicier, ière** *nm/f* grocer.

épidémie [epidemi] *nf* epidemic.

épier [epje] *vt* to spy on, watch closely; (*occasion*) to look out for.

épilepsie [epilɛpsi] *nf* epilepsy.

épiler [epile] *vt* (*jambes*) to remove the hair from; (*sourcils*) to pluck.

épilogue [epilɔg] *nm* (*fig*) conclusion, dénouement.

épiloguer [epilɔge] *vi*: **~ sur** to hold forth on.

épinards [epinar] *nmpl* spinach *sg*.

épine [epin] *nf* thorn, prickle; (*d'oursin etc*) spine; **~ dorsale** backbone.

épingle [epɛ̃gl(ə)] *nf* pin; **~ de nourrice** *ou* **de sûreté** *ou* **double** safety pin.

épingler [epɛ̃gle] *vt* (*badge, décoration*): **~ qch sur** to pin sth on(to); (*fam*) to catch, nick.

épique [epik] *a* epic.

épisode [epizɔd] *nm* episode; **film/roman à ~s** serial; **épisodique** *a* occasional.

épître [epitr(ə)] *nf* epistle.

éploré, e [eplɔre] *a* tearful.

épluche-légumes [eplyʃlegym] *nm inv* (potato) peeler.

éplucher [eplyʃe] *vt* (*fruit, légumes*) to peel; (*fig*) to go over with a fine-tooth comb; **épluchures** *nfpl* peelings.

épointer [epwɛ̃te] *vt* to blunt.

éponge [epɔ̃ʒ] *nf* sponge; **éponger** *vt* (*liquide*) to mop up; (*surface*) to sponge; (*fig: déficit*) to soak up; **s'éponger le front** to mop one's brow.

épopée [epɔpe] *nf* epic.

époque [epɔk] *nf* (*de l'histoire*) age, era; (*de l'année, la vie*) time; **d'~** *a* (*meuble*) period *cpd*.

époumoner [epumɔne]: **s'~** *vi* to shout o.s. hoarse.

épouse [epuz] *nf* wife (*pl* wives).

épouser [epuze] *vt* to marry; (*fig: idées*) to espouse; (: *forme*) to fit.

épousseter [epuste] *vt* to dust.

époustouflant, e [epustuflã, -ãt] *a* staggering, mind-boggling.

épouvantable [epuvãtabl(ə)] *a* appalling, dreadful.

épouvantail [epuvãtaj] *nm* (*à moineaux*) scarecrow.

épouvante [epuvãt] *nf* terror; **film d'~** horror film; **épouvanter** *vt* to terrify.

époux [epu] *nm* husband // *nmpl* (married) couple.

éprendre [eprãdr(ə)]: **s'~ de** *vt* to fall in love with.

épreuve [eprœv] *nf* (*d'examen*) test; (*malheur, difficulté*) trial, ordeal; (*PHOTO*) print; (*TYPO*) proof; (*SPORT*) event; **à l'~ des balles** bulletproof; **à toute ~** unfailing; **mettre à l'~** to put to the test.

épris, e [epri, -iz] *vb voir* **éprendre**.

éprouver [epruve] *vt* (*tester*) to test; (*marquer, faire souffrir*) to afflict, distress; (*ressentir*) to experience.

éprouvette [epruvɛt] *nf* test tube.

épuisé, e [epɥize] *a* exhausted; (*livre*) out of print.

épuisement [epɥizmã] *nm* exhaustion.

épuiser [epɥize] *vt* (*fatiguer*) to exhaust, wear *ou* tire out; (*stock, sujet*) to exhaust; **s'~** *vi* to wear *ou* tire o.s. out, exhaust o.s.; (*stock*) to run out.

épurer [epyre] *vt* (*liquide*) to purify; (*parti etc*) to purge; (*langue, texte*) to refine.

équateur [ekwatœr] *nm* equator; (**la république de) l'É~** Ecuador.

équation [ekwasjɔ̃] *nf* equation.

équerre [ekɛʀ] nf (à dessin) (set) square; (pour fixer) brace; **en ~** at right angles; **à l'~, d'~** straight.

équilibre [ekilibʀ(ə)] nm balance; (d'une balance) equilibrium; **garder/ perdre l'~** to keep/lose one's balance; **être en ~** to be balanced; **équilibré, e** a (fig) well-balanced, stable; **équilibrer** vt to balance; **s'équilibrer** vi (poids) to balance; (fig: défauts etc) to balance each other out.

équipage [ekipaʒ] nm crew.

équipe [ekip] nf team; (bande: parfois péj) bunch.

équipé, e [ekipe] a: **bien/mal ~** well-/ poorly-equipped.

équipée [ekipe] nf escapade.

équipement [ekipmɑ̃] nm equipment; **~s** nmpl amenities, facilities; installations.

équiper [ekipe] vt to equip; (voiture, cuisine) to equip, fit out; **~ qn/qch de** to equip sb/sth with.

équitable [ekitabl(ə)] a fair.

équitation [ekitasjɔ̃] nf (horse-)riding.

équivalent, e [ekivalɑ̃, -ɑ̃t] a, nm equivalent.

équivaloir [ekivalwaʀ]: **~ à** vt to be equivalent to.

équivoque [ekivɔk] a equivocal, ambiguous; (louche) dubious.

érable [eʀabl(ə)] nm maple.

érafler [eʀafle] vt to scratch; **éraflure** nf scratch.

éraillé, e [eʀaje] a (voix) rasping.

ère [ɛʀ] nf era; **en l'an 1050 de notre ~** in the year 1050 A.D.

érection [eʀɛksjɔ̃] nf erection.

éreinter [eʀɛ̃te] vt to exhaust, wear out.

ériger [eʀiʒe] vt (monument) to erect.

ermite [ɛʀmit] nm hermit.

éroder [eʀɔde] vt to erode.

érotique [eʀɔtik] a erotic.

errer [eʀe] vi to wander.

erreur [eʀœʀ] nf mistake, error; (morale) error; **faire ~** to be mistaken; **par ~** by mistake; **~ judiciaire** miscarriage of justice.

érudit, e [eʀydi, -it] nm/f scholar.

éruption [eʀypsjɔ̃] nf eruption; (MÉD) rash.

es vb voir **être**.

ès [ɛs] prép: **licencié ~ lettres/sciences** ≈ Bachelor of Arts/Science.

escabeau, x [ɛskabo] nm (tabouret) stool; (échelle) stepladder.

escadre [ɛskadʀ(ə)] nf (NAVIG) squadron; (AVIAT) wing.

escadrille [ɛskadʀij] nf (AVIAT) flight.

escadron [ɛskadʀɔ̃] nm squadron.

escalade [ɛskalad] nf climbing q; (POL etc) escalation.

escalader [ɛskalade] vt to climb.

escale [ɛskal] nf (NAVIG) call; port of call; (AVIAT) stop(over); **faire ~ à** to

put in at; to stop over at.

escalier [ɛskalje] nm stairs pl; **dans l'~ ou les ~s** on the stairs; **~ roulant** escalator.

escamoter [ɛskamɔte] vt (esquiver) to get round, evade; (faire disparaître) to conjure away.

escapade [ɛskapad] nf: **faire une ~** to go on a jaunt; to run away ou off.

escargot [ɛskaʀgo] nm snail.

escarmouche [ɛskaʀmuʃ] nf skirmish.

escarpé, e [ɛskaʀpe] a steep.

escient [ɛsjɑ̃] nm: **à bon ~** advisedly.

esclaffer [ɛsklafe]: **s'~** vi to guffaw.

esclandre [ɛsklɑ̃dʀ(ə)] nm scene, fracas.

esclavage [ɛsklavaʒ] nm slavery.

esclave [ɛsklav] nm/f slave.

escompter [ɛskɔ̃te] vt (COMM) to discount; (espérer) to expect, reckon upon.

escorte [ɛskɔʀt(ə)] nf escort.

escouade [ɛskwad] nf squad.

escrime [ɛskʀim] nf fencing.

escrimer [ɛskʀime]: **s'~** vi: **s'~ à faire** to wear o.s. out doing.

escroc [ɛskʀo] nm swindler, conman.

escroquer [ɛskʀɔke] vt: **~ qn (de qch)/ qch (à qn)** to swindle sb (out of sth)/sth (out of sb); **escroquerie** nf swindle.

espace [ɛspas] nm space.

espacer [ɛspase] vt to space out; **s'~** vi (visites etc) to become less frequent.

espadon [ɛspadɔ̃] nm swordfish inv.

espadrille [ɛspadʀij] nf rope-soled sandal.

Espagne [ɛspaɲ(ə)] nf: **l'~** Spain; **espagnol, e** a Spanish // nm/f: **Espagnol, e** Spaniard // nm (LING) Spanish.

espagnolette [ɛspaɲɔlɛt] nf (window) catch; **fermé à l'~** resting on the catch.

espèce [ɛspɛs] nf (BIO, BOT, ZOOL) species inv; (gén: sorte) sort, kind, type; (péj): **~ de maladroit!** you clumsy oaf!; **en ~** in cash; **~s** nfpl (COMM) cash sg; **en l'~** ad in the case in point.

espérance [ɛspeʀɑ̃s] nf hope; **~ de vie** life expectancy.

espérer [ɛspeʀe] vt to hope for; **j'espère (bien)** I hope so; **~ que/faire** to hope that/to do; **~ en** to trust in.

espiègle [ɛspjɛgl(ə)] a mischievous.

espion, ne [ɛspjɔ̃, -ɔn] nm/f spy.

espionnage [ɛspjɔnaʒ] nm espionage, spying.

espionner [ɛspjɔne] vt to spy (up)on.

esplanade [ɛsplanad] nf esplanade.

espoir [ɛspwaʀ] nm hope.

esprit [ɛspʀi] nm (pensée, intellect) mind; (humour, ironie) wit; (mentalité, d'une loi etc, fantôme etc) spirit; **faire de l'~** to try to be witty; **reprendre ses ~s** to come to; **perdre l'~** to lose one's mind.

esquimau, de, x [ɛskimo, -od] a, nm/f Eskimo // nm ice lolly (Brit), popsicle

(US).

esquinter [ɛskɛte] *vt* (*fam*) to mess up.

esquisse [ɛskis] *nf* sketch.

esquisser [ɛskise] *vt* to sketch; **s'~** *vi* (*amélioration*) to begin to be detectable; **~ un sourire** to give a vague smile.

esquiver [ɛskive] *vt* to dodge; **s'~** *vi* to slip away.

essai [esɛ] *nm* trying; testing; (*tentative*) attempt, try; (*RUGBY*) try; (*LITTÉRATURE*) essay; **~s** (*AUTO*) trials; **~ gratuit** (*COMM*) free trial; **à l'~** on a trial basis.

essaim [esɛ̃] *nm* swarm.

essayer [eseje] *vt* (*gén*) to try; (*vêtement, chaussures*) to try (on); (*restaurant, méthode, voiture*) to try (out) // *vi* to try; **~ de faire** to try *ou* attempt to do.

essence [esɑ̃s] *nf* (*de voiture*) petrol (*Brit*), gas(oline) (*US*); (*extrait de plante, PHILOSOPHIE*) essence; (*espèce: d'arbre*) species *inv*.

essentiel, le [esɑ̃sjɛl] *a* essential; **c'est l'~** (*ce qui importe*) that's the main thing; **l'~ de** the main part of.

essieu, x [esjø] *nm* axle.

essor [esɔʀ] *nm* (*de l'économie etc*) rapid expansion.

essorer [esɔʀe] *vt* (*en tordant*) to wring (out); (*par la force centrifuge*) to spindry; **essoreuse** *nf* mangle, wringer; spin-dryer.

essouffler [esufle] *vt* to make breathless; **s'~** *vi* to get out of breath; (*fig*) to run out of steam.

essuie-glace [esɥiglas] *nm inv* windscreen (*Brit*) *ou* windshield (*US*) wiper.

essuie-main [esɥimɛ̃] *nm* hand towel.

essuyer [esɥije] *vt* to wipe; (*fig: subir*) to suffer; **s'~** *vi* (*après le bain*) to dry o.s.; **~ la vaisselle** to dry up.

est [ɛst] *vb* [ɛ] *voir* **être** // *nm* east // *a inv* east; (*région*) east(ern); **à l'~** in the east; (*direction*) to the east, east(wards); **à l'~ de** (to the) east of.

estafette [ɛstafɛt] *nf* (*MIL*) dispatch rider.

estaminet [ɛstaminɛ] *nm* tavern.

estampe [ɛstɑ̃p] *nf* print, engraving.

estampille [ɛstɑ̃pij] *nf* stamp.

est-ce que [ɛskə] *ad*: **~ c'est cher/c'était bon?** is it expensive/was it good?; **quand est-ce qu'il part?** when does he leave?, when is he leaving?; *voir aussi* que.

esthéticienne [ɛstetisjɛn] *nf* beautician.

esthétique [ɛstetik] *a* attractive; aesthetically pleasing.

estimation [ɛstimasjɔ̃] *nf* valuation; assessment.

estime [ɛstim] *nf* esteem, regard.

estimer [ɛstime] *vt* (*respecter*) to es-

teem; (*expertiser*) to value; (*évaluer*) to assess, estimate; (*penser*): **~ que/être** to consider that/o.s. to be.

estival, e, aux [ɛstival, -o] *a* summer *cpd*.

estivant, e [ɛstivɑ̃, -ɑ̃t] *nm/f* (summer) holiday-maker.

estomac [ɛstɔma] *nm* stomach.

estomaqué, e [ɛstɔmake] *a* flabbergasted.

estomper [ɛstɔ̃pe] *vt* (*fig*) to blur, dim; **s'~** *vi* to soften; to become blurred.

estrade [ɛstʀad] *nf* platform, rostrum.

estragon [ɛstʀagɔ̃] *nm* tarragon.

estropier [ɛstʀɔpje] *vt* to cripple, maim; (*fig*) to twist, distort.

et [e] *cj* and; **~ lui?** what about him?; **~ alors!** so what!

étable [etabl(ə)] *nf* cowshed.

établi [etabli] *nm* (work)bench.

établir [etabliʀ] *vt* (*papiers d'identité, facture*) to make out; (*liste, programme*) to draw up; (*entreprise, camp, gouvernement, artisan*) to set up; (*réputation, usage, fait, culpabilité*) to establish; **s'~** *vi* (*se faire: entente etc*) to be established; **s'~** (**à son compte**) to set up in business; **s'~ à/près de** to settle in/near.

établissement [etablismɑ̃] *nm* making out; drawing up; setting up, establishing; (*entreprise, institution*) establishment; **~ scolaire** school, educational establishment.

étage [etaʒ] *nm* (*d'immeuble*) storey, floor; (*de fusée*) stage; (*GÉO: de culture, végétation*) level; **à l'~** upstairs; **au 2ème ~** on the 2nd (*Brit*) *ou* 3rd (*US*) floor; **de bas ~** a low.

étagère [etaʒɛʀ] *nf* (*rayon*) shelf; (*meuble*) shelves *pl*.

étai [etɛ] *nm* stay, prop.

étain [etɛ̃] *nm* tin; (*ORFÈVRERIE*) pewter *q*.

étais *etc vb voir* **être**.

étal [etal] *nm* stall.

étalage [etalaʒ] *nm* display; display window; **faire ~ de** to show off, parade.

étaler [etale] *vt* (*carte, nappe*) to spread (out); (*peinture, liquide*) to spread; (*échelonner: paiements, vacances*) to spread, stagger; (*marchandises*) to display; (*richesses, connaissances*) to parade; **s'~** *vi* (*liquide*) to spread out; (*fam*) to fall flat on one's face; **s'~ sur** (*suj: paiements etc*) to be spread out over.

étalon [etalɔ̃] *nm* (*mesure*) standard; (*cheval*) stallion.

étamer [etame] *vt* (*casserole*) to tin(plate); (*glace*) to silver.

étanche [etɑ̃ʃ] *a* (*récipient*) watertight; (*montre, vêtement*) waterproof.

étancher [etɑ̃ʃe] *vt*: **~ sa soif** to quench

one's thirst.

étang [etɑ̃] *nm* pond.

étant [etɑ̃] *vb voir* **être, donné**.

étape [etap] *nf* stage; (*lieu d'arrivée*) stopping place; (; CYCLISME) staging point; **faire ~ à** to stop off at.

état [eta] *nm* (POL, *condition*) state; (*liste*) inventory, statement; **en mauvais ~** in poor condition; **en ~ (de marche)** in (working) order; **remettre en ~** to repair; **hors d'~** out of order; **être en ~/ hors d'~ de faire** to be in a/in no fit state to do; **en tout ~ de cause** in any event; **être dans tous ses ~s** to be in a state; **faire ~ de** (*alléguer*) to put forward; **en ~ d'arrestation** under arrest; **~ civil** civil status; **~ des lieux** inventory of fixtures; **~s d'âme** moods; **étatiser** *vt* to bring under state control.

état-major [etamaʒɔʀ] *nm* (MIL) staff.

États-Unis [etazyni] *nmpl:* **les ~ the** United States.

étau, x [eto] *nm* vice (*Brit*), vise (*US*).

étayer [eteje] *vt* to prop *ou* shore up.

et c(a)etera [etseteʀa], **etc.** *ad* et cetera, and so on, etc.

été [ete] *pp de* **être** // *nm* summer.

éteignoir [etɛɲwaʀ] *nm* (candle) extinguisher; (*péj*) killjoy, wet blanket.

éteindre [etɛ̃dʀ(ə)] *vt* (*lampe, lumière, radio*) to turn *ou* switch off; (*cigarette, incendie, bougie*) to put out, extinguish; (JUR: *dette*) to extinguish; **s'~** *vi* to go out; to go off; (*mourir*) to pass away; **éteint, e** *a* (*fig*) lacklustre, dull; (*volcan*) extinct.

étendard [etɑ̃daʀ] *nm* standard.

étendre [etɑ̃dʀ(ə)] *vt* (*pâte, liquide*) to spread; (*carte etc*) to spread out; (*linge*) to hang up; (*bras, jambes, par terre: blessé*) to stretch out; (*diluer*) to dilute, thin; (*fig: agrandir*) to extend; **s'~** *vi* (*augmenter, se propager*) to spread; (*terrain, forêt etc*) to stretch; (*s'allonger*) to stretch out; (*se coucher*) to lie down; (*fig: expliquer*) to elaborate.

étendu, e [etɑ̃dy] *a* extensive // *nf* (*d'eau, de sable*) stretch, expanse; (*importance*) extent.

éternel, le [etɛʀnɛl] *a* eternal.

éterniser [etɛʀnize]: **s'~** *vi* to last for ages; to stay for ages.

éternité [etɛʀnite] *nf* eternity.

éternuer [etɛʀnɥe] *vi* to sneeze.

êtes *vb voir* **être**.

éthique [etik] *a* ethical.

ethnie [etni] *nf* ethnic group.

éthylisme [etilism(ə)] *nm* alcoholism.

étiez *vb voir* **être**.

étinceler [etɛ̃sle] *vi* to sparkle.

étincelle [etɛ̃sɛl] *nf* spark.

étioler [etjɔle]: **s'~** *vi* to wilt.

étiqueter [etikte] *vt* to label.

étiquette [etikɛt] *nf* label; (*protocole*): **l'~** etiquette.

étirer [etiʀe] *vt* to stretch; **s'~** *vi* (*personne*) to stretch; (*convoi, route*): **s'~ sur** to stretch out over.

étoffe [etɔf] *nf* material, fabric.

étoffer [etɔfe] *vt*, **s'~** *vi* to fill out.

étoile [etwal] *nf* star; **à la belle ~** in the open; **~ filante** shooting star; **~ de mer** starfish; **étoilé, e** *a* starry.

étole [etɔl] *nf* stole.

étonnant, e [etɔnɑ̃, -ɑ̃t] *a* amazing.

étonner [etɔne] *vt* to surprise, amaze; **s'~ que/de** to be amazed that/at; **cela m'étonnerait (que)** (*j'en doute*) I'd be very surprised (if).

étouffée, e [etufe]: **à l'~** *ad* (CULIN) steamed; braised.

étouffer [etufe] *vt* to suffocate; (*bruit*) to muffle; (*scandale*) to hush up // *vi* to suffocate; **s'~** *vi* (*en mangeant etc*) to choke.

étourderie [etuʀdəʀi] *nf* heedlessness *q*; thoughtless blunder.

étourdi, e [etuʀdi] *a* (*distrait*) scatterbrained, heedless.

étourdir [etuʀdiʀ] *vt* (*assommer*) to stun, daze; (*griser*) to make dizzy *ou* giddy; **étourdissement** *nm* dizzy spell.

étourneau, x [etuʀno] *nm* starling.

étrange [etʀɑ̃ʒ] *a* strange.

étranger, ère [etʀɑ̃ʒe, -ɛʀ] *a* foreign; (*pas de la famille, non familier*) strange // *nm/f* foreigner; stranger // *nm:* **à l'~** abroad; **de l'~** from abroad; **~ à** (*fig*) unfamiliar to; irrelevant to.

étranglement [etʀɑ̃gləmɑ̃] *nm* (*d'une vallée etc*) constriction.

étrangler [etʀɑ̃gle] *vt* to strangle; **s'~** *vi* (*en mangeant etc*) to choke.

étrave [etʀav] *nf* stem.

être [etʀ(ə)] ♦ *nm* being; **~ humain** human being

♦ *vb avec attribut* **1** (*état, description*) to be; **il est instituteur** he is a teacher; **vous êtes grand/intelligent/ fatigué** you are *ou* you're tall/clever/tired

2 (+ *à: appartenir*) to be; **le livre est à Paul** the book is Paul's *ou* belongs to Paul; **c'est à moi/eux** it is *ou* it's mine/ theirs

3 (+ *de: provenance*) to be; **il est de Paris** he is from Paris; (; *appartenance*): **il est des nôtres** he is one of us

4 (*date*): **nous sommes le 10 janvier** it's the 10th of January (today)

♦ *vi* to be; **je ne serai pas ici demain** I won't be here tomorrow

♦ *vb auxiliaire* **1** to have; to be; **être arrivé/allé** to have arrived/gone; **il est parti** he has left, he is gone

2 (*forme passive*) to be; **être fait par** to be made by; **il a été promu** he has been promoted

3 (+ *à: obligation*): **c'est à réparer** it needs repairing; **c'est à essayer** it should be tried

♦ *vb impersonnel* **1**: il est + *adjectif* it is + *adjective*; **il est impossible de le faire** it's impossible to do it **2** (*heure, date*): il est 10 heures, c'est 10 heures it is *ou* it's 10 o'clock **3** (*emphatique*): c'est moi it's me; c'est à lui de le faire it's up to him to do it.

étreindre [etʀɛ̃dʀ(ə)] *vt* to clutch, grip; (*amoureusement, amicalement*) to embrace; s'~ *vi* to embrace.

étrenner [etʀene] *vt* to use (*ou* wear) for the first time.

étrennes [etʀen] *nfpl* Christmas box *sg*.

étrier [etʀije] *nm* stirrup.

étriller [etʀije] *vt* (*cheval*) to curry; (*fam: battre*) to slaughter (*fig*).

étriqué, e [etʀike] *a* skimpy.

étroit, e [etʀwa, -wat] *a* narrow; (*vêtement*) tight; (*fig: serré*) close, tight; à l'~ cramped; ~ d'esprit narrow-minded.

étude [etyd] *nf* studying; (*ouvrage, rapport*) study; (*de notaire: bureau*) office; (*: charge*) practice; (*SCOL: salle de travail*) study room; ~s (*SCOL*) studies; être à l'~ (*projet etc*) to be under consideration; **faire des** ~s (de droit/ médecine) to study (law/medicine).

étudiant, e [etydjã, -ãt] *nm/f* student.

étudié, e [etydje] *a* (*démarche*) studied; (*système*) carefully designed; (*prix*) keen.

étudier [etydje] *vt, vi* to study.

étui [etyi] *nm* case.

étuve [etyv] *nf* steamroom.

étuvée [etyve]: à l'~ *ad* braised.

eu, eue [y] *pp de* avoir.

euh [ø] *excl* er.

Europe [øʀɔp] *nf*: l'~ Europe; **européen, ne** *a*, *nm/f* European.

eus *etc vb voir* avoir.

eux [ø] *pronom* (*sujet*) they; (*objet*) them.

évacuer [evakɥe] *vt* to evacuate.

évader [evade]: s'~ *vi* to escape.

évangile [evãʒil] *nm* gospel.

évanouir [evanwiʀ]: s'~ *vi* to faint; (*disparaître*) to vanish, disappear.

évanouissement [evanwismã] *nm* (*syncope*) fainting fit; (*dans un accident*) loss of consciousness.

évaporer [evapɔʀe]: s'~ *vi* to evaporate.

évaser [evaze] *vt* (*tuyau*) to widen, open out; (*jupe, pantalon*) to flare.

évasif, ive [evazif, -iv] *a* evasive.

évasion [evazjɔ̃] *nf* escape.

évêché [eveʃe] *nm* bishopric; bishop's palace.

éveil [evɛj] *nm* awakening; être en ~ to be alert.

éveillé, e [eveje] *a* awake; (*vif*) alert, sharp.

éveiller [eveje] *vt* to (a)waken; s'~ *vi* to (a)waken; (*fig*) to be aroused.

événement [evɛnmã] *nm* event.

éventail [evãtaj] *nm* fan; (*choix*) range.

éventaire [evãtɛʀ] *nm* stall, stand.

éventer [evãte] *vt* (*secret*) to uncover; s'~ *vi* (*parfum*) to go stale.

éventrer [evãtʀe] *vt* to disembowel; (*fig*) to tear *ou* rip open.

éventualité [evãtɥalite] *nf* eventuality; possibility; **dans l'~ de** in the event of.

éventuel, le [evãtɥɛl] *a* possible; ~**lement** *ad* possibly.

évêque [evɛk] *nm* bishop.

évertuer [evɛʀtɥe]: s'~ *vi*: s'~ à faire to try very hard to do.

éviction [eviksjɔ̃] *nf* ousting; (*de locataire*) eviction.

évidemment [evidamã] *ad* obviously.

évidence [evidãs] *nf* obviousness; obvious fact; **de toute** ~ quite obviously *ou* evidently; **en** ~ conspicuous; **mettre en** ~ to highlight; to bring to the fore.

évident, e [evidã, -ãt] *a* obvious, evident.

évider [evide] *vt* to scoop out.

évier [evje] *nm* (kitchen) sink.

évincer [evɛ̃se] *vt* to oust.

éviter [evite] *vt* to avoid; ~ de faire/que qch ne se passe to avoid doing/sth happening; ~ qch à qn to spare sb sth.

évolué, e [evɔlɥe] *a* advanced.

évoluer [evɔlɥe] *vi* (*enfant, maladie*) to develop; (*situation, moralement*) to evolve, develop; (*aller et venir: danseur etc*) to move about, circle; **évolution** *nf* development; evolution; **évolutions** *nfpl* movements.

évoquer [evɔke] *vt* to call to mind, evoke; (*mentionner*) to mention.

ex... [eks] *préfixe* ex-.

exact, e [ɛgzakt] *a* (*précis*) exact, accurate, precise; (*correct*) correct; (*ponctuel*) punctual; **l'heure** ~e the right *ou* exact time; ~**ement** *ad* exactly, accurately, precisely; correctly; (*c'est cela même*) exactly.

ex aequo [ɛgzeko] *a* equally placed.

exagéré, e [ɛgzaʒeʀe] *a* (*prix etc*) excessive.

exagérer [ɛgzaʒeʀe] *vt* to exaggerate // *vi* (*abuser*) to go too far; to overstep the mark; (*déformer les faits*) to exaggerate.

exalter [ɛgzalte] *vt* (*enthousiasmer*) to excite, elate; (*glorifier*) to exalt.

examen [ɛgzamɛ̃] *nm* examination; (*SCOL*) exam, examination; à l'~ under consideration; (*COMM*) on approval.

examiner [ɛgzamine] *vt* to examine.

exaspérant, e [ɛgzaspeʀã, -ãt] *a* exasperating.

exaspérer [ɛgzaspeʀe] *vt* to exasperate; to exacerbate.

exaucer [ɛgzose] *vt* (*vœu*) to grant.

excédent [ɛksedã] *nm* surplus; **en** ~ surplus; ~ **de bagages** excess luggage.

excéder [ɛksede] *vt* (*dépasser*) to exceed; (agacer) to exasperate.

excellence [ɛksɛlãs] nf (titre) Excellency.

excellent, e [ɛksɛlã, -ãt] a excellent.

excentrique [ɛksãtʀik] a eccentric; (quartier) outlying.

excepté, e [ɛksɛpte] a, prép: les élèves ∼s, ∼ les élèves except for the pupils; ∼ si except if.

exception [ɛksɛpsjõ] nf exception; à l'∼ de except for, with the exception of; d'∼ (mesure, loi) special, exceptional; **exceptionnel, le** a exceptional.

excès [ɛksɛ] nm surplus // nmpl excesses; à l'∼ to excess; ∼ de vitesse speeding q; **excessif, ive** a excessive.

excitant, e [ɛksitã, -ãt] a exciting // nm stimulant.

excitation [ɛksitasjõ] nf (état) excitement.

exciter [ɛksite] vt to excite; (suj: café etc) to stimulate; s'∼ vi to get excited.

exclamation [ɛksklamasjõ] nf exclamation.

exclamer [ɛksklame]: s'∼ vi to exclaim.

exclure [ɛksklyʀ] vt (faire sortir) to expel; (ne pas compter) to exclude, leave out; (rendre impossible) to exclude, rule out; ce n'est pas exclu it's not impossible, I don't rule that out; **exclusif, ive** a exclusive; **exclusion** nf expulsion; à l'exclusion de with the exclusion ou exception of; **exclusivité** nf (COMM) exclusive rights pl; film passant en exclusivité a film showing only at.

excursion [ɛkskyʀsjõ] nf (en autocar) excursion, trip; (à pied) walk, hike.

excuse [ɛkskyz] nf excuse; ∼s nfpl apology sg, apologies.

excuser [ɛkskyze] vt to excuse; s'∼ (de) to apologize (for); 'excusez-moi' 'I'm sorry'; (pour attirer l'attention) 'excuse me'.

exécrable [ɛgzekʀabl(ə)] a atrocious.

exécrer [ɛgzekʀe] vt to loathe, abhor.

exécuter [ɛgzekyte] vt (prisonnier) to execute; (tâche etc) to execute, carry out; (MUS: jouer) to perform, execute; (INFORM) to run; s'∼ vi to comply; **exécutif, ive** a, nm (POL) executive; **exécution** nf execution; carrying out; mettre à exécution to carry out.

exemplaire [ɛgzãplɛʀ] nm copy.

exemple [ɛgzãpl(ə)] nm example; par ∼ for instance, for example; donner l'∼ to set an example; prendre ∼ sur to take as a model; à l'∼ de just like.

exempt, e [ɛgzã, -ãt] a: ∼ de (dispensé de) exempt from; (sans) free from.

exercer [ɛgzɛʀse] vt (pratiquer) to exercise, practise; (prérogative) to exercise; (influence, contrôle) to exert; (former) to exercise, train; s'∼ vi (sportif, musicien) to practise; (se faire sentir: pression etc) to be exerted.

exercice [ɛgzɛʀsis] nm (tâche, travail) exercise; l'∼ exercise; (MIL) drill; en ∼ (juge) in office; (médecin) practising.

exhaustif, ive [ɛgzostif, -iv] a exhaustive.

exhiber [ɛgzibe] vt (montrer: papiers, certificat) to present, produce; (péj) to display, flaunt; s'∼ vi to parade; (suj: exhibitionniste) to expose o.s.

exhorter [ɛgzɔʀte] vt to urge.

exigeant, e [ɛgziʒã, -ãt] a demanding; (péj) hard to please.

exigence [ɛgziʒãs] nf demand, requirement.

exiger [ɛgziʒe] vt to demand, require.

exigu, ë [ɛgzigy] a (lieu) cramped, tiny.

exil [ɛgzil] nm exile; ∼er vt to exile; s'∼er vi to go into exile.

existence [ɛgzistãs] nf existence.

exister [ɛgziste] vi to exist; il existe un/des there is a/are (some).

exonérer [ɛgzɔneʀe] vt: ∼ de to exempt from.

exorbité, e [ɛgzɔʀbite] a: yeux ∼s bulging eyes.

exotique [ɛgzɔtik] a exotic.

expatrier [ɛkspatʀije] vt: s'∼ to leave one's country.

expectative [ɛkspɛktativ] nf: être dans l'∼ to be still waiting.

expédient [ɛkspedjã] nm (péj) expedient; vivre d'∼s to live by one's wits.

expédier [ɛkspedje] vt (lettre, paquet) to send; (troupes) to dispatch; (péj: travail etc) to dispose of, dispatch; **expéditeur, trice** nm/f sender.

expédition [ɛkspedisjõ] nf sending; (scientifique, sportive, MIL) expedition.

expérience [ɛkspeʀjãs] nf (de la vie) experience; (scientifique) experiment.

expérimenté, e [ɛkspeʀimãte] a experienced.

expérimenter [ɛkspeʀimãte] vt to test out, experiment with.

expert, e [ɛkspɛʀ, -ɛʀt(ə)] a, nm expert; ∼ en assurances insurance valuer; ∼-comptable nm ≈ chartered accountant (Brit), ≈ certified public accountant (US).

expertise [ɛkspɛʀtiz] nf valuation; assessment; valuer's (ou assessor's) report; (JUR) (forensic) examination.

expertiser [ɛkspɛʀtize] vt (objet de valeur) to value; (voiture accidentée etc) to assess damage to.

expier [ɛkspje] vt to expiate, atone for.

expirer [ɛkspiʀe] vi (prendre fin, mourir) to expire; (respirer) to breathe out.

explicatif, ive [ɛksplikatif, -iv] a explanatory.

explication [ɛksplikasjõ] nf explanation; (discussion) argument; ∼ de texte (SCOL) critical analysis.

explicite [ɛksplisit] a explicit.

expliquer [ɛksplike] vt to explain; s'~ to explain (o.s.); (*discuter*) to discuss things; to have it out; **son erreur s'explique** one can understand his mistake.

exploit [ɛksplwa] nm exploit, feat.

exploitation [ɛksplwatɑsjɔ̃] nf exploitation; running; ~ **agricole** farming concern.

exploiter [ɛksplwate] vt (*mine*) to exploit, work; (*entreprise, ferme*) to run, operate; (*clients, ouvriers, erreur, don*) to exploit.

explorer [ɛksplɔre] vt to explore.

exploser [ɛksploze] vi to explode, blow up; (*engin explosif*) to go off; (*fig: joie, colère*) to burst out, explode; **explosif, ive** a, nm explosive; **explosion** nf explosion.

exportateur, trice [ɛkspɔrtatœr, -tris] a export cpd, exporting // nm exporter.

exportation [ɛkspɔrtɑsjɔ̃] nf exportation; export.

exporter [ɛkspɔrte] vt to export.

exposant [ɛkspozɑ̃] nm exhibitor.

exposé, e [ɛkspoze] nm talk // a: ~ **au sud** facing south; **bien** ~ well situated.

exposer [ɛkspoze] vt (*marchandise*) to display; (*peinture*) to exhibit, show; (*parler de*) to explain, set out; (*mettre en danger, orienter, PHOTO*) to expose; **exposition** nf (*manifestation*) exhibition; (*PHOTO*) exposure.

exprès [ɛksprɛ] ad (*délibérément*) on purpose; (*spécialement*) specially.

exprès, esse [ɛksprɛs] a (*ordre, défense*) express, formal // a inv, ad (*PTT*) express.

express [ɛksprɛs] a, nm: (**café**) ~ espresso (coffee); (**train**) ~ fast train.

expressément [ɛksprɛsemɑ̃] ad expressly; specifically.

expression [ɛksprɛsjɔ̃] nf expression.

exprimer [ɛksprime] vt (*sentiment, idée*) to express; (*jus, liquide*) to press out; s'~ vi (*personne*) to express o.s.

exproprier [ɛksprɔprije] vt to buy up by compulsory purchase, expropriate.

expulser [ɛkspylse] vt to expel; (*locataire*) to evict; (*SPORT*) to send off.

exquis, e [ɛkski, -iz] a exquisite; delightful.

exsangue [ɛksɑ̃g] a bloodless, drained of blood.

extase [ɛkstaz] nf ecstasy; **s'extasier sur** to go into raptures over.

extension [ɛkstɑ̃sjɔ̃] nf (*d'un muscle, ressort*) stretching; (*fig*) extension; expansion.

exténuer [ɛkstenɥe] vt to exhaust.

extérieur, e [ɛksterjœr] a (*porte, mur etc*) outer, outside; (*au dehors: escalier, w.-c.*) outside; (*commerce*) foreign; (*influences*) external; (*apparent: calme, gaieté etc*) surface cpd // nm (*d'une maison, d'un récipient etc*) outside, exterior; (*apparence*) exterior; (*d'un groupe social*): **l'**~ the outside world; **à l'**~ outside; (*à l'étranger*) abroad; ~**ement** ad on the outside; (*en apparence*) on the surface.

exterminer [ɛkstɛrmine] vt to exterminate, wipe out.

externat [ɛkstɛrna] nm day school.

externe [ɛkstɛrn] a external, outer // nm/f (*MÉD*) non-resident medical student (*Brit*), extern (*US*); (*SCOL*) day pupil.

extincteur [ɛkstɛ̃ktœr] nm (fire) extinguisher.

extinction [ɛkstɛ̃ksjɔ̃] nf: ~ **de voix** loss of voice.

extorquer [ɛkstɔrke] vt to extort.

extra [ɛkstra] a inv first-rate; top-quality // nm inv extra help.

extrader [ɛkstrade] vt to extradite.

extraire [ɛkstrɛr] vt to extract; **extrait** nm extract.

extraordinaire [ɛkstraɔrdinɛr] a extraordinary; (*POL: mesures etc*) special.

extravagant, e [ɛkstravagɑ̃, -ɑ̃t] a extravagant; wild.

extraverti, e [ɛkstraverti] a extrovert.

extrême [ɛkstrɛm] a, nm extreme; ~**ment** ad extremely; ~**-onction** nf last rites pl; **E**~**-Orient** nm Far East.

extrémité [ɛkstremite] nf end; (*situation*) straits pl, plight; (*geste désespéré*) extreme action; ~**s** nfpl (*pieds et mains*) extremities; **à la dernière** ~ on the point of death.

exutoire [ɛgzytwar] nm outlet, release.

F

F abr de **franc**.

fa [fa] nm inv (*MUS*) F; (*en chantant la gamme*) fa.

fable [fabl(ə)] nf fable.

fabricant [fabrikɑ̃] nm manufacturer.

fabrication [fabrikɑsjɔ̃] nf manufacture.

fabrique [fabrik] nf factory.

fabriquer [fabrike] vt to make; (*industriellement*) to manufacture; (*fig*): **qu'est-ce qu'il fabrique?** what is he doing?

fabulation [fabylɑsjɔ̃] nf fantasizing.

fac [fak] abr f (*fam: SCOL*) de **faculté**.

façade [fasad] nf front, façade.

face [fas] nf face; (*fig: aspect*) side // a: **le côté** ~ heads; **perdre la** ~ to lose face; **en** ~ **de** prép opposite; (*fig*) in front of; **de** ~ ad from the front; **face on**; ~ **à** prép facing; (*fig*) faced with, in the face of; **faire** ~ **à** to face; ~ **à** ~ ad facing each other // nm inv encounter.

facétieux, euse [fasesjø, -øz] a mischievous.

fâché, e [fɑʃe] a angry; (*désolé*) sorry.

fâcher [faʃe] *vt* to anger; **se ~** *vi* to get angry; **se ~ avec** (*se brouiller*) to fall out with.

fâcheux, euse [faʃø, -øz] *a* unfortunate, regrettable.

facile [fasil] *a* easy; (*accommodant*) easy-going; **~ment** *ad* easily; **facilité** *nf* easiness; (*disposition, don*) aptitude; **facilités** *nfpl* facilities; **facilités de paiement** easy terms; **faciliter** *vt* to make easier.

façon [fasɔ̃] *nf* (*manière*) way; (*d'une robe etc*) making-up; cut; **~s** *nfpl* (*péj*) fuss *sg*; **de quelle ~?** (in) what way?; **de ~ à/à ce que so as to/that; de toute ~** anyway, in any case.

façonner [fasɔne] *vt* (*fabriquer*) to manufacture; (*travailler: matière*) to shape, fashion; (*fig*) to mould, shape.

facteur, trice [faktœʀ, -tʀis] *nm/f* postman/woman (*Brit*), mailman/woman (*US*) // *nm* (*MATH, fig: élément*) factor; **~ d'orgues** organ builder; **~ de pianos** piano maker.

factice [faktis] *a* artificial.

faction [faksjɔ̃] *nf* faction; (*MIL*) guard *ou* sentry (duty); watch.

facture [faktyʀ] *nf* (*à payer: gén*) bill; (: *COMM*) invoice; (*d'un artisan, artiste*) technique, workmanship; **facturer** *vt* to invoice.

facultatif, ive [fakyltatif, -iv] *a* optional; (*arrêt de bus*) request *cpd*.

faculté [fakylte] *nf* (*intellectuelle, d'université*) faculty; (*pouvoir, possibilité*) power.

fade [fad] *a* insipid.

fagot [fago] *nm* bundle of sticks.

faible [fɛbl(ə)] *a* weak; (*voix, lumière, vent*) faint; (*rendement, intensité, revenu etc*) low // *nm* weak point; (*pour quelqu'un*) weakness, soft spot; **~ d'esprit** feeble-minded; **faiblesse** *nf* weakness; **faiblir** *vi* to weaken; (*lumière*) to dim; (*vent*) to drop.

faïence [fajɑ̃s] *nf* earthenware *q*; piece of earthenware.

faignant, e [fɛɲɑ̃, -ɑ̃t] *nm/f* = **fainéant, e**.

faille [faj] *vb voir* **falloir** // *nf* (*GÉO*) fault; (*fig*) flaw, weakness.

faillir [fajiʀ] *vi*: **j'ai failli tomber** I almost *ou* very nearly fell.

faillite [fajit] *nf* bankruptcy.

faim [fɛ̃] *nf* hunger; **avoir ~** to be hungry; **rester sur sa ~** (*aussi fig*) to be left wanting more.

fainéant, e [fɛneɑ̃, -ɑ̃t] *nm/f* idler, loafer.

faire [fɛʀ] ♦ *vt* **1** (*fabriquer, être l'auteur de*) to make; **~ du vin/une offre/un film** to make wine/an offer/a film; **~ du bruit** to make a noise

2 (*effectuer: travail, opération*) to do; **que faites-vous?** (*quel métier etc*) what

do you do?; (*quelle activité: au moment de la question*) what are you doing?; **~ la lessive** to do the washing

3 (*études*) to do; (*sport, musique*) to play; **~ du droit/du français** to do law/French; **~ du rugby/piano** to play rugby/the piano

4 (*simuler*): **~ le malade/l'ignorant** to act the invalid/the fool

5 (*transformer, avoir un effet sur*): **~ de qn un frustré/avocat** to make sb frustrated/a lawyer; **ça ne me fait rien** (*m'est égal*) I don't care *ou* mind; (*me laisse froid*) it has no effect on me; **ça ne fait rien** it doesn't matter; **~ que** (*impliquer*) to mean that

6 (*calculs, prix, mesures*): **2 et 2 font 4** 2 and 2 are *ou* make 4; **ça fait 10 m/15 F** it's 10 m/15 F; **je vous le fais 10 F** I'll let you have it for 10 F

7: **qu'a-t-il fait de sa valise?** what has he done with his case?

8: **ne ~ que**: **il ne fait que critiquer** (*sans cesse*) all he (ever) does is criticize; (*seulement*) he's only criticizing

9 (*dire*) to say; **'vraiment?' fit-il** 'really?' he said

10 (*maladie*) to have; **~ du diabète** to have diabetes *sg*

♦ *vi* **1** (*agir, s'y prendre*) to act, do; **il faut ~ vite** we (*ou* you *etc*) must act quickly; **comment a-t-il fait pour?** how did he manage to?; **faites comme chez vous** make yourself at home

2 (*paraître*) to look; **~ vieux/démodé** to look old/old-fashioned; **ça fait bien** it looks good

♦ *vb substitut* to do; **ne le casse pas comme je l'ai fait** don't break it as I did; **je peux le voir? - faites!** can I see it? - please do!

♦ *vb impersonnel* **1**: **il fait beau** *etc* the weather is fine *etc*; *voir* **jour, froid** *etc*

2 (*temps écoulé, durée*): **ça fait 2 ans qu'il est parti** it's 2 years since he left; **ça fait 2 ans qu'il y est** he's been there for 2 years

♦ *vb semi-auxiliaire*: **~ + infinitif 1** (*action directe*) to make; **~ tomber/bouger qch** to make sth fall/move; **~ démarrer un moteur/chauffer de l'eau** to start up an engine/heat some water; **cela fait dormir** it makes you sleep; **~ travailler les enfants** to make the children work *ou* get the children to work

2 (*indirectement, par un intermédiaire*): **~ réparer qch** to get *ou* have sth repaired; **~ punir les enfants** to have the children punished

se faire *vi* **1** (*vin, fromage*) to mature

2: **cela se fait beaucoup/ne se fait pas** it's done a lot/not done

3: **se ~ + nom ou pronom**: **se ~ une jupe** to make o.s. a skirt; **se ~ des amis** to make friends; **se ~ du souci** to worry;

il ne s'en fait pas he doesn't worry
4: se ~ + *adjectif* (*devenir*): se ~ vieux
to be getting old; (*délibérément*): se ~
beau to do o.s. up
5: se ~ à (*s'habituer*) to get used to; je
n'arrive pas à me ~ à la nourriture/au
climat I can't get used to the food/
climate
6: se ~ + *infinitif*: se ~ examiner la
vue/opérer to have one's eyes tested/have
an operation; se ~ couper les cheveux to
get one's hair cut; il va se ~ tuer/punir
he's going to get himself killed/get (himself) punished; il s'est fait aider he got
somebody to help him; il s'est fait aider
par Simon he got Simon to help him; se
~ faire un vêtement to get a garment
made for o.s.
7 (*impersonnel*): comment se fait-il/
faisait-il que? how is it/was it that?
faire-part [fɛʀpaʀ] *nm inv* announcement (*of birth, marriage etc*).
faisable [fəzabl(ə)] *a* feasible.
faisan, e [fəzɑ̃, -an] *nm/f* pheasant.
faisandé, e [fəzɑ̃de] *a* high (*bad*).
faisceau, x [fɛso] *nm* (*de lumière etc*)
beam; (*de branches etc*) bundle.
faisons *vb voir* **faire**.
fait [fɛ] *nm* (*événement*) event, occurrence; (*réalité, donnée*) fact; être le ~
de (*causé par*) to be the work of; être au
~ (de) to be informed (of); au ~ (*à propos*) by the way; en venir au ~ to get to
the point; de ~ a (*opposé à: de droit*) de
facto // *ad* in fact; du ~ de ceci/qu'il a
menti because of *ou* on account of this/
his having lied; de ce ~ for this reason;
en ~ in fact; en ~ de repas by way of a
meal; prendre ~ et cause pour qn to
support sb, side with sb; prendre qn sur
le ~ to catch sb in the act; ~ divers
news item; les ~s et gestes de qn sb's
actions *ou* doings.
fait, e [fɛ, fɛt] *a* (*mûr: fromage, melon*)
ripe; c'est en ~ de that's the end of.
faîte [fɛt] *nm* top; (*fig*) pinnacle, height.
faites *vb voir* **faire**.
fait-tout *nm inv*, **faitout** *nm* [fɛtu] stew-
pot.
falaise [falɛz] *nf* cliff.
fallacieux, euse [falasjø, -øz] *a* falla-
cious; deceptive; illusory.
falloir [falwaʀ] *vb impersonnel*: il va ~
100 F we'll *ou* I'll need 100 F; il doit ~
du temps that must take time; il me faudrait 100 F I would need 100 F; il vous
faut tourner à gauche après l'église you
have to turn left past the church; nous
avons ce qu'il (nous) faut we have what
we need; il faut qu'il parte/a fallu qu'il
parte (*obligation*) he has to *ou* must
leave/had to leave; il faut le faire it
had to be done // s'en ~: il s'en est
fallu de 100 F/5 minutes we (*ou* they)
were 100 F short/5 minutes late (*ou* ear-

ly); il s'en faut de beaucoup qu'il soit
is far from being; il s'en est fallu de peu
que cela n'arrive it very nearly happened; ou peu s'en faut or as good as.
falot, e [falo, -ɔt] *a* dreary, colourless.
falsifier [falsifje] *vt* to falsify; to doctor.
famé, e [fame] *a*: mal ~ disreputable, of
ill repute.
famélique [famelik] *a* half-starved.
fameux, euse [famø, -øz] *a* (*illustre*)
famous; (*bon: repas, plat etc*) first-rate,
first-class; (*valeur intensive*) real, downright.
familial, e, aux [familjal, -o] *a* family
cpd // *nf* (*AUTO*) estate car (*Brit*), station wagon (*US*).
familiarité [familjaʀite] *nf* informality;
familiarity; ~s *nfpl* familiarities.
familier, ère [familje, -ɛʀ] *a* (*connu,
impertinent*) familiar; (*dénotant une
certaine intimité*) informal, friendly;
(*LING*) informal, colloquial // *nm* regular (visitor).
famille [famij] *nf* family; il a de la ~ à
Paris he has relatives in Paris.
famine [famin] *nf* famine.
fanal, aux [fanal, -o] *nm* beacon; lantern.
fanatique [fanatik] *a* fanatical // *nm/f* fanatic; **fanatisme** *nm* fanaticism.
faner [fane]: se ~ *vi* to fade.
fanfare [fɑ̃faʀ] *nf* (*orchestre*) brass
band; (*musique*) fanfare.
fanfaron, ne [fɑ̃faʀɔ̃, -ɔn] *nm/f* braggart.
fange [fɑ̃ʒ] *nf* mire.
fanion [fanjɔ̃] *nm* pennant.
fantaisie [fɑ̃tezi] *nf* (*spontanéité*) fancy,
imagination; (*caprice*) whim; extravagance // *a*: bijou/pain (de) ~ costume
jewellery/fancy bread; **fantaisiste** *a*
(*péj*) unorthodox, eccentric // *nm/f* (*de
music-hall*) variety artist *ou* entertainer.
fantasme [fɑ̃tasm(ə)] *nm* fantasy.
fantasque [fɑ̃task(ə)] *a* whimsical, capricious; fantastic.
fantastique [fɑ̃tastik] *a* fantastic.
fantôme [fɑ̃tom] *nm* ghost, phantom.
faon [fɑ̃] *nm* fawn.
farce [faʀs(ə)] *nf* (*viande*) stuffing; (*blague*) practical joke; (*THÉÂTRE*) farce;
farcir *vt* (*viande*) to stuff.
fard [faʀ] *nm* make-up.
fardeau, x [faʀdo] *nm* burden.
farder [faʀde] *vt* to make up.
farfelu, e [faʀfəly] *a* hare-brained.
farine [faʀin] *nf* flour; **farineux, euse** *a*
(*sauce, pomme*) floury // *nmpl* (*aliments*) starchy foods.
farouche [faʀuʃ] *a* shy, timid; savage,
wild; fierce.
fart [faʀ(t)] *nm* (ski) wax.
fascicule [fasikyl] *nm* volume.
fasciner [fasine] *vt* to fascinate.
fascisme [faʃism(ə)] *nm* fascism.

fasse *etc vb voir* **faire.**

faste [fast(ə)] *nm* splendour // *a*: **c'est un jour ~** it's his (*ou* our) lucky day.

fastidieux, euse [fastidjø, -øz] *a* tedious, tiresome.

fastueux, euse [fastyø, -øz] *a* sumptuous, luxurious.

fat [fa] *am* conceited, smug.

fatal, e [fatal] *a* fatal; (*inévitable*) inevitable; **~ité** *nf* fate; fateful coincidence; inevitability.

fatidique [fatidik] *a* fateful.

fatigant, e [fatigɑ̃, -ɑ̃t] *a* tiring; (*agaçant*) tiresome.

fatigue [fatig] *nf* tiredness, fatigue.

fatigué, e [fatige] *a* tired.

fatiguer [fatige] *vt* to tire, make tired; (*TECH*) to put a strain on, strain; (*fig: importuner*) to wear out // *vi* (*moteur*) to labour, strain; **se ~** to get tired; to tire o.s. (out).

fatras [fatra] *nm* jumble, hotchpotch.

fatuité [fatɥite] *nf* conceitedness, smugness.

faubourg [fobur] *nm* suburb.

fauché, e [foʃe] *a* (*fam*) broke.

faucher [foʃe] *vt* (*herbe*) to cut; (*champs, blés*) to reap; (*fig*) to cut down; to mow down.

faucille [fosij] *nf* sickle.

faucon [fokɔ̃] *nm* falcon, hawk.

faudra *vb voir* **falloir.**

faufiler [fofile] *vt* to tack, baste; **se ~** *vi*: **se ~ dans** to edge one's way into; **se ~ parmi/entre** to thread one's way among/between.

faune [fon] *nf* (*ZOOL*) wildlife, fauna.

faussaire [fosɛr] *nm* forger.

fausse [fos] *a voir* **faux.**

faussement [fosmɑ̃] *ad* (*accuser*) wrongly, wrongfully; (*croire*) falsely.

fausser [fose] *vt* (*objet*) to bend, buckle; (*fig*) to distort.

fausseté [foste] *nf* wrongness; falseness.

faut *vb voir* **falloir.**

faute [fot] *nf* (*erreur*) mistake, error; (*péché, manquement*) misdemeanour; (*FOOTBALL etc*) offence; (*TENNIS*) fault; **c'est de sa/ma ~** it's his/my fault; **être en ~** to be in the wrong; **~ de** (*temps, argent*) for ou through lack of; **sans ~** *ad* without fail; **~ de frappe** typing error; **~ professionnelle** professional misconduct *q*.

fauteuil [fotœj] *nm* armchair; **~ d'orchestre** seat in the front stalls; **~ roulant** wheelchair.

fauteur [fotœr] *nm*: **~ de troubles** trouble-maker.

fautif, ive [fotif, -iv] *a* (*incorrect*) incorrect, inaccurate; (*responsable*) at fault, in the wrong; guilty.

fauve [fov] *nm* wildcat // *a* (*couleur*) fawn.

faux [fo] *nf* scythe.

faux, fausse [fo, fos] *a* (*inexact*) wrong; (*piano, voix*) out of tune; (*falsifié*) fake; forged; (*sournois, postiche*) false // *ad* (*MUS*) out of tune // *nm* (*copie*) fake, forgery; (*opposé au vrai*): **le ~** falsehood; **faire ~ bond à qn** to stand sb up; **~ frais** *nmpl* extras, incidental expenses; **~ pas** tripping *q*; (*fig*) faux pas; **~ témoignage** (*délit*) perjury; **fausse alerte** false alarm; **fausse couche** miscarriage; **~-filet** *nm* sirloin; **~-fuyant** *nm* equivocation; **~-monnayeur** *nm* counterfeiter, forger.

faveur [favœr] *nf* favour; **traitement de ~** preferential treatment; **à la ~ de** under cover of; **thanks to; en ~ de** in favour of.

favorable [favɔrabl(ə)] *a* favourable.

favori, te [favɔri, -it] *a, nm/f* favourite; **~s** *nmpl* (*barbe*) sideboards (*Brit*), sideburns.

favoriser [favɔrize] *vt* to favour.

fébrile [febril] *a* feverish, febrile.

fécond, e [fekɔ̃, -ɔ̃d] *a* fertile; **féconder** *vt* to fertilize; **fécondité** *nf* fertility.

fécule [fekyl] *nf* potato flour.

fédéral, e, aux [federal, -o] *a* federal.

fée [fe] *nf* fairy; **~rie** *nf* enchantment; **~rique** *a* magical, fairytale *cpd*.

feignant, e [fɛɲɑ̃, -ɑ̃t] *nm/f* = **fainéant, e.**

feindre [fɛ̃dr(ə)] *vt* to feign // *vi* to dissemble; **~ de faire** to pretend to do.

feinte [fɛ̃t] *nf* (*SPORT*) dummy.

fêler [fele] *vt* to crack.

félicitations [felisitasjɔ̃] *nfpl* congratulations.

féliciter [felisite] *vt*: **~ qn (de)** to congratulate sb (on); **se ~ (de)** to congratulate o.s. (on).

félin, e [felɛ̃, -in] *a* feline // *nm* (*big*) cat.

fêlure [felyr] *nf* crack.

femelle [fəmɛl] *a, nf* female.

féminin, e [feminɛ̃, -in] *a* feminine; (*sexe*) female; (*équipe, vêtements etc*) women's // *nm* feminine; **féministe** *a* feminist.

femme [fam] *nf* woman; (*épouse*) wife (*pl* wives); **~ de chambre, ~ de ménage** cleaning lady.

fémur [femyr] *nm* femur, thighbone.

fendre [fɑ̃dr(ə)] *vt* (*couper en deux*) to split; (*fissurer*) to crack; (*fig: traverser*) to cut through; to cleave through; **se ~** *vi* to crack.

fenêtre [fənɛtr(ə)] *nf* window.

fenouil [fənuj] *nm* fennel.

fente [fɑ̃t] *nf* (*fissure*) crack; (*de boîte à lettres etc*) slit.

féodal, e, aux [feɔdal, -o] *a* feudal.

fer [fɛr] *nm* iron; (*de cheval*) shoe; **~ à cheval** horseshoe; **~ forgé** wrought iron; **~ (à repasser)** iron.

ferai *etc vb voir* **faire**.
fer-blanc [fɛʀblɑ̃] *nm* tin(plate).
férié, e [feʀje] *a*: jour ~ public holiday.
ferions *etc vb voir* **faire**.
férir [feʀiʀ]: sans coup ~ *ad* without meeting any opposition.
ferme [fɛʀm(ə)] *a* firm // *ad (travailler etc)* hard // *nf (exploitation)* farm; *(maison)* farmhouse.
fermé, e [fɛʀme] *a* closed, shut; *(gaz, eau etc)* off; *(fig: personne)* uncommunicative; *(: milieu)* exclusive.
fermenter [fɛʀmɑ̃te] *vi* to ferment.
fermer [fɛʀme] *vt* to close, shut; *(cesser l'exploitation de)* to close down, shut down; *(eau, lumière, électricité, robinet)* to put off, turn off; *(aéroport, route)* to close // *vi* to close, shut; to close down, shut down; se ~ *vi (yeux)* to close, shut; *(fleur, blessure)* to close up.
fermeté [fɛʀməte] *nf* firmness.
fermeture [fɛʀmətyʀ] *nf* closing; shutting; closing *ou* shutting down; putting *ou* turning off; *(dispositif)* catch; fastening, fastener; ~ éclair ® *ou* à glissière zip (fastener) *(Brit)*, zipper *(US)*.
fermier, ière [fɛʀmje, -jɛʀ] *nm* farmer // *nf* woman farmer; farmer's wife.
fermoir [fɛʀmwaʀ] *nm* clasp.
féroce [feʀɔs] *a* ferocious, fierce.
ferons *vb voir* **faire**.
ferraille [fɛʀɑj] *nf* scrap iron; mettre à la ~ to scrap.
ferré, e [feʀe] *a* hobnailed; steel-tipped; *(fam)*: ~ en well up on, hot at.
ferrer [feʀe] *vt (cheval)* to shoe.
ferronnerie [fɛʀɔnʀi] *nf* ironwork.
ferroviaire [feʀɔvjɛʀ] *a* rail(way) *cpd (Brit)*, rail(road) *cpd (US)*.
ferry(-boat) [feʀe(bot)] *nm* ferry.
fertile [fɛʀtil] *a* fertile; ~ en incidents eventful, packed with incidents.
féru, e [feʀy] *a*: ~ de with a keen interest in.
férule [feʀyl] *nf*: être sous la ~ de qn to be under sb's (iron) rule.
fervent, e [fɛʀvɑ̃, -ɑ̃t] *a* fervent.
fesse [fɛs] *nf* buttock; **fessée** *nf* spanking.
festin [fɛstɛ̃] *nm* feast.
festival [fɛstival] *nm* festival.
festoyer [fɛstwaje] *vi* to feast.
fêtard [fetaʀ] *nm (péj)* high liver, merry-maker.
fête [fɛt] *nf (religieuse)* feast; *(publique)* holiday; *(en famille etc)* celebration; *(kermesse)* fête, fair, festival; *(du nom)* feast day, name day; faire la ~ to live it up; faire ~ à qn to give sb a warm welcome; les ~s (de fin d'année) the festive season; la salle/le comité des ~s the village hall/festival committee; ~ foraine (fun) fair; la F~ Nationale the national holiday; **fêter** *vt* to celebrate; *(personne)* to have a celebration for.

fétu [fety] *nm*: ~ de paille wisp of straw.
feu [fø] *a inv*: ~ son père his late father.
feu, x [fø] *nm (gén)* fire; *(signal lumineux)* light; *(de cuisinière)* ring; *(sensation de brûlure)* burning *(sensation)*; ~x *nmpl (éclat, lumière)* fire *sg*; *(AUTO)* (traffic) lights; au ~! *(incendie)* fire!; à ~ doux/vif over a slow/brisk heat; à petit ~ *(CULIN)* over a gentle heat; *(fig)* slowly; faire ~ to fire; prendre ~ to catch fire; mettre le ~ à to set fire to; faire du ~ to make a fire; avez-vous du ~? *(pour cigarette)* have you (got) a light?; ~ rouge/vert/orange red/green/amber *(Brit)* ou yellow *(US)* light; ~ arrière rear light; ~ d'artifice firework; *(spectacle)* fireworks *pl*; ~ de joie bonfire; ~x de brouillard fog-lamps; ~x de croisement dipped *(Brit)* ou dimmed *(US)* headlights; ~x de position sidelights; ~x de route headlights.
feuillage [fœjaʒ] *nm* foliage, leaves *pl*.
feuille [fœj] *nf (d'arbre)* leaf *(pl leaves)*; *(de papier)* sheet; ~ d'impôts tax form; ~ de maladie medical expenses claim form; ~ de paie pay slip; ~ de vigne *(BOT)* vine leaf; *(sur statue)* fig leaf; ~ volante loose sheet.
feuillet [fœjɛ] *nm* leaf *(pl leaves)*.
feuilleté, e [fœjte] *a (CULIN)* flaky; *(verre)* laminated.
feuilleter [fœjte] *vt (livre)* to leaf through.
feuilleton [fœjtɔ̃] *nm* serial.
feuillu, e [fœjy] *a* leafy // *nm* broad-leaved tree.
feutre [føtʀ(ə)] *nm* felt; *(chapeau)* felt hat; *(aussi: stylo-~)* felt-tip pen; **feutré, e** *a* feltlike; *(pas, voix)* muffled.
fève [fɛv] *nf* broad bean.
février [fevʀije] *nm* February.
fi [fi] *excl*: faire ~ de to snap one's fingers at.
fiable [fjabl(ə)] *a* reliable.
fiacre [fjakʀ(ə)] *nm* (hackney) cab *ou* carriage.
fiançailles [fjɑ̃sɑj] *nfpl* engagement *sg*.
fiancé, e [fjɑ̃se] *nm/f* fiancé/fiancée // *a*: être ~ (à) to be engaged (to).
fiancer [fjɑ̃se]: se ~ *vi* to become engaged.
fibre [fibʀ(ə)] *nf* fibre; ~ de verre fibreglass, glass fibre.
ficeler [fisle] *vt* to tie up.
ficelle [fisɛl] *nf* string *q*; piece *ou* length of string.
fiche [fiʃ] *nf (pour fichier)* (index) card; *(formulaire)* form; *(ÉLEC)* plug.
ficher [fiʃe] *vt (dans un fichier)* to file; *(POLICE)* to put on file; *(planter)* to stick, drive; *(fam)* to do; to give; to stick *ou* shove; fiche(-moi) le camp *(fam)* clear off; fiche-moi la paix *(fam)* leave me alone; se ~ de *(fam)* to make fun of; not to care about.

fichier [fiʃje] *nm* file; card index.

fichu, e [fiʃy] *pp de* **ficher** (*fam*) // *a* (*fam*: *fini, inutilisable*) bust, done for; (: *intensif*) wretched, darned // *nm* (*foulard*) (head)scarf (*pl* scarves); **mal ~** (*fam*) feeling lousy; useless.

fictif, ive [fiktif, -iv] *a* fictitious.

fiction [fiksjɔ̃] *nf* fiction; (*fait imaginé*) invention.

fidèle [fidɛl] *a* faithful // *nm/f* (REL): **les ~s** the faithful; (*à l'église*) the congregation.

fief [fjɛf] *nm* fief; (*fig*) preserve; stronghold.

fier [fje]: **se ~ à** *vt* to trust.

fier, fière [fjɛʀ] *a* proud; **~té** *nf* pride.

fièvre [fjɛvʀ(ə)] *nf* fever; **avoir de la ~/ 39 de ~** to have a high temperature/a temperature of 39°C; **fiévreux, euse** *a* feverish.

fifre [fifʀ(ə)] *nm* fife; fife-player.

figer [fiʒe] *vt* to congeal; (*fig: personne*) to freeze, root to the spot; **se ~** *vi* to congeal; to freeze; (*institutions etc*) to become set, stop evolving.

figue [fig] *nf* fig; **figuier** *nm* fig tree.

figurant, e [figyʀɑ̃, -ɑ̃t] *nm/f* (THÉÂTRE) walk-on; (CINÉMA) extra.

figure [figyʀ] *nf* (*visage*) face; (*image, tracé, forme, personnage*) figure; (*illustration*) picture, diagram; **faire ~ de** to look like.

figuré, e [figyʀe] *a* (*sens*) figurative.

figurer [figyʀe] *vi* to appear // *vt* to represent; **se ~ que** to imagine that.

fil [fil] *nm* (*brin, fig: d'une histoire*) thread; (*du téléphone*) cable, wire; (*textile de lin*) linen; (*d'un couteau*) edge; **au ~ des années** with the passing of the years; **au ~ de l'eau** with the stream *ou* current; **coup de ~** phone call; **~ à coudre** (sewing) thread; **~ électrique** electric wire; **~ de fer** wire; **~ de fer barbelé** barbed wire; **~ à pêche** fishing line; **~ à plomb** plumbline.

filament [filamɑ̃] *nm* (ÉLEC) filament; (*de liquide*) trickle, thread.

filandreux, euse [filɑ̃dʀø, -øz] *a* stringy.

filasse [filas] *a inv* white blond.

filature [filatyʀ] *nf* (*fabrique*) mill; (*policière*) shadowing *q*, tailing *q*.

file [fil] *nf* line; (AUTO) lane; **~ (d'attente)** queue (Brit), line (US); **en ~ indienne** in single file; **à la ~** *ad* (*d'affilée*) in succession.

filer [file] *vt* (*tissu, toile*) to spin; (*prendre en filature*) to shadow, tail; (*fam: donner*): **~ qch à qn** to slip sb sth // *vi* (*bas, liquide, pâte*) to run; (*aller vite*) to fly past; (*fam: partir*) to make off; **~ doux** to toe the line.

filet [filɛ] *nm* net; (CULIN) fillet; (*d'eau, de sang*) trickle; **~ (à provisions)** string bag.

filiale [filjal] *nf* (COMM) subsidiary.

filière [filjɛʀ] *nf*: **passer par la ~** to go through the (administrative) channels; **suivre la ~** (*dans sa carrière*) to work one's way up (through the hierarchy).

filiforme [filifɔʀm(ə)] *a* spindly; threadlike.

filigrane [filigʀan] *nm* (*d'un billet, timbre*) watermark; **en ~** (*fig*) showing just beneath the surface.

fille [fij] *nf* girl; (*opposé à fils*) daughter; **vieille ~** old maid; **~-mère** *nf* (*péj*) unmarried mother; **fillette** *nf* (little) girl.

filleul, e [fijœl] *nm/f* godchild, godson/daughter.

film [film] *nm* (*pour photo*) (roll of) film; (*œuvre*) film, picture, movie; (*couche*) film; **~ muet/parlant** silent/talking picture *ou* movie; **~ d'animation** animated film; **~ policier** thriller.

filon [filɔ̃] *nm* vein, lode; (*fig*) lucrative line, money spinner.

fils [fis] *nm* son; **~ de famille** moneyed young man; **~ à papa** daddy's boy.

filtre [filtʀ(ə)] *nm* filter; **~ à air** (AUTO) air filter; **filtrer** *vt* to filter; (*fig: candidats, visiteurs*) to screen // *vi* to filter (through).

fin [fɛ̃] *nf* end; **~s** *nfpl* (*but*) ends; **prendre ~** to come to an end; **mettre ~ à** to put an end to; **à la ~** in the end, eventually; **sans ~** a endless // *ad* endlessly.

fin, e [fɛ̃, fin] *a* (*papier, couche, fil*) thin; (*cheveux, poudre, pointe, visage*) fine; (*taille*) neat, slim; (*esprit, remarque*) subtle; shrewd // *ad* (*moudre, couper*) finely // *nf* (*alcool*) liqueur brandy; **~ prêt** quite ready; **un ~ tireur** a crack shot; **avoir la vue/l'ouïe ~e** to have sharp *ou* keen eyes/ears; **vin ~** fine wine; **~ gourmet** gourmet; **une ~ mouche** (*fig*) a sharp customer; **~es herbes** mixed herbs.

final, e [final] *a, nf* final // *nm* (MUS) finale; **quarts de ~e** quarter finals; **8èmes/16èmes de ~e** 2nd/1st round (*in 5 round knock-out competition*); **~ement** *ad* finally, in the end; (*après tout*) after all.

finance [finɑ̃s] *nf* finance; **~s** *nfpl* (*situation*) finances; (*activités*) finance *sg*; **moyennant ~** for a fee; **financer** *vt* to finance; **financier, ière** *a* financial.

finaud, e [fino, -od] *a* wily.

finesse [fines] *nf* thinness; fineness; neatness; slimness; subtlety; shrewdness.

fini, e [fini] *a* finished; (MATH) finite; (*intensif*): **un menteur ~** a liar through and through // *nm* (*d'un objet manufacturé*) finish.

finir [finiʀ] *vt* to finish // *vi* to finish, end; **~ quelque part/par faire** to end *ou* finish up somewhere/doing; ~ **de faire** to finish doing; (*cesser*) to stop doing; **il finit par m'agacer** he's beginning to get on my nerves; ~ **en pointe/tragédie** to end in a point/in tragedy; **en** ~ **avec** to be *ou* have done with; **il va mal** ~ he will come to a bad end.

finition [finisjɔ̃] *nf* finishing; finish.

finlandais, e [fɛ̃lɑ̃dɛ, -ɛz] *a* Finnish // *nm/f*: F~, e Finn.

Finlande [fɛ̃lɑ̃d] *nf*: **la** ~ Finland.

fiole [fjɔl] *nf* phial.

fioriture [fjɔrityʀ] *nf* embellishment, flourish.

firme [firm(ə)] *nf* firm.

fis *vb voir* **faire**.

fisc [fisk] *nm* tax authorities *pl*; ~**al, e, aux** *a* tax *cpd*, fiscal; ~**alité** *nf* tax system; (*charges*) taxation.

fissure [fisyʀ] *nf* crack.

fissurer [fisyʀe] *vt*, **se** ~ *vi* to crack.

fiston [fistɔ̃] *nm* (*fam*) son, lad.

fit *vb voir* **faire**.

fixation [fiksasjɔ̃] *nf* fixing; fastening; setting; (*de ski*) binding; (*PSYCH*) fixation.

fixe [fiks(ə)] *a* fixed; (*emploi*) steady, regular // *nm* (*salaire*) basic salary; **à heure** ~ at a set time; **menu à prix** ~ set menu.

fixé, e [fikse] *a*: **être** ~ (**sur**) (*savoir à quoi s'en tenir*) to have made up one's mind (about); **to know for certain** (about).

fixer [fikse] *vt* (*attacher*): ~ **qch (à/sur)** to fix *ou* fasten sth (to/onto); (*déterminer*) to fix, set; (*CHIMIE, PHOTO*) to fix; (*regarder*) to stare at; **se** ~ *vi* (*s'établir*) to settle down; **se** ~ **sur** (*suj: attention*) to focus on.

flacon [flakɔ̃] *nm* bottle.

flageller [flaʒele] *vt* to flog, scourge.

flageoler [flaʒɔle] *vi* (*jambes*) to sag.

flageolet [flaʒɔle] *nm* (*MUS*) flageolet; (*CULIN*) dwarf kidney bean.

flagrant, e [flagʀɑ̃, -ɑ̃t] *a* flagrant, blatant; **en** ~ **délit** in the act.

flair [flɛʀ] *nm* sense of smell; (*fig*) intuition; **flairer** *vt* (*humer*) to sniff (at); (*détecter*) to scent.

flamand, e [flamɑ̃, -ɑ̃d] *a, nm* (*LING*) Flemish // *nm/f*: F~, e Fleming; **les** F~**s** the Flemish.

flamant [flamɑ̃] *nm* flamingo.

flambant [flɑ̃bɑ̃] *ad*: ~ **neuf** brand new.

flambé, e [flɑ̃be] *a* (*CULIN*) flambé // *nf* blaze; (*fig*) flaring-up, explosion.

flambeau, x [flɑ̃bo] *nm* (flaming) torch.

flamber [flɑ̃be] *vi* to blaze (up).

flamboyer [flɑ̃bwaje] *vi* to blaze (up); to flame.

flamme [flam] *nf* flame; (*fig*) fire, fervour; **en** ~**s** on fire, ablaze.

flan [flɑ̃] *nm* (*CULIN*) custard tart *ou* pie.

flanc [flɑ̃] *nm* side; (*MIL*) flank; **prêter le** ~ **à** (*fig*) to lay o.s. open to.

flancher [flɑ̃ʃe] *vi* to fail, pack up; to quit.

flanelle [flanɛl] *nf* flannel.

flâner [flane] *vi* to stroll; **flânerie** *nf* stroll.

flanquer [flɑ̃ke] *vt* to flank; (*fam: mettre*) to chuck, shove; (*: jeter*): ~ **par terre/à la porte** to fling to the ground/chuck out.

flaque [flak] *nf* (*d'eau*) puddle; (*d'huile, de sang etc*) pool.

flash, *pl* flashes [flaʃ] *nm* (*PHOTO*) flash; ~ (**d'information**) newsflash.

flasque [flask(ə)] *a* flabby.

flatter [flate] *vt* to flatter; **se** ~ **de qch** to pride o.s. on sth; **flatterie** *nf* flattery *q*; **flatteur, euse** *a* flattering // *nm/f* flatterer.

fléau, x [fleo] *nm* scourge.

flèche [flɛʃ] *nf* arrow; (*de clocher*) spire; (*de grue*) jib; **monter en** ~ (*fig*) to soar, rocket; **partir en** ~ to be off like a shot; **fléchette** *nf* dart; **fléchettes** *nfpl* (*jeu*) darts *sg*.

fléchir [fleʃiʀ] *vt* (*corps, genou*) to bend; (*fig*) to sway, weaken // *vi* (*poutre*) to sag, bend; (*fig*) to weaken, flag; to yield.

flemmard, e [flemaʀ, -aʀd(ə)] *nm/f* lazybones *sg*, loafer.

flétrir [fletʀiʀ] *vt*, **se** ~ *vi* to wither.

fleur [flœʀ] *nf* flower; (*d'un arbre*) blossom; **en** ~ (*arbre*) in blossom; **à** ~ **de terre** just above the ground.

fleurer [flœʀe] *vt*: ~ **la lavande** to have the scent of lavender.

fleuri, e [flœʀi] *a* in flower *ou* bloom; surrounded by flowers; (*fig*) flowery; florid.

fleurir [flœʀiʀ] *vi* (*rose*) to flower; (*arbre*) to blossom; (*fig*) to flourish // *vt* (*tombe*) to put flowers on; (*chambre*) to decorate with flowers.

fleuriste [flœʀist(ə)] *nm/f* florist.

fleuron [flœʀɔ̃] *nm* jewel (*fig*).

fleuve [flœv] *nm* river.

flexible [flɛksibl(ə)] *a* flexible.

flexion [flɛksjɔ̃] *nf* flexing, bending.

flic [flik] *nm* (*fam: péj*) cop.

flipper [flipœʀ] *nm* pinball (machine).

flirter [flœʀte] *vi* to flirt.

flocon [flɔkɔ̃] *nm* flake.

floraison [flɔʀɛzɔ̃] *nf* flowering; blossoming; flourishing.

flore [flɔʀ] *nf* flora.

florissant, e [flɔʀisɑ̃, -ɑ̃t] *vb voir* **fleurir**.

flot [flo] *nm* flood, stream; ~**s** *nmpl* (*de la mer*) waves; **être à** ~ (*NAVIG*) to be afloat; (*fig*) to be on an even keel; **entrer à** ~**s** to stream *ou* pour in.

flotte [flɔt] *nf* (*NAVIG*) fleet; (*fam*) water; rain.

flottement [flɔtmɑ̃] *nm* (*fig*) wavering, hesitation.

flotter [flɔte] *vi* to float; (*nuage, odeur*) to drift; (*drapeau*) to fly; (*vêtements*) to hang loose; (*monnaie*) to float // *vt* to float; **faire ~** to float; **flotteur** *nm* float.

flou, e [flu] *a* fuzzy, blurred; (*fig*) woolly, vague.

flouer [flue] *vt* to swindle.

fluctuation [flyktɥasjɔ̃] *nf* fluctuation.

fluet, te [flɥɛ, -ɛt] *a* thin, slight.

fluide [flɥid] *a* fluid; (*circulation etc*) flowing freely // *nm* fluid; (*force*) (mysterious) power.

fluor [flyɔr] *nm* fluorine.

fluorescent, e [flyɔresɑ̃, -ɑ̃t] *a* fluorescent.

flûte [flyt] *nf* flute; (*verre*) flute glass; (*pain*) long loaf (*pl* loaves); **~!** drat it!; **~ à bec** recorder.

flux [fly] *nm* incoming tide; (*écoulement*) flow; **le ~ et le reflux** the ebb and flow.

FM *sigle f* (= *fréquence modulée*) FM.

foc [fɔk] *nm* jib.

foi [fwa] *nf* faith; **sous la ~ du serment** under *ou* on oath; **ajouter ~ à** to lend credence to; **digne de ~** reliable; **sur la ~ de** on the word *ou* strength of; **être de bonne/mauvaise ~** to be sincere/ insincere; **ma ~...** well....

foie [fwa] *nm* liver.

foin [fwɛ̃] *nm* hay; **faire du ~** (*fig: fam*) to kick up a row.

foire [fwar] *nf* fair; (*fête foraine*) (fun) fair; **faire la ~** (*fig: fam*) to whoop it up; **~ (exposition)** trade fair.

fois [fwa] *nf* time; **une/deux ~** once/ twice; **2 ~ 2 2 times 2; quatre ~ plus grand (que)** four times as big (as); **une ~ (passé)** once; (*futur*) sometime; **une ~ pour toutes** once and for all; **une ~ que** once; **des ~ (parfois)** sometimes; **à la ~ (ensemble)** at once.

foison [fwazɔ̃] *nf*: **une ~ de** an abundance of; **à ~** *ad* in plenty.

foisonner [fwazɔne] *vi* to abound.

fol [fɔl] *a voir* **fou.**

folâtrer [fɔlatre] *vi* to frolic (about).

folie [fɔli] *nf* (*d'une décision, d'un acte*) madness, folly; (*état*) madness, insanity; (*acte*) folly; **la ~ des grandeurs** delusions of grandeur; **faire des ~s** (*en dépenses*) to be extravagant.

folklorique [fɔlklɔrik] *a* folk *cpd*; (*fam*) weird.

folle [fɔl] *a, nf voir* **fou; ~ment** *ad* (*très*) madly, wildly.

foncé, e [fɔ̃se] *a* dark.

foncer [fɔ̃se] *vi* to go darker; (*fam: aller vite*) to tear *ou* belt along; **~ sur** to charge at.

foncier, ère [fɔ̃sje, -ɛr] *a* (*honnêteté etc*) basic, fundamental; (*malhonnêteté etc*) deep-rooted; (*COMM*) real estate *cpd*.

fonction [fɔ̃ksjɔ̃] *nf* (*rôle,* MATH, LING) function; (*emploi, poste*) post, position; **~s** (*professionnelles*) duties; **entrer en ~s** to take up one's post *ou* duties; to take up office; **voiture de ~** company car; **être ~ de** (*dépendre de*) to depend on; **en ~ de** (*par rapport à*) according to; **faire ~ de** to serve as; **la ~ publique** (*Brit*) service.

fonctionnaire [fɔ̃ksjɔnɛr] *nm/f* state employee, local authority employee; (*dans l'administration*) ≈ civil servant.

fonctionner [fɔ̃ksjɔne] *vi* to work, function; (*entreprise*) to operate, function.

fond [fɔ̃] *nm voir aussi* **fonds;** (*d'un récipient, trou*) bottom; (*d'une salle, scène*) back; (*d'un tableau, décor*) background; (*opposé à la forme*) content; (*SPORT*): **le ~** long distance (running); **sans ~** bottomless; **au ~ de** at the bottom of; at the back of; **à ~** *ad* (*connaître, soutenir*) thoroughly; (*appuyer, visser*) right down *ou* home; **à ~ (de train)** *ad* (*fam*) full tilt; **dans le ~, au ~** *ad* (*en somme*) basically, really; **de ~ en comble** *ad* from top to bottom; **~ sonore** background noise; background music; **~ de teint** (make-up) foundation.

fondamental, e, aux [fɔ̃damɑ̃tal, -o] *a* fundamental.

fondant, e [fɔ̃dɑ̃, -ɑ̃t] *a* (*neige*) melting; (*poire*) that melts in the mouth.

fondateur, trice [fɔ̃datœr, -tris] *nm/f* founder.

fondation [fɔ̃dɑsjɔ̃] *nf* founding; (*établissement*) foundation; **~s** *nfpl* (*d'une maison*) foundations.

fondé, e [fɔ̃de] *a* (*accusation etc*) well-founded; **être ~ à** to have grounds for *ou* good reason to // *nm*: **~ de pouvoir** authorized representative.

fondement [fɔ̃dmɑ̃] *nm* (*derrière*) behind; **~s** *nmpl* foundations; **sans ~** *a* (*rumeur etc*) groundless, unfounded.

fonder [fɔ̃de] *vt* to found; (*fig*) to base; **se ~ sur** (*suj: personne*) to base o.s. on.

fonderie [fɔ̃dri] *nf* smelting works *sg*.

fondre [fɔ̃dr(ə)] *vt* (*aussi:* **faire ~**) to melt; (*dans l'eau*) to dissolve; (*fig: mélanger*) to merge, blend // *vi* to melt; to dissolve; (*fig*) to melt away; (*se précipiter*): **~ sur** to swoop down on; **~ en larmes** to burst into tears.

fonds [fɔ̃] *nm* (*de bibliothèque*) collection; (*COMM*): **~ (de commerce)** business // *nmpl* (*argent*) funds; **à ~ perdus** *ad* with little or no hope of getting the money back.

fondu, e [fɔ̃dy] *a* (*beurre, neige*) melted; (*métal*) molten // *nf* (*CULIN*) fondue.

font *vb voir* **faire.**

fontaine [fɔ̃tɛn] *nf* fountain; (*source*) spring.

fonte [fɔ̃t] *nf* melting; (*métal*) cast iron; **la ~ des neiges** the (spring) thaw.

fonts baptismaux [fɔbatismo] *nmpl* (baptismal) font *sg*.

foot [fut] *nm (fam)* football.

football [futbol] *nm* football, soccer; **~eur** *nm* footballer.

footing [futiaj] *nm* jogging; **faire du ~** to go jogging.

for [fɔʀ] *nm*: **dans son ~ intérieur** in one's heart of hearts.

forain, e [fɔʀɛ̃, -ɛn] *a* fairground *cpd* // *nm* stallholder; fairground entertainer.

forçat [fɔʀsa] *nm* convict.

force [fɔʀs(ə)] *nf* strength; *(puissance: surnaturelle etc)* power; (PHYSIQUE, MÉCANIQUE) force; **~s** *nfpl (physiques)* strength *sg*; (MIL) forces; **à ~ d'insister** by dint of insisting; **as he (ou I etc) kept on insisting; de ~** *ad* forcibly, by force; **être de ~ à faire** to be up to doing; **de première ~** first class; **~ d'âme** fortitude; **les ~s de l'ordre** the police.

forcé, e [fɔʀse] *a* forced; unintended; inevitable.

forcément [fɔʀsemɑ̃] *ad* necessarily; inevitably; *(bien sûr)* of course.

forcené, e [fɔʀsəne] *nm/f* maniac.

forcer [fɔʀse] *vt (porte, serrure, plante)* to force; *(moteur, voix)* to strain // *vi* (SPORT) to overtax o.s.; **~ la dose/ l'allure** to overdo it/increase the pace; **se ~ (pour faire)** to force o.s. (to do).

forcir [fɔʀsiʀ] *vi (grossir)* to broaden out; *(vent)* to freshen.

forer [fɔʀe] *vt* to drill, bore.

forestier, ère [fɔʀɛstje, -ɛʀ] *a* forest *cpd*.

forêt [fɔʀɛ] *nf* forest.

foreuse [fɔʀøz] *nf* (electric) drill.

forfait [fɔʀfɛ] *nm* (COMM) fixed *ou* set price; all-in deal *ou* price; *(crime)* infamy; **déclarer ~** to withdraw; **travailler à ~** to work for a lump sum; **forfaitaire** *a* inclusive; set.

forfanterie [fɔʀfɑ̃tʀi] *nf* boastfulness *q*.

forge [fɔʀʒ(ə)] *nf* forge, smithy.

forger [fɔʀʒe] *vt* to forge; *(fig: personnalité)* to form; (: *prétexte)* to contrive, make up.

forgeron [fɔʀʒəʀɔ̃] *nm* (black)smith.

formaliser [fɔʀmalize]: **se ~** *vi*: **se ~ (de)** to take offence (at).

format [fɔʀma] *nm* size.

formater [fɔʀmate] *vt (disque)* to format.

formation [fɔʀmasjɔ̃] *nf* forming; training; (MUS) group; (MIL, AVIAT, GÉO) formation; **~ permanente** continuing education; **~ professionnelle** vocational training.

forme [fɔʀm(ə)] *nf (gén)* form; *(d'un objet)* shape, form; **~s** *nfpl (bonnes manières)* proprieties; *(d'une femme)* figure *sg*; **en ~ de poire** pear-shaped; **être en ~** (SPORT *etc)* to be on form; **en**

bonne et due ~ in due form.

formel, le [fɔʀmɛl] *a (preuve, décision)* definite, positive; *(logique)* formal; **~lement** *ad (absolument)* positively.

former [fɔʀme] *vt* to form; *(éduquer)* to train; **se ~** *vi* to form.

formidable [fɔʀmidabl(ə)] *a* tremendous.

formulaire [fɔʀmylɛʀ] *nm* form.

formule [fɔʀmyl] *nf (gén)* formula; *(formulaire)* form; **~ de politesse** polite phrase; letter ending.

formuler [fɔʀmyle] *vt (émettre: réponse, vœux)* to formulate; *(expliciter: sa pensée)* to express.

fort, e [fɔʀ, fɔʀt(ə)] *a* strong; *(intensité, rendement)* high, great; *(corpulent)* stout; *(doué)* good, able // *ad (serrer, frapper)* hard; *(sonner)* loud(ly); *(beaucoup)* greatly, very much; *(très)* very // *nm (édifice)* fort; *(point fort)* strong point, forte; **se faire ~ de ...** to claim one can ...; **au plus ~ de** *(au milieu de)* in the thick of; at the height of; **~e tête** rebel.

fortifiant [fɔʀtifjɑ̃] *nm* tonic.

fortifier [fɔʀtifje] *vt* to strengthen, fortify; (MIL) to fortify.

fortiori [fɔʀtjɔʀi]: **à ~** *ad* all the more so.

fortuit, e [fɔʀtɥi, -it] *a* fortuitous, chance *cpd*.

fortune [fɔʀtyn] *nf* fortune; **faire ~** to make one's fortune; **de ~** *a* makeshift; chance *cpd*.

fortuné, e [fɔʀtyne] *a* wealthy.

fosse [fos] *nf (grand trou)* pit; *(tombe)* grave; **~ (d'orchestre)** (orchestra) pit *pl*; **~ septique** septic tank.

fossé [fose] *nm* ditch; *(fig)* gulf, gap.

fossette [fosɛt] *nf* dimple.

fossile [fosil] *nm* fossil.

fossoyeur [foswajœʀ] *nm* gravedigger.

fou(fol), folle [fu, fɔl] *a* mad; *(déréglé etc)* wild, erratic; *(fam: extrême, très grand)* terrific, tremendous // *nm/f* madman/woman // *nm (du roi)* jester; **être ~ de** to be mad *ou* crazy about; **faire le ~** to act the fool; **avoir le ~ rire** to have the giggles.

foudre [fudʀ(ə)] *nf*: **la ~** lightning; **~s** *nfpl (colère)* wrath *sg*.

foudroyant, e [fudʀwajɑ̃, -ɑ̃t] *a* lightning *cpd*, stunning; *(maladie, poison)* violent.

foudroyer [fudʀwaje] *vt* to strike down; **être foudroyé(e)** to be struck by lightning; **~ qn du regard** to glare at sb.

fouet [fwɛ] *nm* whip; (CULIN) whisk; **de plein ~** *ad (se heurter)* head on; **~ter** *vt* to whip; to whisk.

fougère [fuʒɛʀ] *nf* fern.

fougue [fug] *nf* ardour, spirit.

fouille [fuj] *nf* search; **~s** *nfpl (archéologiques)* excavations.

fouiller [fuje] *vt* to search; (*creuser*) to dig // *vi* to rummage.

fouillis [fuji] *nm* jumble, muddle.

fouiner [fwine] *vi* (*péj*): ~ **dans** to nose around *ou* about in.

foulard [fular] *nm* scarf (*pl* scarves).

foule [ful] *nf* crowd; **la** ~ crowds *pl*; **les** ~**s** the masses; **une** ~ **de** masses of.

foulée [fule] *nf* stride.

fouler [fule] *vt* to press; (*sol*) to tread upon; **se** ~ *vi* (*fam*) to overexert o.s.; **se** ~ **la cheville** to sprain one's ankle; ~ **aux pieds** to trample underfoot.

foulure [fulyr] *nf* sprain.

four [fur] *nm* oven; (*de potier*) kiln; (*THÉÂTRE: échec*) flop.

fourbe [furb(ə)] *a* deceitful.

fourbu, e [furby] *a* exhausted.

fourche [furʃ(ə)] *nf* pitchfork; (*de bicyclette*) fork.

fourchette [furʃɛt] *nf* fork; (*STATISTIQUE*) bracket, margin.

fourgon [furgɔ̃] *nm* van; (*RAIL*) wag(g)on.

fourmi [furmi] *nf* ant; ~**s** *nfpl* (*fig*) pins and needles; ~**lière** *nf* ant-hill.

fourmiller [furmije] *vi* to swarm.

fournaise [furnɛz] *nf* blaze; (*fig*) furnace, oven.

fourneau, x [furno] *nm* stove.

fournée [furne] *nf* batch.

fourni, e [furni] *a* (*barbe, cheveux*) thick; (*magasin*): **bien** ~ (**en**) well stocked (with).

fournir [furnir] *vt* to supply; (*preuve, exemple*) to provide, supply; (*effort*) to put in; **fournisseur, euse** *nm/f* supplier.

fourniture [furnityr] *nf* supply(ing); ~**s** *nfpl* supplies.

fourrage [furaʒ] *nm* fodder.

fourrager, ère [furaʒe, -ɛr] *a* fodder *cpd*.

fourré, e [fure] *a* (*bonbon etc*) filled; (*manteau etc*) fur-lined // *nm* thicket.

fourreau, x [furo] *nm* sheath.

fourrer [fure] *vt* (*fam*) to stick, shove; **se** ~ **dans/sous** to get into/under.

fourre-tout [furtu] *nm inv* (*sac*) hold-all; (*péj*) junk room (*ou* cupboard); (*fig*) rag-bag.

fourrière [furjɛr] *nf* pound.

fourrure [furyr] *nf* fur; (*sur l'animal*) coat.

fourvoyer [furvwaje]: **se** ~ *vi* to go astray, stray.

foutre [futr(ə)] *vt* (*fam!*) = **ficher** (*fam*); **foutu, e** *a* (*fam!*) = **fichu, e** *a*.

foyer [fwaje] *nm* (*de cheminée*) hearth; (*famille*) family; (*maison*) home; (*de jeunes etc*) (social) club; hostel; (*salon*) foyer; (*OPTIQUE, PHOTO*) focus *sg*; **lunettes à double** ~ bi-focal glasses.

fracas [fraka] *nm* din; crash; roar.

fracasser [frakase] *vt* to smash.

fraction [fraksjɔ̃] *nf* fraction;

fractionner *vt* to divide (up), split (up).

fracture [fraktyr] *nf* fracture; ~ **du crâne** fractured skull; ~ **de la jambe** broken leg.

fracturer [fraktyre] *vt* (*coffre, serrure*) to break open; (*os, membre*) to fracture.

fragile [fraʒil] *a* fragile, delicate; (*fig*) frail; **fragilité** *nf* fragility.

fragment [fragmɑ̃] *nm* (*d'un objet*) fragment, piece; (*d'un texte*) passage, extract.

fraîche [frɛʃ] *a voir* **frais; fraîcheur** *nf* coolness; freshness; **fraîchir** *vi* to get cooler; (*vent*) to freshen.

frais, fraîche [frɛ, frɛʃ] *a* fresh; (*froid*) cool // *ad* (*récemment*) newly, fresh(ly); **il fait** ~ it's cool; **servir** ~ serve chilled // *nm*: **mettre au** ~ to put in a cool place; **prendre le** ~ to take a breath of cool air // *nmpl* (*débours*) expenses; (*COMM*) costs; charges; **faire des** ~ to spend; to go to a lot of expense; **faire les** ~ **de** to bear the brunt of; ~ **généraux** overheads; ~ **de scolarité** school fees (*Brit*), tuition (*US*).

fraise [frɛz] *nf* strawberry; (*TECH*) countersink (bit); (*de dentiste*) drill; ~ **des bois** wild strawberry.

framboise [frɑ̃bwaz] *nf* raspberry.

franc, franche [frɑ̃, frɑ̃ʃ] *a* (*personne*) frank, straightforward; (*visage*) open; (*net: refus, couleur*) clear; (: *coupure*) clean; (*intensif*) downright; (*exempt*): ~ **de port** postage paid // *ad*: **parler** ~ to be frank *ou* candid // *nm* franc.

français, e [frɑ̃sɛ, -ɛz] *a* French // *nm/f*: **F**~, **e** Frenchman/woman // *nm* (*LING*) French; **les** ~ the French.

France [frɑ̃s] *nf*: **la** ~ France.

franche [frɑ̃ʃ] *a voir* **franc;** ~**ment** *ad* frankly; clearly; (*tout à fait*) downright.

franchir [frɑ̃ʃir] *vt* (*obstacle*) to clear, get over; (*seuil, ligne, rivière*) to cross; (*distance*) to cover.

franchise [frɑ̃ʃiz] *nf* frankness; (*douanière, d'impôt*) exemption; (*ASSURANCES*) excess.

franciser [frɑ̃size] *vt* to gallicize, Frenchify.

franc-maçon [frɑ̃masɔ̃] *nm* freemason.

franco [frɑ̃ko] *ad* (*COMM*): ~ (**de port**) postage paid.

francophone [frɑ̃kɔfɔn] *a* French-speaking; ~**phonie** *nf* French-speaking communities.

franc-parler [frɑ̃parle] *nm inv* outspokenness.

franc-tireur [frɑ̃tirœr] *nm* (*MIL*) irregular; (*fig*) freelance.

frange [frɑ̃ʒ] *nf* fringe.

frangipane [frɑ̃ʒipan] *nf* almond paste.

franquette [frɑ̃kɛt]: **à la bonne** ~ *ad* without any fuss.

frappe [frap] *nf* (*d'une dactylo, pianiste, machine à écrire*) touch; (*BOXE*) punch.

frappé, e [fʀape] a iced.

frapper [fʀape] vt to hit, strike; (étonner) to strike; (monnaie) to strike, stamp; se ~ vi (s'inquiéter) to get worked up; ~ **dans ses mains** to clap one's hands; ~ **du poing sur** to bang one's fist on; **frappé de stupeur** dumbfounded.

frasques [fʀask(ə)] nfpl escapades.

fraternel, le [fʀatɛʀnɛl] a brotherly, fraternal.

fraternité [fʀatɛʀnite] nf brotherhood.

fraude [fʀod] nf fraud; (SCOL) cheating; **passer qch en ~** to smuggle sth in (ou out); ~ **fiscale** tax evasion; **frauder** vi, vt to cheat; **frauduleux, euse** a fraudulent.

frayer [fʀeje] vt to open up, clear // vi to spawn; (fréquenter): ~ **avec** to mix with.

frayeur [fʀejœʀ] nf fright.

fredonner [fʀədɔne] vt to hum.

freezer [fʀizœʀ] nm freezing compartment.

frein [fʀɛ̃] nm brake; ~ **à main** handbrake; ~s **à disques/tambour** disc/drum brakes.

freiner [fʀene] vi to brake // vt (progrès etc) to check.

frelaté, e [fʀəlate] a adulterated; (fig) tainted.

frêle [fʀɛl] a frail, fragile.

frelon [fʀəlɔ̃] nm hornet.

frémir [fʀemiʀ] vi to tremble, shudder; to shiver; to quiver.

frêne [fʀɛn] nm ash.

frénétique [fʀenetik] a frenzied, frenetic.

fréquemment [fʀekamɑ̃] ad frequently.

fréquent, e [fʀekɑ̃, -ɑ̃t] a frequent.

fréquentation [fʀekɑ̃tasjɔ̃] nf frequenting; seeing; ~s nfpl company sg.

fréquenté, e [fʀekɑ̃te] a: **très ~** (very) busy; **mal ~** patronized by disreputable elements.

fréquenter [fʀekɑ̃te] vt (lieu) to frequent; (personne) to see; se ~ to see each other.

frère [fʀɛʀ] nm brother.

fresque [fʀɛsk(ə)] nf (ART) fresco.

fret [fʀɛ] nm freight.

fréter [fʀete] vt to charter.

frétiller [fʀetije] vi to wriggle; to quiver; (chien) to wag its tail.

fretin [fʀətɛ̃] nm: **menu ~** small fry.

friable [fʀijabl(ə)] a crumbly.

friand, e [fʀijɑ̃, -ɑ̃d] a: ~ **de** very fond of.

friandise [fʀijɑ̃diz] nf sweet.

fric [fʀik] nm (fam) cash, bread.

friche [fʀiʃ]: **en ~ a, ad** (lying) fallow.

friction [fʀiksjɔ̃] nf (massage) rub, rubdown; (TECH, fig) friction; **frictionner** vt to rub (down); to massage.

frigidaire [fʀiʒidɛʀ] nm ® refrigerator.

frigide [fʀiʒid] a frigid.

frigo [fʀigo] nm fridge.

frigorifier [fʀigɔʀifje] vt to refrigerate; **frigorifique** a refrigerating.

frileux, euse [fʀilø, -øz] a sensitive to (the) cold.

frimer [fʀime] vi to put on an act.

frimousse [fʀimus] nf (sweet) little face.

fringale [fʀɛ̃gal] nf: **avoir la ~** to be ravenous.

fringant, e [fʀɛ̃gɑ̃, -ɑ̃t] a dashing.

fripé, e [fʀipe] a crumpled.

fripon, ne [fʀipɔ̃, -ɔn] a roguish, mischievous // nm/f rascal, rogue.

fripouille [fʀipuj] nf scoundrel.

frire [fʀiʀ] vt, vi: **faire ~** to fry.

frisé, e [fʀize] a curly; curly-haired.

frisson [fʀisɔ̃] nm shudder, shiver; quiver; **frissonner** vi to shudder, shiver; to quiver.

frit, e [fʀi, fʀit] pp de **frire** // nf: (pommes) ~es chips (Brit), French fries; **friteuse** nf chip pan; **friture** nf (huile) (deep) fat; (plat): **friture (de poissons)** fried fish; (RADIO) crackle.

frivole [fʀivɔl] a frivolous.

froid, e [fʀwa, fʀwad] a, nm cold; **il fait ~** it's cold; **avoir/prendre ~** to be/catch cold; **être en ~ avec** to be on bad terms with; **froidement** ad (accueillir) coldly; (décider) coolly.

froisser [fʀwase] vt to crumple (up), crease; (fig) to hurt, offend; se ~ vi to crumple, crease; to take offence; se ~ **un muscle** to strain a muscle.

frôler [fʀole] vt to brush against; (suj: projectile) to skim past; (fig) to come very close to.

fromage [fʀɔmaʒ] nm cheese; ~ **blanc** soft white cheese; **fromager, ère** nm/f cheese merchant.

froment [fʀɔmɑ̃] nm wheat.

froncer [fʀɔ̃se] vt to gather; ~ **les sourcils** to frown.

frondaisons [fʀɔ̃dɛzɔ̃] nfpl foliage sg.

fronde [fʀɔ̃d] nf sling; (fig) rebellion, rebelliousness.

front [fʀɔ̃] nm forehead, brow; (MIL) front; **de ~** ad (se heurter) head-on; (rouler) together (i.e. 2 or 3 abreast); (simultanément) at once; **faire ~ à** to face up to; ~ **de mer** (sea) front.

frontalier, ère [fʀɔ̃talje, -ɛʀ] a border cpd, frontier cpd // nm/f: (travailleurs) ~s commuters from across the border.

frontière [fʀɔ̃tjɛʀ] nf frontier, border; (fig) frontier, boundary.

fronton [fʀɔ̃tɔ̃] nm pediment.

frotter [fʀɔte] vi to rub, scrape // vt to rub; (pour nettoyer) to rub (up); to scrub; ~ **une allumette** to strike a match.

fructifier [fʀyktifje] vi to yield a profit; **faire ~** to turn to good account.

fructueux, euse [fʀyktɥø, -øz] a fruitful; profitable.

fruit [fʀɥi] nm fruit gén q; ~s de mer seafood(s); ~s secs dried fruit sg; **fruité, e** a fruity; **fruitier, ère** a: arbre fruitier fruit tree // nm/f fruiterer (Brit), fruit merchant (US).

fruste [fʀyst(ə)] a unpolished, uncultivated.

frustrer [fʀystʀe] vt to frustrate.

fuel(-oil) [fjul(ɔjl)] nm fuel oil; heating oil.

fugace [fygas] a fleeting.

fugitif, ive [fyʒitif, -iv] a (lueur, amour) fleeting; (prisonnier etc) fugitive, runaway // nm/f fugitive.

fugue [fyg] nf: faire une ~ to run away, abscond.

fuir [fɥiʀ] vt to flee from; (éviter) to shun // vi to run away; (gaz, robinet) to leak.

fuite [fɥit] nf flight; (écoulement, divulgation) leak; **être en** ~ to be on the run; **mettre en** ~ to put to flight.

fulgurant, e [fylgyʀɑ̃, -ɑ̃t] a lightning cpd, dazzling.

fulminer [fylmine] vi to thunder forth.

fumé, e [fyme] a (CULIN) smoked; (verre) tinted // nf smoke.

fume-cigarette [fymsigaʀɛt] nm inv cigarette holder.

fumer [fyme] vi to smoke; (soupe) to steam // vt to smoke; (terre, champ) to manure.

fûmes etc vb voir **être**.

fumet [fymɛ] nm aroma.

fumeur, euse [fymœʀ, -øz] nm/f smoker.

fumeux, euse [fymø, -øz] a (péj) woolly, hazy.

fumier [fymje] nm manure.

fumiste [fymist(ə)] nm/f (péj) shirker; phoney.

fumisterie [fymistəʀi] nf (péj) fraud, con.

funambule [fynɑ̃byl] nm tightrope walker.

funèbre [fynɛbʀ(ə)] a funeral cpd; (fig) doleful; funereal.

funérailles [fyneʀaj] nfpl funeral sg.

funeste [fynɛst(ə)] a disastrous; deathly.

fur [fyʀ]: **au** ~ **et à mesure** ad as one goes along; **au** ~ **et à mesure que** as.

furet [fyʀɛ] nm ferret.

fureter [fyʀte] vi (péj) to nose about.

fureur [fyʀœʀ] nf fury; (passion): ~ **de** passion for; **faire** ~ to be all the rage.

furibond, e [fyʀibɔ̃, -ɔ̃d] a furious.

furie [fyʀi] nf fury; (femme) shrew, vixen; **en** ~ (mer) raging; **furieux, euse** a furious.

furoncle [fyʀɔ̃kl(ə)] nm boil.

furtif, ive [fyʀtif, -iv] a furtive.

fus vb voir **être**.

fusain [fyzɛ̃] nm (ART) charcoal.

fuseau, x [fyzo] nm (pour filer) spindle; (pantalon) (ski) pants; ~ **horaire** time zone.

fusée [fyze] nf rocket; ~ **éclairante** flare.

fuselé, e [fyzle] a slender; tapering.

fuser [fyze] vi (rires etc) to burst forth.

fusible [fyzibl(ə)] nm (ÉLEC: fil) fuse wire; (: fiche) fuse.

fusil [fyzi] nm (de guerre, à canon rayé) rifle, gun; (de chasse, à canon lisse) shotgun, gun; **fusillade** [-jad] nf gunfire q, shooting q; shooting battle; **fusiller** vt to shoot; ~**-mitrailleur** nm machine gun.

fusionner [fyzjɔne] vi to merge.

fustiger [fystiʒe] vt to denounce.

fut vb voir **être**.

fût [fy] vb voir **être** // nm (tonneau) barrel, cask.

futaie [fytɛ] nf forest, plantation.

futile [fytil] a futile; frivolous.

futur, e [fytyʀ] a, nm future.

fuyant, e [fɥijɑ̃, -ɑ̃t] vb voir **fuir** // a (regard etc) evasive; (lignes etc) receding; (perspective) vanishing.

fuyard, e [fɥijaʀ, -aʀd(ə)] nm/f runaway.

G

gabarit [gabaʀi] nm (fig) size; calibre.

gâcher [gɑʃe] vt (gâter) to spoil, ruin; (gaspiller) to waste.

gâchette [gɑʃɛt] nf trigger.

gâchis [gɑʃi] nm waste q.

gadoue [gadu] nf sludge.

gaffe [gaf] nf (instrument) boat hook; (erreur) blunder; **faire** ~ (fam) to be careful.

gage [gaʒ] nm (dans un jeu) forfeit; (fig: de fidélité) token; ~s nmpl (salaire) wages; (garantie) guarantee sg; **mettre en** ~ to pawn.

gager [gaʒe] vt to bet, wager.

gageure [gaʒyʀ] nf: c'est une ~ it's attempting the impossible.

gagnant, e [gaɲɑ̃, -ɑ̃t] nm/f winner.

gagne-pain [gaɲpɛ̃] nm inv job.

gagner [gaɲe] vt to win; (somme d'argent, revenu) to earn; (aller vers, atteindre) to reach; (envahir) to overcome; to spread to // vi to win; (fig) to gain; ~ **du temps/de la place** to gain time/save space; ~ **sa vie** to earn one's living.

gai, e [ge] a gay, cheerful; (un peu ivre) merry.

gaieté [gete] nf cheerfulness; ~s nfpl (souvent ironique) delights; **de** ~ **de cœur** with a light heart.

gaillard, e [gajaʀ, -aʀd(ə)] a (grivois) bawdy, ribald // nm (strapping) fellow.

gain [gɛ̃] nm (revenu) earnings pl;

(bénéfice: gén pl) profits *pl; (au jeu: gén pl)* winnings *pl; (fig: de temps, place)* saving; **avoir ~ de cause** to win the case; *(fig)* to be proved right.

gaine [gɛn] *nf (corset)* girdle; *(fourreau)* sheath.

galant, e [galã, -ãt] *a (courtois)* courteous, gentlemanly; *(entreprenant)* flirtatious, gallant; *(aventure, poésie)* amorous.

galbe [galb(ə)] *nm* curve(s); shapeliness.

galère [galɛʀ] *nf* galley.

galérer [galeʀe] *vi (fam)* to slog away, work hard.

galerie [galʀi] *nf* gallery; *(THÉÂTRE)* circle; *(de voiture)* roof rack; *(fig: spectateurs)* audience; **~ marchande** shopping arcade; **~ de peinture** (private) art gallery.

galet [galɛ] *nm* pebble; *(TECH)* wheel.

galette [galɛt] *nf* flat cake.

Galles [gal]: **le pays de ~** Wales.

gallois, e [galwa, -waz] *a, nm (langue)* Welsh // *nm/f:* **G~, e** Welshman/woman.

galon [galɔ̃] *nm (MIL)* stripe; *(décoratif)* piece of braid.

galop [galo] *nm* gallop.

galoper [galɔpe] *vi* to gallop.

galopin [galɔpɛ̃] *nm* urchin, ragamuffin.

galvauder [galvode] *vt* to debase.

gambader [gɑ̃bade] *vi (animal, enfant)* to leap about.

gamelle [gamɛl] *nf* mess tin; billy can.

gamin, e [gamɛ̃, -in] *nm/f* kid // *a* mischievous, playful.

gamme [gam] *nf (MUS)* scale; *(fig)* range.

gammé, e [game] *a:* **croix ~e** swastika.

gant [gɑ̃] *nm* glove; **~ de toilette** (face) flannel *(Brit)*, face cloth.

garage [gaʀaʒ] *nm* garage; **garagiste** *nm/f* garage owner; garage mechanic.

garant, e [gaʀɑ̃, -ɑ̃t] *nm/f* guarantor // *nm* guarantee; **se porter ~ de** to vouch for; to be answerable for.

garantie [gaʀɑ̃ti] *nf* guarantee; *(gage)* security, surety; **(bon de) ~** guarantee *ou* warranty slip.

garantir [gaʀɑ̃tiʀ] *vt* to guarantee; *(protéger):* **~ de** to protect from.

garçon [gaʀsɔ̃] *nm* boy; *(célibataire)* bachelor; *(serveur):* **~ (de café)** waiter; **~ de courses** messenger; **garçonnet** *nm* small boy; **garçonnière** *nf* bachelor flat.

garde [gaʀd(ə)] *nm (de prisonnier)* guard; *(de domaine etc)* warden; *(soldat, sentinelle)* guardsman // *nf* guarding; looking after; *(soldats, BOXE, ESCRIME)* guard; *(faction)* watch; *(TYPO):* **(page de) ~** endpaper; flyleaf; **de ~ a, ad** on duty; **monter la ~** to stand guard; **mettre en ~** to warn; **prendre ~ (à)** to be careful (of); **~ champêtre** *nm* rural policeman; **~ du corps** *nm* body-

guard; **~ des enfants** *nf (après divorce)* custody of the children; **~ des Sceaux** *nm* ≈ Lord Chancellor *(Brit)*, ≈ Attorney General *(US)*; **~ à vue** *nf (JUR)* ≈ police custody; **être/se mettre au ~-à-vous** to be at/stand to attention.

garde... [gaʀd(ə)] *préfixe:* **~-barrière** *nm/f* level-crossing keeper; **~-boue** *nm inv* mudguard; **~-chasse** *nm* gamekeeper; **~-fou** *nm* railing, parapet; **~-malade** *nf* home nurse; **~-manger** *nm inv* meat safe; pantry, larder.

garder [gaʀde] *vt (conserver)* to keep; *(surveiller: enfants)* to look after; *(: immeuble, lieu, prisonnier)* to guard; **~ le lit/la chambre** to stay in bed/indoors; **se ~** *vi (aliment: se conserver)* to keep; **se ~ de faire** to be careful not to do; **pêche/chasse gardée** private fishing/hunting (ground).

garderie [gaʀdəʀi] *nf* day nursery, crèche.

garde-robe [gaʀdərɔb] *nf* wardrobe.

gardien, ne [gaʀdjɛ̃, -jɛn] *nm/f (garde)* guard; *(de prison)* warder; *(de domaine, réserve)* warden; *(de musée etc)* attendant; *(de phare, cimetière)* keeper; *(d'immeuble)* caretaker; *(fig)* guardian; **~ de but** goalkeeper; **~ de nuit** night watchman; **~ de la paix** policeman.

gare [gaʀ] *nf* (railway) station, train station *(US)* // *excl* watch out!; **~ routière** bus station.

garer [gaʀe] *vt* to park; **se ~** *vi* to park; *(pour laisser passer)* to draw into the side.

gargariser [gaʀgaʀize]: **se ~** *vi* to gargle; **gargarisme** *nm* gargling *q*; gargle.

gargote [gaʀgɔt] *nf* cheap restaurant.

gargouille [gaʀguj] *nf* gargoyle.

gargouiller [gaʀguje] *vi* to gurgle.

garnement [gaʀnəmɑ̃] *nm* rascal, scallywag.

garni, e [gaʀni] *a (plat)* served with vegetables *(and chips or pasta or rice)* // *nm* furnished accommodation *q*.

garnir [gaʀniʀ] *vt (orner)* to decorate; to trim; *(approvisionner)* to fill, stock; *(protéger)* to fit.

garnison [gaʀnizɔ̃] *nf* garrison.

garniture [gaʀnityʀ] *nf (CULIN)* vegetables *pl;* filling; *(décoration)* trimming; *(protection)* fittings *pl;* **~ de frein** brake lining.

garrot [gaʀo] *nm (MÉD)* tourniquet.

gars [gɑ] *nm* lad; guy.

Gascogne [gaskɔɲ] *nf* Gascony; **le golfe de ~** the Bay of Biscay.

gas-oil [gazɔjl] *nm* diesel (oil).

gaspiller [gaspije] *vt* to waste.

gastronomique [gastʀɔmɔmik] *a* gastronomic.

gâteau, x [gɑto] *nm* cake; **~ sec** biscuit.

gâter [gɑte] *vt* to spoil; **se ~** *vi (dent, fruit)* to go bad; *(temps, situation)* to change for the worse.

gâterie [gɑtʀi] *nf* little treat.

gâteux, euse [gɑtø, -øz] *a* senile.

gauche [goʃ] *a* left, left-hand; *(maladroit)* awkward, clumsy // *nf* (POL) left (wing); à ~ on the left; *(direction)* (to the) left; **gaucher, ère** *a* left-handed; **gauchiste** *nm/f* leftist.

gaufre [gofʀ(ə)] *nf* waffle.

gaufrette [gofʀɛt] *nf* wafer.

gaulois, e [golwa, -waz] *a* Gallic; *(grivois)* bawdy // *nm/f*: G~, e Gaul.

gausser [gose]: se ~ de *vt* to deride.

gaver [gave] *vt* to force-feed; *(fig)*: ~ de to cram with, fill up with.

gaz [gɑz] *nm inv* gas.

gaze [gɑz] *nf* gauze.

gazéifié, e [gazeifje] *a* aerated.

gazette [gazɛt] *nf* news sheet.

gazeux, euse [gazø, -øz] *a* gaseous; *(boisson)* fizzy; *(eau)* sparkling.

gazoduc [gazɔdyk] *nm* gas pipeline.

gazon [gazɔ̃] *nm (herbe)* turf; grass; *(pelouse)* lawn.

gazouiller [gazuje] *vi* to chirp; *(enfant)* to babble.

geai [ʒɛ] *nm* jay.

géant, e [ʒeɑ̃, -ɑ̃t] *a* gigantic, giant; *(COMM)* giant-size // *nm/f* giant.

geindre [ʒɛ̃dʀ(ə)] *vi* to groan, moan.

gel [ʒɛl] *nm* frost; freezing.

gélatine [ʒelatin] *nf* gelatine.

gelée [ʒəle] *nf* jelly; *(gel)* frost.

geler [ʒəle] *vt, vi* to freeze; **il gèle** it's freezing; **gelures** *nfpl* frostbite *sg*.

gélule [ʒelyl] *nf* (MÉD) capsule.

Gémeaux [ʒemo] *nmpl*: les ~ Gemini.

gémir [ʒemiʀ] *vi* to groan, moan.

gemme [ʒɛm] *nf* gem(stone).

gênant, e [ʒenɑ̃, -ɑ̃t] *a* annoying; embarrassing.

gencive [ʒɑ̃siv] *nf* gum.

gendarme [ʒɑ̃daʀm(ə)] *nm* gendarme; **~rie** *nf* military police force in countryside and small towns; their police station or barracks.

gendre [ʒɑ̃dʀ(ə)] *nm* son-in-law.

gêne [ʒɛn] *nf (à respirer, bouger)* discomfort, difficulty; *(dérangement)* bother, trouble; *(manque d'argent)* financial difficulties *pl ou* straits *pl*; *(confusion)* embarrassment.

gêné, e [ʒene] *a* embarrassed.

gêner [ʒene] *vt (incommoder)* to bother; *(encombrer)* to hamper; to be in the way; *(embarrasser)*: ~ qn to make sb feel ill-at-ease; se ~ *vi* to put o.s. out.

général, e, aux [ʒeneʀal, -o] *a, nm* general // *nf*: *(répétition)* ~e final dress rehearsal; en ~ usually, in general; **~ement** *ad* generally.

généraliser [ʒeneʀalize] *vt, vi* to generalize; se ~ *vi* to become widespread.

généraliste [ʒeneʀalist(ə)] *nm/f* general practitioner, G.P.

générateur, trice [ʒeneʀatœʀ, -tʀis] *a*: ~ de which causes // *nf* generator.

génération [ʒeneʀasjɔ̃] *nf* generation.

généreux, euse [ʒeneʀø, -øz] *a* generous.

générique [ʒeneʀik] *nm* (CINÉMA) credits *pl*, credit titles *pl*.

générosité [ʒeneʀozite] *nf* generosity.

genêt [ʒənɛ] *nm* broom *q (shrub)*.

génétique [ʒenetik] *a* genetic.

Genève [ʒənɛv] *n* Geneva.

génial, e, aux [ʒenjal, -o] *a* of genius; *(fam: formidable)* fantastic, brilliant.

génie [ʒeni] *nm* genius; (MIL): le ~ the Engineers *pl*; ~ civil civil engineering.

genièvre [ʒənjɛvʀ(ə)] *nm* juniper.

génisse [ʒenis] *nf* heifer.

genou, x [ʒnu] *nm* knee; à ~x on one's knees; se mettre à ~x to kneel down.

genre [ʒɑ̃ʀ] *nm* kind, type, sort; *(allure)* manner; (LING) gender.

gens [ʒɑ̃] *nmpl (f in some phrases)* people *pl*.

gentil, le [ʒɑ̃ti, -ij] *a* kind; *(enfant: sage)* good; *(endroit etc)* nice; **gentillesse** *nf* kindness; **gentiment** *ad* kindly.

géographie [ʒeɔgʀafi] *nf* geography.

geôlier [ʒolje] *nm* jailer.

géologie [ʒeɔlɔʒi] *nf* geology.

géomètre [ʒeɔmɛtʀ(ə)] *nm/f*: (arpenteur-)~ (land) surveyor.

géométrie [ʒeɔmetʀi] *nf* geometry; **géométrique** *a* geometric.

gérance [ʒeʀɑ̃s] *nf* management; **mettre en ~** to appoint a manager for.

géranium [ʒeʀanjɔm] *nm* geranium.

gérant, e [ʒeʀɑ̃, -ɑ̃t] *nm/f* manager/manageress.

gerbe [ʒɛʀb(ə)] *nf (de fleurs)* spray; *(de blé)* sheaf *(pl sheaves)*; *(fig)* shower, burst.

gercé, e [ʒeʀse] *a* chapped.

gerçure [ʒeʀsyʀ] *nf* crack.

gérer [ʒeʀe] *vt* to manage.

germain, e [ʒeʀmɛ̃, -ɛn] *a*: cousin ~ first cousin.

germe [ʒeʀm(ə)] *nm* germ.

germer [ʒeʀme] *vi* to sprout; to germinate.

gésir [ʒeziʀ] *vi* to be lying (down); *voir aussi* ci-gît.

geste [ʒɛst(ə)] *nm* gesture; move; motion.

gestion [ʒɛstjɔ̃] *nf* management.

gibecière [ʒibsjɛʀ] *nf* gamebag.

gibet [ʒibɛ] *nm* gallows *pl*.

gibier [ʒibje] *nm (animaux)* game; *(fig)* prey.

giboulée [ʒibule] *nf* sudden shower.

gicler [ʒikle] *vi* to spurt, squirt.

gifle [ʒifl(ə)] *nf* slap (in the face); **gifler** *vt* to slap (in the face).

gigantesque [ʒigɑ̃tɛsk(ə)] *a* gigantic.

gigogne [ʒigɔɲ] *a*: lits ~s truckle *(Brit)*

ou trundle beds.

gigot [ʒigo] *nm* leg (of mutton *ou* lamb).

gigoter [ʒigɔte] *vi* to wriggle (about).

gilet [ʒile] *nm* waistcoat; (*pull*) cardigan; (*de corps*) vest; ~ **pare-balles** bulletproof jacket; ~ **de sauvetage** life jacket.

gingembre [ʒɛ̃ʒɑ̃bʀ(ə)] *nm* ginger.

girafe [ʒiʀaf] *nf* giraffe.

giratoire [ʒiʀatwaʀ] *a*: **sens** ~ roundabout.

girouette [ʒiʀwɛt] *nf* weather vane *ou* cock.

gisait *etc vb voir* **gésir**.

gisement [ʒizmɑ̃] *nm* deposit.

gît *vb voir* **gésir**.

gitan, e [ʒitɑ̃, -an] *nm/f* gipsy.

gîte [ʒit] *nm* home; shelter; ~ (**rural**) holiday cottage *ou* apartment.

givre [ʒivʀ(ə)] *nm* (hoar) frost.

glabre [glabʀ(ə)] *a* hairless; cleanshaven.

glace [glas] *nf* ice; (*crème glacée*) ice cream; (*verre*) sheet of glass; (*miroir*) mirror; (*de voiture*) window.

glacé, e [glase] *a* icy; (*boisson*) iced.

glacer [glase] *vt* to freeze; (*boisson*) to chill, ice; (*gâteau*) to ice; (*papier, tissu*) to glaze; (*fig*): ~ **qn** to chill sb; to make sb's blood run cold.

glacial, e [glasjal] *a* icy.

glacier [glasje] *nm* (*GÉO*) glacier; (*marchand*) ice-cream maker.

glacière [glasjɛʀ] *nf* icebox.

glaçon [glasɔ̃] *nm* icicle; (*pour boisson*) ice cube.

glaise [glɛz] *nf* clay.

gland [glɑ̃] *nm* acorn; (*décoration*) tassel.

glande [glɑ̃d] *nf* gland.

glaner [glane] *vt, vi* to glean.

glapir [glapiʀ] *vi* to yelp.

glas [glɑ] *nm* knell, toll.

glauque [glok] *a* dull blue-green.

glissant, e [glisɑ̃, -ɑ̃t] *a* slippery.

glissement [glismɑ̃] *nm*: ~ **de terrain** landslide.

glisser [glise] *vi* (*avancer*) to glide *ou* slide along; (*coulisser, tomber*) to slide; (*déraper*) to slip; (*être glissant*) to be slippery // *vt* to slip; **se** ~ **dans** to slip into.

global, e, aux [glɔbal, -o] *a* overall.

globe [glɔb] *nm* globe.

globule [glɔbyl] *nm* (*du sang*) corpuscle.

globuleux, euse [glɔbylø, -øz] *a*: **yeux** ~ protruding eyes.

gloire [glwaʀ] *nf* glory; (*mérite*) distinction, credit; (*personne*) celebrity; **glorieux, euse** *a* glorious.

glousser [gluse] *vi* to cluck; (*rire*) to chuckle.

glouton, ne [glutɔ̃, -ɔn] *a* gluttonous.

gluant, e [glyɑ̃, -ɑ̃t] *a* sticky, gummy.

glycine [glisin] *nf* wisteria.

go [go]: **tout de** ~ *ad* straight out.

G.O. *sigle* = **grandes ondes**.

gobelet [gɔblɛ] *nm* tumbler; beaker; (*à dés*) cup.

gober [gɔbe] *vt* to swallow.

godasse [gɔdas] *nf* (*fam*) shoe.

godet [gɔdɛ] *nm* pot.

goéland [gɔelɑ̃] *nm* (sea)gull.

goélette [gɔelɛt] *nf* schooner.

goémon [gɔemɔ̃] *nm* wrack.

gogo [gɔgo]: **à** ~ *ad* galore.

goguenard, e [gɔgnaʀ, -aʀd(ə)] *a* mocking.

goinfre [gwɛ̃fʀ(ə)] *nm* glutton.

golf [gɔlf] *nm* golf; golf course.

golfe [gɔlf(ə)] *nm* gulf; bay.

gomme [gɔm] *nf* (*à effacer*) rubber (*Brit*), eraser; **gommer** *vt* to rub out (*Brit*), erase.

gond [gɔ̃] *nm* hinge; **sortir de ses** ~**s** (*fig*) to fly off the handle.

gondoler [gɔ̃dɔle]: **se** ~ *vi* to warp; to buckle.

gonflé, e [gɔ̃fle] *a* swollen; bloated.

gonfler [gɔ̃fle] *vt* (*pneu, ballon*) to inflate, blow up; (*nombre, importance*) to inflate // *vi* to swell (up); (*CULIN*: *pâte*) to rise.

gonzesse [gɔ̃zɛs] *nf* (*fam*) chick, bird (*Brit*).

goret [gɔʀɛ] *nm* piglet.

gorge [gɔʀʒ(ə)] *nf* (*ANAT*) throat; (*poitrine*) breast.

gorgé, e [gɔʀʒe] *a*: ~ **de** filled with; (*eau*) saturated with // *nf* mouthful; sip; gulp.

gorille [gɔʀij] *nm* gorilla; (*fam*) bodyguard.

gosier [gozje] *nm* throat.

gosse [gɔs] *nm/f* kid.

goudron [gudʀɔ̃] *nm* tar; **goudronner** *vt* to tar(mac) (*Brit*), asphalt (*US*).

gouffre [gufʀ(ə)] *nm* abyss, gulf.

goujat [guʒa] *nm* boor.

goulot [gulo] *nm* neck; **boire au** ~ to drink from the bottle.

goulu, e [guly] *a* greedy.

gourd, e [guʀ, guʀd(ə)] *a* numb (with cold).

gourde [guʀd(ə)] *nf* (*récipient*) flask; (*fam*) (clumsy) clot *ou* oaf // *a* oafish.

gourdin [guʀdɛ̃] *nm* club, bludgeon.

gourmand, e [guʀmɑ̃, -ɑ̃d] *a* greedy; **gourmandise** *nf* greed; (*bonbon*) sweet.

gousse [gus] *nf*: ~ **d'ail** clove of garlic.

goût [gu] *nm* taste; **de bon** ~ tasteful; **de mauvais** ~ tasteless; **prendre** ~ **à** to develop a taste *ou* a liking for.

goûter [gute] *vt* (*essayer*) to taste; (*apprécier*) to enjoy // *vi* to have (afternoon) tea // *nm* (afternoon) tea.

goutte [gut] *nf* drop; (*MÉD*) gout; (*alcool*) brandy.

goutte-à-goutte [gutagut] *nm* (*MÉD*) drip; **tomber** ~ to drip.

gouttière [gutjɛʀ] nf gutter.
gouvernail [guvɛʀnaj] nm rudder; (barre) helm, tiller.
gouvernante [guvɛʀnɑ̃t] nf governess.
gouverne [guvɛʀn(ə)] nf: pour sa ~ for his guidance.
gouvernement [guvɛʀnəmɑ̃] nm government; **gouvernemental, e, aux** a government cpd; pro-government.
gouverner [guvɛʀne] vt to govern.
grâce [gʀɑs] nf grace; favour; (JUR) pardon; ~s nfpl (REL) grace sg; **faire ~ à qn de qch** to spare sb sth; **rendre ~(s) à** to give thanks to; **demander ~** to beg for mercy; ~ **à** prép thanks to; **gracier** vt to pardon; **gracieux, euse** a graceful.
grade [gʀad] nm rank; **monter en ~** to be promoted.
gradé [gʀade] nm officer.
gradin [gʀadɛ̃] nm tier; step; ~s nmpl (de stade) terracing sg.
graduel, le [gʀadɥɛl] a gradual; progressive.
graduer [gʀadɥe] vt (effort etc) to increase gradually; (règle, verre) to graduate.
grain [gʀɛ̃] nm (gén) grain; (NAVIG) squall; ~ **de beauté** beauty spot; ~ **de café** coffee bean; ~ **de poivre** peppercorn; ~ **de poussière** speck of dust; ~ **de raisin** grape.
graine [gʀɛn] nf seed.
graissage [gʀɛsaʒ] nm lubrication, greasing.
graisse [gʀɛs] nf fat; (lubrifiant) grease; **graisser** vt to lubricate, grease; (tacher) to make greasy.
grammaire [gʀamɛʀ] nf grammar; **grammatical, e, aux** a grammatical.
gramme [gʀam] nm gramme.
grand, e [gʀɑ̃, gʀɑ̃d] a (haut) tall; (gros, vaste, large) big, large; (long) long; (sens abstraits) great // ad: ~ **ouvert** wide open; **au ~ air** in the open (air); **les ~s blessés** the severely injured; ~ **ensemble** housing scheme; ~ **magasin** department store; ~**e personne** grown-up; ~**e surface** hypermarket; ~**es écoles** prestige schools of university level; ~**es lignes** (RAIL) main lines; ~**es vacances** summer holidays; **grand-chose** nm/f inv: **pas grand-chose** not much; **Grande-Bretagne** nf (Great) Britain; **grandeur** nf (dimension) size; magnitude; (fig) greatness; **grandeur nature** life-size; **grandir** vi to grow // vt: **grandir qn** (suj: vêtement, chaussure) to make sb look taller; ~**-mère** nf grandmother; ~**-messe** nf high mass; ~**-peine**: **à ~-peine** ad with difficulty; ~**père** nm grandfather; ~**-route** nf main road; ~**-rue** nf high street; ~**s-parents** nmpl grandparents.
grange [gʀɑ̃ʒ] nf barn.

granit(e) [gʀanit] nm granite.
graphique [gʀafik] a graphic // nm graph.
grappe [gʀap] nf cluster; ~ **de raisin** bunch of grapes.
grappiller [gʀapije] vt to glean.
grappin [gʀapɛ̃] nm grapnel; **mettre le ~ sur** (fig) to get one's claws on.
gras, se [gʀɑ, gʀɑs] a (viande, soupe) fatty; (personne) fat; (surface, main) greasy; (plaisanterie) coarse; (TYPO) bold // nm (CULIN) fat; **faire la ~se matinée** to have a lie-in (Brit), sleep late (US); ~**sement** ad: ~**sement payé** handsomely paid; ~**souillet, te** a podgy, plump.
gratifier [gʀatifje] vt: ~ **qn de** to favour sb with; to reward sb with.
gratiné, e [gʀatine] a (CULIN) au gratin.
gratis [gʀatis] ad free.
gratitude [gʀatityd] nf gratitude.
gratte-ciel [gʀatsjɛl] nm inv skyscraper.
gratte-papier [gʀatpapje] nm inv (péj) penpusher.
gratter [gʀate] vt (frotter) to scrape; (enlever) to scrape off; (bras, bouton) to scratch.
gratuit, e [gʀatɥi, -ɥit] a (entrée, billet) free; (fig) gratuitous.
gravats [gʀava] nmpl rubble sg.
grave [gʀav] a (maladie, accident) serious, bad; (sujet, problème) serious, grave; (air) grave, solemn; (voix, son) deep, low-pitched; ~**ment** ad seriously; gravely.
graver [gʀave] vt to engrave.
gravier [gʀavje] nm gravel q; **gravillons** nmpl loose gravel sg.
gravir [gʀaviʀ] vt to climb (up).
gravité [gʀavite] nf seriousness; gravity.
graviter [gʀavite] vi to revolve.
gravure [gʀavyʀ] nf engraving; (reproduction) print; plate.
gré [gʀe] nm: **à son ~** to his liking; as he pleases; **au ~ de** according to, following; **contre le ~ de qn** against sb's will; **de son (plein) ~** of one's own free will; **bon ~ mal ~** like it or not; **de ~ ou de force** whether one likes it or not; **savoir ~ à qn de qch** to be grateful to sb for sth.
grec, grecque [gʀɛk] a Greek; (classique: vase etc) Grecian // nm/f Greek.
Grèce [gʀɛs] nf: **la ~** Greece.
gréement [gʀemɑ̃] nm rigging.
greffer [gʀefe] vt (BOT, MÉD: tissu) to graft; (MÉD: organe) to transplant.
greffier [gʀefje] nm clerk of the court.
grêle [gʀɛl] a (very) thin // nf hail.
grêlé, e [gʀele] a pockmarked.
grêler [gʀele] vb impersonnel: **il grêle** it's hailing.
grêlon [gʀelɔ̃] nm hailstone.

grelot [grəlo] *nm* little bell.
grelotter [grələte] *vi* to shiver.
grenade [grənad] *nf* (*explosive*) grenade; (*BOT*) pomegranate.
grenat [grəna] *a inv* dark red.
grenier [grənje] *nm* attic; (*de ferme*) loft.
grenouille [grənuj] *nf* frog.
grès [grɛ] *nm* sandstone; (*poterie*) stoneware.
grésiller [grezije] *vi* to sizzle; (*RADIO*) to crackle.
grève [grɛv] *nf* (*d'ouvriers*) strike; (*plage*) shore; **se mettre en/faire ~** to go on/be on strike; **~ de la faim** hunger strike; **~ du zèle** work-to-rule (*Brit*), slowdown (*US*).
grever [grəve] *vt* to put a strain on.
gréviste [grevist(ə)] *nm/f* striker.
gribouiller [gribuje] *vt* to scribble, scrawl.
grief [grijef] *nm* grievance; **faire ~ à qn de** to reproach sb for.
grièvement [grijevmɑ̃] *ad* seriously.
griffe [grif] *nf* claw; (*fig*) signature.
griffer [grife] *vt* to scratch.
griffonner [grifone] *vt* to scribble.
grignoter [griɲote] *vt* to nibble *ou* gnaw at.
gril [gril] *nm* steak *ou* grill pan.
grillade [grijad] *nf* grill.
grillage [grijaʒ] *nm* (*treillis*) wire netting; wire fencing.
grille [grij] *nf* (*clôture*) railings; (*portail*) (metal) gate; (*d'égout*) (metal) grate; (*fig*) grid.
grille-pain [grijpɛ̃] *nm inv* toaster.
griller [grije] *vt* (*aussi:* **faire ~:** *pain*) to toast; (: *viande*) to grill; (*fig: ampoule etc*) to burn out, blow.
grillon [grijɔ̃] *nm* cricket.
grimace [grimas] *nf* grimace; (*pour faire rire*): **faire des ~s** to pull *ou* make faces.
grimer [grime] *vt* to make up.
grimper [grɛ̃pe] *vi, vt* to climb.
grincer [grɛ̃se] *vi* (*porte, roue*) to grate; (*plancher*) to creak; **~ des dents** to grind one's teeth.
grincheux, euse [grɛ̃ʃø, -øz] *a* grumpy.
grippe [grip] *nf* flu, influenza; **grippé, e** *a*: **être grippé** to have flu.
gris, e [gri, griz] *a* grey; (*ivre*) tipsy; **faire ~e mine** to pull a miserable *ou* wry face.
grisaille [grizaj] *nf* greyness, dullness.
griser [grize] *vt* to intoxicate.
grisonner [grizone] *vi* to be going grey.
grisou [grizu] *nm* firedamp.
grive [griv] *nf* thrush.
grivois, e [grivwa, -waz] *a* saucy.
Groenland [grɔenlɑ̃d] *nm* Greenland.
grogner [grɔɲe] *vi* to growl; (*fig*) to grumble.

groin [grwɛ̃] *nm* snout.
grommeler [grɔmle] *vi* to mutter to o.s.
gronder [grɔ̃de] *vi* to rumble; (*fig: révolte*) to be brewing // *vt* to scold.
gros, se [gro, gros] *a* big, large; (*obèse*) fat; (*travaux, dégâts*) extensive; (*large: trait, fil*) thick, heavy // *ad*: **risquer/ gagner ~** to risk/win a lot // *nm* (*COMM*): **le ~** the wholesale business; **prix de ~** wholesale price; **par ~ temps/ ~se mer** in rough weather/heavy seas; **le ~ de** the main body of; the bulk of; **en ~** roughly; (*COMM*) wholesale; **~ lot** jackpot; **~ mot** coarse word; **~ plan** (*PHOTO*) close-up; **~ sel** cooking salt; **~se caisse** big drum.
groseille [grozɛj] *nf*: **~ (rouge)/ (blanche)** red/white currant; **~ à maquereau** gooseberry.
grosse [gros] *a voir* **gros**.
grossesse [grosɛs] *nf* pregnancy.
grosseur [grosœr] *nf* size; fatness; (*tumeur*) lump.
grossier, ière [grosje, -jɛr] *a* coarse; (*travail*) rough; crude; (*évident: erreur*) gross.
grossir [grosir] *vi* (*personne*) to put on weight; (*fig*) to grow, get bigger; (*rivière*) to swell // *vt* to increase; to exaggerate; (*au microscope*) to magnify; (*suj: vêtement*): **~ qn** to make sb look fatter.
grossiste [grosist(ə)] *nm/f* wholesaler.
grosso modo [grosomodo] *ad* roughly.
grotte [grɔt] *nf* cave.
grouiller [gruje] *vi* to mill about; to swarm about; **~ de** to be swarming with.
groupe [grup] *nm* group.
groupement [grupmɑ̃] *nm* grouping; group.
grouper [grupe] *vt* to group; **se ~** *vi* to get together.
grue [gry] *nf* crane.
grumeaux [grymo] *nmpl* lumps.
gué [ge] *nm* ford; **passer à ~** to ford.
guenilles [gənij] *nfpl* rags.
guenon [gənɔ̃] *nf* female monkey.
guépard [gepar] *nm* cheetah.
guêpe [gɛp] *nf* wasp.
guêpier [gepje] *nm* (*fig*) trap.
guère [gɛr] *ad* (*avec adjectif, adverbe*): **ne ... ~** hardly; (*avec verbe*): **ne ... ~** *tournure négative* + much; hardly ever; *tournure négative* + (very) long; **il n'y a ~ que/de** there's hardly anybody (*ou* anything) but/hardly any.
guéridon [geridɔ̃] *nm* pedestal table.
guérilla [gerija] *nf* guerrilla warfare.
guérir [gerir] *vt* (*personne, maladie*) to cure; (*membre, plaie*) to heal // *vi* to recover, be cured; to heal; **guérison** *nf* curing; healing; recovery.
guérite [gerit] *nf* sentry box.
guerre [gɛr] *nf* war; (*méthode*): **~ atomique** atomic warfare *q*; **en ~ at**

war; **faire la ~ à** to wage war against; **de ~ lasse** finally; **~ d'usure** war of attrition; **guerrier, ière** *a* warlike // *nm/f* warrior.

guet [gɛ] *nm*: **faire le ~** to be on the watch *ou* look-out.

guet-apens [gɛtapɑ̃] *nm* ambush.

guetter [gete] *vt* (*épier*) to watch (intently); (*attendre*) to watch (out) for; to be lying in wait for.

gueule [gœl] *nf* mouth; (*fam*) face; mouth; **ta ~!** (*fam*) shut up!; **~ de bois** (*fam*) hangover.

gueuler [gœle] *vi* (*fam*) to bawl.

gui [gi] *nm* mistletoe.

guichet [giʃɛ] *nm* (*de bureau, banque*) counter, window; (*d'une porte*) wicket, hatch; **les ~s** (*à la gare, au théâtre*) the ticket office.

guide [gid] *nm* guide.

guider [gide] *vt* to guide.

guidon [gidɔ̃] *nm* handlebars *pl*.

guignol [giɲɔl] *nm* ≈ Punch and Judy show; (*fig*) clown.

guillemets [gijmɛ] *nmpl*: **entre ~** in inverted commas.

guillotiner [gijɔtine] *vt* to guillotine.

guindé, e [gɛ̃de] *a* stiff, starchy.

guirlande [giʀlɑ̃d] *nf* garland; (*de papier*) paper chain.

guise [giz] *nf*: **à votre ~** as you wish *ou* please; **en ~ de** by way of.

guitare [gitaʀ] *nf* guitar.

gymnase [ʒimnɑz] *nm* gym(nasium).

gymnastique [ʒimnastik] *nf* gymnastics *sg*; (*au réveil etc*) keep-fit exercises *pl*.

gynécologie [ʒinekɔlɔʒi] *nf* gynaecology; **gynécologue** *nm/f* gynaecologist.

H

habile [abil] *a* skilful; (*malin*) clever; **~té** *nf* skill, skilfulness; cleverness.

habilité, e [abilite] *a*: **~ à faire** entitled to do, empowered to do.

habillé, e [abije] *a* dressed; (*chic*) dressy; (*TECH*): **~ de** covered with; encased in.

habillement [abijmɑ̃] *nm* clothes *pl*.

habiller [abije] *vt* to dress; (*fournir en vêtements*) to clothe; **s'~** *vi* to dress (o.s.); (*se déguiser, mettre des vêtements chic*) to dress up.

habit [abi] *nm* outfit; **~s** *nmpl* (*vêtements*) clothes; **~ (de soirée)** tails *pl*; evening dress.

habitant, e [abitɑ̃, -ɑ̃t] *nm/f* inhabitant; (*d'une maison*) occupant.

habitation [abitasjɔ̃] *nf* living; residence, home; house; **~s à loyer modéré (HLM)** low-rent housing *sg*.

habiter [abite] *vt* to live in; (*suj: sentiment*) to dwell in // *vi*: **~ à/dans** to live in *ou* at/in.

habitude [abityd] *nf* habit; **avoir l'~ de faire** to be in the habit of doing; (*expérience*) to be used to doing; **d'~** usually; **comme d'~** as usual.

habitué, e [abitɥe] *nm/f* regular visitor; regular (customer).

habituel, le [abitɥel] *a* usual.

habituer [abitɥe] *vt*: **~ qn à** to get sb used to; **s'~ à** to get used to.

'hache [aʃ] *nf* axe.

'hacher [aʃe] *vt* (*viande*) to mince; (*persil*) to chop.

'hachis [aʃi] *nm* mince *q*.

'hachoir [aʃwaʀ] *nm* chopper; (*meat*) mincer; chopping board.

'hagard, e [agaʀ, -aʀd(ə)] *a* wild, distraught.

'haie [ɛ] *nf* hedge; (*SPORT*) hurdle; (*fig: rang*) line, row.

'haillons [ajɔ̃] *nmpl* rags.

'haine [ɛn] *nf* hatred.

'haïr [aiʀ] *vt* to detest, hate.

'hâlé, e [ɑle] *a* (sun)tanned, sunburnt.

haleine [alɛn] *nf* breath; **hors d'~** out of breath; **tenir en ~** to hold spellbound; to keep in suspense; **de longue ~** *a* longterm.

'haler [ale] *vt* to haul in; to tow.

'haleter [alte] *vt* to pant.

'hall [ol] *nm* hall.

'halle [al] *nf* (covered) market; **~s** *nfpl* central food market *sg*.

hallucinant, e [alysinɑ̃, -ɑ̃t] *a* staggering.

hallucination [alysinasjɔ̃] *nf* hallucination.

'halte [alt(ə)] *nf* stop, break; stopping place; (*RAIL*) halt // *excl* stop!; **faire ~** to stop.

haltère [altɛʀ] *nm* dumbbell, barbell; (poids et) **~s** *nmpl* (*activité*) weight lifting *sg*.

'hamac [amak] *nm* hammock.

'hameau, x [amo] *nm* hamlet.

hameçon [amsɔ̃] *nm* (fish) hook.

'hanche [ɑ̃ʃ] *nf* hip.

'handicapé, e [ɑ̃dikape] *nm/f* physically (*ou* mentally) handicapped person; **~ moteur** spastic.

'hangar [ɑ̃gaʀ] *nm* shed; (*AVIAT*) hangar.

'hanneton [antɔ̃] *nm* cockchafer.

'hanter [ɑ̃te] *vt* to haunt.

'hantise [ɑ̃tiz] *nf* obsessive fear.

'happer [ape] *vt* to snatch; (*suj: train etc*) to hit.

'haras [aʀɑ] *nm* stud farm.

'harassant, e [aʀasɑ̃, -ɑ̃t] *a* exhausting.

'harceler [aʀsəle] *vt* (*MIL, CHASSE*) to harass, harry; (*importuner*) to plague.

'hardi, e [aʀdi] *a* bold, daring.

'hareng [aʀɑ̃] *nm* herring.

'hargne [aʀɲ(ə)] *nf* aggressiveness.

'haricot [aʀiko] *nm* bean; **~ blanc** haricot bean; ~ vert green bean.

harmonica [aʀmɔnika] *nm* mouth organ.

harmonie [aʀmɔni] *nf* harmony.

'harnacher [ˈaʀnaʃe] *vt* to harness.

'harnais [ˈaʀnɛ] *nm* harness.

'harpe [ˈaʀp(ə)] *nf* harp.

'harponner [ˈaʀpɔne] *vt* to harpoon; (*fam*) to collar.

'hasard [ˈazaʀ] *nm*: le ~ chance, fate; un ~ a coincidence; a stroke of luck; au ~ aimlessly; at random; haphazardly; par ~ by chance; à tout ~ just in case; on the off chance (*Brit*).

'hasarder [ˈazaʀde] *vt* (*mot*) to venture; (*fortune*) to risk.

'hâte [ˈɑt] *nf* haste; à la ~ hurriedly, hastily; en ~ posthaste, with all possible speed; avoir ~ de to be eager *ou* anxious to; **'hâter** *vt* to hasten; se hâter *vi* to hurry.

'hâtif, ive [ˈɑtif, -iv] *a* hurried; hasty; (*légume*) early.

'hausse [ˈos] *nf* rise, increase.

'hausser [ˈose] *vt* to raise; ~ les épaules to shrug (one's shoulders).

'haut, e [ˈo, ˈot] *a* high; (*grand*) tall; (*son, voix*) high(-pitched) // *ad* high // *nm* top (part); de 3 m de ~ 3 m high, 3 m in height; des ~s et des bas ups and downs; en ~ lieu in high places; à ~e voix, (tout) ~ aloud, out loud; du ~ de from the top of; de ~ en bas from top to bottom; downwards; plus ~ higher up, further up; (*dans un texte*) above; (*parler*) louder; en ~ up above; at (*ou* to) the top; (*dans une maison*) upstairs; en ~ de at the top of.

'hautain, e [ˈotɛ̃, -ɛn] *a* haughty.

'hautbois [ˈobwa] *nm* oboe.

'haut-de-forme [ˈodfɔʀm(ə)] *nm* top hat.

'hauteur [ˈotœʀ] *nf* height; (*fig*) loftiness; haughtiness; à la ~ de (*sur la même ligne*) level with; by; (*fig*) equal to; à la ~ (*fig*) up to it.

'haut-fond [ˈofɔ̃] *nm* shallow, shoal.

'haut-fourneau [ˈofuʀno] *nm* blast *ou* smelting furnace.

'haut-le-cœur [ˈolkœʀ] *nm inv* retch, heave.

'haut-parleur [ˈopaʀlœʀ] *nm* (loud)speaker.

'havre [ˈavʀ(ə)] *nm* haven.

'Haye [ˈɛ] *n*: la ~ the Hague.

'hayon [ˈejɔ̃] *nm* tailgate.

hebdo [ɛbdo] *nm* (*fam*) weekly.

hebdomadaire [ɛbdɔmadɛʀ] *a, nm* weekly.

héberger [ebɛʀʒe] *vt* to accommodate, lodge; (*réfugiés*) to take in.

hébété, e [ebete] *a* dazed.

hébreu, x [ebʀø] *am, nm* Hebrew.

hécatombe [ekatɔ̃b] *nf* slaughter.

hectare [ɛktaʀ] *nm* hectare.

'hein [ˈɛ̃] *excl* eh?

'hélas [ˈelas] *excl* alas! // *ad* unfortunately.

'héler [ˈele] *vt* to hail.

hélice [elis] *nf* propeller.

hélicoptère [elikɔptɛʀ] *nm* helicopter.

helvétique [ɛlvetik] *a* Swiss.

hémicycle [emisikl(ə)] *nm* semicircle; (*POL*): l'~ ≈ the benches (of the Commons) (*Brit*), ≈ the floor (of the House of Representatives) (*US*).

hémorragie [emɔʀaʒi] *nf* bleeding *q*, haemorrhage.

hémorroïdes [emɔʀɔid] *nfpl* piles, haemorrhoids.

'hennir [ˈenir] *vi* to neigh, whinny.

herbe [ɛʀb(ə)] *nf* grass; (*CULIN, MÉD*) herb; en ~ unripe; (*fig*) budding; **herbicide** *nm* weed-killer; **herboriste** *nm/f* herbalist.

'hère [ˈɛʀ] *nm*: pauvre ~ poor wretch.

héréditaire [eʀeditɛʀ] *a* hereditary.

'hérisser [ˈeʀise] *vt*: ~ qn (*fig*) to ruffle sb; se ~ *vi* to bristle, bristle up.

'hérisson [ˈeʀisɔ̃] *nm* hedgehog.

héritage [eʀitaʒ] *nm* inheritance; (*fig*) heritage; legacy.

hériter [eʀite] *vi*: ~ de qch (de qn) to inherit sth (from sb); **héritier, ière** *nm/f* heir/heiress.

hermétique [ɛʀmetik] *a* airtight; watertight; (*fig*) abstruse; impenetrable.

hermine [ɛʀmin] *nf* ermine.

'hernie [ˈɛʀni] *nf* hernia.

héroïne [eʀɔin] *nf* heroine; (*drogue*) heroin.

'héron [ˈeʀɔ̃] *nm* heron.

'héros [ˈeʀo] *nm* hero.

hésitation [ezitasjɔ̃] *nf* hesitation.

hésiter [ezite] *vi*: ~ (à faire) to hesitate (to do).

hétéroclite [eteʀɔklit] *a* heterogeneous; (*objets*) sundry.

'hêtre [ˈɛtʀ(ə)] *nm* beech.

heure [œʀ] *nf* hour; (*SCOL*) period; (*moment*) time; c'est l'~ it's time; quelle ~ est-il? what time is it? 2 ~s (du matin) 2 o'clock (in the morning); être à l'~ to be on time; (*montre*) to be right; mettre à l'~ to set right; à toute ~ at any time; 24 ~s sur 24 round the clock, 24 hours a day; à l'~ qu'il est at this time (of day); by now; sur l'~ at once; ~s supplémentaires overtime *sg*.

heureusement [œʀøzmɑ̃] *ad* (*par bonheur*) fortunately, luckily.

heureux, euse [œʀø, -øz] *a* happy; (*chanceux*) lucky, fortunate; (*judicieux*) felicitous, fortunate.

'heurt [ˈœʀ] *nm* (*choc*) collision; ~s (*fig*) clashes.

'heurter [ˈœʀte] *vt* (*mur*) to strike, hit; (*personne*) to collide with; (*fig*) to go against, upset; se ~ à *vt* (*fig*) to come up against; **'heurtoir** *nm* door knocker.

hexagone [ɛgzagɔn] *nm* hexagon; (*la France*) France (*because of its roughly hexagonal shape*).

hiberner [ibɛʀne] *vi* to hibernate.

'hibou, x ['ibu] *nm* owl.

'hideux, euse ['idø, -øz] *a* hideous.

hier [jɛʀ] *ad* yesterday; **toute la journée d'~** all day yesterday; **toute la matinée d'~** all yesterday morning.

'hiérarchie ['jeʀaʀʃi] *nf* hierarchy.

hilare [ilaʀ] *a* mirthful.

hippique [ipik] *a* equestrian, horse *cpd*.

hippodrome [ipɔdʀom] *nm* racecourse.

hippopotame [ipɔpɔtam] *nm* hippopotamus.

hirondelle [iʀɔ̃dɛl] *nf* swallow.

hirsute [iʀsyt] *a* hairy; shaggy; tousled.

'hisser ['ise] *vt* to hoist, haul up.

histoire [istwaʀ] *nf* (*science, événements*) history; (*anecdote, récit, mensonge*) story; (*affaire*) business *q*; ~**s** *nfpl* (*chichis*) fuss *q*; (*ennuis*) trouble *sg*; **historique** *a* historical; (*important*) historic.

hiver [ivɛʀ] *nm* winter; ~**nal, e, aux** *a* winter *cpd*; wintry; ~**ner** *vi* to winter.

HLM *sigle m ou f voir* **habitation.**

'hobby ['ɔbi] *nm* hobby.

'hocher ['ɔʃe] *vt*: ~ **la tête** to nod; (*signe négatif ou dubitatif*) to shake one's head.

'hochet ['ɔʃe] *nm* rattle.

'hockey ['ɔkɛ] *nm*: ~ (**sur glace/gazon**) (ice/field) hockey.

'hold-up ['ɔldœp] *nm inv* hold-up.

'hollandais, e ['ɔlɑ̃dɛ, -ɛz] *a, nm* (*LING*) Dutch // *nm/f*: H~, e Dutchman/woman; **les** H~ the Dutch.

'Hollande ['ɔlɑ̃d] *nf*: **la** ~ Holland.

'homard ['ɔmaʀ] *nm* lobster.

homéopathique [ɔmeɔpatik] *a* homoeopathic.

homicide [ɔmisid] *nm* murder; ~ **involontaire** manslaughter.

hommage [ɔmaʒ] *nm* tribute; ~**s** *nmpl*: **présenter ses** ~**s** to pay one's respects; **rendre** ~ **à** to pay tribute *ou* homage to.

homme [ɔm] *nm* man; ~ **d'affaires** businessman; ~ **d'État** statesman; ~ **de main** hired man; ~ **de paille** stooge; ~**-grenouille** *nm* frogman.

homogène [ɔmɔʒɛn] *a* homogeneous.

homologue [ɔmɔlɔg] *nm/f* counterpart, opposite number.

homologué, e [ɔmɔlɔge] *a* (*SPORT*) officially recognized, ratified; (*tarif*) authorized.

homonyme [ɔmɔnim] *nm* (*LING*) homonym; (*d'une personne*) namesake.

homosexuel, le [ɔmɔsɛksɥɛl] *a* homosexual.

'Hongrie ['ɔ̃gʀi] *nf*: **la** ~ Hungary; **'hongrois, e** *a, nm/f* Hungarian.

honnête [ɔnɛt] *a* (*intègre*) honest; (*juste, satisfaisant*) fair; ~**ment** *ad*

honestly; ~**té** *nf* honesty.

honneur [ɔnœʀ] *nm* honour; (*mérite*) credit; **en l'~** **de** in honour of; (*événement*) on the occasion of; **faire** ~ **à** (*engagements*) to honour; (*famille*) to be a credit to; (*fig: repas etc*) to do justice to.

honorable [ɔnɔʀabl(ə)] *a* worthy, honourable; (*suffisant*) decent.

honoraire [ɔnɔʀɛʀ] *a* honorary; ~**s** *nmpl* fees *pl*; **professeur** ~ professor emeritus.

honorer [ɔnɔʀe] *vt* to honour; (*estimer*) to hold in high regard; (*faire honneur à*) to do credit to; **s'~ de** to pride o.s. upon; **honorifique** *a* honorary.

'honte ['ɔ̃t] *nf* shame; **avoir** ~ **de** to be ashamed of; **faire** ~ **à qn** to make sb (feel) ashamed; **'honteux, euse** *a* ashamed; (*conduite, acte*) shameful, disgraceful.

hôpital, aux [ɔpital, -o] *nm* hospital.

'hoquet ['ɔkɛ] *nm*: **avoir le** ~ to have (the) hiccoughs; **'hoqueter** ['ɔkte] *vi* to hiccough.

horaire [ɔʀɛʀ] *a* hourly // *nm* timetable, schedule; ~ **souple** flexitime; ~**s** *nmpl* (*d'employé*) hours.

horizon [ɔʀizɔ̃] *nm* horizon; (*paysage*) landscape, view.

horizontal, e, aux [ɔʀizɔ̃tal, -o] *a* horizontal.

horloge [ɔʀlɔʒ] *nf* clock; **horloger, ère** *nm/f* watchmaker; clockmaker; ~**rie** *nf* watch-making; watchmaker's (shop); clockmaker's (shop).

'hormis ['ɔʀmi] *prép* save.

horoscope [ɔʀɔskɔp] *nm* horoscope.

horreur [ɔʀœʀ] *nf* horror; **avoir** ~ **de** to loathe *ou* detest; **horrible** *a* horrible.

horripiler [ɔʀipile] *vt* to exasperate.

'hors ['ɔʀ] *prép* except (for); ~ **de** out of; ~ **pair** outstanding; ~ **de propos** inopportune; **être** ~ **de soi** to be beside o.s.; ~**-bord** *nm inv* speedboat (with outboard motor); ~**-concours** *a* ineligible to compete; ~**-d'œuvre** *nm inv* hors d'œuvre; ~**-jeu** *nm inv* offside; ~**-la-loi** *nm inv* outlaw; ~**-taxe** *a* (*boutique, articles*) duty-free.

hospice [ɔspis] *nm* (*de vieillards*) home.

hospitalier, ière [ɔspitalje, -jɛʀ] *a* (*accueillant*) hospitable; (*MÉD: service, centre*) hospital *cpd*.

hospitalité [ɔspitalite] *nf* hospitality.

hostie [ɔsti] *nf* host (*REL*).

hostile [ɔstil] *a* hostile; **hostilité** *nf* hostility.

hôte [ot] *nm* (*maître de maison*) host; (*invité*) guest.

hôtel [otɛl] *nm* hotel; **aller à l'~** to stay in a hotel; ~ (**particulier**) (private) mansion; ~ **de ville** town hall; **hôtelier, ière** *a* hotel *cpd* // *nm/f* hotelier; ~**lerie** *nf* hotel business; (*auberge*) inn.

hôtesse [otɛs] nf hostess; ~ de l'air air stewardess.

'**hotte** ['ɔt] nf (panier) basket (carried on the back); (de cheminée) hood; ~ aspirante cooker hood.

'**houblon** ['ublɔ̃] nm (BOT) hop; (pour la bière) hops pl.

'**houille** ['uj] nf coal; ~ blanche hydro-electric power.

'**houle** ['ul] nf swell.

'**houlette** ['ulɛt] nf: sous la ~ de under the guidance of.

'**houleux, euse** ['ulø, -øz] a heavy, swelling; (fig) stormy, turbulent.

'**houspiller** ['uspije] vt to scold.

'**housse** ['us] nf cover; dust cover; loose ou stretch cover.

'**houx** ['u] nm holly.

'**hublot** ['yblo] nm porthole.

'**huche** ['yʃ] nf: ~ à pain bread bin.

'**huer** ['ɥe] vt to boo.

huile [ɥil] nf oil; ~ de foie de morue cod-liver oil; **huiler** vt to oil; **huileux, euse** a oily.

huis [ɥi] nm: à ~ clos in camera.

huissier [ɥisje] nm usher; (JUR) ≈ bailiff.

'**huit** ['ɥit] num eight; samedi en ~ a week on Saturday; une huitaine de jours a week or so; '**huitième** num eighth.

huître [ɥitr(ə)] nf oyster.

humain, e [ymɛ̃, -ɛn] a human; (compatissant) humane // nm human (being); **humanité** nf humanity.

humble [œ̃bl(ə)] a humble.

humecter [ymɛkte] vt to dampen.

'**humer** ['yme] vt to smell; to inhale.

humeur [ymœr] nf mood; (tempérament) temper; (irritation) bad temper; de bonne/mauvaise ~ in a good/bad mood.

humide [ymid] a damp; (main, yeux) moist; (climat, chaleur) humid; (saison, route) wet.

humilier [ymilje] vt to humiliate.

humilité [ymilite] nf humility, humbleness.

humoristique [ymɔristik] a humorous; humoristic.

humour [ymur] nm humour; avoir de l'~ to have a sense of humour; ~ noir sick humour.

'**hurlement** ['yrləmɑ̃] nm howling q, howl, yelling q, yell.

'**hurler** ['yrle] vi to howl, yell.

hurluberlu [yrlybɛrly] nm (péj) crank.

'**hutte** ['yt] nf hut.

hydratant, e [idratɑ̃, -ɑ̃t] a (crème) moisturizing.

hydrate [idrat] nm: ~s de carbone carbohydrates.

hydraulique [idrolik] a hydraulic.

hydravion [idravjɔ̃] nm seaplane.

hydrogène [idrɔʒɛn] nm hydrogen.

hydroglisseur [idrɔglisœr] nm hydro-plane.

hygiénique [iʒjenik] a hygienic.

hymne [imn(ə)] nm hymn; ~ national national anthem.

hypermarché [ipɛrmarʃe] nm hyper-market.

hypermétrope [ipɛrmetrɔp] a long-sighted.

hypnotiser [ipnɔtize] vt to hypnotize.

hypocrite [ipɔkrit] a hypocritical.

hypothèque [ipɔtɛk] nf mortgage.

hypothèse [ipɔtɛz] nf hypothesis.

hystérique [isterik] a hysterical.

I

iceberg [isbɛrg] nm iceberg.

ici [isi] ad here; jusqu'~ as far as this; until now; d'~ là by then; in the mean-time; d'~ peu before long.

idéal, e, aux [ideal, -o] a ideal // nm ideal; ideals pl.

idée [ide] nf idea; avoir dans l'~ que to have an idea that; ~s noires black ou dark thoughts.

identifier [idɑ̃tifje] vt to identify; s'~ à (héros etc) to identify with.

identique [idɑ̃tik] a: ~ (à) identical (to).

identité [idɑ̃tite] nf identity.

idiot, e [idjo, idjɔt] a idiotic // nm/f idiot.

idole [idɔl] nf idol.

if [if] nm yew.

ignare [iɲar] a ignorant.

ignifugé, e [iɲifyʒe] a fireproof(ed).

ignoble [iɲɔbl(ə)] a vile.

ignorant, e [iɲɔrɑ̃, -ɑ̃t] a ignorant.

ignorer [iɲɔre] vt (ne pas connaître) not to know, be unaware ou ignorant of; (être sans expérience de: plaisir, guerre etc) not to know about, have no experience of; (bouder: personne) to ignore.

il [il] pronom he; (animal, chose, en tournure impersonnelle) it; ~s they; voir aussi avoir.

île [il] nf island; les ~s anglo-normandes the Channel Islands; les ~s Britanniques the British Isles.

illégal, e, aux [ilegal, -o] a illegal.

illégitime [ileʒitim] a illegitimate.

illettré, e [iletre] a, nm/f illiterate.

illimité, e [ilimite] a unlimited.

illisible [ilizibl(ə)] a illegible; (roman) unreadable.

illumination [ilyminasjɔ̃] nf illumination, floodlighting; (idée) flash of inspiration.

illuminer [ilymine] vt to light up; (monument, rue: pour une fête) to illuminate, floodlight.

illusion [ilyzjɔ̃] nf illusion; se faire des ~s to delude o.s.; faire ~ to delude ou fool people; **illusionniste** nm/f conjuror.

illustration 106 **important**

illustration [ilystʀasjɔ̃] *nf* illustration.
illustre [ilystʀ(ə)] *a* illustrious.
illustré, e [ilystʀe] *a* illustrated // *nm* illustrated magazine; comic.
illustrer [ilystʀe] *vt* to illustrate; s'~ to become famous, win fame.
îlot [ilo] *nm* small island, islet; (*de maisons*) block.
ils [il] *pronom voir* **il**.
image [imaʒ] *nf* (*gén*) picture; (*comparaison, ressemblance, OPTIQUE*) image; ~ **de marque** brand image; (*fig*) public image.
imagination [imaʒinasjɔ̃] *nf* imagination; (*chimère*) fancy; **avoir de l'~** to be imaginative.
imaginer [imaʒine] *vt* to imagine; (*inventer: expédient*) to devise, think up; s'~ *vt* (*se figurer: scène etc*) to imagine, picture; s'~ **que** to imagine that.
imbécile [ɛ̃besil] *a* idiotic // *nm/f* idiot.
imberbe [ɛ̃bɛʀb(ə)] *a* beardless.
imbiber [ɛ̃bibe] *vt* to moisten, wet; s'~ **de** to become saturated with.
imbu, e [ɛ̃by] *a*: ~ **de** full of.
imitateur, trice [imitatœʀ, -tʀis] *nm/f* (*gén*) imitator; (*MUSIC-HALL*) impersonator.
imitation [imitasjɔ̃] *nf* imitation; (*sketch*) imitation, impression; impersonation.
imiter [imite] *vt* to imitate; (*contrefaire*) to forge; (*ressembler à*) to look like.
immaculé, e [imakyle] *a* spotless; immaculate.
immatriculation [imatʀikylasjɔ̃] *nf* registration.
immatriculer [imatʀikyle] *vt* to register; **faire/se faire ~** to register.
immédiat, e [imedja, -at] *a* immediate // *nm*: **dans l'~** for the time being; **immédiatement** *ad* immediately.
immense [imɑ̃s] *a* immense.
immerger [imɛʀʒe] *vt* to immerse, submerge.
immeuble [imœbl(ə)] *nm* building; ~ **locatif** block of rented flats (*Brit*), rental building (*US*).
immigration [imigʀasjɔ̃] *nf* immigration.
immigré, e [imigʀe] *nm/f* immigrant.
imminent, e [iminɑ̃, -ɑ̃t] *a* imminent.
immiscer [imise]: s'~ *vi*: s'~ **dans** to interfere in *ou* with.
immobile [imɔbil] *a* still, motionless; (*fig*) unchanging.
immobilier, ière [imɔbilje, -jɛʀ] *a* property *cpd* // *nm*: **l'~** the property business.
immobiliser [imɔbilize] *vt* (*gén*) to immobilize; (*circulation, véhicule, affaires*) to bring to a standstill; s'~ (*personne*) to stand still; (*machine, véhicule*) to come to a halt.
immonde [imɔ̃d] *a* foul.

immondices [imɔ̃dis] *nmpl* refuse *sg*; filth *sg*.
immoral, e, aux [imɔʀal, -o] *a* immoral.
immuable [imɥabl(ə)] *a* immutable; unchanging.
immunisé, e [imynize] *a*: ~ **contre** immune to.
immunité [imynite] *nf* immunity.
impact [ɛ̃pakt] *nm* impact.
impair, e [ɛ̃pɛʀ] *a* odd // *nm* faux pas, blunder.
impardonnable [ɛ̃paʀdɔnabl(ə)] *a* unpardonable, unforgivable.
imparfait, e [ɛ̃paʀfɛ, -ɛt] *a* imperfect.
impartial, e, aux [ɛ̃paʀsjal, -o] *a* impartial, unbiased.
impartir [ɛ̃paʀtiʀ] *vt* to assign; to bestow.
impasse [ɛ̃pɑs] *nf* dead-end, cul-de-sac; (*fig*) deadlock.
impassible [ɛ̃pasibl(ə)] *a* impassive.
impatience [ɛ̃pasjɑ̃s] *nf* impatience.
impatient, e [ɛ̃pasjɑ̃, -ɑ̃t] *a* impatient; **impatienter** *vt* to irritate, annoy; s'**impatienter** to get impatient.
impayable [ɛ̃pɛjabl(ə)] *a* (*drôle*) priceless.
impeccable [ɛ̃pekabl(ə)] *a* faultless, impeccable; spotlessly clean; impeccably dressed; (*fam*) smashing.
impensable [ɛ̃pɑ̃sabl(ə)] *a* unthinkable; unbelievable.
impératif, ive [ɛ̃peʀatif, -iv] *a* imperative // *nm* (*LING*) imperative; ~s *nmpl* requirements; demands.
impératrice [ɛ̃peʀatʀis] *nf* empress.
impérial, e, aux [ɛ̃peʀjal, -o] *a* imperial // *nf* top deck.
impérieux, euse [ɛ̃peʀjø, -øz] *a* (*caractère, ton*) imperious; (*obligation, besoin*) pressing, urgent.
impérissable [ɛ̃peʀisabl(ə)] *a* undying; imperishable.
imperméable [ɛ̃pɛʀmeabl(ə)] *a* waterproof; (*GÉO*) impermeable; (*fig*): ~ **à** impervious to // *nm* raincoat.
impertinent, e [ɛ̃pɛʀtinɑ̃, -ɑ̃t] *a* impertinent.
impétueux, euse [ɛ̃petɥø, -øz] *a* fiery.
impie [ɛ̃pi] *a* impious, ungodly.
impitoyable [ɛ̃pitwajabl(ə)] *a* pitiless, merciless.
implanter [ɛ̃plɑ̃te] *vt* (*usine, industrie, usage*) to establish; (*colons etc*) to settle; (*idée, préjugé*) to implant.
impliquer [ɛ̃plike] *vt* to imply; ~ **qn** (*dans*) to implicate sb (in).
impoli, e [ɛ̃pɔli] *a* impolite, rude.
importance [ɛ̃pɔʀtɑ̃s] *nf* importance; **sans ~** unimportant.
important, e [ɛ̃pɔʀtɑ̃, -ɑ̃t] *a* important; (*en quantité*) considerable, sizeable; extensive; (*péj: airs, ton*) self-important // *nm*: **l'~** the important thing.

importateur, trice [ɛ̃pɔʀtatœʀ, -tʀis] *nm/f* importer.

importation [ɛ̃pɔʀtasjɔ̃] *nf* importation; introduction; (*produit*) import.

importer [ɛ̃pɔʀte] *vt* (*COMM*) to import; (*maladies, plantes*) to introduce // *vi* (*être important*) to matter; **il importe qu'il fasse** it is important that he should do; **peu m'importe** I don't mind; I don't care; **peu importe (que)** it doesn't matter (if); *voir aussi* **n'importe**.

importun, e [ɛ̃pɔʀtœ̃, -yn] *a* irksome, importunate; (*arrivée, visite*) inopportune, ill-timed // *nm* intruder; **importuner** *vt* to bother.

imposant, e [ɛ̃pozɑ̃, -ɑ̃t] *a* imposing.

imposer [ɛ̃poze] *vt* (*taxer*) to tax; ~ **qch à qn** to impose sth on sb; **s'~** (*être nécessaire*) to be imperative; (*montrer sa prominence*) to stand out, emerge; (*artiste: se faire connaître*) to win recognition; **en ~ à** to impress.

imposition [ɛ̃pozisjɔ̃] *nf* (*ADMIN*) taxation.

impossible [ɛ̃pɔsibl(ə)] *a* impossible; **il m'est ~ de le faire** it is impossible for me to do it, I can't possibly do it; **faire l'~** to do one's utmost.

impôt [ɛ̃po] *nm* tax; (*taxes*) taxation; taxes *pl*; ~**s** *nmpl* (*contributions*) (income) tax *sg*; **payer 1000 F d'~s** to pay 1,000 F in tax; ~ **sur le chiffre d'affaires** corporation (*Brit*) *ou* corporate (*US*) tax; ~ **foncier** land tax; ~ **sur le revenu** income tax.

impotent, e [ɛ̃pɔtɑ̃, -ɑ̃t] *a* disabled.

impraticable [ɛ̃pʀatikabl(ə)] *a* (*projet*) impracticable, unworkable; (*piste*) impassable.

imprécis, e [ɛ̃pʀesi, -iz] *a* imprecise.

imprégner [ɛ̃pʀeɲe] *vt* (*tissu, tampon*) to soak, impregnate; (*lieu, air*) to fill; **s'~ de** (*fig*) to absorb.

imprenable [ɛ̃pʀənabl(ə)] *a* (*forteresse*) impregnable; **vue ~** unimpeded outlook.

impression [ɛ̃pʀesjɔ̃] *nf* impression; (*d'un ouvrage, tissu*) printing; **faire bonne ~** to make a good impression.

impressionnant, e [ɛ̃pʀesjɔnɑ̃, -ɑ̃t] *a* impressive; upsetting.

impressionner [ɛ̃pʀesjɔne] *vt* (*frapper*) to impress; (*troubler*) to upset.

imprévisible [ɛ̃pʀevizibl(ə)] *a* unforeseeable.

imprévoyant, e [ɛ̃pʀevwajɑ̃, -ɑ̃t] *a* lacking in foresight; (*en matière d'argent*) improvident.

imprévu, e [ɛ̃pʀevy] *a* unforeseen, unexpected // *nm* unexpected incident; **en cas d'~** if anything unexpected happens.

imprimante [ɛ̃pʀimɑ̃t] *nf* printer; ~ **matricielle** dot-matrix printer.

imprimé [ɛ̃pʀime] *nm* (*formulaire*) printed form; (*POSTES*) printed matter *q*.

imprimer [ɛ̃pʀime] *vt* to print; (*empreinte etc*) to imprint; (*publier*) to publish; (*communiquer: mouvement, impulsion*) to impart, transmit; **imprimerie** *nf* printing; (*établissement*) printing works *sg*; **imprimeur** *nm* printer.

impromptu, e [ɛ̃pʀɔ̃pty] *a* impromptu; sudden.

impropre [ɛ̃pʀɔpʀ(ə)] *a* inappropriate; ~ **à** unsuitable for.

improviser [ɛ̃pʀɔvize] *vt, vi* to improvise.

improviste [ɛ̃pʀɔvist(ə)]: **à l'~** *ad* unexpectedly, without warning.

imprudence [ɛ̃pʀydɑ̃s] *nf* carelessness *q*; imprudence *q*.

imprudent, e [ɛ̃pʀydɑ̃, -ɑ̃t] *a* (*conducteur, geste, action*) careless; (*remarque*) unwise, imprudent; (*projet*) foolhardy.

impudent, e [ɛ̃pydɑ̃, -ɑ̃t] *a* impudent; brazen.

impudique [ɛ̃pydik] *a* shameless.

impuissant, e [ɛ̃pɥisɑ̃, -ɑ̃t] *a* helpless; (*sans effet*) ineffectual; (*sexuellement*) impotent; ~ **à faire** powerless to do.

impulsif, ive [ɛ̃pylsif, -iv] *a* impulsive.

impulsion [ɛ̃pylsjɔ̃] *nf* (*ÉLEC, instinct*) impulse; (*élan, influence*) impetus.

impunément [ɛ̃pynemɑ̃] *ad* with impunity.

imputer [ɛ̃pyte] *vt* (*attribuer*) to ascribe, impute; (*COMM*): ~ **à** *ou* **sur** to charge to.

inabordable [inabɔʀdabl(ə)] *a* (*cher*) prohibitive.

inaccessible [inaksesibl(ə)] *a* inaccessible; unattainable; (*insensible*): ~ **à** impervious to.

inachevé, e [inaʃve] *a* unfinished.

inadapté, e [inadapte] *a* (*gén*): ~ **à** not adapted to, unsuited to; (*PSYCH*) maladjusted.

inadmissible [inadmisibl(ə)] *a* inadmissible.

inadvertance [inadvɛʀtɑ̃s]: **par ~** *ad* inadvertently.

inaltérable [inalteʀabl(ə)] *a* (*matière*) stable; (*fig*) unchanging; ~ **à** unaffected by.

inamovible [inamɔvibl(ə)] *a* fixed; (*JUR*) irremovable.

inanimé, e [inanime] *a* (*matière*) inanimate; (*évanoui*) unconscious; (*sans vie*) lifeless.

inanition [inanisjɔ̃] *nf*: **tomber d'~** to faint with hunger (and exhaustion).

inaperçu, e [inapɛʀsy] *a*: **passer ~** to go unnoticed.

inappréciable [inapʀesjabl(ə)] *a* (*service*) invaluable.

inapte [inapt(ə)] *a*: ~ **à** incapable of; (*MIL*) unfit for.

inattaquable [inatakabl(ə)] *a* (*texte, preuve*) irrefutable.

inattendu, e [inatɑ̃dy] *a* unexpected.

inattentif, ive [inatɑ̃tif, -iv] *a* inattentive; ~ **à** (*dangers, détails*) heedless of; **inattention** *nf*: **faute d'inattention** careless mistake.

inaugurer [inɔgyʀe] *vt* (*monument*) to unveil; (*exposition, usine*) to open; (*fig*) to inaugurate.

inavouable [inavwabl(ə)] *a* shameful; undisclosable.

inavoué, e [inavwe] *a* unavowed.

incandescence [ɛ̃kɑ̃desɑ̃s] *nf*: **porter à** ~ to heat white-hot.

incapable [ɛ̃kapabl(ə)] *a* incapable; ~ **de faire** incapable of doing; (*empêché*) unable to do.

incapacité [ɛ̃kapasite] *nf* incapability; (*JUR*) incapacity.

incarner [ɛ̃kaʀne] *vt* to embody, personify; (*THÉÂTRE*) to play.

incartade [ɛ̃kaʀtad] *nf* prank.

incassable [ɛ̃kɑsabl(ə)] *a* unbreakable.

incendiaire [ɛ̃sɑ̃djɛʀ] *a* incendiary; (*fig: discours*) inflammatory // *nm/f* fire-raiser, arsonist.

incendie [ɛ̃sɑ̃di] *nm* fire; ~ **criminel** arson *q*; ~ **de forêt** forest fire.

incendier [ɛ̃sɑ̃dje] *vt* (*mettre le feu à*) to set fire to, set alight; (*brûler complètement*) to burn down.

incertain, e [ɛ̃sɛʀtɛ̃, -ɛn] *a* uncertain; (*temps*) uncertain, unsettled; (*imprécis: contours*) indistinct, blurred; **incertitude** *nf* uncertainty.

incessamment [ɛ̃sɛsamɑ̃] *ad* very shortly.

incidemment [ɛ̃sidamɑ̃] *ad* in passing.

incident [ɛ̃sidɑ̃] *nm* incident; ~ **de parcours** minor hitch *ou* setback; ~ **technique** technical difficulties *pl*.

incinérer [ɛ̃sineʀe] *vt* (*ordures*) to incinerate; (*mort*) to cremate.

incisive [ɛ̃siziv] *nf* incisor.

inclinaison [ɛ̃klinɛzɔ̃] *nf* (*déclivité: d'une route etc*) incline; (: *d'un toit*) slope; (*état penché*) tilt.

inclination [ɛ̃klinɑsjɔ̃] *nf*: ~ **de (la) tête** nod (of the head); ~ **(de buste)** bow.

incliner [ɛ̃kline] *vt* (*tête, bouteille*) to tilt // *vi*: ~ **à qch/à faire** to incline towards sth/doing; **s'**~ **(devant)** to bow (before); (*céder*) to give in *ou* yield (to); ~ **la tête** *ou* **le front** to give a slight bow.

inclure [ɛ̃klyʀ] *vt* to include; (*joindre à un envoi*) to enclose; **jusqu'au 10 mars inclus** until 10th March inclusive.

incoercible [ɛ̃kɔɛʀsibl(ə)] *a* uncontrollable.

incohérent, e [ɛ̃kɔeʀɑ̃, -ɑ̃t] *a* inconsistent; incoherent.

incollable [ɛ̃kɔlabl(ə)] *a*: **il est** ~ he's got all the answers.

incolore [ɛ̃kɔlɔʀ] *a* colourless.

incomber [ɛ̃kɔ̃be]: ~ **à** *vt* (*suj: devoirs, responsabilité*) to rest upon; (: *frais, travail*) to be the responsibility of.

incommensurable [ɛ̃kɔmɑ̃syʀabl(ə)] *a* immeasurable.

incommode [ɛ̃kɔmɔd] *a* inconvenient; (*posture, siège*) uncomfortable.

incommoder [ɛ̃kɔmɔde] *vt*: ~ **qn** to inconvenience sb; (*embarrasser*) to make sb feel uncomfortable.

incompétent, e [ɛ̃kɔ̃petɑ̃, -ɑ̃t] *a* incompetent.

incompris, e [ɛ̃kɔ̃pʀi, -iz] *a* misunderstood.

inconcevable [ɛ̃kɔ̃svabl(ə)] *a* incredible.

inconciliable [ɛ̃kɔ̃siljabl(ə)] *a* irreconcilable.

inconditionnel, le [ɛ̃kɔ̃disjɔnɛl] *a* unconditional; (*partisan*) unquestioning.

inconduite [ɛ̃kɔ̃dɥit] *nf* wild behaviour *q*.

incongru, e [ɛ̃kɔ̃gʀy] *a* unseemly.

inconnu, e [ɛ̃kɔny] *a* unknown; new, strange (*ou* artist *etc*) // *nm/f* stranger; unknown person (*ou* artist *etc*) // *nm*: **l'**~ the unknown // *nf* unknown.

inconsciemment [ɛ̃kɔ̃sjamɑ̃] *ad* unconsciously.

inconscient, e [ɛ̃kɔ̃sjɑ̃, -ɑ̃t] *a* unconscious; (*irréfléchi*) thoughtless, reckless // *nm* (*PSYCH*): **l'**~ the unconscious; ~ **de** unaware of.

inconsidéré, e [ɛ̃kɔ̃sideʀe] *a* ill-considered.

inconsistant, e [ɛ̃kɔ̃sistɑ̃, -ɑ̃t] *a* flimsy, weak; runny.

incontestable [ɛ̃kɔ̃tɛstabl(ə)] *a* indisputable.

inconvenant, e [ɛ̃kɔ̃vnɑ̃, -ɑ̃t] *a* unseemly, improper.

inconvénient [ɛ̃kɔ̃venjɑ̃] *nm* (*d'une situation, d'un projet*) disadvantage, drawback; (*d'un remède, changement etc*) inconvenience; **si vous n'y voyez pas d'**~ if you have no objections.

incorporer [ɛ̃kɔʀpɔʀe] *vt*: ~ **(à)** to mix in (with); (*paragraphe etc*): ~ **(dans)** to incorporate (in); (*MIL: appeler*) to recruit, call up.

incorrect, e [ɛ̃kɔʀɛkt] *a* (*impropre, inconvenant*) improper; (*défectueux*) faulty; (*inexact*) incorrect; (*impoli*) impolite; (*déloyal*) underhand.

incrédule [ɛ̃kʀedyl] *a* incredulous; (*REL*) unbelieving.

increvable [ɛ̃kʀəvabl(ə)] *a* (*fam*) tireless.

incriminer [ɛ̃kʀimine] *vt* (*personne*) to incriminate; (*action, conduite*) to bring under attack; (*bonne foi, honnêteté*) to call into question.

incroyable [ɛ̃kʀwajabl(ə)] *a* incredible; unbelievable.

incruster [ɛ̃kʀyste] *vt* (*ART*) to inlay; **s'**~ *vi* (*invité*) to take root; (*radiateur etc*) to become coated with fur *ou* scale.

incubateur [ɛ̃kybatœʀ] *nm* incubator.
inculpé, e [ɛ̃kylpe] *nm/f* accused.
inculper [ɛ̃kylpe] *vt*: ~ **(de)** to charge (with).
inculquer [ɛ̃kylke] *vt*: ~ **qch à** to inculcate sth in *ou* instil sth into.
inculte [ɛ̃kylt(ə)] *a* uncultivated; (*esprit, peuple*) uncultured; (*barbe*) unkempt.
Inde [ɛ̃d] *nf*: l'~ India.
indécis, e [ɛ̃desi, -iz] *a* indecisive; (*perplexe*) undecided.
indéfendable [ɛ̃defɑ̃dabl(ə)] *a* indefensible.
indéfini, e [ɛ̃defini] *a* (*imprécis, incertain*) undefined; (*illimité*, LING) indefinite; ~**ment** *ad* indefinitely; ~**ssable** *a* indefinable.
indélicat, e [ɛ̃delika, -at] *a* tactless; dishonest.
indemne [ɛ̃dɛmn(ə)] *a* unharmed.
indemniser [ɛ̃dɛmnize] *vt*: ~ **qn (de)** to compensate sb (for).
indemnité [ɛ̃dɛmnite] *nf* (*dédommagement*) compensation *q*; (*allocation*) allowance; ~ **de licenciement** redundancy payment.
indépendamment [ɛ̃depɑ̃damɑ̃] *ad* independently; ~ **de** (*abstraction faite de*) irrespective of; (*en plus de*) over and above.
indépendance [ɛ̃depɑ̃dɑ̃s] *nf* independence.
indépendant, e [ɛ̃depɑ̃dɑ̃, -ɑ̃t] *a* independent; ~ **de** independent of.
indescriptible [ɛ̃dɛskʀiptibl(ə)] *a* indescribable.
indétermination [ɛ̃detɛʀminasjɔ̃] *nf* indecision; indecisiveness.
indéterminé, e [ɛ̃detɛʀmine] *a* unspecified; indeterminate.
index [ɛ̃dɛks] *nm* (*doigt*) index finger; (*d'un livre etc*) index; **mettre à l'~** to blacklist.
indexé, e [ɛ̃dɛkse] *a* (ÉCON): ~ **(sur)** index-linked (to).
indicateur [ɛ̃dikatœʀ] *nm* (POLICE) informer; (*livre*) guide; directory; (TECH) gauge; indicator; ~ **des chemins de fer** railway timetable.
indicatif, ive [ɛ̃dikatif, -iv] *a*: **à titre** ~ for (your) information // *nm* (LING) indicative; (RADIO) theme *ou* signature tune; (TÉL) dialling code.
indication [ɛ̃dikasjɔ̃] *nf* indication; (*renseignement*) information *q*; ~**s** *nfpl* (*directives*) instructions.
indice [ɛ̃dis] *nm* (*marque, signe*) indication, sign; (POLICE: *lors d'une enquête*) clue; (JUR: *présomption*) piece of evidence; (SCIENCE, ÉCON, TECH) index.
indicible [ɛ̃disibl(ə)] *a* inexpressible.
indien, ne [ɛ̃djɛ̃, -jɛn] *a, nm/f* Indian.
indifféremment [ɛ̃difeʀamɑ̃] *ad* (*sans distinction*) equally (well); indiscriminately.

indifférence [ɛ̃difeʀɑ̃s] *nf* indifference.
indifférent, e [ɛ̃difeʀɑ̃, -ɑ̃t] *a* (*peu intéressé*) indifferent.
indigence [ɛ̃diʒɑ̃s] *nf* poverty.
indigène [ɛ̃diʒɛn] *a* native, indigenous; local // *nm/f* native.
indigeste [ɛ̃diʒɛst(ə)] *a* indigestible.
indigestion [ɛ̃diʒɛstjɔ̃] *nf* indigestion *q*.
indigne [ɛ̃diɲ] *a* unworthy.
indigner [ɛ̃diɲe] *vt*: s'~ **(de/contre)** to be indignant (at).
indiqué, e [ɛ̃dike] *a* (*date, lieu*) given; (*adéquat, conseillé*) suitable.
indiquer [ɛ̃dike] *vt* (*désigner*): ~ **qch/qn à qn** to point sth/sb out to sb; (*suj: pendule, aiguille*) to show; (*suj: étiquette, plan*) to show, indicate; (*faire connaître: médecin, restaurant*): ~ **qch/qn à qn** to tell sb of sth/sb; (*renseigner sur*) to point out, tell; (*déterminer: date, lieu*) to give, state; (*dénoter*) to indicate, point to.
indirect, e [ɛ̃diʀɛkt] *a* indirect.
indiscipline [ɛ̃disiplin] *nf* lack of discipline; **indiscipliné, e** *a* undisciplined; (*fig*) unmanageable.
indiscret, ète [ɛ̃diskʀɛ, -ɛt] *a* indiscreet.
indiscutable [ɛ̃diskytabl(ə)] *a* indisputable.
indispensable [ɛ̃dispɑ̃sabl(ə)] *a* indispensable; essential.
indisposer [ɛ̃dispoze] *vt* (*incommoder*) to upset; (*déplaire à*) to antagonize.
indistinct, e [ɛ̃distɛ̃, -ɛ̃kt(ə)] *a* indistinct; **indistinctement** *ad* (*voir, prononcer*) indistinctly; (*sans distinction*) indiscriminately.
individu [ɛ̃dividy] *nm* individual.
individuel, le [ɛ̃dividɥɛl] *a* (*gén*) individual; (*opinion, livret, contrôle, avantages*) personal; **chambre** ~**le** single room; **maison** ~**le** detached house.
indolore [ɛ̃dɔlɔʀ] *a* painless.
indomptable [ɛ̃dɔ̃tabl(ə)] *a* untameable; (*fig*) invincible, indomitable.
Indonésie [ɛ̃donezi] *nf* Indonesia.
indu, e [ɛ̃dy] *a*: **à des heures** ~**es** at some ungodly hour.
induire [ɛ̃dɥiʀ] *vt*: ~ **qn en erreur** to lead sb astray, mislead sb.
indulgent, e [ɛ̃dylʒɑ̃, -ɑ̃t] *a* (*parent, regard*) indulgent; (*juge, examinateur*) lenient.
indûment [ɛ̃dymɑ̃] *ad* wrongfully; without due cause.
industrie [ɛ̃dystʀi] *nf* industry; **industriel, le** *a* industrial // *nm* industrialist; manufacturer.
inébranlable [inebʀɑ̃labl(ə)] *a* (*masse, colonne*) solid; (*personne, certitude, foi*) steadfast, unwavering.
inédit, e [inedi, -it] *a* (*correspondance etc*) hitherto unpublished; (*spectacle, moyen*) novel, original.

ineffaçable |inɛfasabl(ə)| a indelible.

inefficace |inɛfikas| a (remède, moyen) ineffective; (machine, employé) inefficient.

inégal, e, aux |inɛgal, -o| a unequal; uneven.

inégalable |inɛgalabl(ə)| a matchless.

inégalé, e |inɛgalɛ| a unmatched, unequalled.

inerte |inɛʀt(ə)| a lifeless; inert.

inestimable |inɛstimabl(ə)| a priceless; (fig: bienfait) invaluable.

inévitable |inɛvitabl(ə)| a unavoidable; (fatal, habituel) inevitable.

inexact, e |inɛgzakt| a inaccurate, inexact; unpunctual.

in extenso |inɛkstɛ̃so| ad in full.

in extremis |inɛkstʀɛmis| ad at the last minute // a last-minute.

infaillible |ɛ̃fajibl(ə)| a infallible.

infâme |ɛ̃fɑm| a vile.

infanticide |ɛ̃fɑ̃tisid| nm/f childmurderer/eress // nm (meurtre) infanticide.

infarctus |ɛ̃faʀktys| nm: ~ (du myocarde) coronary (thrombosis).

infatigable |ɛ̃fatigabl(ə)| a tireless.

infect, e |ɛ̃fɛkt| a vile; foul; (repas, vin) revolting.

infecter |ɛ̃fɛkte| vt (atmosphère, eau) to contaminate; (MÉD) to infect; s'~ to become infected ou septic; **infection** [-sjɔ̃] nf infection.

inférieur, e |ɛ̃feʀjœʀ| a lower; (en qualité, intelligence) inferior; ~ à (somme, quantité) less ou smaller than; (moins bon que) inferior to.

infernal, e, aux |ɛ̃fɛʀnal, -o| a (chaleur, rythme) infernal; (méchanceté, complot) diabolical.

infidèle |ɛ̃fidɛl| a unfaithful.

infiltrer |ɛ̃filtʀe| s'~ vi: s'~ dans to penetrate into; (liquide) to seep into; (fig: noyauter) to infiltrate.

infime |ɛ̃fim| a minute, tiny; (inférieur) lowly.

infini, e |ɛ̃fini| a infinite // nm infinity; à l'~ (MATH) to infinity; (agrandir, varier) infinitely; (interminablement) endlessly; **infinité** nf: une infinité de an infinite number of.

infinitif |ɛ̃finitif| nm infinitive.

infirme |ɛ̃fiʀm(ə)| a disabled // nm/f disabled person; ~ de guerre war cripple.

infirmer |ɛ̃fiʀme| vt to invalidate.

infirmerie |ɛ̃fiʀməʀi| nf sick bay.

infirmier, ière |ɛ̃fiʀmje, -jɛʀ| nm/f nurse; **infirmière chef** sister; **infirmière visiteuse** ≈ district nurse.

infirmité |ɛ̃fiʀmite| nf disability.

inflammable |ɛ̃flamabl(ə)| a (in)flammable.

inflation |ɛ̃flasjɔ̃| nf inflation.

inflexion |ɛ̃flɛksjɔ̃| nf inflexion; ~ de la tête slight nod (of the head).

infliger |ɛ̃fliʒe| vt: ~ qch (à qn) to inflict sth (on sb); (amende, sanction) to impose sth (on sb).

influence |ɛ̃flyɑ̃s| nf influence; (d'un médicament) effect; **influencer** vt to influence; **influent, e** a influential.

influer |ɛ̃flye| : ~ sur vt to have an influence upon.

informaticien, ne |ɛ̃fɔʀmatisjɛ̃, -jɛn| nm/f computer scientist.

information |ɛ̃fɔʀmasjɔ̃| nf (renseignement) piece of information; (PRESSE, TV: nouvelle) item of news; ~s (TV) news sg; (diffusion de renseignements, INFORM) information; (JUR) inquiry, investigation; **voyage d'~** fact-finding trip.

informatique |ɛ̃fɔʀmatik| nf (technique) data processing; (science) computer science // a computer cpd; **informatiser** vt to computerize.

informe |ɛ̃fɔʀm(ə)| a shapeless.

informer |ɛ̃fɔʀme| vt: ~ qn (de) to inform sb (of); s'~ (de/si) to inquire ou find out (about/whether ou if).

infortune |ɛ̃fɔʀtyn| nf misfortune.

infraction |ɛ̃fʀaksjɔ̃| nf offence; ~ à violation ou breach of; **être en ~** to be in breach of the law.

infranchissable |ɛ̃fʀɑ̃ʃisabl(ə)| a impassable; (fig) insuperable.

infrastructure |ɛ̃fʀastʀyktyʀ| nf (AVIAT, MIL) ground installations pl; (ÉCON: touristique etc) infrastructure.

infuser |ɛ̃fyze| vt, vi (thé) to brew; (tisane) to infuse; **infusion** nf (tisane) herb tea.

ingénier |ɛ̃ʒenje| : s'~ vi: s'~ à faire to strive to do.

ingénierie |ɛ̃ʒenjəʀi| nf engineering.

ingénieur |ɛ̃ʒenjœʀ| nm engineer; ~ du son sound engineer.

ingénieux, euse |ɛ̃ʒenjø, -øz| a ingenious, clever.

ingénu, e |ɛ̃ʒeny| a ingenuous, artless.

ingérer |ɛ̃ʒeʀe| : s'~ vi: s'~ dans to interfere in.

ingrat, e |ɛ̃gʀa, -at| a (personne) ungrateful; (sol) poor; (travail, sujet) thankless; (visage) unprepossessing.

ingrédient |ɛ̃gʀedjɑ̃| nm ingredient.

ingurgiter |ɛ̃gyʀʒite| vt to swallow.

inhabitable |inabitabl(ə)| a uninhabitable.

inhérent, e |ineʀɑ̃, -ɑ̃t| a: ~ à inherent in.

inhibition |inibisjɔ̃| nf inhibition.

inhumain, e |inymɛ̃, -ɛn| a inhuman.

inhumer |inyme| vt to inter, bury.

inimitié |inimitje| nf enmity.

initial, e, aux |inisjal, -jo| a, nf initial.

initiateur, trice |inisjatœʀ, -tʀis| nm/f initiator; (d'une mode, technique) innovator, pioneer.

initiative |inisjativ| nf initiative.

initier |inisje| vt: ~ qn à to initiate sb

into; (*faire découvrir: art, jeu*) to introduce sb to.

injecté, e [ɛ̃ʒɛkte] *a*: yeux ~s de sang bloodshot eyes.

injecter [ɛ̃ʒɛkte] *vt* to inject; **injection** [-sjɔ̃] *nf* injection; **à injection** *a* (*AUTO*) fuel injection *cpd*.

injure [ɛ̃ʒyʀ] *nf* insult, abuse *q*.

injurier [ɛ̃ʒyʀje] *vt* to insult, abuse; **injurieux, euse** *a* abusive, insulting.

injuste [ɛ̃ʒyst(ə)] *a* unjust, unfair; **injustice** *nf* injustice.

inlassable [ɛ̃lɑsabl(ə)] *a* tireless.

inné, e [ine] *a* innate, inborn.

innocent, e [inɔsɑ̃, -ɑ̃t] *a* innocent; **innocenter** *vt* to clear, prove innocent.

innombrable [inɔ̃bʀabl(ə)] *a* innumerable.

innommable [inɔmabl(ə)] *a* unspeakable.

innover [inɔve] *vi* to break new ground.

inoccupé, e [inɔkype] *a* unoccupied.

inoculer [inɔkyle] *vt* (*volontairement*) to inoculate; (*accidentellement*) to infect.

inodore [inɔdɔʀ] *a* (*gaz*) odourless; (*fleur*) scentless.

inoffensif, ive [inɔfɑ̃sif, -iv] *a* harmless, innocuous.

inondation [inɔ̃dɑsjɔ̃] *nf* flooding *q*; flood.

inonder [inɔ̃de] *vt* to flood; (*fig*) to inundate, overrun.

inopérant, e [inɔpeʀɑ̃, -ɑ̃t] *a* inoperative, ineffective.

inopiné, e [inɔpine] *a* unexpected, sudden.

inopportun, e [inɔpɔʀtœ̃, -yn] *a* illtimed, untimely; inappropriate.

inoubliable [inublijabl(ə)] *a* unforgettable.

inouï, e [inwi] *a* unheard-of, extraordinary.

inox(ydable) [inɔks(idabl(ə))] *a* stainless.

inqualifiable [ɛ̃kalifjabl(ə)] *a* unspeakable.

inquiet, ète [ɛ̃kjɛ, -ɛt] *a* anxious.

inquiétant, e [ɛ̃kjetɑ̃, -ɑ̃t] *a* worrying, disturbing.

inquiéter [ɛ̃kjete] *vt* to worry; (*harceler*) to harass; s'~ to worry; s'~ de to worry about; (*s'enquérir de*) to inquire about.

inquiétude [ɛ̃kjetyd] *nf* anxiety.

insaisissable [ɛ̃sezizabl(ə)] *a* elusive.

insatisfait, e [ɛ̃satisfɛ, -ɛt] *a* (*non comblé*) unsatisfied; unfulfilled; (*mécontent*) dissatisfied.

inscription [ɛ̃skʀipsjɔ̃] *nf* inscription; (*voir s'inscrire*) enrolment; registration.

inscrire [ɛ̃skʀiʀ] *vt* (*marquer: sur son calepin etc*) to note *ou* write down; (: *sur un mur, une affiche etc*) to write; (: *dans la pierre, le métal*) to inscribe;

(*mettre: sur une liste, un budget etc*) to put down; ~ qn à (*club, école etc*) to enrol sb at; s'~ (*pour une excursion etc*) to put one's name down; s'~ (à) (*club, parti*) to join; (*université*) to register *ou* enrol (at); (*examen, concours*) to register (for); s'~ en faux contre to challenge.

insecte [ɛ̃sɛkt(ə)] *nm* insect; **insecticide** *nm* insecticide.

insensé, e [ɛ̃sɑ̃se] *a* mad.

insensibiliser [ɛ̃sɑ̃sibilize] *vt* to anaesthetize.

insensible [ɛ̃sɑ̃sibl(ə)] *a* (*nerf, membre*) numb; (*dur, indifférent*) insensitive; (*imperceptible*) imperceptible.

insérer [ɛ̃seʀe] *vt* to insert; s'~ dans to fit into; to come within.

insigne [ɛ̃siɲ] *nm* (*d'un parti, club*) badge // *a* distinguished; ~s *nmpl* (*d'une fonction*) insignia *pl*.

insignifiant, e [ɛ̃siɲifjɑ̃, -ɑ̃t] *a* insignificant; trivial.

insinuer [ɛ̃sinɥe] *vt* to insinuate, imply; s'~ dans (*fig*) to creep into.

insister [ɛ̃siste] *vi* to insist; (*s'obstiner*) to keep on; ~ sur (*détail, note*) to stress.

insolation [ɛ̃sɔlɑsjɔ̃] *nf* (*MÉD*) sunstroke *q*.

insolent, e [ɛ̃sɔlɑ̃, -ɑ̃t] *a* insolent.

insolite [ɛ̃sɔlit] *a* strange, unusual.

insomnie [ɛ̃sɔmni] *nf* insomnia *q*, sleeplessness *q*.

insondable [ɛ̃sɔ̃dabl(ə)] *a* unfathomable.

insonoriser [ɛ̃sɔnɔʀize] *vt* to soundproof.

insouciant, e [ɛ̃susjɑ̃, -ɑ̃t] *a* carefree; (*imprévoyant*) heedless.

insoumis, e [ɛ̃sumi, -iz] *a* (*caractère, enfant*) rebellious, refractory; (*contrée, tribu*) unsubdued.

insoupçonnable [ɛ̃supsɔnabl(ə)] *a* unsuspected; (*personne*) above suspicion.

insoutenable [ɛ̃sutnabl(ə)] *a* (*argument*) untenable; (*chaleur*) unbearable.

inspecter [ɛ̃spɛkte] *vt* to inspect.

inspecteur, trice [ɛ̃spɛktœʀ, -tʀis] *nm/f* inspector; ~ d'Académie (regional) director of education; ~ des finances ≈ tax inspector (*Brit*), ≈ Internal Revenue Service agent (*US*).

inspection [ɛ̃spɛksjɔ̃] *nf* inspection.

inspirer [ɛ̃spiʀe] *vt* (*gén*) to inspire // *vi* (*aspirer*) to breathe in; s'~ de (*suj: artiste*) to draw one's inspiration from.

instable [ɛ̃stabl(ə)] *a* (*meuble, équilibre*) unsteady; (*population, temps*) unsettled; (*régime, caractère*) unstable.

installation [ɛ̃stalɑsjɔ̃] *nf* putting in *ou* up; fitting out; settling in; (*appareils etc*) fittings *pl*, installations *pl*; ~s *nfpl* equipment; facilities.

installer [ɛ̃stale] *vt* (*loger*): ~ qn to get sb settled; (*placer*) to put, place; (*meuble, gaz, électricité*) to put in; (*rideau,* *étagère, tente*) to put up; (*appartement*) to fit out; **s'~** (*s'établir: artisan, dentiste etc*) to set o.s. up; (*se loger*) to settle (o.s.); (*emménager*) to settle in; (*sur un siège, à un emplacement*) to settle (down); (*fig: maladie, grève*) to take a firm hold.

instamment [ɛ̃stamɑ̃] *ad* urgently.

instance [ɛ̃stɑ̃s] *nf* (ADMIN: *autorité*) authority; **~s** *nfpl* (*prières*) entreaties; **affaire en ~** matter pending; **être en ~ de divorce** to be awaiting a divorce.

instant [ɛ̃stɑ̃] *nm* moment, instant; **dans un ~** in a moment; **à l'~** this instant; **à tout** *ou* **chaque ~** at any moment; constantly; **pour l'~** for the moment, for the time being; **par ~s** at times; **de tous les ~s** perpetual.

instantané, e [ɛ̃stɑ̃tane] *a* (*lait, café*) instant; (*explosion, mort*) instantaneous // *nm* snapshot.

instar [ɛ̃staR]: **à l'~ de** *prép* following the example of, like.

instaurer [ɛ̃stɔre] *vt* to institute.

instinct [ɛ̃stɛ̃] *nm* instinct.

instituer [ɛ̃stitɥe] *vt* to set up.

institut [ɛ̃stity] *nm* institute; **~ de beauté** beauty salon; **I~ Universitaire de Technologie (IUT)** ≈ polytechnic.

instituteur, trice [ɛ̃stitytœR, -tRis] *nm/f* (primary school) teacher.

institution [ɛ̃stitysjɔ̃] *nf* institution; (*collège*) private school.

instruction [ɛ̃stRyksjɔ̃] *nf* (*enseignement, savoir*) education; (JUR) (preliminary) investigation and hearing; **~s** *nfpl* directions, instructions; **~ civique** civics *sg*.

instruire [ɛ̃stRɥiR] *vt* (*élèves*) to teach; (*recrues*) to train; (JUR: *affaire*) to conduct the investigation for; **s'~** to educate o.s.; **instruit, e** *a* educated.

instrument [ɛ̃stRymɑ̃] *nm* instrument; **~ à cordes/vent** stringed/wind instrument; **~ de mesure** measuring instrument; **~ de musique** musical instrument; **~ de travail** (working) tool.

insu [ɛ̃sy] *nm*: **à l'~ de qn** without sb knowing (it).

insubmersible [ɛ̃sybmɛRsibl(ə)] *a* unsinkable.

insubordination [ɛ̃sybɔRdinasjɔ̃] *nf* rebelliousness; (MIL) insubordination.

insuccès [ɛ̃syksɛ] *nm* failure.

insuffisant, e [ɛ̃syfizɑ̃, -ɑ̃t] *a* insufficient; (*élève, travail*) inadequate.

insuffler [ɛ̃syfle] *vt* to blow; to inspire.

insulaire [ɛ̃sylɛR] *a* island *cpd*; (*attitude*) insular.

insuline [ɛ̃sylin] *nf* insulin.

insulte [ɛ̃sylt(ə)] *nf* insult; **insulter** *vt* to insult.

insupportable [ɛ̃sypɔRtabl(ə)] *a* unbearable.

insurger [ɛ̃syRʒe]: **s'~** *vi*: **s'~ (contre** to rise up *ou* rebel (against).

insurmontable [ɛ̃syRmɔ̃tabl(ə)] *a* (*difficulté*) insuperable; (*aversion*) unconquerable.

intact, e [ɛ̃takt] *a* intact.

intangible [ɛ̃tɑ̃ʒibl(ə)] *a* intangible; (*principe*) inviolable.

intarissable [ɛ̃taRisabl(ə)] *a* inexhaustible.

intégral, e, aux [ɛ̃tegRal, -o] *a* complete.

intégrant, e [ɛ̃tegRɑ̃, -ɑ̃t] *a*: **faire partie ~e de** to be an integral part of.

intègre [ɛ̃tegR(ə)] *a* upright.

intégrer [ɛ̃tegRe] *vt* to integrate; **s'~ à/ dans** to become integrated into.

intellectuel, le [ɛ̃telɛktɥel] *a* intellectual // *nm/f* intellectual; (*péj*) highbrow.

intelligence [ɛ̃teliʒɑ̃s] *nf* intelligence; (*compréhension*): **l'~ de** the understanding of; (*complicité*): **regard d'~** glance of complicity; (*accord*): **vivre en bonne ~ avec qn** to be on good terms with sb.

intelligent, e [ɛ̃teliʒɑ̃, -ɑ̃t] *a* intelligent.

intempéries [ɛ̃tɑ̃peRi] *nfpl* bad weather *sg*.

intempestif, ive [ɛ̃tɑ̃pestif, -iv] *a* untimely.

intenable [ɛ̃tnabl(ə)] *a* (*chaleur*) unbearable.

intendant, e [ɛ̃tɑ̃dɑ̃, -ɑ̃t] *nm/f* (MIL) quartermaster; (SCOL) bursar; (*d'une propriété*) steward.

intense [ɛ̃tɑ̃s] *a* intense; **intensif, ive** *a* intensive.

intenter [ɛ̃tɑ̃te] *vt*: **~ un procès contre** *ou* **à** to start proceedings against.

intention [ɛ̃tɑ̃sjɔ̃] *nf* intention; (JUR) intent; **avoir l'~ de faire** to intend to do; **à l'~ de** *prép* for; (*renseignement*) for the benefit of; (*film, ouvrage*) aimed at; **à cette ~** with this aim in view; **intentionné, e** *a*: **bien intentionné** well-meaning *ou* -intentioned; **mal intentionné** ill-intentioned.

intercaler [ɛ̃teRkale] *vt* to insert.

intercepter [ɛ̃teRsɛpte] *vt* to intercept; (*lumière, chaleur*) to cut off.

interchangeable [ɛ̃teRʃɑ̃ʒabl(ə)] *a* interchangeable.

interclasse [ɛ̃teRklas] *nm* (SCOL) break (between classes).

interdiction [ɛ̃teRdiksjɔ̃] *nf* ban.

interdire [ɛ̃teRdiR] *vt* to forbid; (ADMIN) to ban, prohibit; (: *journal, livre*) to ban; **~ à qn de faire** to forbid sb to do, prohibit sb from doing; (*suj: empêchement*) to prevent sb from doing.

interdit, e [ɛ̃teRdi, -it] *a* (*stupéfait*) taken aback // *nm* prohibition.

intéressant, e [ɛ̃teRɛsɑ̃, -ɑ̃t] *a* interesting.

intéressé, e [ɛ̃teRese] *a* (*parties*) involved, concerned; (*amitié, motifs*) self-interested.

intéresser [ɛ̃teʀese] *vt (captiver)* to interest; *(toucher)* to be of interest to; *(ADMIN: concerner)* to affect, concern; s'~ à to be interested in.
intérêt [ɛ̃teʀɛ] *nm (aussi COMM)* interest; *(égoïsme)* self-interest; **avoir** ~ à **faire** to do well to do.
intérieur, e [ɛ̃teʀjœʀ] *a (mur, escalier, poche)* inside; *(commerce, politique)* domestic; *(cour, calme, vie)* inner; *(navigation)* inland // *nm (d'une maison, d'un récipient etc)* inside; *(d'un pays, aussi: décor, mobilier)* interior; *(POL)*: **l'I~** the Interior; **à l'~ (de)** inside; *(fig)* within.
intérim [ɛ̃teʀim] *nm* interim period; **assurer l'~ (de)** to deputize (for); **par ~** *a* interim.
intérioriser [ɛ̃teʀjɔʀize] *vt* to internalize.
interlocuteur, trice [ɛ̃tɛʀlɔkytœʀ, -tʀis] *nm/f* speaker; **son ~** the person he was speaking to.
interloquer [ɛ̃tɛʀlɔke] *vt* to take aback.
intermède [ɛ̃tɛʀmɛd] *nm* interlude.
intermédiaire [ɛ̃tɛʀmedjɛʀ] *a* intermediate; middle; half-way // *nm/f* intermediary; *(COMM)* middleman; **sans ~** directly; **par l'~ de** through.
intermittence [ɛ̃tɛʀmitɑ̃s] *nf*: **par ~** sporadically, intermittently.
internat [ɛ̃tɛʀna] *nm (SCOL)* boarding school.
international, e, aux [ɛ̃tɛʀnasjɔnal, -o] *a, nm/f* international.
interne [ɛ̃tɛʀn(ə)] *a* internal // *nm/f (SCOL)* boarder; *(MÉD)* houseman.
interner [ɛ̃tɛʀne] *vt (POL)* to intern; *(MÉD)* to confine to a mental institution.
interpeller [ɛ̃tɛʀpele] *vt (appeler)* to call out to; *(apostropher)* to shout at; *(POLICE)* to take in for questioning; *(POL)* to question.
interphone [ɛ̃tɛʀfɔn] *nm* intercom.
interposer [ɛ̃tɛʀpoze] *vt* to interpose; **s'~** *vi* to intervene; **par personnes interposées** through a third party.
interprète [ɛ̃tɛʀpʀɛt] *nm/f* interpreter; *(porte-parole)* spokesman.
interpréter [ɛ̃tɛʀpʀete] *vt* to interpret.
interrogateur, trice [ɛ̃teʀɔgatœʀ, -tʀis] *a* questioning, inquiring.
interrogatif, ive [ɛ̃teʀɔgatif, -iv] *a (LING)* interrogative.
interrogation [ɛ̃teʀɔgasjɔ̃] *nf* question; *(SCOL)* (written *ou* oral) test.
interrogatoire [ɛ̃teʀɔgatwaʀ] *nm (POLICE)* questioning *q*; *(JUR)* cross-examination.
interroger [ɛ̃teʀɔʒe] *vt* to question; *(INFORM)* to consult; *(SCOL)* to test.
interrompre [ɛ̃teʀɔ̃pʀ(ə)] *vt (gén)* to interrupt; *(travail, voyage)* to break off, interrupt; **s'~** to break off.
interrupteur [ɛ̃teʀyptœʀ] *nm* switch.
interruption [ɛ̃teʀypsjɔ̃] *nf* interruption;

(pause) break.
interstice [ɛ̃tɛʀstis] *nm* crack; slit.
interurbain [ɛ̃tɛʀyʀbɛ̃] *nm (TÉL)* long-distance call service // *a (TÉL)* long-distance.
intervalle [ɛ̃tɛʀval] *nm (espace)* space; *(de temps)* interval; **dans l'~** in the meantime.
intervenir [ɛ̃tɛʀvəniʀ] *vi (gén)* to intervene; *(survenir)* to take place; ~ **auprès de qn** to intervene with sb.
intervention [ɛ̃tɛʀvɑ̃sjɔ̃] *nf* intervention; *(discours)* paper; ~ **chirurgicale** (surgical) operation.
intervertir [ɛ̃tɛʀvɛʀtiʀ] *vt* to invert (the order of), reverse.
interview [ɛ̃tɛʀvju] *nf* interview.
intestin, e [ɛ̃tɛstɛ̃, -in] *a* internal // *nm* intestine.
intime [ɛ̃tim] *a* intimate; *(vie, journal)* private; *(conviction)* inmost; *(dîner, cérémonie)* quiet // *nm/f* close friend.
intimer [ɛ̃time] *vt (JUR)* to notify; ~ **à qn l'ordre de faire** to order sb to do.
intimité [ɛ̃timite] *nf*: **dans l'~** in private; *(sans formalités)* with only a few friends, quietly.
intitulé, e [ɛ̃tityle] *a* entitled.
intolérable [ɛ̃tɔleʀabl(ə)] *a* intolerable.
intoxication [ɛ̃tɔksikasjɔ̃] *nf*: ~ **alimentaire** food poisoning.
intoxiquer [ɛ̃tɔksike] *vt* to poison; *(fig)* to brainwash.
intraduisible [ɛ̃tʀadɥizibl(ə)] *a* untranslatable; *(fig)* inexpressible.
intraitable [ɛ̃tʀɛtabl(ə)] *a* inflexible, uncompromising.
intransigeant, e [ɛ̃tʀɑ̃ziʒɑ̃, -ɑ̃t] *a* intransigent; *(morale)* uncompromising.
intransitif, ive [ɛ̃tʀɑ̃zitif, -iv] *a (LING)* intransitive.
intrépide [ɛ̃tʀepid] *a* dauntless.
intrigue [ɛ̃tʀig] *nf (scénario)* plot.
intriguer [ɛ̃tʀige] *vi* to scheme // *vt* to puzzle, intrigue.
intrinsèque [ɛ̃tʀɛ̃sɛk] *a* intrinsic.
introduction [ɛ̃tʀɔdyksjɔ̃] *nf* introduction.
introduire [ɛ̃tʀɔdɥiʀ] *vt* to introduce; *(visiteur)* to show in; *(aiguille, clef)*: ~ **qch dans** to insert *ou* introduce sth into; **s'~ dans** to gain entry into; to get o.s. accepted into; *(eau, fumée)* to get into.
introuvable [ɛ̃tʀuvabl(ə)] *a* which cannot be found; *(COMM)* unobtainable.
introverti, e [ɛ̃tʀɔvɛʀti] *nm/f* introvert.
intrus, e [ɛ̃tʀy, -yz] *nm/f* intruder.
intrusion [ɛ̃tʀyzjɔ̃] *nf* intrusion; interference.
intuition [ɛ̃tɥisjɔ̃] *nf* intuition.
inusable [inyzabl(ə)] *a* hard-wearing.
inusité, e [inyzite] *a* rarely used.
inutile [inytil] *a* useless; *(superflu)* unnecessary; **inutilisable** *a* unusable.
invalide [ɛ̃valid] *a* disabled // *nm*: ~ **de**

guerre disabled ex-serviceman.
invasion [ɛ̃vazjɔ̃] *nf* invasion.
invectiver [ɛ̃vɛktive] *vt* to hurl abuse at.
invendable [ɛ̃vɑ̃dabl(ə)] *a* unsaleable; unmarketable; **invendus** *nmpl* unsold goods.
inventaire [ɛ̃vɑ̃tɛʀ] *nm* inventory; (*COMM: liste*) stocklist; (*: opération*) stocktaking *q*; (*fig*) survey.
inventer [ɛ̃vɑ̃te] *vt* to invent; (*subterfuge*) to devise, invent; (*histoire, excuse*) to make up, invent; **inventeur** *nm* inventor; **inventif, ive** *a* inventive; **invention** [-sjɔ̃] *nf* invention.
inverse [ɛ̃vɛʀs] *a* reverse; opposite; inverse // *nm* inverse, reverse; **dans l'ordre** ~ in the reverse order; **en sens** ~ in (*ou* from) the opposite direction; **~ment** *ad* conversely; **inverser** *vt* to invert, reverse; (*ÉLEC*) to reverse.
investir [ɛ̃vɛstiʀ] *vt* to invest; **investissement** *nm* investment; **investiture** *nf* investiture; (*à une élection*) nomination.
invétéré, e [ɛ̃vetere] *a* (*habitude*) ingrained; (*bavard, buveur*) inveterate.
invisible [ɛ̃vizibl(ə)] *a* invisible.
invitation [ɛ̃vitasjɔ̃] *nf* invitation.
invité, e [ɛ̃vite] *nm/f* guest.
inviter [ɛ̃vite] *vt* to invite; ~ **qn à faire** (*suj: chose*) to induce *ou* tempt sb to do.
involontaire [ɛ̃vɔlɔ̃tɛʀ] *a* (*mouvement*) involuntary; (*insulte*) unintentional; (*complice*) unwitting.
invoquer [ɛ̃vɔke] *vt* (*Dieu, muse*) to call upon, invoke; (*prétexte*) to put forward (as an excuse); (*loi, texte*) to refer to.
invraisemblable [ɛ̃vʀɛsɑ̃blabl(ə)] *a* unlikely, improbable; incredible.
iode [jɔd] *nm* iodine.
irai *etc vb voir* **aller**.
Irak [iʀak] *nm* Iraq.
Iran [iʀɑ̃] *nm* Iran.
irions *etc vb voir* **aller**.
irlandais, e [iʀlɑ̃dɛ, -ɛz] *a* Irish // *nm/f*: **I~,** e Irishman/woman; **les I~** the Irish.
Irlande [iʀlɑ̃d] *nf* Ireland; ~ **du Nord** Northern Ireland.
ironie [iʀɔni] *nf* irony; **ironique** *a* ironical; **ironiser** *vi* to be ironical.
irons *etc vb voir* **aller**.
irradier [iʀadje] *vi* to radiate // *vt* (*aliment*) to irradiate.
irraisonné, e [iʀɛzɔne] *a* irrational, unreasoned.
irrationnel, le [iʀasjɔnɛl] *a* irrational.
irréalisable [iʀealizabl(ə)] *a* unrealizable; impracticable.
irrécupérable [iʀekypeʀabl(ə)] *a* unreclaimable, beyond repair; (*personne*) beyond redemption.
irrécusable [iʀekyzabl(ə)] *a* unimpeachable; incontestable.
irréductible [iʀedyktibl(ə)] *a* indomitable, implacable.

irréel, le [iʀeɛl] *a* unreal.
irréfléchi, e [iʀefleʃi] *a* thoughtless.
irrégularité [iʀegylaʀite] *nf* irregularity; unevenness *q*.
irrégulier, ière [iʀegylje, -jɛʀ] *a* irregular; uneven; (*élève, athlète*) erratic.
irrémédiable [iʀemedjabl(ə)] *a* irreparable.
irréprochable [iʀepʀɔʃabl(ə)] *a* irreproachable, beyond reproach; (*tenue*) impeccable.
irrésistible [iʀezistibl(ə)] *a* irresistible; (*preuve, logique*) compelling.
irrespectueux, euse [iʀɛspɛktyø, -øz] *a* disrespectful.
irriguer [iʀige] *vt* to irrigate.
irritable [iʀitabl(ə)] *a* irritable.
irriter [iʀite] *vt* to irritate.
irruption [iʀypsjɔ̃] *nf* irruption *q*; **faire** ~ **dans** to burst into.
islamic [islamik] *a* Islamic.
Islande [islɑ̃d] *nf* Iceland.
isolant, e [izɔlɑ̃, -ɑ̃t] *a* insulating; (*insonorisant*) soundproofing.
isolation [izɔlasjɔ̃] *nf* insulation.
isolé, e [izɔle] *a* isolated; insulated.
isoler [izɔle] *vt* to isolate; (*prisonnier*) to put in solitary confinement; (*ville*) to cut off, isolate; (*ÉLEC*) to insulate; **isoloir** *nm* polling booth.
Israël [isʀaɛl] *nm* Israel; **israélien, ne** *a, nm/f* Israeli; **israélite** *a* Jewish // *nm/ f* Jew/Jewess.
issu, e [isy] *a*: ~ **de** descended from; (*fig*) stemming from // *nf* (*ouverture, sortie*) exit; (*solution*) way out, solution; (*dénouement*) outcome; **à l'~e de** at the conclusion *ou* close of; **rue sans ~e** dead end.
Italie [itali] *nf* Italy; **italien, ne** *a, nm, nf* Italian.
italique [italik] *nm*: **en** ~ **in** italics.
itinéraire [itineʀɛʀ] *nm* itinerary, route.
IUT *sigle m voir* **institut**.
ivoire [ivwaʀ] *nm* ivory.
ivre [ivʀ(ə)] *a* drunk; ~ **de** (*colère, bonheur*) wild with; **ivresse** *nf* drunkenness; **ivrogne** *nm/f* drunkard.

J

jachère [ʒaʃɛʀ] *nf*: (**être**) **en** ~ (to lie) fallow.
jacinthe [ʒasɛ̃t] *nf* hyacinth.
jack [ʒak] *nm* jack plug.
jadis [ʒadis] *ad* in times past, formerly.
jaillir [ʒajiʀ] *vi* (*liquide*) to spurt out; (*fig*) to burst out; to flood out.
jais [ʒɛ] *nm* jet; **(d'un noir) de** ~ jet-black.
jalon [ʒalɔ̃] *nm* range pole; (*fig*) milestone; **jalonner** *vt* to mark out; (*fig*) to mark, punctuate.
jalousie [ʒaluzi] *nf* jealousy; (*store*) (ve-

netian) blind.

jaloux, se [ʒalu, -uz] *a* jealous.

jamais [ʒamɛ] *ad* never; (*sans négation*) ever; ne ... ~ never; à ~ for ever.

jambe [ʒɑ̃b] *nf* leg.

jambon [ʒɑ̃bɔ̃] *nm* ham.

jante [ʒɑ̃t] *nf* (wheel) rim.

janvier [ʒɑ̃vje] *nm* January.

Japon [ʒapɔ̃] *nm* Japan; **japonais, e** *a, nm, nf* Japanese.

japper [ʒape] *vi* to yap, yelp.

jaquette [ʒakɛt] *nf* (*de cérémonie*) morning coat; (*de dame*) jacket.

jardin [ʒardɛ̃] *nm* garden; ~ **d'enfants** nursery school; **jardinage** *nm* gardening; **jardinier, ière** *nm/f* gardener // (*de fenêtre*) window box.

jarre [ʒaʀ] *nf* (earthenware) jar.

jarret [ʒaʀɛ] *nm* back of knee, ham; (*CULIN*) knuckle, shin.

jarretelle [ʒaʀtɛl] *nf* suspender (*Brit*), garter (*US*).

jarretière [ʒaʀtjɛʀ] *nf* garter.

jaser [ʒaze] *vi* to chatter, prattle; (*indiscrètement*) to gossip.

jatte [ʒat] *nf* basin, bowl.

jauge [ʒoʒ] *nf* (*instrument*) gauge; **jauger** *vt* (*fig*) to size up.

jaune [ʒon] *a, nm* yellow // *ad* (*fam*) **rire** ~ to laugh on the other side of one's face; ~ **d'œuf** (egg) yolk; **jaunir** *vi, vt* to turn yellow.

jaunisse [ʒonis] *nf* jaundice.

Javel [ʒavɛl] *nf voir* **eau**.

javelot [ʒavlo] *nm* javelin.

jazz [dʒaz] *nm* jazz.

J.-C. *sigle voir* **Jésus-Christ**.

je, j' [ʒ(ə)] *pronom* I.

jean [dʒin] *nm* jeans *pl*.

Jésus-Christ [ʒezykri(st)] *n* Jesus Christ; **600 avant/après** ~ **ou J.-C.** 600 B.C./A.D.

jet [ʒɛ] *nm* (*lancer*) throwing *q*, throw; (*jaillissement*) jet; spurt; (*de tuyau*) nozzle; (*avion*) [dʒɛt] jet; **du premier** ~ at the first attempt *or* shot; ~ **d'eau** fountain; spray.

jetable [ʒətabl(ə)] *a* disposable.

jetée [ʒəte] *nf* jetty; pier.

jeter [ʒəte] *vt* (*gén*) to throw; (*se défaire de*) to throw away *ou* out; (*son, lueur etc*) to give out; ~ **qch à qn** to throw sth to sb; (*de façon agressive*) to throw sth at sb; ~ **un coup d'œil (à)** to take a look (at); ~ **un sort à qn** to cast a spell on sb; **se** ~ **dans** (*fleuve*) to flow into.

jeton [ʒətɔ̃] *nm* (*au jeu*) counter; (*de téléphone*) token.

jette *etc vb voir* **jeter**.

jeu, x [ʒø] *nm* (*divertissement, TECH: d'une pièce*) play; (*TENNIS: partie, FOOTBALL etc: façon de jouer*) game; (*THÉÂTRE etc*) acting; (*au casino*): **le** ~ gambling; (*fonctionnement*) working, interplay; (*série d'objets, jouet*) set;

(*CARTES*) hand; **en** ~ at stake; at work; **remettre en** ~ to throw in; **entrer/mettre en** ~ to come/bring into play; ~ **de cartes** pack of cards; ~ **d'échecs** chess set; ~ **de hasard** game of chance; ~ **de mots** pun.

jeudi [ʒødi] *nm* Thursday.

jeun [ʒœ̃]: **à** ~ *ad* on an empty stomach.

jeune [ʒœn] *a* young; ~ **fille** *nf* girl; ~ **homme** *nm* young man.

jeûne [ʒøn] *nm* fast.

jeunesse [ʒœnɛs] *nf* youth; (*aspect*) youthfulness; youngness.

joaillerie [ʒɔajʀi] *nf* jewel trade; jewellery; **joaillier, ière** *nm/f* jeweller.

joie [ʒwa] *nf* joy.

joindre [ʒwɛ̃dʀ(ə)] *vt* to join; (*à une lettre*): ~ **qch à** to enclose sth with; (*contacter*) to contact, get in touch with; ~ **les mains** to put one's hands together; **se** ~ **à** to join.

joint, e [ʒwɛ̃, ʒwɛ̃t] *a*: **pièce** ~**e** enclosure // *nm* joint; (*ligne*) join; ~ **de culasse** cylinder head gasket; ~ **de robinet** washer.

joli, e [ʒɔli] *a* pretty, attractive; **c'est du** ~! (*ironique*) that's very nice!; **c'est bien** ~, **mais...** that's all very well but...

jonc [ʒɔ̃] *nm* (bul)rush.

joncher [ʒɔ̃ʃe] *vt* (*suj: choses*) to be strewed on.

jonction [ʒɔ̃ksjɔ̃] *nf* joining; (**point de**) ~ junction.

jongleur, euse [ʒɔ̃glœʀ, -øz] *nm/f* juggler.

jonquille [ʒɔ̃kij] *nf* daffodil.

Jordanie [ʒɔʀdani] *nf*: **la** ~ Jordan.

joue [ʒu] *nf* cheek; **mettre en** ~ to take aim at.

jouer [ʒwe] *vt* to play; (*somme d'argent, réputation*) to stake, wager; (*pièce, rôle*) to perform; (*film*) to show; (*simuler: sentiment*) to affect, feign // *vi* to play; (*THÉÂTRE, CINÉMA*) to act, perform; (*bois, porte: se voiler*) to warp; (*clef, pièce: avoir du jeu*) to be loose; ~ **sur** (*miser*) to gamble on; ~ **de** (*MUS*) to play; ~ **des coudes** to use one's elbows; ~ **à** (*jeu, sport, roulette*) to play; ~ **avec** (*risquer*) to gamble with; **se** ~ **de** (*difficultés*) to make light of; to deceive; ~ **un tour à qn** to play a trick on sb; ~ **serré** to play a close game; ~ **de malchance** to be dogged with ill-luck.

jouet [ʒwɛ] *nm* toy; **être le** ~ **de** (*illusion etc*) to be the victim of.

joueur, euse [ʒwœʀ, -øz] *nm/f* player; **être beau** ~ to be a good loser.

joufflu, e [ʒufly] *a* chubby-cheeked.

joug [ʒu] *nm* yoke.

jouir [ʒwiʀ]: ~ **de** *vt* to enjoy; **jouissance** *nf* pleasure; (*JUR*) use.

joujou [ʒuʒu] *nm* (*fam*) toy.

jour [ʒuʀ] *nm* day; (*opposé à la nuit*)

day, daytime; (*clarté*) daylight; (*fig: aspect*) light; (*ouverture*) opening; **au ~ le ~** from day to day; **de nos ~s** these days; **il fait ~** it's daylight; **au grand ~** (*fig*) in the open; **mettre au ~** to disclose; **mettre à ~** to update; **donner le ~ à** to give birth to; **voir le ~** to be born.

journal, aux [ʒuʀnal, -o] *nm* (*news*)paper; (*personnel*) journal, diary; **~ parlé/télévisé** radio/television news *sg*; **~ de bord** log.

journalier, ière [ʒuʀnalje, -jɛʀ] *a* daily; (*banal*) everyday.

journalisme [ʒuʀnalism(ə)] *nm* journalism; **journaliste** *nm/f* journalist.

journée [ʒuʀne] *nf* day; **la ~ continue** the 9 to 5 working day.

journellement [ʒuʀnɛlmɑ̃] *ad* daily.

joyau, x [ʒwajo] *nm* gem, jewel.

joyeux, euse [ʒwajø, -øz] *a* joyful, merry; **~ Noël!** merry Christmas!; **~ anniversaire!** happy birthday!

jubiler [ʒybile] *vi* to be jubilant, exult.

jucher [ʒyʃe] *vt, vi* to perch.

judas [ʒyda] *nm* (*trou*) spy-hole.

judiciaire [ʒydisjɛʀ] *a* judicial.

judicieux, euse [ʒydisjø, -øz] *a* judicious.

judo [ʒydo] *nm* judo.

juge [ʒyʒ] *nm* judge; **~ d'instruction** examining (*Brit*) *ou* committing (*US*) magistrate; **~ de paix** justice of the peace.

jugé [ʒyʒe]: **au ~** *ad* by guesswork.

jugement [ʒyʒmɑ̃] *nm* judgment; (*JUR: au pénal*) sentence; (*: au civil*) decision.

juger [ʒyʒe] *vt* to judge; **~ qn/qch satisfaisant** to consider sb/sth (to be) satisfactory; **~ bon de faire** to see fit to do; **~ de** *vt* to appreciate.

juif, ive [ʒɥif, -iv] *a* Jewish // *nm/f* Jew/ Jewess.

juillet [ʒɥijɛ] *nm* July.

juin [ʒɥɛ̃] *nm* June.

jumeau, elle, x [ʒymo, -ɛl] *a, nm/f* twin; **jumelles** *nfpl* binoculars.

jumeler [ʒymle] *vt* to twin.

jumelle [ʒymɛl] *a, nf voir* **jumeau**.

jument [ʒymɑ̃] *nf* mare.

jungle [ʒɔ̃gl(ə)] *nf* jungle.

jupe [ʒyp] *nf* skirt.

jupon [ʒypɔ̃] *nm* waist slip.

juré, e [ʒyʀe] *nm/f* juror.

jurer [ʒyʀe] *vt* (*obéissance etc*) to swear, vow // *vi* (*dire des jurons*) to swear, curse; (*dissoner*): **~** (*avec*) to clash (with); (*s'engager*): **~ de faire/que** to swear *ou* vow to do/that; (*affirmer*): **~ que** to swear *ou* vouch that; **~ de qch** (*s'en porter garant*) to swear to sth.

juridique [ʒyʀidik] *a* legal.

juron [ʒyʀɔ̃] *nm* curse, swearword.

jury [ʒyʀi] *nm* jury; board.

jus [ʒy] *nm* juice; (*de viande*) gravy, (meat) juice; **~ de fruit** fruit juice.

jusque [ʒysk(ə)]: **jusqu'à** *prép* (*endroit*) as far as, (up) to; (*moment*) until, till; (*limite*) up to; **~ sur/dans** up to; (*y compris*) even on/in; **jusqu'à ce que** until; **jusqu'à présent** until now.

juste [ʒyst(ə)] *a* (*équitable*) just, fair; (*légitime*) just, justified; (*exact, vrai*) right; (*étroit, insuffisant*) tight // *ad* right; tight; (*chanter*) in tune; (*seulement*) just; **~ assez/au-dessus** just enough/above; **au ~** exactly; **le ~ milieu** the happy medium; **~ment** *ad* rightly; justly; (*précisément*) just, precisely; **justesse** *nf* (*précision*) accuracy; (*d'une remarque*) aptness; (*d'une opinion*) soundness; **de justesse** just.

justice [ʒystis] *nf* (*équité*) fairness, justice; (*ADMIN*) justice; **rendre la ~** to dispense justice; **rendre ~ à qn** to do sb justice.

justicier, ière [ʒystisje, -jɛʀ] *nm/f* judge, righter of wrongs.

justifier [ʒystifje] *vt* to justify; **~ de** *vt* to prove.

juteux, euse [ʒytø, -øz] *a* juicy.

juvénile [ʒyvenil] *a* young, youthful.

K

K [ka] *nm* (*INFORM*) K.

kaki [kaki] *a inv* khaki.

kangourou [kɑ̃guʀu] *nm* kangaroo.

karaté [kaʀate] *nm* karate.

karting [kaʀtiŋ] *nm* go-carting, karting.

kermesse [kɛʀmɛs] *nf* bazaar, (charity) fête; village fair.

kidnapper [kidnape] *vt* to kidnap.

kilogramme [kilɔgʀam] *nm*, **kilo** *nm* kilogramme.

kilométrage [kilɔmetʀaʒ] *nm* number of kilometres travelled, ≈ mileage.

kilomètre [kilɔmɛtʀ(ə)] *nm* kilometre.

kilométrique [kilɔmetʀik] *a* (*distance*) in kilometres.

kinésithérapeute [kineziteʀapøt] *nm/f* physiotherapist.

kiosque [kjɔsk(ə)] *nm* kiosk, stall.

klaxon [klaksɔn] *nm* horn; **klaxonner** *vi, vt* to hoot (*Brit*), honk (*US*).

km. *abr de* **kilomètre**; **~/h** (= *kilomètres/heure*) ≈ m.p.h. (= *miles per hour*).

Ko [kao] *nm* (*INFORM*: = *kilo-octet*) K.

K.-O. [kao] *a inv* (knocked) out.

kyste [kist(ə)] *nm* cyst.

L

l' [l] *dét voir* **le**.

la [la] *dét voir* **le** // *nm* (*MUS*) A; (*en chantant la gamme*) la.

là [la] *ad* (*voir aussi* **-ci**, **celui**) there; (*ici*) here; (*dans le temps*) then; **elle n'est pas ~** she isn't here; **c'est ~ que**

this is where; ~ où where; de ~ (*fig*)
hence; par ~ (*fig*) by that; tout est ~
(*fig*) that's what it's all about; **~-bas** *ad*
there.

label [label] *nm* stamp, seal.

labeur [labœʀ] *nm* toil *q*, toiling *q*.

labo [labo] *abr m* (= *laboratoire*) lab.

laboratoire [labɔʀatwaʀ] *nm* laboratory; ~ **de langues** language laboratory.

laborieux, euse [labɔʀjø, -øz] *a*
(*tâche*) laborious; **classes ~euses** working classes.

labour [labuʀ] *nm* ploughing *q*; ~**s** *nmpl*
ploughed fields; **cheval de** ~ plough- *ou*
cart-horse; **bœuf de** ~ ox (*pl* oxen).

labourer [labuʀe] *vt* to plough; (*fig*) to
make deep gashes *ou* furrows in.

labyrinthe [labiʀɛ̃t] *nm* labyrinth, maze.

lac [lak] *nm* lake.

lacer [lase] *vt* to lace *ou* do up.

lacérer [laseʀe] *vt* to tear to shreds.

lacet [lasɛ] *nm* (*de chaussure*) lace; (*de
route*) sharp bend; (*piège*) snare.

lâche [lɑʃ] *a* (*poltron*) cowardly; (*des-
serré*) loose, slack // *nm/f* coward.

lâcher [lɑʃe] *nm* (*de ballons, oiseaux*)
release // *vt* to let go of; (*ce qui tombe,
abandonner*) to drop; (*oiseau, animal:
libérer*) to release, set free; (*fig: mot,
remarque*) to let slip, come out with;
(*SPORT: distancer*) to leave behind // *vi*
(*fil, amarres*) to break, give way;
(*freins*) to fail; ~ **les amarres** (*NAVIG*)
to cast off (the moorings); ~ **les chiens**
to unleash the dogs; ~ **prise** to let go.

lâcheté [lɑʃte] *nf* cowardice; lowness.

lacrymogène [lakʀimɔʒɛn] *a*: **gaz** ~
teargas.

lacté, e [lakte] *a* (*produit, régime*) milk
cpd.

lacune [lakyn] *nf* gap.

là-dedans [ladədɑ̃] *ad* inside (there), in
it; (*fig*) in that; **là-dessous** *ad* underneath, under there; (*fig*) behind that;
là-dessus *ad* on there; (*fig*) at that
point; about that.

ladite [ladit] *dét voir* **ledit**.

lagune [lagyn] *nf* lagoon.

là-haut [la'o] *ad* up there.

laïc [laik] *a, nm/f* = **laïque**.

laid, e [lɛ, lɛd] *a* ugly; **laideur** *nf* ugli-
ness *q*.

lainage [lɛnaʒ] *nm* woollen garment;
woollen material.

laine [lɛn] *nf* wool.

laïque [laik] *a* lay, civil; (*SCOL*) state
cpd // *nm/f* layman/woman.

laisse [lɛs] *nf* (*de chien*) lead, leash;
tenir en ~ to keep on a lead *ou* leash.

laisser [lese] *vt* to leave // *vb auxiliaire*:
~ **qn faire** to let sb do; **se** ~ **aller** to let
o.s. go; **laisse-toi faire** let me (*ou* him)
do it; **~-aller** *nm* carelessness, sloven-
liness; **laissez-passer** *nm inv* pass.

lait [lɛ] *nm* milk; **frère/sœur de** ~ foster

brother/sister; ~ **condensé/concentré**
evaporated/condensed milk; **laiterie** *nf*
dairy; **laitier, ière** *a* dairy *cpd* // *nm/f*
milkman/dairywoman.

laiton [lɛtɔ̃] *nm* brass.

laitue [lety] *nf* lettuce.

laïus [lajys] *nm* (*péj*) spiel.

lambeau, x [lɑ̃bo] *nm* scrap; **en ~x** in
tatters, tattered.

lambris [lɑ̃bʀi] *nm* panelling *q*.

lame [lam] *nf* blade; (*vague*) wave; (*lamelle*) strip; ~ **de fond** ground swell *q*;
~ **de rasoir** razor blade.

lamelle [lamɛl] *nf* thin strip *ou* blade.

lamentable [lamɑ̃tabl(ə)] *a* appalling;
pitiful.

lamenter [lamɑ̃te]: **se** ~ *vi*: **se** ~ **(sur)**
to moan (over).

lampadaire [lɑ̃padɛʀ] *nm* (*de salon*)
standard lamp; (*dans la rue*) street
lamp.

lampe [lɑ̃p(ə)] *nf* lamp; (*TECH*) valve;
~ **de poche** torch (*Brit*), flashlight (*US*);
~ **à souder** blowlamp.

lampion [lɑ̃pjɔ̃] *nm* Chinese lantern.

lance [lɑ̃s] *nf* spear; ~ **d'incendie** fire
hose.

lancée [lɑ̃se] *nf*: **être/continuer sur sa** ~
to be under way/keep going.

lancement [lɑ̃smɑ̃] *nm* launching.

lance-pierres [lɑ̃spjɛʀ] *nm inv* catapult.

lancer [lɑ̃se] *nm* (*SPORT*) throwing *q*,
throw // *vt* to throw; (*émettre, projeter*)
to throw out, send out; (*produit, fusée,
bateau, artiste*) to launch; (*injure*) to
hurl, fling; (*proclamation, mandat
d'arrêt*) to issue; ~ **qch à qn** to throw
sth to sb; (*de façon agressive*) to throw
sth at sb; **se** ~ *vi* (*prendre de l'élan*) to
build up speed; (*se précipiter*): **se** ~ **sur**
ou **contre** to rush at; **se** ~ **dans** (*discussion*) to launch into; (*aventure*) to embark on; ~ **du poids** *nm* putting the shot.

lancinant, e [lɑ̃sinɑ̃, -ɑ̃t] *a* (*regrets etc*)
haunting; (*douleur*) shooting.

landau [lɑ̃do] *nm* pram (*Brit*), baby carriage (*US*).

lande [lɑ̃d] *nf* moor.

langage [lɑ̃gaʒ] *nm* language.

langer [lɑ̃ʒe] *vt* to change (the nappy
(*Brit*) *ou* diaper (*US*) of).

langouste [lɑ̃gust(ə)] *nf* crayfish *inv*;
langoustine *nf* Dublin Bay prawn.

langue [lɑ̃g] *nf* (*ANAT, CULIN*) tongue;
(*LING*) language; **tirer la** ~ **(à)** to stick
out one's tongue (at); **de** ~ **française**
French-speaking; ~ **maternelle** native
language, mother tongue; ~ **verte** slang;
~ **vivante** modern language.

langueur [lɑ̃gœʀ] *nf* languidness.

languir [lɑ̃giʀ] *vi* to languish; (*conversation*) to flag; **faire** ~ **qn** to keep sb waiting.

lanière [lanjɛʀ] *nf* (*de fouet*) lash; (*de
valise, bretelle*) strap.

lanterne [lɑ̃tɛʀn(ə)] nf (portable) lantern; (électrique) light, lamp; (de voiture) (side)light.

laper [lape] vt to lap up.

lapidaire [lapidɛʀ] a stone cpd; (fig) terse.

lapin [lapɛ̃] nm rabbit; (peau) rabbitskin; (fourrure) cony.

Laponie [laponi] nf Lapland.

laps [laps] nm: ~ de temps space of time, time q.

laque [lak] nf lacquer; (brute) shellac; (pour cheveux) hair spray.

laquelle [lakɛl] pronom voir **lequel**.

larcin [laʀsɛ̃] nm theft.

lard [laʀ] nm (graisse) fat; (bacon) (streaky) bacon.

lardon [laʀdɔ̃] nm: ~s chopped bacon.

large [laʀʒ(ə)] a wide; broad; (fig) generous // ad: calculer/voir ~ to allow extra/think big // nm (largeur): 5 m de ~ 5 m wide ou in width; (mer): le ~ the open sea; au ~ de off; ~ d'esprit broadminded; ~**ment** ad widely; greatly; easily; generously; **largesse** nf generosity; largesses liberalities; **largeur** nf (qu'on mesure) width; (impression visuelle) wideness, width; breadth; broadness.

larguer [laʀge] vt to drop: ~ les amarres to cast off (the moorings).

larme [laʀm(ə)] nf tear; (fig) drop; en ~s in tears; **larmoyer** vi (yeux) to water; (se plaindre) to whimper.

larvé, e [laʀve] a (fig) latent.

laryngite [laʀɛ̃ʒit] nf laryngitis.

las, lasse [la, las] a weary.

laser [lazɛʀ] nm: (rayon) ~ laser (beam); chaîne ~ compact disc (player); disque ~ compact disc.

lasse [las] af voir **las**.

lasser [lase] vt to weary, tire; se ~ de to grow weary ou tired of.

latéral, e, aux [lateʀal, -o] a side cpd, lateral.

latin, e [latɛ̃, -in] a, nm, nf Latin.

latitude [latityd] nf latitude.

latte [lat] nf lath, slat; (de plancher) board.

lauréat, e [lɔʀea, -at] nm/f winner.

laurier [lɔʀje] nm (BOT) laurel; (CULIN) bay leaves pl; ~s nmpl (fig) laurels.

lavable [lavabl(ə)] a washable.

lavabo [lavabo] nm washbasin; ~s nmpl toilet sg.

lavage [lavaʒ] nm washing q, wash; ~ de cerveau brainwashing q.

lavande [lavɑ̃d] nf lavender.

lave [lav] nf lava q.

lave-glace [lavglas] nm windscreen (Brit) ou windshield (US) washer.

laver [lave] vt to wash; (tache) to wash off; se ~ vi to have a wash, wash; se ~ les mains/dents to wash one's hands/ clean one's teeth; ~ qn de (accusation) to clear sb of; **laverie** nf: laverie (automatique) launderette.

lavette [lavɛt] nf dish cloth; (fam) drip.

laveur, euse [lavœʀ, -øz] nm/f cleaner.

lave-vaisselle [lavvesɛl] nm inv dishwasher.

lavoir [lavwaʀ] nm wash house.

laxatif, ive [laksatif, -iv] a, nm laxative.

le(l'), la, les [l(ə), la, le] ♦ article défini
1 the; le livre/la pomme/l'arbre the book/the apple/the tree; les étudiants the students
2 (noms abstraits): le courage/l'amour/ la jeunesse courage/love/youth
3 (indiquant la possession): se casser la jambe etc to break one's leg etc; levez la main put your hand up; avoir les yeux gris/le nez rouge to have grey eyes/a red nose
4 (temps): le matin/soir in the morning/ evening; mornings/evenings; le jeudi etc (d'habitude) on Thursdays etc; (ce jeudi-là etc) on (the) Thursday
5 (distribution, évaluation) a, an; 10 F le mètre/kilo 10 F a ou per metre/kilo; le tiers/quart de a third/quarter of
♦ pronom 1 (personne: mâle) him; (: femelle) her; (: pluriel) them; je le/la/ les vois I can see her/her/them
2 (animal, chose: sing) it; (: pl) them; je le (ou la) vois I can see it; je les vois I can see them
3 (remplaçant une phrase): je ne le savais pas I didn't know (about it); il était riche et ne l'est plus he was once rich but no longer is.

lécher [leʃe] vt to lick; (laper: lait, eau) to lick ou lap up; ~ les vitrines to go window-shopping.

leçon [l(ə)sɔ̃] nf lesson; faire la ~ à (fig) to give a lecture to; ~s de conduite driving lessons.

lecteur, trice [lɛktœʀ, -tʀis] nm/f reader; (d'université) foreign language assistant // nm (TECH): ~ de cassettes cassette player; ~ de disquette disk drive.

lecture [lɛktyʀ] nf reading.

ledit [lədi], **ladite** [ladit], mpl **lesdits** [ledi], fpl **lesdites** [ledit] dét the aforesaid.

légal, e, aux [legal, -o] a legal.

légende [leʒɑ̃d] nf (mythe) legend; (de carte, plan) key; (de dessin) caption.

léger, ère [leʒe, -ɛʀ] a light; (bruit, retard) slight; (superficiel) thoughtless; (volage) free and easy; flighty; à la légère ad (parler, agir) rashly, thoughtlessly; **légèrement** ad lightly; thoughtlessly; slightly.

législatif, ive [leʒislatif, -iv] a legislative; **législatives** nfpl general election sg.

législature [leʒislatyʀ] nf legislature; term (of office).

légitime [leʒitim] a (JUR) lawful, legitimate; (*fig*) rightful, legitimate; **en état de ~ défense** in self-defence.

legs [lɛg] *nm* legacy.

léguer [lege] *vt*: **~ qch à qn** (*JUR*) to bequeath sth to sb; (*fig*) to hand sth down *ou* pass sth on to sb.

légume [legym] *nm* vegetable.

lendemain [lɑ̃dmɛ̃] *nm*: **le ~** the next *ou* following day; **le ~ matin/soir** the next *ou* following morning/evening; **le ~ de** the day after; **sans ~** short-lived.

lent, e [lɑ̃, lɑ̃t] *a* slow; **lentement** *ad* slowly; **lenteur** *nf* slowness *q*.

lentille [lɑ̃tij] *nf* (*OPTIQUE*) lens *sg*; (*CULIN*) lentil.

léopard [leɔpaʀ] *nm* leopard.

lèpre [lɛpʀ(ə)] *nf* leprosy.

lequel [ləkɛl], **laquelle** [lakɛl], *mpl* **lesquels**, *fpl* **lesquelles** [lekɛl] (*avec à, de*: **auquel, duquel** etc) *pronom* (*interrogatif*) which, which one; (*relatif: personne: sujet*) who; (*: objet, après préposition*) whom; (*: chose*) which // *a*: **auquel cas** in which case.

les [lɛ] *dét voir* **le.**

lesbienne [lɛsbjɛn] *nf* lesbian.

lesdits [ledi], **lesdites** [ledit] *dét voir* **ledit.**

léser [leze] *vt* to wrong.

lésiner [lezine] *vi*: **~ (sur)** to skimp (on).

lésion [lezjɔ̃] *nf* lesion, damage *q*.

lesquels, lesquelles [lekɛl] *pronom voir* **lequel.**

lessive [lesiv] *nf* (*poudre*) washing powder; (*linge*) washing *q*, wash.

lessiver [lesive] *vt* to wash.

lest [lɛst] *nm* ballast.

leste [lɛst(ə)] *a* sprightly, nimble.

lettre [lɛtʀ(ə)] *nf* letter; **~s** *nfpl* literature *sg*; (*SCOL*) arts (subjects); **à la ~** literally; **en toutes ~s** in full.

lettré, e [letʀe] *a* well-read.

leucémie [løsemi] *nf* leukaemia.

leur [lœʀ] ♦ *a possessif* their; **~ maison** their house; **~s amis** their friends ♦ *pronom* (*objet indirect*) (to) them; **je ~ ai dit la vérité** I told them the truth; **je le ~ ai donné** I gave it to them, I gave them it **2** (*possessif*): **le(la) ~, les ~s** theirs.

leurre [lœʀ] *nm* (*appât*) lure; (*fig*) delusion; snare.

leurrer [lœʀe] *vt* to delude, deceive.

levain [ləvɛ̃] *nm* leaven.

levé, e [ləve] *a*: **être ~** to be up.

levée [ləve] *nf* (*POSTES*) collection; (*CARTES*) trick; **~ de boucliers** general outcry.

lever [ləve] *vt* (*vitre, bras* etc) to raise; (*soulever de terre, supprimer: interdiction, siège*) to lift; (*séance*) to close; (*impôts, armée*) to levy // *vi* to rise // *nm*: **au ~** on getting up; **se ~** *vi* to get up; (*soleil*) to rise; (*jour*) to

break; (*brouillard*) to lift; **~ du jour** daybreak; **~ de rideau** curtain raiser; **~ de soleil** sunrise.

levier [ləvje] *nm* lever.

lèvre [lɛvʀ(ə)] *nf* lip.

lévrier [levʀije] *nm* greyhound.

levure [ləvyʀ] *nf* yeast; **~ chimique** baking powder.

lexique [lɛksik] *nm* vocabulary; lexicon.

lézard [lezaʀ] *nm* lizard.

lézarde [lezaʀd(ə)] *nf* crack.

liaison [ljɛzɔ̃] *nf* link; (*amoureuse*) affair; (*PHONÉTIQUE*) liaison; **entrer/être en ~ avec** to get/be in contact with.

liane [ljan] *nf* creeper.

liant, e [ljɑ̃, -ɑ̃t] *a* sociable.

liasse [ljas] *nf* wad, bundle.

Liban [libɑ̃] *nm*: **le ~** (the) Lebanon; **libanais, e** *a, nm/f* Lebanese.

libeller [libele] *vt* (*chèque, mandat*): **~ (au nom de)** to make out (to); (*lettre*) to word.

libellule [libelyl] *nf* dragonfly.

libéral, e, aux [libeʀal, -o] *a, nm/f* liberal.

libérer [libeʀe] *vt* (*délivrer*) to free, liberate; (*: moralement, PSYCH*) to liberate; (*relâcher, dégager: gaz*) to release; to discharge; **se ~** *vi* (*de rendez-vous*) to get out of previous engagements.

liberté [libɛʀte] *nf* freedom; (*loisir*) free time; **~s** *nfpl* (*privautés*) liberties; **mettre/être en ~** to set/be free; **en ~ provisoire/surveillée/conditionnelle** on bail/probation/parole; **~s individuelles** personal freedom *sg*.

libraire [libʀɛʀ] *nm/f* bookseller.

librairie [libʀɛʀi] *nf* bookshop.

libre [libʀ(ə)] *a* free; (*route*) clear; (*place* etc) vacant; empty; not engaged; not taken; (*SCOL*) non-state; **de ~** (*place*) free; **~ de qch/de faire** free from sth/to do; **~ arbitre** free will; **~-échange** *nm* free trade; **~-service** *nm* self-service store.

Libye [libi] *nf*: **la ~** Libya.

licence [lisɑ̃s] *nf* (*permis*) permit; (*diplôme*) degree; (*liberté*) liberty; licence (*Brit*), license (*US*); licentiousness; **licencié, e** *nm/f* (*SCOL*): **licencié ès lettres/en droit;** ≈ Bachelor of Arts/Law; (*SPORT*) member of a sports federation.

licencier [lisɑ̃sje] *vt* (*renvoyer*) to dismiss; (*débaucher*) to make redundant; to lay off.

licite [lisit] *a* lawful.

lie [li] *nf* dregs *pl*, sediment.

lié, e [lje] *a*: **très ~ avec** very friendly with *ou* close to; **~ par** (*serment*) bound by.

liège [ljɛʒ] *nm* cork.

lien [ljɛ̃] *nm* (*corde, fig: affectif*) bond; (*rapport*) link, connection; **~ de parenté** family tie.

lier [lje] *vt* (*attacher*) to tie up; (*joindre*)

to link up; (*fig: unir, engager*) to bind; (*CULIN*) to thicken; ~ **qch à** to tie *ou* link sth to; ~ **conversation avec** to strike up a conversation with; **se** ~ **avec** to make friends with.

lierre [ljɛʀ] *nm* ivy.

liesse [ljɛs] *nf*: **être en** ~ to be celebrating *ou* jubilant.

lieu, x [ljø] *nm* place // *nmpl* (*habitation*) premises; (*endroit: d'un accident etc*) scene *sg*; **en** ~ **sûr** in a safe place; **en premier/dernier** ~ in the first place/ lastly; **avoir** ~ to take place; **avoir** ~ **de faire** to have grounds for doing; **tenir** ~ **de** to take the place of; to serve as; **donner** ~ **à** to give rise to; **au** ~ **de** instead of.

lieu-dit *nm* (*pl* **lieux-dits**) [ljødi] locality.

lieutenant [ljøtnɑ̃] *nm* lieutenant.

lièvre [ljɛvʀ(ə)] *nm* hare.

ligament [ligamɑ̃] *nm* ligament.

ligne [liɲ] *nf* (*gén*) line; (*TRANSPORTS: liaison*) service; (*: trajet*) route; (*silhouette*) figure; **entrer en** ~ **de compte** to come into it.

lignée [liɲe] *nf* line; lineage; descendants *pl*.

ligoter [ligɔte] *vt* to tie up.

ligue [lig] *nf* league; **liguer** *vt*: **se liguer contre** (*fig*) to combine against.

lilas [lila] *nm* lilac.

limace [limas] *nf* slug.

limaille [limaj] *nf*: ~ **de fer** iron filings *pl*.

limande [limɑ̃d] *nf* dab.

lime [lim] *nf* file; ~ **à ongles** nail file; **limer** *vt* to file.

limier [limje] *nm* bloodhound; (*détective*) sleuth.

limitation [limitasjɔ̃] *nf*: ~ **de vitesse** speed limit.

limite [limit] *nf* (*de terrain*) boundary; (*partie ou point extrême*) limit; **vitesse/ charge** ~ maximum speed/load; **cas** ~ borderline case; **date** ~ deadline.

limiter [limite] *vt* (*restreindre*) to limit, restrict; (*délimiter*) to border.

limitrophe [limitʀɔf] *a* border *cpd*.

limoger [limɔʒe] *vt* to dismiss.

limon [limɔ̃] *nm* silt.

limonade [limɔnad] *nf* lemonade.

lin [lɛ̃] *nm* flax.

linceul [lɛ̃sœl] *nm* shroud.

linge [lɛ̃ʒ] *nm* (*serviettes etc*) linen; (*pièce de tissu*) cloth; (*aussi*: ~ **de corps**) underwear; (*aussi*: ~ **de toilette**) towel; (*lessive*) washing.

lingerie [lɛ̃ʒʀi] *nf* lingerie, underwear.

lingot [lɛ̃go] *nm* ingot.

linguistique [lɛ̃gɥistik] *a* linguistic // *nf* linguistics *sg*.

lion, ne [ljɔ̃, ljɔn] *nm/f* lion/lioness; (*signe*): **le L~** Leo; **lionceau, x** *nm* lion cub.

liqueur [likœʀ] *nf* liqueur.

liquide [likid] *a* liquid // *nm* liquid; (*COMM*): **en** ~ in ready money *ou* cash.

liquider [likide] *vt* (*société, biens, témoin gênant*) to liquidate; (*compte, problème*) to settle; (*COMM: articles*) to clear, sell off.

liquidités [likidite] *nfpl* (*COMM*) liquid assets.

lire [liʀ] *nf* (*monnaie*) lira // *vt, vi* to read.

lis [lis] *nm* = **lys**.

lisible [lizibl(ə)] *a* legible.

lisière [lizjɛʀ] *nf* (*de forêt*) edge; (*de tissu*) selvage.

lisons *vb voir* **lire**.

lisse [lis] *a* smooth.

liste [list(ə)] *nf* list; **faire la** ~ **de** to list; ~ **électorale** electoral roll.

listing [listiŋ] *nm* (*INFORM*) printout.

lit [li] *nm* (*gén*) bed; **faire son** ~ to make one's bed; **aller/se mettre au** ~ to go to/ get into bed; ~ **de camp** campbed; ~ **d'enfant** cot (*Brit*), crib (*US*).

literie [litʀi] *nf* bedding, bedclothes *pl*.

litière [litjɛʀ] *nf* litter.

litige [litiʒ] *nm* dispute.

litre [litʀ(ə)] *nm* litre; (*récipient*) litre measure.

littéraire [literɛʀ] *a* literary.

littéral, e, aux [literal, -o] *a* literal.

littérature [literatyʀ] *nf* literature.

littoral, aux [litɔral, -o] *nm* coast.

liturgie [lityʀʒi] *nf* liturgy.

livide [livid] *a* livid, pallid.

livraison [livʀɛzɔ̃] *nf* delivery.

livre [livʀ(ə)] *nm* book // *nf* (*poids, monnaie*) pound; ~ **de bord** logbook; ~ **de poche** paperback (*pocket size*).

livré, e [livʀe] *a*: ~ **à soi-même** left to o.s. *ou* one's own devices // *nf* livery.

livrer [livʀe] *vt* (*COMM*) to deliver; (*otage, coupable*) to hand over; (*secret, information*) to give away; **se** ~ **à** (*se confier*) to confide in; (*se rendre, s'abandonner*) to give o.s. up to; (*faire: pratiques, actes*) to indulge in; (*travail*) to engage in; (*: sport*) to practise; (*: enquête*) to carry out.

livret [livʀɛ] *nm* booklet; (*d'opéra*) libretto (*pl* s); ~ **de caisse d'épargne** (*savings*) bank-book; ~ **de famille** (*official*) family record book; ~ **scolaire** (*school*) report book.

livreur, euse [livʀœʀ, -øz] *nm/f* delivery boy *ou* man/girl *ou* woman.

local, e, aux [lɔkal, -o] *a* local // *nm* (*salle*) premises *pl* // *nmpl* premises.

localiser [lɔkalize] *vt* (*repérer*) to locate, place; (*limiter*) to confine.

localité [lɔkalite] *nf* locality.

locataire [lɔkatɛʀ] *nm/f* tenant; (*de chambre*) lodger.

location [lɔkasjɔ̃] *nf* (*par le locataire, le loueur*) renting; (*par le propriétaire*) renting out, letting; (*THÉÂTRE*) booking

office; '~ de voitures' 'car rental'.
locomotive [lɔkɔmɔtiv] *nf* locomotive,
engine; (*fig*) pacesetter, pacemaker.
locution [lɔkysjɔ̃] *nf* phrase.
loge [lɔʒ] *nf* (*THÉÂTRE: d'artiste*) dressing room; (*: de spectateurs*) box; (*de
concierge, franc-maçon*) lodge.
logement [lɔʒmɑ̃] *nm* accommodation
q; flat (*Brit*), apartment (*US*); housing
q.
loger [lɔʒe] *vt* to accommodate // *vi* to
live; **trouver à se ~** to find accommodation; **se ~ dans** (*suj: balle, flèche*) to
lodge itself in; **logeur, euse** *nm/f*
landlord/landlady.
logiciel [lɔʒisjɛl] *nm* software.
logique [lɔʒik] *a* logical // *nf* logic.
logis [lɔʒi] *nm* home; abode, dwelling.
loi [lwa] *nf* law; **faire la ~** to lay down
the law.
loin [lwɛ̃] *ad* far; (*dans le temps*) a long
way off; a long time ago; **plus ~**
further; **~ de** far from; **au ~** far off; **de
~ ad** from a distance; (*fig: de beaucoup*) by far; **il vient de ~** (*fig*) he's
come a long way.
lointain, e [lwɛ̃tɛ̃, -ɛn] *a* faraway, distant; (*dans le futur, passé*) distant, far-
off; (*cause, parenté*) remote, distant //
nm: **dans le ~** in the distance.
loir [lwaʀ] *nm* dormouse (*pl* -mice).
loisir [lwaziʀ] *nm*: **heures de ~** spare
time; **~s** *nmpl* leisure *sg*; leisure activ-
ities; **avoir le ~ de faire** to have the
time *ou* opportunity to do; **à ~** at leisure; at one's pleasure.
londonien, ne [lɔ̃dɔnjɛ̃, -jɛn] *a* London
cpd, of London // *nm/f*: **L~, ne** Londoner.
Londres [lɔ̃dʀ(ə)] *n* London.
long, longue [lɔ̃, lɔ̃g] *a* long // *ad*: **en
savoir ~** to know a great deal // *nm*: de
3 m de ~ ~ 3 m long, 3 m in length // *nf*: **à
la longue** in the end; **ne pas faire ~ feu**
not to last long; (**tout**) **le ~ de** (all)
along; **tout au ~ de** (*année, vie*) throughout; **de ~ en large** (*marcher*) to and fro,
up and down.
longer [lɔ̃ʒe] *vt* to go (*ou* walk *ou* drive)
along(side); (*suj: mur, route*) to border.
longiligne [lɔ̃ʒiliɲ] *a* long-limbed.
longitude [lɔ̃ʒityd] *nf* longitude.
longitudinal, e, aux [lɔ̃ʒitydinal, -o] *a*
(*running*) lengthways.
longtemps [lɔ̃tɑ̃] *ad* (for) a long time,
(for) long; **avant ~** before long; **pour/
pendant ~** for a long time; **mettre ~ à
faire** to take a long time to do.
longue [lɔ̃g] *af voir* **long**; **~ment** *ad* for
a long time.
longueur [lɔ̃gœʀ] *nf* length; **~s** *nfpl*
(*fig: d'un film etc*) tedious parts; **en ~**
ad lengthwise; **tirer en ~** to drag on; **à
~ de journée** all day long; **~ d'onde**
wavelength.
longue-vue [lɔ̃gvy] *nf* telescope.

lopin [lɔpɛ̃] *nm*: **~ de terre** patch of
land.
loque [lɔk] *nf* (*personne*) wreck; **~s** *nfpl*
(*habits*) rags.
loquet [lɔkɛ] *nm* latch.
lorgner [lɔʀɲe] *vt* to eye; (*fig*) to have
one's eye on.
lors [lɔʀ]: **~ de** *prép* at the time of; during; **~ même que** even though.
lorsque [lɔʀsk(ə)] *cj* when, as.
losange [lɔzɑ̃ʒ] *nm* diamond; (*GÉOM*)
lozenge.
lot [lo] *nm* (*part*) share; (*de loterie*)
prize; (*fig: destin*) fate, lot; (*COMM, IN-
FORM*) batch.
loterie [lɔtʀi] *nf* lottery; raffle.
loti, e [lɔti] *a*: **bien/mal ~** well-/badly off.
lotion [lɔsjɔ̃] *nf* lotion.
lotir [lɔtiʀ] *vt* (*terrain*) to divide into
plots; to sell by lots; **lotissement** *nm*
housing development; plot, lot.
loto [lɔto] *nm* lotto; numerical lottery.
louable [lwabl(ə)] *a* commendable.
louanges [lwɑ̃ʒ] *nfpl* praise *sg*.
loubard [lubaʀ] *nm* (*fam*) lout.
louche [luʃ] *a* shady, fishy, dubious // *nf*
ladle.
loucher [luʃe] *vi* to squint.
louer [lwe] *vt* (*maison: suj: propriétaire*) to let, rent (out); (*: locataire*) to
rent; (*voiture etc*) to hire out (*Brit*),
rent (out); to hire, rent; (*réserver*) to
book; (*faire l'éloge de*) to praise; **'à
louer'** 'to let' (*Brit*), 'for rent' (*US*).
loup [lu] *nm* wolf (*pl* wolves).
loupe [lup] *nf* magnifying glass.
louper [lupe] *vt* (*manquer*) to miss.
lourd, e [luʀ, luʀd(ə)] *a, ad* heavy; **~
de** (*conséquences, menaces*) charged
with; **lourdaud, e** *a* (*péj*) clumsy.
loutre [lutʀ(ə)] *nf* otter.
louve [luv] *nf* she-wolf.
louveteau, x [luvto] *nm* wolf-cub;
(*scout*) cub (scout).
louvoyer [luvwaje] *vi* (*NAVIG*) to tack;
(*fig*) to hedge, evade the issue.
lover [lɔve]: **se ~** *vi* to coil up.
loyal, e, aux [lwajal, -o] *a* (*fidèle*)
loyal, faithful; (*fair-play*) fair; **loyauté**
nf loyalty, faithfulness; fairness.
loyer [lwaje] *nm* rent.
lu, e [ly] *pp de* **lire**.
lubie [lybi] *nf* whim, craze.
lubrifiant [lybʀifjɑ̃] *nm* lubricant.
lubrifier [lybʀifje] *vt* to lubricate.
lubrique [lybʀik] *a* lecherous.
lucarne [lykaʀn(ə)] *nf* skylight.
lucratif, ive [lykʀatif, -iv] *a* lucrative;
profitable; **à but non ~** non profit-
making.
lueur [lɥœʀ] *nf* (*chatoyante*) glimmer *q*;
(*métallique, mouillée*) gleam *q*;
(*rougeoyante, chaude*) glow *q*; (*pâle*)
(faint) light; (*fig*) glimmer; gleam.
luge [lyʒ] *nf* sledge (*Brit*), sled (*US*).

lugubre [lygybʀ(ə)] a gloomy; dismal.

lui [lɥi] pronom **1** (objet indirect: mâle) (to) him; (: femelle) (to) her; (: chose, animal) (to) it; **je ~ ai parlé** I have spoken to him (ou to her); **il ~ a offert un cadeau** he gave him (ou her) a present **2** (après préposition, comparatif: personne) him; (: chose, animal) it; **elle est contente de ~** she is pleased with him; **je la connais mieux que ~** I know her better than he does; I know her better than him **3** (sujet, forme emphatique) he; **~, il est à Paris** HE is in Paris **4**: **~-même** himself; itself.

luire [lɥiʀ] vi to shine; to glow.

lumière [lymjɛʀ] nf light; **~s** nfpl (d'une personne) wisdom sg; **mettre en ~** (fig) to highlight; **~ du jour/soleil** day/sunlight.

luminaire [lyminɛʀ] nm lamp, light.

lumineux, euse [lyminø, -øz] a (émettant de la lumière) luminous; (éclairé) illuminated; (ciel, couleur) bright; (relatif à la lumière: rayon etc) of light, light cpd; (fig: regard) radiant.

lunaire [lynɛʀ] a lunar, moon cpd.

lunatique [lynatik] a whimsical, temperamental.

lundi [lœdi] nm Monday; **~ de Pâques** Easter Monday.

lune [lyn] nf moon; **~ de miel** honeymoon.

lunette [lynɛt] nf: **~s** nfpl glasses, spectacles; (protectrices) goggles; **~ arrière** (AUTO) rear window; **~s noires** dark glasses; **~s de soleil** sunglasses.

lus etc vb voir **lire**.

lustre [lystʀ(ə)] nm (de plafond) chandelier; (fig: éclat) lustre.

lustrer [lystʀe] vt to shine.

lut vb voir **lire**.

luth [lyt] nm lute.

lutin [lytɛ̃] nm imp, goblin.

lutte [lyt] nf (conflit) struggle; (sport) wrestling; **lutter** vi to fight, struggle.

luxe [lyks(ə)] nm luxury; **de ~** a luxury cpd.

Luxembourg [lyksɑ̃buʀ] nm: **le ~** Luxembourg.

luxer [lykse] vt: **se ~ l'épaule** to dislocate one's shoulder.

luxueux, euse [lyksɥø, -øz] a luxurious.

luxure [lyksyʀ] nf lust.

lycée [lise] nm secondary school; **lycéen, ne** nm/f secondary school pupil.

lyrique [liʀik] a lyrical; (OPÉRA) lyric; **artiste ~** opera singer.

lys [lis] nm lily.

M

M abr de **Monsieur**.

m' [m] pronom voir **me**.

ma [ma] dét voir **mon**.

macaron [makaʀɔ̃] nm (gâteau) macaroon; (insigne) (round) badge.

macaronis [makaʀɔni] nmpl macaroni sg.

macédoine [masedwan] nf: **~ de fruits** fruit salad.

macérer [maseʀe] vi, vt to macerate; (dans du vinaigre) to pickle.

mâcher [maʃe] vt to chew; **ne pas ~ ses mots** not to mince one's words.

machin [maʃɛ̃] nm (fam) thing(umajig).

machinal, e, aux [maʃinal, -o] a mechanical, automatic.

machination [maʃinasjɔ̃] nf scheming, frame-up.

machine [maʃin] nf machine; (locomotive) engine; (fig: rouages) machinery; **~ à laver/coudre** washing/sewing machine; **~ à écrire** typewriter; **~ à sous** fruit machine; **~ à vapeur** steam engine; **~rie** nf machinery, plant; (d'un navire) engine room; **machinisme** nm mechanization; **machiniste** nm (de bus, métro) driver.

mâchoire [maʃwaʀ] nf jaw; **~ de frein** brake shoe.

mâchonner [maʃone] vt to chew (at).

maçon [masɔ̃] nm bricklayer; builder.

maçonnerie [masɔnʀi] nf (murs) brickwork; masonry, stonework; (activité) bricklaying; building.

maculer [makyle] vt to stain.

Madame [madam], pl **Mesdames** [medam] nf: **~ X** Mrs X ['mɪsɪz]; **occupez-vous de ~/Monsieur/Mademoiselle** please serve this lady/gentleman/ (young) lady; **bonjour ~/Monsieur/ Mademoiselle** good morning; (ton déférent) good morning Madam/Sir/Madam; (le nom est connu) good morning Mrs/ Mr/Miss X; **~/Monsieur/Mademoiselle!** (pour appeler) Madam/Sir/Miss!; **~/ Monsieur/Mademoiselle** (sur lettre) Dear Madam/Sir/Madam; **chère ~/cher Monsieur/chère Mademoiselle** Dear Mrs/ Mr/Miss X; **Mesdames** Ladies.

Mademoiselle [madmwazɛl], pl **Mesdemoiselles** [medmwazɛl] nf Miss; voir aussi **Madame**.

madère [madɛʀ] nm Madeira (wine).

magasin [magazɛ̃] nm (boutique) shop; (entrepôt) warehouse; (d'une arme) magazine; **en ~** (COMM) in stock.

magazine [magazin] nm magazine.

magicien, ne [maʒisjɛ̃, -jɛn] nm/f magician.

magie [maʒi] nf magic; **magique** a magic; (enchanteur) magical.

magistral, e, aux [maʒistʀal, -o] *a*
(*œuvre, adresse*) masterly; (*ton*) authoritative; (*ex cathedra*): enseignement
~ lecturing, lectures *pl.*

magistrat [maʒistʀa] *nm* magistrate.

magnétique [maɲetik] *a* magnetic.

magnétiser [maɲetize] *vt* to magnetize;
(*fig*) to mesmerize, hypnotize.

magnétophone [maɲetɔfɔn] *nm* tape
recorder; ~ à **cassettes** cassette recorder.

magnétoscope [maɲetɔskɔp] *nm*
video-tape recorder.

magnifique [maɲifik] *a* magnificent.

magot [mago] *nm* (*argent*) pile (of
money); nest egg.

magouille [maguj] *nf* scheming.

mai [mɛ] *nm* May.

maigre [mɛgʀ(ə)] *a* (very) thin, skinny;
(*viande*) lean; (*fromage*) low-fat; (*végétation*) thin, sparse; (*fig*) poor, meagre,
skimpy // *ad*: **faire** ~ not to eat meat;
jours ~s days of abstinence, fish days;
maigreur *nf* thinness; **maigrir** *vi* to get
thinner, lose weight.

maille [maj] *nf* stitch; ~ **à l'endroit/à
l'envers** plain/purl stitch; **avoir** ~ **à
partir avec qn** to have a brush with sb.

maillet [majɛ] *nm* mallet.

maillon [majɔ̃] *nm* link.

maillot [majo] *nm* (*aussi*: ~ **de corps**)
vest; (*de danseur*) leotard; (*de sportif*)
jersey; ~ **de bain** swimsuit; (*d'homme*)
bathing trunks *pl.*

main [mɛ̃] *nf* hand; **à la** ~ in one's hand;
se donner la ~ to hold hands; **donner** *ou*
tendre la ~ **à qn** to hold out one's hand
to sb; **se serrer la** ~ to shake hands;
serrer la ~ **à qn** to shake hands with sb;
sous la ~ to *ou* at hand; **attaque à** ~
armée armed attack; **à** ~ **droite/gauche**
to the right/left; **à remettre en** ~s **propres** to be delivered personally; **de
première** ~ (*COMM: voiture etc*) secondhand with only one previous owner; **mettre la dernière** ~ **à** to put the finishing
touches to; **se faire/perdre la** ~ to get
one's hand in/lose one's touch; **avoir qch
bien en** ~ to have (got) the hang of
sth.

main-d'œuvre [mɛ̃dœvʀ(ə)] *nf* manpower, labour.

main-forte [mɛ̃fɔʀt(ə)] *nf*: **prêter** ~ **à
qn** to come to sb's assistance.

mainmise [mɛ̃miz] *nf* seizure; (*fig*): ~
sur complete hold on.

maint, e [mɛ̃, mɛ̃t] *a* many a; ~s _
many; **à** ~**es reprises** time and (time)
again.

maintenant [mɛ̃tnɑ̃] *ad* now; (*actuellement*) nowadays.

maintenir [mɛ̃tniʀ] *vt* (*retenir, soutenir*)
to support; (*contenir: foule etc*) to hold
back; (*conserver, affirmer*) to maintain;
se ~ *vi* to hold; to keep steady; to persist.

maintien [mɛ̃tjɛ̃] *nm* maintaining; (*attitude*) bearing.

maire [mɛʀ] *nm* mayor.

mairie [meʀi] *nf* (*bâtiment*) town hall;
(*administration*) town council.

mais [mɛ] *cj* but; ~ **non!** of course not!;
~ **enfin** but after all; (*indignation*) look
here!; ~ **encore**? is that all?

maïs [mais] *nm* maize (*Brit*), corn (*US*).

maison [mɛzɔ̃] *nf* house; (*chez-soi*)
home; (*COMM*) firm // *a inv* (*CULIN*)
home-made; made by the chef; (*fig*) inhouse, own; **à la** ~ at home; (*direction*)
home; ~ **close** *ou* **de passe** brothel; ~ **de
correction** reformatory; **des jeunes** ≈
youth club; ~ **mère** parent company; ~
de repos convalescent home; ~ **de santé**
mental home; **maisonnée** *nf* household,
family; **maisonnette** *nf* small house,
cottage.

maître, esse [mɛtʀ(ə), mɛtʀɛs] *nm/f*
master/mistress; (*SCOL*) teacher,
schoolmaster/mistress // *nm* (*peintre etc*)
master; (*titre*): **M~ (Me)** Maître, *term
of address gen for a barrister* // *nf*
(*amante*) mistress // *a* (*principal, essentiel*) main; **être** ~ **de** (*soi-même, situation*) to be in control of; **une maîtresse
femme** a managing woman; ~ **chanteur**
blackmailer; ~/**maîtresse d'école**
schoolmaster/mistress; ~ **d'hôtel** (*domestique*) butler; (*d'hôtel*) head waiter;
~ **de maison** host; ~ **nageur** lifeguard;
maîtresse de maison hostess; housewife
(*pl* wives).

maîtrise [mɛtʀiz] *nf* (*aussi*: ~ **de soi**)
self-control, self-possession; (*habileté*)
skill, mastery; (*suprématie*) mastery,
command; (*diplôme*) ≈ master's
degree.

maîtriser [mɛtʀize] *vt* (*cheval, incendie*)
to (bring under) control; (*sujet*) to master; (*émotion*) to control, master; **se** ~
to control o.s.

majestueux, euse [maʒɛstɥø, -øz] *a*
majestic.

majeur, e [maʒœʀ] *a* (*important*) major; (*JUR*) of age; (*fig*) adult // *nm*
(*doigt*) middle finger; **en** ~ **e partie** for
the most part.

majorer [maʒɔʀe] *vt* to increase.

majoritaire [maʒɔʀitɛʀ] *a* majority
cpd.

majorité [maʒɔʀite] *nf* (*gén*) majority;
(*parti*) party in power; **en** ~ mainly.

majuscule [maʒyskyl] *a, nf*: (**lettre**) ~
capital (letter).

mal, maux [mal, mo] *nm* (*opposé au
bien*) evil; (*tort, dommage*) harm;
(*douleur physique*) pain, ache; (*maladie*) illness, sickness *q* // *ad* badly // *a*
bad, wrong; **être** ~ to be uncomfortable;
être ~ **avec qn** to be on bad terms with
sb; **être au plus** ~ (*malade*) to be at

death's door; (*brouillé*) to be at daggers drawn; **il a ~ compris** he misunderstood; **dire/penser du ~ de** to speak/think ill of; **ne voir aucun ~ à** to see no harm in, see nothing wrong in; **craignant ~ faire** fearing he was doing the wrong thing; **faire du ~ à qn** to hurt sb; to harm sb; **se faire ~** to hurt o.s.; **se donner du ~ pour faire qch** to go to a lot of trouble to do sth; **ça fait ~** it hurts; **j'ai ~ au dos** my back hurts; **avoir ~ à la tête/à la gorge/aux dents** to have a headache/a sore throat/toothache; **avoir le ~ du pays** to be homesick; **prendre ~** to be taken ill, feel unwell; **~ de mer** seasickness; **~ en point** *a inv* in a bad state; **maux de ventre** stomach ache *sg*; *voir* **coeur.**

malade [malad] *a* ill, sick; (*poitrine, jambe*) bad; (*plante*) diseased // *nm/f* invalid, sick person; (*à l'hôpital etc*) patient; **tomber ~** to fall ill; **être ~ du cœur** to have heart trouble *ou* a bad heart; **~ mental** mentally sick *ou* ill person.

maladie [maladi] *nf* (*spécifique*) disease, illness; (*mauvaise santé*) illness, sickness; **maladif, ive** *a* sickly; (*curiosité, besoin*) pathological.

maladresse [maladʀɛs] *nf* clumsiness *q*; (*gaffe*) blunder.

maladroit, e [maladʀwa, -wat] *a* clumsy.

malaise [malɛz] *nm* (*MÉD*) feeling of faintness; feeling of discomfort; (*fig*) uneasiness, malaise.

malaisé, e [maleze] *a* difficult.

malappris, e [malapʀi, -iz] *nm/f* ill-mannered *ou* boorish person.

malaria [malaʀja] *nf* malaria.

malaxer [malakse] *vt* to knead; to mix.

malchance [malʃɑ̃s] *nf* misfortune, ill luck *q*; **par ~** unfortunately.

mâle [mɑl] *a* (*aussi* ÉLEC, TECH) male; (*viril: voix, traits*) manly // *nm* male.

malédiction [malediksjɔ̃] *nf* curse.

malencontreux, euse [malɑ̃kɔ̃tʀø, -øz] *a* unfortunate, untoward.

malentendu [malɑ̃tɑ̃dy] *nm* misunderstanding.

malfaçon [malfasɔ̃] *nf* fault.

malfaisant, e [malfəzɑ̃, -ɑ̃t] *a* evil, harmful.

malfaiteur [malfɛtœʀ] *nm* lawbreaker, criminal; burglar; thief (*pl* thieves).

malgache [malgaʃ] *a, nm/f* Madagascan, Malagasy // *nm* (*langue*) Malagasy.

malgré [malgʀe] *prép* in spite of, despite; **~ tout** *ad* all the same.

malheur [malœʀ] *nm* (*situation*) adversity, misfortune; (*événement*) misfortune; disaster, tragedy; **faire un ~** to be a smash hit; **malheureusement** *ad* unfortunately; **malheureux, euse** *a* (*triste*) unhappy, miserable; (*infortuné,*

regrettable) unfortunate; (*malchanceux*) unlucky; (*insignifiant*) wretched // *nm/f* poor soul; unfortunate creature; **les malheureux** the destitute.

malhonnête [malɔnɛt] *a* dishonest.

malice [malis] *nf* mischievousness; (*méchanceté*): **par ~** out of malice *ou* spite; **sans ~** guileless; **malicieux, euse** *a* mischievous.

malin, igne [malɛ̃, -iɲ] *a* (*futé: f gén*: **maline**) smart, shrewd; (*MÉD*) malignant.

malingre [malɛ̃gʀ(ə)] *a* puny.

malle [mal] *nf* trunk.

mallette [malɛt] *nf* (small) suitcase; overnight case; attaché case.

malmener [malməne] *vt* to manhandle; (*fig*) to give a rough handling to.

malodorant, e [malɔdɔʀɑ̃, -ɑ̃t] *a* foul-*ou* ill-smelling.

malotru [malɔtʀy] *nm* lout, boor.

malpropre [malpʀɔpʀ(ə)] *a* dirty.

malsain, e [malsɛ̃, -ɛn] *a* unhealthy.

malt [malt] *nm* malt.

Malte [malt(ə)] *nf* Malta.

maltraiter [maltʀete] *vt* (*brutaliser*) to manhandle, ill-treat.

malveillance [malvɛjɑ̃s] *nf* (*animosité*) ill will; (*intention de nuire*) malevolence; (*JUR*) malicious intent *q*.

malversation [malvɛʀsasjɔ̃] *nf* embezzlement.

maman [mamɑ̃] *nf* mum(my), mother.

mamelle [mamɛl] *nf* teat.

mamelon [mamlɔ̃] *nm* (*ANAT*) nipple; (*colline*) knoll, hillock.

mamie [mami] *nf* (*fam*) granny.

mammifère [mamifɛʀ] *nm* mammal.

manche [mɑ̃ʃ] *nf* (*de vêtement*) sleeve; (*d'un jeu, tournoi*) round; (*GÉO*): **la M~** the Channel // *nm* (*d'outil, casserole*) handle; (*de pelle, pioche etc*) shaft; **~ à balai** *nm* broomstick; (*AVIAT, INFORM*) joystick.

manchette [mɑ̃ʃɛt] *nf* (*de chemise*) cuff; (*coup*) forearm blow; (*titre*) headline.

manchon [mɑ̃ʃɔ̃] *nm* (*de fourrure*) muff.

manchot [mɑ̃ʃo] *nm* one-armed man; armless man; (*ZOOL*) penguin.

mandarine [mɑ̃daʀin] *nf* mandarin (orange), tangerine.

mandat [mɑ̃da] *nm* (*postal*) postal *ou* money order; (*d'un député etc*) mandate; (*procuration*) power of attorney, proxy; (*POLICE*) warrant; **~ d'amener** summons *sg*; **~ d'arrêt** warrant for arrest; **mandataire** *nm/f* representative; proxy.

mander [mɑ̃de] *vt* to summon.

manège [manɛʒ] *nm* riding school; (*à la foire*) roundabout, merry-go-round; (*fig*) game, ploy.

manette [manɛt] *nf* lever, tap; **~ de jeu**

joystick.

mangeable [mãʒabl(ə)] *a* edible, eatable.

mangeoire [mãʒwaʀ] *nf* trough, manger.

manger [mãʒe] *vt* to eat; (*ronger: suj: rouille etc*) to eat into *ou* away // *vi* to eat.

mangue [mãg] *nf* mango.

maniable [manjabl(ə)] *a* (*outil*) handy; (*voiture, voilier*) easy to handle.

maniaque [manjak] *a* finicky, fussy; suffering from a mania // *nm/f* maniac.

manie [mani] *nf* mania; (*tic*) odd habit.

manier [manje] *vt* to handle.

manière [manjɛʀ] *nf* (*façon*) way, manner; **~s** *nfpl* (*attitude*) manners; (*chichis*) fuss *sg*; **de ~ à** so as to; **de telle ~ que** in such a way that; **de cette ~** in this way *ou* manner; **d'une certaine ~** in a way; **d'une ~ générale** generally speaking, as a general rule; **de toute ~** in any case.

maniéré, e [manjeʀe] *a* affected.

manifestant, e [manifɛstɑ̃, -ɑ̃t] *nm/f* demonstrator.

manifestation [manifɛstasjɔ̃] *nf* (*de joie, mécontentement*) expression, demonstration; (*symptôme*) outward sign; (*fête etc*) event; (*POL*) demonstration.

manifeste [manifɛst(ə)] *a* obvious, evident // *nm* manifesto (*pl* s).

manifester [manifɛste] *vt* (*volonté, intentions*) to show, indicate; (*joie, peur*) to express, show // *vi* to demonstrate; **se ~ vi** (*émotion*) to show *ou* express itself; (*difficultés*) to arise; (*symptômes*) to appear; (*témoin etc*) to come forward.

manigance [manigãs] *nf* scheme.

manipuler [manipyle] *vt* to handle; (*fig*) to manipulate.

manivelle [manivɛl] *nf* crank.

mannequin [mankɛ̃] *nm* (*COUTURE*) dummy; (*MODE*) model.

manœuvre [manœvʀ(ə)] *nf* (*gén*) manœuvre (*Brit*), maneuver (*US*) // *nm* labourer.

manœuvrer [manœvʀe] *vt* to manœuvre (*Brit*), maneuver (*US*); (*levier, machine*) to operate // *vi* to manœuvre.

manoir [manwaʀ] *nm* manor *ou* country house.

manque [mãk] *nm* (*insuffisance*): **~ de** lack of; (*vide*) emptiness, gap; (*MÉD*) withdrawal; **~s** *nmpl* (*lacunes*) faults, defects.

manqué, e [mãke] *a* failed; **garçon ~** tomboy.

manquer [mãke] *vi* (*faire défaut*) to be lacking; (*être absent*) to be missing; (*échouer*) to fail // *vt* to miss // *vb impersonnel*: **il (nous) manque encore 100 F** we are still 100 F short; **il manque des pages (au livre)** there are some pages missing *ou* some pages are missing

(*from the book*); **il/cela me manque** I miss him/this; **~ à** *vt* (*règles etc*) to be in breach of, fail to observe; **~ de** *vt* to lack; **il a manqué (de) se tuer** he very nearly got killed.

mansarde [mãsaʀd(ə)] *nf* attic.

mansuétude [mãsɥetyd] *nf* leniency.

manteau, x [mãto] *nm* coat; **~ de cheminée** mantelpiece.

manucure [manykyʀ] *nf* manicurist.

manuel, le [manɥɛl] *a* manual // *nm* (*ouvrage*) manual, handbook.

manufacture [manyfaktyʀ] *nf* factory.

manufacturé, e [manyfaktyʀe] *a* manufactured.

manuscrit, e [manyskʀi, -it] *a* handwritten // *nm* manuscript.

manutention [manytãsjɔ̃] *nf* (*COMM*) handling; (*local*) storehouse.

mappemonde [mapmɔ̃d] *nf* (*plane*) map of the world; (*sphère*) globe.

maquereau, x [makʀo] *nm* (*ZOOL*) mackerel *inv*; (*fam*) pimp.

maquette [makɛt] *nf* (*d'un décor, bâtiment, véhicule*) (scale) model; (*d'une page illustrée*) paste-up.

maquillage [makijaʒ] *nm* making up; faking; (*crème etc*) make-up.

maquiller [makije] *vt* (*personne, visage*) to make up; (*truquer: passeport, statistique*) to fake; (: *voiture volée*) to do over (*respray etc*); **se ~ vi** to make up (one's face).

maquis [maki] *nm* (*GÉO*) scrub; (*MIL*) maquis, underground fighting *q*.

maraîcher, ère [maʀɛʃe, maʀɛʃɛʀ] *a*: **cultures maraîchères** market gardening *sg* // *nm/f* market gardener.

marais [maʀɛ] *nm* marsh, swamp.

marasme [maʀasm(ə)] *nm* stagnation, slump.

marathon [maʀatɔ̃] *nm* marathon.

marâtre [maʀɑtʀ(ə)] *nf* cruel mother.

maraudeur [maʀodœʀ] *nm* prowler.

marbre [maʀbʀ(ə)] *nm* (*pierre, statue*) marble; (*d'une table, commode*) marble top; **marbrer** *vt* to mottle, blotch.

marc [maʀ] *nm* (*de raisin, pommes*) marc; **~ de café** coffee grounds *pl ou* dregs *pl*.

marchand, e [maʀʃɑ̃, -ɑ̃d] *nm/f* shopkeeper, tradesman/woman; (*au marché*) stallholder // *a*: **prix/valeur ~(e)** market price/value; **~ de charbon/vins** coal/wine merchant; **~/e de couleurs** ironmonger (*Brit*), hardware dealer (*US*); **~/e de fruits** fruiterer (*Brit*), fruit seller (*US*); **~/e de journaux** newsagent; **~/e de légumes** greengrocer (*Brit*), produce dealer (*US*); **~/e de quatre saisons** costermonger (*Brit*), street vendor (selling fresh fruit and vegetables); **~/e de tableaux** art dealer.

marchander [maʀʃɑ̃de] *vi* to bargain, haggle.

marchandise [maʁʃɑ̃diz] *nf* goods *pl*, merchandise *q*.

marche [maʁʃ(ə)] *nf* (*d'escalier*) step; (*activité*) walking; (*promenade, trajet, allure*) walk; (*démarche*) walk, gait; (*MIL etc, MUS*) march; (*fonctionnement*) running; (*progression*) progress; course; **ouvrir/fermer la** ~ to lead the way/bring up the rear; **dans le sens de la** ~ (*RAIL*) facing the engine; **en** ~ (*monter etc*) while the vehicle is moving *ou* in motion; **mettre en** ~ to start; **se mettre en** ~ (*personne*) to get moving; (*machine*) to start; ~ **arrière** reverse (gear); **faire** ~ **arrière** to reverse; (*fig*) to backtrack, back-pedal; ~ **à suivre** (correct) procedure; (*sur notice*) (step by step) instructions *pl*.

marché [maʁʃe] *nm* (*lieu, COMM, ÉCON*) market; (*ville*) trading centre; (*transaction*) bargain, deal; **M~ commun** Common Market; **faire du** ~ **noir** to buy and sell on the black market; ~ **aux puces** flea market.

marchepied [maʁʃəpje] *nm* (*RAIL*) step; (*fig*) stepping stone.

marcher [maʁʃe] *vi* to walk; (*MIL*) to march; (*aller: voiture, train, affaires*) to go; (*prospérer*) to go well; (*fonctionner*) to work, run; (*fam*) to go along, agree; to be taken in; ~ **sur** to walk on; (*mettre le pied sur*) to step on ou in; (*MIL*) to march upon; ~ **dans** (*herbe etc*) to walk in *ou* on; (*flaque*) to step in; **faire** ~ **qn** to pull sb's leg; to lead sb up the garden path; **marcheur, euse** *nm/f* walker.

mardi [maʁdi] *nm* Tuesday; **M~ gras** Shrove Tuesday.

mare [maʁ] *nf* pond; ~ **de sang** pool of blood.

marécage [maʁekaʒ] *nm* marsh, swamp.

maréchal, aux [maʁeʃal, -o] *nm* marshal.

marée [maʁe] *nf* tide; (*poissons*) fresh (sea) fish; ~ **haute/basse** high/low tide; ~ **montante/descendante** rising/ebb tide.

marémotrice [maʁemɔtʁis] *af* tidal.

margarine [maʁgaʁin] *nf* margarine.

marge [maʁʒ(ə)] *nf* margin; **en** ~ **de** (*fig*) on the fringe of; cut off from; ~ **bénéficiaire** profit margin.

marguerite [maʁgəʁit] *nf* marguerite, (oxeye) daisy; (*d'imprimante*) daisy-wheel.

mari [maʁi] *nm* husband.

mariage [maʁjaʒ] *nm* (*union, état, fig*) marriage; (*noce*) wedding; ~ **civil/ religieux** registry office (*Brit*) *ou* civil/ church wedding.

marié, e [maʁje] *a* married // *nm/f* (bride)groom/bride; **les ~s** the bride and groom; **les (jeunes) ~s** the newly-weds.

marier [maʁje] *vt* to marry; (*fig*) to blend; **se** ~ (**avec**) to marry.

marin, e [maʁɛ̃, -in] *a* sea *cpd*, marine // *nm* sailor // *nf* navy; ~**e de guerre** navy; ~**e marchande** merchant navy.

marine [maʁin] *af, nf voir* **marin** // *a inv* navy (blue) // *nm* (*MIL*) marine.

marionnette [maʁjɔnɛt] *nf* puppet.

maritime [maʁitim] *a* sea *cpd*, maritime.

mark [maʁk] *nm* mark.

marmelade [maʁməlad] *nf* stewed fruit, compote; ~ **d'oranges** marmalade.

marmite [maʁmit] *nf* (cooking-)pot.

marmonner [maʁmɔne] *vt, vi* to mumble, mutter.

marmotter [maʁmɔte] *vt* to mumble.

Maroc [maʁɔk] *nm*: **le** ~ Morocco; **ma- rocain, e** *a, nm/f* Moroccan.

maroquinerie [maʁɔkinʁi] *nf* leather craft; fine leather goods *pl*.

marquant, e [maʁkɑ̃, -ɑ̃t] *a* outstanding.

marque [maʁk(ə)] *nf* mark; (*SPORT, JEU: décompte des points*) score; (*COMM: de produits*) brand; make; (*: de disques*) label; **de** ~ *a* (*COMM*) brand-name *cpd*; proprietary; (*fig*) high-class; distinguished; ~ **déposée** registered trademark; ~ **de fabrique** trademark.

marquer [maʁke] *vt* to mark; (*inscrire*) to write down; (*bétail*) to brand; (*SPORT: but etc*) to score; (*: joueur*) to mark; (*accentuer: taille etc*) to emphasize; (*manifester: refus, intérêt*) to show // *vi* (*événement, personnalité*) to stand out, be outstanding; (*SPORT*) to score; ~ **les points** (*tenir la marque*) to keep the score.

marqueterie [maʁkɛtʁi] *nf* inlaid work, marquetry.

marquis, e [maʁki, -iz] *nm/f* marquis *ou* marquess/marchioness // *nf* (*auvent*) glass canopy *ou* awning.

marraine [maʁɛn] *nf* godmother.

marrant, e [maʁɑ̃, -ɑ̃t] *a* (*fam*) funny.

marre [maʁ] *ad* (*fam*): **en avoir** ~ **de** to be fed up with.

marrer [maʁe]: **se** ~ *vi* (*fam*) to have a (good) laugh.

marron [maʁɔ̃] *nm* (*fruit*) chestnut // *a inv* brown; **marronnier** *nm* chestnut (tree).

mars [maʁs] *nm* March.

marsouin [maʁswɛ̃] *nm* porpoise.

marteau, x [maʁto] *nm* hammer; (*de porte*) knocker; ~**-piqueur** *nm* pneumatic drill.

marteler [maʁtəle] *vt* to hammer.

martien, ne [maʁsjɛ̃, -jɛn] *a* Martian, of *ou* from Mars.

martinet [maʁtinɛ] *nm* (*fouet*) small whip; (*ZOOL*) swift.

martyr, e [maʁtiʁ] *nm/f* martyr.

martyre [maʁtiʁ] *nm* martyrdom; (*fig: sens affaibli*) agony, torture.

martyriser [maʀtiʀize] vt (REL) to martyr; (fig) to bully; (enfant) to batter, beat.

marxiste [maʀksist(ə)] a, nm/f Marxist.

masculin, e [maskylɛ̃, -in] a masculine; (sexe, population) male; (équipe, vêtements) men's; (viril) manly // nm masculine.

masque [mask(ə)] nm mask.

masquer [maske] vt (cacher: paysage, porte) to hide, conceal; (dissimuler: vérité, projet) to mask, obscure.

massacre [masakʀ(ə)] nm massacre, slaughter.

massacrer [masakʀe] vt to massacre, slaughter; (fig: texte etc) to murder.

massage [masaʒ] nm massage.

masse [mas] nf (aussi: péj): la ~ the masses pl; (ÉLEC) earth; (maillet) sledgehammer; **une ~ de** (fam) masses ou loads of; **en ~** ad (en bloc) in bulk; (en foule) en masse // a (exécutions, production) mass cpd.

masser [mase] vt (assembler) to gather; (pétrir) to massage; **se ~** vi to gather; **masseur, euse** nm/f masseur/masseuse.

massif, ive [masif, -iv] a (porte) solid, massive; (visage) heavy, large; (bois, or) solid; (dose) massive; (déportations etc) mass cpd // nm (montagneux) massif; (de fleurs) clump, bank.

massue [masy] nf club, bludgeon.

mastic [mastik] nm (pour vitres) putty; (pour fentes) filler.

mastiquer [mastike] vt (aliment) to chew, masticate; (fente) to fill; (vitre) to putty.

mat, e [mat] a (couleur, métal) mat(t); (bruit, son) dull // a inv (ÉCHECS): **être ~** to be checkmate.

mât [mɑ] nm (NAVIG) mast; (poteau) pole, post.

match [matʃ] nm match; **faire ~ nul** to draw; **~ aller** first leg; **~ retour** second leg, return match.

matelas [matla] nm mattress; **~ pneumatique** air bed ou mattress.

matelassé, e [matlase] a padded; quilted.

matelot [matlo] nm sailor, seaman.

mater [mate] vt (personne) to bring to heel, subdue; (révolte) to put down.

matérialiste [mateʀjalist(ə)] a materialistic.

matériaux [mateʀjo] nmpl material(s).

matériel, le [mateʀjɛl] a material // nm equipment q; (de camping etc) gear q; **~ d'exploitation** (COMM) plant.

maternel, le [mateʀnɛl] a (amour, geste) motherly, maternal; (grand-père, oncle) maternal // nf (aussi: école **~le**) (state) nursery school.

maternité [mateʀnite] nf (établissement) maternity hospital; (état de mère) motherhood, maternity; (gros-

sesse) pregnancy.

mathématique [matematik] a mathematical; **~s** nfpl (science) mathematics sg.

matière [matjɛʀ] nf (PHYSIQUE) matter; (COMM, TECH) material, matter q; (fig: d'un livre etc) subject matter, material; (SCOL) subject; **en ~ de** as regards; **~s grasses** fat content sg; **~s premières** raw materials.

matin [matɛ̃] nm, ad morning; **du ~ au soir** from morning till night; **de bon** ou **grand ~** early in the morning; **matinal, e, aux** a (toilette, gymnastique) morning cpd; (de bonne heure) early; **être matinal** (personne) to be up early; to be an early riser.

matinée [matine] nf morning; (spectacle) matinée.

matou [matu] nm tom(cat).

matraque [matʀak] nf club; (de policier) truncheon (Brit), billy (US).

matricule [matʀikyl] nf (aussi: **registre ~**) roll, register // nm (aussi: **numéro ~**: MIL) regimental number; (: ADMIN) reference number.

matrimonial, e, aux [matʀimɔnjal, -o] a marital, marriage cpd.

maudire [modiʀ] vt to curse.

maudit, e [modi, -it] a (fam: satané) blasted, confounded.

maugréer [mogʀee] vi to grumble.

maussade [mosad] a sullen.

mauvais, e [mɔvɛ, -ɛz] a bad; (faux): **le ~ numéro/moment** the wrong number/moment; (méchant, malveillant) malicious, spiteful // ad: **il fait ~** the weather is bad; **la mer est ~e** the sea is rough; **~ plaisant** hoaxer; **~e herbe** weed; **~e langue** gossip, scandalmonger (Brit); **~e passe** difficult situation; bad patch; **~e tête** rebellious ou headstrong customer.

maux [mo] nmpl voir **mal**.

maximum [maksimɔm] a, nm maximum; **au ~** ad (le plus possible) to the full; as much as one can; (tout au plus) at the (very) most ou maximum.

mayonnaise [majɔnɛz] nf mayonnaise.

mazout [mazut] nm (fuel) oil.

Me abr de **Maître**.

me, m' [m(ə)] pronom me; (réfléchi) myself.

mec [mɛk] nm (fam) bloke, guy.

mécanicien, ne [mekanisjɛ̃, -jɛn] nm/f mechanic; (RAIL) (train ou engine) driver.

mécanique [mekanik] a mechanical // nf (science) mechanics sg; (technologie) mechanical engineering; (mécanisme) mechanism; engineering; works pl; **ennui ~** engine trouble q.

mécanisme [mekanism(ə)] nm mechanism.

méchamment [meʃamɑ̃] ad nastily,

maliciously, spitefully.

méchanceté [meʃɑ̃ste] *nf* nastiness, maliciousness; nasty *ou* spiteful *ou* malicious remark (*ou* action).

méchant, e [meʃɑ̃, -ɑ̃t] *a* nasty, malicious, spiteful; (*enfant: pas sage*) naughty; (*animal*) vicious; (*avant le nom: valeur péjorative*) nasty; miserable; (*: intensive*) terrific.

mèche [mɛʃ] *nf* (*de lampe, bougie*) wick; (*d'un explosif*) fuse; (*de vilebrequin, perceuse*) bit; (*de cheveux*) lock; de ~ avec in league with.

mécompte [mekɔ̃t] *nm* miscalculation; (*déception*) disappointment.

méconnaissable [mekɔnɛsabl(ə)] *a* unrecognizable.

méconnaître [mekɔnɛtʀ(ə)] *vt* (*ignorer*) to be unaware of; (*mésestimer*) to misjudge.

mécontent, e [mekɔ̃tɑ̃, -ɑ̃t] *a*: ~ (de) discontented *ou* dissatisfied *ou* displeased (with); (*contrarié*) annoyed (at); **mécontentement** *nm* dissatisfaction, discontent, displeasure; annoyance.

médaille [medaj] *nf* medal.

médaillon [medajɔ̃] *nm* (*portrait*) medallion; (*bijou*) locket.

médecin [medsɛ̃] *nm* doctor; ~ légiste forensic surgeon.

médecine [medsin] *nf* medicine; ~ légale forensic medicine.

média [medja] *nmpl*: les ~ the media.

médiatique [medjatik] *a* media *cpd*.

médical, e, aux [medikal, -o] *a* medical.

médicament [medikamɑ̃] *nm* medicine, drug.

médiéval, e, aux [medjeval, -o] *a* medieval.

médiocre [medjɔkʀ(ə)] *a* mediocre, poor.

médire [mediʀ] *vi*: ~ de to speak ill of; **médisance** *nf* scandalmongering (*Brit*); piece of scandal *ou* of malicious gossip.

méditer [medite] *vt* (*approfondir*) to meditate on, ponder (over); (*combiner*) to meditate // *vi* to meditate.

Méditerranée [mediterane] *nf*: (mer) ~ the Mediterranean (Sea); **méditerranéen, ne** *a*, *nm/f* Mediterranean.

méduse [medyz] *nf* jellyfish.

meeting [mitiaj] *nm* (*POL, SPORT*) rally.

méfait [mefɛ] *nm* (*faute*) misdemeanour, wrongdoing; ~s *nmpl* (*ravages*) ravages, damage *sg*.

méfiance [mefjɑ̃s] *nf* mistrust, distrust.

méfiant, e [mefjɑ̃, -ɑ̃t] *a* mistrustful, distrustful.

méfier [mefje]: se ~ *vi* to be wary; to be careful; se ~ de to mistrust, distrust, be wary of; (*faire attention*) to be careful about.

mégarde [megaʀd(ə)] *nf*: par ~ accidentally; by mistake.

mégère [meʒɛʀ] *nf* shrew.

mégot [mego] *nm* cigarette end.

meilleur, e [mɛjœʀ] *a*, *ad* better; (*valeur superlative*) best // *nm*: le ~ (*celui qui ...*) the best (one); (*ce qui ...*) the best // *nf*: la ~e the best (one); le ~ des deux the better of the two; de ~e heure earlier; ~ **marché** cheaper.

mélancolie [melɑ̃kɔli] *nf* melancholy, gloom; **mélancolique** *a* melancholic, melancholy.

mélange [melɑ̃ʒ] *nm* mixture.

mélanger [melɑ̃ʒe] *vt* (*substances*) to mix; (*vins, couleurs*) to blend; (*mettre en désordre*) to mix up, muddle (up).

mélasse [melas] *nf* treacle, molasses *sg*.

mêlée [mele] *nf* mêlée, scramble; (*RUGBY*) scrum(mage).

mêler [mele] *vt* (*substances, odeurs, races*) to mix; (*embrouiller*) to muddle (up), mix up; se ~ *vi* to mix; to mingle; se ~ à (*suj: personne*) to join; to mix with; (*: odeurs etc*) to mingle with; se ~ de (*suj: personne*) to meddle with, interfere in; ~ qn à (*affaire*) to get sb mixed up ou involved in.

mélodie [melɔdi] *nf* melody.

melon [məlɔ̃] *nm* (*BOT*) (honeydew) melon; (*aussi*: chapeau ~) bowler (hat).

membre [mɑ̃bʀ(ə)] *nm* (*ANAT*) limb; (*personne, pays, élément*) member // *a* member.

mémé [meme] *nf* (*fam*) granny.

même [mɛm] ♦ *a* **1** (*avant le nom*) same; en ~ temps at the same time

2 (*après le nom: renforcement*): il est la loyauté ~ he is loyalty itself; ce sont ses paroles/celles-là ~s they are his very words/the very ones

♦ *pronom*: le(la) ~ the same one

♦ *ad* **1** (*renforcement*): il n'a ~ pas pleuré he didn't even cry; ~ lui l'a dit even HE said it; ici ~ at this very place

2: à ~: à ~ la bouteille straight from the bottle; à ~ la peau next to the skin; être à ~ de faire to be in a position to do, be able to do

3: de ~: faire de ~ to do likewise; lui de ~ so does (*ou* did *ou* is) he; de ~ que just as; il en va de ~ pour the same goes for.

mémento [memɛ̃to] *nm* (*agenda*) appointments diary; (*ouvrage*) summary.

mémoire [memwaʀ] *nf* memory // *nm* (*ADMIN, JUR*) memorandum (*pl* a); (*SCOL*) dissertation, paper; ~s *nmpl* memoirs; à la ~ de to the *ou* in memory of; pour ~ *ad* for the record; de ~ *ad* from memory; ~ **morte/vive** (*INFORM*) ROM/RAM.

menace [mənas] *nf* threat.

menacer [mənase] *vt* to threaten.

ménage [menaʒ] *nm* (*travail*) housekeeping, housework; (*couple*) (married) couple; (*famille*, *ADMIN*) household; **faire le ~** to do the housework.

ménagement [menaʒmã] *nm* care and attention; **~s** *nmpl* (*égards*) consideration *sg*, attention *sg*.

ménager [menaʒe] *vt* (*traiter*) to handle with tact; to treat considerately; (*utiliser*) to use sparingly; to use with care; (*prendre soin de*) to take (great) care of, look after; (*organiser*) to arrange; (*installer*) to put in; to make; **~ qch à qn** (*réserver*) to have sth in store for sb.

ménager, ère [menaʒe, -ɛʀ] *a* household *cpd*, domestic // *nf* housewife (*pl* wives).

mendiant, e [mãdjã, -ãt] *nm/f* beggar.

mendier [mãdje] *vi* to beg // *vt* to beg (for).

menées [məne] *nfpl* intrigues.

mener [məne] *vt* to lead; (*enquête*) to conduct; (*affaires*) to manage // *vi*: **~ (à la marque)** to lead, be in the lead; **~ à/dans** (*emmener*) to take to/into; **~ qch à terme** *ou* **à bien** to see sth through (to a successful conclusion), complete sth successfully.

meneur, euse [mənœʀ, -øz] *nm/f* leader; (*péj*) agitator; **~ de jeu** host, quizmaster.

méningite [menẽʒit] *nf* meningitis *q*.

ménopause [menɔpoz] *nf* menopause.

menottes [mənɔt] *nfpl* handcuffs.

mensonge [mãsɔ̃ʒ] *nm* lie; lying *q*; **mensonger, ère** *a* false.

mensualité [mãsɥalite] *nf* monthly payment; monthly salary.

mensuel, le [mãsɥɛl] *a* monthly.

mensurations [mãsyʀasjɔ̃] *nfpl* measurements.

mentalité [mãtalite] *nf* mentality.

menteur, euse [mãtœʀ, -øz] *nm/f* liar.

menthe [mãt] *nf* mint.

mention [mãsjɔ̃] *nf* (*note*) note, comment; (*SCOL*): **~ bien** *etc* ≈ grade B *etc* (*ou* upper 2nd class *etc*) pass (*Brit*), ≈ pass with (high) honors (*US*); **mentionner** *vt* to mention.

mentir [mãtiʀ] *vi* to lie; to be lying.

menton [mãtɔ̃] *nm* chin.

menu, e [məny] *a* slim, slight; tiny; (*frais, difficulté*) minor // *ad* (*couper, hacher*) very fine // *nm* menu; **par le ~** (*raconter*) in minute detail; **~e monnaie** small change.

menuiserie [mənɥizʀi] *nf* (*travail*) joinery, carpentry; woodwork; (*local*) joiner's workshop; (*ouvrage*) woodwork *q*.

menuisier [mənɥizje] *nm* joiner, carpenter.

méprendre [mepʀãdʀ(ə)]: **se ~** *vi*: se **~ sur** to be mistaken (about).

mépris [mepʀi] *nm* (*dédain*) contempt, scorn; (*indifférence*): **le ~ de** contempt *ou* disregard for; **au ~ de** regardless of, in defiance of.

méprisable [mepʀizabl(ə)] *a* contemptible, despicable.

méprise [mepʀiz] *nf* mistake, error; misunderstanding.

mépriser [mepʀize] *vt* to scorn, despise; (*gloire, danger*) to scorn, spurn.

mer [mɛʀ] *nf* sea; (*marée*) tide; **en ~** at sea; **prendre la ~** to put out to sea; **en haute** *ou* **pleine ~** off shore, on the open sea; **la ~ du Nord/Rouge** the North/Red Sea.

mercantile [mɛʀkãtil] *a* (*péj*) mercenary.

mercenaire [mɛʀsənɛʀ] *nm* mercenary, hired soldier.

mercerie [mɛʀsəʀi] *nf* haberdashery (*Brit*), notions (*US*); haberdasher's shop (*Brit*), notions store (*US*).

merci [mɛʀsi] *excl* thank you // *nf*: **à la ~ de qn/qch** at sb's mercy/the mercy of sth; **~ de** thank you for; **sans ~** merciless(ly).

mercredi [mɛʀkʀədi] *nm* Wednesday.

mercure [mɛʀkyʀ] *nm* mercury.

merde [mɛʀd(ə)] (*fam!*) *nf* shit (*!*) // *excl* (bloody) hell (*!*).

mère [mɛʀ] *nf* mother; **~ célibataire** unmarried mother.

méridional, e, aux [meʀidjɔnal, -o] *a* southern // *nm/f* Southerner.

meringue [məʀɛ̃g] *nf* meringue.

mérite [meʀit] *nm* merit; **le ~ (de ceci) lui revient** the credit (for this) is his.

mériter [meʀite] *vt* to deserve.

merlan [mɛʀlã] *nm* whiting.

merle [mɛʀl(ə)] *nm* blackbird.

merveille [mɛʀvɛj] *nf* marvel, wonder; **faire ~** to work wonders; **à ~** perfectly, wonderfully.

merveilleux, euse [mɛʀvɛjø, -øz] *a* marvellous, wonderful.

mes [me] *dét voir* **mon**.

mésange [mezãʒ] *nf* tit(mouse) (*pl* mice).

mésaventure [mezavãtyʀ] *nf* misadventure, misfortune.

Mesdames *voir* **Madame**.

Mesdemoiselles *voir* **Mademoiselle**.

mésentente [mezãtãt] *nf* dissension, disagreement.

mesquin, e [mɛskɛ̃, -in] *a* mean, petty.

message [mesaʒ] *nm* message; **messager, ère** *nm/f* messenger.

messe [mes] *nf* mass; **aller à la ~** to go to mass; **~ de minuit** midnight mass.

Messieurs [mesjø] *nmpl voir* **Monsieur**.

mesure [məzyʀ] *nf* (*évaluation, dimension*) measurement; (*étalon, récipient, contenu*) measure; (*MUS*: *cadence*) time, tempo; (: *division*) bar; (*retenue*) moderation; (*disposition*) measure, step; **sur ~** (*costume*) made-to-measure; **à la ~ de** (*fig*) worthy of; on the same scale as; **dans la ~ où** insofar as, inasmuch as; **à**

~ que as; être en ~ de to be in a position to.

mesurer [məzyʀe] vt to measure; (juger) to weigh up, assess; (limiter) to limit, ration; (modérer) to moderate; se ~ avec to have a confrontation with; to tackle; il mesure 1 m 80 he's 1 m 80 tall.

met vb voir **mettre**.

métal, aux [metal, -o] nm metal; ~**lique** a metallic.

météo [meteo] nf weather report; ≈ Met Office (Brit), ≈ National Weather Service (US).

météorologie [meteɔʀɔlɔʒi] nf meteorology.

méthode [metɔd] nf method; (livre, ouvrage) manual, tutor.

métier [metje] nm (profession: gén) job; (: manuel) trade; (artisanal) craft; (technique, expérience) (acquired) skill ou technique; (aussi: ~ à tisser) (weaving) loom.

métis, se [metis] a, nm/f half-caste, half-breed.

métisser [metise] vt to cross.

métrage [metʀaʒ] nm (de tissu) length, ≈ yardage; (CINÉMA) footage, length; long/moyen/court ~ full-length/medium-length/short film.

mètre [mɛtʀ(ə)] nm metre; (règle) (metre) rule; (ruban) tape measure; **métrique** a metric.

métro [metʀo] nm underground (Brit), subway.

métropole [metʀɔpɔl] nf (capitale) metropolis; (pays) home country.

mets [mɛ] nm dish.

metteur [metœʀ] nm: ~ en scène (THÉÂTRE) producer; (CINÉMA) director; ~ en ondes producer.

mettre [mɛtʀ(ə)] vt **1** (placer) to put; ~ en bouteille/en sac to bottle/put in bags ou sacks
2 (vêtements: revêtir) to put on; (: porter) to wear; mets ton gilet put your cardigan on; je ne mets plus mon manteau I no longer wear my coat
3 (faire fonctionner: chauffage, électricité) to put on; (: reveil, minuteur) to set; (installer: gaz, eau) to put in, lay on; ~ en marche to start up
4 (consacrer): ~ du temps à faire qch to take time to do sth ou over sth
5 (noter, écrire) to say, put (down); qu'est-ce qu'il a mis sur la carte? what did he say ou write on the card?; mettez au pluriel ... put ... into the plural
6 (supposer): mettons que ... let's suppose ou say that ...
7: y a ~du sien to pull one's weight
se mettre vi **1** (se placer): vous pouvez vous ~ là you can sit (ou stand) there; où ça se met? where does it go?; se ~ au lit to get into bed; se ~ au piano to sit down at the piano; se ~ de l'encre

sur les doigts to get ink on one's fingers
2 (s'habiller): se ~ en maillot de bain to get into ou put on a swimsuit; n'avoir rien à se ~ to have nothing to wear
3: se ~ à to begin, start; se ~ à faire to begin ou start doing ou to do; se ~ au piano to start learning the piano; se ~ au travail/à l'étude to get down to work/one's studies.

meuble [mœbl(ə)] nm piece of furniture; furniture q // a (terre) loose, friable; **meublé** nm furnished flatlet (Brit) ou room; **meubler** vt to furnish; (fig): meubler qch (de) to fill sth (with).

meugler [møgle] vi to low, moo.

meule [møl] nf (à broyer) millstone; (à aiguiser) grindstone; (de foin, blé) stack; (de fromage) round.

meunier, ière [mønje, -jɛʀ] nm miller // nf miller's wife.

meure etc vb voir **mourir**.

meurtre [mœʀtʀ(ə)] nm murder; **meurtrier, ière** a (arme etc) deadly; (fureur, instincts) murderous // nm/f murderer/eress // nf (ouverture) loophole.

meurtrir [mœʀtʀiʀ] vt to bruise; (fig) to wound; **meurtrissure** nf bruise; (fig) scar.

meus etc vb voir **mouvoir**.

meute [møt] nf pack.

Mexico [mɛksiko] n Mexico City.

Mexique [mɛksik] nm: le ~ Mexico.

MF sigle f voir **modulation**.

Mgr abr de **Monseigneur**.

mi [mi] nm (MUS) E; (en chantant la gamme) mi.

mi... [mi] préfixe half(-); mid-; à la ~-janvier in mid-January; à ~-jambes/-corps (up ou down) to the knees/waist; à ~-hauteur/-pente halfway up ou down/up ou down the hill.

miauler [mijole] vi to mew.

miche [miʃ] nf round ou cob loaf.

mi-chemin [miʃmɛ̃]: à ~ ad halfway, midway.

mi-clos, e [miklo, -kloz] a half-closed.

micro [mikʀo] nm mike, microphone; (INFORM) micro.

microbe [mikʀɔb] nm germ, microbe.

micro-onde [mikʀɔ̃d] nf: four à ~s microwave oven.

micro-ordinateur [mikʀɔɔʀdinatœʀ] nm microcomputer.

microscope [mikʀɔskɔp] nm microscope.

midi [midi] nm midday, noon; (moment du déjeuner) lunchtime; à ~ at 12 (o'clock) ou midday ou noon; (sud) south; en plein ~ (right) in the middle of the day; facing south; le M~ the South (of France), the Midi.

mie [mi] nf crumb (of the loaf).

miel [mjɛl] nm honey.

mien, ne [mjɛ̃, mjɛn] pronom: le(la) ~(ne), les ~s mine; les ~s my family.

miette [mjɛt] *nf* (*de pain, gâteau*) crumb; (*fig: de la conversation etc*) scrap; **en ~s** (*fig*) in pieces *ou* bits.

mieux [mjø] ♦ *ad* **1** (*d'une meilleure façon*): **~** (**que**) better (than); **elle travaille/mange ~** she works/eats better; **elle va ~** she is better
2 (*de la meilleure façon*) best; **ce que je sais le ~** what I know best; **les livres les ~ faits** the best made books
3: **de ~ en ~** better and better
♦ *a* **1** (*plus à l'aise, en meilleure forme*) better; **se sentir ~** to feel better
2 (*plus satisfaisant*) better; **c'est ~ ainsi** it's better like this; **c'est le ~ des deux** it's the better of the two; **le(la) ~, les ~** the best; **demandez-lui, c'est ~** ask him, it's the best thing
3 (*plus joli*) better-looking
4: **au ~** at best; **au ~ avec** on the best of terms with; **pour le ~** for the best
♦ *nm* **1** (*progrès*) improvement
2: **de mon/ton ~** as best I/you can (*ou* could); **faire de son ~** to do one's best.

mièvre [mjɛvʀ(ə)] *a* mawkish (*Brit*), sickly sentimental.

mignon, ne [miɲɔ̃, -ɔn] *a* sweet, cute.

migraine [migʀɛn] *nf* headache; migraine.

mijoter [miʒɔte] *vt* to simmer; (*préparer avec soin*) to cook lovingly; (*affaire, projet*) to plot, cook up // *vi* to simmer.

mil [mil] *num* = **mille**.

milieu, x [miljø] *nm* (*centre*) middle; (*fig*) middle course *ou* way; happy medium; (*BIO, GÉO*) environment; (*entourage social*) milieu; background; circle; (*pègre*): **le ~** the underworld; **au ~ de** in the middle of; **au beau *ou* en plein ~** (**de**) right in the middle (of).

militaire [militɛʀ] *a* military, army *cpd* // *nm* serviceman.

militant, e [militɑ̃, -ɑ̃t] *a, nm/f* militant.

militer [milite] *vi* to be a militant; **~ pour/contre** (*suj: faits, raisons etc*) to militate in favour of/against.

mille [mil] *num* a *ou* one thousand // *nm* (*mesure*): **~** (**marin**) nautical mile; **mettre dans le ~** to hit the bull's-eye; to be bang on target; **~feuille** *nm* cream *ou* vanilla slice; **millénaire** *nm* millennium // *a* thousand-year-old; (*fig*) ancient; **~-pattes** *nm inv* centipede.

millésime [milezim] *nm* year; **millésimé, e** *a* vintage *cpd*.

millet [mijɛ] *nm* millet.

milliard [miljaʀ] *nm* milliard, thousand million (*Brit*), billion (*US*); **milliardaire** *nm/f* multimillionaire (*Brit*), billionaire (*US*).

millier [milje] *nm* thousand; **un ~** (**de**) a thousand or so, about a thousand; **par ~s** in (their) thousands, by the thousand.

milligramme [miligʀam] *nm* milli-gramme.

millimètre [milimɛtʀ(ə)] *nm* millimetre.

million [miljɔ̃] *nm* million; **deux ~s de** two million; **millionnaire** *nm/f* millionaire.

mime [mim] *nm/f* (*acteur*) mime(r) // *nm* (*art*) mime, miming.

mimer [mime] *vt* to mime; (*singer*) to mimic, take off.

mimique [mimik] *nf* (*funny*) face; (*signes*) gesticulations *pl*, sign language *q*.

minable [minabl(ə)] *a* shabby(-looking); pathetic.

mince [mɛ̃s] *a* thin; (*personne, taille*) slim, slender; (*fig: profit, connaissances*) slight, small, weak // *excl*: **~ alors!** drat it!, darn it! (*US*); **minceur** *nf* thinness; slimness, slenderness.

mine [min] *nf* (*physionomie*) expression, look; (*extérieur*) exterior, appearance; (*de crayon*) lead; (*gisement, exploitation, explosif, fig*) mine; **avoir bonne ~** (*personne*) to look well; (*ironique*) to look an utter idiot; **avoir mauvaise ~** to look unwell *ou* poorly; **faire ~ de faire** to make a pretence of doing; to make as if to do; **~ de rien** *ad* with a casual air; although you wouldn't think so.

miner [mine] *vt* (*saper*) to undermine, erode; (*MIL*) to mine.

minerai [minʀɛ] *nm* ore.

minéral, e, aux [mineʀal, -o] *a, nm* mineral.

minéralogique [mineʀalɔʒik] *a*: **numéro ~** registration number.

minet, te [minɛ, -ɛt] *nm/f* (*chat*) pussy-cat; (*péj*) young trendy.

mineur, e [minœʀ] *a* minor // *nm/f* (*JUR*) minor, person under age // *nm* (*travailleur*) miner.

miniature [minjatyʀ] *a, nf* miniature.

minibus [minibys] *nm* minibus.

mini-cassette [minikasɛt] *nf* cassette (recorder).

minier, ière [minje, -jɛʀ] *a* mining.

mini-jupe [miniʒyp] *nf* mini-skirt.

minime [minim] *a* minor, minimal.

minimiser [minimize] *vt* to minimize; (*fig*) to play down.

minimum [minimɔm] *a, nm* minimum; **au ~** (*au moins*) at the very least.

ministère [ministɛʀ] *nm* (*aussi REL*) ministry; (*cabinet*) government; **~ public** (*JUR*) Prosecution, State Prosecutor; **ministériel, le** *a* cabinet *cpd*; ministerial.

ministre [ministʀ(ə)] *nm* (*aussi REL*) minister; **~ d'État** senior minister.

Minitel [minitɛl] *nm* ® *videotext terminal and service*.

minorité [minɔʀite] *nf* minority; **être en ~** to be in the *ou* a minority; **mettre en ~** (*POL*) to defeat.

minoterie [minɔtʀi] *nf* flour-mill.
minuit [minɥi] *nm* midnight.
minuscule [minyskyl] *a* minute, tiny // *nf*: (lettre) ~ small letter.
minute [minyt] *nf* minute; (*JUR: original*) minute, draft; **à la ~** (just) this instant; there and then; **minuter** *vt* to time; **minuterie** *nf* time switch.
minutieux, euse [minysjø, -øz] *a* meticulous; minutely detailed.
mirabelle [miʀabɛl] *nf* (cherry) plum.
miracle [miʀakl(ə)] *nm* miracle.
mirage [miʀaʒ] *nm* mirage.
mire [miʀ] *nf*: **point de ~** target; (*fig*) focal point; **ligne de ~** line of sight.
miroir [miʀwaʀ] *nm* mirror.
miroiter [miʀwate] *vi* to sparkle, shimmer; **faire ~ qch à qn** to paint sth in glowing colours for sb, dangle sth in front of sb's eyes.
mis, e [mi, miz] *pp de* **mettre** // *a*: **bien ~** well dressed // *nf* (argent: au jeu) stake; (tenue) clothing; attire; **être de ~e** to be acceptable *ou* in season; ~e **à feu** blast-off; ~e **de fonds** capital outlay; ~e **en plis** set; ~e **au point** (*fig*) clarification (voir aussi **point**); ~e **en scène** production.
miser [mize] *vt* (enjeu) to stake, bet; ~ **sur** *vt* (cheval, numéro) to bet on; (*fig*) to bank *ou* count on.
misérable [mizeʀabl(ə)] *a* (lamentable, malheureux) pitiful, wretched; (pauvre) poverty-stricken; (insignifiant, mesquin) miserable // *nm/f* wretch; (miséreux) poor wretch.
misère [mizɛʀ] *nf* (extreme) poverty, destitution; ~**s** *nfpl* woes, miseries; little troubles; **salaire de ~** starvation wage.
miséricorde [mizeʀikɔʀd(ə)] *nf* mercy, forgiveness.
missile [misil] *nm* missile.
mission [misjɔ̃] *nf* mission; **partir en ~** (*ADMIN, POL*) to go on an assignment; **missionnaire** *nm/f* missionary.
mit *vb voir* **mettre**.
mité, e [mite] *a* moth-eaten.
mi-temps [mitã] *nf inv* (*SPORT: période*) half (pl halves); (: pause) half-time; **à ~ a, ad** part-time.
mitigé, e [mitiʒe] *a* lukewarm; mixed.
mitonner [mitɔne] *vt* to cook with loving care; (*fig*) to cook up quietly.
mitoyen, ne [mitwajɛ̃, -ɛn] *a* common, party *cpd*.
mitrailler [mitʀaje] *vt* to machine-gun; (*fig: photographier*) to take shot after shot of; to pelt, bombard; **mitraillette** *nf* submachine gun; **mitrailleuse** *nf* machine gun.
mi-voix [mivwa]: **à ~** *ad* in a low *ou* hushed voice.
mixage [miksaʒ] *nm* (*CINÉMA*) (sound) mixing.
mixer [miksœʀ] *nm* (food) mixer.

mixte [mikst(ə)] *a* (gén) mixed; (*SCOL*) mixed, coeducational; **à usage ~** dual-purpose.
mixture [mikstyʀ] *nf* mixture; (*fig*) concoction.
MLF *sigle m* = *Mouvement de libération de la femme*.
Mlle, *pl* **Mlles** *abr de* **Mademoiselle**.
MM *abr de* **Messieurs**.
Mme, *pl* **Mmes** *abr de* **Madame**.
Mo *abr de* **métro**.
mobile [mɔbil] *a* mobile; (pièce de machine) moving; (élément de meuble etc) movable // *nm* (motif) motive; (œuvre d'art) mobile.
mobilier, ière [mɔbilje, -jɛʀ] *a* (*JUR*) personal // *nm* furniture.
mobiliser [mɔbilize] *vt* (*MIL, gén*) to mobilize.
moche [mɔʃ] *a* (*fam*) ugly; rotten.
modalité [mɔdalite] *nf* form, mode; ~**s** *nfpl* (d'un accord etc) clauses, terms.
mode [mɔd] *nf* fashion // *nm* (manière) form, mode; **à la ~** fashionable, in fashion; ~ **d'emploi** directions *pl* (for use).
modèle [mɔdɛl] *a, nm* model; (qui pose: de peintre) sitter; ~ **déposé** registered design; ~ **réduit** small-scale model.
modeler [mɔdle] *vt* (*ART*) to model, mould; (suj: vêtement, érosion) to mould, shape.
modem [mɔdɛm] *nm* modem.
modéré, e [mɔdeʀe] *a, nm/f* moderate.
modérer [mɔdeʀe] *vt* to moderate; **se ~** *vi* to restrain o.s.
moderne [mɔdɛʀn(ə)] *a* modern // *nm* modern style; modern furniture; **moderniser** *vt* to modernize.
modeste [mɔdɛst(ə)] *a* modest; **modestie** *nf* modesty.
modifier [mɔdifje] *vt* to modify, alter; **se ~** *vi* to alter.
modique [mɔdik] *a* modest.
modiste [mɔdist(ə)] *nf* milliner.
modulation [mɔdylasjɔ̃] *nf*: ~ **de fréquence** (**FM** *ou* **MF**) frequency modulation.
module [mɔdyl] *nm* module.
moelle [mwal] *nf* marrow.
moelleux, euse [mwalø, -øz] *a* soft; (au goût, à l'ouïe) mellow.
moellon [mwalɔ̃] *nm* rubble stone.
mœurs [mœʀ] *nfpl* (conduite) morals; (manières) manners; (pratiques sociales, mode de vie) habits.
mohair [mɔɛʀ] *nm* mohair.
moi [mwa] *pronom var* me; (emphatique): ~, **je** ... for my part, I ..., I myself ....
moignon [mwaɲɔ̃] *nm* stump.
moi-même [mwamɛm] *pronom* myself; (emphatique) I myself.
moindre [mwɛ̃dʀ(ə)] *a* lesser; lower; **le(la) ~**, **les ~s** the least, the slightest.
moine [mwan] *nm* monk, friar.
moineau, x [mwano] *nm* sparrow.

moins [mwɛ̃] ♦ *ad* **1** (*comparatif*): ~ (que) less (than); ~ **grand que** less tall than, not as tall as; ~ **je travaille, mieux je me porte** the less I work, the better I feel **2** (*superlatif*): **le ~** (the) least; **c'est ce que j'aime le ~** it's what I like (the) least; **le(la) ~ doué(e)** the least gifted; **au ~, du ~** at least; **pour le ~** at the very least **3**: ~ **de** (*quantité*) less (than); (*nombre*) fewer (than); ~ **de sable/d'eau** less sand/water; ~ **de livres/gens** fewer books/people; ~ **de 2 ans** less than 2 years; ~ **de midi** not yet midday **4**: **de ~, en ~**: **100 F/3 jours de ~** 100 F/3 days less; **3 livres en ~** 3 books fewer; **3 books too few**; **de l'argent en ~** less money; **le soleil en ~** but for the sun, minus the sun; **de ~ en ~** less and less **5**: **à ~ de, à ~ que** unless; **à ~ de faire** unless we do (*ou* he does *etc*); **à ~ que tu ne fasses** unless you do; **à ~ d'un accident** barring any accident ♦ *prép*: **4 ~ 2** 4 minus 2; **il est ~ 5** it's 5 to; **il fait ~ 5** it's 5 (degrees) below (freezing), it's minus 5.

mois [mwa] *nm* month; ~ **double** (*COMM*) extra month's salary.

moisi [mwazi] *nm* mould, mildew; **odeur de ~** musty smell.

moisir [mwazir] *vi* to go mouldy; (*fig*) to rot; to hang about.

moisissure [mwazisyr] *nf* mould *q*.

moisson [mwasɔ̃] *nf* harvest; **moissonner** *vt* to harvest, reap; **moissonneuse** *nf* (*machine*) harvester.

moite [mwat] *a* sweaty, sticky.

moitié [mwatje] *nf* half (*pl* halves); **la ~** half; **la ~ de** half (of); **la ~ du temps/ des gens** half the time/the people; **à la ~ de** halfway through; **à ~** half (*avant le verbe*); **half-** (*avant l'adjectif*); **de ~** by half; ~ ~ half-and-half.

mol [mɔl] *a voir* **mou.**

molaire [mɔlɛr] *nf* molar.

molester [mɔlɛste] *vt* to manhandle, maul (about).

molette [mɔlɛt] *nf* toothed *ou* cutting wheel.

molle [mɔl] *af voir* **mou**; ~**ment** *ad* softly; (*péj*) sluggishly; (*protester*) feebly.

mollet [mɔlɛ] *nm* calf (*pl* calves) // *am*: **œuf ~** soft-boiled egg.

molletonné, e [mɔltɔne] *a* fleece-lined.

mollir [mɔlir] *vi* to give way; to relent; to go soft.

môme [mom] *nm/f* (*fam*: *enfant*) brat; (: *fille*) chick.

moment [mɔmɑ̃] *nm* moment; **ce n'est pas le ~** this is not the (right) time; **à un certain ~** at some point; **à un donné** at a certain point; **pour un bon ~** for a good while; **pour le ~** for the moment, for the time being; **au ~ de** at the time of; **au ~ où** as; at a time when; **à tout ~** at any time *ou* moment; constantly, continually; **en ce ~** at the moment; at present; **sur le ~** at the time; **par ~s** now and then, at times; **du ~ où** *ou* **que** seeing that, since; **momentané, e** *a* temporary, momentary.

momie [mɔmi] *nf* mummy.

mon [mɔ̃], **ma** [ma], *pl* **mes** [me] *dét* my.

Monaco [mɔnako] *nm*: **le ~** Monaco.

monarchie [mɔnarʃi] *nf* monarchy.

monastère [mɔnastɛr] *nm* monastery.

monceau, x [mɔ̃so] *nm* heap.

mondain, e [mɔ̃dɛ̃, -ɛn] *a* society *cpd*; social; fashionable // *nf*: **la M~e, la police ~e** ≈ the vice squad.

monde [mɔ̃d] *nm* world; (*haute société*): **le ~** (high) society; (*milieu*): **être du même ~** to move in the same circles; (*gens*): **il y a du ~** (*beaucoup de gens*) there are a lot of people; (*quelques personnes*) there are some people; **beaucoup/peu de ~** many/few people; **le meilleur etc du ~** the best *etc* in the world *ou* on earth; **mettre au ~** to bring into the world; **pas le moins du ~** not in the least; **se faire un ~ de qch** to make a great deal of fuss about sth; **mondial, e, aux** *a* (*population*) world *cpd*; (*influence*) world-wide; **mondialement** *ad* throughout the world.

monégasque [mɔnegask(ə)] *a* Monegasque, of *ou* from Monaco.

monétaire [mɔnetɛr] *a* monetary.

moniteur, trice [mɔnitœr, -tris] *nm/f* (*SPORT*) instructor/instructress; (*de colonie de vacances*) supervisor // *nm* (*écran*) monitor.

monnaie [mɔnɛ] *nf* (*pièce*) coin; (*ÉCON, gén*: *moyen d'échange*) currency; (*petites pièces*): **avoir de la ~** to have (some) change; **faire de la ~** to get (some) change; **avoir/faire la ~ de 20 F** to have change of/get change for 20 F; **rendre à qn la ~** (**sur 20 F**) to give sb the change (out of *ou* from 20 F); **monnayer** *vt* to convert into cash; (*talent*) to capitalize on.

monologue [mɔnɔlɔg] *nm* monologue, soliloquy; **monologuer** *vi* to soliloquize.

monopole [mɔnɔpɔl] *nm* monopoly.

monotone [mɔnɔtɔn] *a* monotonous.

monseigneur [mɔ̃sɛɲœr] *nm* (*archevêque, évêque*) Your (*ou* His) Grace; (*cardinal*) Your (*ou* His) Eminence.

Monsieur [məsjø], *pl* **Messieurs** [mesjø] *titre* Mr ['mistə*] // *nm* (*homme quelconque*): **un/le m~** a/the gentleman; *voir aussi* **Madame.**

monstre [mɔ̃str(ə)] *nm* monster // *a*: **un travail ~** a fantastic amount of work; an enormous job.

mont [mɔ̃] *nm*: par ~s et par vaux up hill and down dale; **le M~ Blanc** Mont Blanc.

montage [mɔ̃taʒ] *nm* putting up; mounting; setting; assembly; (*PHOTO*) photomontage; (*CINÉMA*) editing.

montagnard, e [mɔ̃taɲaʀ, -aʀd(ə)] *a* mountain *cpd* // *nm/f* mountain-dweller.

montagne [mɔ̃taɲ] *nf* (*cime*) mountain; (*région*): **la ~** the mountains *pl*; **~s russes** big dipper *sg*, switchback *sg*.

montagneux, euse [mɔ̃taɲø, -øz] *a* mountainous; hilly.

montant, e [mɔ̃tɑ̃, -ɑ̃t] *a* rising; (*robe, corsage*) high-necked // *nm* (*somme, total*) (sum) total, (total) amount; (*de fenêtre*) upright; (*de lit*) post.

mont-de-piété [mɔ̃dpjete] *nm* pawnshop.

monte-charge [mɔ̃tʃaʀʒ(ə)] *nm inv* goods lift, hoist.

montée [mɔ̃te] *nf* rising, rise; ascent, climb; (*chemin*) way up; (*côte*) hill; **au milieu de la ~** halfway up.

monter [mɔ̃te] *vt* (*escalier, côte*) to go (*ou* come) up; (*valise, paquet*) to take (*ou* bring) up; (*cheval*) to mount; (*étagère*) to raise; (*tente, échafaudage*) to put up; (*machine*) to assemble; (*bijou*) to mount, set; (*COUTURE*) to set in; to sew on; (*CINÉMA*) to edit; (*THÉÂTRE*) to put on, stage; (*société etc*) to set up // *vi* to go (*ou* come) up; (*avion etc*) to climb, go up; (*chemin, niveau, température*) to go up, rise; (*passager*) to get on; (*à cheval*): **~ bien/mal** to ride well/badly; **~ à pied** to walk up, go up on foot; **~ à bicyclette/en voiture** to cycle/drive up, go up by bicycle/by car; **~ dans le train/l'avion** to get into the train/plane, board the train/plane; **~ sur** to climb up onto; **~ à cheval** to get on *ou* mount a horse; **se ~ à** (*frais etc*) to add up to, come to.

monticule [mɔ̃tikyl] *nm* mound.

montre [mɔ̃tʀ(ə)] *nf* watch; **faire ~ de** to show, display; **contre la ~** (*SPORT*) against the clock; **~-bracelet** *nf* wrist watch.

montrer [mɔ̃tʀe] *vt* to show; **~ qch à qn** to show sb sth.

monture [mɔ̃tyʀ] *nf* (*bête*) mount; (*d'une bague*) setting; (*de lunettes*) frame.

monument [mɔnymɑ̃] *nm* monument; **~ aux morts** war memorial.

moquer [mɔke]: **se ~ de** *vt* to make fun of, laugh at; (*fam: se désintéresser de*) not to care about; (*tromper*): **se ~ de qn** to take sb for a ride.

moquette [mɔkɛt] *nf* fitted carpet.

moqueur, euse [mɔkœʀ, -øz] *a* mocking.

moral, e, aux [mɔʀal, -o] *a* moral // *nm* morale // *nf* (*conduite*) morals *pl*; (*règles*) moral code, ethic; (*valeurs*) moral

standards *pl*, morality; (*science*) ethics *sg*, moral philosophy; (*conclusion: d'une fable etc*) moral; **avoir le ~ à zéro** to be really down; **faire la ~e à** to lecture, preach at; **~ité** *nf* morality; (*conduite*) morals *pl*; (*conclusion, enseignement*) moral.

morceau, x [mɔʀso] *nm* piece, bit; (*d'une œuvre*) passage, extract; (*MUS*) piece; (*CULIN: de viande*) cut; **mettre en ~x** to pull to pieces *ou* bits.

morceler [mɔʀsəle] *vt* to break up, divide up.

mordant, e [mɔʀdɑ̃, -ɑ̃t] *a* scathing, cutting; biting.

mordiller [mɔʀdije] *vt* to nibble at, chew at.

mordre [mɔʀdʀ(ə)] *vt* to bite; (*suj: lime, vis*) to bite into // *vi* (*poisson*) to bite; **~ sur** (*fig*) to go over into, overlap into; **~ à l'hameçon** to bite, rise to the bait.

mordu, e [mɔʀdy] *nm/f*: **un ~ du jazz** a jazz fanatic.

morfondre [mɔʀfɔ̃dʀ(ə)]: **se ~** *vi* to mope.

morgue [mɔʀg(ə)] *nf* (*arrogance*) haughtiness; (*lieu: de la police*) morgue; (*: à l'hôpital*) mortuary.

morne [mɔʀn(ə)] *a* dismal, dreary.

mors [mɔʀ] *nm* bit.

morse [mɔʀs(ə)] *nm* (*ZOOL*) walrus; (*TÉL*) Morse (code).

morsure [mɔʀsyʀ] *nf* bite.

mort [mɔʀ] *nf* death.

mort, e [mɔʀ, mɔʀt(ə)] *pp de* **mourir** // *a* dead // *nm/f* (*défunt*) dead man/woman; (*victime*): **il y a eu plusieurs ~s** several people were killed, there were several killed // *nm* (*CARTES*) dummy; **~ ou vif** dead or alive; **~ de peur/fatigue** frightened to death/dead tired.

mortalité [mɔʀtalite] *nf* mortality, death rate.

mortel, le [mɔʀtɛl] *a* (*poison etc*) deadly, lethal; (*accident, blessure*) fatal; (*REL*) mortal; (*fig*) deathly; deadly boring.

mortier [mɔʀtje] *nm* (*gén*) mortar.

mort-né, e [mɔʀne] *a* (*enfant*) stillborn.

mortuaire [mɔʀtɥɛʀ] *a* funeral *cpd*.

morue [mɔʀy] *nf* (*ZOOL*) cod *inv*.

mosaïque [mɔzaik] *nf* (*ART*) mosaic; (*fig*) patchwork.

Moscou [mɔsku] *n* Moscow.

mosquée [mɔske] *nf* mosque.

mot [mo] *nm* word; (*message*) line, note; (*bon mot etc*) saying; sally; **~ à ~** *a, ad* word for word; **~s croisés** crossword (puzzle) *sg*; **~ d'ordre** watchword; **~ de passe** password.

motard [mɔtaʀ] *nm* biker; (*policier*) motorcycle cop.

motel [mɔtɛl] *nm* motel.

moteur, trice [mɔtœʀ, -tʀis] *a* (*ANAT*,

PHYSIOL) motor; *(TECH)* driving; *(AUTO)*: **à 4 roues motrices** 4-wheel drive // *nm* engine, motor; **à ~** power-driven, motor *cpd*.

motif [mɔtif] *nm (cause)* motive; *(décoratif)* design, pattern, motif; *(d'un tableau)* subject, motif; **~s** *nmpl (JUR)* grounds *pl*; **sans ~** *a* groundless.

motiver [mɔtive] *vt (justifier)* to justify, account for; *(ADMIN, JUR, PSYCH)* to motivate.

moto [mɔto] *nf* (motor)bike; **~cyclisme** *nm* motorcycle racing; **~cycliste** *nm/f* motorcyclist.

motorisé, e [mɔtɔrize] *a (troupe)* motorized; *(personne)* having transport *ou* a car.

motrice [mɔtris] *a voir* **moteur**.

motte [mɔt] *nf*: **~ de terre** lump of earth, clod (of earth); **~ de gazon** turf, sod; **~ de beurre** lump of butter.

mou(mol), molle [mu, mɔl] *a* soft; *(péj)* flabby; sluggish // *nm (abats)* lights *pl*, lungs *pl*; *(de la corde)*: **avoir du ~** to be slack.

mouche [muʃ] *nf* fly.

moucher [muʃe] *vt (enfant)* to blow the nose of; *(chandelle)* to snuff (out); **se ~** *vi* to blow one's nose.

moucheron [muʃRɔ̃] *nm* midge.

moucheté, e [muʃte] *a* dappled; flecked.

mouchoir [muʃwaR] *nm* handkerchief, hanky; **~ en papier** tissue, paper hanky.

moudre [mudR(ə)] *vt* to grind.

moue [mu] *nf* pout; **faire la ~** to pout; *(fig)* to pull a face.

mouette [mwet] *nf* (sea)gull.

moufle [mufl(ə)] *nf (gant)* mitt(en).

mouillé, e [muje] *a* wet.

mouiller [muje] *vt (humecter)* to wet, moisten; *(tremper)*: **~ qn/qch** to make sb/sth wet; *(couper, diluer)* to water down; *(mine etc)* to lay // *vi (NAVIG)* to lie *ou* be at anchor; **se ~** to get wet; *(fam)* to commit o.s.; to get o.s. involved.

moule [mul] *nf* mussel // *nm (creux, CULIN)* mould; *(modèle plein)* cast; **~ à gâteaux** *nm* cake tin *(Brit)* ou pan *(US)*.

moulent *vb voir* **moudre, mouler**.

mouler [mule] *vt (suj: vêtement)* to hug, fit closely round; **~ qch sur** *(fig)* to model sth on.

moulin [mulɛ̃] *nm* mill; **~ à café/à poivre** coffee/pepper mill; **~ à légumes** (vegetable) shredder; **~ à paroles** *(fig)* chatterbox; **~ à vent** windmill.

moulinet [mulinɛ] *nm (de treuil)* winch; *(de canne à pêche)* reel; *(mouvement)*: **faire des ~s avec qch** to whirl sth around.

moulinette [mulinɛt] *nf* (vegetable) shredder.

moulu, e [muly] *pp de* **moudre**.

moulure [mulyR] *nf (ornement)* moulding.

mourant, e [muRɑ̃, -ɑ̃t] *a* dying.

mourir [muRiR] *vi* to die; *(civilisation)* to die out; **~ de froid/faim** to die of exposure/hunger; **~ de faim/d'ennui** *(fig)* to be starving/be bored to death; **~ d'envie de faire** to be dying to do.

mousse [mus] *nf (BOT)* moss; *(écume: sur eau, bière)* froth, foam; *(: shampooing)* lather; *(CULIN)* mousse // *nm (NAVIG)* ship's boy; **bas ~** stretch stockings; **~ carbonique** (fire-fighting) foam; **~ à raser** shaving foam.

mousseline [muslin] *nf* muslin; chiffon.

mousser [muse] *vi* to foam; to lather.

mousseux, euse [musø, -øz] *a* frothy // *nm*: **(vin) ~** sparkling wine.

mousson [musɔ̃] *nf* monsoon.

moustache [mustaʃ] *nf* moustache; **~s** *(du chat)* whiskers *pl*.

moustiquaire [mustikɛR] *nf* mosquito net *(ou* screen).

moustique [mustik] *nm* mosquito.

moutarde [mutard(ə)] *nf* mustard.

mouton [mutɔ̃] *nm (ZOOL, péj)* sheep *inv*; *(peau)* sheepskin; *(CULIN)* mutton.

mouvant, e [muvɑ̃, -ɑ̃t] *a* unsettled; changing; shifting.

mouvement [muvmɑ̃] *nm (gén, aussi: mécanisme)* movement; *(fig)* activity; impulse; gesture; *(MUS: rythme)* tempo *(pl* s); **en ~** in motion; on the move; **mouvementé, e** *a (vie, poursuite)* eventful; *(réunion)* turbulent.

mouvoir [muvwaR] *vt (levier, membre)* to move; **se ~** *vi* to move.

moyen, ne [mwajɛ̃, -ɛn] *a* average; *(tailles, prix)* medium; *(de grandeur moyenne)* medium-sized // *nm (façon)* means *sg*, way // *nf* average; *(MATH)* mean; *(SCOL: à l'examen)* pass mark; *(AUTO)* average speed; **~s** *(capacités)* means; **au ~ de** by means of; **par tous les ~s** by every possible means, every possible way; **par ses propres ~s** all by oneself; **en ~ne** on (an) average; **~ de transport** means of transport; **~ âge** Middle Ages; **~ne d'âge** average age.

moyennant [mwajɛnɑ̃] *prép (somme)* for; *(service, conditions)* in return for; *(travail, effort)* with.

Moyen-Orient [mwajɛnɔRjɑ̃] *nm*: **le ~** the Middle East.

moyeu, x [mwajø] *nm* hub.

MST *sigle f (= maladie sexuellement transmissible)* sexually transmitted disease.

mû, mue [my] *pp de* **mouvoir**.

muer [mɥe] *vi (oiseau, mammifère)* to moult; *(serpent)* to slough; *(jeune garçon)*: **il mue** his voice is breaking; **se ~ en** to transform into.

muet, te [mɥe, -ɛt] *a* dumb; *(fig)*: **~**

d'admiration *etc* speechless with admiration *etc*; (*joie, douleur, CINÉMA*) silent; (*carte*) blank // *nm/f* mute.
mufle [myfl(ə)] *nm* muzzle; (*goujat*) boor.
mugir [myʒiʀ] *vi* (*taureau*) to bellow; (*vache*) to low; (*fig*) to howl.
muguet [mygɛ] *nm* lily of the valley.
mule [myl] *nf* (*ZOOL*) (she-)mule.
mulet [mylɛ] *nm* (*ZOOL*) (he-)mule.
multiple [myltipl(ə)] *a* multiple, numerous; (*varié*) many, manifold // *nm* (*MATH*) multiple.
multiplication [myltiplikasjɔ̃] *nf* multiplication.
multiplier [myltiplije] *vt* to multiply; se ~ *vi* to multiply; to increase in number.
municipal, e, aux [mynisipal, -o] *a* municipal; town *cpd*, ≈ borough *cpd*.
municipalité [mynisipalite] *nf* (*corps municipal*) town council, corporation.
munir [myniʀ] *vt*: ~ qn/qch de to equip sb/sth with.
munitions [mynisjɔ̃] *nfpl* ammunition *sg*.
mur [myʀ] *nm* wall; ~ du son sound barrier.
mûr, e [myʀ] *a* ripe; (*personne*) mature // *nf* blackberry; mulberry.
muraille [myʀaj] *nf* (high) wall.
mural, e, aux [myʀal, -o] *a* wall *cpd*; mural.
murer [myʀe] *vt* (*enclos*) to wall (in); (*porte, issue*) to wall up; (*personne*) to wall up ou in.
muret [myʀɛ] *nm* low wall.
mûrir [myʀiʀ] *vi* (*fruit, blé*) to ripen; (*abcès, furoncle*) to come to a head; (*fig: idée, personne*) to mature // *vt* to ripen; to (make) mature.
murmure [myʀmyʀ] *nm* murmur; ~s (*plaintes*) murmurings, mutterings; **murmurer** *vi* to murmur; (*se plaindre*) to mutter, grumble.
muscade [myskad] *nf* (*aussi*: noix ~) nutmeg.
muscat [myska] *nm* muscat grape; muscatel (wine).
muscle [myskl(ə)] *nm* muscle; **musclé, e** *a* muscular; (*fig*) strong-arm.
museau, x [myzo] *nm* muzzle.
musée [myze] *nm* museum; art gallery.
museler [myzle] *vt* to muzzle; **muselière** *nf* muzzle.
musette [myzɛt] *nf* (*sac*) lunchbag // *a inv* (*orchestre etc*) accordion *cpd*.
musical, e, aux [myzikal, -o] *a* musical.
music-hall [myzikol] *nm* variety theatre; (*genre*) variety.
musicien, ne [myzisjɛ̃, -jɛn] *a* musical // *nm/f* musician.
musique [myzik] *nf* music; (*fanfare*) band; ~ de chambre chamber music.
musulman, e [myzylmɑ̃, -an] *a, nm/f*

Moslem, Muslim.
mutation [mytasjɔ̃] *nf* (*ADMIN*) transfer.
mutilé, e [mytile] *nm/f* disabled person (*through loss of limbs*).
mutiler [mytile] *vt* to mutilate, maim.
mutin, e [mytɛ̃, -in] *a* (*air, ton*) mischievous, impish // *nm/f* (*MIL, NAVIG*) mutineer.
mutinerie [mytinʀi] *nf* mutiny.
mutisme [mytism(ə)] *nm* silence.
mutuel, le [mytɥɛl] *a* mutual // *nf* mutual benefit society.
myope [mjɔp] *a* short-sighted.
myosotis [mjozɔtis] *nm* forget-me-not.
myrtille [miʀtij] *nf* bilberry.
mystère [mistɛʀ] *nm* mystery; **mystérieux, euse** *a* mysterious.
mystifier [mistifje] *vt* to fool; to mystify.
mythe [mit] *nm* myth.
mythologie [mitɔlɔʒi] *nf* mythology.

N

n' [n] *ad voir* **ne.**
nacelle [nasɛl] *nf* (*de ballon*) basket.
nacre [nakʀ(ə)] *nf* mother of pearl; **nacré, e** *a* pearly.
nage [naʒ] *nf* swimming; style of swimming, stroke; **traverser/s'éloigner à la** ~ to swim across/away; **en** ~ bathed in perspiration.
nageoire [naʒwaʀ] *nf* fin.
nager [naʒe] *vi* to swim; **nageur, euse** *nm/f* swimmer.
naguère [nagɛʀ] *ad* formerly.
naïf, ïve [naif, naiv] *a* naïve.
nain, e [nɛ̃, nɛn] *nm/f* dwarf.
naissance [nɛsɑ̃s] *nf* birth; **donner** ~ **à** to give birth to; (*fig*) to give rise to.
naître [nɛtʀ(ə)] *vi* to be born; (*fig*): ~ **de** to arise from, be born out of; **il est né en 1960** he was born in 1960; **faire** ~ (*fig*) to give rise to, arouse.
nana [nana] *nf* (*fam: fille*) chick, bird (*Brit*).
nantir [nɑ̃tiʀ] *vt*: ~ qn de to provide sb with; **les nantis** (*péj*) the well-to-do.
nappe [nap] *nf* tablecloth; (*fig*) sheet; layer; ~ron *nm* table-mat.
naquit *etc vb voir* **naître.**
narguer [naʀge] *vt* to taunt.
narine [naʀin] *nf* nostril.
narquois, e [naʀkwa, -waz] *a* derisive, mocking.
narrer [naʀe] *vt* to tell the story of, recount.
naseau, x [nazo] *nm* nostril.
natal, e [natal] *a* native.
natalité [natalite] *nf* birth rate.
natation [natasjɔ̃] *nf* swimming.
natif, ive [natif, -iv] *a* native.
nation [nasjɔ̃] *nf* nation.
national, e, aux [nasjɔnal, -o] *a* national // *nf*: (*route*) ~e ≈ A road (*Brit*),

≈ state highway (*US*); **~iser** *vt* to nationalize; **~ité** *nf* nationality.

natte [nat] *nf* (*tapis*) mat; (*cheveux*) plait.

naturaliser [natyʀalize] *vt* to naturalize.

nature [natyʀ] *nf* nature // *a, ad* (*CULIN*) plain, without seasoning or sweetening; (*café, thé*) black, without sugar; **payer en ~** to pay in kind; **~ morte** still-life; **naturel, le** *a* (*gén, aussi: enfant*) natural // *nm* naturalness; disposition, nature; (*autochtone*) native; **naturellement** *ad* naturally; (*bien sûr*) of course.

naufrage [nofʀaʒ] *nm* (*ship*)wreck; (*fig*) wreck; **faire ~** to be shipwrecked.

nauséabond, e [nozeabɔ̃, -ɔ̃d] *a* foul, nauseous.

nausée [noze] *nf* nausea.

nautique [notik] *a* nautical, water *cpd*.

nautisme [notism] *nm* water sports.

navet [navɛ] *nm* turnip.

navette [navɛt] *nf* shuttle; **faire la ~ (entre)** to go to and fro *ou* shuttle (between).

navigable [navigabl(ə)] *a* navigable.

navigateur [navigatœʀ] *nm* (*NAVIG*) seafarer, sailor; (*AVIAT*) navigator.

navigation [navigasjɔ̃] *nf* navigation, sailing; shipping.

naviguer [navige] *vi* to navigate, sail.

navire [naviʀ] *nm* ship.

navrer [navʀe] *vt* to upset, distress; **je suis navré** I'm so sorry.

ne, n' [n(ə)] *ad voir* **pas, plus, jamais** *etc*; (*explétif*) *non traduit*.

né, e [ne] *pp* (*voir* **naître**): **~ en 1960** born in 1960; **~e Scott** née Scott.

néanmoins [neɑ̃mwɛ̃] *ad* nevertheless.

néant [neɑ̃] *nm* nothingness; **réduire à ~** to bring to nought; (*espoir*) to dash.

nécessaire [nesesɛʀ] *a* necessary // *nm* necessary; (*sac*) kit; **~ de couture** sewing kit; **~ de toilette** toilet bag; **nécessité** *nf* necessity; **nécessiter** *vt* to require; **nécessiteux, euse** *a* needy.

nécrologique [nekʀɔlɔʒik] *a*: **article ~** obituary; **rubrique ~** obituary column.

néerlandais, e [neɛʀlɑ̃dɛ, -ɛz] *a* Dutch.

nef [nɛf] *nf* (*d'église*) nave.

néfaste [nefast(ə)] *a* baneful; ill-fated.

négatif, ive [negatif, iv] *a* negative // *nm* (*PHOTO*) negative.

négligé, e [negliʒe] *a* (*en désordre*) slovenly // *nm* (*tenue*) negligee.

négligent, e [negliʒɑ̃, -ɑ̃t] *a* careless, negligent.

négliger [negliʒe] *vt* (*épouse, jardin*) to neglect; (*tenue*) to be careless about; (*avis, précautions*) to disregard; **~ de faire** to fail to do, not bother to do.

négoce [negɔs] *nm* trade.

négociant [negɔsjɑ̃] *nm* merchant.

négociation [negɔsjasjɔ̃] *nf* negotiation.

négocier [negɔsje] *vi, vt* to negotiate.

nègre [nɛgʀ(ə)] *nm* Negro; ghost (*writer*).

négresse [negʀɛs] *nf* Negro woman.

neige [nɛʒ] *nf* snow; **neiger** *vi* to snow; **neigeux, euse** *a* snowy, snow-covered.

nénuphar [nenyfaʀ] *nm* water-lily.

néon [neɔ̃] *nm* neon.

néophyte [neɔfit] *nm/f* novice.

néo-zélandais, e [neozelɑ̃dɛ, -ɛz] *a* New Zealand *cpd* //: **N~, e** *nm/f* New Zealander.

nerf [nɛʀ] *nm* nerve; (*fig*) spirit; stamina; **nerveux, euse** *a* nervous; (*voiture*) nippy, responsive; (*tendineux*) sinewy; **nervosité** *nf* excitability; state of agitation; nervousness.

nervure [nɛʀvyʀ] *nf* vein.

n'est-ce pas [nɛspa] *ad* isn't it?, won't you? *etc, selon le verbe qui précède*.

net, nette [nɛt] *a* (*sans équivoque, distinct*) clear; (*évident*) definite; (*propre*) neat, clean; (*COMM: prix, salaire*) net // *ad* (*refuser*) flatly; **s'arrêter ~** to stop dead // *nm*: **mettre au ~** to copy out; **nettement** *ad* clearly, distinctly; **~teté** *nf* clearness.

nettoyage [nɛtwajaʒ] *nm* cleaning; **~ à sec** dry cleaning.

nettoyer [nɛtwaje] *vt* to clean; (*fig*) to clean out.

neuf [nœf] *num* nine.

neuf, neuve [nœf, nœv] *a* new // *nm*: **repeindre à ~** to redecorate; **remettre à ~** to do up (as good as new), refurbish.

neutre [nøtʀ(ə)] *a* neutral; (*LING*) neuter // *nm* (*LING*) neuter.

neuve [nœv] *a voir* **neuf**.

neuvième [nœvjɛm] *num* ninth.

neveu, x [nəvø] *nm* nephew.

névrosé, e [nevʀoze] *a, nm/f* neurotic.

nez [ne] *nm* nose; **~ à ~ avec** face to face with; **avoir du ~** to have flair.

ni [ni] *cj*: **~ l'un ~ l'autre** ne sont neither one nor the other are; **il n'a rien dit ~ fait** he hasn't said or done anything.

niais, e [njɛ, -ɛz] *a* silly, thick.

niche [niʃ] *nf* (*du chien*) kennel; (*de mur*) recess, niche.

nicher [niʃe] *vi* to nest.

nid [ni] *nm* nest; **~ de poule** pothole.

nièce [njɛs] *nf* niece.

nier [nje] *vt* to deny.

nigaud, e [nigo, -od] *nm/f* booby, fool.

Nil [nil] *nm*: **le ~** the Nile.

n'importe [nɛ̃pɔʀt(ə)] *ad*: **~ qui/quoi/où** anybody/anything/anywhere; **~ quand** any time; **~ quel/quelle** any; **~ lequel/laquelle** any (one); **~ comment** (*sans soin*) carelessly.

niveau, x [nivo] *nm* level; (*des élèves, études*) standard; **de ~ (avec)** level (with); **~ (à bulle)** spirit level; **le ~ de la mer** sea level; **~ de vie** standard of living.

niveler [nivle] *vt* to level.

NN *abr* (= *nouvelle norme*) *revised standard of hotel classification.*

noble [nɔbl(ə)] *a* noble; **noblesse** *nf* nobility; (*d'une action etc*) nobleness.

noce [nɔs] *nf* wedding; (*gens*) wedding party (*ou* guests *pl*); **faire la ~** (*fam*) to go on a binge; **~s d'or/d'argent** golden/silver wedding.

nocif, ive [nɔsif, -iv] *a* harmful, noxious.

noctambule [nɔktãbyl] *nm* night-bird.

nocturne [nɔktyRn(ə)] *a* nocturnal // *nf* late-night opening.

Noël [nɔɛl] *nm* Christmas.

nœud [nø] *nm* (*de corde, du bois, NAVIG*) knot; (*ruban*) bow; (*fig: liens*) bond, tie; **~ papillon** bow tie.

noir, e [nwaR] *a* black; (*obscur, sombre*) dark // *nm/f* black man/woman, Negro/Negro woman // *nm*: **dans le ~** in the dark; **travail au ~** moonlighting // *nf* (*MUS*) crotchet (*Brit*), quarter note (*US*); **~ceur** *nf* blackness; darkness; **~cir** *vt, vi* to blacken.

noisette [nwazɛt] *nf* hazelnut.

noix [nwa] *nf* walnut; (*CULIN*): **une ~ de beurre** a knob of butter; **~ de cajou** cashew nut; **~ de coco** coconut.

nom [nɔ̃] *nm* name; (*LING*) noun; **~ d'emprunt** assumed name; **~ de famille** surname; **~ de jeune fille** maiden name.

nombre [nɔ̃bR(ə)] *nm* number; **venir en ~** to come in large numbers; **depuis ~ d'années** for many years; **ils sont au ~ de 3** there áre 3 of them; **au ~ de mes amis** among my friends.

nombreux, euse [nɔ̃bRø, -øz] *a* many, numerous; (*avec nom sg: foule etc*) large; **peu ~** few; small.

nombril [nɔ̃bRi] *nm* navel.

nommer [nɔme] *vt* (*baptiser, mentionner*) to name; (*qualifier*) to call; (*élire*) to appoint, nominate; **se ~**: **il se nomme Pascal** his name's Pascal, he's called Pascal.

non [nɔ̃] *ad* (*réponse*) no; (*avec loin, sans, seulement*) not; **~ que, ~ pas que** not that; **moi ~ plus** neither do I, I don't either.

non-alcoolisé, e [nɔnalkɔlize] *a* non-alcoholic.

non-fumeur [nɔ̃fymœr] *nm* non-smoker.

non-lieu [nɔ̃ljø] *nm*: **il y a eu ~ the case** was dismissed.

non-sens [nɔ̃sãs] *nm* absurdity.

nord [nɔR] *nm* North // *a* northern; north; **au ~** (*situation*) in the north; (*direction*) to the north; **au ~ de** (to the) north of; **~-est** *nm* North-East; **~-ouest** *nm* North-West.

normal, e, aux [nɔRmal, -o] *a* normal // *nf*: **la ~e** the norm, the average; **~ement** *ad* (*en général*) normally; **~iser** *vt* (*COMM, TECH*) to standardize.

normand, e [nɔRmã, -ãd] *a* of Normandy.

Normandie [nɔRmãdi] *nf* Normandy.

norme [nɔRm(ə)] *nf* norm; (*TECH*) standard.

Norvège [nɔRvɛʒ] *nf* Norway; **norvégien, ne** *a, nm, nf* Norwegian.

nos [no] *dét voir* **notre**.

nostalgie [nɔstalʒi] *nf* nostalgia.

notable [nɔtabl(ə)] *a* notable, noteworthy; (*marqué*) noticeable, marked // *nm* prominent citizen.

notaire [nɔtɛR] *nm* notary; solicitor.

notamment [nɔtamã] *ad* in particular, among others.

note [nɔt] *nf* (*écrite, MUS*) note; (*SCOL*) mark (*Brit*), grade; (*facture*) bill; **~ de service** memorandum.

noté, e [nɔte] *a*: **être bien/mal ~** (*employé etc*) to have a good/bad record.

noter [nɔte] *vt* (*écrire*) to write down; (*remarquer*) to note, notice.

notice [nɔtis] *nf* summary, short article; (*brochure*) leaflet, instruction book.

notifier [nɔtifje] *vt*: **~ qch à qn** to notify sb of sth, notify sth to sb.

notion [nɔsjɔ̃] *nf* notion, idea.

notoire [nɔtwaR] *a* widely known; (*en mal*) notorious.

notre, nos [nɔtR(ə), no] *dét* our.

nôtre [nɔtR(ə)] *pronom*: **le/la ~** ours; **les ~s** ours; (*alliés etc*) our own people; **soyez des ~s** join us // *a* ours.

nouer [nwe] *vt* to tie, knot; (*fig: alliance etc*) to strike up.

noueux, euse [nwø, -øz] *a* gnarled.

nouilles [nuj] *nfpl* noodles; pasta *sg*.

nourrice [nuRis] *nf* wet-nurse.

nourrir [nuRiR] *vt* to feed; (*fig: espoir*) to harbour, nurse; **logé nourri** with board and lodging; **nourrissant, e** *a* nourishing, nutritious.

nourrisson [nuRisɔ̃] *nm* (unweaned) infant.

nourriture [nuRityR] *nf* food.

nous [nu] *pronom* (*sujet*) we; (*objet*) us; **~-mêmes** *pronom* ourselves.

nouveau(nouvel), elle, x [nuvo, -ɛl] *a* new // *nm/f* new pupil (*ou* employee) // *nf* (piece of) news *sg*; (*LITTÉRATURE*) short story; **de ~, à ~** again; **je suis sans nouvelles de lui** I haven't heard from him; **~ venu, nouvelle venue** *nm/f* newcomer; **Nouvel An New Year**; **~-né, e** *nm/f* newborn baby; **Nouvelle-Calédonie** *nf* New Caledonia; **Nouvelle-Zélande** *nf* New Zealand; **~té** *nf* novelty; (*COMM*) new film (*ou* book *ou* creation *etc*).

novembre [nɔvãbR(ə)] *nm* November.

novice [nɔvis] *a* inexperienced.

noyade [nwajad] *nf* drowning *q*.

noyau, x [nwajo] *nm* (*de fruit*) stone; (*BIO, PHYSIQUE*) nucleus; (*ÉLEC, GÉO, fig: centre*) core; **~ter** *vt* (*POL*) to infiltrate.

noyer [nwaje] *nm* walnut (tree); (*bois*)

walnut // vt to drown; (fig) to flood; to submerge; se ~ vi to be drowned, drown; (suicide) to drown o.s.

nu, e [ny] a naked; (membres) naked, bare; (chambre, fil, plaine) bare // nm (ART) nude; ~**-pieds** a inv barefoot; ~**tête** a inv bareheaded; **se mettre** ~ to strip; **mettre à** ~ to bare.

nuage [nɥaʒ] nm cloud; **nuageux, euse** a cloudy.

nuance [nɥɑ̃s] nf (de couleur, sens) shade; **il y a une** ~ (entre) there's a slight difference (between); **nuancer** vt (opinion) to bring some reservations ou qualifications to.

nucléaire [nykleɛʀ] a nuclear.

nudiste [nydist(ə)] nm/f nudist.

nuée [nɥe] nf: **une** ~ **de** a cloud ou host ou swarm of.

nues [ny] nfpl: **tomber des** ~ to be taken aback; **porter qn aux** ~ to praise sb to the skies.

nuire [nɥiʀ] vi to be harmful; ~ **à** to harm, do damage to; **nuisible** a harmful; **animal nuisible** pest.

nuit [nɥi] nf night; **il fait** ~ it's dark; **cette** ~ last night; tonight; ~ **blanche** sleepless night; ~ **de noces** wedding night.

nul, nulle [nyl] a (aucun) no; (minime) nil, non-existent; (non valable) null; (péj) useless, hopeless // pronom none, no one; **résultat** ~, **match** ~ draw; ~**le part** ad nowhere; ~**lement** ad by no means.

numérique [nymeʀik] a numerical.

numéro [nymeʀo] nm number; (spectacle) act, turn; ~ **de téléphone** (tele)phone number; ~**ter** vt to number.

nuque [nyk] nf nape of the neck.

nutritif, ive [nytʀitif, -iv] a nutritional; (aliment) nutritious.

nylon [nilɔ̃] nm nylon.

O

oasis [ɔazis] nf oasis (pl oases).

obéir [ɔbeiʀ] vi to obey; ~ **à** to obey; (suj: moteur, véhicule) to respond to; **obéissant, e** a obedient.

objecter [ɔbʒɛkte] vt (prétexter) to plead, put forward as an excuse; ~ (à qn) que to object (to sb) that.

objecteur [ɔbʒɛktœʀ] nm: ~ **de conscience** conscientious objector.

objectif, ive [ɔbʒɛktif, -iv] a objective // nm (OPTIQUE, PHOTO) lens sg, objective; (MIL, fig) objective; ~ **à focale variable** zoom lens.

objection [ɔbʒɛksjɔ̃] nf objection.

objet [ɔbʒɛ] nm object; (d'une discussion, recherche) subject; **être ou faire l'**~ **de** (discussion) to be the subject of; (soins) to be given ou shown;

sans ~ a purposeless; groundless; ~ **d'art** objet d'art; ~**s personnels** personal items; ~**s trouvés** lost property sg (Brit), lost-and-found sg (US).

obligation [ɔbligasjɔ̃] nf obligation; (COMM) bond, debenture; **obligatoire** a compulsory, obligatory.

obligé, e [ɔbliʒe] a (redevable): **être très** ~ **à qn** to be most obliged to sb; **obligeant, e** a obliging; kind.

obliger [ɔbliʒe] vt (contraindre): ~ **qn à faire** to force ou oblige sb to do; (JUR: engager) to bind; (rendre service à) to oblige; **je suis bien obligé** I have to.

oblique [ɔblik] a oblique; **regard** ~ sidelong glance; **en** ~ ad diagonally; **obliquer** vi: **obliquer vers** to turn off towards.

oblitérer [ɔblitere] vt (timbre-poste) to cancel.

obscène [ɔpsɛn] a obscene.

obscur, e [ɔpskyʀ] a dark; (fig) obscure; lowly; ~**cir** vt to darken; (fig) to obscure; **s'**~**cir** vi to grow dark; ~**ité** nf darkness; **dans l'**~**ité** in the dark, in darkness.

obséder [ɔpsede] vt to obsess, haunt.

obsèques [ɔpsɛk] nfpl funeral sg.

observateur, trice [ɔpsɛʀvatœʀ, -tʀis] a observant, perceptive // nm/f observer.

observation [ɔpsɛʀvasjɔ̃] nf observation; (d'un règlement etc) observance; (reproche) reproof.

observatoire [ɔpsɛʀvatwaʀ] nm observatory; (lieu élevé) observation post, vantage point.

observer [ɔpsɛʀve] vt (regarder) to observe, watch; (examiner) to examine; (scientifiquement, aussi: règlement, jeûne etc) to observe; (surveiller) to watch; (remarquer) to observe, notice; **faire** ~ **qch à qn** (dire) to point out sth to sb.

obstacle [ɔpstakl(ə)] nm obstacle; (ÉQUITATION) jump, hurdle; **faire** ~ **à** (lumière) to block out; (projet) to hinder, put obstacles in the path of.

obstiné, e [ɔpstine] a obstinate.

obstiner [ɔpstine]: **s'**~ vi to insist, dig one's heels in; **s'**~ **à faire** to persist (obstinately) in doing; **s'**~ **sur qch** to keep working at sth, labour away at sth.

obstruer [ɔpstʀye] vt to block, obstruct.

obtempérer [ɔptɑ̃peʀe] vi to obey.

obtenir [ɔptəniʀ] vt to obtain, get; (total, résultat) to arrive at, reach; to achieve, obtain; ~ **de pouvoir faire** to obtain permission to do; ~ **de qn qu'il fasse** to get sb to agree to do; **obtention** nf obtaining.

obturateur [ɔptyʀatœʀ] nm (PHOTO) shutter.

obturer [ɔptyʀe] vt to close (up); (dent) to fill.

obus [ɔby] nm shell.

occasion [ɔkɑzjɔ̃] nf (aubaine, possibilité) opportunity; (circonstance) occasion; (COMM: article non neuf) second-hand buy; (: acquisition avantageuse) bargain; à plusieurs ~s on several occasions; être l'~ de to occasion, give rise to; à l'~ ad sometimes, on occasions; some time; d'~ a, ad secondhand; **occasionnel, le** a (fortuit) chance cpd; (non régulier) occasional; casual.

occasionner [ɔkazjɔne] vt to cause, bring about; ~ qch à qn to cause sb sth.

occident [ɔksidɑ̃] nm: l'O~ the West; **occidental, e, aux** western; (POL) Western.

occupation [ɔkypasjɔ̃] nf occupation.

occupé, e [ɔkype] a (MIL, POL) occupied; (personne: affairé, pris) busy; (place, sièges) taken; (toilettes, ligne) engaged.

occuper [ɔkype] vt to occupy; (main-d'œuvre) to employ; s'~ (à qch) to occupy o.s. ou keep o.s. busy (with sth); s'~ de (être responsable de) to be in charge of; (se charger de: affaire) to take charge of, deal with; (: clients etc) to attend to; (s'intéresser à, pratiquer) to be involved in; ça occupe trop de place it takes up too much room.

occurrence [ɔkyrɑ̃s] nf: en l'~ in this case.

océan [ɔseɑ̃] nm ocean; l'~ Indien the Indian Ocean.

octet [ɔktɛt] nm byte.

octobre [ɔktɔbr(ə)] nm October.

octroyer [ɔktrwaje] vt: ~ qch à qn to grant sth to sb, grant sb sth.

oculiste [ɔkylist(ə)] nm/f eye specialist.

odeur [ɔdœr] nf smell.

odieux, euse [ɔdjø, -øz] a hateful.

odorant, e [ɔdɔrɑ̃, -ɑ̃t] a sweet-smelling, fragrant.

odorat [ɔdɔra] nm (sense of) smell.

œil [œj], pl **yeux** [jø] nm eye; à l'~ (fam) for free; à l'~ nu with the naked eye; tenir qn à l'~ to keep an eye ou a watch on sb; avoir l'~ à to keep an eye on; fermer les yeux (sur) (fig) to turn a blind eye (to).

œillade [œjad] nf: lancer une ~ à qn to wink at sb, give sb a wink; faire des ~s à to make eyes at.

œillères [œjɛr] nfpl blinkers (Brit), blinders (US).

œillet [œjɛ] nm (BOT) carnation.

œuf [œf, pl ø] nm egg; ~ dur hard-boiled egg; ~ au plat fried egg; ~s brouillés scrambled eggs; ~ de Pâques Easter egg.

œuvre [œvr(ə)] nf (tâche) task, undertaking; (ouvrage achevé, livre, tableau etc) work; (ensemble de la production artistique) works pl; (organisation charitable) charity // nm (d'un artiste) works pl; (CONSTR): le gros ~ the shell; être à l'~ to be at work; mettre en ~ (moyens) to make use of; ~ d'art work of art.

offense [ɔfɑ̃s] nf insult.

offenser [ɔfɑ̃se] vt to offend, hurt; (principes, Dieu) to offend against; s'~ de to take offence at.

offert, e [ɔfɛr, -ɛrt(ə)] pp de **offrir**.

office [ɔfis] nm (charge) office; (agence) bureau, agency; (REL) service // nm ou nf (pièce) pantry; faire ~ de to act as; to do duty as; d'~ ad automatically; ~ du tourisme tourist bureau.

officiel, le [ɔfisjɛl] a, nm/f official.

officier [ɔfisje] nm officer // vi to officiate; ~ de l'état-civil registrar.

officieux, euse [ɔfisjø, -øz] a unofficial.

officinal, e, aux [ɔfisinal, -o] a: plantes ~es medicinal plants.

officine [ɔfisin] nf (de pharmacie) dispensary; (bureau) agency, office.

offrande [ɔfrɑ̃d] nf offering.

offre [ɔfr(ə)] nf offer; (aux enchères) bid; (ADMIN: soumission) tender; (ÉCON): l'~ supply; ~ d'emploi job advertised; '~s d'emploi' 'situations vacant'; ~ publique d'achat (O.P.A.) take-over bid.

offrir [ɔfrir] vt: ~ (à qn) to offer (to sb); (faire cadeau de) to give (to sb); s'~ vi (occasion, paysage) to present itself // vt (vacances, voiture) to treat o.s. to; ~ (à qn) de faire qch to offer to do sth (for sb); ~ à boire à qn to offer sb a drink; s'~ comme guide/en otage to offer one's services as (a) guide/offer o.s. as hostage.

offusquer [ɔfyske] vt to offend.

ogive [ɔʒiv] nf: ~ nucléaire nuclear warhead.

oie [wa] nf (ZOOL) goose (pl geese).

oignon [ɔɲɔ̃] nm (BOT, CULIN) onion; (de tulipe etc: bulbe) bulb; (MÉD) bunion.

oiseau, x [wazo] nm bird; ~ de proie bird of prey.

oiseux, euse [wazø, -øz] a pointless; trivial.

oisif, ive [wazif, -iv] a idle // nm/f (péj) man/woman of leisure.

oléoduc [ɔleɔdyk] nm (oil) pipeline.

olive [ɔliv] nf (BOT) olive; **olivier** nm olive.

olympique [ɔlɛ̃pik] a Olympic.

ombrage [ɔ̃braʒ] nm (ombre) (leafy) shade; **ombragé, e** a shaded, shady; **ombrageux, euse** a (cheval) skittish, nervous; (personne) touchy, easily offended.

ombre [ɔ̃br(ə)] nf (espace non ensoleillé) shade; (ombre portée, tache) shadow; à l'~ in the shade; tu me fais de l'~ you're in my light; ça nous donne de l'~ it gives us (some) shade; dans l'~ (fig) in obscurity; in the dark; ~ à paupières eyeshadow.

ombrelle [ɔ̃bʀɛl] nf parasol, sunshade.

omelette [ɔmlɛt] nf omelette.

omettre [ɔmɛtʀ(ə)] vt to omit, leave out.

omnibus [ɔmnibys] nm slow ou stopping train.

omoplate [ɔmɔplat] nf shoulder blade.

on [ɔ̃] pronom
1 (indéterminé) you, one; ~ peut le faire ainsi you ou one can do it like this, it can be done like this
2 (quelqu'un): ~ les a attaqués they were attacked; ~ vous demande au téléphone there's a phone call for you, you're wanted on the phone
3 (nous) we; ~ va y aller demain we're going tomorrow
4 (les gens) they; autrefois, ~ croyait ... they used to believe ...
5: ~ ne peut plus ad: ~ ne peut plus stupide as stupid as can be.

oncle [ɔ̃kl(ə)] nm uncle.

onctueux, euse [ɔ̃ktɥø, -øz] a creamy, smooth; (fig) smooth, unctuous.

onde [ɔ̃d] nf (PHYSIQUE) wave; sur les ~s on the radio; mettre en ~s to produce for the radio; sur ~s courtes (o.c.) on short wave sg; moyennes/longues ~s medium/long wave sg.

ondée [ɔ̃de] nf shower.

on-dit [ɔ̃di] nm inv rumour.

ondoyer [ɔ̃dwaje] vi to ripple, wave.

onduler [ɔ̃dyle] vi to undulate; (cheveux) to wave.

onéreux, euse [ɔneʀø, -øz] a costly; à titre ~ in return for payment.

ongle [ɔ̃gl(ə)] nm (ANAT) nail; se faire les ~s to do one's nails.

onguent [ɔ̃gɑ̃] nm ointment.

ont vb voir **avoir**.

O.N.U. [ɔny] sigle f voir **organisation**.

onze [ɔ̃z] num eleven; **onzième** num eleventh.

O.P.A. sigle f voir **offre**.

opale [ɔpal] nf opal.

opaque [ɔpak] a opaque.

opéra [ɔpeʀa] nm opera; (édifice) opera house; ~-**comique** nm light opera.

opérateur, trice [ɔpeʀatœʀ, -tʀis] nm/f operator; ~ (de prise de vues) cameraman.

opération [ɔpeʀasjɔ̃] nf operation; (COMM) dealing.

opératoire [ɔpeʀatwaʀ] a operating; (choc etc) post-operative.

opérer [ɔpeʀe] vt (MÉD) to operate on; (faire, exécuter) to carry out, make // vi (remède: faire effet) to act, work; (procéder) to proceed; (MÉD) to operate; s'~ vi (avoir lieu) to occur, take place; se faire ~ to have an operation.

opiner [ɔpine] vi: ~ de la tête to nod assent.

opinion [ɔpinjɔ̃] nf opinion; l'~ (publique) public opinion.

opportun, e [ɔpɔʀtœ̃, -yn] a timely, opportune; en temps ~ at the appropriate time.

opposant, e [ɔpozɑ̃, -ɑ̃t] a opposing; ~s nmpl opponents.

opposé, e [ɔpoze] a (direction, rive) opposite; (faction) opposing; (couleurs) contrasting; (opinions, intérêts) conflicting; (contre): ~ à opposed to, against // nm: l'~ the other ou opposite side (ou direction); (contraire) the opposite; à l'~ (fig) on the other hand; à l'~ de on the other ou opposite side from; (fig) contrary to, unlike.

opposer [ɔpoze] vt (personnes, armées, équipes) to oppose; (couleurs, termes, tons) to contrast; (comme obstacle, défense) to set sth against; (comme objection) to put sth forward against; s'~ (sens réciproque) to conflict; to clash; to contrast; s'~ à (interdire, empêcher) to oppose; (tenir tête à) to rebel against.

opposition [ɔpozisjɔ̃] nf opposition; par ~ à as opposed to, in contrast with; entrer en ~ avec to come into conflict with; être en ~ avec (idées, conduite) to be at variance with; faire ~ à un chèque to stop a cheque.

oppresser [ɔpʀese] vt to oppress; **oppression** nf oppression; (malaise) feeling of suffocation.

opprimer [ɔpʀime] vt to oppress; (liberté, opinion) to suppress, stifle; (suj: chaleur etc) to suffocate, oppress.

opter [ɔpte] vi: ~ pour to opt for; ~ entre to choose between.

opticien, ne [ɔptisjɛ̃, -ɛn] nm/f optician.

optimiste [ɔptimist(ə)] nm/f optimist // a optimistic.

option [ɔpsjɔ̃] nf option; matière à ~ (SCOL) optional subject.

optique [ɔptik] a (nerf) optic; (verres) optical // nf (PHOTO: lentilles etc) optics pl; (science, industrie) optics sg; (fig: manière de voir) perspective.

opulent, e [ɔpylɑ̃, -ɑ̃t] a wealthy, opulent; (formes, poitrine) ample, generous.

or [ɔʀ] nm gold // cj now, but; en ~ gold cpd; (fig) golden, marvellous.

orage [ɔʀaʒ] nm (thunder)storm; **orageux, euse** a stormy.

oraison [ɔʀɛzɔ̃] nf orison, prayer; ~ funèbre funeral oration.

oral, e, aux [ɔʀal, -o] a, nm oral.

orange [ɔʀɑ̃ʒ] nf, a inv orange; **oranger** nm orange tree.

orateur [ɔʀatœʀ] nm speaker; orator.

orbite [ɔʀbit] nf (ANAT) (eye-)socket; (PHYSIQUE) orbit.

orchestre [ɔʀkɛstʀ(ə)] nm orchestra; (de jazz, danse) band; (places) stalls pl (Brit), orchestra (US); **orchestrer** vt (MUS) to orchestrate; (fig) to mount, stage-manage.

orchidée [ɔʀkide] *nf* orchid.

ordinaire [ɔʀdinɛʀ] *a* ordinary; every-day; standard // *nm* ordinary; (*menus*) everyday fare // *nf* (*essence*) ≈ two-star (petrol) (*Brit*), ≈ regular (gas) (*US*); **d'~** usually, normally; **à l'~** usually, ordinarily.

ordinateur [ɔʀdinatœʀ] *nm* computer; **~ domestique** home computer; **~ individuel** personal computer.

ordonnance [ɔʀdɔnɑ̃s] *nf* organization; layout; (*MÉD*) prescription; (*JUR*) order; (*MIL*) orderly, batman (*Brit*).

ordonné, e [ɔʀdɔne] *a* tidy, orderly; (*MATH*) ordered.

ordonner [ɔʀdɔne] *vt* (*agencer*) to organize, arrange; (*donner un ordre*): **~ à qn de faire** to order sb to do; (*REL*) to ordain; (*MÉD*) to prescribe.

ordre [ɔʀdʀ(ə)] *nm* (*gén*) order; (*propreté et soin*) orderliness, tidiness; (*nature*): **d'~ pratique** of a practical nature; **~s** *nmpl* (*REL*) holy orders; **mettre en ~** to tidy (up), put in order; **à l'~ de qn** payable to sb; **être aux ~s de qn/sous les ~s de qn** to be at sb's disposal/under sb's command; **jusqu'à nouvel ~** until further notice; **dans le même ~ d'idées** in this connection; **donnez-nous un ~ de grandeur** give us some idea as regards size (*ou* the amount); **de premier ~** first-rate; **~ du jour** (*d'une réunion*) agenda; (*MIL*) order of the day; **à l'~ du jour** (*fig*) topical.

ordure [ɔʀdyʀ] *nf* filth *q*; **~s** (*balayures, déchets*) rubbish *sg*, refuse *sg*; **~s ménagères** household refuse.

oreille [ɔʀɛj] *nf* (*ANAT*) ear; (*de marmite, tasse*) handle; **avoir de l'~** to have a good ear (for music).

oreiller [ɔʀeje] *nm* pillow.

oreillons [ɔʀɛjɔ̃] *nmpl* mumps *sg*.

ores [ɔʀ]: **d'~ et déjà** *ad* already.

orfèvrerie [ɔʀfɛvʀəʀi] *nf* goldsmith's (*ou* silversmith's) trade; (*ouvrage*) gold (*ou* silver) plate.

organe [ɔʀgan] *nm* organ; (*porte-parole*) representative, mouthpiece.

organigramme [ɔʀganigʀam] *nm* organization chart; flow chart.

organique [ɔʀganik] *a* organic.

organisateur, trice [ɔʀganizatœʀ, -tʀis] *nm/f* organizer.

organisation [ɔʀganizasjɔ̃] *nf* organization; **O~ des Nations Unies** (**O.N.U.**) United Nations (Organization) (**UN, UNO**); **O~ du traité de l'Atlantique Nord** (**O.T.A.N.**) North Atlantic Treaty Organization (**NATO**).

organiser [ɔʀganize] *vt* to organize; (*mettre sur pied: service etc*) to set up; **s'~** to get organized.

organisme [ɔʀganism(ə)] *nm* (*BIO*) organism; (*corps, ADMIN*) body.

organiste [ɔʀganist(ə)] *nm/f* organist.

orgasme [ɔʀgasm(ə)] *nm* orgasm, climax.

orge [ɔʀʒ(ə)] *nf* barley.

orgie [ɔʀʒi] *nf* orgy.

orgue [ɔʀg(ə)] *nm* organ; **~s** *nfpl* organ *sg*.

orgueil [ɔʀgœj] *nm* pride; **orgueilleux, euse** *a* proud.

Orient [ɔʀjɑ̃] *nm*: **l'~** the East, the Orient.

oriental, e, aux [ɔʀjɑ̃tal, -o] *a* oriental, eastern; (*frontière*) eastern.

orientation [ɔʀjɑ̃tasjɔ̃] *nf* positioning; orientation; (*d'une maison etc*) aspect; (*d'un journal*) leanings *pl*; **avoir le sens de l'~** to have a (good) sense of direction; **~ professionnelle** careers advising; careers advisory service.

orienté, e [ɔʀjɑ̃te] *a* (*fig: article, journal*) slanted; **bien/mal ~** (*appartement*) well/badly positioned; **~ au sud** facing south *ou* with a southern aspect.

orienter [ɔʀjɑ̃te] *vt* (*placer, disposer: pièce mobile*) to adjust, position; (*tourner*) to direct, turn; (*voyageur, touriste, recherches*) to direct; (*fig: élève*) to orientate; **s'~** (*se repérer*) to find one's bearings; **s'~ vers** (*fig*) to turn towards.

originaire [ɔʀiʒinɛʀ] *a*: **être ~ de** to be a native of.

original, e, aux [ɔʀiʒinal, -o] *a* original; (*bizarre*) eccentric // *nm/f* eccentric // *nm* (*document etc, ART*) original; (*dactylographie*) top copy.

origine [ɔʀiʒin] *nf* origin; **dès l'~** at *ou* from the outset; **à l'~** originally; **originel, le** *a* original.

O.R.L. *sigle nm/f de* **oto-rhino-laryngologiste**.

orme [ɔʀm(ə)] *nm* elm.

ornement [ɔʀnəmɑ̃] *nm* ornament; (*fig*) embellishment, adornment.

orner [ɔʀne] *vt* to decorate, adorn.

ornière [ɔʀnjɛʀ] *nf* rut.

orphelin, e [ɔʀfəlɛ̃, -in] *a* orphan(ed) // *nm/f* orphan; **~ de père/mère** fatherless/motherless; **orphelinat** *nm* orphanage.

orteil [ɔʀtɛj] *nm* toe; **gros ~** big toe.

orthographe [ɔʀtɔgʀaf] *nf* spelling; **orthographier** *vt* to spell.

orthopédiste [ɔʀtɔpedist(ə)] *nm/f* orthopaedic specialist.

ortie [ɔʀti] *nf* (stinging) nettle.

os [ɔs, *pl* o] *nm* bone.

osciller [ɔsile] *vi* (*pendule*) to swing; (*au vent etc*) to rock; (*TECH*) to oscillate; (*fig*): **~ entre** to waver *ou* fluctuate between.

osé, e [oze] *a* daring, bold.

oseille [ozɛj] *nf* sorrel.

oser [oze] *vi, vt* to dare; **~ faire** to dare (to) do.

osier [ozje] *nm* willow; **d'~, en ~** wicker(work).

ossature [ɔsatyʀ] nf (ANAT) frame, skeletal structure; (fig) framework.

osseux, euse [ɔsø, -øz] a bony; (tissu, maladie, greffe) bone cpd.

ostensible [ɔstɑ̃sibl(ə)] a conspicuous.

otage [ɔtaʒ] nm hostage; **prendre qn comme ~** to take sb hostage.

O.T.A.N. [ɔtɑ̃] sigle f voir **organisation**.

otarie [ɔtaʀi] nf sea-lion.

ôter [ote] vt to remove; (soustraire) to take away; **~ qch à qn** to take sth (away) from sb; **~ qch de** to remove sth from.

otite [ɔtit] nf ear infection.

oto-rhino(-laryngologiste) [ɔtɔʀino(laʀɛ̃gɔlɔʒist(ə)] nm/f ear nose and throat specialist.

ou [u] cj or; **~ ... ~** either ... or; **~ bien** or (else).

où [u] ♦ pronom relatif **1** (position, situation) where, that (souvent omis); **la chambre ~** il était the room (that) he was in, the room where he was; **la ville ~** je l'ai rencontré the town where I met him; **la pièce d'~** il est sorti the room he came out of; **le village d'~** je viens the village I come from; **les villes par ~** il est passé the towns he went through **2** (temps, état) that (souvent omis); **le jour ~** il est parti the day (that) he left; **au prix ~** c'est at the price it is ♦ ad **1** (interrogation) where; **~ est-il/va-t-il?** where is he/is he going?; **par ~?** which way?; **d'~ vient que ...?** how come ...? **2** (position) where; **je sais ~ il est** I know where he is; **~ que l'on aille** wherever you go.

ouate [wat] nf cotton wool (Brit), cotton (US); (bourre) padding, wadding.

oubli [ubli] nm (acte): **l'~** de forgetting; (étourderie) forgetfulness q; (négligence) omission, oversight; (absence de souvenirs) oblivion.

oublier [ublije] vt (gén) to forget; (ne pas voir: erreurs etc) to miss; (ne pas mettre: virgule, nom) to leave out; (laisser quelque part: chapeau etc) to leave behind; **s'~** to forget o.s.

oubliettes [ublijɛt] nfpl dungeon sg.

oublieux, euse [ublijø, -øz] a forgetful.

ouest [wɛst] nm west // a inv west; (région) western; **à l'~** in the west; (to the) west, westwards; **à l'~ de** (to the) west of.

ouf [uf] excl phew!

oui [wi] ad yes.

oui-dire [widiʀ]: **par ~** ad by hearsay.

ouïe [wi] nf hearing; **~s** nfpl (de poisson) gills.

ouïr [wiʀ] vt to hear; **avoir ouï dire que** to have heard it said that.

ouragan [uʀagɑ̃] nm hurricane.

ourlet [uʀlɛ] nm hem.

ours [uʀs] nm bear; **~ brun/blanc** brown/polar bear; **~ (en peluche)** teddy (bear).

oursin [uʀsɛ̃] nm sea urchin.

ourson [uʀsɔ̃] nm (bear-)cub.

ouste [ust(ə)] excl hop it!

outil [uti] nm tool.

outiller [utije] vt (ouvrier, usine) to equip.

outrage [utʀaʒ] nm insult; **faire subir les derniers ~s à** (femme) to ravish; **~ à la pudeur** indecent conduct q.

outrager [utʀaʒe] vt to offend gravely.

outrance [utʀɑ̃s]: **à ~** ad excessively, to excess.

outre [utʀ(ə)] nf goatskin, water skin // prép besides // ad: **passer ~ à** to disregard, take no notice of; **en ~** besides, moreover; **~ que** apart from the fact that; **~ mesure** immoderately; unduly.

outre-Atlantique [utʀatlɑ̃tik] ad across the Atlantic.

outre-Manche [utʀəmɑ̃ʃ] ad across the Channel.

outremer [utʀəmɛʀ] a inv ultramarine.

outre-mer [utʀəmɛʀ] ad overseas.

outrepasser [utʀəpase] vt to go beyond, exceed.

outrer [utʀe] vt to exaggerate; (choquer) to outrage.

ouvert, e [uvɛʀ, -ɛʀt(ə)] pp de **ouvrir** // a open; (robinet, gaz etc) on; **ouvertement** ad openly.

ouverture [uvɛʀtyʀ] nf opening; (MUS) overture; (PHOTO): **~ (du diaphragme)** aperture; **~s** nfpl (propositions) overtures; **~ d'esprit** open-mindedness.

ouvrable [uvʀabl(ə)] a: **jour ~** working day, weekday.

ouvrage [uvʀaʒ] nm (tâche, de tricot etc, MIL) work q; (texte, livre) work.

ouvragé, e [uvʀaʒe] a finely embroidered (ou worked ou carved).

ouvre-boîte(s) [uvʀəbwat] nm inv tin (Brit) ou can opener.

ouvre-bouteille(s) [uvʀəbutɛj] nm inv bottle-opener.

ouvreuse [uvʀøz] nf usherette.

ouvrier, ière [uvʀje, -jɛʀ] nm/f worker // a working-class; industrial, labour cpd; **classe ouvrière** working class.

ouvrir [uvʀiʀ] vt (gén) to open; (brèche, passage, MÉD: abcès) to open up; (commencer l'exploitation de, créer) to open (up); (eau, électricité, chauffage, robinet) to turn on // vi to open; to open up; **s'~** vi to open; **s'~ à qn** to open one's heart to sb; **~ l'appétit à qn** to whet sb's appetite.

ovaire [ɔvɛʀ] nm ovary.

ovale [ɔval] a oval.

ovni [ɔvni] sigle m (= objet volant non identifié) UFO.

oxyder [ɔkside]: **s'~** vi to become oxidized.

oxygène [ɔksiʒɛn] nm oxygen; (fig):

cure d'~ fresh air cure.

oxygéné, e [ɔksiʒene] a: **eau ~e** hydrogen peroxide.

P

pacifique [pasifik] a peaceful // nm: **le P~, l'océan P~** the Pacific (Ocean).

pacte [pakt(ə)] nm pact, treaty.

pactiser [paktize] vi: **~ avec** to come to terms with.

pagaie [pagɛ] nf paddle.

pagaille [pagaj] nf mess, shambles sg.

page [paʒ] nf page // nm page; **à la ~** (fig) up-to-date.

paie [pɛ] nf = **paye**.

paiement [pɛmã] nm = **payement**.

païen, ne [pajɛ̃, -jɛn] a, nm/f pagan, heathen.

paillard, e [pajaʀ, -aʀd(ə)] a bawdy.

paillasson [pajasɔ̃] nm doormat.

paille [paj] nf straw; (défaut) flaw.

paillettes [pajɛt] nfpl (décoratives) sequins, spangles; **lessive en ~** soapflakes pl.

pain [pɛ̃] nm (substance) bread; (unité) loaf (pl loaves) (of bread); (morceau): **~ de cire** etc bar of wax etc; **~ bis/complet** brown/wholemeal (Brit) ou wholewheat (US) bread; **~ d'épice** gingerbread; **~ grillé** toast; **~ de mie** sandwich loaf; **~ de sucre** sugar loaf.

pair, e [pɛʀ] a (nombre) even // nm peer; **aller de ~** to go hand in hand ou together; **jeune fille au ~** au pair.

paire [pɛʀ] nf pair.

paisible [pezibl(ə)] a peaceful, quiet.

paître [pɛtʀ(ə)] vi to graze.

paix [pɛ] nf peace; (fig) peacefulness, peace; **faire/avoir la ~** to make/have peace.

Pakistan [pakistã] nm: **le ~** Pakistan.

palace [palas] nm luxury hotel.

palais [palɛ] nm palace; (ANAT) palate.

pale [pal] nf (d'hélice, de rame) blade.

pâle [pal] a pale; **bleu ~** pale blue.

Palestine [palɛstin] nf: **la ~** Palestine; **palestinien, ne** a, nm/f Palestinian.

palet [palɛ] nm disc; (HOCKEY) puck.

palette [palɛt] nf (de peintre) palette; (produits) range.

pâleur [palœʀ] nf paleness.

palier [palje] nm (d'escalier) landing; (fig) level, plateau; (TECH) bearing; **par ~s** in stages.

pâlir [paliʀ] vi to turn ou go pale; (couleur) to fade.

palissade [palisad] nf fence.

palliatif [paljatif] nm palliative; (expédient) stopgap measure.

pallier [palje] vt: **~ à**; vt to offset, make up for.

palmarès [palmaʀɛs] nm record (of achievements); (SCOL) prize list;

(SPORT) list of winners.

palme [palm(ə)] nf (symbole) palm; (de plongeur) flipper; **palmé, e** a (pattes) webbed.

palmier [palmje] nm palm tree.

palombe [palɔ̃b] nf woodpigeon.

pâlot, te [palo, -ɔt] a pale, peaky.

palourde [paluʀd(ə)] nf clam.

palper [palpe] vt to feel, finger.

palpitant, e [palpitã, -ãt] a thrilling.

palpiter [palpite] vi (cœur, pouls) to beat; (: plus fort) to pound, throb.

paludisme [palydism(ə)] nm malaria.

pamphlet [pãflɛ] nm lampoon, satirical tract.

pamplemousse [pãpləmus] nm grapefruit.

pan [pã] nm section, piece // excl bang!; **~ de chemise** shirt tail.

panachage [panaʃaʒ] nm blend, mix.

panache [panaʃ] nm plume; (fig) spirit, panache.

panaché, e [panaʃe] a: **glace ~e** mixed-flavour ice cream; **bière ~e** shandy.

pancarte [pãkaʀt(ə)] nf sign, notice; (dans un défilé) placard.

pancréas [pãkʀeas] nm pancreas.

pané, e [pane] a fried in breadcrumbs.

panier [panje] nm basket; **mettre au ~** to chuck away; **~ à provisions** shopping basket.

panique [panik] nf, a panic; **paniquer** vi to panic.

panne [pan] nf (d'un mécanisme, moteur) breakdown; **être/tomber en ~** to have broken down/break down; **être en ~ d'essence** ou **sèche** to have run out of petrol (Brit) ou gas (US); **~ d'électricité** ou **de courant** power ou electrical failure.

panneau, x [pano] nm (écriteau) sign, notice; (de boiserie, de tapisserie etc) panel; **~ d'affichage** notice board; **~ de signalisation** roadsign.

panonceau, x [panɔ̃so] nm sign.

panoplie [panɔpli] nf (jouet) outfit; (d'armes) display; (fig) array.

panorama [panɔʀama] nm panorama.

panse [pãs] nf paunch.

pansement [pãsmã] nm dressing, bandage; **~ adhésif** sticking plaster.

panser [pãse] vt (plaie) to dress, bandage; (bras) to put a dressing on, bandage; (cheval) to groom.

pantalon [pãtalɔ̃] nm (aussi: **~s, paire de ~s**) trousers pl, pair of trousers; **~ de ski** ski pants pl.

pantelant, e [pãtlã, -ãt] a gasping for breath, panting.

panthère [pãtɛʀ] nf panther.

pantin [pãtɛ̃] nm jumping jack; (péj) puppet.

pantois [pãtwa] am: **rester ~** to be flabbergasted.

pantomime [pãtɔmim] nf mime;

(*pièce*) mime show.
pantoufle [pãtufl(ə)] *nf* slipper.
paon [pã] *nm* peacock.
papa [papa] *nm* dad(dy).
pape [pap] *nm* pope.
paperasse [papʀas] *nf* (*péj*) bumf *q*, papers *pl*; ~**rie** *nf* (*péj*) red tape *q*; paperwork *q*.
papeterie [papetʀi] *nf* (*usine*) paper mill; (*magasin*) stationer's (shop).
papier [papje] *nm* paper; (*article*) article; ~**s** (*aussi*: ~**s d'identité**) (identity) papers; ~ (**d')aluminium** aluminium (*Brit*) *ou* aluminum (*US*) foil, tinfoil; ~ **buvard** blotting paper; ~ **carbone** carbon paper; ~ **hygiénique** toilet paper; ~ **journal** newsprint; (*pour emballer*) newspaper; ~ **à lettres** writing paper, notepaper; ~ **peint** wallpaper; ~ **de verre** sandpaper.
papillon [papijɔ̃] *nm* butterfly; (*fam*: *contravention*) (parking) ticket; (*TECH*: *écrou*) wing nut; ~ **de nuit** moth.
papilloter [papijɔte] *vi* to blink, flicker.
paquebot [pakbo] *nm* liner.
pâquerette [pakʀɛt] *nf* daisy.
Pâques [pak] *nm*, *nfpl* Easter.
paquet [pakɛ] *nm* packet; (*colis*) parcel; (*fig*: *tas*): ~ **de pile** *ou* heap of; ~**cadeau** *nm* gift-wrapped parcel.
par [paʀ] *prép* by; *finir etc* ~ to end *etc* with; ~ **amour** out of love; **passer** ~ **Lyon/la côte** to go via *ou* through Lyons/ along by the coast; ~ **la fenêtre** (*jeter, regarder*) out of the window; **3** ~ **jour/ personne** 3 a *ou* per day/head; **2** ~ **2** two at a time; in twos; ~ **ici** this way; (*dans le coin*) round here; ~**ci**, ~**là** here and there.
parabole [paʀabɔl] *nf* (*REL*) parable.
parachever [paʀaʃve] *vt* to perfect.
parachute [paʀaʃyt] *nm* parachute.
parachutiste [paʀaʃytist(ə)] *nm/f* parachutist; (*MIL*) paratrooper.
parade [paʀad] *nf* (*spectacle, défilé*) parade; (*ESCRIME, BOXE*) parry.
paradis [paʀadi] *nm* heaven, paradise.
paradoxe [paʀadɔks(ə)] *nm* paradox.
paraffine [paʀafin] *nf* paraffin.
parages [paʀaʒ] *nmpl*: **dans les** ~ (**de**) in the area *ou* vicinity (of).
paragraphe [paʀagʀaf] *nm* paragraph.
paraître [paʀɛtʀ(ə)] *vb avec attribut* to seem, look, appear // *vi* to appear; (*être visible*) to show; (*PRESSE, ÉDITION*) to be published, come out, appear; (*briller*) to show off // *vb impersonnel*: **il paraît que il seems** *ou* appears that, they say that; **il me paraît que il seems** to me that.
parallèle [paʀalɛl] *a* parallel; (*police, marché*) unofficial // *nm* (*comparaison*): **faire un** ~ **entre** to draw a parallel between; (*GÉO*) parallel // *nf* parallel (line).

paralyser [paʀalize] *vt* to paralyze.
parapet [paʀapɛ] *nm* parapet.
parapher [paʀafe] *vt* to initial; to sign.
paraphrase [paʀafʀaz] *nf* paraphrase.
parapluie [paʀaplɥi] *nm* umbrella.
parasite [paʀazit] *nm* parasite; ~**s** (*TÉL*) interference *sg*.
parasol [paʀasɔl] *nm* parasol, sunshade.
paratonnerre [paʀatɔnɛʀ] *nm* lightning conductor.
paravent [paʀavã] *nm* folding screen.
parc [paʀk] *nm* (*public*) park, gardens *pl*; (*de château etc*) grounds *pl*; (*pour le bétail*) pen, enclosure; (*d'enfant*) playpen; (*MIL*: *entrepôt*) depot; (*ensemble d'unités*) stock; (*de voitures etc*) fleet; ~ **automobile** (*d'un pays*) number of cars on the roads; ~ **de stationnement** car park.
parcelle [paʀsɛl] *nf* fragment, scrap; (*de terrain*) plot, parcel.
parce que [paʀsk(ə)] *cj* because.
parchemin [paʀʃəmɛ̃] *nm* parchment.
parc(o)mètre [paʀk(ɔ)mɛtʀ(ə)] *nm* parking meter.
parcourir [paʀkuʀiʀ] *vt* (*trajet, distance*) to cover; (*article, livre*) to skim *ou* glance through; (*lieu*) to go all over, travel up and down; (*suj*: *frisson, vibration*) to run through.
parcours [paʀkuʀ] *nm* (*trajet*) journey; (*itinéraire*) route; (*SPORT*: *terrain*) course; (: *tour*) round; run; lap.
par-dessous [paʀdəsu] *prép*, *ad* under(neath).
pardessus [paʀdəsy] *nm* overcoat.
par-dessus [paʀdəsy] *prép* over (the top of) // *ad* over (the top); ~ **le marché** on top of all that.
par-devant [paʀdəvã] *prép* in the presence of, before // *ad* at the front; round the front.
pardon [paʀdɔ̃] *nm* forgiveness *q* // *excl* sorry!; (*pour interpeller etc*) excuse me!; **demander** ~ **à qn** (**de**) to apologize to sb (for); **je vous demande** ~ I'm sorry; excuse me.
pardonner [paʀdɔne] *vt* to forgive; ~ **qch à qn** to forgive sb for sth.
pare-balles [paʀbal] *a inv* bulletproof.
pare-boue [paʀbu] *nm inv* mudguard.
pare-brise [paʀbʀiz] *nm inv* windscreen (*Brit*), windshield (*US*).
pare-chocs [paʀʃɔk] *nm inv* bumper.
pareil, le [paʀɛj] *a* (*identique*) the same, alike; (*similaire*) similar; (*tel*): **un courage/livre** ~ such courage/a book, courage/a book like this; **de** ~**s livres** such books; **ses** ~**s** one's fellow men; one's peers; **ne pas avoir son(sa)** ~(**le**) to be second to none; ~ **à** the same as; similar to; **sans** ~ unparalleled, unequalled.
parent, e [paʀã, -ãt] *nm/f*: **un/une** ~/**e** a relative *ou* relation // *a*: **être** ~ **de** to be

related to; ~s *nmpl* (*père et mère*) parents; **parenté** *nf* (*lien*) relationship.

parenthèse [parɑ̃tɛz] *nf* (*ponctuation*) bracket, parenthesis; (*MATH*) bracket; (*digression*) parenthesis, digression; **ouvrir/fermer la** ~ to open/close the brackets; **entre** ~s in brackets; (*fig*) incidentally.

parer [pare] *vt* to adorn; (*CULIN*) to dress, trim; (*éviter*) to ward off.

pare-soleil [parsɔlɛj] *nm inv* sun visor.

paresse [parɛs] *nf* laziness; **paresseux, euse** *a* lazy; (*fig*) slow, sluggish.

parfaire [parfɛr] *vt* to perfect.

parfait, e [parfɛ, -ɛt] *a* perfect // *nm* (*LING*) perfect (tense); **parfaitement** *ad* perfectly // *excl* (most) certainly.

parfois [parfwa] *ad* sometimes.

parfum [parfœ̃] *nm* (*produit*) perfume, scent; (*odeur: de fleur*) scent, fragrance; (*: de tabac, vin*) aroma; (*goût*) flavour; **parfumé, e** *a* (*fleur, fruit*) fragrant; (*femme*) perfumed; **parfumé au café** coffee-flavoured; **parfumer** *vt* (*suj: odeur, bouquet*) to perfume; (*mouchoir*) to put scent *ou* perfume on; (*crème, gâteau*) to flavour; **parfumerie** *nf* (*commerce*) perfumery; (*produits*) perfumes *pl*; (*boutique*) perfume shop.

pari [pari] *nm* bet, wager; (*SPORT*) bet.

paria [parja] *nm* outcast.

parier [parje] *vt* to bet.

Paris [pari] *n* Paris; **parisien, ne** *a* Parisian; (*GÉO, ADMIN*) Paris *cpd* // *nm/f*: **Parisien, ne** Parisian.

paritaire [paritɛr] *a* joint.

parjure [parʒyr] *nm* perjury; **se parjurer** *vi* to forswear *ou* perjure o.s.

parking [parkiɲ] *nm* (*lieu*) car park.

parlant, e [parlɑ̃, -ɑ̃t] *a* (*fig*) graphic, vivid; eloquent; (*CINÉMA*) talking.

parlement [parləmɑ̃] *nm* parliament; **parlementaire** *a* parliamentary // *nm/f* member of parliament.

parlementer [parləmɑ̃te] *vi* to negotiate, parley.

parler [parle] *vi* to speak, talk; (*avouer*) to talk; ~ (**à qn**) **de** to talk *ou* speak (to sb) about; ~ **le/en français** to speak French/in French; ~ **affaires** to talk business; ~ **en dormant** to talk in one's sleep; **sans** ~ **de** (*fig*) not to mention, to say nothing of; **tu parles!** you must be joking!

parloir [parlwar] *nm* (*de prison, d'hôpital*) visiting room; (*REL*) parlour.

parmi [parmi] *prép* among(st).

paroi [parwa] *nf* wall; (*cloison*) partition; ~ **rocheuse** rock face.

paroisse [parwas] *nf* parish.

parole [parɔl] *nf* (*faculté*): **la** ~ speech; (*mot, promesse*) word; ~s (*MUS*) words, lyrics; **tenir** ~ to keep one's word; **prendre la** ~ to speak; **demander la** ~ to ask for permission to speak; **je le crois sur** ~

I'll take his word for it.

parquer [parke] *vt* (*voiture, matériel*) to park; (*bestiaux*) to pen (in *ou* up).

parquet [parkɛ] *nm* (*parquet*) floor; (*JUR*): **le** ~ the Public Prosecutor's department.

parrain [parɛ̃] *nm* godfather; (*d'un nouvel adhérent*) sponsor, proposer.

pars *vb voir* **partir**.

parsemer [parsəme] *vt* (*suj: feuilles, papiers*) to be scattered over; ~ **qch de** to scatter sth with.

part [par] *nf* (*qui revient à qn*) share; (*fraction, partie*) part; (*FINANCE*) (non-voting) share; **prendre** ~ **à** (*débat etc*) to take part in; (*soucis, douleur de qn*) to share in; **faire** ~ **de qch à qn** to announce sth to sb, inform sb of sth; **pour ma** ~ as for me, as far as I'm concerned; **à** ~ **entière** *a* full; **de la** ~ **de** (*au nom de*) on behalf of; (*donné par*) from; **de toute(s)** ~s**(s)** from all sides *ou* quarters; **de** ~ **et d'autre** on both sides, on either side; **de** ~ **en** ~ right through; **d'une** ~ ... **d'autre** ~ on the one hand ... on the other hand; **à** ~ *ad* separately; (*de côté*) aside // *prép* apart from, except for // *a* exceptional, special; **faire la** ~ **des choses** to make allowances.

partage [partaʒ] *nm* dividing up; sharing (out) *q*, share-out; sharing; **recevoir qch en** ~ to receive sth as one's share (*ou* lot).

partager [partaʒe] *vt* to share; (*distribuer, répartir*) to share (out); (*morceler, diviser*) to divide (up); **se** ~ *vt* (*héritage etc*) to share between themselves (*ou* ourselves).

partance [partɑ̃s]: **en** ~ *ad* outbound, due to leave; **en** ~ **pour** (*bound*) for.

partant [partɑ̃] *vb voir* **partir** // *nm* (*SPORT*) starter; (*HIPPISME*) runner.

partenaire [partənɛr] *nm/f* partner.

parterre [partɛr] *nm* (*de fleurs*) (flower) bed; (*THÉÂTRE*) stalls *pl*.

parti [parti] *nm* (*POL*) party; (*décision*) course of action; (*personne à marier*) match; **tirer** ~ **de** to take advantage of, turn to good account; **prendre le** ~ **de qn** to stand up for sb, side with sb; **prendre** ~ (**pour/contre**) to take sides *ou* a stand (for/against); **prendre son** ~ **de** to come to terms with; ~ **pris** bias.

partial, e, aux [parsjal, -o] *a* biased, partial.

participant, e [partisipɑ̃, -ɑ̃t] *nm/f* participant; (*à un concours*) entrant.

participation [partisipɔsjɔ̃] *nf* participation; sharing; (*COMM*) interest; **la** ~ **aux bénéfices** profit-sharing.

participe [partisip] *nm* participle.

participer [partisipe]: ~ **à** *vt* (*course, réunion*) to take part in; (*profits etc*) to share in; (*frais etc*) to contribute to; (*chagrin, succès de qn*) to share (in).

particularité [partikylarite] *nf* particularity; (*distinctive*) characteristic.

particule [partikyl] *nf* particle.

particulier, ière [partikylje, -jɛr] *a* (*personnel, privé*) private; (*spécial*) special, particular; (*caractéristique*) characteristic, distinctive; (*spécifique*) particular // *nm* (*individu: ADMIN*) private individual; ~ **à** peculiar to; **en** ~ *ad* (*surtout*) in particular, particularly; (*en privé*) in private; **particulièrement** *ad* particularly.

partie [parti] *nf* (*gén*) part; (*profession, spécialité*) field, subject; (*JUR etc: protagonistes*) party; (*de cartes, tennis etc*) game; **une** ~ **de campagne/de pêche** an outing in the country/a fishing party *ou* trip; **en** ~ *ad* partly, in part; **faire** ~ **de** to belong to; (*suj: chose*) to be part of; **prendre qn à** ~ to take sb to task; (*malmener*) to set on sb; **en grande** ~ largely, in the main; ~ **civile** (*JUR*) *party claiming damages in a criminal case.*

partiel, le [parsjɛl] *a* partial // *nm* (*SCOL*) class exam.

partir [partir] *vi* (*gén*) to go; (*quitter*) to go, leave; (*s'éloigner*) to go (*ou* drive *etc*) away *ou* off; (*moteur*) to start; ~ **de** (*lieu: quitter*) to start from; (*: commencer à*) to start from; (*date*) to run *ou* start from; **à** ~ **de** from.

partisan, e [partizã, -an] *nm/f* partisan // *a*: **être** ~ **de qch/faire** to be in favour of sth/doing.

partition [partisjɔ̃] *nf* (*MUS*) score.

partout [partu] *ad* everywhere; ~ **où il allait** everywhere *ou* wherever he went; **trente** ~ (*TENNIS*) thirty all.

paru *pp de* **paraître**.

parure [paryr] *nf* (*bijoux etc*) finery *q*; jewellery *q*; (*assortiment*) set.

parution [parysjɔ̃] *nf* publication, appearance.

parvenir [parvənir]: ~ **à** *vt* (*atteindre*) to reach; (*réussir*): ~ **à faire** to manage to do, succeed in doing; **faire** ~ **qch à qn** to have sth sent to sb.

parvis [parvi] *nm* square (*in front of a church*).

pas [pɑ] *ad voir le mot suivant* // *nm* (*allure, mesure*) pace; (*démarche*) tread; (*enjambée, DANSE*) step; (*bruit*) (foot)step; (*trace*) footprint; (*TECH: de vis, d'écrou*) thread; ~ **à** ~ step by step; **au** ~ at walking pace; **à** ~ **de loup** stealthily; **faire les cent** ~ to pace up and down; **faire les premiers** ~ to make the first move; **sur le** ~ **de la porte** on the doorstep.

pas [pɑ] ♦ *nm voir le mot précédent* ♦ *ad* **1** (*en corrélation avec ne, non etc*) not; **il ne pleure** ~ he does not *ou* doesn't cry; he's not *ou* isn't crying; **il n'a** ~ **pleuré/ne pleurera** ~ he did not *ou*

didn't/will not *ou* won't cry; **ils n'ont** ~ **de voiture/d'enfants** they haven't got a car/any children, they have no car/ children; **il m'a dit de ne** ~ **le faire** he told me not to do it; **non** ~ **que ...** not that ...

2 (*employé sans ne etc*): ~ **moi** not me; **not I, I don't** (*ou* can't *etc*); **une pomme** ~ **mûre** an apple which isn't ripe; ~ **plus tard qu'hier** only yesterday; ~ **du tout** not at all

3: ~ **mal** not bad; not badly; ~ **mal de** quite a lot of.

passage [pasaʒ] *nm* (*fait de passer*) *voir* **passer**; (*lieu, prix de la traversée, extrait de livre etc*) passage; (*chemin*) way; **de** ~ (*touristes*) passing through; (*amants etc*) casual; ~ **clouté** pedestrian crossing; '~ **interdit** 'no entry'; ~ **à niveau** level crossing; '~ **protégé'** *right of way over secondary road(s) on your right*; ~ **souterrain** subway (*Brit*), underpass.

passager, ère [pasaʒe, -ɛr] *a* passing // *nm/f* passenger; ~ **clandestin** stowaway.

passant, e [pasã, -ãt] *a* (*rue, endroit*) busy // *nm/f* passer-by; **en** ~ in passing.

passe [pas] *nf* (*SPORT, magnétique, NAVIG*) pass // *nm* (*passe-partout*) master *ou* skeleton key; **être en** ~ **de faire** to be on the way to doing.

passé, e [pase] *a* (*événement, temps*) past; (*couleur, tapisserie*) faded // *prép* after // *nm* past; (*LING*) past (tense); ~ **de mode** out of fashion; ~ **composé** perfect (tense); ~ **simple** past historic.

passe-droit [pasdrwa] *nm* special privilege.

passementerie [pasmãtri] *nf* trimmings *pl*.

passe-montagne [pasmɔ̃taɲ] *nm* balaclava.

passe-partout [paspartu] *nm inv* master *ou* skeleton key // *a inv* all-purpose.

passe-passe [paspas] *nm*: **tour de** ~ trick, sleight of hand *q*.

passeport [paspɔr] *nm* passport.

passer [pase] *vi* (*se rendre, aller*) to go; (*voiture, piétons: défiler*) to pass (by), go by; (*faire une halte rapide: facteur, laitier etc*) to come, call; (*: pour rendre visite*) to call *ou* drop in; (*courant, air, lumière, franchir un obstacle etc*) to get through; (*accusé, projet de loi*): ~ **devant** to come before; (*film, émission*) to be on; (*temps, jours*) to pass, go by; (*couleur, papier*) to fade; (*mode*) to die out; (*douleur*) to pass, go away; (*CARTES*) to pass; (*SCOL*) to go up (to the next class) // *vt* (*frontière, rivière etc*) to cross; (*douane*) to go through; (*examen*) to sit, take; (*visite médicale etc*) to have; (*journée, temps*) to spend; (*donner*): ~ **qch à qn** to pass sth to sb; to give sb sth; (*transmettre*): ~ **qch à**

qn to pass sth on to sb; (*enfiler: vêtement*) to slip on; (*faire entrer, mettre*): (faire) ~ qch dans/par to get sth into/through; (*café*) to pour the water on; (*thé, soupe*) to strain; (*film, pièce*) to show, put on; (*disque*) to play, put on; (*marché, accord*) to agree on; (*tolérer*): ~ qch à qn to let sb get away with sth; se ~ *vi* (*avoir lieu: scène, action*) to take place; (*se dérouler: entretien etc*) to go; (*arriver*): que s'est-il passé? what happened?; (*s'écouler: semaine etc*) to pass, go by; se ~ de *vt* to go ou do without; se ~ les mains sous l'eau/de l'eau sur le visage to put one's hands under the tap/run water over one's face; ~ par to go through; ~ sur *vt* (*faute, détail inutile*) to pass over; ~ avant qch/qn (*fig*) to come before sth/sb; laisser ~ (*air, lumière, personne*) to let through; (*occasion*) to let slip, miss; (*erreur*) to overlook; ~ à la radio/télévision to be on the radio/on television; ~ pour riche to be taken for a rich man; ~ en seconde, ~ la seconde (*AUTO*) to change into second; ~ le balai/l'aspirateur to sweep up/hoover; (*je vous passe M. X* (*je vous mets en communication avec lui*) I'm putting you through to Mr X; (*je lui passe l'appareil*) here is Mr X, I'll hand you over to Mr X.

passerelle [pasʀɛl] *nf* footbridge; (*de navire, avion*) gangway.

passe-temps [pastɑ̃] *nm inv* pastime.

passette [pasɛt] *nf* (tea-)strainer.

passeur, euse [pasœʀ, -øz] *nm/f* smuggler.

passible [pasibl(ə)] *a*: ~ de liable to.

passif, ive [pasif, -iv] *a* passive // *nm* (*LING*) passive; (*COMM*) liabilities *pl*.

passion [pasjɔ̃] *nf* passion; **passionnant, e** *a* fascinating; **passionné, e** *a* passionate; impassioned; **passionner** *vt* (*personne*) to fascinate, grip; se **passionner pour** to take an avid interest in; to have a passion for.

passoire [paswaʀ] *nf* sieve; (*à légumes*) colander; (*à thé*) strainer.

pastèque [pastɛk] *nf* watermelon.

pasteur [pastœʀ] *nm* (*protestant*) minister, pastor.

pastille [pastij] *nf* (*à sucer*) lozenge, pastille; (*de papier etc*) (small) disc.

patate [patat] *nf*: ~ **douce** sweet potato.

patauger [patoʒe] *vi* (*pour s'amuser*) to splash about; (*avec effort*) to wade about.

pâte [pɑt] *nf* (*à tarte*) pastry; (*à pain*) dough; (*à frire*) batter; (*substance molle*) paste; cream; ~s *nfpl* (*macaroni etc*) pasta *sg*; ~ **d'amandes** almond paste; ~ **brisée** shortcrust pastry; ~ **de fruits** crystallized fruit *q*; ~ **à modeler** modelling clay, Plasticine ® (*Brit*).

pâté [pɑte] *nm* (*charcuterie*) pâté;

(*tache*) ink blot; (*de sable*) sandpie; ~ **en croûte** ≈ pork pie; ~ **de maisons** block (of houses).

pâtée [pɑte] *nf* mash, feed.

patente [patɑ̃t] *nf* (*COMM*) trading licence.

patère [patɛʀ] *nf* (coat-)peg.

paternel, le [patɛʀnɛl] *a* (*amour, soins*) fatherly; (*ligne, autorité*) paternal.

pâteux, euse [patø, -øz] *a* thick; pasty.

pathétique [patetik] *a* moving.

patience [pasjɑ̃s] *nf* patience.

patient, e [pasjɑ̃, -ɑ̃t] *a, nm/f* patient.

patienter [pasjɑ̃te] *vi* to wait.

patin [patɛ̃] *nm* skate; (*sport*) skating; ~s (à glace) (ice) skates; ~s à roulettes roller skates.

patinage [patinaʒ] *nm* skating.

patiner [patine] *vi* to skate; (*embrayage*) to slip; (*roue, voiture*) to spin; se ~ *vi* (*meuble, cuir*) to acquire a sheen; **patineur, euse** *nm/f* skater; **patinoire** *nf* skating rink, (ice) rink.

pâtir [pɑtiʀ]: ~ **de** *vt* to suffer because of.

pâtisserie [pɑtisʀi] *nf* (*boutique*) cake shop; (*métier*) confectionery; (*à la maison*) pastry- ou cake-making, baking; ~s *nfpl* (*gâteaux*) pastries, cakes; **pâtissier, ière** *nm/f* pastrycook; confectioner.

patois [patwa] *nm* dialect, patois.

patrie [patʀi] *nf* homeland.

patrimoine [patʀimwan] *nm* inheritance, patrimony; (*culture*) heritage.

patriotique [patʀijɔtik] *a* patriotic.

patron, ne [patʀɔ̃, -ɔn] *nm/f* boss; (*REL*) patron saint // *nm* (*COUTURE*) pattern.

patronat [patʀɔna] *nm* employers *pl*.

patronner [patʀɔne] *vt* to sponsor, support.

patrouille [patʀuj] *nf* patrol.

patte [pat] *nf* (*jambe*) leg; (*pied: de chien, chat*) paw; (: *d'oiseau*) foot; (*languette*) strap.

pâturage [pɑtyʀaʒ] *nm* pasture.

pâture [pɑtyʀ] *nf* food.

paume [pom] *nf* palm.

paumé, e [pome] *nm/f* (*fam*) drop-out.

paumer [pome] *vt* (*fam*) to lose.

paupière [popjɛʀ] *nf* eyelid.

pause [poz] *nf* (*arrêt*) break; (*en parlant, MUS*) pause.

pauvre [povʀ(ə)] *a* poor; ~**té** *nf* (*état*) poverty.

pavaner [pavane]: se ~ *vi* to strut about.

pavé, e [pave] *a* paved; cobbled // *nm* (*bloc*) paving stone; cobblestone; (*pavage*) paving.

pavillon [pavijɔ̃] *nm* (*de banlieue*) small (detached) house; (*kiosque*) lodge; pavilion; (*drapeau*) flag.

pavoiser [pavwaze] *vi* to put out flags; (*fig*) to rejoice, exult.

pavot [pavo] *nm* poppy.

payant, e [pɛjɑ̃, -ɑ̃t] *a* (*spectateurs etc*) paying; (*fig: entreprise*) profitable; **c'est ~** you have to pay, there is a charge.

paye [pɛj] *nf* pay, wages *pl*.

payement [pɛjmɑ̃] *nm* payment.

payer [peje] *vt* (*créancier, employé, loyer*) to pay; (*achat, réparations, fig: faute*) to pay for // *vi* to pay; (*métier*) to be well-paid; (*tactique etc*) to pay off; **il me l'a fait ~ 10 F** he charged me 10 F for it; **~ qch à qn** to buy sth for sb, buy sb sth; **cela ne me paie pas de mine** it doesn't look much.

pays [pei] *nm* country; land; region; village; **du ~** a local.

paysage [peizaʒ] *nm* landscape.

paysan, ne [peizɑ̃, -an] *nm/f* countryman/woman; farmer; (*péj*) peasant // *a* country *cpd*, farming; farmers'.

Pays-Bas [peiba] *nmpl*: **les ~** the Netherlands.

PC *nm* (*INFORM*) PC.

PDG *sigle m voir* **président**.

péage [peaʒ] *nm* toll; (*endroit*) tollgate; **pont à ~** toll bridge.

peau, x [po] *nf* skin; **gants de ~** fine leather gloves; **~ de chamois** (*chiffon*) chamois leather, shammy; **P~-Rouge** *nm/f* Red Indian, redskin.

péché [peʃe] *nm* sin.

pêche [pɛʃ] *nf* (*sport, activité*) fishing; (*poissons péchés*) catch; (*fruit*) peach; **~ à la ligne** (*en rivière*) angling.

pécher [peʃe] *vi* (*REL*) to sin; (*fig: personne*) to err; (*: chose*) to be flawed.

pêcher [peʃe] *nm* peach tree // *vi* to go fishing // *vt* to catch; to fish for.

pécheur, eresse [peʃœr, peʃrɛs] *nm/f* sinner.

pêcheur [peʃœr] *nm* fisherman; angler.

pécule [pekyl] *nm* savings *pl*, nest egg.

pécuniaire [pekynjɛr] *a* financial.

pédagogie [pedagoʒi] *nf* educational methods *pl*, pedagogy; **pédagogique** *a* educational.

pédale [pedal] *nf* pedal.

pédalo [pedalo] *nm* pedal-boat.

pédant, e [pedɑ̃, -ɑ̃t] *a* (*péj*) pedantic.

pédestre [pedɛstr(ə)] *a*: **tourisme ~** hiking.

pédiatre [pedjatr(ə)] *nm/f* paediatrician, child specialist.

pédicure [pedikyr] *nm/f* chiropodist.

pègre [pɛgr(ə)] *nf* underworld.

peignais *etc vb voir* **peindre, peigner**.

peigne [pɛɲ] *nm* comb.

peigner [peɲe] *vt* to comb (the hair of); **se ~** *vi* to comb one's hair.

peignoir [pɛɲwar] *nm* dressing gown; **~ de bain** bathrobe.

peindre [pɛ̃dr(ə)] *vt* to paint; (*fig*) to portray, depict.

peine [pɛn] *nf* (*affliction*) sorrow, sad-

ness *q*; (*mal, effort*) trouble *q*, effort; (*difficulté*) difficulty; (*punition, châtiment*) punishment; (*JUR*) sentence; **faire de la ~ à qn** to distress ou upset sb; **prendre la ~ de faire** to go to the trouble of doing; **se donner de la ~** to make an effort; **ce n'est pas la ~ de faire** there's no point in doing, it's not worth doing; **à ~** *ad* scarcely, hardly, barely; **à ~ ... que** hardly ... than; **défense d'afficher sous ~ d'amende** billposters will be fined; **~ capitale** ou **de mort** capital punishment, death sentence; **peiner** *vi* to work hard; to struggle; (*moteur, voiture*) to labour // *vt* to grieve, sadden.

peintre [pɛ̃tr(ə)] *nm* painter; **~ en bâtiment** house painter.

peinture [pɛ̃tyr] *nf* painting; (*couche de couleur, couleur*) paint; (*surfaces peintes: aussi: ~s*) paintwork; **~ mate/brillante** matt/gloss paint; **'~ fraîche'** 'wet paint'.

péjoratif, ive [peʒɔratif, -iv] *a* pejorative, derogatory.

pelage [pəlaʒ] *nm* coat, fur.

pêle-mêle [pɛlmɛl] *ad* higgledy-piggledy.

peler [pəle] *vt, vi* to peel.

pèlerin [pɛlrɛ̃] *nm* pilgrim.

pelle [pɛl] *nf* shovel; (*d'enfant, de terrassier*) spade; **~ mécanique** mechanical digger.

pellicule [pelikyl] *nf* film; **~s** *nfpl* (*MÉD*) dandruff *sg*.

pelote [pəlɔt] *nf* (*de fil, laine*) ball; (*d'épingles*) pin cushion; **~ basque** pelota.

peloton [pəlɔtɔ̃] *nm* group, squad; (*CYCLISME*) pack; **~ d'exécution** firing squad.

pelotonner [pəlɔtɔne]: **se ~** *vi* to curl (o.s.) up.

pelouse [pəluz] *nf* lawn.

peluche [pəlyʃ] *nf*: **animal en ~** fluffy animal, soft toy.

pelure [pəlyr] *nf* peeling, peel *q*.

pénal, e, aux [penal, -o] *a* penal.

pénalité [penalite] *nf* penalty.

penaud, e [pəno, -od] *a* sheepish, contrite.

penchant [pɑ̃ʃɑ̃] *nm* tendency, propensity; liking, fondness.

pencher [pɑ̃ʃe] *vi* to tilt, lean over // *vt* to tilt; **se ~** *vi* to lean over; (*se baisser*) to bend down; **se ~ sur** to bend over; (*fig: problème*) to look into; **se ~ au dehors** to lean out; **~ pour** to be inclined to favour.

pendaison [pɑ̃dɛzɔ̃] *nf* hanging.

pendant [pɑ̃dɑ̃] *nm*: **faire ~ à** to match; to be the counterpart of // *prép* during; **~ que** while.

pendentif [pɑ̃dɑ̃tif] *nm* pendant.

penderie [pɑ̃dri] *nf* wardrobe.

pendre [pɑ̃dr(ə)] *vt, vi* to hang; **se ~**

(à) (se suicider) to hang o.s. (on); ~ à to hang (down) from; ~ qch à to hang sth (up) on.

pendule [pɑ̃dyl] nf clock // nm pendulum.

pêne [pɛn] nm bolt.

pénétrer [penetʀe] vi, vt to penetrate; ~ dans to enter; (suj: projectile) to penetrate; (: air, eau) to come into, get into.

pénible [penibl(ə)] a (astreignant) hard; (affligeant) painful; (personne, caractère) tiresome; ~**ment** ad with difficulty.

péniche [peniʃ] nf barge.

pénicilline [penisilin] nf penicillin.

péninsule [penɛ̃syl] nf peninsula.

pénis [penis] nm penis.

pénitence [penitɑ̃s] nf (repentir) penitence; (peine) penance.

pénitencier [penitɑ̃sje] nm penitentiary.

pénombre [penɔ̃bʀ(ə)] nf half-light; darkness.

pensée [pɑ̃se] nf thought; (démarche, doctrine) thinking q; (BOT) pansy; en ~ in one's mind.

penser [pɑ̃se] vi to think // vt to think; (concevoir: problème, machine) to think out; ~ à to think of; (songer à: ami, vacances) to think of ou about; (réfléchir à: problème, offre): ~ à qch to think about sth ou think sth over; faire ~ à to remind one of; ~ faire qch to be thinking of doing sth, intend to do sth.

pension [pɑ̃sjɔ̃] nf (allocation) pension; (prix du logement) board and lodgings, bed and board; (maison particulière) boarding house; (hôtel) guesthouse, hotel; (école) boarding school; prendre qn en ~ to take sb (in) as a lodger; mettre en ~ to send to boarding school; ~ alimentaire (d'étudiant) living allowance; (de divorcée) maintenance allowance; alimony; ~ complète full board; ~ de famille boarding house, guesthouse; **pensionnaire** nm/f boarder; guest; **pensionnat** nm boarding school.

pente [pɑ̃t] nf slope; en ~ a sloping.

Pentecôte [pɑ̃tkot] nf: la ~ Whitsun (Brit), Pentecost.

pénurie [penyʀi] nf shortage.

pépé [pepe] nm (fam) grandad.

pépin [pepɛ̃] nm (BOT: graine) pip; (ennui) snag, hitch.

pépinière [pepinjɛʀ] nf nursery.

perçant, e [pɛʀsɑ̃, -ɑ̃t] a sharp, keen; piercing, shrill.

percée [pɛʀse] nf (trouée) opening; (MIL, technologique) breakthrough; (SPORT) break.

perce-neige [pɛʀsənɛʒ] nf inv snowdrop.

percepteur [pɛʀsɛptœʀ] nm tax collector.

perception [pɛʀsɛpsjɔ̃] nf perception;

(d'impôts etc) collection; (bureau) tax office.

percer [pɛʀse] vt to pierce; (ouverture etc) to make; (mystère, énigme) to penetrate // vi to come through; to break through; ~ une dent to cut a tooth.

perceuse [pɛʀsøz] nf drill.

percevoir [pɛʀsəvwaʀ] vt (distinguer) to perceive, detect; (taxe, impôt) to collect; (revenu, indemnité) to receive.

perche [pɛʀʃ(ə)] nf (bâton) pole.

percher [pɛʀʃe] vt: ~ qch sur to perch sth on // vi, se ~ vi (oiseau) to perch; **perchoir** nm perch.

perçois etc vb voir **percevoir**.

percolateur [pɛʀkɔlatœʀ] nm percolator.

perçu, e pp de **percevoir**.

percussion [pɛʀkysjɔ̃] nf percussion.

percuter [pɛʀkyte] vt to strike; (suj: véhicule) to crash into.

perdant, e [pɛʀdɑ̃, -ɑ̃t] nm/f loser.

perdition [pɛʀdisjɔ̃] nf: en ~ (NAVIG) in distress; lieu de ~ den of vice.

perdre [pɛʀdʀ(ə)] vt to lose; (gaspiller: temps, argent) to waste; (personne: moralement etc) to ruin // vi to lose; (sur une vente etc) to lose out; se ~ vi (s'égarer) to get lost, lose one's way; (fig) to go to waste; to disappear, vanish.

perdrix [pɛʀdʀi] nf partridge.

perdu, e [pɛʀdy] pp de **perdre** // a (isolé) out-of-the-way; (COMM: emballage) non-returnable; (malade): il est ~ there's no hope left for him; à vos moments ~s in your spare time.

père [pɛʀ] nm father; ~s (ancêtres) forefathers; ~ de famille father; family man; le ~ Noël Father Christmas.

perfectionné, e [pɛʀfɛksjɔne] a sophisticated.

perfectionner [pɛʀfɛksjɔne] vt to improve, perfect.

perforatrice [pɛʀfɔʀatʀis] nf (pour cartes) card-punch; (de bureau) punch.

perforer [pɛʀfɔʀe] vt to perforate; to punch a hole (ou holes) in; (ticket, bande, carte) to punch.

performant, e [pɛʀfɔʀmɑ̃, -ɑ̃t] a: très ~ high-performance cpd.

perfusion [pɛʀfyzjɔ̃] nf: faire une ~ à qn to put sb on a drip.

péril [peʀil] nm peril.

périmé, e [peʀime] a (out)dated; (ADMIN) out-of-date, expired.

périmètre [peʀimɛtʀ(ə)] nm perimeter.

période [peʀjɔd] nf period; **périodique** a (phases) periodic; (publication) periodical // nm periodical.

péripéties [peʀipesi] nfpl events, episodes.

périphérique [peʀifeʀik] a (quartiers) outlying; (ANAT, TECH) peripheral; (station de radio) operating from outside

France // nm (AUTO) ring road; (IN-FORM) peripheral.

périple [peripl(ə)] nm journey.

périr [perir] vi to die, perish.

périssable [perisabl(ə)] a perishable.

perle [perl(ə)] nf pearl; (de plastique, métal, sueur) bead.

perlé, e [perle] a: grève ~e go-slow.

perler [perle] vi to form in droplets.

permanence [permanãs] nf permanence; (local) (duty) office; emergency service; **assurer une ~** (service public, bureaux) to operate ou maintain a basic service; **être de ~** to be on call ou duty; **en ~** ad permanently; continuously.

permanent, e [permanã, -ãt] a permanent; (spectacle) continuous // nf perm.

perméable [permeabl(ə)] a (terrain) permeable; **~ à** (fig) receptive ou open to.

permettre [permetr(ə)] vt to allow, permit; **~ à qn de faire/qch** to allow sb to do/sth; **se ~ de faire** to take the liberty of doing; **permettez!** excuse me!

permis [permi] nm permit, licence; **~ de chasse** hunting permit; **~ (de conduire)** (driving) licence (Brit), (driver's) license (US); **~ de construire** planning permission (Brit), building permit (US); **~ d'inhumer** burial certificate; **~ de séjour** residence permit; **~ de travail** work permit.

permission [permisjõ] nf permission; (MIL) leave; **en ~** on leave; **avoir la ~ de faire** to have permission to do.

permuter [permyte] vt to change around, permutate // vi to change, swap.

Pérou [peru] nm Peru.

perpétuel, le [perpetɥɛl] a perpetual; (ADMIN etc) permanent; for life.

perpétuité [perpetɥite] nf: **à ~** a, ad for life; **être condamné à ~** to receive a life sentence.

perplexe [perpleks(ə)] a perplexed, puzzled.

perquisitionner [perkizisjɔne] vi to carry out a search.

perron [perõ] nm steps pl (in front of mansion etc).

perroquet [perɔkɛ] nm parrot.

perruche [peryʃ] nf budgerigar (Brit), budgie (Brit), parakeet (US).

perruque [peryk] nf wig.

persan, e [persã, -an] a Persian.

persécuter [persekyte] vt to persecute.

persévérer [persevere] vi to persevere.

persiennes [persjɛn] nfpl (metal) shutters.

persiflage [persiflaʒ] nm mockery q.

persil [persi] nm parsley.

Persique [persik] a: **le golfe ~** the (Persian) Gulf.

persistant, e [persistã, -ãt] a persistent; (feuilles) evergreen.

persister [persiste] vi to persist; **~ à faire qch** to persist in doing sth.

personnage [persɔnaʒ] nm (notable) personality; figure; (individu) character, individual; (THÉÂTRE) character; (PEINTURE) figure.

personnalité [persɔnalite] nf personality; (personnage) prominent figure.

personne [persɔn] nf person // pronom nobody, no one; (quelqu'un) anybody, anyone; **~s** people pl; **il n'y a ~** there's nobody there, there isn't anybody there; **~ âgée** elderly person; **personnel, le** a personal // nm staff, personnel; **personnellement** ad personally.

perspective [perspektiv] nf (ART) perspective; (vue, coup d'œil) view; (point de vue) viewpoint, angle; (chose escomptée, envisagée) prospect; **en ~** in prospect.

perspicace [perspikas] a clear-sighted, gifted with (ou showing) insight.

persuader [persɥade] vt: **~ qn (de/de faire)** to persuade sb (of/to do).

perte [pert(ə)] nf loss; (de temps) waste; (fig: morale) ruin; **à ~** at a loss; **à ~ de vue** as far as the eye can (ou could) see; **~ sèche** dead loss; **~s blanches** (vaginal) discharge sg.

pertinemment [pertinamã] ad to the point; full well.

pertinent, e [pertinã, -ãt] a apt, relevant.

perturbation [pertyrbasjõ] nf disruption; perturbation; **~ (atmosphérique)** atmospheric disturbance.

perturber [pertyrbe] vt to disrupt; (PSYCH) to perturb, disturb.

pervers, e [perver, -ers(ə)] a perverted, depraved; perverse.

pervertir [pervertir] vt to pervert.

pesant, e [pəzã, -ãt] a heavy; (fig) burdensome.

pesanteur [pəzãtœr] nf gravity.

pèse-personne [pezpersɔn] nm (bathroom) scales pl.

peser [pəze] vt, vb avec attribut to weigh // vi to be heavy; (fig) to carry weight; **~ sur** (fig) to lie heavy on; to influence.

pessimiste [pesimist(ə)] a pessimistic // nm/f pessimist.

peste [pest(ə)] nf plague.

pester [peste] vi: **~ contre** to curse.

pétale [petal] nm petal.

pétanque [petãk] nf type of bowls.

pétarader [petarade] vi to backfire.

pétard [petar] nm banger (Brit), firecracker.

péter [pete] vi (fam: casser, sauter) to burst; to bust; (fam!) to fart (!).

pétiller [petije] vi (flamme, bois) to crackle; (mousse, champagne) to bubble; (yeux) to sparkle.

petit, e [pəti, -it] a (gén) small; (main,

objet, colline, en âge: enfant) small, little; *(voyage)* short, little; *(bruit etc)* faint, slight; *(mesquin)* mean // *nmpl* *(d'un animal)* young *pl*; **faire des ~s** to have kittens *(ou* puppies *etc)*; **les tout-petits** the little ones, the tiny tots; **~ à ~** bit by bit, gradually; **~(e) ami/e** boyfriend/girlfriend; **les ~es annonces** the small ads; **~ déjeuner** breakfast; **~ pain** (bread) roll; **~s pois** garden peas; **~-bourgeois, ~e-bourgeoise** *a (péj)* middle-class; **~e-fille** *nf* granddaughter; **~-fils** *nm* grandson; **~s-enfants** *nmpl* grandchildren.

pétition [petisjɔ̃] *nf* petition.

pétrin [petʀɛ̃] *nm* kneading-trough; *(fig)*: **dans le ~** in a jam *ou* fix.

pétrir [petʀiʀ] *vt* to knead.

pétrole [petʀɔl] *nm* oil; *(pour lampe, réchaud etc)* paraffin (oil); **pétrolier, ière** *a* oil *cpd* // *nm* oil tanker.

peu [pø] ♦ *ad* **1** *(modifiant verbe, adjectif, adverbe)*: **il boit ~** he doesn't drink (very) much; **il est ~ bavard** he's not very talkative; **~ avant/après** shortly before/afterwards
2 *(modifiant nom)*: **~ de: ~ de gens/d'arbres** few *ou* not (very) many people/trees; **il a ~ d'espoir** he hasn't (got) much hope, he has little hope; **pour ~ de temps** for (only) a short while
3: **~ à ~** little by little; **à ~ près** just about, more or less; **à ~ près 10 kg/10 F** approximately 10 kg/10 F
♦ *nm* **1**: **le ~ de gens qui** the few people who; **le ~ de sable qui** what little sand, the little sand which
2: **un ~ a** little; **un petit ~ a** little bit; **un ~ d'espoir** a little hope
♦ *pronom*: **~ le savent** few know (it); **avant *ou* sous ~** shortly, before long; **de ~** (only) just.

peuple [pœpl(ə)] *nm* people.

peupler [pœple] *vt (pays, région)* to populate; *(étang)* to stock; *(suj: hommes, poissons)* to inhabit; *(fig: imagination, rêves)* to fill.

peuplier [pøplije] *nm* poplar (tree).

peur [pœʀ] *nf* fear; **avoir ~ (de/de faire/que)** to be frightened *ou* afraid (of/of doing/that); **faire ~ à** to frighten; **de ~ de/que** for fear of/that; **~eux, euse** *a* fearful, timorous.

peut *vb voir* **pouvoir.**

peut-être [pøtɛtʀ(ə)] *ad* perhaps, maybe; **~ que** perhaps, maybe; **~ bien qu'il fera/est** he may well do/be.

peux *etc vb voir* **pouvoir.**

phare [faʀ] *nm (en mer)* lighthouse; *(de véhicule)* headlight; **mettre ses ~s** to put on one's headlights; **~s de recul** reversing lights.

pharmacie [faʀmasi] *nf (magasin)* chemist's *(Brit)*, pharmacy; *(officine)* dispensary; *(de salle de bain)* medicine

cabinet; **pharmacien, ne** *nm/f* pharmacist, chemist *(Brit)*.

phase [faz] *nf* phase.

phénomène [fenɔmɛn] *nm* phenomenon *(pl a)*; *(monstre)* freak.

philanthrope [filɑ̃tʀɔp] *nm/f* philanthropist.

philosophe [filɔzɔf] *nm/f* philosopher // *a* philosophical.

philosophie [filɔzɔfi] *nf* philosophy; **philosophique** *a* philosophical.

phobie [fɔbi] *nf* phobia.

phonétique [fɔnetik] *nf* phonetics *sg*.

phoque [fɔk] *nm* seal; *(fourrure)* sealskin.

phosphorescent, e [fɔsfɔʀesɑ̃, -ɑ̃t] *a* luminous.

photo [fɔto] *nf* photo(graph); **en ~** in *ou* on a photograph; **prendre en ~** to take a photo of; **aimer la/faire de la ~** to like taking/take photos; **~ d'identité** passport photograph.

photo... [fɔto] *préfixe*: **~copie** *nf* photocopying; photocopy; **~copier** *vt* to photocopy; **~graphe** *nm/f* photographer; **~graphie** *nf (procédé, technique)* photography; *(cliché)* photograph; **~graphier** *vt* to photograph.

phrase [fʀaz] *nf (LING)* sentence; *(propos, MUS)* phrase.

physicien, ne [fizisjɛ̃, -ɛn] *nm/f* physicist.

physionomie [fizjɔnɔmi] *nf* face.

physique [fizik] *a* physical // *nm* physique // *nf* physics *sg*; **au ~** physically; **~ment** *ad* physically.

piaffer [pjafe] *vi* to stamp.

piailler [pjaje] *vi* to squawk.

pianiste [pjanist(ə)] *nm/f* pianist.

piano [pjano] *nm* piano.

pianoter [pjanɔte] *vi* to tinkle away (at the piano); *(tapoter)*: **~ sur** to drum one's fingers on.

pic [pik] *nm (instrument)* pick(axe); *(montagne)* peak; *(ZOOL)* woodpecker; **à ~** *ad* vertically; *(fig)* just at the right time.

pichet [piʃɛ] *nm* jug.

picorer [pikɔʀe] *vt* to peck.

picoter [pikɔte] *vt (suj: oiseau)* to peck // *vi (irriter)* to smart, prickle.

pie [pi] *nf* magpie; *(fig)* chatterbox.

pièce [pjɛs] *nf (d'un logement)* room; *(THÉÂTRE)* play; *(de mécanisme, machine)* part; *(de monnaie)* coin; *(COUTURE)* patch; *(document)* document; *(de drap, fragment, de collection)* piece; **dix francs ~** ten francs each; **vendre à la ~** to sell separately; **travailler/payer à la ~** to do piecework/pay piece rate; **un maillot une ~** a one-piece swimsuit; **un deux-~s cuisine** a two-room(ed) flat *(Brit)* *ou* apartment *(US)* with kitchen; **~ à conviction** exhibit; **~ d'eau** ornamental lake *ou* pond; **~ d'identité**:

avez-vous une ~ d'identité? have you got any (means of) identification?; ~ montée tiered cake; ~s détachées spares, (spare) parts; ~s justificatives supporting documents.

pied [pje] *nm* foot (*pl* feet); (*de verre*) stem; (*de table*) leg; (*de lampe*) base; (*plante*) plant; à ~ on foot; à ~ sec without getting one's feet wet; au ~ de la lettre literally; de ~ en cap from head to foot; en ~ (*portrait*) full-length; avoir ~ to be able to touch the bottom, not to be out of one's depth; avoir le ~ marin to be a good sailor; sur ~ (*debout, rétabli*) up and about; mettre sur ~ (*entreprise*) to set up; mettre à ~ to dismiss; to lay off; ~ de vigne vine.

piédestal, aux [pjedɛstal, -o] *nm* pedestal.

pied-noir [pjenwaʀ] *nm Algerian-born Frenchman.*

piège [pjɛʒ] *nm* trap; prendre au ~ to trap; **piéger** *vt* (*avec une bombe*) to booby-trap; lettre/voiture piégée letter-/car-bomb.

pierraille [pjɛʀɑj] *nf* loose stones *pl.*

pierre [pjɛʀ] *nf* stone; ~ à briquet flint; ~ fine semiprecious stone; ~ de taille freestone *q*; ~ tombale tombstone.

pierreries [pjɛʀʀi] *nfpl* gems, precious stones.

piétiner [pjetine] *vi* (*trépigner*) to stamp (one's foot); (*marquer le pas*) to stand about; (*fig*) to be at a standstill // *vt* to trample on.

piéton, ne [pjetɔ̃, -ɔn] *nm/f* pedestrian; **piétonnier, ière** *a*: rue/zone piétonnière pedestrian precinct.

pieu, x [pjø] *nm* post; (*pointu*) stake.

pieuvre [pjœvʀ(ə)] *nf* octopus.

pieux, euse [pjø, -øz] *a* pious.

piffer [pife] *vt* (*fam*): je ne peux pas le ~ I can't stand him.

pigeon [piʒɔ̃] *nm* pigeon.

piger [piʒe] *vi, vt* (*fam*) to understand.

pigiste [piʒist(ə)] *nm/f* freelance(r).

pignon [piɲɔ̃] *nm* (*de mur*) gable; (*d'engrenage*) cog(wheel), gearwheel.

pile [pil] *nf* (*tas*) pile; (*ÉLEC*) battery // *ad* (*s'arrêter etc*) dead; à deux heures ~ at two on the dot; jouer à ~ ou face to toss up (for it); ~ ou face? heads or tails?

piler [pile] *vt* to crush, pound.

pileux, euse [pilø, -øz] *a*: système ~ (body) hair.

pilier [pilje] *nm* pillar.

piller [pije] *vt* to pillage, plunder, loot.

pilon [pilɔ̃] *nm* pestle.

pilote [pilɔt] *nm* pilot; (*de char, voiture*) driver // *a* pilot *cpd*; ~ de ligne/d'essai/ de chasse airline/test/fighter pilot; ~ de course racing driver.

piloter [pilɔte] *vt* to pilot, fly; to drive.

pilule [pilyl] *nf* pill; prendre la ~ to be on the pill.

piment [pimɑ̃] *nm* (*BOT*) pepper, capsicum; (*fig*) spice, piquancy.

pimpant, e [pɛ̃pɑ̃, -ɑ̃t] *a* spruce.

pin [pɛ̃] *nm* pine (tree); (*bois*) pine(wood).

pinard [pinaʀ] *nm* (*fam*) (cheap) wine, plonk (*Brit*).

pince [pɛ̃s] *nf* (*outil*) pliers *pl*; (*de homard, crabe*) pincer, claw; (*COUTURE: pli*) dart; ~ à sucre/glace sugar/ ice tongs *pl*; ~ à épiler tweezers *pl*; ~ à linge clothes peg (*Brit*) ou pin (*US*).

pincé, e [pɛ̃se] *a* (*air*) stiff // *nf*: une ~e de a pinch of.

pinceau, x [pɛ̃so] *nm* (paint)brush.

pincer [pɛ̃se] *vt* to pinch; (*MUS: cordes*) to pluck; (*fam*) to nab.

pincettes [pɛ̃sɛt] *nfpl* (*pour le feu*) (fire) tongs.

pinède [pinɛd] *nf* pinewood, pine forest.

pingouin [pɛ̃gwɛ̃] *nm* penguin.

ping-pong [piŋpɔ̃g] *nm* table tennis.

pingre [pɛ̃gʀ(ə)] *a* niggardly.

pinson [pɛ̃sɔ̃] *nm* chaffinch.

pintade [pɛ̃tad] *nf* guinea-fowl.

pioche [pjɔʃ] *nf* pickaxe; **piocher** *vt* to dig up (with a pickaxe).

piolet [pjɔlɛ] *nm* ice axe.

pion [pjɔ̃] *nm* (*ÉCHECS*) pawn; (*DAMES*) piece.

pionnier [pjɔnje] *nm* pioneer.

pipe [pip] *nf* pipe.

pipeau, x [pipo] *nm* (reed-)pipe.

piquant, e [pikɑ̃, -ɑ̃t] *a* (*barbe, rosier etc*) prickly; (*saveur, sauce*) hot, pungent; (*fig*) racy; biting // *nm* (*épine*) thorn, prickle; (*fig*) spiciness, spice.

pique [pik] *nf* pike; cutting remark // *nm* (*CARTES: couleur*) spades *pl*; (*: carte*) spade.

pique-nique [piknik] *nm* picnic.

piquer [pike] *vt* (*percer*) to prick; (*planter*): ~ qch dans to stick sth into; (*MÉD*) to give a jab to; (*: animal blessé etc*) to put to sleep; (*suj: insecte, fumée, ortie*) to sting; (*suj: poivre*) to burn; (*: froid*) to bite; (*COUTURE*) to machine (stitch); (*intérêt etc*) to arouse; (*fam*) to pick up; (*: voler*) to pinch; (*: arrêter*) to nab // *vi* (*avion*) to go into a dive; se ~ de faire to pride o.s. on doing; ~ un galop/un cent mètres to break into a gallop/put on a sprint.

piquet [pikɛ] *nm* (*pieu*) post, stake; (*de tente*) peg; ~ de grève (strike-)picket; ~ d'incendie fire-fighting squad.

piqûre [pikyʀ] *nf* (*d'épingle*) prick; (*d'ortie*) sting; (*de moustique*) bite; (*MÉD*) injection, shot (*US*); (*COUTURE*) (straight) stitch; straight stitching; faire une ~ à qn to give sb an injection.

pirate [piʀat] *nm, a* pirate; ~ de l'air hijacker.

pire [piʀ] *a* worse; (*superlatif*): le(la) ~ ... the worst ... // *nm*: le ~ (de) the worst (of).

pis [pi] *nm* (*de vache*) udder; (*pire*): le ~ the worst // *a, ad* worse; **pis-aller** *nm inv* stopgap.

piscine [pisin] *nf* (swimming) pool; ~ couverte indoor (swimming) pool.

pissenlit [pisɑ̃li] *nm* dandelion.

pistache [pistaʃ] *nf* pistachio (nut).

piste [pist(ə)] *nf* (*d'un animal, sentier*) track, trail; (*indice*) lead; (*de stade, de magnétophone*) track; (*de cirque*) ring; (*de danse*) floor; (*de patinage*) rink; (*de ski*) run; (*AVIAT*) runway; ~ **cyclable** cycle track.

pistolet [pistɔlɛ] *nm* (*arme*) pistol, gun; (*à peinture*) spray gun; ~ **à air comprimé** airgun; ~**-mitrailleur** *nm* submachine gun.

piston [pistɔ̃] *nm* (*TECH*) piston; **pistonner** *vt* (*candidat*) to pull strings for.

piteux, euse [pitø, -øz] *a* pitiful, sorry (*avant le nom*).

pitié [pitje] *nf* pity; **faire** ~ to inspire pity; **avoir** ~ **de** (*compassion*) to pity, feel sorry for; (*merci*) to have pity *ou* mercy on.

piton [pitɔ̃] *nm* (*clou*) peg; ~ **rocheux** rocky outcrop.

pitoyable [pitwajabl(ə)] *a* pitiful.

pitre [pitʀ(ə)] *nm* clown; **pitrerie** *nf* tomfoolery *q*.

pittoresque [pitɔʀɛsk(ə)] *a* picturesque.

pivot [pivo] *nm* pivot; **pivoter** *vi* to swivel; to revolve.

P.J. *sigle f voir* **police**.

placard [plakaʀ] *nm* (*armoire*) cupboard; (*affiche*) poster, notice; **placarder** *vt* (*affiche*) to put up.

place [plas] *nf* (*emplacement, situation, classement*) place; (*de ville, village*) square; (*espace libre*) room, space; (*de parking*) space; (*siège: de train, cinéma, voiture*) seat; (*emploi*) job; en ~ (*mettre*) in its place; **sur** ~ on the spot; **faire** ~ **à** to give way to; **faire de la** ~ **à** to make room for; **ça prend de la** ~ it takes up a lot of room *ou* space; **à la** ~ **de** in place of, instead of; **il y a** **20** ~**s assises/debout** there are 20 seats/there is standing room for 20.

placement [plasmɑ̃] *nm* placing; (*FINANCE*) investment; **bureau de** ~ employment agency.

placer [plase] *vt* to place; (*convive, spectateur*) to seat; (*capital, argent*) to place, invest; (*dans la conversation*) to put *ou* get in; **se** ~ **au premier rang** *ou* to go and stand (*ou* sit) in the first row.

plafond [plafɔ̃] *nm* ceiling.

plafonner [plafɔne] *vi* to reach one's (*ou* a) ceiling.

plage [plaʒ] *nf* beach; (*fig*) band, brack-

et; (*de disque*) track, band; ~ **arrière** (*AUTO*) parcel *ou* back shelf.

plagiat [plaʒja] *nm* plagiarism.

plaider [plede] *vi* (*avocat*) to plead; (*plaignant*) to go to court, litigate // *vt* to plead; ~ **pour** (*fig*) to speak for; **plaidoyer** *nm* (*JUR*) speech for the defence; (*fig*) plea.

plaie [plɛ] *nf* wound.

plaignant, e [plɛɲɑ̃, -ɑ̃t] *nm/f* plaintiff.

plaindre [plɛ̃dʀ(ə)] *vt* to pity, feel sorry for; **se** ~ *vi* (*gémir*) to moan; (*protester, rouspéter*): **se** ~ (**à qn**) (**de**) to complain (to sb) (about); (*souffrir*): **se** ~ **de** to complain of.

plaine [plɛn] *nf* plain.

plain-pied [plɛ̃pje]: **de** ~ (**avec**) on the same level (as).

plainte [plɛ̃t] *nf* (*gémissement*) moan, groan; (*doléance*) complaint; **porter** ~ to lodge a complaint.

plaire [plɛʀ] *vi* to be a success, be successful; to please; ~ **à**: **cela me plaît** I like it; **se** ~ **quelque part** to like being somewhere *ou* like it somewhere; **s'il vous plaît** please.

plaisance [plɛzɑ̃s] *nf* (*aussi:* **navigation de** ~) (pleasure) sailing, yachting.

plaisant, e [plɛzɑ̃, -ɑ̃t] *a* pleasant; (*histoire, anecdote*) amusing.

plaisanter [plɛzɑ̃te] *vi* to joke; **plaisanterie** *nf* joke; joking *q*.

plaise *etc vb voir* **plaire**.

plaisir [plɛziʀ] *nm* pleasure; **faire** ~ **à qn** (*délibérément*) to be nice to sb, please sb; (*suj: cadeau, nouvelle etc*): **ceci me fait** ~ I'm delighted *ou* very pleased with this; **pour le** *ou* **par** ~ for pleasure.

plaît *vb voir* **plaire**.

plan, e [plɑ̃, -an] *a* flat // *nm* plan; (*GÉOM*) plane; (*fig*) level, plane; (*CINÉMA*) shot; **au premier/second** ~ in the foreground/middle distance; **à l'arrière** ~ in the background; ~ **d'eau** lake; pond.

planche [plɑ̃ʃ] *nf* (*pièce de bois*) plank, (wooden) board; (*illustration*) plate; **les** ~**s** (*THÉÂTRE*) the stage *sg*, the boards; ~ **à repasser** ironing board; ~ **à roulettes** skateboard; ~ **de salut** (*fig*) sheet anchor.

plancher [plɑ̃ʃe] *nm* floor; floorboards *pl*; (*fig*) minimum level // *vi* to work hard.

planer [plane] *vi* to glide; ~ **sur** (*fig*) to hang over; to hover above.

planète [planɛt] *nf* planet.

planeur [planœʀ] *nm* glider.

planification [planifikasjɔ̃] *nf* (economic) planning.

planifier [planifje] *vt* to plan.

planning [planiŋ] *nm* programme, schedule; ~ **familial** family planning.

plant [plɑ̃] *nm* seedling, young plant.

plante [plãt] *nf* plant; ~ **d'appartement** house *ou* pot plant; ~ **du pied** sole (of the foot).

planter [plãte] *vt* (*plante*) to plant; (*enfoncer*) to hammer *ou* drive in; (*tente*) to put up, pitch; (*fam*) to dump; to ditch; **se** ~ (*fam: se tromper*) to get it wrong.

plantureux, euse [plãtyʁø, -øz] *a* copious, lavish; (*femme*) buxom.

plaque [plak] *nf* plate; (*de verglas, d'eczéma*) patch; (*avec inscription*) plaque; ~ **(minéralogique** *ou* **d'immatriculation)** number (*Brit*) *ou* license (*US*) plate; ~ **chauffante** hotplate; ~ **de chocolat** bar of chocolate; ~ **d'identité** identity disc; ~ **tournante** (*fig*) centre.

plaqué, e [plake] *a*: ~ **or/argent** gold-/ silver-plated; ~ **acajou** veneered in mahogany.

plaquer [plake] *vt* (*aplatir*): ~ **qch sur/ contre** to make sth stick *ou* cling to; (*RUGBY*) to bring down; (*fam: laisser tomber*) to drop.

plastic [plastik] *nm* plastic explosive.

plastique [plastik] *a, nm* plastic.

plastiquer [plastike] *vt* to blow up (*with a plastic bomb*).

plat, e [pla, -at] *a* flat; (*cheveux*) straight; (*personne, livre*) dull // *nm* (*récipient, CULIN*) dish; (*d'un repas*): **le premier** ~ the first course; **à** ~ **ventre** *ad* face down; **à** ~ *a* (*pneu, batterie*) flat; (*personne*) dead beat; ~ **cuisiné** pre-cooked meal; ~ **du jour** day's special (*menu*); ~ **de résistance** main course.

platane [platan] *nm* plane tree.

plateau, x [plato] *nm* (*support*) tray; (*GÉO*) plateau; (*de tourne-disques*) turntable; (*CINÉMA*) set; ~ **à fromages** cheeseboard.

plate-bande [platbãd] *nf* flower bed.

plate-forme [platfɔʀm(ə)] *nf* platform; ~ **de forage/pétrolière** drilling/oil rig.

platine [platin] *nm* platinum // *nf* (*d'un tourne-disque*) turntable.

plâtras [plɑtʀa] *nm* rubble *q*.

plâtre [plɑtʀ(ə)] *nm* (*matériau*) plaster; (*statue*) plaster statue; (*MÉD*) (plaster) cast; **avoir un bras dans le** ~ to have an arm in plaster.

plein, e [plɛ̃, -ɛn] *a* full; (*porte, roue*) solid; (*chienne, jument*) big (with young) // *nm*: **faire le** ~ **(d'essence)** to fill up (with petrol); **à** ~**es mains** (*ramasser*) in handfuls; (*empoigner*) firmly; **à** ~ **régime** at maximum revs; (*fig*) full steam; **à** ~ **temps** full-time; **en** ~ **air** in the open air; **en** ~ **soleil** in direct sunlight; **en** ~ **nuit/rue** in the middle of the night/street; **en** ~ **jour** in broad daylight; **en** ~ **sur** right on; ~**-emploi** *nm* full employment.

plénitude [plenityd] *nf* fullness.

pleurer [plœʀe] *vi* to cry; (*yeux*) to wa-

ter // *vt* to mourn (for); ~ **sur** *vt* to lament (over), to bemoan.

pleurnicher [plœʀniʃe] *vi* to snivel, whine.

pleurs [plœʀ] *nmpl*: **en** ~ in tears.

pleut *vb voir* **pleuvoir**.

pleuvoir [pløvwaʀ] *vb impersonnel* to rain // *vi* (*fig*): ~ (**sur**) to shower down (upon); to be showered upon; **il pleut** it's raining.

pli [pli] *nm* fold; (*de jupe*) pleat; (*de pantalon*) crease; (*aussi*: **faux** ~) crease; (*enveloppe*) envelope; (*lettre*) letter; (*CARTES*) trick.

pliant, e [plijã, -ãt] *a* folding // *nm* folding stool, campstool.

plier [plije] *vt* to fold; (*pour ranger*) to fold up; (*table pliante*) to fold down; (*genou, bras*) to bend // *vi* to bend; (*fig*) to yield; **se** ~ **à** to submit to.

plinthe [plɛ̃t] *nf* skirting board.

plisser [plise] *vt* (*rider, chiffonner*) to crease; (*jupe*) to put pleats in.

plomb [plɔ̃] *nm* (*métal*) lead; (*d'une cartouche*) (lead) shot; (*PÊCHE*) sinker; (*sceau*) (lead) seal; (*ÉLEC*) fuse.

plombage [plɔ̃baʒ] *nm* (*de dent*) filling.

plomber [plɔ̃be] *vt* (*canne, ligne*) to weight (with lead); (*dent*) to fill.

plomberie [plɔ̃bʀi] *nf* plumbing.

plombier [plɔ̃bje] *nm* plumber.

plongeant, e [plɔ̃ʒã, -ãt] *a* (*vue*) from above; (*tir, décolleté*) plunging.

plongée [plɔ̃ʒe] *nf* (*SPORT*) diving *q*; (*:* *sans scaphandre*) skin diving.

plongeoir [plɔ̃ʒwaʀ] *nm* diving board.

plongeon [plɔ̃ʒɔ̃] *nm* dive.

plonger [plɔ̃ʒe] *vi* to dive // *vt*: ~ **qch dans** to plunge sth into.

ployer [plwaje] *vt* to bend // *vi* to sag; to bend.

plu *pp de* **plaire, pleuvoir**.

pluie [plɥi] *nf* rain; (*fig*): ~ **de** shower of.

plume [plym] *nf* feather; (*pour écrire*) (pen) nib; (*fig*) pen.

plumer [plyme] *vt* to pluck.

plumier [plymje] *nm* pencil box.

plupart [plypaʀ]: **la** ~ *pronom* the majority, most (of them); **la** ~ **des** most, the majority of; **la** ~ **du temps/d'entre nous** most of the time/of us; **pour la** ~ *ad* for the most part, mostly.

pluriel [plyʀjɛl] *nm* plural.

plus ♦ *vb* [ply] *voir* **plaire**

♦ *ad* **1** [ply] (*forme négative*): **ne ... ** ~ no more, no longer; **je n'ai** ~ **d'argent** I've got no more money *ou* no money left; **il ne travaille** ~ he's no longer working, he doesn't work any more
2 [ply, plyz + *voyelle*] (*comparatif*) more, ...+er; (*superlatif*): **le** ~ **the** most, **the** ...+est; ~ **grand/intelligent (que)** bigger/more intelligent (than); **le** ~

grand/intelligent the biggest/most intelligent; **tout au ~** at the very most
3 [plys] (*davantage*) more; **il travaille ~ (que)** he works more (than); **~ il travaille, ~ il est heureux** the more he works, the happier he is; **~ de pain** more bread; **~ de 10 personnes** more than 10 people, over 10 people; **3 heures de ~ que** 3 hours more than; **de ~** what's more, moreover; **3 kilos en ~** 3 kilos more; **en ~ de** in addition to; **de ~ en ~** more and more; **~ ou moins** more or less; **ni ~ ni moins** no more, no less ♦ *prép* [plys]: **4 ~ 2** 4 plus 2.

plusieurs [plyzjœʀ] *dét, pronom* several; **ils sont ~** there are several of them.

plus-que-parfait [plyskəpaʀfɛ] *nm* pluperfect, past perfect.

plus-value [plyvaly] *nf* appreciation; capital gain; surplus.

plut *vb voir* **plaire**.

plutôt [plyto] *ad* rather; **je ferais ~ ceci** I'd rather *ou* sooner do this; **fais ~ comme ça** try this way instead, you'd better try this way; **~ que (de) faire** rather than *ou* instead of doing.

pluvieux, euse [plyvjø, -øz] *a* rainy, wet.

PMU *sigle m* (= *pari mutuel urbain*) *system of betting on horses*; (*café*) betting agency.

pneu [pnø] *nm* tyre (*Brit*), tire (*US*).

pneumatique [pnømatik] *nm* tyre (*Brit*), tire (*US*).

pneumonie [pnømɔni] *nf* pneumonia.

poche [pɔʃ] *nf* pocket; (*déformation*): **faire une/des ~(s)** to bag; (*sous les yeux*) bag, pouch; **de ~** pocket *cpd*.

pocher [pɔʃe] *vt* (*CULIN*) to poach.

pochette [pɔʃɛt] *nf* (*de timbres*) wallet, envelope; (*d'aiguilles etc*) case; (*mouchoir*) breast pocket handkerchief; **~ de disque** record sleeve.

pochoir [pɔʃwaʀ] *nm* (*ART*) stencil.

poêle [pwal] *nm* stove // *nf*: **~ (à frire)** frying pan.

poêlon [pwalɔ̃] *nm* casserole.

poème [pɔɛm] *nm* poem.

poésie [pɔezi] *nf* (*poème*) poem; (*art*): **la ~** poetry.

poète [pɔɛt] *nm* poet.

poids [pwa] *nm* weight; (*SPORT*) shot; **vendre au ~** to sell by weight; **prendre du ~** to put on weight; **~ lourd** (*camion*) lorry (*Brit*), truck (*US*).

poignard [pwaɲaʀ] *nm* dagger; **poignarder** *vt* to stab, knife.

poigne [pwaɲ] *nf* grip; (*fig*): **à ~** firmhanded.

poignée [pwaɲe] *nf* (*de sel etc, fig*) handful; (*de couvercle, porte*) handle; **~ de main** handshake.

poignet [pwaɲɛ] *nm* (*ANAT*) wrist; (*de chemise*) cuff.

poil [pwal] *nm* (*ANAT*) hair; (*de pinceau, brosse*) bristle; (*de tapis*) strand; (*pelage*) coat; **à ~** *a* (*fam*) starkers; **au ~** *a* (*fam*) hunky-dory; **poilu, e** *a* hairy.

poinçon [pwɛ̃sɔ̃] *nm* awl; bodkin; (*marque*) hallmark; **poinçonner** *vt* to stamp; to hallmark; (*billet*) to punch.

poing [pwɛ̃] *nm* fist.

point [pwɛ̃] *nm* (*marque, signe*) dot; (: *de ponctuation*) full stop, period (*US*); (*moment, de score etc, fig*: question) point; (*endroit*) spot; (*COUTURE, TRICOT*) stitch // **ad = pas; faire le ~** (*NAVIG*) to take a bearing; (*fig*) to take stock (of the situation); **en tout ~** in every respect; **sur le ~ de faire** (just) about to do; **à tel ~ que** so much so that; **mettre au ~** (*mécanisme, procédé*) to develop; (*appareil-photo*) to focus; (*affaire*) to settle; **à ~** (*CULIN*) medium; just right; **à ~ (nommé)** just at the right time; **~ (de côté)** stitch (*pain*); **~ d'eau** spring; water point; **~ d'exclamation** exclamation mark; **~ faible** weak point; **~ final** full stop, period; **~ d'interrogation** question mark; **~ mort** (*AUTO*): **au ~ mort** in neutral; **~ de repère** landmark; (*dans le temps*) point of reference; **~ de vente** retail outlet; **~ de vue** viewpoint; (*fig*: *opinion*) point of view; **~s de suspension** suspension points.

pointe [pwɛ̃t] *nf* point; (*fig*): **une ~ de** a hint of; **être à la ~ de** (*fig*) to be in the forefront of; **sur la ~ des pieds** on tiptoe; **en ~** *ad* (*tailler*) into a point // *a* pointed, tapered; **de ~** *a* (*technique etc*) leading; **heures/jours de ~** peak hours/days; **~ de vitesse** burst of speed.

pointer [pwɛ̃te] *vt* (*cocher*) to tick off; (*employés etc*) to check in; (*diriger: canon, doigt*): **~ vers qch** to point at sth // *vi* (*employé*) to clock in.

pointillé [pwɛ̃tije] *nm* (*trait*) dotted line.

pointilleux, euse [pwɛ̃tijø, -øz] *a* particular, pernickety.

pointu, e [pwɛ̃ty] *a* pointed; (*clou*) sharp; (*voix*) shrill; (*analyse*) precise.

pointure [pwɛ̃tyʀ] *nf* size.

point-virgule [pwɛ̃viʀgyl] *nm* semicolon.

poire [pwaʀ] *nf* pear; (*fam*: *péj*) mug.

poireau, x [pwaʀo] *nm* leek.

poirier [pwaʀje] *nm* pear tree.

pois [pwa] *nm* (*BOT*) pea; (*sur une étoffe*) dot, spot; **à ~** (*cravate etc*) spotted, polka-dot *cpd*.

poison [pwazɔ̃] *nm* poison.

poisse [pwas] *nf* rotten luck.

poisseux, euse [pwasø, -øz] *a* sticky.

poisson [pwasɔ̃] *nm* fish *gén inv*; **les P~s** (*signe*) Pisces; **~ d'avril!** April fool!; **~ rouge** goldfish; **poissonnerie** *nf* fish-shop; **poissonnier, ière** *nm/f* fishmonger (*Brit*), fish merchant (*US*).

poitrine [pwatrin] *nf* chest; *(seins)* bust, bosom; *(CULIN)* breast; ~ **de bœuf** brisket.

poivre [pwavʀ(ə)] *nm* pepper; **poivrier** *nm (ustensile)* pepperpot.

poivron [pwavʀɔ̃] *nm* pepper, capsicum.

pôle [pol] *nm (GÉO, ÉLEC)* pole.

poli, e [pɔli] *a* polite; *(lisse)* smooth; polished.

police [pɔlis] *nf* police; **peine de simple ~** *sentence given by magistrates' or police court;* ~ **d'assurance** insurance policy; ~ **judiciaire (P.J.)** ≈ Criminal Investigation Department *(Brit),* ≈ Federal Bureau of Investigation *(US);* ~ **des mœurs** ≈ vice squad; ~ **secours** ≈ emergency services *pl (Brit),* ≈ paramedics *pl (US).*

policier, ière [pɔlisje, -jɛʀ] *a* police *cpd // nm* policeman; *(aussi:* **roman ~)** detective novel.

polio [pɔljo] *nf* polio.

polir [pɔliʀ] *vt* to polish.

polisson, ne [pɔlisɔ̃, -ɔn] *a* naughty.

politesse [pɔlitɛs] *nf* politeness.

politicien, ne [pɔlitisjɛ̃, -ɛn] *nm/f* politician.

politique [pɔlitik] *a* political *// nf (science, pratique, activité)* politics *sg; (mesures, méthode)* policies *pl;* **politiser** *vt* to politicize.

pollen [pɔlɛn] *nm* pollen.

pollution [pɔlysjɔ̃] *nf* pollution.

Pologne [pɔlɔɲ] *nf:* **la ~** Poland; **polonais, e** *a, nm (LING)* Polish; **Polonais, e** *nm/f* Pole.

poltron, ne [pɔltʀɔ̃, -ɔn] *a* cowardly.

poly... [pɔli] *préfixe:* ~**copier** *vt* to duplicate.

Polynésie [pɔlinezi] *nf:* **la ~** Polynesia.

polyvalent, e [pɔlivalɑ̃, -ɑ̃t] *a* versatile; multi-purpose.

pommade [pɔmad] *nf* ointment, cream.

pomme [pɔm] *nf (BOT)* apple; **tomber dans les ~s** *(fam)* to pass out; ~ **d'Adam** Adam's apple; ~ **d'arrosoir** (sprinkler) rose; ~ **de pin** pine *ou* fir cone; ~ **de terre** potato.

pommeau, x [pɔmo] *nm (boule)* knob; *(de selle)* pommel.

pommette [pɔmɛt] *nf* cheekbone.

pommier [pɔmje] *nm* apple tree.

pompe [pɔ̃p] *nf* pump; *(faste)* pomp (and ceremony); ~ **à essence** petrol pump; ~**s funèbres** funeral parlour *sg,* undertaker's *sg.*

pomper [pɔ̃pe] *vt* to pump; *(évacuer)* to pump out; *(aspirer)* to pump up; *(absorber)* to soak up.

pompeux, euse [pɔ̃pø, -øz] *a* pompous.

pompier [pɔ̃pje] *nm* fireman.

pompiste [pɔ̃pist(ə)] *nm/f* petrol *(Brit) ou* gas *(US)* pump attendant.

poncer [pɔ̃se] *vt* to sand (down).

ponctuation [pɔ̃ktɥasjɔ̃] *nf* punctuation.

ponctuel, le [pɔ̃ktɥɛl] *a (à l'heure, aussi TECH)* punctual; *(fig: opération etc)* one-off, single; *(scrupuleux)* punctilious, meticulous.

ponctuer [pɔ̃ktɥe] *vt* to punctuate.

pondéré, e [pɔ̃deʀe] *a* level-headed, composed.

pondre [pɔ̃dʀ(ə)] *vt* to lay; *(fig)* to produce.

poney [pɔnɛ] *nm* pony.

pont [pɔ̃] *nm* bridge; *(AUTO)* axle; *(NAVIG)* deck; **faire le ~** to take the extra day off; ~ **de graissage** ramp *(in garage);* ~ **suspendu** suspension bridge; **P~s et Chaussées** highways department.

pont-levis [pɔ̃lvi] *nm* drawbridge.

pop [pɔp] *a inv* pop.

populace [pɔpylas] *nf (péj)* rabble.

populaire [pɔpylɛʀ] *a* popular; *(manifestation)* mass *cpd; (milieux, clientèle)* working-class.

population [pɔpylasjɔ̃] *nf* population.

populeux, euse [pɔpylø, -øz] *a* densely populated.

porc [pɔʀ] *nm (ZOOL)* pig; *(CULIN)* pork; *(peau)* pigskin.

porcelaine [pɔʀsəlɛn] *nf* porcelain, china; piece of china(ware).

porcelet [pɔʀsəlɛ] *nm* piglet.

porc-épic [pɔʀkepik] *nm* porcupine.

porche [pɔʀʃ(ə)] *nm* porch.

porcherie [pɔʀʃəʀi] *nf* pigsty.

pore [pɔʀ] *nm* pore.

pornographique [pɔʀnɔgʀafik] *a (abr* **porno)** pornographic.

port [pɔʀ] *nm (NAVIG)* harbour, port; *(ville)* port; *(de l'uniforme etc)* wearing; *(pour lettre)* postage; *(pour colis, aussi: posture)* carriage; ~ **d'arme** *(JUR)* carrying of a firearm.

portail [pɔʀtaj] *nm* gate; *(de cathédrale)* portal.

portant, e [pɔʀtɑ̃, -ɑ̃t] *a:* **bien/mal ~** in good/poor health.

portatif, ive [pɔʀtatif, -iv] *a* portable.

porte [pɔʀt(ə)] *nf* door; *(de ville, forteresse, SKI)* gate; **mettre à la ~** to throw out; ~ **d'entrée** front door; ~ **à ~** *nm* door-to-door selling.

porte... [pɔʀt(ə)] *préfixe:* ~**-à-faux** *nm:* **en ~-à-faux** cantilevered; *(fig)* in an awkward position; ~**-avions** *nm inv* aircraft carrier; ~**-bagages** *nm inv* luggage rack; ~**-clefs** *nm inv* key ring; ~**-documents** *nm inv* attaché *ou* document case.

portée [pɔʀte] *nf (d'une arme)* range; *(fig)* impact, import; scope, capability; *(de chatte etc)* litter; *(MUS)* stave, staff *(pl* staves); **à/hors de ~ (de)** within/out of reach (of); **à ~ de (la) main** within (arm's) reach; **à ~ de voix** within earshot; **à la ~ de qn** *(fig)* at sb's level, within sb's capabilities.

porte-fenêtre [pɔrtfənɛtr(ə)] nf French window.

portefeuille [pɔrtəfœj] nm wallet; (POL, BOURSE) portfolio.

porte-jarretelles [pɔrtʒartɛl] nm inv suspender belt.

portemanteau, x [pɔrtmɑ̃to] nm coat hanger; coat rack.

porte-mine [pɔrtəmin] nm propelling (Brit) ou mechanical (US) pencil.

porte-monnaie [pɔrtmɔnɛ] nm inv purse.

porte-parole [pɔrtparɔl] nm inv spokesman.

porter [pɔrte] vt to carry; (sur soi: vêtement, barbe, bague) to wear; (fig: responsabilité etc) to bear, carry; (inscription, marque, titre, patronyme, suj: arbre: fruits, fleurs) to bear; (apporter): ~ qch quelque part/à qn to take sth somewhere/to sb // vi (voix, regard, canon) to carry; (coup, argument) to hit home; ~ sur (peser) to rest on; (accent) to fall on; (conférence etc) to concern; (heurter) to strike; se ~ vi (se sentir): se ~ bien/mal to be well/unwell; être porté à faire to be apt ou inclined to do; se faire ~ malade to report sick; ~ la main à son chapeau to raise one's hat to one's hat; ~ son effort sur to direct one's efforts towards; ~ à croire to lead one to believe.

porte-serviettes [pɔrtsɛrvjɛt] nm inv towel rail.

porteur [pɔrtœr] nm (de bagages) porter; (de chèque) bearer.

porte-voix [pɔrtəvwa] nm inv megaphone.

portier [pɔrtje] nm doorman.

portière [pɔrtjɛr] nf door.

portillon [pɔrtijɔ̃] nm gate.

portion [pɔrsjɔ̃] nf (part) portion, share; (partie) portion, section.

portique [pɔrtik] nm (RAIL) gantry.

porto [pɔrto] nm port (wine).

portrait [pɔrtrɛ] nm portrait; photograph; **~-robot** nm Identikit ® ou photo-fit ® picture.

portuaire [pɔrtɥɛr] a port cpd, harbour cpd.

portugais, e [pɔrtygɛ, -ɛz] a, nm/f Portuguese.

Portugal [pɔrtygal] nm: le ~ Portugal.

pose [poz] nf laying; hanging; (attitude, d'un modèle) pose; (PHOTO) exposure.

posé, e [poze] a serious.

poser [poze] vt (déposer): ~ qch (sur)/ qn à to put sth down (on)/drop sb at; (placer): ~ qch sur/quelque part to put sth on/somewhere; (installer: moquette, carrelage) to lay; (rideaux, papier peint) to hang; (question) to ask; (principe, conditions) to lay ou set down; (problème) to formulate; (difficulté) to pose // vi (modèle) to pose; se ~ vi

(oiseau, avion) to land; (question) to arise.

positif, ive [pozitif, -iv] a positive.

position [pozisjɔ̃] nf position; **prendre** ~ (fig) to take a stand.

posséder [pɔsede] vt to own, possess; (qualité, talent) to have, possess; (bien connaître: métier, langue) to have mastered, have a thorough knowledge of; (sexuellement, aussi: suj: colère etc) to possess; **possession** nf ownership q; possession.

possibilité [pɔsibilite] nf possibility; **~s** nfpl (moyens) means; (potentiel) potential sg.

possible [pɔsibl(ə)] a possible; (projet, entreprise) feasible // nm: **faire son** ~ to do all one can, do one's utmost; **le plus/ moins de livres** ~ as many/few books as possible; **le plus/moins d'eau** ~ as much/little water as possible; **dès que** ~ as soon as possible.

postal, e, aux [pɔstal, -o] a postal.

poste [pɔst(ə)] nf (service) post, postal service; (administration, bureau) post office // nm (fonction, MIL) post; (TÉL) extension; (de radio etc) set; **mettre à la** ~ to post; **P~s, Télécommunications et Télédiffusion** (P.T.T.) postal and telecommunications service; **~ d'essence** nm petrol ou filling station; **~ d'incendie** nm fire point; **~ de pilotage** nm cockpit; **~** (de police) nm police station; **~ restante** nf poste restante (Brit), general delivery (US); **~ de secours** nm first-aid post; **~ de travail** nm work station.

poster vt [pɔste] to post // nm [pɔstɛr] poster.

postérieur, e [pɔsterjœr] a (date) later; (partie) back // nm (fam) behind.

posthume [pɔstym] a posthumous.

postiche [pɔstiʃ] nm hairpiece.

postuler [pɔstyle] vt (emploi) to apply for, put in for.

posture [pɔstyr] nf posture; position.

pot [po] nm jar, pot; (en plastique, carton) carton; (en métal) tin; **boire ou prendre un** ~ (fam) to have a drink; **~ (de chambre)** (chamber) pot; **~ d'échappement** exhaust pipe; **~ de fleurs** plant pot, flowerpot; (plante) pot plant.

potable [pɔtabl(ə)] a: **eau (non)** ~ (not) drinking water.

potage [pɔtaʒ] nm soup; soup course.

potager, ère [pɔtaʒe, -ɛr] a (plante) edible, vegetable cpd; (jardin) ~ kitchen ou vegetable garden.

pot-au-feu [pɔtofø] nm inv (beef) stew.

pot-de-vin [pɔdvɛ̃] nm bribe.

pote [pɔt] nm (fam) pal.

poteau, x [pɔto] nm post; **~ indicateur** signpost.

potelé, e [pɔtle] a plump, chubby.

potence [pɔtɑ̃s] nf gallows sg.

potentiel, le [pɔtɑ̃sjɛl] a, nm potential.

poterie [pɔtʀi] *nf* pottery; piece of pottery.

potier [pɔtje] *nm* potter.

potins [pɔtɛ̃] *nmpl* gossip *sg*.

potiron [pɔtiʀɔ̃] *nm* pumpkin.

pou, x [pu] *nm* louse (*pl* lice).

poubelle [pubɛl] *nf* (dust)bin.

pouce [pus] *nm* thumb.

poudre [pudʀ(ə)] *nf* powder; (*fard*) (face) powder; (*explosif*) gunpowder; en ~: **café en ~** instant coffee; **lait en ~** dried *ou* powdered milk; **poudrier** *nm* (powder) compact.

pouffer [pufe] *vi*: ~ **(de rire)** to snigger; to giggle.

pouilleux, euse [pujø, -øz] *a* flea-ridden; (*fig*) grubby; seedy.

poulailler [pulaje] *nm* henhouse.

poulain [pulɛ̃] *nm* foal; (*fig*) protégé.

poule [pul] *nf* (*ZOOL*) hen; (*CULIN*) (boiling) fowl.

poulet [pulɛ] *nm* chicken; (*fam*) cop.

poulie [puli] *nf* pulley; block.

pouls [pu] *nm* pulse; **prendre le ~ de qn** to feel sb's pulse.

poumon [pumɔ̃] *nm* lung.

poupe [pup] *nf* stern; **en ~** astern.

poupée [pupe] *nf* doll.

poupon [pupɔ̃] *nm* babe-in-arms; **pouponnière** *nf* crèche, day nursery.

pour [puʀ] *prép* for // *nm*: **le ~ et le contre** the pros and cons; ~ **faire** (so as) to do, in order to do; ~ **avoir fait** for having done; ~ **que** so that, in order that; ~ **100 francs d'essence 100 francs'** worth of petrol; ~ **cent** per cent; ~ **ce qui est de** as for.

pourboire [puʀbwaʀ] *nm* tip.

pourcentage [puʀsɑ̃taʒ] *nm* percentage.

pourchasser [puʀʃase] *vt* to pursue.

pourparlers [puʀpaʀle] *nmpl* talks, negotiations.

pourpre [puʀpʀ(ə)] *a* crimson.

pourquoi [puʀkwa] *ad, cj* why // *nm inv*: **le ~ (de)** the reason (for).

pourrai *etc vb voir* **pouvoir**.

pourri, e [puʀi] *a* rotten.

pourrir [puʀiʀ] *vi* to rot; (*fruit*) to go rotten *ou* bad // *vt* to rot; (*fig*) to spoil thoroughly; **pourriture** *nf* rot.

pourrons *etc vb voir* **pouvoir**.

poursuite [puʀsɥit] *nf* pursuit, chase; ~**s** (*JUR*) legal proceedings.

poursuivre [puʀsɥivʀ(ə)] *vt* to pursue, chase (after); (*relancer*) to hound, harry; (*obséder*) to haunt; (*JUR*) to bring proceedings against, prosecute; (: *au civil*) to sue; (*but*) to strive towards; (*voyage, études*) to carry on with, continue // *vi* to carry on, go on; **se ~** *vi* to go on, continue.

pourtant [puʀtɑ̃] *ad* yet; **c'est ~ facile** (and) yet it's easy.

pourtour [puʀtuʀ] *nm* perimeter.

pourvoir [puʀvwaʀ] *vt*: ~ **qch/qn de** to equip sth/sb with // *vi*: ~ **à** to provide for; (*emploi*) to fill; **se** ~ *vi* (*JUR*): **se** ~ **en cassation** to take one's case to the Court of Appeal.

pourvoyeur [puʀvwajœʀ] *nm* supplier.

pourvu, e [puʀvy] *a*: ~ **de** equipped with; ~ **que** *cj* (*si*) provided that, so long as; (*espérons que*) let's hope (that).

pousse [pus] *nf* growth; (*bourgeon*) shoot.

poussé, e [puse] *a* exhaustive.

poussée [puse] *nf* thrust; (*coup*) push; (*MÉD*) eruption; (*fig*) upsurge.

pousser [puse] *vt* to push; (*inciter*): ~ **qn à** to urge *ou* press sb to + *infinitif*; (*acculer*): ~ **qn à** to drive sb to; (*émettre: cri etc*) to give; (*stimuler*) to urge on; to drive hard; (*poursuivre*) to carry on (further) // *vi* to push; (*croître*) to grow; **se ~** *vi* to move over; **faire ~** (*plante*) to grow.

poussette [pusɛt] *nf* (*voiture d'enfant*) push chair (*Brit*), stroller (*US*).

poussière [pusjɛʀ] *nf* dust; (*grain*) speck of dust; **poussiéreux, euse** *a* dusty.

poussin [pusɛ̃] *nm* chick.

poutre [putʀ(ə)] *nf* beam; (*en fer, ciment armé*) girder.

pouvoir [puvwaʀ] ♦ *nm* power; (*POL: dirigeants*): **le ~** those in power; **les ~s publics** the authorities; ~ **d'achat** purchasing power

♦ *vb semi-auxiliaire* **1** (*être en état de*) can, be able to; **je ne peux pas le réparer** I can't *ou* I am not able to repair it; **déçu de ne pas ~ le faire** disappointed not to be able to do it

2 (*avoir la permission*) can, may, be allowed to; **vous pouvez aller au cinéma** you can *ou* may go to the pictures

3 (*probabilité, hypothèse*) may, might, could; **il a pu avoir un accident** he may *ou* might *ou* could have had an accident; **il aurait pu le dire!** he might *ou* could have said (so)!

♦ *vb impersonnel* may, might, could; **il peut arriver que** it may *ou* might *ou* could happen that

♦ *vt* can, be able to; **j'ai fait tout ce que j'ai pu** I did all I could; **je n'en peux plus** (*épuisé*) I'm exhausted; (*à bout*) I can't take any more

se pouvoir *vi*: **il se peut que** it may *ou* might be that; **cela se pourrait** that's quite possible.

prairie [pʀeʀi] *nf* meadow.

praline [pʀalin] *nf* sugared almond.

praticable [pʀatikabl(ə)] *a* passable, practicable.

praticien, ne [pʀatisjɛ̃, -jɛn] *nm/f* practitioner.

pratique [pʀatik] *nf* practice // *a* practical.

pratiquement [pʀatikmɑ̃] *ad* (*pour ainsi dire*) practically, virtually.
pratiquer [pʀatike] *vt* to practise; (*SPORT etc*) to go (in for); to play; (*intervention, opération*) to carry out; (*ouverture, abri*) to make.
pré [pʀe] *nm* meadow.
préalable [pʀealabl(ə)] *a* preliminary; condition ~ (de) precondition (for), pre-requisite (for); au ~ beforehand.
préambule [pʀeɑ̃byl] *nm* preamble; (*fig*) prelude; sans ~ straight away.
préavis [pʀeavi] *nm* notice; communication avec ~ (*TÉL*) personal *ou* person to person call.
précaution [pʀekosjɔ̃] *nf* precaution; avec ~ cautiously; par ~ as a precaution.
précédemment [pʀesedamɑ̃] *ad* before, previously.
précédent, e [pʀesedɑ̃, -ɑ̃t] *a* previous // *nm* precedent; sans ~ unprecedented; le jour ~ the day before, the previous day.
précéder [pʀesede] *vt* to precede; (*marcher ou rouler devant*) to be in front of.
précepteur, trice [pʀeseptœʀ, -tʀis] *nm/f* (private) tutor.
prêcher [pʀeʃe] *vt* to preach.
précieux, euse [pʀesjø, -øz] *a* precious; invaluable; (*style, écrivain*) -précieux, precious.
précipice [pʀesipis] *nm* drop, chasm; (*fig*) abyss.
précipitamment [pʀesipitamɑ̃] *ad* hurriedly, hastily.
précipitation [pʀesipitasjɔ̃] *nf* (*hâte*) haste; ~s (*pluie*) rain.
précipité, e [pʀesipite] *a* hurried, hasty.
précipiter [pʀesipite] *vt* (*faire tomber*): ~ qn/qch du haut de to throw *ou* hurl sb/sth off *ou* from; (*hâter: marche*) to quicken; (*: départ*) to hasten; se ~ *vi* to speed up; se ~ sur/vers to rush at/towards.
précis, e [pʀesi, -iz] *a* precise; (*tir, mesures*) accurate, precise // *nm* handbook; **précisément** *ad* precisely; **préciser** *vt* (*expliquer*) to be more specific about, clarify; (*spécifier*) to state, specify; se préciser *vi* to become clear(er); **précision** *nf* precision; accuracy; point *ou* detail (*made clear or to be clarified*).
précoce [pʀekɔs] *a* early; (*enfant*) precocious; (*calvitie*) premature.
préconiser [pʀekɔnize] *vt* to advocate.
prédécesseur [pʀedesesœʀ] *nm* predecessor.
prédilection [pʀedilɛksjɔ̃] *nf*: avoir une ~ pour to be partial to; de ~ favourite.
prédire [pʀediʀ] *vt* to predict.
prédominer [pʀedɔmine] *vi* to predominate; (*avis*) to prevail.

préface [pʀefas] *nf* preface.
préfecture [pʀefɛktyʀ] *nf* prefecture; ~ de police police headquarters.
préférable [pʀefeʀabl(ə)] *a* preferable.
préféré, e [pʀefeʀe] *a, nm/f* favourite.
préférence [pʀefeʀɑ̃s] *nf* preference; de ~ preferably.
préférer [pʀefeʀe] *vt*: ~ qn/qch (à) to prefer sb/sth (to), like sb/sth better (than); ~ faire to prefer to do; je préférerais du thé I would rather have tea, I'd prefer tea.
préfet [pʀefɛ] *nm* prefect.
préfixe [pʀefiks(ə)] *nm* prefix.
préhistorique [pʀeistɔʀik] *a* prehistoric.
préjudice [pʀeʒydis] *nm* (*matériel*) loss; (*moral*) harm *q*; porter ~ à to harm, be detrimental to; au ~ de at the expense of.
préjugé [pʀeʒyʒe] *nm* prejudice; avoir un ~ contre to be prejudiced *ou* biased against.
préjuger [pʀeʒyʒe]: ~ de *vt* to prejudge.
prélasser [pʀelase]: se ~ *vi* to lounge.
prélèvement [pʀelɛvmɑ̃] *nm*: faire un ~ de sang to take a blood sample.
prélever [pʀelve] *vt* (*échantillon*) to take; (*argent*): ~ (sur) to deduct (from); (*: sur son compte*): ~ (sur) to withdraw (from).
prématuré, e [pʀematyʀe] *a* premature; (*retraite*) early // *nm* premature baby.
premier, ière [pʀəmje, -jɛʀ] *a* first; (*branche, marche*) bottom; (*fig*) basic; prime; initial // *nf* (*THÉÂTRE*) first night; (*AUTO*) first (gear); (*AVIAT, RAIL etc*) first class; (*CINÉMA*) première; (*exploit*) first; le ~ venu the first person to come along; P~ Ministre Prime Minister; **premièrement** *ad* firstly.
prémonition [pʀemɔnisjɔ̃] *nf* premonition.
prémunir [pʀemyniʀ]: se ~ *vi*: se ~ contre to guard against.
prénatal, e [pʀenatal] *a* (*MÉD*) antenatal.
prendre [pʀɑ̃dʀ(ə)] *vt* to take; (*ôter*): ~ qch à to take sth from; (*aller chercher*) to get, fetch; (*se procurer*) to get; (*malfaiteur, poisson*) to catch; (*passager*) to pick up; (*personnel, aussi: couleur, goût*) to take on; (*locataire*) to take in; (*élève etc: traiter*) to handle; (*voix, ton*) to put on; (*coincer*): se ~ les doigts dans to get one's fingers caught in // *vi* (*liquide, ciment*) to set; (*greffe, vaccin*) to take; (*feu: foyer*) to go; (*: incendie*) to start; (*allumette*) to light; (*se diriger*): ~ à gauche to turn (to the) left; à tout ~ on the whole, all in all; se ~ pour to think one is; s'en ~ à to attack; se ~ d'amitié/d'affection pour to

befriend/become fond of; **s'y** ~ (*procé-der*) to set about it.

preneur [pʀənœʀ] *nm*: être/trouver ~ to be willing to buy/find a buyer.

preniez, prenne *etc vb voir* **prendre**.

prénom [pʀenɔ̃] *nm* first *ou* Christian name.

prénuptial, e, aux [pʀenypsjal, -o] *a* premarital.

préoccupation [pʀeɔkypasjɔ̃] *nf* (*souci*) concern; (*idée fixe*) preoccupation.

préoccuper [pʀeɔkype] *vt* to concern; to preoccupy.

préparatif [pʀepaʀatif] *nmpl* preparations.

préparation [pʀepaʀasjɔ̃] *nf* preparation; (*SCOL*) piece of homework.

préparer [pʀepaʀe] *vt* to prepare; (*café*) to make; (*examen*) to prepare for; (*voyage, entreprise*) to plan; se ~ *vi* (*orage, tragédie*) to brew, be in the air; se ~ (à qch/faire) to prepare (o.s.) *ou* get ready (for sth/to do); ~ qch à qn (*surprise etc*) to have sth in store for sb.

prépondérant, e [pʀepɔ̃deʀɑ̃, -ɑ̃t] *a* major, dominating.

préposé, e [pʀepoze] *a*: ~ à in charge of // *nm/f* employee; official; attendant.

préposition [pʀepozisjɔ̃] *nf* preposition.

près [pʀe] *ad* near, close; ~ de *prép* near (to), close to; (*environ*) nearly, almost; de ~ closely; à 5 kg ~ to within about 5 kg; à cela ~ que apart from the fact that.

présage [pʀezaʒ] *nm* omen.

présager [pʀezaʒe] *vt* to foresee.

presbyte [pʀesbit] *a* long-sighted.

presbytère [pʀesbitɛʀ] *nm* presbytery.

prescription [pʀeskʀipsjɔ̃] *nf* (*instruction*) order, instruction; (*MÉD, JUR*) prescription.

prescrire [pʀeskʀiʀ] *vt* to prescribe.

préséance [pʀeseɑ̃s] *nf* precedence *q*.

présence [pʀezɑ̃s] *nf* presence; (*au bureau etc*) attendance; ~ **d'esprit** presence of mind.

présent, e [pʀezɑ̃, -ɑ̃t] *a, nm* present; à ~ **(que)** now (that).

présentation [pʀezɑ̃tasjɔ̃] *nf* introduction; presentation; (*allure*) appearance.

présenter [pʀezɑ̃te] *vt* to present; (*sympathie, condoléances*) to offer; (*soumettre*) to submit; (*invité, conférencier*): ~ qn (à) to introduce sb (to) // *vi*: ~ **mal/bien** to have an unattractive/a pleasing appearance; se ~ *vi* (*sur convocation*) to report, come; (*à une élection*) to stand; (*occasion*) to arise; se ~ **bien/mal** to look good/not too good; se ~ à (*examen*) to sit.

préservatif [pʀezɛʀvatif] *nm* sheath, condom.

préserver [pʀezɛʀve] *vt*: ~ de to protect from; to save from.

président [pʀezidɑ̃] *nm* (*POL*) presi-

dent; (*d'une assemblée, COMM*) chairman; ~ **directeur général (PDG)** chairman and managing director.

présider [pʀezide] *vt* to preside over; (*dîner*) to be the guest of honour at; ~ à *vt* to direct; to govern.

présomptueux, euse [pʀezɔ̃ptɥø, -øz] *a* presumptuous.

presque [pʀesk(ə)] *ad* almost, nearly; ~ **rien** hardly anything; ~ **pas** hardly (at all); ~ **pas de** hardly any.

presqu'île [pʀeskil] *nf* peninsula.

pressant, e [pʀesɑ̃, -ɑ̃t] *a* urgent; se **faire** ~ to become insistent.

presse [pʀes] *nf* press; (*affluence*): **heures de** ~ busy times.

pressé, e [pʀese] *a* in a hurry; (*air*) hurried; (*besogne*) urgent; **orange** ~**e** fresh orange juice.

pressentiment [pʀesɑ̃timɑ̃] *nm* foreboding, premonition.

pressentir [pʀesɑ̃tiʀ] *vt* to sense; (*prendre contact avec*) to approach.

presse-papiers [pʀespapje] *nm inv* paperweight.

presser [pʀese] *vt* (*fruit, éponge*) to squeeze; (*bouton*) to press; (*allure, affaire*) to speed up; (*inciter*): ~ **qn de faire** to urge *ou* press sb to do // *vi* to be urgent; **rien ne presse** there's no hurry; se ~ *vi* (*se hâter*) to hurry (up); se ~ **contre qn** to squeeze up against sb.

pressing [pʀesiŋ] *nm* steam-pressing; (*magasin*) dry-cleaner's.

pression [pʀesjɔ̃] *nf* pressure; **faire** ~ **sur** to put pressure on; ~ **artérielle** blood pressure.

pressoir [pʀeswaʀ] *nm* (*wine ou oil etc*) press.

pressurer [pʀesyʀe] *vt* (*fig*) to squeeze.

prestance [pʀestɑ̃s] *nf* presence, imposing bearing.

prestataire [pʀestatɛʀ] *nm/f* supplier.

prestation [pʀestasjɔ̃] *nf* (*allocation*) benefit; (*d'une entreprise*) service provided; (*d'un artiste*) performance.

prestidigitateur, trice [pʀestidiʒitatœʀ, -tʀis] *nm/f* conjurer.

prestigieux, euse [pʀestiʒjø, -øz] *a* prestigious.

présumer [pʀezyme] *vt*: ~ **que** to presume *ou* assume that; ~ **de** to overrate.

présupposer [pʀesypoze] *vt* to presuppose.

prêt, e [pʀe, pʀet] *a* ready // *nm* lending *q*; loan; **prêt-à-porter** *nm* ready-to-wear *ou* off-the-peg (*Brit*) clothes *pl*.

prétendant [pʀetɑ̃dɑ̃] *nm* pretender; (*d'une femme*) suitor.

prétendre [pʀetɑ̃dʀ(ə)] *vt* (*affirmer*): ~ **que** to claim that; (*avoir l'intention de*): ~ **faire qch** to mean *ou* intend to do sth; ~ à *vt* (*droit, titre*) to lay claim to; **prétendu, e** *a* (*supposé*) so-called.

prête-nom [pʀetnɔ̃] *nm* (*péj*) figurehead.

prétentieux, euse |prɛɑ̃tɑ̃sjø, -øz| *a* pretentious.

prétention |prɛtɑ̃sjɔ̃| *nf* claim; pretentiousness.

prêter |prɛte| *vt* (*livres, argent*): ~ qch (à) to lend sth (to); (*supposer*): ~ à qn (*caractère, propos*) to attribute to sb // *vi* (*aussi*: se ~: *tissu, cuir*) to give; ~ à (*commentaires etc*) to be open to, give rise to; se ~ à to lend o.s. (*ou itself*) to; (*manigances etc*) to go along with; ~ assistance à to give help to; ~ attention à to pay attention to; ~ serment to take the oath; ~ l'oreille to listen.

prétexte |prɛtɛkst(ə)| *nm* pretext, excuse; **sous aucun ~** on no account; **prétexter** *vt* to give as a pretext *ou* an excuse.

prêtre |prɛtʀ(ə)| *nm* priest.

preuve |prœv| *nf* proof; (*indice*) proof, evidence *q*; faire ~ de to show; faire ses ~s to prove o.s. (*ou* itself).

prévaloir |prevalwaʀ| *vi* to prevail; se ~ de *vt* to take advantage of; to pride o.s. on.

prévenant, e |prevnɑ̃, -ɑ̃t| *a* thoughtful, kind.

prévenir |prevniʀ| *vt* (*avertir*): ~ qn (de) to warn sb (about); (*informer*): ~ qn (de) to tell *ou* inform sb (about); (*éviter*) to avoid, prevent; (*anticiper*) to forestall; to anticipate.

prévention |prevɑ̃sjɔ̃| *nf* prevention; ~ routière road safety.

prévenu, e |prevny| *nm/f* (*JUR*) defendant, accused.

prévision |previzjɔ̃| *nf*: ~s predictions; forecast *sg*; en ~ de in anticipation of; ~s météorologiques weather forecast *sg*.

prévoir |prevwaʀ| *vt* (*deviner*) to foresee; (*s'attendre à*) to expect, reckon on; (*prévenir*) to anticipate; (*organiser*) to plan; (*préparer, réserver*) to allow; prévu pour 10h scheduled for 10 o'clock.

prévoyance |prevwajɑ̃s| *nf*: caisse de ~ contingency fund.

prévoyant, e |prevwajɑ̃, -ɑ̃t| *a* gifted with (*ou* showing) foresight.

prévu, e |prevy| *pp de* **prévoir**.

prier |prije| *vi* to pray // *vt* (*Dieu*) to pray to; (*implorer*) to beg; (*demander*): ~ qn de faire to ask sb to do; se faire ~ to need coaxing *ou* persuading; je vous en prie (*allez-y*) please do; (*de rien*) don't mention it.

prière |prijɛʀ| *nf* prayer; '~ de faire ...' 'please do ...'.

primaire |primɛʀ| *a* primary; (*péj*) simple-minded; simplistic // *nm* (*SCOL*) primary education.

prime |prim| *nf* (*bonification*) bonus; (*subside*) premium; allowance; (*COMM: cadeau*) free gift; (*ASSURANCES,*

BOURSE) premium // *a*: de ~ abord at first glance.

primer |prime| *vt* (*l'emporter sur*) to prevail over; (*récompenser*) to award a prize to // *vi* to dominate; to prevail.

primeurs |primœʀ| *nfpl* early fruits and vegetables.

primevère |primvɛʀ| *nf* primrose.

primitif, ive |primitif, -iv| *a* primitive; (*originel*) original.

prince, esse |prɛ̃s, prɛ̃sɛs| *nm/f* prince/princess.

principal, e, aux |prɛ̃sipal, -o| *a* principal, main // *nm* (*SCOL*) principal, head(master); (*essentiel*) main thing.

principe |prɛ̃sip| *nm* principle; **pour le ~** on principle; **de ~** *a* (*accord, hostilité*) automatic; **par ~** on principle; **en ~** (*habituellement*) as a rule; (*théoriquement*) in principle.

printemps |prɛ̃tɑ̃| *nm* spring.

priorité |prijɔʀite| *nf* (*AUTO*): avoir la ~ (**sur**) to have right of way (over); ~ à droite right of way to vehicles coming from the right.

pris, e |pri, priz| *pp de* **prendre** // *a* (*place*) taken; (*journée, mains*) full; (*billets*) sold; (*personne*) busy; avoir le nez/la gorge ~ (e) to have a stuffy nose/ a hoarse throat; être ~ de panique to be panic-stricken.

prise |priz| *nf* (*d'une ville*) capture; (*PÊCHE, CHASSE*) catch; (*de judo ou catch, point d'appui ou pour empoigner*) hold; (*ELEC: fiche*) plug; (*: femelle*) socket; être aux ~s avec to be grappling with; ~ de courant power point; ~ multiple adaptor; ~ de sang blood test; ~ de terre earth; ~ de vue (*photo*) shot.

priser |prize| *vt* (*tabac, héroïne*) to take; (*estimer*) to prize, value // *vi* to take snuff.

prison |prizɔ̃| *nf* prison; aller/être en ~ to go to/be in prison *ou* jail; faire de la ~ to serve time; **prisonnier, ière** *nm/f* prisoner // *a* captive.

prit *vb voir* **prendre**.

privé, e |prive| *a* private; en ~ in private.

priver |prive| *vt*: ~ qn de to deprive sb of; se ~ de to go *ou* do without.

privilège |privilɛʒ| *nm* privilege.

prix |pri| *nm* (*valeur*) price; (*récompense, SCOL*) prize; **hors de ~** exorbitantly priced; à aucun ~ not at any price; à tout ~ at all costs; ~ d'achat/de vente/de revient purchasing/selling/cost price.

probable |prɔbabl(ə)| *a* likely, probable; ~ment *ad* probably.

probant, e |prɔbɑ̃, -ɑ̃t| *a* convincing.

problème |prɔblɛm| *nm* problem.

procédé |prosede| *nm* (*méthode*) process; (*comportement*) behaviour *q*.

procéder |prosede| *vi* to proceed; to be-

have; ~ à *vt* to carry out.
procès [prɔsɛ] *nm* trial; (*poursuites*) proceedings *pl*; être en ~ avec to be involved in a lawsuit with.
processus [prɔsesys] *nm* process.
procès-verbal, aux [prɔsɛvɛrbal, -o] *nm* (*constat*) statement; (*aussi*: P.V.): avoir un ~ to get a parking ticket; to be booked; (*de réunion*) minutes *pl*.
prochain, e [prɔʃɛ̃, -ɛn] *a* next; (*proche*) impending; near // *nm* fellow man; la ~e fois/semaine ~e next time/week; **prochainement** *ad* soon, shortly.
proche [prɔʃ] *a* nearby; (*dans le temps*) imminent; (*parent, ami*) close; ~s *nmpl* close relatives; être ~ (de) to be near, be close (to); de ~ en ~ gradually; le P~ Orient the Middle East.
proclamer [prɔklame] *vt* to proclaim.
procuration [prɔkyrasjɔ̃] *nf* proxy; power of attorney.
procurer [prɔkyre] *vt*: ~ qch à qn (*fournir*) to obtain sth for sb; (*causer: plaisir etc*) to bring sb sth; se ~ *vt* to get.
procureur [prɔkyrœr] *nm* public prosecutor.
prodige [prɔdiʒ] *nm* marvel, wonder; (*personne*) prodigy.
prodigue [prɔdig] *a* generous; extravagant; **fils** ~ prodigal son.
prodiguer [prɔdige] *vt* (*argent, biens*) to be lavish with; (*soins, attentions*): ~ qch à qn to give sb sth.
producteur, trice [prɔdyktœr, -tris] *nm/f* producer.
production [prɔdyksjɔ̃] *nf* (*gén*) production; (*rendement*) output.
produire [prɔdɥir] *vt* to produce; se ~ *vi* (*acteur*) to perform, appear; (*événement*) to happen, occur.
produit [prɔdɥi] *nm* (*gén*) product; ~s agricoles farm produce *sg*; ~ d'entretien cleaning product.
prof [prɔf] *nm* (*fam*) teacher.
profane [prɔfan] *a* (*REL*) secular // *nm/f* layman.
proférer [prɔfere] *vt* to utter.
professer [prɔfese] *vi* to teach.
professeur [prɔfesœr] *nm* teacher; (*titulaire d'une chaire*) professor; ~ (de faculté) (university) lecturer.
profession [prɔfesjɔ̃] *nf* profession; sans ~ unemployed; **professionnel, le** *a, nm/f* professional.
profil [prɔfil] *nm* profile; (*d'une voiture*) line, contour; de ~ in profile; ~er *vt* to streamline.
profit [prɔfi] *nm* (*avantage*) benefit, advantage; (*COMM, FINANCE*) profit; au ~ de in aid of; tirer ~ de to profit from.
profitable [prɔfitabl(ə)] *a* beneficial; profitable.
profiter [prɔfite] *vi*: ~ de to take advantage of; to make the most of; ~ à to

benefit; to be profitable to.
profond, e [prɔfɔ̃, -ɔ̃d] *a* deep; (*méditation, mépris*) profound; **profondeur** *nf* depth.
progéniture [prɔʒenityr] *nf* offspring *inv*.
programme [prɔgram] *nm* programme; (*TV, RADIO*) programmes *pl*; (*SCOL*) syllabus, curriculum; (*INFORM*) program; **programmer** *vt* (*TV, RADIO*) to put on, show; (*INFORM*) to program; **programmeur, euse** *nm/f* programmer.
progrès [prɔgrɛ] *nm* progress *q*; faire des ~ to make progress.
progresser [prɔgrese] *vi* to progress; (*troupes etc*) to make headway ou progress; **progressif, ive** *a* progressive.
prohiber [prɔibe] *vt* to prohibit, ban.
proie [prwa] *nf* prey *q*.
projecteur [prɔʒektœr] *nm* projector; (*de théâtre, cirque*) spotlight.
projectile [prɔʒektil] *nm* missile.
projection [prɔʒeksjɔ̃] *nf* projection; showing; **conférence avec** ~s lecture with slides (*ou a film*).
projet [prɔʒe] *nm* plan; (*ébauche*) draft; ~ de loi bill.
projeter [prɔʒte] *vt* (*envisager*) to plan; (*film, photos*) to project; (*passer*) to show; (*ombre, lueur*) to throw, cast; (*jeter*) to throw up (*ou off ou out*).
prolixe [prɔliks(ə)] *a* verbose.
prolongations [prɔlɔ̃gasjɔ̃] *nfpl* (*FOOTBALL*) extra time *sg*.
prolongement [prɔlɔ̃ʒmɑ̃] *nm* extension; ~s (*fig*) repercussions, effects; dans le ~ de running on from.
prolonger [prɔlɔ̃ʒe] *vt* (*débat, séjour*) to prolong; (*délai, billet, rue*) to extend; (*suj: chose*) to be a continuation ou an extension of; se ~ *vi* to go on.
promenade [prɔmnad] *nf* walk (*ou drive ou ride*); faire une ~ to go for a walk; une ~ en voiture/à vélo a drive/(bicycle) ride.
promener [prɔmne] *vt* (*chien*) to take out for a walk; (*doigts, regard*): ~ qch sur to run sth over; se ~ *vi* to go for (*ou be out for*) a walk.
promesse [prɔmɛs] *nf* promise.
promettre [prɔmɛtr(ə)] *vt* to promise // *vi* to be ou look promising; ~ à qn de faire to promise sb that one will do.
promiscuité [prɔmiskɥite] *nf* crowding; lack of privacy.
promontoire [prɔmɔ̃twar] *nm* headland.
promoteur, trice [prɔmɔtœr, -tris] *nm/f* (*instigateur*) instigator, promoter; ~ (immobilier) property developer (*Brit*), real estate promoter (*US*).
promotion [prɔmosjɔ̃] *nf* promotion.
promouvoir [prɔmuvwar] *vt* to promote.
prompt, e [prɔ̃, prɔ̃t] *a* swift, rapid.

prôner [pʀone] vt to advocate.

pronom [pʀɔnɔ̃] nm pronoun.

prononcer [pʀonɔ̃se] vt (son, mot, juge-ment) to pronounce; (dire) to utter; (al-locution) to deliver; se ~ vi to reach a decision, give a verdict; se ~ sur to give an opinion on; se ~ contre to come down against; **prononciation** nf pronuncia-tion.

pronostic [pʀonɔstik] nm (MÉD) prog-nosis (pl oses); (fig: aussi: ~s) fore-cast.

propagande [pʀopagɑ̃d] nf propaganda.

propager [pʀopaʒe] vt, se ~ vi to spread.

prophète [pʀofɛt] nm prophet.

prophétie [pʀofesi] nf prophecy.

propice [pʀopis] a favourable.

proportion [pʀopɔʀsjɔ̃] nf proportion; **toute(s) ~(s) gardée(s)** making due al-lowance(s).

propos [pʀopo] nm (paroles) talk q, re-mark; (intention) intention, aim; (su-jet): à quel ~? what about?; à ~ de about, regarding; à tout ~ for no reason at all; à ~ ad by the way; (opportuné-ment) at the right moment.

proposer [pʀopoze] vt (suggérer): ~ qch (à qn)/de faire to suggest sth (to sb)/doing, propose sth (to sb)/to do; (of-frir): ~ qch à qn/de faire to offer sb sth/ to do; (candidat) to put forward; (loi, motion) to propose; se ~ to offer one's services; se ~ de faire to intend ou pro-pose to do; **proposition** nf suggestion; proposal; offer; (LING) clause.

propre [pʀopʀ(ə)] a clean; (net) neat, tidy; (possessif) own; (sens) literal; (particulier): ~ à peculiar to; (appro-prié): ~ à suitable for; (de nature à): ~ à faire likely to do // nm: recopier au ~ to make a fair copy of; **~ment** ad cleanly; neatly, tidily; le village ~ment dit the village itself; à ~ment parler strictly speaking; **~té** nf cleanliness; neatness; tidiness.

propriétaire [pʀopʀijetɛʀ] nm/f owner; (pour le locataire) landlord/lady.

propriété [pʀopʀijete] nf (gén) prop-erty; (droit) ownership; (objet, immeu-ble, terres) property gén q.

propulser [pʀopylse] vt (missile) to pro-pel; (projeter) to hurl, fling.

proroger [pʀoʀoʒe] vt to put back, de-fer; (prolonger) to extend.

proscrire [pʀoskʀiʀ] vt (bannir) to ban-ish; (interdire) to ban, prohibit.

prose [pʀoz] nf prose (style).

prospecter [pʀospɛkte] vt to prospect; (COMM) to canvass.

prospectus [pʀospɛktys] nm leaflet.

prospère [pʀospɛʀ] a prosperous.

prosterner [pʀostɛʀne]: se ~ vi to bow low, prostrate o.s.

prostituée [pʀostitɥe] nf prostitute.

protecteur, trice [pʀotɛktœʀ, -tʀis] a protective; (air, ton: péj) patronizing // nm/f protector.

protection [pʀotɛksjɔ̃] nf protection; (d'un personnage influent: aide) patron-age.

protéger [pʀoteʒe] vt to protect; se ~ de/contre to protect o.s. from.

protéine [pʀotein] nf protein.

protestant, e [pʀotɛstɑ̃, -ɑ̃t] a, nm/f Protestant.

protestation [pʀotɛstasjɔ̃] nf (plainte) protest.

protester [pʀotɛste] vi: ~ (contre) to protest (against ou about); ~ de (son innocence, sa loyauté) to protest.

prothèse [pʀotɛz] nf artificial limb, prosthesis; ~ dentaire denture.

protocole [pʀotɔkɔl] nm (fig) etiquette.

proue [pʀu] nf bow(s pl), prow.

prouesse [pʀuɛs] nf feat.

prouver [pʀuve] vt to prove.

provenance [pʀovnɑ̃s] nf origin; (de mot, coutume) source; avion en ~ de plane (arriving) from.

provenir [pʀovniʀ]: ~ de vt to come from; (résulter de) to be the result of.

proverbe [pʀovɛʀb(ə)] nm proverb.

province [pʀovɛ̃s] nf province.

proviseur [pʀovizœʀ] nm ≈ head-(teacher) (Brit), ≈ principal (US).

provision [pʀovizjɔ̃] nf (réserve) stock, supply; (avance: à un avocat, avoué) re-tainer, retaining fee; (COMM) funds pl (in account); reserve; ~s (vivres) provi-sions, food q.

provisoire [pʀovizwaʀ] a temporary; (JUR) provisional.

provoquer [pʀovɔke] vt (inciter): ~ qn à to incite sb to; (défier) to provoke; (causer) to cause, bring about.

proxénète [pʀoksenɛt] nm procurer.

proximité [pʀoksimite] nf nearness, closeness; (dans le temps) imminence, closeness; à ~ near ou close by; à ~ de near (to), close to.

prude [pʀyd] a prudish.

prudemment [pʀydamɑ̃] ad carefully, cautiously; wisely, sensibly.

prudence [pʀydɑ̃s] nf carefulness; cau-tion; avec ~ carefully; cautiously; par (mesure de) ~ as a precaution.

prudent, e [pʀydɑ̃, -ɑ̃t] a (pas témé-raire) careful, cautious; (: en général) safety-conscious; (sage, conseillé) wise, sensible; (réservé) cautious.

prune [pʀyn] nf plum.

pruneau, x [pʀyno] nm prune.

prunelle [pʀynɛl] nf pupil; eye.

prunier [pʀynje] nm plum tree.

psaume [psom] nm psalm.

pseudonyme [psødɔnim] nm (gén) fictitious name; (d'écrivain) pseudonym, pen name; (de comédien) stage name.

psychanalyste [psikanalist(ə)] nm/f

psychoanalyst.

psychiatre [psikjatʀ(ə)] *nm/f* psychiatrist.

psychiatrique [psikjatʀik] *a* psychiatric.

psychique [psiʃik] *a* psychological.

psychologie [psikɔlɔʒi] *nf* psychology; **psychologique** *a* psychological; **psychologue** *nm/f* psychologist.

P.T.T. *sigle fpl voir* **poste**.

pu *pp de* **pouvoir**.

puanteur [pɥɑ̃tœʀ] *nf* stink, stench.

pub [pyb] *abr f (fam: = publicité)*: la ~ advertising.

public, ique [pyblik] *a* public; *(école, instruction)* state *cpd // nm* public; *(assistance)* audience; **en ~** in public.

publicitaire [pyblisitɛʀ] *a* advertising *cpd*; *(film, voiture)* publicity *cpd*.

publicité [pyblisite] *nf (méthode, profession)* advertising; *(annonce)* advertisement; *(révélations)* publicity.

publier [pyblije] *vt* to publish.

publique [pyblik] *af voir* **public**.

puce [pys] *nf* flea; *(INFORM)* chip; ~s *nfpl (marché)* flea market *sg*.

pucelle [pysɛl] *af*: **être ~** to be a virgin.

pudeur [pydœʀ] *nf* modesty.

pudique [pydik] *a (chaste)* modest; *(discret)* discreet.

puer [pɥe] *(péj) vi* to stink.

puéricultrice [pɥeʀikyltʀis] *nf* p(a)ediatric nurse.

puériculture [pɥeʀikyltyʀ] *nf* p(a)ediatric nursing; infant care.

puéril, e [pɥeʀil] *a* childish.

pugilat [pyʒila] *nm (fist)* fight.

puis [pɥi] *vb voir* **pouvoir** *// ad* then.

puiser [pɥize] *vt*: ~ **(dans)** to draw (from).

puisque [pɥisk(ə)] *cj* since.

puissance [pɥisɑ̃s] *nf* power; **en ~** *a* potential.

puissant, e [pɥisɑ̃, -ɑ̃t] *a* powerful.

puisse *etc vb voir* **pouvoir**.

puits [pɥi] *nm* well; ~ **de mine** mine shaft.

pull(-over) [pul(ɔvœʀ)] *nm* sweater.

pulluler [pylyle] *vi* to swarm.

pulpe [pylp(ə)] *nf* pulp.

pulvérisateur [pylveʀizatœʀ] *nm* spray.

pulvériser [pylveʀize] *vt* to pulverize; *(liquide)* to spray.

punaise [pynɛz] *nf (ZOOL)* bug; *(clou)* drawing pin *(Brit)*, thumbtack *(US)*.

punch [pɔ̃ʃ] *nm (boisson)* punch; [pœnʃ] *(BOXE, fig)* punch.

punir [pyniʀ] *vt* to punish; **punition** *nf* punishment.

pupille [pypij] *nf (ANAT)* pupil *// nm/f (enfant)* ward; ~ **de l'État** child in care.

pupitre [pypitʀ(ə)] *nm (SCOL)* desk; *(REL)* lectern; *(de chef d'orchestre)* rostrum.

pur, e [pyʀ] *a* pure; *(vin)* undiluted;

(whisky) neat; **en ~e perte** to no avail.

purée [pyʀe] *nf*: ~ **(de pommes de terre)** mashed potatoes *pl*; ~ **de marrons** chestnut purée.

purger [pyʀʒe] *vt (radiateur)* to drain; *(circuit hydraulique)* to bleed; *(MÉD, POL)* to purge; *(JUR: peine)* to serve.

purin [pyʀɛ̃] *nm* liquid manure.

pur-sang [pyʀsɑ̃] *nm inv* thoroughbred.

pusillanime [pyzilanim] *a* fainthearted.

putain [pytɛ̃] *nf (fam!)* whore *(!)*.

puzzle [pœzl(ə)] *nm* jigsaw (puzzle).

P.V. *sigle m* = **procès-verbal**.

pyjama [piʒama] *nm* pyjamas *pl*.

pyramide [piʀamid] *nf* pyramid.

Pyrénées [piʀene] *nfpl*: **les ~** the Pyrenees.

Q

QG [kyʒe] *voir* **quartier**.

QI [kyi] *sigle m (= quotient intellectuel)* IQ.

quadragénaire [kadʀaʒenɛʀ] *nm/f* man/woman in his/her forties.

quadriller [kadʀije] *vt (papier)* to mark out in squares; *(POLICE)* to keep under tight control.

quadruple [k(w)adʀypl(ə)] *nm*: **le ~ de** four times as much as; **quadruplés, ées** *nm/fpl* quadruplets, quads.

quai [ke] *nm (de port)* quay; *(de gare)* platform; **être à ~** *(navire)* to be alongside; *(train)* to be in the station.

qualifier [kalifje] *vt*, **se ~** *vi (SPORT)* to qualify; ~ **qch/qn de** to describe sth/sb as.

qualité [kalite] *nf* quality; *(titre, fonction)* position.

quand [kɑ̃] *cj, ad* when; ~ **je serai riche** when I'm rich; ~ **même** all the same; really; ~ **bien même** even though.

quant [kɑ̃]: ~ **à** *prép* as for, as to; regarding.

quant-à-soi [kɑ̃taswa] *nm*: **rester sur son ~** to remain aloof.

quantité [kɑ̃tite] *nf* quantity, amount; *(SCIENCE)* quantity; *(grand nombre)*: **une ou des ~(s)** a great deal of.

quarantaine [kaʀɑ̃tɛn] *nf (MÉD)* quarantine; **avoir la ~** *(âge)* to be around forty; **une ~ (de)** forty or so, about forty.

quarante [kaʀɑ̃t] *num* forty.

quart [kaʀ] *nm (fraction, partie)* quarter; *(surveillance)* watch; **un ~ de beurre** a quarter kilo of butter; **un ~ de vin** a quarter litre of wine; **une livre un ~ ou et** ~ one and a quarter pounds; **le ~ de** a quarter of; ~ **d'heure** quarter of an hour.

quartier [kaʀtje] *nm (de ville)* district, area; *(de bœuf)* quarter; *(de fruit, fromage)* piece; ~s *nmpl (MIL, BLASON)* quarters; **cinéma de ~** local cinema; **avoir ~ libre** (*fig*) to be free; **~ général** (QG) headquarters (HQ).

quartz [kwarts] *nm* quartz.

quasi [kazi] *ad* almost, nearly; **~ment** *ad* almost, nearly.

quatorze [katɔrz(ə)] *num* fourteen.

quatre [katr(ə)] *num* four; **à ~ pattes** on all fours; **tiré à ~ épingles** dressed up to the nines; **faire les ~ cent coups** to get a bit wild; **se mettre en ~ pour qn** to go out of one's way for sb; **~ à ~** (*monter, descendre*) four at a time; **~-vingt-dix** *num* ninety; **~-vingts** *num* eighty; **quatrième** *num* fourth.

quatuor [kwatyɔr] *nm* quartet(te).

que [kə] ♦ *cj* **1** (*introduisant complétive*) that; **il sait ~ tu es là** he knows (that) you're here; **je veux ~ tu acceptes** I want you to accept; **il a dit ~ oui** he said he would (*ou* it was *etc*)

2 (*reprise d'autres conjonctions*): **quand il rentrera et qu'il aura mangé** when he gets back and (when) he has eaten; **si vous y allez ou ~ vous ...** if you go there or if you ...

3 (*en tête de phrase: hypothèse, souhait etc*): **qu'il le veuille ou non** whether he likes it or not; **qu'il fasse ce qu'il voudra!** let him do as he pleases!

4 (*après comparatif*) than; as; *voir* **plus, aussi, autant** *etc*

5 (*seulement*): **ne ... ~** only; **il ne boit ~ de l'eau** he only drinks water

♦ *ad* (*exclamation*): **qu'il** *ou* **qu'est-ce qu'il est bête/court vite!** he's so silly!/he runs so fast!; **~ de livres!** what a lot of books!

♦ *pronom* **1** (*relatif: personne*) whom; (*: chose*) that, which; **l'homme ~ je vois** the man (whom) I see; **le livre ~ tu vois** the book (that *ou* which) you see; **un jour ~ j'étais ...** a day when I was ...

2 (*interrogatif*) what; **~ fais-tu?, qu'est-ce que tu fais?** what are you doing?; **qu'est-ce que c'est?** what is it?, what's that?; **~ faire?** what can one do?

quel, quelle [kɛl] *a* **1** (*interrogatif: personne*) who; (*: chose*) what; which; **~ est cet homme?** who is this man?; **~ est ce livre?** what is this book?; **~ livre/homme?** what book/man?; (*parmi un certain choix*) which book/man?; **~s acteurs préférez-vous?** which actors do you prefer; **dans ~s pays êtes-vous allé?** which *ou* what countries did you go to?

2 (*exclamatif*): **~le surprise!** what a surprise!

3: **~(le) que soit: ~ que soit le coupable** whoever is guilty; **~ que soit votre avis** whatever your opinion.

quelconque [kɛlkɔ̃k] *a* (*médiocre*) indifferent, poor; (*sans attrait*) ordinary, plain; (*indéfini*): **un ami/pretexte ~** some friend/pretext or other.

quelque [kɛlkə] ♦ *a* **1** some; a few; (*tournure interrogative*) any; **~ espoir** some hope; **il a ~s amis** he has a few *ou* some friends; **a-t-il ~s amis?** has he any friends?; **les ~s livres qui** the few books which; **20 kg et ~(s)** a bit over 20 kg

2: **~ ... que:** **~ livre qu'il choisisse** whatever (*ou* whichever) book he chooses

3: **~ chose** something; (*tournure interrogative*) anything; **~ chose d'autre** something else; anything else; **~ part** somewhere; anywhere; **en ~ sorte** as it were

♦ *ad* **1** (*environ*): **~ 100 mètres** some 100 metres

2: **~ peu** rather, somewhat.

quelquefois [kɛlkəfwa] *ad* sometimes.

quelques-uns, -unes [kɛlkəzœ̃, -yn] *pronom* a few, some.

quelqu'un [kɛlkœ̃] *pronom* someone, somebody, *tournure interrogative* + anyone *ou* anybody; **~ d'autre** someone *ou* somebody else; anybody else.

quémander [kemɑ̃de] *vt* to beg for.

qu'en dira-t-on [kɑ̃diratɔ̃] *nm inv*: **le ~** gossip, what people say.

querelle [kərɛl] *nf* quarrel.

quereller [kərele]: **se ~** *vi* to quarrel.

qu'est-ce que (*ou* **qui**) [kɛskə(ki)] *voir* **que, qui**.

question [kɛstjɔ̃] *nf* (*gén*) question; (*fig*) matter; issue; **il a été ~ de we** (*ou* they) spoke about; **de quoi est-il ~?** what is it about?; **il n'en est pas ~** there's no question of it; **hors de ~** out of the question; **remettre en ~** to question.

questionnaire [kɛstjɔnɛr] *nm* questionnaire; **questionner** *vt* to question.

quête [kɛt] *nf* collection; (*recherche*) quest, search; **faire la ~** (*à l'église*) to take the collection; (*artiste*) to pass the hat round; **quêter** *vi* (*à l'église*) to take the collection.

quetsche [kwɛtʃ(ə)] *nf* damson.

queue [kø] *nf* tail; (*fig: du classement*) bottom; (*: de poêle*) handle; (*: de fruit, feuille*) stalk; (*: de train, colonne, file*) rear; **faire la ~** to queue (up); **~ de cheval** ponytail; **~-de-pie** *nf* (*habit*) tails *pl*, tail coat.

qui [ki] *pronom* (*personne*) who, *prép* + whom; (*chose, animal*) which, that; **qu'est-ce ~ est sur la table?** what is on the table?; **~ est-ce qui?** who?; **~ est-ce que?** who?; whom?; **à ~ est ce sac?** whose bag is this?; **à ~ parlais-tu?** who were you talking to?, to whom were you talking?; **amenez ~ vous voulez** bring who you like; **~ que ce soit** whoever it may be.

quiconque [kikɔ̃k] *pronom* (*celui qui*) whoever, anyone who; (*personne*) anyone, anybody.

quiétude [kjetyd] *nf* (*d'un lieu*) quiet, tranquillity; **en toute ~** in complete peace.

quille [kij] *nf*: (jeu de) ~s skittles *sg* (*Brit*), bowling (*US*).

quincaillerie [kɛ̃kajʀi] *nf* (*ustensiles*) hardware; (*magasin*) hardware shop; **quincaillier, ière** *nm/f* hardware dealer.

quinine [kinin] *nf* quinine.

quinquagénaire [kɛ̃kaʒenɛʀ] *nm/f* man/woman in his/her fifties.

quintal, aux [kɛ̃tal, -o] *nm* quintal (*100 kg*).

quinte [kɛ̃t] *nf*: ~ (de toux) coughing fit.

quintuple [kɛ̃typl(ə)] *nm*: le ~ de five times as much as; **quintuplés, ées** *nm/fpl* quintuplets, quins.

quinzaine [kɛ̃zɛn] *nf*: une ~ (de) about fifteen, fifteen or so; une ~ (de jours) a fortnight, two weeks.

quinze [kɛ̃z] *num* fifteen; **demain en** ~ a fortnight *ou* two weeks tomorrow; **dans** ~ **jours** in a fortnight('s time), in two weeks(' time).

quiproquo [kipʀɔko] *nm* misunderstanding.

quittance [kitɑ̃s] *nf* (*reçu*) receipt; (*facture*) bill.

quitte [kit] *a*: être ~ envers qn to be no longer in sb's debt; (*fig*) to be quits with sb; être ~ de (*obligation*) to be clear of; en être ~ à bon compte to have got off lightly; ~ à faire even if it means doing.

quitter [kite] *vt* to leave; (*espoir, illusion*) to give up; (*vêtement*) to take off; se ~ *vi* (*couples, interlocuteurs*) to part; ne quittez pas (*au téléphone*) hold the line.

qui-vive [kiviv] *nm*: être sur le ~ to be on the alert.

quoi [kwa] *pronom* (*interrogatif*) what; ~ de neuf? what's the news?; as-tu de ~ écrire? have you anything to write with?; il n'a pas de ~ se l'acheter he can't afford it; ~ qu'il arrive whatever happens; ~ qu'il en soit be that as it may; ~ que ce soit anything at all; 'il n'y a pas de ~' '(please) don't mention it'; à ~ bon? what's the use?; en ~ puis-je vous aider? how can I help you?

quoique [kwak(ə)] *cj* (al)though.

quolibet [kɔlibɛ] *nm* gibe, jeer.

quote-part [kɔtpaʀ] *nf* share.

quotidien, ne [kɔtidjɛ̃, -ɛn] *a* daily; (*banal*) everyday // *nm* (*journal*) daily (paper).

R

r. *abr de* **route, rue**.

rab [ʀab] *abr m* (*fam*) *de* **rabiot**.

rabâcher [ʀabɑʃe] *vt* to keep on repeating.

rabais [ʀabɛ] *nm* reduction, discount.

rabaisser [ʀabese] *vt* (*rabattre*) to reduce; (*dénigrer*) to belittle.

rabattre [ʀabatʀ(ə)] *vt* (*couvercle,*

siège) to pull down; (*gibier*) to drive; se ~ *vi* (*bords, couvercle*) to fall shut; (*véhicule, coureur*) to cut in; **se ~ sur** *vt* to fall back on.

rabbin [ʀabɛ̃] *nm* rabbi.

rabiot [ʀabjo] *nm* (*fam*) extra, more.

râblé, e [ʀɑble] *a* stocky.

rabot [ʀabo] *nm* plane.

rabougri, e [ʀabugʀi] *a* stunted.

rabrouer [ʀabʀue] *vt* to snub.

racaille [ʀakɑj] *nf* (*péj*) rabble, riffraff.

raccommoder [ʀakɔmɔde] *vt* to mend, repair; (*chaussette etc*) to darn.

raccompagner [ʀakɔ̃paɲe] *vt* to take *ou* see back.

raccord [ʀakɔʀ] *nm* link.

raccorder [ʀakɔʀde] *vt* to join (up), link up; (*suj: pont etc*) to connect, link.

raccourci [ʀakuʀsi] *nm* short cut.

raccourcir [ʀakuʀsiʀ] *vt* to shorten.

raccrocher [ʀakʀoʃe] *vt* (*tableau*) to hang back up; (*récepteur*) to put down // *vi* (*TÉL*) to hang up, ring off; se ~ à *vt* to cling to, hang on to.

race [ʀas] *nf* race; (*d'animaux, fig*) breed; (*ascendance*) stock, race; **de** ~ *a* purebred, pedigree.

rachat [ʀaʃa] *nm* buying; buying back.

racheter [ʀaʃte] *vt* (*article perdu*) to buy another; (*davantage*): ~ du lait/3 œufs to buy more milk/another 3 eggs *ou* 3 more eggs; (*après avoir vendu*) to buy back; (*d'occasion*) to buy; (*COMM: part, firme*) to buy up; (*: pension, rente*) to redeem; se ~ *vi* (*fig*) to make amends.

racial, e, aux [ʀasjal, -o] *a* racial.

racine [ʀasin] *nf* root; ~ carrée/cubique square/cube root.

raciste [ʀasist(ə)] *a, nm/f* raci(al)ist.

racket [ʀakɛt] *nm* racketeering *q*.

racler [ʀɑkle] *vt* (*surface*) to scrape; (*tache, boue*) to scrape off.

racoler [ʀakɔle] *vt* (*attirer: suj: prostituée*) to solicit; (*: parti, marchand*) to tout for.

racontars [ʀakɔ̃taʀ] *nmpl* gossip *sg*.

raconter [ʀakɔ̃te] *vt*: ~ (à qn) (*décrire*) to relate (to sb), tell (sb) about; (*dire*) to tell (sb).

racorni, e [ʀakɔʀni] *a* hard(ened).

radar [ʀadaʀ] *nm* radar.

rade [ʀad] *nf* (*natural*) harbour; **rester en** ~ (*fig*) to be left stranded.

radeau, x [ʀado] *nm* raft.

radiateur [ʀadjatœʀ] *nm* radiator, heater; (*AUTO*) radiator; ~ électrique/à gaz electric/gas heater *ou* fire.

radiation [ʀadjasjɔ̃] *nf* (*voir radier*) striking off *q*; (*PHYSIQUE*) radiation.

radical, e, aux [ʀadikal, -o] *a* radical.

radier [ʀadje] *vt* to strike off.

radieux, euse [ʀadjø, -øz] *a* radiant; brilliant, glorious.

radin, e [ʀadɛ̃, -in] *a* (*fam*) stingy.

radio [ʀadjo] *nf* radio; (*MÉD*) X-ray //

nm radio operator; **à la ~** on the radio.

radio... [ʀadjo] *préfixe*: **~actif, ive** *a* radioactive; **radiodiffuser** *vt* to broadcast; **~graphie** *nf* radiography; *(photo)* X-ray photograph; **~phonique** *a* radio *cpd*; **~télévisé, e** *a* broadcast on radio and television.

radis [ʀadi] *nm* radish.

radoter [ʀadɔte] *vi* to ramble on.

radoucir [ʀadusiʀ]: **se ~** *vi* *(se réchauffer)* to become milder; *(se calmer)* to calm down; to soften.

rafale [ʀafal] *nf* *(vent)* gust (of wind); *(tir)* burst of gunfire.

raffermir [ʀafɛʀmiʀ] *vt*, **se ~** *vi* *(tissus, muscle)* to firm up; *(fig)* to strengthen.

raffiner [ʀafine] *vt* to refine; **raffinerie** *nf* refinery.

raffoler [ʀafɔle]: **~ de** *vt* to be very keen on.

rafle [ʀafl(ə)] *nf* *(de police)* raid.

rafler [ʀafle] *vt* *(fam)* to swipe, nick.

rafraîchir [ʀafʀeʃiʀ] *vt* *(atmosphère, température)* to cool (down); *(aussi:* **mettre à ~)** to chill; *(fig: rénover)* to brighten up; **se ~** *vi* to grow cooler; to freshen up; to refresh o.s; **rafraîchissant, e** *a* refreshing; **rafraîchissement** *nm* cooling; *(boisson)* cool drink; **rafraîchissements** *(boissons, fruits etc)* refreshments.

rage [ʀaʒ] *nf* *(MÉD)*: **la ~** rabies; *(fureur)* rage, fury; **faire ~** to rage; **~ de dents** (raging) toothache.

ragot [ʀago] *nm* *(fam)* malicious gossip *q*.

ragoût [ʀagu] *nm* *(plat)* stew.

raide [ʀɛd] *a* *(tendu)* taut, tight; *(escarpé)* steep; *(droit: cheveux)* straight; *(ankylosé, dur, guindé)* stiff; *(fam)* steep, stiff; flat broke // *ad* *(en pente)* steeply; **~ mort** stone dead; **raidir** *vt* *(muscles)* to stiffen; *(câble)* to pull taut; **se raidir** *vi* to stiffen; to become taut; *(personne)* to tense up; to brace o.s.

raie [ʀɛ] *nf* *(ZOOL)* skate, ray; *(rayure)* stripe; *(des cheveux)* parting.

raifort [ʀɛfɔʀ] *nm* horseradish.

rail [ʀaj] *nm* rail; *(chemins de fer)* railways *pl*; **par ~** by rail.

railler [ʀaje] *vt* to scoff at, jeer at.

rainure [ʀɛnyʀ] *nf* groove; slot.

raisin [ʀɛzɛ̃] *nm* *(aussi:* **~s)** grapes *pl*; **~s secs** raisins.

raison [ʀɛzɔ̃] *nf* reason; **avoir ~** to be right; **donner ~ à qn** to agree with sb; to prove sb right; **se faire une ~** to learn to live with it; **perdre la ~** to become insane; to take leave of one's senses; **~ de plus** all the more reason; **à plus forte ~** all the more so; **en ~ de** because of; according to; in proportion to; **à ~ de** at the rate of; **~ sociale** corporate name; **raisonnable** *a* reasonable, sensible.

raisonnement [ʀɛzɔnmɑ̃] *nm* reasoning; arguing; argument.

raisonner [ʀɛzɔne] *vi* *(penser)* to reason; *(argumenter, discuter)* to argue // *vt* *(personne)* to reason with.

rajeunir [ʀaʒœniʀ] *vt* *(suj: coiffure, robe)*: **~ qn** to make sb look younger; *(suj: cure etc)* to rejuvenate; *(fig)* to give a new look to; to inject new blood into // *vi* to become *(ou* look) younger.

rajouter [ʀaʒute] *vt*: **~ du sel/un œuf** to add some more salt/another egg.

rajuster [ʀaʒyste] *vt* *(vêtement)* to straighten, tidy; *(salaires)* to adjust; *(machine)* to readjust.

ralenti [ʀalɑ̃ti] *nm*: **au ~** *(AUTO)*: **tourner au ~** to tick over, idle; *(CINÉMA)* in slow motion; *(fig)* at a slower pace.

ralentir [ʀalɑ̃tiʀ] *vt, vi*, **se ~** *vi* to slow down.

râler [ʀɑle] *vi* to groan; *(fam)* to grouse, moan (and groan).

rallier [ʀalje] *vt* *(rassembler)* to rally; *(rejoindre)* to rejoin; *(gagner à sa cause)* to win over; **se ~ à** *(avis)* to come over *ou* round to.

rallonge [ʀalɔ̃ʒ] *nf* *(de table)* (extra) leaf *(pl* leaves); *(argent etc)* extra *q*.

rallonger [ʀalɔ̃ʒe] *vt* to lengthen.

rallye [ʀali] *nm* rally; *(POL)* march.

ramassage [ʀamasaʒ] *nm*: **~ scolaire** school bus service.

ramassé, e [ʀamase] *a* *(trapu)* squat.

ramasser [ʀamase] *vt* *(objet tombé ou par terre, fam)* to pick up; *(recueillir)* to collect; *(récolter)* to gather; **se ~** *vi* *(sur soi-même)* to huddle up; to crouch; **ramassis** *nm* *(péj)* bunch; jumble.

rambarde [ʀɑ̃baʀd(ə)] *nf* guardrail.

rame [ʀam] *nf* *(aviron)* oar; *(de métro)* train; *(de papier)* ream.

rameau, x [ʀamo] *nm* (small) branch; **les R~x** *(REL)* Palm Sunday *sg*.

ramener [ʀamne] *vt* to bring back; *(reconduire)* to take back; *(rabattre: couverture, visière)*: **~ qch sur** to pull sth back over; **~ qch à** *(réduire à, aussi MATH)* to reduce sth to.

ramer [ʀame] *vi* to row.

ramollir [ʀamɔliʀ] *vt* to soften; **se ~** *vi* to go soft.

ramoner [ʀamɔne] *vt* to sweep.

rampe [ʀɑ̃p] *nf* *(d'escalier)* banister(s *pl*); *(dans un garage, d'un terrain)* ramp; *(THÉÂTRE)*: **la ~** the footlights *pl*; **~ de lancement** launching pad.

ramper [ʀɑ̃pe] *vi* to crawl.

rancard [ʀɑ̃kaʀ] *nm* *(fam)* date; tip.

rancart [ʀɑ̃kaʀ] *nm*: **mettre au ~** to scrap.

rance [ʀɑ̃s] *a* rancid.

rancœur [ʀɑ̃kœʀ] *nf* rancour.

rançon [ʀɑ̃sɔ̃] *nf* ransom; *(fig)* price.

rancune [ʀɑ̃kyn] *nf* grudge, rancour; **garder ~ à qn (de qch)** to bear sb a grudge (for sth); **sans ~!** no hard feelings!; **rancunier, ière** a vindictive, spiteful.

randonnée [Rɑ̃dɔne] nf ride; (à pied) walk, ramble; hike, hiking q.

rang [Rɑ̃] nm (rangée) row; (grade, classement) rank; **~s** (MIL) ranks; **se mettre en ~s/sur un ~** to get into ou form rows/a line; **au premier ~** in the first row; (fig) ranking first.

rangé, e [Rɑ̃ʒe] a (sérieux) orderly, steady.

rangée [Rɑ̃ʒe] nf row.

ranger [Rɑ̃ʒe] vt (classer, grouper) to order, arrange; (mettre à sa place) to put away; (voiture dans la rue) to park; (mettre de l'ordre dans) to tidy up; (arranger) to arrange; (fig: classer): **~ qn/qch parmi** to rank sb/sth among; **se ~** vi (véhicule, conducteur) to pull over ou in; (piéton) to step aside; (s'assagir) to settle down; **se ~ à** (avis) to come round to.

ranimer [Ranime] vt (personne) to bring round; (forces, courage) to restore; (troupes etc) to kindle new life in; (douleur, souvenir) to revive; (feu) to rekindle.

rapace [Rapas] nm bird of prey.

râpe [Rɑp] nf (CULIN) grater.

râpé, e [Rɑpe] a (tissu) threadbare.

râper [Rɑpe] vt (CULIN) to grate.

rapetisser [Raptise] vt to shorten.

rapide [Rapid] a fast; (prompt) quick // nm express (train); (de cours d'eau) rapid; **~ment** ad fast; quickly.

rapiécer [Rapjese] vt to patch.

rappel [Rapɛl] nm (THÉÂTRE) curtain call; (MÉD: vaccination) booster; (ADMIN: de salaire) back pay q; (d'une aventure, d'un nom) reminder.

rappeler [Raple] vt to call back; (ambassadeur, MIL) to recall; (faire se souvenir): **~ qch à qn** to remind sb of sth; **se ~** vt (se souvenir de) to remember, recall.

rapport [RapɔR] nm (compte rendu) report; (profit) yield, return; revenue; (lien, analogie) relationship; (MATH, TECH) ratio (pl s); **~s** (entre personnes, pays) relations; **avoir ~ à** to have something to do with; **être en ~ avec** (idée de corrélation) to be related to; **être/se mettre en ~ avec qn** to be/get in touch with sb; **par ~ à** in relation to; **~s (sexuels)** (sexual) intercourse sg.

rapporter [RapɔRte] vt (rendre, ramener) to bring back; (apporter davantage) to bring more; (suj: investissement) to yield; (: activité) to bring in; (relater) to report // vi (investissement) to give a good return ou yield; (: activité) to be very profitable; **~ qch à** (fig: rattacher) to relate sth to; **se ~ à** (correspondre à) to relate to; **s'en ~ à** to

rely on; **rapporteur, euse** nm/f (de procès, commission) reporter; (péj) telltale // nm (GÉOM) protractor.

rapprochement [RapRɔʃmɑ̃] nm (de nations, familles) reconciliation; (analogie, rapport) parallel.

rapprocher [RapRɔʃe] vt (chaise d'une table): **~ qch (de)** to bring sth closer (to); (deux objets) to bring closer together; (réunir) to bring together; (comparer) to establish a parallel between; **se ~** vi to draw closer ou nearer; **se ~ de** to come closer to; (présenter une analogie avec) to be close to.

rapt [Rapt] nm abduction.

raquette [Rakɛt] nf (de tennis) racket; (de ping-pong) bat; (à neige) snowshoe.

rare [RaR] a rare; (main-d'œuvre, denrées) scarce; (cheveux, herbe) sparse.

rarement [RaRmɑ̃] ad rarely, seldom.

ras, e [Rɑ, Rɑz] a (tête, cheveux) close-cropped; (poil, herbe) short // ad short; **en ~e campagne** in open country; **à ~ bords** to the brim; **au ~ de** level with; **en avoir ~ le bol** (fam) to be fed up; **~ du cou** a (pull, robe) crew-neck.

rasade [Razad] nf glassful.

raser [Rɑze] vt (barbe, cheveux) to shave off; (menton, personne) to shave; (fam: ennuyer) to bore; (démolir) to raze (to the ground); (frôler) to graze, skim; **se ~** vi to shave; (fam) to be bored (to tears); **rasoir** nm razor.

rassasier [Rasazje] vt to satisfy.

rassemblement [Rasɑ̃bləmɑ̃] nm (groupe) gathering; (POL) union.

rassembler [Rasɑ̃ble] vt (réunir) to assemble, gather; (regrouper, amasser) to gather together, collect; **se ~** vi to gather.

rassis, e [Rasi, -iz] a (pain) stale.

rassurer [RasyRe] vt to reassure; **se ~** vi to be reassured; **rassure-toi** don't worry.

rat [Ra] nm rat.

rate [Rat] nf spleen.

raté, e [Rate] a (tentative) unsuccessful, failed // nm/f failure // nm misfiring q.

râteau, x [Rɑto] nm rake.

râtelier [Rɑtəlje] nm rack; (fam) false teeth pl.

rater [Rate] vi (affaire, projet etc) to go wrong, fail // vt (cible, train, occasion) to miss; (démonstration, plat) to spoil; (examen) to fail.

ration [Rasjɔ̃] nf ration; (fig) share.

ratisser [Ratise] vt (allée) to rake; (feuilles) to rake up; (suj: armée, police) to comb.

R.A.T.P. sigle f (= Régie autonome des transports parisiens) Paris transport authority.

rattacher [Rataʃe] vt (animal, cheveux) to tie up again; (incorporer: ADMIN etc): **~ qch à** to join sth to; (fig: relier): **~ qch à** to link sth with; (: lier): **~ qn à**

to bind *ou* tie sb to.

rattraper [ʀatʀape] *vt* (*fugitif*) to recapture; (*empêcher de tomber*) to catch (hold of); (*atteindre, rejoindre*) to catch up with; (*réparer: imprudence, erreur*) to make up for; se ~ *vi* to make good one's losses; to make up for it; se ~ (à) (*se raccrocher*) to stop o.s. falling (by catching hold of).

rature [ʀatyʀ] *nf* deletion, erasure.

rauque [ʀok] *a* raucous; hoarse.

ravages [ʀavaʒ] *nmpl*: faire des ~ to wreak havoc.

ravaler [ʀavale] *vt* (*mur, façade*) to restore; (*déprécier*) to lower.

ravi, e [ʀavi] *a*: être ~ de/que to be delighted with/that.

ravin [ʀavɛ̃] *nm* gully, ravine.

ravir [ʀaviʀ] *vt* (*enchanter*) to delight; (*enlever*): ~ qch à qn to rob sb of sth; à ~ *ad* beautifully.

raviser [ʀavize]: se ~ *vi* to change one's mind.

ravissant, e [ʀavisã, -ãt] *a* delightful.

ravisseur, euse [ʀavisœʀ, -øz] *nm/f* abductor, kidnapper.

ravitailler [ʀavitaje] *vt* to resupply; (*véhicule*) to refuel; se ~ *vi* to get fresh supplies.

raviver [ʀavive] *vt* (*feu, douleur*) to revive; (*couleurs*) to brighten up.

rayé, e [ʀeje] *a* (à *rayures*) striped.

rayer [ʀeje] *vt* (*érafler*) to scratch; (*barrer*) to cross out; (*d'une liste*) to cross off.

rayon [ʀɛjɔ̃] *nm* (*de soleil etc*) ray; (*GÉOM*) radius; (*de roue*) spoke; (*étagère*) shelf (*pl* shelves); (*de grand magasin*) department; **dans un ~ de** within a radius of; ~ **d'action** range; ~ **de soleil** sunbeam; ~**s X** X-rays.

rayonnement [ʀejɔnmã] *nm* radiation; (*fig*) radiance; influence.

rayonner [ʀejɔne] *vi* (*chaleur, énergie*) to radiate; (*fig*) to shine forth; to be radiant; (*touriste*) to go touring (*from one base*).

rayure [ʀejyʀ] *nf* (*motif*) stripe; (*éraflure*) scratch; (*rainure, d'un fusil*) groove.

raz-de-marée [ʀɑdmaʀe] *nm inv* tidal wave.

ré [ʀe] *nm* (*MUS*) D, (*en chantant la gamme*) re.

réacteur [ʀeaktœʀ] *nm* jet engine.

réaction [ʀeaksjɔ̃] *nf* reaction; **moteur à ~** jet engine.

réadapter [ʀeadapte] *vt* to readjust; (*MÉD*) to rehabilitate; se ~ (à) to readjust (to).

réagir [ʀeaʒiʀ] *vi* to react.

réalisateur, trice [ʀealizatœʀ, -tʀis] *nm/f* (*TV, CINÉMA*) director.

réalisation [ʀealizasjɔ̃] *nf* carrying out; realization; fulfilment; achievement;

production; (*œuvre*) production; creation; work.

réaliser [ʀealize] *vt* (*projet, opération*) to carry out, realize; (*rêve, souhait*) to realize, fulfil; (*exploit*) to achieve; (*achat, vente*) to make; (*film*) to produce; (*se rendre compte de, COMM*: *bien, capital*) to realize; se ~ *vi* to be realized.

réaliste [ʀealist(ə)] *a* realistic.

réalité [ʀealite] *nf* reality; **en ~** in (actual) fact; **dans la ~** in reality.

réanimation [ʀeanimasjɔ̃] *nf* resuscitation; **service de ~** intensive care unit.

réarmer [ʀeaʀme] *vt* (*arme*) to reload // *vi* (*état*) to rearm.

rébarbatif, ive [ʀebaʀbatif, -iv] *a* forbidding.

rebattu, e [ʀəbaty] *a* hackneyed.

rebelle [ʀəbel] *nm/f* rebel // *a* (*troupes*) rebel; (*enfant*) rebellious; (*mèche etc*) unruly; ~ à unamenable to.

rebeller [ʀəbele]: se ~ *vi* to rebel.

rebondi, e [ʀəbɔ̃di] *a* rounded; chubby.

rebondir [ʀəbɔ̃diʀ] *vi* (*ballon: au sol*) to bounce; (*: contre un mur*) to rebound; (*fig*) to get moving again; **rebondissement** *nm* new development.

rebord [ʀəbɔʀ] *nm* edge.

rebours [ʀəbuʀ]: à ~ *ad* the wrong way.

rebrousse-poil [ʀbʀuspwal]: à ~ *ad* the wrong way.

rebrousser [ʀəbʀuse] *vt*: ~ **chemin** to turn back.

rebut [ʀəby] *nm*: mettre au ~ to scrap.

rebuter [ʀəbyte] *vt* to put off.

récalcitrant, e [ʀekalsitʀã, -ãt] *a* refractory.

recaler [ʀəkale] *vt* (*SCOL*) to fail.

récapituler [ʀekapityle] *vt* to recapitulate; to sum up.

receler [ʀəsəle] *vt* (*produit d'un vol*) to receive; (*malfaiteur*) to harbour; (*fig*) to conceal; **receleur, euse** *nm/f* receiver.

récemment [ʀesamã] *ad* recently.

recenser [ʀəsãse] *vt* (*population*) to take a census of; (*inventorier*) to list.

récent, e [ʀesã, -ãt] *a* recent.

récépissé [ʀesepise] *nm* receipt.

récepteur [ʀeseptœʀ] *nm* receiver; ~ (**de radio**) radio set *ou* receiver.

réception [ʀesɛpsjɔ̃] *nf* receiving *q*; (*accueil*) reception, welcome; (*bureau*) reception desk; (*réunion mondaine*) reception, party; **réceptionniste** *nm/f* receptionist.

recette [ʀəsɛt] *nf* (*CULIN*) recipe; (*fig*) formula, recipe; (*COMM*) takings *pl*; ~**s** *nfpl* (*COMM*: rentrées) receipts.

receveur, euse [ʀəsvœʀ, -øz] *nm/f* (*des contributions*) tax collector; (*des postes*) postmaster/mistress; (*d'autobus*) conductor/conductress.

recevoir [ʀəsvwaʀ] *vt* to receive;

(*client, patient*) to see // *vi* to receive visitors; to give parties; to see patients *etc*; se ~ *vi* (*athlète*) to land; **être reçu** (*à un examen*) to pass.

rechange [rəʃɑ̃ʒ]: de ~ *a* (*pièces, roue*) spare; (*fig: solution*) alternative; **des vêtements de** ~ a change of clothes.

rechaper [rəʃape] *vt* to remould, re-tread.

réchapper [reʃape]: ~ de ou à *vt* (*accident, maladie*) to come through.

recharge [rəʃarʒ(ə)] *nf* refill.

recharger [rəʃarʒe] *vt* (*camion, fusil, appareil-photo*) to reload; (*briquet, stylo*) to refill; (*batterie*) to recharge.

réchaud [reʃo] *nm* (portable) stove; plate-warmer.

réchauffer [reʃofe] *vt* (*plat*) to reheat; (*mains, personne*) to warm; se ~ *vi* (*température*) to get warmer.

rêche [rɛʃ] *a* rough.

recherche [rəʃɛrʃ(ə)] *nf* (*action*): la ~ de the search for; (*raffinement*) affectedness, studied elegance; (*scientifique etc*): la ~ research; ~s *nfpl* (*de la police*) investigations; (*scientifiques*) research *sg*; se mettre à la ~ de to go in search of.

recherché, e [rəʃɛrʃe] *a* (*rare, demandé*) much sought-after; (*raffiné*) studied, affected.

rechercher [rəʃɛrʃe] *vt* (*objet égaré, personne*) to look for; (*causes, nouveau procédé*) to try to find; (*bonheur, amitié*) to seek.

rechute [rəʃyt] *nf* (*MÉD*) relapse.

récidiver [residive] *vi* to commit a subsequent offence; (*fig*) to do it again.

récif [resif] *nm* reef.

récipient [resipjɑ̃] *nm* container.

réciproque [resiprɔk] *a* reciprocal.

récit [resi] *nm* story.

récital [resital] *nm* recital.

réciter [resite] *vt* to recite.

réclamation [reklamasjɔ̃] *nf* complaint; ~s (*bureau*) complaints department *sg*.

réclame [reklam] *nf* ad, advert(isement); **article en** ~ special offer.

réclamer [reklame] *vt* (*aide, nourriture etc*) to ask for; (*revendiquer*) to claim, demand; (*nécessiter*) to demand, require // *vi* to complain.

réclusion [reklyzjɔ̃] *nf* imprisonment.

recoin [rəkwɛ̃] *nm* nook, corner; (*fig*) hidden recess.

reçois *etc vb voir* **recevoir**.

récolte [rekɔlt(ə)] *nf* harvesting; gathering; (*produits*) harvest, crop; (*fig*) crop, collection.

récolter [rekɔlte] *vt* to harvest, gather (in); (*fig*) to collect; to get.

recommandé [rəkɔmɑ̃de] *nm* (*POSTES*): **en** ~ by registered mail.

recommander [rəkɔmɑ̃de] *vt* to recommend; (*suj: qualités etc*) to commend;

(*POSTES*) to register; se ~ de qn to give sb's name as a reference.

recommencer [rəkɔmɑ̃se] *vt* (*reprendre: lutte, séance*) to resume, start again; (*refaire: travail, explications*) to start afresh, start (over) again; (*récidiver: erreur*) to make again // *vi* to start again; (*récidiver*) to do it again.

récompense [rekɔ̃pɑ̃s] *nf* reward; (*prix*) award; **récompenser** *vt*: **récompenser qn (de ou pour)** to reward sb (for).

réconcilier [rekɔ̃silje] *vt* to reconcile; se ~ (avec) to be reconciled (with).

reconduire [rəkɔ̃dɥir] *vt* (*raccompagner*) to take ou see back; (*JUR, POL: renouveler*) to renew.

réconfort [rekɔ̃fɔr] *nm* comfort.

réconforter [rekɔ̃fɔrte] *vt* (*consoler*) to comfort; (*revigorer*) to fortify.

reconnaissance [rəkɔnɛsɑ̃s] *nf* recognition; acknowledgement; (*gratitude*) gratitude, gratefulness; (*MIL*) reconnaissance, recce.

reconnaissant, e [rəkɔnɛsɑ̃, -ɑ̃t] *a* grateful.

reconnaître [rəkɔnɛtr(ə)] *vt* to recognize; (*MIL: lieu*) to reconnoitre; (*JUR: enfant, dette, droit*) to acknowledge; ~ que to admit ou acknowledge that; ~ qn/qch à to recognize sb/sth by.

reconstituer [rəkɔ̃stitɥe] *vt* (*monument ancien*) to recreate; (*fresque, vase brisé*) to piece together, reconstitute; (*événement, accident*) to reconstruct; (*fortune, patrimoine*) to rebuild.

reconstruire [rəkɔ̃strɥir] *vt* to rebuild.

record [rəkɔr] *nm, a* record.

recoupement [rəkupmɑ̃] *nm*: **par** ~ by cross-checking.

recouper [rəkupe]: se ~ *vi* (*témoignages*) to tie ou match up.

recourbé, e [rəkurbe] *a* curved; hooked; bent.

recourir [rəkurir]: ~ à *vt* (*ami, agence*) to turn ou appeal to; (*force, ruse, emprunt*) to resort to.

recours [rəkur] *nm* (*JUR*) appeal; **avoir** ~ à = **recourir à**; **en dernier** ~ as a last resort; ~ **en grâce** plea for clemency.

recouvrer [rəkuvre] *vt* (*vue, santé etc*) to recover, regain; (*impôts*) to collect; (*créance*) to recover.

recouvrir [rəkuvrir] *vt* (*couvrir à nouveau*) to re-cover; (*couvrir entièrement, aussi fig*) to cover; (*cacher, masquer*) to conceal, hide; se ~ *vi* (*se superposer*) to overlap.

récréation [rekreasjɔ̃] *nf* recreation, entertainment; (*SCOL*) break.

récrier [rekrije]: se ~ *vi* to exclaim.

récriminations [rekriminasjɔ̃] *nfpl* remonstrations, complaints.

recroqueviller [rəkrɔkvije]: se ~ *vi* (*feuilles*) to curl ou shrivel up; (*per-*

sonne) to huddle up.

recrudescence [ʀəkʀydesɑ̃s] *nf* fresh outbreak.

recrue [ʀəkʀy] *nf* recruit.

recruter [ʀəkʀyte] *vt* to recruit.

rectangle [ʀɛktɑ̃gl(ə)] *nm* rectangle; **rectangulaire** *a* rectangular.

recteur [ʀɛktœʀ] *nm* ≈ (regional) director of education (*Brit*), ≈ state superintendent of education (*US*).

rectifier [ʀɛktifje] *vt* (*tracé, virage*) to straighten; (*calcul, adresse*) to correct; (*erreur, faute*) to rectify.

rectiligne [ʀɛktiliɲ] *a* straight; (*GÉOM*) rectilinear.

reçu, e [ʀəsy] *pp de* **recevoir** // *a* (*admis, consacré*) accepted // *nm* (*COMM*) receipt.

recueil [ʀəkœj] *nm* collection.

recueillir [ʀəkœjiʀ] *vt* to collect; (*voix, suffrages*) to win; (*accueillir: réfugiés, chat*) to take in; **se ~** *vi* to gather one's thoughts; to meditate.

recul [ʀəkyl] *nm* retreat; recession; decline; (*d'arme à feu*) recoil, kick; **avoir un mouvement de ~** to recoil; **prendre du ~** to stand back.

reculé, e [ʀəkyle] *a* remote.

reculer [ʀəkyle] *vi* to move back, back away; (*AUTO*) to reverse, back (up); (*fig*) to (be on the) decline; to be losing ground; (*: se dérober*) to shrink back // *vt* to move back; to reverse, back (up); (*fig: possibilités, limites*) to extend; (*: date, décision*) to postpone.

reculons [ʀəkylɔ̃]: **à ~** *ad* backwards.

récupérer [ʀekypeʀe] *vt* to recover, get back; (*heures de travail*) to make up; (*déchets*) to salvage; (*délinquant etc*) to rehabilitate // *vi* to recover.

récurer [ʀekyʀe] *vt* to scour.

récuser [ʀekyze] *vt* to challenge; **se ~** *vi* to decline to give an opinion.

reçut *vb voir* **recevoir**.

recycler [ʀəsikle] *vt* (*SCOL*) to reorientate; (*employés*) to retrain; (*TECH*) to recycle.

rédacteur, trice [ʀedaktœʀ, -tʀis] *nm/f* (*journaliste*) writer; subeditor; (*d'ouvrage de référence*) editor, compiler; **~ en chef** chief editor; **~ publicitaire** copywriter.

rédaction [ʀedaksjɔ̃] *nf* writing; (*rédacteurs*) editorial staff; (*bureau*) editorial office(s); (*SCOL: devoir*) essay, composition.

reddition [ʀedisjɔ̃] *nf* surrender.

redemander [ʀədmɑ̃de] *vt* to ask again for; to ask for more of.

redescendre [ʀədesɑ̃dʀ(ə)] *vi* to go back down // *vt* (*pente etc*) to go down.

redevable [ʀədvabl(ə)] *a*: **être ~ de qch à qn** (*somme*) to owe sb sth; (*fig*) to be indebted to sb for sth.

redevance [ʀədvɑ̃s] *nf* (*TÉL*) rental

charge; (*TV*) licence fee.

rédiger [ʀediʒe] *vt* to write; (*contrat*) to draw up.

redire [ʀədiʀ] *vt* to repeat; **trouver à ~ à** to find fault with.

redoublé, e [ʀəduble] *a*: **à coups ~s** even harder, twice as hard.

redoubler [ʀəduble] *vi* (*tempête, violence*) to intensify; (*SCOL*) to repeat a year; **~ de** *vt* to be twice as + *adjectif*.

redoutable [ʀədutabl(ə)] *a* formidable, fearsome.

redouter [ʀədute] *vt* to fear; (*appréhender*) to dread.

redresser [ʀədʀese] *vt* (*arbre, mât*) to set upright; (*pièce tordue*) to straighten out; (*situation, économie*) to put right; **se ~** *vi* (*objet penché*) to right itself; (*personne*) to sit (*ou* stand) up (straight).

réduction [ʀedyksjɔ̃] *nf* reduction.

réduire [ʀeduiʀ] *vt* to reduce; (*prix, dépenses*) to cut, reduce; (*MÉD: fracture*) to set; **se ~ à** (*revenir à*) to boil down to; **se ~ en** (*se transformer en*) to be reduced to.

réduit [ʀedui] *nm* tiny room; recess.

rééducation [ʀeedykasjɔ̃] *nf* (*d'un membre*) re-education; (*de délinquants, d'un blessé*) rehabilitation; **~ de la parole** speech therapy.

réel, le [ʀeɛl] *a* real.

réellement [ʀeɛlmɑ̃] *ad* really.

réévaluer [ʀeevalɥe] *vt* to revalue.

réexpédier [ʀeɛkspedje] *vt* (*à l'envoyeur*) to return, send back; (*au destinataire*) to send on, forward.

refaire [ʀəfɛʀ] *vt* (*faire de nouveau, recommencer*) to do again; (*réparer, restaurer*) to do up.

réfection [ʀefɛksjɔ̃] *nf* repair.

réfectoire [ʀefɛktwaʀ] *nm* refectory.

référence [ʀefeʀɑ̃s] *nf* reference; **~s** (*recommandations*) reference *sg*.

référer [ʀefeʀe]: **se ~ à** *vt* to refer to; **en ~ à qn** to refer the matter to sb.

réfléchi, e [ʀefleʃi] *a* (*caractère*) thoughtful; (*action*) well-thought-out; (*LING*) reflexive.

réfléchir [ʀefleʃiʀ] *vt* to reflect // *vi* to think; **~ à** *ou* **sur** to think about.

reflet [ʀəflɛ] *nm* reflection; (*sur l'eau etc*) sheen *q*, glint.

refléter [ʀəflete] *vt* to reflect; **se ~** *vi* to be reflected.

réflexe [ʀeflɛks(ə)] *nm, a* reflex.

réflexion [ʀeflɛksjɔ̃] *nf* (*de la lumière etc, pensée*) reflection; (*fait de penser*) thought; (*remarque*) remark; **~ faite, à la ~** on reflection.

refluer [ʀəflɥe] *vi* to flow back; (*foule*) to surge back.

reflux [ʀəfly] *nm* (*de la mer*) ebb.

réforme [ʀefɔʀm(ə)] *nf* reform; (*REL*): **la R~** the Reformation.

réformer [RefɔRme] vt to reform; (MIL) to declare unfit for service.

refouler [Rəfule] vt (envahisseurs) to drive back; (liquide) to force back; (fig) to suppress; (PSYCH) to repress.

réfractaire [RefRaktɛR] a: être ~ à to resist.

refrain [RəfRɛ̃] nm (MUS) refrain, chorus; (air, fig) tune.

refréner, réfréner [Rəfrene, RefRene] vt to curb, check.

réfrigérateur [RefRiʒeRatœR] nm refrigerator, fridge.

refroidir [RəfRwadiR] vt to cool // vi to cool (down); se ~ vi (prendre froid) to catch a chill; (temps) to get cooler ou colder; (fig) to cool (off); **refroidissement** nm (grippe etc) chill.

refuge [Rəfyʒ] nm refuge; (pour piétons) (traffic) island.

réfugié, e [Refyʒje] a, nm/f refugee.

réfugier [Refyʒje]: se ~ vi to take refuge.

refus [Rəfy] nm refusal; ce n'est pas de ~ I won't say no, it's welcome.

refuser [Rəfyze] vt to refuse; (SCOL: candidat) to fail; ~ qch à qn to refuse sb sth; ~ du monde to have to turn people away; se ~ à faire to refuse to do.

regagner [Rəgaɲe] vt (argent, faveur) to win back; (lieu) to get back to; ~ le temps perdu to make up (for) lost time.

regain [Rəgɛ̃] nm (renouveau): un ~ de renewed + nom.

régal [Regal] nm treat.

régaler [Regale]: se ~ vi to have a delicious meal; (fig) to enjoy o.s.

regard [RəgaR] nm (coup d'œil) look, glance; (expression) look (in one's eye); au ~ de (loi, morale) from the point of view of; en ~ (vis à vis) opposite; en ~ de in comparison with.

regardant, e [RəgaRdã, -ãt] a: très/peu ~ (sur) quite fussy/very free (about); (économe) very tight-fisted/quite generous (with).

regarder [RəgaRde] vt (examiner, observer, lire) to look at; (film, télévision, match) to watch; (envisager: situation, avenir) to view; (considérer: son intérêt etc) to be concerned with; (être orienté vers): ~ (vers) to face; (concerner) to concern // vi to look; ~ à vt (dépense) to be fussy with ou over; ~ qn/qch comme to regard sb/sth as.

régie [Reʒi] nf (COMM, INDUSTRIE) state-owned company; (THÉÂTRE, CINÉMA) production; (RADIO, TV) control room.

regimber [Rəʒɛ̃be] vi to balk, jib.

régime [Reʒim] nm (POL) régime; (ADMIN: carcéral, fiscal etc) system; (MÉD) diet; (TECH) (engine) speed; (fig) rate, pace; (de bananes, dattes) bunch; se mettre au/suivre un ~ to go on/be on a diet.

régiment [Reʒimã] nm regiment; (fig: fam): un ~ de an army of.

région [Reʒjɔ̃] nf region; **régional, e, aux** a regional.

régir [ReʒiR] vt to govern.

régisseur [ReʒisœR] nm (d'un domaine) steward; (CINÉMA, TV) assistant director; (THÉÂTRE) stage manager.

registre [RəʒistR(ə)] nm (livre) register; logbook; ledger; (MUS, LING) register.

réglage [Reglaʒ] nm adjustment; tuning.

règle [Regl(ə)] nf (instrument) ruler; (loi, prescription) rule; ~s nfpl (PHYSIOL) period sg; en ~ (papiers d'identité) in order; ~ générale as a (general) rule; ~ à calcul slide rule.

réglé, e [Regle] a well-ordered; steady; (papier) ruled; (arrangé) settled.

règlement [Regləmã] nm (paiement) settlement; (arrêté) regulation; (règles, statuts) regulations pl, rules pl; **réglementaire** a conforming to the regulations; (tenue) regulation cpd.

réglementer [Regləmãte] vt to regulate.

régler [Regle] vt (mécanisme, machine) to regulate, adjust; (moteur) to tune; (thermostat etc) to set, adjust; (conflit, facture) to settle; (fournisseur) to settle up with.

réglisse [Reglis] nf liquorice.

règne [Rɛɲ] nm (d'un roi etc, fig) reign; (BIO): le ~ végétal/animal the vegetable/animal kingdom.

régner [Reɲe] vi (roi) to rule, reign; (fig) to reign.

regorger [RəgɔRʒe] vi: ~ de to overflow with, be bursting with.

regret [RəgRɛ] nm regret; à ~ with regret; avec ~ regretfully; être au ~ de devoir faire to regret having to do.

regrettable [RəgRɛtabl(ə)] a regrettable.

regretter [RəgRɛte] vt to regret; (personne) to miss; je regrette I'm sorry.

regrouper [RəgRupe] vt (grouper) to group together; (contenir) to include, comprise; se ~ vi to gather (together).

régulier, ière [Regylje, -jɛR] a (gén) regular; (vitesse, qualité) steady; (répartition, pression, paysage) even; (TRANSPORTS: ligne, service) scheduled, regular; (légal, réglementaire) lawful, in order; (fam: correct) straight, on the level; **régulièrement** ad regularly; steadily; evenly; normally.

rehausser [Rəose] vt to heighten, raise.

rein [Rɛ̃] nm kidney; ~s nmpl (dos) back sg.

reine [Rɛn] nf queen.

reine-claude [Rɛnklod] nf greengage.

réintégrer [Reɛ̃tegRe] vt (lieu) to return to; (fonctionnaire) to reinstate.

rejaillir [RəʒajiR] vi to splash up; ~ sur to splash up onto; (fig) to rebound on; to fall upon.

rejet [Rəʒɛ] nm (action, aussi MÉD) rejection.

rejeter [Rəʒte] vt (relancer) to throw back; (vomir) to bring ou throw up; (écarter) to reject; (déverser) to throw out, discharge; ~ **la responsabilité de qch sur qn** to lay the responsibility for sth at sb's door.

rejoindre [Rəʒwɛ̃dR(ə)] vt (famille, régiment) to rejoin, return to; (lieu) to get (back) to; (suj: route etc) to meet, join; (rattraper) to catch up (with); se ~ vi to meet; **je te rejoins au café** I'll see ou meet you at the café.

réjouir [ReʒwiR] vt to delight; se ~ vi to be delighted; to rejoice; **réjouissances** nfpl (joie) rejoicing sg; (fête) festivities.

relâche [Rəlaʃ]: **faire** ~ vi (CINÉMA) to be closed; **sans** ~ ad without respite ou a break.

relâché, e [Rəlaʃe] a loose, lax.

relâcher [Rəlaʃe] vt to release; (étreinte) to loosen; se ~ vi to loosen; (discipline) to become slack ou lax; (élève etc) to slacken off.

relais [Rəlɛ] nm (SPORT): (**course de**) ~ relay (race); **équipe de** ~ shift team; (SPORT) relay team; **prendre le** ~ (**de**) to take over (from); ~ **routier** ≈ transport café (Brit), ≈ truck stop (US).

relancer [Rəlãse] vt (balle) to throw back; (moteur) to restart; (fig) to boost, revive; (personne): ~ **qn** to pester sb.

relater [Rəlate] vt to relate, recount.

relatif, ive [Rəlatif, -iv] a relative.

relation [Rəlasjɔ̃] nf (récit) account, report; (rapport) relation(ship); ~s nmpl (rapports) relations; relationship sg; (connaissances) connections; **être/entrer en** ~(**s**) **avec** to be/get in contact with.

relaxer [Rəlakse] vt to relax; (JUR) to discharge; se ~ vi to relax.

relayer [Rəleje] vt (collaborateur, coureur etc) to relieve; se ~ vi (dans une activité) to take it in turns.

reléguer [Rəlege] vt to relegate.

relent(s) [Rəlã] nm(pl) (foul) smell.

relevé, e [Rəlve] a (manches) rolled-up; (sauce) highly-seasoned // nm (lecture) reading; (liste) statement; list; (facture) account; ~ **de compte** bank statement.

relève [Rəlɛv] nf relief; relief team (ou troops pl); **prendre la** ~ to take over.

relever [Rəlve] vt (statue, meuble) to stand up again; (personne tombée) to help up; (vitre, niveau de vie) to raise; (col) to turn up; (style, conversation) to elevate; (plat, sauce) to season; (sentinelle, équipe) to relieve; (fautes, points) to pick out; (constater: traces etc) to find, pick up; (répliquer à: remarque) to react to, reply to; (: défi) to accept, take up; (noter: adresse etc) to

take down, note; (: plan) to sketch; (: cotes etc) to plot; (compteur) to read; (ramasser: cahiers) to collect, take in; ~ **de** vt (maladie) to be recovering from; (être du ressort de) to be a matter for; (ADMIN: dépendre de) to come under; (fig) to pertain to; se ~ vi (se remettre debout) to get up; ~ **qn de** (fonctions) to relieve sb of; ~ **la tête** to look up; to hold up one's head.

relief [Rəljɛf] nm relief; ~**s** nmpl (restes) remains; **mettre en** ~ (fig) to bring out, highlight.

relier [Rəlje] vt to link up; (livre) to bind; ~ **qch à** to link sth to.

religieux, euse [Rəliʒjø, -øz] a religious // nm monk // nf nun; (gâteau) cream bun.

religion [Rəliʒjɔ̃] nf religion; (piété, dévotion) faith.

relire [RəliR] vt (à nouveau) to reread, read again; (vérifier) to read over.

reliure [RəljyR] nf binding.

reluire [RəlɥiR] vi to gleam.

remanier [Rəmanje] vt to reshape, recast; (POL) to reshuffle.

remarquable [Rəmarkabl(ə)] a remarkable.

remarque [Rəmark(ə)] nf remark; (écrite) note.

remarquer [Rəmarke] vt (voir) to notice; se ~ vi to be noticeable; **faire** ~ (à qn) **que** to point out (to sb) that; **faire** ~ **qch** (à qn) to point sth out (to sb); **remarquez, ...** mind you ....

remblai [Rãblɛ] nm embankment.

rembourrer [Rãbure] vt to stuff; (dossier, vêtement, souliers) to pad.

remboursement [Rãbursəmã] nm repayment; **envoi contre** ~ cash on delivery.

rembourser [Rãburse] vt to pay back, repay.

remède [Rəmɛd] nm (médicament) medicine; (traitement, fig) remedy, cure.

remémorer [Rəmemore]: se ~ vt to recall, recollect.

remerciements [Rəmɛrsimã] nmpl thanks.

remercier [Rəmɛrsje] vt to thank; (congédier) to dismiss; ~ **qn de/d'avoir fait** to thank sb for/for having done.

remettre [RəmɛtR(ə)] vt (vêtement): ~ **qch** to put sth back on; (replacer): ~ **qch quelque part** to put sth back somewhere; (ajouter): ~ **du sel/un sucre** to add more salt/another lump of sugar; (ajourner): ~ **qch** (à) to postpone sth (until); ~ **qch à qn** (rendre, restituer) to give sth back to sb; (donner, confier: paquet, argent) to hand over sth to sb, deliver sth to sb; (: prix, décoration) to present sb with sth; se ~ vi to get better, recover; se ~ **de** to recover from, get over; s'en ~ à to leave it (up) to.

remise [Rəmiz] *nf* delivery; presentation; (*rabais*) discount; (*local*) shed; ~ en jeu (*FOOTBALL*) throw-in; ~ de peine reduction of sentence.

remontant [Rəmɔ̃tɑ̃] *nm* tonic, pick-me-up.

remonte-pente [Rəmɔ̃tpɑ̃t] *nm* skilift.

remonter [Rəmɔ̃te] *vi* to go back up; (*jupe*) to ride up // *vt* (*pente*) to go up; (*fleuve*) to sail (*ou* swim *etc*) up; (*manches, pantalon*) to roll up; (*col*) to turn up; (*niveau, limite*) to raise; (*fig: personne*) to buck up; (*moteur, meuble*) to put back together, reassemble; (*montre, mécanisme*) to wind up; ~ le moral à qn to raise sb's spirits; ~ à (*dater de*) to date *ou* go back to.

remontrance [Rəmɔ̃tRɑ̃s] *nf* reproof, reprimand.

remontrer [Rəmɔ̃tRe] *vt* (*fig*): en ~ à to prove one's superiority over.

remords [RəmɔR] *nm* remorse *q*; avoir des ~ to feel remorse.

remorque [RəmɔRk(ə)] *nf* trailer; être en ~ to be on tow; **remorquer** *vt* to tow; **remorqueur** *nm* tug(boat).

remous [Rəmu] *nm* (*d'un navire*) (back)wash *q*; (*de rivière*) swirl, eddy // *nmpl* (*fig*) stir *sg*.

remparts [Rɑ̃paR] *nmpl* walls, ramparts.

remplaçant, e [Rɑ̃plasɑ̃, -ɑ̃t] *nm/f* replacement, stand-in; (*THÉÂTRE*) understudy; (*SCOL*) supply teacher.

remplacement [Rɑ̃plasmɑ̃] *nm* replacement; (*job*) replacement work *q*.

remplacer [Rɑ̃plase] *vt* to replace; (*tenir lieu de*) to take the place of; ~ qch/qn par to replace sth/sb with.

rempli, e [Rɑ̃pli] *a* (*emploi du temps*) full, busy; ~ de full of, filled with.

remplir [Rɑ̃pliR] *vt* to fill (up); (*questionnaire*) to fill out *ou* up; (*obligations, fonction, condition*) to fulfil; se ~ *vi* to fill up.

remporter [Rɑ̃pɔRte] *vt* (*marchandise*) to take away; (*fig*) to win, achieve.

remuant, e [Rəmɥɑ̃, -ɑ̃t] *a* restless.

remue-ménage [Rəmymenaʒ] *nm inv* commotion.

remuer [Rəmɥe] *vt* to move; (*café, sauce*) to stir // *vi*, se ~ *vi* to move.

rémunérer [RemyneRe] *vt* to remunerate.

renard [RənaR] *nm* fox.

renchérir [Rɑ̃ʃeRiR] *vi* (*fig*): ~ (sur) to add something (to).

rencontre [RɑkɔtR(ə)] *nf* meeting; (*imprévue*) encounter; aller à la ~ de qn to go and meet sb.

rencontrer [RɑkɔtRe] *vt* to meet; (*mot, expression*) to come across; (*difficultés*) to meet with; se ~ *vi* to meet; (*véhicules*) to collide.

rendement [Rɑ̃dmɑ̃] *nm* (*d'un*

travailleur, d'une machine) output; (*d'une culture*) yield; (*d'un investissement*) return; à plein ~ at full capacity.

rendez-vous [Rɑ̃devu] *nm* (*rencontre*) appointment; (: *d'amoureux*) date; (*lieu*) meeting place; **donner ~ à qn** to arrange to meet sb; **avoir/prendre ~** (avec) to have/make an appointment (with).

rendre [RɑdR(ə)] *vt* (*livre, argent etc*) to give back, return; (*otages, visite etc*) to return; (*sang, aliments*) to bring up; (*exprimer, traduire*) to render; (*faire devenir*): ~ qn célèbre/qch possible to make sb famous/sth possible; se ~ *vi* (*capituler*) to surrender, give o.s. up; (*aller*): se ~ **quelque part** to go somewhere; se ~ **compte de qch** to realize sth.

rênes [Rɛn] *nfpl* reins.

renfermé, e [RɑfɛRme] *a* (*fig*) withdrawn // *nm*: sentir le ~ to smell stuffy.

renfermer [RɑfɛRme] *vt* to contain.

renflement [Rɑ̃fləmɑ̃] *nm* bulge.

renflouer [Rɑ̃flue] *vt* to refloat; (*fig*) to set back on its (*ou* his/her *etc*) feet.

renfoncement [Rɑ̃fɔ̃smɑ̃] *nm* recess.

renforcer [RɑfɔRse] *vt* to reinforce.

renfort [RɑfɔR]: ~s *nmpl* reinforcements; à grand ~ de with a great deal of.

renfrogné, e [RɑfRɔɲe] *a* sullen.

rengaine [Rɑ̃gɛn] *nf* (*péj*) old tune.

renier [Rənje] *vt* (*parents*) to disown, repudiate; (*foi*) to renounce.

renifler [Rənifle] *vi*, *vt* to sniff.

renne [Rɛn] *nm* reindeer *inv*.

renom [Rənɔ̃] *nm* reputation; (*célébrité*) renown; **renommé, e** *a* celebrated, renowned // *nf* fame.

renoncer [Rənɔ̃se] *vi*: ~ à *vt* to give up; ~ à faire to give up the idea of doing.

renouer [Rənwe] *vt*: ~ avec (*tradition*) to revive; (*habitude*) to take up again; ~ avec qn to take up with sb again.

renouveler [Rənuvle] *vt* to renew; (*exploit, méfait*) to repeat; se ~ *vi* (*incident*) to recur, happen again; **renouvellement** *nm* renewal; recurrence.

rénover [Renɔve] *vt* (*immeuble*) to renovate, do up; (*enseignement*) to reform; (*quartier*) to redevelop.

renseignement [Rɑ̃sɛɲmɑ̃] *nm* information *q*, piece of information; (*guichet des*) ~s information desk.

renseigner [Rɑ̃seɲe] *vt*: ~ qn (sur) to give information to sb (about); se ~ *vi* to ask for information, make inquiries.

rentable [Rɑ̃tabl(ə)] *a* profitable.

rente [Rɑ̃t] *nf* income; pension; government stock *ou* bond; **rentier, ière** *nm/f* person of private means.

rentrée [RɑtRe] *nf*: ~ (d'argent) cash *q* coming in; la ~ (des classes) the start of the new school year.

rentrer [ʀɑ̃tʀe] *vi* (*entrer de nouveau*) to go (*ou* come) back in; (*entrer*) to go (*ou* come) in; (*revenir chez soi*) to go (*ou* come) (back) home; (*air, clou: pénétrer*) to go in; (*revenu, argent*) to come in // *vt* (*foins*) to bring in; (*véhicule*) to put away; (*chemise dans pantalon etc*) to tuck in; (*griffes*) to draw in; (*fig: larmes, colère etc*) to hold back; ~ le ventre to pull in one's stomach; ~ dans (*heurter*) to crash into; ~ dans l'ordre to be back to normal; ~ dans ses frais to recover one's expenses.

renversant, e [ʀɑ̃vɛʀsɑ̃, -ɑ̃t] *a* astounding.

renverse [ʀɑ̃vɛʀs(ə)]: à la ~ *ad* backwards.

renverser [ʀɑ̃vɛʀse] *vt* (*faire tomber: chaise, verre*) to knock over, overturn; (*piéton*) to knock down; (*liquide, contenu*) to spill, upset; (*retourner*) to turn upside down; (*: ordre des mots etc*) to reverse; (*fig: gouvernement etc*) to overthrow; (*stupéfier*) to bowl over; se ~ *vi* to fall over; to overturn; to spill.

renvoi [ʀɑ̃vwa] *nm* (*référence*) cross-reference; (*éructation*) belch.

renvoyer [ʀɑ̃vwaje] *vt* to send back; (*congédier*) to dismiss; (*lumière*) to reflect; (*son*) to echo; (*ajourner*): ~ qch (à) to put sth off *ou* postpone sth (until); ~ qn à (*fig*) to refer sb to.

repaire [ʀəpɛʀ] *nm* den.

répandre [ʀepɑ̃dʀ(ə)] *vt* (*renverser*) to spill; (*étaler, diffuser*) to spread; (*lumière*) to shed; (*chaleur, odeur*) to give off; se ~ *vi* to spill; to spread; **répandu, e** *a* (*opinion, usage*) widespread.

réparation [ʀepaʀɑsjɔ̃] *nf* repair.

réparer [ʀepaʀe] *vt* to repair; (*fig: offense*) to make up for, atone for; (*: oubli, erreur*) to put right.

repartie [ʀəpaʀti] *nf* retort; avoir de la ~ to be quick at repartee.

repartir [ʀəpaʀtiʀ] *vi* to set off again; to leave again; (*fig*) to get going again; ~ à zéro to start from scratch (again).

répartir [ʀepaʀtiʀ] *vt* (*pour attribuer*) to share out; (*pour disperser, disposer*) to divide up; (*poids, chaleur*) to distribute; se ~ *vt* (*travail, rôles*) to share out between themselves; **répartition** *nf* sharing out; dividing up; distribution.

repas [ʀəpa] *nm* meal.

repasser [ʀəpase] *vi* to come (*ou* go) back // *vt* (*vêtement, tissu*) to iron; (*examen*) to retake, resit; (*film*) to show again; (*leçon, rôle: revoir*) to go over (again).

repêcher [ʀəpeʃe] *vt* (*noyé*) to recover the body of; (*candidat*) to pass (*by inflating marks*).

repentir [ʀəpɑ̃tiʀ] *nm* repentance; se ~ *vi* to repent; se ~ de to repent of.

répercuter [ʀepɛʀkyte] *vt* (*information, hausse des prix*) to pass on; se ~ *vi* (*bruit*) to reverberate; (*fig*): se ~ sur to have repercussions on.

repère [ʀəpɛʀ] *nm* mark; (*monument etc*) landmark.

repérer [ʀəpeʀe] *vt* (*erreur, connaissance*) to spot; (*abri, ennemi*) to locate; se ~ *vi* to find one's way about.

répertoire [ʀepɛʀtwaʀ] *nm* (*liste*) (alphabetical) list; (*carnet*) index notebook; (*d'un artiste*) repertoire.

répéter [ʀepete] *vt* to repeat; (*préparer: leçon: aussi vi*) to learn, go over; (*THÉÂTRE*) to rehearse; se ~ *vi* (*redire*) to repeat o.s.; (*se reproduire*) to be repeated, recur.

répétition [ʀepetisjɔ̃] *nf* repetition; (*THÉÂTRE*) rehearsal; ~ générale final dress rehearsal.

répit [ʀepi] *nm* respite.

replet, ète [ʀəplɛ, -ɛt] *a* chubby.

replier [ʀəplije] *vt* (*rabattre*) to fold down *ou* over; se ~ *vi* (*troupes, armée*) to withdraw, fall back.

réplique [ʀeplik] *nf* (*repartie, fig*) reply; (*THÉÂTRE*) line; (*copie*) replica.

répliquer [ʀeplike] *vi* to reply; (*riposter*) to retaliate.

répondre [ʀepɔ̃dʀ(ə)] *vi* to answer, reply; (*freins, mécanisme*) to respond; ~ à *vt* to reply to, answer; (*avec impertinence*): ~ à qn to answer sb back; (*affection, salut*) to return; (*provocation, suj: mécanisme etc*) to respond to; (*correspondre à: besoin*) to answer; (*: conditions*) to meet; (*: description*) to match; ~ de to answer for.

réponse [ʀepɔ̃s] *nf* answer, reply; en ~ à in reply to.

reportage [ʀəpɔʀtaʒ] *nm* (*bref*) report; (*écrit: documentaire*) story; article; (*en direct*) commentary; (*genre, activité*): le ~ reporting.

reporter *nm* [ʀəpɔʀtɛʀ] reporter // *vt* [ʀəpɔʀte] (*total*): ~ qch sur to carry sth forward *ou* over to; (*ajourner*): ~ qch (à) to postpone sth (until); (*transférer*): ~ qch sur to transfer sth to; se ~ à (*époque*) to think back to; (*document*) to refer to.

repos [ʀəpo] *nm* rest; (*fig*) peace (and quiet); peace of mind; (*MIL*): ~! stand at ease!; en ~ at rest; de tout ~ safe.

reposant, e [ʀəpozɑ̃, -ɑ̃t] *a* restful.

reposer [ʀəpoze] *vt* (*verre, livre*) to put down; (*délasser*) to rest; (*problème*) to reformulate // *vi* (*liquide, pâte*) to settle, rest; ~ sur to be built on; (*fig*) to rest on; se ~ *vi* to rest; se ~ sur qn to rely on sb.

repoussant, e [ʀəpusɑ̃, -ɑ̃t] *a* repulsive.

repousser [ʀəpuse] *vi* to grow again // *vt* to repel, repulse; (*offre*) to turn down, reject; (*tiroir, personne*) to push back; (*différer*) to put back.

reprendre [ʀəpʀɑ̃dʀ(ə)] *vt* (*prisonnier, ville*) to recapture; (*objet prêté, donné*) to take back; (*chercher*): **je viendrai te ~ à 4h** I'll come and fetch you at 4; (*se resservir de*): **~ du pain/un œuf** to take (*ou* eat) more bread/another egg; (*firme, entreprise*) to take over; (*travail, promenade*) to resume; (*emprunter: argument, idée*) to take up, use; (*refaire: article etc*) to go over again; (*jupe etc*) to alter; (*émission, pièce*) to put on again; (*réprimander*) to tell off; (*corriger*) to correct // *vi* (*classes, pluie*) to start (up) again; (*activités, travaux, combats*) to resume, start (up) again; (*affaires, industrie*) to pick up; (*dire*): **reprit-il** he went on; **se ~** *vi* (*se ressaisir*) to recover; **s'y ~** to make another attempt; **~ des forces** to recover one's strength; **~ courage** to take new heart; **~ la route** to set off again; **~ haleine** *ou* **son souffle** to get one's breath back.

représailles [ʀəpʀezaj] *nfpl* reprisals.

représentant, e [ʀəpʀezɑ̃tɑ̃, -ɑ̃t] *nm/f* representative.

représentation [ʀəpʀezɑ̃tasjɔ̃] *nf* (*symbole, image*) representation; (*spectacle*) performance.

représenter [ʀəpʀezɑ̃te] *vt* to represent; (*donner: pièce, opéra*) to perform; **se ~** *vt* (*se figurer*) to imagine; to visualize.

répression [ʀepʀesjɔ̃] *nf* (*voir réprimer*) suppression; repression.

réprimer [ʀepʀime] *vt* (*émotions*) to suppress; (*peuple etc*) to repress.

repris [ʀəpʀi] *nm*: **~ de justice** ex-prisoner, ex-convict.

reprise [ʀəpʀiz] *nf* (*recommencement*) resumption; recovery; (*TV*) repeat; (*CINÉMA*) rerun; (*AUTO*) acceleration *q*; (*COMM*) trade-in, part exchange; **à plusieurs ~s** on several occasions.

repriser [ʀəpʀize] *vt* to darn; to mend.

reproche [ʀəpʀɔʃ] *nm* (*remontrance*) reproach; **faire des ~s à qn** to reproach sb; **sans ~(s)** beyond reproach.

reprocher [ʀəpʀɔʃe] *vt*: **~ qch à qn** to reproach *ou* blame sb for sth; **~ qch à** (*machine, théorie*) to have sth against.

reproduction [ʀəpʀɔdyksjɔ̃] *nf* reproduction.

reproduire [ʀəpʀɔdɥiʀ] *vt* to reproduce; **se ~** *vi* (*BIO*) to reproduce; (*recommencer*) to recur, re-occur.

reptile [ʀɛptil] *nm* reptile.

repu, e [ʀəpy] *a* satisfied, sated.

républicain, e [ʀepyblikɛ̃, -ɛn] *a, nm/f* republican.

république [ʀepyblik] *nf* republic.

répugnant, e [ʀepyɲɑ̃, -ɑ̃t] *a* repulsive; loathsome.

répugner [ʀepyɲe]: **~ à** *vt*: **~ à qn** to

repel *ou* disgust sb; **~ à faire** to be loath *ou* reluctant to do.

réputation [ʀepytasjɔ̃] *nf* reputation; **réputé, e** *a* renowned.

requérir [ʀəkeʀiʀ] *vt* (*nécessiter*) to require, call for; (*JUR: peine*) to call for, demand.

requête [ʀəkɛt] *nf* request; (*JUR*) petition.

requin [ʀəkɛ̃] *nm* shark.

requis, e [ʀəki, -iz] *a* required.

R.E.R. *sigle m* (= *réseau express régional*) Greater Paris high speed train service.

rescapé, e [ʀɛskape] *nm/f* survivor.

rescousse [ʀɛskus] *nf*: **aller à la ~ de qn** to go to sb's aid *ou* rescue.

réseau, x [ʀezo] *nm* network.

réservation [ʀezɛʀvasjɔ̃] *nf* booking, reservation.

réserve [ʀezɛʀv(ə)] *nf* (*retenue*) reserve; (*entrepôt*) storeroom; (*restriction, d'Indiens*) reservation; (*de pêche, chasse*) reserve; **sous ~ de** subject to; **sans ~** *ad* unreservedly; **de ~** (*provisions etc*) in reserve.

réservé, e [ʀezɛʀve] *a* (*discret*) reserved; (*chasse, pêche*) private.

réserver [ʀezɛʀve] *vt* (*gén*) to reserve; (*chambre, billet etc*) to book, reserve; (*garder*): **~ qch pour/à** to keep *ou* save sth for; **~ qch à qn** to reserve (*ou* book) sth for sb.

réservoir [ʀezɛʀvwaʀ] *nm* tank.

résidence [ʀezidɑ̃s] *nf* residence; **~ secondaire** second home; **(en) ~ surveillée** (under) house arrest; **résidentiel, le** *a* residential.

résider [ʀezide] *vi*: **~ à/dans/en** to reside in; **~ dans** (*fig*) to lie in.

résidu [ʀezidy] *nm* residue *q*.

résigner [ʀeziɲe]: **se ~** *vi*: **se ~ (à qch/à faire)** to resign o.s. (to sth/to doing).

résilier [ʀezilje] *vt* to terminate.

résistance [ʀezistɑ̃s] *nf* resistance; (*de réchaud, bouilloire: fil*) element.

résistant, e [ʀezistɑ̃, -ɑ̃t] *a* (*personne*) robust, tough; (*matériau*) strong, hard-wearing.

résister [ʀeziste] *vi* to resist; **~ à** *vt* (*assaut, tentation*) to resist; (*effort, souffrance*) to withstand; (*désobéir à*) to stand up to, oppose.

résolu, e [ʀezɔly] *pp de* **résoudre** // *a*: **être ~ à qch/faire** to be set upon sth/ doing.

résolution [ʀezɔlysjɔ̃] *nf* solving; (*fermeté, décision*) resolution.

résolve *etc vb voir* **résoudre**.

résonner [ʀezɔne] *vi* (*cloche, pas*) to reverberate, resound; (*salle*) to be resonant; **~ de** to resound with.

résorber [ʀezɔʀbe]: **se ~** *vi* (*fig*) to be reduced; to be absorbed.

résoudre [ʀezudʀ(ə)] *vt* to solve; **se ~ à**

faire to bring o.s. to do.

respect [ʀɛspɛ] nm respect; **tenir en ~** to keep at bay.

respecter [ʀɛspɛkte] vt to respect.

respectueux, euse [ʀɛspɛktɥø, -øz] a respectful; **~ de** respectful of.

respiration [ʀɛspiʀasjɔ̃] nf breathing q; **~ artificielle** artificial respiration.

respirer [ʀɛspiʀe] vi to breathe; (fig) to get one's breath; to breathe again // vt to breathe (in), inhale; (manifester: santé, calme etc) to exude.

resplendir [ʀɛsplɑ̃diʀ] vi to shine; (fig): **~ (de)** to be radiant (with).

responsabilité [ʀɛspɔ̃sabilite] nf responsibility; (légale) liability.

responsable [ʀɛspɔ̃sabl(ə)] a responsible // nm/f (du ravitaillement etc) person in charge; (de parti, syndicat) official; **~ de** responsible for; (chargé de) in charge of, responsible for.

ressaisir [ʀəseziʀ]: **se ~** vi to regain one's self-control.

ressasser [ʀəsase] vt to keep going over.

ressemblance [ʀəsɑ̃blɑ̃s] nf resemblance, similarity, likeness.

ressemblant, e [ʀəsɑ̃blɑ̃, -ɑ̃t] a (portrait) lifelike, true to life.

ressembler [ʀəsɑ̃ble]: **~ à** vt to be like; to resemble; (visuellement) to look like; **se ~** vi to be (ou look) alike.

ressemeler [ʀəsəmle] vt to (re)sole.

ressentiment [ʀəsɑ̃timɑ̃] nm resentment.

ressentir [ʀəsɑ̃tiʀ] vt to feel; **se ~ de** to feel (ou show) the effects of.

resserrer [ʀəseʀe] vt (nœud, boulon) to tighten (up); (fig: liens) to strengthen; **se ~** vi (vallée) to narrow.

resservir [ʀəseʀviʀ] vi to do ou serve again // vt: **~ qn (d'un plat)** to give sb a second helping (of a dish).

ressort [ʀəsɔʀ] nm (pièce) spring; (force morale) spirit; (recours): **en dernier ~** as a last resort; (compétence): **être du ~ de** to fall within the competence of.

ressortir [ʀəsɔʀtiʀ] vi to go (ou come) out (again); (contraster) to stand out; **~ de** to emerge from; **faire ~** (fig: souligner) to bring out.

ressortissant, e [ʀəsɔʀtisɑ̃, -ɑ̃t] nm/f national.

ressource [ʀəsuʀs(ə)] nf: **avoir la ~ de** to have the possibility of; **leur seule ~ était de** the only course open to them was to; **~s** nfpl resources.

ressusciter [ʀesysite] vt (fig) to revive, bring back // vi to rise (from the dead).

restant, e [ʀɛstɑ̃, -ɑ̃t] a remaining // nm: **le ~ (de)** the remainder (of); **un ~ de** (de trop) some left-over.

restaurant [ʀɛstɔʀɑ̃] nm restaurant.

restauration [ʀɛstɔʀasjɔ̃] nf restoration; (hôtellerie) catering; **~ rapide** fast food.

restaurer [ʀɛstɔʀe] vt to restore; **se ~** vi to have something to eat.

reste [ʀɛst(ə)] nm (restant): **le ~ (de)** the rest (of); (de trop): **un ~ (de)** some left over; (vestige): **un ~ de** a remnant ou last trace of; (MATH) remainder; **~s** nmpl left-overs; (d'une cité etc, dépouille mortelle) remains; **du ~, au ~** ad besides, moreover.

rester [ʀɛste] vi to stay, remain; (subsister) to remain, be left; (durer) to last, live on // vb impersonnel: **il reste du pain/2 œufs** there's some bread/there are 2 eggs left (over); **il me reste assez de temps** I have enough time left; **ce qui reste à faire** what remains to be done; **restons-en là** let's leave it at that.

restituer [ʀɛstitɥe] vt (objet, somme): **~ qch (à qn)** to return sth (to sb); (TECH) to release; (: son) to reproduce.

restoroute [ʀɛstɔʀut] nm motorway (Brit) ou highway (US) restaurant.

restreindre [ʀɛstʀɛ̃dʀ(ə)] vt to restrict, limit.

restriction [ʀɛstʀiksjɔ̃] nf restriction; **~s** (mentales) reservations.

résultat [ʀezylta] nm result; (d'élection etc) results pl.

résulter [ʀezylte]: **~ de** vt to result from, be the result of.

résumé [ʀezyme] nm summary, résumé.

résumer [ʀezyme] vt (texte) to summarize; (récapituler) to sum up; **se ~ à** to come down to.

résurrection [ʀezyʀɛksjɔ̃] nf resurrection; (fig) revival.

rétablir [ʀetabliʀ] vt to restore, reestablish; **se ~** vi (guérir) to recover; (silence, calme) to return, be restored; **rétablissement** nm restoring; recovery; (SPORT) pull-up.

retaper [ʀətape] vt (maison, voiture etc) to do up; (fam: revigorer) to buck up; (redactylographier) to retype.

retard [ʀətaʀ] nm (d'une personne attendue) lateness q; (sur l'horaire, un programme) delay; (fig: scolaire, mental etc) backwardness; **en ~ (de 2 heures)** (2 hours) late; **avoir du ~** to be late; (sur un programme) to be behind (schedule); **prendre du ~** (train, avion) to be delayed; (montre) to lose (time); **sans ~** ad without delay.

retardement [ʀətaʀdəmɑ̃]: **à ~** a delayed action cpd; **bombe à ~** time bomb.

retarder [ʀətaʀde] vt (sur un horaire): **~ qn (d'une heure)** to delay sb (an hour); (départ, date): **~ qch (de 2 jours)** to put sth back (2 days), delay sth (for ou by 2 days); (horloge) to put back // vi (montre) to be slow; to lose (time).

retenir [ʀətniʀ] vt (garder, retarder) to keep, detain; (maintenir: objet qui glisse, fig: colère, larmes) to hold back;

(: *objet suspendu*) to hold; (*fig: empêcher d'agir*): ~ **qn** (*de faire*) to hold sb back (from doing); (*se rappeler*) to retain; (*réserver*) to reserve; (*accepter*) to accept; (*prélever*): ~ **qch** (**sur**) to deduct sth (from); se ~ *vi* (*se raccrocher*): se ~ à to hold onto; (*se contenir*): se ~ **de faire** to restrain o.s. from doing; ~ **son souffle** to hold one's breath.

retentir [Rətɑ̃tiʀ] *vi* to ring out; (*salle*): ~ **de** to ring *ou* resound with.

retentissant, e [Rətɑ̃tisɑ̃, -ɑ̃t] *a* resounding; (*fig*) impact-making.

retentissement [Rətɑ̃tismɑ̃] *nm* repercussion; effect, impact; stir.

retenue [Rətny] *nf* (*prélèvement*) deduction; (*SCOL*) detention; (*modération*) (self-)restraint; (*réserve*) reserve, reticence.

réticence [Retisɑ̃s] *nf* hesitation, reluctance *q*.

rétine [Retin] *nf* retina.

retiré, e [Rətiʀe] *a* secluded; remote.

retirer [Rətiʀe] *vt* to withdraw; (*vêtement, lunettes*) to take off, remove; (*extraire*): ~ **qch de** to take sth out of, remove sth from; (*reprendre: bagages, billets*) to collect, pick up.

retombées [Rətɔ̃be] *nfpl* (*radioactives*) fallout *sg*; (*fig*) fallout; spin-offs.

retomber [Rətɔ̃be] *vi* (*à nouveau*) to fall again; (*atterrir: après un saut etc*) to land; (*tomber, redescendre*) to fall back; (*pendre*) to fall, hang (down); (*échoir*): ~ **sur qn** to fall on sb.

rétorquer [Retɔʀke] *vt*: ~ (**à qn**) **que** to retort (to sb) that.

retors, e [Rətɔʀ, -ɔʀs(ə)] *a* wily.

rétorsion [Retɔʀsjɔ̃] *nf*: **mesures de ~** reprisals.

retoucher [Rətuʃe] *vt* (*photographie*) to touch up; (*texte, vêtement*) to alter.

retour [RətuʀR] *nm* return; **au ~** when we (*ou* they *etc*) get (*ou* got) back; (*en route*) on the way back; **être de ~ (de)** to be back (from); **par ~ du courrier** by return of post.

retourner [RətuʀRne] *vt* (*dans l'autre sens: matelas, crêpe, foin, terre*) to turn (over); (: *caisse*) to turn upside down; (: *sac, vêtement*) to turn inside out; (*émouvoir: personne*) to shake; (*renvoyer, restituer*): ~ **qch à qn** to return sth to sb // *vi* (*aller, revenir*): ~ **quelque part/à** to go back *ou* return somewhere/to; ~ **à** (*état, activité*) to return to, go back to; **se** ~ *vi* to turn over; (*tourner la tête*) to turn round; **se** ~ **contre** (*fig*) to turn against; **savoir de quoi il retourne** to know what it is all about.

retracer [RətʀRase] *vt* to relate, recount.

retrait [RətʀRɛ] *nm* (*voir retirer*) withdrawal; collection; **en ~ set back**; ~ **du permis** (**de conduire**) disqualification

from driving (*Brit*), revocation of driver's license (*US*).

retraite [RətʀRɛt] *nf* (*d'une armée, REL*) *refuge*) retreat; (*d'un employé*) retirement; (*revenu*) pension; **prendre sa ~** to retire; ~ **anticipée** early retirement; **retraité, e** *a* retired // *nm/f* pensioner.

retrancher [RətʀRɑ̃ʃe] *vt* (*passage, détails*) to take out, remove; (*nombre, somme*): ~ **qch de** to take *ou* deduct sth from; (*couper*) to cut off; **se ~ derrière/dans** to take refuge behind/in.

retransmettre [RətʀRɑ̃smɛtʀ(ə)] *vt* (*RADIO*) to broadcast; (*TV*) to show.

rétrécir [RetʀResiʀ] *vt* (*vêtement*) to take in // *vi* to shrink; **se** ~ *vi* to narrow.

rétribution [RetʀRibysjɔ̃] *nf* payment.

rétro [RetʀRo] *a inv*: **la mode ~** the nostalgia vogue.

rétrograde [RetʀRogʀad] *a* reactionary, backward-looking.

rétrograder [RetʀRogʀade] *vi* (*économie*) to regress; (*AUTO*) to change down.

rétroprojecteur [RetʀRopʀRɔʒɛktœʀ] *nm* overhead projector.

rétrospective [RetʀRospɛktiv] *nf*; retrospective exhibition/season; ~**ment** *ad* in retrospect.

retrousser [RətʀRuse] *vt* to roll up.

retrouvailles [RətʀRuvaj] *nfpl* reunion *sg*.

retrouver [RətʀRuve] *vt* (*fugitif, objet perdu*) to find; (*occasion*) to find again; (*calme, santé*) to regain; (*revoir*) to see again; (*rejoindre*) to meet (again), join; **se** ~ *vi* to meet; (*s'orienter*) to find one's way; **se** ~ **quelque part** to find o.s. somewhere; **s'y** ~ (*rentrer dans ses frais*) to break even.

rétroviseur [RetʀRovizœʀ] *nm* (rearview) mirror.

réunion [Reynjɔ̃] *nf* bringing together; joining; (*séance*) meeting.

réunir [Reyniʀ] *vt* (*convoquer*) to call together; (*rassembler*) to gather together; (*cumuler*) to combine; (*rapprocher*) to bring together (again), reunite; (*rattacher*) to join (together); **se** ~ *vi* (*se rencontrer*) to meet.

réussi, e [Reysi] *a* successful.

réussir [Reysiʀ] *vi* to succeed, be successful; (*à un examen*) to pass; (*plante, culture*) to thrive, do well // *vt* to make a success of; ~ **à faire** to succeed in doing; ~ **à qn** to go right for sb; (*aliment*) to agree with sb.

réussite [Reysit] *nf* success; (*CARTES*) patience.

revaloir [Rəvalwaʀ] *vt*: **je vous revaudrai cela** I'll repay you some day; (*en mal*) I'll pay you back for this.

revaloriser [Rəvalɔʀize] *vt* (*monnaie*) to revalue; (*salaires*) to raise the level of.

revanche [Rəvɑ̃ʃ] *nf* revenge; **en ~ on the other hand.**

rêve [rɛv] *nm* dream; *(activité psychique)*: le ~ dreaming.

revêche [rəvɛʃ] *a* surly, sour-tempered.

réveil [rɛvɛj] *nm (d'un dormeur)* waking up *q*; *(fig)* awakening; *(pendule)* alarm (clock); *(MIL)* reveille; **au ~** on waking (up).

réveille-matin [rɛvɛjmatɛ̃] *nm inv* alarm clock.

réveiller [reveje] *vt (personne)* to wake up; *(fig)* to awaken, revive; **se ~** *vi* to wake up; *(fig)* to reawaken.

réveillon [revɛjɔ̃] *nm* Christmas Eve; *(de la Saint-Sylvestre)* New Year's Eve; **réveillonner** *vi* to celebrate Christmas Eve *(ou* New Year's Eve).

révélateur, trice [revelatœr, -tris] *a*: ~ *(de qch)* revealing (sth) // *nm (PHOTO)* developer.

révéler [revele] *vt (gén)* to reveal; *(faire connaître au public)*: ~ **qn/qch** to make sb/sth widely known, bring sb/sth to the public's notice; **se ~** *vi* to be revealed, reveal itself // *vb avec attribut* to prove (to be).

revenant, e [rəvnɑ̃, -ɑ̃t] *nm/f* ghost.

revendeur, euse [rəvɑ̃dœr, -øz] *nm/f (détaillant)* retailer; *(d'occasions)* secondhand dealer.

revendication [rəvɑ̃dikasjɔ̃] *nf* claim, demand; **journée de ~** day of action.

revendiquer [rəvɑ̃dike] *vt* to claim, demand; *(responsabilité)* to claim.

revendre [rəvɑ̃dr(ə)] *vt (d'occasion)* to resell; *(détailler)* to sell; **à ~** *ad (en abondance)* to spare.

revenir [rəvnir] *vi* to come back; *(CULIN)*: **faire ~** to brown; *(coûter)*: ~ **cher/à 100 F (à qn)** to cost (sb) a lot/100 F; ~ **à** *(études, projet)* to return to, go back to; *(équivaloir à)* to amount to; ~ **à qn** *(part, honneur)* to go to sb, be sb's; *(souvenir, nom)* to come back to sb; ~ **de** *(fig: maladie, étonnement)* to recover from; ~ **sur** *(question, sujet)* to go back over; *(engagement)* to go back on; ~ **à la charge** to return to the attack; ~ **à soi** to come round; **n'en pas ~**: **je n'en reviens pas** I can't get over it; ~ **sur ses pas** to retrace one's steps; **cela revient à dire que/au même** it amounts to saying that/the same thing.

revenu [rəvny] *nm* income; *(de l'État)* revenue; *(d'un capital)* yield; **~s** *nmpl* income *sg*.

rêver [rɛve] *vi, vt* to dream; ~ **de/à** to dream of.

réverbère [reverbɛr] *nm* street lamp *ou* light.

réverbérer [reverbere] *vt* to reflect.

révérence [reverɑ̃s] *nf (salut)* bow; *(: de femme)* curtsey.

rêverie [rɛvri] *nf* daydreaming *q*, daydream.

revers [rəvɛr] *nm (de feuille, main)* back; *(d'étoffe)* wrong side; *(de pièce, médaille)* back, reverse; *(TENNIS, PING-PONG)* backhand; *(de veston)* lapel; *(de pantalon)* turn-up; *(fig: échec)* setback.

revêtement [rəvɛtmɑ̃] *nm (de paroi)* facing; *(des sols)* flooring; *(de chaussée)* surface; *(de tuyau etc: enduit)* coating.

revêtir [rəvetir] *vt (habit)* to don, put on; *(fig)* to take on; ~ **qn de** *(fig)* to endow *ou* invest sb with; ~ **qch de** to cover sth with; *(fig)* to cloak sth in.

rêveur, euse [rɛvœr, -øz] *a* dreamy // *nm/f* dreamer.

revient [rəvjɛ̃] *vb voir* **revenir**.

revigorer [rəvigɔre] *vt* to invigorate, brace up; to revive, buck up.

revirement [rəvirmɑ̃] *nm* change of mind; *(d'une situation)* reversal.

réviser [revize] *vt (texte, SCOL: matière)* to revise; *(machine, installation, moteur)* to overhaul, service; *(JUR: procès)* to review.

révision [revizjɔ̃] *nf* revision; auditing *q*; overhaul; servicing *q*; review; **la ~ des 10000 km** *(AUTO)* the 10,000 km service.

revivre [rəvivr(ə)] *vi (reprendre des forces)* to come alive again; *(traditions)* to be revived // *vt (épreuve, moment)* to relive.

revoir [rəvwar] *vt* to see again; *(réviser)* to revise // *nm*: **au ~** goodbye.

révoltant, e [revɔltɑ̃, -ɑ̃t] *a* a revolting; appalling.

révolte [revɔlt(ə)] *nf* rebellion, revolt.

révolter [revɔlte] *vt* to revolt; to outrage, appal; **se ~** *(contre)* to rebel (against).

révolu, e [revɔly] *a* past; *(ADMIN)*: **âgé de 18 ans ~s** over 18 years of age; **après 3 ans ~s** when 3 full years have passed.

révolution [revɔlysjɔ̃] *nf* revolution; **révolutionnaire** *a, nm/f* revolutionary.

revolver [revɔlvɛr] *nm* gun; *(à barillet)* revolver.

révoquer [revɔke] *vt (fonctionnaire)* to dismiss; *(arrêt, contrat)* to revoke.

revue [rəvy] *nf (inventaire, examen, MIL)* review; *(périodique)* review, magazine; *(de music-hall)* variety show; **passer en ~** to review; to go through.

rez-de-chaussée [redʃose] *nm inv* ground floor.

RF *sigle* = République Française.

RFA *sigle f* = République fédérale d'Allemagne.

Rhin [rɛ̃] *nm*: **le ~** the Rhine.

rhinocéros [rinɔserɔs] *nm* rhinoceros.

Rhône [ron] *nm*: **le ~** the Rhone.

rhubarbe [rybarb(ə)] *nf* rhubarb.

rhum [rɔm] *nm* rum.

rhumatisme [rymatism(ə)] *nm* rheumatism *q*.

rhume [rym] *nm* cold; ~ **de cerveau** head cold; **le ~ des foins** hay fever.

ri [ʀi] *pp de* **rire**.

riant, e [ʀjɑ̃, -ɑ̃t] *a* smiling, cheerful.

ricaner [ʀikane] *vi (avec méchanceté)* to snigger; *(bêtement)* to giggle.

riche [ʀiʃ] *a (gén)* rich; *(personne, pays)* rich, wealthy; ~ en rich in; ~ de full of; rich in; **richesse** *nf* wealth; *(fig)* richness; **richesses** *nfpl* wealth *sg*; treasures.

ricin [ʀisɛ̃] *nm:* huile de ~ castor oil.

ricocher [ʀikɔʃe] *vi:* ~ (sur) to rebound (off); *(sur l'eau)* to bounce (on *ou* off).

ricochet [ʀikɔʃe] *nm:* faire des ~s to skip stones; par ~ *ad* on the rebound; *(fig)* as an indirect result.

rictus [ʀiktys] *nm* grin; *(snarling)* grimace.

ride [ʀid] *nf* wrinkle; *(fig)* ripple.

rideau, x [ʀido] *nm* curtain; *(POL):* le ~ de fer the Iron Curtain.

rider [ʀide] *vt* to wrinkle; *(eau)* to ripple; se ~ *vi* to become wrinkled.

ridicule [ʀidikyl] *a* ridiculous // *nm:* le ~ ridicule; **se ridiculiser** *vi* to make a fool of o.s.

rien [ʀjɛ̃] ♦ *pronom*

1: (ne) ... ~ nothing, *tournure négative* + anything; qu'est-ce que vous avez? - ~ what have you got? - nothing; il n'a ~ dit/fait he said/did nothing; he hasn't said/done anything; il n'a ~ *(n'est pas blessé)* he's all right; de ~! not at all!

2 *(quelque chose):* a-t-il jamais ~ fait pour nous? has he ever done anything for us?

3: ~ de: ~ d'intéressant nothing interesting; ~ d'autre nothing else; ~ du tout nothing at all

4: ~ que just, only; nothing but; ~ que pour lui faire plaisir only *ou* just to please him; ~ que la vérité nothing but the truth; ~ que cela that alone

♦ *nm:* un petit ~ *(cadeau)* a little something; des ~s trivia *pl*; un ~ de a hint of; en un ~ de temps in no time at all.

rieur, euse [ʀjœʀ, -øz] *a* cheerful.

rigide [ʀiʒid] *a* stiff; *(fig)* rigid; strict.

rigole [ʀigɔl] *nf (conduit)* channel; *(filet d'eau)* rivulet.

rigoler [ʀigɔle] *vi (rire)* to laugh; *(s'amuser)* to have (some) fun; *(plaisanter)* to be joking *ou* kidding.

rigolo, ote [ʀigɔlo, -ɔt] *a (fam)* funny // *nm/f* comic; *(péj)* fraud, phoney.

rigoureux, euse [ʀiguʀø, -øz] *a (morale)* rigorous, strict; *(personne)* stern, strict; *(climat, châtiment)* rigorous, harsh; *(interdiction, neutralité)* strict.

rigueur [ʀigœʀ] *nf* rigour; strictness; harshness; être de ~ to be the rule; à la ~ at a pinch; possibly; tenir ~ à qn de qch to hold sth against sb.

rime [ʀim] *nf* rhyme.

rinçage [ʀɛ̃saʒ] *nm* rinsing (out); *(opération)* rinse.

rincer [ʀɛ̃se] *vt* to rinse; *(récipient)* to rinse out.

ring [ʀiaŋ] *nm* (boxing) ring.

ringard, e [ʀɛ̃gaʀ, -aʀd(ə)] *a* old-fashioned.

rions *vb voir* **rire**.

riposter [ʀipɔste] *vi* to retaliate // *vt:* ~ que to retort that; ~ à *vt* to counter; to reply to.

rire [ʀiʀ] *vi* to laugh; *(se divertir)* to have fun // *nm* laugh; le ~ laughter; ~ de *vt* to laugh at; pour ~ *(pas sérieusement)* for a joke *ou* a laugh.

risée [ʀize] *nf:* être la ~ de to be the laughing stock of.

risible [ʀizibl(ə)] *a* laughable.

risque [ʀisk(ə)] *nm* risk; le ~ danger; à ses ~s et périls at his own risk.

risqué, e [ʀiske] *a* risky; *(plaisanterie)* risqué, daring.

risquer [ʀiske] *vt* to risk; *(allusion, question)* to venture, hazard; ça ne risque rien it's quite safe; ~ de: il risque de se tuer he could get himself killed; ce qui risque de se produire what might *ou* could well happen; il ne risque pas de recommencer there's no chance of him doing that again; se ~ à faire *(tenter)* to venture *ou* dare to do.

rissoler [ʀisɔle] *vi, vt:* (faire) ~ to brown.

ristourne [ʀistuʀn(ə)] *nf* rebate.

rite [ʀit] *nm* rite; *(fig)* ritual.

rivage [ʀivaʒ] *nm* shore.

rival, e, aux [ʀival, -o] *a, nm/f* rival.

rivaliser [ʀivalize] *vi:* ~ avec to rival, vie with; *(être comparable)* to hold its own against, compare with.

rivalité [ʀivalite] *nf* rivalry.

rive [ʀiv] *nf* shore; *(de fleuve)* bank.

river [ʀive] *vt (clou, pointe)* to clinch; *(plaques)* to rivet together.

riverain, e [ʀivʀɛ̃, -ɛn] *nm/f* riverside *(ou* lakeside) resident; local resident.

rivet [ʀive] *nm* rivet.

rivière [ʀivjɛʀ] *nf* river.

rixe [ʀiks(ə)] *nf* brawl, scuffle.

riz [ʀi] *nm* rice.

R.N. *sigle f de* **route nationale**.

robe [ʀɔb] *nf* dress; *(de juge, d'ecclésiastique)* robe; *(de professeur)* gown; *(pelage)* coat; ~ de soirée/de mariée evening/wedding dress; ~ de chambre dressing gown; ~ de grossesse maternity dress.

robinet [ʀɔbinɛ] *nm* tap.

robot [ʀɔbo] *nm* robot.

robuste [ʀɔbyst(ə)] *a* robust, sturdy.

roc [ʀɔk] *nm* rock.

rocaille [ʀɔkaj] *nf* loose stones *pl*; rocky *ou* stony ground; *(jardin)* rockery, rock garden.

roche [ʀɔʃ] *nf* rock.

rocher [ʀɔʃe] *nm* rock.

rocheux, euse [ʀɔʃø, -øz] *a* rocky.

rodage [Rɔdaʒ] *nm*: en ~ running in.

roder [Rɔde] *vt* (AUTO) to run in.

rôder [Rode] *vi* to roam about; (*de façon suspecte*) to lurk (about *ou* around); **rôdeur, euse** *nm/f* prowler.

rogne [Rɔɲ] *nf*: être en ~ to be in a temper.

rogner [Rɔɲe] *vt* to clip; ~ sur (*fig*) to cut down *ou* back on.

rognons [Rɔɲɔ̃] *nmpl* kidneys.

roi [Rwa] *nm* king; le jour *ou* la fête des R~s, les R~s Twelfth Night.

roitelet [Rwatlɛ] *nm* wren.

rôle [Rol] *nm* role; (*contribution*) part.

romain, e [Rɔmɛ̃, -ɛn] *a, nm/f* Roman.

roman, e [Rɔmɑ̃, -an] *a* (ARCHIT) Romanesque // *nm* novel; ~ d'espionnage spy novel *ou* story; ~ photo romantic picture story.

romance [Rɔmɑ̃s] *nf* ballad.

romancer [Rɔmɑ̃se] *vt* to make into a novel; to romanticize.

romancier, ière [Rɔmɑ̃sje, -jɛR] *nm/f* novelist.

romanesque [Rɔmanɛsk(ə)] *a* (*fantastique*) fantastic; storybook *cpd*; (*sentimental*) romantic.

roman-feuilleton [Rɔmɑ̃fœjtɔ̃] *nm* serialized novel.

romanichel, le [Rɔmaniʃɛl] *nm/f* gipsy.

romantique [Rɔmɑ̃tik] *a* romantic.

romarin [RɔmaRɛ̃] *nm* rosemary.

rompre [Rɔ̃pR(ə)] *vt* to break; (*entretien, fiançailles*) to break off // *vi* (*fiancés*) to break it off; **se ~** *vi* to break; (MÉD) to burst, rupture.

rompu, e [Rɔ̃py] *a*: ~ à with wide experience of; inured to.

ronces [Rɔ̃s] *nfpl* brambles.

ronchonner [Rɔ̃ʃɔne] *vi* (*fam*) to grouse, grouch.

rond, e [Rɔ̃, Rɔ̃d] *a* round; (*joues, mollets*) well-rounded; (*fam: ivre*) tight // *nm* (*cercle*) ring; (*fam: sou*): je n'ai plus un ~ I haven't a penny left // *nf* (*gén: de surveillance*) rounds *pl*, patrol; (*danse*) round (dance); (MUS) semibreve (Brit), whole note (US); en ~ (*s'asseoir, danser*) in a ring; à la ~e (*alentour*): à 10 km à la ~e for 10 km round; **rondelet, te** *a* plump.

rondelle [Rɔ̃dɛl] *nf* (TECH) washer; (*tranche*) slice, round.

rondement [Rɔ̃dmɑ̃] *ad* briskly; frankly.

rondin [Rɔ̃dɛ̃] *nm* log.

rond-point [Rɔ̃pwɛ̃] *nm* roundabout.

ronéotyper [Rɔneɔtipe] *vt* to duplicate.

ronfler [Rɔ̃fle] *vi* to snore; (*moteur, poêle*) to hum; to roar.

ronger [Rɔ̃ʒe] *vt* to gnaw (at); (*suj: vers, rouille*) to eat into; **se ~ les sangs** to worry o.s. sick; **se ~ les ongles** to bite one's nails; **rongeur** *nm* rodent.

ronronner [Rɔ̃Rɔne] *vi* to purr.

roquet [Rɔkɛ] *nm* nasty little lap-dog.

roquette [Rɔkɛt] *nf* rocket.

rosace [Rozas] *nf* (*vitrail*) rose window.

rosbif [Rɔsbif] *nm*: du ~ roasting beef; (*cuit*) roast beef; un ~ a joint of beef.

rose [Roz] *nf* rose // *a* pink.

rosé, e [Roze] *a* pinkish; (*vin*) ~ rosé.

roseau, x [Rozo] *nm* reed.

rosée [Roze] *nf* dew.

roseraie [RozRɛ] *nf* rose garden.

rosier [Rozje] *nm* rosebush, rose tree.

rosse [Rɔs] *nf* (*péj: cheval*) nag // *a* nasty, vicious.

rossignol [Rɔsiɲɔl] *nm* (ZOOL) nightingale.

rot [Ro] *nm* belch; (*de bébé*) burp.

rotatif, ive [Rɔtatif, -iv] *a* rotary.

rotation [Rɔtasjɔ̃] *nf* rotation; (*fig*) rotation, swap-around; turnover.

roter [Rɔte] *vi* (*fam*) to burp, belch.

rôti [Roti] *nm*: du ~ roasting meat; (*cuit*) roast meat; un ~ de bœuf/porc a joint of beef/pork.

rotin [Rɔtɛ̃] *nm* rattan (cane); **fauteuil en ~** cane (arm)chair.

rôtir [Rotir] *vi, vt* (*aussi*: faire ~) to roast; **rôtisserie** *nf* steakhouse; roast meat counter (*ou* shop); **rôtissoire** *nf* (roasting) spit.

rotule [Rɔtyl] *nf* kneecap, patella.

roturier, ière [RɔtyRje, -jɛR] *nm/f* commoner.

rouage [Rwaʒ] *nm* cog(wheel), gearwheel; (*de montre*) part; (*fig*) cog.

roucouler [Rukule] *vi* to coo.

roue [Ru] *nf* wheel; ~ dentée cogwheel; ~ de secours spare wheel.

roué, e [Rwe] *a* wily.

rouer [Rwe] *vt*: ~ qn de coups to give sb a thrashing.

rouet [Rwɛ] *nm* spinning wheel.

rouge [Ruʒ] *a, nm/f* red // *nm* red; (*fard*) rouge; (*vin*) ~ red wine; sur la liste ~ ex-directory (Brit), unlisted (US); passer au ~ (*signal*) to go red; (*automobiliste*) to go through a red light; ~ (à lèvres) lipstick; ~-gorge *nm* robin (redbreast).

rougeole [Ruʒɔl] *nf* measles *sg*.

rougeoyer [Ruʒwaje] *vi* to glow red.

rouget [Ruʒɛ] *nm* mullet.

rougeur [RuʒœR] *nf* redness.

rougir [RuʒiR] *vi* (*de honte, timidité*) to blush, flush; (*de plaisir, colère*) to flush; (*fraise, tomate*) to go *ou* turn red; (*ciel*) to redden.

rouille [Ruj] *nf* rust.

rouillé, e [Ruje] *a* rusty.

rouiller [Ruje] *vt* to rust // *vi* to rust, go rusty; **se ~** *vi* to rust.

roulant, e [Rulɑ̃, -ɑ̃t] *a* (*meuble*) on wheels; (*surface, trottoir*) moving.

rouleau, x [Rulo] *nm* (*de papier, tissu,*

SPORT) roll; (*de machine à écrire*) roller, platen; (*à mise en plis, à peinture, vague*) roller; ~ **compresseur** steamroller; ~ **à pâtisserie** rolling pin.

roulement [Rulmɑ̃] *nm* (*bruit*) rumbling *q*, rumble; (*rotation*) rotation; turnover; **par** ~ on a rota (*Brit*) *ou* rotation (*US*) basis; ~ (**à billes**) ball bearings *pl*; ~ **de tambour** drum roll.

rouler [Rule] *vt* to roll; (*papier, tapis*) to roll up; (*CULIN: pâte*) to roll out; (*fam*) to do, con // *vi* (*bille, boule*) to roll; (*voiture, train*) to go, run; (*automobiliste*) to drive; (*cycliste*) to ride; (*bateau*) to roll; (*tonnerre*) to rumble, roll; se ~ **dans** (*boue*) to roll in; (*couverture*) to roll o.s. (up) in.

roulette [Rulɛt] *nf* (*de table, fauteuil*) castor; (*de pâtissier*) pastry wheel; (*jeu*): **la** ~ roulette; **à** ~**s** on castors.

roulis [Ruli] *nm* roll(ing).

roulotte [Rulɔt] *nf* caravan.

Roumanie [Rumani] *nf* Rumania.

rouquin, e [Rukɛ̃, -in] *nm/f* (*péj*) redhead.

rouspéter [Ruspete] *vi* (*fam*) to moan.

rousse [Rus] *a voir* **roux**.

roussi [Rusi] *nm*: ça sent le ~ there's a smell of burning; (*fig*) I can smell trouble.

roussir [RusiR] *vt* to scorch // *vi* (*feuilles*) to go *ou* turn brown; (*CULIN*): **faire** ~ to brown.

route [Rut] *nf* road; (*fig: chemin*) way; (*itinéraire, parcours*) route; (*fig: voie*) road, path; **par** (**la**) ~ by road; **il y a 3h de** ~ it's a 3-hour ride *ou* journey; **en** ~ *ad* on the way; **mettre en** ~ to start up; **se mettre en** ~ to set off; **faire** ~ **vers** to head towards; ~ **nationale** ≈ A road (*Brit*), ≈ state highway (*US*); **routier, ière** *a* road *cpd* // *nm* (*camionneur*) (long-distance) lorry (*Brit*) *ou* truck (*US*) driver; (*restaurant*) ≈ transport café (*Brit*), ≈ truck stop (*US*) // *nf* (*voiture*) touring car.

routine [Rutin] *nf* routine; **routinier, ière** *a* (*péj*) humdrum; addicted to routine.

rouvrir [RuvRiR] *vt, vi*, **se** ~ *vi* to reopen, open again.

roux, rousse [Ru, Rus] *a* red; (*personne*) red-haired // *nm/f* redhead.

royal, e, aux [Rwajal, -o] *a* royal; (*fig*) princely.

royaume [Rwajom] *nm* kingdom; (*fig*) realm; **le R~Uni** the United Kingdom.

royauté [Rwajote] *nf* (*dignité*) kingship; (*régime*) monarchy.

ruban [Rybɑ̃] *nm* (*gén*) ribbon; (*d'acier*) strip; ~ **adhésif** adhesive tape.

rubéole [Rybeɔl] *nf* German measles *sg*, rubella.

rubis [Rybi] *nm* ruby.

rubrique [RybRik] *nf* (*titre, catégorie*)

heading; (*PRESSE: article*) column.

ruche [Ryʃ] *nf* hive.

rude [Ryd] *a* (*barbe, toile*) rough; (*métier, tâche*) hard, tough; (*climat*) severe, harsh; (*bourru*) harsh, rough; (*fruste*) rugged, tough; (*fam*) jolly good; ~**ment** *ad*; (*fam: très*) terribly; (*: beaucoup*) terribly hard.

rudimentaire [Rydimɑ̃tɛR] *a* rudimentary, basic.

rudoyer [Rydwaje] *vt* to treat harshly.

rue [Ry] *nf* street.

ruée [Rɥe] *nf* rush.

ruelle [Rɥɛl] *nf* alley(-way).

ruer [Rɥe] *vi* (*cheval*) to kick out; **se** ~ *vi*: **se** ~ **sur** to pounce on; **se** ~ **vers/dans/hors de** to rush *ou* dash towards/into/out of.

rugby [Rygbi] *nm* Rugby (football).

rugir [RyʒiR] *vi* to roar.

rugueux, euse [Rygø, -øz] *a* rough.

ruine [Rɥin] *nf* ruin; ~**s** *nfpl* ruins.

ruiner [Rɥine] *vt* to ruin.

ruisseau, x [Rɥiso] *nm* stream, brook.

ruisseler [Rɥisle] *vi* to stream.

rumeur [RymœR] *nf* (*bruit confus*) rumbling; hubbub *q*; murmur(ing); (*nouvelle*) rumour.

ruminer [Rymine] *vt* (*herbe*) to ruminate; (*fig*) to ruminate on *ou* over, chew over.

rupture [RyptyR] *nf* (*de câble, digue*) breaking; (*de tendon*) rupture, tearing; (*de négociations etc*) breakdown; (*de contrat*) breach; (*séparation, désunion*) break-up, split.

rural, e, aux [RyRal, -o] *a* rural, country *cpd*.

ruse [Ryz] *nf*: **la** ~ cunning, craftiness; trickery; **une** ~ a trick, a ruse; **rusé, e** *a* cunning, crafty.

russe [Rys] *a, nm, nf* Russian.

Russie [Rysi] *nf*: **la** ~ Russia.

rustique [Rystik] *a* rustic.

rustre [RystR(ə)] *nm* boor.

rutilant, e [Rytilɑ̃, -ɑ̃t] *a* gleaming.

rythme [Ritm(ə)] *nm* rhythm; (*vitesse*) rate; (*: de la vie*) pace, tempo.

S

s' [s] *pronom voir* **se**.

sa [sa] *dét voir* **son**.

S.A. *sigle voir* **société**.

sable [sabl(ə)] *nm* sand; ~**s mouvants** quicksand(s).

sablé [sable] *nm* shortbread biscuit.

sabler [sable] *vt* to sand; (*contre le verglas*) to grit; ~ **le champagne** to drink champagne.

sablier [sablije] *nm* hourglass; (*de cuisine*) egg timer.

sablonneux, euse [sablɔnø, -øz] *a* sandy.

saborder [sabɔʀde] *vt (navire)* to scuttle; *(fig)* to wind up, shut down.

sabot [sabo] *nm* clog; *(de cheval, bœuf)* hoof; ~ de frein brake shoe.

saboter [sabɔte] *vt* to sabotage.

sac [sak] *nm* bag; *(à charbon etc)* sack; mettre à ~ to sack; ~ à provisions/de voyage shopping/travelling bag; ~ de couchage sleeping bag; ~ à dos rucksack; ~ à main handbag.

saccade [sakad] *nf* jerk.

saccager [sakaʒe] *vt (piller)* to sack; *(dévaster)* to create havoc in.

saccharine [sakaʀin] *nf* saccharin(e).

sacerdoce [saseʀdɔs] *nm* priesthood; *(fig)* calling, vocation.

sache *etc vb voir* **savoir**.

sachet [saʃɛ] *nm* (small) bag; *(de lavande, poudre, shampooing)* sachet; ~ de thé tea bag.

sacoche [sakɔʃ] *nf (gén)* bag; *(de bicyclette)* saddlebag.

sacre [sakʀ(ə)] *nm* coronation; consecration.

sacré, e [sakʀe] *a* sacred; *(fam: satané)* blasted; *(: fameux)*: un ~ ... a heck of a ...

sacrement [sakʀəmɑ̃] *nm* sacrament.

sacrifice [sakʀifis] *nm* sacrifice.

sacrifier [sakʀifje] *vt* to sacrifice; ~ à *vt* to conform to.

sacristie [sakʀisti] *nf* sacristy; *(culte protestant)* vestry.

sadique [sadik] *a* sadistic.

sage [saʒ] *nf* a wise; *(enfant)* good // *nm* wise man; sage.

sage-femme [saʒfam] *nf* midwife *(pl* wives).

sagesse [saʒɛs] *nf* wisdom.

Sagittaire [saʒitɛʀ] *nm*: le ~ Sagittarius.

Sahara [saaʀa] *nm*: le ~ the Sahara (desert).

saignant, e [sɛɲɑ̃, -ɑ̃t] *a (viande)* rare.

saignée [seɲe] *nf (fig)* heavy losses *pl*.

saigner [seɲe] *vi* to bleed // *vt* to bleed; *(animal)* to kill (by bleeding); ~ du nez to have a nosebleed.

saillie [saji] *nf (sur un mur etc)* projection; *(trait d'esprit)* witticism.

saillir [sajiʀ] *vi* to project, stick out; *(veine, muscle)* to bulge.

sain, e [sɛ̃, sɛn] *a* healthy; *(lectures)* wholesome; ~ et sauf safe and sound, unharmed; ~ d'esprit sound in mind, sane.

saindoux [sɛ̃du] *nm* lard.

saint, e [sɛ̃, sɛ̃t] *a* holy; *(fig)* saintly // *nm/f* saint; le S~ Esprit the Holy Spirit ou Ghost; la S~e Vierge the Blessed Virgin; la S~Sylvestre New Year's Eve; **sainteté** *nf* holiness.

sais *etc vb voir* **savoir**.

saisie [sezi] *nf* seizure; ~ (de données) (data) capture.

saisir [seziʀ] *vt* to take hold of, grab; *(fig: occasion)* to seize; *(comprendre)* to grasp; *(entendre)* to get, catch; *(données)* to capture; *(suj: émotions)* to take hold of, come over; *(CULIN)* to fry quickly; *(JUR: biens, publication)* to seize; *(: juridiction)*: ~ un tribunal d'une affaire to submit *ou* refer a case to a court; se ~ de *vt* to seize; **saisissant, e** *a* startling, striking.

saison [sɛzɔ̃] *nf* season; morte ~ slack season; **saisonnier, ière** *a* seasonal.

sait *vb voir* **savoir**.

salade [salad] *nf (BOT)* lettuce *etc*; *(CULIN)* (green) salad; *(fam)* tangle, muddle; ~ de fruits fruit salad; **saladier** *nm* (salad) bowl.

salaire [salɛʀ] *nm (annuel, mensuel)* salary; *(hebdomadaire, journalier)* pay, wages *pl*; *(fig)* reward; ~ de base basic salary *(ou* wage); ~ minimum interprofessionnel de croissance (SMIC) *index-linked guaranteed minimum wage.*

salarié, e [salaʀje] *nm/f* salaried employee; wage-earner.

salaud [salo] *nm (fam!)* sod *(!)*, bastard *(!)*.

sale [sal] *a* dirty, filthy.

salé, e [sale] *a (liquide, saveur)* salty; *(CULIN)* salted; *(fig)* spicy; steep.

saler [sale] *vt* to salt.

saleté [salte] *nf (état)* dirtiness; *(crasse)* dirt, filth; *(tache etc)* dirt *q*; *(fig)* dirty trick; rubbish *q*; filth *q*.

salière [saljɛʀ] *nf* saltcellar.

salin, e [salɛ̃, -in] *a* saline // *nf* saltworks *sg*; salt marsh.

salir [saliʀ] *vt* to (make) dirty; *(fig)* to soil the reputation of; se ~ *vi* to get dirty; **salissant, e** *a (tissu)* which shows the dirt; *(métier)* dirty, messy.

salle [sal] *nf* room; *(d'hôpital)* ward; *(de restaurant)* dining room; *(d'un cinéma)* auditorium; *(: public)* audience; faire ~ comble to have a full house; ~ d'attente waiting room; ~ de bain(s) bathroom; ~ de classe classroom; ~ commune *(d'hôpital)* ward; ~ de concert concert hall; ~ de consultation consulting room; ~ d'eau shower-room; ~ d'embarquement *(à l'aéroport)* departure lounge; ~ de jeux games room; playroom; ~ à manger dining room; ~ d'opération *(d'hôpital)* operating theatre; ~ de séjour living room; ~ de spectacle theatre; cinema; ~ des ventes saleroom.

salon [salɔ̃] *nm* lounge, sitting room; *(mobilier)* lounge suite; *(exposition)* exhibition, show; ~ de thé tearoom.

salopard [salɔpaʀ] *nm (fam!)* bastard *(!)*.

salope [salɔp] *nf (fam!)* bitch *(!)*.

saloperie [salɔpʀi] *nf (fam!)* filth *q*; dirty trick; rubbish *q*.

salopette [salɔpɛt] *nf* dungarees *pl*;

(d'ouvrier) overall(s).

salsifis [salsifi] nm salsify.

salubre [salybʀ(ə)] a healthy, salubrious.

saluer [salɥe] vt (pour dire bonjour, fig) to greet; (pour dire au revoir) to take one's leave; (MIL) to salute.

salut [saly] nm (sauvegarde) safety; (REL) salvation; (geste) wave; (parole) greeting; (MIL) salute // excl (fam) hi (there).

salutations [salytɑsjɔ̃] nfpl greetings; recevez mes ~ distinguées ou respectueuses yours faithfully.

samedi [samdi] nm Saturday.

SAMU [samy] sigle f (= service d'assistance médicale d'urgence) ≈ ambulance (service) (Brit), ≈ paramedics pl (US).

sanction [sɑ̃ksjɔ̃] nf sanction; (fig) penalty; **sanctionner** vt (loi, usage) to sanction; (punir) to punish.

sandale [sɑ̃dal] nf sandal.

sandwich [sɑ̃dwitʃ] nm sandwich.

sang [sɑ̃] nm blood; **en ~** covered in blood; **se faire du mauvais ~** to fret, get in a state.

sang-froid [sɑ̃fʀwa] nm calm, sang-froid; **de ~** in cold blood.

sanglant, e [sɑ̃glɑ̃, -ɑ̃t] a bloody, covered in blood; (combat) bloody.

sangle [sɑ̃gl(ə)] nf strap.

sanglier [sɑ̃glije] nm (wild) boar.

sanglot [sɑ̃glo] nm sob.

sangsue [sɑ̃sy] nf leech.

sanguin, e [sɑ̃gɛ̃, -in] a blood cpd; (fig) fiery.

sanguinaire [sɑ̃ginɛʀ] a bloodthirsty; bloody.

sanisette [sanizɛt] nf (automatic) public toilet.

sanitaire [sanitɛʀ] a health cpd; **~s** nmpl bathroom sg.

sans [sɑ̃] prép without; **~ qu'il s'en aperçoive** without him ou his noticing; **~-abri** nmpl homeless; **~-façon** a inv fuss-free; free and easy; **~-gêne** a inv inconsiderate; **~-logis** nmpl homeless.

santé [sɑ̃te] nf health; **en bonne ~** in good health; **boire à la ~ de qn** to drink (to) sb's health; **'à la ~ de'** 'here's to'; **à ta/votre ~!** cheers!

saoudien, ne [saudjɛ̃, -jɛn] a Saudi Arabian // nm/f: S~(ne) Saudi Arabian.

saoul, e [su, sul] a = soûl, e.

saper [sape] vt to undermine, sap.

sapeur [sapœʀ] nm sapper; **~-pompier** nm fireman.

saphir [safiʀ] nm sapphire.

sapin [sapɛ̃] nm fir (tree); (bois) fir; **~ de Noël** Christmas tree.

sarcastique [saʀkastik] a sarcastic.

sarcler [saʀkle] vt to weed.

Sardaigne [saʀdɛɲ] nf: la ~ Sardinia.

sardine [saʀdin] nf sardine.

S.A.R.L. sigle voir **société**.

sas [sas] nm (de sous-marin, d'engin spatial) airlock; (d'écluse) lock.

satané, e [satane] a confounded.

satellite [satelit] nm satellite.

satin [satɛ̃] nm satin.

satire [satiʀ] nf satire; **satirique** a satirical.

satisfaction [satisfaksjɔ̃] nf satisfaction.

satisfaire [satisfɛʀ] vt to satisfy; **~ à** vt (engagement) to fulfil; (revendications, conditions) to satisfy, meet; to comply with; **satisfaisant, e** a satisfactory; (qui fait plaisir) satisfying; **satisfait, e** a satisfied; **satisfait de** happy ou satisfied with.

saturer [satyʀe] vt to saturate.

sauce [sos] nf sauce; (avec un rôti) gravy; **saucière** nf sauceboat.

saucisse [sosis] nf sausage.

saucisson [sosisɔ̃] nm (slicing) sausage.

sauf [sof] prép except; **~ si** (à moins que) unless; **~ erreur** if I'm not mistaken; **~ avis contraire** unless you hear to the contrary.

sauf, sauve [sof, sov] a unharmed, unhurt; (fig: honneur) intact, saved; **laisser la vie sauve à qn** to spare sb's life.

sauge [soʒ] nf sage.

saugrenu, e [sogʀəny] a preposterous.

saule [sol] nm willow (tree).

saumon [somɔ̃] nm salmon inv.

saumure [somyʀ] nf brine.

sauna [sona] nm sauna.

saupoudrer [sopudʀe] vt: **~ qch de** to sprinkle sth with.

saur [sɔʀ] am: **hareng ~** smoked ou red herring, kipper.

saurai etc vb voir **savoir**.

saut [so] nm jump; (discipline sportive) jumping; **faire un ~ chez qn** to pop over to sb's (place); **au ~ du lit** on getting out of bed; **~ en hauteur/longueur** high/long jump; **~ à la corde** skipping; **~ à la perche** pole vaulting; **~ périlleux** somersault.

saute [sot] nf sudden change.

saute-mouton [sotmutɔ̃] nm: **jouer à ~** to play leapfrog.

sauter [sote] vi to jump, leap; (exploser) to blow up, explode; (: fusibles) to blow; (se rompre) to snap, burst; (se détacher) to pop out (ou off) // vt to jump (over), leap (over); (fig: omettre) to skip, miss (out); **faire ~** to blow up; to burst open; (CULIN) to sauté; **~ au cou de qn** to fly into sb's arms.

sauterelle [sotʀɛl] nf grasshopper.

sautiller [sotije] vi to hop; to skip.

sautoir [sotwaʀ] nm: **~ (de perles)** string of pearls.

sauvage [sovaʒ] a (gén) wild; (peuplade) savage; (farouche) unsociable;

(*barbare*) wild, savage; (*non officiel*) unauthorized, unofficial // *nm/f* savage; (*timide*) unsociable type.

sauve [sov] *af voir* **sauf**.

sauvegarde [sovgard(ə)] *nf* safeguard; **sauvegarder** *vt* to safeguard; (*INFORM: enregistrer*) to save; (: *copier*) to back up.

sauve-qui-peut [sovkipø] *excl* run for your life!

sauver [sove] *vt* to save; (*porter secours à*) to rescue; (*récupérer*) to salvage, rescue; **se ~** *vi* (*s'enfuir*) to run away; (*fam: partir*) to be off; **sauvetage** *nm* rescue; **sauveteur** *nm* rescuer; **sauvette: à la sauvette** *ad* (*vendre*) without authorization; (*se marier etc*) hastily, hurriedly; **sauveur** *nm* saviour (*Brit*), savior (*US*).

savais *etc vb voir* **savoir**.

savamment [savamɑ̃] *ad* (*avec érudition*) learnedly; (*habilement*) skilfully, cleverly.

savant, e [savɑ̃, -ɑ̃t] *a* scholarly, learned; (*calé*) clever // *nm* scientist.

saveur [savœʀ] *nf* flavour; (*fig*) savour.

savoir [savwaʀ] *vt* to know; (*être capable de*): **il sait nager** he can swim // *nm* knowledge; **se ~** *vi* (*être connu*) to be known; **à ~** *ad* that is, namely; **faire ~ qch à qn** to let sb know sth; **pas que je sache** not as far as I know.

savon [savɔ̃] *nm* (*produit*) soap; (*morceau*) bar of soap; (*fam*): **passer un ~ à qn** to give sb a good dressing-down; **savonnette** *nf* bar of soap; **savonneux, euse** *a* soapy.

savons *vb voir* **savoir**.

savourer [savure] *vt* to savour.

savoureux, euse [savurø, -øz] *a* tasty; (*fig*) spicy, juicy.

saxo(phone) [saksɔ(fɔn)] *nm* sax(o-phone).

scabreux, euse [skabrø, -øz] *a* risky; (*indécent*) improper, shocking.

scandale [skɑ̃dal] *nm* scandal; (*tapage*): **faire du ~** to make a scene, create a disturbance; **faire ~** to scandalize people; **scandaleux, euse** *a* scandalous, outrageous.

scandinave [skɑ̃dinav] *a*, *nm/f* Scandinavian.

Scandinavie [skɑ̃dinavi] *nf* Scandinavia.

scaphandre [skafɑ̃dʀ(ə)] *nm* (*de plongeur*) diving suit; (*de cosmonaute*) space-suit.

scarabée [skaʀabe] *nm* beetle.

sceau, x [so] *nm* seal; (*fig*) stamp, mark.

scélérat, e [seleʀa, -at] *nm/f* villain.

sceller [sele] *vt* to seal.

scénario [senaʀjo] *nm* (*CINÉMA*) scenario; script; (*fig*) scenario.

scène [sɛn] *nf* (*gén*) scene; (*estrade, fig: théâtre*) stage; **entrer en ~** to come on

stage; **mettre en ~** (*THÉÂTRE*) to stage; (*CINÉMA*) to direct; (*fig*) to present, introduce.

sceptique [sɛptik] *a* sceptical.

schéma [ʃema] *nm* (*diagramme*) diagram, sketch; (*fig*) outline; pattern; **schématique** *a* diagrammatic(al), schematic; (*fig*) oversimplified.

sciatique [sjatik] *nf* sciatica.

scie [si] *nf* saw; **~ à découper** fretsaw; **~ à métaux** hacksaw.

sciemment [sjamɑ̃] *ad* knowingly.

science [sjɑ̃s] *nf* science; (*savoir*) knowledge; (*savoir-faire*) art, skill; **~s naturelles** (*SCOL*) natural science *sg*, biology *sg*; **scientifique** *a* scientific // *nm/f* scientist; science student.

scier [sje] *vt* to saw; (*retrancher*) to saw off; **scierie** *nf* sawmill.

scinder [sɛ̃de] *vt*, **se ~** *vi* to split (up).

scintiller [sɛ̃tije] *vi* to sparkle.

scission [sisjɔ̃] *nf* split.

sciure [sjyʀ] *nf*: **~ (de bois)** sawdust.

sclérose [skleʀoz] *nf*: **~ en plaques** multiple sclerosis.

scolaire [skɔlɛʀ] *a* school *cpd*; (*péj*) schoolish; **scolariser** *vt* to provide with schooling (*ou* schools); **scolarité** *nf* schooling.

scooter [skutœʀ] *nm* (motor) scooter.

score [skɔʀ] *nm* score.

scorpion [skɔʀpjɔ̃] *nm* (*signe*): **le S~** Scorpio.

Scotch [skɔtʃ] *nm* ® adhesive tape.

scout, e [skut] *a*, *nm* scout.

script [skʀipt] *nm* printing; (*CINÉMA*) (shooting) script; **~-girl** [-gœʀl] *nf* continuity girl.

scrupule [skʀypyl] *nm* scruple.

scruter [skʀyte] *vt* to scrutinize; (*l'obscurité*) to peer into.

scrutin [skʀytɛ̃] *nm* (*vote*) ballot; (*ensemble des opérations*) poll.

sculpter [skylte] *vt* to sculpt; (*suj: érosion*) to carve; **sculpteur** *nm* sculptor.

sculpture [skyltyʀ] *nf* sculpture; **~ sur bois** wood carving.

se, s' [s(ə)] *pronom* **1** (*emploi réfléchi*) oneself, *m* himself, *f* herself, *sujet non humain* itself; *pl* themselves; **~ voir comme l'on est** to see o.s. as one is

2 (*réciproque*) one another, each other; **ils s'aiment** they love one another *ou* each other

3 (*passif*): **cela ~ répare facilement** it is easily repaired

4 (*possessif*): **~ casser la jambe/laver les mains** to break one's leg/wash one's hands; *autres emplois pronominaux: voir le verbe en question*.

séance [seɑ̃s] *nf* (*d'assemblée, récréative*) meeting, session; (*de tribunal*) sitting, session; (*musicale, CINÉMA, THÉÂTRE*) performance; **~ tenante** forthwith.

seau, x [so] nm bucket, pail.

sec, sèche [sɛk, sɛʃ] a dry; (raisins, figues) dried; (cœur, personne: insensible) hard, cold // nm: tenir au ~ to keep in a dry place // à ~ hard; je le bois ~ I drink it straight ou neat; à ~ a dried up.

sécateur [sekatœʀ] nm secateurs pl (Brit), shears pl.

sèche [sɛʃ] af voir **sec**.

sèche-cheveux [sɛʃʃəvø] nm inv hairdrier.

sécher [seʃe] vt to dry; (dessécher: peau, blé) to dry (out); (: étang) to dry up // vi to dry; to dry out; to dry up; (fam: candidat) to be stumped; se ~ (après le bain) to dry o.s.

sécheresse [seʃʀɛs] nf dryness; (absence de pluie) drought.

séchoir [seʃwaʀ] nm drier.

second, e [səgɔ̃, -ɔ̃d] a second // nm (assistant) second in command; (NAVIG) first mate // nf second; **voyager en ~e** to travel second-class; **de ~e main** secondhand; **secondaire** a secondary; **seconder** vt to assist.

secouer [səkwe] vt to shake; (passagers) to rock; (traumatiser) to shake (up).

secourir [səkuʀiʀ] vt (aller sauver) to (go and) rescue; (prodiguer des soins à) to help, assist; (venir en aide à) to assist, aid; **secourisme** nm first aid; life saving.

secours [səkuʀ] nm help, aid, assistance // nmpl aid sg; au ~! help!; appeler au ~ to shout ou call for help; **porter** ~ à qn to give sb assistance, help sb; les **premiers** ~ first aid sg.

secousse [səkus] nf jolt, bump; (électrique) shock; (fig: psychologique) jolt, shock; ~ **sismique** ou **tellurique** earth tremor.

secret, ète [səkʀɛ, -ɛt] a secret; (fig: renfermé) reticent, reserved // nm secret; (discrétion absolue): le ~ secrecy; au ~ in solitary confinement.

secrétaire [səkʀetɛʀ] nm/f secretary // nm (meuble) writing desk; ~ **de direction** private ou personal secretary; ~ **d'État** junior minister; **secrétariat** nm (profession) secretarial work; (bureau) office; (: d'organisation internationale) secretariat.

secteur [sɛktœʀ] nm sector; (ADMIN) district; (ÉLEC): **branché sur le** ~ plugged into the mains (supply).

section [sɛksjɔ̃] nf section; (de parcours d'autobus) fare stage; (MIL: unité) platoon; **sectionner** vt to sever.

Sécu [seky] abr f de **sécurité sociale**.

séculaire [sekylɛʀ] a secular; (très vieux) age-old.

sécuriser [sekyʀize] vt to give (a feeling of) security to.

sécurité [sekyʀite] nf safety; security; **système de** ~ safety system; **être en** ~ to be safe; **la** ~ **routière** road safety; **la** ~ **sociale** ≈ (the) Social Security (Brit), ≈ Welfare (US).

sédition [sedisjɔ̃] nf insurrection; sedition.

séduction [sedyksjɔ̃] nf seduction; (charme, attrait) appeal, charm.

séduire [seduiʀ] vt to charm; (femme: abuser de) to seduce; **séduisant, e** a (femme) seductive; (homme, offre) very attractive.

ségrégation [segʀegɑsjɔ̃] nf segregation.

seigle [sɛgl(ə)] nm rye.

seigneur [sɛɲœʀ] nm lord.

sein [sɛ̃] nm breast; (entrailles) womb; **au** ~ **de** prép (équipe, institution) within; (flots, bonheur) in the midst of.

séisme [seism(ə)] nm earthquake.

seize [sɛz] num sixteen; **seizième** num sixteenth.

séjour [seʒuʀ] nm stay; (pièce) living room; ~**ner** vi to stay.

sel [sɛl] nm salt; (fig) wit; spice; ~ **de cuisine/de table** cooking/table salt.

sélection [selɛksjɔ̃] nf selection; **sélectionner** vt to select.

self-service [sɛlfsɛʀvis] a, nm selfservice.

selle [sɛl] nf saddle; ~**s** nfpl (MÉD) stools; **seller** vt to saddle.

sellette [sɛlɛt] nf: **être sur la** ~ to be on the carpet.

selon [səlɔ̃] prép according to; (en se conformant à) in accordance with; ~ **que** according to whether; ~ **moi** as I see it.

semaine [səmɛn] nf week; **en** ~ during the week, on weekdays.

semblable [sɑ̃blabl(ə)] a similar; (de ce genre): **de** ~**s mésaventures** such mishaps // nm fellow creature ou man; ~ **à** similar to, like.

semblant [sɑ̃blɑ̃] nm: **un** ~ **de vérité** a semblance of truth; **faire** ~ **(de faire)** to pretend (to do).

sembler [sɑ̃ble] vb avec attribut to seem // vb impersonnel: **il semble (bien) que/ inutile de** it (really) seems ou appears that/useless to; **il me semble que** it seems to me that; I think (that); **comme bon lui semble** as he sees fit.

semelle [səmɛl] nf sole; (intérieure) insole, inner sole.

semence [səmɑ̃s] nf (graine) seed.

semer [səme] vt to sow; (fig: éparpiller) to scatter; (: confusion) to spread; (: poursuivants) to lose, shake off; **semé de** (difficultés) riddled with.

semestre [səmɛstʀ(ə)] nm half-year; (SCOL) semester.

séminaire [seminɛʀ] nm seminar.

semi-remorque [səmiʀəmɔʀk(ə)] nm

articulated lorry (*Brit*), semi (trailer) (*US*).

semonce [səmɔ̃s] *nf*: **un coup de ~ a** shot across the bows.

semoule [səmul] *nf* semolina.

sempiternel, le [sɛpitɛʀnɛl] *a* eternal, never-ending.

sénat [sena] *nm* Senate; **sénateur** *nm* Senator.

sens [sɑ̃s] *nm* (PHYSIOL, *instinct*) sense; (*signification*) meaning, sense; (*direction*) direction; **à mon ~** to my mind; **reprendre ses ~** to regain consciousness; **dans le ~ des aiguilles d'une montre** clockwise; **~ commun** common sense; **~ dessus dessous** upside down; **~ interdit, ~ unique** one-way street.

sensass [sɑ̃sas] *a* (*fam*) fantastic.

sensation [sɑ̃sasjɔ̃] *nf* sensation; **à ~** (*péj*) sensational.

sensé, e [sɑ̃se] *a* sensible.

sensibiliser [sɑ̃sibilize] *vt*: **~ qn à** to make sb sensitive to.

sensibilité [sɑ̃sibilite] *nf* sensitivity.

sensible [sɑ̃sibl(ə)] *a* sensitive; (*aux sens*) perceptible; (*appréciable: différence, progrès*) appreciable, noticeable; **~ment** *ad* (*notablement*) appreciably, noticeably; (*à peu près*): **ils ont ~ment le même poids** they weigh approximately the same; **~rie** *nf* sentimentality; squeamishness.

sensuel, le [sɑ̃sɥɛl] *a* sensual; sensuous.

sentence [sɑ̃tɑ̃s] *nf* (*jugement*) sentence; (*adage*) maxim.

sentier [sɑ̃tje] *nm* path.

sentiment [sɑ̃timɑ̃] *nm* feeling; **recevez mes ~s respectueux** yours faithfully; **sentimental, e, aux** *a* sentimental; (*vie, aventure*) love *cpd*.

sentinelle [sɑ̃tinɛl] *nf* sentry.

sentir [sɑ̃tiʀ] *vt* (*par l'odorat*) to smell; (*par le goût*) to taste; (*au toucher, fig*) to feel; (*répandre une odeur de*) to smell of; (: *ressemblance*) to smell like; (*avoir la saveur de*) to taste of; to taste like // *vi* to smell; **~ mauvais** to smell bad; **se ~ bien** to feel good; **se ~ mal** (*être indisposé*) to feel unwell ou ill; **se ~ le courage/la force de faire** to feel brave/strong enough to do; **il ne peut pas le ~** (*fam*) he can't stand him.

séparation [sepaʀasjɔ̃] *nf* separation; (*cloison*) division, partition; **~ de corps** legal separation.

séparé, e [sepaʀe] *a* (*appartements, pouvoirs*) separate; (*époux*) separated; **~ment** *ad* separately.

séparer [sepaʀe] *vt* (*gén*) to separate; (*suj: divergences etc*) to divide; to drive apart; (: *différences, obstacles*) to stand between; (*détacher*): **~ qch de** to pull sth (off) from; (*diviser*): **~ qch par** to divide sth (up) with; **une pièce en deux** to divide a room into two; **se ~** *vi*

(*époux, amis, adversaires*) to separate, part; (*se diviser: route, tige etc*) to divide; (*se détacher*): **se ~ (de)** to split off (from); to come off; **se ~ de** (*époux*) to separate ou part from; (*employé, objet personnel*) to part with.

sept [sɛt] *num* seven.

septembre [sɛptɑ̃bʀ(ə)] *nm* September.

septentrional, e, aux [sɛptɑ̃tʀijɔnal, -o] *a* northern.

septicémie [sɛptisemi] *nf* blood poisoning, septicaemia.

septième [sɛtjɛm] *num* seventh.

septique [sɛptik] *a*: **fosse ~** septic tank.

sépulture [sepyltyʀ] *nf* burial; burial place, grave.

séquelles [sekɛl] *nfpl* after-effects; (*fig*) aftermath *sg*; consequences.

séquestrer [sekɛstʀe] *vt* (*personne*) to confine illegally; (*biens*) to impound.

serai *etc vb voir* **être**.

serein, e [səʀɛ̃, -ɛn] *a* serene; (*jugement*) dispassionate.

serez *vb voir* **être**.

sergent [sɛʀʒɑ̃] *nm* sergeant.

série [seʀi] *nf* (*de questions, d'accidents*) series *inv*; (*de clés, casseroles, outils*) set; (*catégorie: SPORT*) rank; class; **en ~** in quick succession; (COMM) mass *cpd*; **de ~** a standard; **hors ~** (COMM) custom-built; (*fig*) outstanding.

sérieusement [seʀjøzmɑ̃] *ad* seriously; reliably; responsibly.

sérieux, euse [seʀjø, -øz] *a* serious; (*élève, employé*) serious, responsible; (*client, maison*) reliable, dependable // *nm* seriousness; reliability; **garder son ~** to keep a straight face; **prendre qch/qn au ~** to take sth/sb seriously.

serin [səʀɛ̃] *nm* canary.

seringue [səʀɛ̃g] *nf* syringe.

serions *vb voir* **être**.

serment [sɛʀmɑ̃] *nm* (*juré*) oath; (*promesse*) pledge, vow.

sermon [sɛʀmɔ̃] *nm* sermon.

serpent [sɛʀpɑ̃] *nm* snake; **~ à sonnettes** rattlesnake.

serpenter [sɛʀpɑ̃te] *vi* to wind.

serpentin [sɛʀpɑ̃tɛ̃] *nm* (*tube*) coil; (*ruban*) streamer.

serpillière [sɛʀpijɛʀ] *nf* floorcloth.

serre [sɛʀ] *nf* (AGR) greenhouse; **~s** *nfpl* (*griffes*) claws, talons.

serré, e [seʀe] *a* (*réseau*) dense; (*écriture*) close; (*habits*) tight; (*fig: lutte, match*) tight, close-fought; (*passagers etc*) (tightly) packed.

serrer [seʀe] *vt* (*tenir*) to grip ou hold tight; (*comprimer, coincer*) to squeeze; (*poings, mâchoires*) to clench; (*suj: vêtement*) to be too tight for; to fit tightly; (*rapprocher*) to close up, move closer together; (*ceinture, nœud, frein, vis*) to tighten // *vi*: **~ à droite** to keep ou get over to the right; **se ~** *vi* (*se rap-*

procher) to squeeze up; **se ~ contre qn** to huddle up to sb; **~ la main à qn** to shake sb's hand; **~ qn dans ses bras** to hug sb, clasp sb in one's arms.

serrure [seʀyʀ] *nf* lock.

serrurier [seʀyʀje] *nm* locksmith.

sert *etc vb voir* **servir**.

sertir [seʀtiʀ] *vt* (*pierre*) to set.

servante [seʀvɑ̃t] *nf* (maid)servant.

serveur, euse [seʀvœʀ, -øz] *nm/f* waiter/waitress.

serviable [seʀvjabl(ə)] *a* obliging, willing to help.

service [seʀvis] *nm* (*gén*) service; (*série de repas*): **premier ~** first sitting; (*assortiment de vaisselle*) set, service; (*bureau: de la vente etc*) department, section; (*travail*): **pendant le ~** on duty; **~s** *nmpl* (*travail, ÉCON*) services; **faire le ~** to serve; **rendre ~ à** to help; **rendre un ~ à qn** to do sb a favour; **mettre en ~** to put into service *ou* operation; **hors ~** out of order; **~ après vente** after-sales service; **~ militaire** military service; **~ d'ordre** police (*ou* stewards) in charge of maintaining order; **~s secrets** secret service *sg*.

serviette [seʀvjet] *nf* (*de table*) (table) napkin, serviette; (*de toilette*) towel; (*porte-documents*) briefcase; **~ hygiénique** sanitary towel.

servir [seʀviʀ] *vt* (*gén*) to serve; (*au restaurant*) to wait on; (*au magasin*) to serve, attend to; (*fig: aider*): **~ qn** to aid sb; **to serve sb's interests**; (*COMM: rente*) to pay // *vi* (*TENNIS*) to serve; (*CARTES*) to deal; **vous êtes servi?** are you being served?; **se ~** *vi* (*prendre d'un plat*) to help o.s.; **se ~ de** (*plat*) to help o.s. to; (*voiture, outil, relations*) to use; **~ à qn** (*diplôme, livre*) to be of use to sb; **~ à qch/faire** (*outil etc*) to be used for sth/doing; **à quoi cela sert-il (de faire)?** what's the use (of doing)?; **cela ne sert à rien** it's no use; **~ (à qn)** to serve as (for sb); **~ à dîner (à qn)** to serve dinner (to sb).

serviteur [seʀvitœʀ] *nm* servant.

servitude [seʀvityd] *nf* servitude; (*fig*) constraint.

ses [se] *dét voir* **son**.

seuil [sœj] *nm* doorstep; (*fig*) threshold.

seul, e [sœl] *a* (*sans compagnie*) alone; (*avec nuance affective: isolé*) lonely; (*unique*): **un ~ livre** only one book, a single book; **le ~ livre** the only book; **~ ce livre, ce livre ~** this book alone, only this book // *ad* (*vivre*) alone, on one's own; **parler tout ~** to talk to oneself; **faire qch (tout) ~** to do sth (all) on one's own *ou* (all) by oneself // *nm, nf*: **il en reste un(e) ~(e)** there's only one left; **à lui (tout) ~** single-handed, on his own.

seulement [sœlmɑ̃] *ad* only; **non ~ ... mais aussi** *ou* **encore** not only ... but

also.

sève [sɛv] *nf* sap.

sévère [sevɛʀ] *a* severe.

sévices [sevis] *nmpl* (physical) cruelty *sg*, ill treatment *sg*.

sévir [seviʀ] *vi* (*punir*) to use harsh measures, crack down; (*suj: fléau*) to rage, be rampant.

sevrer [səvʀe] *vt* (*enfant etc*) to wean.

sexe [sɛks(ə)] *nm* sex; (*organe mâle*) member.

sexuel, le [sɛksɥel] *a* sexual.

seyant, e [sejɑ̃, -ɑ̃t] *a* becoming.

shampooing [ʃɑ̃pwɛ̃] *nm* shampoo; **se faire un ~** to shampoo one's hair.

short [ʃɔʀt] *nm* (pair of) shorts *pl*.

si [si] ♦ *nm* (*MUS*) B; (*en chantant la gamme*) ti
♦ *ad* **1** (*oui*) yes
2 (*tellement*) so; **~ gentil/rapidement** so kind/fast; (*tant et*) **~ bien que** so much so that; **~ rapide qu'il soit** however fast he may be
♦ *cj* if; **~ tu veux** if you want; **je me demande ~** I wonder if *ou* whether; **~ seulement** if only.

Sicile [sisil] *nf*: **la ~** Sicily.

SIDA [sida] *sigle m* (= *syndrome immuno-déficitaire acquis*) AIDS *sg*.

sidéré, e [sideʀe] *a* staggered.

sidérurgie [sideʀyʀʒi] *nf* steel industry.

siècle [sjɛkl(ə)] *nm* century; (*époque*) age.

siège [sjɛʒ] *nm* seat; (*d'entreprise*) head office; (*d'organisation*) headquarters *pl*; (*MIL*) siege; **~ social** registered office.

siéger [sjeʒe] *vi* to sit.

sien, ne [sjɛ̃, sjɛn] *pronom*: **le(la) ~(ne), les ~s(~nes)** his; hers; its; **faire des ~nes** (*fam*) to be up to one's (usual) tricks; **les ~s** (*sa famille*) one's family.

sieste [sjɛst(ə)] *nf* (afternoon) snooze *ou* nap, siesta; **faire la ~** to have a snooze *ou* nap.

sieur [sjœʀ] *nm*: **le ~ Thomas** Master Thomas.

sifflement [sifləmɑ̃] *nm* whistle, whistling *q*; wheezing *q*; hissing *q*.

siffler [sifle] *vi* (*gén*) to whistle; (*en respirant*) to wheeze; (*serpent, vapeur*) to hiss // *vt* (*chanson*) to whistle; (*chien etc*) to whistle for; (*fille*) to whistle at; (*pièce, orateur*) to hiss, boo; (*faute*) to blow one's whistle at; (*fin du match, départ*) to blow one's whistle for; (*fam: verre*) to guzzle.

sifflet [sifle] *nm* whistle; **coup de ~** whistle.

siffloter [siflɔte] *vi, vt* to whistle.

sigle [sigl(ə)] *nm* acronym.

signal, aux [siɲal, -o] *nm* (*signe convenu, appareil*) signal; (*indice, écriteau*) sign; **donner le ~ de** to give the signal for; **~ d'alarme** alarm signal; **signaux (lumineux)** (*AUTO*) traffic signals.

signalement [siɲalmɑ̃] *nm* description, particulars *pl*.

signaler [siɲale] *vt* to indicate; to announce; to report; (*faire remarquer*): ~ qch à qn/(à qn) que to point out sth to sb/(to sb) that; se ~ (par) to distinguish o.s. (by).

signaliser [siɲalize] *vt* to put up road-signs on; to put signals on.

signature [siɲatyʀ] *nf* signature (*action*), signing.

signe [siɲ] *nm* sign; (*TYPO*) mark; faire un ~ de la main to give a sign with one's hand; faire ~ à qn (*fig*) to get in touch with sb; faire ~ à qn d'entrer to motion (to) sb to come in.

signer [siɲe] *vt* to sign; se ~ *vi* to cross o.s.

signet [siɲe] *nm* bookmark.

significatif, ive [siɲifikatif, -iv] *a* significant.

signification [siɲifikɑsjɔ̃] *nf* meaning.

signifier [siɲifje] *vt* (*vouloir dire*) to mean; (*faire connaître*): ~ qch (à qn) to make sth known (to sb); (*JUR*): ~ qch à qn to serve notice of sth on sb.

silence [silɑ̃s] *nm* silence; (*MUS*) rest; garder le ~ to keep silent, say nothing; passer sous ~ to pass over (in silence); **silencieux, euse** *a* quiet, silent // *nm* silencer.

silex [sileks] *nm* flint.

silhouette [silwet] *nf* outline, silhouette; (*lignes, contour*) outline; (*figure*) figure.

silicium [silisjɔm] *nm* silicon; **plaquette de ~** silicon chip.

sillage [sijaʒ] *nm* wake; (*fig*) trail.

sillon [sijɔ̃] *nm* furrow; (*de disque*) groove; **sillonner** *vt* to criss-cross.

simagrées [simagʀe] *nfpl* fuss *sg*; airs and graces.

similaire [similɛʀ] *a* similar; **similicuir** *nm* imitation leather; **similitude** *nf* similarity.

simple [sɛ̃pl(ə)] *a* (*gén*) simple; (*non multiple*) single; ~s *nmpl* (*MÉD*) medicinal plants; ~ messieurs *nm* (*TENNIS*) men's singles *sg*; un ~ particulier an ordinary citizen; ~ d'esprit *nm/f* simpleton; ~ soldat private.

simulacre [simylakʀ(ə)] *nm* (*péj*): un ~ de a pretence of.

simuler [simyle] *vt* to sham, simulate.

simultané, e [simyltane] *a* simultaneous.

sincère [sɛ̃sɛʀ] *a* sincere; genuine; **sincérité** *nf* sincerity.

sine qua non [sinekwanɔn] *a*: condition ~ indispensable condition.

singe [sɛ̃ʒ] *nm* monkey; (*de grande taille*) ape.

singer [sɛ̃ʒe] *vt* to ape, mimic.

singeries [sɛ̃ʒʀi] *nfpl* antics; (*simagrées*) airs and graces.

singulariser [sɛ̃gylaʀize] *vt* to mark out; se ~ *vi* to call attention to o.s.

singularité [sɛ̃gylaʀite] *nf* peculiarity.

singulier, ière [sɛ̃gylje, -jɛʀ] *a* remarkable, singular // *nm* singular.

sinistre [sinistʀ(ə)] *a* sinister // *nm* (*incendie*) blaze; (*catastrophe*) disaster; (*ASSURANCES*) damage (*giving rise to a claim*); **sinistré, e** *a* disaster-stricken // *nm/f* disaster victim.

sinon [sinɔ̃] *cj* (*autrement, sans quoi*) otherwise, or else; (*sauf*) except, other than; (*si ce n'est*) if not.

sinueux, euse [sinɥø, -øz] *a* winding; (*fig*) tortuous.

sinus [sinys] *nm* (*ANAT*) sinus; (*GÉOM*) sine; **sinusite** *nf* sinusitis.

siphon [sifɔ̃] *nm* (*tube, d'eau gazeuse*) siphon; (*d'évier etc*) U-bend.

sirène [siʀɛn] *nf* siren; ~ d'alarme air-raid siren; fire alarm.

sirop [siʀo] *nm* (*à diluer: de fruit etc*) syrup; (*boisson*) fruit drink; (*pharmaceutique*) syrup, mixture.

siroter [siʀɔte] *vt* to sip.

sis, e [si, siz] *a* located.

sismique [sismik] *a* seismic.

site [sit] *nm* (*paysage, environnement*) setting; (*d'une ville etc: emplacement*) site; ~ (pittoresque) beauty spot; ~s touristiques places of interest.

sitôt [sito] *ad*: ~ parti as soon as he *etc* had left; ~ après straight after; pas de ~ not for a long time.

situation [sitɥɑsjɔ̃] *nf* (*gén*) situation; (*d'un édifice, d'une ville*) situation, position; location.

situé, e [sitɥe] *a*: bien ~ well situated; ~ à situated at.

situer [sitɥe] *vt* to site, situate; (*en pensée*) to set, place; se ~ *vi*: se ~ à/près de to be situated at/near.

six [sis] *num* six; **sixième** *num* sixth.

ski [ski] *nm* (*objet*) ski; (*sport*) skiing; faire du ~ to ski; ~ de fond cross-country skiing; ~ nautique water-skiing; ~ de piste downhill skiing; ~ de randonnée cross-country skiing; **skier** *vi* to ski; **skieur, euse** *nm/f* skier.

slip [slip] *nm* (*sous-vêtement*) pants *pl*, briefs *pl*; (*de bain: d'homme*) trunks *pl*; (: *du bikini*) (bikini) briefs *pl*.

slogan [slɔgã] *nm* slogan.

S.M.I.C. [smik] *sigle m voir* **salaire**.

smoking [smɔkiaj] *nm* dinner *ou* evening suit.

S.N.C.F. *sigle f* (= *société nationale des chemins de fer français*) French railways.

snob [snɔb] *a* snobbish // *nm/f* snob.

sobre [sɔbʀ(ə)] *a* temperate, abstemious; (*élégance, style*) sober; ~ de (*gestes, compliments*) sparing of.

sobriquet [sɔbʀikɛ] *nm* nickname.

social, e, aux [sɔsjal, -o] *a* social.

socialisme [sɔsjalism(ə)] *nm* socialism;

socialiste *nm/f* socialist.

société [sɔsjete] *nf* society; (*sportive*) club; (*COMM*) company; **la ~ d'abondance/de consommation** the affluent/consumer society; **~ anonyme (S.A.)** ≈ limited (*Brit*) *ou* incorporated (*US*) company; **~ à responsabilité limitée (S.A.R.L.)** *type of limited liability company (with non-negotiable shares)*.

sociologie [sɔsjɔlɔʒi] *nf* sociology.

socle [sɔkl(ə)] *nm* (*de colonne, statue*) plinth, pedestal; (*de lampe*) base.

socquette [sɔkɛt] *nf* ankle sock.

sœur [sœʀ] *nf* sister; (*religieuse*) nun, sister.

soi [swa] *pronom* oneself; **cela va de ~** that *ou* it goes without saying; **~-disant** *a inv* so-called // *ad* supposedly.

soie [swa] *nf* silk; (*de porc, sanglier: poil*) bristle; **~rie** *nf* (*tissu*) silk.

soif [swaf] *nf* thirst; **avoir ~** to be thirsty; **donner ~ à qn** to make sb thirsty.

soigné, e [swaɲe] *a* (*tenue*) well-groomed, neat; (*travail*) careful, meticulous; (*fam*) whopping; stiff.

soigner [swaɲe] *vt* (*malade, maladie: suj: docteur*) to treat; (*suj: infirmière, mère*) to nurse, look after; (*blessé*) to tend; (*travail, détails*) to take care over; (*jardin, chevelure, invités*) to look after.

soigneux, euse [swaɲø, -øz] *a* (*propre*) tidy, neat; (*méticuleux*) painstaking, careful; **~ de** careful with.

soi-même [swamɛm] *pronom* oneself.

soin [swɛ̃] *nm* (*application*) care; (*propreté, ordre*) tidiness, neatness; **~s** *nmpl* (*à un malade, blessé*) treatment *sg*, medical attention *sg*; (*attentions, prévenance*) care and attention *sg*; (*hygiène*) care *sg*; **prendre ~ de** to take care of, look after; **prendre ~ de faire** to take care to do; **les premiers ~s** first aid *sg*; **aux bons ~s de** c/o, care of.

soir [swaʀ] *nm* evening; **ce ~** this evening, tonight; **demain ~** tomorrow evening, tomorrow night.

soirée [swaʀe] *nf* evening; (*réception*) party.

soit [swa] *vb voir* **être** // *cj* (*à savoir*) namely; (*ou*): **~ ... ~** either ... or // *ad* so be it, very well; **~ que ... ~ que** *ou* **que** whether ... or whether.

soixantaine [swasɑ̃tɛn] *nf*: **une ~ (de)** sixty or so, about sixty; **avoir la ~ (âge)** to be around sixty.

soixante [swasɑ̃t] *num* sixty; **~-dix** seventy.

soja [sɔʒa] *nm* soya; (*graines*) soya beans *pl*.

sol [sɔl] *nm* ground; (*de logement*) floor; (*revêtement*) flooring *q*; (*territoire, AGR, GÉO*) soil; (*MUS*) G; (: *en chantant la gamme*) so(h).

solaire [sɔlɛʀ] *a* solar, sun *cpd*.

soldat [sɔlda] *nm* soldier.

solde [sɔld(ə)] *nf* pay // *nm* (*COMM*) balance; **~s** *nmpl ou nfpl* (*COMM*) sale goods; sales; **en ~** at sale price.

solder [sɔlde] *vt* (*compte*) to settle; (*marchandise*) to sell at sale price, sell off; **se ~ par** (*fig*) to end in; **article soldé (à) 10 F** item reduced to 10 F.

sole [sɔl] *nf* sole *inv* (*fish*).

soleil [sɔlɛj] *nm* sun; (*lumière*) sun(light); (*temps ensoleillé*) sun-(shine); (*BOT*) sunflower; **il fait du ~** it's sunny; **au ~** in the sun.

solennel, le [sɔlanɛl] *a* solemn; ceremonial; **solennité** *nf* (*d'une fête*) solemnity.

solfège [sɔlfɛʒ] *nm* rudiments *pl* of music; (*exercices*) ear training *q*.

solidaire [sɔlidɛʀ] *a* (*personnes*) who stand together, who show solidarity; (*pièces mécaniques*) interdependent; **être ~ de** (*collègues*) to stand by; **solidarité** *nf* solidarity; interdependence; **par solidarité (avec)** in sympathy (with).

solide [sɔlid] *a* solid; (*mur, maison, meuble*) solid, sturdy; (*connaissances, argument*) sound; (*personne, estomac*) robust, sturdy // *nm* solid.

soliste [sɔlist(ə)] *nm/f* soloist.

solitaire [sɔlitɛʀ] *a* (*sans compagnie*) solitary, lonely; (*lieu*) lonely // *nm/f* recluse; loner.

solitude [sɔlityd] *nf* loneliness; (*paix*) solitude.

solive [sɔliv] *nf* joist.

sollicitations [sɔlisitasjɔ̃] *nfpl* entreaties, appeals; enticements; (*TECH*) stress *sg*.

solliciter [sɔlisite] *vt* (*personne*) to appeal to; (*emploi, faveur*) to seek; (*suj: occupations, attractions etc*): **~ qn** to appeal to sb's curiosity *etc*; to entice sb; to make demands on sb's time.

sollicitude [sɔlisityd] *nf* concern.

soluble [sɔlybl(ə)] *a* soluble.

solution [sɔlysjɔ̃] *nf* solution; **~ de facilité** easy way out.

solvable [sɔlvabl(ə)] *a* solvent.

sombre [sɔ̃bʀ(ə)] *a* dark; (*fig*) gloomy.

sombrer [sɔ̃bʀe] *vi* (*bateau*) to sink; **~ dans** (*misère, désespoir*) to sink into.

sommaire [sɔmɛʀ] *a* (*simple*) basic; (*expéditif*) summary // *nm* summary.

sommation [sɔmasjɔ̃] *nf* (*JUR*) summons *sg*; (*avant de faire feu*) warning.

somme [sɔm] *nf* (*MATH*) sum; (*fig*) amount; (*argent*) sum, amount // *nm*: **faire un ~** to have a (short) nap; **en ~ ad** all in all; **~ toute** *ad* all in all.

sommeil [sɔmɛj] *nm* sleep; **avoir ~ to** be sleepy; **sommeiller** *vi* to doze; (*fig*) to lie dormant.

sommelier [sɔməlje] *nm* wine waiter.

sommer [sɔme] vt: ~ qn de faire to command ou order sb to do; (JUR) to summon sb to do.

sommes vb voir **être**.

sommet [sɔme] nm top; (d'une montagne) summit, top; (fig: de la perfection, gloire) height.

sommier [sɔmje] nm (bed) base.

sommité [sɔmite] nf prominent person, leading light.

somnambule [sɔmnãbyl] nm/f sleepwalker.

somnifère [sɔmnifɛr] nm sleeping drug q (ou pill).

somnoler [sɔmnɔle] vi to doze.

somptueux, euse [sõptɥø, -øz] a sumptuous; lavish.

son [sõ], **sa** [sa], pl **ses** [se] dét (antécédent humain mâle) his; (: femelle) her; (: valeur indéfinie) one's, his/her; (: non humain) its.

son [sõ] nm sound; (de blé) bran.

sondage [sõdaʒ] nm: ~ (d'opinion) (opinion) poll.

sonde [sõd] nf (NAVIG) lead ou sounding line; (MÉD) probe; catheter; feeding tube; (TECH) borer, driller; (pour fouiller etc) probe.

sonder [sõde] vt (NAVIG) to sound; (atmosphère, plaie, bagages etc) to probe; (TECH) to bore, drill; (fig) to sound out; to probe.

songe [sõʒ] nm dream.

songer [sõʒe] vi: ~ à (penser à) to think of; ~ que to consider that; to think that; **songeur, euse** a pensive.

sonnant, e [sɔnã, -ãt] a: à 8 heures ~es on the stroke of 8.

sonné, e [sɔne] a (fam) cracked; il est midi ~ it's gone twelve.

sonner [sɔne] vi to ring // vt (cloche) to ring; (glas, tocsin) to sound; (portier, infirmière) to ring for; (messe) to ring the bell for; ~ **faux** (instrument) to sound out of tune; (rire) to ring false; ~ **les heures** to strike the hours.

sonnerie [sɔnri] nf (son) ringing; (sonnette) bell; (mécanisme d'horloge) striking mechanism; ~ **d'alarme** alarm bell.

sonnette [sɔnɛt] nf bell; ~ **d'alarme** alarm bell; ~ **de nuit** night-bell.

sono [sɔno] abr f de **sonorisation**.

sonore [sɔnɔr] a (voix) sonorous, ringing; (salle, métal) resonant; (ondes, film, signal) sound cpd.

sonorisation [sɔnɔrizasjõ] nf (installations) public address system, P.A. system.

sonorité [sɔnɔrite] nf (de piano, violon) tone; (de voix, mot) sonority; (d'une salle) resonance; acoustics pl.

sont vb voir **être**.

sophistiqué, e [sɔfistike] a sophisticated.

sorbet [sɔrbɛ] nm water ice, sorbet.

sorcellerie [sɔrsɛlri] nf witchcraft q.

sorcier, ière [sɔrsje, -jɛr] nm/f sorcerer/witch ou sorceress.

sordide [sɔrdid] a sordid; squalid.

sornettes [sɔrnɛt] nfpl twaddle sg.

sort [sɔr] nm (fortune, destinée) fate; (condition, situation) lot; (magique) curse, spell; tirer au ~ to draw lots.

sorte [sɔrt(ə)] nf sort, kind; de la ~ ad in that way; de (telle) ~ que, en ~ que so that; so much so that; faire en ~ que to see to it that.

sortie [sɔrti] nf (issue) way out, exit; (MIL) sortie; (fig: verbale) outburst; sally; (promenade) outing; (le soir: au restaurant etc) night out; (COMM: somme): ~s items of expenditure; outgoings sans sg; ~ **de bain** (vêtement) bathrobe; ~ **de secours** emergency exit.

sortilège [sɔrtilɛʒ] nm (magic) spell.

sortir [sɔrtir] vi (gén) to come out; (partir, se promener, aller au spectacle etc) to go out; (numéro gagnant) to come up // vt (gén) to take out; (produit, ouvrage, modèle) to bring out; (INFORM) to output; (: sur papier) to print out; (fam: expulser) to throw out; ~ **de** (gén) to leave; (endroit) to go (ou come) out of, leave; (rainure etc) to come out of; (cadre, compétence) to be outside; se ~ **de** (affaire, situation) to get out of; s'en ~ (malade) to pull through; (d'une difficulté etc) to get through.

sosie [sozi] nm double.

sot, sotte [so, sɔt] a silly, foolish // nm/f fool; **sottise** nf silliness, foolishness; silly ou foolish thing.

sou [su] nm: près de ses ~s tight-fisted; sans le ~ penniless.

soubresaut [subrəso] nm start; jolt.

souche [suʃ] nf (d'arbre) stump; (de carnet) counterfoil (Brit), stub; de vieille ~ of old stock.

souci [susi] nm (inquiétude) worry; (préoccupation) concern; (BOT) marigold; se faire du ~ to worry.

soucier [susje]: se ~ **de** vt to care about.

soucieux, euse [susjø, -øz] a concerned, worried.

soucoupe [sukup] nf saucer; ~ **volante** flying saucer.

soudain, e [sudɛ̃, -ɛn] a (douleur, mort) sudden // ad suddenly, all of a sudden.

soude [sud] nf soda.

souder [sude] vt (avec fil à souder) to solder; (par soudure autogène) to weld; (fig) to bind together.

soudoyer [sudwaje] vt (péj) to bribe.

soudure [sudyr] nf soldering; welding; (joint) soldered joint; weld.

souffert, e [sufɛr, -ɛrt(ə)] pp de **souffrir**.

souffle [sufl(ə)] nm (en expirant) breath; (en soufflant) puff, blow;

(*respiration*) breathing; (*d'explosion, de ventilateur*) blast; (*du vent*) blowing; **être à bout de** ~ to be out of breath; **un** ~ **d'air** *ou* **de vent** a breath of air, a puff of wind.

soufflé, e [sufle] *a* (*fam: stupéfié*) staggered // *nm* (*CULIN*) soufflé.

souffler [sufle] *vi* (*gén*) to blow; (*haleter*) to puff (and blow) // *vt* (*feu, bougie*) to blow out; (*chasser: poussière etc*) to blow away; (*TECH: verre*) to blow; (*suj: explosion*) to destroy (with its blast); (*dire*): ~ **qch à qn** to whisper sth to sb; (*fam: voler*): ~ **qch à qn** to pinch sth from sb.

soufflet [sufle] *nm* (*instrument*) bellows *pl*; (*gifle*) slap (in the face).

souffleur [suflœR] *nm* (*THÉÂTRE*) prompter.

souffrance [sufRɑ̃s] *nf* suffering; **en** ~ (*marchandise*) awaiting delivery; (*affaire*) pending.

souffrant, e [sufRɑ̃, -ɑ̃t] *a* unwell.

souffre-douleur [sufRədulœR] *nm inv* butt, underdog.

souffrir [sufRiR] *vi* to suffer; to be in pain // *vt* to suffer, endure; (*supporter*) to bear, stand; (*admettre: exception etc*) to allow *ou* admit of; ~ **de** (*maladie, froid*) to suffer from.

soufre [sufR(ə)] *nm* sulphur.

souhait [swɛ] *nm* wish; **tous nos** ~**s de** good wishes *ou* our best wishes for; **riche** *etc* **à** ~ as rich *etc* as one could wish; **à vos** ~**s!** bless you!

souhaitable [swɛtabl(ə)] *a* desirable.

souhaiter [swete] *vt* to wish for; ~ **la bonne année à qn** to wish sb a happy New Year.

souiller [suje] *vt* to dirty, soil; (*fig*) to sully, tarnish.

soûl, e [su, sul] *a* drunk // *nm*: **tout son** ~ to one's heart's content.

soulagement [sulaʒmɑ̃] *nm* relief.

soulager [sulaʒe] *vt* to relieve.

soûler [sule] *vt*: ~ **qn** to get sb drunk; (*suj: boisson*) to make sb drunk; (*fig*) to make sb's head spin *ou* reel; **se** ~ *vi* to get drunk.

soulever [sulve] *vt* to lift; (*vagues, poussière*) to send up; (*peuple*) to stir up (to revolt); (*enthousiasme*) to arouse; (*question, débat*) to raise; **se** ~ *vi* (*peuple*) to rise up; (*personne couchée*) to lift o.s. up; **cela me soulève le cœur** it makes me feel sick.

soulier [sulje] *nm* shoe.

souligner [suliɲe] *vt* to underline; (*fig*) to emphasize; to stress.

soumettre [sumɛtR] *vt* (*pays*) to subject, subjugate; (*rebelle*) to put down, subdue; ~ **qn/qch à** to subject sb/sth to; ~ **qch à qn** (*projet etc*) to submit sth to sb; **se** ~ (**à**) to submit (to).

soumis, e [sumi, -iz] *a* submissive;

revenus ~ **à l'impôt** taxable income.

soumission [sumisjɔ̃] *nf* submission; (*docilité*) submissiveness; (*COMM*) tender.

soupape [supap] *nf* valve.

soupçon [supsɔ̃] *nm* suspicion; (*petite quantité*): **un** ~ **de** a hint *ou* touch of; **soupçonner** *vt* to suspect; **soupçonneux, euse** *a* suspicious.

soupe [sup] *nf* soup; ~ **au lait** *a inv* quick-tempered.

souper [supe] *vi* to have supper // *nm* supper.

soupeser [supəze] *vt* to weigh in one's hand(s); (*fig*) to weigh up.

soupière [supjɛR] *nf* (soup) tureen.

soupir [supiR] *nm* sigh; (*MUS*) crotchet rest.

soupirail, aux [supiRaj, -o] *nm* (small) basement window.

soupirer [supiRe] *vi* to sigh; ~ **après qch** to yearn for sth.

souple [supl(ə)] *a* supple; (*fig: règlement, caractère*) flexible; (*: démarche, taille*) lithe, supple.

source [suRs(ə)] *nf* (*point d'eau*) spring; (*d'un cours d'eau, fig*) source; **de bonne** ~ on good authority.

sourcil [suRsij] *nm* (eye)brow.

sourciller [suRsije] *vi*: **sans** ~ without turning a hair *ou* batting an eyelid.

sourcilleux, euse [suRsijø, -øz] *a* pernickety.

sourd, e [suR, suRd(ə)] *a* deaf; (*bruit, voix*) muffled; (*douleur*) dull; (*lutte*) silent, hidden // *nm/f* deaf person.

sourdine [suRdin] *nf* (*MUS*) mute; **en** ~ *ad* softly, quietly.

sourd-muet, sourde-muette [suRmɥɛ, suRdmɥɛt] *a* deaf-and-dumb // *nm/f* deaf-mute.

souriant, e [suRjɑ̃, -ɑ̃t] *a* cheerful.

souricière [suRisjɛR] *nf* mousetrap; (*fig*) trap.

sourire [suRiR] *nm* smile // *vi* to smile; ~ **à qn** to smile at sb; (*fig*) to appeal to sb; to smile on sb; **garder le** ~ to keep smiling.

souris [suRi] *nf* mouse (*pl* mice).

sournois, e [suRnwa, -waz] *a* deceitful, underhand.

sous [su] *prép* (*gén*) under; ~ **la pluie/le soleil** in the rain/sunshine; ~ **terre** *a, ad* underground; ~ **peu** *ad* shortly, before long.

sous-alimenté, e [suzalimɑ̃te] *a* undernourished.

sous-bois [subwa] *nm inv* undergrowth.

souscrire [suskRiR]: ~ **à** *vt* to subscribe to.

sous-directeur, trice [sudiRɛktœR, -tRis] *nm/f* assistant manager/ manageress.

sous-entendre [suzɑ̃tɑ̃dR(ə)] *vt* to imply, infer; **sous-entendu, e** *a* implied;

(*LING*) understood // *nm* innuendo, insinuation.

sous-estimer [suzɛstime] *vt* to underestimate.

sous-jacent, e [suʒasɑ̃, -ɑ̃t] *a* underlying.

sous-louer [sulwe] *vt* to sublet.

sous-main [sumɛ̃] *nm inv* desk blotter; en ~ *ad* secretly.

sous-marin, e [sumaʀɛ̃, -in] *a* (*flore, volcan*) submarine; (*navigation, pêche, explosif*) underwater // *nm* submarine.

sous-officier [suzɔfisje] *nm* ≈ non-commissioned officer (N.C.O.).

sous-produit [supʀɔdɥi] *nm* by-product; (*fig: péj*) pale imitation.

soussigné, e [susiɲe] *a*: je ~ I the undersigned.

sous-sol [susɔl] *nm* basement.

sous-titre [sutitʀ(ə)] *nm* subtitle.

soustraction [sustʀaksjɔ̃] *nf* subtraction.

soustraire [sustʀɛʀ] *vt* to subtract, take away; (*dérober*): ~ qch à qn to remove sth from sb; ~ qn à (*danger*) to shield sb from; se ~ à (*autorité etc*) to elude, escape from.

sous-traitant [sutʀɛtɑ̃] *nm* subcontractor.

sous-vêtements [suvɛtmɑ̃] *nmpl* underwear *sg*.

soutane [sutan] *nf* cassock, soutane.

soute [sut] *nf* hold.

soutènement [sutɛnmɑ̃] *nm*: mur de ~ retaining wall.

souteneur [sutnœʀ] *nm* procurer.

soutenir [sutniʀ] *vt* to support; (*assaut, choc*) to stand up to, withstand; (*intérêt, effort*) to keep up; (*assurer*): ~ que to maintain that; ~ la comparaison avec to bear *ou* stand comparison with; **soutenu, e** *a* (*efforts*) sustained, unflagging; (*style*) elevated.

souterrain, e [sutɛʀɛ̃, -ɛn] *a* underground // *nm* underground passage.

soutien [sutjɛ̃] *nm* support; ~ de famille breadwinner.

soutien-gorge [sutjɛ̃gɔʀʒ(ə)] *nm* bra.

soutirer [sutiʀe] *vt*: ~ qch à qn to squeeze *ou* get sth out of sb.

souvenir [suvniʀ] *nm* (*réminiscence*) memory; (*objet*) souvenir // *vb*: se ~ de *vt* to remember; se ~ que to remember that; en ~ de in memory *ou* remembrance of.

souvent [suvɑ̃] *ad* often; peu ~ seldom, infrequently.

souverain, e [suvʀɛ̃, -ɛn] *a* sovereign; (*fig: mépris*) supreme // *nm/f* sovereign, monarch.

soviétique [sɔvjetik] *a* Soviet // *nm/f*: S~ Soviet citizen.

soyeux, euse [swajø, øz] *a* silky.

soyons *etc vb voir* **être**.

spacieux, euse [spasjø, -øz] *a* spa-

cious; roomy.

spaghettis [spageti] *nmpl* spaghetti *sg*.

sparadrap [spaʀadʀa] *nm* sticking plaster (*Brit*), bandaid ® (*US*).

spatial, e, aux [spasjal, -o] *a* (*AVIAT*) space *cpd*.

speaker, ine [spikœʀ, -kʀin] *nm/f* announcer.

spécial, e, aux [spesjal, -o] *a* special; (*bizarre*) peculiar; **~ement** *ad* especially, particularly; (*tout exprès*) specially.

spécialiser [spesjalize]: se ~ *vi* to specialize.

spécialiste [spesjalist(ə)] *nm/f* specialist.

spécialité [spesjalite] *nf* speciality; (*SCOL*) special field.

spécifier [spesifje] *vt* to specify, state.

spécimen [spesimɛn] *nm* specimen; (*revue etc*) specimen *ou* sample copy.

spectacle [spɛktakl(ə)] *nm* (*tableau, scène*) sight; (*représentation*) show; (*industrie*) show business; **spectaculaire** *a* spectacular.

spectateur, trice [spɛktatœʀ, -tʀis] *nm/f* (*CINÉMA etc*) member of the audience; (*SPORT*) spectator; (*d'un événement*) onlooker, witness.

spéculer [spekyle] *vi* to speculate; ~ sur (*COMM*) to speculate in; (*réfléchir*) to speculate on.

spéléologie [speleɔlɔʒi] *nf* potholing.

sperme [spɛʀm(ə)] *nm* semen, sperm.

sphère [sfɛʀ] *nf* sphere.

spirale [spiʀal] *nf* spiral.

spirituel, le [spiʀitɥɛl] *a* spiritual; (*fin, piquant*) witty.

spiritueux [spiʀitɥø] *nm* spirit.

splendide [splɑ̃did] *a* splendid; magnificent.

spontané, e [spɔ̃tane] *a* spontaneous.

sport [spɔʀ] *nm* sport // *a inv* (*vêtement*) casual; faire du ~ to do sport; ~s d'hiver winter sports; **sportif, ive** *a* (*journal, association, épreuve*) sports *cpd*; (*allure, démarche*) athletic; (*attitude, esprit*) sporting.

spot [spɔt] *nm* (*lampe*) spot(light); (*annonce*): ~ (*publicitaire*) commercial (break).

square [skwaʀ] *nm* public garden(s).

squelette [skəlɛt] *nm* skeleton; **squelettique** *a* scrawny; (*fig*) skimpy.

stabiliser [stabilize] *vt* to stabilize; (*terrain*) to consolidate.

stable [stabl(ə)] *a* stable, steady.

stade [stad] *nm* (*SPORT*) stadium; (*phase, niveau*) stage.

stage [staʒ] *nm* training period; training course; **stagiaire** *nm/f*, *a* trainee.

stalle [stal] *nf* stall, box.

stand [stɑ̃d] *nm* (*d'exposition*) stand; (*de foire*) stall; ~ de tir (*à la foire, SPORT*) shooting range.

standard [stãdaʀ] *a inv* standard // *nm* switchboard; **standardiste** *nm/f* switchboard operator.

standing [stãdiaj] *nm* standing; **immeuble de grand ~** block of luxury flats (*Brit*), condo(minium) (*US*).

starter [staʀtɛʀ] *nm* (*AUTO*) choke.

station [stusjɔ̃] *nf* station; (*de bus*) stop; (*de villégiature*) resort; (*posture*): **la ~ debout** standing, an upright posture; **~ de ski** ski resort; **~ de taxis** taxi rank (*Brit*) *ou* stand (*US*).

stationnement [stasjɔnmã] *nm* parking.

stationner [stasjɔne] *vi* to park.

station-service [stasjɔ̃sɛʀvis] *nf* service station.

statistique [statistik] *nf* (*science*) statistics *sg*; (*rapport, étude*) statistic // *a* statistical.

statue [staty] *nf* statue.

statuer [statɥe] *vi*: **~ sur** to rule on, give a ruling on.

statut [staty] *nm* status; **~s** *nmpl* (*JUR*, *ADMIN*) statutes; **statutaire** *a* statutory.

Sté *abr de* **société**.

steak [stɛk] *nm* steak.

sténo... [stenɔ] *préfixe*: **~(dactylo)** *nf* shorthand typist (*Brit*), stenographer (*US*); **~(graphie)** *nf* shorthand.

stéréo(phonique) [steʀeɔ(fɔnik)] *a* stereo(phonic).

stérile [steʀil] *a* sterile; (*terre*) barren; (*fig*) fruitless, futile.

stérilet [steʀilɛ] *nm* coil, loop.

stériliser [steʀilize] *vt* to sterilize.

stigmates [stigmat] *nmpl* scars, marks.

stimulant [stimylã] *nm* (*fig*) stimulus (*pl* i), incentive.

stimuler [stimyle] *vt* to stimulate.

stipuler [stipyle] *vt* to stipulate.

stock [stɔk] *nm* stock; **~ d'or** (*FINANCE*) gold reserves *pl*; **~er** *vt* to stock.

stop [stɔp] *nm* (*AUTO*: *écriteau*) stop sign; (: *signal*) brake-light.

stopper [stɔpe] *vt* to stop, halt; (*COUTURE*) to mend // *vi* to stop, halt.

store [stɔʀ] *nm* blind; (*de magasin*) shade, awning.

strabisme [sʀabism(ə)] *nm* squinting.

strapontin [sʀapɔ̃tɛ̃] *nm* jump *ou* foldaway seat.

stratégie [sʀateʒi] *nf* strategy; **stratégique** *a* strategic.

stressant, e [sʀesã, -ãt] *a* stressful.

strict, e [sʀikt(ə)] *a* strict; (*tenue, décor*) severe, plain; **son droit le plus ~** his most basic right; **le ~ nécessaire/ minimum** the bare essentials/minimum.

strie [sʀi] *nf* streak.

strophe [sʀɔf] *nf* verse, stanza.

structure [sʀyktyʀ] *nf* structure; **~s d'accueil** reception facilities.

studieux, euse [stydjø, -øz] *a* studious;

devoted to study.

studio [stydjo] *nm* (*logement*) (one-roomed) flatlet (*Brit*) *ou* apartment (*US*); (*d'artiste, TV etc*) studio (*pl* s).

stupéfait, e [stypefɛ, -ɛt] *a* astonished.

stupéfiant [stypefjã] *nm* (*MÉD*) drug, narcotic.

stupéfier [stypefje] *vt* to stupefy; (*étonner*) to stun, astonish.

stupeur [stypœʀ] *nf* astonishment.

stupide [stypid] *a* stupid; **stupidité** *nf* stupidity; stupid thing (to do *ou* say).

style [stil] *nm* style; **meuble de ~** piece of period furniture.

stylé, e [stile] *a* well-trained.

stylo [stilo] *nm*: **~ (à encre)** (fountain) pen; **~ (à) bille** ball-point pen.

su, e [sy] *pp de* **savoir** // *nm*: **au ~ de** with the knowledge of.

suave [sɥav] *a* sweet; (*goût*) mellow.

subalterne [sybaltɛʀn(ə)] *a* (*employé, officier*) junior; (*rôle*) subordinate, subsidiary // *nm/f* subordinate.

subconscient [sypkɔ̃sjã] *nm* subconscious.

subir [sybiʀ] *vt* (*affront, dégâts*) to suffer; (*influence, charme*) to be under; (*opération, châtiment*) to undergo.

subit, e [sybi, -it] *a* sudden; **subitement** *ad* suddenly, all of a sudden.

subjectif, ive [sybʒɛktif, -iv] *a* subjective.

subjonctif [sybʒɔ̃ktif] *nm* subjunctive.

submerger [sybmɛʀʒe] *vt* to submerge; (*fig*) to overwhelm.

subordonné, e [sybɔʀdɔne] *a*, *nm/f* subordinate; **~ à** subordinate to; subject to, depending on.

subornation [sybɔʀnɑsjɔ̃] *nf* bribing.

subrepticement [sybʀɛptismã] *ad* surreptitiously.

subside [sypsid] *nm* grant.

subsidiaire [sypsidjɛʀ] *a*: **question ~** deciding question.

subsister [sybziste] *vi* (*rester*) to remain, subsist; (*vivre*) to live; (*survivre*) to live on.

substance [sypstãs] *nf* substance.

substituer [sypstitɥe] *vt*: **~ qn/qch à** to substitute sb/sth for; **se ~ à qn** (*évincer*) to substitute o.s. for sb.

substitut [sypstity] *nm* (*JUR*) deputy public prosecutor; (*succédané*) substitute.

subtil, e [syptil] *a* subtle.

subtiliser [syptilize] *vt*: **~ qch (à qn)** to spirit sth away (from sb).

subvenir [sybvəniʀ] : **~ à** *vt* to meet.

subvention [sybvãsjɔ̃] *nf* subsidy, grant; **subventionner** *vt* to subsidize.

suc [syk] *nm* (*BOT*) sap; (*de viande, fruit*) juice.

succédané [syksedane] *nm* substitute.

succéder [syksede] : **~ à** *vt* (*directeur, roi etc*) to succeed; (*venir après: dans*

une série) to follow, succeed; **se ~** *vi*
(accidents, années) to follow one another.

succès [syksɛ] *nm* success; avoir du **~**
to be a success, be successful; **~ de librairie** bestseller; **~ (féminins)** con-
quests; **à ~** successful.

succession [syksesjɔ̃] *nf (série, POL)*
succession; *(JUR: patrimoine)* estate, inheritance.

succomber [sykɔ̃be] *vi* to die, succumb;
(fig): **~ à** to give way to, succumb to.

succursale [sykyrsal] *nf* branch.

sucer [syse] *vt* to suck.

sucette [sysɛt] *nf (bonbon)* lollipop; *(de
bébé)* dummy *(Brit)*, pacifier *(US)*.

sucre [sykʀ(ə)] *nm (substance)* sugar;
(morceau) lump of sugar, sugar lump *ou*
cube; **~ en morceaux/cristallisé/en poudre** lump/granulated/caster sugar; **~
d'orge** barley sugar; **sucré, e** *a (produit
alimentaire)* sweetened; *(au goût)*
sweet; *(péj)* sugary, honeyed; **sucrer** *vt*
(thé, café) to sweeten, put sugar in; **su-
creries** *nfpl (bonbons)* sweets, sweet
things; **sucrier** *nm (récipient)* sugar
bowl.

sud [syd] *nm:* **le ~** the south // *a inv*
south; *(côte)* south, southern; **au ~** *(situation)* in the south; *(direction)* to the
south; **au ~ de** (to the) south of; **~
africain, e** *a, nm/f* South African; **~
américain, e** *a, nm/f* South American.

sud-est [sydɛst] *nm, a inv* south-east.

sud-ouest [sydwɛst] *nm, a inv* south-
west.

Suède [sɥɛd] *nf:* **la ~** Sweden; **suédois,
e** *a* Swedish // *nm/f:* **Suédois, e** Swede //
nm (LING) Swedish.

suer [sɥe] *vi* to sweat; *(suinter)* to ooze.

sueur [sɥœr] *nf* sweat; **en ~** sweating, in
a sweat.

suffire [syfir] *vi (être assez):* **~ (à qn/
pour qch/pour faire)** to be enough *ou*
sufficient (for sb/for sth/to do); **cela suffit
pour les irriter/qu'ils se fâchent** it's
enough to annoy them/for them to get
angry; **il suffit d'une négligence/qu'on
oublie pour que ...** it only takes one act
of carelessness/one only needs to forget
for ....

suffisamment [syfizamɑ̃] *ad* sufficiently, enough; **~ de** sufficient, enough.

suffisant, e [syfizɑ̃, -ɑ̃t] *a (temps, ressources)* sufficient; *(résultats)* satisfactory; *(vaniteux)* self-important,
bumptious.

suffixe [syfiks(ə)] *nm* suffix.

suffoquer [syfɔke] *vt* to choke, suffocate; *(stupéfier)* to stagger, astound // *vi*
to choke, suffocate.

suffrage [syfraʒ] *nm (POL: voix)* vote;
(du public etc) approval *q.*

suggérer [syʒere] *vt* to suggest;
suggestion *nf* suggestion.

suicide [sɥisid] *nm* suicide.

suicider [sɥiside]: **se ~** *vi* to commit suicide.

suie [sɥi] *nf* soot.

suinter [sɥɛ̃te] *vi* to ooze.

suis *vb voir* **être; suivre.**

suisse [sɥis] *a* Swiss // *nm:* **S~** Swiss *pl
inv*; *(bedeau)* ≈ verger // *nf:* **la S~** Switzerland; **la S~ romande/allemande**
French-speaking/German-speaking Switzerland; **Suissesse** *nf* Swiss (woman *ou*
girl).

suite [sɥit] *nf (continuation):* d'énu-
mération etc)* rest, remainder; *(: de
feuilleton)* continuation; *(: second film
etc sur le même thème)* sequel; *(série:
de maisons, succès)*: **une ~ de** a series
ou succession of; *(MATH)* series *sg;
(conséquence)* result; *(ordre, liaison logique)* coherence; *(appartement, MUS)*
suite; *(escorte)* retinue, suite; **~s** *nfpl
(d'une maladie etc)* effects; **prendre la
~ de** *(directeur etc)* to succeed, take
over from; **donner ~ à** *(requête, projet)*
to follow up; **faire ~ à** to follow;
(faisant) **~ à votre lettre du** further to
your letter of the; **de ~** *ad (d'affilée)* in
succession; *(immédiatement)* at once;
par la ~ afterwards, subsequently; **à la
~** one after the other; **à la ~ de** *(derrière)* behind; *(en conséquence de)* following; **par ~ de** owing to, as a result of.

suivant, e [sɥivɑ̃, -ɑ̃t] *a* next, following;
(ci-après): **l'exercice ~** the following exercise // *prép (selon)* according to; **au ~!**
next!

suivi, e [sɥivi] *a (régulier)* regular; *(co-
hérent)* consistent, coherent; **très/peu ~**
(cours) well-/poorly-attended.

suivre [sɥivr(ə)] *vt (gén)* to follow;
(SCOL: cours) to attend; *(: programme)*
to keep up with; *(COMM: article)* to continue to stock // *vi* to follow; *(élève)* to
attend; to keep up; **se ~** *vi (accidents
etc)* to follow one after the other; *(raisonnement)* to be coherent; **faire ~**
(lettre) to forward; **~ son cours** *(suj:
enquête etc)* to run *ou* take its course; **'à
~'** 'to be continued'.

sujet, te [syʒɛ, -ɛt] *a:* **être ~ à** *(vertige
etc)* to be liable *ou* subject to // *nm/f
(d'un souverain)* subject // *nm* subject;
au ~ de *prép* about; **~ à caution** *a* questionable; **~ de conversation** topic *ou* subject of conversation; **~ d'examen** *(SCOL)*
examination question; examination paper.

summum [sɔmɔm] *nm:* **le ~ de** the
height of.

superbe [sypɛʀb(ə)] *a* magnificent, superb.

super(carburant) [sypɛʀ(kaʀbyʀɑ̃)] *nm*
≈ 4-star petrol *(Brit)*, ≈ high-octane
gasoline *(US)*.

supercherie [sypɛʀʃəʀi] *nf* trick.

superficie [sypɛʀfisi] *nf* (surface) area; (*fig*) surface.

superficiel, le [sypɛʀfisjɛl] *a* superficial.

superflu, e [sypɛʀfly] *a* superfluous.

supérieur, e [sypeʀjœʀ] *a* (*lèvre, étages, classes*) upper; (*plus élevé: température, niveau*): ~ (à) higher (than); (*meilleur: qualité, produit*): ~ (à) superior (to); (*excellent, hautain*) superior // *nm, nf* superior; à l'étage ~ on the next floor up; **supériorité** *nf* superiority.

superlatif [sypɛʀlatif] *nm* superlative.

supermarché [sypɛʀmaʀʃe] *nm* supermarket.

superposer [sypɛʀpoze] *vt* (*faire chevaucher*) to superimpose; **lits superposés** bunk beds.

superproduction [sypɛʀpʀɔdyksjɔ̃] *nf* (*film*) spectacular.

superpuissance [sypɛʀpɥisãs] *nf* super-power.

superstitieux, euse [sypɛʀstisjø, -øz] *a* superstitious.

superviser [sypɛʀvize] *vt* to supervise.

suppléant, e [sypleã, -ãt] *a* (*juge, fonctionnaire*) deputy *cpd*; (*professeur*) supply *cpd* // *nm/f* deputy; supply teacher.

suppléer [syplee] *vt* (*ajouter: mot manquant etc*) to supply, provide; (*compenser: lacune*) to fill in; (: *défaut*) to make up for; (*remplacer*) to stand in for; ~ à *vt* to make up for; to substitute for.

supplément [syplemã] *nm* supplement; (*de frites etc*) extra portion; **un ~ de travail** extra *ou* additional work; **ceci est en ~** (*au menu etc*) this is extra, there is an extra charge for this; **supplémentaire** *a* additional, further; (*train, bus*) relief *cpd*, extra.

supplications [syplikasjɔ̃] *nfpl* pleas, entreaties.

supplice [syplis] *nm* (*peine corporelle*) torture *q*; form of torture; (*douleur physique, morale*) torture, agony.

supplier [syplije] *vt* to implore, beseech.

supplique [syplik] *nf* petition.

support [sypɔʀ] *nm* support; (*pour livre, outils*) stand.

supportable [sypɔʀtabl(ə)] *a* (*douleur*) bearable.

supporter *nm* [sypɔʀtɛʀ] supporter, fan // *vt* [sypɔʀte] (*poids, poussée*) to support; (*conséquences, épreuve*) to bear, endure; (*défauts, personne*) to put up with; (*suj: chose: chaleur etc*) to withstand; (*suj: personne: chaleur, vin*) to be able to take.

supposé, e [sypoze] *a* (*nombre*) estimated; (*auteur*) supposed.

supposer [sypoze] *vt* to suppose; (*impliquer*) to presuppose; à ~ **que** supposing (that).

suppositoire [sypozitwaʀ] *nm* suppository.

suppression [sypʀesjɔ̃] *nf* removal; deletion; cancellation; suppression.

supprimer [sypʀime] *vt* (*cloison, cause, anxiété*) to remove; (*clause, mot*) to delete; (*congés, service d'autobus etc*) to cancel; (*emplois, privilèges, témoin gênant*) to do away with.

supputer [sypyte] *vt* to calculate.

suprême [sypʀɛm] *a* supreme.

sur, e [syʀ] *a* sour.

sur [syʀ] *prép* **1** (*position*) on; (*pardessus*) over; (*au-dessus*) above; **pose-le ~ la table** put it on the table; **je n'ai pas d'argent ~ moi** I haven't any money on me

2 (*direction*) towards; **en allant ~ Paris** going towards Paris; ~ **votre droite** on *ou* to your right

3 (*à propos de*) on, about; **un livre/une conférence ~ Balzac** a book/lecture on *ou* about Balzac

4 (*proportion, mesures*) out of; by; **un ~ 10** one in 10; (*SCOL*) one out of 10; **4 m ~ 2** 4 m by 2

sur ce *ad* hereupon.

sûr, e [syʀ] *a* sure, certain; (*digne de confiance*) reliable; (*sans danger*) safe; ~ **de soi** self-confident; **le plus ~ est de** the safest thing is to; ~ **et certain** absolutely certain.

suranné, e [syʀane] *a* outdated, outmoded.

surbaissé, e [syʀbese] *a* lowered, low.

surcharge [syʀʃaʀʒ(ə)] *nf* (*de passagers, marchandises*) excess load; (*correction*) alteration.

surcharger [syʀʃaʀʒe] *vt* to overload.

surchoix [syʀʃwa] *a inv* top-quality.

surclasser [syʀklase] *vt* to outclass.

surcroît [syʀkʀwa] *nm*: **un ~ de** additional + *nom*; **par** *ou* **de ~** moreover; **en ~** in addition.

surdité [syʀdite] *nf* deafness.

surélever [syʀɛlve] *vt* to raise, heighten.

sûrement [syʀmã] *ad* reliably; safely, securely; (*certainement*) certainly.

surenchère [syʀãʃɛʀ] *nf* (*aux enchères*) higher bid; (*sur prix fixe*) overbid; (*fig*) overstatement; outbidding tactics *pl*; **surenchérir** *vi* to bid higher; (*fig*) to try and outbid each other.

surent *vb voir* **savoir**.

surestimer [syʀɛstime] *vt* to overestimate.

sûreté [syʀte] *nf* (*voir sûr*) reliability; safety; (*JUR*) guaranty; surety; **mettre en ~** to put in a safe place; **pour plus de ~** as an extra precaution; **to be on the safe side.**

surf [syʀf] *nm* surfing.

surface [syʀfas] *nf* surface; (*superficie*) surface area; **faire ~** to surface; **en ~** *ad* near the surface; (*fig*) superficially.

surfait, e [syʀfɛ, -ɛt] *a* overrated.

surfin, e [syʀfɛ̃, -in] a superfine.

surgelé, e [syʀʒəle] a (deep-)frozen.

surgir [syʀʒiʀ] vi to appear suddenly; (jaillir) to shoot up; (fig: problème, conflit) to arise.

surhumain, e [syʀymɛ̃, -ɛn] a superhuman.

surimpression [syʀɛ̃pʀesjɔ̃] nf (PHOTO) double exposure; en ~ superimposed.

sur-le-champ [syʀləʃɑ̃] ad immediately.

surlendemain [syʀlɑ̃dmɛ̃] nm: le ~ (soir) two days later (in the evening); le ~ de two days after.

surligneur [syʀliɲœʀ] nm highlighter (pen).

surmener [syʀməne] vt, se ~ vi to overwork.

surmonter [syʀmɔ̃te] vt (suj: coupole etc) to top; (vaincre) to overcome.

surnager [syʀnaʒe] vi to float.

surnaturel, le [syʀnatyʀɛl] a, nm supernatural.

surnom [syʀnɔ̃] nm nickname.

surnombre [syʀnɔ̃bʀ(ə)] nm: être en ~ to be too many (ou one too many).

surpeuplé, e [syʀpœple] a overpopulated.

sur-place [syʀplas] nm: faire du ~ to mark time.

surplomber [syʀplɔ̃be] vi to be overhanging // vt to overhang; to tower above.

surplus [syʀply] nm (COMM) surplus; (reste): ~ de bois wood left over.

surprenant, e [syʀpʀənɑ̃, -ɑ̃t] a amazing.

surprendre [syʀpʀɑ̃dʀ(ə)] vt (étonner, prendre à l'improviste) to surprise; (tomber sur: intrus etc) to catch; (fig) to detect; to chance upon; to overhear.

surpris, e [syʀpʀi, -iz] a: ~ (de/que) surprised (at/that).

surprise [syʀpʀiz] nf surprise; faire une ~ à qn to give sb a surprise.

surprise-partie [syʀpʀizpaʀti] nf party.

sursaut [syʀso] nm start, jump; ~ de (énergie, indignation) sudden fit ou burst of; en ~ ad with a start; **sursauter** vi to (give a) start, jump.

surseoir [syʀswaʀ]: ~ à vt to defer.

sursis [syʀsi] nm (JUR: gén) suspended sentence; (à l'exécution capitale, aussi fig) reprieve; (MIL) deferment.

surtaxe [syʀtaks(ə)] nf surcharge.

surtout [syʀtu] ad (avant tout, d'abord) above all; (spécialement, particulièrement) especially; ~, ne dites rien! whatever you do don't say anything!; ~ pas! certainly ou definitely not!; ~ que ... especially as ...

surveillance [syʀvɛjɑ̃s] nf watch; (PO-LICE, MIL) surveillance; sous ~ médicale under medical supervision.

surveillant, e [syʀvɛjɑ̃, -ɑ̃t] nm/f (de prison) warder; (SCOL) monitor; (de travaux) supervisor, overseer.

surveiller [syʀveje] vt (enfant, élèves, bagages) to watch, keep an eye on; (malade) to watch over; (prisonnier, suspect) to keep (a) watch on; (territoire, bâtiment) to (keep) watch over; (travaux, cuisson) to supervise; (SCOL: examen) to invigilate; se ~ vi to keep a check ou watch on o.s.; ~ son langage/sa ligne to watch one's language/figure.

survenir [syʀvəniʀ] vi (incident, retards) to occur, arise; (événement) to take place; (personne) to appear, arrive.

survêt(ement) [syʀvɛt(mɑ̃)] nm tracksuit.

survie [syʀvi] nf survival; (REL) afterlife.

survivant, e [syʀvivɑ̃, -ɑ̃t] nm/f survivor.

survivre [syʀvivʀ(ə)] vi to survive; ~ à vt (accident etc) to survive; (personne) to outlive.

survoler [syʀvɔle] vt to fly over; (fig: livre) to skim through.

survolté, e [syʀvɔlte] a (fig) worked up.

sus [sy(s)]: en ~ de prép in addition to, over and above; en ~ ad in addition; à ~ excl: ~ au tyran! at the tyrant!

susceptible [sysɛptibl(ə)] a touchy, sensitive; ~ d'amélioration that can be improved, open to improvement; ~ de faire able to do; liable to do.

susciter [sysite] vt (admiration) to arouse; (obstacles, ennuis): (à qn) to create (for sb).

suspect, e [syspɛ(kt), -ɛkt(ə)] a suspicious; (témoignage, opinions) suspect // nm/f suspect.

suspecter [syspɛkte] vt to suspect; (honnêteté de qn) to question, have one's suspicions about.

suspendre [syspɑ̃dʀ(ə)] vt (accrocher: vêtement): ~ qch (à) to hang sth up (on); (fixer: lustre etc): ~ qch à to hang sth from; (interrompre, démettre) to suspend; (remettre) to defer; se ~ à to hang from.

suspendu, e [syspɑ̃dy] a (accroché): ~ à hanging on (ou from); (perché): ~ au-dessus de suspended over.

suspens [syspɑ̃]: en ~ ad (affaire) in abeyance; tenir en ~ to keep in suspense.

suspense [syspɑ̃s] nm suspense.

suspension [syspɑ̃sjɔ̃] nf suspension; ~ d'audience adjournment.

sut vb voir savoir.

suture [sytyʀ] nf: point de ~ stitch.

svelte [svɛlt(ə)] a slender, svelte.

S.V.P. sigle (= s'il vous plaît) please.

syllabe [silab] nf syllable.

sylviculture [silvikyltyʀ] nf forestry.

symbole [sɛ̃bɔl] nm symbol; **symbolique** a symbolic(al); (geste, of-

frande) token *cpd*; (*salaire, dommage-intérêts*) nominal; **symboliser** *vt* to symbolize.

symétrique [simetrik] *a* symmetrical.

sympa [sɛ̃pa] *a abr de* **sympathique**.

sympathie [sɛ̃pati] *nf* (*inclination*) liking; (*affinité*) fellow feeling; (*condoléances*) sympathy; **accueillir avec ~** (*projet*) to receive favourably; **croyez à toute ma ~** you have my deepest sympathy.

sympathique [sɛ̃patik] *a* nice, friendly; likeable; pleasant.

sympathisant, e [sɛ̃patizɑ̃, -ɑ̃t] *nm/f* sympathizer.

sympathiser [sɛ̃patize] *vi* (*voisins etc*: *s'entendre*) to get on (*Brit*) *ou* along (*US*) (well).

symphonie [sɛ̃fɔni] *nf* symphony.

symptôme [sɛ̃ptom] *nm* symptom.

synagogue [sinagɔg] *nf* synagogue.

syncope [sɛ̃kɔp] *nf* (*MÉD*) blackout; **tomber en ~** to faint, pass out.

syndic [sɛ̃dik] *nm* managing agent.

syndical, e, aux [sɛ̃dikal, -o] *a* (trade-)union *cpd*; **~iste** *nm/f* trade unionist.

syndicat [sɛ̃dika] *nm* (*d'ouvriers, employés*) (trade) union; (*autre association d'intérêts*) union, association; **~ d'initiative** tourist office.

syndiqué, e [sɛ̃dike] *a* belonging to a (trade) union; **non ~** non-union.

syndiquer [sɛ̃dike]: **se ~** *vi* to form a trade union; (*adhérer*) to join a trade union.

synonyme [sinɔnim] *a* synonymous // *nm* synonym; **~ de** synonymous with.

syntaxe [sɛ̃taks] *nf* syntax.

synthèse [sɛ̃tɛz] *nf* synthesis (*pl* es).

synthétique [sɛ̃tetik] *a* synthetic.

Syrie [siri] *nf*: **la ~** Syria.

systématique [sistematik] *a* systematic.

système [sistɛm] *nm* system; **le ~ D** resourcefulness.

T

t' [t(ə)] *pronom voir* **te**.

ta [ta] *dét voir* **ton**.

tabac [taba] *nm* tobacco; tobacconist's (shop); **~ blond/brun** light/dark tobacco; **~ à priser** snuff.

table [tabl(ə)] *nf* table; **à ~!** dinner *etc* is ready!; **se mettre à ~** to sit down to eat; (*fig*: *fam*) to come clean; **mettre la ~** to lay the table; **faire ~ rase de** to make a clean sweep of; **~ des matières** (table of) contents *pl*; **~ de nuit** *ou* **de chevet** bedside table.

tableau, x [tablo] *nm* painting; (*reproduction, fig*) picture; (*panneau*) board; (*schéma*) table, chart; **~ d'affi-**

chage notice board; **~ de bord** dashboard; (*AVIAT*) instrument panel; **~ noir** blackboard.

tabler [table] *vi*: **~ sur** to bank on.

tablette [tablɛt] *nf* (*planche*) shelf (*pl* shelves); **~ de chocolat** bar of chocolate.

tableur [tablœr] *nm* spreadsheet.

tablier [tablije] *nm* apron.

tabouret [taburɛ] *nm* stool.

tac [tak] *nm*: **du ~ au ~** tit for tat.

tache [taʃ] *nf* (*saleté*) stain, mark; (*ART, de couleur, lumière*) spot; splash, patch.

tâche [taʃ] *nf* task; **travailler à la ~** to do piecework.

tacher [taʃe] *vt* to stain, mark; (*fig*) to sully, stain.

tâcher [taʃe] *vi*: **~ de faire** to try *ou* endeavour to do.

tacot [tako] *nm* (*péj*) banger (*Brit*), (old) heap.

tact [takt] *nm* tact; **avoir du ~** to be tactful.

tactique [taktik] *a* tactical // *nf* (*technique*) tactics *sg*; (*plan*) tactic.

taie [tɛ] *nf*: **~ (d'oreiller)** pillowslip, pillowcase.

taille [taj] *nf* cutting; pruning; (*milieu du corps*) waist; (*hauteur*) height; (*grandeur*) size; **de ~ à faire** capable of doing; **de ~** a sizeable.

taille-crayon(s) [tajkrɛjɔ̃] *nm* pencil sharpener.

tailler [taje] *vt* (*pierre, diamant*) to cut; (*arbre, plante*) to prune; (*vêtement*) to cut out; (*crayon*) to sharpen.

tailleur [tajœr] *nm* (*couturier*) tailor; (*vêtement*) suit; **en ~** (*assis*) cross-legged.

taillis [taji] *nm* copse.

taire [tɛr] *vt* to keep to o.s., conceal // *vi*: **faire ~ qn** to make sb be quiet; (*fig*) to silence sb; **se ~** *vi* to be silent *ou* quiet.

talc [talk] *nm* talc, talcum powder.

talent [talɑ̃] *nm* talent.

talon [talɔ̃] *nm* heel; (*de chèque, billet*) stub, counterfoil (*Brit*); **~s plats/aiguilles** flat/stiletto heels.

talonner [talɔne] *vt* to follow hard behind; (*fig*) to hound.

talus [taly] *nm* embankment.

tambour [tɑ̃bur] *nm* (*MUS, aussi TECH*) drum; (*musicien*) drummer; (*porte*) revolving door(s *pl*).

tamis [tami] *nm* sieve.

Tamise [tamiz] *nf*: **la ~** the Thames.

tamisé, e [tamize] *a* (*fig*) subdued, soft.

tamiser [tamize] *vt* to sieve, sift.

tampon [tɑ̃pɔ̃] *nm* (*de coton, d'ouate*) wad, pad; (*amortisseur*) buffer; (*bouchon*) plug, stopper; (*cachet, timbre*) stamp; (*mémoire*) **~** (*INFORM*) buffer; **~** (**hygiénique**) tampon;

tamponner *vt* (*timbres*) to stamp; (*heurter*) to crash *ou* ram into;

tamponneuse *a*: autos tamponneuses dodgems.

tandis [tɑ̃di]: ~ **que** *cj* while.

tanguer [tɑ̃ge] *vi* to pitch (and toss).

tanière [tanjɛʀ] *nf* lair, den.

tanné, e [tane] *a* weather-beaten.

tanner [tane] *vt* to tan.

tant [tɑ̃] *ad* so much; ~ **de** (*sable, eau*) so much; (*gens, livres*) so many; ~ **que** *cj* as long as; ~ **que** (*comparatif*) as much as; ~ **mieux** that's great; so much the better; ~ **pis** never mind; too bad.

tante [tɑ̃t] *nf* aunt.

tantôt [tɑ̃to] *ad* (*parfois*): ~ ... ~ now ... now; (*cet après-midi*) this afternoon.

tapage [tapaʒ] *nm* uproar, din.

tapageur, euse [tapaʒœʀ, -øz] *a* loud, flashy; noisy.

tape [tap] *nf* slap.

tape-à-l'œil [tapalœj] *a inv* flashy, showy.

taper [tape] *vt* (*porte*) to bang, slam; (*dactylographier*) to type (out); (*fam: emprunter*): ~ **qn de 10 F** to touch sb for 10 F // *vi* (*soleil*) to beat down; ~ **sur qn** to thump sb; (*fig*) to run sb down; ~ **sur qch** to hit sth; to bang on sth; ~ **à** (*porte etc*) to knock on; ~ **dans** *vt* (*se servir*) to dig into; ~ **des mains/pieds** to clap one's hands/stamp one's feet; ~ **à** (*à la machine*) to type; **se** ~ **un travail** to land o.s. with a job.

tapi, e [tapi] *a* crouching, cowering; hidden away.

tapis [tapi] *nm* carpet; (*de table*) cloth; **mettre sur le** ~ (*fig*) to bring up for discussion; ~ **roulant** conveyor belt; ~ **de sol** (*de tente*) groundsheet.

tapisser [tapise] *vt* (*avec du papier peint*) to paper; (*recouvrir*): ~ **qch** (**de**) to cover sth (with).

tapisserie [tapisʀi] *nf* (*tenture, broderie*) tapestry; (*papier peint*) wallpaper.

tapissier, ière [tapisje, -jɛʀ] *nm/f*: ~(-**décorateur**) upholsterer (and decorator).

tapoter [tapɔte] *vt* to pat, tap.

taquiner [takine] *vt* to tease.

tarabiscoté, e [taʀabiskɔte] *a* overornate, fussy.

tard [taʀ] *ad* late; **plus** ~ **later** (on); **au plus** ~ at the latest; **sur le** ~ late in life.

tarder [taʀde] *vi* (*chose*) to be a long time coming; (*personne*): ~ **à faire** to delay doing; **il me tarde d'être** I am longing to be; **sans** (**plus**) ~ without (further) delay.

tardif, ive [taʀdif, -iv] *a* late.

targuer [taʀge]: **se** ~ **de** *vt* to boast about.

tarif [taʀif] *nm* (*liste*) price list; tariff; (*barème*) rates *pl*; fares *pl*; tariff; (*prix*) rate; fare.

tarir [taʀiʀ] *vi* to dry up, run dry.

tarte [taʀt(ə)] *nf* tart.

tartine [taʀtin] *nf* slice of bread; ~ **de miel** slice of bread and honey; **tartiner** *vt* to spread; **fromage à tartiner** cheese spread.

tartre [taʀtʀ(ə)] *nm* (*des dents*) tartar; (*de chaudière*) fur, scale.

tas [tɑ] *nm* heap, pile; (*fig*): **un** ~ **de** heaps of, lots of; **en** ~ in a heap *ou* pile; **formé sur le** ~ trained on the job.

tasse [tɑs] *nf* cup; ~ **à café** coffee cup.

tassé, e [tɑse] *a*: **bien** ~ (*café etc*) strong.

tasser [tɑse] *vt* (*terre, neige*) to pack down; (*entasser*): ~ **qch dans** to cram sth into; **se** ~ *vi* (*terrain*) to settle; (*fig*) to sort itself out, settle down.

tâter [tɑte] *vt* to feel; (*fig*) to try out; ~ **de** (*prison etc*) to have a taste of; **se** ~ (*hésiter*) to be in two minds.

tatillon, ne [tatijɔ̃, -ɔn] *a* pernickety.

tâtonnement [tɑtɔnmɑ̃] *nm*: **par** ~**s** (*fig*) by trial and error.

tâtonner [tɑtɔne] *vi* to grope one's way along.

tâtons [tɑtɔ̃]: **à** ~ *ad*: **chercher/avancer à** ~ to grope around for/grope one's way forward.

tatouer [tatwe] *vt* to tattoo.

taudis [todi] *nm* hovel, slum.

taule [tol] *nf* (*fam*) nick (*fam*), prison.

taupe [top] *nf* mole.

taureau, x [tɔʀo] *nm* bull; (*signe*): **le T~** Taurus.

tauromachie [tɔʀɔmaʃi] *nf* bullfighting.

taux [to] *nm* rate; (*d'alcool*) level; ~ **d'intérêt** interest rate.

taxe [taks] *nf* tax; (*douanière*) duty; ~ **de séjour** tourist tax; ~ **à la valeur ajoutée** (**T.V.A.**) value added tax (**V.A.T.**).

taxer [takse] *vt* (*personne*) to tax; (*produit*) to put a tax on, tax; (*fig*): ~ **qn de** to call sb + *attribut*; to accuse sb of, tax sb with.

taxi [taksi] *nm* taxi.

tchao [tʃao] *excl* (*fam*) bye(-bye)!

Tchécoslovaquie [tʃekɔslɔvaki] *nf* Czechoslovakia; **tchèque** *a, nm, nf* Czech.

te, t' [t(ə)] *pronom* you; (*réfléchi*) yourself.

technicien, ne [tɛknisjɛ̃, -jɛn] *nm/f* technician.

technique [tɛknik] *a* technical // *nf* technique; ~**ment** *ad* technically.

technologie [tɛknɔlɔʒi] *nf* technology; **technologique** *a* technological.

teck [tɛk] *nm* teak.

teignais *etc vb voir* **teindre**.

teindre [tɛ̃dʀ(ə)] *vt* to dye.

teint, e [tɛ̃, tɛ̃t] *a* dyed // *nm* (*du visage*) complexion; colour // *nf* shade; **grand** ~ *a inv* colourfast.

teinté, e [tɛ̃te] *a*: ~ **de** (*fig*) tinged with.

teinter [tɛ̃te] *vt* to tint; (*bois*) to stain;

teinture *nf* dyeing; (*substance*) dye; (*MÉD*) tincture.

teinturerie [tɛ̃tyʀʀi] *nf* dry cleaner's.

teinturier [tɛ̃tyʀje] *nm* dry cleaner.

tel, telle [tɛl] *a* (*pareil*) such; (*comme*): ~ un/des ... like a/like ...; (*indéfini*) such-and-such a, a given; (*intensif*): un ~/de ~s ... such (a)/such ...; rien de ~ nothing like it, no such thing; ~ que *cj* like, such as; ~ quel as it is *ou* stands (*ou* was *etc*).

télé [tele] *abr f* (= *télévision*) TV, telly (*Brit*); (*poste*) TV (set), telly; à la ~ on TV, on telly.

télé... [tele] *préfixe*: ~benne, ~cabine *nf* (*benne*) cable car; ~commande *nf* remote control; ~copie *nf* fax; ~distribution *nf* cable TV; ~férique *nm* = ~phérique; ~gramme *nm* telegram.

télégraphe [telegraf] *nm* telegraph; **télégraphier** *vt* to telegraph, cable.

téléguider [telegide] *vt* to operate by remote control, radio-control.

téléjournal [teleʒuʀnal] *nm* TV news magazine programme.

télématique [telematik] *nf* telematics *sg*.

téléobjectif [teleɔbʒɛktif] *nm* telephoto lens *sg*.

téléphérique [telefeʀik] *nm* cable-car.

téléphone [telefɔn] *nm* telephone; avoir le ~ to be on the (tele)phone; au ~ on the phone; **téléphoner** *vi* to telephone, ring; to make a phone call; téléphoner à to phone, call up; **téléphonique** *a* (tele)phone *cpd*.

télescope [teleskɔp] *nm* telescope.

télescoper [teleskɔpe] *vt* to smash up; se ~ (*véhicules*) to concertina.

téléscripteur [teleskʀiptœʀ] *nm* teleprinter.

télésiège [telesjɛʒ] *nm* chairlift.

téléski [teleski] *nm* ski-tow.

téléspectateur, trice [telespɛktatœʀ, -tʀis] *nm/f* (television) viewer.

téléviseur [televizœʀ] *nm* television set.

télévision [televizjɔ̃] *nf* television; à la ~ on television.

télex [telɛks] *nm* telex.

telle [tɛl] *a voir* **tel**.

tellement [tɛlmɑ̃] *ad* (*tant*) so much; (*si*) so; ~ de (*sable*, *eau*) so much; (*gens*, *livres*) so many; il s'est endormi ~ il était fatigué he was so tired (that) he fell asleep; **pas** ~ not (all) that much; not (all) that + *adjectif*.

téméraire [temeʀɛʀ] *a* reckless, rash; **témérité** *nf* recklessness, rashness.

témoignage [temwaɲaʒ] *nm* (*JUR*: *déclaration*) testimony *q*, evidence *q*; (: *faits*) evidence *q*; (*rapport*, *récit*) account; (*fig*: *d'affection etc*) token, mark; expression.

témoigner [temwaɲe] *vt* (*intérêt*, *grati-*

tude) to show // *vi* (*JUR*) to testify, give evidence; ~ de *vt* to bear witness to, testify to.

témoin [temwɛ̃] *nm* witness; (*fig*) testimony // *a* control *cpd*, test *cpd*; appartement ~ show flat (*Brit*); être ~ de to witness; ~ oculaire eyewitness.

tempe [tɑ̃p] *nf* temple.

tempérament [tɑ̃peʀamɑ̃] *nm* temperament, disposition; à ~ (*vente*) on deferred (payment) terms; (*achat*) by instalments, hire purchase *cpd*.

température [tɑ̃peʀatyʀ] *nf* temperature; avoir *ou* faire de la ~ to be running *ou* have a temperature.

tempéré, e [tɑ̃peʀe] *a* temperate.

tempête [tɑ̃pɛt] *nf* storm; ~ de sable/neige sand/snowstorm.

temple [tɑ̃pl(ə)] *nm* temple; (*protestant*) church.

temporaire [tɑ̃pɔʀɛʀ] *a* temporary.

temps [tɑ̃] *nm* (*atmosphérique*) weather; (*durée*) time; (*époque*) time, times *pl*; (*LING*) tense; (*MUS*) beat; (*TECH*) stroke; **il fait beau/mauvais** ~ the weather is fine/bad; avoir le ~/tout le ~ to have time/plenty of time; en ~ de paix/guerre in peacetime/wartime; en ~ utile *ou* voulu in due time *ou* course; de ~ en ~, de ~ à autre from time to time; à ~ (*partir*, *arriver*) in time; à ~ partiel *ad*, *a* part-time; dans le ~ at one time; de tout ~ always; ~ d'arrêt pause, halt; ~ mort (*COMM*) slack period.

tenable [tənabl(ə)] *a* bearable.

tenace [tənas] *a* tenacious, persistent.

tenailler [tənaje] *vt* (*fig*) to torment.

tenailles [tənaj] *nfpl* pincers.

tenais *etc vb voir* **tenir**.

tenancier, ière [tənɑ̃sje, -jɛʀ] *nm/f* manager/manageress.

tenant, e [tənɑ̃, -ɑ̃t] *nm/f* (*SPORT*): ~ du titre title-holder.

tendance [tɑ̃dɑ̃s] *nf* (*opinions*) leanings *pl*, sympathies *pl*; (*inclination*) tendency; (*évolution*) trend; avoir ~ à to have a tendency to, tend to.

tendeur [tɑ̃dœʀ] *nm* (*attache*) elastic strap.

tendre [tɑ̃dʀ(ə)] *a* tender; (*bois*, *roche*, *couleur*) soft // *vt* (*élastique*, *peau*) to stretch, draw tight; (*muscle*) to tense; (*donner*): ~ qch à to hold sth out to sb; to offer sb sth; (*fig: piège*) to set, lay; se ~ *vi* (*corde*) to tighten; (*relations*) to become strained; ~ à qch/à faire to tend towards sth/to do; ~ l'oreille to prick up one's ears; ~ la main/le bras to hold out one's hand/stretch out one's arm; ~ment *ad* tenderly; **tendresse** *nf* tenderness.

tendu, e [tɑ̃dy] *pp de* **tendre** // *a* tight; tensed; strained.

ténèbres [tenɛbʀ(ə)] *nfpl* darkness *sg*.

teneur [tənœʀ] *nf* content; (*d'une lettre*)

terms *pl*, content.

tenir [təniʀ] *vt* to hold; (*magasin, hôtel*) to run; (*promesse*) to keep // *vi* to hold; (*neige, gel*) to last; se ~ *vi* (*avoir lieu*) to be held, take place; (*être: personne*) to stand; se ~ droit to stand up (*ou* sit up) straight; bien se ~ to behave well; se ~ à qch to hold on to sth; s'en ~ à qch to confine o.s. to sth; to stick to sth; ~ à *vt* to be attached to; to care about; to depend on; to stem from; ~ à faire to want to do; ~ de *vt* to partake of; to take after; ça ne tient qu'à lui it is entirely up to him; ~ qn pour to take sb for; ~ qch de qn (*histoire*) to have heard *ou* learnt sth from sb; (*qualité, défaut*) to have inherited *ou* got sth from sb; ~ les comptes to keep the books; ~ le coup to hold out; ~ au chaud to keep hot; tiens/tenez, voilà le stylo there's the pen!; tiens, Alain! look, here's Alain!; tiens? (*surprise*) really?

tennis [tenis] *nm* tennis; (*court*) tennis court // *nmpl ou fpl* (*aussi*: **chaussures de ~**) tennis *ou* gym shoes; ~ de table table tennis; ~**man** *nm* tennis player.

tension [tɑ̃sjɔ̃] *nf* tension; (*fig*) tension; strain; (*MÉD*) blood pressure; faire *ou* avoir de la ~ to have high blood pressure.

tentation [tɑ̃tasjɔ̃] *nf* temptation.

tentative [tɑ̃tativ] *nf* attempt, bid.

tente [tɑ̃t] *nf* tent.

tenter [tɑ̃te] *vt* (*éprouver, attirer*) to tempt; (*essayer*): ~ qch/de faire to attempt *ou* try sth/to do; ~ sa chance to try one's luck.

tenture [tɑ̃tyʀ] *nf* hanging.

tenu, e [təny] *pp de* **tenir** // *a* (*maison, comptes*): bien ~ well-kept; (*obligé*): ~ de faire under an obligation to do // *nf* (*action de tenir*) running; keeping; holding; (*vêtements*) clothes *pl*, gear; (*allure*) dress *q*, appearance; (*comportement*) manners *pl*, behaviour; en petite ~e scantily dressed *ou* clad; ~e de route (*AUTO*) road-holding; ~e de soirée evening dress.

ter [tɛʀ] *a*: 16 ~ 16b *ou* B.

térébenthine [teʀebɑ̃tin] *nf*: (essence de) ~ (oil of) turpentine.

terme [tɛʀm(ə)] *nm* term; (*fin*) end; à court/long ~ *a* short-/long-term *ou* -range // *ad* in the short/long term; avant ~ (*MÉD*) *ad* prematurely; mettre un ~ à to put an end *ou* a stop to.

terminaison [tɛʀminɛzɔ̃] *nf* (*LING*) ending.

terminal, e, aux [tɛʀminal, -o] *a* final // *nm* terminal // *nf* (*SCOL*) ≈ sixth form *ou* year (*Brit*), ≈ twelfth grade (*US*).

terminer [tɛʀmine] *vt* to end; (*travail, repas*) to finish; se ~ *vi* to end.

terne [tɛʀn(ə)] *a* dull.

ternir [tɛʀniʀ] *vt* to dull; (*fig*) to sully,

tarnish; se ~ *vi* to become dull.

terrain [tɛʀɛ̃] *nm* (*sol, fig*) ground; (*COMM*) land *q*, plot (of land); site; sur le ~ (*fig*) on the field; ~ de football/ rugby football/rugby pitch (*Brit*) *ou* field (*US*); ~ d'aviation airfield; ~ de camping campsite; ~ de golf golf course; ~ de jeu games field; playground; ~ de sport sports ground; ~ vague waste ground *q*.

terrasse [tɛʀas] *nf* terrace; à la ~ (*café*) outside.

terrassement [tɛʀasmɑ̃] *nm* earthmoving, earthworks *pl*; embankment.

terrasser [tɛʀase] *vt* (*adversaire*) to floor; (*suj: maladie etc*) to lay low.

terre [tɛʀ] *nf* (*gén, aussi* ÉLEC) earth; (*substance*) soil, earth; (*opposé à mer*) land *q*; (*contrée*) land; ~s *nfpl* (*terrains*) lands, land *sg*; en ~ (*pipe, poterie*) clay *cpd*; à ~ *ou* par ~ (*mettre, être*) on the ground (*ou* floor); (*jeter, tomber*) to the ground, down; ~ cuite earthenware; terracotta; la ~ ferme dry land; ~ glaise clay; ~ à ~ *a inv* down-to-earth.

terreau [tɛʀo] *nm* compost.

terre-plein [tɛʀplɛ̃] *nm* platform.

terrer [tɛʀe]: se ~ *vi* to hide away; to go to ground.

terrestre [tɛʀɛstʀ(ə)] *a* (*surface*) earth's, of the earth; (*BOT, ZOOL, MIL*) land *cpd*; (*REL*) earthly, worldly.

terreur [tɛʀœʀ] *nf* terror *q*.

terrible [tɛʀibl(ə)] *a* terrible, dreadful; (*fam*) terrific.

terrien, ne [tɛʀjɛ̃, -jɛn] *a*: propriétaire ~ landowner // *nm/f* (*non martien etc*) earthling.

terrier [tɛʀje] *nm* burrow, hole; (*chien*) terrier.

terril [tɛʀil] *nm* slag heap.

terrine [tɛʀin] *nf* (*récipient*) terrine; (*CULIN*) pâté.

territoire [tɛʀitwaʀ] *nm* territory.

terroir [tɛʀwaʀ] *nm* (*AGR*) soil; region.

terrorisme [tɛʀɔʀism(ə)] *nm* terrorism; **terroriste** *nm/f* terrorist.

tertiaire [tɛʀsjɛʀ] *a* tertiary // *nm* (*ÉCON*) service industries *pl*.

tertre [tɛʀtʀ(ə)] *nm* hillock, mound.

tes [te] *dét voir* **ton**.

tesson [tesɔ̃] *nm*: ~ de bouteille piece of broken bottle.

test [tɛst] *nm* test.

testament [tɛstamɑ̃] *nm* (*JUR*) will; (*REL*) Testament; (*fig*) legacy.

tester [tɛste] *vt* to test.

testicule [tɛstikyl] *nm* testicle.

tétanos [tetanos] *nm* tetanus.

têtard [tɛtaʀ] *nm* tadpole.

tête [tɛt] *nf* head; (*cheveux*) hair *q*; (*visage*) face; de ~ *a* (*wagon etc*) front *cpd* // *ad* (*calculer*) in one's head, mentally; tenir ~ à qn to stand up to sb; la

~ **en bas** with one's head down; **la ~ la première** (*tomber*) headfirst; **faire une ~** (*FOOTBALL*) to head the ball; **faire la ~** (*fig*) to sulk; **en ~** (*SPORT*) in the lead; at the front; **en ~ à ~** in private, alone together; **de la ~ aux pieds** from head to toe; **~ de lecture** (playback) head; **~ de liste** (*POL*) chief candidate; **~ de série** (*TENNIS*) seeded player, seed; **~-à-queue** *nm inv*: **faire un ~-à-queue** to spin round.

téter [tete] *vt*: **~ (sa mère)** to suck at one's mother's breast, feed.

tétine [tetin] *nf* teat; (*sucette*) dummy (*Brit*), pacifier (*US*).

têtu, e [tety] *a* stubborn, pigheaded.

texte [tɛkst(ə)] *nm* text.

textile [tɛkstil] *a* textile *cpd* // *nm* textile; textile industry.

texture [tɛkstyʀ] *nf* texture.

TGV *sigle m* (= *train à grande vitesse*) high-speed train.

thé [te] *nm* tea; **prendre le ~** to have tea; **faire le ~** to make the tea.

théâtral, e, aux [teɑtʀal, -o] *a* theatrical.

théâtre [teɑtʀ(ə)] *nm* theatre; (*œuvres*) plays *pl*, dramatic works *pl*; (*fig: lieu*): **le ~ de** the scene of; (*péj*) histrionics *pl*, playacting; **faire du ~** to be on the stage; to do some acting.

théière [tejɛʀ] *nf* teapot.

thème [tɛm] *nm* theme; (*SCOL: traduction*) prose (composition).

théologie [teɔlɔʒi] *nf* theology.

théorie [teɔʀi] *nf* theory; **théorique** *a* theoretical.

thérapie [teʀapi] *nf* therapy.

thermal, e, aux [tɛʀmal, -o] *a*: **station ~e** spa; **cure ~e** water cure.

thermes [tɛʀm(ə)] *nmpl* thermal baths.

thermomètre [tɛʀmɔmɛtʀ(ə)] *nm* thermometer.

thermos ® [tɛʀmos] *nm ou nf*: **(bouteille) ~** vacuum *ou* Thermos ® flask.

thermostat [tɛʀmɔsta] *nm* thermostat.

thèse [tɛz] *nf* thesis (*pl* theses).

thon [tɔ̃] *nm* tuna (fish).

thym [tɛ̃] *nm* thyme.

tibia [tibja] *nm* shinbone, tibia; shin.

tic [tik] *nm* tic, (nervous) twitch; (*de langage etc*) mannerism.

ticket [tikɛ] *nm* ticket; **~ de quai** platform ticket.

tiède [tjɛd] *a* lukewarm; tepid; (*vent, air*) mild, warm; **tiédir** *vi* to cool; to grow warmer.

tien, tienne [tjɛ̃, tjɛn] *pronom*: **le ~ (la tienne), les ~s (tiennes)** yours; **à la tienne!** cheers!

tiens [tjɛ̃] *vb, excl voir* **tenir**.

tiercé [tjɛʀse] *nm* system of forecast betting giving first 3 horses.

tiers, tierce [tjɛʀ, tjɛʀs(ə)] *a* third //

nm (*JUR*) third party; (*fraction*) third; **le ~ monde** the third world.

tige [tiʒ] *nf* stem; (*baguette*) rod.

tignasse [tiɲas] *nf* (*péj*) mop of hair.

tigre [tigʀ(ə)] *nm* tiger.

tigré, e [tigʀe] *a* striped; spotted.

tilleul [tijœl] *nm* lime (tree), linden (tree); (*boisson*) lime(-blossom) tea.

timbale [tɛ̃bal] *nf* (metal) tumbler; **~s** *nfpl* (*MUS*) timpani, kettledrums.

timbre [tɛ̃bʀ(ə)] *nm* (*tampon*) stamp; (*aussi*: **~-poste**) (postage) stamp; (*MUS: de voix, instrument*) timbre, tone.

timbré, e [tɛ̃bʀe] *a* (*fam*) daft.

timbrer [tɛ̃bʀe] *vt* to stamp.

timide [timid] *a* shy; timid; (*timoré*) timid, timorous; **~ment** *ad* shyly; timidly; **timidité** *nf* shyness; timidity.

tins *etc vb voir* **tenir**.

tintamarre [tɛ̃tamaʀ] *nm* din, uproar.

tinter [tɛ̃te] *vi* to ring, chime; (*argent, clefs*) to jingle.

tir [tiʀ] *nm* (*sport*) shooting; (*fait ou manière de tirer*) firing *q*; (*stand*) shooting gallery; **~ à l'arc** archery; **~ au pigeon** clay pigeon shooting.

tirage [tiʀaʒ] *nm* (*action*) printing; (*PHOTO*) print; (*de journal*) circulation; (*de livre*) (print-)run; edition; (*de cheminée*) draught; (*de loterie*) draw; (*désaccord*) friction; **~ au sort** drawing lots.

tirailler [tiʀaje] *vt* to pull at, tug at // *vi* to fire at random.

tirant [tiʀɑ̃] *nm*: **~ d'eau** draught.

tire [tiʀ] *nf*: **vol à la ~** pickpocketing.

tiré, e [tiʀe] *a* (*traits*) drawn // *nm* (*COMM*) drawee; **~ par les cheveux** far-fetched.

tire-au-flanc [tiʀoflɑ̃] *nm inv* (*péj*) skiver.

tire-bouchon [tiʀbuʃɔ̃] *nm* corkscrew.

tirelire [tiʀliʀ] *nf* moneybox.

tirer [tiʀe] *vt* (*gén*) to pull; (*extraire*): **~ qch de** to take *ou* pull sth out of; to get sth out of; to extract sth from; (*tracer: ligne, trait*) to draw, trace; (*fermer: rideau*) to draw, close; (*choisir: carte, conclusion, avantage COMM: chèque*) to draw; (*en faisant feu: balle, coup*) to fire; (*: animal*) to shoot; (*journal, livre, photo*) to print; (*FOOTBALL: corner etc*) to take // *vi* (*faire feu*) to fire; (*faire du tir, FOOTBALL*) to shoot; (*cheminée*) to draw; **se ~** *vi* (*fam*) to push off; **s'en ~** to pull through, get off; **~ sur** to pull on *ou* at; to shoot *ou* fire at; (*pipe*) to draw on; (*fig: avoisiner*) to verge *ou* border on; **~ qn de** (*embarras etc*) to help *ou* get sb out of; **~ à l'arc/la carabine** to shoot with a bow and arrow/with a rifle.

tiret [tiʀɛ] *nm* dash.

tireur, euse [tiʀœʀ, -øz] *nm/f* gunman; (*COMM*) drawer; **~ d'élite** marksman.

tiroir [tiʀwaʀ] *nm* drawer; **~-caisse** *nm*

till.

tisane [tizan] *nf* herb tea.

tisonnier [tizɔnje] *nm* poker.

tisser [tise] *vt* to weave; **tisserand** *nm* weaver.

tissu [tisy] *nm* fabric, material, cloth *q*; (*ANAT, BIO*) tissue.

tissu-éponge [tisyepɔ̃ʒ] *nm* (terry) towelling *q*.

titre [titʀ(ə)] *nm* (*gén*) title; (*de journal*) headline; (*diplôme*) qualification; (*COMM*) security; **en ~** (*champion*) official; **à juste ~** with just cause, rightly; **à quel ~?** on what grounds?; **à aucun ~** on no account; **au même ~** (**que**) in the same way (as); **à ~ d'information** for (your) information; **à ~ gracieux** free of charge; **à ~ d'essai** on a trial basis; **à ~ privé** in a private capacity; **~ de propriété** title deed; **~ de transport** ticket.

tituber [titybe] *vi* to stagger (along).

titulaire [tityleʀ] (*ADMIN*) *a* appointed, with tenure // *nm* incumbent; **être ~ de** (*poste*) to hold; (*permis*) to be the holder of.

toast [tost] *nm* slice *ou* piece of toast; (*de bienvenue*) (welcoming) toast; **porter un ~ à qn** to propose *ou* drink a toast to sb.

toboggan [tɔbɔgɑ̃] *nm* toboggan; (*jeu*) slide.

tocsin [tɔksɛ̃] *nm* alarm (bell).

toge [tɔʒ] *nf* toga; (*de juge*) gown.

toi [twa] *pronom* you.

toile [twal] *nf* (*matériau*) cloth *q*; (*bâche*) piece of canvas; (*tableau*) canvas; **~ d'araignée** cobweb; **~ cirée** oilcloth; **~ de fond** (*fig*) backdrop.

toilette [twalɛt] *nf* wash; (*habits*) outfit; dress *q*; **~s** *nfpl* (*w.-c.*) toilet *sg*; **faire sa ~** to have a wash, get washed; **articles de ~** toiletries.

toi-même [twamɛm] *pronom* yourself.

toiser [twaze] *vt* to eye up and down.

toison [twazɔ̃] *nf* (*de mouton*) fleece; (*cheveux*) mane.

toit [twa] *nm* roof; **~ ouvrant** sunroof.

toiture [twatyʀ] *nf* roof.

tôle [tol] *nf* (*plaque*) steel *ou* iron sheet; **~ ondulée** corrugated iron.

tolérable [tɔleʀabl(ə)] *a* tolerable, bearable.

tolérant, e [tɔleʀɑ̃, -ɑ̃t] *a* tolerant.

tolérer [tɔleʀe] *vt* to tolerate; (*ADMIN*: *hors taxe etc*) to allow.

tollé [tɔle] *nm* outcry.

tomate [tɔmat] *nf* tomato.

tombe [tɔ̃b] *nf* (*sépulture*) grave; (*avec monument*) tomb.

tombeau, x [tɔ̃bo] *nm* tomb.

tombée [tɔ̃be] *nf*: **à la ~ de la nuit** at the close of day, at nightfall.

tomber [tɔ̃be] *vi* to fall; **laisser ~** to drop; **~ sur** *vt* (*rencontrer*) to come across; (*attaquer*) to set about; **~ de**

fatigue/sommeil to drop from exhaustion/be falling asleep on one's feet; **ça tombe bien** that's come at the right time; **il est bien tombé** he's been lucky.

tome [tɔm] *nm* volume.

ton, ta, *pl* **tes** [tɔ̃, ta, te] *dét* your.

ton [tɔ̃] *nm* (*gén*) tone; (*MUS*) key; (*couleur*) shade, tone; **de bon ~** in good taste.

tonalité [tɔnalite] *nf* (*au téléphone*) dialling tone; (*MUS*) key; (*fig*) tone.

tondeuse [tɔ̃døz] *nf* (*à gazon*) (lawn)mower; (*du coiffeur*) clippers *pl*; (*pour la tonte*) shears *pl*.

tondre [tɔ̃dʀ(ə)] *vt* (*pelouse, herbe*) to mow; (*haie*) to cut, clip; (*mouton, toison*) to shear; (*cheveux*) to crop.

tonifier [tɔnifje] *vt* (*peau, organisme*) to tone up.

tonique [tɔnik] *a* fortifying // *nm* tonic.

tonne [tɔn] *nf* metric ton, tonne.

tonneau, x [tɔno] *nm* (*à vin, cidre*) barrel; (*NAVIG*) ton; **faire des ~x** (*voiture, avion*) to roll over.

tonnelle [tɔnɛl] *nf* bower, arbour.

tonner [tɔne] *vi* to thunder; **il tonne** it is thundering, there's some thunder.

tonnerre [tɔnɛʀ] *nm* thunder.

tonus [tɔnys] *nm* dynamism.

top [tɔp] *nm*: **au 3ème ~** at the 3rd stroke.

topinambour [tɔpinɑ̃buʀ] *nm* Jerusalem artichoke.

toque [tɔk] *nf* (*de fourrure*) fur hat; **~ de jockey/juge** jockey's/judge's cap; **~ de cuisinier** chef's hat.

toqué, e [tɔke] *a* (*fam*) cracked.

torche [tɔʀʃ(ə)] *nf* torch.

torchon [tɔʀʃɔ̃] *nm* cloth, duster; (*à vaisselle*) tea towel *ou* cloth.

tordre [tɔʀdʀ(ə)] *vt* (*chiffon*) to wring; (*barre, fig: visage*) to twist; **se ~** *vi* (*barre*) to bend; (*roue*) to twist, buckle; (*ver, serpent*) to writhe; **se ~ le pied/bras** to twist one's foot/arm.

tordu, e [tɔʀdy] *a* (*fig*) warped, twisted.

tornade [tɔʀnad] *nf* tornado.

torpille [tɔʀpij] *nf* torpedo; **torpiller** *vt* to torpedo.

torréfier [tɔʀefje] *vt* to roast.

torrent [tɔʀɑ̃] *nm* torrent.

torse [tɔʀs(ə)] *nm* (*ANAT*) torso; chest.

torsion [tɔʀsjɔ̃] *nf* twisting; torsion.

tort [tɔʀ] *nm* (*défaut*) fault; **~s** *nmpl* (*JUR*) fault *sg*; **avoir ~** to be wrong; **être dans son ~** to be in the wrong; **donner ~ à qn** to lay the blame on sb; (*fig*) to prove sb wrong; **causer du ~ à** to harm; to be harmful *ou* detrimental to; **à ~** wrongly; **à ~ et à travers** wildly.

torticolis [tɔʀtikɔli] *nm* stiff neck.

tortiller [tɔʀtije] *vt* to twist; to twiddle; **se ~** *vi* to wriggle, squirm.

tortionnaire [tɔʀsjɔnɛʀ] *nm* torturer.
tortue [tɔʀty] *nf* tortoise.
tortueux, euse [tɔʀtɥø, -øz] *a (rue)* twisting; *(fig)* tortuous.
torture [tɔʀtyʀ] *nf* torture; **torturer** *vt* to torture; *(fig)* to torment.
tôt [to] *ad* early; ~ **ou tard** sooner or later; **si** ~ so early; *(déjà)* so soon; **au plus** ~ at the earliest; **il eut** ~ **fait de faire** he soon did.
total, e, aux [tɔtal, -o] *a, nm* total; **au** ~ **in total** *ou* all; **faire le** ~ to work out the total, add up; **~ement** *ad* totally, completely; **~iser** *vt* total (up).
totalité [tɔtalite] *nf*: **la** ~ **de** all of, the total amount *(ou number)* of; **the whole** + *sg*; **en** ~ entirely.
toubib [tubib] *nm (fam)* doctor.
touchant, e [tuʃɑ̃, -ɑ̃t] *a* touching.
touche [tuʃ] *nf (de piano, de machine à écrire)* key; *(PEINTURE etc)* stroke, touch; *(fig: de nostalgie)* touch, hint; *(FOOTBALL: aussi:* **remise en ~)** throw-in; *(aussi:* **ligne de ~)** touch-line.
toucher [tuʃe] *nm* touch // *vt* to touch; *(palper)* to feel; *(atteindre: d'un coup de feu etc)* to hit; *(concerner)* to concern, affect; *(contacter)* to reach, contact; *(recevoir: récompense)* to receive, get; *(: salaire)* to draw, get; *(: chèque)* to cash; **au** ~ to the touch; **se** ~ *(être en contact)* to touch; **~ à** to touch; *(concerner)* to have to do with, concern; **je vais lui en** ~ **un mot** I'll have a word with him about it; **~ à sa fin** to be drawing to a close.
touffe [tuf] *nf* tuft.
touffu, e [tufy] *a* thick, dense.
toujours [tuʒuʀ] *ad* always; *(encore)* still; *(constamment)* forever; ~ **plus** more and more; **pour** ~ forever; ~ **est-il que** the fact remains that; **essaie** ~ *(you can)* try anyway.
toupet [tupɛ] *nm (fam)* cheek.
toupie [tupi] *nf* (spinning) top.
tour [tuʀ] *nf* tower; *(immeuble)* high-rise block *(Brit) ou* building *(US)*; *(ÉCHECS)* castle, rook // *nm (excursion)* stroll, walk; run, ride; trip; *(SPORT: aussi:* ~ **de piste)** lap; *(d'être servi ou de jouer etc, tournure, de vis ou clef)* turn; *(de roue etc)* revolution; *(circonférence)*: **de 3 m de** ~ 3 m round, with a circumference *ou* girth of 3 m; *(POL: aussi:* ~ **de scrutin)** ballot; *(ruse, de prestidigitation)* trick; *(de potier)* wheel; *(à bois, métaux)* lathe; **faire le** ~ **de** to go round; *(à pied)* to walk round; **c'est au** ~ **de Renée** it's Renée's turn; **à** ~ **de rôle,** ~ **à** ~ in turn; ~ **de taille/tête** waist/head measurement; ~ **de chant** song recital; ~ **de contrôle** *nf* control tower; ~ **de garde** spell of duty; ~ **d'horizon** *(fig)* general survey.
tourbe [tuʀb(ə)] *nf* peat.

tourbillon [tuʀbijɔ̃] *nm* whirlwind; *(d'eau)* whirlpool; *(fig)* whirl, swirl; **tourbillonner** *vi* to whirl (round).
tourelle [tuʀɛl] *nf* turret.
tourisme [tuʀism(ə)] *nm* tourism; **agence de** ~ tourist agency; **faire du** ~ to go sightseeing; to go touring; **touriste** *nm/f* tourist; **touristique** *a* tourist *cpd*; *(région)* touristic.
tourment [tuʀmɑ̃] *nm* torment.
tourmenter [tuʀmɑ̃te] *vt* to torment; **se** ~ *vi* to fret, worry o.s.
tournant [tuʀnɑ̃] *nm (de route)* bend; *(fig)* turning point.
tournebroche [tuʀnəbʀɔʃ] *nm* roasting spit.
tourne-disque [tuʀnədisk(ə)] *nm* record player.
tournée [tuʀne] *nf (du facteur etc)* round; *(d'artiste, politicien)* tour; *(au café)* round (of drinks).
tourner [tuʀne] *vt* to turn; *(sauce, mélange)* to stir; *(contourner)* to get round; *(CINÉMA)* to shoot; to make // *vi* to turn; *(moteur)* to run; *(compteur)* to tick away; *(lait etc)* to turn (sour); **se** ~ *vi* to turn round; **se** ~ **vers** to turn to; to turn towards; **bien** ~ to turn out well; ~ **autour de** to go round; *(péj)* to hang round; ~ **à/en** to turn into; ~ **le dos à** to turn one's back on; to have one's back to; ~ **de l'œil** to pass out.
tournesol [tuʀnəsɔl] *nm* sunflower.
tournevis [tuʀnəvis] *nm* screwdriver.
tourniquet [tuʀnikɛ] *nm (pour arroser)* sprinkler; *(portillon)* turnstile; *(présentoir)* revolving stand, spinner.
tournoi [tuʀnwa] *nm* tournament.
tournoyer [tuʀnwaje] *vi* to whirl round; to swirl round.
tournure [tuʀnyʀ] *nf (LING)* turn of phrase; form; phrasing; *(évolution)*: **la** ~ **de qch** the way sth is developing; *(aspect)*: **la** ~ **de the look of;** ~ **d'esprit** turn *ou* cast of mind; **la** ~ **des événements** the turn of events.
tourte [tuʀt(ə)] *nf* pie.
tous *dét* [tu] , *pronom* [tus] *voir* **tout**.
Toussaint [tusɛ̃] *nf*: **la** ~ All Saints' Day.
tousser [tuse] *vi* to cough.
tout, e, *pl* **tous, toutes** [tu, tut, tus] ♦ *a* **1** *(avec article sing)* all; ~ **le lait** all the milk; ~**e la nuit** all night, the whole night; ~ **le livre** the whole book; ~ **un pain** a whole loaf; ~ **le temps** all the time; the whole time; **c'est** ~ **le contraire** it's quite the opposite
2 *(avec article pl)* every; all; **tous les livres** all the books; **toutes les nuits** every night; **toutes les fois** every time; **toutes les trois/deux semaines** every third/other *ou* second week, every three/two weeks; **tous les deux** both *ou* each of us *(ou* them *ou* you); **toutes les 3** all 3 of us *(ou*

them *ou* you)

3 (*sans article*): à ~ âge at any age; **pour** ~**e nourriture, il avait ...** his only food was ...

♦ *pronom* everything, all; **il a** ~ **fait** he's done everything; **je les vois tous** I can see them all *ou* all of them; **nous y sommes tous allés** all of us went, we all went; **en** ~ **in** all; ~ **ce qu'il sait** all he knows

♦ *nm* whole; **le** ~ all of it (*ou* them); **le** ~ **est de ...** the main thing is to ...; **pas du** ~ not at all

♦ *ad* **1** (*très, complètement*) very; ~ **près** very near; **le** ~ **premier** the very first; ~ **seul** all alone; **le livre** ~ **entier** the whole book; ~ **en haut** right at the top; ~ **droit** straight ahead **2:** ~ **en** while; ~ **en travaillant** while working, as he *etc* works **3:** ~ **d'abord** first of all; ~ **à coup** suddenly; ~ **à fait** absolutely; ~ **à l'heure** a short while ago; (*futur*) in a short while, shortly; **à** ~ **à l'heure!** see you later!; ~ **de même** all the same; ~ **le monde** *pronom* everybody; ~ **de suite** immediately, straight away; ~ **terrain, tous terrains** *a inv* all-terrain.

toutefois [tutfwa] *ad* however.

toux [tu] *nf* cough.

toxicomane [tɔksikɔman] *nm/f* drug addict.

trac [tʀak] *nm* nerves *pl*.

tracasser [tʀakase] *vt* to worry, bother; to harass.

trace [tʀas] *nf* (*empreintes*) tracks *pl*; (*marques, aussi fig*) mark; (*restes, vestige*) trace; (*indice*) sign; ~**s de pas** footprints.

tracé [tʀase] *nm* line; layout.

tracer [tʀase] *vt* to draw; (*mot*) to trace; (*piste*) to open up.

tract [tʀakt] *nm* tract, pamphlet.

tractations [tʀaktɑsjɔ̃] *nfpl* dealings, bargaining *sg*.

tracteur [tʀaktœʀ] *nm* tractor.

traction [tʀaksjɔ̃] *nf:* ~ **avant/arrière** front-wheel/rear-wheel drive.

tradition [tʀadisjɔ̃] *nf* tradition; **traditionnel, le** *a* traditional.

traducteur, trice [tʀadyktœʀ, -tʀis] *nm/f* translator.

traduction [tʀadyksjɔ̃] *nf* translation.

traduire [tʀadɥiʀ] *vt* to translate; (*exprimer*) to render, convey.

trafic [tʀafik] *nm* traffic; ~ **d'armes** arms dealing; **trafiquant, e** *nm/f* trafficker; dealer; **trafiquer** *vt* (*péj*) to doctor, tamper with.

tragédie [tʀaʒedi] *nf* tragedy.

tragique [tʀaʒik] *a* tragic.

trahir [tʀaiʀ] *vt* to betray; (*fig*) to give away, reveal; **trahison** *nf* betrayal; (*JUR*) treason.

train [tʀɛ̃] *nm* (*RAIL*) train; (*allure*)

pace; (*fig: ensemble*) set; **mettre qch en** ~ to get sth under way; **mettre qn en** ~ to put sb in good spirits; **se mettre en** ~ to get started; to warm up; **se sentir en** ~ to feel in good form; ~ **d'atterrissage** undercarriage; ~**autos-couchettes** car-sleeper train; ~ **électrique** (*jouet*) (electric) train set; ~ **de vie** style of living.

traîne [tʀɛn] *nf* (*de robe*) train; **être à la** ~ to be in tow; to lag behind

traîneau, x [tʀɛno] *nm* sleigh, sledge.

traînée [tʀene] *nf* streak, trail; (*péj*) slut.

traîner [tʀene] *vt* (*remorque*) to pull; (*enfant, chien*) to drag *ou* trail along // *vi* (*être en désordre*) to lie around; (*marcher*) to dawdle (along); (*vagabonder*) to hang about; (*agir lentement*) to idle about; (*durer*) to drag on; **se** ~ *vi* to drag o.s. along; ~ **les pieds** to drag one's feet.

train-train [tʀɛ̃tʀɛ̃] *nm* humdrum routine.

traire [tʀɛʀ] *vt* to milk.

trait [tʀɛ] *nm* (*ligne*) line; (*de dessin*) stroke; (*caractéristique*) feature, trait; ~**s** *nmpl* (*du visage*) features; **d'un** ~ (*boire*) in one gulp; **de** ~ *a* (*animal*) draught; **avoir** ~ **à** to concern; ~ **d'union** hyphen; (*fig*) link.

traitant, e [tʀɛtɑ̃, -ɑ̃t] *a:* **votre médecin** ~ your usual *ou* family doctor; **crème** ~**e** conditioning cream.

traite [tʀɛt] *nf* (*COMM*) draft; (*AGR*) milking; **d'une** ~ without stopping; **la** ~ **des noirs** the slave trade.

traité [tʀɛte] *nm* treaty.

traitement [tʀɛtmɑ̃] *nm* treatment; processing; (*salaire*) salary; ~ **de données/ texte** data/word processing.

traiter [tʀɛte] *vt* (*gén*) to treat; (*TECH, INFORM*) to process; (*affaire*) to deal with, handle; (*qualifier*): ~ **qn d'idiot** to call sb a fool // *vi* to deal; ~ **de** *vt* to deal with.

traiteur [tʀɛtœʀ] *nm* caterer.

traître, esse [tʀɛtʀ(ə), -tʀɛs] *a* (*dangereux*) treacherous // *nm* traitor.

trajectoire [tʀaʒɛktwaʀ] *nf* path.

trajet [tʀaʒɛ] *nm* journey; (*itinéraire*) route; (*fig*) path, course.

trame [tʀam] *nf* (*de tissu*) weft; (*fig*) framework; texture.

tramer [tʀame] *vt* to plot, hatch.

trampolino [tʀɑ̃polino] *nm* trampoline.

tramway [tʀamwɛ] *nm* tram(way); tram(car) (*Brit*), streetcar (*US*).

tranchant, e [tʀɑ̃ʃɑ̃, -ɑ̃t] *a* sharp; (*fig*) peremptory // *nm* (*d'un couteau*) cutting edge; (*de la main*) edge.

tranche [tʀɑ̃ʃ] *nf* (*morceau*) slice; (*arête*) edge; (*partie*) section; (*série*) block; issue; bracket.

tranché, e [tʀɑ̃ʃe] *a* (*couleurs*) distinct, sharply contrasted; (*opinions*) clear-cut, definite // nf trench.

trancher [trɑ̃ʃe] vt to cut, sever; (fig: résoudre) to settle // vi to take a decision; ~ avec to contrast sharply with.

tranquille [trɑ̃kil] a calm, quiet; (enfant, élève) quiet; (rassuré) easy in one's mind, with one's mind at rest; se tenir ~ (enfant) to be quiet; laisse-moi/laisse-ça ~ leave me/it~ alone; **tranquillité** nf quietness; peace (and quiet).

transat [trɑ̃zat] nm deckchair.

transborder [trɑ̃sbɔrde] vt to tran(s)ship.

transférer [trɑ̃sfere] vt to transfer; **transfert** nm transfer.

transfigurer [trɑ̃sfigyre] vt to transform.

transformation [trɑ̃sfɔrmasjɔ̃] nf transformation; (RUGBY) conversion.

transformer [trɑ̃sfɔrme] vt to transform, alter; (matière première, appartement, RUGBY) to convert; ~ en to transform into; to turn into; to convert into.

transfusion [trɑ̃sfyzjɔ̃] nf: ~ sanguine blood transfusion.

transgresser [trɑ̃sgrese] vt to contravene, disobey.

transi, e [trɑ̃zi] a numb (with cold), chilled to the bone.

transiger [trɑ̃ziʒe] vi to compromise.

transistor [trɑ̃zistɔr] nm transistor.

transit [trɑ̃zit] nm transit; ~er vi to pass in transit.

transitif, ive [trɑ̃zitif, -iv] a transitive.

transition [trɑ̃zisjɔ̃] nf transition; **transitoire** a transitional; transient.

translucide [trɑ̃slysid] a translucent.

transmetteur [trɑ̃smetœr] nm transmitter.

transmettre [trɑ̃smetr(ə)] vt (passer): ~ qch à qn to pass sth on to sb; (TECH, TÉL, MÉD) to transmit; (TV, RADIO: retransmettre) to broadcast.

transmission [trɑ̃smisjɔ̃] nf transmission.

transparaître [trɑ̃sparɛtr(ə)] vi to show (through).

transparence [trɑ̃sparɑ̃s] nf transparence; par ~ (regarder) against the light; (voir) showing through.

transparent, e [trɑ̃sparɑ̃, -ɑ̃t] a transparent.

transpercer [trɑ̃spɛrse] vt to go through, pierce.

transpiration [trɑ̃spirasjɔ̃] nf perspiration.

transpirer [trɑ̃spire] vi to perspire.

transplanter [trɑ̃splɑ̃te] vt (MÉD, BOT) to transplant; (personne) to uproot.

transport [trɑ̃spɔr] nm transport; ~s en commun public transport sg.

transporter [trɑ̃spɔrte] vt to carry, move; (COMM) to transport, convey; **transporteur** nm haulage contractor

(Brit), trucker (US).

transversal, e, aux [trɑ̃svɛrsal, -o] a transverse, cross(-); cross-country; running at right angles.

trapèze [trapez] nm (au cirque) trapeze.

trappe [trap] nf trap door.

trapu, e [trapy] a squat, stocky.

traquenard [traknar] nm trap.

traquer [trake] vt to track down; (harceler) to hound.

traumatiser [tromatize] vt to traumatize.

travail, aux [travaj, -o] nm (gén) work; (tâche, métier) work q, job; (ÉCON, MÉD) labour // nmpl (de réparation, agricoles etc) work sg; (sur route) roadworks pl; (de construction) building (work); être sans ~ (employé) to be out of work ou unemployed; ~ (au) noir moonlighting; travaux des champs farmwork sg; travaux dirigés (SCOL) supervised practical work sg; travaux forcés hard labour sg; travaux manuels (SCOL) handicrafts; travaux ménagers housework sg.

travailler [travaje] vi to work; (bois) to warp // vt (bois, métal) to work; (objet d'art, discipline, fig: influencer) to work on; cela le travaille it is on his mind; ~ à to work on; (fig: contribuer à) to work towards; **travailleur, euse** a hardworking // nm/f worker; **travailliste** a ≈ Labour cpd.

travée [trave] nf row; (ARCHIT) bay; span.

travers [travɛr] nm fault, failing; en ~ (de) across; au ~ (de) through; de ~ a askew // ad sideways; (fig) the wrong way; à ~ through; regarder de ~ (fig) to look askance at.

traverse [travɛrs(ə)] nf (de voie ferrée) sleeper; chemin de ~ shortcut.

traversée [travɛrse] nf crossing.

traverser [travɛrse] vt (gén) to cross; (ville, tunnel, aussi: percer, fig) to go through; (suj: ligne, trait) to run across.

traversin [travɛrsɛ̃] nm bolster.

travestir [travɛstir] vt (vérité) to misrepresent; se ~ vi to dress up; to dress as a woman.

trébucher [trebyʃe] vi: ~ (sur) to stumble (over), trip (against).

trèfle [trɛfl(ə)] nm (BOT) clover; (CARTES: couleur) clubs pl; (: carte) club.

treille [trɛj] nf vine arbour; climbing vine.

treillis [trɛji] nm (métallique) wiremesh.

treize [trɛz] num thirteen; **treizième** num thirteenth.

tréma [trema] nm diaeresis.

tremblement [trɑ̃bləmɑ̃] nm: ~ de terre earthquake.

trembler [tʀɑ̃ble] vi to tremble, shake; ~ de (froid, fièvre) to shiver ou tremble with; (peur) to shake ou tremble with; ~ pour qn to fear for sb.

trémousser [tʀemuse]: se ~ vi to jig about, wriggle about.

trempe [tʀɑ̃p] nf (fig): de cette/sa ~ of this/his calibre.

trempé, e [tʀɑ̃pe] a soaking (wet), drenched; (TECH) tempered.

tremper [tʀɑ̃pe] vt to soak, drench; (aussi: faire ~, mettre à ~) to soak; (plonger): ~ qch dans to dip sth in(to) // vi to soak; (fig): ~ dans to be involved ou have a hand in; se ~ vi to have a quick dip; **trempette** nf: faire **trempette** to go paddling.

tremplin [tʀɑ̃plɛ̃] nm springboard; (SKI) ski-jump.

trentaine [tʀɑ̃tɛn] nf: une ~ (de) thirty or so, about thirty; avoir la ~ (âge) to be around thirty.

trente [tʀɑ̃t] num thirty; **trentième** num thirtieth.

trépied [tʀepje] nm tripod.

trépigner [tʀepiɲe] vi to stamp (one's feet).

très [tʀɛ] ad very; much + pp, highly + pp.

trésor [tʀezɔʀ] nm treasure; (ADMIN) finances pl; funds pl; T~ (public) public revenue.

trésorerie [tʀezɔʀʀi] nf (gestion) accounts pl; (bureaux) accounts department; difficultés de ~ cash problems, shortage of cash ou funds.

trésorier, ière [tʀezɔʀje, -jɛʀ] nm/f treasurer.

tressaillir [tʀesajiʀ] vi to shiver, shudder; to quiver.

tressauter [tʀesote] vi to start, jump.

tresse [tʀɛs] nf braid, plait.

tresser [tʀese] vt (cheveux) to braid, plait; (fil, jonc) to plait; (corbeille) to weave; (corde) to twist.

tréteau, x [tʀeto] nm trestle.

treuil [tʀœj] nm winch.

trêve [tʀɛv] nf (MIL, POL) truce; (fig) respite; ~ de ... enough of this ....

tri [tʀi] nm sorting out q; selection; (POSTES) sorting; sorting office.

triangle [tʀijɑ̃gl(ə)] nm triangle.

tribord [tʀibɔʀ] nm: à ~ to starboard, on the starboard side.

tribu [tʀiby] nf tribe.

tribunal, aux [tʀibynal, -o] nm (JUR) court; (MIL) tribunal.

tribune [tʀibyn] nf (estrade) platform, rostrum; (débat) forum; (d'église, de tribunal) gallery; (de stade) stand.

tribut [tʀiby] nm tribute.

tributaire [tʀibytɛʀ] a: être ~ de to be dependent on.

tricher [tʀiʃe] vi to cheat.

tricolore [tʀikɔlɔʀ] a three-coloured; (français) red, white and blue.

tricot [tʀiko] nm (technique, ouvrage) knitting q; (tissu) knitted fabric; (vêtement) jersey, sweater.

tricoter [tʀikɔte] vt to knit.

trictrac [tʀiktʀak] nm backgammon.

tricycle [tʀisikl(ə)] nm tricycle.

triennal, e, aux [tʀiɛnal, -o] a three-yearly; three-year.

trier [tʀije] vt to sort out; (POSTES, fruits) to sort.

trimestre [tʀimɛstʀ(ə)] nm (SCOL) term; (COMM) quarter; **trimestriel, le** a quarterly; (SCOL) end-of-term.

tringle [tʀɛ̃gl(ə)] nf rod.

trinquer [tʀɛ̃ke] vi to clink glasses.

triomphe [tʀijɔ̃f] nm triumph.

triompher [tʀijɔ̃fe] vi to triumph, win; ~ de to triumph over, overcome.

tripes [tʀip] nfpl (CULIN) tripe sg.

triple [tʀipl(ə)] a triple; treble // nm: le ~ (de) (comparaison) three times as much (as); en ~ exemplaire in triplicate; **triplés, ées** nm/fpl triplets; **tripler** vi, vt to triple, treble.

tripoter [tʀipɔte] vt to fiddle with.

trique [tʀik] nf cudgel.

triste [tʀist(ə)] a sad; (péj): personnage/affaire sorry individual/affair; **tristesse** nf sadness.

trivial, e, aux [tʀivjal, -o] a coarse, crude; (commun) mundane.

troc [tʀɔk] nm barter.

trognon [tʀɔɲɔ̃] nm (de fruit) core; (de légume) stalk.

trois [tʀwa] num three; **troisième** num third; ~-quarts nmpl: les ~-quarts de three-quarters of.

trombe [tʀɔ̃b] nf: des ~s d'eau a downpour; en ~ like a whirlwind.

trombone [tʀɔ̃bɔn] nm (MUS) trombone; (de bureau) paper clip.

trompe [tʀɔ̃p] nf (d'éléphant) trunk; (MUS) trumpet, horn.

tromper [tʀɔ̃pe] vt to deceive; (vigilance, poursuivants) to elude; se ~ vi to make a mistake, be mistaken; se ~ de voiture/jour to take the wrong car/get the day wrong; se ~ de 3 cm/20 F to be out by 3 cm/20 F; **tromperie** nf deception, trickery q.

trompette [tʀɔ̃pɛt] nf trumpet; en ~ (nez) turned-up.

tronc [tʀɔ̃] nm (BOT, ANAT) trunk; (d'église) collection box.

tronçon [tʀɔ̃sɔ̃] nm section.

tronçonner [tʀɔ̃sɔne] vt to saw up.

trône [tʀon] nm throne.

trop [tʀo] ad vb +, too much, too + adjectif, adverbe; ~ (nombreux) too many; ~ peu (nombreux) too few; ~ (souvent) too often; ~ (longtemps) (for) too long; ~ de (nombre) too many; (quantité) too much; de ~, en ~: des livres en ~ a few books too many; du lait en ~ too much milk; **3 livres/3 F de** ~ 3 books too many/3 F too much.

tropical, e, aux [tʀɔpikal, -o] *a* tropical.

tropique [tʀɔpik] *nm* tropic.

trop-plein [tʀɔplɛ̃] *nm (tuyau)* overflow *ou* outlet *(pipe)*; *(liquide)* overflow.

troquer [tʀɔke]: ~ **qch contre** to barter *ou* trade sth for; *(fig)* to swap sth for.

trot [tʀo] *nm* trot.

trotter [tʀɔte] *vi* to trot; *(fig)* to scamper along *(ou* about).

trottiner [tʀɔtine] *vi (fig)* to scamper along *(ou* about).

trottinette [tʀɔtinɛt] *nf* (child's) scooter.

trottoir [tʀɔtwaʀ] *nm* pavement; **faire le** ~ *(péj)* to walk the streets; ~ **roulant** moving walkway, travellator.

trou [tʀu] *nm* hole; *(fig)* gap; *(COMM)* deficit; ~ **d'air** air pocket; ~ **de mémoire** blank, lapse of memory; **le** ~ **de la serrure** the keyhole.

trouble [tʀubl(ə)] *a (liquide)* cloudy; *(image, mémoire)* indistinct, hazy; *(affaire)* shady, murky // *nm (désarroi)* agitation; *(embarras)* confusion; *(zizanie)* unrest, discord; ~**s** *nmpl (POL)* disturbances, troubles, unrest *sg*; *(MÉD)* trouble *sg*, disorders.

troubler [tʀuble] *vt (embarrasser)* to confuse, disconcert; *(émouvoir)* to agitate; to disturb; *(perturber: ordre etc)* to disrupt; *(liquide)* to make cloudy; **se** ~ *vi (personne)* to become flustered *ou* confused.

trouée [tʀue] *nf* gap; *(MIL)* breach.

trouer [tʀue] *vt* to make a hole *(ou* holes) in; *(fig)* to pierce.

trouille [tʀuj] *nf (fam)*: **avoir la** ~ to be scared to death.

troupe [tʀup] *nf* troop; ~ **(de théâtre)** (theatrical) company.

troupeau, x [tʀupo] *nm (de moutons)* flock; *(de vaches)* herd.

trousse [tʀus] *nf* case, kit; *(d'écolier)* pencil case; *(de docteur)* instrument case; **aux** ~**s de** *(fig)* on the heels *ou* tail of; ~ **à outils** toolkit; ~ **de toilette** toilet bag.

trousseau, x [tʀuso] *nm (de mariée)* trousseau; ~ **de clefs** bunch of keys.

trouvaille [tʀuvaj] *nf* find.

trouver [tʀuve] *vt* to find; *(rendre visite)*: **aller/venir** ~ **qn** to go/come and see sb; **je trouve que** I find *ou* think that; ~ **à boire/critiquer** to find something to drink/criticize; **se** ~ *vi (être)* to be; *(être soudain)* to find o.s.; **il se trouve que** it happens that, it turns out that; **se** ~ **bien** to feel well; **se** ~ **mal** to pass out.

truand [tʀyɑ̃] *nm* villain, crook.

truander [tʀyɑ̃de] *vt* to cheat.

truc [tʀyk] *nm (astuce)* way, device; *(de*

cinéma, prestidigitateur) trick effect; *(chose)* thing, thingumajig; **avoir le** ~ to have the knack.

truchement [tʀyʃmɑ̃] *nm*: **par le** ~ **de qn** through (the intervention of) sb.

truelle [tʀyɛl] *nf* trowel.

truffe [tʀyf] *nf* truffle; *(nez)* nose.

truffé [tʀyfe] *a*: ~ **de** *(fig)* peppered with; bristling with.

truie [tʀyi] *nf* sow.

truite [tʀyit] *nf* trout *inv*.

truquer [tʀyke] *vt (élections, serrure, dés)* to fix; *(CINÉMA)* to use special effects in.

T.S.V.P. *sigle* (= *tournez s.v.p.*) P.T.O.

T.T.C. *sigle* = *toutes taxes comprises*.

tu [ty] *pronom* you.

tu, e [ty] *pp de* **taire**.

tuba [tyba] *nm (MUS)* tuba; *(SPORT)* snorkel.

tube [tyb] *nm* tube; pipe; *(chanson, disque)* hit song *ou* record.

tuer [tɥe] *vt* to kill; **se** ~ *vi* to be killed; *(suicide)* to kill o.s.; **tuerie** *nf* slaughter *q*.

tue-tête [tytɛt]: **à** ~ *ad* at the top of one's voice.

tueur [tɥœʀ] *nm* killer; ~ **à gages** hired killer.

tuile [tɥil] *nf* tile; *(fam)* spot of bad luck, blow.

tulipe [tylip] *nf* tulip.

tuméfié, e [tymefje] *a* puffy, swollen.

tumeur [tymœʀ] *nf* growth, tumour.

tumulte [tymylt(ə)] *nm* commotion.

tumultueux, euse [tymyltɥø, -øz] *a* stormy, turbulent.

tunique [tynik] *nf* tunic.

Tunisie [tynizi] *nf*: **la** ~ Tunisia; **tunisien, ne** *a, nm/f* Tunisian.

tunnel [tynɛl] *nm* tunnel.

turbulences [tyʀbylɑ̃s] *nfpl (AVIAT)* turbulence *sg*.

turbulent, e [tyʀbylɑ̃, -ɑ̃t] *a* boisterous, unruly.

turc, turque [tyʀk(ə)] *a* Turkish // *nm/f*: **T**~, **Turque** Turk/Turkish woman // *nm (LING)* Turkish.

turf [tyʀf] *nm* racing; ~**iste** *nm/f* racegoer.

Turquie [tyʀki] *nf*: **la** ~ Turkey.

turquoise [tyʀkwaz] *nf, a inv* turquoise.

tus *etc vb voir* **taire**.

tutelle [tytɛl] *nf (JUR)* guardianship; *(POL)* trusteeship; **sous la** ~ **de** *(fig)* under the supervision of.

tuteur [tytœʀ] *nm (JUR)* guardian; *(de plante)* stake, support.

tutoyer [tytwaje] *vt*: ~ **qn** to address sb as 'tu'.

tuyau, x [tɥijo] *nm* pipe; *(flexible)* tube; *(fam)* tip; *gen q*; ~ **d'arrosage** hosepipe; ~ **d'échappement** exhaust pipe; ~**terie** *nf* piping *q*.

T.V.A. *sigle f voir* **taxe**.

tympan [tɛ̃pɑ̃] *nm* (ANAT) eardrum.
type [tip] *nm* type; (*fam*) chap, guy // *a* typical, standard.
typé [tipe] *a* ethnic (*euph*).
typhoïde [tifɔid] *nf* typhoid.
typique [tipik] *a* typical.
tyran [tiʀɑ̃] *nm* tyrant.
tzigane [dzigan] *a* gipsy, tzigane.

U

ulcère [ylsɛʀ] *nm* ulcer.
ulcérer [ylseʀe] *vt* (*fig*) to sicken, appal.
ultérieur, e [ylteʀjœʀ] *a* later, subsequent; **remis à une date ~e** postponed to a later date.
ultime [yltim] *a* final.
ultra... [yltʀa] *préfixe*: **~moderne/ -rapide** ultra-modern/-fast.
un, une [œ̃, yn] ♦ *article indéfini* a; (*devant voyelle*) an; **~ garçon/vieillard** a boy/an old man; **une fille** a girl
♦ *pronom* one; **l'~ des meilleurs** one of the best; **l'~ ...**, **l'autre** (the) one ..., the other; **les ~s ...**, **les autres** some ..., others; **l'~ et l'autre** both (of them); **l'~ ou l'autre** either (of them); **l'~ l'autre, les ~s les autres** each other, one another; **pas ~ seul** not a single one; **~ par ~** one by one
♦ *num* one; **une pomme seulement** one apple only.
unanime [ynanim] *a* unanimous; **unanimité** *nf*: **à l'unanimité** unanimously.
uni, e [yni] *a* (*ton, tissu*) plain; (*surface*) smooth, even; (*famille*) close(-knit); (*pays*) united.
unifier [ynifje] *vt* to unite, unify.
uniforme [ynifɔʀm(ə)] *a* (*mouvement*) regular, uniform; (*surface, ton*) even; (*objets, maisons*) uniform // *nm* uniform; **uniformiser** *vt* to make uniform; (*systèmes*) to standardize.
union [ynjɔ̃] *nf* union; **~ de consommateurs** consumers' association; **l'U~ soviétique** the Soviet Union.
unique [ynik] *a* (*seul*) only; (*le même*): **un prix/système ~** a single price/system; (*exceptionnel*) unique; **fils/fille ~** only son/daughter, only child; **~ment** *ad* only, solely; (*juste*) only, merely.
unir [yniʀ] *vt* (*nations*) to unite; (*éléments, couleurs*) to combine; (*en mariage*) to unite, join together; **~ qch à** to unite sth with; to combine sth with; **s'~** to unite; (*en mariage*) to be joined together.
unité [ynite] *nf* (*harmonie, cohésion*) unity; (*COMM, MIL, de mesure, MATH*) unit.
univers [ynivɛʀ] *nm* universe.
universel, le [ynivɛʀsɛl] *a* universal; (*esprit*) all-embracing.

universitaire [ynivɛʀsitɛʀ] *a* university *cpd*; (*diplôme, études*) academic, university *cpd* // *nm/f* academic.
université [ynivɛʀsite] *nf* university.
urbain, e [yʀbɛ̃, -ɛn] *a* urban, city *cpd*, town *cpd*; (*poli*) urbane; **urbanisme** *nm* town planning.
urgence [yʀʒɑ̃s] *nf* urgency; (MÉD *etc*) emergency; **d'~** *a* emergency *cpd* // *ad* as a matter of urgency.
urgent, e [yʀʒɑ̃, -ɑ̃t] *a* urgent.
urine [yʀin] *nf* urine; **urinoir** *nm* (public) urinal.
urne [yʀn(ə)] *nf* (*électorale*) ballot box; (*vase*) urn.
URSS [*fareois:* yʀs] *sigle f*: **l'~** the USSR.
urticaire [yʀtikɛʀ] *nf* nettle rash.
us [ys] *nmpl*: **~ et coutumes** (habits and) customs.
USA *sigle mpl*: **les ~** the USA.
usage [yzaʒ] *nm* (*emploi, utilisation*) use; (*coutume*) custom; (LING): **l'~** usage; **à l'~ de** (*pour*) for (use of); **en ~** in use; **hors d'~** out of service; wrecked; **à ~ interne** to be taken; **à ~ externe** for external use only.
usagé, e [yzaʒe] *a* (*usé*) worn; (*d'occasion*) used.
usager, ère [yzaʒe, -ɛʀ] *nm/f* user.
usé, e [yze] *a* worn; (*banal*) hackneyed.
user [yze] *vt* (*outil*) to wear down; (*vêtement*) to wear out; (*matière*) to wear away; (*consommer: charbon etc*) to use; **s'~** *vi* to wear; to wear out; (*fig*) to decline; **~ de** *vt* (*moyen, procédé*) to use, employ; (*droit*) to exercise.
usine [yzin] *nf* factory; **~ marémotrice** tidal power station.
usiner [yzine] *vt* (TECH) to machine.
usité, e [yzite] *a* common.
ustensile [ystɑ̃sil] *nm* implement; **~ de cuisine** kitchen utensil.
usuel, le [yzɥɛl] *a* everyday, common.
usure [yzyʀ] *nf* wear; worn state.
ut [yt] *nm* (MUS) C.
utérus [yteʀys] *nm* uterus, womb.
utile [ytil] *a* useful.
utilisation [ytilizasjɔ̃] *nf* use.
utiliser [ytilize] *vt* to use.
utilitaire [ytilitɛʀ] *a* utilitarian; (*objets*) practical.
utilité [ytilite] *nf* usefulness *q*; use; **reconnu d'~ publique** state-approved.

V

va *vb voir* **aller**.
vacance [vakɑ̃s] *nf* (ADMIN) vacancy; **~s** *nfpl* holiday(s *pl*), vacation *sg*; **prendre des/ses ~s** to take a holiday/one's holiday(s); **aller en ~s** to go on holiday; **vacancier, ière** *nm/f* holiday-maker.
vacant, e [vakɑ̃, -ɑ̃t] *a* vacant.

vacarme [vakaʀm(ə)] *nm* row, din.

vaccin [vaksɛ̃] *nm* vaccine; *(opération)* vaccination; **vaccination** *nf* vaccination; **vacciner** *vt* to vaccinate; *(fig)* to make immune.

vache [vaʃ] *nf* (ZOOL) cow; *(cuir)* cowhide // *a* *(fam)* rotten, mean; **vachement** *ad* *(fam)* damned, hellish.

vaciller [vasije] *vi* to sway, wobble; *(bougie, lumière)* to flicker; *(fig)* to be failing, falter.

va-et-vient [vaevjɛ̃] *nm* *inv* *(de personnes, véhicules)* comings and goings *pl*, to-ings and fro-ings *pl*.

vagabond [vagabɔ̃] *nm* *(rôdeur)* tramp, vagrant; *(voyageur)* wanderer.

vagabonder [vagabɔ̃de] *vi* to roam, wander.

vagin [vaʒɛ̃] *nm* vagina.

vague [vag] *nf* wave // *a* vague; *(regard)* faraway; *(manteau, robe)* loose(-fitting); *(quelconque)*: **un ~ bureau/cousin** some office/cousin or other; **~ de fond** *nf* ground swell.

vaillant, e [vajɑ̃, -ɑ̃t] *a* *(courageux)* gallant; *(robuste)* hale and hearty.

vaille *vb voir* **valoir**.

vain, e [vɛ̃, vɛn] *a* vain; **en ~** *ad* in vain.

vaincre [vɛ̃kʀ(ə)] *vt* to defeat; *(fig)* to conquer, overcome; **vaincu, e** *nm/f* defeated party; **vainqueur** *nm* victor; *(SPORT)* winner.

vais *vb voir* **aller**.

vaisseau, x [vɛso] *nm* (ANAT) vessel; *(NAVIG)* ship, vessel; **~ spatial** spaceship.

vaisselier [vɛsəlje] *nm* dresser.

vaisselle [vɛsɛl] *nf* *(service)* crockery; *(plats etc à laver)* (dirty) dishes *pl*; *(lavage)* washing-up *(Brit)*, dishes *pl*.

val, vaux *ou* **vals** [val, vo] *nm* valley.

valable [valabl(ə)] *a* valid; *(acceptable)* decent, worthwhile.

valent *etc vb voir* **valoir**.

valet [valɛ] *nm* valet; *(CARTES)* jack.

valeur [valœʀ] *nf* *(gén)* value; *(mérite)* worth, merit; *(COMM: titre)* security; **mettre en ~** *(terrain, région)* to develop; *(fig)* to highlight; to show off to advantage; **avoir de la ~** to be valuable; **sans ~** worthless; **prendre de la ~** to go up *ou* gain in value.

valide [valid] *a* *(en bonne santé)* fit; *(valable)* valid; **valider** *vt* to validate.

valions *vb voir* **valoir**.

valise [valiz] *nf* (suit)case.

vallée [vale] *nf* valley.

vallon [valɔ̃] *nm* small valley.

valoir [valwaʀ] *vi* *(être valable)* to hold, apply // *vt* *(prix, valeur, effort)* to be worth; *(causer)*: **~ qch à qn** to earn sb sth; **se ~** *vi* to be of equal merit; *(péj)* to be two of a kind; **faire ~** *(droits, prérogatives)* to assert; **faire ~ que** to point

out that; **à ~ sur** to be deducted from; **vaille que vaille** somehow or other; **cela ne me dit rien qui vaille** I don't like the look of it at all; **ce climat ne me vaut rien** this climate doesn't suit me; **~ la peine** to be worth the trouble *ou* worth it; **~ mieux: il vaut mieux se taire** it's better to say nothing; **ça ne vaut rien** it's worthless; **que vaut ce candidat?** how good is this applicant?

valoriser [valɔʀize] *vt* (ÉCON) to develop (the economy of); (PSYCH) to increase the standing of.

valse [vals(ə)] *nf* waltz.

valu, e [valy] *pp de* **valoir**.

vandale [vɑ̃dal] *nm/f* vandal; **vandalisme** *nm* vandalism.

vanille [vanij] *nf* vanilla.

vanité [vanite] *nf* vanity; **vaniteux, euse** *a* vain, conceited.

vanne [van] *nf* gate; *(fig)* joke.

vannerie [vanʀi] *nf* basketwork.

vantail, aux [vɑ̃taj, -o] *nm* door, leaf *(pl* leaves).

vantard, e [vɑ̃taʀ, -aʀd(ə)] *a* boastful.

vanter [vɑ̃te] *vt* to speak highly of, vaunt; **se ~** *vi* to boast, brag; **se ~ de** to pride o.s. on; *(péj)* to boast of.

vapeur [vapœʀ] *nf* steam; *(émanation)* vapour, fumes *pl*; **~s** *nfpl* *(bouffées)* vapours; **à ~** steam-powered, steam *cpd*; **cuit à la ~** steamed.

vapocuiseur [vapɔkɥizœʀ] *nm* pressure cooker.

vaporeux, euse [vapɔʀø, -øz] *a* *(flou)* hazy, misty; *(léger)* filmy.

vaporisateur [vapɔʀizatœʀ] *nm* spray.

vaporiser [vapɔʀize] *vt* *(parfum etc)* to spray.

varappe [vaʀap] *nf* rock climbing.

vareuse [vaʀøz] *nf* *(blouson)* pea jacket; *(d'uniforme)* tunic.

variable [vaʀjabl(ə)] *a* variable; *(temps, humeur)* changeable; *(divers: résultats)* varied, various.

varice [vaʀis] *nf* varicose vein.

varicelle [vaʀisɛl] *nf* chickenpox.

varié, e [vaʀje] *a* varied; *(divers)* various.

varier [vaʀje] *vi* to vary; *(temps, humeur)* to change // *vt* to vary.

variété [vaʀjete] *nf* variety.

variole [vaʀjɔl] *nf* smallpox.

vas *vb voir* **aller**.

vase [vaz] *nm* vase // *nf* silt, mud.

vaseux, euse [vazø, -øz] *a* silty, muddy; *(fig: confus)* woolly, hazy; *(: fatigué)* peaky; woozy.

vasistas [vazistas] *nm* fanlight.

vaste [vast(ə)] *a* vast, immense.

vaudrai *etc vb voir* **valoir**.

vaurien, ne [voʀjɛ̃, -ɛn] *nm/f* good-for-nothing, guttersnipe.

vaut *vb voir* **valoir**.

vautour [votuʀ] *nm* vulture.

vautrer [votʀe]: se ~ *vi*: se ~ dans/sur to wallow in/sprawl on.

vaux [vo] *pl de* **val** // *vb voir* **valoir**.

veau, x [vo] *nm* (*ZOOL*) calf (*pl* calves); (*CULIN*) veal; (*peau*) calfskin.

vécu, e [veky] *pp de* **vivre**.

vedette [vədɛt] *nf* (*artiste etc*) star; (*canot*) patrol boat; launch.

végétal, e, aux [veʒetal, -o] *a* vegetable // *nm* vegetable, plant.

végétarien, ne [veʒetaʀjɛ̃, -ɛn] *a, nm/f* vegetarian.

végétation [veʒetasjɔ̃] *nf* vegetation; ~s *nfpl* (*MÉD*) adenoids.

véhicule [veikyl] *nm* vehicle; ~ utilitaire commercial vehicle.

veille [vɛj] *nf* (*garde*) watch; (*PSYCH*) wakefulness; (*jour*): **la ~ (de)** the day before; **la ~ au soir** the previous evening; **à la ~ de** on the eve of.

veillée [veje] *nf* (*soirée*) evening; (*réunion*) evening gathering; ~ (**mortuaire**) watch.

veiller [veje] *vi* to stay up; to be awake; to be on watch // *vt* (*malade, mort*) to watch over, sit up with; ~ **à** *vt* to attend to, see to; ~ **à ce que** to make sure that; ~ **sur** *vt* to keep a watch on; **veilleur de nuit** *nm* night watchman.

veilleuse [vɛjøz] *nf* (*lampe*) night light; (*AUTO*) sidelight; (*flamme*) pilot light; **en ~** *a, ad* (*lampe*) dimmed.

veine [vɛn] *nf* (*ANAT, du bois etc*) vein; (*filon*) vein, seam; (*fam: chance*): **avoir de la ~** to be lucky.

velléités [veleite] *nfpl* vague impulses.

vélo [velo] *nm* bike, cycle; **faire du ~** to go cycling.

vélomoteur [velomɔtœʀ] *nm* moped.

velours [vəluʀ] *nm* velvet; ~ **côtelé** corduroy.

velouté, e [vəlute] *a* (*au toucher*) velvety; (*à la vue*) soft, mellow; (*au goût*) smooth, mellow.

velu, e [vəly] *a* hairy.

venais *etc vb voir* **venir**.

venaison [vənɛzɔ̃] *nf* venison.

vendange [vɑ̃dɑ̃ʒ] *nf* (*opération, période: aussi:* ~s) grape harvest; (*raisins*) grape crop, grapes *pl*.

vendanger [vɑ̃dɑ̃ʒe] *vi* to harvest the grapes.

vendeur, euse [vɑ̃dœʀ, -øz] *nm/f* (*de magasin*) shop assistant; (*COMM*) salesman/woman // *nm* (*JUR*) vendor, seller; ~ **de journaux** newspaper seller.

vendre [vɑ̃dʀ(ə)] *vt* to sell; ~ **qch à qn** to sell sb sth; **'à ~'** 'for sale'.

vendredi [vɑ̃dʀədi] *nm* Friday; **V~ saint** Good Friday.

vénéneux, euse [venenø, -øz] *a* poisonous.

vénérien, ne [veneʀjɛ̃, -ɛn] *a* venereal.

vengeance [vɑ̃ʒɑ̃s] *nf* vengeance *q*, revenge *q*.

venger [vɑ̃ʒe] *vt* to avenge; **se ~** *vi* to avenge o.s.; **se ~ de qch** to avenge o.s. for sth; to take one's revenge for sth; **se ~ de qn** to take revenge on sb; **se ~ sur** to take revenge on; to have it out on.

venimeux, euse [vənimø, -øz] *a* poisonous, venomous; (*fig: haineux*) venomous, vicious.

venin [vənɛ̃] *nm* venom, poison.

venir [vəniʀ] *vi* to come; ~ **de** to come from; ~ **de faire**: **je viens d'y aller/de le voir** I've just been there/seen him; **s'il vient à pleuvoir** if it should rain; **j'en viens à croire que** I have come to believe that; **faire ~** (*docteur, plombier*) to call (out).

vent [vɑ̃] *nm* wind; **il y a du ~** it's windy; **c'est du ~** it's all hot air; **au ~** to windward; **sous le ~** to leeward; **avoir le ~ debout/arrière** to head into the wind/ have the wind astern; **dans le ~** (*fam*) trendy.

vente [vɑ̃t] *nf* sale; **la ~** (*activité*) selling; (*secteur*) sales *pl*; **mettre en ~** to put on sale; (*objets personnels*) to put up for sale; ~ **de charité** jumble sale; ~ **aux enchères** auction sale.

venteux, euse [vɑ̃tø, -øz] *a* windy.

ventilateur [vɑ̃tilatœʀ] *nm* fan.

ventiler [vɑ̃tile] *vt* to ventilate; (*total, statistiques*) to break down.

ventouse [vɑ̃tuz] *nf* (*de caoutchouc*) suction pad; (*ZOOL*) sucker.

ventre [vɑ̃tʀ(ə)] *nm* (*ANAT*) stomach; (*fig*) belly; **avoir mal au ~** to have stomach ache (*Brit*) *ou* a stomach ache (*US*).

ventriloque [vɑ̃tʀilɔk] *nm/f* ventriloquist.

venu, e [vəny] *pp de* **venir** // *a*: **être mal ~ à** *ou* **de faire** to have no grounds for doing, be in no position to do // *nf* coming.

ver [vɛʀ] *nm voir aussi* **vers**; worm; (*des fruits etc*) maggot; (*du bois*) woodworm *q*; ~ **luisant** glow-worm; ~ **à soie** silkworm; ~ **solitaire** tapeworm; ~ **de terre** earthworm.

verbaliser [vɛʀbalize] *vi* (*POLICE*) to book *ou* report an offender.

verbe [vɛʀb(ə)] *nm* verb.

verdeur [vɛʀdœʀ] *nf* (*vigueur*) vigour, vitality; (*crudité*) forthrightness.

verdict [vɛʀdik(t)] *nm* verdict.

verdir [vɛʀdiʀ] *vi, vt* to turn green.

verdure [vɛʀdyʀ] *nf* greenery.

véreux, euse [veʀø, -øz] *a* worm-eaten; (*malhonnête*) shady, corrupt.

verge [vɛʀʒ(ə)] *nf* (*ANAT*) penis; (*baguette*) stick, cane.

verger [vɛʀʒe] *nm* orchard.

verglacé, e [vɛʀglase] *a* icy, iced-over.

verglas [vɛʀgla] *nm* (black) ice.

vergogne [vɛʀgɔɲ]: **sans ~** *ad* shamelessly.

véridique [veʀidik] *a* truthful.

vérification [veʀifikɑsjɔ̃] *nf* checking *q,* check.

vérifier [veʀifje] *vt* to check; *(corroborer)* to confirm, bear out.

véritable [veʀitabl(ə)] *a* real; *(ami, amour)* true.

vérité [veʀite] *nf* truth; *(d'un portrait romanesque)* lifelikeness; *(sincérité)* truthfulness, sincerity.

vermeil, le [veʀmɛj] *a* ruby red.

vermine [veʀmin] *nf* vermin *pl.*

vermoulu, e [veʀmuly] *a* worm-eaten, with woodworm.

verni, e [veʀni] *a (fam)* lucky; **cuir ~** patent leather.

vernir [veʀniʀ] *vt (bois, tableau, ongles)* to varnish; *(poterie)* to glaze.

vernis [veʀni] *nm (enduit)* varnish; glaze; *(fig)* veneer; **~ à ongles** nail polish *ou* varnish.

vernissage [veʀnisaʒ] *nm* varnishing; glazing; *(d'une exposition)* preview.

vérole [veʀɔl] *nf (variole)* smallpox.

verrai *etc vb voir* **voir.**

verre [veʀ] *nm* glass; *(de lunettes)* lens *sg;* **boire** *ou* **prendre un ~** to have a drink; **~s de contact** contact lenses.

verrerie [veʀʀi] *nf (fabrique)* glassworks *sg;* *(activité)* glass-making; *(objets)* glassware.

verrière [veʀjɛʀ] *nf (grand vitrage)* window; *(toit vitré)* glass roof.

verrons *etc vb voir* **voir.**

verrou [veʀu] *nm (targette)* bolt; *(fig)* constriction; **mettre qn sous les ~s** to put sb behind bars; **verrouillage** *nm* locking; **verrouiller** *vt* to bolt; to lock.

verrue [veʀy] *nf* wart.

vers [veʀ] *nm* line // *nmpl (poésie)* verse *sg* // *prép (en direction de)* toward(s); *(près de)* around (about); *(temporel)* about, around.

versant [veʀsɑ̃] *nm* slopes *pl,* side.

versatile [veʀsatil] *a* fickle, changeable.

verse [veʀs(ə)]: **à ~** *ad:* **Il pleut à ~** it's pouring (with rain).

Verseau [veʀso] *nm:* **le ~** Aquarius.

versement [veʀsəmɑ̃] *nm* payment; **en 3 ~s** in 3 instalments.

verser [veʀse] *vt (liquide, grains)* to pour; *(larmes, sang)* to shed; *(argent)* to pay // *vi (véhicule)* to overturn; *(fig):* **~ dans** to lapse into.

verset [veʀse] *nm* verse.

version [veʀsjɔ̃] *nf* version; *(SCOL)* translation *(into the mother tongue).*

verso [veʀso] *nm* back; **voir au ~** see over(leaf).

vert, e [veʀ, veʀt(ə)] *a* green; *(vin)* young; *(vigoureux)* sprightly; *(cru)* forthright // *nm* green.

vertèbre [veʀtɛbʀ(ə)] *nf* vertebra *(pl* ae).

vertement [veʀtəmɑ̃] *ad (réprimander)* sharply.

vertical, e, aux [veʀtikal, -o] *a, nf* vertical; **à la ~e** *ad* vertically; **~ement** *ad* vertically.

vertige [veʀtiʒ] *nm (peur du vide)* vertigo; *(étourdissement)* dizzy spell; *(fig)* fever; **vertigineux, euse** *a* breathtaking.

vertu [veʀty] *nf* virtue; **en ~ de** *prép* in accordance with; **~eux, euse** *a* virtuous.

verve [veʀv(ə)] *nf* witty eloquence; **être en ~** to be in brilliant form.

verveine [veʀvɛn] *nf (BOT)* verbena, vervain; *(infusion)* verbena tea.

vésicule [vezikyl] *nf* vesicle; **~ biliaire** gall-bladder.

vessie [vesi] *nf* bladder.

veste [vɛst(ə)] *nf* jacket; **~ droite/ croisée** single-/double-breasted jacket.

vestiaire [vɛstjɛʀ] *nm (au théâtre etc)* cloakroom; *(de stade etc)* changing-room *(Brit),* locker-room *(US).*

vestibule [vɛstibyl] *nm* hall.

vestige [vɛstiʒ] *nm* relic; *(fig)* vestige; **~s** *nmpl* remains.

veston [vɛstɔ̃] *nm* jacket.

vêtement [vɛtmɑ̃] *nm* garment, item of clothing; **~s** *nmpl* clothes.

vétérinaire [veteʀinɛʀ] *nm/f* vet, veterinary surgeon.

vêtir [vetiʀ] *vt* to clothe, dress.

veto [veto] *nm* veto; **opposer un ~ à** to veto.

vêtu, e [vɛty] *pp de* **vêtir.**

vétuste [vetyst(ə)] *a* ancient, timeworn.

veuf, veuve [vœf, vœv] *a* widowed // *nm* widower // *nf* widow.

veuille, veuillez *etc vb voir* **vouloir.**

veule [vøl] *a* spineless.

veux *vb voir* **vouloir.**

vexations [vɛksasjɔ̃] *nfpl* humiliations.

vexer [vɛkse] *vt* to hurt, upset; **se ~** *vi* to be hurt, get upset.

viabiliser [vjabilize] *vt* to provide with services *(water etc).*

viable [vjabl(ə)] *a* viable.

viager, ère [vjaʒe, -ɛʀ] *a:* **rente viagère** life annuity.

viande [vjɑ̃d] *nf* meat.

vibrer [vibʀe] *vi* to vibrate; *(son, voix)* to be vibrant; *(fig)* to be stirred; **faire ~** to (cause to) vibrate; to stir, thrill.

vice [vis] *nm* vice; *(défaut)* fault; **~ de forme** legal flaw *ou* irregularity.

vice... [vis] *préfixe* vice-.

vichy [viʃi] *nm (toile)* gingham.

vicié, e [visje] *a (air)* polluted, tainted; *(JUR)* invalidated.

vicieux, euse [visjø, -øz] *a (pervers)* dirty(-minded); nasty; *(fautif)* incorrect, wrong.

vicinal, e, aux [visinal, -o] *a:* **chemin ~** by-road, byway.

victime [viktim] *nf* victim; *(d'accident)*

casualty.

victoire [viktwar] *nf* victory.

vidange [vidɑ̃ʒ] *nf* (*d'un fossé, réservoir*) emptying; (*AUTO*) oil change; (*de lavabo: bonde*) waste outlet; ~s *nfpl* (*matières*) sewage *sg*; **vidanger** *vt* to empty.

vide [vid] *a* empty // *nm* (*PHYSIQUE*) vacuum; (*espace*) (empty) space, gap; (*futilité, néant*) void; **avoir peur du** ~ to be afraid of heights; **emballé sous** ~ vacuum packed; **à** ~ *ad* (*sans occupants*) empty; (*sans charge*) unladen.

vidéo [video] *nf* video // *a*: **cassette** ~ video cassette.

vide-ordures [vidɔrdyr] *nm inv* (rubbish) chute.

vide-poches [vidpɔʃ] *nm inv* tidy; (*AUTO*) glove compartment.

vider [vide] *vt* to empty; (*CULIN: volaille, poisson*) to gut, clean out; **se** ~ *vi* to empty; ~ **les lieux** to quit *ou* vacate the premises; **videur** *nm* (*de boîte de nuit*) bouncer.

vie [vi] *nf* life (*pl* lives); **être en** ~ to be alive; **sans** ~ lifeless; **à** ~ for life.

vieil [vjɛj] *am voir* **vieux.**

vieillard [vjɛjar] *nm* old man; **les** ~s old people, the elderly.

vieille [vjɛj] *a, nf voir* **vieux.**

vieilleries [vjɛjri] *nfpl* old things.

vieillesse [vjɛjɛs] *nf* old age.

vieillir [vjɛjir] *vi* (*prendre de l'âge*) to grow old; (*population, vin*) to age; (*doctrine, auteur*) to become dated // *vt* to age; **vieillissement** *nm* growing old; ageing.

Vienne [vjɛn] *nf* Vienna.

vienne, viens *etc vb voir* **venir.**

vierge [vjɛrʒ(ə)] *a* virgin; (*page*) clean, blank // *nf* virgin; (*signe*): **la V**~ Virgo; ~ **de** (*sans*) free from, unsullied by.

Viet-Nam, Vietnam [vjɛtnam] *nm* Vietnam.

vietnamien, ne [vjɛtnamjɛ̃, -jɛn] *a, nm/f* Vietnamese.

vieux(vieil), vieille [vjø, vjɛj] *a* old // *nm/f* old man/woman // *nmpl* old people; **mon** ~/**ma vieille** (*fam*) old man/girl; **prendre un coup de** ~ to put years on; ~ **garçon** *nm* bachelor; ~ **jeu** *a inv* old-fashioned.

vif, vive [vif, viv] *a* (*animé*) lively; (*alerte, brusque, aigu*) sharp; (*lumière, couleur*) brilliant; (*air*) crisp; (*vent, émotion*) keen; (*fort: regret, déception*) great, deep; (*vivant*): **brûlé** ~ burnt alive; **de vive voix** personally; **piquer qn au** ~ to cut sb to the quick; **à** ~ (*plaie*) open; **avoir les nerfs à** ~ to be on edge.

vigie [viʒi] *nf* look-out; look-out post.

vigne [viɲ] *nf* (*plante*) vine; (*plantation*) vineyard.

vigneron [viɲrɔ̃] *nm* wine grower.

vignette [viɲɛt] *nf* (*motif*) vignette; (*de marque*) manufacturer's label *ou* seal; (*ADMIN*) ≈ (road) tax disc (*Brit*), ≈ license plate sticker (*US*); price label (*on medicines for reimbursement by Social Security*).

vignoble [viɲɔbl(ə)] *nm* (*plantation*) vineyard; (*vignes d'une région*) vineyards *pl.*

vigoureux, euse [vigurø, -øz] *a* vigorous, robust.

vigueur [vigœr] *nf* vigour; **entrer en** ~ to come into force; **en** ~ current.

vil, e [vil] *a* vile, base; **à** ~ **prix** at a very low price.

vilain, e [vilɛ̃, -ɛn] *a* (*laid*) ugly; (*affaire, blessure*) nasty; (*pas sage: enfant*) naughty.

vilebrequin [vilbrəkɛ̃] *nm* (*outil*) (bit-)brace.

villa [vila] *nf* (detached) house.

village [vilaʒ] *nm* village; **villageois, e** *a* village *cpd* // *nm/f* villager.

ville [vil] *nf* town; (*importante*) city; (*administration*): **la** ~ ≈ the Corporation; ≈ the (town) council.

villégiature [vileʒjatyr] *nf* holiday; (holiday) resort.

vin [vɛ̃] *nm* wine; **avoir le** ~ **gai** to get happy after a few drinks; ~ **d'honneur** reception (*with wine and snacks*); ~ **ordinaire** table wine; ~ **de pays** local wine.

vinaigre [vinɛgr(ə)] *nm* vinegar; **vinaigrette** *nf* vinaigrette, French dressing.

vindicatif, ive [vɛ̃dikatif, -iv] *a* vindictive.

vineux, euse [vinø, -øz] *a* win(e)y.

vingt [vɛ̃] *num* twenty; **vingtaine** *nf*: **une vingtaine (de)** about twenty, twenty or so; **vingtième** *num* twentieth.

vinicole [vinikɔl] *a* wine *cpd*, wine-growing.

vins *etc vb voir* **venir.**

vinyle [vinil] *nm* vinyl.

viol [vjɔl] *nm* (*d'une femme*) rape; (*d'un lieu sacré*) violation.

violacé, e [vjɔlase] *a* purplish, mauvish.

violemment [vjɔlamɑ̃] *ad* violently.

violence [vjɔlɑ̃s] *nf* violence.

violent, e [vjɔlɑ̃, -ɑ̃t] *a* violent; (*remède*) drastic.

violer [vjɔle] *vt* (*femme*) to rape; (*sépulture, loi, traité*) to violate.

violet, te [vjɔlɛ, -ɛt] *a, nm* purple, mauve // *nf* (*fleur*) violet.

violon [vjɔlɔ̃] *nm* violin; (*fam: prison*) lock-up.

violoncelle [vjɔlɔ̃sɛl] *nm* cello.

violoniste [vjɔlɔnist(ə)] *nm/f* violinist.

vipère [viper] *nf* viper, adder.

virage [viraʒ] *nm* (*d'un véhicule*) turn; (*d'une route, piste*) bend; (*fig: POL*) about-turn.

virée [vire] *nf* (*courte*) run; (: *à pied*) walk; (*longue*) trip; hike, walking tour.

virement [viʀmɑ̃] *nm* (*COMM*) transfer.

virent *vb voir aussi* **voir**.

virer [viʀe] *vt* (*COMM*): ~ **qch (sur)** to transfer sth (into) // *vi* to turn; (*CHIMIE*) to change colour; ~ **de bord** to tack.

virevolter [viʀvɔlte] *vi* to twirl around.

virgule [viʀgyl] *nf* comma; (*MATH*) point.

viril, e [viʀil] *a* (*propre à l'homme*) masculine; (*énergique, courageux*) manly, virile.

virtuel, le [viʀtɥɛl] *a* potential; (*théorique*) virtual.

virtuose [viʀtɥoz] *nm/f* (*MUS*) virtuoso; (*gén*) master.

virus [viʀys] *nm* virus.

vis *vb* [vi] *voir* **voir**, **vivre** // *nf* [vis] screw.

visa [viza] *nm* (*sceau*) stamp; (*validation de passeport*) visa.

visage [vizaʒ] *nm* face.

vis-à-vis [vizavi] *ad* face to face // *nm* person opposite; house *etc* opposite; ~ **de** *prép* opposite; (*fig*) vis-à-vis; **en** ~ facing each other.

viscéral, e, aux [viseʀal, -o] *a* (*fig*) deep-seated, deep-rooted.

visée [vize]: ~**s** *nfpl* (*intentions*) designs.

viser [vize] *vi* to aim // *vt* to aim at; (*concerner*) to be aimed *ou* directed at; (*apposer un visa sur*) to stamp, visa; ~ **à qch/faire** to aim at sth/at doing *ou* to do.

viseur [vizœʀ] *nm* (*d'arme*) sights *pl*; (*PHOTO*) viewfinder.

visibilité [vizibilite] *nf* visibility.

visible [vizibl(ə)] *a* visible; (*disponible*): **est-il** ~? can he see me?, will he see visitors?

visière [vizjɛʀ] *nf* (*de casquette*) peak; (*qui s'attache*) eyeshade.

vision [vizjɔ̃] *nf* vision; (*sens*) (eye)sight, vision; (*fait de voir*): **la** ~ **de** the sight of.

visite [vizit] *nf* visit; (*visiteur*) visitor; (*médicale, à domicile*) visit, call; **la** ~ (*MÉD*) medical examination; **faire une** ~ **à qn** to call on sb, pay sb a visit; **rendre** ~ **à qn** to visit sb, pay sb a visit; **être en** ~ (*chez qn*) to be visiting (sb); **heures de** ~ (*hôpital, prison*) visiting hours.

visiter [vizite] *vt* to visit; (*musée, ville*) to visit, go round; **visiteur, euse** *nm/f* visitor.

vison [vizɔ̃] *nm* mink.

visser [vise] *vt*: ~ **qch** (*fixer, serrer*) to screw sth on.

visuel, le [vizɥɛl] *a* visual.

vit *vb voir* **voir**; **vivre**.

vital, e, aux [vital, -o] *a* vital.

vitamine [vitamin] *nf* vitamin.

vite [vit] *ad* (*rapidement*) quickly, fast; (*sans délai*) quickly; soon; **faire** ~ to act quickly; to be quick.

vitesse [vitɛs] *nf* speed; (*AUTO*: disposi-

tif) gear; **prendre qn de** ~ to outstrip sb; get ahead of sb; **prendre de la** ~ to pick up *ou* gather speed; **à toute** ~ at full *ou* top speed.

viticole [vitikɔl] *a* wine *cpd*, wine-growing.

viticulteur [vitikyltœʀ] *nm* wine grower.

vitrage [vitʀaʒ] *nm* glass *q*; (*rideau*) net curtain.

vitrail, aux [vitʀaj, -o] *nm* stained-glass window.

vitre [vitʀ(ə)] *nf* (*window*) pane; (*de portière, voiture*) window.

vitré, e [vitʀe] *a* glass *cpd*.

vitrer [vitʀe] *vt* to glaze.

vitreux, euse [vitʀø, -øz] *a* (*terne*) glassy.

vitrine [vitʀin] *nf* (*devanture*) (shop) window; (*étalage*) display; (*petite armoire*) display cabinet; ~ **publicitaire** display case, showcase.

vitupérer [vitypeʀe] *vi* to rant and rave.

vivace *a* [vivas] (*arbre, plante*) hardy; (*fig*) indestructible, inveterate.

vivacité [vivasite] *nf* liveliness, vivacity; sharpness; brilliance.

vivant, e [vivɑ̃, -ɑ̃t] *a* (*qui vit*) living, alive; (*animé*) lively; (*preuve, exemple*) living // *nm*: **du** ~ **de qn** in sb's lifetime.

vivats [viva] *nmpl* cheers.

vive [viv] *af voir* **vif** // *vb voir* **vivre** // *excl*: ~ **le roi!** long live the king!; ~**ment** *ad* vivaciously; sharply // *excl*: ~**ment les vacances!** roll on the holidays!

viveur [vivœʀ] *nm* (*péj*) high liver, pleasure-seeker.

vivier [vivje] *nm* fish tank; fishpond.

vivifiant, e [vivifjɑ̃, -ɑ̃t] *a* invigorating.

vivions *vb voir* **vivre**.

vivre [vivʀ(ə)] *vi, vt* to live; ~**s** *nmpl* provisions, food supplies; **il vit encore** he is still alive; **se laisser** ~ to take life as it comes; **ne plus** ~ (*être anxieux*) to live on one's nerves; **il a vécu** (*eu une vie aventureuse*) he has seen life; **être facile à** ~ to be easy to get on with; **faire** ~ **qn** (*pourvoir à sa subsistance*) to provide (a living) for sb.

vlan [vlɑ̃] *excl* wham!, bang!

vocable [vɔkabl(ə)] *nm* term.

vocabulaire [vɔkabylɛʀ] *nm* vocabulary.

vocation [vɔkɑsjɔ̃] *nf* vocation, calling.

vociférer [vɔsifeʀe] *vi, vt* to scream.

vodka [vɔdka] *nf* vodka.

vœu, x [vø] *nm* wish; (*à Dieu*) vow; **faire** ~ **de** to take a vow of; ~**x de bonne année** best wishes for the New Year.

vogue [vɔg] *nf* fashion, vogue.

voguer [vɔge] *vi* to sail.

voici [vwasi] *prép* (*pour introduire, désigner*) here is + *sg*, here are + *pl*; **et** ~ **que ...** and now it (*ou* he) ...; *voir aussi* **voilà**.

voie [vwa] *nf* way; *(RAIL)* track, line; *(AUTO)* lane; **être en bonne ~** to be going well; **mettre qn sur la ~** to put sb on the right track; **être en ~ d'achèvement/de rénovation** to be nearing completion/in the process of renovation; **par ~ buccale** *ou* **orale** orally; **à ~ étroite** narrow-gauge; **~ d'eau** *(NAVIG)* leak; **~ ferrée** track; railway line; **~ de garage** *(RAIL)* siding.

voilà [vwala] *prép (en désignant)* there is + *sg*, there are + *pl*; **les ~** *ou* **voici** here *ou* there they are; **en ~ un** here's one, there's one; **~ deux ans** two years ago; **~** *ou* **voici deux ans que** it's two years since; **et ~!** there we are!; **~ tout** that's all; **'~** *ou* **voici'** *(en offrant etc)* 'there *ou* here you are'.

voile [vwal] *nm* veil; *(tissu léger)* net // *nf* sail; *(sport)* sailing.

voiler [vwale] *vt* to veil; *(fausser: roue)* to buckle; *(: bois)* to warp; **se ~** *vi (lune, regard)* to mist over; *(voix)* to become husky; *(roue, disque)* to buckle; *(planche)* to warp.

voilier [vwalje] *nm* sailing ship; *(de plaisance)* sailing boat.

voilure [vwalyr] *nf (de voilier)* sails *pl*.

voir [vwar] *vi, vt* to see; **se ~** *vt*: **se ~ critiquer/transformer** to be criticized/transformed; **cela se voit** *(cela arrive)* it happens; *(c'est visible)* that's obvious, it shows; **~ venir** *(fig)* to wait and see; **faire ~ qch à qn** to show sb sth; **en faire ~ à qn** *(fig)* to give sb a hard time; **ne pas pouvoir ~ qn** *(fig)* not to be able to stand sb; **voyons!** let's see now; *(indignation etc)* come (along) now!; **avoir quelque chose à ~ avec** to have something to do with.

voire [vwar] *ad* indeed; nay; or even.

voisin, e [vwazɛ̃, -in] *a (proche)* neighbouring; *(contigu)* next; *(ressemblant)* connected // *nm/f* neighbour; **voisinage** *nm (proximité)* proximity; *(environs)* vicinity; *(quartier, voisins)* neighbourhood.

voiture [vwatyr] *nf* car; *(wagon)* coach, carriage; **~ d'enfant** pram *(Brit)*, baby carriage *(US)*; **~ de sport** sports car; **~-lit** *nf* sleeper.

voix [vwa] *nf* voice; *(POL)* vote; **à haute ~** aloud; **à ~ basse** in a low voice; **à 2/4 ~** *(MUS)* in 2/4 parts; **avoir ~ au chapitre** to have a say in the matter.

vol [vɔl] *nm (mode de locomotion)* flying; *(trajet, voyage, groupe d'oiseaux)* flight; *(larcin)* theft; **à ~ d'oiseau** as the crow flies; **au ~: attraper qch au ~** to catch sth as it flies past; **au ~** in flight; **~ libre** hang-gliding; **~ à main armée** armed robbery; **~ à voile** gliding.

volage [vɔlaʒ] *a* fickle.

volaille [vɔlaj] *nf (oiseaux)* poultry *pl*; *(viande)* poultry *q*; *(oiseau)* fowl.

volant, e [vɔlɑ̃, -ɑ̃t] *a voir* **feuille** *etc* // *nm (d'automobile)* (steering) wheel; *(de commande)* wheel; *(objet lancé)* shuttlecock; *(bande de tissu)* flounce.

volcan [vɔlkɑ̃] *nm* volcano.

volée [vɔle] *nf (TENNIS)* volley; **~ de coups/de flèches** volley of blows/arrows; **à la ~: rattraper à la ~** to catch in mid air; **à toute ~** *(sonner les cloches)* vigorously; *(lancer un projectile)* with full force.

voler [vɔle] *vi (avion, oiseau, fig)* to fly; *(voleur)* to steal // *vt (objet)* to steal; *(personne)* to rob; **~ qch à qn** to steal sth from sb.

volet [vɔlɛ] *nm (de fenêtre)* shutter; *(de feuillet, document)* section.

voleter [vɔlte] *vi* to flutter (about).

voleur, euse [vɔlœr, -øz] *nm/f* thief *(pl* thieves) // *a* thieving.

volontaire [vɔlɔ̃tɛr] *a* voluntary; *(caractère, personne: décidé)* self-willed // *nm/f* volunteer.

volonté [vɔlɔ̃te] *nf (faculté de vouloir)* will; *(énergie, fermeté)* will(power); *(souhait, désir)* wish; **à ~** as much as one likes; **bonne ~** goodwill, willingness; **mauvaise ~** lack of goodwill, unwillingness.

volontiers [vɔlɔ̃tje] *ad (de bonne grâce)* willingly; *(avec plaisir)* willingly, gladly; *(habituellement, souvent)* readily, willingly.

volt [vɔlt] *nm* volt.

volte-face [vɔltəfas] *nf inv* about-turn.

voltige [vɔltiʒ] *nf (ÉQUITATION)* trick riding; *(au cirque)* acrobatics *sg*.

voltiger [vɔltiʒe] *vi* to flutter (about).

volume [vɔlym] *nm* volume; *(GÉOM: solide)* solid; **volumineux, euse** *a* voluminous, bulky.

volupté [vɔlypte] *nf* sensual delight *ou* pleasure.

vomir [vɔmir] *vi* to vomit, be sick // *vt* to vomit, bring up; *(fig)* to belch out, spew out; *(exécrer)* to loathe, abhor.

vont [vɔ̃] *vb voir* **aller**.

vos [vo] *dét voir* **votre**.

vote [vɔt] *nm* vote; **~ par correspondance/procuration** postal/proxy vote.

voter [vɔte] *vi* to vote // *vt (loi, décision)* to vote for.

votre [vɔtr(ə)], *pl* **vos** [vo] *dét vour*.

vôtre [votr(ə)] *pronom*: **le ~, la ~, les ~s** yours; **les ~s** *(fig)* your family *ou* folks; **à la ~** *(toast)* your (good) health!

voudrai *etc vb voir* **vouloir**.

voué, e [vwe] *a*: **~ à** doomed to.

vouer [vwe] *vt*: **~ qch à** *(Dieu/un saint)* to dedicate sth to; **~ sa vie à** *(étude, cause etc)* to devote one's life to; **~ une amitié éternelle à qn** to vow undying friendship to sb.

vouloir [vulwar] ♦ *nm*: **le bon ~ de qn** sb's goodwill; sb's pleasure
♦ *vt* **1** *(exiger, désirer)* to want; **~**

faire/que qn fasse to want to do/sb to do;
voulez-vous du thé? would you like *ou* do
you want some tea?; **que me veut-il?**
what does he want with me?; **sans le ~**
(*involontairement*) without meaning to,
unintentionally; **je voudrais ceci/faire** I
would *ou* I'd like this/to do
2 (*consentir*): **je veux bien** (*bonne volonté*) I'll be happy to; (*concession*) fair
enough, that's fine; **oui, si on veut** (*en
quelque sorte*) yes, if you like; **veuillez
attendre** please wait; **veuillez agréer ...**
(*formule épistolaire*) yours faithfully
3: **en ~ à: en ~ à qn** to bear sb a
grudge; **s'en ~** (**de**) to be annoyed with
o.s. (for); **il en veut à mon argent** he's
after my money
4: **~ de: l'entreprise ne veut plus de lui**
the firm doesn't want him any more; **elle
ne veut pas de son aide** she doesn't want
his help
5: **~ dire** to mean.
voulu, e [vuly] *a* (*requis*) required,
requisite; (*délibéré*) deliberate, intentional.
vous [vu] *pronom you*; (*objet indirect*)
(to) you; (*réfléchi*) yourself (*pl* yourselves); (*réciproque*) each other; **~-
même** yourself; **~-mêmes** yourselves.
voûte [vut] *nf* vault.
voûter [vute] *vt*: **se ~** *vi* (*dos, personne*)
to become stooped.
vouvoyer [vuvwaje] *vt*: **~ qn** to address
sb as 'vous'.
voyage [vwajaʒ] *nm* journey, trip; (*fait
de voyager*): **le ~** travel(ling); **partir/
être en ~** to go off/be away on a journey
ou trip; **faire bon ~** to have a good journey; **~ d'agrément/d'affaires** pleasure/
business trip; **~ de noces** honeymoon; **~
organisé** package tour.
voyager [vwajaʒe] *vi* to travel; **voyageur, euse** *nm/f* traveller; (*passager*)
passenger.
voyant, e [vwajã, -ãt] *a* (*couleur*) loud,
gaudy // *nm* (*signal*) (warning) light // *nf*
clairvoyant.
voyelle [vwajɛl] *nf* vowel.
voyons *etc vb voir voir*.
voyou [vwaju] *nm* lout, hoodlum; (*enfant*) guttersnipe.
vrac [vʀak]: **en ~** *ad* higgledy-piggledy;
(*COMM*) in bulk.
vrai, e [vʀe] *a* (*véridique: récit, faits*)
true; (*non factice, authentique*) real; **à
~ dire** to tell the truth.
vraiment [vʀɛmã] *ad* really.
vraisemblable [vʀɛsãblabl(ə)] *a* likely,
probable.
vraisemblance [vʀɛsãblãs] *nf* likelihood; (*romanesque*) verisimilitude.
vrille [vʀij] *nf* (*de plante*) tendril; (*outil*)
gimlet; (*spirale*) spiral; (*AVIAT*) spin.
vrombir [vʀɔ̃biʀ] *vi* to hum.
vu [vy] *prép* (*en raison de*) in view of; **~**

que in view of the fact that.
vu, e [vy] *pp de* **voir** // *a*: **bien/mal ~**
(*fig*) well/poorly thought of; good/bad
form.
vue [vy] *nf* (*fait de voir*): **la ~ de** the
sight of; (*sens, faculté*) (eye)sight;
(*panorama, image, photo*) view; **~s** *nfpl*
(*idées*) views; (*dessein*) designs; **hors de
~** out of sight; **tirer à ~** to shoot on
sight; **à ~ d'œil** *ad* visibly; at a quick
glance; **en ~** (*visible*) in sight; (*COMM*)
in the public eye; **en ~ de faire** with a
view to doing.
vulgaire [vylgɛʀ] *a* (*grossier*) vulgar,
coarse; (*trivial*) commonplace, mundane; (*péj: quelconque*): **de ~s touristes**
common tourists; (*BOT, ZOOL: non latin*) common; **vulgariser** *vt* to popular-
ize.
vulnérable [vylneʀabl(ə)] *a* vulnerable.

W X Y Z

wagon [vagɔ̃] *nm* (*de voyageurs*) carriage; (*de marchandises*) truck, wagon;
~-citerne *nm* tanker; **~-lit** *nm* sleeper,
sleeping car; **~-restaurant** *nm* restaurant *ou* dining car.
wallon, ne [valɔ̃, -ɔn] *a* Walloon.
waters [watɛʀ] *nmpl* toilet *sg*.
watt [wat] *nm* watt.
w.-c. [vese] *nmpl* toilet *sg*, lavatory *sg*.
week-end [wikɛnd] *nm* weekend.
western [wɛstɛʀn] *nm* western.
whisky, *pl* whiskies [wiski] *nm* whisky.
xérès [gzeʀɛs] *nm* sherry.
xylophone [ksilɔfɔn] *nm* xylophone.
y [i] *ad* (*à cet endroit*) there; (*dessus*) on
it (*ou* them); (*dedans*) in it (*ou* them) //
pronom (*about ou on ou of*) it : *vérifier
la syntaxe du verbe employé*; **j'~** pense
I'm thinking about it; *voir aussi* **aller,
avoir.**
yacht [jɔt] *nm* yacht.
yaourt [jauʀt] *nm* yoghourt.
yeux [jø] *pl de* **œil**.
yoga [jɔga] *nm* yoga.
yoghourt [jɔguʀt] *nm* = **yaourt**.
yougoslave [jugɔslav] *a, nm/f* Yugo-
slav(ian).
Yougoslavie [jugɔslavi] *nf* Yugoslavia.
zèbre [zɛbʀ(ə)] *nm* (*ZOOL*) zebra.
zébré, e [zebʀe] *a* striped, streaked.
zèle [zɛl] *nm* zeal; **faire du ~** (*péj*) to be
over-zealous.
zéro [zeʀo] *nm* zero, nought (*Brit*); **au-
dessous de ~** below zero (Centigrade) *ou*
freezing; **partir de ~** to start from
scratch; **trois (buts) à ~** 3 (goals) to nil.
zeste [zɛst(ə)] *nm* peel, zest.
zézayer [zezeje] *vi* to have a lisp.
zigzag [zigzag] *nm* zigzag.
zinc [zɛ̃g] *nm* (*CHIMIE*) zinc; (*comptoir*)
bar, counter.

zizanie [zizani] *nf*: semer la ~ to stir up ill-feeling.

zodiaque [zɔdjak] *nm* zodiac.

zona [zona] *nm* shingles *sg*.

zone [zon] *nf* zone, area; *(quartiers)*: la ~ the slum belt; ~ **bleue** ≈ restricted parking area.

zoo [zoo] *nm* zoo.

zoologie [zɔɔlɔʒi] *nf* zoology; **zoologique** *a* zoological.

zut [zyt] *excl* dash (it)! *(Brit)*, nuts! *(US)*.

A

A [eɪ] *n* (MUS) la *m*; (AUT): ~ **road** route nationale.

a (*before vowel or silent h*: **an**) [ə, æn] *indefinite article* **1** un(e); ~ **book** un livre; **an apple** une pomme; **she's** ~ **doctor** elle est médecin

2 (*instead of the number 'one'*) un(e); ~ **year ago** il y a un an; ~ **hundred/thousand** *etc* **pounds** cent/mille *etc* livres **3** (*in expressing ratios, prices etc*): **3** ~ **day/week** 3 par jour/semaine; **10 km an hour** 10 km à l'heure; **30p** ~ **kilo** 30p le kilo.

A.A. *n abbr* =Alcoholics Anonymous; (*Brit*: =Automobile Association) ≈TCF *m*.

A.A.A. *n abbr* (US: =American Automobile Association) ≈TCF *m*.

aback [ə'bæk] *ad*: **to be taken** ~ être stupéfait(e).

abandon [ə'bændən] *vt* abandonner // *n* abandon *m*; **with** ~ avec désinvolture.

abashed [ə'bæʃt] *a* confus(e), embarrassé(e).

abate [ə'beɪt] *vi* s'apaiser, se calmer.

abbey ['æbɪ] *n* abbaye *f*.

abbot ['æbət] *n* père supérieur.

abbreviation [əbri:vɪ'eɪʃən] *n* abréviation *f*.

abdicate ['æbdɪkeɪt] *vt, vi* abdiquer.

abdomen ['æbdəmɛn] *n* abdomen *m*.

abduct [æb'dʌkt] *vt* enlever.

aberration [æbə'reɪʃən] *n* anomalie *f*.

abet [ə'bɛt] *vt see* **aid**.

abeyance [ə'beɪəns] *n*: **in** ~ (*law*) en désuétude; (*matter*) en suspens.

abide [ə'baɪd] *vt*: **I can't** ~ **it/him** je ne peux pas le souffrir *or* supporter; **to** ~ **by** *vt fus* observer, respecter.

ability [ə'bɪlɪtɪ] *n* compétence *f*; capacité *f*; (*skill*) talent *m*.

abject ['æbdʒɛkt] *a* (*poverty*) sordide; (*apology*) plat(e).

ablaze [ə'bleɪz] *a* en feu, en flammes.

able ['eɪbl] *a* compétent(e); **to be** ~ **to do sth** pouvoir faire qch, être capable de faire qch; **ably** *ad* avec compétence *or* talent, habilement.

abnormal [æb'nɔ:məl] *a* anormal(e).

aboard [ə'bɔ:d] *ad* à bord // *prep* à bord de.

abode [ə'bəud] *n*: **of no fixed** ~ sans domicile fixe.

abolish [ə'bɒlɪʃ] *vt* abolir.

aborigine [æbə'rɪdʒɪnɪ] *n* aborigène *m/f*.

abort [ə'bɔ:t] *vt* faire avorter; ~**ion** [ə'bɔ:ʃən] *n* avortement *m*; **to have an** ~**ion** se faire avorter; ~**ive** *a* manqué(e).

abound [ə'baund] *vi* abonder; **to** ~ **in** abonder en, regorger de.

about [ə'baut] ♦ *ad* **1** (*approximately*) environ, à peu près; ~ **a hundred/thousand** *etc* environ cent/mille *etc*, une centaine/un millier *etc*; **it takes** ~ **10 hours** ça prend environ *or* à peu près 10 heures; **at** ~ **2 o'clock** vers 2 heures; **I've just** ~ **finished** j'ai presque fini

2 (*referring to place*) çà et là, de côté et d'autre; **to run** ~ courir çà et là; **to walk** ~ se promener, aller et venir

3: **to be** ~ **to do sth** être sur le point de faire qch

♦ *prep* **1** (*relating to*) au sujet de, à propos de; **a book** ~ **London** un livre sur Londres; **what is it** ~? de quoi s'agit-il?; **we talked** ~ **it** nous en avons parlé; **what** *or* **how** ~ **doing this?** et si nous faisions ceci?

2 (*referring to place*) dans; **to walk** ~ **the town** se promener dans la ville.

about turn *n* demi-tour *m*.

above [ə'bʌv] *ad* au-dessus // *prep* au-dessus de; **mentioned** ~ mentionné ci-dessus; ~ **all** par-dessus tout, surtout; ~**board** *a* franc(franche), loyal(e), honnête.

abrasive [ə'breɪzɪv] *a* abrasif(ive); (*fig*) caustique, agressif(ive).

abreast [ə'brɛst] *ad* de front; **to keep** ~ **of** se tenir au courant de.

abridge [ə'brɪdʒ] *vt* abréger.

abroad [ə'brɔ:d] *ad* à l'étranger.

abrupt [ə'brʌpt] *a* (*steep, blunt*) abrupt(e); (*sudden, gruff*) brusque.

abscess ['æbsɪs] *n* abcès *m*.

abscond [əb'skɒnd] *vi* disparaître, s'enfuir.

absence ['æbsəns] *n* absence *f*.

absent ['æbsənt] *a* absent(e); ~**ee** [-'ti:] *n* absent/e; ~**-minded** *a* distrait(e).

absolute ['æbsəlu:t] *a* absolu(e); ~**ly** [-'lu:tlɪ] *ad* absolument.

absolve [əb'zɒlv] *vt*: **to** ~ **sb (from)** (*sin etc*) absoudre qn (de); **to** ~ **sb from** (*oath*) délier qn de.

absorb [əb'zɔ:b] *vt* absorber; **to be** ~**ed in a book** être plongé dans un livre; ~**ent cotton** *n* (US) coton *m* hydrophile.

absorption [əb'zɔ:pʃən] *n* absorption *f*; amortissement *m*; intégration *f*; (*fig*) concentration f.

abstain [əb'steɪn] vi: to ~ **(from)** s'abstenir (de).

abstemious [əb'stiːmɪəs] a sobre, frugal(e).

abstract ['æbstrækt] a abstrait(e).

absurd [əb'səːd] a absurde.

abuse n [ə'bjuːs] abus m, insultes fpl, injures fpl // vt [ə'bjuːz] abuser de; **abusive** a grossier(ère), injurieux(euse).

abysmal [ə'bɪzməl] a exécrable; (ignorance etc) sans bornes.

abyss [ə'bɪs] n abîme m, gouffre m.

AC abbr (=alternating current) courant alternatif.

academic [ækə'dɛmɪk] a universitaire; (pej: issue) oiseux(euse), purement théorique // n universitaire m/f.

academy [ə'kædəmɪ] n (learned body) académie f; (school) collège m; ~ of music conservatoire m.

accelerate [æk'sɛləreɪt] vt, vi accélérer; **accelerator** n accélérateur m.

accent ['æksɛnt] n accent m.

accept [ək'sɛpt] vt accepter; ~able a acceptable; ~ance n acceptation f.

access ['æksɛs] n accès m; ~ible [æk'sɛsəbl] a accessible.

accessory [æk'sɛsərɪ] n accessoire m; toilet accessories npl articles mpl de toilette.

accident ['æksɪdənt] n accident m; (chance) hasard m; by ~ par hasard; accidentellement; ~al [-'dɛntl] a accidentel(le); ~ally [-'dɛntəlɪ] ad accidentellement; ~-prone a sujet(te) aux accidents.

acclaim [ə'kleɪm] n acclamation f.

accommodate [ə'kɔmədeɪt] vt loger, recevoir; (oblige, help) obliger.

accommodating [ə'kɔmədeɪtɪŋ] a obligeant(e), arrangeant(e).

accommodation [əkɔmə'deɪʃən] n (US: ~s) logement m.

accompany [ə'kʌmpənɪ] vt accompagner.

accomplice [ə'kʌmplɪs] n complice m/f.

accomplish [ə'kʌmplɪʃ] vt accomplir; ~ment n accomplissement m; réussite f, résultat m; ~ments npl talents mpl.

accord [ə'kɔːd] n accord m // vt accorder; of his own ~ de son plein gré; ~ance n: in ~ance with conformément à; ~ing to prep selon; ~ingly ad en conséquence.

accordion [ə'kɔːdɪən] n accordéon m.

accost [ə'kɔst] vt aborder.

account [ə'kaunt] n (COMM) compte m; (report) compte rendu; récit m; ~s npl comptabilité f, comptes; of little ~ de peu d'importance; on ~ en acompte; on no ~ en aucun cas; on ~ of à cause de; to take into ~, take ~ of tenir compte de; to ~ for vt fus expliquer, rendre compte de; ~able a responsable.

accountancy [ə'kauntənsɪ] n comptabilité f.

accountant [ə'kauntənt] n comptable m/f.

account number n (at bank etc) numéro m de compte.

accumulate [ə'kjuːmjuleɪt] vt accumuler, amasser // vi s'accumuler, s'amasser.

accuracy ['ækjurəsɪ] n exactitude f, précision f.

accurate ['ækjurɪt] a exact(e), précis(e); ~ly ad avec précision.

accusation [ækju'zeɪʃən] n accusation f.

accuse [ə'kjuːz] vt accuser; ~d n accusé/e.

accustom [ə'kʌstəm] vt accoutumer, habituer; ~ed a (usual) habituel(le); ~ed to habitué(e) or accoutumé(e) à.

ace [eɪs] n as m.

ache [eɪk] n mal m, douleur f // vi (be sore) faire mal, être douloureux(euse); my head ~s j'ai mal à la tête.

achieve [ə'tʃiːv] vt (aim) atteindre; (victory, success) remporter, obtenir; (task) accomplir; ~ment n exploit m, réussite f.

acid ['æsɪd] a, n acide (m); ~ rain n pluies fpl acides.

acknowledge [ək'nɔlɪdʒ] vt (letter: also: ~ receipt of) accuser réception de; (fact) reconnaître; ~ment n accusé m de réception.

acne ['æknɪ] n acné m.

acorn ['eɪkɔːn] n gland m.

acoustic [ə'kuːstɪk] a acoustique; ~s n, npl acoustique f.

acquaint [ə'kweɪnt] vt: to ~ sb with sth mettre qn au courant de qch; to be ~ed with (person) connaître; ~ance n connaissance f.

acquire [ə'kwaɪə*] vt acquérir.

acquit [ə'kwɪt] vt acquitter; to ~ o.s. well bien se comporter, s'en tirer très honorablement; ~tal n acquittement m.

acre ['eɪkə*] n acre f (= 4047 m²).

acrid ['ækrɪd] a âcre.

acrobat ['ækrəbæt] n acrobate m/f.

across [ə'krɔs] prep (on the other side) de l'autre côté de; (crosswise) en travers de // ad de l'autre côté; en travers; to run/swim ~ traverser en courant/à la nage; ~ from en face de.

acrylic [ə'krɪlɪk] a, n acrylique (m).

act [ækt] n acte m, action f; (THEATRE) acte; (in music-hall etc) numéro m; (LAW) loi f // vi agir; (THEATRE) jouer; (pretend) jouer la comédie // vt (part) jouer, tenir; to ~ as servir de; ~ing a suppléant(e), par intérim // n (of actor) jeu m; (activity): to do some ~ing faire du théâtre (or du cinéma).

action ['ækʃən] n action f; (MIL) combat(s) m(pl); (LAW) procès m, action en justice; out of ~ hors de combat; hors d'usage; to take ~ agir, prendre des mesures; ~ **replay** *n* (*TV*) répétition *f* d'une séquence.

activate ['æktɪveɪt] *vt* (*mechanism*) actionner, faire fonctionner; (*CHEM*, *PHYSICS*) activer.

active ['æktɪv] *a* actif(ive); (*volcano*) en activité; ~**ly** *ad* activement.

activity [æk'tɪvɪtɪ] *n* activité *f*.

actor ['æktə*] *n* acteur *m*.

actress ['æktrɪs] *n* actrice *f*.

actual ['æktjuəl] *a* réel(le), véritable; ~**ly** *ad* réellement, véritablement; en fait.

acumen ['ækjumən] *n* perspicacité *f*.

acute [ə'kju:t] *a* aigu(ë); (*mind*, *observer*) pénétrant(e).

ad [æd] *n abbr of* **advertisement**.

A.D. *ad abbr* (= *Anno Domini*) ap. J.-C.

adamant ['ædəmənt] *a* inflexible.

adapt [ə'dæpt] *vt* adapter // *vi*: to ~ (to) s'adapter (à); ~**able** *a* (*device*) adaptable; (*person*) qui s'adapte facilement; ~**er** *or* ~**or** *n* (*ELEC*) adapteur *m*.

add [æd] *vt* ajouter; (*figures: also*: to ~ up) additionner // *vi*: to ~ to (*increase*) ajouter à, accroître; it doesn't ~ up (*fig*) cela ne rime à rien.

adder ['ædə*] *n* vipère *f*.

addict ['ædɪkt] *n* intoxiqué/e; (*fig*) fanatique *m/f*; ~**ed** [ə'dɪktɪd] *a*: to be ~**ed** to (*drink etc*) être adonné(e) à; (*fig: football etc*) être un(e) fanatique de; ~**ion** [ə'dɪkʃən] *n* (*MED*) dépendance *f*; ~**ive** *a* qui crée une dépendance.

addition [ə'dɪʃən] *n* addition *f*; in ~ de plus; de surcroît; in ~ to en plus de; ~**al** *a* supplémentaire.

additive ['ædɪtɪv] *n* additif *m*.

address [ə'drɛs] *n* adresse *f*; (*talk*) discours *m*, allocution *f* // *vt* adresser; (*speak to*) s'adresser à.

adept ['ædɛpt] *a*: ~ at expert(e) à *or* en.

adequate ['ædɪkwɪt] *a* adéquat(e); suffisant(e); compétent(e).

adhere [əd'hɪə*] *vi*: to ~ to adhérer à; (*fig: rule, decision*) se tenir à.

adhesive [əd'hi:zɪv] *a* adhésif(ive) // *n* adhésif *m*; ~ **tape** *n* (*Brit*) ruban adhésif; (*US*: *MED*) sparadrap *m*.

adjective ['ædʒɛktɪv] *n* adjectif *m*.

adjoining [ə'dʒɔɪnɪŋ] *a* voisin(e), adjacent(e), attenant(e).

adjourn [ə'dʒə:n] *vt* ajourner // *vi* suspendre la séance; lever la séance; clore la session; (*go*) se retirer.

adjudicate [ə'dʒu:dɪkeɪt] *vi* se prononcer.

adjust [ə'dʒʌst] *vt* ajuster, régler; rajuster // *vi*: to ~ (to) s'adapter (à); ~**able** *a* réglable.

ad-lib [æd'lɪb] *vt*, *vi* improviser // *ad*: ad lib à volonté, à discrétion.

administer [əd'mɪnɪstə*] *vt* adminis-

trer; (*justice*) rendre.

administration [ədmɪnɪs'treɪʃən] *n* administration *f*.

administrative [əd'mɪnɪstrətɪv] *a* administratif(ive).

admiral ['ædmərəl] *n* amiral *m*; **A~ty** *n* (*Brit: also*: **A~ty Board**) ministère *m* de la Marine.

admiration [ædmə'reɪʃən] *n* admiration *f*.

admire [əd'maɪə*] *vt* admirer.

admission [əd'mɪʃən] *n* admission *f*; (*to exhibition, night club etc*) entrée *f*; (*confession*) aveu *m*.

admit [əd'mɪt] *vt* laisser entrer; admettre; (*agree*) reconnaître, admettre; to ~ to *vt fus* reconnaître, avouer; ~**tance** *n* admission *f*, (droit *m* d')entrée *f*; ~**tedly** *ad* il faut en convenir.

admonish [əd'mɔnɪʃ] *vt* donner un avertissement à; réprimander.

ad nauseam [æd'nɔ:zɪəm] *ad* (*repeat, talk*) à satiété.

ado [ə'du:] *n*: without (any) more ~ sans plus de cérémonies.

adolescence [ædəu'lɛsns] *n* adolescence *f*.

adolescent [ædəu'lɛsnt] *a*, *n* adolescent(e).

adopt [ə'dɔpt] *vt* adopter; ~**ed** *a* adoptif(ive), adopté(e); ~**ion** [ə'dɔpʃən] *n* adoption *f*.

adore [ə'dɔ:*] *vt* adorer.

adorn [ə'dɔ:n] *vt* orner.

Adriatic (Sea) [eɪdrɪ'ætɪk('si:)] *n* Adriatique *f*.

adrift [ə'drɪft] *ad* à la dérive.

adult ['ædʌlt] *n* adulte *m/f*.

adultery [ə'dʌltərɪ] *n* adultère *m*.

advance [əd'vɑ:ns] *n* avance *f* // *vt* avancer // *vi* s'avancer; in ~ en avance, d'avance; ~**d** *a* avancé(e); (*SCOL*: *studies*) supérieur(e).

advantage [əd'vɑ:ntɪdʒ] *n* (*also TENNIS*) avantage *m*; to take ~ of profiter de.

advent ['ædvənt] *n* avènement *m*, venue *f*; **A~** Avent *m*.

adventure [əd'vɛntʃə*] *n* aventure *f*.

adverb ['ædvə:b] *n* adverbe *m*.

adverse ['ædvə:s] *a* contraire, adverse; ~ to hostile à.

advert ['ædvə:t] *n abbr* (*Brit*) *of* **advertisement**.

advertise ['ædvətaɪz] *vi* (*vt*) faire de la publicité *or* de la réclame (pour); mettre une annonce (pour vendre); to ~ **for** (*staff*) faire paraître une annonce pour trouver.

advertisement [əd'və:tɪsmənt] *n* (*COMM*) réclame *f*, publicité *f*; (*in classified ads*) annonce *f*.

advertiser ['ædvətaɪzə*] *n* (*in newspaper etc*) annonceur *m*.

advertising ['ædvətaɪzɪŋ] *n* publicité *f*,

réclame f.

advice [əd'vaɪs] n conseils mpl; (notification) avis m; piece of ~ conseil; to take legal ~ consulter un avocat.

advisable [əd'vaɪzəbl] a recommandable, indiqué(e).

advise [əd'vaɪz] vt conseiller; to ~ sb of sth aviser or informer qn de qch; to ~ against sth/doing sth déconseiller qch/conseiller de ne pas faire qch; ~dly [-'vaɪzədlɪ] ad (deliberately) délibérément; ~r n conseiller/ère; advisory [-ərɪ] a consultatif(ive).

advocate n ['ædvəkɪt] (upholder) défenseur m, avocat/e ♦ vt ['ædvəkeɪt] recommander, prôner; to be an ~ of être partisan/e de.

aerial ['ɛərɪəl] n antenne f // a aérien(ne).

aerobics [ɛə'rəubɪks] n aérobic m.

aeroplane ['ɛərəpleɪn] n (Brit) avion m.

aerosol ['ɛərəsɔl] n aérosol m.

aesthetic [ɪs'θɛtɪk] a esthétique.

afar [ə'fɑ:*] ad: from ~ de loin.

affair [ə'fɛə*] n affaire f; (also: love ~) liaison f; aventure f.

affect [ə'fɛkt] vt affecter.

affection [ə'fɛkʃən] n affection f; ~ate a affectueux(euse).

affirmation [æfə'meɪʃən] n affirmation f, assertion f.

affix [ə'fɪks] vt apposer, ajouter.

afflict [ə'flɪkt] vt affliger.

affluence ['æfluəns] n abondance f, opulence f.

affluent ['æfluənt] a abondant(e), opulent(e); (person) dans l'aisance, riche.

afford [ə'fɔ:d] vt se permettre; avoir les moyens d'acheter or d'entretenir; (provide) fournir, procurer.

afield [ə'fi:ld] ad: far ~ loin.

afloat [ə'fləut] a, ad à flot; to stay ~ surnager.

afoot [ə'fut] ad: there is something ~ il se prépare quelque chose.

afraid [ə'freɪd] a effrayé(e); to be ~ of or to avoir peur de; I am ~ that je crains que + sub.

afresh [ə'frɛʃ] ad de nouveau.

Africa ['æfrɪkə] n Afrique f; ~n a africain(e) // n Africain/e.

aft [ɑ:ft] ad à l'arrière, vers l'arrière.

after ['ɑ:ftə*] prep, ad après // cj après que, après avoir or être + pp; what/who are you ~? que/qui cherchez-vous?; ~ he left/having done après qu'il fut parti/après avoir fait; ask ~ him demandez de ses nouvelles; ~ all après tout; ~ you! après vous, Monsieur (or Madame etc); ~-effects npl répercussions fpl; (of illness) séquelles fpl, suites fpl; ~life n vie future; ~math n conséquences fpl; in the ~math of dans les mois or années etc qui suivirent, au lendemain de;

~noon n après-midi m or f; ~s n (col: dessert) dessert m; ~-sales service n (Brit: for car, washing machine etc) service m après-vente (S.A.V.); ~-shave (lotion) n after-shave m; ~thought n: I had an ~thought il m'est venu une idée après coup; ~wards ad après.

again [ə'gɛn] ad de nouveau; to do sth ~ refaire qch; not ~ ne — plus; ~ and ~ à plusieurs reprises.

against [ə'gɛnst] prep contre.

age [eɪdʒ] n âge m // vt, vi vieillir; it's been ~s since ça fait une éternité que — ne; he is 20 years of ~ il a 20 ans; to come of ~ atteindre sa majorité; ~d 10 âgé de 10 ans; the ~d ['eɪdʒɪd] les personnes âgées; ~ group n tranche f d'âge; ~ limit n limite f d'âge.

agency ['eɪdʒənsɪ] n agence f; through or by the ~ of par l'entremise or l'action de.

agenda [ə'dʒɛndə] n ordre m du jour.

agent ['eɪdʒənt] n agent m.

aggregate ['ægrɪgeɪt] n ensemble m, total m.

aggressive [ə'grɛsɪv] a agressif(ive).

aggrieved [ə'gri:vd] a chagriné(e), affligé(e).

aghast [ə'gɑ:st] a consterné(e), atterré(e).

agitate ['ædʒɪteɪt] vt rendre inquiet(ète) or agité(e); agiter; to ~ for faire campagne pour.

ago [ə'gəu] ad: 2 days ~ il y a deux jours; not long ~ il n'y a pas longtemps; how long ~? il y a combien de temps (de cela)?

agog [ə'gɔg] a en émoi.

agonizing ['ægənaɪzɪŋ] a angoissant(e); déchirant(e).

agony ['ægənɪ] n grande souffrance or angoisse.

agree [ə'gri:] vt (price) convenir de // vi: to ~ (with) (person) être d'accord (avec); (statements etc) concorder (avec); (LING) s'accorder (avec); to ~ to do accepter de or consentir à faire; to ~ to sth consentir à qch; to ~ that (admit) convenir or reconnaître que; garlic doesn't ~ with me je ne supporte pas l'ail; ~able a agréable; (willing) consentant(e), d'accord; ~d a (time, place) convenu(e); ~ment n accord m; in ~ment d'accord.

agricultural [ægrɪ'kʌltʃərəl] a agricole.

agriculture ['ægrɪkʌltʃə*] n agriculture f.

aground [ə'graund] ad: to run ~ s'échouer.

ahead [ə'hɛd] ad en avant; devant; ~ of devant; (fig: schedule etc) en avance sur; ~ of time en avance; go right or straight ~ allez tout droit; they were (right) ~ of us ils nous précédaient (de

peu), ils étaient (juste) devant nous.
aid [eɪd] *n* aide *f* // *vt* aider; **in ~ of** en faveur de; **to ~ and abet** (*LAW*) se faire le complice de.
aide [eɪd] *n* (*person*) collaborateur/trice, assistant/e.
AIDS [eɪdz] *n abbr* (=*acquired immune deficiency syndrome*) SIDA *m*.
ailing ['eɪlɪŋ] *a* malade.
ailment ['eɪlmənt] *n* petite maladie, affection *f*.
aim [eɪm] *vt*: **to ~** sth at (*such as gun, camera*) braquer *or* pointer qch sur, diriger qch contre; (*missile*) lancer qch à *or* contre *or* en direction de; (*remark, blow*) destiner *or* adresser qch à // *vi* (*also*: **to take ~**) viser // **n** but *m*; **to ~ at** viser; (*fig*) viser (à); avoir pour but *or* ambition; **to ~ to do** avoir l'intention de faire; **~less** *a* sans but.
ain't [eɪnt] (*col*) **=am not, aren't, isn't**.
air [ɛə*] *n* air *m* // *vt* aérer; (*grievances, ideas*) exposer (librement) // *cpd* (*currents, attack etc*) aérien(ne); **to throw** sth into the **~** jeter qch en l'air; **to be on the ~** (*RADIO, TV: programme*) être diffusé(e); (: *station*) diffuser; **~bed** *n* matelas *m* pneumatique; **~borne** *a* en vol; aéroporté(e); **~conditioning** *n* climatisation *f*; **~craft** *n, pl inv* avion *m*; **~craft carrier** *n* porte-avions *m inv*; **~field** *n* terrain *m* d'aviation; **A~ Force** *n* Armée *f* de l'air; **~ freshener** *n* désodorisant *m*; **~gun** *n* fusil *m* à air comprimé; **~ hostess** *n* (*Brit*) hôtesse *f* de l'air; **~ letter** *n* (*Brit*) aérogramme *m*; **~lift** *n* pont aérien; **~line** *n* ligne aérienne, compagnie *f* d'aviation; **~liner** *n* avion *m* de ligne; **~lock** *n* sas *m*; **~mail** *n*: **by ~mail** par avion; **~ mattress** *n* matelas *m* pneumatique; **~plane** *n* (*US*) avion *m*; **~port** *n* aéroport *m*; **~ raid** *n* attaque aérienne; **~sick** *a*: **to be ~sick** avoir le mal de l'air; **~strip** *n* terrain *m* d'atterrissage; **~ terminal** *n* aérogare *f*; **~tight** *a* hermétique; **~ traffic controller** *n* aiguilleur *m* du ciel; **~y** *a* bien aéré(e); (*manners*) dégagé(e).
aisle [aɪl] *n* (*of church*) allée centrale; nef latérale.
ajar [ə'dʒɑ:*] *a* entrouvert(e).
akin [ə'kɪn] *a*: **~ to** (*similar*) qui tient de *or* ressemble à.
alacrity [ə'lækrɪtɪ] *n* empressement *m*.
alarm [ə'lɑ:m] *n* alarme *f* // *vt* alarmer; **~ clock** *n* réveille-matin *m*, réveil *m*.
alas [ə'lɑ:s] *excl* hélas!
albeit [ɔ:l'bi:ɪt] *cj* (*although*) bien que + *sub*, encore que + *sub*.
album ['ælbəm] *n* album *m*; (*L.P.*) 33 tours *m inv*.
alcohol ['ælkəhɔl] *n* alcool *m*; **~ic** [-'hɔlɪk] *a, n* alcoolique (*m/f*).
alderman ['ɔ:ldəmən] *n* conseiller

municipal (*en Angleterre*).
ale [eɪl] *n* bière *f*.
alert [ə'lə:t] *a* alerte, vif(vive); vigilant(e) // *n* alerte *f* // *vt* alerter; (*fig*) éveiller l'attention de; **on the ~** sur le qui-vive; (*MIL*) en état d'alerte.
algebra ['ældʒɪbrə] *n* algèbre *m*.
Algeria [æl'dʒɪərɪə] *n* Algérie *f*.
alias ['eɪlɪəs] *ad* alias // *n* faux nom, nom d'emprunt.
alibi ['ælɪbaɪ] *n* alibi *m*.
alien ['eɪlɪən] *n* étranger/ère // *a*: **~ (to)** étranger(ère) (à); (*fig*); **~ate** *vt* aliéner; s'aliéner.
alight [ə'laɪt] *a, ad* en feu // *vi* mettre pied à terre; (*passenger*) descendre; (*bird*) se poser.
alike [ə'laɪk] *a* semblable, pareil(le) // *ad* de même; **to look ~** se ressembler.
alimony ['ælɪmənɪ] *n* (*payment*) pension *f* alimentaire.
alive [ə'laɪv] *a* vivant(e); (*active*) plein(e) de vie.
all [ɔ:l] ♦ *a* (*singular*) tout(e); (*plural*) tous(toutes); **~ day** tout le jour; **~ night** toute la nuit; **~ men** tous les hommes; **~ five** tous les cinq; **~ the food** toute la nourriture; **~ the books** tous les livres; **~ the time** tout le temps; **~ his life** toute sa vie
♦ *pronoun* **1** tout; I ate it **~**, I ate **~** of it j'ai tout mangé; **~ of us** went nous y sommes tous allés; **~ of the boys** went tous les garçons y sont allés
2 (*in phrases*): **above ~** surtout, par-dessus tout; **after ~** après tout; **at ~**: **not at ~** (*in answer to question*) pas du tout; (*in answer to thanks*) je vous en prie!; **I'm not at ~ tired** je ne suis pas du tout fatigué(e); **anything at ~ will do** n'importe quoi fera l'affaire; **~ in ~** tout bien considéré, en fin de compte
♦ *ad*: **~ alone** tout(e) seul(e); **it's not as hard as ~ that** ce n'est pas si difficile que ça; **~ the more/the better** d'autant plus/mieux; **~ but** presque, pratiquement; **the score is** 2 **~** le score est 2 partout.
allay [ə'leɪ] *vt* (*fears*) apaiser, calmer.
all clear *n* (*after attack etc, also fig*) fin *f* d'alerte.
allege [ə'lɛdʒ] *vt* alléguer, prétendre; **~dly** [ə'lɛdʒɪdlɪ] *ad* à ce que l'on prétend, paraît-il.
allegiance [ə'li:dʒəns] *n* fidélité *f*, obéissance *f*.
allergic [ə'lə:dʒɪk] *a*: **~ to** allergique à.
allergy ['ælədʒɪ] *n* allergie *f*.
alleviate [ə'li:vɪeɪt] *vt* soulager, adoucir.
alley ['ælɪ] *n* ruelle *f*; (*in garden*) allée *f*.
alliance [ə'laɪəns] *n* alliance *f*.
allied ['ælaɪd] *a* allié(e).
all-in ['ɔ:lɪn] *a* (*Brit: also ad: charge*) tout compris; **~ wrestling** *n* catch *m*.
all-night ['ɔ:l'naɪt] *a* ouvert(e) *or* qui

dure toute la nuit.

allocate ['æləkeıt] *vt* (*share out*) répartir, distribuer; (*duties*): to ~ sth to assigner *or* attribuer qch à; (*sum, time*): to ~ sth to allouer qch à; to ~ sth for affecter qch à.

allot [ə'lɔt] *vt* (*share out*) répartir, distribuer; (*time*): to ~ sth to allouer qch à; (*duties*): to ~ sth to assigner qch à; ~**ment** *n* (*share*) part *f*; (*garden*) lopin *m* de terre (*loué à la municipalité*).

all-out ['ɔ:laut] *a* (*effort etc*) total(e) // *ad*: all out à fond.

allow [ə'lau] *vt* (*practice, behaviour*) permettre, autoriser; (*sum to spend etc*) accorder; allouer; (*sum, time estimated*) compter, prévoir; (*concede*): to ~ that convenir que; to ~ sb to do permettre à qn de faire, autoriser qn à faire; he is ~ed to — on lui permet de —; to ~ for *vt fus* tenir compte de; ~**ance** *n* (*money received*) allocation *f*; subside *m*; indemnité *f*; (*TAX*) somme *f* déductible du revenu imposable, abattement *m*; to make ~**ances for** tenir compte de.

alloy ['ælɔı] *n* alliage *m*.

all right ['ɔ:l'raıt] *ad* (*feel, work*) bien; (*as answer*) d'accord.

all-round ['ɔ:l'raund] *a* compétent(e) dans tous les domaines; (*athlete etc*) complet(ète).

all-time ['ɔ:l'taım] *a* (*record*) sans précédent, absolu(e).

allude [ə'lu:d] *vi*: to ~ to faire allusion à.

alluring [ə'ljuərıŋ] *a* séduisant(e), alléchant(e).

ally ['ælaı] *n* allié *m*.

almighty [ɔ:l'maıtı] *a* tout-puissant.

almond ['ɑ:mənd] *n* amande *f*.

almost ['ɔ:lməust] *ad* presque.

alms [ɑ:mz] *npl* aumône(s) *f(pl)*.

aloft [ə'lɔft] *ad* en haut, en l'air; (*NAUT*) dans la mâture.

alone [ə'ləun] *a, ad* seul(e); to leave sb ~ laisser qn tranquille; to leave sth ~ ne pas toucher à qch; let ~ — sans parler de —; encore moins —.

along [ə'lɔŋ] *prep* le long de // *ad*: is he coming ~? vient-il avec nous?; he was hopping/limping ~ il venait *or* avançait en sautillant/boitant; ~ with en compagnie de; avec, en plus de; all ~ (*all the time*) depuis le début; ~**side** *prep* le long de; au côté de // *ad* bord à bord; côte à côte.

aloof [ə'lu:f] *a, ad* à distance, à l'écart.

aloud [ə'laud] *ad* à haute voix.

alphabet ['ælfəbet] *n* alphabet *m*; ~**ical** [-'betıkəl] *a* alphabétique.

alpine ['ælpaın] *a* alpin(e), alpestre.

Alps [ælps] *npl*: the ~ les Alpes *fpl*.

already [ɔ:l'redı] *ad* déjà.

alright ['ɔ:l'raıt] *ad* (*Brit*) = **all right**.

Alsatian [æl'seıʃən] *n* (*dog*) berger

allemand.

also ['ɔ:lsəu] *ad* aussi.

altar ['ɔltə*] *n* autel *m*.

alter ['ɔltə*] *vt, vi* changer, modifier.

alternate *a* [ɔl'tɔ:nıt] alterné(e), alternant(e), alternatif(ive) // *vi* ['ɔltə:neıt] alterner; on ~ days un jour sur deux, tous les deux jours; **alternating** *a* (*current*) alternatif(ive).

alternative [ɔl'tɔ:nətıv] *a* (*solutions*) interchangeable, possible; (*solution*) autre, de remplacement // *n* (*choice*) alternative *f*; (*other possibility*) solution *f* de remplacement *or* de rechange, autre possibilité *f*; ~**ly** *ad*: ~**ly** one could une autre *or* l'autre solution serait de.

alternator ['ɔltə:neıtə*] *n* (*AUT*) alternateur *m*.

although [ɔ:l'ðəu] *cj* bien que + *sub*.

altitude ['æltıtju:d] *n* altitude *f*.

alto ['æltəu] *n* (*female*) contralto *m*; (*male*) haute-contre *f*.

altogether [ɔ:ltə'geðə*] *ad* entièrement, tout à fait; (*on the whole*) tout compte fait; (*in all*) en tout.

aluminium [ælju'mınıəm] , (*US*) **aluminum** [ə'lu:mınəm] *n* aluminium *m*.

always ['ɔ:lweız] *ad* toujours.

am [æm] *vb see* **be**.

a.m. *ad abbr* (=*ante meridiem*) du matin.

amalgamate [ə'mælgəmeıt] *vt, vi* fusionner.

amateur ['æmətə*] *n* amateur *m* // *a* (*SPORT*) amateur *inv*; ~**ish** *a* (*pej*) d'amateur.

amaze [ə'meız] *vt* stupéfier; to be ~d (at) être surpris(e) *or* étonné(e) (de); ~**ment** *n* stupéfaction *f*, stupeur *f*; **amazing** *a* étonnant(e); exceptionnel(le).

ambassador [æm'bæsədə*] *n* ambassadeur *m*.

amber ['æmbə*] *n* ambre *m*; at ~ (*Brit AUT*) à l'orange.

ambiguous [æm'bıgjuəs] *a* ambigu(ë).

ambition [æm'bıʃən] *n* ambition *f*.

ambitious [æm'bıʃəs] *a* ambitieux(euse).

amble ['æmbl] *vi* (*also*: to ~ along) aller d'un pas tranquille.

ambulance ['æmbjuləns] *n* ambulance *f*.

ambush ['æmbuʃ] *n* embuscade *f* // *vt* tendre une embuscade à.

amenable [ə'mi:nəbl] *a*: ~ to (*advice etc*) disposé(e) à écouter *or* suivre.

amend [ə'mend] *vt* (*law*) amender; (*text*) corriger; to make ~s réparer ses torts, faire amende honorable.

amenities [ə'mi:nıtız] *npl* aménagements *mpl* (*prévus pour le loisir des habitants*).

America [ə'merıkə] *n* Amérique *f*; ~**n** *a* américain(e) // *n* Américain/e.

amiable ['eımıəbl] *a* aimable, affable.

amicable ['æmɪkəbl] *a* amical(e).

amid(st) [ə'mɪd(st)] *prep* parmi, au milieu de.

amiss [ə'mɪs] *a, ad*: there's something ~ il y a quelque chose qui ne va pas *or* qui cloche; to take sth ~ prendre qch mal *or* de travers.

ammonia [ə'məunɪə] *n* (*gas*) ammoniac *m*; (*liquid*) ammoniaque *f*.

ammunition [æmju'nɪʃən] *n* munitions *fpl*.

amok [ə'mɔk] *ad*: to run ~ être pris(e) d'un accès de folie furieuse.

among(st) [ə'mʌŋ(st)] *prep* parmi, entre.

amorous ['æmərəs] *a* amoureux(euse).

amount [ə'maunt] *n* (*sum*) somme *f*, montant *m*; (*quantity*) quantité *f* // *vi*: to ~ to (*total*) s'élever à; (*be same as*) équivaloir à, revenir à.

amp(ère) ['æmp(ɛə*)] *n* ampère *m*.

ample ['æmpl] *a* ample; spacieux(euse); (*enough*): this is ~ c'est largement suffisant; to have ~ time/room avoir bien assez de temps/place.

amplifier ['æmplɪfaɪə*] *n* amplificateur *m*.

amuck [ə'mʌk] *ad* =**amok.**

amuse [ə'mju:z] *vt* amuser; ~ment *n* amusement *m*; ~ment arcade *n* salle *f* de jeu.

an [æn] *indefinite article see* **a.**

anaemic [ə'ni:mɪk] *a* anémique.

anaesthetic [æns'θɛtɪk] *a, n* anesthésique (*m*).

analog(ue) ['ænlɔg] *a* (*watch, computer*) analogique.

analyse ['ænəlaɪz] *vt* (*Brit*) analyser.

analysis, *pl* **analyses** [ə'næləsɪs, -sɪ:z] *n* analyse *f*.

analyst ['ænəlɪst] *n* (*POL etc*) spécialiste *m/f*; (*US*) psychanalyste *m/f*.

analyze ['ænəlaɪz] *vt* (*US*) =**analyse.**

anarchist ['ænəkɪst] *a, n* anarchiste (*m/f*).

anarchy ['ænəkɪ] *n* anarchie *f*.

anathema [ə'næθɪmə] *n*: it is ~ to him il a cela en abomination.

anatomy [ə'nætəmɪ] *n* anatomie *f*.

ancestor ['ænsɪstə*] *n* ancêtre *m*, aïeul *m*.

anchor ['æŋkə*] *n* ancre *f* // *vi* (*also*: to drop ~) jeter l'ancre, mouiller // *vt* mettre à l'ancre; to weigh ~ lever l'ancre.

anchovy ['æntʃəvɪ] *n* anchois *m*.

ancient ['eɪnʃənt] *a* ancien(ne), antique; (*fig*) d'un âge vénérable, antique.

ancillary [æn'sɪlərɪ] *a* auxiliaire.

and [ænd] *cj* et; ~ so on et ainsi de suite; try ~ come tâchez de venir; he talked ~ talked il n'a pas arrêté de parler; better ~ better de mieux en mieux.

anew [ə'nju:] *ad* à nouveau.

angel ['eɪndʒəl] *n* ange *m*.

anger ['æŋgə*] *n* colère *f* // *vt* mettre en colère, irriter.

angina [æn'dʒaɪnə] *n* angine *f* de poitrine.

angle ['æŋgl] *n* angle *m*; from their ~ de leur point de vue; ~r *n* pêcheur/euse à la ligne.

Anglican ['æŋglɪkən] *a, n* anglican(e).

angling ['æŋglɪŋ] *n* pêche *f* à la ligne.

Anglo- ['æŋgləu] *prefix* anglo(-).

angry ['æŋgrɪ] *a* en colère, furieux(euse); to be ~ with sb/at sth être furieux contre qn/de qch; to get ~ se fâcher, se mettre en colère; to make sb ~ mettre qn en colère.

anguish ['æŋgwɪʃ] *n* angoisse *f*.

angular ['æŋgjulə*] *a* anguleux(euse).

animal ['ænɪməl] *n* animal *m* // *a* animal(e).

animate *vt* ['ænɪmeɪt] animer // *a* ['ænɪmɪt] animé(e), vivant(e); ~d *a* animé(e).

aniseed ['ænɪsi:d] *n* anis *m*.

ankle ['æŋkl] *n* cheville *f*; ~ **sock** *n* socquette *f*.

annex *n* ['ænɛks] (*also*: *Brit*: **annexe**) annexe *f* // *vt* [ə'nɛks] annexer.

anniversary [ænɪ'və:sərɪ] *n* anniversaire *m*.

announce [ə'nauns] *vt* annoncer; (*birth, death*) faire part de; ~ment *n* annonce *f*; (*for births etc: in newspaper*) avis *m* de faire-part; (: *letter, card*) faire-part *m*; ~r *n* (*RADIO, TV: between programmes*) speaker/ine; (: *in a programme*) présentateur/trice.

annoy [ə'nɔɪ] *vt* agacer, ennuyer, contrarier; don't get ~ed! ne vous fâchez pas!; ~ance *n* mécontentement *m*, contrariété *f*; ~ing *a* ennuyeux(euse), agaçant(e), contrariant(e).

annual ['ænjuəl] *a* annuel(le) // *n* (*BOT*) plante annuelle; (*book*) album *m*.

annul [ə'nʌl] *vt* annuler; (*law*) abroger.

annum ['ænəm] *n see* **per.**

anonymous [ə'nɔnɪməs] *a* anonyme.

anorak ['ænəræk] *n* anorak *m*.

another [ə'nʌðə*] *a*: ~ **book** (*one more*) un autre livre, encore un livre, un livre de plus; (*a different one*) un autre livre // *pronoun* un(e) autre, encore un(e), un(e) de plus; *see also* **one.**

answer ['ɑ:nsə*] *n* réponse *f*; solution *f* // *vi* répondre // *vt* (*reply to*) répondre à; (*problem*) résoudre; (*prayer*) exaucer; to ~ the phone répondre (au téléphone); in ~ to your letter suite à *or* en réponse à votre lettre; to ~ the bell *or* the door aller *or* venir ouvrir (la porte); to ~ back *vi* répondre, répliquer; to ~ for *vt fus* répondre de, se porter garant de; être responsable de; to ~ to *vt fus* (*description*) répondre *or* correspondre à; ~able *a*: ~able (to sb/for sth) responsable (devant qn/de qch); ~ing

machine n répondeur m automatique.
ant [ænt] n fourmi f.
antagonism [æn'tægənɪzəm] n antagonisme m.
antagonize [æn'tægənaɪz] vt éveiller l'hostilité de, contrarier.
Antarctic [ænt'ɑːktɪk] n: the ~ l'Antarctique m.
antenatal ['æntɪ'neɪtl] a prénatal(e); ~ **clinic** n service m de consultation prénatale.
anthem ['ænθəm] n motet m; **national ~** hymne national.
anthology [æn'θɒlədʒɪ] n anthologie f.
antibiotic ['æntɪbaɪ'ɒtɪk] a, n antibiotique (m).
antibody ['æntɪbɒdɪ] n anticorps m.
anticipate [æn'tɪsɪpeɪt] vt s'attendre à; prévoir; (wishes, request) aller au devant de, devancer.
anticipation [æntɪsɪ'peɪʃən] n attente f.
anticlimax ['æntɪ'klaɪmæks] n réalisation décevante d'un événement que l'on escomptait important, intéressant etc.
anticlockwise ['æntɪ'klɒkwaɪz] a, ad dans le sens inverse des aiguilles d'une montre.
antics ['æntɪks] npl singeries fpl.
antifreeze ['æntɪfriːz] n antigel m.
antihistamine [æntɪ'hɪstəmiːn] n antihistaminique m.
antiquated ['æntɪkweɪtɪd] a vieilli(e), suranné(e), vieillot(te).
antique [æn'tiːk] n objet m d'art ancien, meuble ancien or d'époque, antiquité f // a ancien(ne); (pre-mediaeval) antique; ~ **shop** n magasin m d'antiquités.
anti-Semitism [æntɪ'semɪtɪzəm] n antisémitisme m.
antiseptic [æntɪ'septɪk] a, n antiseptique (m).
antisocial ['æntɪ'səʊʃəl] a peu liant(e), sauvage, insociable; (against society) anti-social(e).
antlers ['æntləz] npl bois mpl, ramure f.
anvil ['ænvɪl] n enclume f.
anxiety [æŋ'zaɪətɪ] n anxiété f; (keenness): ~ **to do** grand désir or impatience f de faire.
anxious ['æŋkʃəs] a anxieux(euse), (très) inquiet(ète); (keen): ~ **to do/that** qui tient beaucoup à faire/à ce que; impatient(e) de faire/que.
any ['enɪ] ♦ a 1 (in questions etc: singular) du, de l', de la; (: plural) des; **have you ~ butter/children/ink?** avez-vous du beurre/des enfants/de l'encre?
2 (with negative) de, d'; **I haven't ~ money/books** je n'ai pas d'argent/de livres
3 (no matter which) n'importe quel(le); **choose ~ book you like** vous pouvez choisir n'importe quel livre
4 (in phrases): **in ~ case** de toute façon; **~ day now** d'un jour à l'autre; **at**

~ moment à tout moment, d'un instant à l'autre; **at ~ rate** en tout cas
♦ pronoun **1** (in questions etc) en; **have you got ~?** est-ce que vous en avez?; **can ~ of you sing?** est-ce que parmi vous il y en a qui chantent?
2 (with negative) en; **I haven't ~** (of them) je n'en ai pas, je n'en ai aucun
3 (no matter which one(s)) n'importe lequel (or laquelle); **take ~ of those books (you like)** vous pouvez prendre n'importe lequel de ces livres
♦ ad **1** (in questions etc): **do you want ~ more soup/sandwiches?** voulez-vous encore de la soupe/des sandwichs?; **are you feeling ~ better?** est-ce que vous vous sentez mieux?
2 (with negative): **I can't hear him ~ more** je ne l'entends plus; **don't wait ~ longer** n'attendez pas plus longtemps.
anybody ['enɪbɒdɪ] pronoun n'importe qui; (in interrogative sentences) quelqu'un; (in negative sentences): **I don't see ~** je ne vois personne.
anyhow ['enɪhaʊ] ad (at any rate) de toute façon, quand même; (haphazard) n'importe comment.
anyone ['enɪwʌn] pronoun = **anybody**.
anything ['enɪθɪŋ] pronoun (see anybody) n'importe quoi; quelque chose; **ne — rien.**
anyway ['enɪweɪ] ad de toute façon.
anywhere ['enɪweə*] ad (see anybody) n'importe où; quelque part; **I don't see him ~** je ne le vois nulle part.
apart [ə'pɑːt] ad (to one side) à part; de côté; à l'écart; (separately) séparément; **with one's legs ~** les jambes écartées; **10 miles ~** à 10 milles l'un de l'autre; **to take ~** démonter; **~ from** prep à part, excepté.
apartheid [ə'pɑːteɪt] n apartheid m.
apartment [ə'pɑːtmənt] n (US) appartement m, logement m; ~ **building** n (US) immeuble m; maison divisée en appartements.
ape [eɪp] n (grand) singe // vt singer.
aperture ['æpətʃjʊə*] n orifice m, ouverture f; (PHOT) ouverture (du diaphragme).
apex ['eɪpeks] n sommet m.
apiece [ə'piːs] ad (for each person) chacun(e).
apologetic [əpɒlə'dʒetɪk] a (tone, letter) d'excuse.
apologize [ə'pɒlədʒaɪz] vi: **to ~ (for sth to sb)** s'excuser (de qch auprès de qn), présenter des excuses (à qn pour qch).
apology [ə'pɒlədʒɪ] n excuses fpl.
apostle [ə'pɒsl] n apôtre m.
apostrophe [ə'pɒstrəfɪ] n apostrophe f.
appalling [ə'pɔːlɪŋ] a épouvantable; (stupidity) consternant(e).
apparatus [æpə'reɪtəs] n appareil m, dispositif m; (in gymnasium) agrès mpl.

apparel [ə'pærl] n (US) habillement m.
apparent [ə'pærənt] a apparent(e); ~**ly**
ad apparemment.
appeal [ə'pi:l] vi (LAW) faire or
interjeter appel // n (LAW) appel m;
(request) prière f; appel m; (charm) attrait m, charme m; **to** ~ **to** for demander
(instamment); implorer; **to** ~ **to** (subj:
person) faire appel à; (subj: thing)
plaire à; **it doesn't** ~ **to me** cela ne
m'attire pas; ~**ing** a (nice) at-
trayant(e); (touching) attendrissant(e).
appear [ə'piə*] vi apparaître, se montrer; (LAW) comparaître; (publication)
paraître, sortir, être publié(e); (seem)
paraître, sembler; **it would** ~ **that** il
semble que; **to** ~ **in Hamlet** jouer dans
Hamlet; **to** ~ **on TV** passer à la télé;
~**ance** n apparition f; parution f; (look,
aspect) apparence f, aspect m.
appease [ə'pi:z] vt apaiser, calmer.
appendicitis [əpendɪ'saɪtɪs] n
appendicite f.
appendix, pl **appendices** [ə'pendiks,
-si:z] n appendice m.
appetite ['æpɪtaɪt] n appétit m.
appetizer ['æpɪtaɪzə*] n amuse-gueule
m.
applaud [ə'plɔ:d] vt, vi applaudir.
applause [ə'plɔ:z] n applaudissements
mpl.
apple ['æpl] n pomme f; ~ **tree** n
pommier m.
appliance [ə'plaɪəns] n appareil m.
applicant ['æplɪkənt] n: ~ (**for**) (post)
candidat/e (à).
application [æplɪ'keɪʃən] n application
f; (for a job, a grant etc) demande f;
candidature f; ~ **form** n formulaire m
de demande.
applied [ə'plaɪd] a appliqué(e).
apply [ə'plaɪ] vt (paint, ointment): **to** ~
(**to**) appliquer (sur); (theory, technique): **to** ~ (**to**) appliquer (à) // vi: **to**
~ **to** (ask) s'adresser à; (be suitable for,
relevant to) s'appliquer à, se rapporter
à; être valable pour; **to** ~ (**for**) (permit,
grant) faire une demande (en vue
d'obtenir); (job) poser sa candidature
(pour), faire une demande d'emploi
(concernant); **to** ~ **the brakes** actionner
les freins, freiner; **to** ~ **o.s.** to s'appliquer à.
appoint [ə'pɔɪnt] vt nommer, engager;
(date, place) fixer, désigner; ~**ment** n
nomination f; rendez-vous m; **to make
an** ~**ment** (**with**) prendre rendez-vous
(avec).
appraisal [ə'preɪzl] n évaluation f.
appreciate [ə'pri:ʃɪeɪt] vt (like) apprécier, faire cas de; être reconnais-
sant(e) de; (assess) évaluer; (be aware
of) comprendre; se rendre compte de //
vi (FINANCE) prendre de la valeur.
appreciation [əpri:ʃɪ'eɪʃən] n ap-

préciation f; reconnaissance f; (COMM)
hausse f, valorisation f.
appreciative [ə'pri:ʃɪətɪv] a (person)
sensible; (comment) élogieux(euse).
apprehensive [æprɪ'hensɪv] a
inquiet(ète), appréhensif(ive).
apprentice [ə'prentɪs] n apprenti m;
~**ship** n apprentissage m.
approach [ə'prəʊtʃ] vi approcher // vt
(come near) approcher de; (ask, apply
to) s'adresser à; (subject, passer-by)
aborder // n approche f; accès m, abord
m; démarche f (auprès de qn); démarche (intellectuelle); ~**able** a accessible.
appropriate a [ə'prəʊprɪɪt] a oppor-
tun(e); qui convient, approprié(e) // vt
[ə'prəʊprɪeɪt] (take) s'approprier.
approval [ə'pru:vəl] n approbation f; **on**
~ (COMM) à l'examen.
approve [ə'pru:v] vt approuver; **to** ~
of vt fus approuver; ~**d school** n
(Brit) centre m d'éducation surveillée.
approximate a [ə'prɒksɪmɪt] ap-
proximatif(ive); ~**ly** ad approximativement.
apricot ['eɪprɪkɔt] n abricot m.
April ['eɪprəl] n avril m; ~ **Fool's Day**
le premier avril.
apron ['eɪprən] n tablier m.
apt [æpt] a (suitable) approprié(e);
(likely): ~ **to do** susceptible de faire;
ayant tendance à faire.
aqualung ['ækwəlʌŋ] n scaphandre m
autonome.
aquarium [ə'kwɛərɪəm] n aquarium
m.
Aquarius [ə'kwɛərɪəs] n le Verseau.
Arab ['ærəb] n Arabe m/f.
Arabian [ə'reɪbɪən] a arabe.
Arabic ['ærəbɪk] a arabe // n arabe m; ~
numerals chiffres mpl arabes.
arbitrary ['ɑ:bɪtrərɪ] a arbitraire.
arbitration [ɑ:bɪ'treɪʃən] n arbitrage m.
arcade [ɑ:'keɪd] n arcade f; (passage
with shops) passage m, galerie f.
arch [ɑ:tʃ] n arche f; (of foot) cambrure
f, voûte f plantaire // vt arquer, cambrer
// a malicieux(euse).
archaeologist [ɑ:kɪ'ɔlədʒɪst] n archéologue m/f.
archaeology [ɑ:kɪ'ɔlədʒɪ] n archéologie
f.
archbishop [ɑ:tʃ'bɪʃəp] n archevêque
m.
arch-enemy ['ɑ:tʃ'enəmɪ] n ennemi m
de toujours or par excellence.
archeology etc [ɑ:kɪ'ɔlədʒɪ] (US) =**archaeology** etc.
archer ['ɑ:tʃə*] n archer m; ~**y** n tir m
à l'arc.
architect ['ɑ:kɪtekt] n architecte m;
~**ure** ['ɑ:kɪtektʃə*] n architecture f.
archives ['ɑ:kaɪvz] npl archives fpl.
archway ['ɑ:tʃweɪ] n voûte f, porche m
voûté or cintré.

Arctic ['ɑ:ktɪk] *a* arctique // *n*: the ~ l'Arctique *m*.

ardent ['ɑ:dənt] *a* fervent(e).

are [ɑ:*] *vb see* **be**.

area ['ɛərɪə] *n* (GEOM) superficie *f*; (*zone*) région *f*; (: *smaller*) secteur *m*.

aren't [ɑ:nt] =**are not**.

Argentina [ɑ:dʒən'ti:nə] *n* Argentine *f*; **Argentinian** [-'tɪnɪən] *a* argentin(e) // *n* Argentin/e.

arguably ['ɑ:gjuəblɪ] *ad*: it is ~ — on peut soutenir que c'est —.

argue ['ɑ:gju:] *vi* (*quarrel*) se disputer; (*reason*) argumenter; **to ~ that** objecter *or* alléguer que, donner comme argument que.

argument ['ɑ:gjumənt] *n* (*reasons*) argument *m*; (*quarrel*) dispute *f*, discussion *f*; (*debate*) discussion *f*, controverse *f*; **~ative** [-'mɛntətɪv] *a* ergoteur(euse), raisonneur(euse).

Aries ['ɛərɪz] *n* le Bélier.

arise, *pt* **arose**, *pp* **arisen** [ə'raɪz, ə'rəuz, ə'rɪzn] *vi* survenir, se présenter; **to ~ from** résulter de.

aristocrat ['ærɪstəkræt] *n* aristocrate *m/f*.

arithmetic [ə'rɪθmətɪk] *n* arithmétique *f*.

ark [ɑ:k] *n*: **Noah's A~** l'Arche *f* de Noé.

arm [ɑ:m] *n* bras *m* // *vt* armer; **~s** *npl* (*weapons*, HERALDRY) armes *fpl*; **~ in ~** bras dessus bras dessous.

armaments ['ɑ:məmənts] *npl* armements *mpl*.

arm: **~chair** *n* fauteuil *m*; **~ed** *a* armé(e); **~ed robbery** *n* vol *m* à main armée.

armour, (US) **armor** ['ɑ:mə*] *n* armure *f*; (*also*: **~-plating**) blindage *m*; (MIL: *tanks*) blindés *mpl*; **~ed car** *n* véhicule blindé; **~y** *n* arsenal *m*.

armpit ['ɑ:mpɪt] *n* aisselle *f*.

armrest ['ɑ:mrɛst] *n* accoudoir *m*.

army ['ɑ:mɪ] *n* armée *f*.

aroma [ə'rəumə] *n* arôme *m*.

arose [ə'rəuz] *pt of* **arise**.

around [ə'raund] *ad* (tout) autour; dans les parages // *prep* autour de; (*fig*: *about*) environ; vers.

arouse [ə'rauz] *vt* (*sleeper*) éveiller; (*curiosity*, *passions*) éveiller, susciter, exciter.

arrange [ə'reɪndʒ] *vt* arranger; (*programme*) arrêter, convenir de; **to ~ to do sth** prévoir de faire qch; **~ment** *n* arrangement *m*; (*plans etc*): **~ments** dispositions *fpl*.

array [ə'reɪ] *n*: **~ of** déploiement *m* or étalage *m* de.

arrears [ə'rɪəz] *npl* arriéré *m*; **to be in ~ with one's rent** devoir un arriéré de loyer.

arrest [ə'rɛst] *vt* arrêter; (*sb's attention*) retenir, attirer // *n* arrestation *f*; **under ~** en état d'arrestation.

arrival [ə'raɪvəl] *n* arrivée *f*; (COMM) arrivage *m*; (*person*) arrivant/e; **new ~** nouveau venu, nouvelle venue.

arrive [ə'raɪv] *vi* arriver.

arrogant ['ærəgənt] *a* arrogant(e).

arrow ['ærəu] *n* flèche *f*.

arse [ɑ:s] *n* (*col!*) cul *m* (*!*).

arson ['ɑ:sn] *n* incendie criminel.

art [ɑ:t] *n* art *m*; (*craft*) métier *m*; **A~s** *npl* (SCOL) les lettres *fpl*.

artefact ['ɑ:tɪfækt] *n* objet fabriqué.

artery ['ɑ:tərɪ] *n* artère *f*.

art gallery *n* musée *m* d'art; (*small and private*) galerie *f* de peinture.

arthritis [ɑ:'θraɪtɪs] *n* arthrite *f*.

artichoke ['ɑ:tɪtʃəuk] *n* artichaut *m*; **Jerusalem ~** topinambour *m*.

article ['ɑ:tɪkl] *n* article *m*; (Brit LAW: *training*): **~s** *npl* ≈stage *m*; **~ of clothing** vêtement *m*.

articulate *a* [ɑ:'tɪkjulɪt] (*person*) qui s'exprime clairement et aisément; (*speech*) bien articulé(e), prononcé(e) clairement // *vi* [ɑ:'tɪkjuleɪt] articuler, parler distinctement; **~d lorry** *n* (Brit) (*camion*) semi-remorque *m*.

artificial [ɑ:tɪ'fɪʃəl] *a* artificiel(le).

artist ['ɑ:tɪst] *n* artiste *m/f*; **~ic** [ɑ:'tɪstɪk] *a* artistique; **~ry** *n* art *m*, talent *m*.

artless ['ɑ:tlɪs] *a* naïf(naïve), simple, ingénu(e).

art school *n* ≈école *f* des beaux-arts.

as [æz] ♦ *cj* **1** (*referring to time*) comme, alors que; à mesure que; **he came in ~ I was leaving** il est arrivé comme je partais; **~ the years went by** à mesure que les années passaient; **~ from tomorrow** à partir de demain

2 (*in comparisons*): **~ big** ~ aussi grand que; **twice ~ big** ~ deux fois plus grand que; **~ much** *or* **many** ~ autant que; **much money/many books** ~ autant d'argent/de livres que; **~ soon** ~ dès que

3 (*since*, *because*) comme, puisque; **he left early, ~ he had to be home by 10** comme il *or* puisqu'il devait être de retour avant 10h il est parti tôt

4 (*referring to manner*, *way*) comme; **do ~ you wish** faites comme vous voudrez

5 (*concerning*): **~ for** *or* **to that** quant à cela, pour ce qui est de cela

6: **~ if** *or* **though** comme si; **he looked ~ if he was ill** il avait l'air d'être malade; *see also* **long, such, well**

♦ *prep*: **he works** ~ **a driver** il travaille comme chauffeur; **~ chairman of the company, he —** en tant que président de la compagnie, il —; **dressed up** ~ **a cowboy** déguisé en cowboy; **he gave me it** ~ **a present** il me l'a offert, il m'en a fait cadeau.

a.s.a.p. *abbr* (=*as soon as possible*) dès

que possible.
ascend [ə'sɛnd] vt gravir.
ascent [ə'sɛnt] n ascension f.
ascertain [æsə'teɪn] vt s'assurer de, vérifier; établir.
ash [æʃ] n (dust) cendre f; (also: ~ tree) frêne m.
ashamed [ə'ʃeɪmd] a honteux(euse), confus(e); to be ~ of avoir honte de.
ashen ['æʃn] a (pale) cendreux(euse), blême.
ashore [ə'ʃɔ:•] ad à terre.
ashtray ['æʃtreɪ] n cendrier m.
Ash Wednesday n mercredi m des cendres.
Asia ['eɪʃə] n Asie f; ~n n Asiatique m/f // a asiatique.
aside [ə'saɪd] ad de côté; à l'écart // n aparté m.
ask [ɑ:sk] vt demander; (invite) inviter; to ~ sb sth/to do sth demander à qn qch/ de faire qch; to ~ sb about sth questionner qn au sujet de qch; se renseigner auprès de qn au sujet de qch; to ~ (sb) a question poser une question (à qn); to ~ sb out to dinner inviter qn au restaurant; to ~ after vt fus demander des nouvelles de; to ~ for vt fus demander.
askance [ə'skɑːns] ad: to look ~ at sb regarder qn de travers or d'un œil désapprobateur.
askew [ə'skju:] ad de travers, de guinguois.
asleep [ə'sli:p] a endormi(e); to be ~ dormir, être endormi; to fall ~ s'endormir.
asparagus [əs'pærəgəs] n asperges fpl.
aspect ['æspɛkt] n aspect m; (direction in which a building etc faces) orientation f, exposition f.
aspersions [əs'pə:ʃənz] npl: to cast ~ on dénigrer.
aspire [əs'paɪə•] vi: to ~ to aspirer à.
aspirin ['æsprɪn] n aspirine f.
ass [æs] n âne m; (col) imbécile m/f; (US col!) cul m (!).
assailant [ə'seɪlənt] n agresseur m; assaillant m.
assassinate [ə'sæsɪneɪt] vt assassiner;
assassination [əsæsɪ'neɪʃən] n assassinat m.
assault [ə'sɔ:lt] n (MIL) assaut m; (gen: attack) agression f // vt attaquer; (sexually) violenter.
assemble [ə'sɛmbl] vt assembler // vi s'assembler, se rassembler.
assembly [ə'sɛmblɪ] n (meeting) rassemblement m; (construction) assemblage m; ~ line n chaîne f de montage.
assent [ə'sɛnt] n assentiment m, consentement m.
assert [ə'sə:t] vt affirmer, déclarer; établir.
assess [ə'sɛs] vt évaluer, estimer; (tax,

damages, établir or fixer le montant de; (property etc: for tax) calculer la valeur imposable de; ~ment n évaluation f, estimation f; ~or n expert m (en matière d'impôt et d'assurance).
asset ['æsɛt] n avantage m, atout m; ~s npl capital m; avoir(s) m(pl); actif m.
assign [ə'saɪn] vt (date) fixer, arrêter; (task): to ~ sth to assigner qch à; (resources): to ~ sth to affecter qch à; (cause, meaning): to ~ sth to attribuer qch à; ~ment n tâche f, mission f.
assist [ə'sɪst] vt aider, assister; secourir; ~ance n aide f, assistance f; secours mpl; ~ant n assistant/e, adjoint/e; (Brit: also: shop ~ant) vendeur/euse.
associate a, n [ə'səuʃɪɪt] associé(e) // vb [ə'səuʃɪeɪt] vt associer // vi: to ~ with sb fréquenter qn.
association [əsəusɪ'eɪʃən] n association f.
assorted [ə'sɔ:tɪd] a assorti(e).
assortment [ə'sɔ:tmənt] n assortiment m.
assume [ə'sju:m] vt supposer; (responsibilities etc) assumer; (attitude, name) prendre, adopter; ~d name n nom m d'emprunt.
assumption [ə'sʌmpʃən] n supposition f, hypothèse f.
assurance [ə'ʃuərəns] n assurance f.
assure [ə'ʃuə•] vt assurer.
astern [ə'stə:n] ad à l'arrière.
asthma ['æsmə] n asthme m.
astonish [ə'stɔnɪʃ] vt étonner, stupéfier; ~ment n étonnement m.
astound [ə'staund] vt stupéfier, sidérer.
astray [ə'streɪ] ad: to go ~ s'égarer; (fig) quitter le droit chemin.
astride [ə'straɪd] ad à cheval // prep à cheval sur.
astrology [əs'trɔlədʒɪ] n astrologie f.
astronaut ['æstrənɔ:t] n astronaute m/f.
astronomy [əs'trɔnəmɪ] n astronomie f.
astute [əs'tju:t] a astucieux(euse).
asylum [ə'saɪləm] n asile m.
at [æt] prep
1 (referring to position, direction) à; ~ the top au sommet; ~ home/school à la maison or chez soi/à l'école; ~ the baker's à la boulangerie, chez le boulanger; to look ~ sth regarder qch
2 (referring to time) à; ~ 4 o'clock à 4 heures; ~ Christmas à Noël; ~ night la nuit; ~ times par moments, parfois
3 (referring to rates, speed etc) à; ~ £1 a kilo une livre le kilo; two ~ a time deux à la fois; ~ 50 km/h à 50 km/h
4 (referring to manner): ~ a stroke d'un seul coup; ~ peace en paix
5 (referring to activity): to be ~ work être à l'œuvre, travailler; to play ~ cowboys jouer aux cowboys; to be good ~ sth être bon en qch

6 (referring to cause): shocked/ surprised/annoyed ~ sth choqué par/ étonné de/agacé par qch; I went ~ his suggestion j'y suis allé sur son conseil.

ate [eɪt] pt of **eat**.

atheist ['eɪθɪɪst] n athée m/f.

Athens ['æθɪnz] n Athènes.

athlete ['æθliːt] n athlète m/f.

athletic [æθ'letɪk] a athlétique; ~s n athlétisme m.

Atlantic [ət'læntɪk] a atlantique // n: the ~ (Ocean) l'Atlantique m, l'océan m Atlantique.

atlas ['ætləs] n atlas m.

atmosphere ['ætməsfɪə*] n atmosphère f.

atom ['ætəm] n atome m; ~ic [ə'tɒmɪk] a atomique; ~(ic) bomb n bombe f atomique; ~izer ['ætəmaɪzə*] n atomiseur m.

atone [ə'təun] vi: to ~ for expier, racheter.

atrocious [ə'trəuʃəs] a (very bad) atroce, exécrable.

attach [ə'tætʃ] vt (gen) attacher; (document, letter) joindre; (employee, troops) affecter; to be ~ed to sb/sth (to like) être attaché à qn/qch.

attaché case [ə'tæʃeɪ-] n mallette f, attaché-case m.

attachment [ə'tætʃmənt] n (tool) accessoire m; (love): ~ (to) affection f (pour), attachement m (à).

attack [ə'tæk] vt attaquer; (task etc) s'attaquer à // n attaque f; (also: heart ~) crise f cardiaque.

attain [ə'teɪn] vt (also: to ~ to) parvenir à, atteindre; acquérir; ~ments npl connaissances fpl, résultats mpl.

attempt [ə'tempt] n tentative f // vt essayer, tenter; to make an ~ on sb's life attenter à la vie de qn.

attend [ə'tend] vt (course) suivre; (meeting, talk) assister à; (school, church) aller à, fréquenter; (patient) soigner, s'occuper de; to ~ to vt fus (needs, affairs etc) s'occuper de; (customer) s'occuper de, servir; ~ance n (being present) présence f; (people present) assistance f; ~ant n employé/ e; gardien/ne // a concomitant(e), qui accompagne or s'ensuit.

attention [ə'tenʃən] n attention f; ~! (MIL) garde-à-vous!; for the ~ of (ADMIN) à l'attention de.

attentive [ə'tentɪv] a attentif(ive); (kind) prévenant(e).

attic ['ætɪk] n grenier m, combles mpl.

attitude ['ætɪtjuːd] n attitude f, manière f; pose f, maintien m.

attorney [ə'təːnɪ] n (lawyer) avoué m; (having proxy) mandataire m; A~ General n (Brit) ≈procureur général; (US) ≈garde m des Sceaux, ministre m de la Justice.

attract [ə'trækt] vt attirer; ~ion [ə'trækʃən] n (gen pl: pleasant things) attraction f, attrait m; (PHYSICS) attraction f; (fig: towards sth) attirance f; ~ive a séduisant(e), attrayant(e).

attribute n ['ætrɪbjuːt] attribut m // vt [ə'trɪbjuːt]: to ~ sth to attribuer qch à.

attrition [ə'trɪʃən] n: war of ~ guerre f d'usure.

aubergine ['əubəʒiːn] n aubergine f.

auction ['ɔːkʃən] n (also: sale by ~) vente f aux enchères // vt (also: to sell by ~) vendre aux enchères; (also: to put up for ~) mettre aux enchères; ~eer [-'nɪə*] n commissaire-priseur m.

audience ['ɔːdɪəns] n (people) assistance f, auditoire m; auditeurs mpl; spectateurs mpl; (interview) audience f.

audio-visual [ɔːdɪəu'vɪzjuəl] a audio-visuel(le); ~ aids npl supports or moyens audiovisuels.

audit ['ɔːdɪt] vt vérifier, apurer.

audition [ɔː'dɪʃən] n audition f.

auditor ['ɔːdɪtə*] n vérificateur m des comptes.

augur ['ɔːgə*] vi: it ~s well c'est bon signe or de bon augure.

August ['ɔːgəst] n août m.

aunt [ɑːnt] n tante f; ~ie, ~y n diminutive of **aunt**.

au pair ['əu'pɛə*] n (also: ~ girl) jeune fille f au pair.

aura ['ɔːrə] n atmosphère f.

auspicious [ɔːs'pɪʃəs] a de bon augure, propice.

austerity [ɔ'sterɪtɪ] n austérité f.

Australia [ɔs'treɪlɪə] n Australie f; ~n a australien(ne) // n Australien/ne.

Austria ['ɔstrɪə] n Autriche f; ~n a autrichien(ne) // n Autrichien/ne.

authentic [ɔː'θentɪk] a authentique.

author ['ɔːθə*] n auteur m.

authoritarian [ɔːθɒrɪ'tɛərɪən] a autoritaire.

authoritative [ɔː'θɒrɪtətɪv] a (account) digne de foi; (study, treatise) qui fait autorité; (manner) autoritaire.

authority [ɔː'θɒrɪtɪ] n autorité f; (permission) autorisation (formelle); the authorities npl les autorités fpl, l'administration f.

authorize ['ɔːθəraɪz] vt autoriser.

auto ['ɔːtəu] n (US) auto f, voiture f.

autobiography [ɔːtəbaɪ'ɒgrəfɪ] n autobiographie f.

autograph ['ɔːtəgrɑːf] n autographe m // vt signer, dédicacer.

automatic [ɔːtə'mætɪk] a automatique // n (gun) automatique m; (Brit AUT) voiture f à transmission automatique; ~ally ad automatiquement.

automation [ɔːtə'meɪʃən] n automatisation f.

automobile ['ɔːtəməbiːl] n (US) automobile f.

autonomy [ɔːˈtɒnəmɪ] *n* autonomie *f*.
autumn [ˈɔːtəm] *n* automne *m*.
auxiliary [ɔːgˈzɪlɪərɪ] *a*, *n* auxiliaire *(m/ f)*.
Av. *abbr of* **avenue**.
avail [əˈveɪl] *vt*: to ~ o.s. of user de; profiter de // *n*: to no ~ sans résultat, en vain, en pure perte.
available [əˈveɪləbl] *a* disponible.
avalanche [ˈævəlɑːnʃ] *n* avalanche *f*.
Ave. *abbr of* **avenue**.
avenge [əˈvɛndʒ] *vt* venger.
avenue [ˈævənjuː] *n* avenue *f*.
average [ˈævərɪdʒ] *n* moyenne *f* // *a* moyen(ne) // *vt* (*a certain figure*) atteindre or faire *etc* en moyenne; on ~ en moyenne; **to ~ out** *vi*: to ~ out at représenter en moyenne, donner une moyenne de.
averse [əˈvɜːs] *a*: to be ~ to sth/doing éprouver une forte répugnance envers qch/à faire.
avert [əˈvɜːt] *vt* prévenir, écarter; (*one's eyes*) détourner.
aviary [ˈeɪvɪərɪ] *n* volière *f*.
avocado [ævəˈkɑːdəu] *n* (*also: Brit* ~ **pear**) avocat *m*.
avoid [əˈvɔɪd] *vt* éviter.
await [əˈweɪt] *vt* attendre.
awake [əˈweɪk] *a* éveillé(e); (*fig*) en éveil // *vb* (*pt* **awoke**, *pp* **awoken**, **awaked**) *vt* éveiller // *vi* s'éveiller; to be ~ être réveillé(e); ne pas dormir; **~ning** [əˈweɪknɪŋ] *n* réveil *m*.
award [əˈwɔːd] *n* récompense *f*, prix *m* // *vt* (*prize*) décerner; (*LAW: damages*) accorder.
aware [əˈwɛə*] *a*: ~ of (*conscious*) conscient(e) de; (*informed*) au courant de; **to become** ~ **of** avoir conscience de, prendre conscience de; se rendre compte de; **~ness** *n* le fait d'être conscient, au courant *etc*.
awash [əˈwɒʃ] *a* recouvert(e) (d'eau); ~ with inondé(e) de.
away [əˈweɪ] *a*, *ad* (au) loin; absent(e); two kilometres ~ à (une distance de) deux kilomètres, à deux kilomètres de distance; two hours ~ by car à deux heures de voiture *or* de route; the holiday was two weeks ~ il restait deux semaines jusqu'aux vacances; ~ **from** loin de; he's ~ **for a week** il est parti (pour) une semaine; **to take** ~ *vt* emporter; **to pedal/work/laugh** *etc* ~ *la particule indique la constance et l'énergie de l'action*: il pédalait *etc* tant qu'il pouvait; **to fade** *etc* ~ *la particule renforce l'idée de la disparition, l'éloignement*; ~ **game** *n* (*SPORT*) match *m* à l'extérieur.
awe [ɔː] *n* respect mêlé de crainte, effroi mêlé d'admiration; **~-inspiring**, **~some** *a* impressionnant(e).
awful [ˈɔːfəl] *a* affreux(euse); **~ly** *ad*

(*very*) terriblement, vraiment.
awhile [əˈwaɪl] *ad* un moment, quelque temps.
awkward [ˈɔːkwəd] *a* (*clumsy*) gauche, maladroit(e); (*inconvenient*) malaisé(e), d'emploi malaisé, peu pratique; (*embarrassing*) gênant(e), délicat(e).
awning [ˈɔːnɪŋ] *n* (*of tent*) auvent *m*; (*of shop*) store *m*; (*of hotel etc*) marquise *f* (de toile).
awoke, awoken [əˈwəuk, -kən] *pt, pp of* **awake**.
awry [əˈraɪ] *ad*, *a* de travers; **to go** ~ mal tourner.
axe, (*US*) **ax** [æks] *n* hache *f* // *vt* (*employee*) renvoyer; (*project etc*) abandonner; (*jobs*) supprimer.
axis, *pl* **axes** [ˈæksɪs, -siːz] *n* axe *m*.
axle [ˈæksl] *n* (*also:* ~-**tree**) essieu *m*.
ay(e) [aɪ] *excl* (*yes*) oui.

B

B [biː] *n* (*MUS*) si *m*.
B.A. *abbr see* **bachelor**.
baby [ˈbeɪbɪ] *n* bébé *m*; ~ **carriage** *n* (*US*) voiture *f* d'enfant; **~-sit** *vi* garder les enfants; **~-sitter** *n* baby-sitter *m/f*.
bachelor [ˈbætʃələ*] *n* célibataire *m*; B~ **of Arts/Science** (**B.A./B.Sc.**) ≈ licencié/e ès or en lettres/sciences.
back [bæk] *n* (*of person, horse*) dos *m*; (*of hand*) dos, revers *m*; (*of house*) derrière *m*; (*of car, train*) arrière *m*; (*of chair*) dossier *m*; (*of page*) verso *m*; (*FOOTBALL*) arrière *m* // *vt* (*candidate: also:* ~ **up**) soutenir, appuyer; (*horse: at races*) parier *or* miser sur; (*car*) (faire) reculer // *vi* reculer; (*car etc*) faire marche arrière // *a* (*in compounds*) de derrière, à l'arrière; ~ **seats/wheels** (*AUT*) sièges *mpl*/roues *fpl* arrière; ~ **payments/rent** arriéré *m* de paiements/ loyer // *ad* (*not forward*) en arrière; (*returned*): he's ~ il est rentré, il est de retour; he ran ~ il est revenu en courant; (*restitution*): **throw the ball** ~ renvoie la balle; **can I have it** ~? puis-je le ravoir?; (*again*): he called ~ il a rappelé; **to** ~ **down** vi rabattre de ses prétentions; **to** ~ **out** *vi* (*of promise*) se dédire; **to** ~ **up** *vt* (*candidate etc*) soutenir, appuyer; (*COMPUT*) sauvegarder; **~bencher** *n* (*Brit*) membre du parlement sans portefeuille; **~bone** *n* colonne vertébrale, épine dorsale; **~-cloth** *n* toile *f* de fond; **~date** *vt* (*letter*) antidater; **~dated** pay rise augmentation *f* avec effet rétroactif; **~drop** *n* = **~-cloth**; **~fire** *vi* (*AUT*) pétarader; (*plans*) mal tourner; **~ground** *n* arrière-plan *m*; (*of events*) situation *f*, conjoncture *f*; (*basic knowledge*) éléments *mpl* de base;

(*experience*) formation *f*; family ~**ground** milieu familial; ~**hand** *n* (*TENNIS: also:* ~**hand stroke**) revers *m*; ~**handed** *a* (*fig*) déloyal(e); équivoque; ~**hander** *n* (*Brit: bribe*) pot-de-vin *m*; ~**ing** *n* (*fig*) soutien *m*, appui *m*; ~**lash** *n* contre-coup *m*, répercussion *f*; ~**log** *n:* ~**log of work** travail *m* en retard; ~ **number** *n* (*of magazine etc*) vieux numéro; ~**pack** *n* sac *m* à dos; ~ **pay** *n* rappel *m* de salaire; ~**side** *n* (*col*) derrière *m*, postérieur *m*; ~**stage** *ad* derrière la scène, dans la coulisse; ~**stroke** *n* dos crawlé; ~**up** *a* (*train, plane*) supplémentaire, de réserve; (*COMPUT*) de sauvegarde // *n* (*support*) appui *m*, soutien *m*; (*also:* ~**up file**) sauvegarde *f*; ~**ward** *a* (*movement*) en arrière; (*person, country*) arriéré(e); attardé(e); ~**wards** *ad* (*move, go*) en arrière; (*read a list*) à l'envers, à rebours; (*fall*) à la renverse; (*walk*) à reculons; ~**water** *n* (*fig*) coin reculé; bled perdu; ~**yard** *n* arrière-cour *f*.

bacon ['beɪkən] *n* bacon *m*, lard *m*.

bad [bæd] *a* mauvais(e); (*child*) vilain(e); (*meat, food*) gâté(e), avarié(e); his ~ **leg** sa jambe malade; **to go** ~ (*meat, food*) se gâter; (*milk*) tourner.

bade [bæd] *pt of* **bid**.

badge [bædʒ] *n* insigne *m*; (*of policeman*) plaque *f*.

badger ['bædʒə*] *n* blaireau *m*.

badly ['bædlɪ] *ad* (*work, dress etc*) mal; ~ **wounded** grièvement blessé; **he needs it** ~ il en a absolument besoin; ~ **off** *a, ad* dans la gêne.

badminton ['bædmɪntən] *n* badminton *m*.

bad-tempered ['bæd'tɛmpəd] *a* ayant mauvais caractère; de mauvaise humeur.

baffle ['bæfl] *vt* (*puzzle*) déconcerter.

bag [bæg] *n* sac *m*; (*of hunter*) gibecière *f*; chasse *f* // *vt* (*col: take*) empocher; s'approprier; ~**s of** (*col: lots of*) des masses de; ~**gage** *n* bagages *mpl*; ~**gy** *a* avachi(e), qui fait des poches; ~**pipes** *npl* cornemuse *f*.

bail [beɪl] *n* caution *f* // *vt* (*prisoner: also:* **grant** ~ **to**) mettre en liberté sous caution; (*boat: also:* ~ **out**) écoper; **on** ~ (*prisoner*) sous caution; **to** ~ **out** *vt* (*prisoner*) payer la caution de; *see also* **bale**.

bailiff ['beɪlɪf] *n* huissier *m*.

bait [beɪt] *n* appât *m* // *vt* appâter; (*fig*) tourmenter.

bake [beɪk] *vt* (faire) cuire au four // *vi* cuire (au four); faire de la pâtisserie; ~**d beans** *npl* haricots blancs à la sauce tomate; ~**r** *n* boulanger *m*; ~**ry** *n* boulangerie *f*; boulangerie industrielle; **baking** *n* cuisson *f*.

balance ['bæləns] *n* équilibre *m*; (*COMM: sum*) solde *m*; (*scales*) balance *f* // *vt* mettre *or* faire tenir en équilibre; (*pros and cons*) peser; (*budget*) équilibrer; (*account*) balancer; (*compensate*) compenser, contrebalancer; ~ **of trade/payments** balance commerciale/des comptes *or* paiements; ~**d** *a* (*personality, diet*) équilibré(e); ~ **sheet** *n* bilan *m*.

balcony ['bælkənɪ] *n* balcon *m*.

bald [bɔːld] *a* chauve; (*tyre*) lisse.

bale [beɪl] *n* balle *f*, ballot *m*; **to** ~ **out** *vi* (*of a plane*) sauter en parachute.

baleful ['beɪful] *a* funeste, maléfique.

ball [bɔːl] *n* boule *f*; (*football*) ballon *m*; (*for tennis, golf*) balle *f*; (*dance*) bal *m*.

ballast ['bæləst] *n* lest *m*.

ball bearings *npl* roulement *m* à billes.

ballerina [bælə'riːnə] *n* ballerine *f*.

ballet ['bæleɪ] *n* ballet *m*; (*art*) danse *f* (classique).

balloon [bə'luːn] *n* ballon *m*; (*in comic strip*) bulle *f*.

ballot ['bælət] *n* scrutin *m*.

ball-point pen ['bɔːlpɔɪnt-] *n* stylo *m* à bille.

ballroom ['bɔːlrum] *n* salle *f* de bal.

balm [bɑːm] *n* baume *m*.

ban [bæn] *n* interdiction *f* // *vt* interdire.

banana [bə'nɑːnə] *n* banane *f*.

band [bænd] *n* bande *f*; (*at a dance*) orchestre *m*; (*MIL*) musique *f*, fanfare *f*; **to** ~ **together** *vi* se liguer.

bandage ['bændɪdʒ] *n* bandage *m*, pansement *m*.

bandaid ['bændeɪd] *n* (*US*) pansement adhésif.

bandwagon ['bændwægən] *n:* **to jump on the** ~ (*fig*) monter dans *or* prendre le train en marche.

bandy ['bændɪ] *vt* (*jokes, insults*) échanger.

bandy-legged ['bændɪ'lɛgɪd] *a* aux jambes arquées.

bang [bæŋ] *n* détonation *f*; (*of door*) claquement *m*; (*blow*) coup (violent) // *vt* frapper (violemment); (*door*) claquer // *vi* détoner; claquer.

bangle ['bæŋgl] *n* bracelet *m*.

bangs [bæŋz] *npl* (*US: fringe*) frange *f*.

banish ['bænɪʃ] *vt* bannir.

banister(s) ['bænɪstə(z)] *n(pl)* rampe *f* (d'escalier).

bank [bæŋk] *n* banque *f*; (*of river, lake*) bord *m*, rive *f*; (*of earth*) talus *m*, remblai *m* // *vi* (*AVIAT*) virer sur l'aile; **to** ~ **on** *vt fus* miser *or* tabler sur; ~ **account** *n* compte *m* en banque; ~ **card** *n* carte *f* d'identité bancaire; ~**er** *n* banquier *m*; ~**er's card** *n* (*Brit*) = ~ **card**; **B**~ **holiday** *n* (*Brit*) jour férié (*où les banques sont fermées*); ~**ing** *n* opérations *fpl* bancaires; profession *f* de banquier; ~**note** *n* billet *m* de banque;

~ **rate** n taux m de l'escompte.

bankrupt ['bæŋkrʌpt] a en faillite; **to go ~** faire faillite; **~cy** n faillite f.

bank statement n relevé m de compte.

banner ['bænə*] n bannière f.

baptism ['bæptɪzəm] n baptême m.

bar [bɑ:*] n barre f; (of window etc) barreau m; (of chocolate) tablette f, plaque f; (fig) obstacle m; mesure f d'exclusion; (pub) bar m; (counter: in pub) comptoir m, bar; (MUS) mesure f // vt (road) barrer; (window) munir de barreaux; (person) exclure; (activity) interdire; **~ of soap** savonnette f; **the B~** (LAW) le barreau; **behind ~s** (prisoner) sous les verrous; **~ none** sans exception.

barbaric [bɑ:'bærɪk] a barbare.

barbecue ['bɑ:bɪkju:] n barbecue m.

barbed wire ['bɑ:bd-] n fil m de fer barbelé.

barber ['bɑ:bə*] n coiffeur m (pour hommes).

bar code n (on goods) code m à barres.

bare [bɛə*] a nu(e) // vt mettre à nu, dénuder; (teeth) montrer; **~back** ad à cru, sans selle; **~faced** a impudent(e), effronté(e); **~foot** a, ad nu-pieds, (les) pieds nus; **~ly** ad à peine.

bargain ['bɑ:gɪn] n (transaction) marché m; (good buy) affaire f, occasion f // vi (haggle) marchander; (trade) négocier, traiter; **into the ~** par-dessus le marché; **to ~ for** vt fus: he got more than he **~ed** for il ne s'attendait pas à un coup pareil.

barge [bɑ:dʒ] n péniche f; **to ~ in** vi (walk in) faire irruption; (interrupt talk) intervenir mal à propos; **to ~ into** vt fus rentrer dans.

bark [bɑ:k] n (of tree) écorce f; (of dog) aboiement m // vi aboyer.

barley ['bɑ:lɪ] n orge f.

barmaid ['bɑ:meɪd] n serveuse f (de bar), barmaid f.

barman ['bɑ:mən] n serveur m (de bar), barman m.

barn [bɑ:n] n grange f.

barometer [bə'rɒmɪtə*] n baromètre m.

baron ['bærən] n baron m; **~ess** n baronne f.

barracks ['bærəks] npl caserne f.

barrage ['bærɑ:ʒ] n (MIL) tir m de barrage; (dam) barrage m; (fig) pluie f.

barrel ['bærəl] n tonneau m; (of gun) canon m.

barren ['bærən] a stérile; (hills) aride.

barricade [bærɪ'keɪd] n barricade f.

barrier ['bærɪə*] n barrière f.

barring ['bɑ:rɪŋ] prep sauf.

barrister ['bærɪstə*] n (Brit) avocat (plaidant).

barrow ['bærəu] n (cart) charrette f à bras.

bartender ['bɑ:tɛndə*] n (US) serveur

m (de bar), barman m.

barter ['bɑ:tə*] vt: **to ~ sth for** échanger qch contre.

base [beɪs] n base f // vt: **to ~ sth on** baser or fonder qch sur // a vil(e), bas(se).

baseball ['beɪsbɔ:l] n base-ball m.

basement ['beɪsmənt] n sous-sol m.

bases ['beɪsi:z] npl of **basis**; ['beɪsɪz] npl of **base**.

bash [bæʃ] vt (col) frapper, cogner.

bashful ['bæʃful] a timide; modeste.

basic ['beɪsɪk] a fondamental(e), de base; réduit(e) au minimum, rudimentaire; **~ally** [-lɪ] ad fondamentalement, à la base; en fait, au fond.

basil ['bæzl] n basilic m.

basin ['beɪsn] n (vessel, also GEO) cuvette f, bassin m; (also: **wash~**) lavabo m.

basis, pl **bases** ['beɪsɪs, -si:z] n base f.

bask [bɑ:sk] vi: **to ~ in the sun** se chauffer au soleil.

basket ['bɑ:skɪt] n corbeille f; (with handle) panier m; **~ball** n basket-ball m.

bass [beɪs] n (MUS) basse f.

bassoon [bə'su:n] n basson m.

bastard ['bɑ:stəd] n enfant naturel(le), bâtard/e; (col!) salaud m (!).

bat [bæt] n chauve-souris f; (for baseball etc) batte f; (Brit: for table tennis) raquette f // vt: he didn't **~ an eyelid** il n'a pas sourcillé or bronché.

batch [bætʃ] n (of bread) fournée f; (of papers) liasse f.

bated ['beɪtɪd] a: **with ~ breath** en retenant son souffle.

bath [bɑ:θ, pl bɑ:ðz] n see also **baths**; bain m; (bathtub) baignoire f // vt baigner, donner un bain à; **to have a ~** prendre un bain.

bathe [beɪð] vi se baigner // vt baigner.

bathing ['beɪðɪŋ] n baignade f; **~ cap** n bonnet m de bain; **~ costume**, (US) **~ suit** n maillot m (de bain).

bath: ~robe n peignoir m de bain; **~room** n salle f de bains.

baths [bɑ:ðz] npl établissement m de bains(-douches).

bath towel n serviette f de bain.

baton ['bætən] n bâton m; (MUS) baguette f; (club) matraque f.

batter ['bætə*] vt battre // n pâte f à frire; **~ed** a (hat, pan) cabossé(e).

battery ['bætərɪ] n batterie f; (of torch) pile f.

battle ['bætl] n bataille f, combat m // vi se battre, lutter; **~field** n champ m de bataille; **~ship** n cuirassé m.

bawdy ['bɔ:dɪ] a paillard(e).

bawl [bɔ:l] vi hurler, brailler.

bay [beɪ] n (of sea) baie f; **to hold sb at ~** tenir qn à distance or en échec.

bay window n baie vitrée.

bazaar [bə'zɑ:*] *n* bazar *m*; vente *f* de charité.

b. & b. B. & B. *abbr see* **bed.**

BBC *n abbr* (= *British Broadcasting Corporation*) office de la radiodiffusion et télévision britannique.

B.C. *ad abbr* (= *before Christ*) av. J.C.

be [bi:], *pt* **was, were,** *pp* **been** ♦ *auxiliary vb* **1** (*with present participle: forming continuous tenses*): **what are you doing?** que faites-vous?; **they're coming tomorrow** ils viennent demain; **I've been waiting for you for 2 hours** je t'attends depuis 2 heures

2 (*with pp: forming passives*) être; **to ~ killed** être tué(e); **he was nowhere to ~ seen** on ne le voyait nulle part

3 (*in tag questions*): **it was fun, wasn't it?** c'était drôle, n'est-ce pas?; **she's back, is she?** elle est rentrée, n'est-ce pas *or* alors?

4 (+ *to + infinitive*): **the house is to ~ sold** la maison doit être vendue; **he's not to open it** il ne doit pas l'ouvrir

♦ *vb + complement* **1** (*gen*) être; **I'm English** je suis anglais(e); **I'm tired** je suis fatigué(e); **I'm hot/cold** j'ai chaud/froid; **I'm a doctor** il est médecin; **2 and 2 are 4** 2 et 2 font 4

2 (*of health*) aller; **how are you?** comment allez-vous?; **I'm better now** je vais mieux maintenant; **he's very ill** il est très malade

3 (*of age*) avoir; **how old are you?** quel âge avez-vous?; **I'm sixteen (years old)** j'ai seize ans

4 (*cost*) coûter; **how much was the meal?** combien a coûté le repas?; **that'll ~ £5, please** ça fera 5 livres, s'il vous plaît

♦ *vi* **1** (*exist, occur etc*) être, exister; **the best singer that ever was** le meilleur chanteur qui ait jamais existé; **~ that as it may** quoi qu'il en soit; **so ~ it** soit

2 (*referring to place*) être, se trouver; **I won't ~ here tomorrow** je ne serai pas là demain; **Edinburgh is in Scotland** Édimbourg est *or* se trouve en Écosse

3 (*referring to movement*) aller; **where have you been?** où êtes-vous allé(s)?

♦ *impersonal vb* **1** (*referring to time, distance*) être; **it's 5 o'clock** il est 5 heures; **it's the 28th of April** c'est le 28 avril; **it's 10 km to the village** le village est à 10 km

2 (*referring to the weather*) faire; **it's too hot/cold** il fait trop chaud/froid; **it's windy** il y a du vent

3 (*emphatic*): **it's me/the postman** c'est moi/le facteur.

beach [bi:tʃ] *n* plage *f* // *vt* échouer.

beacon ['bi:kən] *n* (*lighthouse*) fanal *m*; (*marker*) balise *f*.

bead [bi:d] *n* perle *f*.

beak [bi:k] *n* bec *m*.

beaker ['bi:kə*] *n* gobelet *m*.

beam [bi:m] *n* poutre *f*; (*of light*) rayon *m* // *vi* rayonner.

bean [bi:n] *n* haricot *m*; (*of coffee*) grain *m*; **runner ~** haricot *m* (à rames); **broad ~** fève *f*; **~sprouts** *npl* germes *mpl* de soja.

bear [bɛə*] *n* ours *m* // *vb* (*pt* **bore,** *pp* **borne**) *vt* porter; (*endure*) supporter // *vi*: **to ~ right/left** obliquer à droite/gauche, se diriger vers la droite/gauche; **to ~ out** *vt* corroborer, confirmer; **to ~ up** *vi* (*person*) tenir le coup.

beard [bɪəd] *n* barbe *f*.

bearer ['bɛərə*] *n* porteur *m*.

bearing ['bɛərɪŋ] *n* maintien *m*, allure *f*; (*connection*) rapport *m*; **~s** *npl* (*also:* **ball ~s**) roulement *m* (à billes); **to take a ~** faire le point; **to find one's ~s** s'orienter.

beast [bi:st] *n* bête *f*; **~ly** *a* infect(e).

beat [bi:t] *n* battement *m*; (*MUS*) temps *m*, mesure *f*; (*of policeman*) ronde *f* // *vt* (*pt* **beat,** *pp* **beaten**) battre; **off the ~en track** hors des chemins *or* sentiers battus; **to ~ time** battre la mesure; **~ it!** (*col*) fiche(-moi) le camp!; **to ~ off** *vt* repousser; **to ~ up** *vt* (*col: person*) tabasser; (*eggs*) battre; **~ing** *n* raclée *f*.

beautiful ['bju:tɪful] *a* beau(belle); **~ly** *ad* admirablement.

beauty ['bju:tɪ] *n* beauté *f*; **~ salon** *n* institut *m* de beauté; **~ spot** *n* grain *m* de beauté; (*Brit TOURISM*) site naturel (d'une grande beauté).

beaver ['bi:və*] *n* castor *m*.

became [bɪ'keɪm] *pt of* **become.**

because [bɪ'kɔz] *cj* parce que; **~ of** *prep* à cause de.

beck [bɛk] *n*: **to be at sb's ~ and call** être à l'entière disposition de qn.

beckon ['bɛkən] *vt* (*also:* **~ to**) faire signe (de venir) à.

become [bɪ'kʌm] *vt* (*irg: like* **come**) devenir; **to ~ thin** maigrir.

becoming [bɪ'kʌmɪŋ] *a* (*behaviour*) convenable, bienséant(e); (*clothes*) seyant(e).

bed [bɛd] *n* lit *m*; (*of flowers*) parterre *m*; (*of coal, clay*) couche *f*; **to go to ~** aller se coucher; **single ~** lit à une place; **double ~** grand lit; **~ and breakfast (b. & b.)** *n* (*terms*) chambre et petit déjeuner; **~clothes** *npl* couvertures *fpl* et draps *mpl*; **~ding** *n* literie *f*.

bedlam ['bɛdləm] *n* chahut *m*, cirque *m*.

bedraggled [bɪ'drægld] *a* dépenaillé(e), les vêtements en désordre.

bed: ~ridden *a* cloué(e) au lit; **~room** *n* chambre *f* (à coucher); **~side** *n*: **at sb's ~side** au chevet de qn; **~sit(ter)** *n* (*Brit*) chambre meublée, studio *m*;

~**spread** n couvre-lit m, dessus-de-lit m; ~**time** n heure f du coucher.

bee [bi:] n abeille f.

beech [bi:tʃ] n hêtre m.

beef [bi:f] n bœuf m; **roast** ~ rosbif m; ~**burger** n hamburger m; ~**eater** n hallebardier de la Tour de Londres.

beehive ['bi:haɪv] n ruche f.

beeline ['bi:laɪn] n: **to make a** ~ **for** se diriger tout droit vers.

been [bi:n] pp of **be**.

beer [bɪə*] n bière f.

beetle ['bi:tl] n scarabée m.

beetroot ['bi:tru:t] n (Brit) betterave f.

before [bɪ'fɔ:*] prep (in time) avant; (in space) devant // cj avant que + sub; avant de // ad avant; ~ **going** avant de partir; ~ **she goes** avant qu'elle (ne) parte; **the week** ~ la semaine précédente or d'avant; **I've seen it** ~ je l'ai déjà vu; ~**hand** ad au préalable, à l'avance.

beg [bɛg] vi mendier // vt mendier; (favour) quémander, solliciter; (entreat) supplier.

began [bɪ'gæn] pt of **begin**.

beggar ['bɛgə*] n mendiant/e.

begin [bɪ'gɪn], pt **began**, pp **begun** vt, vi commencer; **to** ~ **doing** or **to do sth** commencer à or de faire qch; ~**ner** n débutant/e; ~**ning** n commencement m, début m.

begun [bɪ'gʌn] pp of **begin**.

behalf [bɪ'hɑ:f] n: **on** ~ **of** de la part de; au nom de; pour le compte de.

behave [bɪ'heɪv] vi se conduire, se comporter; (well: also: ~ **o.s.**) se conduire bien or comme il faut.

behaviour, (US) **behavior** [bɪ'heɪvjə*] n comportement m, conduite f.

behead [bɪ'hɛd] vt décapiter.

beheld [bɪ'hɛld] pt, pp of **behold**.

behind [bɪ'haɪnd] prep derrière; (time) en retard sur // ad derrière; en retard // n derrière m; **to be** ~ (schedule) être en retard; ~ **the scenes** dans les coulisses.

behold [bɪ'həuld] vt (irg: like hold) apercevoir, voir.

beige [beɪʒ] a beige.

being ['bi:ɪŋ] n être m; **to come into** ~ prendre naissance.

Beirut [beɪ'ru:t] n Beyrouth.

belated [bɪ'leɪtɪd] a tardif(ive).

belch [bɛltʃ] vi avoir un renvoi, roter // vt (also: ~ **out**: smoke etc) vomir, cracher.

belfry ['bɛlfrɪ] n beffroi m.

Belgian ['bɛldʒən] a belge, de Belgique // n Belge m/f.

Belgium ['bɛldʒəm] n Belgique f.

belie [bɪ'laɪ] vt démentir.

belief [bɪ'li:f] n (opinion) conviction f; (trust, faith) foi f; (acceptance as true) croyance f.

believe [bɪ'li:v] vt, vi croire; **to** ~ **in** (God) croire en; (method, ghosts) croire

à; ~**r** n (in idea, activity): ~**r in** partisan/e de; (REL) croyant/e.

belittle [bɪ'lɪtl] vt déprécier, rabaisser.

bell [bɛl] n cloche f; (small) clochette f, grelot m; (on door) sonnette f; (electric) sonnerie f.

bellow ['bɛləu] vi mugir.

bellows ['bɛləuz] npl soufflet m.

belly ['bɛlɪ] n ventre m.

belong [bɪ'lɔŋ] vi: **to** ~ **to** appartenir à; (club etc) faire partie de; **this book** ~**s here** ce livre a ici; ~**ings** npl affaires fpl, possessions fpl.

beloved [bɪ'lʌvɪd] a (bien-)aimé(e).

below [bɪ'ləu] prep sous, au-dessous de // ad en dessous; en contre-bas; **see** ~ voir plus bas or plus loin or ci-dessous.

belt [bɛlt] n ceinture f; (TECH) courroie f // vt (thrash) donner une raclée à; ~**way** n (US AUT) route f de ceinture; (: motorway) périphérique m.

bemused [bɪ'mju:zd] a stupéfié(e).

bench [bɛntʃ] n banc m; (in workshop) établi m; **the B**~ (LAW) la magistrature, la Cour.

bend [bɛnd] vb (pt, pp **bent**) vt courber; (leg, arm) plier // vi se courber // n (Brit: in road) virage m, tournant m; (in pipe, river) coude m; **to** ~ **down** vi se baisser; **to** ~ **over** vi se pencher.

beneath [bɪ'ni:θ] prep sous, au-dessous de; (unworthy of) indigne de // ad dessous, au-dessous, en bas.

benefactor ['bɛnɪfæktə*] n bienfaiteur m.

beneficial [bɛnɪ'fɪʃəl] a salutaire; avantageux(euse).

benefit ['bɛnɪfɪt] n avantage m, profit m; (allowance of money) allocation f // vt faire du bien à, profiter à // vi: **he'll** ~ **from it** cela lui fera du bien, il y gagnera or s'en trouvera bien.

benevolent [bɪ'nɛvələnt] a bienveillant(e).

benign [bɪ'naɪn] a (person, smile) bienveillant(e), affable; (MED) bénin(igne).

bent [bɛnt] pt, pp of **bend** // n inclination f, penchant m // a (col: dishonest) véreux(euse); **to be** ~ **on** être résolu(e) à.

bequest [bɪ'kwɛst] n legs m.

bereaved [bɪ'ri:vd] n: **the** ~ la famille du disparu.

beret ['bɛreɪ] n béret m.

berm [bə:m] n (US AUT) accotement m.

berry ['bɛrɪ] n baie f.

berserk [bə'sə:k] a: **to go** ~ être pris(e) d'une rage incontrôlable; se déchaîner.

berth [bə:θ] n (bed) couchette f; (for ship) poste m d'amarrage, mouillage m // vi (in harbour) venir à quai; (at anchor) mouiller.

beseech [bɪ'si:tʃ], pt, pp **besought** vt implorer, supplier.

beset, *pt*, *pp* **beset** [bɪ'sɛt] *vt* assaillir.
beside [bɪ'saɪd] *prep* à côté de; **to be ~ o.s. (with anger)** être hors de soi; **that's ~ the point** cela n'a rien à voir.
besides [bɪ'saɪdz] *ad* en outre, de plus // *prep* en plus de; excepté.
besiege [bɪ'siːdʒ] *vt* (*town*) assiéger; (*fig*) assaillir.
besought [bɪ'sɔːt] *pt*, *pp of* **beseech**.
best [bɛst] *a* meilleur(e) // *ad* le mieux; **the ~ part of** (*quantity*) le plus clair de, la plus grande partie de; **at ~** au mieux; **to make the ~ of sth** s'accommoder de qch (du mieux que l'on peut); **to do one's ~** faire de son mieux; **to the ~ of my knowledge** pour autant que je sache; **to the ~ of my ability** du mieux que je pourrai; **~ man** *n* garçon *m* d'honneur.
bestow [bɪ'stəu] *vt* accorder; (*title*) conférer.
bet [bɛt] *n* pari *m* // *vt*, *vi* (*pt*, *pp* **bet** or **betted**) parier.
betray [bɪ'treɪ] *vt* trahir; **~al** *n* trahison *f*.
better ['bɛtə*] *a* meilleur(e) // *ad* mieux // *vt* améliorer // *n*: **to get the ~ of** triompher de, l'emporter sur; **you had ~ do it** vous feriez mieux de le faire; **he thought ~ of it** il s'est ravisé; **to get ~** aller mieux; s'améliorer; **~ off** *a* plus à l'aise financièrement; (*fig*): **you'd be ~ off this way** vous vous en trouveriez mieux ainsi.
betting ['bɛtɪŋ] *n* paris *mpl*; **~ shop** *n* (*Brit*) bureau *m* de paris.
between [bɪ'twiːn] *prep* entre // *ad* au milieu; dans l'intervalle.
beverage ['bɛvərɪdʒ] *n* boisson *f* (*gén sans alcool*).
bevy ['bɛvɪ] *n*: **a ~ of** un essaim or une volée de.
beware [bɪ'wɛə*] *vi*: **to ~ (of)** prendre garde (à).
bewildered [bɪ'wɪldəd] *a* dérouté(e), ahuri(e).
bewitching [bɪ'wɪtʃɪŋ] *a* enchanteur(teresse).
beyond [bɪ'jɔnd] *prep* (*in space*) au-delà de; (*exceeding*) au-dessus de // *ad* au-delà; **~ doubt** hors de doute.
bias ['baɪəs] *n* (*prejudice*) préjugé *m*, parti pris; (*preference*) prévention *f*; **~(s)ed** *a* partial(e), montrant un parti pris.
bib [bɪb] *n* bavoir *m*, bavette *f*.
Bible ['baɪbl] *n* Bible *f*.
bicarbonate of soda [baɪ'kɑːbənɪt-] *n* bicarbonate *m* de soude.
bicker ['bɪkə*] *vi* se chamailler.
bicycle ['baɪsɪkl] *n* bicyclette *f*.
bid [bɪd] *n* offre *f*; (*at auction*) enchère *f*; (*attempt*) tentative *f* // *vb* (*pt* **bid** or **bade**, *pp* **bid** or **bidden**) *vi* faire une enchère or offre // *vt* faire une enchère or offre de; **to ~ sb good day** souhaiter le

bonjour à qn; **~der** *n*: **the highest ~der** le plus offrant; **~ding** *n* enchères *fpl*.
bide [baɪd] *vt*: **to ~ one's time** attendre son heure.
bifocals [baɪ'fəuklz] *npl* verres *mpl* à double foyer, lunettes bifocales.
big [bɪg] *a* grand(e); gros(se).
big dipper [-'dɪpə*] *n* montagnes *fpl* russes.
bigheaded ['bɪg'hɛdɪd] *a* prétentieux(euse).
bigot ['bɪgət] *n* fanatique *m/f*, sectaire *m/f*; **~ed** *a* fanatique, sectaire; **~ry** *n* fanatisme *m*, sectarisme *m*.
big top *n* grand chapiteau.
bike [baɪk] *n* vélo *m*, bécane *f*.
bikini [bɪ'kiːnɪ] *n* bikini *m*.
bilingual [baɪ'lɪŋgwəl] *a* bilingue.
bill [bɪl] *n* note *f*, facture *f*; (*POL*) projet *m* de loi; (*US: banknote*) billet *m* (de banque); (*of bird*) bec *m*; **'post no ~s'** 'défense d'afficher'; **to fit** or **fill the ~** (*fig*) faire l'affaire; **~board** *n* panneau *m* d'affichage.
billet ['bɪlɪt] *n* cantonnement *m* (chez l'habitant).
billfold ['bɪlfəuld] *n* (*US*) portefeuille *m*.
billiards ['bɪljədz] *n* (jeu *m* de) billard *m*.
billion ['bɪljən] *n* (*Brit*) billion *m* (*million de millions*); (*US*) milliard *m*.
bin [bɪn] *n* boîte *f*; (*also: dust~*) poubelle *f*; (*for coal*) coffre *m*.
bind [baɪnd], *pt*, *pp* **bound** *vt* attacher; (*book*) relier; (*oblige*) obliger, contraindre; **~ing** *n* (*of book*) reliure *f* // *a* (*contract*) constituant une obligation.
binge [bɪndʒ] *n* (*col*): **to go on a ~** aller faire la bringue.
bingo ['bɪŋgəu] *n* sorte de jeu de loto pratiqué dans des établissements publics.
binoculars [bɪ'nɔkjuləz] *npl* jumelles *fpl*.
bio... [baɪə'...] *prefix*: **~chemistry** *n* biochimie *f*; **~graphy** [baɪ'ɔgrəfɪ] *n* biographie *f*; **~logical** *a* biologique; **~logy** [baɪ'ɔlədʒɪ] *n* biologie *f*.
birch [bəːtʃ] *n* bouleau *m*.
bird [bəːd] *n* oiseau *m*; (*Brit col: girl*) nana *f*; **~'s-eye view** *n* vue *f* à vol d'oiseau; (*fig*) vue d'ensemble or générale; **~ watcher** *n* ornithologue *m/f* amateur.
Biro ['baɪərəu] *n* ® stylo *m* à bille.
birth [bəːθ] *n* naissance *f*; **~ certificate** *n* acte *m* de naissance; **~ control** *n* limitation *f* des naissances; méthode(s) contraceptive(s); **~day** *n* anniversaire *m*; **~ rate** *n* (taux *m* de) natalité *f*.
biscuit ['bɪskɪt] *n* (*Brit*) biscuit *m*.
bisect [baɪ'sɛkt] *vt* couper or diviser en deux.
bishop ['bɪʃəp] *n* évêque *m*.
bit [bɪt] *pt of* **bite** // *n* morceau *m*; (*of*

tool) mèche *f*; (*of horse*) mors *m*; (*COMPUT*) élément *m* binaire; **a ~ of** un peu de; **a ~ mad** un peu fou; **~ by ~** petit à petit.

bitch [bɪtʃ] *n* (*dog*) chienne *f*; (*col*!) salope *f* (!), garce *f*.

bite [baɪt] *vt, vi* (*pt* **bit**, *pp* **bitten**) mordre // *n* morsure *f*; (*insect ~*) piqûre *f*; (*mouthful*) bouchée *f*; let's have a ~ (to eat) mangeons un morceau; to ~ one's nails se ronger les ongles.

bitter ['bɪtə*] *a* amer(ère); (*wind, criticism*) cinglant(e) // *n* (*Brit: beer*) bière *f* (*à forte teneur en houblon*); **~ness** *n* amertume *f*; goût amer.

blab [blæb] *vi* jaser, trop parler.

black [blæk] *a* noir(e) // *n* (*colour*) noir *m*; (*person*): **B~** noir/e *m/f*; // *vt* (*shoes*) cirer; (*Brit INDUSTRY*) boycotter; **to give sb a ~ eye** pocher l'œil à qn, faire un œil au beurre noir à qn; **~ and blue** *a* couvert(e) de bleus; **to be in the ~** (*in credit*) être créditeur(trice); **~berry** *n* mûre *f*; **~bird** *n* merle *m*; **~board** *n* tableau noir; **~currant** *n* cassis *m*; **~en** *vt* noircir; **~ ice** *n* verglas *m*; **~leg** *n* (*Brit*) briseur *m* de grève, jaune *m*; **~list** *n* liste noire; **~mail** *n* chantage *m* // *vt* faire chanter; soumettre au chantage; **~ market** *n* marché noir; **~out** *n* panne *f* d'électricité; (*fainting*) syncope *f*; **the B~ Sea** *n* la mer Noire; **~ sheep** *n* brebis galeuse; **~smith** *n* forgeron *m*; **~ spot** *n* (*AUT*) point noir.

bladder ['blædə*] *n* vessie *f*.

blade [bleɪd] *n* lame *f*; (*of oar*) plat *m*; **~ of grass** brin *m* d'herbe.

blame [bleɪm] *n* faute *f*, blâme *m* // *vt*: **to ~ sb/sth for sth** attribuer à qn/qch la responsabilité de qch; reprocher qch à qn/qch; **who's to ~?** qui est le fautif *or* coupable *or* responsable?

bland [blænd] *a* affable; (*taste*) doux(douce), fade.

blank [blæŋk] *a* blanc(blanche); (*look*) sans expression, dénué(e) d'expression // *n* espace *m* vide, blanc *m*; (*cartridge*) cartouche *f* à blanc; **~ cheque** *n* chèque *m* en blanc.

blanket ['blæŋkɪt] *n* couverture *f*.

blare [blɛə*] *vi* beugler.

blast [blɑ:st] *n* souffle *m*; explosion *f* // *vt* faire sauter *or* exploser; **~-off** *n* (*SPACE*) lancement *m*.

blatant ['bleɪtənt] *a* flagrant(e), criant(e).

blaze [bleɪz] *n* (*fire*) incendie *m*; (*fig*) flamboiement *m* // *vi* (*fire*) flamber; (*fig*) flamboyer, resplendir // *vt*: **to ~ a trail** (*fig*) montrer la voie.

blazer ['bleɪzə*] *n* blazer *m*.

bleach [bli:tʃ] *n* (*also*: household ~) eau *f* de Javel // *vt* (*linen*) blanchir; **~ed** *a* (*hair*) oxygéné(e), décoloré(e); **~ers** *npl* (*US SPORT*) gradins *mpl* (*en plein*

soleil).

bleak [bli:k] *a* morne, désolé(e).

bleary-eyed ['blɪərɪ'aɪd] *a* aux yeux pleins de sommeil.

bleat [bli:t] *vi* bêler.

bleed, *pt*, *pp* **bled** [bli:d, blɛd] *vt, vi* saigner; **my nose is ~ing** je saigne du nez.

bleeper ['bli:pə*] *n* (*device*) bip *m*.

blemish ['blɛmɪʃ] *n* défaut *m*.

blend [blɛnd] *n* mélange *m* // *vt* mélanger // *vi* (*colours etc*) se mélanger, se fondre, s'allier.

bless, *pt*, *pp* **blessed** *or* **blest** [blɛs, blɛst] *vt* bénir; **~ing** *n* bénédiction *f*; bienfait *m*.

blew [blu:] *pt of* **blow**.

blight [blaɪt] *vt* (*hopes etc*) anéantir, briser.

blimey ['blaɪmɪ] *excl* (*Brit col*) mince alors!

blind [blaɪnd] *a* aveugle // *n* (*for window*) store *m* // *vt* aveugler; **~ alley** *n* impasse *f*; **~ corner** *n* (*Brit*) virage *m* sans visibilité; **~fold** *n* bandeau *m* // *a, ad* les yeux bandés // *vt* bander les yeux à; **~ly** *ad* aveuglément; **~ness** *n* cécité *f*; (*fig*) aveuglement *m*; **~ spot** *n* (*AUT etc*) angle mort.

blink [blɪŋk] *vi* cligner des yeux; (*light*) clignoter; **~ers** *npl* œillères *fpl*.

bliss [blɪs] *n* félicité *f*, bonheur *m* sans mélange.

blister ['blɪstə*] *n* (*on skin*) ampoule *f*, cloque *f*; (*on paintwork*) boursouflure *f* // *vi* (*paint*) se boursoufler, se cloquer.

blithely ['blaɪðlɪ] *ad* joyeusement.

blitz [blɪts] *n* bombardement (aérien).

blizzard ['blɪzəd] *n* blizzard *m*, tempête *f* de neige.

bloated ['bləutɪd] *a* (*face*) bouffi(e); (*stomach*) gonflé(e).

blob [blɔb] *n* (*drop*) goutte *f*; (*stain, spot*) tache *f*.

block [blɔk] *n* bloc *m*; (*in pipes*) obstruction *f*; (*toy*) cube *m*; (*of buildings*) pâté *m* (de maisons) // *vt* bloquer; **~ade** [-'keɪd] *n* blocus *m* // *vt* faire le blocus de; **~age** *n* obstruction *f*; **~buster** *n* (*film, book*) grand succès; **~ of flats** *n* (*Brit*) immeuble (locatif); **~ letters** *npl* majuscules *fpl*.

bloke [bləuk] *n* (*Brit col*) type *m*.

blonde [blɔnd] *a, n* blond(e).

blood [blʌd] *n* sang *m*; **~ donor** *n* donneur/euse de sang; **~ group** *n* groupe sanguin; **~hound** *n* limier *m*; **~ poisoning** *n* empoisonnement *m* du sang; **~ pressure** *n* tension *f* (artérielle); **~shed** *n* effusion *f* de sang, carnage *m*; **~shot** *a*: **~shot eyes** yeux injectés de sang; **~stream** *n* sang *m*, système sanguin; **~ test** *n* prise *f* de sang; **~thirsty** *a* sanguinaire; **~y** *a* sanglant(e); (*Brit col*!): **this ~y ... ce**

foutu ..., ce putain de ... (!); **~y strong/ good** vachement or sacrément fort/bon; **~y-minded** a (Brit col) contrariant(e), obstiné(e).

bloom [blu:m] n fleur f; (fig) épanouissement m // vi être en fleur; (fig) s'épanouir; être florissant(e).

blossom ['blɔsəm] n fleur(s) f(pl) // vi être en fleurs; (fig) s'épanouir.

blot [blɔt] n tache f // vt tachér; **to ~out** vt (memories) effacer; (view) cacher, masquer; (nation, city) annihiler.

blotchy ['blɔtʃɪ] a (complexion) couvert(e) de marbrures.

blotting paper ['blɔtɪŋ-] n buvard m.

blouse [blauz] n (feminine garment) chemisier m, corsage m.

blow [bləu] n coup m // vb (pt blew, pp blown [blu:, bləun]) vi souffler // vt (fuse) faire sauter; **to ~ one's nose** se moucher; **to ~ a whistle** siffler; **to ~ away** vt chasser, faire s'envoler; **to ~ down** vt faire tomber, renverser; **to ~ off** vt emporter; **to ~ out** vi éclater, sauter; **to ~ over** vi s'apaiser; **to ~ up** vi exploser, sauter // vt faire sauter; (tyre) gonfler; (PHOT) agrandir; **~-dry** n brushing m; **~lamp** n (Brit) chalumeau m; **~-out** n (of tyre) éclatement m; **~-torch** n = **~lamp**.

blue [blu:] a bleu(e); **~ film/joke** film m/ histoire f pornographique; **to come out of the ~** (fig) être complètement inattendu; **to have the ~s** avoir le cafard; **~bottle** n mouche f à viande; **~ jeans** npl bluejeans mpl; **~print** n (fig) projet m, plan directeur.

bluff [blʌf] vi bluffer // n bluff m; **to call sb's ~** mettre qn au défi d'exécuter ses menaces.

blunder ['blʌndə*] n gaffe f, bévue f // vi faire une gaffe ou une bévue.

blunt [blʌnt] a émoussé(e), peu tranchant(e); (person) brusque, ne mâchant pas ses mots // vt émousser.

blur [blə:*] n tache ou masse floue ou confuse // vt brouiller, rendre flou(e).

blurb [blə:b] n notice f publicitaire; (for book) texte m de présentation.

blurt [blə:t]: **to ~ out** vt (reveal) lâcher; (say) balbutier, dire d'une voix entrecoupée.

blush [blʌʃ] vi rougir // n rougeur f.

blustery ['blʌstərɪ] a (weather) à bourrasques.

boar [bɔ:*] n sanglier m.

board [bɔ:d] n planche f; (on wall) panneau m; (committee) conseil m, comité m; (in firm) conseil d'administration // vt (ship) monter à bord de; (train) monter dans; (NAUT, AVIAT): **on ~** à bord; **full ~** (Brit) pension complète; **half ~** (Brit) demi-pension f; **~ and lodging** n chambre f avec pension; **which goes by the ~** (fig) qu'on

laisse tomber, qu'on abandonne; **to ~ up** vt (door) condamner (au moyen de planches, de tôle); **~er** n pensionnaire m/f; (SCOL) interne m/f, pensionnaire; **~ing card** n (AVIAT, NAUT) carte f d'embarquement; **~ing house** n pension f; **~ing school** n internat m, pensionnat m; **~ room** n salle f du conseil d'administration.

boast [bəust] vi: **to ~ (about or of)** se vanter (de) // vt s'enorgueillir de // n vantardise f; sujet m d'orgueil or de fierté.

boat [bəut] n bateau m; (small) canot m; barque f; **~er** n (hat) canotier m; **~swain** ['bəusn] n maître m d'équipage.

bob [bɔb] vi (boat, cork on water: also: **~ up and down**) danser, se balancer // n (Brit col) = **shilling**; **to ~ up** vi surgir or apparaître brusquement.

bobby ['bɔbɪ] n (Brit col) ≈ agent m (de police).

bobsleigh ['bɔbsleɪ] n bob m.

bode [bəud] vi: **to ~ well/ill (for)** être de bon/mauvais augure (pour).

bodily ['bɔdɪlɪ] a corporel(le) // ad physiquement; dans son entier or ensemble; en personne.

body ['bɔdɪ] n corps m; (of car) carrosserie f; (of plane) fuselage m; (fig: society) organe m, organisme m; (fig: quantity) ensemble m, masse f; (of wine) corps m; **~-building** n culturisme m; **~guard** n garde m du corps; **~work** n carrosserie f.

bog [bɔg] n tourbière f // vt: **to get ~ged down** (fig) s'enliser.

boggle ['bɔgl] vi: **the mind ~s** c'est incroyable, on en reste sidéré.

bogus ['bəugəs] a bidon inv; fantôme.

boil [bɔɪl] vt (faire) bouillir // vi bouillir // n (MED) furoncle m; **to come to the** (Brit) or a (US) **~** bouillir; **to ~ down** vi (fig): **to ~ down to** se réduire or ramener à; **to ~ over** vi déborder; **~ed egg** n œuf m à la coque; **~ed potatoes** npl pommes fpl à l'anglaise or à l'eau; **~er** n chaudière f; **~er suit** n (Brit) bleu m de travail, combinaison f; **~ing point** n point m d'ébullition.

boisterous ['bɔɪstərəs] a bruyant(e), tapageur(euse).

bold [bəuld] a hardi(e), audacieux(euse); (pej) effronté(e); (outline, colour) franc(franche), tranché(e), marqué(e).

bollard ['bɔləd] n (Brit AUT) borne lumineuse or de signalisation.

bolster ['bəulstə*] n traversin m; **to ~ up** vt soutenir.

bolt [bəult] n verrou m; (with nut) boulon m // ad: **~ upright** droit(e) comme un piquet // vt verrouiller; (food) engloutir // vi se sauver, filer (comme une flèche).

bomb [bɔm] *n* bombe *f* // *vt* bombarder; ~ **disposal unit** *n* section *f* de déminage; ~**er** *n* (AVIAT) bombardier *m*; ~**shell** *n* (*fig*) bombe *f*.

bona fide ['bəunə'faɪd*] *a* de bonne foi; (*offer*) sérieux(euse).

bond [bɔnd] *n* lien *m*; (*binding promise*) engagement *m*, obligation *f*; (COMM) obligation; **in** ~ (*of goods*) en douane.

bondage ['bɔndɪdʒ] *n* esclavage *m*.

bone [bəun] *n* os *m*; (*of fish*) arête *f* // *vt* désosser; ôter les arêtes de; ~ **idle** *a*, ~ **lazy** *a* fainéant(e).

bonfire ['bɔnfaɪə*] *n* feu *m* (de joie); (*for rubbish*) feu.

bonnet ['bɔnɪt] *n* bonnet *m*; (*Brit: of car*) capot *m*.

bonus ['bəunəs] *n* prime *f*, gratification *f*.

bony ['bəunɪ] *a* (*arm, face,* MED: *tissue*) osseux(euse); (*meat*) plein(e) d'os; (*fish*) plein d'arêtes.

boo [bu:] *excl* hou!, peuh! // *vt* huer.

booby trap ['bu:bɪ-] *n* engin piégé.

book [buk] *n* livre *m*; (*of stamps etc*) carnet *m*; (COMM): ~**s** comptes *mpl*, comptabilité *f* // *vt* (*ticket*) prendre; (*seat, room*) réserver; (*driver*) dresser un procès-verbal à; (*football player*) prendre le nom de; ~**case** *n* bibliothèque *f* (*meuble*); ~**ing office** *n* (*Brit*) bureau *m* de location; ~**-keeping** *n* comptabilité *f*; ~**let** *n* brochure *f*; ~**maker** *n* bookmaker *m*; ~**seller** *n* libraire *m/f*; ~**shop** *n*, ~**store** *n* librairie *f*.

boom [bu:m] *n* (*noise*) grondement *m*; (*busy period*) boom *m*, vague *f* de prospérité // *vi* gronder; prospérer.

boon [bu:n] *n* bénédiction *f*, grand avantage *m*.

boost [bu:st] *n* stimulant *m*, remontant *m* // *vt* stimuler; ~**er** *n* (MED) rappel *m*.

boot [bu:t] *n* botte *f*; (*for hiking*) chaussure *f* (de marche); (*for football etc*) soulier *m*; (*Brit: of car*) coffre *m* // *vt* (COMPUT) remettre à zéro; **to** ~ (*in addition*) par-dessus le marché, en plus.

booth [bu:ð] *n* (*at fair*) baraque (foraine); (*of cinema, telephone etc*) cabine *f*; (*also:* **voting** ~) isoloir *m*.

booty ['bu:tɪ] *n* butin *m*.

booze [bu:z] *n* (*col*) boissons *fpl* alcooliques, alcool *m*.

border ['bɔ:də*] *n* bordure *f*; bord *m*; (*of a country*) frontière *f*; **the B**~**s** la région frontière entre l'Écosse et l'Angleterre; **to** ~ **on** *vt fus* être voisin(e) de, toucher à; ~**line** *n* (*fig*) ligne *f* de démarcation; ~**line case** *n* cas *m* limite.

bore [bɔ:*] *pt of* **bear** // *vt* (*hole*) percer; (*person*) ennuyer, raser // *n* (*person*) raseur/euse; (*of gun*) calibre

m; **to be** ~**d** s'ennuyer; ~**dom** *n* ennui *m*; **boring** *a* ennuyeux(euse).

born [bɔ:n] *a*: **to be** ~ naître; **I was** ~ **in 1960** je suis né en 1960.

borne [bɔ:n] *pp of* **bear**.

borough ['bʌrə] *n* municipalité *f*.

borrow ['bɔrəu] *vt*: **to** ~ **sth** (**from sb**) emprunter qch (à qn).

bosom ['buzəm] *n* poitrine *f*; (*fig*) sein *m*.

boss [bɔs] *n* patron/ne *m* // *vt* commander; ~**y** *a* autoritaire.

bosun ['bəusn] *n* maître *m* d'équipage.

botany ['bɔtənɪ] *n* botanique *f*.

botch [bɔtʃ] *vt* (*also:* ~ **up**) saboter, bâcler.

both [bəuθ] *a* les deux, l'un(e) et l'autre // *pronoun:* ~ (*of them*) les deux, tous(toutes) (les) deux, l'un(e) et l'autre; ~ **of us went, we** ~ **went** nous y sommes allés (tous) les deux // *ad*: **they sell** ~ **the fabric and the finished curtains** ils vendent (et) le tissu et les rideaux (finis), ils vendent à la fois le tissu et les rideaux (finis).

bother ['bɔðə*] *vt* (*worry*) tracasser; (*needle, bait*) importuner, ennuyer; (*disturb*) déranger // *vi* (*also:* ~ **o.s.**) se tracasser, se faire du souci // *n*: **it's a** ~ **to have to do** c'est vraiment ennuyeux d'avoir à faire; **it's no** ~ aucun problème; **to** ~ **doing** prendre la peine de faire.

bottle ['bɔtl] *n* bouteille *f*; (*baby's*) biberon *m* // *vt* mettre en bouteille(s); **to** ~ **up** *vt* refouler, contenir; ~**neck** *n* étranglement *m*; ~**-opener** *n* ouvre-bouteille *m*.

bottom ['bɔtəm] *n* (*of container, sea etc*) fond *m*; (*buttocks*) derrière *m*; (*of page, list*) bas *m*; (*of chair*) siège *m* // *a* du fond; du bas.

bough [bau] *n* branche *f*, rameau *m*.

bought [bɔ:t] *pt, pp of* **buy**.

boulder ['bəuldə*] *n* gros rocher.

bounce [bauns] *vi* (*ball*) rebondir; (*cheque*) être refusé (*étant sans provision*) // *vt* faire rebondir // *n* (*rebound*) rebond *m*; ~**r** *n* (*col*) videur *m*.

bound [baund] *pt, pp of* **bind** // *n* (*gen pl*) limite *f*; (*leap*) bond *m* // *vi* (*leap*) bondir; (*limit*) borner // *a*: **to be** ~ **to do sth** (*obliged*) être obligé(e) ou avoir obligation de faire qch; **he's** ~ **to fail** (*likely*) il est sûr d'échouer, son échec est inévitable ou assuré; ~ **for** à destination de; **out of** ~**s** dont l'accès est interdit.

boundary ['baundrɪ] *n* frontière *f*.

bout [baut] *n* période *f*; (*of malaria etc*) accès *m*, crise *f*, attaque *f*; (BOXING *etc*) combat *m*, match *m*.

bow *n* [bəu] nœud *m*; (*weapon*) arc *m*; (MUS) archet *m*; [bau] (*with body*) révérence f, inclination f (du buste or corps); (NAUT: also: ~s) proue f // vi [bau] faire une révérence, s'incliner; (yield): to ~ to or before s'incliner devant, se soumettre à.

bowels [bauəlz] npl intestins mpl; (fig) entrailles fpl.

bowl [bəul] n (for eating) bol m; (for washing) cuvette f; (ball) boule f; (of pipe) fourneau m // vi (CRICKET) lancer (la balle); ~s n (jeu m de) boules fpl.

bow-legged ['bəu'lɛgid] a aux jambes arquées.

bowler ['bəulə*] n (CRICKET) lanceur m (de la balle); (Brit: also: ~ hat) (chapeau m) melon m.

bowling ['bəuliŋ] n (game) jeu m de boules; jeu m de quilles; ~ alley n bowling m; ~ green n terrain m de boules (gazonné et carré).

bow tie n nœud m papillon.

box [bɔks] n boîte f; (also: cardboard ~) carton m; (THEATRE) loge f // vt mettre en boîte; (SPORT) boxer avec // vi boxer, faire de la boxe; ~er n (person) boxeur m; ~ing n (SPORT) boxe f; B~ing Day n (Brit) le lendemain de Noël; ~ing gloves npl gants mpl de boxe; ~ing ring n ring m; ~ office n bureau m de location; ~ room n débarras m; chambrette f.

boy [bɔi] n garçon m.

boycott ['bɔikɔt] n boycottage m // vt boycotter.

boyfriend ['bɔifrɛnd] n (petit) ami.

B.R. abbr of **British Rail.**

bra [brɑ:] n soutien-gorge m.

brace [breis] n attache f, agrafe f; (on teeth) appareil m (dentaire); (tool) vilbrequin m // vt consolider, soutenir; ~s npl (Brit) bretelles fpl; to ~ o.s. (fig) se préparer mentalement.

bracelet ['breislit] n bracelet m.

bracing ['breisiŋ] a tonifiant(e), tonique.

bracken ['brækən] n fougère f.

bracket ['brækit] n (TECH) tasseau m, support m; (group) classe f, tranche f; (also: brace ~) accolade f; (also: round ~) parenthèse f; (also: square ~) crochet m // vt mettre entre parenthèse(s).

brag [bræg] vi se vanter.

braid [breid] n (trimming) galon m; (of hair) tresse f, natte f.

brain [brein] n cerveau m; ~s npl cervelle f; he's got ~s il est intelligent; ~child n invention personnelle; ~wash vt faire subir un lavage de cerveau à; ~wave n idée géniale; ~y a intelligent(e), doué(e).

brake [breik] n (on vehicle) frein m // vt, vi freiner; ~ fluid n liquide m de freins; ~ light n feu m de stop.

bramble ['bræmbl] n (bush) ronce f; (berry) mûre f sauvage.

bran [bræn] n son m.

branch [brɑ:ntʃ] n branche f; (COMM) succursale f // vi bifurquer.

brand [brænd] n marque (commerciale) // vt (cattle) marquer (au fer rouge).

brand-new ['brænd'nju:] a tout(e) neuf(neuve), flambant neuf(neuve).

brandy ['brændi] n cognac m, fine f.

brash [bræʃ] a effronté(e).

brass [brɑ:s] n cuivre m (jaune), laiton m; the ~ (MUS) les cuivres; ~ band n fanfare f.

brassière ['bræsiə*] n soutien-gorge m.

brat [bræt] n (pej) mioche m/f, môme m/f.

brave [breiv] a courageux(euse), brave // n guerrier indien // vt braver, affronter; ~ry n bravoure f, courage m.

brawl [brɔ:l] n rixe f, bagarre f.

brawn [brɔ:n] n muscle m; (meat) fromage m de tête.

bray [brei] vi braire.

brazen ['breizn] a impudent(e), effronté(e) // vt: to ~ it out payer d'effronterie, crâner.

brazier ['breiziə*] n brasero m.

Brazil [brə'zil] n Brésil m.

breach [bri:tʃ] vt ouvrir une brèche dans // n (gap) brèche f; (breaking): ~ of contract rupture f de contract; ~ of the peace attentat m à l'ordre public.

bread [brɛd] n pain m; ~ and butter n tartines (beurrées); (fig) subsistance f; ~bin, (US) ~box n boîte f à pain; (bigger) huche f à pain; ~crumbs npl miettes fpl de pain; (CULIN) chapelure f, panure f; ~line n: to be on the ~line être sans le sou or dans l'indigence.

breadth [brɛtθ] n largeur f.

breadwinner ['brɛdwinə*] n soutien m de famille.

break [breik] vb (pt broke, pp broken) vt casser, briser; (promise) rompre; (law) violer // vi (se) casser, se briser; (weather) tourner // n (gap) brèche f; (fracture) cassure f; (rest) interruption f, arrêt m; (: short) pause f; (: at school) récréation f; (chance) chance f, occasion f favorable; to ~ one's leg etc se casser la jambe etc; to ~ a record battre un record; to ~ the news to sb annoncer la nouvelle à qn; to ~ down vt (figures, data) décomposer, analyser // vi s'effondrer; (MED) faire une dépression (nerveuse); (AUT) tomber en panne; to ~ even vi rentrer dans ses frais; to ~ free or loose vi se dégager, s'échapper; to ~ in vt (horse etc) dresser // vi (burglar) entrer par effraction; to ~ into vt fus (house) s'introduire or pénétrer par effraction dans; to ~ off vi (speaker) s'interrompre; (branch) se rompre; to ~ open vt (door etc) forcer, fracturer; to ~ out vi éclater, se déclarer; to ~ out in spots se couvrir de boutons; to ~ up vi (*partnership*) cesser, prendre fin; (*friends*) se séparer // *vt* fracasser, casser; (*fight etc*) interrompre, faire cesser; **~age** *n* casse *f*; **~down** *n* (*AUT*) panne *f*; (*in communications*) rupture *f*; (*MED: also:* **nervous ~down**) dépression (nerveuse); **~down van** *n* (*Brit*) dépanneuse *f*; **~er** *n* brisant *m*.

breakfast ['brɛkfəst] *n* petit déjeuner *m*.

break: **~-in** *n* cambriolage *m*; **~ing and entering** *n* (*LAW*) effraction *f*; **~through** *n* percée *f*; **~water** *n* brise-lames *m inv*, digue *f*.

breast [brɛst] *n* (*of woman*) sein *m*; (*chest*) poitrine *f*; **~-feed** *vt, vi* (*irg: like* feed) allaiter; **~-stroke** *n* brasse *f*.

breath [brɛθ] *n* haleine *f*, souffle *m*; out of **~** à bout de souffle, essoufflé(e).

Breathalyser ['brɛθəlaɪzə*] *n* ® alcootest *m*.

breathe [briːð] *vt, vi* respirer; **to ~ in** *vt, vi* aspirer, inspirer; **to ~ out** *vt, vi* expirer; **~r** *n* moment *m* de repos *or* de répit; **breathing** *n* respiration *f*.

breathless ['brɛθlɪs] *a* essoufflé(e), haletant(e); oppressé(e).

breath-taking ['brɛθteɪkɪŋ] *a* stupéfiant(e), à vous couper le souffle.

breed [briːd] *vb* (*pt, pp* **bred** [brɛd]) *vt* élever, faire l'élevage de // *vi* se reproduire // *n* race *f*, variété *f*; **~ing** *n* reproduction *f*; élevage *m*; (*upbringing*) éducation *f*.

breeze [briːz] *n* brise *f*.

breezy ['briːzɪ] *a* frais(fraîche); aéré(e); désinvolte, jovial(e).

brevity ['brɛvɪtɪ] *n* brièveté *f*.

brew [bruː] *vt* (*tea*) faire infuser; (*beer*) brasser; (*plot*) tramer, préparer // *vi* (*tea*) infuser; (*beer*) fermenter; (*fig*) se préparer, couver; **~er** *n* brasseur *m*; **~ery** *n* brasserie *f* (*fabrique*).

bribe [braɪb] *n* pot-de-vin *m* // *vt* acheter; soudoyer; **~ry** *n* corruption *f*.

brick [brɪk] *n* brique *f*; **~layer** *n* maçon *m*; **~works** *n* briqueterie *f*.

bridal ['braɪdl] *a* nuptial(e).

bride [braɪd] *n* mariée *f*, épouse *f*; **~groom** *n* marié *m*, époux *m*; **~smaid** *n* demoiselle *f* d'honneur.

bridge [brɪdʒ] *n* pont *m*; (*NAUT*) passerelle *f* (de commandement); (*of nose*) arête *f*; (*CARDS, DENTISTRY*) bridge *m* // *vt* (*river*) construire un pont sur; (*gap*) combler.

bridle ['braɪdl] *n* bride *f* // *vt* refréner, mettre la bride à; (*horse*) brider; **~ path** *n* piste *or* allée cavalière.

brief [briːf] *a* bref(brève) // *n* (*LAW*) dossier *m*, cause *f* // *vt* donner des instructions à; **~s** *npl* slip *m*; **~case** *n* serviette *f*; porte-documents *m inv*; **~ing** *n* instructions *fpl*; **~ly** *ad* brièvement.

bright [braɪt] *a* brillant(e); (*room,*

weather) clair(e); (*person*) intelligent(e), doué(e); (*colour*) vif(vive); **~en** (*also:* **~en up**) *vt* (*room*) éclaircir; égayer // *vi* s'éclaircir; (*person*) retrouver un peu de sa gaieté.

brilliance ['brɪljəns] *n* éclat *m*.

brilliant ['brɪljənt] *a* brillant(e).

brim [brɪm] *n* bord *m*.

brine [braɪn] *n* eau salée; (*CULIN*) saumure *f*.

bring [brɪŋ], *pt, pp* **brought** *vt* (*thing*) apporter; (*person*) amener; **to ~ about** *vt* provoquer, entraîner; **to ~ back** *vt* rapporter; ramener; **to ~ down** *vt* abaisser; faire s'effondrer; **to ~ forward** *vt* avancer; **to ~ off** *vt* (*task, plan*) réussir, mener à bien; **to ~ out** *vt* (*meaning*) faire ressortir, mettre en relief; **to ~ round** *or* **to ~ to** (*unconscious person*) ranimer; **to ~ up** *vt* élever; (*question*) soulever; (*food: vomit*) vomir, rendre.

brink [brɪŋk] *n* bord *m*.

brisk [brɪsk] *a* vif(vive).

bristle ['brɪsl] *n* poil *m* // *vi* se hérisser.

Britain ['brɪtən] *n* (*also:* **Great ~**) Grande-Bretagne *f*.

British ['brɪtɪʃ] *a* britannique; **the ~** *npl* les Britanniques *mpl*; **the ~ Isles** *npl* les Îles *fpl* Britanniques; **B~ Rail (B.R.)** *n* compagnie ferroviaire britannique, ≈ S.N.C.F. *f*.

Briton ['brɪtən] *n* Britannique *m/f*.

Brittany ['brɪtənɪ] *n* Bretagne *f*.

brittle ['brɪtl] *a* cassant(e), fragile.

broach [brəutʃ] *vt* (*subject*) aborder.

broad [brɔːd] *a* large; (*distinction*) général(e); (*accent*) prononcé(e); **in ~ daylight** en plein jour; **~cast** *n* émission *f* // *vb* (*pt, pp* **broadcast**) *vt* radiodiffuser; téléviser // *vi* émettre; **~en** *vt* élargir // *vi* s'élargir; **~ly** *ad* en gros, généralement; **~-minded** *a* large d'esprit.

broccoli ['brɔkəlɪ] *n* brocoli *m*.

brochure ['brəuʃuə*] *n* prospectus *m*, dépliant *m*.

broil [brɔɪl] *vt* griller.

broke [brəuk] *pt of* **break** // *a* (*col*) fauché(e).

broken ['brəukn] *pp of* **break** // *a:* **~ leg** *etc* jambe *etc* cassée; **in ~ English** dans un anglais approximatif *or* hésitant; **~-hearted** *a* (*ayant*) le cœur brisé.

broker ['brəukə*] *n* courtier *m*.

brolly ['brɔlɪ] *n* (*Brit col*) pépin *m*, parapluie *m*.

bronchitis [brɔŋ'kaɪtɪs] *n* bronchite *f*.

bronze [brɔnz] *n* bronze *m*.

brooch [brəutʃ] *n* broche *f*.

brood [bruːd] *n* couvée *f* // *vi* (*hen, storm*) couver; (*person*) méditer (sombrement), ruminer.

brook [bruːk] *n* ruisseau *m*.

broom [brum] *n* balai *m*; **~stick** *n*

manche *m* à balai.

Bros. *abbr* = *Brothers*.

broth [brɔθ] *n* bouillon *m* de viande et de légumes.

brothel ['brɔθl] *n* maison close, bordel *m*.

brother ['brʌðə*] *n* frère *m*; ~-**in-law** *n* beau-frère *m*.

brought [brɔːt] *pt, pp of* **bring**.

brow [brau] *n* front *m*; *(rare, gen:* eye~*)* sourcil *m*; *(of hill)* sommet *m*.

brown [braun] *a* brun(e), marron *inv* // *n (colour)* brun *m* // *vt* brunir; *(CULIN)* faire dorer, faire roussir; ~ **bread** *n* pain *m* bis.

brownie ['braunɪ] *n* jeannette *f*, éclaireuse (cadette).

brown paper *n* papier *m* d'emballage.

brown sugar *n* cassonade *f*.

browse [brauz] *vi (among books)* bouquiner, feuilleter les livres.

bruise [bruːz] *n* bleu *m*, ecchymose *f*, contusion *f* // *vt* contusionner, meurtrir.

brunette [bruːˈnet] *n (femme)* brune.

brunt [brʌnt] *n:* the ~ of *(attack, criticism etc)* le plus gros de.

brush [brʌʃ] *n* brosse *f*; *(quarrel)* accrochage *m*, prise *f* de bec // *vt* brosser; *(also:* ~ *past,* ~ *against)* effleurer, frôler; **to** ~ **aside** *vt* écarter, balayer; **to** ~ **up** *vt (knowledge)* rafraîchir, réviser; ~**wood** *n* broussailles *fpl*, taillis *m*.

Brussels ['brʌslz] *n* Bruxelles; ~ **sprout** *n* chou *m* de Bruxelles.

brutal ['bruːtl] *a* brutal(e).

brute [bruːt] *n* brute *f* // *a:* **by** ~ **force** par la force.

B.Sc. *abbr see* **bachelor**.

bubble ['bʌbl] *n* bulle *f* // *vi* bouillonner, faire des bulles; *(sparkle, fig)* pétiller; ~ **bath** *n* bain moussant.

buck [bʌk] *n* mâle *m (d'un lapin, lièvre, daim etc)*; *(US col)* dollar *m* // *vi* ruer, lancer une ruade; **to pass the** ~ **(to sb)** se décharger de la responsabilité (sur qn); **to** ~ **up** *vi (cheer up)* reprendre du poil de la bête, se remonter.

bucket ['bʌkɪt] *n* seau *m*.

buckle ['bʌkl] *n* boucle *f* // *vt* boucler, attacher; *(warp)* tordre, gauchir; *(: wheel)* voiler.

bud [bʌd] *n* bourgeon *m*; *(of flower)* bouton *m* // *vi* bourgeonner; *(flower)* éclore.

Buddhism ['budɪzəm] *n* bouddhisme *m*.

budding ['bʌdɪŋ] *a (poet etc)* en herbe; *(passion etc)* naissant(e).

buddy ['bʌdɪ] *n (US)* copain *m*.

budge [bʌdʒ] *vt* faire bouger // *vi* bouger.

budgerigar ['bʌdʒərɪgɑ:*] *n* perruche *f*.

budget ['bʌdʒɪt] *n* budget *m* // *vi:* **to** ~ **for sth** inscrire qch au budget.

budgie ['bʌdʒɪ] *n* = **budgerigar**.

buff [bʌf] *a (couleur f)* chamois *m* // *n (enthusiast)* mordu/e.

buffalo, *pl* ~ *or* ~**es** ['bʌfələu] *n* buffle *m*; *(US)* bison *m*.

buffer ['bʌfə*] *n* tampon *m*; *(COMPUT)* mémoire *f* tampon.

buffet *n* ['bufeɪ] *(food, Brit: bar)* buffet *m* // *vt* ['bʌfɪt] gifler, frapper; secouer, ébranler; ~ **car** *n (Brit RAIL)* voiture-buffet *f*.

bug [bʌg] *n (insect)* punaise *f*; *(: gen)* insecte *m*, bestiole *f*; *(fig: germ)* virus *m*, microbe *m*; *(: spy device)* dispositif *m* d'écoute (électronique), micro clandestin // *vt* garnir de dispositifs d'écoute.

bugle ['bjuːgl] *n* clairon *m*.

build [bɪld] *n (of person)* carrure *f*, charpente *f* // *vt (pt, pp* **built)** construire, bâtir; **to** ~ **up** *vt* accumuler, amasser; accroître; ~**er** *n* entrepreneur *m*; ~**ing** *n* construction *f*; bâtiment *m*, construction; *(habitation, offices)* immeuble *m*; ~**ing society** *n (Brit)* société *f* de crédit immobilier.

built [bɪlt] *pt, pp of* **build**; ~-**in** *a (cupboard)* encastré(e); *(device)* incorporé(e); *(fig)* inné(e); ~-**up area** *n* agglomération (urbaine); zone urbanisée.

bulb [bʌlb] *n (BOT)* bulbe *m*, oignon *m*; *(ELEC)* ampoule *f*.

bulge [bʌldʒ] *n* renflement *m*, gonflement *m* // *vi* faire saillie; présenter un renflement; **to be bulging with** être plein(e) à craquer de.

bulk [bʌlk] *n* masse *f*, volume *m*; **in** ~ *(COMM)* en vrac; **the** ~ **of** la plus grande *or* grosse partie de; ~**y** *a* volumineux(euse), encombrant(e).

bull [bul] *n* taureau *m*; ~**dog** *n* bouledogue *m*.

bulldozer ['buldəuzə*] *n* bulldozer *m*.

bullet ['bulɪt] *n* balle *f (de fusil etc)*.

bulletin ['bulɪtɪn] *n* bulletin *m*, communiqué *m*.

bulletproof ['bulɪtpruːf] *a (car)* blindé(e); *(vest etc)* pare-balles *inv*.

bullfight ['bulfaɪt] *n* corrida *f*, course *f* de taureaux; ~**er** *n* torero *m*; ~**ing** *n* tauromachie *f*.

bullion ['buljən] *n* or *m or* argent *m* en lingots.

bullock ['bulək] *n* bœuf *m*.

bullring ['bulrɪŋ] *n* arènes *fpl*.

bull's-eye ['bulzaɪ] *n* centre *m (de la cible)*.

bully ['bulɪ] *n* brute *f*, tyran *m* // *vt* tyranniser, rudoyer; *(frighten)* intimider.

bum [bʌm] *n (col: backside)* derrière *m*; *(tramp)* vagabond/e, traîne-savates *m/f inv*.

bumblebee ['bʌmblbiː] *n* bourdon *m*.

bump [bʌmp] *n (blow)* coup *m*, choc *m*;

(*jolt*) cahot *m*; (*on road etc, on head*) bosse *f* // *vt* heurter, cogner; **to ~ into** *vt* fus rentrer dans, tamponner; **~er** *n* pare-chocs *m inv* // *a*: **~er crop/harvest** récolte/moisson exceptionnelle.

bumptious ['bʌmpʃəs] *a* suffisant(e), prétentieux(euse).

bumpy ['bʌmpɪ] *a* cahoteux(euse).

bun [bʌn] *n* petit pain au lait; (*of hair*) chignon *m*.

bunch [bʌntʃ] *n* (*of flowers*) bouquet *m*; (*of keys*) trousseau *m*; (*of bananas*) régime *m*; (*of people*) groupe *m*; **~ of grapes** grappe *f* de raisin.

bundle ['bʌndl] *n* paquet *m* // *vt* (*also:* **~ up**) faire un paquet de; (*put:*) **to ~ sth/sb into** fourrer or enfourner qch/qn dans.

bungalow ['bʌŋgələu] *n* bungalow *m*.

bungle ['bʌŋgl] *vt* bâcler, gâcher.

bunion ['bʌnjən] *n* oignon *m* (*au pied*).

bunk [bʌŋk] *n* couchette *f*; **~ beds** *npl* lits superposés.

bunker ['bʌŋkə*] *n* (*coal store*) soute *f* à charbon; (*MIL, GOLF*) bunker *m*.

bunny ['bʌnɪ] *n* (*also:* **~ rabbit**) Jeannot *m* lapin.

bunting ['bʌntɪŋ] *n* pavoisement *m*, drapeaux *mpl*.

buoy [bɔɪ] *n* bouée *f*; **to ~ up** *vt* faire flotter; (*fig*) soutenir, épauler; **~ant** *a* (*carefree*) gai(e), plein(e) d'entrain.

burden ['bə:dn] *n* fardeau *m*, charge *f* // *vt* charger; (*oppress*) accabler, surcharger.

bureau, *pl* **~x** [bjuə'rəu, -z] *n* (*Brit: writing desk*) bureau *m*, secrétaire *m*; (*US: chest of drawers*) commode *f*; (*office*) bureau, office *m*.

bureaucracy [bjuə'rɔkrəsɪ] *n* bureaucratie *f*.

burglar ['bə:glə*] *n* cambrioleur *m*; **~ alarm** *n* sonnerie *f* d'alarme; **~y** *n* cambriolage *m*.

Burgundy ['bə:gəndɪ] *n* Bourgogne *f*.

burial ['berɪəl] *n* enterrement *m*.

burly ['bə:lɪ] *a* de forte carrure, costaud(e).

Burma ['bə:mə] *n* Birmanie *f*.

burn [bə:n] *vt, vi* (*pt, pp* **burned** or **burnt**) brûler // *n* brûlure *f*; **to ~ down** *vt* incendier, détruire par le feu; **~er** *n* brûleur *m*.

burnt [bə:nt] *pt, pp of* **burn**.

burrow ['bʌrəu] *n* terrier *m* // *vt* creuser.

bursar ['bə:sə*] *n* économe *m/f*; (*Brit: student*) boursier/ère; **~y** *n* (*Brit*) bourse *f* (d'études).

burst [bə:st] *vb* (*pt, pp* **burst**) *vt* crever; faire éclater // *vi* éclater; (*tyre*) crever // *n* explosion *f*; (*also:* **~ pipe**) rupture *f*; fuite *f*; **to ~ into flames** s'enflammer soudainement; **to ~ out laughing** éclater de rire; **to ~ into tears** fondre en

larmes; **to be ~ing with** être plein (à craquer) de; regorger de; **to ~ into** *vt* fus (*room etc*) faire irruption dans; **to ~ open** *vi* s'ouvrir violemment or soudainement.

bury ['berɪ] *vt* enterrer.

bus, **~es** [bʌs, 'bʌsɪz] *n* autobus *m*.

bush [buʃ] *n* buisson *m*; (*scrub land*) brousse *f*; **to beat about the ~** tourner autour du pot.

bushy ['buʃɪ] *a* broussailleux(euse), touffu(e).

busily ['bɪzɪlɪ] *ad* activement.

business ['bɪznɪs] *n* (*matter, firm*) affaire *f*; (*trading*) affaires *fpl*; (*job, duty*) travail *m*; **to be away on ~** être en déplacement d'affaires; **it's none of my ~** cela ne me regarde pas, ce ne sont pas mes affaires; **he means ~** il ne plaisante pas, il est sérieux; **~like** *a* sérieux(euse); efficace; **~man/woman** *n* homme/femme d'affaires; **~ trip** *n* voyage *m* d'affaires.

busker ['bʌskə*] *n* (*Brit*) musicien ambulant.

bus-stop ['bʌsstɔp] *n* arrêt *m* d'autobus.

bust [bʌst] *n* buste *m* // *a* (*col: broken*) fichu(e), fini(e); **to go ~** faire faillite.

bustle ['bʌsl] *n* remue-ménage *m*, affairement *m* // *vi* s'affairer, se démener.

busy ['bɪzɪ] *a* occupé(e); (*shop, street*) très fréquenté(e) // *vt*: **to ~ o.s.** s'occuper; **~body** *n* mouche *f* du coche, âme *f* charitable; **~ signal** *n* (*US TEL*) tonalité *f* occupé *inv*.

but [bʌt] ♦ *cj* mais; **I'd love to come, ~ I'm busy** j'aimerais venir mais je suis occupé ♦ *prep* (*apart from, except*) sauf, excepté; **we've had nothing ~ trouble** nous n'avons eu que des ennuis; **no-one ~ him can do it** lui seul peut le faire; **~ for you/your help** sans toi/ton aide; **anything ~ that** tout sauf or excepté ça, tout mais pas ça

♦ *ad* (*just, only*) ne ... que; **she's ~ a child** elle n'est qu'une enfant; **had I ~ known** si seulement j'avais su; **all ~ finished** pratiquement terminé.

butcher ['butʃə*] *n* boucher *m* // *vt* massacrer; (*cattle etc for meat*) tuer.

butler ['bʌtlə*] *n* maître m d'hôtel.

butt [bʌt] *n* (*cask*) gros tonneau; (*thick end*) (gros) bout *m*; (*of gun*) crosse *f*; (*of cigarette*) mégot *m*; (*Brit fig: target*) cible *f* // *vt* donner un coup de tête à; **to ~ in** *vi* (*interrupt*) s'immiscer dans la conversation.

butter ['bʌtə*] *n* beurre *m* // *vt* beurrer; **~cup** *n* bouton *m* d'or.

butterfly ['bʌtəflaɪ] *n* papillon *m*; (*SWIMMING: also:* **~ stroke**) brasse *f* papillon *inv*.

buttocks ['bʌtəks] *npl* fesses *fpl*.

button ['bʌtn] *n* bouton *m* // *vt* (*also:* **~**

up) boutonner // *vi* se boutonner.
buttress ['bʌtrɪs] *n* contrefort *m*.
buxom ['bʌksəm] *a* aux formes
avantageuses *or* épanouies.
buy [baɪ] *vb* (*pt, pp* **bought**) *vt* acheter;
to ~ sb sth/sth from sb acheter qch à qn;
to ~ sb a drink offrir un verre *or* à boire
à qn; ~**er** *n* acheteur/euse.
buzz [bʌz] *n* bourdonnement *m*; (*col:
phone call*) coup *m* de fil // *vi*
bourdonner.
buzzer ['bʌzə*] *n* timbre *m* électrique.
buzz word *n* (*col*) mot *m* à la mode.
by [baɪ] ♦ *prep* **1** (*referring to cause,
agent*) par, de; killed ~ lightning tué par
la foudre; surrounded ~ a fence entouré
d'une barrière; a painting ~ Picasso un
tableau de Picasso
2 (*referring to method, manner,
means*): ~ bus/car en autobus/voiture; ~
train par le *or* en train; to pay ~ cheque
payer par chèque; ~ saving hard, he ...
à force d'économiser, il ...
3 (*via, through*) par; we came ~ Dover
nous sommes venus par Douvres
4 (*close to, past*) à côté de; the house ~
the school la maison à côté de l'école; a
holiday ~ the sea des vacances au bord
de la mer; she sat ~ his bed elle était
assise à son chevet; she went ~ me elle
est passée à côté de moi; I go ~ the post
office every day je passe devant la poste
tous les jours
5 (*with time: not later than*) avant; (:
during): ~ daylight à la lumière du
jour; by night la nuit, de nuit; ~ 4
o'clock avant 4 heures; ~ this time tomorrow d'ici demain à la même heure;
~ the time I got here it was too late
lorsque je suis arrivé c'était déjà trop
tard
6 (*amount*) à; ~ the kilo/metre au kilo/
au mètre; paid ~ the hour payé à
l'heure
7 (*MATH, measure*): to divide/multiply
~ 3 diviser/multiplier par 3; a room 3
metres ~ 4 une pièce de 3 mètres sur 4;
it's broader ~ a metre c'est plus large
d'un mètre; one ~ one un à un; little ~
little petit à petit, peu à peu
8 (*according to*) d'après, selon; it's 3
o'clock ~ my watch il est 3 heures
d'après ma montre; it's all right ~ me
je n'ai rien contre
9: (all) ~ oneself *etc* tout(e) seul(e)
10: ~ the way au fait, à propos
♦ *ad* **1** see go, pass *etc*
2: ~ and ~ un peu plus tard, bientôt; ~
and large dans l'ensemble.
bye-(bye) ['baɪ('baɪ)] *excl* au revoir!,
salut!
by(e)-law ['baɪlɔ:] *n* arrêté municipal.
by-election ['baɪɪlɛkʃən] *n* (*Brit*)
élection (législative) partielle.
bygone ['baɪgɔn] *a* passé(e) // *n*: let ~s

be ~s passons l'éponge, oublions le
passé.
bypass ['baɪpɑ:s] *n* (route *f* de)
contournement *m*; (*MÉD*) pontage *m* // *vt*
éviter.
by-product ['baɪprɔdʌkt] *n* sous-produit
m, dérivé *m*; (*fig*) conséquence *f*
secondaire, retombée *f*.
bystander ['baɪstændə*] *n* spectateur/
trice, badaud/e.
byte [baɪt] *n* (*COMPUT*) octet *m*.
byway ['baɪweɪ] *n* chemin *m* (écarté).
byword ['baɪwə:d] *n*: to be a ~ for être
synonyme de (*fig*).
by-your-leave ['baɪjɔ:'li:v] *n*: without
so much as a ~ sans même demander la
permission.

C

C [si:] *n* (*MUS*) do *m*.
C.A. *abbr of* **chartered accountant**.
cab [kæb] *n* taxi *m*; (*of train, truck*)
cabine *f*; (*horse-drawn*) fiacre *m*.
cabaret ['kæbəreɪ] *n* attractions *fpl*,
spectacle *m* de cabaret.
cabbage ['kæbɪdʒ] *n* chou *m*.
cabin ['kæbɪn] *n* cabane *f*, hutte *f*; (*on
ship*) cabine *f*.
cabinet ['kæbɪnɪt] *n* (*POL*) cabinet *m*;
(*furniture*) petit meuble à tiroirs et
rayons; (*also: display* ~) vitrine *f*, petite
armoire vitrée; ~-**maker** *n* ébéniste *m*.
cable ['keɪbl] *n* câble *m* // *vt* câbler, télégraphier; ~-**car** *n* téléphérique *m*; ~
television *n* télévision *f* par câble.
cache [kæʃ] *n* cachette *f*.
cackle ['kækl] *vi* caqueter.
cactus, *pl* **cacti** ['kæktəs, -taɪ] *n* cactus
m.
cadet [kə'dɛt] *n* (*MIL*) élève *m* officier.
cadge [kædʒ] *vt* se faire donner.
café ['kæfeɪ] *n* ≈ café(-restaurant) *m*
(*sans alcool*).
cage [keɪdʒ] *n* cage *f*.
cagey ['keɪdʒɪ] *a* (*col*) réticent(e),
méfiant(e).
cagoule [kə'gu:l] *n* K-way *m* ®.
Cairo ['kaɪərəu] *n* le Caire.
cajole [kə'dʒəul] *vt* couvrir de flatteries
or de gentillesses.
cake [keɪk] *n* gâteau *m*; ~ of soap
savonnette *f*; ~**d** *a*: ~**d with** raidi(e)
par, couvert(e) d'une croûte de.
calculate ['kælkjuleɪt] *vt* calculer; **calculation** [-'leɪʃən] *n* calcul *m*; **calculator** *n* machine *f* à calculer, calculatrice
f.
calendar ['kæləndə*] *n* calendrier *m*; ~
year *n* année civile.
calf [kɑ:f], *pl* **calves** *n* (*of cow*) veau *m*;
(*of other animals*) petit *m*; (*also*: ~**skin**)
veau *m*, vachette *f*; (*ANAT*) mollet *m*.
calibre, (*US*) **caliber** ['kælɪbə*] *n* cali-

bre *m*.

call [kɔ:l] *vt* (*gen, also TEL*) appeler // *vi* appeler; (*visit: also:* ~ **in,** ~ **round**): to ~ (**for**) passer (prendre) // *n* (*shout*) appel *m*, cri *m*; (*visit*) visite *f*; (*also:* **telephone** ~) coup *m* de téléphone; communication *f*; **she's** ~**ed Suzanne** elle s'appelle Suzanne; **to be on** ~ être de permanence; **to** ~ **back** *vi* (*return*) repasser; (*TEL*) rappeler; **to** ~ **for** *vt fus* demander; **to** ~ **off** *vt* annuler; **to** ~ **on** *vt fus* (*visit*) rendre visite à, passer voir; (*request*): **to** ~ **on sb to do** inviter qn à faire; **to** ~ **out** *vi* pousser un cri or des cris; **to** ~ **up** *vt* (*MIL*) appeler, mobiliser; ~**box** *n* (*Brit*) cabine *f* téléphonique; ~**er** *n* personne *f* qui appelle; visiteur *m*; ~ **girl** *n* call-girl *f*; ~**-in** *n* (*US: phone-in*) programme *m* à ligne ouverte; ~**ing** *n* vocation *f*; (*trade, occupation*) état *m*; ~**ing card** *n* (*US*) carte *f* de visite.

callous ['kæləs] *a* dur(e), insensible.

calm [kɑ:m] *a* calme // *n* calme *m* // *vt* calmer, apaiser; **to** ~ **down** *vi* se calmer, s'apaiser // *vt* calmer, apaiser.

Calor gas ['kælə*-] *n* ® butane *m*, butagaz *m* ®.

calorie ['kælərɪ] *n* calorie *f*.

calves [kɑ:vz] *npl of* **calf**.

camber ['kæmbə*] *n* (*of road*) bombement *m*.

Cambodia [kæm'bəudjə] *n* Cambodge *m*.

came [keɪm] *pt of* **come**.

camel ['kæməl] *n* chameau *m*.

cameo ['kæmɪəu] *n* camée *m*.

camera ['kæmərə] *n* appareil-photo *m*; (*also:* ciné-~, movie ~) caméra *f*; **in** ~ à huis clos, en privé; ~**man** *n* caméraman *m*.

camouflage ['kæməflɑ:ʒ] *n* camouflage *m* // *vt* camoufler.

camp [kæmp] *n* camp *m* // *vi* camper.

campaign [kæm'peɪn] *n* (*MIL, POL etc*) campagne *f* // *vi* (*also fig*) faire campagne.

campbed ['kæmp'bɛd] *n* (*Brit*) lit *m* de camp.

camper ['kæmpə*] *n* campeur/euse.

camping ['kæmpɪŋ] *n* camping *m*; **to go** ~ faire du camping.

campsite ['kæmpsaɪt] *n* campement *m*.

campus ['kæmpəs] *n* campus *m*.

can [kæn] *auxiliary vb see next headword* // *n* (*of milk, oil, water*) bidon *m*; (*tin*) boîte *f* de conserve // *vt* mettre en conserve.

can [kæn] ♦ *n, vt see previous headword* ♦ *auxiliary vb* (*negative* **cannot**, **can't**; *conditional and pt* **could**) **1** (*be able to*) pouvoir; **you** ~ **do it if you try** vous pouvez le faire si vous essayez; **I** ~**'t hear you** je ne t'entends pas **2** (*know how to*) savoir; **I** ~ **swim/play**

tennis/drive je sais nager/jouer au tennis/conduire; ~ **you speak French?** parlez-vous français? **3** (*may*) pouvoir; ~ **I use your phone?** puis-je me servir de votre téléphone? **4** (*expressing disbelief, puzzlement etc*): **it** ~**'t be true!** ce n'est pas possible!; **what CAN he want?** qu'est-ce qu'il peut bien vouloir? **5** (*expressing possibility, suggestion etc*): **he could be in the library** il est peut-être dans la bibliothèque; **she could have been delayed** il se peut qu'elle ait été retardée.

Canada ['kænədə] *n* Canada *m*.

Canadian [kə'neɪdɪən] *a* canadien(ne) // *n* Canadien/ne.

canal [kə'næl] *n* canal *m*.

canary [kə'nɛərɪ] *n* canari *m*, serin *m*.

cancel ['kænsəl] *vt* annuler; (*train*) supprimer; (*party, appointment*) décommander; (*cross out*) barrer; rayer; (*stamp*) oblitérer; ~**lation** [-'leɪʃən] *n* annulation *f*; suppression *f*; oblitération *f*; (*TOURISM*) réservation annulée.

cancer ['kænsə*] *n* cancer *m*; **C~** (*sign*) le Cancer.

candid ['kændɪd] *a* (très) franc(franche), sincère.

candidate ['kændɪdeɪt] *n* candidat/e.

candle ['kændl] *n* bougie *f*; (*of tallow*) chandelle *f*; (*in church*) cierge *m*; **by** ~**light** à la lumière d'une bougie; (*dinner*) aux chandelles; ~**stick** *n* (*also:* ~ **holder**) bougeoir *m*; (*bigger, ornate*) chandelier *m*.

candour, (*US*) **candor** ['kændə*] *n* (grande) franchise or sincérité.

candy ['kændɪ] *n* sucre candi; (*US*) bonbon *m*; ~**-floss** *n* (*Brit*) barbe *f* à papa.

cane [keɪn] *n* canne *f* // *vt* (*Brit SCOL*) administrer des coups de bâton à.

canister ['kænɪstə*] *n* boîte *f*.

cannabis ['kænəbɪs] *n* (*drug*) cannabis *m*; (*also:* ~ **plant**) chanvre indien.

canned ['kænd] *a* (*food*) en boîte, en conserve.

cannon, *pl* ~ or ~**s** ['kænən] *n* (*gun*) canon *m*.

cannot ['kænɔt] = **can not**.

canny ['kænɪ] *a* madré(e), finaud(e).

canoe [kə'nu:] *n* pirogue *f*; (*SPORT*) canoë *m*.

canon ['kænən] *n* (*clergyman*) chanoine *m*; (*standard*) canon *m*.

can opener [-'əupnə*] *n* ouvre-boîte *m*.

canopy ['kænəpɪ] *n* baldaquin *m*; dais *m*.

can't [kænt] = **can not**.

cantankerous [kæn'tæŋkərəs] *a* querelleur(euse), acariâtre.

canteen [kæn'ti:n] *n* cantine *f*; (*Brit: of cutlery*) ménagère *f*.

canter ['kæntə*] n petit galop.
canvas ['kænvəs] n (gen) toile f.
canvassing ['kænvəsɪŋ] n (POL) prospection électorale, démarchage électoral; (COMM) démarchage, prospection.
canyon ['kænjən] n cañon m, gorge (profonde).
cap [kæp] n casquette f; (of pen) capuchon m; (of bottle) capsule f // vt capsuler; (outdo) surpasser.
capability [keɪpə'bɪlɪtɪ] n aptitude f, capacité f.
capable ['keɪpəbl] a capable.
capacity [kə'pæsɪtɪ] n capacité f, contenance f; aptitude f.
cape [keɪp] n (garment) cape f; (GEO) cap m.
capital ['kæpɪtl] n (also: ~ city) capitale f; (money) capital m; (also: ~ letter) majuscule f; ~ **gains tax** n impôt m sur les plus-values; ~**ism** n capitalisme m; ~**ist** a, n capitaliste (m/f); ~**ize**: to ~ize on vt fus profiter de; ~ **punishment** n peine capitale.
Capricorn ['kæprɪkɔ:n] n le Capricorne.
capsize [kæp'saɪz] vt faire chavirer // vi chavirer.
capsule ['kæpsju:l] n capsule f.
captain ['kæptɪn] n capitaine m.
caption ['kæpʃən] n légende f.
captive ['kæptɪv] a, n captif(ive).
capture ['kæptʃə*] vt capturer, prendre; (attention) capter // n capture f; (data ~) saisie f de données.
car [ka:*] n voiture f, auto f.
carafe [kə'ræf] n carafe f.
caramel ['kærəməl] n caramel m.
caravan ['kærəvæn] n caravane f; ~ **site** n (Brit) camping m pour caravanes.
carbohydrates [ka:bəu'haɪdreɪts] npl (foods) aliments mpl riches en hydrate de carbone.
carbon ['ka:bən] n carbone m; ~ **paper** n papier m carbone.
carburettor, (US) **carburetor** [ka:bju-'retə*] n carburateur m.
card [ka:d] n carte f; ~**board** n carton m; ~ **game** n jeu m de cartes.
cardiac ['ka:dɪæk] a cardiaque.
cardigan ['ka:dɪgən] n cardigan m.
cardinal ['ka:dɪnl] a cardinal(e) // n cardinal m.
card index ['ka:dɪndɛks] n fichier m (alphabétique).
care [kɛə*] n soin m, attention f; (worry) souci m // vi: to ~ **about** se soucier de, s'intéresser à; ~ **of** (c/o) chez, aux bons soins de; in sb's ~ à la garde de qn, confié à qn; to take ~ (to do) faire attention (à faire); to take ~ of vt s'occuper de, prendre soin de; to ~ for vt fus s'occuper de; (like) aimer; I don't ~ ça m'est bien égal, peu m'importe.

career [kə'rɪə*] n carrière f // vi (also: ~ along) aller à toute allure.
carefree ['kɛəfri:] a sans souci, insouciant(e).
careful ['kɛəful] a soigneux(euse); (cautious) prudent(e); (be) ~! (fais) attention!; ~**ly** ad avec soin, soigneusement; prudemment.
careless ['kɛəlɪs] a négligent(e); (heedless) insouciant(e).
caress [kə'rɛs] n caresse f // vt caresser.
caretaker ['kɛəteɪkə*] n gardien/ne, concierge m/f.
car-ferry ['ka:fɛrɪ] n (on sea) ferry(-boat) m; (on river) bac m.
cargo, pl ~es ['ka:gəu] n cargaison f, chargement m.
car hire n location f de voiture.
Caribbean [kærɪ'bi:ən] a: the ~ (Sea) la mer des Antilles or Caraïbes.
caring ['kɛərɪŋ] a (person) bienveillant(e); (society, organization) humanitaire.
carnal ['ka:nl] a charnel(le).
carnation [ka:'neɪʃən] n œillet m.
carnival ['ka:nɪvəl] n (public celebration) carnaval m; (US: funfair) fête foraine.
carol ['kærəl] n: (Christmas) ~ chant m de Noël.
carp [ka:p] n (fish) carpe f; to ~ **at** vt fus critiquer.
car park ['ka:pa:k] n (Brit) parking m, parc m de stationnement.
carpenter ['ka:pɪntə*] n charpentier m.
carpentry ['ka:pɪntrɪ] n charpenterie f, métier m de charpentier; (woodwork: at school etc) menuiserie f.
carpet ['ka:pɪt] n tapis m // vt recouvrir (d'un tapis); ~ **slippers** npl pantoufles fpl; ~ **sweeper** n balai m mécanique.
carriage ['kærɪdʒ] n voiture f; (of goods) transport m; (: cost) port m; (of typewriter) chariot m; (bearing) maintien m, port m; ~ **return** n (on typewriter etc) retour m de chariot; ~**way** n (Brit: part of road) chaussée f.
carrier ['kærɪə*] n transporteur m, camionneur m; (MED) porteur/euse; (NAUT) porte-avions m inv; ~ **bag** n (Brit) sac m en papier or en plastique.
carrot ['kærət] n carotte f.
carry ['kærɪ] vt (subj: person) porter; (: vehicle) transporter; (a motion, bill) voter, adopter; (involve: responsibilities etc) comporter, impliquer // vi (sound) porter; to be or get carried away (fig) s'emballer, s'enthousiasmer; to ~ **on** vi: to ~ on with sth/doing continuer qch/à faire // vt entretenir, poursuivre; to ~ **out** vt (orders) exécuter; (investigation) effectuer; ~**cot** n porte-bébé m; ~**-on** n (col: fuss) histoires fpl.
cart [ka:t] n charrette f // vt transporter.

carton ['kɑːtən] n (box) carton m; (of yogurt) pot m (en carton); (of cigarettes) cartouche f.

cartoon [kɑː'tuːn] n (PRESS) dessin m (humoristique); (satirical) caricature f; (comic strip) bande dessinée; (CINEMA) dessin animé.

cartridge ['kɑːtrɪdʒ] n (for gun, pen) cartouche f; (for camera) chargeur m; (music tape) cassette f.

carve [kɑːv] vt (meat) découper; (wood, stone) tailler, sculpter; **to ~ up** vt découper; (fig: country) morceler; **carving** n (in wood etc) sculpture f; **carving knife** n couteau m à découper.

car wash n station f de lavage (de voitures).

case [keɪs] n cas m; (LAW) affaire f, procès m; (box) caisse f, boîte f, étui m; (Brit: also: suit~) valise f; he hasn't put forward his ~ very well ses arguments ne sont guère convaincants; **in ~ of** en cas de; **in ~** he au cas où il; **just in ~** à tout hasard.

cash [kæʃ] n argent m; (COMM) argent liquide, numéraire m; liquidités fpl; (COMM: in payment) argent comptant, espèces fpl // vt encaisser; **to pay (in) ~** payer (en argent) comptant; **~ on delivery (C.O.D.)** (COMM) payable or paiement à la livraison; **~book** n livre m de caisse; **~ card** n carte f de retrait; **~ desk** n (Brit) caisse f; **~ dispenser** n. guichet m automatique de banque.

cashew [kæ'ʃuː] n. (also: ~ **nut**) noix f de cajou.

cashier [kæ'ʃɪə*] n caissier/ère.

cashmere ['kæʃmɪə*] n cachemire m.

cash register n caisse enregistreuse.

casing ['keɪsɪŋ] n revêtement (protecteur), enveloppe (protectrice).

casino [kə'siːnəu] n casino m.

cask [kɑːsk] n tonneau m.

casket ['kɑːskɪt] n coffret m; (US: coffin) cercueil m.

casserole ['kæsərəul] n cocotte f; (food) ragoût m (en cocotte).

cassette [kæ'set] n cassette f, musicassette f; **~ player** n lecteur m de cassettes; **~ recorder** n magnétophone m à cassettes.

cast [kɑːst] vb (pt, pp **cast**) vt (throw) jeter; (shed) perdre; se dépouiller de; (metal) couler, fondre; (THEATRE): **to ~ sb as Hamlet** attribuer à qn le rôle d'Hamlet // n (THEATRE) distribution f; (mould) moule m; (also: **plaster ~**) plâtre m; **to ~ one's vote** voter, exprimer son suffrage; **to ~ off** vi (NAUT) larguer les amarres.

castaway ['kɑːstəwəɪ] n naufragé/e.

caster sugar ['kɑːstə*-] n (Brit) sucre m semoule.

casting ['kɑːstɪŋ] a: **~ vote** (Brit) voix

prépondérante (pour départager).

cast iron n fonte f.

castle ['kɑːsl] n château-fort m; (manor) château m.

castor ['kɑːstə*] n (wheel) roulette f; **~ oil** n huile f de ricin.

castrate [kæs'treɪt] vt châtrer.

casual ['kæʒjul] a (by chance) de hasard, fait(e) au hasard, fortuit(e); (irregular: work etc) temporaire; (unconcerned) désinvolte; **~ wear** n vêtements mpl sport inv; **~ly** ad avec désinvolture, négligemment; fortuitement.

casualty ['kæʒjultɪ] n accidenté/e, blessé/e; (dead) victime f, mort/e.

cat [kæt] n chat m.

catalogue, (US) catalog ['kætələɡ] n catalogue m // vt cataloguer.

catalyst ['kætəlɪst] n catalyseur m.

catapult ['kætəpʌlt] n lance-pierres m inv, fronde m; (HISTORY) catapulte f.

catarrh [kə'tɑː*] n rhume m chronique, catarrhe f.

catastrophe [kə'tæstrəfɪ] n catastrophe f.

catch [kætʃ] vb (pt, pp **caught**) vt (ball, train, thief, cold) attraper; (person: by surprise) prendre, surprendre; (understand) saisir; (get entangled) accrocher // vi (fire) prendre // n (fish etc caught) prise f; (thief etc caught) capture f; (trick) attrape f; (TECH) loquet m; cliquet m; **to ~ sb's attention** or **eye** attirer l'attention de qn; **to ~ fire** prendre feu; **to ~ sight of** apercevoir; **to ~ on** vi saisir; (grow popular) prendre; **to ~ up** vi se rattraper, combler son retard // vt (also: **~ up with**) rattraper.

catching ['kætʃɪŋ] a (MED) contagieux(euse).

catchment area ['kætʃmənt-] n (Brit SCOL) aire f de recrutement; (GEO) bassin m hydrographique.

catch phrase n slogan m; expression toute faite.

catchy ['kætʃɪ] a (tune) facile à retenir.

category ['kætɪɡərɪ] n catégorie f.

cater ['keɪtə*] vi (provide food): **to ~ (for)** préparer des repas (pour), se charger de la restauration (pour); **to ~ for** vt fus (Brit: needs) satisfaire, pourvoir à; (: readers, consumers) s'adresser à, pourvoir aux besoins de; **~er** n traiteur m; fournisseur m; **~ing** n restauration f; approvisionnement m, ravitaillement m.

caterpillar ['kætəpɪlə*] n chenille f; **~ track** n chenille f.

cathedral [kə'θiːdrəl] n cathédrale f.

catholic ['kæθəlɪk] a éclectique; universel(le); libéral(e); **C~** a, n (REL) catholique (m/f).

cat's-eye [kæts'aɪ] n (Brit AUT) (clou m à) catadioptre m.

cattle ['kætl] *npl* bétail *m*, bestiaux *mpl*.

catty ['kætɪ] *a* méchant(e).

caucus ['kɔ:kəs] *n* (*POL: group*) comité local d'un parti politique; (*: US*) comité électoral (pour désigner des candidats).

caught [kɔ:t] *pt, pp of* **catch**.

cauliflower ['kɔlɪflauə*'] *n* chou-fleur *m*.

cause [kɔ:z] *n* cause *f* // *vt* causer.

caution ['kɔ:ʃən] *n* prudence *f*; (*warning*) avertissement *m* // *vt* avertir, donner un avertissement à.

cautious ['kɔ:ʃəs] *a* prudent(e).

cavalry ['kævəlrɪ] *n* cavalerie *f*.

cave [keɪv] *n* caverne *f*, grotte *f*; **to ~ in** *vi* (*roof etc*) s'effondrer; **~man** *n* homme *m* des cavernes.

caviar(e) ['kævɪɑ:*'] *n* caviar *m*.

cavort [kə'vɔ:t] *vi* cabrioler, faire des cabrioles.

CB *n abbr* (= *Citizens' Band (Radio)*) CB *f*.

CBI *n abbr* (= *Confederation of British Industries*) groupement du patronat.

cc *abbr* = *carbon copy, cubic centimetres*.

cease [si:s] *vt, vi* cesser; **~fire** *n* cessez-le-feu *m*; **~less** *a* incessant(e), continuel(le).

cedar ['si:də*'] *n* cèdre *m*.

ceiling ['si:lɪŋ] *n* plafond *m*.

celebrate ['sɛlɪbreɪt] *vt, vi* célébrer; **~d** *a* célèbre; **celebration** [-'breɪʃən] *n* célébration *f*.

celery ['sɛlərɪ] *n* céleri *m* (en branches).

cell [sɛl] *n* (*gen*) cellule *f*; (*ELEC*) élément *m* (*de pile*).

cellar ['sɛlə*'] *n* cave *f*.

'cello ['tʃɛləu] *n* violoncelle *m*.

Celt [kɛlt, sɛlt] *n* Celte *m/f*.

Celtic ['kɛltɪk, 'sɛltɪk] *a* celte.

cement [sə'mɛnt] *n* ciment *m* // *vt* cimenter; **~ mixer** *n* bétonnière *f*.

cemetery ['sɛmɪtrɪ] *n* cimetière *m*.

censor ['sɛnsə*'] *n* censeur *m* // *vt* censurer; **~ship** *n* censure *f*.

censure ['sɛnʃə*'] *vt* blâmer, critiquer.

census ['sɛnsəs] *n* recensement *m*.

cent [sɛnt] *n* (*US: coin*) cent *m* (= *1:100 du dollar*); *see also* **per**.

centenary [sɛn'ti:nərɪ] *n* centenaire *m*.

center ['sɛntə*'] *n* (*US*) = **centre**.

centi... ['sɛntɪ] *prefix*: **~grade** *a* centigrade; **~metre**, (*US*) **~meter** *n* centimètre *m*.

centipede ['sɛntɪpi:d] *n* mille-pattes *m inv*.

central ['sɛntrəl] *a* central(e); **C~ America** *n* Amérique centrale; **~ heating** *n* chauffage central.

centre ['sɛntə*'] *n* centre *m* // *vt* centrer; (*PHOT*) cadrer; **~-forward** *n* (*SPORT*) avant-centre *m*; **~-half** *n* (*SPORT*) demi-centre *m*.

century ['sɛntjurɪ] *n* siècle *m*; **20th ~**

XXe siècle.

ceramic [sɪ'ræmɪk] *a* céramique.

cereal ['si:rɪəl] *n* céréale *f*.

ceremony ['sɛrɪmənɪ] *n* cérémonie *f*; **to stand on ~** faire des façons.

certain ['sə:tən] *a* certain(e); **to make ~ of** s'assurer de; **for ~** certainement, sûrement; **~ly** *ad* certainement; **~ty** *n* certitude *f*.

certificate [sə'tɪfɪkɪt] *n* certificat *m*.

certified ['sə:tɪfaɪd]: **~ mail** *n* (*US*): **by ~ mail** en recommandé, avec avis de réception; **~ public accountant** *n* (*US*) expert-comptable *m*.

cervical ['sə:vɪkl] *a*: **~ cancer** cancer *m* du col de l'utérus; **~ smear** frottis vaginal.

cervix ['sə:vɪks] *n* col *m* de l'utérus.

cesspit ['sɛspɪt] *n* fosse *f* d'aisance.

cf. *abbr* (= *compare*) cf., voir.

ch. *abbr* (= *chapter*) chap.

chafe [tʃeɪf] *vt* irriter, frotter contre.

chaffinch ['tʃæfɪntʃ] *n* pinson *m*.

chain [tʃeɪn] *n* (*gen*) chaîne *f* // *vt* (*also:* **~ up**) enchaîner, attacher (avec une chaîne); **~ reaction** *n* réaction *f* en chaîne; **to ~ smoke** *vi* fumer cigarette sur cigarette; **~ store** *n* magasin *m* à succursales multiples.

chair [tʃeə*'] *n* chaise *f*; (*armchair*) fauteuil *m*; (*of university*) chaire *f* // *vt* (*meeting*) présider; **~lift** *n* télésiège *m*; **~man** *n* président *m*.

chalice ['tʃælɪs] *n* calice *m*.

chalk [tʃɔ:k] *n* craie *f*.

challenge ['tʃælɪndʒ] *n* défi *m* // *vt* défier; (*statement, right*) mettre en question, contester; **to ~ sb to do** mettre qn au défi de faire; **challenging** *a* de défi, provocateur(trice).

chamber ['tʃeɪmbə*'] *n* chambre *f*; **~ of commerce** chambre de commerce; **~maid** *n* femme *f* de chambre; **~ music** *n* musique *f* de chambre.

champagne [ʃæm'peɪn] *n* champagne *m*.

champion ['tʃæmpɪən] *n* champion/ne; **~ship** *n* championnat *m*.

chance [tʃɑ:ns] *n* hasard *m*; (*opportunity*) occasion *f*, possibilité *f*; (*hope, likelihood*) chance *f* // *vt*: **to ~ it** risquer (le coup), essayer // *a* fortuit(e), de hasard; **to take a ~** prendre un risque; **by ~** par hasard.

chancellor ['tʃɑ:nsələ*'] *n* chancelier *m*; **C~ of the Exchequer** *n* (*Brit*) chancelier de l'Échiquier.

chandelier [ʃændə'lɪə*'] *n* lustre *m*.

change [tʃeɪndʒ] *vt* (*alter, replace, COMM: money*) changer; (*switch, substitute: gear, hands, trains, clothes, one's name etc*) changer de; (*transform*): **to ~ sb into** changer or transformer qn en // *vi* (*gen*) changer; (*change clothes*) se changer; (*be transformed*): **to ~ into** se

changer *or* transformer en // *n*
changement *m*; (*money*) monnaie *f*; **to
~ one's mind** changer d'avis; **a ~ of
clothes** des vêtements de rechange; **for a
~ pour** changer; **~able** *a* (*weather*)
variable; **~ machine** *n* distributeur *m*
de monnaie; **~over** *n* (*to new system*)
changement *m*, passage *m*.

changing ['tʃeɪndʒɪŋ] *a* changeant(e);
~ room *n* (*Brit*: *in shop*) salon *m*
d'essayage; (: *SPORT*) vestiaire *m*.

channel ['tʃænl] *n* (*TV*) chaîne *f*; (*wave-
band, groove, fig: medium*) canal *m*; (*of
river, sea*) chenal *m* // *vt* canaliser;
through the usual ~s en suivant la filière
habituelle; **the (English) C~** la Manche;
the C~ Islands les îles de la Manche,
les îles anglo-normandes.

chant [tʃɑːnt] *n* chant *m*; mélopée *f*;
psalmodie *f* // *vt* chanter, scander;
psalmodier.

chaos ['keɪɔs] *n* chaos *m*.

chap [tʃæp] *n* (*Brit col: man*) type *m*.

chapel ['tʃæpəl] *n* chapelle *f*.

chaplain ['tʃæplɪn] *n* aumônier *m*.

chapped [tʃæpt] *a* (*skin, lips*) gercé(e).

chapter ['tʃæptə*] *n* chapitre *m*.

char [tʃɑː*] *vt* (*burn*) carboniser // *n*
(*Brit*) = **charlady**.

character ['kærɪktə*] *n* caractère *m*; (*in
novel, film*), personnage *m*; (*eccentric*)
numéro *m*, phénomène *m*; **~istic**
[-'rɪstɪk] *a, n* caractéristique (*f*).

charcoal ['tʃɑːkəʊl] *n* charbon *m* de
bois.

charge [tʃɑːdʒ] *n* accusation *f*; (*LAW*)
inculpation *f*; (*cost*) prix (demandé); (*of
gun, battery, MIL: attack*) charge *f* // *vt*
(*LAW*): **to ~ sb (with)** inculper qn (de);
(*gun, battery, MIL: enemy*) charger;
(*customer, sum*) faire payer // *vi* (*gen
with: up, along etc*) foncer; **~s** *npl*:
bank ~s frais *mpl* de banque; **is there a
~?** doit-on payer?; **to reverse the ~s**
(*TEL*) téléphoner en PCV; **to take ~ of**
se charger de; **to be in ~ of** être
responsable de, s'occuper de; **to ~ an expense (up) to sb** mettre une dépense sur
le compte de qn; **~ card** *f* carte *f* de
client (*émise par un grand magasin*).

charity ['tʃærɪtɪ] *n* charité *f*; institution *f*
charitable *or* de bienfaisance, œuvre *f*
(de charité).

charlady ['tʃɑːleɪdɪ] *n* (*Brit*) femme *f* de
ménage.

charm [tʃɑːm] *n* charme *m* // *vt*
charmer, enchanter; **~ing** *a* char-
mant(e).

chart [tʃɑːt] *n* tableau *m*, diagramme *m*;
graphique *m*; (*map*) carte marine *f* // *vt*
dresser *or* établir la carte de.

charter ['tʃɑːtə*] *vt* (*plane*) affréter // *n*
(*document*) charte *f*; **~ed accountant**
n (*Brit*) expert-comptable *m*; **~ flight** *n*
charter *m*.

chase [tʃeɪs] *vt* poursuivre, pourchasser
// *n* poursuite *f*, chasse *f*.

chasm ['kæzəm] *n* gouffre *m*, abîme *m*.

chat [tʃæt] *vi* (*also:* **have a ~**) bavarder,
causer // *n* conversation *f*; **~ show** *n*
(*Brit*) entretien télévisé.

chatter ['tʃætə*] *vi* (*person*) bavarder //
n bavardage *m*; **my teeth are ~ing** je
claque des dents; **~box** *n* moulin *m* à
paroles.

chatty ['tʃætɪ] *a* (*style*) familier(ère);
(*person*) enclin(e) à bavarder.

chauffeur ['ʃəʊfə*] *n* chauffeur *m* (de
maître).

chauvinist ['ʃəʊvɪnɪst] *n* (*male ~*)
phallocrate *m*; (*nationalist*) chauvin/e.

cheap [tʃiːp] *a* bon marché *inv*, pas
cher(chère); (*joke*) facile, d'un goût
douteux; (*poor quality*) à bon marché,
de qualité médiocre // *ad* à bon marché,
pour pas cher; **~en** *vt* rabaisser, déprécier; **~er** *a* moins cher(chère); **~ly**
ad à bon marché, à bon compte.

cheat [tʃiːt] *vi* tricher // *vt* tromper,
duper; (*rob*) escroquer // *n* tricheur/
euse; escroc *m*; (*trick*) duperie *f*,
tromperie *f*.

check [tʃɛk] *vt* vérifier; (*passport, ticket*) contrôler; (*halt*) enrayer; (*restrain*)
maîtriser // *n* vérification *f*; contrôle *m*;
(*curb*) frein *m*; (*bill*) addition *f*; (*pattern: gen pl*) carreaux *mpl*; (*US*) =
cheque // *a* (*also:* **~ed:** *pattern, cloth*) à
carreaux; **to ~ in** *vi* (*in hotel*) remplir
sa fiche (d'hôtel); (*at airport*) se
présenter à l'enregistrement // *vt*
(*luggage*) (faire) enregistrer; **to ~ out**
vi (*in hotel*) régler sa note // *vt*
(*luggage*) retirer; **to ~ up** *vi*: **to ~ up
(on sth)** vérifier (qch); **to ~ up on sb** se
renseigner sur le compte de qn; **~ered**
a (*US*) = **chequered**; **~ers** *n* (*US*) jeu
m de dames; **~in (desk)** *n* enregistrement *m*; **~ing account** *n* (*US: current account*) compte courant; **~mate** *n*
échec et mat *m*; **~out** *n* caisse *f*;
~point *n* contrôle *m*; **~room** *n* (*US:
left-luggage office*) consigne *f*; **~up** *n*
(*MED*) examen médical, check-up *m*.

cheek [tʃiːk] *n* joue *f*; (*impudence*)
toupet *m*, culot *m*; **~bone** *n* pommette
f; **~y** *a* effronté(e), culotté(e).

cheep [tʃiːp] *vi* piauler.

cheer [tʃɪə*] *vt* acclamer, applaudir;
(*gladden*) réjouir, réconforter // *vi* applaudir // *n* (*gen pl*) acclamations *fpl*,
applaudissements *mpl*; bravos *mpl*,
hourras *mpl*; **~s!** (à votre) santé!; **to ~
up** *vi* se dérider, reprendre courage // *vt*
remonter le moral à *or* de, dérider,
égayer; **~ful** *a* gai(e), joyeux(euse).

cheerio ['tʃɪərɪ'əʊ] *excl* (*Brit*) salut!, au
revoir!

cheese [tʃiːz] *n* fromage *m*; **~board** *n*
plateau *m* à fromages.

cheetah ['tʃiːtə] n guépard m.

chef [ʃɛf] n chef (cuisinier).

chemical ['kɛmɪkəl] a chimique // n produit m chimique.

chemist ['kɛmɪst] n (Brit: pharmacist) pharmacien/ne; (scientist) chimiste m/f; **~ry** n chimie f; **~'s** (shop) n (Brit) pharmacie f.

cheque [tʃɛk] n (Brit) chèque m; **~book** n chéquier m, carnet m de chèques; **~ card** n carte f (d'identité) bancaire.

chequered ['tʃɛkəd] a (fig) varié(e).

cherish ['tʃɛrɪʃ] vt chérir; (hope etc) entretenir.

cherry ['tʃɛrɪ] n cerise f.

chess [tʃɛs] n échecs mpl; **~board** n échiquier m; **~man** n pièce f (de jeu d'échecs).

chest [tʃɛst] n poitrine f; (box) coffre m, caisse f; **~ of drawers** n commode f.

chestnut ['tʃɛsnʌt] n châtaigne f; (also: ~ tree) châtaignier m.

chew [tʃuː] vt mâcher; **~ing gum** n chewing-gum m.

chic [ʃiːk] a chic inv, élégant(e).

chick [tʃɪk] n poussin m; (US col) pépée f.

chicken ['tʃɪkɪn] n poulet m; **to ~ out** vi (col) se dégonfler; **~pox** n varicelle f.

chicory ['tʃɪkərɪ] n (for coffee) chicorée f; (salad) endive f.

chief [tʃiːf] n chef m // a principal(e); **~ executive** n directeur général; **~ly** ad principalement, surtout.

chiffon ['ʃɪfɔn] n mousseline f de soie.

chilblain ['tʃɪlbleɪn] n engelure f.

child, pl **~ren** [tʃaɪld, 'tʃɪldrən] n enfant m/f; **~birth** n accouchement m; **~hood** n enfance f; **~ish** a puéril(e), enfantin(e); **~like** a innocent(e), pur(e); **~ minder** n (Brit) garde f d'enfants.

Chile ['tʃɪlɪ] n Chili m.

chill [tʃɪl] n froid m; (MED) refroidissement m, coup m de froid // a froid(e), glacial(e) // vt faire frissonner; refroidir; (CULIN) mettre au frais, rafraîchir.

chil(l)i ['tʃɪlɪ] n piment m (rouge).

chilly ['tʃɪlɪ] a froid(e), glacé(e); (sensitive to cold) frileux(euse); **to feel ~** avoir froid.

chime [tʃaɪm] n carillon m // vi carillonner, sonner.

chimney ['tʃɪmnɪ] n cheminée f; **~ sweep** n ramoneur m.

chimpanzee [tʃɪmpæn'ziː] n chimpanzé m.

chin [tʃɪn] n menton m.

China ['tʃaɪnə] n Chine f.

china ['tʃaɪnə] n porcelaine f; (vaisselle f en) porcelaine.

Chinese [tʃaɪ'niːz] a chinois(e) // n, pl inv Chinois/e; (LING) chinois m.

chink [tʃɪŋk] n (opening) fente f, fissure f; (noise) tintement m.

chip [tʃɪp] n (gen pl: CULIN) frite f; (: US: also: potato ~) chip m; (of wood) copeau m; (of glass, stone) éclat m; (also: micro~) puce f // vt (cup, plate) ébrécher; **to ~ in** vi mettre son grain de sel.

chiropodist [kɪ'rɔpədɪst] n (Brit) pédicure m/f.

chirp [tʃəːp] vi pépier, gazouiller.

chisel ['tʃɪzl] n ciseau m.

chit [tʃɪt] n mot m, note f.

chitchat ['tʃɪttʃæt] n bavardage m.

chivalry ['ʃɪvəlrɪ] n chevalerie f; esprit m chevaleresque.

chives [tʃaɪvz] npl ciboulette f, civette f.

chock [tʃɔk] n cale f; **~-a-block**, **~-full** a plein(e) à craquer.

chocolate ['tʃɔklɪt] n chocolat m.

choice [tʃɔɪs] n choix m // a de choix.

choir ['kwaɪə*] n chœur m, chorale f; **~boy** n jeune choriste m.

choke [tʃəuk] vi étouffer // vt étrangler; étouffer; (block) boucher, obstruer // n (AUT) starter m.

choose [tʃuːz], pt **chose**, pp **chosen** vt choisir; **to ~ to do** décider de faire, juger bon de faire.

choosy ['tʃuːzɪ] a: **(to be) ~** (faire le) difficile.

chop [tʃɔp] vt (wood) couper (à la hache); (CULIN: also: ~ up) couper (fin), émincer, hacher (en morceaux) // n coup m (de hache, du tranchant de la main); (CULIN) côtelette f; **~s** npl (jaws) mâchoires fpl; babines fpl.

chopper ['tʃɔpə*] n (helicopter) hélicoptère m, hélico m.

choppy ['tʃɔpɪ] a (sea) un peu agité(e).

chopsticks ['tʃɔpstɪks] npl baguettes fpl.

chord [kɔːd] n (MUS) accord m.

chore [tʃɔː*] n travail m de routine; **household ~s** travaux mpl du ménage.

chortle ['tʃɔːtl] vi glousser.

chorus ['kɔːrəs] n chœur m; (repeated part of song, also fig) refrain m.

chose [tʃəuz] pt of **choose**.

chosen ['tʃəuzn] pp of **choose**.

Christ [kraɪst] n Christ m.

christen ['krɪsn] vt baptiser.

Christian ['krɪstɪən] a, n chrétien(ne); **~ity** [-'ænɪtɪ] n christianisme m; chrétienté f; **~ name** n prénom m.

Christmas ['krɪsməs] n Noël m or f; **Merry ~!** joyeux Noël!; **~ card** n carte f de Noël; **~ Day** n le jour de Noël; **~ Eve** n la veille de Noël; la nuit de Noël; **~ tree** n arbre m de Noël.

chrome [krəum], **chromium** ['krəumɪəm] n chrome m.

chronic ['krɔnɪk] a chronique.

chronicle ['krɔnɪkl] n chronique f.

chronological [krɔnə'lɔdʒɪkəl] a

chronologique.

chrysanthemum [krɪ'sænθəməm] n chrysanthème m.

chubby ['tʃʌbɪ] a potelé(e), rondelet(te).

chuck [tʃʌk] vt lancer, jeter; **to ~ out** vt flanquer dehors or à la porte; **to ~ (up)** vt (Brit) lâcher, plaquer.

chuckle ['tʃʌkl] vi glousser.

chug [tʃʌg] vi faire teuf-teuf; souffler.

chum [tʃʌm] n copain/copine.

chunk [tʃʌŋk] n gros morceau; (of bread) quignon m.

church [tʃɜ:tʃ] n église f; **~yard** n cimetière m.

churlish ['tʃɜ:lɪʃ] a grossier(ère); hargneux(euse).

churn [tʃɜ:n] n (for butter) baratte f; (for transport: also: **milk ~**) (grand) bidon à lait; **to ~ out** vt débiter.

chute [ʃu:t] n glissoire f; (also: rubbish ~) vide-ordures m inv; (Brit: children's slide) toboggan m.

chutney ['tʃʌtnɪ] n condiment m à base de fruits.

CIA n abbr (US: = Central Intelligence Agency) CIA f.

CID n abbr (Brit: = Criminal Investigation Department) ≈ P.J. f (= police judiciaire).

cider ['saɪdə*] n cidre m.

cigar [sɪ'gɑ:*] n cigare m.

cigarette [sɪgə'ret] n cigarette f; **~ case** n étui m à cigarettes; **~ end** n mégot m.

cinder ['sɪndə*] n cendre f.

Cinderella [sɪndə'relə] n Cendrillon.

cine ['sɪnɪ]: **~-camera** n (Brit) caméra f; **~-film** n (Brit) film m.

cinema ['sɪnəmə] n cinéma m.

cinnamon ['sɪnəmən] n cannelle f.

cipher ['saɪfə*] n code secret; (fig: faceless employee etc) numéro m.

circle ['sɜ:kl] n cercle m; (in cinema) balcon m // vi faire or décrire des cercles // vt (surround) entourer, encercler; (move round) faire le tour de, tourner autour de.

circuit ['sɜ:kɪt] n circuit m; **~ous** [sə:'kjuɪtəs] a indirect(e), qui fait un détour.

circular ['sɜ:kjulə*] a, n circulaire (f).

circulate ['sɜ:kjuleɪt] vi circuler // vt faire circuler; **circulation** [-'leɪʃən] n circulation f; (of newspaper) tirage m.

circumflex ['sɜ:kəmfleks] n (also: ~ accent) accent m circonflexe.

circumstances ['sɜ:kəmstənsɪz] npl circonstances fpl; (financial condition) moyens mpl, situation financière.

circumvent [sɜ:kəm'vent] vt tourner.

circus ['sɜ:kəs] n cirque m.

cistern ['sɪstən] n réservoir m (d'eau); (in toilet) réservoir de la chasse d'eau.

citizen ['sɪtɪzn] n (POL) citoyen/ne; (resident): **the ~s of this town** les

habitants de cette ville; **~ship** n citoyenneté f.

citrus fruit ['sɪtrəs-] n agrume m.

city ['sɪtɪ] n ville f, cité f; **the C~** la Cité de Londres (centre des affaires).

civic ['sɪvɪk] a civique; **~ centre** n (Brit) centre administratif (municipal).

civil ['sɪvɪl] a civil(e); poli(e), civil; **~ engineer** n ingénieur civil; **~ian** [sɪ'vɪlɪən] a, n civil(e).

civilization [sɪvɪlaɪ'zeɪʃən] n civilisation f.

civilized ['sɪvɪlaɪzd] a civilisé(e); (fig) où règnent les bonnes manières, empreint(e) d'une courtoisie de bon ton.

civil: **~ law** n code civil; (study) droit civil; **~ servant** n fonctionnaire m/f; **C~ Service** n fonction publique, administration f; **~ war** n guerre civile.

clad [klæd] a: **~ (in)** habillé(e) (de).

claim [kleɪm] vt revendiquer; demander, prétendre à; déclarer, prétendre // vi (for insurance) faire une déclaration de sinistre // n revendication f; demande f; prétention f, déclaration f; (right) droit m, titre m; (insurance) ~ demande f d'indemnisation, déclaration f de sinistre; **~ant** n (ADMIN, LAW) requérant/e.

clairvoyant [kleə'vɔɪənt] n voyant/e, extra-lucide m/f.

clam [klæm] n palourde f.

clamber ['klæmbə*] vi grimper, se hisser.

clammy ['klæmɪ] a humide et froid(e) (au toucher), moite.

clamour, (US) **clamor** ['klæmə*] vi: **to ~ for** réclamer à grands cris.

clamp [klæmp] n étau m à main; agrafe f, crampon m // vt serrer; cramponner; **to ~ down on** vt fus sévir contre, prendre des mesures draconiennes à l'égard de.

clan [klæn] n clan m.

clang [klæŋ] n bruit m or fracas m métallique.

clap [klæp] vi applaudir; **~ping** n applaudissements mpl.

claret ['klærət] n (vin m de) bordeaux m (rouge).

clarinet [klærɪ'net] n clarinette f.

clarity ['klærɪtɪ] n clarté f.

clash [klæʃ] n choc m; (fig) conflit m // vi se heurter; être or entrer en conflit.

clasp [klɑ:sp] n fermoir m // vt serrer, étreindre.

class [klɑ:s] n (gen) classe f // vt classer, classifier.

classic ['klæsɪk] a classique // n (author, work) classique m; **~al** a classique.

classified ['klæsɪfaɪd] a (information) secret(ète); **~ advertisements**, **~ ads** npl petites annonces.

classmate ['klɑ:smeɪt] n camarade m/f de classe.

classroom ['klɑ:srum] n (salle f de) classe f.

clatter ['klætə*] n cliquetis m // vi cliqueter.

clause [klɔ:z] n clause f; (LING) proposition f.

claw [klɔ:] n griffe f; (of bird of prey) serre f; (of lobster) pince f; **to ~ at** vt essayer de griffer or déchirer.

clay [kleɪ] n argile f.

clean [kli:n] a propre; (clear, smooth) net(te) // vt nettoyer; **to ~ out** vt nettoyer (à fond); **to ~ up** vt nettoyer; (fig) remettre de l'ordre dans; **~er** n (person) nettoyeur/euse, femme f de ménage; (also: **dry ~er**) teinturier/ière; (product) détachant m; **~ing** n nettoyage m; **~liness** ['klɛnlɪnɪs] n propreté f.

cleanse [klɛnz] vt nettoyer; purifier; **~r** n détergent m; (for face) démaquillant m; **cleansing department** n (Brit) service m de voirie.

clean-shaven ['kli:n'ʃeɪvn] a rasé(e) de près.

clear [klɪə*] a clair(e); (road, way) libre, dégagé(e) // vt dégager, déblayer, débarrasser; faire évacuer; (COMM: goods) liquider; (cheque) compenser; (LAW: suspect) innocenter; (obstacle) franchir or sauter sans heurter // vi (weather) s'éclaircir; (fog) se dissiper // ad: **~ of** à distance de, à l'écart de; **to ~ the table** débarrasser la table, desservir; **to ~ up** vi s'éclaircir, se dissiper // vt ranger, mettre en ordre; (mystery) éclaircir, résoudre; **~ance** n (removal) déblayage m; (free space) dégagement m; (permission) autorisation f; **~-cut** a précis(e), nettement défini(e); **~ing** n (in forest) clairière f; **~ing bank** n (Brit) banque f qui appartient à une chambre de compensation; **~ly** ad clairement; de toute évidence; **~way** n (Brit) route f à stationnement interdit.

cleaver ['kli:və*] n fendoir m, couperet m.

clef [klɛf] n (MUS) clé f.

cleft [klɛft] n (in rock) crevasse f, fissure f.

clench [klɛntʃ] vt serrer.

clergy ['klə:dʒɪ] n clergé m; **~man** n ecclésiastique m.

clerical ['klɛrɪkəl] a de bureau, d'employé de bureau; (REL) clérical(e), du clergé.

clerk [klɑ:k, (US) klə:rk] n employé/e de bureau; (US: salesman/woman) vendeur/euse.

clever ['klɛvə*] a (mentally) intelligent(e); (deft, crafty) habile, adroit(e); (device, arrangement) ingénieux(euse), astucieux(euse).

click [klɪk] vi faire un bruit sec or un dé-

clic // vt: **to ~ one's tongue** faire claquer sa langue; **to ~ one's heels** claquer des talons.

client ['klaɪənt] n client/e.

cliff [klɪf] n falaise f.

climate ['klaɪmɪt] n climat m.

climax ['klaɪmæks] n apogée m, point culminant; (sexual) orgasme m.

climb [klaɪm] vi grimper, monter // vt gravir, escalader, monter sur // n montée f, escalade f; **~down** n reculade f, dérobade f; **~er** n (also: **rock ~er**) grimpeur/euse, varappeur/euse; **~ing** n (also: **rock ~ing**) escalade f, varappe f.

clinch [klɪntʃ] vt (deal) conclure, sceller.

cling [klɪŋ], pt, pp **clung** vi: **to ~ (to)** se cramponner (à), s'accrocher (à); (of clothes) coller (à).

clinic ['klɪnɪk] n centre médical.

clink [klɪŋk] vi tinter, cliqueter.

clip [klɪp] n (for hair) barrette f; (also: **paper ~**) trombone m; (holding hose etc) collier m or bague f (métallique) de serrage // vt (also: **~ together**) attacher; (hair, nails) couper; (hedge) tailler; **~pers** npl tondeuse f; (also: **nail ~pers**) coupe-ongles m inv; **~ping** n (from newspaper) coupure f de journal.

cloak [kləuk] n grande cape // vt (fig) masquer, cacher; **~room** n (for coats etc) vestiaire m; (Brit: W.C.) toilettes fpl.

clock [klɔk] n (large) horloge f; (small) pendule f; **to ~ in** or **on** vi pointer (en arrivant); **to ~ off** or **out** vi pointer (en partant); **~wise** ad dans le sens des aiguilles d'une montre; **~work** n mouvement m (d'horlogerie); rouages mpl, mécanisme m // a mécanique.

clog [klɔg] n sabot m // vt boucher, encrasser // vi se boucher, s'encrasser.

cloister ['klɔɪstə*] n cloître m.

close a, ad and derivatives [kləus] a (near): **~ (to)** près (de), proche (de); (writing, texture) serré(e); (watch) étroit(e), strict(e); (examination) attentif(ive), minutieux(euse); (weather) lourd(e), étouffant(e) // ad près, à proximité; **~ to** prep près de; **~ by**, **~ at hand** a, ad tout(e) près; **a ~ friend** un ami intime; **to have a ~ shave** (fig) l'échapper belle // vb and derivatives [kləuz] vt fermer // vi (shop etc) fermer; (lid, door etc) se fermer; (end) se terminer, se conclure // n (end) conclusion f; **to ~ down** vt, vi fermer (définitivement); **~d** a fermé(e); **~d shop** n organisation f qui n'admet que des travailleurs syndiqués; **~-knit** a (family, community) très uni(e); **~ly** ad (examine, watch) de près.

closet ['klɔzɪt] n (cupboard) placard m, réduit m.

close-up ['kləusʌp] n gros plan.

closure ['kləuʒə*] n fermeture f.

clot [klɔt] *n* (*gen: blood* ~) caillot *m*; (*col: person*) ballot *m* // *vi* (*blood*) former des caillots; (*: external bleeding*) se coaguler.

cloth [klɔθ] *n* (*material*) tissu *m*, étoffe *f*; (*also: tea*~) torchon *m*; lavette *f*.

clothe [kləuð] *vt* habiller, vêtir; ~**s** *npl* vêtements *mpl*, habits *mpl*; ~**s brush** *n* brosse *f* à habits; ~**s line** *n* corde *f* (à linge); ~**s peg**, (*US*) ~**s pin** *n* pince *f* à linge.

clothing ['kləuðɪŋ] *n* =**clothes**.

cloud [klaud] *n* nuage *m*; ~**y** *a* nuageux(euse), couvert(e); (*liquid*) trouble.

clout [klaut] *vt* flanquer une taloche à.

clove [kləuv] *n* clou *m* de girofle; ~ **of garlic** gousse *f* d'ail.

clover ['kləuvə*] *n* trèfle *m*.

clown [klaun] *n* clown *m* // *vi* (*also:* ~ **about**, ~ **around**) faire le clown.

cloying ['klɔɪɪŋ] *a* (*taste, smell*) écœurant(e).

club [klʌb] *n* (*society*) club *m*; (*weapon*) massue *f*, matraque *f*; (*also: golf* ~) club // *vt* matraquer // *vi*: **to** ~ **together** s'associer; ~**s** *npl* (*CARDS*) trèfle *m*; ~ **car** *n* (*US RAIL*) wagon-restaurant *m*; ~**house** *n* pavillon *m*.

cluck [klʌk] *vi* glousser.

clue [klu:] *n* indice *m*; (*in crosswords*) définition *f*; **I haven't a** ~ je n'en ai pas la moindre idée.

clump [klʌmp] *n*: ~ **of trees** bouquet *m* d'arbres.

clumsy ['klʌmzɪ] *a* (*person*) gauche, maladroit(e); (*object*) malcommode, peu maniable.

clung [klʌŋ] *pt, pp of* **cling**.

cluster ['klʌstə*] *n* (petit) groupe // *vi* se rassembler.

clutch [klʌtʃ] *n* (*grip, grasp*) étreinte *f*, prise *f*; (*AUT*) embrayage *m* // *vt* agripper, serrer fort; **to** ~ **at** se cramponner à.

clutter ['klʌtə*] *vt* encombrer.

CND *abbr* = *Campaign for Nuclear Disarmament*.

Co. *abbr of* **county, company**.

c/o *abbr* (= *care of*) c/o, aux bons soins de.

coach [kəutʃ] *n* (*bus*) autocar *m*; (*horse-drawn*) diligence *f*; (*of train*) voiture *f*, wagon *m*; (*SPORT: trainer*) entraîneur/euse // *vt* entraîner; ~ **trip** *n* excursion *f* en car.

coal [kəul] *n* charbon *m*; ~ **face** *n* front *m* de taille; ~**field** *n* bassin houiller.

coalition [kəuə'lɪʃən] *n* coalition *f*.

coalman, coal merchant ['kəulmən, 'kəuləʃ'tʃənt] *n* charbonnier *m*, marchand *m* de charbon.

coalmine ['kəulmaɪn] *n* mine *f* de charbon.

coarse [kɔ:s] *a* grossier(ère), rude.

coast [kəust] *n* côte *f* // *vi* (*with cycle etc*) descendre en roue libre; ~**al** *a* côtier(ère); ~**guard** *n* garde-côte *m*; ~**line** *n* côte *f*, littoral *m*.

coat [kəut] *n* manteau *m*; (*of animal*) pelage *m*, poil *m*; (*of paint*) couche *f* // *vt* couvrir, enduire; ~ **of arms** *n* blason *m*, armoiries *fpl*; ~ **hanger** *n* cintre *m*; ~**ing** *n* couche *f*, enduit *m*.

coax [kəuks] *vt* persuader par des cajoleries.

cob [kɔb] *n see* **corn**.

cobbler ['kɔblə*] *n* cordonnier *m*.

cobbles, cobblestones ['kɔblz, 'kɔblstəunz] *npl* pavés (ronds).

cobweb ['kɔbwɛb] *n* toile *f* d'araignée.

cocaine [kə'keɪn] *n* cocaïne *f*.

cock [kɔk] *n* (*rooster*) coq *m*; (*male bird*) mâle *m* // *vt* (*gun*) armer; ~**erel** *n* jeune coq *m*; ~**-eyed** *a* (*fig*) de travers; qui louche; qui ne tient pas debout (*fig*).

cockle ['kɔkl] *n* coque *f*.

cockney ['kɔknɪ] *n* cockney *m/f* (*habitant des quartiers populaires de l'East End de Londres*), ≈ faubourien/ne.

cockpit ['kɔkpɪt] *n* (*in aircraft*) poste *m* de pilotage, cockpit *m*.

cockroach ['kɔkrəutʃ] *n* cafard *m*.

cocktail ['kɔkteɪl] *n* cocktail *m*; ~ **cabinet** *n* (meuble-)bar *m*; ~ **party** *n* cocktail *m*.

cocoa ['kəukəu] *n* cacao *m*.

coconut ['kəukənʌt] *n* noix *f* de coco.

cod [kɔd] *n* morue (fraîche), cabillaud *m*.

C.O.D. *abbr of* **cash on delivery**.

code [kəud] *n* code *m*.

cod-liver oil *n* huile *f* de foie de morue.

coercion [kəu'ə:ʃən] *n* contrainte *f*.

coffee ['kɔfɪ] *n* café *m*; ~ **bar** *n* (*Brit*) café *m*; ~ **break** *n* pause-café *f*; ~**pot** *n* cafetière *f*; ~ **table** *n* (petite) table basse.

coffin ['kɔfɪn] *n* cercueil *m*.

cog [kɔg] *n* dent *f* (d'engrenage).

cogent ['kəudʒənt] *a* puissant(e), convaincant(e).

coil [kɔɪl] *n* rouleau *m*, bobine *f*; (*one loop*) anneau *m*, spire *f*; (*contraceptive*) stérilet *m* // *vt* enrouler.

coin [kɔɪn] *n* pièce *f* de monnaie // *vt* (*word*) inventer; ~**age** *n* monnaie *f*, système *m* monétaire; ~**-box** *n* (*Brit*) cabine *f* téléphonique.

coincide [kəuɪn'saɪd] *vi* coïncider; ~**nce** [kəu'ɪnsɪdəns] *n* coïncidence *f*.

coke [kəuk] *n* coke *m*.

colander ['kɔləndə*] *n* passoire *f* (à légumes).

cold [kəuld] *a* froid(e) // *n* froid *m*; (*MED*) rhume *m*; **it's** ~ il fait froid; **to be** ~ avoir froid; **to catch** ~ prendre *or* attraper froid; **to catch a** ~ attraper un rhume; **in** ~ **blood** de sang-froid; ~ **sore** *n* bouton *m* de fièvre.

coleslaw ['kəulslɔ:] n sorte de salade de chou cru.

colic ['kɒlɪk] n colique(s) f(pl).

collapse [kə'læps] vi s'effondrer, s'écrouler // n effondrement m, écroulement m.

collapsible [kə'læpsəbl] a pliant(e), télescopique.

collar ['kɒlə*] n (of coat, shirt) col m; ~**bone** n clavicule f.

collateral [kə'lætərl] n nantissement m.

colleague ['kɒli:g] n collègue m/f.

collect [kə'lɛkt] vt rassembler; ramasser; (as a hobby) collectionner; (Brit: call and pick up) (passer) prendre; (mail) faire la levée de, ramasser; (money owed) encaisser; (donations, subscriptions) recueillir // vi se rassembler; s'amasser; **to call ~** (US TEL) téléphoner en PCV; ~**ion** [kə'lɛkʃən] n collection f; levée f; (for money) collecte f, quête f.

collector [kə'lɛktə*] n collectionneur m; (of taxes) percepteur m.

college ['kɒlɪdʒ] n collège m.

collide [kə'laɪd] vi: **to ~ (with)** entrer en collision (avec).

collie ['kɒlɪ] n (dog) colley m.

colliery ['kɒlɪərɪ] n mine f de charbon, houillère f.

collision [kə'lɪʒən] n collision f, heurt m.

colloquial [kə'ləukwɪəl] a familier(ère).

colon ['kəulən] n (sign) deux-points mpl; (MED) côlon m.

colonel ['kə:nl] n colonel m.

colonial [kə'ləunɪəl] a colonial(e).

colony ['kɒlənɪ] n colonie f.

colour, (US) **color** ['kʌlə*] n couleur f // vt colorer; peindre; (with crayons) colorier; (news) fausser, exagérer // vi (blush) rougir; ~**s** npl (of party, club) couleurs fpl; ~ **bar** n discrimination raciale (dans un établissement etc); ~**blind** a daltonien(ne); ~**ed** a coloré(e); (photo) en couleur // n: ~**eds** personnes fpl de couleur; ~ **film** n (for camera) pellicule f (en) couleur; ~**ful** a coloré(e), vif(vive); (personality) pittoresque, haut(e) en couleurs; ~**ing** n colorant m; (complexion) teint m; ~ **scheme** n combinaison f de(s) couleurs; ~ **television** n télévision f en couleur.

colt [kəult] n poulain m.

column ['kɒləm] n colonne f; ~**ist** ['kɒləmnɪst] n rédacteur/trice d'une rubrique.

coma ['kəumə] n coma m.

comb [kəum] n peigne m // vt (hair) peigner; (area) ratisser, passer au peigne fin.

combat ['kɒmbæt] n combat m // vt combattre, lutter contre.

combination [kɒmbɪ'neɪʃən] n (gen) ombinaison f.

combine vb [kəm'baɪn] vt combiner; (one quality with another) joindre (à), allier (à) // vi s'associer; (CHEM) se combiner // n ['kɒmbaɪn] association f; (ECON) trust m; ~ **(harvester)** n moissonneuse-batteuse(-lieuse) f.

come [kʌm], pt **came**, pp **come** vi venir; arriver; **to ~ to** (decision etc) parvenir or arriver à; **to ~ undone/loose** se défaire/desserrer; **to ~ about** vi se produire, arriver; **to ~ across** vt fus rencontrer par hasard, tomber sur; **to ~ along** vi = **to come on**; **to ~ away** vi partir, s'en aller, se détacher; **to ~ back** vi revenir; **to ~ by** vt fus (acquire) obtenir, se procurer; **to ~ down** vi descendre; (prices) baisser; (buildings) s'écrouler; être démoli(e); **to ~ forward** vi s'avancer; se présenter, s'annoncer; **to ~ from** vt fus être originaire de; venir de; **to ~ in** vi entrer; **to ~ in for** vt fus (criticism etc) être l'objet de; **to ~ into** vt fus (money) hériter de; **to ~ off** vi (button) se détacher; (stain) s'enlever; (attempt) réussir; **to ~ on** vi (pupil, work, project) faire des progrès, avancer; (lights, electricity) s'allumer; (central heating) se mettre en marche; ~ **on!** viens!; allons!, allez!; **to ~ out** vi sortir; (book) paraître; (strike) cesser le travail, se mettre en grève; **to ~ round** vi (after faint, operation) revenir à soi, reprendre connaissance; **to ~ to** vi revenir à soi; **to ~ up** vi monter; **to ~ up against** vt fus (resistance, difficulties) rencontrer; **to ~ up with** vt fus: he came up with an idea il a eu une idée, il a proposé quelque chose; **to ~ upon** vt fus tomber sur; ~**back** n (THEATRE etc) rentrée f.

comedian [kə'mi:dɪən] n (in music hall etc) comique m; (THEATRE) comédien m.

comedown ['kʌmdaun] n déchéance f.

comedy ['kɒmɪdɪ] n comédie f.

comeuppance [kʌm'ʌpəns] n: **to get one's ~** recevoir ce qu'on mérite.

comfort ['kʌmfət] n confort m, bien-être m; (solace) consolation f, réconfort m // vt consoler, réconforter; ~**s** npl aises fpl; ~**able** a confortable; ~**ably** ad (sit) confortablement; (live) à l'aise; ~ **station** n (US) toilettes fpl.

comic ['kɒmɪk] a (also: ~**al**) comique // n comique m; (magazine) illustré m; ~ **strip** n bande dessinée.

coming ['kʌmɪŋ] n arrivée f // a prochain(e), à venir; ~**(s) and going(s)** n(pl) va-et-vient m inv.

comma ['kɒmə] n virgule f.

command [kə'ma:nd] n ordre m, commandement m; (MIL: authority) commandement; (mastery) maîtrise f // vt (troops) commander; (be able to get) (pouvoir) disposer de, avoir à sa disposition; (*deserve*) avoir droit à; **~eer** [kɔmən'dɪə*] *vt* réquisitionner (par la force); **~er** *n* chef *m*; (MIL) commandant *m*.

commando [kə'mɑːndəu] *n* commando *m*; membre *m* d'un commando.

commemorate [kə'mɛmərert] *vt* commémorer.

commence [kə'mɛns] *vt, vi* commencer.

commend [kə'mɛnd] *vt* louer; recommander.

commensurate [kə'mɛnʃərrt] *a*: ~ with en proportion de, proportionné(e) à.

comment ['kɔmɛnt] *n* commentaire *m* / *vi*: to ~ (on) faire des remarques (sur); **~ary** ['kɔməntərɪ] *n* commentaire *m*, (SPORT) reportage *m* (en direct); **~ator** ['kɔməntertə*] *n* commentateur *m*; reporter *m*.

commerce ['kɔməːs] *n* commerce *m*.

commercial [kə'məːʃəl] *a* commercial(e) / *n* (TV: *also*: ~ **break**) annonce *f* publicitaire, spot *m* (publicitaire).

commiserate [kə'mɪzərert] *vi*: to ~ with sb témoigner de la sympathie pour qn.

commission [kə'mɪʃən] *n* (*committee, fee*) commission *f* / *vt* (MIL) nommer (à un commandement); (*work of art*) commander, charger un artiste de l'exécution de; out of ~ (NAUT) hors de service; **~aire** [kəmɪʃə'nɛə*] *n* (*Brit*: *at shop, cinema etc*) portier *m* (en uniforme); **~er** *n* membre *m* d'une commission; (POLICE) préfet *m* (de police).

commit [kə'mɪt] *vt* (*act*) commettre; (*to sb's care*) confier (à); to ~ o.s. (to do) s'engager (à faire); to ~ suicide se suicider; **~ment** *n* engagement *m*; (*obligation*) responsabilité(s) *f(pl)*.

committee [kə'mɪtɪ] *n* comité *m*.

commodity [kə'mɔdɪtɪ] *n* produit *m*, marchandise *f*, article *m*; (*food*) denrée *f*.

common ['kɔmən] *a* (*gen, also pej*) commun(e); (*usual*) courant(e) / *n* terrain communal; **the C~s** *npl* (*Brit*) la chambre des Communes; **in** ~ en commun; **~er** *n* roturier/ière; **~ law** *n* droit coutumier; **~ly** *ad* communément, généralement; couramment; **C~ Market** *n* Marché commun; **~place** *a* banal(e), ordinaire; **~room** *n* salle commune; (SCOL) salle des professeurs; ~ **sense** *n* bon sens; **the C~wealth** *n* le Commonwealth.

commotion [kə'məuʃən] *n* désordre *m*, tumulte *m*.

communal ['kɔmjuːnl] *a* (*life*) communautaire; (*for common use*) commun(e).

commune *n* ['kɔmjuːn] (*group*) communauté *f* / *vi* [kə'mjuːn]: to ~ with

converser intimement avec; communier avec.

communicate [kə'mjuːnɪkert] *vt, vi* communiquer.

communication [kəmjuːnɪ'kerʃən] *n* communication *f*; ~ **cord** *n* (*Brit*) sonnette *f* d'alarme.

communion [kə'mjuːnɪən] *n* (*also*: Holy C~) communion *f*.

communism ['kɔmjunɪzəm] *n* communisme *m*; **communist** *a, n* communiste *(m/f)*.

community [kə'mjuːnɪtɪ] *n* communauté *f*; ~ **centre** *n* foyer socio-éducatif, centre *m* de loisirs; ~ **chest** *n* (US) fonds commun.

commutation ticket [kɔmju 'terʃən-] *n* (US) carte *f* d'abonnement.

commute [kə'mjuːt] *vi* faire le trajet journalier (de son domicile à un lieu de travail assez éloigné) // *vt* (LAW) commuer; **~r** *n* banlieusard/e (qui ... see *vi*).

compact *a* [kəm'pækt] compact(e) // *n* ['kɔmpækt] (*also*: **powder** ~) poudrier *m*; ~ **disk** *n* disque compact.

companion [kəm'pænɪən] *n* compagnon/compagne; **~ship** *n* camaraderie *f*.

company ['kʌmpənɪ] *n* (*also* COMM, MIL, THEATRE) compagnie *f*; **to keep sb** ~ tenir compagnie à qn; ~ **secretary** *n* (COMM) secrétaire général (*d'une société*).

comparative [kəm'pærətɪv] *a* comparatif(ive); (*relative*) relatif(ive); **~ly** *ad* (*relatively*) relativement.

compare [kəm'pɛə*] *vt*: to ~ sth/sb with/to comparer qch/qn avec *or* et/à // *vi*: to ~ (with) se comparer (à); être comparable (à); **comparison** [-'pærɪsn] *n* comparaison *f*.

compartment [kəm'pɑːtmənt] *n* (*also* RAIL) compartiment *m*.

compass ['kʌmpəs] *n* boussole *f*; **~es** *npl* compas *m*.

compassion [kəm'pæʃən] *n* compassion *f*, humanité *f*.

compatible [kəm'pætɪbl] *a* compatible.

compel [kəm'pɛl] *vt* contraindre, obliger; **~ling** *a* (*fig: argument*) irrésistible.

compendium [kəm'pɛndɪəm] *n* abrégé *m*.

compensate ['kɔmpənsert] *vt* indemniser, dédommager // *vi*: to ~ for compenser; **compensation** [-'serʃən] *n* compensation *f*; (*money*) dédommagement *m*, indemnité *f*.

compete [kəm'piːt] *vi* (*take part*) concourir; (*vie*): to ~ (with) rivaliser (avec), faire concurrence (à).

competence ['kɔmpɪtəns] *n* compétence *f*, aptitude *f*.

competent ['kɔmpɪtənt] *a* compé-

tent(e), capable.
competition [kɔmpɪ'tɪʃən] n compétition f, concours m; (ECON) concurrence f.
competitive [kəm'pɛtɪtɪv] a (ECON)
concurrentiel(le); (sport) de compétition.
competitor [kəm'pɛtɪtə*] n concur-
rent/e.
complacency [kəm'pleɪsnsɪ] n
contentement m de soi, vaine complaisance.
complain [kəm'pleɪn] vi: to ~ (about)
se plaindre (de); (in shop etc) réclamer
(au sujet de); ~t n plainte f; réclamation f; (MED) affection f.
complement ['kɔmplɪmənt] n complément m; (especially of ship's crew etc)
effectif complet // ['kɔmplɪmɛnt] vt
(enhance) compléter; ~ary [kɔmplɪ-
'mɛntərɪ] a complémentaire.
complete [kəm'pliːt] a complet(ète) //
vt achever, parachever; (a form) remplir; ~ly ad complètement; **completion**
n achèvement m.
complex ['kɔmplɛks] a, n complexe
(m).
complexion [kəm'plɛkʃən] n (of face)
teint m; (of event etc) aspect m,
caractère m.
compliance [kəm'plaɪəns] n (submission) docilité f; (agreement): ~ with le
fait de se conformer à.
complicate ['kɔmplɪkeɪt] vt compli-
quer; ~d a compliqué(e); **complication** [-'keɪʃən] n complication f.
compliment n ['kɔmplɪmənt] compliment m // vt ['kɔmplɪmɛnt]
complimenter; ~s npl compliments mpl,
hommages mpl; vœux mpl; to pay sb a
~ faire un compliment or adresser un
compliment à qn; ~ary [-'mɛntərɪ] a flatteur(euse); (free)
à titre gracieux; ~ary ticket n billet m
de faveur.
comply [kəm'plaɪ] vi: to ~ with se
soumettre à, se conformer à.
component [kəm'pəʊnənt] n composant
m, élément m.
compose [kəm'pəʊz] vt composer; to ~
o.s. se calmer, se maîtriser; prendre une
contenance; ~d a calme, posé(e); ~r n
(MUS) compositeur n.
composition [kɔmpə'zɪʃən] n composition f.
composure [kəm'pəʊʒə*] n calme m,
maîtrise f de soi.
compound ['kɔmpaʊnd] n (CHEM,
LING) composé m; (enclosure) enclos m,
enceinte f // a composé(e); ~ fracture n
fracture compliquée.
comprehend [kɔmprɪ'hɛnd] vt comprendre; **comprehension** [-'hɛnʃən] n
compréhension f.
comprehensive [kɔmprɪ'hɛnsɪv] a
(très) complet(ète); ~ **policy** n

(INSURANCE) assurance f tous risques;
~ **(school)** n (Brit) école secondaire
non sélective avec libre circulation d'une
section à l'autre, ≈ C.E.S. m.
compress vt [kəm'prɛs] comprimer // n
['kɔmprɛs] (MED) compresse f.
comprise [kəm'praɪz] vt (also: be ~d
of) comprendre.
compromise ['kɔmprəmaɪz] n compromis m // vt compromettre // vi transiger,
accepter un compromis.
compulsion [kəm'pʌlʃən] n contrainte
f, force f.
compulsive [kəm'pʌlsɪv] a (PSYCH)
compulsif(ive).
compulsory [kəm'pʌlsərɪ] a obligatoire.
computer [kəm'pjuːtə*] n ordinateur
m; (mechanical) calculatrice f; ~ize vt
traiter or automatiser par ordinateur; ~
programmer n programmeur/euse; ~
programming n programmation f; ~
science, computing n informatique f.
comrade ['kɔmrɪd] n camarade m/f.
con [kɔn] vt duper; escroquer // n escroquerie f.
conceal [kən'siːl] vt cacher, dissimuler.
conceit [kən'siːt] n vanité f, suffisance f,
prétention f; ~ed a vaniteux(euse),
suffisant(e).
conceive [kən'siːv] vt, vi concevoir.
concentrate ['kɔnsəntreɪt] vi se concentrer // vt concentrer.
concentration [kɔnsən'treɪʃən] n
concentration f; ~ **camp** n camp m de
concentration.
concept ['kɔnsɛpt] n concept m.
concern [kən'sɜːn] n affaire f; (COMM)
entreprise f, firme f; (anxiety)
inquiétude f, souci m // vt concerner; to
be ~ed (about) s'inquiéter (de), être
inquiet (au sujet de); ~ing prep en ce
qui concerne, à propos de.
concert ['kɔnsət] n concert m; ~ed
[kən'sɜːtɪd] a concerté(e); ~ **hall** n
salle f de concert.
concertina [kɔnsə'tiːnə] n concertina m
// vi se télescoper, se caramboler.
concerto [kən'tʃɜːtəʊ] n concerto m.
conclude [kən'kluːd] vt conclure; **conclusion** [-'kluːʒən] n conclusion f; **conclusive** [-'kluːsɪv] a concluant(e),
définitif(ive).
concoct [kən'kɔkt] vt confectionner,
composer; ~ion [-'kɔkʃən] n mélange
m.
concourse ['kɔnkɔːs] n (hall) hall m,
salle f des pas perdus.
concrete ['kɔnkriːt] n béton m // a
concret(ète); en béton.
concur [kən'kɜː*] vi être d'accord.
concurrently [kən'kʌrntlɪ] ad simultanément.
concussion [kən'kʌʃən] n (MED)
commotion (cérébrale).
condemn [kən'dɛm] vt condamner.

condensation [kɔndɛn'seɪʃən] *n* condensation *f*.

condense [kən'dɛns] *vi* se condenser // *vt* condenser; **~d milk** *n* lait concentré (sucré).

condition [kən'dɪʃən] *n* condition *f* // *vt* déterminer, conditionner; **on ~ that** à condition que + *sub*, à condition de; **~al** *a* conditionnel(le); **~er** *n* (*for hair*) baume démêlant.

condolences [kən'dəulənsɪz] *npl* condoléances *fpl*.

condom ['kɔndəm] *n* préservatif *m*.

condominium [kɔndə'mɪnɪəm] *n* (*US: building*) immeuble *m* (en copropriété); (*: rooms*) appartement *m* (dans un immeuble en copropriété).

condone [kən'dəun] *vt* fermer les yeux sur, approuver (tacitement).

conducive [kən'djuːsɪv] *a*: **~ to** favorable à, qui contribue à.

conduct *n* ['kɔndʌkt] conduite *f* // *vt* [kən'dʌkt] conduire; (*manage*) mener, diriger; (*MUS*) diriger; **to ~ o.s.** se conduire, se comporter; **~ed tour** *n* voyage organisé; visite guidée; **~or** *n* (*of orchestra*) chef *m* d'orchestre; (*on bus*) receveur *m*; (*US: on train*) chef *m* de train; (*ELEC*) conducteur *m*; **~ress** *n* (*on bus*) receveuse *f*.

cone [kəun] *n* cône *m*; (*for ice-cream*) cornet *m*; (*BOT*) pomme *f* de pin, cône.

confectioner [kən'fɛkʃənə*] *n* (*of cakes*) pâtissier/ière; (*of sweets*) confiseur/euse; **~'s** (**shop**) *n* confiserie(-pâtisserie); **~y** *n* pâtisserie *f*; confiserie *f*.

confer [kən'fəː*] *vt*: **to ~ sth on** conférer qch à // *vi* conférer, s'entretenir.

conference ['kɔnfərns] *n* conférence *f*.

confess [kən'fɛs] *vt* confesser, avouer // *vi* se confesser; **~ion** [-'fɛʃən] *n* confession *f*.

confetti [kən'fɛtɪ] *n* confettis *mpl*.

confide [kən'faɪd] *vi*: **to ~ in** s'ouvrir à, se confier à.

confidence ['kɔnfɪdns] *n* confiance *f*; (*also: self-~*) assurance *f*, confiance en soi; (*secret*) confidence *f*; **in ~** (*speak, write*) en confidence, confidentiellement; **~ trick** *n* escroquerie *f*; **confident** *a* sûr(e), assuré(e); **confidential** [kɔnfɪ-'dɛnʃəl] *a* confidentiel(le).

confine [kən'faɪn] *vt* limiter, borner; (*shut up*) confiner, enfermer; **~s** ['kɔnfaɪnz] *npl* confins *mpl*, bornes *fpl*; **~d** *a* (*space*) restreint(e), réduit(e); **~ment** *n* emprisonnement *m*, détention *f*; (*MIL*) consigne *f* (au quartier); (*MED*) accouchement *m*.

confirm [kən'fəːm] *vt* (*report, REL*) confirmer; (*appointment*) ratifier; **~ation** [kɔnfə'meɪʃən] *n* confirmation *f*; **~ed** *a* invétéré(e), incorrigible.

confiscate ['kɔnfɪskeɪt] *vt* confisquer.

conflict *n* ['kɔnflɪkt] conflit *m*, lutte *f* // *vi* [kən'flɪkt] être *or* entrer en conflit; (*opinions*) s'opposer, se heurter; **~ing** *a* contradictoire.

conform [kən'fɔːm] *vi*: **to ~ (to)** se conformer (à).

confound [kən'faund] *vt* confondre.

confront [kən'frʌnt] *vt* confronter, mettre en présence; (*enemy, danger*) affronter, faire face à; **~ation** [kɔnfrən-'teɪʃən] *n* confrontation *f*.

confuse [kən'fjuːz] *vt* embrouiller; (*one thing with another*) confondre; **~d** *a* (*person*) dérouté(e), désorienté(e); **confusing** *a* peu clair(e), déroutant(e); **confusion** [-'fjuːʒən] *n* confusion *f*.

congeal [kən'dʒiːl] *vi* (*blood*) se coaguler.

congenial [kən'dʒiːnɪəl] *a* sympathique, agréable.

congested [kən'dʒɛstɪd] *a* (*MED*) congestionné(e); (*fig*) surpeuplé(e); congestionné; bloqué(e).

congestion [kən'dʒɛstʃən] *n* congestion *f*; (*fig*) encombrement *m*.

congratulate [kən'grætjuleɪt] *vt*: **to ~ sb (on)** féliciter qn (de); **congratulations** [-'leɪʃənz] *npl* félicitations *fpl*.

congregate ['kɔŋgrɪgeɪt] *vi* se rassembler, se réunir.

congregation [kɔŋgrɪ'geɪʃən] *n* assemblée *f* (des fidèles).

congress ['kɔŋgrɛs] *n* congrès *m*; **~man** *n* (*US*) membre *m* du Congrès.

conjunction [kən'dʒʌŋkʃən] *n* conjonction *f*.

conjunctivitis [kəndʒʌŋktɪ'vaɪtɪs] *n* conjonctivite *f*.

conjure ['kʌndʒə*] *vt* faire apparaître (par la prestidigitation) // *vi* faire des tours de passe-passe; **to ~ up** *vt* (*ghost, spirit*) faire apparaître; (*memories*) évoquer; **~r** *n* prestidigitateur *m*, illusionniste *m/f*.

conk out [kɔŋk-] *vi* (*col*) tomber *or* rester en panne.

conman ['kɔnmæn] *n* escroc *m*.

connect [kə'nɛkt] *vt* joindre, relier; (*ELEC*) connecter; (*fig*) établir un rapport entre, faire un rapprochement entre // *vi* (*train*): **to ~ with** assurer la correspondance avec; **to be ~ed with** avoir un rapport avec; avoir des rapports avec, être en relation avec; (*related*) être allié(e) à, être parent/e de; **~ion** [-ʃən] *n* relation *f*, lien *m*; (*ELEC*) connexion *f*; (*TEL*) communication *f*; **in ~ion with** à propos de.

connive [kə'naɪv] *vi*: **to ~ at** se faire le complice de.

conquer ['kɔŋkə*] *vt* conquérir; (*feelings*) vaincre, surmonter.

conquest ['kɔŋkwɛst] *n* conquête *f*.

cons [kɔnz] *npl* see **convenience, pro**.

conscience ['kɔnʃəns] *n* conscience *f*.

conscientious [kɔnʃɪ'ɛnʃəs] *a* consciencieux(euse); (*scruple, objection*) de conscience.

conscious ['kɔnʃəs] *a* conscient(e); **~ness** *n* conscience *f*; (*MED*) connaissance *f*.

conscript ['kɔnskrɪpt] *n* conscrit *m*.

consent [kən'sɛnt] *n* consentement *m* // *vi*: **to ~ (to)** consentir (à).

consequence ['kɔnsɪkwəns] *n* suites *fpl*, conséquence *f*; importance *f*.

consequently ['kɔnsɪkwəntlɪ] *ad* par conséquent, donc.

conservation [kɔnsə'veɪʃən] *n* préservation *f*, protection *f*.

conservative [kən'sə:vətɪv] *a* conservateur(trice); (*cautious*) prudent(e); **C~** *a*, *n* (*Brit POL*) conservateur(trice).

conservatory [kən'sə:vətrɪ] *n* (*greenhouse*) serre *f*.

conserve [kən'sə:v] *vt* conserver, préserver; (*supplies, energy*) économiser // *n* confiture *f*, conserve *f* (de fruits).

consider [kən'sɪdə*] *vt* considérer, réfléchir à; (*take into account*) penser à, prendre en considération; (*regard, judge*) considérer, estimer; **to ~ doing sth** envisager de faire qch.

considerable [kən'sɪdərəbl] *a* considérable; **considerably** *ad* nettement.

considerate [kən'sɪdərɪt] *a* prévenant(e), plein(e) d'égards.

consideration [kənsɪdə'reɪʃən] *n* considération *f*; (*reward*) rétribution *f*, rémunération *f*.

considering [kən'sɪdərɪŋ] *prep* étant donné.

consign [kən'saɪn] *vt* expédier, livrer; **~ment** *n* arrivage *m*, envoi *m*.

consist [kən'sɪst] *vi*: **to ~ of** consister en, se composer de.

consistency [kən'sɪstənsɪ] *n* consistance *f*; (*fig*) cohérence *f*.

consistent [kən'sɪstənt] *a* logique, cohérent(e); **~ with** compatible avec, en accord avec.

consolation [kɔnsə'leɪʃən] *n* consolation *f*.

consonant ['kɔnsənənt] *n* consonne *f*.

conspicuous [kən'spɪkjuəs] *a* voyant(e), qui attire la vue *or* l'attention.

conspiracy [kən'spɪrəsɪ] *n* conspiration *f*, complot *m*.

constable ['kʌnstəbl] *n* (*Brit*) ≈ agent *m* de police, gendarme *m*; **chief ~** ≈ préfet *m* de police.

constabulary [kən'stæbjuləri] *n* ≈ police *f*, gendarmerie *f*.

constant ['kɔnstənt] *a* constant(e); incessant(e); **~ly** *ad* constamment, sans cesse.

constipated ['kɔnstɪpeɪtɪd] *a* constipé(e).

constipation [kɔnstɪ'peɪʃən] *n* constipation *f*.

constituency [kən'stɪtjuənsɪ] *n* circonscription électorale.

constituent [kən'stɪtjuənt] *n* électeur/trice; (*part*) élément constitutif, composant *m*.

constitution [kɔnstɪ'tju:ʃən] *n* constitution *f*; **~al** *a* constitutionnel(le).

constraint [kən'streɪnt] *n* contrainte *f*.

construct [kən'strʌkt] *vt* construire; **~ion** [-ʃən] *n* construction *f*; **~ive** *a* constructif(ive).

construe [kən'stru:] *vt* analyser, expliquer.

consul ['kɔnsl] *n* consul *m*; **~ate** ['kɔnsjulɪt] *n* consulat *m*.

consult [kən'sʌlt] *vt* consulter // *vi* consulter; se consulter; **~ant** *n* (*MED*) médecin consultant; (*other specialist*) consultant *m*, (*expert-*)conseil *m*; **~ing room** *n* (*Brit MED*) cabinet *m* de consultation.

consume [kən'sju:m] *vt* consommer; **~r** *n* consommateur/trice; **~r goods** *npl* biens *mpl* de consommation; **~r society** *n* société *f* de consommation.

consummate ['kɔnsʌmeɪt] *vt* consommer.

consumption [kən'sʌmpʃən] *n* consommation *f*; (*MED*) consomption *f* (pulmonaire).

cont. *abbr* = **continued**.

contact ['kɔntækt] *n* contact *m*; (*person*) connaissance *f*, relation *f* // *vt* se mettre en contact *or* en rapport avec; **~ lenses** *npl* verres *mpl* de contact.

contagious [kən'teɪdʒəs] *a* contagieux(euse).

contain [kən'teɪn] *vt* contenir; **to ~ o.s.** se contenir, se maîtriser; **~er** *n* récipient *m*; (*for shipping etc*) container *m*.

contaminate [kən'tæmɪneɪt] *vt* contaminer.

cont'd *abbr* = **continued**.

contemplate ['kɔntəmpleɪt] *vt* contempler; (*consider*) envisager.

contemporary [kən'tɛmpərərɪ] *a* contemporain(e); (*design, wallpaper*) moderne // *n* contemporain/e.

contempt [kən'tɛmpt] *n* mépris *m*, dédain *m*; **~ of court** (*LAW*) outrage *m* à l'autorité de la justice; **~uous** *a* dédaigneux(euse), méprisant(e).

contend [kən'tɛnd] *vt*: **to ~ that** soutenir *or* prétendre que // *vi*: **to ~ with** rivaliser avec, lutter avec; **~er** *n* prétendant/e; adversaire *m/f*.

content [kən'tɛnt] *a* content(e), satisfait(e) // *vt* contenter, satisfaire // *n* ['kɔntɛnt] contenu *m*; teneur *f*; **~s** *npl* contenu; (**table of**) **~s** table *f* des matières; **~ed** *a* content(e), satisfait(e).

contention [kən'tɛnʃən] *n* dispute *f*,

contestation f; (*argument*) assertion f, affirmation f.

contest n ['kɔntest] combat m, lutte f; (*competition*) concours m // vt [kən'test] contester, discuter; (*compete for*) disputer; **~ant** [kən'testənt] n concurrent/e; (*in fight*) adversaire m/f.

context ['kɔntekst] n contexte m.

continent ['kɔntinənt] n continent m; **the C~** (*Brit*) l'Europe continentale; **~al** [-'nentl] a continental(e) // n Européen/ne (continental(e)); **~al quilt** n (*Brit*) couette f.

contingency [kən'tindʒənsi] n éventualité f, événement imprévu; **~ plan** n plan m d'urgence.

continual [kən'tinjuəl] a continuel(le).

continuation [kəntinju'eiʃən] n continuation f; (*after interruption*) reprise f; (*of story*) suite f.

continue [kən'tinju:] vi continuer // vt continuer; (*start again*) reprendre.

continuous [kən'tinjuəs] a continu(e), permanent(e); **~ stationery** n papier m en continu.

contort [kən'tɔ:t] vt tordre, crisper.

contour ['kɔntuə*] n contour m, profil m; (*also:* **~ line**) courbe f de niveau.

contraband ['kɔntrəbænd] n contrebande f.

contraceptive [kɔntrə'septiv] a contraceptif(ive), anticonceptionnel(le) // n contraceptif m.

contract n ['kɔntrækt] contrat m // vb [kən'trækt] vi (*become smaller*) se contracter, se resserrer; (*COMM*): **to ~ to do sth** s'engager (par contrat) à faire qch; **~ion** [-ʃən] n contraction f; **~or** n entrepreneur m.

contradict [kɔntrə'dikt] vt contredire; (*be contrary to*) démentir, être en contradiction avec.

contraption [kən'træpʃən] n (*pej*) machin m, truc m.

contrary ['kɔntrəri] a contraire, opposé(e); [kən'treəri] (*perverse*) contrariant(e), entêté(e) // n contraire m; **on the ~** au contraire; **unless you hear to the ~** sauf avis contraire.

contrast n ['kɔntra:st] contraste m // vt [kən'tra:st] mettre en contraste, contraster.

contribute [kən'tribju:t] vi contribuer // vt: **to ~ £10/an article to** donner 10 livres/un article à; **to ~ to** (*gen*) contribuer à; (*newspaper*) collaborer à; **contribution** [kɔntri'bju:ʃən] n contribution f; **contributor** n (*to newspaper*) collaborateur/trice.

contrive [kən'traiv] vt combiner, inventer // vi: **to ~ to do** s'arranger pour faire, trouver le moyen de faire.

control [kən'trəul] vt maîtriser; (*check*) contrôler // n contrôle m, autorité f; maîtrise f; **~s** npl commandes fpl; every-

thing is under **~** tout va bien, j'ai (or il a *etc*) la situation en main; **to be in ~ of** être maître de, maîtriser; être responsable de; **the car went out of ~** j'ai (or il a *etc*) perdu le contrôle du véhicule; **~ panel** n tableau m de commande; **~ room** n salle f des commandes; (*RADIO, TV*) régie f; **~ tower** n (*AVIAT*) tour f de contrôle.

controversial [kɔntrə'və:ʃl] a discutable, controversé(e).

controversy ['kɔntrəvə:si] n controverse f, polémique f.

convalesce [kɔnvə'les] vi relever de maladie, se remettre (d'une maladie).

convene [kən'vi:n] vt convoquer, assembler // vi se réunir, s'assembler.

convenience [kən'vi:niəns] n commodité f; **at your ~** quand or comme cela vous convient; **all modern ~s, all mod cons** avec tout le confort moderne, tout confort.

convenient [kən'vi:niənt] a commode.

convent ['kɔnvənt] n couvent m.

convention [kən'venʃən] n convention f; **~al** a conventionnel(le).

conversant [kən'və:snt] a: **to be ~ with** s'y connaître en; être au courant de.

conversation [kɔnvə'seiʃən] n conversation f.

converse ['kɔnvə:s] n contraire m, inverse m // vi [kən'və:s] s'entretenir; **~ly** [-'və:sli] ad inversement, réciproquement.

convert vt [kən'və:t] (*REL, COMM*) convertir; (*alter*) transformer, aménager // n ['kɔnvə:t] converti/e; **~ible** a convertible // n (*voiture f*) décapotable f.

convey [kən'vei] vt transporter; (*thanks*) transmettre; (*idea*) communiquer; **~or belt** n convoyeur m, tapis roulant.

convict vt [kən'vikt] déclarer (or reconnaître) coupable // n ['kɔnvikt] forçat m, convict m; **~ion** [-ʃən] n condamnation f; (*belief*) conviction f.

convince [kən'vins] vt convaincre, persuader; **convincing** a persuasif(ive), convaincant(e).

convoluted [kɔnvə'lu:tid] a (*argument*) compliqué(e).

convulse [kən'vʌls] vt ébranler; **to be ~d with laughter** se tordre de rire.

coo [ku:] vi roucouler.

cook [kuk] vt (faire) cuire // vi cuire; (*person*) faire la cuisine // n cuisinier/ière; **~book** n livre m de cuisine; **~er** n cuisinière f; **~ery** n cuisine f; **~ery book** n (*Brit*) = **~book**; **~ie** n (*US*) biscuit m, petit gâteau sec; **~ing** n cuisine f.

cool [ku:l] a frais(fraîche); (*not afraid*) calme; (*unfriendly*) froid(e); (*impertinent*) effronté(e) // vt, vi rafraîchir, refroidir.

coop [ku:p] *n* poulailler *m* // *vt*: to ~ up (*fig*) cloîtrer, enfermer.

cooperate [kəu'ɔpəreɪt] *vi* coopérer, collaborer; **cooperation** [-'reɪʃən] *n* coopération *f*, collaboration *f*.

cooperative [kəu'ɔpərətɪv] *a* coopératif(ive) // *n* coopérative *f*.

coordinate *vt* [kəu'ɔ:dɪneɪt] coordonner // *n* [kəu'ɔ:dɪnət] (*MATH*) coordonnée *f*; ~s *npl* (*clothes*) ensemble *m*, coordonnés *mpl*.

cop [kɔp] *n* (*col*) flic *m*.

cope [kəup] *vi* se débrouiller; to ~ with faire face à; s'occuper de.

copper [kɔpə*] *n* cuivre *m*; (*col*: *policeman*) flic *m*; ~s *npl* petite monnaie.

coppice ['kɔpɪs] *n*, **copse** [kɔps] *n* taillis *m*.

copy ['kɔpɪ] *n* copie *f*; (*book etc*) exemplaire *m* // *vt* copier; ~right *n* droit *m* d'auteur, copyright *m*.

coral ['kɔrəl] *n* corail *m*.

cord [kɔ:d] *n* corde *f*; (*fabric*) velours côtelé; whipcord *m*; corde *f*.

cordial ['kɔ:dɪəl] *a* cordial(e), chaleureux(euse) // *n* sirop *m*; cordial *m*.

cordon ['kɔ:dn] *n* cordon *m*; to ~ off *vt* boucler (*par cordon de police*).

corduroy ['kɔ:dərɔɪ] *n* velours côtelé.

core [kɔ:*] *n* (*of fruit*) trognon *m*, cœur *m*; (*TECH*) noyau *m* // *vt* enlever le trognon *or* le cœur de.

cork [kɔ:k] *n* liège *m*; (*of bottle*) bouchon *m*; ~screw *n* tire-bouchon *m*.

corn [kɔ:n] *n* (*Brit*: *wheat*) blé *m*; (*US*: *maize*) maïs *m*; (*on foot*) cor *m*; ~ on the cob (*CULIN*) épi *m* de maïs au naturel.

corned beef ['kɔ:nd-] *n* corned-beef *m*.

corner ['kɔ:nə*] *n* coin *m*; (*AUT*) tournant *m*, virage *m* // *vt* acculer, mettre au pied du mur; coincer; (*COMM*: *market*) accaparer // *vi* prendre un virage; ~stone *n* pierre *f* angulaire.

cornet ['kɔ:nɪt] *n* (*MUS*) cornet *m* à pistons; (*Brit*: *of ice-cream*) cornet (de glace).

cornflakes ['kɔ:nfleɪks] *npl* cornflakes *mpl*.

cornflour ['kɔ:nflauə*] *n* (*Brit*) farine *f* de maïs, maizena *f* ®.

cornstarch ['kɔ:nsta:tʃ] *n* (*US*) = **cornflour**.

Cornwall ['kɔ:nwəl] *n* Cornouailles *f*.

corny ['kɔ:nɪ] *a* (*col*) rebattu(e), galvaudé(e).

coronary ['kɔrənərɪ] *n*: ~ (**thrombosis**) infarctus *m* (du myocarde), thrombose *f* coronaire.

coronation [kɔrə'neɪʃən] *n* couronnement *m*.

coronet ['kɔrənɪt] *n* couronne *f*.

corporal ['kɔ:pərl] *n* caporal *m*, brigadier *m* // *a*: ~ **punishment** châtiment corporel.

corporate ['kɔ:pərɪt] *a* en commun; constitué(e) (en corporation).

corporation [kɔ:pə'reɪʃən] *n* (*of town*) municipalité *f*, conseil municipal; (*COMM*) société *f*.

corps [kɔ:*], *pl* **corps** [kɔ:z] *n* corps *m*.

corpse [kɔ:ps] *n* cadavre *m*.

correct [kə'rekt] *a* (*accurate*) correct(e), exact(e); (*proper*) correct, convenable // *vt* corriger; ~**ion** [-ʃən] *n* correction *f*.

correspond [kɔrɪs'pɔnd] *vi* correspondre; ~**ence** *n* correspondance *f*; ~**ence course** *n* cours *m* par correspondance; ~**ent** *n* correspondant/e.

corridor ['kɔrɪdɔ:*] *n* couloir *m*, corridor *m*.

corrode [kə'rəud] *vt* corroder, ronger // *vi* se corroder.

corrugated ['kɔrəgeɪtɪd] *a* plissé(e); cannelé(e); ondulé(e); ~ **iron** *n* tôle ondulée.

corrupt [kə'rʌpt] *a* corrompu(e) // *vt* corrompre; ~**ion** [-ʃən] *n* corruption *f*.

Corsica ['kɔ:sɪkə] *n* Corse *f*.

cortège [kɔ:'teɪʒ] *n* cortège *m* (*gén funèbre*).

cosh [kɔʃ] *n* (*Brit*) matraque *f*.

cosmetic [kɔz'metɪk] *n* produit *m* de beauté, cosmétique *m*.

cosset ['kɔsɪt] *vt* choyer, dorloter.

cost [kɔst] *n* coût *m* // *vb* (*pt*, *pp* cost) *vi* coûter // *vt* établir *or* calculer le prix de revient de; ~s *npl* (*LAW*) dépens *mpl*; it ~s £5/too much cela coûte cinq livres/ trop cher; at all ~s coûte que coûte, à tout prix.

co-star ['kəusta:*] *n* partenaire *m/f*.

cost-effective [kɔstɪ'fektɪv] *a* rentable.

costly ['kɔstlɪ] *a* coûteux(euse).

cost-of-living [kɔstəv'lɪvɪŋ] *a*: ~ **allowance** indemnité *f* de vie chère; ~ **index** indexe *m* du coût de la vie.

cost price *n* (*Brit*) prix coûtant *or* de revient.

costume ['kɔstju:m] *n* costume *m*; (*lady's suit*) tailleur *m*; (*Brit*: *also*: **swimming** ~) maillot *m* (de bain); ~ **jewellery** *n* bijoux *mpl* de fantaisie.

cosy, (*US*) **cozy** ['kəuzɪ] *a* douillet(te).

cot [kɔt] *n* (*Brit*: *child's*) lit *m* d'enfant, petit lit; (*US*: *campbed*) lit de camp.

cottage ['kɔtɪdʒ] *n* petite maison (à la campagne), cottage *m*; ~ **cheese** *n* fromage blanc (*maigre*); ~ **industry** *n* industrie familiale *or* artisanale; ~ **pie** *n* ≈ hachis *m* Parmentier.

cotton ['kɔtn] *n* coton *m*; ~ **candy** *n* (*US*) barbe *f* à papa; ~ **wool** *n* (*Brit*) ouate *f*, coton *m* hydrophile.

couch [kautʃ] *n* canapé *m*; divan *m* // *vt* formuler, exprimer.

couchette [ku:'ʃet] *n* couchette *f*.

cough [kɔf] *vi* tousser // *n* toux *f*; ~ **drop** *n* pastille *f* pour *or* contre la toux.

could [kud] *pt of* **can**; **~n't = could not.**

council ['kaunsl] *n* conseil *m*; **city** *or* **town ~** conseil municipal; **~ estate** *n* (*Brit*) (quartier *m* or zone *f* de) logements loués à/par la municipalité; **~ house** *n* (*Brit*) maison *f* (à loyer modéré) louée par la municipalité; **~lor** *n* conseiller/ère.

counsel ['kaunsl] *n* avocat/e; consultation *f*, délibération *f*; **~lor** *n* conseiller/ère.

count [kaunt] *vt, vi* compter // *n* compte *m*; (*nobleman*) comte *m*; **to ~ on** *vt fus* compter sur; **~down** *n* compte *m* à rebours.

countenance ['kauntɪnəns] *n* expression *f* // *vt* approuver.

counter ['kauntə*] *n* comptoir *m*; (*in post office, bank*) guichet *m*; (*in game*) jeton *m* // *vt* aller à l'encontre de, opposer; (*blow*) parer // *ad*: ~ **to** à l'encontre de; contrairement à; **~act** *vt* neutraliser, contrebalancer; **~espionage** *n* contre-espionnage *m*.

counterfeit ['kauntəfɪt] *n* faux *m*, contrefaçon *f* // *vt* contrefaire // *a* faux (fausse).

counterfoil ['kauntəfɔɪl] *n* talon *m*, souche *f*.

countermand [kauntə'ma:nd] *vt* annuler.

counterpart ['kauntəpa:t] *n* (*of document etc*) double *m*; (*of person*) homologue *m/f*.

countess ['kauntɪs] *n* comtesse *f*.

countless ['kauntlɪs] *a* innombrable.

country ['kʌntrɪ] *n* pays *m*; (*native land*) patrie *f*; (*as opposed to town*) campagne *f*; (*region*) région *f*, pays; ~ **dancing** *n* (*Brit*) danse *f* folklorique; ~ **house** *n* manoir *m*, (petit) château; **~man** *n* (*national*) compatriote *m*; (*rural*) habitant *m* de la campagne, campagnard *m*; **~side** *n* campagne *f*.

county ['kauntɪ] *n* comté *m*.

coup, **~s** [ku:, -z] *n* beau coup; (*also*: ~ **d'état**) coup d'État.

couple ['kʌpl] *n* couple *m* // *vt* (*carriages*) atteler; (*TECH*) coupler; (*ideas, names*) associer; **a ~ of** deux.

coupon ['ku:pɔn] *n* coupon *m*, bonprime *m*, bon-réclame *m*; (*COMM*) coupon.

courage ['kʌrɪdʒ] *n* courage *m*.

courgette [kuə'ʒɛt] *n* (*Brit*) courgette *f*.

courier ['kurɪə*] *n* messager *m*, courrier *m*; (*for tourists*) accompagnateur/trice.

course [kɔ:s] *n* cours *m*; (*of ship*) route *f*; (*for golf*) terrain *m*; (*part of meal*) plat *m*; **first ~** entrée *f*; **of ~** *ad* bien sûr; ~ **of action** parti *m*, ligne *f* de conduite; ~ **of lectures** série *f* de conférences; ~ **of treatment** (*MED*) traitement *m*.

court [kɔ:t] *n* cour *f*; (*LAW*) cour, tribunal *m*; (*TENNIS*) court *m* // *vt* (*woman*) courtiser, faire la cour à; **to take to ~** actionner *or* poursuivre en justice.

courteous ['kə:tɪəs] *a* courtois(e), poli(e).

courtesy ['kə:təsɪ] *n* courtoisie *f*, politesse *f*; **by ~ of** avec l'aimable autorisation de.

court-house ['kɔ:thaus] *n* (*US*) palais *m* de justice.

courtier ['kɔ:tɪə*] *n* courtisan *m*, dame *f* de cour.

court-martial, *pl* **courts-martial** ['kɔ:t'ma:ʃəl] *n* cour martiale, conseil *m* de guerre.

courtroom ['kɔ:trum] *n* salle *f* de tribunal.

courtyard ['kɔ:tja:d] *n* cour *f*.

cousin ['kʌzn] *n* cousin/e; **first ~** cousin/e germain(e).

cove [kəuv] *n* petite baie, anse *f*.

covenant ['kʌvənənt] *n* contrat *m*, engagement *m*.

cover ['kʌvə*] *vt* couvrir // *n* (*for bed, of book*, *COMM*) couverture *f*; (*of pan*) couvercle *m*; (*over furniture*) housse *f*; (*shelter*) abri *m*; **to take ~** (*shelter*) se mettre à l'abri; **under ~** à l'abri; **under ~ of darkness** à la faveur de la nuit; **under separate ~** (*COMM*) sous pli séparé; **to ~ up for sb** couvrir qn; **~age** *n* reportage *m*; (*INSURANCE*) couverture *f*; ~ **charge** *n* couvert *m* (*supplément à payer*); **~ing** *n* couverture *f*, enveloppe *f*; **~ing letter**, (*US*) ~ **letter** *n* lettre explicative; ~ **note** *n* (*INSURANCE*) police *f* provisoire.

covert ['kʌvət] *a* (*threat*) voilé(e), caché(e); (*attack*) indirect(e); (*glance*) furtif(ive).

cover-up ['kʌvərʌp] *n* tentative *f* pour étouffer une affaire.

covet ['kʌvɪt] *vt* convoiter.

cow [kau] *n* vache *f* // *cpd* femelle // *vt* effrayer, intimider.

coward ['kauəd] *n* lâche *m/f*; **~ice** [-ɪs] *n* lâcheté *f*; **~ly** *a* lâche.

cowboy ['kaubɔɪ] *n* cow-boy *m*.

cower ['kauə*] *vi* se recroqueviller; trembler.

coxswain ['kɔksn] *n* (*abbr*: **cox**) barreur *m*; (*of ship*) patron *m*.

coy [kɔɪ] *a* faussement effarouché(e) *or* timide.

cozy ['kəuzɪ] *a* (*US*) = **cosy.**

CPA *n abbr* (*US*) *of* **certified public accountant.**

crab [kræb] *n* crabe *m*; ~ **apple** *n* pomme *f* sauvage.

crack [kræk] *n* fente *f*, fissure *f*; fêlure *f*; lézarde *f*; (*noise*) craquement *m*, coup (sec); (*joke*) plaisanterie *f*; (*col*: *attempt*): **to have a ~ at** essayer // *vt* fendre, fissurer; fêler; lézarder; (*whip*) faire claquer; (*nut*) casser // a (*athlete*) de première classe, d'élite; **to ~ down on** *vt fus* mettre un frein à; **to ~ up** *vi* être au bout de son rouleau, flancher; **~er** *n* pétard *m*; biscuit (salé), craquelin *m*.

crackle ['krækl] *vi* crépiter, grésiller.

cradle ['kreɪdl] *n* berceau *m*.

craft [krɑːft] *n* métier (artisanal); (*cunning*) ruse *f*, astuce *f*; (*boat*) embarcation *f*, barque *f*; **~sman** *n* artisan *m*, ouvrier (qualifié); **~smanship** *n* métier *m*, habileté *f*; **~y** *a* rusé(e), malin(igne), astucieux(euse).

crag [kræg] *n* rocher escarpé.

cram [kræm] *vt* (*fill*): **to ~ sth with** bourrer qch de; (*put*): **to ~ sth into** fourrer qch dans // *vi* (*for exams*) bachoter.

cramp [kræmp] *n* crampe *f* // *vt* gêner, entraver; **~ed** *a* à l'étroit, très serré(e).

cranberry ['krænbəri] *n* canneberge *f*.

crane [kreɪn] *n* grue *f*.

crank [kræŋk] *n* manivelle *f*; (*person*) excentrique *m/f*; **~shaft** *n* vilebrequin *m*.

cranny ['kræni] *n see* **nook**.

crash [kræʃ] *n* fracas *m*; (*of car, plane*) collision *f* // *vt* (*plane*) écraser // *vi* (*plane*) s'écraser; (*two cars*) se percuter, s'emboutir; (*fig*) s'effondrer; **to ~ into** se jeter *or* se fracasser contre; **~ course** *n* cours intensif; **~ helmet** *n* casque (protecteur); **~ landing** *n* atterrissage forcé *or* en catastrophe.

crate [kreɪt] *n* cageot *m*.

cravat(e) [krə'væt] *n* foulard (noué autour du cou).

crave [kreɪv] *vt, vi*: **to ~ (for)** avoir une envie irrésistible de.

crawl [krɔːl] *vi* ramper; (*vehicle*) avancer au pas // *n* (*SWIMMING*) crawl *m*.

crayfish ['kreɪfɪʃ] *n* (*pl inv*) (*freshwater*) écrevisse *f*; (*saltwater*) langoustine *f*.

crayon ['kreɪən] *n* crayon *m* (de couleur).

craze [kreɪz] *n* engouement *m*.

crazy ['kreɪzi] *a* fou(folle); **~ paving** *n* dallage irrégulier (en pierres plates).

creak [kriːk] *vi* grincer; craquer.

cream [kriːm] *n* crème *f* // *a* (*colour*) crème *inv*; **~ cake** *n* (petit) gâteau à la crème; **~ cheese** *n* fromage *m* à la crème, fromage blanc; **~y** *a* crémeux(euse).

crease [kriːs] *n* pli *m* // *vt* froisser, chiffonner // *vi* se froisser, se chiffonner.

create [kriː'eɪt] *vt* créer; **creation** [-ʃən] *n* création *f*; **creative** *a* créateur(trice).

creature ['kriːtʃə*] *n* créature *f*.

crèche, creche [krɛʃ] *n* garderie *f*, crèche *f*.

credence ['kriːdns] *n*: **to lend** *or* **give ~ to** ajouter foi à.

credentials [krɪ'dɛnʃlz] *npl* (*papers*) références *fpl*.

credit ['krɛdɪt] *n* crédit *m* // *vt* (*COMM*) créditer; (*believe*: *also*: **give ~ to**) ajouter foi à, croire; **~s** *npl* (*CINEMA*) générique *m*; **to ~ sb with** (*fig*) prêter *or* attribuer à qn; **to be in ~** (*person, bank account*) être créditeur(trice); **~ card** *n* carte *f* de crédit; **~or** *n* créancier/ière.

creed [kriːd] *n* croyance *f*; credo *m*, principes *mpl*.

creek [kriːk] *n* crique *f*, anse *f*; (*US*) ruisseau *m*, petit cours d'eau.

creep [kriːp], *pt, pp* **crept** *vi* ramper; (*fig*) se faufiler, se glisser; (*plant*) grimper; **~er** *n* plante grimpante; **~y** *a* (*frightening*) qui fait frissonner, qui donne la chair de poule.

cremate [krɪ'meɪt] *vt* incinérer.

crematorium, *pl* **crematoria** [krɛmə-'tɔːrɪəm, -'tɔːrɪə] *n* four *m* crématoire.

crêpe [kreɪp] *n* crêpe *m*; **~ bandage** *n* (*Brit*) bande *f* Velpeau ®.

crept [krɛpt] *pt, pp of* **creep**.

crescent ['krɛsnt] *n* croissant *m*; rue *f* (en arc de cercle).

cress [krɛs] *n* cresson *m*.

crest [krɛst] *n* crête *f*; **~fallen** *a* déconfit(e), découragé(e).

crevice ['krɛvɪs] *n* fissure *f*, lézarde *f*, fente *f*.

crew [kruː] *n* équipage *m*; **to have a ~-cut** avoir les cheveux en brosse; **~-neck** *n* col ras.

crib [krɪb] *n* lit *m* d'enfant // *vt* (*col*) copier.

crick [krɪk] *n* crampe *f*.

cricket ['krɪkɪt] *n* (*insect*) grillon *m*, cri-cri *m inv*; (*game*) cricket *m*.

crime [kraɪm] *n* crime *m*; **criminal** ['krɪmɪnl] *a, n* criminel(le).

crimson ['krɪmzn] *a* cramoisi(e).

cringe [krɪndʒ] *vi* avoir un mouvement de recul; (*fig*) s'humilier, ramper.

crinkle ['krɪŋkl] *vt* froisser, chiffonner.

cripple ['krɪpl] *n* boiteux/euse, infirme *m/f* // *vt* estropier, paralyser.

crisis, *pl* **crises** ['kraɪsɪs, -siːz] *n* crise *f*.

crisp [krɪsp] *a* croquant(e); (*fig*) vif(vive); brusque; **~s** *npl* (*Brit*) (pommes) chips *fpl*.

criss-cross ['krɪskrɔs] *a* entrecroisé(e).

criterion, *pl* **criteria** [kraɪ'tɪərɪən, -'tɪərɪə] *n* critère *m*.

critic ['krɪtɪk] *n* critique *m/f*; **~al** *a* critique; **~ally** *ad* (*examine*) d'un œil critique; (*speak etc*) sévèrement; **~ally ill** gravement malade; **~ism** ['krɪtɪsɪzm] *n* critique *f*; **~ize** ['krɪtɪsaɪz] *vt* critiquer.

croak [krəuk] *vi* (*frog*) coasser; (*raven*) croasser.

crochet ['krəuʃeɪ] *n* travail *m* au crochet.

crockery ['krɔkərɪ] *n* vaisselle *f*.

crocodile ['krɔkədaɪl] *n* crocodile *m*.

crocus ['krəukəs] *n* crocus *m*.

croft [krɔft] *n* (*Brit*) petite ferme.

crony ['krəunɪ] *n* copain/copine.

crook [kruk] *n* escroc *m*; (*of shepherd*) houlette *f*; **~ed** ['krukɪd] *a* courbé(e), tordu(e); (*action*) malhonnête.

crop [krɔp] *n* (*produce*) culture *f*; (*amount produced*) récolte *f*; (*riding ~*) cravache *f*; **to ~ up** *vi* surgir, se présenter, survenir.

cross [krɔs] *n* croix *f*; (BIOL) croisement *m* // *vt* (*street etc*) traverser; (*arms, legs,* BIOL) croiser; (*cheque*) barrer // *a* en colère, fâché(e); **to ~ o.s.** se signer, faire le signe de (la) croix; **to ~ out** *vt* barrer, biffer; **to ~ over** *vi* traverser; **~bar** *n* barre transversale; **~country (race)** *n* cross(-country) *m*; **~-examine** *vt* (LAW) faire subir un examen contradictoire à; **~-eyed** *a* qui louche; **~fire** *n* feux croisés; **~ing** *n* croisement *m*, carrefour *m*; (*sea passage*) traversée *f*; (*also:* pedestrian **~ing**) passage clouté; **~ing guard** *n* (US) *contractuel/le qui fait traverser la rue aux enfants*; **~ purposes** *npl*: **to be at ~ purposes** ne pas parler de la même chose; **~reference** *n* renvoi *m*, référence *f*; **~roads** *n* carrefour *m*; **~ section** *n* (BIOL) coupe transversale; (*in population*) échantillon *m*; **~walk** *n* (US) passage clouté; **~wind** *n* vent *m* de travers; **~wise** *ad* en travers; **~word** *n* mots croisés *mpl*.

crotch [krɔtʃ] *n* (*of garment*) entrejambes *m inv*.

crotchety ['krɔtʃɪtɪ] *a* (*person*) grognon(ne), grincheux(euse).

crouch [krautʃ] *vi* s'accroupir; se tapir; se ramasser.

crow [krəu] *n* (*bird*) corneille *f*; (*of cock*) chant *m* du coq, cocorico *m* // *vi* (*cock*) chanter; (*fig*) pavoiser, chanter victoire.

crowbar ['krəuba:*] *n* levier *m*.

crowd [kraud] *n* foule *f* // *vt* bourrer, remplir // *vi* affluer, s'attrouper, s'entasser; **~ed** *a* bondé(e), plein(e); **~ed with** plein de.

crown [kraun] *n* couronne *f*; (*of head*) sommet *m* de la tête, calotte crânienne; (*of hat*) fond *m*; (*of hill*) sommet *m* // *vt* couronner; **~ jewels** *npl* joyaux *mpl* de la Couronne; **~ prince** *n* prince héritier.

crow's feet *npl* pattes *fpl* d'oie (*fig*).

crucial ['kru:ʃl] *a* crucial(e), décisif(ive).

crucifixion [kru:sɪ'fɪkʃən] *n* crucifiement *m*, crucifixion *f*.

crude [kru:d] *a* (*materials*) brut(e); non raffiné(e); (*fig: basic*) rudimentaire, sommaire; (*: vulgar*) cru(e), grossier(ère); **~ (oil)** *n* (pétrole) brut *m*.

cruel ['kruəl] *a* cruel(le); **~ty** *n* cruauté *f*.

cruet ['kru:ɪt] *n* huilier *m*; vinaigrier *m*.

cruise [kru:z] *n* croisière *f* // *vi* (*ship*) croiser; (*car*) rouler; (*aircraft*) voler; (*taxi*) être en maraude; **~r** *n* croiseur *m*.

crumb [krʌm] *n* miette *f*.

crumble ['krʌmbl] *vt* émietter // *vi* s'émietter; (*plaster etc*) s'effriter; (*land, earth*) s'ébouler; (*building*) s'écrouler, crouler; (*fig*) s'effondrer; **crumbly** *a* friable.

crumpet ['krʌmpɪt] *n* petite crêpe (épaisse).

crumple ['krʌmpl] *vt* froisser, friper.

crunch [krʌntʃ] *vt* croquer; (*underfoot*) faire craquer, écraser; faire crisser // *n* (*fig*) instant *m* or moment *m* critique, moment de vérité; **~y** *a* croquant(e), croustillant(e).

crusade [kru:'seɪd] *n* croisade *f*.

crush [krʌʃ] *n* foule *f*, cohue *f* // *vt* écraser; (*crumple*) froisser.

crust [krʌst] *n* croûte *f*.

crutch [krʌtʃ] *n* béquille *f*.

crux [krʌks] *n* point crucial.

cry [kraɪ] *vi* pleurer; (*shout: also: ~ out*) crier // *n* cri *m*; **to ~ off** *vi* se dédire; se décommander.

cryptic ['krɪptɪk] *a* énigmatique.

crystal ['krɪstl] *n* cristal *m*; **~-clear** *a* clair(e) comme de l'eau de roche.

cub [kʌb] *n* petit *m* (*d'un animal*); (*also: ~ scout*) louveteau *m*.

Cuba ['kju:bə] *n* Cuba *m*.

cubbyhole ['kʌbɪhəul] *n* cagibi *m*.

cube [kju:b] *n* cube *m* // *vt* (MATH) élever au cube; **cubic** *a* cubique; **cubic metre** *etc* mètre *m etc* cube; **cubic capacity** *n* cylindrée *f*.

cubicle ['kju:bɪkl] *n* box *m*, cabine *f*.

cuckoo ['kuku:] *n* coucou *m*; **~ clock** *n* (pendule *f* à) coucou *m*.

cucumber ['kju:kʌmbə*] *n* concombre *m*.

cuddle ['kʌdl] *vt* câliner, caresser // *vi* se blottir l'un contre l'autre.

cue [kju:] *n* (*snooker ~*) queue *f* de billard; (THEATRE etc) signal *m*.

cuff [kʌf] *n* (*Brit: of shirt, coat etc*) poignet *m*, manchette *f*; (*US: of trousers*) revers *m*; **off the ~** *ad* de chic, à l'improviste; **~link** *n* bouton *m* de manchette.

cul-de-sac ['kʌldəsæk] *n* cul-de-sac *m*, impasse *f*.

cull [kʌl] *vt* sélectionner.

culminate ['kʌlmɪneɪt] *vi*: **to ~ in** finir or se terminer par; (*end in*) mener à; **culmination** [-'neɪʃən] *n* point culminant.

culottes [kju:'lɔts] *npl* jupe-culotte *f*.

culpable ['kʌlpəbl] *a* coupable.

culprit ['kʌlprɪt] *n* coupable *m/f*.

cult [kʌlt] *n* culte *m*.

cultivate ['kʌltɪveɪt] *vt* (*also fig*) cultiver; **cultivation** [-'veɪʃən] *n* culture *f*.

cultural ['kʌltʃərəl] *a* culturel(le).

culture ['kʌltʃə*] *n* (*also fig*) culture *f*; ~**d** *a* cultivé(e) (*fig*).

cumbersome ['kʌmbəsəm] *a* encombrant(e), embarrassant(e).

cunning ['kʌnɪŋ] *n* ruse *f*, astuce *f* // *a* rusé(e), malin(igne).

cup [kʌp] *n* tasse *f*; (*prize, event*) coupe *f*; (*of bra*) bonnet *m*.

cupboard ['kʌbəd] *n* placard *m*.

cup-tie ['kʌptaɪ] *n* (*Brit*) match *m* de coupe.

curate ['kjuərɪt] *n* vicaire *m*.

curator [kjuə'reɪtə*] *n* conservateur *m* (*d'un musée etc*).

curb [kə:b] *vt* refréner, mettre un frein à // *n* frein *m* (*fig*); (*US*) = **kerb**.

curdle ['kə:dl] *vi* (se) cailler.

cure [kjuə*] *vt* guérir; (*CULIN*) saler; fumer; sécher // *n* remède *m*.

curfew ['kə:fju:] *n* couvre-feu *m*.

curio ['kjuərɪəu] *n* bibelot *m*, curiosité *f*.

curiosity [kjuərɪ'ɔsɪtɪ] *n* curiosité *f*.

curious ['kjuərɪəs] *a* curieux(euse).

curl [kə:l] *n* boucle *f* (de cheveux) // *vt, vi* boucler; (*tightly*) friser; **to ~ up** *vi* s'enrouler; se pelotonner; ~**er** *n* bigoudi *m*, rouleau *m*.

curly ['kə:lɪ] *a* bouclé(e); frisé(e).

currant ['kʌrnt] *n* raisin *m* de Corinthe, raisin sec.

currency ['kʌrnsɪ] *n* monnaie *f*; **to gain** ~ (*fig*) s'accréditer.

current ['kʌrnt] *n* courant *m* // *a* courant(e); ~ **account** *n* (*Brit*) compte courant; ~ **affairs** *npl* (questions *fpl* d'actualité *f*; ~**ly** *ad* actuellement.

curriculum, *pl* ~**s** *or* **curricula** [kə'rɪkjuləm, -lə] *n* programme *m* d'études; ~ **vitae (CV)** *n* curriculum vitae (C.V.) *m*.

curry ['kʌrɪ] *n* curry *m* // *vt*: **to ~ favour with** chercher à gagner la faveur *or* à s'attirer les bonnes grâces de.

curse [kə:s] *vi* jurer, blasphémer // *vt* maudire // *n* malédiction *f*; fléau *m*.

cursor ['kə:sə*] *n* (*COMPUT*) curseur *m*.

cursory ['kə:sərɪ] *a* superficiel(le), hâtif(ive).

curt [kə:t] *a* brusque, sec(sèche).

curtail [kə:'teɪl] *vt* (*visit etc*) écourter; (*expenses etc*) réduire.

curtain ['kə:tn] *n* rideau *m*.

curts(e)y ['kə:tsɪ] *n* révérence *f* // *vi* faire une révérence.

curve [kə:v] *n* courbe *f*; (*in the road*) tournant *m*, virage *m* // *vi* se courber;

(*road*) faire une courbe.

cushion ['kuʃən] *n* coussin *m* // *vt* (*shock*) amortir.

custard ['kʌstəd] *n* (*for pouring*) crème anglaise.

custodian [kʌs'təudɪən] *n* gardien/ne; (*of collection etc*) conservateur/trice.

custody ['kʌstədɪ] *n* (*of child*) garde *f*; (*for offenders*) détention préventive.

custom ['kʌstəm] *n* coutume *f*, usage *m*; (*LAW*) droit coutumier, coutume; (*COMM*) clientèle *f*; ~**ary** *a* habituel(le).

customer ['kʌstəmə*] *n* client/e.

customized ['kʌstəmaɪzd] *a* (*car etc*) construit(e) sur commande.

custom-made ['kʌstəm'meɪd] *a* (*clothes*) fait(e) sur mesure; (*other goods*) hors série, fait(e) sur commande.

customs ['kʌstəmz] *npl* douane *f*; ~ **officer** *n* douanier *m*.

cut [kʌt] *vb* (*pt, pp* **cut**) *vt* couper; (*meat*) découper; (*shape, make*) tailler; couper; creuser; graver; (*reduce*) réduire // *vi* couper; (*intersect*) se couper // *n* (*gen*) coupure *f*; (*of clothes*) coupe *f*; (*of jewel*) taille *f*; (*in salary etc*) réduction *f*; (*of meat*) morceau *m*; **to ~ a tooth** percer une dent; **to ~ down** *vt fus* (*tree etc*) couper, abattre; (*reduce: also*: ~ **down on**) réduire; **to ~ off** *vt* couper; (*fig*) isoler; **to ~ out** *vt* ôter; découper; tailler; **to ~ up** *vt* (*paper, meat*) découper; ~**back** *n* réduction *f*.

cute [kju:t] *a* mignon(ne), adorable; (*clever*) rusé(e), astucieux(euse).

cuticle ['kju:tɪkl] *n* (*on nail*): ~ **remover** *n* repousse-peaux *m inv*.

cutlery ['kʌtlərɪ] *n* couverts *mpl*.

cutlet ['kʌtlɪt] *n* côtelette *f*.

cut: ~**out** *n* coupe-circuit *m inv*; (*cardboard* ~) découpage *m*; ~**-price**, (*US*) ~**-rate** *a* au rabais, à prix réduit; ~**throat** *n* assassin *m* // *a* acharné(e).

cutting ['kʌtɪŋ] *a* tranchant(e), coupant(e); (*fig*) cinglant(e), mordant(e) // *n* (*Brit: from newspaper*) coupure *f* (de journal).

CV *n abbr of* **curriculum vitae**.

cwt *abbr of* **hundredweight(s)**.

cyanide ['saɪənaɪd] *n* cyanure *m*.

cycle ['saɪkl] *n* cycle *m* // *vi* faire de la bicyclette.

cycling ['saɪklɪŋ] *n* cyclisme *m*.

cyclist ['saɪklɪst] *n* cycliste *m/f*.

cygnet ['sɪgnɪt] *n* jeune cygne *m*.

cylinder ['sɪlɪndə*] *n* cylindre *m*; ~**head gasket** *n* joint *m* de culasse.

cymbals ['sɪmblz] *npl* cymbales *fpl*.

cynic ['sɪnɪk] *n* cynique *m/f*; ~**al** *a* cynique; ~**ism** ['sɪnɪsɪzəm] *n* cynisme *m*.

Cypriot ['sɪprɪət] *a* cypriote, chypriote // *n* Cypriote *m/f*, Chypriote *m/f*.

Cyprus ['saɪprəs] *n* Chypre *f*.

cyst [sɪst] n kyste m.

cystitis [sɪs'taɪtɪs] n cystite f.

czar [zɑ:*] n tsar m.

Czech [tʃɛk] a tchèque // n Tchèque m/f; (LING) tchèque m.

Czechoslovakia [tʃɛkəslə'vækɪə] n Tchécoslovaquie f; **~n** a tchécoslovaque // n Tchécoslovaque m/f.

D

D [di:] n (MUS) ré m.

dab [dæb] vt (eyes, wound) tamponner; (paint, cream) appliquer (par petites touches or rapidement).

dabble ['dæbl] vi: to ~ in faire or se mêler or s'occuper un peu de.

dad, daddy [dæd, 'dædɪ] n papa m.

daffodil ['dæfədɪl] n jonquille f.

daft [dɑ:ft] a idiot(e), stupide.

dagger ['dægə*] n poignard m.

daily ['deɪlɪ] a quotidien(ne), journalier(ère) // n quotidien m // ad tous les jours.

dainty ['deɪntɪ] a délicat(e), mignon(ne).

dairy ['dɛərɪ] n (shop) crémerie f, laiterie f; (on farm) laiterie // a laitier(ère); ~ **produce** n produits laitiers.

dais ['deɪɪs] n estrade f.

daisy ['deɪzɪ] n pâquerette f; ~ **wheel** n (on printer) marguerite f.

dale [deɪl] n vallon m.

dam [dæm] n barrage m // vt endiguer.

damage ['dæmɪdʒ] n dégâts mpl, dommages mpl; (fig) tort m // vt endommager, abîmer; (fig) faire du tort à; ~**s** npl (LAW) dommages-intérêts mpl.

damn [dæm] vt condamner; (curse) maudire // n (col): I don't give a ~ je m'en fous // a (col: also: ~ed): this ~ ... ce sacré or foutu ...; ~ (it)! zut!

damp [dæmp] a humide // n humidité f // vt (also: ~en: cloth, rag) humecter; (enthusiasm etc) refroidir.

damson ['dæmzən] n prune f de Damas.

dance [dɑ:ns] n danse f; (ball) bal m // vi danser; ~ **hall** n salle f de bal, dancing m; ~**r** n danseur/euse.

dancing ['dɑ:nsɪŋ] n danse f.

dandelion ['dændɪlaɪən] n pissenlit m.

dandruff ['dændrəf] n pellicules fpl.

Dane [deɪn] n Danois/e.

danger ['deɪndʒə*] n danger m; there is a ~ of fire il y a (un) risque d'incendie; in ~ en danger; he was in ~ of falling il risquait de tomber; ~**ous** a dangereux(euse).

dangle ['dæŋgl] vt balancer; (fig) faire miroiter // vi pendre, se balancer.

Danish ['deɪnɪʃ] a danois(e) // n (LING) danois m.

dapper ['dæpə*] a pimpant(e).

dare [dɛə*] vt: to ~ sb to do défier qn or mettre qn au défi de faire // vi: to ~ (to) do sth oser faire qch; I ~ say (I suppose) il est probable (que); ~**devil** n casse-cou m inv; **daring** a hardi(e), audacieux(euse) // n audace f, hardiesse f.

dark [dɑ:k] a (night, room) obscur(e), sombre; (colour, complexion) foncé(e), sombre; (fig) sombre // n: in the ~ dans le noir; in the ~ about (fig) ignorant tout de; after ~ après la tombée de la nuit; ~**en** vt obscurcir, assombrir // vi s'obscurcir, s'assombrir; ~ **glasses** npl lunettes noires; ~**ness** n obscurité f; ~ **room** n chambre noire.

darling ['dɑ:lɪŋ] a, n chéri(e).

darn [dɑ:n] vt repriser.

dart [dɑ:t] n fléchette f // vi: to ~ towards se précipiter or s'élancer vers; to ~ away/along partir/passer comme une flèche; ~**s** n jeu m de fléchettes; ~**board** n cible f (de jeu de fléchettes).

dash [dæʃ] n (sign) tiret m; (small quantity) goutte f, larme f // vt (missile) jeter or lancer violemment; (hopes) anéantir // vi: to ~ towards se précipiter or se ruer vers; to ~ away or off vi partir à toute allure.

dashboard ['dæʃbɔ:d] n (AUT) tableau m de bord.

dashing ['dæʃɪŋ] a fringant(e).

data ['deɪtə] npl données fpl; ~**base** n base f de données; ~ **processing** n traitement m (électronique) de l'information.

date [deɪt] n date f; rendez-vous m; (fruit) datte f // vt dater; ~ of birth date de naissance; to ~ ad à ce jour; out of ~ périmé(e); up to ~ à la page; mis(e) à jour; moderne; ~**d** a démodé(e).

daub [dɔ:b] vt barbouiller.

daughter ['dɔ:tə*] n fille f; ~**-in-law** n belle-fille f, bru f.

daunting ['dɔ:ntɪŋ] a intimidant(e), décourageant(e).

dawdle ['dɔ:dl] vi traîner, lambiner.

dawn [dɔ:n] n aube f, aurore f // vi (day) se lever, poindre; (fig) naître, se faire jour; it ~**ed on him that ... il lui vint à l'esprit que ...

day [deɪ] n jour m; (as duration) journée f; (period of time, age) époque f, temps m; the ~ before la veille, le jour précédent; the ~ after, the following ~ le lendemain, le jour suivant; the ~ after tomorrow après-demain; the ~ before yesterday avant-hier; by ~ de jour; ~**break** n point m du jour; ~**dream** vi rêver (tout éveillé); ~**light** n (lumière f du) jour m; ~ **return** n (Brit) billet m d'aller-retour (valable pour la journée); ~**time** n jour m, journée f; ~**-to-~** a journalier(ère).

daze [deɪz] vt (subj: drug) hébéter; (: blow) étourdir // n: in a ~ hébété(e);

étourdi(e).

dazzle ['dæzl] vt éblouir, aveugler.

DC abbr (= direct current) courant continu.

deacon ['di:kən] n diacre m.

dead [dɛd] a mort(e); (numb) engourdi(e), insensible // ad absolument, complètement; **he was shot** ~ il a été tué d'un coup de revolver; ~ **on time** à l'heure pile; ~ **tired** éreinté(e), complètement fourbu(e); **to stop** ~ s'arrêter pile or net; **the** ~ les morts; ~**en** vt (blow, sound) amortir; (make numb) endormir, rendre insensible; ~ **end** n impasse f; ~ **heat** n (SPORT): **to finish in a** ~ **heat** terminer ex-aequo; ~**line** n date f or heure f limite; ~**lock** n impasse f (fig); ~ **loss** n: **to be a** ~ **loss** (col: person) n'être bon(bonne) à rien; (thing) ne rien valoir; ~**ly** a mortel(le); (weapon) meurtrier(ère); ~**pan** a impassible.

deaf [dɛf] a sourd(e); ~**en** vt rendre sourd; (fig) assourdir; ~**ness** n surdité f; ~-**mute** n sourd/e-muet/te.

deal [di:l] n affaire f, marché m // vt (pt, pp **dealt** [dɛlt]) (blow) porter; (cards) donner, distribuer; **a great** ~ **(of)** beaucoup (de); **to** ~ **in** vt fus faire le commerce de; **to** ~ **with** vt fus (COMM) traiter avec; (handle) s'occuper or se charger de; (be about: book etc) traiter de; ~**er** n marchand m; ~**ings** npl (COMM) transactions fpl; (relations) relations fpl, rapports mpl.

dean [di:n] n (REL, Brit SCOL) doyen m; (US SCOL) conseiller/ère (principal(e)) d'éducation.

dear [dɪə*] a cher(chère); (expensive) cher, coûteux(euse) // n: **my** ~ mon cher/ma chère; ~ **me!** mon Dieu!; **D**~ **Sir/Madam** (in letter) Monsieur/ Madame; ~**ly** ad (love) tendrement; (pay) cher.

death [dɛθ] n mort f; (ADMIN) décès m; ~ **certificate** n acte m de décès; ~ **duties** npl (Brit) droits mpl de succession; ~**ly** a de mort; ~ **penalty** n peine f de mort; ~ **rate** n (taux m de) mortalité f.

debar [dɪ'ba:*] vt: **to** ~ **sb from doing** interdire à qn de faire.

debase [dɪ'beɪs] vt (currency) déprécier, dévaloriser; (person) abaisser, avilir.

debate [dɪ'beɪt] n discussion f, débat m // vt discuter, débattre.

debit ['dɛbɪt] n débit m // vt: **to** ~ **a sum to sb** or **to sb's account** porter une somme au débit de qn, débiter qn d'une somme.

debt [dɛt] n dette f; **to be in** ~ avoir des dettes, être endetté(e); ~**or** n débiteur/ trice.

debunk [dɪ'bʌŋk] vt (theory, claim)

montrer le ridicule de.

decade ['dɛkeɪd] n décennie f, décade f.

decadence ['dɛkədəns] n décadence f.

decaffeinated [dɪ'kæfɪneɪtɪd] a décaféiné(e).

decanter [dɪ'kæntə*] n carafe f.

decay [dɪ'keɪ] n décomposition f, pourrissement m; (fig) déclin m, délabrement m; (also: **tooth** ~) carie f (dentaire) // vi (rot) se décomposer, pourrir; (fig) se délabrer; décliner; se détériorer.

deceased [dɪ'si:st] n défunt/e.

deceit [dɪ'si:t] n tromperie f, supercherie f; ~**ful** a trompeur(euse).

deceive [dɪ'si:v] vt tromper.

December [dɪ'sɛmbə*] n décembre m.

decent ['di:sənt] a décent(e), convenable; **they were very** ~ **about it** ils se sont montrés très chics.

deception [dɪ'sɛpʃən] n tromperie f.

deceptive [dɪ'sɛptɪv] a trompeur(euse).

decide [dɪ'saɪd] vt (person) décider; (question, argument) trancher, régler // vi se décider, décider; **to** ~ **to do/that** décider de faire/que; **to** ~ **on** décider, se décider pour; ~**d** a (resolute) résolu(e), décidé(e); (clear, definite) net(te), marqué(e); ~**dly** [-dɪdlɪ] ad résolument; incontestablement, nettement.

deciduous [dɪ'sɪdjuəs] a à feuilles caduques.

decimal ['dɛsɪməl] a décimal(e) // n décimale f; ~ **point** n ≈ virgule f.

decipher [dɪ'saɪfə*] vt déchiffrer.

decision [dɪ'sɪʒən] n décision f.

decisive [dɪ'saɪsɪv] a décisif(ive).

deck [dɛk] n (NAUT) pont m; (of bus): **top** ~ impériale f; (of cards) jeu m; ~**chair** n chaise longue.

declaration [dɛklə'reɪʃən] n déclaration f.

declare [dɪ'klɛə*] vt déclarer.

decline [dɪ'klaɪn] n (decay) déclin m; (lessening) baisse f // vi refuser, décliner // vi décliner; être en baisse, baisser.

decorate ['dɛkəreɪt] vt (adorn, give a medal to) décorer; (paint and paper) peindre et tapisser; **decoration** [-'reɪʃən] n (medal etc, adornment) décoration f; **decorator** n peintre m en bâtiment.

decoy ['di:kɔɪ] n piège m.

decrease n ['di:kri:s] diminution f // vt, vi [di:'kri:s] diminuer.

decree [dɪ'kri:] n (POL, REL) décret m; (LAW) arrêt m, jugement m; ~ **nisi** n jugement m provisoire de divorce.

dedicate ['dɛdɪkeɪt] vt consacrer; (book etc) dédier.

dedication [dɛdɪ'keɪʃən] n (devotion) dévouement m.

deduce [dɪ'dju:s] vt déduire, conclure.

deduct [dɪ'dʌkt] vt: **to** ~ **sth (from)**

déduire qch (de), retrancher qch (de); (from wage etc) prélever qch (sur), retenir qch (sur); **~ion** [dɪ'dʌkʃən] n (deducting, deducing) déduction f; (from wage etc) prélèvement m, retenue f.

deed [diːd] n action f, acte m; (LAW) acte notarié, contrat m.

deep [diːp] a (water, sigh, sorrow, thoughts) profond(e); (voice) grave; 4 metres ~ de 4 mètres de profondeur // ad: spectators stood 20 ~ il y avait 20 rangs de spectateurs; **~en** vt (hole) approfondir // vi s'approfondir; (darkness) s'épaissir; **~-freeze** n congélateur m // vt surgeler; **~-fry** vt faire frire (en friteuse); **~ly** ad (breathe) profondément; (interested, moved) vivement; (grateful) profondément, infiniment; **~-sea diving** n plongée sous-marine.

deer [dɪə*] n (pl inv): the ~ les cervidés mpl (ZOOL); (red) ~ cerf m; (fallow) ~ daim m; (roe) ~ chevreuil m.

deface [dɪ'feɪs] vt dégrader; barbouiller; rendre illisible.

default [dɪ'fɔːlt] vi (LAW) faire défaut; (gen) manquer à ses engagements // n (COMPUT: also: ~ value) valeur f par défaut; **by ~** (LAW) par défaut, par contumace; (SPORT) par forfait.

defeat [dɪ'fiːt] n défaite f // vt (team, opponents) battre; (fig: plans, efforts) faire échouer.

defect n ['diːfɛkt] défaut m // vi [dɪ'fɛkt]: **to ~ to the enemy** passer à l'ennemi; **~ive** [dɪ'fɛktɪv] a défectueux(euse).

defence [dɪ'fɛns] n défense f; **in ~ of** pour défendre; **~less** a sans défense.

defend [dɪ'fɛnd] vt défendre; **~ant** n défendeur/deresse; (in criminal case) accusé/e, prévenu/e; **~er** n défenseur m.

defense [dɪ'fɛns] n (US) = **defence**.

defer [dɪ'fə:*] vt (postpone) différer, ajourner // vi: **to ~ to** déférer à, s'en remettre à.

defiance [dɪ'faɪəns] n défi m; **in ~ of** au mépris de.

defiant [dɪ'faɪənt] a provocant(e), de défi; (person) rebelle, intraitable.

deficiency [dɪ'fɪʃənsɪ] n insuffisance f, déficience f; carence f.

deficit ['dɛfɪsɪt] n déficit m.

defile vb [dɪ'faɪl] vt souiller // vi défiler // n ['diːfaɪl] défilé m n.

define [dɪ'faɪn] vt définir.

definite ['dɛfɪnɪt] a (fixed) défini(e), (bien) déterminé(e); (clear, obvious) net(te), manifeste; **he was ~ about it** il a été catégorique; il était sûr de son fait; **~ly** ad sans aucun doute.

definition [dɛfɪ'nɪʃən] n définition f.

deflate [diː'fleɪt] vt dégonfler.

deflect [dɪ'flɛkt] vt détourner, faire dévier.

deformed [dɪ'fɔːmd] a difforme.

defraud [dɪ'frɔːd] vt frauder; **to ~ sb of sth** escroquer qch à qn.

defrost [diː'frɔst] vt (fridge) dégivrer; **~er** n (US: demister) dispositif m antibuée inv.

deft [dɛft] a adroit(e), preste.

defunct [dɪ'fʌŋkt] a défunt(e).

defuse [diː'fjuːz] vt désamorcer.

defy [dɪ'faɪ] vt défier; (efforts etc) résister à.

degenerate vi [dɪ'dʒɛnəreɪt] dégénérer // a [dɪ'dʒɛnərɪt] dégénéré(e).

degree [dɪ'griː] n degré m; grade m (universitaire); **a (first) ~ in maths** une licence en maths; **by ~s** (gradually) par degrés; **to some ~** jusqu'à un certain point, dans une certaine mesure.

dehydrated [diːhaɪ'dreɪtɪd] a déshydraté(e); (milk, eggs) en poudre.

de-ice [diː'aɪs] vt (windscreen) dégivrer.

deign [deɪn] vi: **to ~ to do** daigner faire.

deity ['diːɪtɪ] n divinité f; dieu m, déesse f.

dejected [dɪ'dʒɛktɪd] a abattu(e), déprimé(e).

delay [dɪ'leɪ] vt retarder // vi s'attarder // n délai m, retard m.

delectable [dɪ'lɛktəbl] a délicieux(euse).

delegate n ['dɛlɪgɪt] délégué/e // vt ['dɛlɪgeɪt] déléguer.

delete [dɪ'liːt] vt rayer, supprimer.

deliberate a [dɪ'lɪbərɪt] (intentional) délibéré(e); (slow) mesuré(e) // vi [dɪ'lɪbəreɪt] délibérer, réfléchir; **~ly** ad (on purpose) exprès, délibérément.

delicacy ['dɛlɪkəsɪ] n délicatesse f; (food) mets fin or délicat, friandise f.

delicate ['dɛlɪkɪt] a délicat(e).

delicatessen [dɛlɪkə'tɛsn] n épicerie fine.

delicious [dɪ'lɪʃəs] a délicieux(euse).

delight [dɪ'laɪt] n (grande) joie, grand plaisir // vt enchanter; **~ed** a: **~ed (at** or **with/to do)** ravi(e) (de/de faire); **~ful** a adorable; merveilleux(euse); délicieux(euse).

delinquent [dɪ'lɪŋkwənt] a, n délinquant(e).

delirious [dɪ'lɪrɪəs] a: **to be ~** délirer.

deliver [dɪ'lɪvə*] vt (mail) distribuer; (goods) livrer; (message) remettre; (speech) prononcer; (warning, ultimatum) lancer; (free) délivrer; (MED) accoucher; **~y** n distribution f; livraison f; (of speaker) élocution f; (MED) accouchement m.

delude [dɪ'luːd] vt tromper, leurrer.

delusion [dɪ'luːʒən] n illusion f.

delve [dɛlv] vi: **to ~ into** fouiller dans.

demand [dɪ'mɑːnd] vt réclamer, exiger // n exigence f; (claim) revendication f; (ECON) demande f; **in ~** demandé(e), recherché(e); **on ~** sur demande; **~ing** a (boss) exigeant(e); (work) astreignant(e).

demean [dɪˈmiːn] *vt*: to ~ o.s. s'abaisser.

demeanour, (*US*) **demeanor** [dɪˈmiː-nə*] *n* comportement *m*; maintien *m*.

demented [dɪˈmɛntɪd] *a* dément(e), fou(folle).

demise [dɪˈmaɪz] *n* décès *m*.

demister [diːˈmɪstə*] *n* (*AUT*) dispositif *m* anti-buée *inv*.

demo [ˈdɛməu] *n abbr* (*col: = demonstration*) manif *f*.

democracy [dɪˈmɔkrəsɪ] *n* démocratie *f*.

democrat [ˈdɛməkræt] *n* démocrate *m/f*; **~ic** [dɛməˈkrætɪk] *a* démocratique.

demolish [dɪˈmɔlɪʃ] *vt* démolir.

demonstrate [ˈdɛmənstreɪt] *vt* démontrer, prouver // *vi*: to ~ (**for/against**) manifester (en faveur de/contre); **demonstration** [-ˈstreɪʃən] *n* démonstration *f*, manifestation *f*; **demonstrator** *n* (*POL*) manifestant/e.

demote [dɪˈməut] *vt* rétrograder.

demure [dɪˈmjuə*] *a* sage, réservé(e); d'une modestie affectée.

den [dɛn] *n* tanière *f*, antre *m*.

denatured alcohol [diːˈneɪtʃəd-] *n* (*US*) alcool *m* à brûler.

denial [dɪˈnaɪəl] *n* démenti *m*; dénégation *f*.

denim [ˈdɛnɪm] *n* coton émerisé; **~s** *npl* (blue-)jeans *mpl*.

Denmark [ˈdɛnmɑːk] *n* Danemark *m*.

denomination [dɪnɔmɪˈneɪʃən] *n* (*money*) valeur *f*; (*REL*) confession *f*; culte *m*.

denounce [dɪˈnauns] *vt* dénoncer.

dense [dɛns] *a* dense; (*stupid*) obtus(e), dur(e) *or* lent(e) à la comprenette.

density [ˈdɛnsɪtɪ] *n* densité *f*.

dent [dɛnt] *n* bosse *f* // *vt* (*also:* make a ~ in) cabosser.

dental [ˈdɛntl] *a* dentaire; ~ **surgeon** *n* (chirurgien/ne) dentiste.

dentist [ˈdɛntɪst] *n* dentiste *m/f*; **~ry** *n* art *m* dentaire.

denture(s) [ˈdɛntʃə(z)] *n(pl)* dentier *m*.

deny [dɪˈnaɪ] *vt* nier; (*refuse*) refuser.

deodorant [diːˈəudərənt] *n* désodorisant *m*, déodorant *m*.

depart [dɪˈpɑːt] *vi* partir; to ~ **from** (*fig: differ from*) s'écarter de.

department [dɪˈpɑːtmənt] *n* (*COMM*) rayon *m*; (*SCOL*) section *f*; (*POL*) ministère *m*, département *m*; ~ **store** *n* grand magasin.

departure [dɪˈpɑːtʃə*] *n* départ *m*; (*fig*): ~ **from** écart *m* par rapport à; a new ~ une nouvelle voie; ~ **lounge** *n* (at airport) salle *f* de départ.

depend [dɪˈpɛnd] *vi*: to ~ **on** dépendre de; (*rely on*) compter sur; it ~**s** cela dépend; ~**ing on the result** ... selon le résultat ...; ~**able** *a* sûr(e), digne de confiance; ~**ant** *n* personne *f* à charge;

~**ent** *a*: to be ~**ent (on)** dépendre (de) // *n* = ~**ant**.

depict [dɪˈpɪkt] *vt* (*in picture*) représenter; (*in words*) (dé)peindre, décrire.

depleted [dɪˈpliːtɪd] *a* (considérablement) réduit(e) *or* diminué(e).

deploy [dɪˈplɔɪ] *vt* déployer.

deport [dɪˈpɔːt] *vt* déporter; expulser.

deportment [dɪˈpɔːtmənt] *n* maintien *m*, tenue *f*.

deposit [dɪˈpɔzɪt] *n* (*CHEM*, *COMM*, *GEO*) dépôt *m*; (*of ore, oil*) gisement *m*; (*part payment*) arrhes *fpl*, acompte *m*; (*on bottle etc*) consigne *f*; (*for hired goods etc*) cautionnement *m*, garantie *f* // *vt* déposer; mettre *or* laisser en dépôt; fournir *or* donner en acompte; laisser en garantie; ~ **account** *n* compte *m* de dépôt.

depot [ˈdɛpəu] *n* dépôt *m*.

depress [dɪˈprɛs] *vt* déprimer; (*press down*) appuyer sur, abaisser; ~**ed** *a* (*person*) déprimé(e), abattu(e); (*area*) en déclin, touché(e) par le sous-emploi; ~**ing** *a* déprimant(e); ~**ion** [dɪˈprɛʃən] *n* dépression *f*.

deprivation [dɛprɪˈveɪʃən] *n* privation *f*; (*loss*) perte *f*.

deprive [dɪˈpraɪv] *vt*: to ~ **sb of** priver qn de; enlever à qn; ~**d** *a* déshérité(e).

depth [dɛpθ] *n* profondeur *f*; in the ~**s of** au fond de; au cœur de; au plus profond de.

deputize [ˈdɛpjutaɪz] *vi*: to ~ **for** assurer l'intérim de.

deputy [ˈdɛpjutɪ] *a*: ~ **head** directeur adjoint, sous-directeur *m* // *n* (*replacement*) suppléant/e, intérimaire *m/f*; (*second in command*) adjoint/e.

derail [dɪˈreɪl] *vt*: to be ~**ed** dérailler.

derby [ˈdɑːbɪ] *n* (*US: bowler hat*) (chapeau *m*) melon *m*.

derelict [ˈdɛrɪlɪkt] *a* abandonné(e), à l'abandon.

deride [dɪˈraɪd] *vt* railler.

derisory [dɪˈraɪsrɪ] *a* (*sum*) dérisoire; (*smile, person*) moqueur(euse).

derive [dɪˈraɪv] *vt*: to ~ **sth from** tirer qch de; trouver qch dans // *vi*: to ~ **from** provenir de, dériver de.

derogatory [dɪˈrɔgətərɪ] *a* désobligeant(e); péjoratif(ive).

derv [dəːv] *n* (*Brit*) gas-oil *m*.

descend [dɪˈsɛnd] *vt, vi* descendre; to ~ **from** descendre de, être issu de.

descent [dɪˈsɛnt] *n* descente *f*; (*origin*) origine *f*.

describe [dɪsˈkraɪb] *vt* décrire; **description** [-ˈkrɪpʃən] *n* description *f*; (*sort*) sorte *f*, espèce *f*.

desecrate [ˈdɛsɪkreɪt] *vt* profaner.

desert *n* [ˈdɛzət] désert *m* // *vb* [dɪˈzəːt] *vt* déserter, abandonner // *vi* (*MIL*) déserter; ~**er** *n* déserteur *m*; ~ **island** *n* île déserte; ~**s** *npl*: to get one's just ~**s**

n'avoir que ce qu'on mérite.

deserve [dɪ'zɜ:v] *vt* mériter; **deserving** *a* (*person*) méritant(e); (*action, cause*) méritoire.

design [dɪ'zaɪn] *n* (*sketch*) plan *m*, dessin *m*; (*layout, shape*) conception *f*, ligne *f*; (*pattern*) dessin *m*, motif(s) *m(pl)*; (*COMM*) esthétique industrielle; (*intention*) dessein *m* // *vt* dessiner; concevoir; **to have** ~**s on** avoir des visées sur.

designer [dɪ'zaɪnə*] *n* (*ART, TECH*) dessinateur/trice; (*fashion*) modéliste *m/f*.

desire [dɪ'zaɪə*] *n* désir *m* // *vt* désirer, vouloir.

desk [dɛsk] *n* (*in office*) bureau *m*; (*for pupil*) pupitre *m*; (*Brit: in shop, restaurant*) caisse *f*; (*in hotel, at airport*) réception *f*.

desolate ['dɛsəlɪt] *a* désolé(e).

despair [dɪs'pɛə*] *n* désespoir *m* // *vi:* **to** ~ **of** désespérer de.

despatch [dɪs'pætʃ] *n, vt* = **dispatch**.

desperate ['dɛspərɪt] *a* désespéré(e); (*fugitive*) prêt(e) à tout; ~**ly** *ad* désespérément; (*very*) terriblement, extrêmement.

desperation [dɛspə'reɪʃən] *n* désespoir *m*; **in** ~ à bout de nerf; en désespoir de cause.

despicable [dɪs'pɪkəbl] *a* méprisable.

despise [dɪs'paɪz] *vt* mépriser, dédaigner.

despite [dɪs'paɪt] *prep* malgré, en dépit de.

despondent [dɪs'pɔndənt] *a* découragé(e), abattu(e).

dessert [dɪ'zɜ:t] *n* dessert *m*; ~**spoon** *n* cuiller *f* à dessert.

destination [dɛstɪ'neɪʃən] *n* destination *f*.

destiny ['dɛstɪnɪ] *n* destinée *f*, destin *m*.

destitute ['dɛstɪtjuːt] *a* indigent(e).

destroy [dɪs'trɔɪ] *vt* détruire; ~**er** *n* (*NAUT*) contre-torpilleur *m*.

destruction [dɪs'trʌkʃən] *n* destruction *f*.

detach [dɪ'tætʃ] *vt* détacher; ~**ed** *a* (*attitude*) détaché(e); ~**ed house** *n* pavillon *m*, maison(nette) (individuelle); ~**ment** *n* (*MIL*) détachement *m*; (*fig*) détachement, indifférence *f*.

detail ['diːteɪl] *n* détail *m* // *vt* raconter en détail, énumérer; **in** ~ en détail; ~**ed** *a* détaillé(e).

detain [dɪ'teɪn] *vt* retenir; (*in captivity*) détenir; (*in hospital*) hospitaliser.

detect [dɪ'tɛkt] *vt* déceler, percevoir; (*MED, POLICE*) dépister; (*MIL, RADAR, TECH*) détecter; ~**ion** [dɪ'tɛkʃən] *n* découverte *f*; dépistage *m*; détection *f*; ~**ive** *n* agent *m* de la sûreté, policier *m*; private ~**ive** détective privé; ~**ive story** *n* roman policier.

detention [dɪ'tɛnʃən] *n* détention *f*; (*SCOL*) retenue *f*, consigne *f*.

deter [dɪ'tɜ:*] *vt* dissuader.

detergent [dɪ'tɜ:dʒənt] *n* détersif *m*, détergent *m*.

deteriorate [dɪ'tɪərɪəreɪt] *vi* se détériorer, se dégrader.

determine [dɪ'tɜ:mɪn] *vt* déterminer; **to** ~ **to do** résoudre de faire, se déterminer à faire; ~**d** *a* (*person*) déterminé(e).

deterrent [dɪ'tɛrənt] *n* effet *m* de dissuasion; force *f* de dissuasion.

detour ['diːtuə*] *n* détour *m*; (*US AUT: diversion*) déviation *f*.

detract [dɪ'trækt] *vt:* **to** ~ **from** (*quality, pleasure*) diminuer; (*reputation*) porter atteinte à.

detriment ['dɛtrɪmənt] *n:* **to the** ~ **of** au détriment de, au préjudice de; ~**al** [dɛtrɪ'mɛntl] *a:* ~**al to** préjudiciable *or* nuisible à.

devaluation [dɪvælju'eɪʃən] *n* dévaluation *f*.

devastating ['dɛvəsteɪtɪŋ] *a* dévastateur(trice).

develop [dɪ'vɛləp] *vt* (*gen*) développer; (*habit*) contracter; (*resources*) mettre en valeur, exploiter // *vi* se développer; (*situation, disease: evolve*) évoluer; (*facts, symptoms: appear*) se manifester, se produire; ~**ing country** pays *m* en voie de développement; ~**ment** *n* développement *m*; (*of affair, case*) rebondissement *m*, fait(s) nouveau(x).

device [dɪ'vaɪs] *n* (*apparatus*) engin *m*, dispositif *m*.

devil ['dɛvl] *n* diable *m*; démon *m*.

devious ['diːvɪəs] *a* (*means*) détourné(e); (*person*) sournois(e), dissimulé(e).

devise [dɪ'vaɪz] *vt* imaginer, concevoir.

devoid [dɪ'vɔɪd] *a:* ~ **of** dépourvu(e) de, dénué(e) de.

devolution [diːvə'luːʃən] *n* (*POL*) décentralisation *f*.

devote [dɪ'vəut] *vt:* **to** ~ **sth to** consacrer qch à; ~**d** *a* dévoué(e); **to be** ~**d to** (*book etc*) être consacré(e) à; ~**e** [dɛvəu'tiː] *n* (*REL*) adepte *m/f*; (*MUS, SPORT*) fervent/e.

devotion [dɪ'vəuʃən] *n* dévouement *m*, attachement *m*; (*REL*) dévotion *f*, piété *f*.

devour [dɪ'vauə*] *vt* dévorer.

devout [dɪ'vaut] *a* pieux(euse), dévot(e).

dew [djuː] *n* rosée *f*.

DHSS *n abbr* (*Brit:* = *Department of Health and Social Security*) ≈ ministère de la Santé et de la Sécurité Sociale.

diabetes [daɪə'biːtiːz] *n* diabète *m*; **diabetic** [-'bɛtɪk] *a, n* diabétique (*m/f*).

diabolical [daɪə'bɔlɪkl] *a* (*col: weather*) atroce; (*: behaviour*) infernal(e).

diagnosis, *pl* **diagnoses** [daɪəg'nəusɪs, -siːz] *n* diagnostic *m*.

diagonal [daɪ'ægənl] a diagonal(e) // n diagonale f.

diagram ['daɪəgræm] n diagramme m, schéma m; graphique m.

dial ['daɪəl] n cadran m // vt (number) faire, composer.

dialect ['daɪəlekt] n dialecte m.

dialling: ~ **code**, (US) **dial code** n indicatif m (téléphonique); ~ **tone**, (US) **dial tone** n tonalité f.

dialogue ['daɪələg] n dialogue m.

diameter [daɪ'æmɪtə*] n diamètre m.

diamond ['daɪəmənd] n diamant m; (shape) losange m; ~s npl (CARDS) carreau m.

diaper ['daɪəpə*] n (US) couche f.

diaphragm ['daɪəfræm] n diaphragme m.

diarrhoea, (US) **diarrhea** [daɪə'rɪːə] n diarrhée f.

diary ['daɪərɪ] n (daily account) journal m; (book) agenda m.

dice [daɪs] n (pl inv) dé m // vt (CULIN) couper en dés et en cubes.

dictate vt [dɪk'teɪt] dicter // n ['dɪkteɪt] injonction f.

dictation [dɪk'teɪʃən] n dictée f.

dictator [dɪk'teɪtə*] n dictateur m; ~**ship** n dictature f.

dictionary ['dɪkʃənrɪ] n dictionnaire m.

did [dɪd] pt of **do**.

didn't = **did not**.

die [daɪ] vi mourir; to be dying for sth avoir une envie folle de qch; to be dying to do sth mourir d'envie de faire qch; **to** ~ **away** vi s'éteindre; **to** ~ **down** vi se calmer, s'apaiser; **to** ~ **out** vi disparaître, s'éteindre.

diehard ['daɪhɑːd] n réactionnaire m/f, jusqu'au-boutiste m/f.

Diesel ['diːzəl]: ~ **engine** n moteur m diesel; ~ **(oil)** n carburant m diesel.

diet ['daɪət] n alimentation f; (restricted food) régime m // vi (also: be on a ~) suivre un régime.

differ ['dɪfə*] vi: to ~ from sth être différent de; différer de; to ~ from sb over sth ne pas être d'accord avec qn au sujet de qch; ~**ence** n différence f; (quarrel) différend m, désaccord m; ~**ent** a différent(e); ~**entiate** [-'renʃɪeɪt] vi se différencier; to ~entiate between faire une différence entre.

difficult ['dɪfɪkəlt] a difficile; ~**y** n difficulté f.

diffident ['dɪfɪdənt] a qui manque de confiance or d'assurance.

dig [dɪg] vt (pt, pp **dug**) (hole) creuser; (garden) bêcher // n (prod) coup m de coude; (fig) coup de griffe or de patte; **to** ~ **in** vi (MIL: also: ~ o.s. in) se retrancher; (col: eat) attaquer (un repas etc); **to** ~ **into** (snow, soil) creuser; to ~ one's nails into enfoncer ses ongles dans; **to** ~ **up** vt déterrer.

digest vt [daɪ'dʒest] digérer // n ['daɪdʒest] sommaire m, résumé m; ~**ion** [dɪ'dʒestʃən] n digestion f.

digit ['dɪdʒɪt] n chiffre m (de 0 à 9); (finger) doigt m; ~**al** a digital(e); à affichage numérique or digital.

dignified ['dɪgnɪfaɪd] a digne.

dignity ['dɪgnɪtɪ] n dignité f.

digress [daɪ'gres] vi: to ~ from s'écarter de, s'éloigner de.

digs [dɪgz] npl (Brit col) piaule f, chambre meublée.

dilapidated [dɪ'læpɪdeɪtɪd] a délabré(e).

dilemma [daɪ'lemə] n dilemme m.

diligent ['dɪlɪdʒənt] a appliqué(e), assidu(e).

dilute [daɪ'luːt] vt diluer.

dim [dɪm] a (light, eyesight) faible; (memory, outline) vague, indécis(e); (stupid) borné(e), obtus(e) // vt (light) réduire, baisser.

dime [daɪm] n (US) = 10 cents.

dimension [daɪ'menʃən] n dimension f.

diminish [dɪ'mɪnɪʃ] vt, vi diminuer.

diminutive [dɪ'mɪnjutɪv] a minuscule, tout(e) petit(e) // n (LING) diminutif m.

dimmers ['dɪməz] npl (US AUT) phares mpl code inv; feux mpl de position.

dimple ['dɪmpl] n fossette f.

din [dɪn] n vacarme m.

dine [daɪn] vi dîner; ~**r** n (person) dîneur/euse; (RAIL) = **dining car**.

dinghy ['dɪŋgɪ] n youyou m; (also: rubber ~) canot m pneumatique; (also: sailing ~) voilier m, dériveur m.

dingy ['dɪndʒɪ] a miteux(euse), minable.

dining ['daɪnɪŋ] cpd: ~ **car** n (Brit) wagon-restaurant m; ~ **room** n salle f à manger.

dinner ['dɪnə*] n dîner m; (public) banquet m; ~'s ready! à table!; ~ **jacket** n smoking m; ~ **party** n dîner m; ~ **time** n heure f du dîner.

dint [dɪnt] n: by ~ of (doing) à force de (faire).

dip [dɪp] n déclivité f; (in sea) baignade f, bain m // vt tremper, plonger; (Brit AUT: lights) mettre en code, baisser // vi plonger.

diploma [dɪ'pləumə] n diplôme m.

diplomacy [dɪ'pləuməsɪ] n diplomatie f.

diplomat ['dɪpləmæt] n diplomate m; ~**ic** [dɪplə'mætɪk] a diplomatique.

dipstick ['dɪpstɪk] n (AUT) jauge f de niveau d'huile.

dire [daɪə*] a terrible, extrême, affreux(euse).

direct [daɪ'rekt] a direct(e) // vt diriger, orienter; can you ~ me to ...? pouvez-vous m'indiquer le chemin de ...?

direction [dɪ'rekʃən] n direction f; sense of ~ sens m de l'orientation; ~**s** npl (advice) indications fpl; ~**s for use** mode m d'emploi.

directly [dɪ'rektlɪ] ad (in straight line)

directement, tout droit; (*at once*) tout de suite, immédiatement.

director [dɪ'rɛktə*] *n* directeur *m*; administrateur *m*; (*THEATRE*) metteur *m* en scène; (*CINEMA*, *TV*) réalisateur/trice.

directory [dɪ'rɛktərɪ] *n* annuaire *m*.

dirt [də:t] *n* saleté *f*; crasse *f*; ~**-cheap** *a* (ne) coûtant presque rien; ~**y** *a* sale // *vt* salir; ~**y trick** coup tordu.

disability [dɪsə'bɪlɪtɪ] *n* invalidité *f*, infirmité *f*.

disabled [dɪs'eɪbld] *a* infirme, invalide; (*maimed*) mutilé(e); (*through illness, old age*) impotent(e).

disadvantage [dɪsəd'vɑ:ntɪdʒ] *n* désavantage *m*, inconvénient *m*.

disagree [dɪsə'gri:] *vi* (*differ*) ne pas concorder; (*be against, think otherwise*): to ~ (**with**) ne pas être d'accord (avec); ~**able** *a* désagréable; ~**ment** *n* désaccord *m*, différend *m*.

disappear [dɪsə'pɪə*] *vi* disparaître; ~**ance** *n* disparition *f*.

disappoint [dɪsə'pɔɪnt] *vt* décevoir; ~**ed** *a* déçu(e); ~**ing** *a* décevant(e); ~**ment** *n* déception *f*.

disapproval [dɪsə'pru:vəl] *n* désapprobation *f*.

disapprove [dɪsə'pru:v] *vi*: to ~ **of** désapprouver.

disarm [dɪs'ɑ:m] *vt* désarmer; ~**ament** *n* désarmement *m*.

disarray [dɪsə'reɪ] *n*: in ~ (*army, organization*) en déroute; (*hair, clothes*) en désordre.

disaster [dɪ'zɑ:stə*] *n* catastrophe *f*, désastre *m*.

disband [dɪs'bænd] *vt* démobiliser; disperser // *vi* se séparer; se disperser.

disbelief ['dɪsbə'li:f] *n* incrédulité *f*.

disc [dɪsk] *n* disque *m*; (*COMPUT*) = disk.

discard [dɪs'kɑ:d] *vt* (*old things*) se défaire de; (*fig*) écarter, renoncer à.

discern [dɪ'sə:n] *vt* discerner, distinguer; ~**ing** *a* judicieux(euse), perspicace.

discharge *vt* [dɪs'tʃɑ:dʒ] (*duties*) s'acquitter de; (*waste etc*) déverser; décharger; (*ELEC*, *MED*) émettre; (*patient*) renvoyer (chez lui); (*employee, soldier*) congédier, licencier; (*defendant*) relaxer, élargir // *n* ['dɪstʃɑ:dʒ] (*ELEC*, *MED*) émission *f*; (*dismissal*) renvoi *m*; licenciement *m*; élargissement *m*.

discipline ['dɪsɪplɪn] *n* discipline *f*.

disc jockey *n* disque-jockey *m*.

disclaim [dɪs'kleɪm] *vt* désavouer, dénier.

disclose [dɪs'kləʊz] *vt* révéler, divulguer; **disclosure** [-'kləʊʒə*] *n* révélation *f*, divulgation *f*.

disco ['dɪskəʊ] *n abbr of* **discothèque**.

discomfort [dɪs'kʌmfət] *n* malaise *m*,

gêne *f*; (*lack of comfort*) m[...] confort.

disconcert [dɪskən'sə:t] *vt* déc[...]

disconnect [dɪskə'nɛkt] *vt* [...] (*ELEC, RADIO*) débrancher; (*ga[...] couper.

disconsolate [dɪs'kɒnsəlɪt] *a* inc[...] ble.

discontent [dɪskən'tɛnt] *n* méco[...] tement *m*; ~**ed** *a* mécontent(e).

discontinue [dɪskən'tɪnju:] *vt* ces[...] interrompre.

discord ['dɪskɔ:d] *n* discorde [...] dissension *f*; (*MUS*) dissonance *f*.

discothèque ['dɪskəʊtɛk] *n* discothèque *f*.

discount *n* ['dɪskaʊnt] remise *f*, rabais *m* // *vt* [dɪs'kaʊnt] ne pas tenir compte de.

discourage [dɪs'kʌrɪdʒ] *vt* décourager.

discover [dɪs'kʌvə*] *vt* découvrir; ~**y** *n* découverte *f*.

discredit [dɪs'krɛdɪt] *vt* mettre en doute; discréditer.

discreet [dɪ'skri:t] *a* discret(ète).

discrepancy [dɪ'skrɛpənsɪ] *n* divergence *f*, contradiction *f*.

discriminate [dɪ'skrɪmɪneɪt] *vi*: to ~ between établir une distinction entre, faire la différence entre; to ~ against pratiquer une discrimination contre; **discriminating** *a* qui a du discernement; **discrimination** [-'neɪʃən] *n* discrimination *f*; (*judgment*) discernement *m*.

discuss [dɪ'skʌs] *vt* discuter de; (*debate*) discuter; ~**ion** [dɪ'skʌʃən] *n* discussion *f*.

disdain [dɪs'deɪn] *n* dédain *m*.

disease [dɪ'zi:z] *n* maladie *f*.

disembark [dɪsɪm'bɑ:k] *vt*, *vi* débarquer.

disengage [dɪsɪn'geɪdʒ] *vt* dégager; (*TECH*) déclencher; to ~ the clutch (*AUT*) débrayer.

disfigure [dɪs'fɪgə*] *vt* défigurer.

disgrace [dɪs'greɪs] *n* honte *f*; (*disfavour*) disgrâce *f* // *vt* déshonorer, couvrir de honte; ~**ful** *a* scandaleux(euse), honteux(euse).

disgruntled [dɪs'grʌntld] *a* mécontent(e).

disguise [dɪs'gaɪz] *n* déguisement *m* // *vt* déguiser; in ~ déguisé(e).

disgust [dɪs'gʌst] *n* dégoût *m*, aversion *f* // *vt* dégoûter, écœurer; ~**ing** *a* dégoûtant(e); révoltant(e).

dish [dɪʃ] *n* plat *m*; to do *or* wash the ~**es** faire la vaisselle; to ~ **up** *vt* servir; ~**cloth** *n* (*for drying*) torchon *m*; (*for washing*) lavette *f*.

dishearten [dɪs'hɑ:tn] *vt* décourager.

dishevelled [dɪ'ʃɛvəld] *a* ébouriffé(e); décoiffé(e); débraillé(e).

dishonest [dɪs'ɒnɪst] *a* malhonnête.

dishonour, (*US*) **dishonor** [dɪs'ɒnə*] *n*

déshonneur *m*; ~**able** *a* déshonorant(e).

ish towel *n* (*US*) torchon *m*.

ishwasher ['dɪʃwɔʃə*] *n* lave-vaisselle *m*; (*person*) plongeur/euse.

disillusion [dɪsɪ'luːʒən] *vt* désabuser, désenchanter.

disincentive [dɪsɪn'sɛntɪv] *n*: to be a ~ être démotivant(e); to be a ~ to sb démotiver qn.

disinfect [dɪsɪn'fɛkt] *vt* désinfecter; ~**ant** *n* désinfectant *m*.

disintegrate [dɪs'ɪntɪgreɪt] *vi* se désintégrer.

disinterested [dɪs'ɪntrəstɪd] *a* désintéressé(e).

disjointed [dɪs'dʒɔɪntɪd] *a* décousu(e), incohérent(e).

disk [dɪsk] *n* (*COMPUT*) disquette *f*; single-/double-sided ~ disquette une face/double face; ~ **drive** *n* lecteur *m* de disque *or* disquette, drive *m*; ~**ette** *n* (*US*) = **disk**.

dislike [dɪs'laɪk] *n* aversion *f*, antipathie *f* // *vt* ne pas aimer.

dislocate ['dɪsləkeɪt] *vt* disloquer; déboiter; désorganiser.

dislodge [dɪs'lɔdʒ] *vt* déplacer, faire bouger; (*enemy*) déloger.

disloyal [dɪs'lɔɪəl] *a* déloyal(e).

dismal ['dɪzml] *a* lugubre, maussade.

dismantle [dɪs'mæntl] *vt* démonter; (*fort, warship*) démanteler.

dismay [dɪs'meɪ] *n* consternation *f*.

dismiss [dɪs'mɪs] *vt* congédier, renvoyer; (*idea*) écarter; (*LAW*) rejeter // *vi* (*MIL*) rompre les rangs; ~**al** *n* renvoi *m*.

dismount [dɪs'maunt] *vi* mettre pied à terre.

disobedience [dɪsə'biːdɪəns] *n* désobéissance *f*.

disobedient [dɪsə'biːdɪənt] *a* désobéissant(e).

disobey [dɪsə'beɪ] *vt* désobéir à.

disorder [dɪs'ɔːdə*] *n* désordre *m*; (*rioting*) désordres *mpl*; (*MED*) troubles *mpl*; ~**ly** *a* en désordre; désordonné(e).

disorientated [dɪs'ɔːrɪɛnteɪtɪd] *a* désorienté(e).

disown [dɪs'əun] *vt* renier.

disparaging [dɪs'pærɪdʒɪŋ] *a* désobligeant(e).

dispassionate [dɪs'pæʃənət] *a* calme, froid(e); impartial(e), objectif(ive).

dispatch [dɪs'pætʃ] *vt* expédier, envoyer // *n* envoi *m*, expédition *f*; (*MIL, PRESS*) dépêche *f*.

dispel [dɪs'pɛl] *vt* dissiper, chasser.

dispensary [dɪs'pɛnsərɪ] *n* pharmacie *f*; (*in chemist's*) officine *f*.

dispense [dɪs'pɛns] *vt* distribuer, administrer; to ~ with *vt fus* se passer de; ~**r** *n* (*container*) distributeur *m*; **dispensing chemist** *n* (*Brit*) pharmacie *f*.

disperse [dɪs'pəːs] *vt* disperser; (*knowledge*) disséminer // *vi* se disperser.

dispirited [dɪs'pɪrɪtɪd] *a* découragé(e), déprimé(e).

displace [dɪs'pleɪs] *vt* déplacer.

display [dɪs'pleɪ] . *n* étalage *m*; déploiement *m*; affichage *m*; (*screen*) écran *m* de visualisation, visuel *m*; (*of feeling*) manifestation *f*; (*pej*) ostentation *f* // *vt* montrer; (*goods*) mettre à l'étalage, exposer; (*results, departure times*) afficher; (*pej*) faire étalage de.

displease [dɪs'pliːz] *vt* mécontenter, contrarier; ~**d with** mécontent(e) de; **displeasure** [-'plɛʒə*] *n* mécontentement *m*.

disposable [dɪs'pəuzəbl] *a* (*pack etc*) jetable; (*income*) disponible; ~ **nappy** *n* couche *f* à jeter, couche-culotte *f*.

disposal [dɪs'pəuzl] *n* (*availability, arrangement*) disposition *f*; (*of property*) disposition *f*, cession *f*; (*of rubbish*) évacuation *f*, destruction *f*; at one's ~ à sa disposition.

dispose [dɪs'pəuz] *vt* disposer; to ~ of *vt* (*time, money*) disposer de; (*unwanted goods*) se débarrasser de, se défaire de; (*problem*) expédier; ~**d** *a*: ~**d to do** disposé(e) à faire; **disposition** [-'zɪʃən] *n* disposition *f*; (*temperament*) naturel *m*.

disprove [dɪs'pruːv] *vt* réfuter.

dispute [dɪs'pjuːt] *n* discussion *f*; (*also*: **industrial** ~) conflit *m* // *vt* contester; (*matter*) discuter; (*victory*) disputer.

disqualify [dɪs'kwɔlɪfaɪ] *vt* (*SPORT*) disqualifier; to ~ **sb for sth/from doing** rendre qn inapte à qch/à faire; signifier à qn l'interdiction de faire; to ~ **sb** (**from driving**) retirer à qn son permis (de conduire).

disquiet [dɪs'kwaɪət] *n* inquiétude *f*, trouble *m*.

disregard [dɪsrɪ'gɑːd] *vt* ne pas tenir compte de.

disrepair [dɪsrɪ'pɛə*] *n* mauvais état; to fall into ~ (*building*) tomber en ruine.

disreputable [dɪs'rɛpjutəbl] *a* (*person*) de mauvaise réputation; (*behaviour*) déshonorant(e).

disrupt [dɪs'rʌpt] *vt* (*plans*) déranger; (*conversation*) interrompre.

dissatisfaction [dɪssætɪs'fækʃən] *n* mécontentement *m*, insatisfaction *f*.

dissect [dɪ'sɛkt] *vt* disséquer.

dissent [dɪ'sɛnt] *n* dissentiment *m*, différence *f* d'opinion.

dissertation [dɪsə'teɪʃən] *n* mémoire *m*.

disservice [dɪs'səːvɪs] *n*: to do sb a ~ rendre un mauvais service à qn; desservir qn.

dissimilar [dɪ'sɪmɪlə*] *a*: ~ (**to**) dissemblable (à), différent(e) (de).

dissipate ['dɪsɪpeɪt] *vt* dissiper; (*energy, efforts*) disperser.

dissolute ['dɪsəluːt] *a* débauché(e), dissolu(e).

dissolve [dɪ'zɔlv] *vt* dissoudre // *vi* se dissoudre, fondre; (*fig*) disparaître.

distance ['dɪstns] *n* distance *f*; **in the ~** au loin.

distant ['dɪstnt] *a* lointain(e), éloigné(e); (*manner*) distant(e), froid(e).

distaste [dɪs'teɪst] *n* dégoût *m*; **~ful** *a* déplaisant(e), désagréable.

distended [dɪs'tɛndɪd] *a* (*stomach*) dilaté(e).

distil [dɪs'tɪl] *vt* distiller; **~lery** *n* distillerie *f*.

distinct [dɪs'tɪŋkt] *a* distinct(e); (*preference, progress*) marqué(e); **as ~ from** par opposition à; **~ion** [dɪs'tɪŋkʃən] *n* distinction *f*; (*in exam*) mention *f* très bien; **~ive** *a* distinctif(ive).

distinguish [dɪs'tɪŋgwɪʃ] *vt* distinguer; différencier; **~ed** *a* (*eminent*) distingué(e); **~ing** *a* (*feature*) distinctif(ive), caractéristique.

distort [dɪs'tɔːt] *vt* déformer.

distract [dɪs'trækt] *vt* distraire, déranger; **~ed** *a* éperdu(e), égaré(e); **~ion** [dɪs'trækʃən] *n* distraction *f*; égarement *m*.

distraught [dɪs'trɔːt] *a* éperdu(e).

distress [dɪs'trɛs] *n* détresse *f*; (*pain*) douleur *f* // *vt* affliger; **~ing** *a* douloureux(euse), pénible.

distribute [dɪs'trɪbjuːt] *vt* distribuer; **distribution** [-'bjuːʃən] *n* distribution *f*; **distributor** *n* distributeur *m*.

district ['dɪstrɪkt] *n* (*of country*) région *f*; (*of town*) quartier *m*; (ADMIN) district *m*; **~ attorney** *n* (*US*) ≈ procureur *m* de la République; **~ nurse** *n* (*Brit*) infirmière visiteuse.

distrust [dɪs'trʌst] *n* méfiance *f*, doute *m* // *vt* se méfier de.

disturb [dɪs'tɔːb] *vt* troubler; (*inconvenience*) déranger; **~ance** *n* dérangement *m*; (*political etc*) troubles *mpl*; (*by drunks etc*) tapage *m*; **~ed** *a* (*worried, upset*) agité(e), troublé(e); **to be emotionally ~ed** avoir des problèmes affectifs; **~ing** *a* troublant(e), inquiétant(e).

disuse [dɪs'juːs] *n*: **to fall into ~** tomber en désuétude.

disused [dɪs'juːzd] *a* désaffecté(e).

ditch [dɪtʃ] *n* fossé *m* // *vt* (*col*) abandonner.

dither ['dɪðə*] *vi* hésiter.

ditto ['dɪtəu] *ad* idem.

dive [daɪv] *n* plongeon *m*; (*of submarine*) plongée *f*; (AVIAT) piqué *m*; (*pej*) bouge *m* // *vi* plonger; **~r** *n* plongeur *m*.

diversion [daɪ'vɔːʃən] *n* (Brit AUT) déviation *f*; (*distraction*, MIL) diversion *f*.

divert [daɪ'vɔːt] *vt* (*traffic*) dévier; (*river*) détourner; (*amuse*) divertir.

divide [dɪ'vaɪd] *vt* diviser; (*separate*) séparer // *vi* se diviser; **~d highway** *n* (*US*) route *f* à quatre voies.

dividend ['dɪvɪdɛnd] *n* dividende *m*.

divine [dɪ'vaɪn] *a* divin(e).

diving ['daɪvɪŋ] *n* plongée (sousmarine); **~ board** *n* plongeoir *m*.

divinity [dɪ'vɪnɪtɪ] *n* divinité *f*; théologie *f*.

division [dɪ'vɪʒən] *n* division *f*; séparation *f*.

divorce [dɪ'vɔːs] *n* divorce *m* // *vt* divorcer d'avec; **~d** *a* divorcé(e); **~e** [-'siː] *n* divorcé.e.

D.I.Y. *n abbr* (Brit) of **do-it-yourself**.

dizzy ['dɪzɪ] *a* (*height*) vertigineux(euse); **to make sb ~** donner le vertige à qn; **to feel ~** avoir la tête qui tourne.

DJ *n abbr* of **disc jockey**.

do [duː] ♦ *n* (*col: party etc*) soirée *f*, fête *f*

♦ *vb* (*pt* **did**, *pp* **done**) **1** (*in negative constructions*) *non traduit*; **I don't understand** je ne comprends pas

2 (*to form questions*) *non traduit*; **didn't you know?** vous ne le saviez pas?; **why didn't you come?** pourquoi n'êtes-vous pas venu?

3 (*for emphasis, in polite expressions*): **she does seem rather late** je trouve qu'elle est bien en retard; **~ sit down/help yourself** asseyez-vous/servez-vous je vous en prie

4 (*used to avoid repeating vb*): **she swims better than I ~** elle nage mieux que moi; **~ you agree? - yes, I ~/no, I don't** vous êtes d'accord? - oui/non; **she lives in Glasgow - so ~ I** elle habite Glasgow - moi aussi; **who broke it? - I did** qui l'a cassé? - c'est moi

5 (*in question tags*): **he laughed, didn't he?** il a ri, n'est-ce pas?; **I don't know him, ~ I?** je ne le connais pas, je crois

♦ *vt* (*gen: carry out, perform etc*) faire; **what are you doing tonight?** qu'est-ce que vous faites ce soir?; **to ~ the cooking/washing-up** faire la cuisine/la vaisselle; **to ~ one's teeth/hair/nails** se brosser les dents/se coiffer/se faire les ongles; **the car was ~ing 100** la voiture faisait du 100 (à l'heure)

♦ *vi* **1** (*act, behave*) faire; **~ as I ~** faites comme moi

2 (*get on, fare*) marcher; **the firm is ~ing well** l'entreprise marche bien; **how ~ you ~?** comment allez-vous?; (*on being introduced*) enchanté(e)!

3 (*suit*) aller; **will it ~?** est-ce que ça ira?

4 (*be sufficient*) suffire, aller; **will £10 ~?** est-ce que 10 livres suffiront?; **that'll**

~ ça suffit, ça ira; **that'll** ~! (*in annoyance*) ça va *ou* suffit comme ça!; **to make** ~ **(with)** se contenter (de)
to do away with *vt fus* supprimer
to do up *vt* (*laces, dress*) attacher; (*buttons*) boutonner; (*zip*) fermer; (*renovate: room*) refaire; (*: house*) remettre à neuf
to do with *vt fus* (*need*): **I could** ~ **with a drink/some help** quelque chose à boire/un peu d'aide ne serait pas de refus; (*be connected*): **that has nothing to** ~ **with you** cela ne vous concerne pas; **I won't have anything to** ~ **with it** je ne veux pas m'en mêler
to do without *vi* s'en passer ♦ *vt fus* se passer de.

dock [dɔk] *n* dock *m*; (*LAW*) banc *m* des accusés // *vi* se mettre à quai; **~er** *n* docker *m*; **~yard** *n* chantier *m* de construction navale.

doctor ['dɔktə*] *n* médecin *m*, docteur *m*; (*Ph.D. etc*) docteur // *vt* (*fig*) falsifier; (*drink*) frelater; **D~ of Philosophy (Ph.D.)** *n* doctorat *m*; titulaire *m/f* d'un doctorat.

doctrine ['dɔktrin] *n* doctrine *f*.

document ['dɔkjumənt] *n* document *m*; **~ary** [-'mɛntəri] *a, n* documentaire (*m*).

dodge [dɔdʒ] *n* truc *m*; combine *f* // *vt* esquiver, éviter.

doe [dəu] *n* (*deer*) biche *f*; (*rabbit*) lapine *f*.

does [dʌz] *vb see* do; **doesn't** = does not.

dog [dɔg] *n* chien/ne *m* // *vt* suivre de près; poursuivre, harceler; ~ **collar** *n* collier *m* de chien; (*fig*) faux-col *m* d'ecclésiastique; **~-eared** *a* corné(e).

dogged ['dɔgid] *a* obstiné(e), opiniâtre.

dogsbody ['dɔgzbɔdi] *n* bonne *f* à tout faire, tâcheron *m*.

doings ['duiŋz] *npl* activités *fpl*.

do-it-yourself [du:itjɔ:'self] *n* bricolage *m*.

doldrums ['dɔldrəmz] *npl*: **to be in the** ~ avoir le cafard; être dans le marasme.

dole [dəul] *n* (*Brit: payment*) allocation *f* de chômage; **on the** ~ au chômage; **to** ~ **out** *vt* donner au compte-goutte.

doleful ['dəulful] *a* triste, lugubre.

doll [dɔl] *n* poupée *f*; **to** ~ **o.s. up** se faire beau(belle).

dollar ['dɔlə*] *n* dollar *m*.

dolphin ['dɔlfin] *n* dauphin *m*.

domestic [də'mɛstik] *a* (*duty, happiness*) familial(e); (*policy, affairs, flights*) intérieur(e); (*animal*) domestique.

dominant ['dɔminənt] *a* dominant(e).

dominate ['dɔmineit] *vt* dominer; **domineering** [-'niəriŋ] *a* dominateur(trice), autoritaire.

dominion [də'miniən] *n* domination *f*; territoire *m*; dominion *m*.

domino, ~es ['dɔminəu] *n* domino *m*; **~es** *n* (*game*) dominos *mpl*.

don [dɔn] *n* (*Brit*) professeur *m* d'université.

donate [də'neit] *vt* faire don de, donner.

done [dʌn] *pp of* do.

donkey ['dɔŋki] *n* âne *m*.

donor ['dəunə*] *n* (*of blood etc*) donneur/euse; (*to charity*) donateur/trice.

don't [dəunt] *vb* = do not.

doodle ['du:dl] *vi* griffonner, gribouiller.

doom [du:m] *n* destin *m*; ruine *f* // *vt*: **to be ~ed (to failure)** être voué(e) à l'échec; **~sday** *n* le Jugement dernier.

door [dɔ:*] *n* porte *f*; **~bell** *n* sonnette *f*; **~man** *n* (*in hotel*) portier *m*; (*in block of flats*) concierge *m*; **~mat** *n* paillasson *m*; **~step** *n* pas *m* de (la) porte, seuil *m*; **~way** *n* (embrasure *f* de) porte *f*.

dope [dəup] *n* (*col*) drogue *f* // *vt* (*horse etc*) doper.

dopey ['dəupi] *a* (*col*) à moitié endormi(e).

dormant ['dɔ:mənt] *a* assoupi(e), en veilleuse; (*rule, law*) inappliqué(e).

dormitory ['dɔ:mitri] *n* dortoir *m*.

dose [dəus] *n* dose *f*; (*bout*) attaque *f*.

doss house ['dɔs-] *n* (*Brit*) asile *m* de nuit.

dot [dɔt] *n* point *m* // *vt*: **~ted with** parsemé(e) de; **on the** ~ à l'heure tapante.

dote [dəut]: **to** ~ **on** *vt fus* être fou(folle) de.

dot-matrix printer ['dɔt'meitriks-] *n* imprimante matricielle.

dotted line ['dɔtid-] *n* ligne pointillée.

double ['dʌbl] *a* double // *ad* (*fold*) en deux; (*twice*): **to cost** ~ **(sth)** coûter le double (de qch) *ou* deux fois plus (que qch) // *n* double *m*; (*CINEMA*) doublure *f* // *vt* doubler; (*fold*) plier en deux // *vi* doubler; **on the** ~, (*Brit*) **at the** ~ au pas de course; **~s** *n* (*TENNIS*) double *m*; ~ **bass** *n* contrebasse *f*; ~ **bed** *n* grand lit; **~-breasted** *a* croisé(e); **~cross** *vt* doubler, trahir; **~decker** *n* autobus *m* à impériale; ~ **glazing** *n* (*Brit*) double vitrage *m*; ~ **room** *n* chambre *f* pour deux personnes; **doubly** *ad* doublement, deux fois plus.

doubt [daut] *n* doute *m* // *vt* douter de; **to** ~ **that** douter que; **~ful** *a* douteux(euse); (*person*) incertain(e); **~less** *ad* sans doute, sûrement.

dough [dəu] *n* pâte *f*; **~nut** *n* beignet *m*.

douse [dauz] *vt* (*drench*) tremper, inonder; (*extinguish*) éteindre.

dove [dʌv] *n* colombe *f*.

Dover ['dəuvə*] *n* Douvres.

dovetail ['dʌvteɪl] vi (fig) concorder.

dowdy ['daudɪ] a démodé(e); mal fagoté(e).

down [daun] n (fluff) duvet m // ad en bas // prep en bas de // vt (col: drink) vider; ~ **with X!** à bas X!; ~**-and-out** n clochard/e; ~**-at-heel** a éculé(e); (fig) miteux(euse); ~**cast** a démoralisé(e); ~**fall** n chute f; ruine f; ~**hearted** a découragé(e); ~**hill** ad: **to go** ~hill descendre; ~ **payment** n acompte m; ~**pour** n pluie torrentielle, déluge m; ~**right** a franc(franche); (refusal) catégorique; ~**stairs** ad au rez-de-chaussée; à l'étage inférieur; ~**stream** ad en aval; ~**-to-earth** a terre à terre inv; ~**town** ad en ville; ~ **under** ad en Australie (or Nouvelle Zélande); ~**ward** ['daunwəd] a, ad, ~**wards** ['daunwədz] ad vers le bas.

dowry ['daurɪ] n dot f.

doz. abbr of **dozen**.

doze [dəuz] vi sommeiller; **to** ~ **off** vi s'assoupir.

dozen ['dʌzn] n douzaine f; **a** ~ **books** une douzaine de livres; ~**s of** des centaines or des milliers de.

Dr. abbr of **doctor, drive** (n).

drab [dræb] a terne, morne.

draft [drɑːft] n brouillon m; (COMM) traite f; (US MIL) contingent m; (: call-up) conscription f // vt faire le brouillon de; see also **draught**.

draftsman n (US) = **draughtsman**.

drag [dræg] vt traîner; (river) draguer // vi traîner // n (col) raseur/euse; corvée f; (women's clothing): **in** ~ (en) travesti; **to** ~ **on** vi s'éterniser.

dragon ['drægn] n dragon m.

dragonfly ['drægənflaɪ] n libellule f.

drain [dreɪn] n égout m; (on resources) saignée f // vt. (land, marshes) drainer, assécher; (vegetables) égoutter; (reservoir etc) vider // vi (water) s'écouler; ~**age** n système m d'égouts; ~**ing board**, (US) ~**board** n égouttoir m; ~**pipe** n tuyau m d'écoulement.

dram [dræm] n petit verre.

drama ['drɑːmə] n (art) théâtre m, art m dramatique; (play) pièce f; (event) drame m; ~**tic** [drə'mætɪk] a dramatique; spectaculaire; ~**tist** ['dræmətɪst] n auteur m dramatique; ~**tize** vt (events) dramatiser; (adapt: for TV/cinema) adapter pour la télévision/pour l'écran.

drank [dræŋk] pt of **drink**.

drape [dreɪp] vt draper; ~**s** npl (US) rideaux mpl; ~**r** n (Brit) marchand/e de nouveautés.

drastic ['dræstɪk] a sévère; énergique.

draught [drɑːft] (US) **draft** [drɑːft] n courant m d'air; (NAUT) tirant m d'eau; ~**s** n (Brit) (jeu m de) dames fpl; **on** ~ (beer) à la pression; ~**board** n (Brit)

damier m.

draughtsman, (US) **draftsman** ['drɑːftsmən] n dessinateur/trice (industriel(le)).

draw [drɔː] vb (pt **drew**, pp **drawn**) vt tirer; (attract) attirer; (picture) dessiner; (line, circle) tracer; (money) retirer // vi (SPORT) faire match nul // n match nul; tirage m au sort; loterie f; **to** ~ **near** vi s'approcher; approcher; **to** ~ **out** vi (lengthen) s'allonger // vt (money) retirer; **to** ~ **up** vi (stop) s'arrêter // vt (document) établir, dresser; ~**back** n inconvénient m, désavantage m; ~**bridge** n pont-levis m.

drawer [drɔː*] n tiroir m; ['drɔːə*] (of cheque) tireur m.

drawing ['drɔːɪŋ] n dessin m; ~ **board** n planche f à dessin; ~ **pin** n (Brit) punaise f; ~ **room** n salon m.

drawl [drɔːl] n accent traînant.

drawn [drɔːn] pp of **draw**.

dread [drɛd] n épouvante f, effroi m // vt redouter, appréhender; ~**ful** a épouvantable, affreux(euse).

dream [driːm] n rêve m // vt, vi (pt, pp **dreamed** or **dreamt** [drɛmt]) rêver; ~**y** a rêveur(euse).

dreary ['drɪərɪ] a triste; monotone.

dredge [drɛdʒ] vt draguer.

dregs [drɛgz] npl lie f.

drench [drɛntʃ] vt tremper.

dress [drɛs] n robe f; (clothing) habillement m, tenue f // vi s'habiller // vt habiller; (wound) panser; (food) préparer; **to get** ~**ed** s'habiller; **to** ~ **up** vi s'habiller; (in fancy dress) se déguiser; ~ **circle** n (Brit) premier balcon; ~**er** n (THEATRE) habilleur/euse; (furniture) vaisselier m; ~**ing** n (MED) pansement m; (CULIN) sauce f, assaisonnement m; ~**ing gown** n (Brit) robe f de chambre; ~**ing room** n (THEATRE) loge f; (SPORT) vestiaire m; ~**ing table** n coiffeuse f; ~**maker** n couturière f; ~ **rehearsal** n (répétition) générale f; ~**y** a (col: clothes) (qui fait) habillé(e).

drew [druː] pt of **draw**.

dribble ['drɪbl] vi tomber goutte à goutte; (baby) baver // vt (ball) dribbler.

dried [draɪd] a (fruit, beans) sec(sèche); (eggs, milk) en poudre.

drier ['draɪə*] n = **dryer**.

drift [drɪft] n (of current etc) force f; direction f; (of sand etc) amoncellement m; (of snow) rafale f; coulée f; (: on ground) congère f; (general meaning) sens général // vi (boat) aller à la dérive, dériver; (sand, snow) s'amonceler, s'entasser; ~**wood** n bois flotté.

drill [drɪl] n perceuse f; (bit) foret m; (of dentist) roulette f, fraise f; (MIL) exercice *m* // *vt* percer // *vi* (*for oil*) faire un *or* des forage(s).

drink [drɪŋk] *n* boisson *f* // *vt*, *vi* (*pt* **drank**, *pp* **drunk**) boire; **to have a ~** boire quelque chose, boire un verre; prendre l'apéritif; **a ~ of water** un verre d'eau; **~er** *n* buveur/euse; **~ing water** *n* eau *f* potable.

drip [drɪp] *n* bruit *m* d'égouttement; goutte *f*; (*MED*) goutte-à-goutte *m inv*; perfusion *f* // *vi* tomber goutte à goutte; (*washing*) s'égoutter; (*wall*) suinter; **~-dry** *a* (*shirt*) sans repassage // **~ping** *n* graisse *f* de rôti.

drive [draɪv] *n* promenade *f* or trajet *m* en voiture; (*also:* **~way**) allée *f*; (*energy*) dynamisme *m*, énergie *f*; (*PSYCH*) besoin *m*, pulsion *f*; (*push*) effort (*concerté*); campagne *f*; (*SPORT*) drive *m*; (*TECH*) entraînement *m*; traction *f*; transmission *f*; (*also:* disk **~**) lecteur *m* de disquette // *vb* (*pt* **drove**, *pp* **driven**) *vt* conduire; (*nail*) enfoncer; (*push*) chasser, pousser; (*TECH: motor*) actionner; entraîner // *vi* (*AUT: at controls*) conduire; (*: travel*) aller en voiture; **left-/right-hand ~** conduite *f* à gauche/droite; **to ~ sb mad** rendre qn fou(folle).

drivel [ˈdrɪvl] *n* (*col*) idioties *fpl*.

driven [ˈdrɪvn] *pp* of **drive**.

driver [ˈdraɪvə*] *n* conducteur/trice; (*of taxi, bus*) chauffeur *m*; **~'s license** *n* (*US*) permis *m* de conduire.

driveway [ˈdraɪvwɛɪ] *n* allée *f*.

driving [ˈdraɪvɪŋ] *n* conduite *f*; **~ instructor** *n* moniteur *m* d'auto-école; **~ lesson** *n* leçon *f* de conduite; **~ licence** *n* (*Brit*) permis *m* de conduire; **~ mirror** *n* rétroviseur *m*; **~ school** *n* auto-école *f*; **~ test** *n* examen *m* du permis de conduire.

drizzle [ˈdrɪzl] *n* bruine *f*, crachin *m*.

droll [drəul] *a* drôle.

drone [drəun] *n* bourdonnement *m*.

drool [dru:l] *vi* baver.

droop [dru:p] *vi* s'affaisser; tomber.

drop [drɔp] *n* goutte *f*; (*fall*) baisse *f*; (*also:* **parachute ~**) saut *m*; (*of cliff*) dénivellation *f*; à-pic *m* // *vt* laisser tomber; (*voice, eyes, price*) baisser; (*set down from car*) déposer // *vi* tomber; **~s** *npl* (*MED*) gouttes; **to ~ off** *vi* (*sleep*) s'assoupir // *vt* (*passenger*) déposer; **to ~ out** *vi* (*withdraw*) se retirer; (*student etc*) abandonner, décrocher; **~-out** *n* marginal/e; (*from studies*) drop-out *m/f*; **~pings** *npl* crottes *fpl*.

drought [draut] *n* sécheresse *f*.

drove [drəuv] *pt* of **drive**.

drown [draun] *vt* noyer // *vi* se noyer.

owsy [ˈdrauzɪ] *a* somnolent(e).

dgery [ˈdrʌdʒərɪ] *n* corvée *f*.

drug [drʌg] *n* médicament *m*; (*narcotic*) drogue *f* // *vt* droguer **~ addict** *n* toxicomane *m/f*; **~gist** *n* (*US*) pharmacien/ne-droguiste; **~store** *n* (*US*) pharmacie-droguerie *f*, drugstore *m*.

drum [drʌm] *n* tambour *m*; (*for oil, petrol*) bidon *m* // *vi* tambouriner; **~s** *npl* batterie *f*; **~mer** *n* (joueur *m* de) tambour *m*.

drunk [drʌŋk] *pp* of **drink** // *a* ivre, soûl(e) // *n* (*also:* **~ard**) soûlard/e; homme/femme soûl(e); **~en** *a* ivre, soûl(e); ivrogne, d'ivrogne.

dry [draɪ] *a* sec(sèche); (*day*) sans pluie // *vt* sécher; (*clothes*) faire sécher // *vi* sécher; **to ~ up** *vi* se tarir; **~-cleaner's** *n* teinturerie *f*; **~er** *n* séchoir *m*; (*US: spin-dryer*) essoreuse *f*; **~ goods store** *n* (*US*) magasin *m* de nouveautés; **~ness** *n* sécheresse *f*; **~ rot** *n* pourriture sèche (*du bois*).

dual [ˈdjuəl] *a* double; **~ carriageway** *n* (*Brit*) route *f* à quatre voies *or* à chaussées séparées.

dubbed [dʌbd] *a* (*CINEMA*) doublé(e); (*nicknamed*) surnommé(e).

dubious [ˈdjuːbɪəs] *a* hésitant(e), incertain(e); (*reputation, company*) douteux(euse).

duchess [ˈdʌtʃɪs] *n* duchesse *f*.

duck [dʌk] *n* canard *m* // *vi* se baisser vivement, baisser subitement la tête; **~ling** *n* caneton *m*.

duct [dʌkt] *n* conduite *f*, canalisation *f*; (*ANAT*) conduit *m*.

dud [dʌd] *n* (*shell*) obus non éclaté; (*object, tool*): **it's a ~** c'est de la camelote, ça ne marche pas // *a* (*Brit: cheque*) sans provision; (*: note, coin*) faux(fausse).

due [djuː] *a* dû(due); (*expected*) attendu(e); (*fitting*) qui convient // *n* dû *m* // *ad*: **~ north** droit vers le nord; **~s** *npl* (*for club, union*) cotisation *f*; (*in harbour*) droits *mpl* (de port); **in ~ course** en temps utile *or* voulu; finalement; **~ to** dû(due) à; causé(e) par; **he's ~ to finish tomorrow** normalement il doit finir demain.

duet [djuːˈɛt] *n* duo *m*.

duffel [ˈdʌfl] *a*: **~ bag** sac *m* marin; **~ coat** duffel-coat *m*.

dug [dʌg] *pt*, *pp* of **dig**.

duke [djuːk] *n* duc *m*.

dull [dʌl] *a* ennuyeux(euse); terne; (*sound, pain*) sourd(e); (*weather, day*) gris(e), maussade; (*blade*) émoussé(e) // *vt* (*pain, grief*) atténuer; (*mind, senses*) engourdir.

duly [ˈdjuːlɪ] *ad* (*on time*) en temps voulu; (*as expected*) comme il se doit.

dumb [dʌm] *a* muet(te); (*stupid*) bête; **dumbfounded** [dʌmˈfaundɪd] *a* sidéré(e).

dummy ['dʌmɪ] *n* (*tailor's model*) mannequin *m*; (*SPORT*) feinte *f*; (*Brit: for baby*) tétine *f* // *a* faux(fausse), factice.

dump [dʌmp] *n* tas *m* d'ordures; (*place*) décharge (publique); (*MIL*) dépôt *m* // *vt* (*put down*) déposer; déverser; (*get rid of*) se débarrasser de; **~ing** *n* (*ECON*) dumping *m*; (*of rubbish*): 'no **~ing**' 'décharge interdite'.

dumpling ['dʌmplɪŋ] *n* boulette *f* (de pâte).

dumpy ['dʌmpɪ] *a* courtaud(e), boulot(te).

dunce [dʌns] *n* âne *m*, cancre *m*.

dung [dʌŋ] *n* fumier *m*.

dungarees [dʌŋgə'riːz] *npl* bleu(s) *m(pl)*; salopette *f*.

dungeon ['dʌndʒən] *n* cachot *m*.

Dunkirk [dʌn'kɜːk] *n* Dunkerque.

duplex ['djuːpleks] *n* (*US*) maison jumelée; (*: apartment*) duplex *m*.

duplicate *n* ['djuːplɪkət] double *m*, copie exacte // *vt* ['djuːplɪkeɪt] faire un double de; (*on machine*) polycopier.

durable ['djuərəbl] *a* durable; (*clothes, metal*) résistant(e), solide.

duration [djuə'reɪʃən] *n* durée *f*.

duress [djuə'res] *n*: **under ~** sous la contrainte.

during ['djuərɪŋ] *prep* pendant, au cours de.

dusk [dʌsk] *n* crépuscule *m*.

dust [dʌst] *n* poussière *f* // *vt* (*furniture*) essuyer, épousseter; (*cake etc*): **to ~ with** saupoudrer de; **~bin** *n* (*Brit*) poubelle *f*; **~er** *n* chiffon *m*; **~ jacket** *n* jacquette *f*; **~man** *n* (*Brit*) boueux *m*, éboueur *m*; **~y** *a* poussiéreux(euse).

Dutch [dʌtʃ] *a* hollandais(e), néerlandais(e) // *n* (*LING*) hollandais *m*; the **~** *npl* les Hollandais; **to go ~** partager les frais; **~man/woman** *n* Hollandais/e.

dutiful ['djuːtɪful] *a* (*child*) respectueux(euse).

duty ['djuːtɪ] *n* devoir *m*; (*tax*) droit *m*, taxe *f*; **duties** *npl* fonctions *fpl*; **on ~** de service; (*at night etc*) de garde; **off ~** libre, pas de service *or* de garde; **~-free** *a* exempté(e) de douane, hors-taxe.

duvet ['duːveɪ] *n* (*Brit*) couette *f*.

dwarf [dwɔːf] *n* nain/e // *vt* écraser.

dwell, *pt*, *pp* **dwelt** [dwel, dwelt] *vi* demeurer; **to ~ on** *vt fus* s'étendre sur; **~ing** *n* habitation *f*, demeure *f*.

dwindle ['dwɪndl] *vi* diminuer, décroître.

dye [daɪ] *n* teinture *f* // *vt* teindre.

dying ['daɪɪŋ] *a* mourant(e), agonisant(e).

dyke [daɪk] *n* (*Brit*) digue *f*.

dynamic [daɪ'næmɪk] *a* dynamique.

dynamite ['daɪnəmaɪt] *n* dynamite *f*.

dynamo ['daɪnəməu] *n* dynamo *f*.

dyslexia [dɪs'leksɪə] *n* dyslexie *f*.

E

E [iː] *n* (*MUS*) mi *m*.

each [iːtʃ] *a* chaque // *pronoun* chacun(e); **~ one** chacun(e); **they hate ~ other** ils se détestent (mutuellement); **you are jealous of ~ other** vous êtes jaloux l'un de l'autre; **they have 2 books ~** ils ont 2 livres chacun.

eager ['iːgə*] *a* impatient(e); avide; ardent(e), passionné(e); **to be ~ for** désirer vivement, être avide de.

eagle ['iːgl] *n* aigle *m*.

ear [ɪə*] *n* oreille *f*; (*of corn*) épi *m*; **~ache** *n* douleurs *fpl* aux oreilles; **~drum** *n* tympan *m*.

earl [ɜːl] *n* comte *m*.

earlier ['ɜːlɪə*] *a* (*date etc*) plus rapproché(e); (*edition etc*) plus ancien(ne), antérieur(e) // *ad* plus tôt.

early ['ɜːlɪ] *ad* tôt, de bonne heure; (*ahead of time*) en avance // *a* précoce; anticipé(e); qui se manifeste (*or* se fait) tôt *or* de bonne heure; **to have an ~ night** se coucher tôt *or* de bonne heure; **in the ~ or ~ in the spring/19th century** au début *or* commencement du printemps/19ème siècle; **~ retirement** *n* retraite anticipée.

earmark ['ɪəmɑːk] *vt*: **to ~ sth for** réserver *or* destiner qch à.

earn [ɜːn] *vt* gagner; (*COMM: yield*) rapporter.

earnest ['ɜːnɪst] *a* sérieux(euse); **in ~** *ad* sérieusement, pour de bon.

earnings ['ɜːnɪŋz] *npl* salaire *m*; gains *mpl*.

earphones ['ɪəfəunz] *npl* écouteurs *mpl*.

earring ['ɪərɪŋ] *n* boucle *f* d'oreille.

earshot ['ɪəʃɔt] *n*: **out of/within ~** hors de portée/à portée de la voix.

earth [ɜːθ] *n* (*gen*; *also ELEC*: *Brit*) terre *f*; (*of fox etc*) terrier *m* // *vt* (*Brit*: *ELEC*) relier à la terre; **~enware** *n* poterie *f*; faïence *f*; **~quake** *n* tremblement *m* de terre, séisme *m*; **~y** *a* (*fig*) terre à terre *inv*; truculent(e).

ease [iːz] *n* facilité *f*, aisance *f* // *vt* (*soothe*) calmer; (*loosen*) relâcher, détendre; (*help pass*): **to ~ sth in/out** faire pénétrer/sortir qch délicatement *or* avec douceur; faciliter la pénétration/la sortie de qch; **at ~** à l'aise; (*MIL*) au repos; **to ~ off** *or* **up** *vi* diminuer; ralentir; se détendre.

easel ['iːzl] *n* chevalet *m*.

east [iːst] *n* est *m* // *a* d'est // *ad* à l'est, vers l'est; **the E~** l'Orient *m*.

Easter ['iːstə*] *n* Pâques *fpl*; **~ egg** *n* œuf *m* de Pâques.

easterly ['iːstəlɪ] *a* d'est.

eastern ['iːstən] *a* de l'est, oriental(e).

East Germany n Allemagne f de l'Est.
eastward(s) ['i:stwəd(z)] ad vers l'est, à l'est.
easy ['i:zı] a facile; (manner) aisé(e) // ad: **to take it** or **things** ~ ne pas se fatiguer; ne pas (trop) s'en faire; ~ **chair** n fauteuil m; ~**-going** a accommodant(e), facile à vivre.
eat, pt **ate**, pp **eaten** [i:t, eıt, 'i:tn] vt, vi manger; **to** ~ **into**, **to** ~ **away at** vt fus ronger, attaquer.
eaves [i:vz] npl avant-toit m.
eavesdrop ['i:vzdrɔp] vi: **to** ~ **(on a conversation)** écouter (une conversation) de façon indiscrète.
ebb [eb] n reflux m // vi refluer; (fig: also: ~ **away**) décliner.
ebony ['ebənı] n ébène f.
eccentric [ık'sentrık] a, n excentrique (m/f).
echo, ~**es** ['ekəu] n écho m // vt répéter; faire chorus avec // vi résonner; faire écho.
eclipse [ı'klıps] n éclipse f.
ecology [ı'kɔlədʒı] n écologie f.
economic [i:kə'nɔmık] a économique; (business etc) rentable; ~**al** a économique; (person) économe; ~**s** n économie f politique.
economize [ı'kɔnəmaız] vi économiser, faire des économies.
economy [ı'kɔnəmı] n économie f.
ecstasy ['ekstəsı] n extase f.
eczema ['eksımə] n eczéma m.
edge [edʒ] n bord m; (of knife etc) tranchant m, fil m // vt border; **on** ~ (fig) = edgy; **to** ~ **away from** s'éloigner furtivement de; ~**ways** ad latéralement; **he couldn't get a word in** ~**ways** il ne pouvait pas placer un mot.
edgy ['edʒı] a crispé(e), tendu(e).
edible ['edıbl] a comestible; (meal) mangeable.
edict ['i:dıkt] n décret m.
Edinburgh ['edınbərə] n Édimbourg.
edit ['edıt] vt éditer; ~**ion** [ı'dıʃən] n édition f; ~**or** n (in newspaper) rédacteur/trice; rédacteur/trice en chef; (of sb's work) éditeur/trice; ~**orial** [-'tɔ:rıəl] a de la rédaction, éditorial(e) // n éditorial m.
educate ['edjukeıt] vt instruire; éduquer.
education [edju'keıʃən] n éducation f; (schooling) enseignement m, instruction f; ~**al** a pédagogique; scolaire; instructif(ive).
EEC n abbr (= European Economic Community) C.E.E. f (= Communauté économique européenne).
eel [i:l] n anguille f.
eerie ['ıərı] a inquiétant(e), spectral(e), surnaturel(le).
effect [ı'fekt] n effet m // vt effectuer; ~**s** npl (THEATRE) effets mpl; **to take** ~

(law) entrer en vigueur, prendre effet; (drug) agir, faire son effet; **in** ~ en fait; ~**ive** a efficace; ~**ively** ad efficacement; (in reality) effectivement; ~**iveness** n efficacité f.
effeminate [ı'femınıt] a efféminé(e).
efficiency [ı'fıʃənsı] n efficacité f; rendement m.
efficient [ı'fıʃənt] a efficace.
effort ['efət] n effort m.
effusive [ı'fju:sıv] a expansif(ive); chaleureux(euse).
e.g. ad abbr (= exempli gratia) par exemple, p. ex.
egg [eg] n œuf m; **to** ~ **on** vt pousser; ~**cup** n coquetier m; ~**plant** n (esp US) aubergine f; ~**shell** n coquille f d'œuf.
ego ['i:gəu] n moi m.
egotism ['egəutızəm] n égotisme m.
egotist ['egəutıst] n égocentrique m/f.
Egypt ['i:dʒıpt] n Égypte f; ~**ian** [ı'dʒıpʃən] a égyptien(ne) // n Égyptien/ne.
eiderdown ['aıdədaun] n édredon m.
eight [eıt] num huit; ~**een** num dix-huit; ~**th** a, n huitième (m); ~**y** num quatre-vingt(s).
Eire ['eərə] n République f d'Irlande.
either ['aıðə*] a l'un ou l'autre; (both, each) chaque; **on** ~ **side** de chaque côté // pronoun: ~ **(of them)** l'un ou l'autre; **I don't like** ~ je n'aime ni l'un ni l'autre // ad non plus; **no, I don't** ~ moi non plus // cj: ~ **good** or **bad** ou bon ou mauvais, soit bon soit mauvais.
eject [ı'dʒekt] vt expulser; éjecter.
eke [i:k]: **to** ~ **out** vt faire durer; augmenter.
elaborate a [ı'læbərıt] compliqué(e), recherché(e), minutieux(euse) // vb [ı'læbəreıt] vt élaborer // vi entrer dans les détails.
elapse [ı'læps] vi s'écouler, passer.
elastic [ı'læstık] a, n élastique (m); ~ **band** n (Brit) élastique m.
elated [ı'leıtıd] a transporté(e) de joie.
elbow ['elbəu] n coude m.
elder ['eldə*] a aîné(e) // n (tree) sureau m; **one's** ~**s** ses aînés; ~**ly** a âgé(e) // npl: **the** ~**ly** les personnes âgées.
eldest ['eldıst] a, n: **the** ~ **(child)** l'aîné(e) (des enfants).
elect [ı'lekt] vt élire; **to** ~ **to do** choisir de faire // a: **the president** ~ le président désigné; ~**ion** [ı'lekʃən] n élection f; ~**ioneering** [ılekʃə'nıərıŋ] n propagande électorale, manœuvres électorales; ~**or** n électeur/trice; ~**orate** n électorat m.
electric [ı'lektrık] a électrique; ~**al** a électrique; ~ **blanket** n couverture chauffante; ~ **fire** n radiateur m électrique.
electrician [ılek'trıʃən] n électricien m.

electricity [ɪlek'trɪsɪtɪ] n électricité f.
electrify [ɪ'lektrɪfaɪ] vt (RAIL) électrifier; (audience) électriser.
electronic [ɪlek'trɒnɪk] a électronique; **~s** n électronique f.
elegant ['elɪgənt] a élégant(e).
element ['elɪmənt] n (gen) élément m; (of heater, kettle etc) résistance f; **~ary** [-'mentərɪ] a élémentaire; (school, education) primaire.
elephant ['elɪfənt] n éléphant m.
elevate ['elɪveɪt] vt élever.
elevator ['elɪveɪtə*] n élévateur m, monte-charge m inv; (US: lift) ascenseur m.
eleven [ɪ'levn] num onze; **~ses** npl (Brit) ≈ pause-café f; **~th** a onzième.
elicit [ɪ'lɪsɪt] vt: **to ~ (from)** obtenir (de), arracher (à).
eligible ['elɪdʒəbl] a éligible; (for membership) admissible.
elm [elm] n orme m.
elongated ['i:lɒŋgeɪtɪd] a étiré(e), allongé(e).
elope [ɪ'ləup] vi (lovers) s'enfuir (ensemble).
eloquent ['elɒkwənt] a éloquent(e).
else [els] ad d'autre; **something ~** quelque chose d'autre, autre chose; **somewhere ~** ailleurs, autre part; **everywhere ~** partout ailleurs; **nobody ~** personne d'autre; **where ~?** à quel autre endroit?; **little ~** pas grand-chose d'autre; **~where** ad ailleurs, autre part.
elude [ɪ'lu:d] vt échapper à; (question) éluder.
elusive [ɪ'lu:sɪv] a insaisissable.
emaciated [ɪ'meɪsɪeɪtɪd] a émacié(e), décharné(e).
emancipate [ɪ'mænsɪpeɪt] vt émanciper.
embankment [ɪm'bæŋkmənt] n (of road, railway) remblai m, talus m; (riverside) berge f, quai m; (dyke) digue f.
embark [ɪm'bɑ:k] vi: **to ~ (on)** (s')embarquer (à bord de or sur) // vt embarquer; **to ~ on** (fig) se lancer or s'embarquer dans; **~ation** [embɑ:'keɪʃən] n embarquement m.
embarrass [ɪm'bærəs] vt embarrasser, gêner; **~ed** a gêné(e); **~ing** a gênant(e), embarrassant(e); **~ment** n embarras m, gêne f.
embassy ['embəsɪ] n ambassade f.
embed [ɪm'bed] vt enfoncer; sceller.
embers ['embəz] npl braise f.
embezzle [ɪm'bezl] vt détourner.
embitter [ɪm'bɪtə*] vt aigrir; envenimer.
embody [ɪm'bɒdɪ] vt (features) réunir, comprendre; (ideas) formuler, exprimer.
embossed [ɪm'bɒst] a repoussé(e); gaufré(e).

embrace [ɪm'breɪs] vt embrasser, étreindre; (include) embrasser, couvrir // vi s'étreindre, s'embrasser // n étreinte f.
embroider [ɪm'brɔɪdə*] vt broder; (fig: story) enjoliver; **~y** n broderie f.
emerald ['emərəld] n émeraude f.
emerge [ɪ'mə:dʒ] vi apparaître, surgir.
emergence [ɪ'mə:dʒəns] n apparition f.
emergency [ɪ'mə:dʒənsɪ] n urgence f; **in an ~** en cas d'urgence; **~ cord** n (US) sonnette f d'alarme; **~ exit** n sortie f de secours; **~ landing** n atterrissage forcé; **the ~ services** npl (fire, police, ambulance) les services mpl d'urgence.
emery board ['emərɪ-] n lime f à ongles (en carton émerisé).
emigrate ['emɪgreɪt] vi émigrer.
eminent ['emɪnənt] a éminent(e).
emit [ɪ'mɪt] vt émettre.
emotion [ɪ'məuʃən] n émotion f; **~al** a (person) émotif(ive), très sensible; (scene) émouvant(e); (tone, speech) qui fait appel aux sentiments.
emperor ['empərə*] n empereur m.
emphasis, pl **-ases** ['emfəsɪs, -si:z] n accent m; force f, insistance f.
emphasize ['emfəsaɪz] vt (syllable, word, point) appuyer or insister sur; (feature) souligner, accentuer.
emphatic [em'fætɪk] a (strong) énergique, vigoureux(euse); (unambiguous, clear) catégorique; **~ally** ad avec vigueur or énergie; catégoriquement.
empire ['empaɪə*] n empire m.
employ [ɪm'plɔɪ] vt employer; **~ee** [-'i:] n employé(e); **~er** n employeur/euse; **~ment** n emploi m; **~ment agency** n agence f or bureau m de placement.
empower [ɪm'pauə*] vt: **to ~ sb to do** autoriser or habiliter qn à faire.
empress ['emprɪs] n impératrice f.
empty ['emptɪ] a vide; (threat, promise) en l'air, vain(e) // vt vider // vi se vider; (liquid) s'écouler // n (bottle) bouteille f vide; **~-handed** a les mains vides.
emulate ['emjuleɪt] vt rivaliser avec, imiter.
emulsion [ɪ'mʌlʃən] n émulsion f; **~ (paint)** n peinture mate.
enable [ɪ'neɪbl] vt: **to ~ sb to do** permettre à qn de faire.
enact [ɪn'ækt] vt (law) promulguer; (play) jouer, représenter.
enamel [ɪ'næməl] n émail m.
encased [ɪn'keɪst] a: **~ in** enfermé(e) dans, recouvert(e) de.
enchant [ɪn'tʃɑ:nt] vt enchanter; **~ing** a ravissant(e), enchanteur(eresse).
encl. abbr (= enclosed) annexe(s).
enclose [ɪn'kləuz] vt (land) clôturer; (letter etc): **to ~ (with)** joindre (à); **please find ~d** veuillez trouver ci-joint.
enclosure [ɪn'kləuʒə*] n enceinte f;

(COMM) annexe f.
encompass [ɪn'kʌmpəs] vt encercler, entourer; (include) contenir, inclure.
encore [ɔŋ'kɔː*] excl, n bis (m).
encounter [ɪn'kauntə*] n rencontre f // vt rencontrer.
encourage [ɪn'kʌrɪdʒ] vt encourager; ~ment n encouragement m.
encroach [ɪn'krəutʃ] vi: to ~ (up)on empiéter sur.
encyclop(a)edia [ɛnsaɪkləu'piːdɪə] n encyclopédie f.
end [ɛnd] n (gen, also: aim) fin f; (of table, street etc) bout m, extrémité f // vt terminer; (also: bring to an ~, put an ~ to) mettre fin à // vi se terminer, finir; in the ~ finalement; on ~ (object) debout, dressé(e); to stand on ~ (hair) se dresser sur la tête; for 5 hours on ~ durant 5 heures d'affilée or de suite; to ~ up vi: to ~ up in finir or se terminer par; (place) finir or aboutir à.
endanger [ɪn'deɪndʒə*] vt mettre en danger.
endearing [ɪn'dɪərɪŋ] a attachant(e).
endeavour, (US) **endeavor** [ɪn'devə*] n tentative f, effort m // vi: to ~ to do tenter or s'efforcer de faire.
ending ['ɛndɪŋ] n dénouement m, conclusion f; (LING) terminaison f.
endive ['ɛndaɪv] n chicorée f.
endless ['ɛndlɪs] a sans fin, interminable; (patience, resources) inépuisable, sans limites.
endorse [ɪn'dɔːs] vt (cheque) endosser; (approve) appuyer, approuver, sanctionner; ~ment n (on driving licence) contravention portée au permis de conduire.
endow [ɪn'dau] vt (provide with money) faire une donation à, doter; (equip): to ~ with gratifier de, doter de.
endure [ɪn'djuə*] vt supporter, endurer // vi durer.
enemy ['ɛnəmɪ] a, n ennemi(e).
energetic [ɛnə'dʒɛtɪk] a énergique; actif(ive); qui fait se dépenser (physiquement).
energy ['ɛnədʒɪ] n énergie f.
enforce [ɪn'fɔːs] vt (LAW) appliquer, faire respecter; ~d a forcé(e).
engage [ɪn'geɪdʒ] vt engager; (MIL) engager le combat avec // vi (TECH) s'enclencher, s'engrener; to ~ in se lancer dans; ~d a (Brit: busy, in use) occupé(e); (betrothed) fiancé(e); to get ~d se fiancer; ~d tone n (Brit TEL) tonalité f occupé or pas libre; ~ment n obligation f, engagement m; rendez-vous m inv; (to marry) fiançailles fpl; (MIL) combat m; ~ment ring n bague f de fiançailles.
engaging [ɪn'geɪdʒɪŋ] a engageant(e), attirant(e).
engender [ɪn'dʒɛndə*] vt produire, causer.

engine ['ɛndʒɪn] n (AUT) moteur m; (RAIL) locomotive f; ~ driver n mécanicien m.
engineer [ɛndʒɪ'nɪə*] n ingénieur m; (US RAIL) mécanicien m; ~ing n engineering m, ingénierie f; (of bridges, ships) génie m; (of machine) mécanique f.
England ['ɪŋglənd] n Angleterre f.
English ['ɪŋglɪʃ] a anglais(e) // n (LING) anglais m; the ~ npl les Anglais; the ~ Channel n la Manche; ~man/woman n Anglais/e.
engraving [ɪn'greɪvɪŋ] n gravure f.
engrossed [ɪn'grəust] a: ~ in absorbé(e) par, plongé(e) dans.
engulf [ɪn'gʌlf] vt engloutir.
enhance [ɪn'haːns] vt rehausser, mettre en valeur.
enjoy [ɪn'dʒɔɪ] vt aimer, prendre plaisir à; (have: health, fortune) jouir de; (: success) connaître; to ~ o.s. s'amuser; ~able a agréable; ~ment n plaisir m.
enlarge [ɪn'laːdʒ] vt accroître, (PHOT) agrandir // vi: to ~ on (subject) s'étendre sur.
enlighten [ɪn'laɪtn] vt éclairer; ~ed a éclairé(e); ~ment n: the E~ment (HISTORY) ≈ le Siècle des lumières.
enlist [ɪn'lɪst] vt recruter; (support) s'assurer // vi s'engager.
enmity ['ɛnmɪtɪ] n inimitié f.
enormous [ɪ'nɔːməs] a énorme.
enough [ɪ'nʌf] a, n: ~ time/books assez or suffisamment de temps/livres; have you got ~? (en) avez-vous assez? // ad: big ~ assez or suffisamment grand; he has not worked ~ il n'a pas assez or suffisamment travaillé; ~! assez!, ça suffit!; that's ~, thanks cela suffit or c'est assez, merci; I've had ~ of him j'en ai assez de lui; ... which, funnily ~ ... qui, chose curieuse.
enquire [ɪn'kwaɪə*] vt, vi = **inquire**.
enrage [ɪn'reɪdʒ] vt mettre en fureur or en rage, rendre furieux(euse).
enrol [ɪn'rəul] vt inscrire // vi s'inscrire; ~ment n inscription f.
ensign n (NAUT) ['ɛnsən] enseigne f, pavillon m; (MIL) ['ɛnsaɪn] porte-étendard m.
ensue [ɪn'sjuː] vi s'ensuivre, résulter.
ensure [ɪn'ʃuə*] vt assurer; garantir; to ~ that s'assurer que.
entail [ɪn'teɪl] vt entraîner, nécessiter.
entangle [ɪn'tæŋgl] vt emmêler, embrouiller.
enter ['ɛntə*] vt (room) entrer dans, pénétrer dans; (club, army) entrer à; (competition) s'inscrire à or pour; (sb for a competition) (faire) inscrire; (write down) inscrire, noter; (COMPUT) entrer, introduire // vi entrer; to ~ for vt fus s'inscrire à, se présenter pour or à; to ~ into vt fus (explanation) se

lancer dans; (*debate*) prendre part à; (*agreement*) conclure; **to ~ (up)on** *vt fus* commencer.

enterprise ['entəpraiz] *n* entreprise *f*; (*esprit m* d')initiative *f*; **free ~** libre entreprise; **private ~** entreprise privée.

enterprising ['entəpraiziŋ] *a* entreprenant(e), dynamique.

entertain [entə'tein] *vt* amuser, distraire; (*invite*) recevoir (à dîner); (*idea, plan*) envisager; **~er** *n* artiste *m/f* de variétés; **~ing** *a* amusant(e), distrayant(e); **~ment** *n* (*amusement*) distraction *f*, divertissement *m*, amusement *m*; (*show*) spectacle *m*.

enthralled [in'θrɔ:ld] *a* captivé(e).

enthusiasm [in'θu:ziæzəm] *n* enthousiasme *m*.

enthusiast [in'θu:ziæst] *n* enthousiaste *m/f*; **~ic** [-'æstik] *a* enthousiaste; **to be ~ic about** être enthousiasmé(e) par.

entice [in'tais] *vt* attirer, séduire.

entire [in'taiə*] *a* (*tout*) entier(ère); **~ly** *ad* entièrement, complètement; **~ty** [in'taiərəti] *n*: **in its ~ty** dans sa totalité.

entitle [in'taitl] *vt* (*allow*): **to ~ sb to do** donner (le) droit à qn de faire; **to ~ sb to sth** donner droit à qch à qn; **~d** *a* (*book*) intitulé(e); **to be ~d to do** avoir le droit de *or* être habilité à faire.

entrance *n* ['entrns] entrée *f* // *vt* [in'tra:ns] enchanter, ravir; **to gain ~ to** (*university etc*) être admis à; **~ examination** *n* examen *m* d'entrée; **~ fee** *n* droit *m* d'inscription; (*to museum etc*) prix *m* d'entrée; **~ ramp** *n* (*US AUT*) bretelle *f* d'accès.

entrant ['entrnt] *n* participant/e; concurrent/e.

entreat [en'tri:t] *vt* supplier.

entrenched [en'trentʃt] *a* retranché(e).

entrepreneur [ɔntrəprə'nə:*] *n* entrepreneur *m*.

entrust [in'trʌst] *vt*: **to ~ sth to** confier qch à.

entry ['entri] *n* entrée *f*; (*in register*) inscription *f*; **no ~** défense d'entrer, entrée interdite; (*AUT*) sens interdit; **~ form** *n* feuille *f* d'inscription; **~ phone** *n* interphone *m* (à l'entrée d'un immeuble).

envelop [in'veləp] *vt* envelopper.

envelope ['envələup] *n* enveloppe *f*.

envious ['enviəs] *a* envieux(euse).

environment [in'vaiərnmənt] *n* milieu *m*; environnement *m*; **~al** [-'mentl] *a* écologique; du milieu.

envisage [in'vizidʒ] *vt* envisager; prévoir.

envoy ['envɔi] *n* envoyé/e.

envy ['envi] *n* envie *f* // *vt* envier; **to ~ sb sth** envier qch à qn.

epic ['epik] *n* épopée *f* // *a* épique.

epidemic [epi'demik] *n* épidémie *f*.

epilepsy ['epilepsi] *n* épilepsie *f*.

episode ['episəud] *n* épisode *m*.

epistle [i'pisl] *n* épître *f*.

epitome [i'pitəmi] *n* résumé *m*; quintessence *f*, type *m*; **epitomize** *vt* résumer; illustrer, incarner.

equable ['ekwəbl] *a* égal(e); de tempérament égal.

equal ['i:kwl] *a* égal(e) // *n* égal/e // *vt* égaler; **~ to** (*task*) à la hauteur de; **~ity** [i:'kwɔliti] *n* égalité *f*; **~ize** *vt, vi* égaliser; **~izer** *n* but égalisateur; **~ly** *ad* également; (*just as*) tout aussi.

equanimity [ekwə'nimiti] *n* égalité *f* d'humeur.

equate [i'kweit] *vt*: **to ~ sth with** comparer qch à; assimiler qch à; **equation** [i'kweiʃən] *n* (*MATH*) équation *f*.

equator [i'kweitə*] *n* équateur *m*.

equilibrium [i:kwi'libriəm] *n* équilibre *m*.

equip [i'kwip] *vt* équiper; **to be well ~ped** (*office etc*) être bien équipé(e); **he is well ~ped for the job** il a les compétences *or* les qualités requises pour ce travail; **~ment** *n* équipement *m*; (*electrical etc*) appareillage *m*, installation *f*.

equities ['ekwitiz] *npl* (*Brit COMM*) actions cotées en Bourse.

equivalent [i'kwivəlnt] *a*: **~ (to)** équivalent(e) (à) // *n* équivalent *m*.

equivocal [i'kwivəkl] *a* équivoque; (*open to suspicion*) douteux(euse).

era ['iərə] *n* ère *f*, époque *f*.

eradicate [i'rædikeit] *vt* éliminer.

erase [i'reiz] *vt* effacer; **~r** *n* gomme *f*.

erect [i'rekt] *a* droit(e) // *vt* construire; (*monument*) ériger; élever; (*tent etc*) dresser; **~ion** [i'rekʃən] *n* érection *f*.

ermine ['ə:min] *n* hermine *f*.

erode [i'rəud] *vt* éroder; (*metal*) ronger.

erotic [i'rɔtik] *a* érotique.

err [ə:*] *vi* se tromper; (*REL*) pécher.

errand ['ernd] *n* course *f*, commission *f*.

erratic [i'rætik] *a* irrégulier(ère); inconstant(e).

error ['erə*] *n* erreur *f*.

erupt [i'rʌpt] *vi* entrer en éruption; (*fig*) éclater; **~ion** [i'rʌpʃən] *n* éruption *f*.

escalate ['eskəleit] *vi* s'intensifier.

escalator ['eskəleitə*] *n* escalier roulant.

escapade [eskə'peid] *n* fredaine *f*; équipée *f*.

escape [i'skeip] *n* évasion *f*; fuite *f*; (*of gas etc*) échappement *m*; fuite *f* // *vi* s'échapper, fuir; (*from jail*) s'évader; (*fig*) s'en tirer; (*leak*) s'échapper; fuir // *vt* échapper à; **to ~ from** (*person*) échapper à; (*place*) s'échapper de; (*fig*) fuir; **escapism** *n* évasion *f* (*fig*).

escort *n* ['eskɔ:t] escorte *f* // *vt* [i'skɔ:t] escorter.

Eskimo ['eskiməu] *n* Esquimau/de.

especially [ɪ'spɛʃlɪ] *ad* particulièrement; surtout; exprès.

espionage ['ɛspɪənɑ:ʒ] *n* espionnage *m*.

Esquire [ɪ'skwaɪə*] *n* (*abbr* Esq.): J. Brown, ~ Monsieur J. Brown.

essay ['ɛseɪ] *n* (*SCOL*) dissertation *f*; (*LITERATURE*) essai *m*.

essence ['ɛsns] *n* essence *f*.

essential [ɪ'sɛnʃl] *a* essentiel(le); (*basic*) fondamental(e) // *n*: ~s éléments essentiels; ~**ly** *ad* essentiellement.

establish [ɪ'stæblɪʃ] *vt* établir; (*business*) fonder, créer; (*one's power etc*) asseoir, affermir; ~**ment** *n* établissement *m*; création *f*; the E~ment les pouvoirs établis; l'ordre établi; les milieux dirigeants.

estate [ɪ'steɪt] *n* domaine *m*, propriété *f*; biens *mpl*, succession *f*; ~ **agent** *n* agent immobilier; ~ **car** *n* (*Brit*) break *m*.

esteem [ɪ'sti:m] *n* estime *f* // *vt* estimer; apprécier.

esthetic [ɪs'θɛtɪk] *a* (*US*) = **aesthetic**.

estimate *n* ['ɛstɪmət] estimation *f*; (*COMM*) devis *m* // *vt* ['ɛstɪmeɪt] estimer; **estimation** [-'meɪʃən] *n* opinion *f*; estime *f*.

estranged [ɪ'streɪndʒd] *a* séparé(e); dont on s'est séparé(e).

etc *abbr* (= et cetera) etc.

etching ['ɛtʃɪŋ] *n* eau-forte *f*.

eternal [ɪ'tə:nl] *a* éternel(le).

eternity [ɪ'tə:nɪtɪ] *n* éternité *f*.

ethical ['ɛθɪkl] *a* moral(e).

ethics ['ɛθɪks] *n* éthique *f* // *npl* moralité *f*.

Ethiopia [i:θɪ'əupɪə] *n* Éthiopie *f*.

ethnic ['ɛθnɪk] *a* ethnique.

ethos ['i:θɔs] *n* génie *m*.

etiquette ['ɛtɪkɛt] *n* convenances *fpl*, étiquette *f*.

Eurocheque ['juərəutʃɛk] *n* eurochèque *m*.

Europe ['juərəp] *n* Europe *f*; ~**an** [-'pi:ən] *a* européen(ne) // *n* Européen/ne.

evacuate [ɪ'vækjueɪt] *vt* évacuer.

evade [ɪ'veɪd] *vt* échapper à; (*question etc*) éluder; (*duties*) se dérober à.

evaporate [ɪ'væpəreɪt] *vi* s'évaporer // *vt* faire évaporer; ~**d milk** *n* lait condensé non sucré.

evasion [ɪ'veɪʒən] *n* dérobade *f*; fauxfuyant *m*.

eve [i:v] *n*: on the ~ of à la veille de.

even ['i:vn] *a* régulier(ère), égal(e); (*number*) pair(e) // *ad* même; ~ if même si + *indic*; ~ though quand (bien) même + *cond*, alors même que + *cond*; ~ more encore plus; ~ so quand même; not ~ pas même; to get ~ with sb prendre sa revanche sur qn; to ~ out *vi* s'égaliser.

evening ['i:vnɪŋ] *n* soir *m*; (*as duration,*

event) soirée *f*; in the ~ le soir; ~ **class** *n* cours *m* du soir; ~ **dress** *n* (*man's*) habit *m* de soirée, smoking *m*; (*woman's*) robe *f* de soirée.

event [ɪ'vɛnt] *n* événement *m*; (*SPORT*) épreuve *f*; in the ~ of en cas de; ~**ful** *a* mouvementé(e).

eventual [ɪ'vɛntʃuəl] *a* final(e); ~**ity** [-'ælɪtɪ] *n* possibilité *f*, éventualité *f*; ~**ly** *ad* finalement.

ever ['ɛvə*] *ad* jamais; (*at all times*) toujours; the best ~ le meilleur qu'on ait jamais vu; have you ~ seen it? l'as-tu déjà vu?, as-tu eu l'occasion *or* t'est-il arrivé de le voir?; ~ since *ad* depuis // *cj* depuis que; ~**green** *n* arbre *m* à feuilles persistantes; ~**lasting** *a* éternel(le).

every ['ɛvrɪ] *a* chaque; ~ day tous les jours, chaque jour; ~ other/third day tous les deux/trois jours; ~ other car une voiture sur deux; ~ now and then de temps en temps; ~**body** *pronoun* tout le monde, tous *pl*; ~**day** *a* quotidien(ne); de tous les jours; ~**one** = ~**body**; ~**thing** *pronoun* tout; ~**where** *ad* partout.

evict [ɪ'vɪkt] *vt* expulser.

evidence ['ɛvɪdns] *n* (*proof*) preuve(s) *f(pl)*; (*of witness*) témoignage *m*; (*sign*): to show ~ of donner des signes de; to give ~ témoigner, déposer.

evident ['ɛvɪdnt] *a* évident(e); ~**ly** *ad* de toute évidence.

evil ['i:vl] *a* mauvais(e) // *n* mal *m*.

evoke [ɪ'vəuk] *vt* évoquer.

evolution [i:və'lu:ʃən] *n* évolution *f*.

evolve [ɪ'vɔlv] *vt* élaborer // *vi* évoluer, se transformer.

ewe [ju:] *n* brebis *f*.

ex- [ɛks] *prefix* ex-.

exact [ɪg'zækt] *a* exact(e) // *vt*: to ~ sth (from) extorquer qch (à); exiger qch (de); ~**ing** *a* exigeant(e); (*work*) fatigant(e); ~**ly** *ad* exactement.

exaggerate [ɪg'zædʒəreɪt] *vt*, *vi* exagérer; **exaggeration** [-'reɪʃən] *n* exagération *f*.

exalted [ɪg'zɔ:ltɪd] *a* élevé(e); (*person*) haut placé(e); (*elated*) exalté(e).

exam [ɪg'zæm] *n* *abbr* (*SCOL*) of **examination**.

examination [ɪgzæmɪ'neɪʃən] *n* (*SCOL*, *MED*) examen *m*.

examine [ɪg'zæmɪn] *vt* (*gen*) examiner; (*SCOL*, *LAW*: *person*) interroger; (*at customs*: *luggage*) inspecter; ~**r** *n* examinateur/trice.

example [ɪg'zɑ:mpl] *n* exemple *m*; for ~ par exemple.

exasperate [ɪg'zɑ:spəreɪt] *vt* exaspérer; **exasperation** [ɪgzɑ:spə'reɪʃən] *n* exaspération *f*, irritation *f*.

excavate ['ɛkskəveɪt] *vt* excaver; (*object*) mettre au jour.

exceed [ɪk'siːd] *vt* dépasser; (*one's powers*) outrepasser; **~ingly** *ad* excessivement.

excellent ['ɛksələnt] *a* excellent(e).

except [ɪk'sɛpt] *prep* (*also*: ~ **for**, **~ing**) sauf, excepté, à l'exception de // *vt* excepter; ~ **if/when** sauf si/quand; ~ **that** excepté que, si ce n'est que; **~ion** [ɪk'sɛpʃən] *n* exception *f*; **to take ~ion to** s'offusquer de; **~ional** [ɪk'sɛpʃənl] *a* exceptionnel(le).

excerpt ['ɛksəːpt] *n* extrait *m*.

excess [ɪk'sɛs] *n* excès *m*; ~ **baggage** *n* excédent *m* de bagages; ~ **fare** *n* supplément *m*; **~ive** *a* excessif(ive).

exchange [ɪks'tʃeɪndʒ] *n* échange *m*; (*also*: **telephone ~**) central *m* // *vt*: **to ~ (for)** échanger (contre); ~ **rate** *n* taux *m* des changes.

Exchequer [ɪks'tʃɛkə*] *n*: **the ~** (*Brit*) l'Échiquier *m*, ≈ le ministère des Finances.

excise ['ɛksaɪz] *n* taxe *f*.

excite [ɪk'saɪt] *vt* exciter; **to get ~d** s'exciter; **~ment** *n* excitation *f*; **exciting** *a* passionnant(e).

exclaim [ɪk'skleɪm] *vi* s'exclamer; **exclamation** [ɛksklə'meɪʃən] *n* exclamation *f*; **exclamation mark** *n* point *m* d'exclamation.

exclude [ɪk'skluːd] *vt* exclure.

exclusive [ɪk'skluːsɪv] *a* exclusif(ive); (*club*, *district*) sélect(e); (*item of news*) en exclusivité; ~ **of VAT** TVA non comprise.

excruciating [ɪk'skruːʃɪeɪtɪŋ] *a* atroce, déchirant(e).

excursion [ɪk'skəːʃən] *n* excursion *f*.

excuse *n* [ɪk'skjuːs] excuse *f* // *vt* [ɪk'skjuːz] excuser; **to ~ sb from** (*activity*) dispenser qn de; ~ **me!** excusez-moi!, pardon!; **now if you will ~ me,** ... maintenant, si vous (le) permettez ....

ex-directory ['ɛksdɪ'rɛktərɪ] *a* (*Brit*) sur la liste rouge.

execute ['ɛksɪkjuːt] *vt* exécuter.

execution [ɛksɪ'kjuːʃən] *n* exécution *f*; **~er** *n* bourreau *m*.

executive [ɪg'zɛkjutɪv] *n* (*COMM*) cadre *m*; (*POL*) exécutif *m* // *a* exécutif(ive).

exemplify [ɪg'zɛmplɪfaɪ] *vt* illustrer.

exempt [ɪg'zɛmpt] *a*: ~ **from** exempté(e) *or* dispensé(e) de // *vt*: **to ~ sb from** exempter *or* dispenser qn de.

exercise ['ɛksəsaɪz] *n* exercice *m* // *vt* exercer; (*patience etc*) faire preuve de; (*dog*) promener // *vi* prendre de l'exercice; ~ **book** *n* cahier *m*.

exert [ɪg'zəːt] *vt* exercer, employer; **to ~ o.s.** se dépenser; **~ion** [-ʃən] *n* effort *m*.

exhaust [ɪg'zɔːst] *n* (*also*: ~ **fumes**) gaz *mpl* d'échappement; (*also*: ~ **pipe**) tuyau *m* d'échappement // *vt* épuiser; **~ed** *a* épuisé(e); **~ion** [ɪg'zɔːstʃən] *n* épuisement *m*; **nervous ~ion** fatigue nerveuse; surmenage mental; **~ive** *a* très complet(ète).

exhibit [ɪg'zɪbɪt] *n* (*ART*) pièce *f or* objet *m* exposé(e); (*LAW*) pièce à conviction // *vt* exposer; (*courage*, *skill*) faire preuve de; **~ion** [ɛksɪ'bɪʃən] *n* exposition *f*.

exhilarating [ɪg'zɪləreɪtɪŋ] *a* grisant(e); stimulant(e).

exile ['ɛksaɪl] *n* exil *m*; (*person*) exilé/e // *vt* exiler.

exist [ɪg'zɪst] *vi* exister; **~ence** *n* existence *f*; **to be in ~ence** exister; **~ing** *a* actuel(le).

exit ['ɛksɪt] *n* sortie *f* // *vi* (*COMPUT*, *THEATRE*) sortir; ~ **ramp** *n* (*US AUT*) bretelle *f* d'accès.

exodus ['ɛksədəs] *n* exode *m*.

exonerate [ɪg'zɔnəreɪt] *vt*: **to ~ from** disculper de.

exotic [ɪg'zɔtɪk] *a* exotique.

expand [ɪk'spænd] *vt* agrandir; accroître, étendre // *vi* (*trade etc*) se développer, s'accroître; s'étendre; (*gas*, *metal*) se dilater.

expanse [ɪk'spæns] *n* étendue *f*.

expansion [ɪk'spænʃən] *n* développement *m*, accroissement *m*; dilatation *f*.

expect [ɪk'spɛkt] *vt* (*anticipate*) s'attendre à, s'attendre à ce que + *sub*; (*count on*) compter sur, escompter; (*hope for*) espérer; (*require*) demander, exiger; (*suppose*) supposer; (*await*, *also baby*) attendre // *vi*: **to be ~ing** être enceinte; **to ~ sb to do** s'attendre à ce que qn fasse; attendre de qn qu'il fasse; **~ancy** *n* (*anticipation*) attente *f*; **life ~ancy** espérance *f* de vie; **~ant mother** *n* future maman; **~ation** [ɛkspɛk'teɪʃən] *n* attente *f*, prévisions *fpl*; espérance(s) *f(pl)*.

expedience, expediency [ɪk'spiːdɪəns, ɪk'spiːdɪənsɪ] *n*: **for the sake of ~** parce que c'est plus commode.

expedient [ɪk'spiːdɪənt] *a* indiqué(e), opportun(e); commode // *n* expédient *m*.

expedition [ɛkspə'dɪʃən] *n* expédition *f*.

expel [ɪk'spɛl] *vt* chasser, expulser; (*SCOL*) renvoyer, exclure.

expend [ɪk'spɛnd] *vt* consacrer; (*use up*) dépenser; **~able** *a* remplaçable; **~iture** [ɪk'spɛndɪtʃə*] *n* dépense *f*; dépenses *fpl*.

expense [ɪk'spɛns] *n* dépense *f*; frais *mpl*; (*high cost*) coût *m*; **~s** *npl* (*COMM*) frais *mpl*; **at the ~ of** aux dépens de; ~ **account** *n* (note *f* de) frais *mpl*.

expensive [ɪk'spɛnsɪv] *a* cher(chère), coûteux(euse); **to be ~** coûter cher.

experience [ɪk'spɪərɪəns] *n* expérience *f* // *vt* connaître; éprouver; **~d** *a* expérimenté(e).

experiment [ɪk'spɛrɪmənt] *n* expérience *f* // *vi* faire une expérience; **to ~ with**

expérimenter.
expert ['ɛkspə:t] *a* expert(e) // *n* expert *m*; **~ise** [-'ti:z] *n* (grande) compétence.
expire [ık'spaıə*] *vi* expirer; **expiry** *n* expiration *f*.
explain [ık'spleın] *vt* expliquer; **explanation** [ɛksplə'neıʃən] *n* explication *f*; **explanatory** [ık'splænətrı] *a* explicatif(ive).
explicit [ık'splısıt] *a* explicite; *(definite)* formel(le).
explode [ık'spləud] *vi* exploser // *vt* faire exploser.
exploit *n* ['ɛksplɔıt] exploit *m* // *vt* [ık'splɔıt] exploiter; **~ation** [-'teıʃən] *n* exploitation *f*.
exploratory [ık'splɔrətrı] *a* *(fig: talks)* préliminaire.
explore [ık'splɔ:*] *vt* explorer; *(possibilities)* étudier, examiner; **~r** *n* explorateur/trice.
explosion [ık'spləuʒən] *n* explosion *f*.
explosive [ık'spləusıv] *a* explosif(ive) // *n* explosif *m*.
exponent [ık'spəunənt] *n* *(of school of thought etc)* interprète *m*, représentant *m*.
export *vt* [ɛk'spɔ:t] exporter // *n* ['ɛkspɔ:t] exportation *f* // *cpd* d'exportation; **~er** *n* exportateur *m*.
expose [ık'spəuz] *vt* exposer; *(unmask)* démasquer, dévoiler; **~d** *a* *(position)* exposé(e).
exposure [ık'spəuʒə*] *n* exposition *f*; *(PHOT)* (temps *m* de) pose *f*; *(: shot)* pose; **suffering from ~** *(MED)* souffrant des effets du froid et de l'épuisement; **~ meter** *n* posemètre *m*.
expound [ık'spaund] *vt* exposer.
express [ık'sprɛs] *a* *(definite)* formel(le), exprès(esse) *(Brit: letter etc)* exprès *inv* // *n* *(train)* rapide *m* // *ad* *(send)* exprès // *vt* exprimer; **~ion** [ık'sprɛʃən] *n* expression *f*; **~ly** *ad* expressément, formellement; **~way** *n* *(US: urban motorway)* voie *f* express (à plusieurs files).
exquisite [ɛk'skwızıt] *a* exquis(e).
extend [ık'stɛnd] *vt* *(visit, street)* prolonger; *(building)* agrandir; *(offer)* présenter, offrir // *vi* *(land)* s'étendre.
extension [ık'stɛnʃən] *n* prolongation *f*; agrandissement *m*; *(building)* annexe *f*; *(to wire, table)* rallonge *f*; *(telephone: in offices)* poste *m*; *(: in private house)* téléphone *m* supplémentaire.
extensive [ık'stɛnsıv] *a* étendu(e), vaste; *(damage, alterations)* considérable; *(inquiries)* approfondi(e); *(use)* largement répandu(e); **he's travelled ~ly** il a beaucoup voyagé.
extent [ık'stɛnt] *n* étendue *f*; **to some ~** dans une certaine mesure; **to what ~?** dans quelle mesure?, jusqu'à quel point?; **to the ~ of ...** au point de ....

extenuating [ık'stɛnjueıtıŋ] *a*: **~ circumstances** circonstances atténuantes.
exterior [ɛk'stıərıə*] *a* extérieur(e), du dehors // *n* extérieur *m*; dehors *m*.
external [ɛk'stə:nl] *a* externe.
extinct [ık'stıŋkt] *a* éteint(e).
extinguish [ık'stıŋgwıʃ] *vt* éteindre; **~er** *n* extincteur *m*.
extort [ık'stɔ:t] *vt*: **to ~ sth (from)** extorquer qch (à); **~ionate** [ık'stɔ:ʃnət] *a* exorbitant(e).
extra ['ɛkstrə] *a* supplémentaire, de plus // *ad* *(in addition)* en plus // *n* supplément *m*; *(THEATRE)* figurant/e.
extra... ['ɛkstrə] *prefix* extra....
extract *vt* [ık'strækt] extraire; *(tooth)* arracher; *(money, promise)* soutirer // *n* ['ɛkstrækt] extrait *m*.
extracurricular ['ɛkstrəkə'rıkjulə*] *a* parascolaire.
extradite ['ɛkstrədaıt] *vt* extrader.
extramarital [ɛkstrə'mærıtl] *a* extraconjugal(e).
extramural [ɛkstrə'mjuərl] *a* hors-faculté *inv*.
extraordinary [ık'strɔ:dnrı] *a* extraordinaire.
extravagance [ık'strævəgəns] *n* prodigalités *fpl*; *(thing bought)* folie *f*, dépense excessive *or* exagérée.
extravagant [ık'strævəgənt] *a* extravagant(e); *(in spending)* prodigue, dépensier(ère); dispendieux(euse).
extreme [ık'stri:m] *a*, *n* extrême *(m)*; **~ly** *ad* extrêmement.
extricate ['ɛkstrıkeıt] *vt*: **to ~ sth (from)** dégager qch (de).
extrovert ['ɛkstrəvə:t] *n* extraverti/e.
eye [aı] *n* œil *m* (*pl* yeux); *(of needle)* trou *m*, chas *m* // *vt* examiner; **to keep an ~ on** surveiller; **~ball** *n* globe *m* oculaire; **~bath** *n* œillère *f* *(pour bains d'œil)*; **~brow** *n* sourcil *m*; **~brow pencil** *n* crayon *m* à sourcils; **~drops** *npl* gouttes *fpl* pour les yeux; **~lash** *n* cil *m*; **~lid** *n* paupière *f*; **~liner** *n* eye-liner *m*; **~opener** *n* révélation *f*; **~shadow** *n* ombre *f* à paupières; **~sight** *n* vue *f*; **~sore** *n* horreur *f*, chose *f* qui dépare *or* enlaidit; **~ witness** *n* témoin *m* oculaire.

F

F [ɛf] *n* *(MUS)* fa *m*.
fable ['feıbl] *n* fable *f*.
fabric ['fæbrık] *n* tissu *m*.
fabrication [fæbrı'keıʃən] *n* invention(s) *f(pl)*, fabulation *f*; fait *m* *(or preuve f)* forgé(e) de toutes pièces.
fabulous ['fæbjuləs] *a* fabuleux(euse); *(col: super)* formidable.
face [feıs] *n* visage *m*, figure *f*; expression *f*; *(of clock)* cadran *m*; *(of*

building) façade f; (side, surface) face f // vt faire face à; ~ **down** (person) à plat ventre; (card) face en dessous; **to make** or **pull a** ~ faire une grimace; **in the** ~ **of** (difficulties etc) face à, devant; **on the** ~ **of it** à première vue; ~ **to** ~ face à face; **to** ~ **up to** vt fus faire face à, affronter; ~ **cloth** n (Brit) gant m de toilette; ~ **cream** n crème f pour le visage; ~ **lift** n lifting m; (of building etc) ravalement m, retapage m.

face value n (of coin) valeur nominale; **to take sth at** ~ (fig) prendre qch pour argent comptant.

facilities [fə'sɪlɪtɪz] npl installations fpl, équipement m; **credit** ~ facilités fpl de paiement.

facing ['feɪsɪŋ] prep face à, en face de // n (of wall etc) revêtement m; (SEWING) revers m.

facsimile [fæk'sɪmɪlɪ] n (document) télécopie f; (machine) télécopieur m.

fact [fækt] n fait m; **in** ~ en fait.

factor ['fæktə*] n facteur m.

factory ['fæktərɪ] n usine f, fabrique f.

factual ['fæktjʊəl] a basé(e) sur les faits.

faculty ['fækəltɪ] n faculté f; (US: teaching staff) corps enseignant.

fad [fæd] n manie f; engouement m.

fade [feɪd] vi se décolorer, passer; (light, sound, hope) s'affaiblir, disparaître; (flower) se faner.

fag [fæg] n (col: cigarette) sèche f.

fail [feɪl] vt (exam) échouer à; (candidate) recaler; (subj: courage, memory) faire défaut à // vi échouer; (supplies) manquer; (eyesight, health, light) baisser, s'affaiblir; **to** ~ **to do sth** (neglect) négliger de faire qch; (be unable) ne pas arriver or parvenir à faire qch; **without** ~ à coup sûr; sans faute; ~**ing** n défaut m // prep faute de; ~**ure** ['feɪljə*] n échec m; (person) raté/e; (mechanical etc) défaillance f.

faint [feɪnt] a faible; (recollection) vague; (mark) à peine visible // n évanouissement m // vi s'évanouir; **to feel** ~ défaillir.

fair [feə*] a équitable, juste, impartial(e); (hair) blond(e); (skin, complexion) pâle, blanc(blanche); (weather) beau(belle); (good enough) assez bon(ne); (sizeable) considérable // ad (play) franc-jeu // n foire f; (Brit: funfair) fête (foraine); ~**ly** ad équitablement; (quite) assez; ~**ness** n justice f, équité f, impartialité f.

fairy ['feərɪ] n fée f; ~ **tale** n conte m de fées.

faith [feɪθ] n foi f; (trust) confiance f; (sect) culte m, religion f; ~**ful** a fidèle; ~**fully** ad fidèlement.

fake [feɪk] n (painting etc) faux m; (photo) trucage m; (person) imposteur m // a faux(fausse); simulé(e) // vt

simuler; (photo) truquer; (story) fabriquer.

falcon ['fɔ:lkən] n faucon m.

fall [fɔ:l] n chute f; (US: autumn) automne m // vi (pt fell, pp fallen) tomber; ~**s** npl (waterfall) chute f d'eau, cascade f; **to** ~ **flat** vi (on one's face) tomber de tout son long, s'étaler; (joke) tomber à plat; (plan) échouer; **to** ~ **back** vi reculer, se retirer; **to** ~ **back on** vt fus se rabattre sur; **to** ~ **behind** vi prendre du retard; **to** ~ **down** vi (person) tomber; (building, hopes) s'effondrer, s'écrouler; **to** ~ **for** vt fus (trick) se laisser prendre à; (person) tomber amoureux de; **to** ~ **in** vi s'effondrer; (MIL) se mettre en rangs; **to** ~ **off** vi tomber; (diminish) baisser, diminuer; **to** ~ **out** vi (friends etc) se brouiller; **to** ~ **through** vi (plan, project) tomber à l'eau.

fallacy ['fæləsɪ] n erreur f, illusion f.

fallen ['fɔ:lən] pp of **fall**.

fallout ['fɔ:laʊt] n retombées (radioactives); ~ **shelter** n abri m anti-atomique.

fallow ['fæləʊ] a en jachère; en friche.

false [fɔ:ls] a faux(fausse); **under** ~ **pretences** sous un faux prétexte; ~ **teeth** npl (Brit) fausses dents.

falter ['fɔ:ltə*] vi chanceler, vaciller.

fame [feɪm] n renommée f, renom m.

familiar [fə'mɪlɪə*] a familier(ère); **to be** ~ **with** (subject) connaître; ~**ity** [fəmɪlɪ'ærɪtɪ] n familiarité f.

family ['fæmɪlɪ] n famille f.

famine ['fæmɪn] n famine f.

famished ['fæmɪʃt] a affamé(e).

famous ['feɪməs] a célèbre; ~**ly** ad (get on) fameusement, à merveille.

fan [fæn] n (folding) éventail m; (ELEC) ventilateur m; (person) fan m, admirateur/trice; supporter m/f // vt éventer; (fire, quarrel) attiser; **to** ~ **out** vi se déployer (en éventail).

fanatic [fə'nætɪk] n fanatique m/f.

fan belt n courroie f de ventilateur.

fanciful ['fænsɪfʊl] a fantaisiste.

fancy ['fænsɪ] n fantaisie f, envie f; imagination f // a (de) fantaisie inv // vt (feel like, want) avoir envie de; (imagine) imaginer; **to take a** ~ **to** se prendre d'affection pour; s'enticher de; ~ **dress** n déguisement m, travesti m; ~-**dress ball** n bal masqué or costumé.

fang [fæŋ] n croc m; (of snake) crochet m.

fantastic [fæn'tæstɪk] a fantastique.

fantasy ['fæntəsɪ] n imagination f, fantaisie f; fantasme m; chimère f.

far [fɑ:*] a: **the** ~ **side/end** l'autre côté/ bout // ad loin; ~ **away** au loin, dans le lointain; ~ **better** beaucoup mieux; ~ **from** loin de; **by** ~ de loin, de beaucoup; **go as** ~ **as the farm** allez jusqu'à la ferme; as ~ as I know pour autant que je sache; ~away *a* lointain(e).

farce [fɑ:s] *n* farce *f*.

farcical ['fɑ:sɪkəl] *a* grotesque.

fare [fɛə*] *n* (*on trains, buses*) prix *m* du billet; (*in taxi*) prix de la course; (*food*) table *f*, chère *f*; **half ~** demi-tarif; **full ~** plein tarif.

Far East *n*: the ~ l'Extrême-Orient *m*.

farewell [fɛə'wɛl] *excl, n* adieu *(m)*.

farm [fɑ:m] *n* ferme *f* // *vt* cultiver; **~er** *n* fermier/ère; cultivateur/trice; **~hand** *n* ouvrier/ère agricole; **~house** *n* (maison *f* de) ferme *f*; **~ing** *n* agriculture *f*; ~ **worker** *n* = **~hand**; **~yard** *n* cour *f* de ferme.

far-reaching ['fɑ:'ri:tʃɪŋ] *a* d'une grande portée.

fart [fɑ:t] (*col!*) *n* pet *m* // *vi* péter.

farther ['fɑ:ðə*] *ad* plus loin // *a* plus éloigné(e), plus lointain(e).

farthest ['fɑ:ðɪst] *superlative of* **far**.

fascinate ['fæsɪneɪt] *vt* fasciner; **fascinating** *a* fascinant(e).

fascism ['fæʃɪzəm] *n* fascisme *m*.

fashion ['fæʃən] *n* mode *f*; (*manner*) façon *f*, manière *f* // *vt* façonner; **in ~** à la mode; **out of ~** démodé(e); **~able** *a* à la mode; ~ **show** *n* défilé *m* de mannequins *or* de mode.

fast [fɑ:st] *a* rapide; (*clock*): **to be ~** avancer; (*dye, colour*) grand *or* bon teint *inv* // *ad* vite, rapidement; (*stuck, held*) solidement // *n* jeûne *m* // *vi* jeûner; ~ **asleep** profondément endormi.

fasten ['fɑ:sn] *vt* attacher, fixer; (*coat*) attacher, fermer // *vi* se fermer, s'attacher; **~er, ~ing** *n* fermeture *f*, attache *f*.

fast food *n* fast food *m*, restauration *f* rapide.

fastidious [fæs'tɪdɪəs] *a* exigeant(e), difficile.

fat [fæt] *a* gros(se) // *n* graisse *f*; (*on meat*) gras *m*.

fatal ['feɪtl] *a* mortel(le); fatal(e); désastreux(euse); **~ity** [fə'tælɪtɪ] *n* (*road death etc*) victime *f*, décès *m*.

fate [feɪt] *n* destin *m*; (*of person*) sort *m*; **~ful** *a* fatidique.

father ['fɑ:ðə*] *n* père *m*; **~-in-law** *n* beau-père *m*; **~ly** *a* paternel(le).

fathom ['fæðəm] *n* brasse *f* (= *1828 mm*) // *vt* (*mystery*) sonder, pénétrer.

fatigue [fə'ti:g] *n* fatigue *f*; (*MIL*) corvée *f*.

fatten ['fætn] *vt, vi* engraisser.

fatty ['fætɪ] *a* (*food*) gras(se) // *n* (*col*) gros/grosse.

fatuous ['fætjuəs] *a* stupide.

faucet ['fɔ:sɪt] *n* (*US*) robinet *m*.

fault [fɔ:lt] *n* faute *f*; (*defect*) défaut *m*; (*GEO*) faille *f* // *vt* trouver des défauts à, prendre en défaut; **it's my ~** c'est de ma faute; **to find ~ with** trouver à redire *or*

à critiquer à; **at ~** fautif(ive), coupable; **to a ~** à l'excès; **~less** *a* sans fautes; impeccable; irréprochable; **~y** *a* défectueux(euse).

fauna ['fɔ:nə] *n* faune *f*.

faux pas ['fəu'pɑ:] *n* impair *m*, bévue *f*, gaffe *f*.

favour, (*US*) **favor** ['feɪvə*] *n* faveur *f*; (*help*) service *m* // *vt* (*proposition*) être en faveur de; (*pupil etc*) favoriser; (*team, horse*) donner gagnant; **to do sb a ~** rendre un service à qn; **to find ~ with** trouver grâce aux yeux de; **in ~ of** en faveur de; **~able** *a* favorable; (*price*) avantageux(euse); **~ite** [-rɪt] *a, n* favori(te).

fawn [fɔ:n] *n* faon *m* // *a* (*also*: **~-coloured**) fauve // *vi*: **to ~ (up)on** flatter servilement.

fax [fæks] *n* (*document*) télécopie *f*; (*machine*) télécopieur *m*.

FBI *n abbr* (*US*: = *Federal Bureau of Investigation*) F.B.I. *m*.

fear [fɪə*] *n* crainte *f*, peur *f* // *vt* craindre; **for ~ of** de peur que + *sub or* de + *infinitive*; **~ful** *a* craintif(ive); (*sight, noise*) affreux(euse), épouvantable.

feasible ['fi:zəbl] *a* faisable, réalisable.

feast [fi:st] *n* festin *m*, banquet *m*; (*REL*: *also*: ~ **day**) fête *f* // *vi* festoyer.

feat [fi:t] *n* exploit *m*, prouesse *f*.

feather ['fɛðə*] *n* plume *f*.

feature ['fi:tʃə*] *n* caractéristique *f*; (*article*) chronique *f*, rubrique *f* // *vt* (*subj*: *film*) avoir pour vedette(s) // *vi* figurer (en bonne place); **~s** *npl* (*of face*) traits *mpl*; ~ **film** *n* film principal.

February ['fɛbruərɪ] *n* février *m*.

fed [fɛd] *pt, pp of* **feed**.

federal ['fɛdərəl] *a* fédéral(e).

fed-up [fɛd'ʌp] *a*: **to be ~** en avoir marre *or* plein le dos.

fee [fi:] *n* rémunération *f*; (*of doctor, lawyer*) honoraires *mpl*; (*of school, college etc*) frais *mpl* de scolarité; (*for examination*) droits *mpl*.

feeble ['fi:bl] *a* faible.

feed [fi:d] *n* (*of baby*) tétée *f*; (*of animal*) fourrage *m*; pâture *f*; (*on printer*) mécanisme *m* d'alimentation // *vt* (*pt, pp* **fed**) nourrir; (*Brit*: *baby*) allaiter; donner le biberon à; (*horse etc*) donner à manger à; (*machine*) alimenter; (*data, information*): **to ~ into** fournir à; **to ~ on** *vt fus* se nourrir de; **~back** *n* feed-back *m*; **~ing bottle** *n* (*Brit*) biberon *m*.

feel [fi:l] *n* sensation *f* // *vt* (*pt, pp* **felt**) toucher; tâter, palper; (*cold, pain*) sentir; (*grief, anger*) ressentir, éprouver; (*think, believe*): **to ~ (that)** trouver que; **to ~ hungry/cold** avoir faim/froid; **to ~ lonely/better** se sentir seul/mieux; **I don't ~ well** je ne me sens pas bien; **to ~ like** (*want*) avoir envie de; **to ~ about** *or* **around** *vi* fouiller, tâtonner; **~er** *n* (*of insect*) antenne *f*; **to put out ~ers** *or* **a ~er** tâter le terrain; **~ing** *n* sensation *f*, sentiment *m*.

feet [fiːt] *npl of* **foot**.

feign [feɪn] *vt* feindre, simuler.

fell [fel] *pt of* **fall** // *vt* (*tree*) abattre.

fellow ['fɛləu] *n* type *m*; compagnon *m*; (*of learned society*) membre *m* // *cpd*: ~ **countryman** *n* compatriote *m*; ~ **men** *npl* semblables *mpl*; **~ship** *n* association *f*; amitié *f*, camaraderie *f*; *sorte de bourse universitaire.*

felony ['fɛlənɪ] *n* crime *m*, forfait *m*.

felt [fɛlt] *pt*, *pp of* **feel** // *n* feutre *m*; **~-tip pen** *n* stylo-feutre *m*.

female ['fiːmeɪl] *n* (*ZOOL*) femelle *f*; (*pej*: *woman*) bonne femme // *a* (*BIOL*, *ELEC*) femelle; (*sex*, *character*) féminin(e); (*vote etc*) des femmes.

feminine ['fɛmɪnɪn] *a* féminin(e).

feminist ['fɛmɪnɪst] *n* féministe *m/f*.

fence [fɛns] *n* barrière *f*; (*col*: *person*) receleur/euse // *vt* (*also*: ~ **in**) clôturer // *vi* faire de l'escrime; **fencing** *n* escrime *m*.

fend [fɛnd] *vi*: **to ~ for o.s.** se débrouiller (tout seul); **to ~ off** *vt* (*attack etc*) parer.

fender ['fɛndə*] *n* garde-feu *m inv*; (*US*) garde-boue *m inv*; pare-chocs *m inv*.

ferment *vi* [fə'mɛnt] fermenter // *n* ['fəːmɛnt] agitation *f*, effervescence *f*.

fern [fəːn] *n* fougère *f*.

ferocious [fə'rəuʃəs] *a* féroce.

ferret ['fɛrɪt] *n* furet *m*.

ferry ['fɛrɪ] *n* (*small*) bac *m*; (*large*: *also*: **~boat**) ferry(-boat) *m* // *vt* transporter.

fertile ['fəːtaɪl] *a* fertile; (*BIOL*) fécond(e); **fertilizer** ['fəːtɪlaɪzə*] *n* engrais *m*.

fester ['fɛstə*] *vi* suppurer.

festival ['fɛstɪvəl] *n* (*REL*) fête *f*; (*ART*, *MUS*) festival *m*.

festive ['fɛstɪv] *a* de fête; **the ~ season** (*Brit*: *Christmas*) la période des fêtes.

festivities [fɛs'tɪvɪtɪz] *npl* réjouissances *fpl*.

festoon [fɛ'stuːn] *vt*: **to ~ with** orner de.

fetch [fɛtʃ] *vt* aller chercher; (*sell for*) se vendre.

fetching ['fɛtʃɪŋ] *a* charmant(e).

fête [feɪt] *n* fête *f*, kermesse *f*.

feud [fjuːd] *n* dispute *f*, dissension *f*.

feudal ['fjuːdl] *a* féodal(e).

fever ['fiːvə*] *n* fièvre *f*; **~ish** *a* fiévreux(euse), fébrile.

few [fjuː] *a* peu de; **they were ~** ils étaient peu (nombreux); **a ~** *a* quelques // *pronoun* quelques-uns; **~er** *a* moins de; moins (nombreux).

fiancé [fɪ'ãːŋseɪ] *n* fiancé *m*; **~e** *n* fiancée *f*.

fib [fɪb] *n* bobard *m*.

fibre, (*US***) fiber** ['faɪbə*] *n* fibre *f*; **~-glass** *n* fibre de verre.

fickle ['fɪkl] *a* inconstant(e), volage, capricieux(euse).

fiction ['fɪkʃən] *n* romans *mpl*, littérature *f* romanesque; fiction *f*; **~al** *a* fictif(ive).

fictitious [fɪk'tɪʃəs] *a* fictif(ive), imaginaire.

fiddle ['fɪdl] *n* (*MUS*) violon *m*; (*cheating*) combine *f*; escroquerie *f* // *vt* (*Brit*: *accounts*) falsifier, maquiller; **to ~ with** *vt fus* tripoter.

fidget ['fɪdʒɪt] *vi* se trémousser, remuer.

field [fiːld] *n* champ *m*; (*fig*) domaine *m*, champ; (*SPORT*: *ground*) terrain *m*; ~ **marshal** *n* maréchal *m*; **~work** *n* travaux *mpl* pratiques (sur le terrain).

fiend [fiːnd] *n* démon *m*.

fierce [fɪəs] *a* (*look*) féroce, sauvage; (*wind*, *attack*) (très) violent(e); (*fighting*, *enemy*) acharné(e).

fiery ['faɪərɪ] *a* ardent(e), brûlant(e); fougueux(euse).

fifteen [fɪf'tiːn] *num* quinze.

fifth [fɪfθ] *a*, *n* cinquième (*m*).

fifty ['fɪftɪ] *num* cinquante; **~-~** *a*: **a ~-~ chance** *etc* une chance *etc* sur deux // *ad* moitié-moitié.

fig [fɪg] *n* figue *f*.

fight [faɪt] *n* bagarre *f*; (*MIL*) combat *m*; (*against cancer etc*) lutte *f* // *vb* (*pt*, *pp* **fought**) *vt* se battre contre; (*cancer*, *alcoholism*) combattre, lutter contre // *vi* se battre; **~er** *n* lutteur *m* (*fig*); (*plane*) chasseur *m*; **~ing** *n* combats *mpl*.

figment ['fɪgmənt] *n*: **a ~ of the imagination** une invention.

figurative ['fɪgjurətɪv] *a* figuré(e).

figure ['fɪgə*] *n* (*DRAWING*, *GEOM*) figure *f*; (*number*, *cipher*) chiffre *m*; (*body*, *outline*) silhouette *f*, ligne *f*, formes *fpl* // *vt* (*US*) supposer // *vi* (*appear*) figurer; (*US*: *make sense*) s'expliquer; **to ~ out** *vt* arriver à comprendre; calculer; **~head** *n* (*NAUT*) figure *f* de proue; (*pej*) prête-nom *m*; ~ **of speech** *n* figure *f* de rhétorique.

file [faɪl] *n* (*tool*) lime *f*; (*dossier*) dossier *m*; (*folder*) dossier *m*, chemise *f*; (*with hinges*) classeur *m*; (*COMPUT*) fichier *m*; (*row*) file *f* // *vt* (*nails*, *wood*) limer; (*papers*) classer; (*LAW*: *claim*) faire enregistrer; déposer // *vi*: **to ~ in/out** entrer/sortir l'un derrière l'autre; **to ~ past** défiler devant.

filing ['faɪlɪŋ] *n* (travaux *mpl* de) classement *m*; ~ **cabinet** *n* classeur *m* (*meuble*).

fill [fɪl] *vt* remplir // *n*: **to eat one's ~** manger à sa faim; **to ~ in** *vt* (*hole*) boucher; (*form*) remplir; **to ~ up** *vt* remplir; ~ **it up, please** (AUT) le plein, s'il vous plaît.

fillet ['fɪlɪt] n filet m; ~ **steak** n filet m de bœuf, tournedos m.

filling ['fɪlɪŋ] n (CULIN) garniture f, farce f; (for tooth) plombage m; ~ **station** n station f d'essence.

film [fɪlm] n film m; (PHOT) pellicule f, film // vt (scene) filmer; ~ **star** n vedette f de cinéma; ~**strip** n (film m pour) projection f fixe.

filter ['fɪltə*] n filtre m // vt filtrer; ~ **lane** n (Brit AUT) voie f de sortie; ~**tipped** a à bout filtre.

filth [fɪlθ] n saleté f; ~**y** a sale, dé-goûtant(e); (language) ordurier(ère).

fin [fɪn] n (of fish) nageoire f.

final ['faɪnl] a final(e), dernier(ère); définitif(ive) // n (SPORT) finale f; ~**s** npl (SCOL) examens mpl de dernière année; ~**e** [fɪ'nɑːlɪ] n finale m; ~**ize** vt mettre au point; ~**ly** ad (lastly) en dernier lieu; (eventually) enfin, finalement.

finance [faɪ'næns] n finance f; ~**s** npl finances fpl // vt financer.

financial [faɪ'nænʃəl] a financier(ère).

find [faɪnd] vt (pt, pp found) trouver; (lost object) retrouver // n trouvaille f, découverte f; to ~ **sb guilty** (LAW) dé-clarer qn coupable; **to ~ out** vt se renseigner sur; (truth, secret) décou-vrir; (person) démasquer; **to ~ out about** se renseigner sur; (by chance) ap-prendre; ~**ings** npl (LAW) conclusions fpl, verdict m; (of report) constatations fpl.

fine [faɪn] a beau(belle); excellent(e); (thin, subtle) fin(e) // ad (well) très bien; (small) fin, finement // n (LAW) amende f; contravention f // vt (LAW) condamner à une amende; donner une contravention à; **to be ~** (weather) faire beau; ~ **arts** npl beaux-arts mpl.

finery ['faɪnərɪ] n parure f.

finger ['fɪŋgə*] n doigt m // vt palper, toucher; **little/index ~** auriculaire m/ index m; ~**nail** n ongle m (de la main); ~**print** n empreinte digitale; ~**tip** n bout m du doigt.

finicky ['fɪnɪkɪ] a tatillon(ne), méticu-leux(euse); minutieux(euse).

finish ['fɪnɪʃ] n fin f; (SPORT) arrivée f; (polish etc) finition f // vt finir, terminer // vi finir, se terminer; (session) s'achever; **to ~ doing sth** finir de faire qch; **to ~ third** arriver or terminer troisième; **to ~ off** vt finir, terminer; (kill) achever; **to ~ up** vi, vt finir; ~**ing line** n ligne f d'arrivée; ~**ing school** n institution privée (pour jeunes filles).

finite ['faɪnaɪt] a fini(e); (verb) conjugué(e).

Finland ['fɪnlənd] n Finlande f.

Finn [fɪn] n Finnois/e; Finlandais/e;

~**ish** a finnois(e); finlandais(e) // n (LING) finnois m.

fir [fəː*] n sapin m.

fire ['faɪə*] n feu m; incendie m // vt (discharge): **to ~ a gun** tirer un coup de feu; (fig) enflammer, animer; (dismiss) mettre à la porte, renvoyer // vi tirer, faire feu; **on ~** en feu; ~ **alarm** n avertisseur m d'incendie; ~**arm** n arme f à feu; ~ **brigade**, (US) ~ **department** n (régiment m de sapeurs-)pompiers mpl; ~ **engine** n pompe f à incendie; ~ **escape** n es-calier m de secours; ~ **extinguisher** n extincteur m; ~**man** n pompier m; ~**place** n cheminée f; ~**side** n foyer m, coin m du feu; ~ **station** n ca-serne f de pompiers; ~**wood** n bois m de chauffage; ~**work** n feu m d'artifice; ~**works** npl (display) feu(x) d'artifice.

firing ['faɪərɪŋ] n (MIL) feu m, tir m; ~ **squad** n peloton m d'exécution.

firm [fəːm] a ferme // n compagnie f, firme f; ~**ly** ad fermement.

first [fəːst] a premier(ère) // ad (before others) le premier, la première; (before other things) en premier, d'abord; (when listing reasons etc) en premier lieu, premièrement // n (person: in race) premier/ère; (SCOL) mention f très bien; (AUT) première f; **at ~** au commencement, au début; ~ **of all** tout d'abord, pour commencer; ~ **aid** n premiers secours or soins; ~**-aid kit** n trousse f à pharmacie; ~**-class** a de première classe; ~**-hand** a de première main; ~ **lady** n (US) femme f du président; ~**ly** ad premièrement, en premier lieu; ~ **name** n prénom m; ~**-rate** a excellent(e).

fish [fɪʃ] n (pl inv) poisson m; poissons mpl // vt, vi pêcher; **to go ~ing** aller à la pêche; ~**erman** n pêcheur m; ~ **farm** n établissement m piscicole; ~ **fingers** npl (Brit) bâtonnets de poisson (congelés); ~**ing boat** n barque f de pêche; ~**ing line** n ligne f (de pêche); ~**ing rod** n canne f à pêche; ~**monger** n marchand de poisson; ~**monger's (shop)** n poissonnerie f; ~ **sticks** npl (US) = ~ **fingers**; ~**y** a (fig) suspect(e), louche.

fist [fɪst] n poing m.

fit [fɪt] a (MED, SPORT) en (bonne) forme; (proper) convenable; appro-prié(e) // vt (subj: clothes) aller à; (adjust) ajuster; (put in, attach) installer, poser; adapter; (equip) équiper, garnir, munir // vi (clothes) aller; (parts) s'adapter; (in space, gap) entrer, s'adapter // n (MED) accès m, crise f; (of coughing) quinte f; ~ **to** en état de; ~ **for** digne de; apte à; **a ~ of anger** un accès de colère; **this dress is a tight/good ~** cette robe est un peu juste/

(me) va très bien; **by ~s and starts** par à-coups; **to ~ in** vi s'accorder; s'adapter; **to ~ out** (Brit: also: **~ up**) vt équiper; **~ful** a intermittent(e); **~ment** n meuble encastré, élément m; **~ness** n (MED) forme f physique; (of remark) à-propos m, justesse f; **~ted carpet** n moquette f; **~ted kitchen** n cuisine équipée; **~ter** n monteur m; (DRESSMAKING) essayeur/euse; **~ting** a approprié(e) // n (of dress) essayage m; (of piece of equipment) pose f, installation f; **~ting room** n cabine f d'essayage; **~tings** npl installations fpl.

five [faɪv] num cinq; **~r** n (col: Brit) billet m de cinq livres; (: US) billet de cinq dollars.

fix [fɪks] vt fixer; arranger; (mend) réparer // n: **to be in a ~** être dans le pétrin; **to ~ up** vt (meeting) arranger; **to ~ sb up with** faire avoir qch à qn; **~ation** [-'eɪʃən] n (PSYCH) fixation f; (fig) obsession f; **~ed** [fɪkst] a (prices etc) fixe; **~ture** ['fɪkstʃə*] n installation f (fixe); (SPORT) rencontre f (au programme).

fizz [fɪz] vi pétiller.

fizzle ['fɪzl] vi pétiller; **to ~ out** vi rater.

fizzy ['fɪzɪ] a pétillant(e); gazeux(euse).

flabbergasted ['flæbəga:stɪd] a sidéré(e), ahuri(e).

flabby ['flæbɪ] a mou(molle).

flag [flæg] n drapeau m; (also: **~stone**) dalle f // vi faiblir; fléchir; **to ~ down** vt héler, faire signe (de s'arrêter) à.

flagpole ['flægpəul] n mât m.

flair [flɛə*] n flair m.

flak [flæk] n (MIL) tir antiaérien; (col: criticism) critiques fpl.

flake [fleɪk] n (of rust, paint) écaille f; (of snow, soap powder) flocon m // vi (also: **~ off**) s'écailler.

flamboyant [flæm'bɔɪənt] a flamboyant(e), éclatant(e); (person) haut(e) en couleur.

flame [fleɪm] n flamme f.

flamingo [flə'mɪŋgəu] n flamant m (rose).

flammable ['flæməbl] a inflammable.

flan [flæn] n (Brit) tarte f.

flank [flæŋk] n flanc m // vt flanquer.

flannel ['flænl] n (Brit: also: **face ~**) gant m de toilette; (fabric) flanelle f; **~s** npl pantalon m de flanelle.

flap [flæp] n (of pocket, envelope) rabat m // vt (wings) battre (de) // vi (sail, flag) claquer; (col: also: **be in a ~**) paniquer.

flare [flɛə*] n fusée éclairante; (in skirt etc) évasement m; **to ~ up** vi s'embraser; (fig: person) se mettre en colère, s'emporter; (: revolt) éclater.

flash [flæʃ] n éclair m; (also: **news ~**) flash m (d'information); (PHOT) flash //

vt (switch on) allumer (brièvement); (send: message) câbler // vi briller; jeter des éclairs; (light on ambulance etc) clignoter; **in a ~** en un clin d'œil; **to ~ one's headlights** faire un appel de phares; **he ~ed by** or **past** il passa (devant nous) comme un éclair; **~bulb** n ampoule f de flash; **~cube** n cubeflash m; **~light** n lampe f de poche.

flashy ['flæʃɪ] a (pej) tape-à-l'œil inv, tapageur(euse).

flask [fla:sk] n flacon m, bouteille f; (also: **vacuum ~**) bouteille f thermos ®.

flat [flæt] a plat(e); (tyre) dégonflé(e), à plat; (denial) catégorique; (MUS) bémolisé(e); (: voice) faux(fausse) // n (Brit: apartment) appartement m; (AUT) crevaison f; (MUS) bémol m; **to work ~ out** travailler d'arrache-pied; **~ly** ad catégoriquement; **~ten** vt (also: **~ten out**) aplatir.

flatter ['flætə*] vt flatter; **~ing** a flatteur(euse); **~y** n flatterie f.

flaunt [flɔ:nt] vt faire étalage de.

flavour, (US) **flavor** ['fleɪvə*] n goût m, saveur f; (of ice cream etc) parfum m // vt parfumer; **vanilla-~ed** à l'arôme de vanille, vanillé(e); **~ing** n arôme m (synthétique).

flaw [flɔ:] n défaut m.

flax [flæks] n lin m; **~en** a blond(e).

flea [fli:] n puce f.

fleck [flɛk] n tacheture f; moucheture f.

flee, pt, pp **fled** [fli:, flɛd] vt fuir, s'enfuir de // vi fuir, s'enfuir.

fleece [fli:s] n toison f // vt (col) voler, filouter.

fleet [fli:t] n flotte f; (of lorries etc) parc m, convoi m.

fleeting ['fli:tɪŋ] a fugace, fugitif(ive); (visit) très bref(brève).

Flemish ['flɛmɪʃ] a flamand(e).

flesh [flɛʃ] n chair f; **~ wound** n blessure superficielle.

flew [flu:] pt of **fly**.

flex [flɛks] n fil m or câble m électrique (souple) // vt fléchir; (muscles) tendre; **~ible** a flexible.

flick [flɪk] n petite tape; chiquenaude f; sursaut m; **to ~ through** vt fus feuilleter.

flicker ['flɪkə*] vi vaciller.

flier ['flaɪə*] n aviateur m.

flight [flaɪt] n vol m; (escape) fuite f; (also: **~ of steps**) escalier m; **~ attendant** n (US) steward m, hôtesse f de l'air; **~ deck** n (AVIAT) poste m de pilotage; (NAUT) pont m d'envol.

flimsy ['flɪmzɪ] a (partition, fabric) peu solide, mince; (excuse) pauvre, mince.

flinch [flɪntʃ] vi tressaillir; **to ~ from** se dérober à, reculer devant.

fling [flɪŋ], pt, pp **flung** vt jeter, lancer.

flint [flɪnt] n silex m; (in lighter) pierre f (à briquet).

flip [flɪp] n chiquenaude f.

flippant ['flɪpənt] a désinvolte, irré-vérencieux(euse).

flipper ['flɪpə*] n (of seal etc) nageoire f; (for swimming) palme f.

flirt [flə:t] vi flirter // n flirteuse f.

flit [flɪt] vi voleter.

float [fləut] n flotteur m; (in procession) char m; (money) réserve f // vi flotter // vt faire flotter; (loan, business) lancer.

flock [flɔk] n troupeau m; (of people) foule f.

flog [flɔg] vt fouetter.

flood [flʌd] n inondation f; (of words, tears etc) flot m, torrent m // vt inonder; **~ing** n inondation f; **~light** n projecteur m // vt éclairer aux projecteurs, illuminer.

floor [flɔ:*] n sol m; (storey) étage m; (fig: at meeting): the ~ l'assemblée f, les membres mpl de l'assemblée // vt terrasser; **on the ~** par terre; **ground ~**, (US) **first ~** rez-de-chaussée m; **first ~**, (US) **second ~** premier étage; **~board** n planche f (du plancher); **~ show** n spectacle m de variétés.

flop [flɔp] n fiasco m.

floppy ['flɔpɪ] a lâche, flottant(e); **~ (disk)** n (COMPUT) disquette f.

flora ['flɔ:rə] n flore f.

florid ['flɔrɪd] a (complexion) fleuri(e); (style) plein(e) de fioritures.

florist ['flɔrɪst] n fleuriste m/f.

flounce [flauns] n volant m.

flounder ['flaundə*] vi patauger // n (ZOOL) flet m.

flour ['flauə*] n farine f.

flourish ['flʌrɪʃ] vi prospérer // n fioriture f; (of trumpets) fanfare f.

flout [flaut] vt se moquer de, faire fi de.

flow [fləu] n flot m; courant m; circulation f; (tide) flux m // vi couler; (traffic) s'écouler; (robes, hair) flotter; **~ chart** n organigramme m.

flower ['flauə*] n fleur f // vi fleurir; **~ bed** n plate-bande f; **~pot** n pot m (à fleurs); **~y** a fleuri(e).

flown [fləun] pp of **fly**.

flu [flu:] n grippe f.

fluctuate ['flʌktjueɪt] vi varier, fluctuer.

fluency ['flu:ənsɪ] n facilité f.

fluent ['flu:ənt] a (speech) coulant(e), aisé(e); **he speaks ~ French** il parle le français couramment.

fluff [flʌf] n duvet m; peluche f; **~y** a duveteux(euse); pelucheux(euse).

fluid ['flu:ɪd] a, n fluide (m).

fluke [flu:k] n (col: luck) coup m de veine.

flung [flʌŋ] pt, pp of **fling**.

fluoride ['fluəraɪd] n fluor m.

flurry ['flʌrɪ] n (of snow) rafale f, bourrasque f; **~ of activity/excitement** affairement m/excitation f soudain(e).

flush [flʌʃ] n rougeur f; excitation f; (fig: of youth, beauty etc) éclat m // vt nettoyer à grande eau // vi rougir // a: **~ with** au ras de, de niveau avec; **to ~ the toilet** tirer la chasse (d'eau); **to ~ out** vt débusquer; **~ed** a (tout(e)) rouge.

flustered ['flʌstəd] a énervé(e).

flute [flu:t] n flûte f.

flutter ['flʌtə*] n agitation f; (of wings) battement m // vi battre des ailes, voleter.

flux [flʌks] n: **in a state of ~** fluctuant sans cesse.

fly [flaɪ] n (insect) mouche f; (on trousers: also: **flies**) braguette f // vb (pt flew, pp flown) vt piloter; (passengers, cargo) transporter (par avion); (distances) parcourir // vi voler; (passengers) aller en avion; (escape) s'enfuir, fuir; (flag) se déployer; **to ~ away** or **off** vi (bird, insect) s'envoler; **~ing** n (activity) aviation f // a: **~ing visit** visite f éclair inv; **with ~ing colours** haut la main; **~ing saucer** n soucoupe volante; **~ing start** n: **to get off to a ~ing start** faire un excellent départ; **~over** n (Brit: bridge) saut-de-mouton m; **~sheet** n (for tent) double toit m.

foal [fəul] n poulain m.

foam [fəum] n écume f; (on beer) mousse f; (also: **plastic ~**) mousse cellulaire or de plastique // vi écumer; (soapy water) mousser; **~ rubber** n caoutchouc m mousse.

fob [fɔb] vt: **to ~ sb off with** refiler à qn; se débarrasser de qn avec.

focus ['fəukəs] n (pl: ~es) foyer m; (of interest) centre m // vt (field glasses etc) mettre au point // vi: **to ~ (on)** (with camera) régler la mise au point (sur); (person) fixer son regard (sur); **in ~** au point; **out of ~** pas au point.

fodder ['fɔdə*] n fourrage m.

foe [fəu] n ennemi m.

fog [fɔg] n brouillard m; **~gy** a: it's **~gy** il y a du brouillard; **~lamp** n (AUT) phare m anti-brouillard.

foil [fɔɪl] vt déjouer, contrecarrer // n feuille f de métal; (kitchen ~) papier m d'alu(minium); (FENCING) fleuret m.

fold [fəuld] n (bend, crease) pli m; (AGR) parc m à moutons; (fig) bercail m // vt plier; **to ~ up** vi (business) fermer boutique // vt (map etc) plier, re-plier; **~er** n (for papers) chemise f; classeur m; (brochure) dépliant m; **~ing** a (chair, bed) pliant(e).

foliage ['fəulɪɪdʒ] n feuillage m.

folk [fəuk] npl gens mpl // a folklorique; **~s** npl famille f, parents mpl; **~lore** ['fəuklɔ:*] n folklore m; **~ song** n chanson f folklorique.

follow ['fɔləu] vt suivre // vi suivre; (result) s'ensuivre; **he ~ed suit** il fit de même; **to ~ up** vt (victory) tirer parti de; (letter, offer) donner suite à; (case)

suivre; **~er** n disciple m/f, partisan/e;
~ing a suivant(e) // n partisans mpl,
disciples mpl.

folly ['fɒlɪ] n inconscience f; sottise f.

fond [fɒnd] a (memory, look) tendre,
affectueux(euse); **to be ~ of** aimer
beaucoup.

fondle ['fɒndl] vt caresser.

food [fuːd] n nourriture f; **~ mixer** n
mixeur m; **~ poisoning** n intoxication f
alimentaire; **~ processor** n robot m de
cuisine; **~stuffs** npl denrées fpl
alimentaires.

fool [fuːl] n idiot/e; (HISTORY: of king)
bouffon m, fou m; (CULIN) purée f de
fruits à la crème // vt berner, duper // vi
(also: **~ around**) faire l'idiot or
l'imbécile; **~hardy** a téméraire, im-
prudent(e); **~ish** a idiot(e), stupide; im-
prudent(e); écervelé(e); **~proof** a
(plan etc) infaillible.

foot [fut] n (pl: feet) pied m; (measure)
pied (= 304 mm; 12 inches); (of animal)
patte f // vt (bill) casquer, payer; **on ~** à
pied; **~age** n (CINEMA: length) ≈ métrage m; (: material) séquences fpl;
~ball n ballon m (de football); (sport:
Brit) football m; (: US) football
américain; **~baller** (Brit) = **~ball
player**; **~ball ground** n terrain m de
football; **~ball player** n joueur m de
football; **~brake** n frein m à pied;
~bridge n passerelle f; **~hills** npl
contreforts mpl; **~hold** n prise f (de
pied); **~ing** n (fig) position f; **to lose
one's ~ing** perdre pied; **~lights** npl
rampe f; **~man** n laquais m; **~note** n
note f (en bas de page); **~path** n
sentier m; (in street) trottoir m; **~print**
n trace f (de pied); **~step** n pas m;
~wear n chaussure(s) f(pl).

for [fɔː*] ♦ prep **1** (indicating destination, intention, purpose) pour; **the train
~ London** le train pour or (à destination)
de Londres; **he went ~ the paper** il est
allé chercher le journal; **it's time ~
lunch** c'est l'heure du déjeuner; **what's it
~?** ça sert à quoi?; **what ~?** (why)
pourquoi?
2 (on behalf of, representing) pour; **the
MP ~ Hove** le député de Hove; **to work
~ sb/sth** travailler pour qn/qch; **G ~
George** G comme Georges
3 (because of) pour; **~ this reason** pour
cette raison; **~ fear of being criticized**
de peur d'être critiqué
4 (with regard to) pour; **it's cold ~ July**
il fait froid pour juillet; **a gift ~ languages** un don pour les langues
5 (in exchange for): **I sold it ~ £5** je l'ai
vendu 5 livres; **to pay 50 pence ~ a ticket** payer 50 pence un billet
6 (in favour of) pour; **are you ~ or
against us?** êtes-vous pour ou contre
nous?

7 (referring to distance) pendant, sur;
there are roadworks ~ 5 km il y a des
travaux sur or pendant 5 km; **we walked
~ miles** nous avons marché pendant des
kilomètres
8 (referring to time) pendant; depuis;
pour; **he was away ~ 2 years** il a été
absent pendant 2 ans; **she will be away
~ a month** elle sera absente (pendant)
un mois; **I have known her ~ years** je la
connais depuis des années; **can you do it
~ tomorrow?** est-ce que tu peux le faire
pour demain?
9 (with infinitive clauses): **it is not ~
me to decide** ce n'est pas à moi de
décider; **it would be best ~ you to leave**
le mieux serait que vous partiez; **there is
still time ~ you to do it** vous avez encore
le temps de le faire; **~ this to be possible ...** pour que cela soit possible ...
10 (in spite of): **~ all his work/efforts**
malgré tout son travail/tous ses efforts;
**~ all his complaints, he's very fond of
her** il a beau se plaindre, il l'aime
beaucoup
♦ cj (since, as: rather formal) car.

forage ['fɒrɪdʒ] n fourrage m.

foray ['fɒreɪ] n incursion f.

forbid [fə'bɪd], pt **forbad(e)** [fə'bæd,
-'beɪd, -'bɪd] vt défendre,
interdire; **to ~ sb to do** défendre or
interdire à qn de faire; **~den** a dé-
fendu(e); **~ding** a d'aspect or d'allure
sévère or sombre.

force [fɔːs] n force f // vt forcer; **the F~s**
npl (Brit) l'armée f; **in ~** en force; **to
come into ~** entrer en vigueur; **~feed**
vt nourrir de force; **~ful** a énergique,
volontaire.

forcibly ['fɔːsəblɪ] ad par la force, de
force; (vigorously) énergiquement.

ford [fɔːd] n gué m.

fore [fɔː*] n: **to the ~** en évidence.

forearm ['fɔːrɑːm] n avant-bras m inv.

foreboding [fɔː'bəudɪŋ] n pressentiment
m (néfaste).

forecast ['fɔːkɑːst] n prévision f // vt
(irg: like cast) prévoir.

forecourt ['fɔːkɔːt] n (of garage) devant
m.

forefathers ['fɔːfɑːðəz] npl ancêtres
mpl.

forefinger ['fɔːfɪŋgə*] n index m.

forefront ['fɔːfrʌnt] n: **in the ~ of** au
premier rang or plan de.

forego vt = **forgo**.

foregone ['fɔːgɒn] a: **it's a ~ conclusion**
c'est à prévoir, c'est couru d'avance.

foreground ['fɔːgraund] n premier plan.

forehead ['fɔrɪd] n front m.

foreign ['fɒrɪn] a étranger(ère); (trade)
extérieur(e); **~er** n étranger/ère; **~
secretary** n (Brit) ministre m des
Affaires étrangères; **F~ Office** n (Brit)
ministère m des Affaires étrangères.

foreleg ['fɔːlɛg] n patte f de devant; jambe antérieure.

foreman ['fɔːmən] n contremaître m.

foremost ['fɔːməust] a le(la) plus en vue; premier(ère) // ad: **first and ~** avant tout, tout d'abord.

forensic [fə'rɛnsɪk] a: ~ **medicine** médecine légale.

forerunner ['fɔːrʌnə*] n précurseur m.

foresee, pt **foresaw**, pp **foreseen** [fɔː'siː, -'sɔː, -'siːn] vt prévoir; **~able** a prévisible.

foreshadow [fɔː'ʃædəu] vt présager, annoncer, laisser prévoir.

foresight ['fɔːsaɪt] n prévoyance f.

forest ['fɔrɪst] n forêt f.

forestall [fɔː'stɔːl] vt devancer.

forestry ['fɔrɪstrɪ] n sylviculture f.

foretaste ['fɔːteɪst] n avant-goût m.

foretell, pt, pp **foretold** [fɔː'tɛl, -'təuld] vt prédire.

forever [fə'rɛvə*] ad pour toujours; (fig) continuellement.

foreword ['fɔːwəːd] n avant-propos m inv.

forfeit ['fɔːfɪt] n prix m, rançon f // vt perdre; (one's life, health) payer de.

forgave [fə'geɪv] pt of **forgive**.

forge [fɔːdʒ] n forge f // vt (signature) contrefaire; (wrought iron) forger; **to ~ documents** fabriquer de faux papiers; **to ~ money** (Brit) fabriquer de la fausse monnaie; **to ~ ahead** vi pousser de l'avant, prendre de l'avance; **~r** n faussaire m; **~ry** n faux m, contrefaçon f.

forget [fə'gɛt], pt **forgot**, pp **forgotten** vt, vi oublier; **~ful** a distrait(e), étourdi(e); **~ful of** oublieux(euse) de; **~-me-not** n myosotis m.

forgive [fə'gɪv], pt **forgave**, pp **forgiven** vt pardonner; **to ~ sb for sth** pardonner qch à qn; **~ness** n pardon m.

forgo [fɔː'gəu], pt **forwent**, pp **forgone** vt renoncer à.

forgot [fə'gɔt] pt of **forget**.

forgotten [fə'gɔtn] pp of **forget**.

fork [fɔːk] n (for eating) fourchette f; (for gardening) fourche f; (of roads) bifurcation f; (of railways) embranchement m // vi (road) bifurquer; **to ~ out** (col: pay) vt allonger, se fendre de // vi casquer; **~-lift truck** n chariot élévateur.

forlorn [fə'lɔːn] a (person) abandonné(e); (place) désert(e); (attempt, hope) désespéré(e).

form [fɔːm] n forme f; (SCOL) classe f; (questionnaire) formulaire m // vt former; **in top ~** en pleine forme.

formal ['fɔːməl] a (offer, receipt) en bonne et due forme; (person) cérémonieux(euse); (dinner) officiel(le); (ART, PHILOSOPHY) formel(le); **~ly** ad officiellement; formellement; cérémo-

nieusement.

format ['fɔːmæt] n format m // vt (COMPUT) formater.

formation [fɔː'meɪʃən] n formation f.

formative ['fɔːmətɪv] a: ~ **years** années fpl d'apprentissage (fig) or de formation.

former ['fɔːmə*] a ancien(ne) (before n), précédent(e); **the ~ ... the latter** le premier ... le second, celui-là ... celui-ci; **~ly** ad autrefois.

formidable ['fɔːmɪdəbl] a redoutable.

formula ['fɔːmjulə] n formule f.

forsake, pt **forsook**, pp **forsaken** [fə'seɪk, -'suk, -'seɪkən] vt abandonner.

fort [fɔːt] n fort m.

forte ['fɔːtɪ] n (point) fort m.

forth [fɔːθ] ad en avant; **to go back and ~** aller et venir; **and so ~** et ainsi de suite; **~coming** a qui va paraître or avoir lieu prochainement; (character) ouvert(e), communicatif(ive); **~right** a franc(franche), direct(e); **~with** ad sur le champ.

fortify ['fɔːtɪfaɪ] vt fortifier; **fortified wine** n vin liquoreux or de liqueur.

fortnight ['fɔːtnaɪt] n quinzaine f, quinze jours mpl; **~ly** a bimensuel(le) // ad tous les quinze jours.

fortunate ['fɔːtʃənɪt] a: **it is ~ that** c'est une chance que; **~ly** ad heureusement.

fortune ['fɔːtʃən] n chance f; (wealth) fortune f; **~teller** n diseuse f de bonne aventure.

forty ['fɔːtɪ] num quarante.

forward ['fɔːwəd] a (ahead of schedule) en avance; (movement, position) en avant, vers l'avant; (not shy) ouvert(e); direct(e); effronté(e) // n (SPORT) avant m // vt (letter) faire suivre; (parcel, goods) expédier; (fig) promouvoir, contribuer au développement or à l'avancement de; **to move ~** avancer; **~(s)** ad en avant.

forwent [fɔː'wɛnt] pt of **forgo**.

fossil ['fɔsl] a, n fossile (m).

foster ['fɔstə*] vt encourager, favoriser; ~ **child** n enfant adopté; ~ **mother** n mère adoptive; mère nourricière.

fought [fɔːt] pt, pp of **fight**.

foul [faul] a (weather, smell, food) infect(e); (language) ordurier(ère); (deed) infâme // n (FOOTBALL) faute f // vt salir, encrasser; (football player) commettre une faute sur.

found [faund] pt, pp of **find** // vt (establish) fonder; **~ation** [-'deɪʃən] n (act) fondation f; (base) fondement m; (also: ~ation cream) fond m de teint; **~ations** npl (of building) fondations fpl.

founder ['faundə*] n fondateur m // vi couler, sombrer.

foundry ['faundrɪ] n fonderie f.

fount [faunt] n source f.

fountain ['fauntɪn] n fontaine f; ~ **pen** n stylo m (à encre).

four [fɔ:*] *num* quatre; **on all** ~s à quatre pattes; **~-poster** *n* (*also*: ~-poster bed) lit *m* à baldaquin; **~some** ['fɔ:səm] *n* partie *f* à quatre; sortie *f* à quatre; **~teen** *num* quatorze; **~th** *num* quatrième.

fowl [faul] *n* volaille *f*.

fox [fɔks] *n* renard *m* // *vt* mystifier.

foyer ['fɔɪeɪ] *n* vestibule *m*; (*THEATRE*) foyer *m*.

fraction ['frækʃən] *n* fraction *f*.

fracture ['fræktʃə*] *n* fracture *f*.

fragile ['frædʒaɪl] *a* fragile.

fragment ['frægmənt] *n* fragment *m*.

fragrant ['freɪgrənt] *a* parfumé(e), odorant(e).

frail [freɪl] *a* fragile, délicat(e).

frame [freɪm] *n* charpente *f*; (*of picture*) cadre *m*; (*of door, window*) encadrement *m*, chambranle *m*; (*of spectacles: also*: ~s) monture *f* // *vt* encadrer; ~ **of mind** *n* disposition *f* d'esprit; **~work** *n* structure *f*.

France [frɑ:ns] *n* France *f*.

franchise ['fræntʃaɪz] *n* (*POL*) droit *m* de vote; (*COMM*) franchise *f*.

frank [fræŋk] *a* franc(franche) // *vt* (*letter*) affranchir; **~ly** *ad* franchement.

frantic ['fræntɪk] *a* frénétique.

fraternity [frə'tɜ:nɪtɪ] *n* (*club*) communauté *f*, confrérie *f*; (*spirit*) fraternité *f*.

fraud [frɔ:d] *n* supercherie *f*, fraude *f*, tromperie *f*; imposteur *m*.

fraught [frɔ:t] *a*: ~ **with** chargé(e) de, plein(e) de.

fray [freɪ] *n* bagarre *f* // *vi* s'effilocher; **tempers were ~ed** les gens commençaient à s'énerver.

freak [fri:k] *n* (*also cpd*) phénomène *m*, créature ou événement exceptionnel par sa rareté, son caractère d'anomalie.

freckle ['frɛkl] *n* tache *f* de rousseur.

free [fri:] *a* libre; (*gratis*) gratuit(e); (*liberal*) généreux(euse), large // *vt* (*prisoner etc*) libérer; (*jammed object or person*) dégager, for ~ *ad* gratuitement; **~dom** ['fri:dəm] *n* liberté *f*; **~-for-all** *n* mêlée générale; **~ gift** *n* prime *f*; **~hold** *n* propriété foncière libre; ~ **kick** *n* coup franc; **~lance** *a* indépendant(e); **~ly** *ad* librement; (*liberally*) libéralement; **~mason** *n* franc-maçon *m*; **~post** *n* franchise postale; **~-range** *a* (*hen, eggs*) de ferme; **~ trade** *n* libre-échange *m*; **~way** *n* (*US*) autoroute *f*; **~wheel** *vi* descendre en roue libre; **~ will** *n* libre arbitre *m*; **of one's own ~ will** de son plein gré.

freeze [fri:z] *vb* (*pt* **froze**, *pp* **frozen**) *vi* geler // *vt* geler; (*food*) congeler; (*prices, salaries*) bloquer, geler // *n* gel *m*; blocage *m*; **~-dried** *a* lyophilisé(e); **~r** *n* congélateur *m*.

freezing ['fri:zɪŋ] *a*: ~ **cold** *a* glacial(e);

~ **point** *n* point *m* de congélation; **3 degrees below** ~ 3 degrés au-dessous de zéro.

freight [freɪt] *n* (*goods*) fret *m*, cargaison *f*; (*money charged*) fret, prix *m* du transport; ~ **train** *n* (*US*) train *m* de marchandises.

French [frɛntʃ] *a* français(e) // *n* (*LING*) français *m*; **the** ~ *npl* les Français; ~ **bean** *n* haricot vert; ~ **fried potatoes**, (*US*) ~ **fries** *npl* (pommes de terre *fpl*) frites *fpl*; **~man** *n* Français *m*; ~ **window** *n* porte-fenêtre *f*; **~woman** *n* Française *f*.

frenzy ['frɛnzɪ] *n* frénésie *f*.

frequent *a* ['fri:kwənt] fréquent(e) // *vt* [frɪ'kwɛnt] fréquenter; **~ly** *ad* fréquemment.

fresh [frɛʃ] *a* frais(fraîche); (*new*) nouveau(nouvelle); (*cheeky*) familier(ère), culotté(e); **~en** *vi* (*wind, air*) fraîchir; **to ~en up** *vi* faire un brin de toilette; **~er** *n* (*Brit SCOL: col*) bizuth *m*, étudiant/e de 1ère année; **~ly** *ad* nouvellement, récemment; **~man** *n* (*US*) = **~er**; **~ness** *n* fraîcheur *f*; **~water** *a* (*fish*) d'eau douce.

fret [frɛt] *vi* s'agiter, se tracasser.

friar ['fraɪə*] *n* moine *m*, frère *m*.

friction ['frɪkʃən] *n* friction *f*.

Friday ['fraɪdɪ] *n* vendredi *m*.

fridge [frɪdʒ] *n* (*Brit*) frigo *m*, frigidaire *m* ®.

fried [fraɪd] *pt, pp* of **fry** // *a* frit(e); ~ **egg** œuf *m* sur le plat.

friend [frɛnd] *n* ami/e; **~ly** *a* amical(e); gentil(le); **~ship** *n* amitié *f*.

frieze [fri:z] *n* frise *f*, bordure *f*.

fright [fraɪt] *n* peur *f*, effroi *m*; **to take** ~ prendre peur, s'effrayer; **~en** *vt* effrayer, faire peur à; **~ened** *a*: **to be ~ened (of)** avoir peur (de); **~ening** *a* effrayant(e); **~ful** *a* affreux(euse).

frigid ['frɪdʒɪd] *a* (*woman*) frigide.

frill [frɪl] *n* (*of dress*) volant *m*; (*of shirt*) jabot *m*.

fringe [frɪndʒ] *n* frange *f*; (*edge: of forest etc*) bordure *f*; (*fig*): **on the** ~ en marge; ~ **benefits** *npl* avantages sociaux ou en nature.

frisk [frɪsk] *vt* fouiller.

frisky ['frɪskɪ] *a* vif(vive), sémillant(e).

fritter ['frɪtə*] *n* beignet *m*; **to ~ away** *vt* gaspiller.

frivolous ['frɪvələs] *a* frivole.

frizzy ['frɪzɪ] *a* crépu(e).

fro [frəu] *see* **to**.

frock [frɔk] *n* robe *f*.

frog [frɔg] *n* grenouille *f*; **~man** *n* homme-grenouille *m*.

frolic ['frɔlɪk] *vi* folâtrer, batifoler.

from [frɔm] *prep* **1** (*indicating starting place, origin etc*) de; **where do you come** ~?, **where are you** ~? d'où venez-vous?; ~ **London to Paris** de Londres à Paris; **a**

letter ~ my sister une lettre de ma sœur; **to drink ~ the bottle** boire à (même) la bouteille
2 (*indicating time*) (à partir) de; **~ one o'clock to** *or* **until** *or* **till two** de une heure à deux heures; **~ January (on)** à partir de janvier
3 (*indicating distance*) de; **the hotel is one kilometre ~ the beach** l'hôtel est à un kilomètre de la plage
4 (*indicating price, number etc*) de; **the interest rate was increased ~ 9% to 10%** le taux d'intérêt a augmenté de 9 à 10%
5 (*indicating difference*) de; **he can't tell red ~ green** il ne peut pas distinguer le rouge du vert
6 (*because of, on the basis of*): **~ what he says** d'après ce qu'il dit; **weak ~ hunger** affaibli par la faim.

front [frʌnt] *n* (*of house, dress*) devant *m*; (*of coach, train*) avant *m*; (*of book*) couverture *f*; (*promenade: also*: **sea ~**) bord *m* de mer; (MIL, POL, METEOROLOGY) front *m*; (*fig: appearances*) contenance *f*, façade *f* // *a* de devant; premier(ère); **in ~ (of)** devant; **~ door** *n* porte *f* d'entrée; (*of car*) portière *f* avant; **~ier** ['frʌntɪə*] *n* frontière *f*; **~ page** *n* première page; **~ room** *n* (*Brit*) pièce *f* de devant, salon *m*; **~-wheel drive** *n* traction *f* avant.

frost [frɔst] *n* gel *m*, gelée *f*; (*also*: **hoar~**) givre *m*; **~bite** *n* gelures *fpl*; **~ed** *a* (*glass*) dépoli(e); **~y** *a* (*window*) couvert(e) de givre; (*welcome*) glacial(e).

froth ['frɔθ] *n* mousse *f*; écume *f*.

frown [fraun] *vi* froncer les sourcils.

froze [frəuz] *pt of* **freeze**; **~n** *pp of* **freeze** // *a* (*food*) congelé(e).

fruit [fru:t] *n* (*pl inv*) fruit *m*; **~erer** *n* fruitier *m*, marchand/e de fruits; **~erer's (shop)** *n* fruiterie *f*; **~ful** *a* fructueux(euse); (*plant, soil*) fécond(e); **~ion** [fru:'ɪʃən] *n*: **to come to ~ion se** réaliser; **~ juice** *n* jus *m* de fruit; **~ machine** *n* (*Brit*) machine *f* à sous; **~ salad** *n* salade *f* de fruits.

frustrate [frʌs'treɪt] *vt* frustrer; (*plot, plans*) faire échouer; **~d** *a* frustré(e).

fry [fraɪ], *pt, pp* **fried** *vt* (faire) frire; **the small ~** le menu fretin; **~ing pan** *n* poêle *f* (à frire).

ft. *abbr of* **foot, feet**.

fuddy-duddy ['fʌdɪdʌdɪ] *n* (*pej*) vieux schnock.

fudge [fʌdʒ] *n* (CULIN) sorte de confiserie à base de sucre, de beurre et de lait.

fuel [fjuəl] *n* (*for heating*) combustible *m*; (*for propelling*) carburant *m*; **~ tank** *n* cuve *f* à mazout, citerne *f*; (*in vehicle*) réservoir *m* de mer à or carburant.

fugitive ['fju:dʒɪtɪv] *n* fugitif/ive.

fulfil [ful'fɪl] *vt* (*function*) remplir; (*order*) exécuter; (*wish, desire*)

satisfaire, réaliser; **~ment** *n* (*of wishes*) réalisation *f*.

full [ful] *a* plein(e); (*details, information*) complet(ète); (*skirt*) ample, large // *ad*: **to know ~ well that** savoir fort bien que; **I'm ~ (up)** j'ai bien mangé; **~ employment** plein emploi; **a ~ two hours** deux bonnes heures; **at ~ speed** à toute vitesse; **in ~** (*reproduce, quote*) intégralement; (*write name etc*) en toutes lettres; **to pay in ~** tout payer; **~ moon** *n* pleine lune; **~-scale** *a* (*attack, war*) complet(ète), total(e); (*model*) grandeur nature *inv*; **~ stop** *n* point *m*; **~-time** *a, ad* (*work*) à plein temps // *n* (SPORT) fin *f* du match; **~y** *ad* entièrement, complètement; **~y-fledged** *a* (*teacher, barrister*) diplômé(e); (*citizen, member*) à part entière.

fulsome ['fulsəm] *a* (*pej: praise, gratitude*) excessif(ive).

fumble ['fʌmbl] *vi* fouiller, tâtonner; **to ~ with** *vt fus* tripoter.

fume [fju:m] *vi* rager; **~s** *npl* vapeurs *fpl*, émanations *fpl*, gaz *mpl*.

fun [fʌn] *n* amusement *m*, divertissement *m*; **to have ~** s'amuser; **for ~** pour rire; **to make ~ of** *vt fus* se moquer de.

function ['fʌŋkʃən] *n* fonction *f*; cérémonie *f*, soirée officielle // *vi* fonctionner; **~al** *a* fonctionnel(le).

fund [fʌnd] *n* caisse *f*, fonds *m*; (*source, store*) source *f*, mine *f*; **~s** *npl* fonds *mpl*.

fundamental [fʌndə'mɛntl] *a* fondamental(e).

funeral ['fju:nərəl] *n* enterrement *m*, obsèques *fpl* (*more formal occasion*); **~ parlour** *n* dépôt *m* mortuaire; **~ service** *n* service *m* funèbre.

fun fair *n* (*Brit*) fête (foraine).

fungus, *pl* **fungi** ['fʌŋgəs, -gaɪ] *n* champignon *m*; (*mould*) moisissure *f*.

funnel ['fʌnl] *n* entonnoir *m*; (*of ship*) cheminée *f*.

funny ['fʌnɪ] *a* amusant(e), drôle; (*strange*) curieux(euse), bizarre.

fur [fə:*] *n* fourrure *f*; (*Brit: in kettle etc*) (dépôt *m* de) tartre *m*; **~ coat** *n* manteau *m* de fourrure.

furious ['fjuərɪəs] *a* furieux(euse); (*effort*) acharné(e).

furlong ['fə:lɔŋ] *n* = 201.17 m (*terme d'hippisme*).

furlough ['fə:ləu] *n* permission *f*, congé *m*.

furnace ['fə:nɪs] *n* fourneau *m*.

furnish ['fə:nɪʃ] *vt* meubler; (*supply*) fournir; **~ings** *npl* mobilier *m*, articles *mpl* d'ameublement.

furniture ['fə:nɪtʃə*] *n* meubles *mpl*, mobilier *m*; **piece of ~** meuble *m*.

furrow ['fʌrəu] *n* sillon *m*.

furry ['fə:rɪ] *a* (*animal*) à fourrure; (*toy*) en peluche.

further ['fə:ðə*] *a* supplémentaire, autre; nouveau(nouvelle); plus loin // *ad* plus loin; (*more*) davantage; (*moreover*) de plus // *vt* faire avancer *or* progresser, promouvoir; ~ **education** *n* enseignement *m* post-scolaire (*recyclage, formation professionnelle*); ~**more** [fə:ðə'mɔ:*] *ad* de plus, en outre.

furthest ['fə:ðɪst] *superlative of* **far**.

fury ['fjuərɪ] *n* fureur *f*.

fuse [fju:z] *n* fusible *m*; (*for bomb etc*) amorce *f*, détonateur *m* // *vt, vi* (*metal*) fondre; (*fig*) fusionner; **the lights have** ~**d** (*Brit*) les plombs ont sauté; ~ **box** *n* boîte *f* à fusibles.

fuss [fʌs] *n* chichis *mpl*, façons *fpl*, embarras *mpl*; (*complaining*) histoire(s) *f(pl)*; **to make a** ~ faire des façons *etc*; ~**y** *a* (*person*) tatillon(ne), difficile; chichiteux(euse); (*dress, style*) tarabiscoté(e).

future ['fju:tʃə*] *a* futur(e) // *n* avenir *m*; (LING) futur *m*; **in (the)** ~ à l'avenir.

fuze [fju:z] (*US*) = **fuse**.

fuzzy ['fʌzɪ] *a* (PHOT) flou(e); (*hair*) crépu(e).

G

G [dʒi:] *n* (MUS) sol *m*.

gabble ['gæbl] *vi* bredouiller; jacasser.

gable ['geɪbl] *n* pignon *m*.

gadget ['gædʒɪt] *n* gadget *m*.

Gaelic ['geɪlɪk] *a, n* (LING) gaélique (*m*).

gag [gæg] *n* bâillon *m*; (*joke*) gag *m* // *vt* bâillonner.

gaiety ['geɪɪtɪ] *n* gaieté *f*.

gaily ['geɪlɪ] *ad* gaiement.

gain [geɪn] *n* gain *m*, profit *m* // *vt* gagner // *vi* (*watch*) avancer; **to** ~ **in/by** gagner en/à; **to** ~ **3lbs (in weight)** prendre 3 livres.

gait [geɪt] *n* démarche *f*.

gal. *abbr of* **gallon**.

gale [geɪl] *n* rafale *f* de vent; coup *m* de vent.

gallant ['gælənt] *a* vaillant(e), brave; (*towards ladies*) empressé(e), galant(e).

gall bladder ['gɔ:lblædə*] *n* vésicule *f* biliaire.

gallery ['gælərɪ] *n* galerie *f*; (*also:* **art** ~) musée *m*; (: *private*) galerie.

galley ['gælɪ] *n* (*ship's kitchen*) cambuse *f*; (*ship*) galère *f*.

Gallic ['gælɪk] *a* gaulois(e), français(e); (*charm*) latin(e).

gallon ['gælən] *n* gallon *m* (= *8 pints; Brit* = 4.543 *l; US* = 3.785 *l*).

gallop ['gæləp] *n* galop *m* // *vi* galoper.

gallows ['gæləuz] *n* potence *f*.

gallstone ['gɔ:lstəun] *n* calcul *m* (biliaire).

galore [gə'lɔ:*] *ad* en abondance, à gogo (*col*).

galvanize ['gælvənaɪz] *vt* galvaniser; (*fig*): **to** ~ **sb into action** galvaniser qn.

gambit ['gæmbɪt] *n* (*fig*): (**opening**) ~ manœuvre *f* stratégique.

gamble ['gæmbl] *n* pari *m*, risque calculé // *vt, vi* jouer; **to** ~ **on** (*fig*) miser sur; ~**r** *n* joueur *m*; **gambling** *n* jeu *m*.

game [geɪm] *n* jeu *m*; (*event*) match *m*; (HUNTING) gibier *m* // *a* brave; (*ready*): **to be** ~ (**for sth/to do**) être prêt(e) (à qch/à faire); **a** ~ **of football/tennis** une partie de football/tennis; **big** ~ *n* gros gibier; ~**keeper** *n* garde-chasse *m*.

gammon ['gæmən] *n* (*bacon*) quartier *m* de lard fumé; (*ham*) jambon fumé.

gamut ['gæmət] *n* gamme *f*.

gang [gæŋ] *n* bande *f*, groupe *m* // *vi*: **to** ~ **up on sb** se liguer contre qn.

gangster ['gæŋstə*] *n* gangster *m*.

gangway ['gæŋweɪ] *n* passerelle *f*; (*Brit: of bus*) couloir central.

gaol [dʒeɪl] *n, vt* (*Brit*) = **jail**.

gap [gæp] *n* trou *m*; (*in time*) intervalle *m*; (*fig*) lacune *f*; (*fig*) vide *m*.

gape [geɪp] *vi* être *or* rester bouche bée; **gaping** *a* (*hole*) béant(e).

garage ['gæra:ʒ] *n* garage *m*.

garbage ['ga:bɪdʒ] *n* ordures *fpl*, détritus *mpl*; ~ **can** *n* (*US*) poubelle *f*, boîte *f* à ordures.

garbled ['ga:bld] *a* déformé(e); faussé(e).

garden ['ga:dn] *n* jardin *m*; ~**er** *n* jardinier *m*; ~**ing** *n* jardinage *m*.

gargle ['ga:gl] *vi* se gargariser.

gargoyle ['ga:gɔɪl] *n* gargouille *f*.

garish ['gɛərɪʃ] *a* criard(e), voyant(e).

garland ['ga:lənd] *n* guirlande *f*; couronne *f*.

garlic ['ga:lɪk] *n* ail *m*.

garment ['ga:mənt] *n* vêtement *m*.

garrison ['gærɪsn] *n* garnison *f*.

garrulous ['gærjuləs] *a* volubile, loquace.

garter ['ga:tə*] *n* jarretière *f*; (*US*) jarretelle *f*.

gas [gæs] *n* gaz *m*; (*US: gasoline*) essence *f* // *vt* asphyxier; (MIL) gazer; ~ **cooker** *n* (*Brit*) cuisinière *f* à gaz; ~ **cylinder** *n* bouteille *f* de gaz; ~ **fire** *n* radiateur *m* à gaz.

gash [gæʃ] *n* entaille *f*; (*on face*) balafre *f*.

gasket ['gæskɪt] *n* (AUT) joint *m* de culasse.

gas mask *n* masque *m* à gaz.

gas meter *n* compteur *m* à gaz.

gasoline ['gæsəli:n] *n* (*US*) essence *f*.

gasp [ga:sp] *vi* haleter; (*fig*) avoir le souffle coupé; **to** ~ **out** *vt* (*say*) dire dans un souffle *or* d'une voix entrecoupée.

gas ring n brûleur m.

gassy ['gæsɪ] a gazeux(euse).

gas tap n bouton m (de cuisinière à gaz); (on pipe) robinet m à gaz.

gate [geɪt] n (of garden) portail m; (of farm) barrière f; (of building) porte f; (of lock) vanne f; ~**crash** vt (Brit) s'introduire sans invitation dans; ~**way** n porte f.

gather ['gæðə*] vt (flowers, fruit) cueillir; (pick up) ramasser; (assemble) rassembler, réunir; recueillir; (understand) comprendre // vi (assemble) se rassembler; to ~ speed prendre de la vitesse; ~**ing** n rassemblement m.

gaudy ['gɔːdɪ] a voyant(e).

gauge [geɪdʒ] n (standard measure) calibre m; (RAIL) écartement m; (instrument) jauge f // vt jauger.

Gaul [gɔːl] n (country) Gaule f; (person) Gaulois/e.

gaunt [gɔːnt] a décharné(e); (grim, desolate) désolé(e).

gauntlet ['gɔːntlɪt] n (fig): to run the ~ through an angry crowd se frayer un passage à travers une foule hostile; to throw down the ~ jeter le gant.

gauze [gɔːz] n gaze f.

gave [geɪv] pt of **give**.

gay [geɪ] a (person) gai(e), réjoui(e); (colour) gai, vif(vive); (col) homosexuel(le).

gaze [geɪz] n regard m fixe // vi: to ~ at fixer du regard.

gazetteer [gæzə'tɪə*] n dictionnaire m géographique.

GB abbr of **Great Britain**.

GCE n abbr (Brit) = General Certificate of Education.

GCSE n abbr (Brit) = General Certificate of Secondary Education.

gear [gɪə*] n matériel m, équipement m; attirail m; (TECH) engrenage m; (AUT) vitesse f // vt (fig: adapt): to ~ sth to adapter qch à; top or (US) **high/low/bottom** ~ quatrième (or cinquième)/deuxième/première vitesse; **in** ~ en prise; ~ **box** n boîte f de vitesse; ~ **lever**, (US) ~ **shift** n levier m de vitesse.

geese [giːs] npl of **goose**.

gel [dʒɛl] n gelée f; (CHEM) colloïde m.

gelignite ['dʒɛlɪgnaɪt] n plastic m.

gem [dʒɛm] n pierre précieuse.

Gemini ['dʒɛmɪnaɪ] n les Gémeaux mpl.

gender ['dʒɛndə*] n genre m.

general ['dʒɛnərl] n général m // a général(e); **in** ~ en général; ~ **delivery** n (US) poste restante; ~ **election** n élection(s) législative(s); ~**ize** vi généraliser; ~**ly** ad généralement; ~ **practitioner (G.P.)** n généraliste m/f.

generate ['dʒɛnəreɪt] vt engendrer; (electricity) produire.

generation [dʒɛnə'reɪʃən] n génération

f.

generator ['dʒɛnəreɪtə*] n générateur m.

generosity [dʒɛnə'rɒsɪtɪ] n générosité f.

generous ['dʒɛnərəs] a généreux(euse); (copious) copieux(euse).

genetic [dʒɪ'nɛtɪk] a génétique.

Geneva [dʒɪ'niːvə] n Genève f.

genial ['dʒiːnɪəl] a cordial(e), chaleureux(euse); (climate) clément(e).

genitals ['dʒɛnɪtlz] npl organes génitaux.

genius ['dʒiːnɪəs] n génie m.

gent [dʒɛnt] n abbr of **gentleman**.

genteel [dʒɛn'tiːl] a de bon ton, distingué(e).

gentle ['dʒɛntl] a doux(douce).

gentleman ['dʒɛntlmən] n monsieur m; (well-bred man) gentleman m.

gently ['dʒɛntlɪ] ad doucement.

gentry ['dʒɛntrɪ] n petite noblesse.

gents [dʒɛnts] n W.-C. mpl (pour hommes).

genuine ['dʒɛnjuɪn] a véritable, authentique; sincère.

geography [dʒɪ'ɒgrəfɪ] n géographie f.

geology [dʒɪ'ɒlədʒɪ] n géologie f.

geometric(al) [dʒɪə'mɛtrɪk(l)] a géométrique.

geometry [dʒɪ'ɒmətrɪ] n géométrie f.

geranium [dʒɪ'reɪnjəm] n géranium m.

geriatric [dʒɛrɪ'ætrɪk] a gériatrique.

germ [dʒɜːm] n (MED) microbe m; (BIO, fig) germe m.

German ['dʒɜːmən] a allemand(e) // n Allemand/e; (LING) allemand m; ~ **measles** n rubéole f.

Germany ['dʒɜːmənɪ] n Allemagne f.

gesture ['dʒɛstjə*] n geste m.

get [gɛt], pt, pp **got**, pp **gotten** (US) vi 1 (become, be) devenir; to ~ old/tired devenir vieux/fatigué, vieillir/se fatiguer; to ~ drunk s'enivrer; to ~ killed se faire tuer; when do I ~ paid? quand est-ce que je serai payé?; it's ~ting late il se fait tard

2 (go): to ~ to/from aller à/de; to ~ home rentrer chez soi; how did you ~ here? comment es-tu arrivé ici?

3 (begin) commencer or se mettre à; I'm ~ting to like him je commence à l'apprécier; let's ~ going or started allons-y

4 (modal auxiliary vb): you've got to do it il faut que vous le fassiez; I've got to tell the police je dois le dire à la police

♦ vt

1: to ~ sth done (do) faire qch; (have done) faire faire qch; to ~ one's hair cut se faire couper les cheveux; to ~ sb to do sth faire faire qch à qn; to ~ sb drunk enivrer qn

2 (obtain: money, permission, results) obtenir, avoir; (find: job, flat) trouver; (fetch: person, doctor, object) aller cher-

cher; **to ~ sth for sb** procurer qch à qn; **~ me Mr Jones, please** (*on phone*) passez-moi Mr Jones, s'il vous plaît; **can I ~ you a drink?** est-ce que je peux vous servir à boire?
3 (*receive: present, letter*) recevoir, avoir; (*acquire: reputation*) avoir; (: *prize*) obtenir; **what did you ~ for your birthday?** qu'est-ce que tu as eu pour ton anniversaire?
4 (*catch*) prendre, saisir, attraper; (*hit: target etc*) atteindre; **to ~ sb by the arm/throat** prendre *or* saisir *or* attraper qn par le bras/à la gorge; **~ him!** arrête-le!
5 (*take, move*) faire parvenir; **do you think we'll ~ it through the door?** on arrivera à le faire passer par la porte?; **I'll ~ you there somehow** je me débrouillerai pour t'y emmener
6 (*catch, take: plane, bus etc*) prendre
7 (*understand*) comprendre, saisir; (*hear*) entendre; **I've got it!** j'ai compris!, je saisis!; **I didn't ~ your name** je n'ai pas entendu votre nom
8 (*have, possess*): **to have got** avoir; **how many have you got?** vous en avez combien?
to get about *vi* se déplacer; (*news*) se répandre
to get along *vi* (*agree*) s'entendre; (*depart*) s'en aller; (*manage*) = **to get by**
to get at *vt fus* (*attack*) s'en prendre à; (*reach*) attraper, atteindre
to get away *vi* partir, s'en aller; (*escape*) s'échapper
to get away with *vt fus* en être quitte pour; se faire passer *or* pardonner
to get back *vi* (*return*) rentrer ♦ *vt* récupérer, recouvrer
to get by *vi* (*pass*) passer; (*manage*) se débrouiller
to get down *vi, vt fus* descendre ♦ *vt* descendre; (*depress*) déprimer
to get down to *vt fus* (*work*) se mettre à (faire)
to get in *vi* rentrer; (*train*) arriver
to get into *vt fus* entrer dans; (*car, train etc*) monter dans; (*clothes*) mettre, enfiler, endosser; **to ~ into bed/a rage** se mettre au lit/en colère
to get off *vi* (*from train etc*) descendre; (*depart: person, car*) s'en aller; (*escape*) s'en tirer ♦ *vt* (*remove: clothes, stain*) enlever ♦ *vt fus* (*train, bus*) descendre de
to get on *vi* (*at exam etc*) se débrouiller; (*agree*): **to ~ on (with)** s'entendre (avec) ♦ *vt fus* monter dans; (*horse*) monter sur
to get out *vi* sortir; (*of vehicle*) descendre ♦ *vt* sortir
to get out of *vt fus* sortir de; (*duty etc*) échapper à, se soustraire à

to get over *vt fus* (*illness*) se remettre de
to get round *vt fus* contourner; (*fig: person*) entortiller
to get through *vi* (*TEL*) avoir la communication; **to ~ through to sb** atteindre qn
to get together *vi* se réunir ♦ *vt* assembler
to get up *vi* (*rise*) se lever ♦ *vt fus* monter
to get up to *vt fus* (*reach*) arriver à; (*prank etc*) faire.
getaway ['gɛtəweɪ] *n* fuite *f*.
get-up ['gɛtʌp] *n* (*col*) accoutrement *m*.
geyser ['giːzə*] *n* chauffe-eau *m inv*; (*GEO*) geyser *m*.
Ghana ['gɑːnə] *n* Ghana *m*.
ghastly ['gɑːstlɪ] *a* atroce, horrible; (*pale*) livide, blême.
gherkin ['gɜːkɪn] *n* cornichon *m*.
ghost [gəust] *n* fantôme *m*, revenant *m*.
giant ['dʒaɪənt] *n* géant/e // *a* géant(e), énorme.
gibberish ['dʒɪbərɪʃ] *n* charabia *m*.
gibe [dʒaɪb] *n* sarcasme *m*.
giblets ['dʒɪblɪts] *npl* abats *mpl*.
Gibraltar [dʒɪ'brɔltə*] *n* Gibraltar *m*.
giddy ['gɪdɪ] *a* (*dizzy*): **to be ~** avoir le vertige; (*height*) vertigineux(euse).
gift [gɪft] *n* cadeau *m*, présent *m*; (*donation, ability*) don *m*; **~ed** *a* doué(e); **~ token** *or* **voucher** *n* chèque-cadeau *m*.
gigantic [dʒaɪ'gæntɪk] *a* gigantesque.
giggle ['gɪgl] *vi* pouffer, ricaner sottement.
gill [dʒɪl] *n* (*measure*) = 0.25 pints (*Brit* = 0.148 l, *US* = 0.118 l*).
gills [gɪlz] *npl* (*of fish*) ouïes *fpl*, branchies *fpl*.
gilt [gɪlt] *n* dorure *f* // *a* doré(e); **~-edged** *a* (*COMM*) de premier ordre.
gimmick ['gɪmɪk] *n* truc *m*.
gin [dʒɪn] *n* (*liquor*) gin *m*.
ginger ['dʒɪndʒə*] *n* gingembre *m*; **~ ale**, **~ beer** *n* boisson gazeuse au gingembre; **~bread** *n* pain *m* d'épices.
gingerly ['dʒɪndʒəlɪ] *ad* avec précaution.
gipsy ['dʒɪpsɪ] *n* gitan/e, bohémien/ne.
giraffe [dʒɪ'rɑːf] *n* girafe *f*.
girder ['gɜːdə*] *n* poutrelle *f*.
girdle ['gɜːdl] *n* (*corset*) gaine *f*.
girl [gɜːl] *n* fille *f*, fillette *f*; (*young unmarried woman*) jeune fille; (*daughter*) fille; **an English ~** une jeune Anglaise; **~friend** *n* (*of girl*) amie *f*; (*of boy*) petite amie.
giro ['dʒaɪrəu] *n* (*bank ~*) virement *m* bancaire; (*post office ~*) mandat *m*.
girth [gɜːθ] *n* circonférence *f*; (*of horse*) sangle *f*.
gist [dʒɪst] *n* essentiel *m*.
give [gɪv] *vb* (*pt* **gave**, *pp* **given**) *vt*

donner // vi (*break*) céder; (*stretch: fabric*) se prêter; **to ~ sb sth, ~ sth to sb** donner qch à qn; **to ~ a cry/sigh** pousser un cri/un soupir; **to ~ away** vt donner; (*give free*) faire cadeau de; (*betray*) donner, trahir; (*disclose*) révéler; (*bride*) conduire à l'autel; **to ~ back** vt rendre; **to ~ in** vi céder // vt donner; **to ~ off** vt dégager; **to ~ out** vt distribuer; annoncer; **to ~ up** vi renoncer // vt renoncer à; **to ~ up smoking** arrêter de fumer; **to ~ o.s. up** se rendre; **to ~ way** vi céder; (*Brit AUT*) céder la priorité.

glacier ['glæsɪə*] n glacier m.

glad [glæd] a content(e).

gladly ['glædlɪ] ad volontiers.

glamorous ['glæmərəs] a séduisant(e).

glamour ['glæmə*] n éclat m, prestige m.

glance [glɑ:ns] n coup m d'œil // vi: **to ~ at** jeter un coup d'œil à; **to ~ off** vt fus (*bullet*) ricocher sur; **glancing** a (*blow*) oblique.

gland [glænd] n glande f.

glare [glɛə*] n lumière éblouissante // vi briller d'un éclat aveuglant; **to ~ at** lancer un or des regard(s) furieux à; **glaring** a (*mistake*) criant(e), qui saute aux yeux.

glass [glɑ:s] n verre m; (*also: looking ~*) miroir m; **~es** npl lunettes fpl; **~ware** n verrerie f; **~y** a (*eyes*) vitreux(euse).

glaze [gleɪz] vt (*door*) vitrer; (*pottery*) vernir // n vernis m.

glazier ['gleɪzɪə*] n vitrier m.

gleam [gli:m] n lueur f; rayon m // vi luire, briller; **~ing** a luisant(e).

glean [gli:n] vt (*information*) recueillir.

glee [gli:] n joie f.

glen [glɛn] n vallée f.

glib [glɪb] a qui a du bagou; facile.

glide [glaɪd] vi glisser; (*AVIAT, birds*) planer; **~r** n (*AVIAT*) planeur m; **gliding** n (*AVIAT*) vol m à voile.

glimmer ['glɪmə*] n lueur f.

glimpse [glɪmps] n vision passagère, aperçu m // vt entrevoir, apercevoir.

glint [glɪnt] vi étinceler.

glisten ['glɪsn] vi briller, luire.

glitter ['glɪtə*] vi scintiller, briller // n scintillement m.

gloat [gləʊt] vi: **to ~ (over)** jubiler (à propos de).

global ['gləʊbl] a mondial(e).

globe [gləʊb] n globe m.

gloom [glu:m] n obscurité f; (*sadness*) tristesse f, mélancolie f; **~y** a sombre, triste, mélancolique.

glorious ['glɔ:rɪəs] a glorieux(euse); splendide.

glory ['glɔ:rɪ] n gloire f; splendeur f // vi: **to ~ in** se glorifier de.

gloss [glɔs] n (*shine*) brillant m, vernis

m; **to ~ over** vt fus glisser sur.

glossary ['glɔsərɪ] n glossaire m.

glossy ['glɔsɪ] a brillant(e), luisant(e).

glove [glʌv] n gant m; **~ compartment** n (*AUT*) boîte f à gants, vide-poches m inv.

glow [gləʊ] vi rougeoyer; (*face*) rayonner // n rougeoiement m.

glower ['glaʊə*] vi: **to ~ (at)** lancer des regards mauvais (à).

glue [glu:] n colle f // vt coller.

glum [glʌm] a maussade, morose.

glut [glʌt] n surabondance f.

glutton ['glʌtn] n glouton/ne; a **~ for work** un bourreau de travail.

gnarled [nɑ:ld] a noueux(euse).

gnat [næt] n moucheron m.

gnaw [nɔ:] vt ronger.

go [gəʊ] vb (pt **went**, pp **gone**) vi aller; (*depart*) partir, s'en aller; (*work*) marcher; (*be sold*): **to ~ for £10** se vendre 10 livres; (*fit, suit*): **to ~ with** aller avec; (*become*): **to ~ pale/mouldy** pâlir/ moisir; (*break etc*) céder // n (pl: **~es**): **to have a ~ (at)** essayer (de faire); **to be on the ~** être en mouvement; **whose ~ is it?** à qui est-ce de jouer?; **he's going to do it** va faire, il est sur le point de faire; **to ~ for a walk** aller se promener; **to ~ dancing** aller danser; **how did it ~?** comment est-ce que ça s'est passé?; **to ~ round the back/by the shop** passer par derrière/devant le magasin; **to ~ about** vi (*rumour*) se répandre // vt fus: **how do I ~ about this?** comment dois-je m'y prendre (pour faire ceci?); **to ~ ahead** vi (*make progress*) avancer; (*get going*) y aller; **to ~ along** vi aller, avancer // vt fus longer, parcourir; **to ~ away** vi partir, s'en aller; **to ~ back** vi rentrer; revenir; (*go again*) retourner; **to ~ back on** vt fus (*promise*) revenir sur; **to ~ by** vi (*years, time*) passer, s'écouler // vt fus se tenir à; en croire; **to ~ down** vi descendre; (*ship*) couler; (*sun*) se coucher // vt fus descendre; **to ~ for** vt fus (*fetch*) aller chercher; (*like*) aimer; (*attack*) s'en prendre à; attaquer; **to ~ in** vi entrer; **to ~ in for** vt fus (*competition*) se présenter à; (*like*) aimer; **to ~ into** vt fus entrer dans; (*investigate*) étudier, examiner; (*embark on*) se lancer dans; **to ~ off** vi partir, s'en aller; (*food*) se gâter; (*explode*) sauter; (*event*) se dérouler // vt fus ne plus aimer; **the gun went off** le coup est parti; **to ~ on** vi continuer; (*happen*) se passer; **to ~ on doing** continuer à faire; **to ~ out** vi sortir; (*fire, light*) s'éteindre; **to ~ over** vt fus (*check*) revoir, vérifier; **to ~ through** vt fus (*town etc*) traverser; **to ~ up** vi monter; (*price*) augmenter // vt fus gravir; **to ~ without** vt fus se passer de.

goad [gəud] vt aiguillonner.

go-ahead ['gəuəhɛd] a dynamique, entreprenant(e) // n feu vert.

goal [gəul] n but m; **~keeper** n gardien m de but; **~-post** n poteau m de but.

goat [gəut] n chèvre f.

gobble ['gɔbl] vt (also: ~ **down**, ~ **up**) engloutir.

god [gɔd] n dieu m; **G~** n Dieu m; **~child** n filleul/e; **~daughter** n filleule f; **~dess** n déesse f; **~father** n parrain m; **~-forsaken** a maudit(e); **~mother** n marraine f; **~send** n aubaine f; **~son** n filleul m.

goggles ['gɔglz] npl lunettes fpl (protectrices) (de motocycliste etc).

going ['gəuɪŋ] n (conditions) état m du terrain // a: **the ~ rate** le tarif (en vigueur).

gold [gəuld] n or m // a en or; **~en** a (made of gold) en or; (gold in colour) doré(e); **~fish** n poisson m rouge; **~-plated** a plaqué(e) or inv; **~smith** n orfèvre m.

golf [gɔlf] n golf m; **~ ball** n balle f de golf; (on typewriter) boule m; **~ club** n club m de golf; (stick) club m, crosse f de golf; **~ course** n terrain m de golf; **~er** n joueur/euse de golf.

gone [gɔn] pp of go // a parti(e).

good [gud] a bon(ne); (kind) gentil(le); (child) sage // n bien m; **~s** npl marchandise f, articles mpl; **~!** bon!, très bien!; **to be ~ at** être bon en; **to be ~ for** être bon à; **it's ~ for you** c'est bon pour vous; **would you be ~ enough to ...?** auriez-vous la bonté or l'amabilité de ...?; **a ~ deal (of)** beaucoup (de); **a ~ many** beaucoup (de); **to make ~** vi (succeed) faire son chemin, réussir // vt (deficit) combler; (losses) compenser; **it's no ~ complaining** cela ne sert à rien de se plaindre; **for ~** pour de bon, une fois pour toutes; **~ morning/afternoon!** bonjour!; **~ evening!** bonsoir!; **~ night!** bonsoir!; (on going to bed) bonne nuit!; **~bye** excl au revoir!; **G~ Friday** n Vendredi saint; **~-looking** a bien inv; **~-natured** a qui a un bon naturel; (discussion) enjoué(e); **~ness** n (of person) bonté f; **for ~ness sake!** je vous en prie!; **~ness gracious!** mon Dieu!; **~s train** n (Brit) train m de marchandises; **~will** n bonne volonté; (COMM) réputation f (auprès de la clientèle).

goose [gu:s], pl **geese** n oie f.

gooseberry ['guzbərɪ] n groseille f à maquereau; **to play ~** tenir la chandelle.

gooseflesh ['gu:sflɛʃ] n, **goose pimples** npl chair f de poule.

gore [gɔ:*] vt encorner // n sang m.

gorge [gɔ:dʒ] n gorge f // vt: **to ~ o.s. (on)** se gorger (de).

gorgeous ['gɔ:dʒəs] a splendide, superbe.

gorilla [gə'rɪlə] n gorille m.

gorse [gɔ:s] n ajoncs mpl.

gory ['gɔ:rɪ] a sanglant(e).

go-slow ['gəu'sləu] n (Brit) grève perlée.

gospel ['gɔspl] n évangile m.

gossip ['gɔsɪp] n bavardages mpl; commérage m, cancans mpl; (person) commère f // vi bavarder; (maliciously) cancaner, faire des commérages.

got [gɔt] pt, pp of get; **~ten** (US) pp of get.

gout [gaut] n goutte f.

govern ['gʌvn] vt gouverner.

governess ['gʌvənɪs] n gouvernante f.

government ['gʌvnmənt] n gouvernement m; (Brit: ministers) ministère m.

governor ['gʌvənə*] n (of state, bank) gouverneur m; (of school, hospital) administrateur m.

gown [gaun] n robe f; (of teacher; Brit: of judge) toge f.

G.P. n abbr of **general practitioner**.

grab [græb] vt saisir, empoigner; (property, power) se saisir de.

grace [greɪs] n grâce f // vt honorer; **5 days' ~** répit m de 5 jours; **to say ~** dire le bénédicité; (after meal) dire les grâces; **~ful** a gracieux(euse), élégant(e); **gracious** ['greɪʃəs] a bienveillant(e); de bonne grâce; miséricordieux(euse).

grade [greɪd] n (COMM) qualité f; calibre m; catégorie f; (in hierarchy) grade m, échelon m; (US SCOL) note f; classe f // vt classer; calibrer; graduer; **~ crossing** n (US) passage m à niveau; **~ school** n (US) école f primaire.

gradient ['greɪdɪənt] n inclinaison f, pente f.

gradual ['grædjuəl] a graduel(le), progressif(ive); **~ly** ad peu à peu, graduellement.

graduate n ['grædjuɪt] diplômé/e d'université // vi ['grædjueɪt] obtenir un diplôme d'université; **graduation** [-'eɪʃən] n cérémonie f de remise des diplômes.

graffiti [grə'fi:tɪ] npl graffiti mpl.

graft [gra:ft] n (AGR, MED) greffe f; (bribery) corruption f // vt greffer; **hard ~** n (col) boulot acharné.

grain [greɪn] n grain m.

gram [græm] n gramme m.

grammar ['græmə*] n grammaire f; **~ school** n (Brit) ≈ lycée m.

grammatical [grə'mætɪkl] a grammatical(e).

gramme [græm] n = gram.

grand [grænd] a magnifique, splendide; noble; **~children** npl petits-enfants mpl; **~dad** n grand-papa m; **~daughter** n petite-fille f; **~father** n grand-père m;

~ma n grand-maman f; ~mother n grand-mère f; ~pa n = ~dad; ~parents npl grand-père m et grand-mère f; ~ piano n piano m à queue; ~son n petit-fils m; ~stand n (SPORT) tribune f.

granite ['grænɪt] n granit m.

granny ['grænɪ] n grand-maman f.

grant [grɑːnt] vt accorder; (a request) accéder à; (admit) concéder // n (SCOL) bourse f; (ADMIN) subside m, subvention f; to take sth for ~ed considérer qch comme acquis.

granulated ['grænjuleɪtɪd] a: ~ sugar n sucre m en poudre.

grape [greɪp] n raisin m.

grapefruit ['greɪpfruːt] n pamplemousse m.

graph [grɑːf] n graphique m, courbe f; ~ic a graphique; (vivid) vivant(e); ~ics n arts mpl graphiques // npl graphisme m.

grapple ['græpl] vi: to ~ with être aux prises avec.

grasp [grɑːsp] vt saisir // n (grip) prise f; (fig) emprise f, pouvoir m; compréhension f, connaissance f; ~ing a avide.

grass [grɑːs] n herbe f; ~hopper n sauterelle f; ~roots a de base; ~ snake n couleuvre f.

grate [greɪt] n grille f de cheminée // vi grincer // vt (CULIN) râper.

grateful ['greɪtful] a reconnaissant(e).

grater ['greɪtə*] n râpe f.

gratify ['grætɪfaɪ] vt faire plaisir à; (whim) satisfaire.

grating ['greɪtɪŋ] n (iron bars) grille f // a (noise) grinçant(e).

gratitude ['grætɪtjuːd] n gratitude f.

gratuity [grə'tjuːɪtɪ] n pourboire m.

grave [greɪv] n tombe f // a grave, sérieux(euse).

gravel ['grævl] n gravier m.

gravestone ['greɪvstəun] n pierre tombale.

graveyard ['greɪvjɑːd] n cimetière m.

gravity ['grævɪtɪ] n (PHYSICS) gravité f; pesanteur f; (seriousness) gravité.

gravy ['greɪvɪ] n jus m (de viande); sauce f.

gray [greɪ] a = grey.

graze [greɪz] vi paître, brouter // vt (touch lightly) frôler, effleurer; (scrape) écorcher // n écorchure f.

grease [griːs] n (fat) graisse f; (lubricant) lubrifiant m // vt graisser; lubrifier; ~proof paper n (Brit) papier sulfurisé; **greasy** a gras(se), graisseux(euse).

great [greɪt] a grand(e); (col) formidable; G~ Britain n Grande-Bretagne f; ~-grandfather n arrière-grand-père m; ~-grandmother n arrière-grand-mère f; ~ly ad très, grandement; (with verbs) beaucoup; ~ness n grandeur f.

Greece [griːs] n Grèce f.

greed [griːd] n (also: ~iness) avidité f; (for food) gourmandise f; ~y a avide; gourmand(e).

Greek [griːk] a grec(grecque) // n Grec/Grecque; (LING) grec m.

green [griːn] a vert(e); (inexperienced) (bien) jeune, naïf(ïve) // n vert m; (stretch of grass) pelouse f; (also: village ~) ≈ place f du village; ~s npl légumes verts; ~ belt n (round town) ceinture verte; ~ card n (AUT) carte verte; ~ery n verdure f; ~gage n reine-claude f; ~grocer n (Brit) marchand m de fruits et légumes; ~house n serre f.

Greenland ['griːnlənd] n Groenland m.

greet [griːt] vt accueillir; ~ing n salutation f; ~ing(s) card n carte f de vœux.

grenade [grə'neɪd] n grenade f.

grew [gruː] pt of **grow**.

grey [greɪ] a gris(e); (dismal) sombre; ~hound n lévrier m.

grid [grɪd] n grille f; (ELEC) réseau m.

grief [griːf] n chagrin m, douleur f.

grievance ['griːvəns] n doléance f, grief m.

grieve [griːv] vi avoir du chagrin; se désoler // vt faire de la peine à, affliger; to ~ for sb (dead person) pleurer qn.

grievous ['griːvəs] a: ~ bodily harm (LAW) coups mpl et blessures fpl.

grill [grɪl] n (on cooker) gril m // vt (Brit) griller; (question) cuisiner.

grille [grɪl] n grillage m; (AUT) calandre f.

grim [grɪm] a sinistre, lugubre.

grimace [grɪ'meɪs] n grimace f // vi grimacer, faire une grimace.

grimy ['graɪmɪ] a crasseux(euse).

grin [grɪn] n large sourire m // vi sourire.

grind [graɪnd] vt (pt, pp ground) écraser; (coffee, pepper etc) moudre; (US: meat) hacher; (make sharp) aiguiser // n (work) corvée f; to ~ one's teeth grincer des dents.

grip [grɪp] n étreinte f, poigne f; prise f; (holdall) sac m de voyage // vt saisir, empoigner; étreindre; to come to ~s with en venir aux prises avec.

gripping ['grɪpɪŋ] a prenant(e), palpitant(e).

grisly ['grɪzlɪ] a sinistre, macabre.

gristle ['grɪsl] n cartilage m (de poulet etc).

grit [grɪt] n gravillon m; (courage) cran m // vt (road) sabler; to ~ one's teeth serrer les dents.

groan [grəun] n gémissement m; grognement m // vi gémir; grogner.

grocer ['grəusə*] n épicier m; ~ies npl provisions fpl.

groin [grɔɪn] n aine f.

groom [gruːm] n palefrenier m; (also:

bride~) marié *m* // *vt* (*horse*) panser; (*fig*): **to ~ sb for** former qn pour.

groove [gru:v] *n* sillon *m*, rainure *f*.

grope [grəup] *vi* tâtonner; **to ~ for** *vt fus* chercher à tâtons.

gross [grəus] *a* grossier(ère); (*COMM*) brut(e); **~ly** *ad* (*greatly*) très, grandement.

grotto [ˈgrɔtəu] *n* grotte *f*.

ground [graund] *pt, pp of* grind // *n* sol *m*, terre *f*; (*land*) terrain *m*, terres *fpl*; (*SPORT*) terrain; (*US: also:* ~ wire) terre; (*reason: gen pl*) raison *f* // *vt* (*plane*) empêcher de décoller, retenir au sol; (*US: ELEC*) équiper d'une prise de terre // *vi* (*ship*) s'échouer; **~s** *npl* (*of coffee etc*) marc *m*; (*gardens etc*) parc *m*, domaine *m*; **on the ~, to the ~** par terre; **to gain/lose ~** gagner/perdre du terrain; **~ cloth** *n* (*US*) = **~sheet**; **~ing** *n* (*in education*) connaissances *fpl* de base; **~less** *a* sans fondement; **~sheet** *n* (*Brit*) tapis *m* de sol; **~ staff** *n* équipage *m* au sol; **~ swell** *n* lame *f* or vague *f* de fond; **~work** *n* préparation *f*.

group [gru:p] *n* groupe *m* // *vt* (*also:* ~ **together**) grouper // *vi* (*also:* ~ **together**) se grouper.

grouse [graus] *n* (*pl inv*) (*bird*) grouse *f* // *vi* (*complain*) rouspéter, râler.

grove [grəuv] *n* bosquet *m*.

grovel [ˈgrɔvl] *vi* ramper.

grow [grəu], *pt* grew, *pp* grown *vi* (*plant*) pousser, croître; (*person*) grandir; (*increase*) augmenter, se développer; (*become*): **to ~ rich/weak** s'enrichir/s'affaiblir // *vt* cultiver, faire pousser; **to ~ up** *vi* grandir; **~er** *n* producteur *m*; **~ing** *a* (*fear, amount*) croissant(e), grandissant(e).

growl [graul] *vi* grogner.

grown [grəun] *pp of* grow // *a* adulte; **~-up** *n* adulte *m/f*, grande personne.

growth [grəuθ] *n* croissance *f*, développement *m*; (*what has grown*) pousse *f*; poussée *f*; (*MED*) grosseur *f*, tumeur *f*.

grub [grʌb] *n* larve *f*; (*col: food*) bouffe *f*.

grubby [ˈgrʌbɪ] *a* crasseux(euse).

grudge [grʌdʒ] *n* rancune *f* // *vt*: **to ~ sb sth** donner qch à qn à contre-cœur; reprocher qch à qn; **to bear sb a ~ (for)** garder rancune *or* en vouloir à qn (de).

gruelling [ˈgruəlɪŋ] *a* exténuant(e).

gruesome [ˈgruːsəm] *a* horrible.

gruff [grʌf] *a* bourru(e).

grumble [ˈgrʌmbl] *vi* rouspéter, ronchonner.

grumpy [ˈgrʌmpɪ] *a* grincheux(euse).

grunt [grʌnt] *vi* grogner.

G-string [ˈdʒiːstrɪŋ] *n* (*garment*) cache-sexe *m inv*.

guarantee [gærənˈtiː] *n* garantie *f* // *vt* garantir.

guard [gɑːd] *n* garde *f*; (*one man*) garde *m*; (*Brit RAIL*) chef *m* de train // *vt* garder, surveiller; **~ed** *a* (*fig*) prudent(e); **~ian** *n* gardien/ne; (*of minor*) tuteur/trice; **~'s van** *n* (*Brit RAIL*) fourgon *m*.

guerrilla [gəˈrɪlə] *n* guérillero *m*; **~ warfare** *n* guérilla *f*.

guess [gɛs] *vi* deviner // *vt* deviner; (*US*) croire, penser // *n* supposition *f*, hypothèse *f*; **~work** *n* hypothèse *f*.

guest [gɛst] *n* invité/e; (*in hotel*) client/e; **~-house** *n* pension *f*; **~ room** *n* chambre *f* d'amis.

guffaw [gʌˈfɔː] *vi* pouffer de rire.

guidance [ˈgaɪdəns] *n* conseils *mpl*.

guide [gaɪd] *n* (*person, book etc*) guide *m*; (*also:* girl ~) guide *f* // *vt* guider; **~book** *n* guide *m*; **~ dog** *n* chien *m* d'aveugle; **~lines** *npl* (*fig*) instructions générales, conseils *mpl*.

guild [gɪld] *n* corporation *f*; cercle *m*, association *f*.

guile [gaɪl] *n* astuce *f*.

guillotine [ˈgɪlətiːn] *n* guillotine *f*.

guilt [gɪlt] *n* culpabilité *f*; **~y** *a* coupable.

guinea pig [ˈgɪnɪpɪg] *n* cobaye *m*.

guise [gaɪz] *n* aspect *m*, apparence *f*.

guitar [gɪˈtɑː*] *n* guitare *f*.

gulf [gʌlf] *n* golfe *m*; (*abyss*) gouffre *m*.

gull [gʌl] *n* mouette *f*.

gullet [ˈgʌlɪt] *n* gosier *m*.

gullible [ˈgʌlɪbl] *a* crédule.

gully [ˈgʌlɪ] *n* ravin *m*; ravine *f*; couloir *m*.

gulp [gʌlp] *vi* avaler sa salive; (*from emotion*) avoir la gorge serrée // *vt* (*also:* ~ **down**) avaler.

gum [gʌm] *n* (*ANAT*) gencive *f*; (*glue*) colle *f*; (*sweet*) boule *f* de gomme; (*also:* chewing-~) chewing-gum *m* // *vt* coller; **~boots** *npl* (*Brit*) bottes *fpl* en caoutchouc.

gun [gʌn] *n* (*small*) revolver *m*, pistolet *m*; (*rifle*) fusil *m*, carabine *f*; (*cannon*) canon *m*; **~boat** *n* canonnière *f*; **~fire** *n* fusillade *f*; **~man** *n* bandit armé; **~ner** *n* artilleur *m*; **~point** *n*: **at ~point** sous la menace du pistolet (*or* fusil); **~powder** *n* poudre *f* à canon; **~shot** *n* coup *m* de feu; **~smith** *n* armurier *m*.

gurgle [ˈgəːgl] *vi* gargouiller.

guru [ˈguruː] *n* gourou *m*.

gush [gʌʃ] *vi* jaillir; (*fig*) se répandre en effusions.

gusset [ˈgʌsɪt] *n* gousset *m*, soufflet *m*.

gust [gʌst] *n* (*of wind*) rafale *f*; (*of smoke*) bouffée *f*.

gusto [ˈgʌstəu] *n* enthousiasme *m*.

gut [gʌt] *n* intestin *m*, boyau *m*; (*MUS etc*) boyau; **~s** *npl* (*courage*) cran *m*.

gutter [ˈgʌtə*] *n* (*of roof*) gouttière *f*;

(*in street*) caniveau *m*.

guy [gaɪ] *n* (*also*: ~**rope**) corde *f*; (*col*: *man*) type *m*; (*figure*) effigie de Guy Fawkes.

guzzle ['gʌzl] *vi* s'empiffrer // *vt* avaler gloutonnement.

gym [dʒɪm] *n* (*also*: gymnasium) gymnase *m*; (*also*: gymnastics) gym *f*; ~ **shoes** *npl* chaussures *fpl* de gym (nastique); ~ **slip** *n* (*Brit*) tunique *f* (d'écolière).

gymnast ['dʒɪmnæst] *n* gymnaste *m/f*; ~**ics** [-'næstɪks] *n*, *npl* gymnastique *f*.

gynaecologist, (*US*) **gynecologist** [gaɪnɪ'kɔlədʒɪst] *n* gynécologue *m/f*.

gypsy ['dʒɪpsɪ] *n* = gipsy.

gyrate [dʒaɪ'reɪt] *vi* tournoyer.

H

haberdashery ['hæbə'dæʃərɪ] *n* (*Brit*) mercerie *f*.

habit ['hæbɪt] *n* habitude *f*; (*costume*) habit *m*, tenue *f*.

habitual [hə'bɪtjuəl] *a* habituel(le); (*drinker, liar*) invétéré(e).

hack [hæk] *vt* hacher, tailler // *n* (*cut*) entaille *f*; (*blow*) coup *m*; (*pej: writer*) nègre *m*.

hackneyed ['hæknɪd] *a* usé(e), rebattu(e).

had [hæd] *pt, pp* of **have**.

haddock, *pl* ~ *or* ~**s** ['hædək] *n* églefin *m*; smoked ~ haddock *m*.

hadn't ['hædnt] = **had not**.

haemorrhage, (*US*) **hemorrhage** ['hemərɪdʒ] *n* hémorragie *f*.

haggle ['hægl] *vi* marchander.

Hague [heɪg] *n*: The ~ La Haye.

hail [heɪl] *n* grêle *f* // *vt* (*call*) héler; (*greet*) acclamer // *vi* grêler; ~**stone** *n* grêlon *m*.

hair [heə*] *n* cheveux *mpl*; (*single hair: on head*) cheveu *m*; (*: on body*) poil *m*; to do one's ~ se coiffer; ~**brush** *n* brosse *f* à cheveux; ~**cut** *n* coupe *f* (de cheveux); ~**do** ['heədu:] *n* coiffure *f*; ~**dresser** *n* coiffeur/euse; ~**dryer** *n* sèche-cheveux *m*; ~**grip** *n* pince *f* à cheveux; ~**pin** *n* épingle *f* à cheveux; ~**pin bend,** (*US*) ~**pin curve** *n* virage *m* en épingle à cheveux; ~**raising** *a* à (vous) faire dresser les cheveux sur la tête; ~ **remover** *n* dépilateur *m*; ~ **spray** *n* laque *f* (pour les cheveux); ~**style** *n* coiffure *f*; ~**y** *a* poilu(e); chevelu(e); (*fig*) effrayant(e).

hake [heɪk] *n* colin *m*, merlu *m*.

half [hɑ:f] *n* (*pl* halves) moitié *f* // *a* demi(e) // *ad* (à) moitié, à demi; ~**-an-hour** une demi-heure; ~ **a dozen** une demi-douzaine; ~ **a pound** une demi-livre, ≈ 250 g; two and a ~ deux et demi; a week and a ~ une semaine et

demie; ~ (of it) la moitié; ~ (of) la moitié de; to cut sth in ~ couper qch en deux; ~ asleep à moitié endormi(e); ~**back** *n* (*SPORT*) demi *m*; ~**breed,** ~**caste** *n* métis/se; ~**hearted** *a* tiède, sans enthousiasme; ~**hour** *n* demi-heure *f*; ~**mast**: at ~**mast** (*flag*) en berne, à mi-mât; ~**penny** ['heɪpnɪ] *n* (*Brit*) demi-penny *m*; (**at**) ~**price** à moitié prix; ~ **term** *n* (*Brit SCOL*) congé *m* de demi-trimestre; ~**time** *n* mi-temps *f*; ~**way** *ad* à mi-chemin.

halibut ['hælɪbət] *n* (*pl inv*) flétan *m*.

hall [hɔ:l] *n* salle *f*; (*entrance way*) hall *m*, entrée *f*; (*corridor*) couloir *m*; (*mansion*) château *m*, manoir *m*; ~ **of residence** *n* (*Brit*) pavillon *m* or résidence *f* universitaire.

hallmark ['hɔ:lmɑ:k] *n* poinçon *m*; (*fig*) marque *f*.

hallo [hə'ləu] *excl* = **hello.**

Hallowe'en [hæləu'i:n] *n* veille *f* de la Toussaint.

hallucination [həlu:sɪ'neɪʃən] *n* hallucination *f*.

hallway ['hɔ:lweɪ] *n* vestibule *m*; couloir *m*.

halo ['heɪləu] *n* (*of saint etc*) auréole *f*; (*of sun*) halo *m*.

halt [hɔ:lt] *n* halte *f*, arrêt *m* // *vt* faire arrêter // *vi* faire halte, s'arrêter.

halve [hɑ:v] *vt* (*apple etc*) partager *or* diviser en deux; (*expense*) réduire de moitié.

halves [hɑ:vz] *npl* of **half.**

ham [hæm] *n* jambon *m*.

hamburger ['hæmbə:gə*] *n* hamburger *m*.

hamlet ['hæmlɪt] *n* hameau *m*.

hammer ['hæmə*] *n* marteau *m* // *vt* (*fig*) éreinter, démolir // *vi* (*on door*) frapper à coups redoublés.

hammock ['hæmək] *n* hamac *m*.

hamper ['hæmpə*] *vt* gêner // *n* panier *m* (d'osier).

hamster ['hæmstə*] *n* hamster *m*.

hand [hænd] *n* main *f*; (*of clock*) aiguille *f*; (*handwriting*) écriture *f*; (*at cards*) jeu *m*; (*worker*) ouvrier/ère *m* // *vt* passer, donner; to give sb a ~ donner un coup de main à qn; at ~ à portée de la main; in ~ en main; (*work*) en cours; to be on ~ (*person*) être disponible; (*emergency services*) se tenir prêt(e) (à intervenir); to ~ (*information etc*) sous la main, à portée de la main; on the one ~ ..., on the other ~ d'une part ..., d'autre part; to ~ in *vt* remettre; to ~ out *vt* distribuer; to ~ over *vt* transmettre; céder; ~**bag** *n* sac *m* à main; ~**book** *n* manuel *m*; ~**brake** *n* frein *m* à main; ~**cuffs** *npl* menottes *fpl*; ~**ful** *n* poignée *f*.

handicap ['hændɪkæp] *n* handicap *m* // *vt* handicaper; **mentally/physically** ~**ped**

a handicapé(e) mentalement/physiquement.

handicraft ['hændɪkrɑːft] *n* travail *m* d'artisanat, technique artisanale.

handiwork ['hændɪwəːk] *n* ouvrage *m*; (*pej*) œuvre *f*.

handkerchief ['hæŋkətʃɪf] *n* mouchoir *m*.

handle ['hændl] *n* (*of door etc*) poignée *f*; (*of cup etc*) anse *f*; (*of knife etc*) manche *m*; (*of saucepan*) queue *f*; (*for winding*) manivelle *f* // *vt* toucher, manier; (*deal with*) s'occuper de; (*treat: people*) prendre; '~ **with care**' 'fragile'; **to fly off the** ~ s'énerver; **~bar(s)** *n(pl)* guidon *m*.

hand: **~-luggage** *n* bagages *mpl* à main; **~made** *a* fait(e) à la main; **~out** *n* documentation *f*, prospectus *m*; **~rail** *n* rampe *f*, main courante; **~shake** *n* poignée *f* de main.

handsome ['hænsəm] *a* beau(belle); généreux(euse); considérable.

handwriting ['hændraɪtɪŋ] *n* écriture *f*.

handy ['hændɪ] *a* (*person*) adroit(e); (*close at hand*) sous la main; (*convenient*) pratique; **handyman** *n* bricoleur *m*; (*servant*) homme *m* à tout faire.

hang [hæŋ], *pt*, *pp* **hung** *vt* accrocher; (*criminal: pt*, *pp* **hanged**) pendre // *vi* pendre; (*hair*, *drapery*) tomber; **to get the ~ of (doing) sth** (*col*) attraper le coup pour faire qch; **to ~ about** *vi* flâner, traîner; **to ~ on** *vi* (*wait*) attendre; **to ~ up** *vi* (*TEL*) raccrocher // *vt* accrocher, suspendre.

hangar ['hæŋə*] *n* hangar *m*.

hanger ['hæŋə*] *n* cintre *m*, portemanteau *m*.

hanger-on [hæŋər'ɔn] *n* parasite *m*.

hang-gliding ['hæŋɡlaɪdɪŋ] *n* vol *m* libre or sur aile delta.

hangover ['hæŋəuvə*] *n* (*after drinking*) gueule *f* de bois.

hang-up ['hæŋʌp] *n* complexe *m*.

hanker ['hæŋkə*] *vi:* **to ~ after** avoir envie de.

hankie, hanky ['hæŋkɪ] *n abbr of* **handkerchief.**

haphazard [hæp'hæzəd] *a* fait(e) au hasard, fait(e) au petit bonheur.

happen ['hæpən] *vi* arriver; se passer, se produire; **as it ~s** justement; **~ing** *n* événement *m*.

happily ['hæpɪlɪ] *ad* heureusement.

happiness ['hæpɪnɪs] *n* bonheur *m*.

happy ['hæpɪ] *a* heureux(euse); **~ with** (*arrangements etc*) satisfait(e) de; **~-birthday!** bon anniversaire!; **~-go-lucky** *a* insouciant(e).

harass ['hærəs] *vt* accabler, tourmenter; **~ment** *n* tracasseries *fpl*.

harbour, (US) harbor ['hɑːbə*] *n* port *m* // *vt* héberger, abriter.

hard [hɑːd] *a* dur(e) // *ad* (*work*) dur; (*think*, *try*) sérieusement; **to look ~ at** regarder fixement; regarder de près; **no ~ feelings!** sans rancune!; **to be ~ of hearing** être dur(e) d'oreille; **to be ~ done by** être traité(e) injustement; **~back** *n* livre relié; **~ cash** *n* espèces *fpl*; **~ disk** *n* (*COMPUT*) disque dur; **~en** *vt* durcir; (*fig*) endurcir // *vi* durcir; **~-headed** *a* réaliste; décidé(e); **~ labour** *n* travaux forcés.

hardly ['hɑːdlɪ] *ad* (*scarcely*) à peine; it's ~ the case ce n'est guère le cas; that can ~ be true cela ne peut tout de même pas être vrai; **~ anywhere/ever** presque nulle part/jamais.

hardship ['hɑːdʃɪp] *n* épreuves *fpl*; privations *fpl*.

hard-up [hɑːd'ʌp] *a* (*col*) fauché(e).

hardware ['hɑːdwɛə*] *n* quincaillerie *f*; (*COMPUT*) matériel *m*; **~ shop** *n* quincaillerie *f*.

hard-wearing [hɑːd'wɛərɪŋ] *a* solide.

hard-working [hɑːd'wəːkɪŋ] *a* travailleur(euse).

hardy ['hɑːdɪ] *a* robuste; (*plant*) résistant(e) au gel.

hare [hɛə*] *n* lièvre *m*; **~-brained** *a* farfelu(e); écervelé(e).

harm [hɑːm] *n* mal *m*; (*wrong*) tort *m* // *vt* (*person*) faire du mal or du tort à; (*thing*) endommager; **out of ~'s way** à l'abri du danger, en lieu sûr; **~ful** *a* nuisible; **~less** *a* inoffensif(ive); sans méchanceté.

harmony ['hɑːmənɪ] *n* harmonie *f*.

harness ['hɑːnɪs] *n* harnais *m* // *vt* (*horse*) harnacher; (*resources*) exploiter.

harp [hɑːp] *n* harpe *f* // *vi:* **to ~ on about** parler tout le temps de.

harrowing ['hærəuɪŋ] *a* déchirant(e).

harsh [hɑːʃ] *a* (*hard*) dur(e); (*severe*) sévère; (*unpleasant: sound*) discordant(e); (*: colour*) criard(e); cru(e); (*: wine*) âpre.

harvest ['hɑːvɪst] *n* (*of corn*) moisson *f*; (*of fruit*) récolte *f*; (*of grapes*) vendange *f* // *vi*, *vt* moissonner; récolter; vendanger.

has [hæz] *vb see* **have.**

hash [hæʃ] *n* (*CULIN*) hachis *m*; (*fig: mess*) gâchis *m*.

hasn't ['hæznt] = **has not.**

hassle ['hæsl] *n* chamaillerie *f*.

haste [heɪst] *n* hâte *f*; précipitation *f*; **~n** ['heɪsn] *vt* hâter, accélérer // *vi* se hâter, s'empresser; **hastily** *ad* à la hâte; précipitamment; **hasty** *a* hâtif(ive); précipité(e).

hat [hæt] *n* chapeau *m*.

hatch [hætʃ] *n* (*NAUT: also:* **~way**) écoutille *f*; (*also:* **service ~**) passe-plats *m inv* // *vi* éclore // *vt* faire éclore; (*plot*) tramer.

hatchback ['hætʃbæk] n (AUT) modèle m avec hayon arrière.
hatchet ['hætʃɪt] n hachette f.
hate [heɪt] vt haïr, détester // n haine f; **~ful** a odieux(euse), détestable.
hatred ['heɪtrɪd] n haine f.
hat trick n (SPORT, also fig) triplé m (3 buts réussis au cours du même match etc).
haughty ['hɔːtɪ] a hautain(e), arrogant(e).
haul [hɔːl] vt traîner, tirer // n (of fish) prise f; (of stolen goods etc) butin m; **~age** n transport routier; **~ier**, (US) **~er** n transporteur (routier), camionneur m.
haunch [hɔːntʃ] n hanche f.
haunt [hɔːnt] vt (subj: ghost, fear) hanter; (: person) fréquenter // n repaire m.
have [hæv], pt, pp had ♦ auxiliary vb **1** (gen) avoir; être; to ~ arrived/gone être arrivé(e)/allé(e); to ~ eaten/slept avoir mangé/dormi; he has been promoted il a été promu
2 (in tag questions): you've done it, ~n't you? vous l'avez fait, n'est-ce pas?
3 (in short answers and questions): no I ~n't!/yes we ~! mais non!/mais si!; so I ~! ah oui!, oui c'est vrai!; I've been there before, ~ you? j'y suis déjà allé, et vous?
♦ modal auxiliary vb (be obliged): to ~ (got) to do sth devoir faire qch; être obligé(e) de faire qch; she has (got) to do it elle doit le faire, il faut qu'elle le fasse; you ~n't to tell her vous ne devez pas le lui dire
♦ vt **1** (possess, obtain): avoir; he has (got) blue eyes/dark hair il a les yeux bleus/les cheveux bruns; may I ~ your address? puis-je avoir votre adresse?
2 (+ noun: take, hold etc): to ~ breakfast/a bath/a shower prendre le petit déjeuner/un bain/une douche; to ~ dinner/lunch dîner/déjeuner; to ~ a swim nager; to ~ a meeting se réunir; to ~ a party organiser une fête
3: to ~ sth done faire faire qch; to ~ one's hair cut se faire couper les cheveux; to ~ sb do sth faire faire qch à qn
4 (experience, suffer) avoir; to ~ a cold/flu avoir un rhume/la grippe; to ~ an operation se faire opérer
5 (col: dupe) avoir; he's been had il s'est fait avoir ou roulé
to have out vt: to ~ it out with sb (settle a problem etc) s'expliquer (franchement) avec qn.
haven ['heɪvn] n port m; (fig) havre m.
haven't ['hævnt] = **have not**.
haversack ['hævəsæk] n sac m à dos.
havoc ['hævək] n ravages mpl.
hawk [hɔːk] n faucon m.

hay [heɪ] n foin m; ~ **fever** n rhume m des foins; **~stack** n meule f de foin.
haywire ['heɪwaɪə*] a (col): to go ~ perdre la tête; mal tourner.
hazard ['hæzəd] n hasard m, chance f; danger m, risque m // vt risquer, hasarder; ~ **warning lights** npl (AUT) feux mpl de détresse.
haze [heɪz] n brume f.
hazelnut ['heɪzlnʌt] n noisette f.
hazy ['heɪzɪ] a brumeux(euse); (idea) vague; (photograph) flou(e).
he [hiː] pronoun il; it is ~ who ... c'est lui qui ...
head [hɛd] n tête f; (leader) chef m // vt (list) être en tête de; (group) être à la tête de; ~s or tails pile ou face; ~ **first** la tête la première; ~ **over heels in love** follement or éperdument amoureux(euse); to ~ **the ball** faire une tête; **to ~ for** vt fus se diriger vers; **~ache** n mal m de tête; **~dress** n coiffure f; **~ing** n titre m; rubrique f; **~lamp** n (Brit) = **~light**; **~land** n promontoire m, cap m; **~light** n phare m; **~line** n titre m; **~long** ad (fall) la tête la première; (rush) tête baissée; **~master** n directeur m, proviseur m; **~mistress** n directrice f; ~ **office** n bureau central; **~-on** a (collision) de plein fouet; **~phones** npl casque m (à écouteurs); **~quarters** npl bureau or siège central; (MIL) quartier général; **~rest** n appui-tête m; **~room** n (in car) hauteur f de plafond; (under bridge) hauteur limite; dégagement m; **~scarf** n foulard m; **~strong** a têtu(e), entêté(e); ~ **waiter** n maître m d'hôtel; **~way** n: to make ~way avancer, faire des progrès; **~wind** n vent m contraire; **~y** a capiteux(euse); enivrant(e).
heal [hiːl] vt, vi guérir.
health [hɛlθ] n santé f; ~ **food shop** n magasin m diététique; **the** H~ **Service** n (Brit) ≈ la Sécurité Sociale; **~y** a (person) en bonne santé; (climate, food, attitude etc) sain(e).
heap [hiːp] n tas m, monceau m // vt entasser, amonceler.
hear, pt, pp **heard** [hɪə*, hɜːd] vt entendre; (news) apprendre; (lecture) assister à, écouter // vi entendre; to ~ **about** avoir des nouvelles de; entendre parler de; to ~ **from** sb recevoir des nouvelles de qn; **~ing** n (sense) ouïe f; (of witnesses) audition f; (of a case) audience f; **~ing aid** n appareil m acoustique; **~say**: by **~say** ad par ouï-dire m.
hearse [hɜːs] n corbillard m.
heart [hɑːt] n cœur m; ~**s** npl (CARDS) cœur; **at** ~ au fond; **by** ~ (learn, know) par cœur; ~ **attack** n crise f cardiaque; **~beat** n battement m de cœur; **~broken** a: to be **~broken** avoir

beaucoup de chagrin; **~burn** n brûlures fpl d'estomac; ~ **failure** n arrêt m du cœur; **~felt** a sincère.

hearth [hɑ:θ] n foyer m, cheminée f.

heartily ['hɑ:tɪlɪ] ad chaleureusement; (laugh) de bon cœur; (eat) de bon appétit; **to agree** ~ être entièrement d'accord.

hearty ['hɑ:tɪ] a chaleureux(euse); robuste; vigoureux(euse).

heat [hi:t] n chaleur f; (fig) ardeur f; feu m; (SPORT: also: **qualifying** ~) éliminatoire f // vt chauffer; **to** ~ **up** vi (liquids) chauffer; (room) se réchauffer // vt réchauffer; **~ed** a chauffé(e); (fig) passionné(e), échauffé(e), excité(e); **~er** n appareil m de chauffage; radiateur m.

heath [hi:θ] n (Brit) lande f.

heathen ['hi:ðn] a, n païen(ne).

heather ['hɛðə*] n bruyère f.

heating ['hi:tɪŋ] n chauffage m.

heatstroke ['hi:tstrəuk] n coup m de chaleur.

heatwave ['hi:tweɪv] n vague f de chaleur.

heave [hi:v] vt soulever (avec effort) // vi se soulever; (retch) avoir des haut-le-cœur // n (push) poussée f.

heaven ['hɛvn] n ciel m, paradis m; **~ly** a céleste, divin(e).

heavily ['hɛvɪlɪ] ad lourdement; (drink, smoke) beaucoup; (sleep, sigh) profondément.

heavy ['hɛvɪ] a lourd(e); (work, sea, rain, eater) gros(se); (drinker, smoker) grand(e); ~ **goods vehicle (HGV)** n poids lourd (PL); **~weight** n (SPORT) poids lourd.

Hebrew ['hi:bru:] a hébraïque // n (LING) hébreu m.

Hebrides ['hɛbrɪdi:z] npl: the ~ les Hébrides fpl.

heckle ['hɛkl] vt interpeller (un orateur).

hectic ['hɛktɪk] a agité(e), trépidant(e).

he'd [hi:d] = **he would, he had.**

hedge [hɛdʒ] n haie f // vi se défiler; **to** ~ **one's bets** (fig) se couvrir.

hedgehog ['hɛdʒhɔg] n hérisson m.

heed [hi:d] vt (also: **take** ~ **of**) tenir compte de, prendre garde à; **~less** a insouciant(e).

heel [hi:l] n talon m // vt (shoe) retalonner.

hefty ['hɛftɪ] a (person) costaud(e); (parcel) lourd(e); (piece, price) gros(se).

heifer ['hɛfə*] n génisse f.

height [haɪt] n (of person) taille f, grandeur f; (of object) hauteur f; (of plane, mountain) altitude f; (high ground) hauteur, éminence f; (fig: of glory) sommet m; (: of stupidity) comble m; **~en** vt hausser, surélever;

(fig) augmenter.

heir [ɛə*] n héritier m; **~ess** n héritière f; **~loom** n meuble m (or bijou m or tableau m) de famille.

held [hɛld] pt, pp of **hold.**

helicopter ['hɛlɪkɔptə*] n hélicoptère m.

hell [hɛl] n enfer m; ~! (col) merde!

he'll [hi:l] = **he will, he shall.**

hellish ['hɛlɪʃ] a infernal(e).

hello [hə'ləu] excl bonjour!; salut! (to sb one addresses as 'tu'); (surprise) tiens!

helm [hɛlm] n (NAUT) barre f.

helmet ['hɛlmɪt] n casque m.

help [hɛlp] n aide f; (charwoman) femme f de ménage; (assistant etc) employé/e // vt aider; ~! au secours!; ~ **yourself** (to bread) servez-vous (de pain); **he can't** ~ **it** il n'y peut rien; **~er** n aide m/f, assistant/e; **~ful** a serviable, obligeant(e); (useful) utile; **~ing** n portion f; **~less** a impuissant(e); faible.

hem [hɛm] n ourlet m // vt ourler; **to** ~ **in** vt cerner.

he-man ['hi:mæn] n macho m.

hemorrhage ['hɛmərɪdʒ] n (US) = **haemorrhage.**

hen [hɛn] n poule f.

hence [hɛns] ad (therefore) d'où, de là; **2 years** ~ d'ici 2 ans; **~forth** ad dorénavant.

henchman ['hɛntʃmən] n (pej) acolyte m, séide m.

henpecked ['hɛnpɛkt] a dominé par sa femme.

her [hə:*] pronoun (direct) la, l' + vowel or h mute; (indirect) lui; (stressed, after prep) elle; see note at **she** // a son(sa), ses pl; see also **me, my.**

herald ['hɛrəld] n héraut m // vt annoncer.

herb [hə:b] n herbe f.

herd [hə:d] n troupeau m.

here [hɪə*] ad ici // excl tiens!, tenez!; ~! présent!; ~ **is,** ~ **are** voici; ~'s **my sister** voici ma sœur; ~ **he/she is** le/la voici; ~ **she comes** la voici qui vient; **~after** ad après, plus tard; ci-après // n: **the ~after** l'au-delà m; **~by** ad (in letter) par la présente.

hereditary [hɪ'rɛdɪtrɪ] a héréditaire.

heresy ['hɛrəsɪ] n hérésie f.

hermit ['hə:mɪt] n ermite m.

hernia ['hə:nɪə] n hernie f.

hero, pl **~es** ['hɪərəu] n héros m.

heroin ['hɛrəuɪn] n héroïne f.

heroine ['hɛrəuɪn] n héroïne f.

heron ['hɛrən] n héron m.

herring ['hɛrɪŋ] n hareng m.

hers [hə:z] pronoun le(la) sien(ne), les siens(siennes); see also **mine.**

herself [hə:'sɛlf] pronoun (reflexive) se; (emphatic) elle-même; (after prep) elle; see also **oneself.**

he's [hi:z] = **he is, he has.**

hesitant ['hezitənt] *a* hésitant(e), indécis(e).

hesitate ['heziteit] *vi*: to ~ (about/to do) hésiter (sur/à faire); **hesitation** ['-teɪʃən] *n* hésitation *f*.

heyday ['heideɪ] *n*: the ~ of l'âge *m* d'or de, les beaux jours de.

HGV *n abbr of* **heavy goods vehicle**.

hi [haɪ] *excl* salut!

hiatus [haɪ'eɪtəs] *n* trou *m*, lacune *f*; (*LING*) hiatus *m*.

hibernate ['haɪbəneɪt] *vi* hiberner.

hiccough, hiccup ['hɪkʌp] *vi* hoqueter // *n* hoquet *m*.

hide [haɪd] *n* (*skin*) peau *f* // *vb* (*pt* **hid**, *pp* **hidden** [hɪd, 'hɪdn]) *vt*: to ~ sth (from sb) cacher qch (à qn) // *vi*: to ~ (from sb) se cacher (de qn); **~-and-seek** *n* cache-cache *m*; **~away** *n* cachette *f*.

hideous ['hɪdɪəs] *a* hideux(euse), atroce.

hiding ['haɪdɪŋ] *n* (*beating*) correction *f*, volée *f* de coups; **to be in ~** (*concealed*) se tenir caché(e).

hierarchy ['haɪərɑːkɪ] *n* hiérarchie *f*.

hi-fi ['haɪfaɪ] *n* hi-fi *f inv* // *a* hi-fi *inv*.

high [haɪ] *a* haut(e); (*speed, respect, number*) grand(e); (*price*) élevé(e); (*wind*) fort(e), violent(e); (*voice*) aigu(aiguë) // *ad* haut, en haut; **20 m ~** haut(e) de 20 m; **~boy** *n* (*US: tallboy*) commode (haute); **~brow** *a*, *n* intellectuel(le); **~chair** *n* chaise haute (*pour enfant*); **~er education** *n* études supérieures; **~-handed** *a* très autoritaire; très cavalier(ère); **~jack** = **hijack**; **~ jump** *n* (*SPORT*) saut *m* en hauteur; **the H~lands** *npl* les Highlands *mpl*; **~light** *n* (*fig: of event*) point culminant // *vt* faire ressortir, souligner; **~ly** *ad* très, fort, hautement; **~ly strung** *a* nerveux(euse), toujours tendu(e); **~ness** *n* hauteur *f*; **Her H~ness** son Altesse *f*; **~-pitched** *a* aigu(aiguë); **~-rise block** *n* tour *f* (d'habitation); **~ school** *n* lycée *m*; (*US*) établissement *m* d'enseignement supérieur; **~ season** *n* (*Brit*) haute saison; **~ street** *n* (*Brit*) grand-rue *f*.

highway ['haɪweɪ] *n* grand'route *f*, route nationale; **H~ Code** *n* (*Brit*) code *m* de la route.

hijack ['haɪdʒæk] *vt* détourner (*par la force*); **~er** *n* pirate *m* de l'air.

hike [haɪk] *vi* aller à pied // *n* excursion *f* à pied, randonnée *f*; (*in prices*) hausse *f*, augmentation *f*; **~r** *n* promeneur/euse, excursionniste *m/f*.

hilarious [hɪ'lɛərɪəs] *a* (*behaviour, event*) désopilant(e).

hill [hɪl] *n* colline *f*; (*fairly high*) montagne *f*; (*on road*) côte *f*; **~side** *n* (*flanc m* de) coteau *m*; **~y** *a* vallonné(e); montagneux(euse).

hilt [hɪlt] *n* (*of sword*) garde *f*; **to the ~** (*fig: support*) à fond.

him [hɪm] *pronoun* (*direct*) le, l' + *vowel or h mute*; (*stressed, indirect, after prep*) lui; *see also* **me**; **~self** *pronoun* (*reflexive*) se; (*emphatic*) lui-même; (*after prep*) lui; *see also* **oneself**.

hind [haɪnd] *a* de derrière // *n* biche *f*.

hinder ['hɪndə*] *vt* gêner; (*delay*) retarder; (*prevent*) **to ~ sb from doing** empêcher qn de faire; **hindrance** ['hɪndrəns] *n* gêne *f*, obstacle *m*.

hindsight ['haɪndsaɪt] *n*: **with ~** avec du recul, rétrospectivement.

Hindu ['hɪndu:] *n* Hindou/e.

hinge [hɪndʒ] *n* charnière *f* // *vi* (*fig*): **to ~ on** dépendre de.

hint [hɪnt] *n* allusion *f*; (*advice*) conseil *m* // *vt*: **to ~ that** insinuer que // *vi*: **to ~ at** faire une allusion à.

hip [hɪp] *n* hanche *f*.

hippopotamus, *pl* **~es** *or* **hippopotami** [hɪpə'pɔtəməs, -'pɔtəmaɪ] *n* hippopotame *m*.

hire ['haɪə*] *vt* (*Brit: car, equipment*) louer; (*worker*) embaucher, engager // *n* location *f*; **for ~** à louer; (*taxi*) libre; **~ purchase (H.P.)** *n* (*Brit*) achat *m* (*or* vente *f*) à tempérament *or* crédit.

his [hɪz] *pronoun* le(la) sien(ne), les siens(siennes) // *a* son(sa), ses *pl*; *see also* **my**, **mine**.

hiss [hɪs] *vi* siffler.

historic(al) [hɪ'stɔrɪk(l)] *a* historique.

history ['hɪstərɪ] *n* histoire *f*.

hit [hɪt] *vt* (*pt, pp* **hit**) frapper; (*knock against*) cogner; (*reach: target*) atteindre, toucher; (*collide with: car*) entrer en collision avec, heurter; (*fig: affect*) toucher; (*find*) tomber sur // *n* coup *m*; (*success*) coup réussi; succès *m*; (*song*) chanson *f* à succès, tube *m*; **to ~ it off with sb** bien s'entendre avec qn; **~-and-run driver** *n* chauffard *m*.

hitch [hɪtʃ] *vt* (*fasten*) accrocher, attacher; (*also*: ~ **up**) remonter d'une saccade // *n* (*difficulty*) anicroche *f*, contretemps *m*; **to ~ a lift** faire du stop.

hitch-hike ['hɪtʃhaɪk] *vi* faire de l'auto-stop; **~r** *n* auto-stoppeur/euse.

hi-tech ['haɪ'tɛk] *a* à la pointe de la technologie, technologiquement avancé(e) // *n* high-tech *m*.

hitherto [hɪðə'tu:] *ad* jusqu'ici.

hive [haɪv] *n* ruche *f*; **to ~ off** *vt* mettre à part, séparer.

H.M.S. *abbr = His (Her) Majesty's Ship*.

hoard [hɔːd] *n* (*of food*) provisions *fpl*, réserves *fpl*; (*of money*) trésor *m* // *vt* amasser.

hoarding ['hɔːdɪŋ] *n* (*Brit: for posters*) panneau *m* d'affichage *or* publicitaire.

hoarfrost ['hɔːfrɔst] *n* givre *m*.

hoarse [hɔːs] *a* enroué(e).

hoax [həʊks] *n* canular *m*.

hob [hɔb] *n* plaque chauffante.

hobble ['hɔbl] *vi* boitiller.

hobby ['hɔbɪ] *n* passe-temps favori; **~-horse** *n* (*fig*) dada *m*.

hobo ['həubəu] *n* (*US*) vagabond *m*.

hockey ['hɔkɪ] *n* hockey *m*.

hoe [həu] *n* houe *f*, binette *f*.

hog [hɔg] *n* sanglier *m* // *vt* (*fig*) accaparer; **to go the whole ~** aller jusqu'au bout.

hoist [hɔɪst] *n* palan *m* // *vt* hisser.

hold [həuld] *vb* (*pt, pp* **held**) *vt* tenir; (*contain*) contenir; (*keep back*) retenir; (*believe*) maintenir; considérer; (*possess*) avoir; détenir // *vi* (*withstand pressure*) tenir (bon); (*be valid*) valoir // *n* prise *f*; (*fig*) influence *f*; (*NAUT*) cale *f*; **~ the line!** (*TEL*) ne quittez pas!; **to ~ one's own** (*fig*) (bien) se défendre; (*sick person*) se maintenir; **to catch** *or* **get** (a) **~ of** saisir; **to get ~ of** (*fig*) trouver; **to ~ back** *vt* retenir; (*secret*) cacher; **to ~ down** *vt* (*person*) maintenir à terre; (*job*) occuper; **to ~ off** *vt* tenir à distance; **to ~ on** *vi* tenir bon; (*wait*) attendre; **~ on!** (*TEL*) ne quittez pas!; **to ~ on to** *vt fus* se cramponner à; (*keep*) conserver, garder; **to ~ out** *vt* offrir // *vi* (*resist*) tenir bon; **to ~ up** *vt* (*raise*) lever; (*support*) soutenir; (*delay*) retarder; **~all** *n* (*Brit*) fourre-tout *m inv*; **~er** *n* (*of ticket, record*) détenteur/trice; (*of office, title etc*) titulaire *m/f*; (*of share*) intérêts *mpl*; (*farm*) ferme *f*; **~up** *n* (*robbery*) hold-up *m*; (*delay*) retard *m*; (*Brit: in traffic*) embouteillage *m*.

hole [həul] *n* trou *m*.

holiday ['hɔlədɪ] *n* vacances *fpl*; (*day off*) jour *m* de congé; (*public*) jour férié; **on ~** en congé; **~ camp** *n* (*for children*) colonie *f* de vacances; (*also:* **~ centre**) camp *m* de vacances; **~-maker** *n* (*Brit*) vacancier/ère; **~ resort** *n* centre *m* de villégiature *or* de vacances.

holiness ['həulɪnɪs] *n* sainteté *f*.

Holland ['hɔlənd] *n* Hollande *f*.

hollow ['hɔləu] *a* creux(euse); (*fig*) faux(fausse) // *n* creux *m*; (*in land*) dépression *f* (de terrain), cuvette *f* // *vt*: **to ~ out** creuser, évider.

holly ['hɔlɪ] *n* houx *m*.

holocaust ['hɔləkɔːst] *n* holocauste *m*.

holster ['həulstə*] *n* étui *m* de revolver.

holy ['həulɪ] *a* saint(e); (*bread, water*) bénit(e); (*ground*) sacré(e); **H~ Ghost** *or* **Spirit** *n* Saint-Esprit *m*.

home [həum] *n* foyer *m*, maison *f*; (*country*) pays natal, patrie *f*; (*institution*) maison // *a* de famille; (*ECON, POL*) national(e), intérieur(e) // *ad* chez soi, à la maison; au pays natal; (*right in: nail etc*) à fond; **at ~** chez soi, à la maison; **to go** (*or* **come**) **~** rentrer (chez soi), rentrer à la maison (*or* au

pays); **make yourself at ~** faites comme chez vous; **~ address** *n* domicile permanent; **~ computer** *n* ordinateur *m* domestique; **~land** *n* patrie *f*; **~less** *a* sans foyer; sans abri; **~ly** *a* simple, sans prétention; accueillant(e); **~-made** *a* fait(e) à la maison; **H~ Office** *n* (*Brit*) Ministère *m* de l'Intérieur; **~ rule** *n* autonomie *f*; **H~ Secretary** *n* (*Brit*) ministre *m* de l'Intérieur; **~sick** *a*: **to be ~sick** avoir le mal du pays; s'ennuyer de sa famille; **~ town** *n* ville natale; **~ward** ['həumwəd] *a* (*journey*) du retour; **~work** *n* devoirs *mpl*.

homogeneous [hɔməu'dʒiːnɪəs] *a* homogène.

homosexual [hɔməu'sɛksjuəl] *a, n* homosexuel(le).

honest ['ɔnɪst] *a* honnête; (*sincere*) franc(franche); **~ly** *ad* honnêtement; franchement; **~y** *n* honnêteté *f*.

honey ['hʌnɪ] *n* miel *m*; **~comb** *n* rayon *m* de miel; **~moon** *n* lune *f* de miel; (*trip*) voyage *m* de noces; **~suckle** *n* (*BOT*) chèvrefeuille *m*.

honk [hɔŋk] *vi* klaxonner.

honorary ['ɔnərərɪ] *a* honoraire; (*duty, title*) honorifique.

honour, (*US***) honor** ['ɔnə*] *vt* honorer // *n* honneur *m*; **~able** *a* honorable; **~s degree** *n* (*SCOL*) licence avec mention.

hood [hud] *n* capuchon *m*; (*Brit AUT*) capote *f*; (*US AUT*) capot *m*.

hoodlum ['huːdləm] *n* truand *m*.

hoodwink ['hudwɪŋk] *vt* tromper.

hoof [huːf] , *pl* **~s** *or* **hooves** *n* sabot *m*.

hook [huk] *n* crochet *m*; (*on dress*) agrafe *f*; (*for fishing*) hameçon *m* // *vt* accrocher; (*dress*) agrafer.

hooligan ['huːlɪgən] *n* voyou *m*.

hoop [huːp] *n* cerceau *m*.

hoot [huːt] *vi* (*AUT*) klaxonner; (*siren*) mugir; **~er** *n* (*Brit AUT*) klaxon *m*; (*NAUT*) sirène *f*.

hoover ® ['huːvə*] (*Brit*) *n* aspirateur *m* // *vt* passer l'aspirateur dans *or* sur.

hooves [huːvz] *npl of* **hoof**.

hop [hɔp] *vi* sauter; (*on one foot*) sauter à cloche-pied.

hope [həup] *vt, vi* espérer // *n* espoir *m*; **I ~ so** je l'espère; **I ~ not** j'espère que non; **~ful** *a* (*person*) plein(e) d'espoir; (*situation*) prometteur(euse), encourageant(e); **~fully** *ad* avec espoir, avec optimisme; avec un peu de chance; **~less** *a* désespéré(e); (*useless*) nul(le).

hops [hɔps] *npl* houblon *m*.

horizon [hə'raɪzn] *n* horizon *m*; **~tal** [hɔrɪ'zɔntl] *a* horizontal(e).

horn [hɔːn] *n* corne *f*; (*MUS: also:* **French ~**) cor *m*; (*AUT*) klaxon *m*.

hornet ['hɔːnɪt] *n* frelon *m*.

horny ['hɔːnɪ] *a* corné(e); (*hands*) calleux(euse); (*col*) en rut, excité(e).

horoscope ['hɔrəskəup] n horoscope m.

horrendous [hə'rɛndəs] a horrible, affreux(euse).

horrible ['hɔrɪbl] a horrible, affreux(euse).

horrid ['hɔrɪd] a méchant(e), désagréable.

horrify ['hɔrɪfaɪ] vt horrifier.

horror ['hɔrə*] n horreur f; ~ **film** n film m d'épouvante.

horse [hɔ:s] n cheval m; ~**back**: on ~back à cheval; ~ **chestnut** n marron m (d'Inde); ~**man/woman** n cavalier/ière; ~**power (h.p.)** n puissance f (en chevaux); ~**-racing** n courses fpl de chevaux; ~**radish** n raifort m; ~**shoe** n fer m à cheval.

hose [həuz] n (also: ~pipe) tuyau m; (also: garden ~) tuyau d'arrosage.

hosiery ['həuzɪərɪ] n (in shop) (rayon m des) bas mpl.

hospitable ['hɔspɪtəbl] a hospitalier(ère).

hospital ['hɔspɪtl] n hôpital m; in ~ à l'hôpital.

hospitality [hɔspɪ'tælɪtɪ] n hospitalité f.

host [həust] n hôte m; (in hotel etc) patron m; (REL) hostie f; (large number): a ~ of une foule de.

hostage ['hɔstɪdʒ] n otage m.

hostel ['hɔstl] n foyer m; (also: youth ~) auberge f de jeunesse.

hostess ['həustɪs] n hôtesse f.

hostile ['hɔstaɪl] a hostile.

hostility [hɔ'stɪlɪtɪ] n hostilité f.

hot [hɔt] a chaud(e); (as opposed to only warm) très chaud; (spicy) fort(e); (fig) acharné(e); brûlant(e); violent(e); passionné(e); to be ~ (person) avoir chaud; (object) être (très) chaud; (weather) faire chaud; ~**bed** n (fig) foyer m, pépinière f; ~ **dog** n hot-dog m.

hotel [həu'tɛl] n hôtel m.

hot: ~**headed** a impétueux(euse); ~**house** n serre chaude; ~ **line** n (POL) téléphone m rouge, ligne directe; ~**ly** ad passionnément, violemment; ~**plate** n (on cooker) plaque chauffante; ~**-water bottle** n bouillotte f.

hound [haund] vt poursuivre avec acharnement // n chien courant.

hour ['auə*] n heure f; ~**ly** a, ad toutes les heures; (rate) horaire; ~**ly paid** a payé(e) à l'heure.

house n [haus] (pl: ~s ['hauzɪz]) maison f; (POL) chambre f; (THEATRE) salle f; auditoire m // vt [hauz] (person) loger, héberger; on the ~ (fig) aux frais de la maison; ~**boat** n bateau (aménagé en habitation); ~**breaking** n cambriolage m (avec effraction); ~**coat** n peignoir m; ~**hold** n famille f, maisonnée f; ménage m; ~**keeper** n

gouvernante f; ~**keeping** n (work) ménage m; ~**keeping** (money) argent m du ménage; ~**warming party** n pendaison f de crémaillère; ~**wife** n ménagère f; femme f au foyer; ~**work** n (travaux mpl du) ménage m.

housing ['hauzɪŋ] n logement m; ~ **development**, (Brit) ~ **estate** n cité f; lotissement m.

hovel ['hɔvl] n taudis m.

hover ['hɔvə*] vi planer; ~**craft** n aéroglisseur m.

how [hau] ad comment; ~ **are you?** comment allez-vous?; ~ **do you do?** bonjour; enchanté(e); ~ **far is it to ...?** combien y a-t-il jusqu'à ...?; ~ **long have you been here?** depuis combien de temps êtes-vous là?; ~ **lovely!** que or comme c'est joli!; ~ **many/much?** combien?; ~ **many people/much milk** combien de gens/lait; ~ **old are you?** quel âge avez-vous?; ~**ever** ad de quelque façon or manière que + sub; (+ adjective) quelque or si ... que + sub; (in questions) comment // cj pourtant, cependant.

howl ['haul] vi hurler.

h.p., H.P. abbr of **hire purchase, horsepower.**

HQ abbr of **headquarters.**

hub [hʌb] n (of wheel) moyeu m; (fig) centre m, foyer m.

hubbub ['hʌbʌb] n brouhaha m.

hub cap n enjoliveur m.

huddle ['hʌdl] vi: to ~ **together** se blottir les uns contre les autres.

hue [hju:] n teinte f, nuance f; ~ **and cry** n tollé (général), clameur f.

huff [hʌf] n: in a ~ fâché(e).

hug [hʌg] vt serrer dans ses bras; (shore, kerb) serrer // n étreinte f.

huge [hju:dʒ] a énorme, immense.

hulk [hʌlk] n (ship) vieux rafiot m; (car, building) carcasse f; (person) mastodonte m, malabar m.

hull [hʌl] n (of ship, nuts) coque f.

hullo [hə'ləu] excl = **hello.**

hum [hʌm] vt (tune) fredonner // vi fredonner; (insect) bourdonner; (plane, tool) vrombir.

human ['hju:mən] a humain(e) // n être humain.

humane [hju:'meɪn] a humain(e), humanitaire.

humanitarian [hju:mænɪ'tɛərɪən] a humanitaire.

humanity [hju:'mænɪtɪ] n humanité f.

humble ['hʌmbl] a humble, modeste // vt humilier.

humbug ['hʌmbʌg] n fumisterie f.

humdrum ['hʌmdrʌm] a monotone, routinier(ère).

humid ['hju:mɪd] a humide.

humiliate [hju:'mɪlɪeɪt] vt humilier; **humiliation** [-'eɪʃən] n humiliation f.

humility [hju:'mılıtı] n humilité f.

humorous ['hju:mərəs] a humoristique; (person) plein(e) d'humour.

humour, (US) humor ['hju:mə*] n humour m; (mood) humeur f // vt (person) faire plaisir à; se prêter aux caprices de.

hump [hʌmp] n bosse f.

hunch [hʌntʃ] n bosse f; (premonition) intuition f; ~**back** n bossu/e; ~**ed** a arrondi(e), voûté(e).

hundred ['hʌndrəd] num cent; ~s of des centaines de; ~**weight** n (Brit) = 50.8 kg; 112 lb; (US) = 45.3 kg; 100 lb.

hung [hʌŋ] pt, pp of **hang**.

Hungary ['hʌŋgərı] n Hongrie f.

hunger ['hʌŋgə*] n faim f // vi: **to ~ for** avoir faim de, désirer ardemment.

hungry ['hʌŋgrı] a affamé(e); **to be ~** avoir faim.

hunk [hʌŋk] n (of bread etc) gros morceau.

hunt [hʌnt] vt (seek) chercher; (SPORT) chasser // vi chasser // n chasse f; ~**er** n chasseur m; ~**ing** n chasse f.

hurdle ['hə:dl] n (SPORT) haie f; (fig) obstacle m.

hurl [hə:l] vt lancer (avec violence).

hurrah, hurray [hu'rɑ:, hu'reı] n hourra m.

hurricane ['hʌrıkən] n ouragan m.

hurried ['hʌrıd] a pressé(e), précipité(e); (work) fait(e) à la hâte; ~**ly** ad précipitamment, à la hâte.

hurry ['hʌrı] n hâte f, précipitation f // vb (also: ~ **up**) vi se presser, se dépêcher // vt (person) faire presser, faire dépêcher; (work) presser; **to be in a ~** être pressé(e); **to do sth in a ~** faire qch en vitesse; **to ~ in/out** entrer/sortir précipitamment.

hurt [hə:t] vb (pt, pp **hurt**) vt (cause pain to) faire mal à; (injure, fig) blesser // vi faire mal // a blessé(e); ~**ful** a (remark) blessant(e).

hurtle ['hə:tl] vi: **to ~ past** passer en trombe; **to ~ down** dégringoler.

husband ['hʌzbənd] n mari m.

hush [hʌʃ] n calme m, silence m // vt faire taire; ~! chut!

husk [hʌsk] n (of wheat) balle f; (of rice, maize) enveloppe f.

husky ['hʌskı] a rauque // n chien m esquimau or de traîneau.

hustle ['hʌsl] vt pousser, bousculer // n bousculade f; ~ **and bustle** n tourbillon m (d'activité).

hut [hʌt] n hutte f; (shed) cabane f.

hutch [hʌtʃ] n clapier m.

hyacinth ['haıəsınθ] n jacinthe f.

hydrant ['haıdrənt] n prise f d'eau; (also: **fire ~**) bouche f d'incendie.

hydraulic [haı'drɔ:lık] a hydraulique.

hydroelectric [haıdrəuı'lcktrık] a hydro-électrique.

hydrofoil ['haıdrəufɔıl] n hydrofoil m.

hydrogen ['haıdrədʒən] n hydrogène m.

hyena [haı'i:nə] n hyène f.

hygiene ['haıdʒi:n] n hygiène f.

hymn [hım] n hymne m; cantique m.

hype [haıp] n (col) campagne f publicitaire.

hypermarket ['haıpəma:kıt] n hypermarché m.

hyphen ['haıfn] n trait m d'union.

hypnotize ['hıpnətaız] vt hypnotiser.

hypocrisy [hı'pɔkrısı] n hypocrisie f.

hypocrite ['hıpəkrıt] n hypocrite m/f; **hypocritical** [-'krıtıkl] a hypocrite.

hypothesis, pl hypotheses [haı'pɔθısıs, -sı:z] n hypothèse f.

hysterical [hı'sterıkl] a hystérique.

hysterics [hı'sterıks] npl (violente) crise de nerfs; (laughter) crise de rire.

I

I [aı] pronoun je; (before vowel) j'; (stressed) moi.

ice [aıs] n glace f; (on road) verglas m // vt (cake) glacer; (drink) faire rafraîchir // vi (also: ~ **up**) geler; (also: ~ **up**) se givrer; ~ **axe** n piolet m; ~**berg** n iceberg m; ~**box** n (US) réfrigérateur m; (Brit) compartiment m à glace; (insulated box) glacière f; ~ **cream** n glace f; ~ **cube** n glaçon m; ~ **hockey** n hockey m sur glace.

Iceland ['aıslənd] n Islande f.

ice: ~ **lolly** n (Brit) esquimau m; ~ **rink** n patinoire f; ~ **skating** n patinage m (sur glace).

icicle ['aısıkl] n glaçon m (naturel).

icing ['aısıŋ] n (AVIAT etc) givrage m; (CULIN) glaçage m; ~ **sugar** n (Brit) sucre m glace.

icy ['aısı] a glacé(e); (road) verglacé(e); (weather, temperature) glacial(e).

I'd [aıd] = **I would, I had**.

idea [aı'dıə] n idée f.

ideal [aı'dıəl] n idéal m // a idéal(e).

identical [aı'dentıkl] a identique.

identification [aıdentıfı'keıʃən] n identification f; **means of ~** pièce f d'identité.

identify [aı'dentıfaı] vt identifier.

identikit picture [aı'dentıkıt-] n portrait-robot m.

identity [aı'dentıtı] n identité f; ~ **card** n carte f d'identité.

idiom ['ıdıəm] n langue f, idiome m; (phrase) expression f idiomatique.

idiosyncrasy [ıdıəu'sıŋkrəsı] n particularité f, caractéristique f.

idiot ['ıdıət] n idiot/e, imbécile m/f; ~**ic** [-'ɔtık] a idiot(e), bête, stupide.

idle ['aıdl] a sans occupation, désœuvré(e); (lazy) oisif(ive), paresseux(euse); (unemployed) au chômage;

(*question, pleasures*) vain(e), futile // *vt*: to ~ **away the time** passer son temps à ne rien faire; **to lie ~** être arrêté, ne pas fonctionner.

idol [ˈaɪdl] *n* idole *f*; ~**ize** *vt* idolâtrer, adorer.

i.e. *ad abbr* (= *id est*) c'est-à-dire.

if [ɪf] *cj* si; ~ **so** si c'est le cas; ~ **not** sinon; ~ **only** si seulement.

ignite [ɪgˈnaɪt] *vt* mettre le feu à, enflammer // *vi* s'enflammer.

ignition [ɪgˈnɪʃən] *n* (AUT) allumage *m*; **to switch on/off the** ~ mettre/couper le contact; ~ **key** *n* (AUT) clé *f* de contact.

ignorant [ˈɪgnərənt] *a* ignorant(e); **to be** ~ **of** (*subject*) ne rien connaître en; (*events*) ne pas être au courant de.

ignore [ɪgˈnɔː*] *vt* ne tenir aucun compte de, ne pas relever; (*person*) faire semblant de ne pas reconnaître, ignorer; (*fact*) méconnaître.

ill [ɪl] *a* (*sick*) malade; (*bad*) mauvais(e) // *n* mal *m* // *ad*: **to speak** *etc* ~ **of** dire *etc* du mal de; **to take** *or* **be taken** ~ tomber malade; ~**-advised** *a* (*decision*) peu judicieux(euse); (*person*) malavisé(e); ~**-at-ease** *a* mal à l'aise.

I'll [aɪl] = **I will**, **I shall**.

illegal [ɪˈliːgl] *a* illégal(e).

illegible [ɪˈledʒɪbl] *a* illisible.

illegitimate [ɪlɪˈdʒɪtɪmət] *a* illégitime.

ill-fated [ɪlˈfeɪtɪd] *a* malheureux(euse); (*day*) néfaste.

ill feeling *n* ressentiment *m*, rancune *f*.

illiterate [ɪˈlɪtərət] *a* illettré(e); (*letter*) plein(e) de fautes.

illness [ˈɪlnɪs] *n* maladie *f*.

ill-treat [ɪlˈtriːt] *vt* maltraiter.

illuminate [ɪˈluːmɪneɪt] *vt* (*room, street*) éclairer; (*building*) illuminer; **illumination** [-ˈneɪʃən] *n* éclairage *m*; illumination *f*.

illusion [ɪˈluːʒən] *n* illusion *f*; **to be under the** ~ **that** s'imaginer *or* croire que.

illustrate [ˈɪləstreɪt] *vt* illustrer; **illustration** [-ˈstreɪʃən] *n* illustration *f*.

ill will *n* malveillance *f*.

I'm [aɪm] = **I am**.

image [ˈɪmɪdʒ] *n* image *f*; (*public face*) image de marque; ~**ry** *n* images *fpl*.

imaginary [ɪˈmædʒɪnərɪ] *a* imaginaire.

imagination [ɪmædʒɪˈneɪʃən] *n* imagination *f*.

imaginative [ɪˈmædʒɪnətɪv] *a* imaginatif(ive); plein(e) d'imagination.

imagine [ɪˈmædʒɪn] *vt* s'imaginer; (*suppose*) imaginer, supposer.

imbalance [ɪmˈbæləns] *n* déséquilibre *m*.

imitate [ˈɪmɪteɪt] *vt* imiter; **imitation** [-ˈteɪʃən] *n* imitation *f*.

immaculate [ɪˈmækjulət] *a* impeccable; (REL) immaculé(e).

immaterial [ɪməˈtɪərɪəl] *a* sans importance, insignifiant(e).

immature [ɪməˈtjuə*] *a* (*fruit*) qui n'est pas mûr(e); (*person*) qui manque de maturité.

immediate [ɪˈmiːdɪət] *a* immédiat(e); ~**ly** *ad* (*at once*) immédiatement; ~**ly next to** juste à côté de.

immense [ɪˈmɛns] *a* immense; énorme.

immerse [ɪˈmɔːs] *vt* immerger, plonger.

immersion heater [ɪˈmɔː∫ən-] *n* (*Brit*) chauffe-eau *m* électrique.

immigrant [ˈɪmɪgrənt] *n* immigrant/e; immigré/e.

immigration [ɪmɪˈgreɪ∫ən] *n* immigration *f*.

imminent [ˈɪmɪnənt] *a* imminent(e).

immoral [ɪˈmɔrl] *a* immoral(e).

immortal [ɪˈmɔːtl] *a*, *n* immortel(le).

immune [ɪˈmjuːn] *a*: ~ **(to)** immunisé(e) (contre).

immunity [ɪˈmjuːnɪtɪ] *n* immunité *f*.

imp [ɪmp] *n* lutin *m*; (*child*) petit diable.

impact [ˈɪmpækt] *n* choc *m*, impact *m*; (*fig*) impact.

impair [ɪmˈpɛə*] *vt* détériorer, diminuer.

impart [ɪmˈpɑːt] *vt* communiquer, transmettre; confier, donner.

impartial [ɪmˈpɑː∫l] *a* impartial(e).

impassable [ɪmˈpɑːsəbl] *a* infranchissable; (*road*) impraticable.

impassive [ɪmˈpæsɪv] *a* impassible.

impatience [ɪmˈpeɪ∫əns] *n* impatience *f*.

impatient [ɪmˈpeɪ∫ənt] *a* impatient(e); **to get** *or* **grow** ~ s'impatienter.

impeccable [ɪmˈpɛkəbl] *a* impeccable, parfait(e).

impede [ɪmˈpiːd] *vt* gêner.

impediment [ɪmˈpɛdɪmənt] *n* obstacle *m*; (*also*: **speech** ~) défaut *m* d'élocution.

impending [ɪmˈpɛndɪŋ] *a* imminent(e).

imperative [ɪmˈpɛrətɪv] *a* nécessaire; urgent(e), pressant(e); (*tone*) impérieux(euse) // *n* (LING) impératif *m*.

imperfect [ɪmˈpɔːfɪkt] *a* imparfait(e); (*goods etc*) défectueux(euse).

imperial [ɪmˈpɪərɪəl] *a* impérial(e); (*measure*) légal(e).

impersonal [ɪmˈpɔːsənl] *a* impersonnel(le).

impersonate [ɪmˈpɔːsəneɪt] *vt* se faire passer pour; (THEATRE) imiter.

impertinent [ɪmˈpɔːtɪnənt] *a* impertinent(e), insolent(e).

impervious [ɪmˈpɔːvɪəs] *a* imperméable; (*fig*): ~ **to** insensible à; inaccessible à.

impetuous [ɪmˈpɛtjuəs] *a* impétueux(euse), fougueux(euse).

impetus [ˈɪmpətəs] *n* impulsion *f*; (*of runner*) élan *m*.

impinge [ɪmˈpɪndʒ]: **to** ~ **on** *vt fus* (*person*) affecter, toucher; (*rights*) empiéter sur.

implement *n* [ˈɪmplɪmənt] outil *m*, instrument *m*; (*for cooking*) ustensile *m* //

vt ['ɪmplɪmɛnt] exécuter, mettre à effet.
implicit [ɪm'plɪsɪt] *a* implicite; (*complete*) absolu(e), sans réserve.
imply [ɪm'plaɪ] *vt* suggérer, laisser entendre; indiquer, supposer.
impolite [ɪmpə'laɪt] *a* impoli(e).
import *vt* [ɪm'pɔ:t] importer // *n* ['ɪmpɔ:t] (*COMM*) importation *f*; (*meaning*) portée *f*, signification *f*.
importance [ɪm'pɔ:tns] *n* importance *f*.
important [ɪm'pɔ:tnt] *a* important(e).
importer [ɪm'pɔ:tə*] *n* importateur/trice.
impose [ɪm'pəuz] *vt* imposer // *vi*: **to ~ on sb** abuser de la gentillesse (*or* crédulité) de qn.
imposing [ɪm'pəuzɪŋ] *a* imposant(e), impressionnant(e).
imposition [ɪmpə'zɪʃən] *n* (*of tax etc*) imposition *f*; **to be an ~ on** (*person*) abuser de la gentillesse *or* la bonté de.
impossible [ɪm'pɔsɪbl] *a* impossible.
impotent ['ɪmpətnt] *a* impuissant(e).
impound [ɪm'paund] *vt* confisquer, saisir.
impoverished [ɪm'pɔvərɪʃt] *a* pauvre, appauvri(e).
impractical [ɪm'præktɪkl] *a* pas pratique; (*person*) qui manque d'esprit pratique.
impregnable [ɪm'prɛgnəbl] *a* (*fortress*) imprenable; (*fig*) inattaquable; irréfutable.
impress [ɪm'prɛs] *vt* impressionner, faire impression sur; (*mark*) imprimer, marquer; **to ~ sth on sb** faire bien comprendre qch à qn.
impression [ɪm'prɛʃən] *n* impression *f*; (*of stamp, seal*) empreinte *f*; **to be under the ~ that** avoir l'impression que.
impressive [ɪm'prɛsɪv] *a* impressionnant(e).
imprint ['ɪmprɪnt] *n* (*PUBLISHING*) notice *f*.
imprison [ɪm'prɪzn] *vt* emprisonner, mettre en prison.
improbable [ɪm'prɔbəbl] *a* improbable; (*excuse*) peu plausible.
improper [ɪm'prɔpə*] *a* incorrect(e); (*unsuitable*) déplacé(e), de mauvais goût; indécent(e).
improve [ɪm'pru:v] *vt* améliorer // *vi* s'améliorer; (*pupil etc*) faire des progrès; **~ment** *n* amélioration *f*; progrès *m*.
improvise ['ɪmprəvaɪz] *vt*, *vi* improviser.
impudent ['ɪmpjudnt] *a* impudent(e).
impulse ['ɪmpʌls] *n* impulsion *f*; **on ~** impulsivement, sur un coup de tête.
impulsive [ɪm'pʌlsɪv] *a* impulsif(ive).
in [ɪn] ♦ *prep* **1** (*indicating place, position*) dans; **~ the house/the fridge** dans la maison/le frigo; **~ the garden** dans le *or* au jardin; **~ town** en ville; **~**

the country à la campagne; **~ school** à l'école; **~ here/there** ici/là
2 (*with place names: of town, region, country*): **~ London** à Londres; **~ England** en Angleterre; **~ Japan** au Japon; **~ the United States** aux États-Unis
3 (*indicating time: during*): **~ spring** au printemps; **~ summer** en été; **~ May/ 1992** en mai/1992; **~ the afternoon** (dans) l'après-midi; **at 4 o'clock ~ the afternoon** à 4 heures de l'après-midi
4 (*indicating time: in the space of*) en; (*: future*) dans; **I did it ~ 3 hours/days** je l'ai fait en 3 heures/jours; **I'll see you ~ 2 weeks** *or* **~ 2 weeks' time** je te verrai dans 2 semaines
5 (*indicating manner etc*) à; **~ a loud/ soft voice** à voix haute/basse; **~ pencil** au crayon; **~ French** en français; **the boy ~ the blue shirt** le garçon à *or* avec la chemise bleue
6 (*indicating circumstances*): **~ the sun** au soleil; **~ the shade** à l'ombre; **~ the rain** sous la pluie
7 (*indicating mood, state*): **~ tears** en larmes; **~ anger** sous le coup de la colère; **~ despair** au désespoir; **~ good condition** en bon état; **to live ~ luxury** vivre dans le luxe
8 (*with ratios, numbers*): **1 ~ 10 (households), 1 (household) ~ 10** (ménage) sur 10; **20 pence ~ the pound** 20 pence par livre sterling; **they lined up ~ twos** ils se mirent en rangs (deux) par deux; **~ hundreds** par centaines
9 (*referring to people, works*) chez; **the disease is common ~ children** c'est une maladie courante chez les enfants; **~ (the works of) Dickens** chez Dickens, dans (l'œuvre de) Dickens
10 (*indicating profession etc*) dans; **to be ~ teaching** être dans l'enseignement
11 (*after superlative*) de; **the best pupil ~ the class** le meilleur élève de la classe
12 (*with present participle*): **~ saying this** en disant ceci
♦ *ad*: **to be ~** (*person: at home, work*) être là; (*train, ship, plane*) être arrivé(e); (*in fashion*) être à la mode; **to ask sb ~** inviter qn à entrer; **to run/ limp etc ~** entrer en courant/boitant etc
♦ *n*: **the ~s and outs (of)** (*of proposal, situation etc*) les tenants et aboutissants (de).

in., ins *abbr of* **inch(es)**.
inability [ɪnə'bɪlɪtɪ] *n* incapacité *f*.
inaccurate [ɪn'ækjurət] *a* inexact(e); (*person*) qui manque de précision.
inadequate [ɪn'ædɪkwət] *a* insuffisant(e), inadéquat(e).
inadvertently [ɪnəd'və:tntlɪ] *ad* par mégarde.
inane [ɪ'neɪn] *a* inepte, stupide.
inanimate [ɪn'ænɪmət] *a* inanimé(e).
inappropriate [ɪnə'prəuprɪət] *a*

inopportun(e), mal à propos; (word, expression) impropre.

inarticulate [ɪnɑːˈtɪkjulət] a (person) qui s'exprime mal; (speech) indistinct(e).

inasmuch as [ɪnəzˈmʌtʃæz] ad dans la mesure où; (seeing that) attendu que.

inauguration [ɪnɔːgjuˈreɪʃən] n inauguration f; (of president, official) investiture f.

in-between [ɪnbɪˈtwiːn] a entre les deux.

inborn [ɪnˈbɔːn] a (feeling) inné(e); (defect) congénital(e).

inbred [ɪnˈbred] a inné(e), naturel(le); (family) consanguin(e).

Inc. abbr of **incorporated**.

incapable [ɪnˈkeɪpəbl] a incapable.

incapacitate [ɪnkəˈpæsɪteɪt] vt: to ~ sb from doing rendre qn incapable de faire.

incense n [ˈɪnsɛns] encens m // vt [ɪnˈsɛns] (anger) mettre en colère.

incentive [ɪnˈsɛntɪv] n encouragement m, raison f de se donner de la peine.

incessant [ɪnˈsɛsnt] a incessant(e); ~ly ad sans cesse, constamment.

inch [ɪntʃ] n pouce m (= 25 mm; 12 in a foot); within an ~ of à deux doigts de; he didn't give an ~ (fig) il n'a pas voulu céder d'un pouce or faire la plus petite concession; to ~ forward vi avancer petit à petit.

incidence [ˈɪnsɪdns] n (of crime, disease) fréquence f.

incident [ˈɪnsɪdnt] n incident m; (in book) péripétie f.

incidental [ɪnsɪˈdɛntl] a accessoire; (unplanned) accidentel(le); ~ to qui accompagne; ~ly [-ˈdɛntəlɪ] ad (by the way) à propos.

incipient [ɪnˈsɪpɪənt] a naissant(e).

inclination [ɪnklɪˈneɪʃən] n inclination f.

incline n [ˈɪnklaɪn] pente f, plan incliné // vb [ɪnˈklaɪn] vt incliner // vi: to ~ to avoir tendance à; to be ~d to être enclin(e) à faire; avoir tendance à faire.

include [ɪnˈkluːd] vt inclure, comprendre; **including** prep y compris.

inclusive [ɪnˈkluːsɪv] a inclus(e), compris(e) // ad: ~ of tax etc taxes etc comprises.

income [ˈɪnkʌm] n revenu m; ~ tax n impôt m sur le revenu.

incompetent [ɪnˈkɔmpɪtnt] a incompétent(e), incapable.

incomplete [ɪnkəmˈpliːt] a incomplet(ète).

incongruous [ɪnˈkɔŋgruəs] a peu approprié(e); (remark, act) incongru(e), déplacé(e).

inconsistency [ɪnkənˈsɪstənsɪ] n (of actions etc) inconséquence f; (of work) irrégularité f; (of statement etc) incohérence f.

inconsistent [ɪnkənˈsɪstnt] a incon-

séquent(e); irrégulier(ère); peu cohérent(e).

inconspicuous [ɪnkənˈspɪkjuəs] a qui passe inaperçu(e); (colour, dress) discret(ète).

inconvenience [ɪnkənˈviːnjəns] n inconvénient m; (trouble) dérangement m // vt déranger.

inconvenient [ɪnkənˈviːnjənt] a malcommode; (time, place) mal choisi(e), qui ne convient pas.

incorporate [ɪnˈkɔːpəreɪt] vt incorporer; (contain) contenir; ~d a: ~d company (US: abbr Inc.) ≈ société f anonyme (S.A.).

incorrect [ɪnkəˈrɛkt] a incorrect(e); (opinion, statement) inexact(e).

increase n [ˈɪnkriːs] augmentation f // vi, vt [ɪnˈkriːs] augmenter.

increasing [ɪnˈkriːsɪŋ] a (number) croissant(e); ~ly ad de plus en plus.

incredible [ɪnˈkrɛdɪbl] a incroyable.

incredulous [ɪnˈkrɛdjuləs] a incrédule.

increment [ˈɪnkrɪmənt] n augmentation f.

incubator [ˈɪnkjubeɪtə*] n incubateur m; (for babies) couveuse f.

incumbent [ɪnˈkʌmbənt] n (REL) titulaire m/f // a: it is ~ on him to ... il lui incombe or appartient de ....

incur [ɪnˈkɔː*] vt (expenses) encourir; (anger, risk) s'exposer à; (debt) contracter; (loss) subir.

indebted [ɪnˈdetɪd] a: to be ~ to sb (for) être redevable à qn (de).

indecent [ɪnˈdiːsnt] a indécent(e), inconvenant(e); ~ assault n (Brit) attentat m à la pudeur; ~ exposure n outrage m (public) à la pudeur.

indecisive [ɪndɪˈsaɪsɪv] a indécis(e); (discussion) peu concluant(e).

indeed [ɪnˈdiːd] ad en effet; d'ailleurs; vraiment; yes ~! certainement!

indefinite [ɪnˈdɛfɪnɪt] a indéfini(e); (answer) vague; (period, number) indéterminé(e); ~ly ad (wait) indéfiniment.

indemnity [ɪnˈdɛmnɪtɪ] n (insurance) assurance f, garantie f; (compensation) indemnité f.

independence [ɪndɪˈpɛndns] n indépendance f.

independent [ɪndɪˈpɛndnt] a indépendant(e); to become ~ s'affranchir.

index [ˈɪndɛks] n (pl: ~es: in book) index m; (: in library etc) catalogue m; (pl: indices [ˈɪndɪsiːz]) (ratio, sign) indice m; ~ card n fiche f; ~ finger n index m; ~-linked, (US) ~ed a indexé(e) (sur le coût de la vie etc).

India [ˈɪndɪə] n Inde f; ~n a indien(ne) // n Indien/ne; Red ~n Indien/ne (d'Amérique).

indicate [ˈɪndɪkeɪt] vt indiquer; **indica-**

tion [-'keɪʃən] *n* indication *f*, signe *m*.
indicative [ɪn'dɪkətɪv] *a* indicatif(ive) // *n* (*LING*) indicatif *m*; ~ **of** symptomatique de.
indicator ['ɪndɪkeɪtə*] *n* (*sign*) indicateur *m*; (*AUT*) clignotant *m*.
indices ['ɪndɪsiːz] *npl of* **index**.
indictment [ɪn'daɪtmənt] *n* accusation *f*.
indifference [ɪn'dɪfrəns] *n* indifférence *f*.
indifferent [ɪn'dɪfrənt] *a* indifférent(e); (*poor*) médiocre, quelconque.
indigenous [ɪn'dɪdʒɪnəs] *a* indigène.
indigestion [ɪndɪ'dʒɛstʃən] *n* indigestion *f*, mauvaise digestion.
indignant [ɪn'dɪgnənt] *a*: ~ (**at** *or* **about** sth/with sb) indigné(e) (de qch/contre qn).
indignity [ɪn'dɪgnɪtɪ] *n* indignité *f*, affront *m*.
indirect [ɪndɪ'rɛkt] *a* indirect(e).
indiscreet [ɪndɪ'skriːt] *a* indiscret(ète); (*rash*) imprudent(e).
indiscriminate [ɪndɪ'skrɪmɪnət] *a* (*person*) qui manque de discernement; (*admiration*) aveugle; (*killings*) commis(e) au hasard.
indisputable [ɪndɪ'spjuːtəbl] *a* incontestable, indiscutable.
individual [ɪndɪ'vɪdjuəl] *n* individu *m* // *a* individuel(le); (*characteristic*) particulier(ère), original(e).
indoctrination [ɪndɔktrɪ'neɪʃən] *n* endoctrinement *m*.
Indonesia [ɪndə'niːzɪə] *n* Indonésie *f*.
indoor ['ɪndɔː*] *a* d'intérieur; (*plant*) d'appartement; (*swimming pool*) couvert(e); (*sport*, *games*) pratiqué(e) en salle; ~**s** [ɪn'dɔːz] *ad* à l'intérieur; (*at home*) à la maison.
induce [ɪn'djuːs] *vt* persuader; (*bring about*) provoquer; ~**ment** *n* incitation *f*; (*incentive*) but *m*; (*pej: bribe*) pot-de-vin *m*.
induction [ɪn'dʌkʃən] *n* (*MED: of birth*) accouchement provoqué; ~ **course** *n* (*Brit*) stage *m* de mise au courant.
indulge [ɪn'dʌldʒ] *vt* (*whim*) céder à, satisfaire; (*child*) gâter // *vi*: **to** ~ **in** sth s'offrir qch, se permettre qch; se livrer à qch; ~**nce** *n* fantaisie *f* (que l'on s'offre); (*leniency*) indulgence *f*; ~**nt** *a* indulgent(e).
industrial [ɪn'dʌstrɪəl] *a* industriel(le); (*injury*) du travail; (*dispute*) ouvrier(ère); ~ **action** *n* action revendicative; ~ **estate** *n* (*Brit*) zone industrielle; ~**ist** *n* industriel *m*; ~ **park** *n* (*US*) = ~ **estate**.
industrious [ɪn'dʌstrɪəs] *a* travailleur(euse).
industry ['ɪndəstrɪ] *n* industrie *f*; (*diligence*) zèle *m*, application *f*.
inebriated [ɪ'niːbrɪeɪtɪd] *a* ivre.
inedible [ɪn'ɛdɪbl] *a* immangeable;

(*plant etc*) non comestible.
ineffective [ɪnɪ'fɛktɪv], **ineffectual** [ɪnɪ'fɛktʃuəl] *a* inefficace; (*person*) incompétent(e).
inefficiency [ɪnɪ'fɪʃənsɪ] *n* inefficacité *f*.
inefficient [ɪnɪ'fɪʃənt] *a* inefficace.
inequality [ɪnɪ'kwɔlɪtɪ] *n* inégalité *f*.
inescapable [ɪnɪ'skeɪpəbl] *a* inéluctable, inévitable.
inevitable [ɪn'ɛvɪtəbl] *a* inévitable; **inevitably** *ad* inévitablement.
inexpensive [ɪnɪk'spɛnsɪv] *a* bon marché *inv*.
inexperienced [ɪnɪks'pɪərɪənst] *a* inexpérimenté(e).
infallible [ɪn'fælɪbl] *a* infaillible.
infamous ['ɪnfəməs] *a* infâme, abominable.
infancy ['ɪnfənsɪ] *n* petite enfance, bas âge; (*fig*) enfance, débuts *mpl*.
infant ['ɪnfənt] *n* (*baby*) nourrisson *m*; (*young child*) petit(e) enfant; ~ **school** *n* (*Brit*) classes *fpl* préparatoires (*entre 5 et 7 ans*).
infatuated [ɪn'fætjueɪtɪd] *a*: ~ **with** entiché(e) de.
infatuation [ɪnfætju'eɪʃən] *n* toquade *f*; engouement *m*.
infect [ɪn'fɛkt] *vt* infecter, contaminer; ~**ion** [ɪn'fɛkʃən] *n* infection *f*; contagion *f*; ~**ious** [ɪn'fɛkʃəs] *a* infectieux(euse); (*also fig*) contagieux(euse).
infer [ɪn'fəː*] *vt* conclure, déduire.
inferior [ɪn'fɪərɪə*] *a* inférieur(e); (*goods*) de qualité inférieure // *n* inférieur/e; (*in rank*) subalterne *m/f*; ~**ity** [ɪnfɪərɪ'ɔrətɪ] *n* infériorité *f*; ~**ity complex** *n* complexe *m* d'infériorité.
inferno [ɪn'fəːnəu] *n* enfer *m*; brasier *m*.
infertile [ɪn'fəːtaɪl] *a* stérile.
in-fighting ['ɪnfaɪtɪŋ] *n* querelles *fpl* internes.
infinite ['ɪnfɪnɪt] *a* infini(e).
infinitive [ɪn'fɪnɪtɪv] *n* infinitif *m*.
infinity [ɪn'fɪnɪtɪ] *n* infinité *f*; (*also MATH*) infini *m*.
infirmary [ɪn'fəːmərɪ] *n* hôpital *m*; (*in school*, *factory*) infirmerie *f*.
infirmity [ɪn'fəːmɪtɪ] *n* infirmité *f*.
inflamed [ɪn'fleɪmd] *a* enflammé(e).
inflammable [ɪn'flæməbl] *a* (*Brit*) inflammable.
inflammation [ɪnflə'meɪʃən] *n* inflammation *f*.
inflatable [ɪn'fleɪtəbl] *a* gonflable.
inflate [ɪn'fleɪt] *vt* (*tyre*, *balloon*) gonfler; (*fig*) grossir; gonfler; faire monter; **inflation** [ɪn'fleɪʃən] *n* (*ECON*) inflation *f*; **inflationary** [ɪn'fleɪʃnərɪ] *a* inflationniste.
inflict [ɪn'flɪkt] *vt*: **to** ~ **on** infliger à.
influence ['ɪnfluəns] *n* influence *f* // *vt* influencer; **under the** ~ **of drink** en état d'ébriété.

influential [ɪnflu'ɛnʃl] *a* influent(e).
influenza [ɪnflu'ɛnzə] *n* grippe *f.*
influx ['ɪnflʌks] *n* afflux *m.*
inform [ɪn'fɔ:m] *vt*: to ~ sb (of) informer *or* avertir qn (de) // *vi*: to ~ on sb dénoncer qn, informer contre qn; to ~ sb about renseigner qn sur, mettre qn au courant de.
informal [ɪn'fɔ:ml] *a* (*person, manner*) simple, sans façon; (*visit, discussion*) dénué(e) de formalités; (*announcement, invitation*) non officiel(le); ~**ity** [-'mælɪtɪ] *n* simplicité *f,* absence *f* de cérémonie; caractère non officiel.
informant [ɪn'fɔ:mənt] *n* informateur/trice.
information [ɪnfə'meɪʃən] *n* information *f;* renseignements *mpl;* (*knowledge*) connaissances *fpl;* a piece of ~ un renseignement; ~ **office** *n* bureau *m* de renseignements.
informative [ɪn'fɔ:mətɪv] *a* instructif(ive).
informer [ɪn'fɔ:mə*] *n* dénonciateur/trice; (*also:* police ~) indicateur/trice.
infringe [ɪn'frɪndʒ] *vt* enfreindre // *vi*: to ~ on empiéter sur; ~**ment** *n:* ~**ment** (of) infraction *f* (à).
infuriating [ɪn'fjuərɪeɪtɪŋ] *a* exaspérant(e).
ingenious [ɪn'dʒi:njəs] *a* ingénieux(euse).
ingenuity [ɪndʒɪ'nju:ɪtɪ] *n* ingéniosité *f.*
ingenuous [ɪn'dʒɛnjuəs] *a* naïf(ïve), ingénu(e).
ingot ['ɪŋgət] *n* lingot *m.*
ingrained [ɪn'greɪnd] *a* enraciné(e).
ingratiate [ɪn'greɪʃɪeɪt] *vt*: to ~ o.s. with s'insinuer dans les bonnes grâces de, se faire bien voir de.
ingredient [ɪn'gri:dɪənt] *n* ingrédient *m;* élément *m.*
inhabit [ɪn'hæbɪt] *vt* habiter.
inhabitant [ɪn'hæbɪtnt] *n* habitant/e.
inhale [ɪn'heɪl] *vt* inhaler; (*perfume*) respirer // *vi* (*in smoking*) avaler la fumée.
inherent [ɪn'hɪərənt] *a:* ~ (in *or* to) inhérent(e) (à).
inherit [ɪn'hɛrɪt] *vt* hériter (de); ~**ance** *n* héritage *m.*
inhibit [ɪn'hɪbɪt] *vt* (PSYCH) inhiber; to ~ sb from doing empêcher *or* retenir qn de faire; ~**ion** [-'bɪʃən] *n* inhibition *f.*
inhuman [ɪn'hju:mən] *a* inhumain(e).
initial [ɪ'nɪʃl] *a* initial(e) // *n* initiale *f* // *vt* parafer; ~**s** *npl* initiales *fpl;* (*as signature*) parafe *m;* ~**ly** *ad* initialement, au début.
initiate [ɪ'nɪʃɪeɪt] *vt* (*start*) entreprendre; amorcer; lancer; (*person*) initier.
initiative [ɪ'nɪʃətɪv] *n* initiative *f.*
inject [ɪn'dʒɛkt] *vt* (*liquid*) injecter; (*person*) faire une piqûre à; ~**ion** [ɪn'dʒɛkʃən] *n* injection *f,* piqûre *f.*

injure ['ɪndʒə*] *vt* blesser; (*wrong*) faire du tort à; (*damage: reputation etc*) compromettre; ~**d** *a* blessé(e).
injury ['ɪndʒərɪ] *n* blessure *f;* (*wrong*) tort *m;* ~ **time** *n* (SPORT) arrêts *mpl* de jeu.
injustice [ɪn'dʒʌstɪs] *n* injustice *f.*
ink [ɪŋk] *n* encre *f.*
inkling ['ɪŋklɪŋ] *n* soupçon *m,* vague idée *f.*
inlaid ['ɪnleɪd] *a* incrusté(e); (*table etc*) marqueté(e).
inland *a* ['ɪnlənd] intérieur(e) // *ad* [ɪn'lænd] à l'intérieur, dans les terres; **I~ Revenue** *n* (*Brit*) fisc *m.*
in-laws ['ɪnlɔ:z] *npl* beaux-parents *mpl;* belle famille.
inlet ['ɪnlɛt] *n* (GEO) crique *f.*
inmate ['ɪnmeɪt] *n* (*in prison*) détenu/e; (*in asylum*) interné/e.
inn [ɪn] *n* auberge *f.*
innate [ɪ'neɪt] *a* inné(e).
inner ['ɪnə*] *a* intérieur(e); ~ **city** *n* centre *m* de zone urbaine; ~ **tube** *n* (*of tyre*) chambre *f* à air.
innings ['ɪnɪŋz] *n* (CRICKET) tour *m* de batte.
innocence ['ɪnəsns] *n* innocence *f.*
innocent ['ɪnəsnt] *a* innocent(e).
innocuous [ɪ'nɔkjuəs] *a* inoffensif(ive).
innuendo, ~**es** [ɪnju'ɛndəu] *n* insinuation *f,* allusion (malveillante).
innumerable [ɪ'nju:mrəbl] *a* innombrable.
inordinately [ɪ'nɔ:dɪnətlɪ] *ad* démesurément.
in-patient ['ɪnpeɪʃənt] *n* malade hospitalisé(e).
input ['ɪnput] *n* (ELEC) énergie *f,* puissance *f;* (*of machine*) consommation *f;* (*of computer*) information fournie.
inquest ['ɪnkwɛst] *n* enquête (criminelle).
inquire [ɪn'kwaɪə*] *vi* demander, s'informer de; to ~ **about** s'informer de, se renseigner sur; to ~ **into** *vt fus* faire une enquête sur; **inquiry** *n* demande *f* de renseignements; (LAW) enquête *f,* investigation *f;* **inquiry office** *n* (*Brit*) bureau *m* de renseignements.
inquisitive [ɪn'kwɪzɪtɪv] *a* curieux(euse).
inroad ['ɪnrəud] *n* incursion *f.*
insane [ɪn'seɪn] *a* fou(folle); (MED) aliéné(e).
insanity [ɪn'sænɪtɪ] *n* folie *f;* (MED) aliénation (mentale).
inscription [ɪn'skrɪpʃən] *n* inscription *f;* dédicace *f.*
inscrutable [ɪn'skru:təbl] *a* impénétrable.
insect ['ɪnsɛkt] *n* insecte *m;* ~**icide** [ɪn'sɛktɪsaɪd] *n* insecticide *m.*
insecure [ɪnsɪ'kjuə*] *a* peu solide; peu

sûr(e); (*person*) anxieux(euse).

insensible [ɪn'sɛnsɪbl] *a* insensible; (*unconscious*) sans connaissance.

insensitive [ɪn'sɛnsɪtɪv] *a* insensible.

insert *vt* [ɪn'səːt] insérer // *n* ['ɪnsəːt] insertion *f*; ~**ion** [ɪn'səːʃən] *n* insertion *f*.

in-service [ɪn'səːvɪs] *a* (*training*) continu(e), en cours d'emploi; (*course*) d'initiation; de perfectionnement; de recyclage.

inshore [ɪn'ʃɔː*] *a* côtier(ère) // *ad* près de la côte; vers la côte.

inside ['ɪn'saɪd] *n* intérieur *m* // *a* intérieur(e) // *ad* à l'intérieur, dedans // *prep* à l'intérieur de; (*of time*): ~ 10 minutes en moins de 10 minutes; ~s *npl* (*col*) intestins *mpl*; ~ **forward** *n* (*SPORT*) intérieur *m*; ~ **lane** *n* (*AUT*: *in Britain*) voie *f* de gauche; ~ **out** *ad* à l'envers; (*know*) à fond; **to turn** ~ **out** retourner.

insight ['ɪnsaɪt] *n* perspicacité *f*; (*glimpse, idea*) aperçu *m*.

insignificant [ɪnsɪg'nɪfɪknt] *a* insignifiant(e).

insincere [ɪnsɪn'sɪə*] *a* hypocrite.

insinuate [ɪn'sɪnjueɪt] *vt* insinuer.

insist [ɪn'sɪst] *vi* insister; **to** ~ **on doing** insister pour faire; **to** ~ **that** insister pour que; (*claim*) maintenir *or* soutenir que; ~**ent** *a* insistant(e), pressant(e).

insole ['ɪnsəul] *n* semelle intérieure; (*fixed part of shoe*) première *f*.

insolent ['ɪnsələnt] *a* insolent(e).

insomnia [ɪn'sɔmnɪə] *n* insomnie *f*.

inspect [ɪn'spɛkt] *vt* inspecter; (*ticket*) contrôler; ~**ion** [ɪn'spɛkʃən] *n* inspection *f*; contrôle *m*; ~**or** *n* inspecteur/trice; (*Brit*: *on buses, trains*) contrôleur/euse.

inspire [ɪn'spaɪə*] *vt* inspirer.

install [ɪn'stɔːl] *vt* installer; ~**ation** [ɪnstə'leɪʃən] *n* installation *f*.

instalment, (*US*) **installment** [ɪn'stɔːlmənt] *n* acompte *m*, versement partiel; (*of TV serial etc*) épisode *m*; **in** ~**s** (*pay*) à tempérament; (*receive*) en plusieurs fois.

instance ['ɪnstəns] *n* exemple *m*; **for** ~ par exemple; **in many** ~**s** dans bien des cas; **in the first** ~ tout d'abord, en premier lieu.

instant ['ɪnstənt] *n* instant *m* // *a* immédiat(e), urgent(e); (*coffee, food*) instantané(e), en poudre; ~**ly** *ad* immédiatement, tout de suite.

instead [ɪn'stɛd] *ad* au lieu de cela; ~ **of** au lieu de; ~ **of sb** à la place de qn.

instep ['ɪnstɛp] *n* cou-de-pied *m*; (*of shoe*) cambrure *f*.

instil [ɪn'stɪl] *vt*: **to** ~ (**into**) inculquer (à); (*courage*) insuffler (à).

instinct ['ɪnstɪŋkt] *n* instinct *m*.

institute ['ɪnstɪtjuːt] *n* institut *m* // *vt* instituer, établir; (*inquiry*) ouvrir; (*proceedings*) entamer.

institution [ɪnstɪ'tjuːʃən] *n* institution *f*; établissement *m* (scolaire); établissement (psychiatrique).

instruct [ɪn'strʌkt] *vt* instruire, former; **to** ~ **sb in sth** enseigner qch à qn; **to** ~ **sb to do** charger qn *or* ordonner à qn de faire; ~**ion** [ɪn'strʌkʃən] *n* instruction *f*; ~**ions** *npl* directives *fpl*; ~**ions** (**for use**) mode *m* d'emploi; ~**or** *n* professeur *m*; (*for skiing, driving*) moniteur *m*.

instrument ['ɪnstrəmənt] *n* instrument *m*; ~**al** [-'mɛntl] *a*: **to be** ~**al in** contribuer à; ~ **panel** *n* tableau *m* de bord.

insufficient [ɪnsə'fɪʃənt] *a* insuffisant(e).

insular ['ɪnsjulə*] *a* insulaire; (*outlook*) étroit(e); (*person*) aux vues étroites.

insulate ['ɪnsjuleɪt] *vt* isoler; (*against sound*) insonoriser; **insulating tape** *n* ruban isolant; **insulation** [-'leɪʃən] *n* isolation *f*; insonorisation *f*.

insulin ['ɪnsjulɪn] *n* insuline *f*.

insult *n* ['ɪnsʌlt] insulte *f*, affront *m* // *vt* [ɪn'sʌlt] insulter, faire un affront à.

insuperable [ɪn'sjuːprəbl] *a* insurmontable.

insurance [ɪn'ʃuərəns] *n* assurance *f*; **fire/life** ~ assurance-incendie/-vie; ~ **policy** *n* police *f* d'assurance.

insure [ɪn'ʃuə*] *vt* assurer.

intact [ɪn'tækt] *a* intact(e).

intake ['ɪnteɪk] *n* (*TECH*) admission *f*; adduction *f*; (*of food*) consommation *f*; (*Brit SCOL*): **an** ~ **of 200 a year** 200 admissions *fpl* par an.

integral ['ɪntɪgrəl] *a* intégral(e); (*part*) intégrant(e).

integrate ['ɪntɪgreɪt] *vt* intégrer // *vi* s'intégrer.

integrity [ɪn'tɛgrɪtɪ] *n* intégrité *f*.

intellect ['ɪntəlɛkt] *n* intelligence *f*; ~**ual** [-'lɛktjuəl] *a*, *n* intellectuel(le).

intelligence [ɪn'tɛlɪdʒəns] *n* intelligence *f*; (*MIL etc*) informations *fpl*, renseignements *mpl*.

intelligent [ɪn'tɛlɪdʒənt] *a* intelligent(e).

intend [ɪn'tɛnd] *vt* (*gift etc*): **to** ~ **sth for** destiner qch à; **to** ~ **to do** avoir l'intention de faire; ~**ed** *a* (*insult*) intentionnel(le); (*journey*) projeté(e); (*effect*) voulu(e).

intense [ɪn'tɛns] *a* intense; (*person*) véhément(e); ~**ly** *ad* intensément; profondément.

intensive [ɪn'tɛnsɪv] *a* intensif(ive); ~ **care unit** *n* service *m* de réanimation.

intent [ɪn'tɛnt] *n* intention *f* // *a* attentif(ive), absorbé(e); **to all** ~**s and purposes** en fait, pratiquement; **to be** ~ **on doing sth** être (bien) décidé à faire qch.

intention [ɪn'tɛnʃən] *n* intention *f*; **~al** *a* intentionnel(le), délibéré(e).

intently [ɪn'tɛntlɪ] *ad* attentivement.

interact [ɪntər'ækt] *vi* avoir une action réciproque.

interchange *n* ['ɪntətʃeɪndʒ] (*exchange*) échange *m*; (*on motorway*) échangeur *m* // *vt* [ɪntə'tʃeɪndʒ] échanger; mettre à la place l'un(e) de l'autre; **~able** *a* interchangeable.

intercom ['ɪntəkɔm] *n* interphone *m*.

intercourse ['ɪntəkɔːs] *n* rapports *mpl*.

interest ['ɪntrɪst] *n* intérêt *m*; (*COMM: stake, share*) intérêts *mpl* // *vt* intéresser; **~ed** *a* intéressé(e); **to be ~ed** in s'intéresser à; **~ing** *a* intéressant(e); **~ rate** *n* taux *m* d'intérêt.

interfere [ɪntə'fɪə*] *vi*: **to ~ in** (*quarrel, other people's business*) se mêler à; **to ~ with** (*object*) tripoter, toucher à; (*plans*) contrecarrer; (*duty*) être en conflit avec.

interference [ɪntə'fɪərəns] *n* (*gen*) intrusion *f*; (*PHYSICS*) interférence *f*; (*RADIO, TV*) parasites *mpl*.

interim ['ɪntərɪm] *a* provisoire; (*post*) intérimaire // *n*: **in the ~** dans l'intérim.

interior [ɪn'tɪərɪə*] *n* intérieur *m* // *a* intérieur(e).

interlock [ɪntə'lɔk] *vi* s'enclencher.

interloper ['ɪntələupə*] *n* intrus/e.

interlude ['ɪntəluːd] *n* intervalle *m*; (*THEATRE*) intermède *m*.

intermediate [ɪntə'miːdɪət] *a* intermédiaire; (*SCOL: course, level*) moyen(ne).

intermission [ɪntə'mɪʃən] *n* pause *f*; (*THEATRE, CINEMA*) entracte *m*.

intern [ɪn'təːn] *vt* interner // *n* ['ɪntəːn] (*US*) interne *m/f*.

internal [ɪn'təːnl] *a* interne; (*dispute, reform etc*) intérieur(e); **~ly** *ad* intérieurement; **'not to be taken ~ly'** 'pour usage externe'; **I~ Revenue Service (IRS)** *n* (*US*) fisc *m*.

international [ɪntə'næʃənl] *a* international(e).

interplay ['ɪntəpleɪ] *n* effet *m* réciproque, jeu *m*.

interpret [ɪn'təːprɪt] *vt* interpréter // *vi* servir d'interprète; **~er** *n* interprète *m/f*.

interrelated [ɪntərɪ'leɪtɪd] *a* en corrélation, en rapport étroit.

interrogate [ɪn'tɛrəugeɪt] *vt* interroger; (*suspect etc*) soumettre à un interrogatoire; **interrogation** [-'geɪʃən] *n* interrogation *f*; interrogatoire *m*; **interrogative** [ɪntə'rɔgətɪv] *a* interrogateur(trice).

interrupt [ɪntə'rʌpt] *vt* interrompre; **~ion** [-'rʌpʃən] *n* interruption *f*.

intersect [ɪntə'sɛkt] *vt* couper, croiser // *vi* (*roads*) se croiser, se couper; **~ion** [-'sɛkʃən] *n* intersection *f*; (*of roads*) croisement *m*.

intersperse [ɪntə'spəːs] *vt*: **to ~ with** parsemer de.

intertwine [ɪntə'twaɪn] *vt* entrelacer // *vi* s'entrelacer.

interval ['ɪntəvl] *n* intervalle *m*; (*Brit: SCOL*) récréation *f*; (: *THEATRE*) entracte *m*; (: *SPORT*) mi-temps *f*; **at ~s** par intervalles.

intervene [ɪntə'viːn] *vi* (*time*) s'écouler (entre-temps); (*event*) survenir; (*person*) intervenir; **intervention** [-'vɛnʃən] *n* intervention *f*.

interview ['ɪntəvjuː] *n* (*RADIO, TV etc*) interview *f*; (*for job*) entrevue *f* // *vt* interviewer; avoir une entrevue avec; **~er** *n* interviewer *m*.

intestine [ɪn'tɛstɪn] *n* intestin *m*.

intimacy ['ɪntɪməsɪ] *n* intimité *f*.

intimate ['ɪntɪmət] *a* intime; (*knowledge*) approfondi(e) // *vt* ['ɪntɪmeɪt] suggérer, laisser entendre; (*announce*) faire savoir.

into ['ɪntu] *prep* dans; **~ pieces/French** en morceaux/français.

intolerable [ɪn'tɔlərəbl] *a* intolérable.

intolerance [ɪn'tɔlərns] *n* intolérance *f*.

intolerant [ɪn'tɔlərnt] *a*: **~ of** intolérant(e) de; (*MED*) intolérant à.

intoxicate [ɪn'tɔksɪkeɪt] *vt* enivrer; **~d** *a* ivre; **intoxication** [-'keɪʃən] *n* ivresse *f*.

intractable [ɪn'træktəbl] *a* (*child, temper*) indocile, insoumis(e); (*problem*) insoluble.

intransitive [ɪn'trænsɪtɪv] *a* intransitif(ive).

intravenous [ɪntrə'viːnəs] *a* intraveineux(euse).

in-tray ['ɪntreɪ] *n* courrier *m* 'arrivée'.

intricate ['ɪntrɪkət] *a* complexe, compliqué(e).

intrigue [ɪn'triːg] *n* intrigue *f* // *vt* intriguer // *vi* intriguer, comploter; **intriguing** *a* fascinant(e).

intrinsic [ɪn'trɪnsɪk] *a* intrinsèque.

introduce [ɪntrə'djuːs] *vt* introduire; **to ~ sb (to sb)** présenter qn (à qn); **to ~ sb to** (*pastime, technique*) initier qn à; **introduction** [-'dʌkʃən] *n* introduction *f*; (*of person*) présentation *f*; **introductory** *a* préliminaire, d'introduction.

intrude [ɪn'truːd] *vi* (*person*) être importun(e); **to ~ on** (*conversation etc*) s'immiscer dans; **~r** *n* intrus/e.

intuition [ɪntjuː'ɪʃən] *n* intuition *f*.

inundate ['ɪnʌndeɪt] *vt*: **to ~ with** inonder de.

invade [ɪn'veɪd] *vt* envahir.

invalid *n* ['ɪnvəlɪd] malade *m/f*; (*with disability*) invalide *m/f* // *a* [ɪn'vælɪd] (*not valid*) invalide, non valide.

invaluable [ɪn'væljuəbl] *a* inestimable, inappréciable.

invariably [ɪn'vɛərɪəblɪ] *ad* invariablement; toujours.

invasion [ɪn'veɪʒən] n invasion f.
invent [ɪn'vɛnt] vt inventer; **~ion** [ɪn'vɛnʃən] n invention f; **~ive** a inventif(ive); **~or** n inventeur/trice.
inventory ['ɪnvəntrɪ] n inventaire m.
invert [ɪn'vɜːt] vt intervertir; (cup, object) retourner; **~ed commas** npl (Brit) guillemets mpl.
invest [ɪn'vɛst] vt investir // vi faire un investissement.
investigate [ɪn'vɛstɪgeɪt] vt étudier, examiner; (crime) faire une enquête sur; **investigation** [-'geɪʃən] n examen m; (of crime) enquête f, investigation f.
investment [ɪn'vɛstmənt] n investissement m, placement m.
investor [ɪn'vɛstə*] n épargnant/e; actionnaire m/f.
invidious [ɪn'vɪdɪəs] a injuste; (task) déplaisant(e).
invigilate [ɪn'vɪdʒɪleɪt] vt surveiller // vi (in exam) être de surveillance.
invigorating [ɪn'vɪgəreɪtɪŋ] a vivifiant(e); stimulant(e).
invisible [ɪn'vɪzɪbl] a invisible; **~ ink** n encre f sympathique.
invitation [ɪnvɪ'teɪʃən] n invitation f.
invite [ɪn'vaɪt] vt inviter; (opinions etc) demander; (trouble) chercher; **inviting** a engageant(e), attrayant(e); (gesture) encourageant(e).
invoice ['ɪnvɔɪs] n facture f.
involuntary [ɪn'vɔləntrɪ] a involontaire.
involve [ɪn'vɔlv] vt (entail) entraîner, nécessiter; (associate): **to ~ sb (in)** impliquer qn (dans), mêler qn (à); faire participer qn (à); **~d** a complexe; **to feel ~d** se sentir concerné(e); **~ment** n mise f en jeu; implication f; **~ment (in)** participation f (à); rôle m (dans).
inward ['ɪnwəd] a (movement) vers l'intérieur; (thought, feeling) profond(e), intime; **~(s)** ad vers l'intérieur.
I/O abbr (COMPUT: = input/output) E/S.
iodine ['aɪəudiːn] n iode m.
iota [aɪ'əutə] n (fig) brin m, grain m.
IOU n abbr (= I owe you) reconnaissance f de dette.
IQ n abbr (= intelligence quotient) Q.I. m (= quotient intellectuel).
IRA n abbr (= Irish Republican Army) IRA f.
Iran [ɪ'rɑːn] n Iran m.
Iraq [ɪ'rɑːk] n Irak m.
irate [aɪ'reɪt] a courroucé(e).
Ireland ['aɪələnd] n Irlande f.
iris, ~es ['aɪrɪs, -ɪz] n iris m.
Irish ['aɪrɪʃ] a irlandais(e) // npl: **the ~** les Irlandais; **~man** n Irlandais m; **~ Sea** n mer f d'Irlande; **~woman** n Irlandaise f.
irksome ['ɜːksəm] a ennuyeux(euse).
iron ['aɪən] n fer m; (for clothes) fer à repasser // a de or en fer // vt (clothes) repasser; **to ~ out** vt

(crease) faire disparaître au fer; (fig) aplanir; faire disparaître; **the ~ curtain** n le rideau de fer.
ironic(al) [aɪ'rɒnɪk(l)] a ironique.
ironing ['aɪənɪŋ] n repassage m; **~ board** n planche f à repasser.
ironmonger ['aɪənmʌŋgə*] n (Brit) quincailler m; **~'s (shop)** n quincaillerie f.
irony ['aɪrənɪ] n ironie f.
irrational [ɪ'ræʃənl] a irrationnel(le); déraisonnable; qui manque de logique.
irregular [ɪ'rɛgjulə*] a irrégulier(ère).
irrelevant [ɪ'rɛləvənt] a sans rapport, hors de propos.
irresistible [ɪrɪ'zɪstɪbl] a irrésistible.
irrespective [ɪrɪ'spɛktɪv]: **~ of** prep sans tenir compte de.
irresponsible [ɪrɪ'spɒnsɪbl] a (act) irréfléchi(e); (person) qui n'a pas le sens des responsabilités.
irrigate ['ɪrɪgeɪt] vt irriguer; **irrigation** [-'geɪʃən] n irrigation f.
irritable ['ɪrɪtəbl] a irritable.
irritate ['ɪrɪteɪt] vt irriter; **irritating** a irritant(e); **irritation** [-'teɪʃən] n irritation f.
IRS n abbr of **Internal Revenue Service**.
is [ɪz] vb see **be**.
Islam ['ɪzlɑːm] n Islam m.
island ['aɪlənd] n île f; (also: **traffic ~**) refuge m (pour piétons); **~er** n habitant/e d'une île, insulaire m/f.
isle [aɪl] n île f.
isn't ['ɪznt] = **is not**.
isolate ['aɪsəleɪt] vt isoler; **~d** a isolé(e).
Israel ['ɪzreɪl] n Israël m; **~i** [ɪz'reɪlɪ] a israélien(ne) // n Israélien/ne.
issue ['ɪʃuː] n question f, problème m; (outcome) résultat m, issue f; (of bank-notes etc) émission f; (of newspaper etc) numéro m; (offspring) descendance f // vt (rations, equipment) distribuer; (orders) donner; (book) faire paraître, publier; (banknotes, cheques, stamps) émettre, mettre en circulation; **at ~** en jeu, en cause; **to take ~ with sb (over)** exprimer son désaccord avec qn (sur).
it [ɪt] pronoun **1** (specific: subject) il(elle); (: direct object) le(la), l'; (: indirect object) lui; **~'s on the table** c'est or il (or elle) est sur la table; **about/from/of ~ en**; I spoke to him about **~** je lui en ai parlé; **what did you learn from ~?** qu'est-ce que vous en avez retiré?; **I'm proud of ~** j'en suis fier; **in/to ~** y; **put the book in ~** mettez-y le livre; **he agreed to ~** il y a consenti; **did you go to ~?** (party, concert etc) est-ce que vous y êtes allé(s)?
2 (impersonal) il; ce; **~'s raining** il pleut; **~'s Friday tomorrow** demain c'est vendredi or nous sommes vendredi; **~'s**

6 o'clock il est 6 heures; who is ~? - ~'s me qui est-ce? - c'est moi.

Italian [ɪ'tæljən] *a* italien(ne) // *n* Italien/ne; (*LING*) italien *m*.

italic [ɪ'tælɪk] *a* italique.

Italy ['ɪtəlɪ] *n* Italie *f*.

itch [ɪtʃ] *n* démangeaison *f* // *vi* (*person*) éprouver des démangeaisons; (*part of body*) démanger; **I'm ~ing to do** l'envie me démange de faire; **~y** *a* qui démange; **to be ~y** = **to** ~.

it'd ['ɪtd] = **it would, it had.**

item ['aɪtəm] *n* (*gen*) article *m*; (*on agenda*) question *f*, point *m*; (*in programme*) numéro *m*; (*also*: **news ~**) nouvelle *f*; **~ize** *vt* détailler, spécifier.

itinerary [aɪ'tɪnərərɪ] *n* itinéraire *m*.

it'll ['ɪtl] = **it will, it shall.**

its [ɪts] *a* son(sa), ses *pl*.

it's [ɪts] = **it is, it has.**

itself [ɪt'sɛlf] *pronoun* (*emphatic*) lui-même(elle-même); (*reflexive*) se.

ITV *n abbr* (*Brit*: = *Independent Television*) *chaîne fonctionnant en concurrence avec la BBC.*

I.U.D. *n abbr* (= *intra-uterine device*) DIU *m* (dispositif intra-utérin), stérilet *m*.

I've [aɪv] = **I have.**

ivory ['aɪvərɪ] *n* ivoire *m*.

ivy ['aɪvɪ] *n* lierre *m*.

J

jab [dʒæb] *vt*: **to ~ sth into** enfoncer *or* planter qch dans // *n* coup *m*; (*MED*: *col*) piqûre *f*.

jack [dʒæk] *n* (*AUT*) cric *m*; (*CARDS*) valet *m*; **to ~ up** *vt* soulever (au cric).

jackal ['dʒækl] *n* chacal *m*.

jackdaw ['dʒækdɔ:] *n* choucas *m*.

jacket ['dʒækɪt] *n* veste *f*, veston *m*.

jack-knife ['dʒæknaɪf] *vi*: **the lorry ~d** la remorque (du camion) s'est mise en travers.

jack plug *n* (*ELEC*) jack *m*.

jackpot ['dʒækpɔt] *n* gros lot.

jaded ['dʒeɪdɪd] *a* éreinté(e), fatigué(e).

jagged ['dʒægɪd] *a* dentelé(e).

jail [dʒeɪl] *n* prison *f* // *vt* emprisonner, mettre en prison; **~er** *n* geôlier/ière.

jam [dʒæm] *n* confiture *f*; (*of shoppers etc*) cohue *f*; (*also*: **traffic ~**) embouteillage *m* // *vt* (*passage etc*) encombrer, obstruer; (*mechanism, drawer etc*) bloquer, coincer; (*RADIO*) brouiller // *vi* (*mechanism, sliding part*) se coincer, se bloquer; (*gun*) s'enrayer; **to ~ sth into** entasser *or* comprimer qch dans; enfoncer qch dans.

jangle ['dʒæŋgl] *vi* cliqueter.

janitor ['dʒænɪtə*] *n* (*caretaker*) huissier *m*; concierge *m*.

January ['dʒænjuərɪ] *n* janvier *m*.

Japan [dʒə'pæn] *n* Japon *m*; **~ese** [dʒæpə'ni:z] *a* japonais(e) // *n* (*pl inv*) Japonais/e; (*LING*) japonais *m*.

jar [dʒɑ:*] *n* (*glass*) pot *m*, bocal *m* // *vi* (*sound*) produire un son grinçant *or* discordant; (*colours etc*) détonner, jurer.

jargon ['dʒɑ:gən] *n* jargon *m*.

jaundice ['dʒɔ:ndɪs] *n* jaunisse *f*; **~d** *a* (*fig*) envieux(euse), désapprobateur(trice).

jaunt [dʒɔ:nt] *n* balade *f*; **~y** *a* enjoué(e); désinvolte.

javelin ['dʒævlɪn] *n* javelot *m*.

jaw [dʒɔ:] *n* mâchoire *f*.

jay [dʒeɪ] *n* geai *m*.

jaywalker ['dʒeɪwɔ:kə*] *n* piéton indiscipliné.

jazz [dʒæz] *n* jazz *m*; **to ~ up** *vt* animer, égayer.

jealous ['dʒɛləs] *a* jaloux(euse); **~y** *n* jalousie *f*.

jeans [dʒi:nz] *npl* (blue-)jean *m*.

jeer [dʒɪə*] *vi*: **to ~ (at)** huer; se moquer cruellement (de), railler.

jelly ['dʒɛlɪ] *n* gelée *f*; **~fish** *n* méduse *f*.

jeopardy ['dʒɛpədɪ] *n*: **to be in ~** être en danger *or* péril.

jerk [dʒə:k] *n* secousse *f*; saccade *f*; sursaut *m*, spasme *m* // *vt* donner une secousse à // *vi* (*vehicles*) cahoter.

jerkin ['dʒə:kɪn] *n* blouson *m*.

jersey ['dʒə:zɪ] *n* tricot *m*.

jest [dʒɛst] *n* plaisanterie *f*.

jet [dʒɛt] *n* (*gas, liquid*) jet *m*; (*AVIAT*) avion *m* à réaction, jet *m*; **~-black** *a* (d'un noir) de jais; **~ engine** *n* moteur *m* à réaction; **~ lag** *n* décalage *m* horaire.

jettison ['dʒɛtɪsn] *vt* jeter par-dessus bord.

jetty ['dʒɛtɪ] *n* jetée *f*, digue *f*.

Jew [dʒu:] *n* Juif *m*.

jewel ['dʒu:əl] *n* bijou *m*, joyau *m*; **~ler** *n* bijoutier/ère, joaillier *m*; **~ler's (shop)** *n* bijouterie *f*, joaillerie *f*; **~lery** *n* bijoux *mpl*.

Jewess ['dʒu:ɪs] *n* Juive *f*.

Jewish ['dʒu:ɪʃ] *a* juif(juive).

jib [dʒɪb] *n* (*NAUT*) foc *m*.

jibe [dʒaɪb] *n* sarcasme *m*.

jiffy ['dʒɪfɪ] *n* (*col*): **in a ~** en un clin d'œil.

jig [dʒɪg] *n* gigue *f*.

jigsaw ['dʒɪgsɔ:] *n* (*also*: **~ puzzle**) puzzle *m*.

jilt [dʒɪlt] *vt* laisser tomber, plaquer.

jingle ['dʒɪŋgl] *n* (*advert*) couplet *m* publicitaire // *vi* cliqueter, tinter.

jinx [dʒɪŋks] *n* (*col*) (mauvais) sort.

jitters ['dʒɪtəz] *npl* (*col*): **to get the ~** avoir la trouille *or* la frousse.

job [dʒɔb] *n* travail *m*; (*employment*) emploi *m*, poste *m*, place *f*; **it's a good ~ that** — c'est heureux *or* c'est une chance que —; **just the ~!** (c'est) juste *or*

exactement ce qu'il faut!; ~ **centre** *n*
(*Brit*) agence *f* pour l'emploi; ~**less** *a*
sans travail, au chômage.

jockey ['dʒɔkɪ] *n* jockey *m* // *vi*: **to ~ for**
position manœuvrer pour être bien placé.

jocular ['dʒɔkjulə*] *a* jovial(e),
enjoué(e); facétieux(euse).

jog [dʒɔg] *vt* secouer // *vi* (*SPORT*) faire
du footing; **to ~ along** *vi* cahoter;
trotter; ~**ging** *n* footing *m*.

join [dʒɔɪn] *vt* unir, assembler; (*become*
member of) s'inscrire à; (*meet*) rejoindre, retrouver; se joindre à // *vi* (*roads*,
rivers) se rejoindre, se rencontrer // *n*
raccord *m*; **to ~ in** *vi* se mettre de la
partie // *vt fus* se mêler à; (*thanks etc*)
s'associer à; **to ~ up** *vi* s'engager.

joiner ['dʒɔɪnə*] *n* menuisier *m*; ~**y** *n*
menuiserie *f*.

joint [dʒɔɪnt] *n* (*TECH*) jointure *f*; joint
m; (*ANAT*) articulation *f*, jointure;
(*Brit*: *CULIN*) rôti *m*; (*col*: *place*) boîte *f*
// *a* commun(e); ~ **account** *n* (*with*
bank etc) compte joint; ~**ly** *ad* ensemble, en commun.

joist [dʒɔɪst] *n* solive *f*.

joke [dʒəuk] *n* plaisanterie *f*; (*also*:
practical ~) farce *f* // *vi* plaisanter; **to**
play a ~ on jouer un tour à, faire une
farce à; ~**r** *n* plaisantin *m*, blagueur/
euse; (*CARDS*) joker *m*.

jolly ['dʒɔlɪ] *a* gai(e), enjoué(e) // *ad*
(*col*) rudement, drôlement.

jolt [dʒəult] *n* cahot *m*, secousse *f* // *vt*
cahoter, secouer.

Jordan ['dʒɔːdən] *n* Jordanie *f*.

jostle ['dʒɔsl] *vt* bousculer, pousser.

jot [dʒɔt] *n*: **not one ~** pas un brin; **to ~**
down *vt* inscrire rapidement, noter;
~**ter** *n* (*Brit*) cahier *m* (de brouillon);
bloc-notes *m*.

journal ['dʒɔːnl] *n* journal *m*; ~**ism** *n*
journalisme *m*; ~**ist** *n* journaliste *m/f*.

journey ['dʒɔːnɪ] *n* voyage *m*; (*distance*
covered) trajet *m* // *vi* voyager.

joy [dʒɔɪ] *n* joie *f*; ~**ful**, ~**ous** *a*
joyeux(euse); ~ **ride** *n* virée *f* (*gén*
avec une voiture volée); ~**stick** *n*
(*AVIAT*, *COMPUT*) manche *m* à balai.

J.P. *n abbr see* **justice.**

Jr, Jun., Junr *abbr of* **junior.**

jubilant ['dʒuːbɪlnt] *a* triomphant(e);
réjoui(e).

judge [dʒʌdʒ] *n* juge *m* // *vt* juger;
judg(e)ment *n* jugement *m*; (*punish-*
ment) châtiment *m*.

judicial [dʒuː'dɪʃl] *a* judiciaire.

judiciary [dʒuː'dɪʃɪərɪ] *n* (pouvoir *m*)
judiciaire *m*.

judo ['dʒuːdəu] *n* judo *m*.

jug [dʒʌg] *n* pot *m*, cruche *f*.

juggernaut ['dʒʌgənɔːt] *n* (*Brit*: *huge*
truck) mastodonte *m*.

juggle ['dʒʌgl] *vi* jongler; ~**r** *n* jongleur
m.

Jugoslav *etc* ['juːgəuslɑːv] = **Yugo-**
slav *etc*.

juice [dʒuːs] *n* jus *m*.

juicy ['dʒuːsɪ] *a* juteux(euse).

jukebox ['dʒuːkbɔks] *n* juke-box *m*.

July [dʒuː'laɪ] *n* juillet *m*.

jumble ['dʒʌmbl] *n* fouillis *m* // *vt* (*also*:
~ **up**) mélanger, brouiller; ~ **sale** *n*
(*Brit*) vente *f* de charité.

jumbo ['dʒʌmbəu] *a*: ~ **jet** avion géant,
gros porteur (à réaction).

jump [dʒʌmp] *vi* sauter, bondir; (*start*)
sursauter; (*increase*) monter en flèche //
vt sauter, franchir // *n* saut *m*, bond *m*;
sursaut *m*.

jumper ['dʒʌmpə*] *n* (*Brit*: *pullover*)
pull-over *m*; (*US*: *dress*) robe-chasuble
f; ~ **cables** *npl* (*US*) = **jump leads.**

jump leads *npl* (*Brit*) câbles *mpl* de
démarrage.

jumpy ['dʒʌmpɪ] *a* nerveux(euse),
agité(e).

junction ['dʒʌŋkʃən] *n* (*Brit*: *of roads*)
carrefour *m*; (*of rails*) embranchement
m.

juncture ['dʒʌŋktʃə*] *n*: **at this ~** à ce
moment-là, sur ces entrefaites.

June [dʒuːn] *n* juin *m*.

jungle ['dʒʌŋgl] *n* jungle *f*.

junior ['dʒuːnɪə*] *a*, *n*: **he's ~ to me** (*by*
2 years), **he's my ~** (**by 2 years**) il est
mon cadet (de 2 ans), il est plus jeune
que moi (de 2 ans); **he's ~ to me**
(*seniority*) il est en dessous de moi (dans
la hiérarchie), j'ai plus d'ancienneté que
lui; ~ **school** *n* (*Brit*) école *f* primaire,
cours moyen.

junk [dʒʌŋk] *n* (*rubbish*) bric-à-brac *m*
inv; ~ **food** *n* snacks *mpl* (vite prêts);
~ **shop** *n* (boutique *f* de) brocanteur *m*.

juror ['dʒuərə*] *n* juré *m*.

jury ['dʒuərɪ] *n* jury *m*.

just [dʒʌst] *a* juste // *ad*: **he's ~ done it/**
left il vient de le faire/partir; ~ **as I ex-**
pected exactement *or* précisément
comme je m'y attendais; ~ **right/two**
o'clock exactement *or* juste ce qu'il faut/
deux heures; **she's ~ as clever as you**
elle est tout aussi intelligente que vous;
it's ~ as well that ... heureusement que
...; ~ **as he was leaving** au moment *or* à
l'instant précis où il partait; ~ **before/**
enough/here juste avant/assez/là; **it's ~**
me/a mistake ce n'est que moi/(rien)
qu'une erreur; ~ **missed/caught** manqué/
attrapé de justesse; ~ **listen to this!**
écoutez un peu ça!

justice ['dʒʌstɪs] *n* justice *f*; **J~ of the**
Peace (J.P.) *n* juge *m* de paix.

justify ['dʒʌstɪfaɪ] *vt* justifier.

jut [dʒʌt] *vi* (*also*: ~ **out**) dépasser, faire
saillie.

juvenile ['dʒuːvənaɪl] *a* juvénile; (*court*,
books) pour enfants // *n* adolescent/e.

K

K abbr (= one thousand) K; (= kilobyte) Ko.

kangaroo [kæŋgə'ru:] n kangourou m.

karate [kə'rɑ:tɪ] n karaté m.

kebab [kə'bæb] n kébab m.

keel [ki:l] n quille f; on an even ~ (fig) à flot.

keen [ki:n] a (interest, desire, competition) vif(vive); (eye, intelligence) pénétrant(e); (edge) effilé(e); (eager) plein(e) d'enthousiasme; to be ~ to do or on doing sth désirer vivement faire qch, tenir beaucoup à faire qch; to be ~ on sth/sb aimer beaucoup qch/qn.

keep [ki:p] vb (pt, pp kept) vt (retain, preserve) garder; (hold back) retenir; (a shop, the books, a diary, a promise) tenir; (feed: one's family etc) entretenir, assurer la subsistance de; (chickens, bees etc) élever // vi (food) se conserver; (remain: in a certain state or place) rester // n (of castle) donjon m; (food etc): enough for his ~ assez pour (assurer) sa subsistance; (col): for ~s pour de bon, pour toujours; to ~ doing sth continuer à faire qch; faire qch continuellement; to ~ sb from doing/sth from happening empêcher qn de faire or que qn (ne) fasse/que qch (n')arrive; to ~ sb happy/a place tidy faire que qn soit content/qu'un endroit reste propre; to ~ sth to o.s. garder qch pour soi, tenir qch secret; to ~ sth (back) from sb cacher qch à qn; to ~ time (clock) être à l'heure, ne pas retarder; **to ~ on** vi continuer; to ~ on doing continuer à faire; **to ~ out** vt empêcher d'entrer; '~ out' 'défense d'entrer'; **to ~ up** vi se maintenir // vt continuer, maintenir; to ~ up with se maintenir au niveau de; ~er n gardien/ne; ~-fit n gymnastique f de maintien; ~ing n (care) garde f; in ~ing with à l'avenant de; en accord avec; ~sake n souvenir m.

keg [kɛg] n barrique f, tonnelet m.

kennel ['kɛnl] n niche f; ~s npl chenil m.

kept [kɛpt] pt, pp of **keep**.

kerb [kə:b] n (Brit) bordure f du trottoir.

kernel ['kə:nl] n amande f; (fig) noyau m.

kettle ['kɛtl] n bouilloire f.

kettle drums npl timbales fpl.

key [ki:] n (gen, MUS) clé f; (of piano, typewriter) touche f // vt (also: ~ in) introduire au clavier; ~board n clavier m; ~ed up a (person) surexcité(e); ~hole n trou m de la serrure; ~note n (fig) note dominante; ~ ring n porte-clés m.

khaki ['kɑ:kɪ] a, n kaki (m).

kick [kɪk] vt donner un coup de pied à // vi (horse) ruer // n coup m de pied; (of rifle) recul m; (thrill): he does it for ~s il le fait parce que ça l'excite, il le fait pour le plaisir; **to ~ off** vi (SPORT) donner le coup d'envoi.

kid [kɪd] n (col: child) gamin/e, gosse m/f; (animal, leather) chevreau m // vi (col) plaisanter, blaguer.

kidnap ['kɪdnæp] vt enlever, kidnapper; ~per n ravisseur/euse; ~ping n enlèvement m.

kidney ['kɪdnɪ] n (ANAT) rein m; (CULIN) rognon m.

kill [kɪl] vt tuer; (fig) faire échouer; détruire; supprimer // n mise f à mort; ~er n tueur/euse; meurtrier/ère; ~ing n meurtre m; tuerie f, massacre m; ~joy n rabat-joie m/f.

kiln [kɪln] n four m.

kilo ['ki:ləʊ] n kilo m; ~byte n (COMPUT) kilo-octet m; ~gram(me) ['kɪləʊgræm] n kilogramme m; ~metre, (US) ~meter ['kɪləmi:tə*] n kilomètre m; ~watt ['kɪləʊwɔt] n kilowatt m.

kilt [kɪlt] n kilt m.

kin [kɪn] n see **next**, **kith**.

kind [kaɪnd] a gentil(le), aimable // n sorte f, espèce f; (species) genre m; to be two of a ~ se ressembler; in ~ (COMM) en nature.

kindergarten ['kɪndəgɑ:tn] n jardin m d'enfants.

kind-hearted [kaɪnd'hɑ:tɪd] a bon(bonne).

kindle ['kɪndl] vt allumer, enflammer.

kindly ['kaɪndlɪ] a bienveillant(e), plein(e) de gentillesse // ad avec bonté; will you ~ ... auriez-vous la bonté or l'obligeance de ....

kindness ['kaɪndnɪs] n bonté f, gentillesse f.

kindred ['kɪndrɪd] a apparenté(e); ~ spirit âme f sœur.

king [kɪŋ] n roi m; ~dom n royaume m; ~fisher n martin-pêcheur m; ~-size a long format inv; format géant inv.

kinky ['kɪŋkɪ] a (fig) excentrique; aux goûts spéciaux.

kiosk ['ki:ɔsk] n kiosque m; (Brit TEL) cabine f (téléphonique).

kipper ['kɪpə*] n hareng fumé et salé.

kiss [kɪs] n baiser m // vt embrasser; to ~ (each other) s'embrasser.

kit [kɪt] n équipement m, matériel m; (set of tools etc) trousse f; (for assembly) kit m.

kitchen ['kɪtʃɪn] n cuisine f; ~ sink n évier m.

kite [kaɪt] n (toy) cerf-volant m.

kith [kɪθ] n: ~ and kin parents et amis mpl.

kitten ['kɪtn] n petit chat, chaton m.

kitty ['kɪtɪ] n (money) cagnotte f.

knack [næk] n: to have the ~ (of doing)

avoir le coup (pour faire); **there's a ~** il
y a un coup à prendre or une combine.

knapsack ['næpsæk] n musette f.

knead [ni:d] vt pétrir.

knee [ni:] n genou m; **~cap** n rotule f.

kneel, pt, pp **knelt** [ni:l, nɛlt] vi (also:
~ **down**) s'agenouiller.

knell [nɛl] n glas m.

knew [nju:] pt of **know**.

knickers ['nɪkəz] npl (Brit) culotte f (de
femme).

knife [naɪf] n (pl **knives**) couteau m // vt
poignarder, frapper d'un coup de
couteau.

knight [naɪt] n chevalier m; (CHESS)
cavalier m; **~hood** n (title): to get a
~hood être fait chevalier.

knit [nɪt] vt tricoter; (fig): to ~ **together**
vt unir // vi (broken bones) se ressouder;
~ting n tricot m; **~ting needle** n
aiguille f à tricoter; **~wear** n tricots
mpl, lainages mpl.

knives [naɪvz] npl of **knife**.

knob [nɔb] n bouton m.

knock [nɔk] vt frapper; heurter; (fig:
col) dénigrer // vi (at door etc): to ~ at/
on frapper à/sur // n coup m; **to ~
down** vt renverser; **to ~ off** vi (col:
finish) s'arrêter (de travailler); **to ~
out** vt assommer; (BOXING) mettre
k.-o.; **to ~ over** vt (person) renverser;
(object) faire tomber; **~er** n (on door)
heurtoir m; **~-kneed** a aux genoux cagneux; **~out** n (BOXING) knock-out m,
K.-O. m.

knot [nɔt] n (gen) nœud m // vt nouer;
~ty a (fig) épineux(euse).

know [nəu] vt (pt **knew**, pp **known**)
savoir; (person, place) connaître; to ~
how to do savoir (comment) faire; to ~
how to swim savoir nager; to ~ **about/of**
sth être au courant de/connaître qch; to
~ **about** or **of** sb avoir entendu parler de
qn; **~-all** n je-sais-tout m/f; **~how** n
savoir-faire m, technique f, compétence
f; **~ing** a (look etc) entendu(e); **~ingly**
ad sciemment; (smile, look) d'un air
entendu.

knowledge ['nɔlɪdʒ] n connaissance f;
(learning) connaissances, savoir m;
~able a bien informé(e).

known [nəun] pp of **know**.

knuckle ['nʌkl] n articulation f (des
phalanges), jointure f.

Koran [kɔ'rɑːn] n Coran m.

Korea [kə'rɪə] n Corée f.

kosher ['kəuʃə*] a kascher inv.

L

lab [læb] n abbr (= laboratory) labo m.

label ['leɪbl] n étiquette f; (brand: of
record) marque f // vt étiqueter.

laboratory [lə'bɔrətəri] n laboratoire m.

labour, (US) **labor** ['leɪbə*] n (task)
travail m; (also: ~ **force**) main-d'œuvre
f; (MED) travail, accouchement m // vi:
to ~ (at) travailler dur (à), peiner
(sur); **in ~** (MED) en travail; **L~, the
L~ party** (Brit) le parti travailliste, les
travaillistes mpl; **~ed** a lourd(e),
laborieux(euse); **~er** n manœuvre m;
(on farm) ouvrier m agricole.

lace [leɪs] n dentelle f; (of shoe etc) lacet
m // vt (shoe) lacer.

lack [læk] n manque m // vt manquer de;
through or **for ~ of** faute de, par
manque de; to be **~ing** manquer, faire
défaut; to be **~ing** in manquer de.

lackadaisical [lækə'deɪzɪkl] a non-
chalant(e), indolent(e).

lacquer ['lækə*] n laque f.

lad [læd] n garçon m, gars m.

ladder ['lædə*] n échelle f; (Brit: in
tights) maille filée f // vt, vi (Brit: tights)
filer.

laden ['leɪdn] a: ~ **(with)** chargé(e)
(de).

ladle ['leɪdl] n louche f.

lady ['leɪdɪ] n dame f; (du
monde); **L~ Smith** lady Smith; **the ladies' (room)** les toilettes fpl des dames;
~bird, (US) **~bug** n coccinelle f; **~-
in-waiting** n dame f d'honneur; **~like** a
distingué(e); **~ship** n: your **~ship**
Madame la comtesse (or la baronne
etc).

lag [læg] vi (also: ~ **behind**) rester en
arrière, traîner // vt (pipes) calorifuger.

lager ['lɑːgə*] n bière blonde.

lagoon [lə'guːn] n lagune f.

laid [leɪd] pt, pp of **lay**; ~ **back** a (col)
relaxe, décontracté(e).

lain [leɪn] pp of **lie**.

lair [lɛə*] n tanière f, gîte m.

laity ['leɪɪtɪ] n laïques mpl.

lake [leɪk] n lac m.

lamb [læm] n agneau m.

lame [leɪm] a boiteux(euse).

lament [lə'mɛnt] vt pleurer, se lamenter
sur.

laminated ['læmɪneɪtɪd] a laminé(e);
(windscreen) (en verre) feuilleté.

lamp [læmp] n lampe f.

lampoon [læm'puːn] n pamphlet m.

lamp: **~post** n (Brit) réverbère m;
~shade n abat-jour m inv.

lance [lɑːns] n lance f // vt (MED)
inciser; ~ **corporal** n (Brit) (soldat m
de) première classe m.

land [lænd] n (as opposed to sea) terre f
(ferme); (country) pays m; (soil) terre;
terrain m; (estate) terre(s), domaine(s)
m(pl) // vi (from ship) débarquer;
(AVIAT) atterrir; (fig: fall) (re)tomber //
vt (obtain) décrocher; (passengers,
goods) débarquer; **to ~ up** vi atterrir,
(finir par) se retrouver; **~ing** n
débarquement m; atterrissage m; (of

staircase) palier *m*; **~ing stage** *n* (*Brit*) débarcadère *m*, embarcadère *m*; **~lady** *n* propriétaire *f*, logeuse *f*; **~lord** *n* propriétaire *m*, logeur *m*; (*of pub etc*) patron *m*; **~mark** *n* (point *m* de) repère *m*; **to be a ~mark** (*fig*) faire date *or* époque; **~owner** *n* propriétaire foncier *or* terrien.

landscape ['lænskeɪp] *n* paysage *m*.

landslide ['lændslaɪd] *n* (*GEO*) glissement *m* (de terrain); (*fig*: *POL*) raz-de-marée (électoral).

lane [leɪn] *n* (*in country*) chemin *m*; (*in town*) ruelle *f*; (*AUT*) voie *f*, file *f*; (*in race*) couloir *m*.

language ['læŋgwɪdʒ] *n* langue *f*; (*way one speaks*) langage *m*; **bad ~** grossièretés *fpl*, langage grossier; **~ laboratory** *n* laboratoire *m* de langues.

languid ['læŋgwɪd] *a* languissant(e); langoureux(euse).

lank [læŋk] *a* (*hair*) raide et terne.

lanky ['læŋkɪ] *a* grand(e) et maigre, efflanqué(e).

lantern ['læntn] *n* lanterne *f*.

lap [læp] *n* (*of track*) tour *m* (de piste); (*of body*): **in *or* on one's ~** sur les genoux // *vt* (*also*: **~ up**) laper // *vi* (*waves*) clapoter.

lapel [lə'pel] *n* revers *m*.

Lapland ['læplænd] *n* Laponie *f*.

lapse [læps] *n* défaillance *f* // *vi* (*LAW*) cesser d'être en vigueur; se périmer; **to ~ into bad habits** prendre de mauvaises habitudes; **~ of time** laps *m* de temps, intervalle *m*.

larceny ['lɑːsənɪ] *n* vol *m*.

lard [lɑːd] *n* saindoux *m*.

larder ['lɑːdə*] *n* garde-manger *m inv*.

large [lɑːdʒ] *a* grand(e); (*person, animal*) gros(grosse); **at ~** (*free*) en liberté; (*generally*) en général; **pour la plupart**; **~ly** *ad* en grande partie.

lark [lɑːk] *n* (*bird*) alouette *f*; (*joke*) blague *f*, farce *f*; **to ~ about** *vi* faire l'idiot, rigoler.

laryngitis [lærɪn'dʒaɪtɪs] *n* laryngite *f*.

laser ['leɪzə*] *n* laser *m*; **~ printer** *n* imprimante *f* laser.

lash [læʃ] *n* coup *m* de fouet; (*also*: *eyelash*) cil *m* // *vt* fouetter; (*tie*) attacher; **to ~ out** *vi*: **to ~ out** (at *or* against sb/sth) attaquer violemment (qn/qch); **to ~ out** (on sth) (*col*: *spend*) se fendre (de qch).

lass [læs] *n* (jeune) fille *f*.

lasso [læ'suː] *n* lasso *m*.

last [lɑːst] *a* dernier(ère) // *ad* en dernier // *vi* durer; **~ week** la semaine dernière; **~ night** hier soir; la nuit dernière; **at ~** enfin; **~ but one** avant-dernier(ère); **~-ditch** *a* (*attempt*) ultime, désespéré(e); **~ing** *a* durable; **~ly** *ad* en dernier lieu, pour finir; **~-minute** *a* de dernière minute.

latch [lætʃ] *n* loquet *m*.

late [leɪt] *a* (*not on time*) en retard; (*far on in day etc*) dernier(ère); tardif(ive); (*recent*) récent(e), dernier; (*former*) ancien(ne); (*dead*) défunt(e) // *ad* tard; (*behind time, schedule*) en retard; **of ~** dernièrement; **in ~ May** vers la fin (du mois) de mai, fin mai; **the ~ Mr X** feu M. X; **~comer** *n* retardataire *m/f*; **~ly** *ad* récemment.

later ['leɪtə*] *a* (*date etc*) ultérieur(e); (*version etc*) plus récent(e) // *ad* plus tard; **~ on** plus tard.

lateral ['lætərəl] *a* latéral(e).

latest ['leɪtɪst] *a* tout(e) dernier(ère); **at the ~** au plus tard.

lathe [leɪð] *n* tour *m*.

lather ['lɑːðə*] *n* mousse *f* (de savon).

Latin ['lætɪn] *n* latin *m* // *a* latin(e); **~ America** *n* Amérique latine; **~-American** *a* d'Amérique latine.

latitude ['lætɪtjuːd] *n* latitude *f*.

latter ['lætə*] *a* deuxième, dernier(ère) // *n*: **the ~** ce dernier, celui-ci; **~ly** *ad* dernièrement, récemment.

lattice ['lætɪs] *n* treillis *m*; treillage *m*.

laudable ['lɔːdəbl] *a* louable.

laugh [lɑːf] *n* rire *m* // *vi* rire; **to ~ at** *vt fus* se moquer de; (*joke*) rire de; **to ~ off** *vt* écarter *or* rejeter par une plaisanterie *or* par une boutade; **~able** *a* risible, ridicule; **~ing stock** *n*: **the ~ing stock of** la risée de; **~ter** *n* rire *m*; rires *mpl*.

launch [lɔːntʃ] *n* lancement *m*; (*boat*) chaloupe *f*; (*also*: **motor ~**) vedette *f* // *vt* (*ship, rocket, plan*) lancer; **~(ing) pad** *n* rampe *f* de lancement.

launder ['lɔːndə*] *vt* blanchir.

launderette [lɔːn'dret], (*US*) **laundromat** ['lɔːndrəmæt] *n* laverie *f* (automatique).

laundry ['lɔːndrɪ] *n* blanchisserie *f*; (*clothes*) linge *m*.

laureate ['lɔːrɪət] *a see* **poet**.

laurel ['lɔrl] *n* laurier *m*.

lava ['lɑːvə] *n* lave *f*.

lavatory ['lævətərɪ] *n* toilettes *fpl*.

lavender ['lævəndə*] *n* lavande *f*.

lavish ['lævɪʃ] *a* copieux(euse); somptueux(euse); (*giving freely*): **~ with** prodigue de // *vt*: **to ~ sth on sb** prodiguer qch à qn; (*money*) dépenser qch sans compter pour qn/qch.

law [lɔː] *n* loi *f*; (*science*) droit *m*; **~-abiding** *a* respectueux(euse) des lois; **~ and order** *n* l'ordre public; **~ court** *n* tribunal *m*, cour *f* de justice; **~ful** *a* légal(e); permis(e).

lawn [lɔːn] *n* pelouse *f*; **~mower** *n* tondeuse *f* à gazon; **~ tennis** *n* tennis *m*.

law school *n* faculté *f* de droit.

lawsuit ['lɔːsuːt] *n* procès *m*.

lawyer ['lɔːjə*] *n* (*consultant, with*

company) juriste *m*; (*for sales, wills etc*) ≈ notaire *m*; (*partner, in court*) ≈ avocat *m*.

lax [læks] *a* relâché(e).

laxative ['læksətıv] *n* laxatif *m*.

laxity ['læksıtı] *n* relâchement *m*.

lay [leı] *pt of* **lie** // *a* laïque; profane // *vt* (*pt, pp* **laid**) poser, mettre; (*eggs*) pondre; (*trap*) tendre; (*plans*) élaborer; **to ~ the table** mettre la table; **to ~ aside** *or* **by** *vt* mettre de côté; **to ~ down** *vt* poser; **to ~ down the law** faire la loi; **to ~ off** *vt* (*workers*) licencier; **to ~ on** *vt* (*water, gas*) mettre, installer; (*provide*) fournir; (*paint*) étaler; **to ~ out** *vt* (*design*) dessiner, concevoir; (*display*) disposer; (*spend*) dépenser; **to ~ up** *vt* (*to store*) amasser; (*car*) remiser; (*ship*) désarmer; (*subj: illness*) forcer à s'aliter; **~about** *n* fainéant/e; **~-by** *n* (*Brit*) aire *f* de stationnement (sur le bas-côté).

layer ['leıə*] *n* couche *f*.

layman ['leımən] *n* laïque *m*; profane *m*.

layout ['leıaut] *n* disposition *f*, plan *m*, agencement *m*; (*PRESS*) mise *f* en page.

laze [leız] *vi* paresser.

lazy ['leızı] *a* paresseux(euse).

lb. *abbr of* **pound** (*weight*).

lead [li:d] *n* (*front position*) tête *f*; (*distance, time ahead*) avance *f*; (*clue*) piste *f*; (*to battery*) raccord *m*; (*ELEC*) fil *m*; (*for dog*) laisse *f*; (*THEATRE*) rôle principal; [led] (*metal*) plomb *m*; (*in pencil*) mine *f* // *vb* (*pt, pp* **led**) *vt* mener, conduire; (*induce*) amener; (*be leader of*) être à la tête de; (*SPORT*) être en tête de // *vi* mener, être en tête; **to ~ sb astray** détourner qn du droit chemin; **to ~ away** *vt* emmener; **to ~ back** *vt*: **to ~ back to** ramener à; **to ~ on** *vt* (*tease*) faire marcher; **to ~ on to** (*induce*) amener à; **to ~ to** *vt fus* mener à; conduire à; aboutir à; **to ~ up to** *vt fus* conduire à.

leaden ['ledn] *a* (*sky, sea*) de plomb; (*heavy: footsteps*) lourd(e).

leader ['li:də*] *n* chef *m*; dirigeant/e, leader *m*; (*in newspaper*) éditorial *m*; **~ship** *n* direction *f*; qualités *fpl* de chef.

leading ['li:dıŋ] *a* de premier plan; principal(e); **~ man/lady** *n* (*THEATRE*) vedette (masculine)/(féminine); **~ light** *n* (*person*) vedette *f*, sommité *f*.

leaf [li:f], *pl* **leaves** *n* feuille *f*; (*of table*) rallonge *f* // *vi*: **to ~ through** sth feuilleter qch; **to turn over a new ~** changer de conduite *or* d'existence.

leaflet ['li:flıt] *n* prospectus *m*, brochure *f*; (*POL, REL*) tract *m*.

league [li:g] *n* ligue *f*; (*FOOTBALL*) championnat *m*; (*measure*) lieue *f*; **to be in ~ with** avoir partie liée avec, être de mèche avec.

leak [li:k] *n* (*out, also fig*) fuite *f*; (*in*) infiltration *f* // *vi* (*pipe, liquid etc*) fuir; (*shoes*) prendre l'eau // *vt* (*liquid*) répandre; (*information*) divulguer; **to ~ out** *vi* fuir; être divulgué(e).

lean [li:n] *a* maigre // *vb* (*pt, pp* **leaned** *or* **leant** [lent]) *vt*: **to ~ sth on sth** appuyer qch sur qch // *vi* (*slope*) pencher; (*rest*): **to ~ against** s'appuyer contre; être appuyé(e) contre; **to ~ on** s'appuyer sur; **to ~ back/forward** *vi* se pencher en arrière/avant; **to ~ out** *vi* se pencher au dehors; **to ~ over** *vi* se pencher; **~-to** *n* appentis *m*.

leap [li:p] *n* bond *m*, saut *m* // *vi* (*pt, pp* **leaped** *or* **leapt** [lept]) bondir, sauter; **~frog** *n* jeu *m* de saute-mouton; **~ year** *n* année *f* bissextile.

learn, *pt, pp* **learned** *or* **learnt** [lə:n, -t] *vt, vi* apprendre; **to ~ how to do sth** apprendre à faire qch; **~ed** ['lə:nıd] *a* érudit(e), savant(e); **~er** *n* débutant/e; (*Brit: also*: **~er driver**) (conducteur/trice) débutant(e); **~ing** *n* savoir *m*.

lease [li:s] *n* bail *m* // *vt* louer à bail.

leash [li:ʃ] *n* laisse *f*.

least [li:st] *a*: **the ~ + noun** le(la) plus petit(e), le(la) moindre; (*smallest amount of*) le moins de; **the ~ + adjective** le(la) moins; **the ~ money** le moins d'argent; **at ~** au moins; **not in the ~** pas le moins du monde.

leather ['leðə*] *n* cuir *m*.

leave [li:v] *vb* (*pt, pp* **left**) *vt* laisser; (*go away from*) quitter // *vi* partir, s'en aller // *n* (*time off*) congé *m*; (*MIL, also: consent*) permission *f*; **to be left** rester; **there's some milk left over** il reste du lait; **on ~** en permission; **to ~ behind** *vt* (*person, object*) laisser; **to ~ out** *vt* oublier, omettre; **~ of absence** *n* congé exceptionnel; (*MIL*) permission spéciale.

leaves [li:vz] *npl of* **leaf**.

Lebanon ['lebənən] *n* Liban *m*.

lecherous ['letʃərəs] *a* lubrique.

lecture ['lektʃə*] *n* conférence *f*; (*SCOL*) cours (magistral) // *vi* donner des cours; enseigner // *vt* (*scold*) sermonner, réprimander; **to ~ on** ou faire un cours (*or* son cours) sur; **to give a ~ on** faire une conférence sur; faire *or* donner un cours sur.

lecturer ['lektʃərə*] *n* (*speaker*) conférencier/ère; (*Brit: at university*) professeur *m* (d'université); ≈ maître assistant, maître de conférences.

led [led] *pt, pp of* **lead**.

ledge [ledʒ] *n* (*of window, on wall*) rebord *m*; (*of mountain*) saillie *f*, corniche *f*.

ledger ['ledʒə*] *n* registre *m*, grand livre.

lee [li:] *n* côté *m* sous le vent.

leech [li:tʃ] *n* sangsue *f*.

leek [li:k] *n* poireau *m*.

leer [lɪə*] *vi*: to ~ at sb regarder qn d'un air mauvais *or* concupiscent.

leeway ['li:weɪ] *n* (*fig*): to have some ~ avoir une certaine liberté d'action.

left [lɛft] *pt, pp of* **leave** // à gauche // *ad* à gauche // *n* gauche *f*; on the ~ to the ~ à gauche; **the L~** (*POL*) la gauche; **~handed** *a* gaucher(ère); **~hand side** *n* gauche *f*, côté *m* gauche; **~luggage (office)** *n* (*Brit*) consigne *f*; **~overs** *npl* restes *mpl*; **~wing** *a* (*POL*) de gauche.

leg [lɛg] *n* jambe *f*; (*of animal*) patte *f*; (*of furniture*) pied *m*; (*CULIN*: *of chicken*) cuisse *f*; **lst/2nd ~** (*SPORT*) match *m* aller/retour; (*of journey*) 1ère/2ème étape.

legacy ['lɛgəsɪ] *n* héritage *m*, legs *m*.

legal ['li:gl] *a* légal(e); ~ **holiday** *n* (*US*) jour férié; ~ **tender** *n* monnaie légale.

legend ['lɛdʒənd] *n* légende *f*.

legible ['lɛdʒəbl] *a* lisible.

legislation [lɛdʒɪs'leɪʃən] *n* législation *f*; **legislature** ['lɛdʒɪslətʃə*] *n* corps législatif.

legitimate [lɪ'dʒɪtɪmət] *a* légitime.

leg-room ['lɛgru:m] *n* place *f* pour les jambes.

leisure ['lɛʒə*] *n* loisir *m*, temps *m* libre; loisirs *mpl*; at ~ (tout) à loisir; à tête reposée; ~ **centre** *n* centre *m* de loisirs; **~ly** *a* tranquille; fait(e) sans se presser.

lemon ['lɛmən] *n* citron *m*; **~ade** [-'neɪd] *n* limonade *f*; ~ **tea** *n* thé *m* au citron.

lend [lɛnd], *pt, pp* **lent** *vt*: to ~ sth (to sb) prêter qch (à qn).

length [lɛŋθ] *n* longueur *f*; (*section: of road, pipe etc*) morceau *m*, bout *m*; at ~ (*at last*) enfin, à la fin; (*lengthily*) longuement; **~en** *vt* allonger, prolonger // *vi* s'allonger; **~ways** *ad* dans le sens de la longueur, en long; **~y** *a* (très) long(longue).

lenient ['li:nɪənt] *a* indulgent(e), clément(e).

lens [lɛnz] *n* lentille *f*; (*of spectacles*) verre *m*; (*of camera*) objectif *m*.

Lent [lɛnt] *n* Carême *m*.

lent [lɛnt] *pt, pp of* **lend**.

lentil ['lɛntl] *n* lentille *f*.

Leo ['li:əu] *n* le Lion.

leotard ['li:əta:d] *n* maillot *m* (*de danseur etc*).

leper ['lɛpə*] *n* lépreux/euse.

leprosy ['lɛprəsɪ] *n* lèpre *f*.

lesbian ['lɛzbɪən] *n* lesbienne *f*.

less [lɛs] *a* moins de // *pronoun, ad* moins; ~ **than that/you** moins que cela/vous; ~ **than half** moins de la moitié; ~ **than ever** moins que jamais; ~ **and** ~ de moins en moins; **the** ~ **he works** ... moins il travaille ....

lessen ['lɛsn] *vi* diminuer, s'amoindrir, s'atténuer // *vt* diminuer, réduire, atténuer.

lesser ['lɛsə*] *a* moindre; **to a** ~ **extent** à un degré moindre.

lesson ['lɛsn] *n* leçon *f*.

lest [lɛst] *cj* de peur de + *infinitive*, de peur que + *sub*.

let [lɛt], *pt, pp* **let** [lɛt] *vt* laisser; (*Brit*: *lease*) louer; to ~ **sb do sth** laisser qn faire qch; to ~ **sb know sth** faire savoir qch à qn, prévenir qn de qch; **he** ~ **me go** il m'a laissé partir; ~'s **go** allons-y; ~ **him come** qu'il vienne; 'to ~' 'à louer'; **to** ~ **down** *vt* (*lower*) baisser; (*dress*) rallonger; (*hair*) défaire; (*disappoint*) décevoir; **to** ~ **go** *vi* lâcher prise // *vt* lâcher; **to** ~ **in** *vt* laisser entrer; (*visitor etc*) faire entrer; **to** ~ **off** *vt* laisser partir; (*firework etc*) faire partir; (*smell etc*) dégager; **to** ~ **on** *vi* (*col*) dire; **to** ~ **out** *vt* laisser sortir; (*dress*) élargir; (*scream*) échapper; **to** ~ **up** *vi* diminuer, s'arrêter.

lethal ['li:θl] *a* mortel(le), fatal(e).

letter ['lɛtə*] *n* lettre *f*; ~ **bomb** *n* lettre piégée; **~box** *n* (*Brit*) boîte *f* aux *or* à lettres; **~ing** *n* lettres *fpl*; caractères *mpl*.

lettuce ['lɛtɪs] *n* laitue *f*, salade *f*.

leukaemia, (*US*) **leukemia** [lu:'ki:mɪə] *n* leucémie *f*.

level ['lɛvl] *a* plat(e), plan(e), uni(e); horizontal(e) // *n* niveau *m*; (*flat place*) terrain plat; (*also*: **spirit ~**) niveau à bulle // *vt* niveler, aplanir; **to be** ~ **with** être au même niveau que; **'A'** ~s *npl* (*Brit*) ≈ baccalauréat *m*; **'O'** ~s *npl* (*Brit*) ≈ B.E.P.C.; **on the** ~ à l'horizontale; (*fig*: *honest*) régulier(ère); **to** ~ **off** *or* **out** *vi* (*prices etc*) se stabiliser; ~ **crossing** *n* (*Brit*) passage *m* à niveau; **~headed** *a* équilibré(e).

lever ['li:və*] *n* levier *m* // *vt*: **to** ~ **up/out** soulever/extraire au moyen d'un levier; **~age** *n*: **~age (on** *or* **with)** prise *f* (sur).

levy ['lɛvɪ] *n* taxe *f*, impôt *m* // *vt* prélever, imposer; percevoir.

lewd [lu:d] *a* obscène, lubrique.

liability [laɪə'bɪlɪtɪ] *n* responsabilité *f*; (*handicap*) handicap *m*; **liabilities** *npl* obligations *fpl*, engagements *mpl*; (*on balance sheet*) passif *m*.

liable ['laɪəbl] *a* (*subject*): ~ **to** sujet(te) à; passible de; (*responsible*): ~ **(for)** responsable (de); (*likely*): ~ **to do** susceptible de.

liaison [li:'eɪzɔn] *n* liaison *f*.

liar ['laɪə*] *n* menteur/euse.

libel ['laɪbl] *n* écrit *m* diffamatoire; diffamation *f* // *vt* diffamer.

liberal ['lɪbərl] *a* libéral(e); (*generous*): ~ **with** prodigue de, généreux(euse) avec.

liberty ['lɪbətɪ] *n* liberté *f*; **to be at ~ to do** être libre de faire.

Libra ['li:brə] *n* la Balance.

librarian [laɪ'brɛərɪən] *n* bibliothécaire *m/f*.

library ['laɪbrərɪ] *n* bibliothèque *f*.

libretto [lɪ'brɛtəu] *n* livret *m*.

Libya ['lɪbɪə] *n* Libye *f*.

lice [laɪs] *npl* of **louse**.

licence, (US**) license** ['laɪsns] *n* autorisation *f*, permis *m*; (COMM) licence *f*; (RADIO, TV) redevance *f*; (*also*: **driving ~, (**US**) driver's ~**) permis *m* (de conduire); (*excessive freedom*) licence; **~ number** *n* numéro *m* d'immatriculation; **~ plate** *n* plaque *f* minéralogique.

license ['laɪsns] *n* (US) = **licence** // *vt* donner une licence à; **~d** *a* (*for alcohol*) patenté(e) pour la vente des spiritueux.

lick [lɪk] *vt* lécher.

licorice ['lɪkərɪs] *n* = **liquorice**.

lid [lɪd] *n* couvercle *m*.

lie [laɪ] *n* mensonge *m* // *vi* mentir; (*pt* lay, *pp* lain) (*rest*) être étendu(e) or allongé(e) or couché(e); (*in grave*) être enterré(e), reposer; (*of object: be situated*) se trouver, être; **to ~ low** (*fig*) se cacher; **to ~ about** *vi* traîner; **to have a ~-down** (*Brit*) s'allonger, se reposer; **to have a ~-in** (*Brit*) faire la grasse matinée.

lieutenant [lɛf'tɛnənt, (US) lu:'tɛnənt] *n* lieutenant *m*.

life [laɪf], *pl* **lives** *n* vie *f*; **~ assurance** *n* (*Brit*) assurance-vie *f*; **~ belt** *n* (*Brit*) bouée *f* de sauvetage; **~boat** *n* canot *m* or chaloupe *f* de sauvetage; **~guard** *n* surveillant *m* de baignade; **~ insurance** = **~ assurance**; **~ jacket** *n* gilet *m* or ceinture *f* de sauvetage; **~less** *a* sans vie, inanimé(e); (*dull*) qui manque de vie or de vigueur; **~like** *a* qui semble vrai(e) or vivant(e); ressemblant(e); **~long** *a* de toute une vie, de toujours; **~ preserver** *n* (US) gilet *m* or ceinture *f* de sauvetage; bouée *f* de sauvetage; **~-saver** *n* surveillant *m* de baignade; **~ sentence** *n* condamnation *f* à vie or à perpétuité; **~-sized** *a* grandeur nature *inv*; **~ span** *n* (durée *f* de) vie *f*; **~style** *n* style *m* or mode *m* de vie; **~ support system** *n* (MED) respirateur artificiel; **~time** *n*: **in his ~time** de son vivant; **once in a ~time** une fois dans la or dans une vie.

lift [lɪft] *vt* soulever, lever; (*steal*) prendre, voler // *vi* (*fog*) se lever // *n* (*Brit: elevator*) ascenseur *m*; **to give sb a ~** (*Brit*) emmener or prendre qn en voiture; **~-off** *n* décollage *m*.

light [laɪt] *n* lumière *f*; (*daylight*) lumière, jour *m*; (*lamp*) lampe *f*; (AUT: traffic ~, rear ~) feu *m*; (: *headlamp*) phare *m*; (*for cigarette etc*): **have you got a ~?** avez-vous du feu? // *vt* (*pt, pp* **lighted** *or* **lit**) (*candle, cigarette, fire*) allumer; (*room*) éclairer // *a* (*room, colour*) clair(e); (*not heavy, also fig*) léger(ère); **to come to ~** être dévoilé(e) or découvert(e); **to ~ up** *vi* s'allumer; (*face*) s'éclairer // *vt* (*illuminate*) éclairer, illuminer; **~ bulb** *n* ampoule *f*; **~en** *vi* s'éclairer // *vt* (*give light to*) éclairer; (*make lighter*) éclaircir; (*make less heavy*) alléger; **~er** *n* (*also*: **cigarette ~er**) briquet *m*; (: *in car*) allume-cigare *m inv*; (*boat*) péniche *f*; **~-headed** *a* étourdi(e), écervelé(e); **~-hearted** *a* gai(e), joyeux(euse), enjoué(e); **~house** *n* phare *m*; **~ing** *n* (*on road*) éclairage *m*; (*in theatre*) éclairages; **~ly** *ad* légèrement; **to get off ~ly** s'en tirer à bon compte; **~ness** *n* clarté *f*; (*in weight*) légèreté *f*.

lightning ['laɪtnɪŋ] *n* éclair *m*, foudre *f*; **~ conductor, (**US**) ~ rod** *n* paratonnerre *m*.

light pen *n* crayon *m* optique.

lightweight ['laɪtweɪt] *a* (*suit*) léger(ère); (*boxer*) poids léger *inv* // *n* (BOXING) poids leger.

like [laɪk] *vt* aimer (bien) // *prep* comme // *a* semblable, pareil(le) // *n*: **the ~** un(e) pareil(le) or semblable; le(la) pareil(le); (*pej*) (d')autres du même genre or acabit; **his ~s and dislikes** ses goûts *mpl* or préférences *fpl*; **I would ~, I'd ~** je voudrais, j'aimerais; **would you ~ a coffee?** voulez-vous du café?; **to be/ look ~ sb/sth** ressembler à qn/qch; **that's just ~ him** c'est bien de lui, ça lui ressemble; **do it ~ this** fais-le comme ceci; **nothing ~ ...** rien de tel que ...; **~able** *a* sympathique, agréable.

likelihood ['laɪklɪhud] *n* probabilité *f*.

likely ['laɪklɪ] *a* probable; plausible; **he's ~ to leave** il va sûrement partir, il risque fort de partir; **not ~!** pas de danger!

likeness ['laɪknɪs] *n* ressemblance *f*.

likewise ['laɪkwaɪz] *ad* de même, pareillement.

liking ['laɪkɪŋ] *n* affection *f*, penchant *m*; goût *m*.

lilac ['laɪlək] *n* lilas *m* // *a* lilas *inv*.

lily ['lɪlɪ] *n* lis *m*; **~ of the valley** *n* muguet *m*.

limb [lɪm] *n* membre *m*.

limber ['lɪmbə*] : **to ~ up** *vi* se dégourdir, se mettre en train.

limbo ['lɪmbəu] *n*: **to be in ~** (*fig*) être tombé(e) dans l'oubli.

lime [laɪm] *n* (*tree*) tilleul *m*; (*fruit*) lime *f*; (GEO) chaux *f*.

limelight ['laɪmlaɪt] *n*: **in the ~** (*fig*) en vedette, au premier plan.

limerick ['lɪmərɪk] *n* poème *m* humoristique (de 5 vers).

limestone ['laɪmstəun] n pierre f à chaux; (GEO) calcaire m.

limit ['lɪmɪt] n limite f // vt limiter; **~ed** a limité(e), restreint(e); **to be ~ed** to se limiter à, ne concerner que; **~ed (liability) company (Ltd)** n (Brit) ≈ société f anonyme (S.A.).

limp [lɪmp] n: **to have a ~** boiter // vi boiter // a mou(molle).

limpet ['lɪmpɪt] n patelle f.

line [laɪn] n (gen) ligne f; (rope) corde f; (wire) fil m; (of poem) vers m; (row, series) rangée f; file f, queue f; (COMM: series of goods) article(s) m(pl) // vt (clothes): **to ~ (with)** doubler (de); (box): **to ~ (with)** garnir or tapisser (de); (subj: trees, crowd) border; **in his ~ of business** dans sa partie, dans son rayon; **in ~ with** en accord avec; **to ~ up** vi s'aligner, se mettre en rang(s) // vt aligner.

lined [laɪnd] a (face) ridé(e), marqué(e); (paper) réglé(e).

linen ['lɪnɪn] n linge m (de corps or de maison); (cloth) lin m.

liner ['laɪnə*] n paquebot m de ligne.

linesman ['laɪnzmən] n (TENNIS) juge m de ligne; (FOOTBALL) juge de touche.

line-up ['laɪnʌp] n file f; (SPORT) (composition f de l')équipe f.

linger ['lɪŋgə*] vi s'attarder; traîner; (smell, tradition) persister.

lingo, ~es ['lɪŋgəu] n (pej) jargon m.

linguistics [lɪŋ'gwɪstɪks] n linguistique f.

lining ['laɪnɪŋ] n doublure f.

link [lɪŋk] n (of a chain) maillon m; (connection) lien m, rapport m // vt relier, lier, unir; **~s** npl (GOLF) (terrain m de) golf m; **to ~ up** vt relier // vi se rejoindre; s'associer.

lino ['laɪnəu] , **linoleum** [lɪ'nəuliəm] n linoléum m.

lion ['laɪən] n lion m; **~ess** n lionne f.

lip [lɪp] n lèvre f; (of cup etc) rebord m; **~read** vi lire sur les lèvres; **~ salve** n pommade f rosat or pour les lèvres; **~ service** n: **to pay ~ service to sth** ne reconnaître le mérite de qch que pour la forme; **~stick** n rouge m à lèvres.

liqueur [lɪ'kjuə*] n liqueur f.

liquid ['lɪkwɪd] n liquide m // a liquide.

liquidize ['lɪkwɪdaɪz] vt (CULIN) passer au mixer; **~r** n mixer m.

liquor ['lɪkə*] n spiritueux m, alcool m; **~ store** n (US) magasin m de vins et spiritueux.

liquorice ['lɪkərɪs] n réglisse f.

lisp [lɪsp] n zézaiement m.

list [lɪst] n liste f; (of ship) inclinaison f // vt (write down) inscrire; faire la liste de; (enumerate) énumérer // vi (ship) gîter, donner de la bande.

listen ['lɪsn] vi écouter; **to ~ to** écouter; **~er** n auditeur/trice.

listless ['lɪstlɪs] a indolent(e), apathique.

lit [lɪt] pt, pp of **light**.

liter ['li:tə*] n (US) = **litre**.

literacy ['lɪtərəsɪ] n degré m d'alphabétisation, fait m de savoir lire et écrire.

literal ['lɪtərl] a littéral(e).

literary ['lɪtərərɪ] a littéraire.

literate ['lɪtərət] a qui sait lire et écrire, instruit(e).

literature ['lɪtərɪtʃə*] n littérature f; (brochures etc) copie f publicitaire, prospectus mpl.

lithe [laɪð] a agile, souple.

litigation [lɪtɪ'geɪʃən] n litige m; contentieux m.

litre, (US) liter ['li:tə*] n litre m.

litter ['lɪtə*] n (rubbish) détritus mpl, ordures fpl; (young animals) portée f; **~ bin** n (Brit) boîte f à ordures, poubelle f; **~ed** a: **~ed with** jonché(e) de, couvert(e) de.

little ['lɪtl] a (small) petit(e); (not much): **it's ~ c'est peu; ~ milk** peu de lait // ad peu; **a ~** un peu (de); **~ by ~** petit à petit, peu à peu.

live vi [lɪv] vivre; (reside) vivre, habiter // a [laɪv] (animal) vivant(e), en vie; (wire) sous tension; (broadcast) (transmis(e)) en direct; **to ~ down** vt faire oublier (avec le temps); **to ~ on** vt fus (food) vivre de // vi survivre; **to ~ together** vi vivre ensemble, cohabiter; **to ~ up to** vt fus se montrer à la hauteur de.

livelihood ['laɪvlɪhud] n moyens mpl d'existence.

lively ['laɪvlɪ] a vif(vive), plein(e) d'entrain.

liven up ['laɪvnʌp] vt animer.

liver ['lɪvə*] n foie m.

livery ['lɪvərɪ] n livrée f.

lives [laɪvz] npl of **life**.

livestock ['laɪvstɔk] n cheptel m, bétail m.

livid ['lɪvɪd] a livide, blafard(e); (furious) furieux(euse), furibond(e).

living ['lɪvɪŋ] a vivant(e), en vie // n: **to earn** or **make a ~** gagner sa vie; **~ conditions** npl conditions fpl de vie; **~ room** n salle f de séjour; **~ wage** n salaire m permettant de vivre (décemment).

lizard ['lɪzəd] n lézard m.

load [ləud] n (weight) poids m; (thing carried) chargement m, charge f; (ELEC, TECH) charge f // vt (also: **~ up**): **to ~ (with)** (lorry, ship) charger (de); (gun, camera) charger (avec); (COMPUT) charger; **a ~ of, ~s of** (fig) un or des tas de, des masses de; **~ed** a (dice) pipé(e); (question) insidieux(euse); (col: rich) bourré(e) de fric; (: drunk) bourré(e); **~ing bay** n aire f de chargement.

loaf [ləuf], pl **loaves** n pain m, miche f //

vi (*also:* **~ about, ~ around**) fainéanter, traîner.

loan [ləun] *n* prêt *m* // *vt* prêter; **on ~** prêté(e), en prêt.

loath [ləuθ] *a*: **to be ~ to do** répugner à faire.

loathe [ləuð] *vt* détester, avoir en horreur.

loaves [ləuvz] *npl of* **loaf**.

lobby ['lɒbɪ] *n* hall *m*, entrée *f*; (POL) groupe *m* de pression, lobby *m* // *vt* faire pression sur.

lobster ['lɒbstə*] *n* homard *m*.

local ['ləukl] *a* local(e) // *n̄* (*pub*) pub *m or* café *m* du coin; **the ~s** *npl* les gens *mpl* du pays *or* du coin; **~ call** *n* communication urbaine; **~ government** *n* administration locale *or* municipale.

locality [ləu'kælɪtɪ] *n* région *f*, environs *mpl*; (*position*) lieu *m*.

locate [ləu'keɪt] *vt* (*find*) trouver, repérer; (*situate*) situer.

location [ləu'keɪʃən] *n* emplacement *m*; **on ~** (CINEMA) en extérieur.

loch [lɒx] *n* lac *m*, loch *m*.

lock [lɒk] *n* (*of door, box*) serrure *f*; (*of canal*) écluse *f*; (*of hair*) mèche *f*, boucle *f* // *vt* (*with key*) fermer à clé; (*immobilize*) bloquer // *vi* (*door etc*) fermer à clé; (*wheels*) se bloquer.

locker ['lɒkə*] *n* casier *m*.

locket ['lɒkɪt] *n* médaillon *m*.

locksmith ['lɒksmɪθ] *n* serrurier *m*.

lock-up ['lɒkʌp] *n* box *m*.

locomotive [ləukə'məutɪv] *n* locomotive *f*.

locum ['ləukəm] *n* (MED) suppléant/e (de médecin).

lodge [lɒdʒ] *n* pavillon *m* (de gardien); (FREEMASONRY) loge *f* // *vi* (*person*): **to ~** (**with**) être logé(e) (chez), être en pension (chez) // *vt* (*appeal etc*) présenter; déposer; **to ~ a complaint** porter plainte; **~r** *n* locataire *m/f*; (*with room and meals*) pensionnaire *m/f*.

lodgings ['lɒdʒɪŋz] *npl* chambre *f*; meublé *m*.

loft [lɒft] *n* grenier *m*.

lofty ['lɒftɪ] *a* élevé(e); (*haughty*) hautain(e).

log [lɒg] *n* (*of wood*) bûche *f*; (*book*) = **logbook**.

logbook ['lɒgbuk] *n* (NAUT) livre *m or* journal *m* de bord; (AVIAT) carnet *m* de vol; (*of car*) ≈ carte grise.

loggerheads ['lɒgəhɛdz] *npl*: **at ~ (with)** à couteaux tirés (avec).

logic ['lɒdʒɪk] *n* logique *f*; **~al** *a* logique.

loin [lɔɪn] *n* (CULIN) filet *m*, longe *f*.

loiter ['lɔɪtə*] *vi* s'attarder; **to ~ (about)** traîner, musarder; (*pej*) rôder.

loll [lɒl] *vi* (*also:* **~ about**) se prélasser, fainéanter.

lollipop ['lɒlɪpɒp] *n* sucette *f*; **~ man/**

lady *n* (*Brit*) contractuel/le qui fait traverser la rue aux enfants.

London ['lʌndən] *n* Londres *m*; **~er** *n* Londonien/ne.

lone [ləun] *a* solitaire.

loneliness ['ləunlɪnɪs] *n* solitude *f*, isolement *m*.

lonely ['ləunlɪ] *a* seul(e); solitaire, isolé(e).

long [lɒŋ] *a* long(longue) // *ad* longtemps // *vi*: **to ~ for sth** avoir très envie de qch; attendre qch avec impatience; **to ~ to do** avoir très envie de faire; attendre avec impatience de faire; **in the ~ run** à la longue; finalement; **so** *or* **as ~ as** pourvu que; **don't be ~** dépêchez-vous; **how ~ is this river/course?** quelle est la longueur de ce fleuve/la durée de ce cours?; **6 metres ~** (long) de 6 mètres; **6 months ~** qui dure 6 mois, de 6 mois; **all night ~** toute la nuit; **he no ~er comes** il ne vient plus; **~ before** longtemps avant; **before ~** (+ *future*) avant peu, dans peu de temps; (+ *past*) peu de temps après; **at ~ last** enfin; **~-distance** *a* (*race*) de fond; (*call*) interurbain(e); **~-hand** *n* écriture normale *or* courante; **~ing** *n* désir *m*, envie *f*, nostalgie *f*.

longitude ['lɒŋgɪtjuːd] *n* longitude *f*.

long: **~ jump** *n* saut *m* en longueur; **~-playing** *a*: **~-playing record (L.P.)** *n* (disque *m*) 33 tours *m inv*; **~-range** *a* à longue portée; **~-sighted** *a* presbyte; (*fig*) prévoyant(e); **~-standing** *a* de longue date; **~-suffering** *a* empreint(e) d'une patience résignée; extrêmement patient(e); **~-term** *a* à long terme; **~ wave** *n* grandes ondes; **~-winded** *a* intarissable, interminable.

loo [luː] *n* (*Brit col*) w.-c. *mpl*, petit coin.

look [luk] *vi* regarder; (*seem*) sembler, paraître, avoir l'air; (*building etc*): **to ~ south/on to the sea** donner au sud/sur la mer // *n* regard *m*; (*appearance*) air *m*, allure *f*, aspect *m*; **~s** *npl* mine *f*; physique *m*, beauté *f*; **to ~ after** *vt fus* s'occuper de, prendre soin de; garder, surveiller; **to ~ at** *vt fus* regarder; **to ~ back** *vi*: **to ~ back** se retourner pour regarder; **to ~ back on** (*event etc*) évoquer, repenser à; **to ~ down on** *vt fus* (*fig*) regarder de haut, dédaigner; **to ~ for** *vt fus* chercher; **to ~ forward to** *vt fus* attendre avec impatience; **we ~ forward to hearing from you** dans l'attente de vous lire; **to ~ into** *vt* examiner, étudier; **to ~ on** *vi* regarder (en spectateur); **to ~ out** *vi* (*beware*): **to ~ out (for)** prendre garde (à), faire attention (à); **to ~ out for** *vt fus* être à la recherche de; guetter; **to ~ round** *vi* regarder derrière soi, se retourner; **to ~ to** *vt fus* veiller à; (*rely on*) compter sur; **to ~ up** *vi* lever les yeux; (*improve*) s'améliorer // *vt* (*word*) chercher;

(friend) passer voir; **to ~ up to** *vt fus* avoir du respect pour; **~-out** *n* poste *m* de guet; guetteur *m*; **to be on the ~-out (for)** guetter.

loom [luːm] *n* métier *m* à tisser // *vi* surgir; *(fig)* menacer.

loony [ˈluːnɪ] *n (col)* timbré/e, cinglé/e.

loop [luːp] *n* boucle *f*; **~hole** *n* porte *f* de sortie *(fig)*; échappatoire *f*.

loose [luːs] *a (knot, screw)* desserré(e); *(stone)* branlant(e); *(clothes)* vague, ample, lâche; *(animal)* en liberté, échappé(e); *(life)* dissolu(e); *(morals, discipline)* relâché(e); *(thinking)* peu rigoureux(euse), vague; *(translation)* approximatif(ive); **~ change** *n* petite monnaie; **~ chippings** *npl (on road)* gravillons *mpl*; **to be at a ~ end** *or (US)* **at ~ ends** ne pas trop savoir quoi faire; **~ly** *ad* sans serrer; approximativement; **~n** *vt* desserrer, relâcher, défaire.

loot [luːt] *n* butin *m* // *vt* piller.

lop [lɔp] : **to ~ off** *vt* couper, trancher.

lop-sided [ˈlɔpˈsaɪdɪd] *a* de travers, asymétrique.

lord [lɔːd] *n* seigneur *m*; **L~** Smith lord Smith; **the L~** le Seigneur; **the (House of) L~s** *(Brit)* la Chambre des Lords; **~ship** *n*: **your L~ship** Monsieur le comte *(or* le baron *or* le Juge).

lore [lɔː*] *n* tradition(s) *f(pl)*.

lorry [ˈlɔrɪ] *n (Brit)* camion *m*; **~ driver** *n (Brit)* camionneur *m*, routier *m*.

lose [luːz], *pt, pp* **lost** *vt* perdre; *(opportunity)* manquer, perdre; *(pursuers)* distancer, semer // *vi* perdre; **to ~ (time) (clock)** retarder; **to get lost** *vi* se perdre; **~r** *n* perdant/e.

loss [lɔs] *n* perte *f*; **to be at a ~** être perplexe *or* embarrassé(e).

lost [lɔst] *pt, pp* de **lose** // *a* perdu(e); **~ property** *n, (US)* **~ and found** *n* objets trouvés.

lot [lɔt] *n (at auctions)* lot *m*; *(destiny)* sort *m*, destinée *f*; **the ~** le tout; tous *mpl*, toutes *fpl*; **a ~** beaucoup; **a ~ of** beaucoup de; **~s of** des tas de; **to draw ~s (for sth)** tirer (qch) au sort.

lotion [ˈləʊʃən] *n* lotion *f*.

lottery [ˈlɔtərɪ] *n* loterie *f*.

loud [laʊd] *a* bruyant(e), sonore, fort(e); *(gaudy)* voyant(e), tapageur(euse) // *ad (speak etc)* fort; **~hailer** *n (Brit)* porte-voix *m inv*; **~ly** *ad* fort, bruyamment; **~speaker** *n* haut-parleur *m*.

lounge [laʊndʒ] *n* salon *m* // *vi* se prélasser, paresser; **~ suit** *n (Brit)* complet *m*; 'tenue de ville'.

louse [laʊs], *pl* **lice** *n* pou *m*.

lousy [ˈlaʊzɪ] *a (fig)* infect(e), moche.

lout [laʊt] *n* rustre *m*, butor *m*.

louvre, *(US)* **louver** [ˈluːvə*] *a (door, window)* à claire-voie.

lovable [ˈlʌvəbl] *a* très sympathique; adorable.

love [lʌv] *n* amour *m* // *vt* aimer; aimer beaucoup; **to be in ~ with** être amoureux(euse) de; **to make ~** faire l'amour; **'15 ~'** *(TENNIS)* '15 à rien *or* zéro'; **~ affair** *n* liaison (amoureuse); **~ life** *n* vie sentimentale.

lovely [ˈlʌvlɪ] *a (très)* joli(e); ravissant(e), charmant(e); agréable.

lover [ˈlʌvə*] *n* amant *m*; *(amateur)*: **a ~ of** un(e) ami(e) de; un(e) amoureux(euse) de.

loving [ˈlʌvɪŋ] *a* affectueux(euse), tendre, aimant(e).

low [ləʊ] *a* bas(basse) // *ad* bas // *n (METEOROLOGY)* dépression *f* // *vi (cow)* mugir; **to feel ~** se sentir déprimé(e); **to turn (down) ~** *vt* baisser; **~-cut** *a (dress)* décolleté(e); **~er** *vt* abaisser, baisser; **~-fat** *a* maigre; **~lands** *npl (GEO)* plaines *fpl*; **~ly** *a* humble, modeste; **~-lying** *a* à faible altitude.

loyal [ˈlɔɪəl] *a* loyal(e), fidèle; **~ty** *n* loyauté *f*, fidélité *f*.

lozenge [ˈlɔzɪndʒ] *n (MED)* pastille *f*; *(GEOM)* losange *m*.

L.P. *n abbr of* **long-playing record**.

L-plates [ˈɛlpleɪts] *npl (Brit)* plaques *fpl* d'apprenti conducteur.

Ltd *abbr see* **limited**.

lubricant [ˈluːbrɪkənt] *n* lubrifiant *m*.

lubricate [ˈluːbrɪkeɪt] *vt* lubrifier, graisser.

luck [lʌk] *n* chance *f*; **bad ~** malchance *f*, malheur *m*; **good ~!** bonne chance!; **~ily** *ad* heureusement, par bonheur; **~y** *a (person)* qui a de la chance; *(coincidence)* heureux(euse); *(number etc)* qui porte bonheur.

ludicrous [ˈluːdɪkrəs] *a* ridicule, absurde.

lug [lʌg] *vt* traîner, tirer.

luggage [ˈlʌgɪdʒ] *n* bagages *mpl*; **~ rack** *n (in train)* porte-bagages *m inv*; *(on car)* galerie *f*.

lukewarm [ˈluːkwɔːm] *a* tiède.

lull [lʌl] *n* accalmie *f* // *vt (child)* bercer; *(person, fear)* apaiser, calmer.

lullaby [ˈlʌləbaɪ] *n* berceuse *f*.

lumbago [lʌmˈbeɪgəʊ] *n* lumbago *m*.

lumber [ˈlʌmbə*] *n* bric-à-brac *m inv*; **~jack** *n* bûcheron *m*.

luminous [ˈluːmɪnəs] *a* lumineux(euse).

lump [lʌmp] *n* morceau *m*; *(in sauce)* grumeau *m*; *(swelling)* grosseur *f* // *vt (also:* **~ together**) réunir, mettre en tas; **~ sum** *n* somme globale *or* forfaitaire.

lunacy [ˈluːnəsɪ] *n* démence *f*, folie *f*.

lunar [ˈluːnə*] *a* lunaire.

lunatic [ˈluːnətɪk] *a, n* fou(folle), dément(e).

lunch [lʌntʃ] *n* déjeuner *m*.

luncheon [ˈlʌntʃən] *n* déjeuner *m*; **~ meat** *n* sorte de saucisson; **~ voucher**

n chèque-repas *m*.
lung [lʌŋ] *n* poumon *m*.
lunge [lʌndʒ] *vi* (*also*: ~ forward) faire un mouvement brusque en avant; **to ~ at** envoyer *or* assener un coup à.
lurch [lɜːtʃ] *vi* vaciller, tituber // *n* écart *m* brusque, embardée *f*; **to leave sb in the ~** laisser qn se débrouiller *or* se dépêtrer tout(e) seul(e).
lure [luə*] *n* appât *m*, leurre *m* // *vt* attirer *or* persuader par la ruse.
lurid ['luərɪd] *a* affreux(euse), atroce.
lurk [lɜːk] *vi* se tapir, se cacher.
luscious ['lʌʃəs] *a* succulent(e); appétissant(e).
lush [lʌʃ] *a* luxuriant(e).
lust [lʌst] *n* luxure *f*; lubricité *f*; désir *m*; (*fig*): ~ **for** soif *f* de; **to ~ after** *vt fus* convoiter, désirer.
lusty ['lʌstɪ] *a* vigoureux(euse), robuste.
Luxembourg ['lʌksəmbəːg] *n* Luxembourg *m*.
luxurious [lʌg'zjuərɪəs] *a* luxueux(euse).
luxury ['lʌkʃərɪ] *n* luxe *m* // *cpd* de luxe.
lying ['laɪɪŋ] *n* mensonge(s) *m(pl)*.
lyric ['lɪrɪk] *a* lyrique; ~**s** *npl* (*of song*) paroles *fpl*; ~**al** *a* lyrique.

M

m. *abbr of* **metre, mile, million**.
M.A. *abbr see* **master**.
mac [mæk] *n* (*Brit*) imper(méable) *m*.
mace [meɪs] *n* masse *f*; (*spice*) macis *m*.
machine [mə'ʃiːn] *n* machine *f* // *vt* (*dress etc*) coudre à la machine; ~ **gun** *n* mitrailleuse *f*; ~**ry** *n* machinerie *f*, machines *fpl*; (*fig*) mécanisme(s) *m(pl)*.
mackerel ['mækrl] *n* (*pl inv*) maquereau *m*.
mackintosh ['mækɪntɔʃ] *n* (*Brit*) imperméable *m*.
mad [mæd] *a* fou(folle); (*foolish*) insensé(e); (*angry*) furieux(euse).
madam ['mædəm] *n* madame *f*.
madden ['mædn] *vt* exaspérer.
made [meɪd] *pt*, *pp of* **make**.
Madeira [mə'dɪərə] *n* (*GEO*) Madère *f*; (*wine*) madère *m*.
made-to-measure ['meɪdtə'mɛʒə*] *a* (*Brit*) fait(e) sur mesure.
madly ['mædlɪ] *ad* follement.
madman ['mædmən] *n* fou *m*, aliéné *m*.
madness ['mædnɪs] *n* folie *f*.
magazine [mægə'ziːn] *n* (*PRESS*) magazine *m*, revue *f*; (*MIL*: *store*) dépôt *m*, arsenal *m*; (*of firearm*) magasin *m*.
maggot ['mægət] *n* ver *m*, asticot *m*.
magic ['mædʒɪk] *n* magie *f* // *a* magique; ~**al** *a* magique; ~**ian** [mə'dʒɪʃən] *n* magicien/ne.
magistrate ['mædʒɪstreɪt] *n* magistrat *m*; juge *m*.

magnet ['mægnɪt] *n* aimant *m*; ~**ic** [-'nɛtɪk] *a* magnétique.
magnificent [mæg'nɪfɪsnt] *a* superbe, magnifique.
magnify ['mægnɪfaɪ] *vt* grossir; (*sound*) amplifier; ~**ing glass** *n* loupe *f*.
magnitude ['mægnɪtjuːd] *n* ampleur *f*.
magpie ['mægpaɪ] *n* pie *f*.
mahogany [mə'hɔgənɪ] *n* acajou *m*.
maid [meɪd] *n* bonne *f*; old ~ (*pej*) vieille fille.
maiden ['meɪdn] *n* jeune fille *f* // *a* (*aunt etc*) non mariée; (*speech, voyage*) inaugural(e); ~ **name** *n* nom *m* de jeune fille.
mail [meɪl] *n* poste *f*; (*letters*) courrier *m* // *vt* envoyer (par la poste); ~**box** *n* (*US*) boîte *f* aux lettres; ~**ing list** *n* liste *f* d'adresses; ~**-order** *n* vente *f or* achat *m* par correspondance.
maim [meɪm] *vt* mutiler.
main [meɪn] *a* principal(e) // *n* (*pipe*) conduite principale, canalisation *f*; the ~**s** (*ELEC*) le secteur; **in the ~** dans l'ensemble; ~**frame** *n* (*COMPUT*) (gros) ordinateur, unité centrale; ~**land** *n* continent *m*; ~**ly** *ad* principalement, surtout; ~ **road** *n* grand-route *f*; ~**stream** *n* courant principal; ~**stay** *n* (*fig*) pilier *m*.
maintain [meɪn'teɪn] *vt* entretenir; (*continue*) maintenir, préserver; (*affirm*) soutenir; **maintenance** ['meɪntənəns] *n* entretien *m*; (*alimony*) pension *f* alimentaire.
maize [meɪz] *n* maïs *m*.
majestic [mə'dʒɛstɪk] *a* majestueux(euse).
majesty ['mædʒɪstɪ] *n* majesté *f*.
major ['meɪdʒə*] *n* (*MIL*) commandant *m* // *a* important(e), principal(e); (*MUS*) majeur(e).
Majorca [mə'jɔːkə] *n* Majorque *f*.
majority [mə'dʒɔrɪtɪ] *n* majorité *f*.
make [meɪk] *vt* (*pt*, *pp* made) faire; (*manufacture*) faire, fabriquer; (*cause to be*): **to ~ sb sad** *etc* rendre qn triste *etc*; (*force*): **to ~ sb do sth** obliger qn à faire qch, faire faire qch à qn; (*equal*): **2 and 2 ~ 4** 2 et 2 font 4 // *n* fabrication *f*; (*brand*) marque *f*; **to ~ a fool of sb** (*ridicule*) ridiculiser qn; (*trick*) avoir *or* duper qn; **to ~ a profit** faire un *or* des bénéfice(s); **to ~ a loss** essuyer une perte; **to ~ it** (*arrive*) arriver; (*achieve sth*) parvenir à qch; **what time do you ~ it?** quelle heure avez-vous?; **to ~ do with** se contenter de; se débrouiller avec; **to ~ for** *vt fus* (*place*) se diriger vers; **to ~ out** *vt* (*write out*) écrire; (: *cheque*) faire; (*understand*) comprendre; (*see*) distinguer; **to ~ up** *vt* (*invent*) inventer, imaginer; (*parcel*) faire // *vi* se réconcilier; (*with cosmetics*) se maquiller, se farder; **to ~ up for** *vt fus*

compenser; racheter; **~-believe** n: a world of ~-believe un pays de chimères; it's just ~-believe c'est pour faire semblant; c'est de l'invention pure; **~r** n fabricant m; **~shift** a provisoire, improvisé(e); **~-up** n maquillage m; **~-up remover** n démaquillant m.

making ['meɪkɪŋ] n (fig): in the ~ en formation or gestation; **to have the ~s of** (actor, athlete etc) avoir l'étoffe de.

malaria [mə'lɛərɪə] n malaria f.

Malaya [mə'leɪə] n Malaisie f.

male [meɪl] n (BIOL, ELEC) mâle m // a (sex, attitude) masculin(e); mâle; (child etc) du sexe masculin.

malevolent [mə'levələnt] a malveillant(e).

malfunction [mæl'fʌŋkʃən] n fonctionnement défectueux.

malice ['mælɪs] n méchanceté f, malveillance f; **malicious** [mə'lɪʃəs] a méchant(e), malveillant(e); (LAW) avec intention criminelle.

malign [mə'laɪn] vt diffamer, calomnier.

malignant [mə'lɪgnənt] a (MED) malin(igne).

mall [mɔːl] n (also: **shopping ~**) centre commercial.

mallet ['mælɪt] n maillet m.

malpractice [mæl'præktɪs] n faute professionnelle; négligence f.

malt [mɔːlt] n malt m // cpd (whisky) pur malt.

Malta ['mɔːltə] n Malte f.

mammal ['mæml] n mammifère m.

mammoth ['mæməθ] n mammouth m // a géant(e), monstre.

man [mæn], pl **men** n homme m; (CHESS) pièce f; (DRAUGHTS) pion m // vt garnir d'hommes; servir, assurer le fonctionnement de; être de service à; **an old ~** un vieillard; **~ and wife** mari et femme.

manage ['mænɪdʒ] vi se débrouiller // vt (be in charge of) s'occuper de; gérer; **to ~ to do** se débrouiller pour faire; réussir à faire; **~able** a maniable; faisable; **~ment** n administration f, direction f; **~r** n directeur m; administrateur m; (of hotel etc) gérant m; (of artist) impresario m; **~ress** [-ə'res] n directrice f; gérante f; **~rial** [-ə'dʒɪərɪəl] a directorial(e); **managing** a: **managing director** directeur général.

mandarin ['mændərɪn] n (also: ~ **orange**) mandarine f; (person) mandarin m.

mandatory ['mændətərɪ] a obligatoire; (powers etc) mandataire.

mane [meɪn] n crinière f.

maneuver etc [mə'nuːvə*] (US) = **manoeuvre** etc.

manfully ['mænfəlɪ] ad vaillamment.

mangle ['mæŋgl] vt déchiqueter; mutiler.

mango, **~es** ['mæŋgəu] n mangue f.

mangy ['meɪndʒɪ] a galeux(euse).

manhandle ['mænhændl] vt malmener.

manhole ['mænhəul] n trou m d'homme.

manhood ['mænhud] n âge m d'homme; virilité f.

man-hour ['mæn'auə*] n heure f de main-d'œuvre.

mania ['meɪnɪə] n manie f; **~c** ['meɪnɪæk] n maniaque m/f.

manic ['mænɪk] a maniaque.

manicure ['mænɪkjuə*] n manucure f; **~ set** n trousse f à ongles.

manifest ['mænɪfest] vt manifester // a manifeste, évident(e).

manifesto [mænɪ'festəu] n manifeste m.

manipulate [mə'nɪpjuleɪt] vt manipuler.

mankind [mæn'kaɪnd] n humanité f, genre humain.

manly ['mænlɪ] a viril(e); courageux(euse).

man-made ['mæn'meɪd] a artificiel(le).

manner ['mænə*] n manière f, façon f; **~s** npl manières; **~ism** n particularité f de langage (or de comportement), tic m.

manoeuvre, (US) **maneuver** [mə'nuːvə*] vt, vi manœuvrer. // n manœuvre f.

manor ['mænə*] n (also: ~ **house**) manoir m.

manpower ['mænpauə*] n main-d'œuvre f.

mansion ['mænʃən] n château m, manoir m.

manslaughter ['mænslɔːtə*] n homicide m involontaire.

mantelpiece ['mæntlpiːs] n cheminée f.

manual ['mænjuəl] a manuel(le) // n manuel m.

manufacture [mænju'fæktʃə*] vt fabriquer // n fabrication f; **~r** n fabricant m.

manure [mə'njuə*] n fumier m; (artificial) engrais m.

manuscript ['mænjuskrɪpt] n manuscrit m.

many ['menɪ] a beaucoup de, de nombreux(euses) // pronoun beaucoup, un grand nombre; **a great ~** un grand nombre (de); **~ a ...** bien des ..., plus d'un(e) ....

map [mæp] n carte f // vt dresser la carte de; **to ~ out** tracer.

maple ['meɪpl] n érable m.

mar [mɑː*] vt gâcher, gâter.

marathon ['mærəθən] n marathon m.

marble ['mɑːbl] n marbre m; (toy) bille f.

March [mɑːtʃ] n mars m.

march [mɑːtʃ] vi marcher au pas; défiler // n marche f; (demonstration) rallye m.

mare [mɛə*] n jument f.

margarine [mɑːdʒə'riːn] n margarine f.

margin ['mɑːdʒɪn] n marge f; **~al**

(seat) n (POL) siège disputé.
marigold ['mærɪgəuld] n souci m.
marijuana [mærɪ'wɑ:nə] n marijuana f.
marine [mə'ri:n] a marin(e) // n fusilier marin; (US) marine m.
marital ['mærɪtl] a matrimonial(e); ~ **status** situation f de famille.
mark [mɑ:k] n marque f; (of skid etc) trace f; (Brit SCOL) note f; (SPORT) cible f; (currency) mark m // vt marquer; (stain) tacher; (Brit SCOL) noter; corriger; **to ~ time** marquer le pas; **to ~ out** vt désigner; **~er** n (sign) jalon m; (bookmark) signet m.
market ['mɑ:kɪt] n marché m // vt (COMM) commercialiser; ~ **garden** n (Brit) jardin maraîcher; **~ing** n marketing m; **~place** n place f du marché; (COMM) marché m; ~ **research** n étude f de marché; **~ value** n valeur marchande; valeur du marché.
marksman ['mɑ:ksmən] n tireur m d'élite.
marmalade ['mɑ:məleɪd] n confiture f d'oranges.
maroon [mə'ru:n] vt (fig): **to be ~ed** (in or at) être bloqué(e) (à) // a bordeaux inv.
marquee [mɑ:'ki:] n chapiteau m.
marriage ['mærɪdʒ] n mariage m; ~ **bureau** n agence matrimoniale; ~ **certificate** n extrait m d'acte de mariage.
married ['mærɪd] a marié(e); (life, love) conjugal(e).
marrow ['mærəu] n moelle f; (vegetable) courge f.
marry ['mærɪ] vt épouser, se marier avec; (subj: father, priest etc) marier // vi (also: **get married**) se marier.
Mars [mɑ:z] n (planet) Mars f.
marsh [mɑ:ʃ] n marais m, marécage m.
marshal ['mɑ:ʃl] n maréchal m; (US: fire, police) ≈ capitaine m // vt rassembler.
martyr ['mɑ:tə*] n martyr/e // vt martyriser; **~dom** n martyre m.
marvel ['mɑ:vl] n merveille f // vi: **to ~ (at)** s'émerveiller (de); **~lous**, (US) **~ous** a merveilleux(euse).
Marxist ['mɑ:ksɪst] a, n marxiste (m/f).
marzipan ['mɑ:zɪpæn] n pâte f d'amandes.
mascara [mæs'kɑ:rə] n mascara m.
masculine ['mæskjulɪn] a masculin(e).
mashed [mæʃt] a: ~ **potatoes** purée f de pommes de terre.
mask [mɑ:sk] n masque m // vt masquer.
mason ['meɪsn] n (also: **stone~**) maçon m; (also: **free~**) franc-maçon m; **~ry** n maçonnerie f.
masquerade [mæskə'reɪd] n bal masqué; (fig) mascarade f // vi: **to ~ as** se faire passer pour.
mass [mæs] n multitude f, masse f; (PHYSICS) masse; (REL) messe f // vi se

masser; **the ~es** les masses.
massacre ['mæsəkə*] n massacre m.
massage ['mæsɑ:ʒ] n massage m // vt masser.
massive ['mæsɪv] a énorme, massif(ive).
mass media ['mæs'mi:dɪə] npl mass-media mpl.
mass-production ['mæsprə'dʌkʃən] n fabrication f en série.
mast [mɑ:st] n mât m.
master ['mɑ:stə*] n maître m; (in secondary school) professeur m; (title for boys): **M~ X** Monsieur X // vt maîtriser; (learn) apprendre à fond; (understand) posséder parfaitement or à fond; ~ **key** n passe-partout m inv; **~ly** a magistral(e); **~mind** n esprit supérieur // vt diriger, être le cerveau de; **M~ of Arts/Science (M.A./M.Sc.)** n ≈ titulaire m/f d'une maîtrise (en lettres/sciences); **~piece** n chef-d'œuvre m; **~y** n maîtrise f; connaissance parfaite.
mat [mæt] n petit tapis; (also: **door~**) paillasson m // a = **matt**.
match [mætʃ] n allumette f; (game) match m, partie f; (fig) égal/e; mariage m; parti m // vt assortir; (go well with) aller bien avec, s'assortir à; (equal) égaler, valoir // vi être assorti(e); **to be a good ~** être bien assorti(e); **~box** n boîte f d'allumettes; **~ing** a assorti(e).
mate [meɪt] n camarade m/f de travail; (col) copain/copine; (animal) partenaire m/f, mâle/femelle; (in merchant navy) second m // vi s'accoupler // vt accoupler.
material [mə'tɪərɪəl] n (substance) matière f, matériau m; (cloth) tissu m, étoffe f // a matériel(le); (important) essentiel(le); **~s** npl matériaux mpl.
maternal [mə'tə:nl] a maternel(le).
maternity [mə'tə:nɪtɪ] n maternité f; ~ **dress** n robe f de grossesse; ~ **hospital** n maternité f.
math [mæθ] n (US) = **maths**.
mathematical [mæθə'mætɪkl] a mathématique.
mathematics [mæθə'mætɪks] n mathématiques fpl.
maths, (US) **math** [mæθs, mæθ] n math(s) fpl.
matinée ['mætɪneɪ] n matinée f.
mating ['meɪtɪŋ] n accouplement m.
matriculation [mətrɪkju'leɪʃən] n inscription f.
matrimonial [mætrɪ'məunɪəl] a matrimonial(e), conjugal(e).
matrimony ['mætrɪmənɪ] n mariage m.
matron ['meɪtrən] n (in hospital) infirmière-chef f; (in school) infirmière; **~ly** a de matrone; imposant(e).
mat(t) [mæt] a mat(e).
matted ['mætɪd] a emmêlé(e).
matter ['mætə*] n question f; (PHYSICS)

matière f, substance f; (*content*) contenu m, fond m; (MED: *pus*) pus m // vi importer; it **doesn't** ~ cela n'a pas d'importance; (*I don't mind*) cela ne fait rien; what's the ~? qu'est-ce qu'il y a?, qu'est-ce qui ne va pas?; **no** ~ **what** quoiqu'il arrive; **as a** ~ **of course** tout naturellement; **as a** ~ **of fact** en fait; ~**-of-fact** à terre à terre, neutre.

mattress ['mætrɪs] n matelas m.

mature [mə'tjuə*] a mûr(e); (*cheese*) fait(e) // vi mûrir; se faire.

maul [mɔːl] vt lacérer.

mauve [məuv] a mauve.

maximum ['mæksɪməm] a maximum // n (*pl* maxima ['mæksɪmə]) maximum m.

May [meɪ] n mai m.

may [meɪ] vi (*conditional*: **might**) (*indicating possibility*): he ~ **come** il se peut qu'il vienne; (*be allowed to*): ~ **I smoke?** puis-je fumer?; (*wishes*): ~ **God bless you!** (que) Dieu vous bénisse!

maybe ['meɪbɪ] ad peut-être; ~ **he'll** ... peut-être qu'il ....

May Day n le Premier mai.

mayhem ['meɪhɛm] n grabuge m.

mayonnaise [meɪə'neɪz] n mayonnaise f.

mayor [mɛə*] n maire m; ~**ess** n maire m; épouse f du maire.

maze [meɪz] n labyrinthe m, dédale m.

M.D. abbr = **Doctor of Medicine.**

me [miː] pronoun me, m' + *vowel*; (*stressed, after prep*) moi; he **heard** ~ il m'a entendu(e); **give** ~ **a book** donnez-moi un livre; **after** ~ après moi.

meadow ['mɛdəu] n prairie f, pré m.

meagre, (US) **meager** ['miːgə*] a maigre.

meal [miːl] n repas m; (*flour*) farine f; ~**time** n l'heure f du repas.

mean [miːn] a (*with money*) avare, radin(e); (*unkind*) mesquin(e), méchant(e); (*average*) moyen(ne) // vt (pt, pp **meant**) (*signify*) signifier, vouloir dire; (*intend*): **to** ~ **to do** avoir l'intention de faire // n moyenne f; ~**s** npl moyens mpl; **by** ~**s of** par l'intermédiaire de; au moyen de; **by all** ~**s** je vous en prie; **to be meant for** sb/sth être destiné(e) à qn/qch; **do you** ~ **it?** vous êtes sérieux?; **what do you** ~? que voulez-vous dire?

meander [mɪ'ændə*] vi faire des méandres; (*fig*) flâner.

meaning ['miːnɪŋ] n signification f, sens m; ~**ful** a significatif(ive); ~**less** a dénué(e) de sens.

meant [mɛnt] pt, pp of **mean.**

meantime ['miːntaɪm] ad, **meanwhile** ['miːnwaɪl] ad (*also*: **in the** ~) pendant ce temps.

measles ['miːzlz] n rougeole f.

measly ['miːzlɪ] a (*col*) minable.

measure ['mɛʒə*] vt, vi mesurer // n mesure f; (*ruler*) règle (graduée); ~**ments** npl mesures fpl; **chest/hip** ~**ment** tour m de poitrine/hanches.

meat [miːt] n viande f; ~**ball** n boulette f de viande; ~**y** a avec beaucoup de viande, plein(e) de viande; (*fig*) substantiel(le).

Mecca ['mɛkə] n la Mecque.

mechanic [mɪ'kænɪk] n mécanicien m; ~**s** n mécanique f // npl mécanisme m; ~**al** a mécanique.

mechanism ['mɛkənɪzəm] n mécanisme m.

medal ['mɛdl] n médaille f; ~**lion** [mɪ'dælɪən] n médaillon m.

meddle ['mɛdl] vi: **to** ~ **in** se mêler de, s'occuper de; **to** ~ **with** toucher à.

media ['miːdɪə] npl media mpl.

mediaeval [mɛdɪ'iːvl] a = **medieval.**

median ['miːdɪən] n (US: *also*: ~ **strip**) bande médiane.

mediate ['miːdɪeɪt] vi s'interposer; servir d'intermédiaire.

Medicaid ['mɛdɪkeɪd] n (US) assistance médicale aux indigents.

medical ['mɛdɪkl] a médical(e).

Medicare ['mɛdɪkɛə*] n (US) assistance médicale aux personnes âgées.

medicated ['mɛdɪkeɪtɪd] a traitant(e), médicamenteux(euse).

medicine ['mɛdsɪn] n médecine f; (*drug*) médicament m.

medieval [mɛdɪ'iːvl] a médiéval(e).

mediocre [miːdɪ'əukə*] a médiocre.

meditate ['mɛdɪteɪt] vi méditer.

Mediterranean [mɛdɪtə'reɪnɪən] a méditerranéen(ne); **the** ~ (**Sea**) la (mer) Méditerranée.

medium ['miːdɪəm] a moyen(ne) // n (*pl* media: **means**) moyen m; (*pl* **mediums**: *person*) médium m; **the happy** ~ le juste milieu; ~ **wave** n ondes moyennes.

medley ['mɛdlɪ] n mélange m.

meek [miːk] a doux(douce), humble.

meet [miːt] pt, pp **met** vt rencontrer; (*by arrangement*) retrouver, rejoindre; (*for the first time*) faire la connaissance de; (*go and fetch*): **I'll** ~ **you** at the station j'irai te chercher à la gare; (*fig*) faire face à; satisfaire à; se joindre à // vi se rencontrer; se retrouver; (*in session*) se réunir; (*join: objects*) se joindre; **to** ~ **with** vt fus rencontrer; ~**ing** n rencontre f; (*session: of club etc*) réunion f; (*interview*) entrevue f; **she's at a** ~**ing** (COMM) elle est en conférence.

megabyte ['mɛgəbaɪt] n (COMPUT) méga-octet m.

megaphone ['mɛgəfəun] n porte-voix m inv.

melancholy ['mɛlənkəlɪ] n mélancolie f // a mélancolique.

mellow ['mɛləu] a velouté(e);

doux(douce); (*colour*) riche et pro-
fond(e); (*fruit*) mûr(e) // *vi* (*person*)
s'adoucir.

melody ['mɛlədɪ] *n* mélodie *f*.

melon ['mɛlən] *n* melon *m*.

melt [mɛlt] *vi* fondre; (*become soft*)
s'amollir; (*fig*) s'attendrir // *vt* faire fondre; (*person*) attendrir; **to ~ away** *vi*
fondre complètement; **to ~ down** *vt*
fondre; **~down** *n* fusion *f* (du cœur
d'un réacteur nucléaire); **~ing pot** *n*
(*fig*) creuset *m*.

member ['mɛmbə*] *n* membre *m*; **M~
of Parliament (MP)** (*Brit*) député *m*;
M~ of the European Parliament (MEP)
(*Brit*) Eurodéputé *m*; **~ship** *n* adhésion
f; statut *m* de membre; (*nombre m de*)
membres *mpl*, adhérents *mpl*; **~ship
card** *n* carte *f* de membre.

memento [mə'mɛntəu] *n* souvenir *m*.

memo ['mɛməu] *n* note *f* (de service).

memoirs ['mɛmwɑ:z] *npl* mémoires
mpl.

memorandum, *pl* **memoranda**
[mɛmə'rændəm, -də] *n* note *f* (de
service); (*DIPLOMACY*) mémorandum
m.

memorial [mɪ'mɔ:rɪəl] *n* mémorial *m* //
a commémoratif(ive).

memorize ['mɛməraɪz] *vt* apprendre
par cœur; retenir.

memory ['mɛmərɪ] *n* mémoire *f*;
(*recollection*) souvenir *m*.

men [mɛn] *npl of* **man**.

menace ['mɛnəs] *n* menace *f* // *vt*
menacer.

mend [mɛnd] *vt* réparer; (*darn*)
raccommoder, repriser // *n* reprise *f*; **on
the ~** en voie de guérison.

menial ['mi:nɪəl] *a* de domestique,
inférieur(e); subalterne.

meningitis [mɛnɪn'dʒaɪtɪs] *n* méningite
f.

menopause ['mɛnəupɔ:z] *n* ménopause
f.

menstruation [mɛnstru'eɪʃən] *n* menstruation *f*.

mental ['mɛntl] *a* mental(e).

mentality [mɛn'tælɪtɪ] *n* mentalité *f*.

mention ['mɛnʃən] *n* mention *f* // *vt*
mentionner, faire mention de; **don't ~ it!**
je vous en prie, il n'y a pas de quoi!

menu ['mɛnju:] *n* (*set ~, COMPUT*)
menu *m*; (*printed*) carte *f*.

MEP *n abbr of* **Member of the
European Parliament**.

mercenary ['mə:sɪnərɪ] *a* mercantile // *n*
mercenaire *m*.

merchandise ['mə:tʃəndaɪz] *n* marchandises *fpl*.

merchant ['mə:tʃənt] *n* négociant *m*,
marchand *m*; **~ bank** *n* (*Brit*) banque *f*
d'affaires; **~ navy**, (*US*) **~ marine** *n*
marine marchande.

merciful ['mə:sɪful] *a* miséricor-

dieux(euse), clément(e).

merciless ['mə:sɪlɪs] *a* impitoyable, sans
pitié.

mercury ['mə:kjurɪ] *n* mercure *m*.

mercy ['mə:sɪ] *n* pitié *f*, merci *f*; (*REL*)
miséricorde *f*; **at the ~ of** à la merci de.

mere [mɪə*] *a* simple; **~ly** *ad* sim-
plement, purement.

merge [mə:dʒ] *vt* unir // *vi* se fondre;
(*COMM*) fusionner; **~r** *n* (*COMM*) fusion
f.

meringue [mə'ræŋ] *n* meringue *f*.

merit ['mɛrɪt] *n* mérite *m*, valeur *f* // *vt*
mériter.

mermaid ['mə:meɪd] *n* sirène *f*.

merry ['mɛrɪ] *a* gai(e); **M~ Christmas!**
Joyeux Noël!; **~-go-round** *n* manège
m.

mesh [mɛʃ] *n* maille *f*; filet *m*.

mesmerize ['mɛzməraɪz] *vt* hypnotiser;
fasciner.

mess [mɛs] *n* désordre *m*, fouillis *m*,
pagaille *f*; (*MIL*) mess *m*, cantine *f*; **to
~ about** *or* **around** *vi* (*col*) perdre son
temps; **to ~ about** *or* **around with**
vt fus (*col*) chambarder, tripoter; **to ~
up** *vt* salir; chambarder; gâcher.

message ['mɛsɪdʒ] *n* message *m*.

messenger ['mɛsɪndʒə*] *n* messager *m*.

Messrs [mɛsrz] *abbr* (*on letters*) MM.

messy ['mɛsɪ] *a* sale; en désordre.

met [mɛt] *pt, pp of* **meet**.

metal ['mɛtl] *n* métal *m*; **~lic**
[-'tælɪk] *a* métallique.

mete [mi:t] : **to ~ out** *vt fus* infliger.

meteorology [mi:tɪə'rɔlədʒɪ] *n* météorologie *f*.

meter ['mi:tə*] *n* (*instrument*) compteur
m; (*US: unit*) = **metre**.

method ['mɛθəd] *n* méthode *f*; **~ical**
[mɪ'θɒdɪkl] *a* méthodique.

Methodist ['mɛθədɪst] *a, n* méthodiste
(*m/f*).

methylated spirit ['mɛθɪleɪtɪd-] *n*
(*Brit: also:* **meths**) alcool *m* à brûler.

metre, (US) meter ['mi:tə*] *n* mètre *m*.

metric ['mɛtrɪk] *a* métrique.

metropolitan [mɛtrə'pɒlɪtən] *a* mé-
tropolitain(e); **the M~ Police** *n* (*Brit*) la
police londonienne.

mettle ['mɛtl] *n* courage *m*.

mew [mju:] *vi* (*cat*) miauler.

mews [mju:z] *n*: **~ cottage** (*Brit*) maisonnette aménagée dans une ancienne
écurie ou remise.

Mexico ['mɛksɪkəu] *n* Mexique *m*.

miaow [mi:'au] *vi* miauler.

mice [maɪs] *npl of* **mouse**.

micro ['maɪkrəu] *n* (*also:* **~computer**)
micro-ordinateur *m*.

microchip ['maɪkrəutʃɪp] *n* puce *f*.

microphone ['maɪkrəfəun] *n* microphone *m*.

microscope ['maɪkrəskəup] *n* microscope *m*.

microwave ['maɪkrəʊweɪv] n (also: ~ oven) four m à micro-ondes.

mid [mɪd] a: ~ **May** la mi-mai; ~ **after-noon** le milieu de l'après-midi; **in** ~ **air** en plein ciel; ~**day** n midi m.

middle ['mɪdl] n milieu m; (waist) ceinture f, taille f // a du milieu; **in the** ~ **of the night** au milieu de la nuit; ~-**aged** a d'un certain âge; **the M**~ **Ages** npl le moyen âge; ~-**class** a ≈ bourgeois(e); **the** ~ **class(es)** n(pl) ≈ les classes moyennes; **M**~ **East** n Proche-Orient m, Moyen-Orient m; ~**man** n intermédiaire m; ~ **name** n deuxième nom m; ~**weight** n (BOXING) poids moyen.

middling ['mɪdlɪŋ] a moyen(ne).

midge [mɪdʒ] n moucheron m.

midget ['mɪdʒɪt] n nain/e.

Midlands ['mɪdləndz] npl comtés du centre de l'Angleterre.

midnight ['mɪdnaɪt] n minuit m.

midriff ['mɪdrɪf] n estomac m, taille f.

midst [mɪdst] n: **in the** ~ **of** au milieu de.

midsummer [mɪd'sʌmə*] n milieu m de l'été.

midway [mɪd'weɪ] a, ad: ~ **(between)** à mi-chemin (entre).

midweek [mɪd'wi:k] n milieu m de la semaine.

midwife, pl **midwives** ['mɪdwaɪf, -vz] n sage-femme f; ~**ry** [-wɪfərɪ] n obsté-trique f.

might [maɪt] vb see **may** // n puissance f, force f; ~**y** a puissant(e).

migraine ['mi:greɪn] n migraine f.

migrant ['maɪgrənt] a (bird) mi-grateur(trice); (person) migrant(e); nomade; (worker) saisonnier(ère).

migrate [maɪ'greɪt] vi émigrer.

mike [maɪk] n abbr (= microphone) mi-cro m.

mild [maɪld] a doux(douce); (reproach) léger(ère); (illness) bénin(igne).

mildew ['mɪldju:] n mildiou m.

mildly ['maɪldlɪ] ad doucement; légè-rement; **to put it** ~ c'est le moins qu'on puisse dire.

mile [maɪl] n mil(l)e m (= 1609 m); ~**age** n distance f en milles, ≈ kilomé-trage m; ~**stone** n borne f; (fig) jalon m.

militant ['mɪlɪtnt] a, n militant(e).

military ['mɪlɪtərɪ] a militaire.

milk [mɪlk] n lait m // vt (cow) traire; (fig) dépouiller, plumer; ~ **chocolate** n chocolat m au lait; ~**man** n laitier m; ~ **shake** n milk-shake m; ~**y** a lacté(e); (colour) laiteux(euse); **M**~**y Way** n Voie lactée.

mill [mɪl] n moulin m; (factory) usine f, fabrique f; (spinning ~) filature f; (flour ~) minoterie f // vt moudre, broyer // vi (also: ~ **about**) grouiller.

miller ['mɪlə*] n meunier m.

millet ['mɪlɪt] n millet m.

milli... ['mɪlɪ] prefix: ~**gram(me)** n milligramme m; ~**metre**, (US) ~**meter** n millimètre m.

millinery ['mɪlɪnərɪ] n modes fpl.

million ['mɪljən] n million m; ~**aire** n millionnaire m.

millstone ['mɪlstəʊn] n meule f.

milometer [maɪ'lɒmɪtə*] n ≈ compteur m kilométrique.

mime [maɪm] n mime m // vt, vi mimer.

mimic ['mɪmɪk] n imitateur/trice // vt imiter, contrefaire; ~**ry** n imitation f.

min. abbr of **minute(s)**, **minimum**.

mince [mɪns] vt hacher // vi (in walking) marcher à petits pas maniérés // n (Brit CULIN) viande hachée, hachis m; ~**meat** n hachis de fruits secs utilisés en pâtisserie; ~ **pie** n sorte de tarte aux fruits secs; ~**r** n hachoir m.

mind [maɪnd] n esprit m // vt (attend to, look after) s'occuper de; (be careful) faire attention à; (object to): **I don't** ~ **the noise** je ne crains pas le bruit, le bruit ne me dérange pas; **I don't** ~ cela ne me dérange pas; **it is on my** ~ cela me préoccupe; **to my** ~ à mon avis or sens; **to be out of one's** ~ ne plus avoir toute sa raison; **to bear sth in** ~ tenir compte de qch; **to make up one's** ~ se décider; ~ **you,** — remarquez —; je vous assure —; **never** ~ ne vous en faites pas; **'**~ **the step'** 'attention à la marche'; ~**er** n (child-~er) gardienne f; (bodyguard) ange gardien (fig); ~**ful** a: ~**ful of** attentif(ive) à, soucieux(euse) de; ~**less** a irréfléchi(e).

mine [maɪn] pronoun le(la) mien(ne), les miens(miennes) // a: **this book is** ~ ce li-vre est à moi // n mine f // vt (coal) ex-traire; (ship, beach) miner.

miner ['maɪnə*] n mineur m.

mineral ['mɪnərəl] a minéral(e) // n minéral m; ~**s** npl (Brit: soft drinks) boissons gazeuses (sucrées); ~ **water** n eau minérale.

minesweeper ['maɪnswi:pə*] n dragueur m de mines.

mingle ['mɪŋgl] vi: **to** ~ **with** se mêler à.

miniature ['mɪnətʃə*] a (en) miniature // n miniature f.

minibus ['mɪnɪbʌs] n minibus m.

minimum ['mɪnɪməm] n, a minimum (m).

mining ['maɪnɪŋ] n exploitation minière // a minier(ère); de mineurs.

miniskirt ['mɪnɪskə:t] n mini-jupe f.

minister ['mɪnɪstə*] n (Brit POL) minis-tre m; (REL) pasteur m // vi: **to** ~ **to sb** donner ses soins à qn; **to** ~ **to sb's needs** pourvoir aux besoins de qn; ~**ial** [-'tɪərɪəl] a (Brit POL) ministériel(le).

ministry ['mɪnɪstrɪ] n (Brit POL) ministère m; (REL): **to go into the** ~

devenir pasteur.

mink [mɪŋk] *n* vison *m*.

minnow ['mɪnəʊ] *n* vairon *m*.

minor ['maɪnə*] *a* petit(e), de peu d'importance; (*MUS*) mineur(e) // *n* (*LAW*) mineur/e.

minority [maɪ'nɔrɪtɪ] *n* minorité *f*.

mint [mɪnt] *n* (*plant*) menthe *f*; (*sweet*) bonbon *m* à la menthe // *vt* (*coins*) battre; **the (Royal) M~**, (*US*) **the (US) M~** ≈ l'hôtel *m* de la Monnaie; **in ~ condition** à l'état de neuf.

minus ['maɪnəs] *n* (*also:* **~ sign**) signe *m* moins // *prep* moins.

minute *a* [maɪ'nju:t] minuscule; (*detail*) minutieux(euse) // *n* ['mɪnɪt] minute *f*; (*official record*) procès-verbal *m*, compte rendu; **~s** *npl* procès-verbal.

miracle ['mɪrəkl] *n* miracle *m*.

mirage ['mɪrɑ:ʒ] *n* mirage *m*.

mire ['maɪə*] *n* bourbe *f*, boue *f*.

mirror ['mɪrə*] *n* miroir *m*, glace *f* // *vt* refléter.

mirth [mə:θ] *n* gaieté *f*.

misadventure [mɪsəd'ventʃə*] *n* mésaventure *f*; **death by ~** décès accidentel.

misapprehension ['mɪsæprɪ'henʃən] *n* malentendu *m*, méprise *f*.

misbehave [mɪsbɪ'heɪv] *vi* se conduire mal.

miscarriage ['mɪskærɪdʒ] *n* (*MED*) fausse couche; **~ of justice** erreur *f* judiciaire.

miscellaneous [mɪsɪ'leɪnɪəs] *a* (*items*) divers(es); (*selection*) varié(e).

mischief ['mɪstʃɪf] *n* (*naughtiness*) sottises *fpl*; (*harm*) mal *m*, dommage *m*; (*maliciousness*) méchanceté *f*; **mischievous** *a* (*naughty*) coquin(e), espiègle; (*harmful*) méchant(e).

misconception ['mɪskən'sepʃən] *n* idée fausse.

misconduct [mɪs'kɔndʌkt] *n* inconduite *f*; **professional ~** faute professionnelle.

misconstrue [mɪskən'stru:] *vt* mal interpréter.

misdeed [mɪs'di:d] *n* méfait *m*.

misdemeanour, (*US*) **misdemeanor** [mɪsdɪ'mi:nə*] *n* écart *m* de conduite; infraction *f*.

miser ['maɪzə*] *n* avare *m/f*.

miserable ['mɪzərəbl] *a* malheureux(euse); (*wretched*) misérable.

miserly ['maɪzəlɪ] *a* avare.

misery ['mɪzərɪ] *n* (*unhappiness*) tristesse *f*; (*pain*) souffrances *fpl*; (*wretchedness*) misère *f*.

misfire [mɪs'faɪə*] *vi* rater; (*car engine*) avoir des ratés.

misfit ['mɪsfɪt] *n* (*person*) inadapté/e.

misfortune [mɪs'fɔ:tʃən] *n* malchance *f*, malheur *m*.

misgiving(s) [mɪs'gɪvɪŋ(z)] *n(pl)* craintes *fpl*, soupçons *mpl*.

misguided [mɪs'gaɪdɪd] *a* malavisé(e).

mishandle [mɪs'hændl] *vt* (*treat roughly*) malmener; (*mismanage*) mal s'y prendre pour faire *or* résoudre *etc*.

mishap ['mɪshæp] *n* mésaventure *f*.

misinterpret [mɪsɪn'tə:prɪt] *vt* mal interpréter.

misjudge [mɪs'dʒʌdʒ] *vt* méjuger, se méprendre sur le compte de.

mislay [mɪs'leɪ] *vt irg* égarer.

mislead [mɪs'li:d] *vt irg* induire en erreur; **~ing** *a* trompeur(euse).

misnomer [mɪs'nəʊmə*] *n* terme *or* qualificatif trompeur *or* peu approprié.

misplace [mɪs'pleɪs] *vt* égarer.

misprint ['mɪsprɪnt] *n* faute *f* d'impression.

Miss [mɪs] *n* Mademoiselle.

miss [mɪs] *vt* (*fail to get*) manquer, rater; (*regret the absence of*): **I ~ him/it** il/cela me manque // *vi* manquer // *n* (*shot*) coup manqué; **to ~ out** *vt* (*Brit*) oublier.

misshapen [mɪs'ʃeɪpən] *a* difforme.

missile ['mɪsaɪl] *n* (*AVIAT*) missile *m*; (*object thrown*) projectile *m*.

missing ['mɪsɪŋ] *a* manquant(e); (*after escape, disaster: person*) disparu(e); **to go ~** disparaître.

mission ['mɪʃən] *n* mission *f*; **~ary** *n* missionnaire *m/f*.

misspent ['mɪs'spent] *a*: **his ~ youth** sa folle jeunesse.

mist [mɪst] *n* brume *f*, brouillard *m* // *vi* (*also:* **~ over**, **~ up**) devenir brumeux(euse); (*Brit: windows*) s'embuer.

mistake [mɪs'teɪk] *n* erreur *f*, faute *f* // *vt* (*irg: like take*) mal comprendre; se méprendre sur; **to make a ~** se tromper, faire une erreur; **by ~** par erreur, par inadvertance; **to ~ for** prendre pour; **~n** *a* (*idea etc*) erroné(e); **to be ~n** faire erreur, se tromper.

mister ['mɪstə*] *n* (*col*) Monsieur *m*; *see* **Mr**.

mistletoe ['mɪsltəʊ] *n* gui *m*.

mistook [mɪs'tuk] *pt of* **mistake**.

mistress ['mɪstrɪs] *n* maîtresse *f*; (*Brit: in primary school*) institutrice *f*; *see* **Mrs**.

mistrust [mɪs'trʌst] *vt* se méfier de.

misty ['mɪstɪ] *a* brumeux(euse).

misunderstand [mɪsʌndə'stænd] *vt, vi irg* mal comprendre; **~ing** *n* méprise *f*, malentendu *m*.

misuse *n* [mɪs'ju:s] mauvais emploi; (*of power*) abus *m* // *vt* [mɪs'ju:z] mal employer; abuser de.

mitigate ['mɪtɪgeɪt] *vt* atténuer.

mitt(en) ['mɪt(n)] *n* mitaine *f*; moufle *f*.

mix [mɪks] *vt* mélanger // *vi* se mélanger // *n* mélange *m*; dosage *m*; **to ~ up** *vt* mélanger; (*confuse*) confondre; **~ed** *a* (*assorted*) assortis(ies); (*school etc*) mixte; **~ed grill** *n* assortiment *m* de

grillades; **~ed-up** a (confused) déso-
rienté(e), embrouillé(e); **~er** n (for
food) batteur m, mixeur m; (person): he
is a good **~er** il est très liant; **~ture** n
assortiment m, mélange m; (MED)
préparation f; **~-up** n confusion f.

moan [məun] n gémissement m // vi
gémir; (col: complain): to **~** (about) se
plaindre (de).

moat [məut] n fossé m, douves fpl.

mob [mɔb] n foule f; (disorderly) cohue
f; (pej): the **~** la populace // vt assaillir.

mobile ['məubaɪl] a mobile // n mobile
m; **~ home** n caravane f.

mock [mɔk] vt ridiculiser, se moquer de
// a faux(fausse); **~ery** n moquerie f,
raillerie f.

mod [mɔd] a see **convenience**.

mode [məud] n mode m.

model ['mɔdl] n modèle m; (person: for
fashion) mannequin m; (: for artist)
modèle // vt modeler // vi travailler
comme mannequin // a (railway: toy)
modèle réduit inv; (child, factory)
modèle; to **~** clothes présenter des
vêtements.

modem ['məudɛm] n modem m.

moderate a, ['mɔdərət] a modéré(e) //
n (POL) modéré/e // vb ['mɔdəreɪt] vi se
modérer, se calmer // vt modérer.

modern ['mɔdən] a moderne; **~ize** n
moderniser.

modest ['mɔdɪst] a modeste; **~y** n
modestie f.

modicum ['mɔdɪkəm] n: a **~** of un
minimum de.

modify ['mɔdɪfaɪ] vt modifier.

mogul ['məugl] n (fig) nabab m.

mohair ['məuhɛə*] n mohair m.

moist [mɔɪst] a humide, moite; **~en**
['mɔɪsn] vt humecter, mouiller légèrement; **~ure** ['mɔɪstʃə*] n humidité f;
(on glass) buée f; **~urizer**
['mɔɪstʃəraɪzə*] n produit hydratant.

molar ['məulə*] n molaire f.

molasses [məu'læsɪz] n mélasse f.

mold [məuld] n, vt (US) = **mould**.

mole [məul] n (animal) taupe f; (spot)
grain m de beauté.

molest [məu'lɛst] vt tracasser;
molester.

mollycoddle ['mɔlɪkɔdl] vt chouchouter,
couver.

molt [məult] vi (US) = **moult**.

molten ['məultən] a fondu(e).

mom [mɔm] n (US) = **mum**.

moment ['məumənt] n moment m,
instant m; importance f; at the **~** à ce
moment; **~ary** a momentané(e),
passager(ère); **~ous** [-'mɛntəs] a
important(e), capital(e).

momentum [məu'mɛntəm] n élan m,
vitesse acquise; to gather **~** prendre de
la vitesse.

mommy ['mɔmɪ] n (US) = **mummy**.

Monaco ['mɔnəkəu] n Monaco m.

monarch ['mɔnək] n monarque m; **~y**
n monarchie f.

monastery ['mɔnəstərɪ] n monastère m.

Monday ['mʌndɪ] n lundi m.

monetary ['mʌnɪtərɪ] a monétaire.

money ['mʌnɪ] n argent m; to make **~**
gagner de l'argent; faire des bénéfices;
rapporter; **~lender** n prêteur/euse; **~
order** n mandat m; **~-spinner** n (col)
mine f d'or (fig).

mongrel ['mʌngrəl] n (dog) bâtard m.

monitor ['mɔnɪtə*] n (SCOL) chef m de
classe; (TV, COMPUT) moniteur m // vt
contrôler.

monk [mʌŋk] n moine m.

monkey ['mʌŋkɪ] n singe m; **~ nut** n
(Brit) cacahuète f; **~ wrench** n clé f à
molette.

mono... ['mɔnəu] prefix: **~chrome** a
monochrome.

monopoly [mə'nɔpəlɪ] n monopole m.

monotone ['mɔnətəun] n ton m (or voix
f) monocorde.

monotonous [mə'nɔtənəs] a monotone.

monsoon [mɔn'su:n] n mousson f.

monster ['mɔnstə*] n monstre m.

monstrous ['mɔnstrəs] a (huge) gigantesque; (atrocious) monstrueux(euse),
atroce.

month [mʌnθ] n mois m; **~ly** a
mensuel(le) // ad mensuellement // n
(magazine) mensuel m, publication
mensuelle.

monument ['mɔnjumənt] n monument
m.

moo [mu:] vi meugler, beugler.

mood [mu:d] n humeur f, disposition f;
to be in a good/bad **~** être de bonne/
mauvaise humeur; **~y** a (variable)
d'humeur changeante, lunatique;
(sullen) morose, maussade.

moon [mu:n] n lune f; **~light** n clair m
de lune; **~lighting** n travail m au noir;
~lit a éclairé(e) par la lune; (night) de
lune.

moor [muə*] n lande f // vt (ship)
amarrer // vi mouiller.

moorland ['muələnd] n lande f.

moose [mu:s] n (pl inv) élan m.

mop [mɔp] n balai m à laver // vt
éponger, essuyer; to **~ up** vt éponger;
~ of hair tignasse f.

mope [məup] vi avoir le cafard, se
morfondre.

moped ['məupɛd] n cyclomoteur m.

moral ['mɔrl] a moral(e) // n morale f;
~s npl moralité f.

morale [mɔ'rɑ:l] n moral m.

morality [mə'rælɪtɪ] n moralité f.

morass [mə'ræs] n marais m, marécage
m.

more [mɔ:*] ♦ a 1 (greater in number
etc) plus (de), davantage; **~** people/work
(than) plus de gens/de travail (que)

2 (additional) encore (de); **do you want (some) ~ tea?** voulez-vous encore du thé?; **I have no** or **I don't have any ~ money** je n'ai plus d'argent; **it'll take a few ~ weeks** ça prendra encore quelques semaines

♦ pronoun plus, davantage; **~ than 10** plus de 10; **it cost ~ than we expected** cela a coûté plus que prévu; **I want ~** j'en veux plus or davantage; **is there any ~?** est-ce qu'il en reste?; **there's no ~** il n'y en a plus; **a little ~** un peu plus; **many/much ~** beaucoup plus, bien davantage

♦ ad: **~ dangerous/easily (than)** plus dangereux/facilement (que); **~ and ~ expensive** de plus en plus cher; **~ or less** plus ou moins; **~ than ever** plus que jamais.

moreover [mɔː'rəuvə*] ad de plus.

morning ['mɔːnɪŋ] n matin m; matinée f; **in the ~** le matin; **7 o'clock in the ~** 7 heures du matin.

Morocco [mə'rɔkəu] n Maroc m.

moron ['mɔːrɔn] n idiot/e, minus m/f.

Morse [mɔːs] n (also: **~ code**) morse m.

morsel ['mɔːsl] n bouchée f.

mortal ['mɔːtl] a, n mortel(le); **~ity** [-'tælɪtɪ] n mortalité f.

mortar ['mɔːtə*] n mortier m.

mortgage ['mɔːgɪdʒ] n hypothèque f; (loan) prêt m (or crédit m) hypothécaire; **~ company** n (US) société f de crédit immobilier.

mortuary ['mɔːtjuərɪ] n morgue f.

mosaic [məu'zeɪɪk] n mosaïque f.

Moscow ['mɔskəu] n Moscou.

Moslem ['mɔzləm] a, n = **Muslim**.

mosque [mɔsk] n mosquée f.

mosquito, ~es [mɔs'kiːtəu] n moustique m.

moss [mɔs] n mousse f.

most [məust] a la plupart de; le plus de // pronoun la plupart // ad le plus; (very) très, extrêmement; **the ~** (also: + adjective) le plus; **~ of** la plus grande partie de; **~ of them** la plupart d'entre eux; **I saw (the) ~** j'en ai vu la plupart; c'est moi qui en ai vu le plus; **at the (very) ~** au plus; **to make the ~ of** profiter au maximum de; **~ly** ad surtout, principalement.

MOT n abbr (Brit: = Ministry of Transport): **the ~ (test)** la visite technique (annuelle) obligatoire des véhicules à moteur.

motel [məu'tɛl] n motel m.

moth [mɔθ] n papillon m de nuit; mite f; **~ball** n boule f de naphtaline.

mother ['mʌðə*] n mère f // vt (care for) dorloter; **~hood** n maternité f; **~-in-law** n belle-mère f; **~ly** a maternel(le); **~-of-pearl** n nacre f; **~-to-be** n future maman; **~ tongue** n langue maternelle.

motion ['məuʃən] n mouvement m; (gesture) geste m; (at meeting) motion f // vt, vi: **to ~ (to) sb to do** faire signe à qn de faire; (telephone, sans mouvement; **~ picture** n film m.

motivated ['məutɪveɪtɪd] a motivé(e).

motive ['məutɪv] n motif m, mobile m.

motley ['mɔtlɪ] a hétéroclite; bigarré(e), bariolé(e).

motor ['məutə*] n moteur m; (Brit col: vehicle) auto f // a moteur(trice); **~bike** n moto f; **~boat** n bateau m à moteur; **~car** n (Brit) automobile f; **~cycle** n vélomoteur m; **~cyclist** n motocycliste m/f; **~ing** n (Brit) tourisme m automobile; **~ist** n automobiliste m/f; **~ racing** n (Brit) course f automobile; **~way** n (Brit) autoroute f.

mottled ['mɔtld] a tacheté(e), marbré(e).

motto, ~es ['mɔtəu] n devise f.

mould, (US) **mold** [məuld] n moule m; (mildew) moisissure f // vt mouler, modeler; (fig) façonner; **~er** vi (decay) moisir; **~y** a moisi(e).

moult, (US) **molt** [məult] vi muer.

mound [maund] n monticule m, tertre m.

mount [maunt] n mont m, montagne f; (horse) monture f; (for jewel etc) monture // vt monter // vi (also: **~ up**) s'élever, monter.

mountain ['mauntɪn] n montagne f // cpd de (la) montagne; **~eer** [-'nɪə*] n alpiniste m/f; **~eering** [-'nɪərɪŋ] n alpinisme m; **~ous** a montagneux(euse); **~side** n flanc m or versant m de la montagne.

mourn [mɔːn] vt pleurer // vi: **to ~ (for)** se lamenter (sur); **~er** n parent/e or ami/e du défunt; personne f en deuil; **~ful** a triste, lugubre; **~ing** n deuil m // cpd (dress) de deuil; **in ~ing** en deuil.

mouse [maus], pl **mice** n (also COMPUT) souris f; **~trap** n souricière f.

mousse [muːs] n mousse f.

moustache [məs'tɑːʃ] n moustache(s) f(pl).

mousy ['mausɪ] a (person) effacé(e); (hair) d'un châtain terne.

mouth, ~s [mauθ, -ðz] n bouche f; (of dog, cat) gueule f; (of river) embouchure f; (of bottle) goulot m; (opening) orifice m; **~ful** n bouchée f; **~ organ** n harmonica m; **~piece** n (of musical instrument) embouchure f; (spokesman) porte-parole m inv; **~wash** n bain m de bouche; **~-watering** a qui met l'eau à la bouche.

movable ['muːvəbl] a mobile.

move [muːv] n (movement) mouvement m; (in game) coup m; (: turn to play) tour m; (change of house) déménagement m // vt déplacer, bouger; (emotion-

ally) émouvoir; *(POL: resolution etc)* proposer // *vi (gen)* bouger, remuer; *(traffic)* circuler; *(also:* ~ **house)** déménager; **to** ~ **towards** se diriger vers; **to** ~ **sb to do sth** pousser *or* inciter qn à faire qch; **to get a** ~ **on** se dépêcher, se remuer; **to** ~ **about** *or* **around** *vi (fidget)* remuer; *(travel)* voyager, se déplacer; **to** ~ **along** *vi* se pousser; **to** ~ **away** *vi* s'en aller, s'éloigner; **to** ~ **back** *vi* revenir, retourner; **to** ~ **forward** *vi* avancer // *vt* avancer; *(people)* faire avancer; **to** ~ **in** *vi (to a house)* emménager; **to** ~ **on** *vi* se remettre en route // *vt (onlookers)* faire circuler; **to** ~ **out** *vi (of house)* déménager; **to** ~ **over** *vi* se pousser, se déplacer; **to** ~ **up** *vi* avancer; *(employee)* avoir de l'avancement.

movement ['mu:vmənt] *n* mouvement *m*.

movie ['mu:vɪ] *n* film *m*; **the** ~**s** le cinéma; ~ **camera** *n* caméra *f*.

moving ['mu:vɪŋ] *a* en mouvement; émouvant(e).

mow, *pt* **mowed**, *pp* **mowed** *or* **mown** [meu, -n] *vt* faucher; *(lawn)* tondre; **to** ~ **down** *vt* faucher; ~**er** *n (also:* **lawnmower)** tondeuse *f* à gazon.

MP *n abbr of* **member of parliament**.

m.p.h. *abbr = miles per hour (60 m.p.h. = 96 km/h).*

Mr, Mr. ['mɪstə*] *n:* ~ **Smith** Monsieur Smith, M. Smith.

Mrs, Mrs. ['mɪsɪz] *n:* ~ **Smith** Madame Smith, Mme Smith.

Ms, Ms. [mɪz] *n (= Miss or Mrs):* ~ **Smith** ≈ Madame Smith, Mme Smith.

M.Sc. *abbr see* **master**.

much [mʌtʃ] *a* beaucoup de // *ad, n or pronoun* beaucoup; **how** ~ **is it?** combien est-ce que ça coûte?; **too** ~ trop (de); **as** ~ as autant de.

muck [mʌk] *n (mud)* boue *f*; *(dirt)* ordures *fpl*; **to** ~ **about** *or* **around** *vi (col)* faire l'imbécile; *(waste time)* traînasser; **to** ~ **up** *vt (col: ruin)* gâcher, esquinter.

mud [mʌd] *n* boue *f*.

muddle ['mʌdl] *n* pagaille *f*; désordre *m*, fouillis *m* // *vt (also:* ~ **up)** brouiller, embrouiller; **to be in a** ~ *(person)* ne plus savoir où l'on en est; **to** ~ **through** *vi* se débrouiller.

muddy ['mʌdɪ] *a* boueux(euse).

mud: ~**guard** *n* garde-boue *m inv*; ~**slinging** *n* médisance *f*, dénigrement *m*.

muff [mʌf] *n* manchon *m* // *vt (chance)* rater, louper.

muffin ['mʌfɪn] *n* petit pain rond et plat.

muffle ['mʌfl] *vt (sound)* assourdir, étouffer; *(against cold)* emmitoufler.

muffler ['mʌflə*] *n (US AUT)* silencieux *m*.

mug [mʌg] *n (cup)* grande tasse *(sans*

soucoupe), chope *f*; *(: for beer)* chope; *(col: face)* bouille *f*; *(: fool)* poire *f* // *vt (assault)* agresser; ~**ging** *n* agression *f*.

muggy ['mʌgɪ] *a* lourd(e), moite.

mule [mju:l] *n* mule *f*.

mull [mʌl]: **to** ~ **over** *vt* réfléchir à.

mulled [mʌld] *a:* ~ **wine** vin chaud.

multi-level ['mʌltɪlevl] *a (US)* = **multistorey**.

multiple ['mʌltɪpl] *a, n* multiple *(m)*; ~ **sclerosis** *n* sclérose *f* en plaques.

multiplication [mʌltɪplɪ'keɪʃən] *n* multiplication *f*.

multiply ['mʌltɪplaɪ] *vt* multiplier // *vi* se multiplier.

multistorey ['mʌltɪ'stɔ:rɪ] *a (Brit: building)* à étages; *(: car park)* à étages *or* niveaux multiples.

mum [mʌm] *n (Brit)* maman *f* // *a:* **to keep** ~ ne pas souffler mot.

mumble ['mʌmbl] *vt, vi* marmotter, marmonner.

mummy ['mʌmɪ] *n (Brit: mother)* maman *f*; *(embalmed)* momie *f*.

mumps [mʌmps] *n* oreillons *mpl*.

munch [mʌntʃ] *vt, vi* mâcher.

mundane [mʌn'deɪn] *a* banal(e), terre à terre *inv*.

municipal [mju:'nɪsɪpl] *a* municipal(e).

mural ['mjuərl] *n* peinture murale.

murder ['mə:də*] *n* meurtre *m*, assassinat *m* // *vt* assassiner; ~**er** *n* meurtrier *m*, assassin *m*; ~**ous** *a* meurtrier(ère).

murky ['mə:kɪ] *a* sombre, ténébreux(euse).

murmur ['mə:mə*] *n* murmure *m* // *vt, vi* murmurer.

muscle ['mʌsl] *n* muscle *m*; **to** ~ **in** *vi* s'imposer, s'immiscer.

muscular ['mʌskjulə*] *a* musculaire; *(person, arm)* musclé(e).

muse [mju:z] *vi* méditer, songer.

museum [mju:'zɪəm] *n* musée *m*.

mushroom ['mʌʃrum] *n* champignon *m*.

music ['mju:zɪk] *n* musique *f*; ~**al** *a* musical(e); *(person)* musicien(ne) // *n (show)* comédie musicale; ~**al instrument** *n* instrument *m* de musique; ~**ian** [-'zɪʃən] *n* musicien/ne.

Muslim ['mʌzlɪm] *a, n* musulman(e).

muslin ['mʌzlɪn] *n* mousseline *f*.

mussel ['mʌsl] *n* moule *f*.

must [mʌst] *auxiliary vb (obligation):* **I** ~ **do it** je dois le faire, il faut que je le fasse; *(probability):* **he** ~ **be there by now** il doit y être maintenant, il y est probablement maintenant; **I** ~ **have made a mistake** j'ai dû me tromper // *n* nécessité *f*, impératif *m*; **it's a** ~ c'est indispensable.

mustard ['mʌstəd] *n* moutarde *f*.

muster ['mʌstə*] *vt* rassembler.

mustn't ['mʌsnt] = **must not**.

musty ['mʌstɪ] *a* qui sent le moisi *or* le

renfermé.

mute [mju:t] *a*, *n* muet(te).

muted ['mju:tɪd] *a* assourdi(e); voilé(e).

mutiny ['mju:tɪnɪ] *n* mutinerie *f*.

mutter ['mʌtə*] *vt*, *vi* marmonner, marmotter.

mutton ['mʌtn] *n* mouton *m*.

mutual ['mju:tʃuəl] *a* mutuel(le), réciproque.

muzzle ['mʌzl] *n* museau *m*; (*protective device*) muselière *f*; (*of gun*) gueule *f*.

my [maɪ] *a* mon(ma), mes *pl*; ~ **house/car/gloves** ma maison/mon auto/mes gants; I've washed ~ **hair/cut** ~ **finger** je me suis lavé les cheveux/coupé le doigt.

myself [maɪ'self] *pronoun* (*reflexive*) me; (*emphatic*) moi-même; (*after prep*) moi; *see also* **oneself**.

mysterious [mɪs'tɪərɪəs] *a* mystérieux(euse).

mystery ['mɪstərɪ] *n* mystère *m*.

mystify ['mɪstɪfaɪ] *vt* mystifier; (*puzzle*) ébahir.

myth [mɪθ] *n* mythe *m*; ~**ology** [mɪ'θɒlədʒɪ] *n* mythologie *f*.

N

n/a *abbr* = *not applicable*.

nab [næb] *vt* pincer, attraper.

nag [næg] *vt* (*person*) être toujours après, reprendre sans arrêt; ~**ging** *a* (*doubt, pain*) persistant(e).

nail [neɪl] *n* (*human*) ongle *m*; (*metal*) clou *m* // *vt* clouer; **to** ~ **sb down to a date/price** contraindre qn à accepter or donner une date/un prix; ~**brush** *n* brosse *f* à ongles; ~**file** *n* lime *f* à ongles; ~ **polish** *n* vernis *m* à ongles; ~ **polish remover** *n* dissolvant *m*; ~ **scissors** *npl* ciseaux *mpl* à ongles; ~ **varnish** *n* (*Brit*) = ~ **polish**.

naïve [naɪ'iːv] *a* naïf(ïve).

naked ['neɪkɪd] *a* nu(e).

name [neɪm] *n* nom *m*; réputation *f* // *vt* nommer; citer; (*price, date*) fixer, donner; **by** ~ par son nom; ~**less** *a* sans nom; (*witness, contributor*) anonyme; ~**ly** *ad* à savoir; ~**sake** *n* homonyme *m*.

nanny ['nænɪ] *n* bonne *f* d'enfants.

nap [næp] *n* (*sleep*) (petit) somme; **to be caught** ~**ping** être pris à l'improviste or en défaut.

nape [neɪp] *n*: ~ **of the neck** nuque *f*.

napkin ['næpkɪn] *n* serviette *f* (de table).

nappy ['næpɪ] *n* (*Brit*) couche *f* (*gen pl*); ~ **rash** *n*: **to have** ~ **rash** avoir les fesses rouges.

narcissus, *pl* **narcisci** [nɑː'sɪsəs, -saɪ] *n* narcisse *m*.

narcotic [nɑː'kɒtɪk] *n* (*drug*) stupéfiant *m*; (*MED*) narcotique *m* // *a* narcotique.

narrative ['nærətɪv] *n* récit *m* // *a* narratif(ive).

narrow ['nærəu] *a* étroit(e); (*fig*) restreint(e), limité(e) // *vi* devenir plus étroit, se rétrécir; **to have a** ~ **escape** l'échapper belle; **to** ~ **sth down to** réduire qch à; ~**ly** *ad*: he ~**ly** missed injury/the tree il a failli se blesser/rentrer dans l'arbre; ~**-minded** *a* à l'esprit étroit, borné(e).

nasty ['nɑːstɪ] *a* (*person*) méchant(e); très désagréable; (*smell*) dégoûtant(e); (*wound, situation*) mauvais(e).

nation ['neɪʃən] *n* nation *f*.

national ['næʃənl] *a* national(e) // *n* (*abroad*) ressortissant/e; (*when home*) national/e; ~ **dress** *n* costume national; **N~ Health Service (NHS)** *n* (*Brit*) service national de santé, ≈ Sécurité Sociale; **N~ Insurance** *n* (*Brit*) ≈ Sécurité Sociale; ~**ism** *n* nationalisme *m*; ~**ity** [-'nælɪtɪ] *n* nationalité *f*; ~**ize** *vt* nationaliser; ~**ly** *ad* du point de vue national; dans le pays entier.

nation-wide ['neɪʃənwaɪd] *a* s'étendant à l'ensemble du pays; (*problem*) à l'échelle du pays entier // *ad* à travers or dans tout le pays.

native ['neɪtɪv] *n* habitant/e du pays, autochtone *m/f*; (*in colonies*) indigène *m/f* // *a* du pays, indigène; (*country*) natal(e); (*ability*) inné(e); **a** ~ **of Russia** une personne originaire de Russie; **a** ~ **speaker of French** une personne de langue maternelle française; ~ **language** *n* langue maternelle.

NATO ['neɪtəu] *n abbr* (= *North Atlantic Treaty Organization*) O.T.A.N. *f*.

natural ['nætʃrəl] *a* naturel(le); ~ **gas** *n* gaz naturel; ~**ize** *vt* naturaliser; (*plant*) acclimater; **to become** ~**ized** (*person*) se faire naturaliser; ~**ly** *ad* naturellement.

nature ['neɪtʃə*] *n* nature *f*; **by** ~ par tempérament, de nature.

naught [nɔːt] *n* = **nought**.

naughty ['nɔːtɪ] *a* (*child*) vilain(e), pas sage; (*story, film*) polisson(ne).

nausea ['nɔːsɪə] *n* nausée *f*; **nauseate** ['nɔːsɪeɪt] *vt* écœurer, donner la nausée à.

naval ['neɪvl] *a* naval(e); ~ **officer** *n* officier *m* de marine.

nave [neɪv] *n* nef *f*.

navel ['neɪvl] *n* nombril *m*.

navigate ['nævɪgeɪt] *vt* diriger, piloter // *vi* naviguer; **navigation** [-'geɪʃən] *n* navigation *f*; **navigator** *n* navigateur *m*.

navvy ['nævɪ] *n* (*Brit*) terrassier *m*.

navy ['neɪvɪ] *n* marine *f*; ~**(-blue)** *a* bleu marine *inv*.

Nazi ['nɑːtsɪ] *n* Nazi/e.

NB *abbr* (= *nota bene*) NB.

near [nɪə*] *a* proche // *ad* près // *prep* (*also*: ~ **to**) près de // *vt* approcher de;

~by [niə'bai] *a* proche // *ad* tout près, à proximité; **~ly** *ad* presque; **I ~ly** fell j'ai failli tomber; **~ miss** *n* collision évitée de justesse; *(when aiming)* coup manqué de peu *or* de justesse; **~side** *n* *(AUT: right-hand drive)* côté *m* gauche; **~-sighted** *a* myope.

neat [ni:t] *a* *(person, work)* soigné(e); *(room etc)* bien tenu(e) *or* rangé(e); *(solution, plan)* habile; *(spirits)* pur(e); **~ly** *ad* avec soin *or* ordre; habilement.

necessarily ['nesisrili] *ad* nécessairement.

necessary ['nesisri] *a* nécessaire.

necessity [ni'sesiti] *n* nécessité *f*; chose nécessaire *or* essentielle.

neck [nek] *n* cou *m*; *(of horse, garment)* encolure *f*; *(of bottle)* goulot *m* // *vi* *(col)* se peloter; **~ and** ~ à égalité.

necklace ['neklis] *n* collier *m*.

neckline ['neklain] *n* encolure *f*.

necktie ['nektai] *n* cravate *f*.

need [ni:d] *n* besoin *m* // *vt* avoir besoin de; **to** ~ **to do** devoir faire; avoir besoin de faire; **you don't** ~ **to go** vous n'avez pas besoin *or* vous n'êtes pas obligé de partir.

needle ['ni:dl] *n* aiguille *f* // *vt* asticoter, tourmenter.

needless ['ni:dlis] *a* inutile.

needlework ['ni:dlwə:k] *n* *(activity)* travaux *mpl* d'aiguille; *(object)* ouvrage *m*.

needn't [ni:dnt] = **need not**.

needy ['ni:di] *a* nécessiteux(euse).

negative ['negətiv] *n* *(PHOT, ELEC)* négatif *m*; *(LING)* terme *m* de négation // *a* négatif(ive).

neglect [ni'glekt] *vt* négliger // *n* *(of person, duty, garden)* le fait de négliger; *(state of ~)* abandon *m*.

negligee ['neglizei] *n* déshabillé *m*.

negligence ['neglidʒəns] *n* négligence *f*.

negotiate [ni'gəuʃieit] *vi, vt* négocier; **negotiation** [-'eiʃən] *n* négociation *f*, pourparlers *mpl*.

Negro ['ni:grəu] *a* *(gen)* noir(e); *(music, arts)* nègre, noir // *n* *(pl:* ~**es)** Noir/e.

neigh [nei] *vi* hennir.

neighbour, (US) neighbor ['neibə*] *n* voisin/e; **~hood** *n* quartier *m*; voisinage *m*; **~ing** *a* voisin(e), avoisinant(e); **~ly** *a* obligeant(e); *(relations)* de bon voisinage.

neither ['naiðə*] *a, pronoun* aucun(e) *(des deux)*, ni l'un(e) ni l'autre // *cj*: **I didn't move and** ~ **did Claude** je n'ai pas bougé, *(et)* Claude non plus; ..., ~ **did I refuse** ..., *(et or* mais) je n'ai pas non plus refusé // *ad*: ~ **good nor bad** ni bon ni mauvais.

neon ['ni:ɔn] *n* néon *m*; ~ **light** *n* lampe *f* au néon.

nephew ['nevju:] *n* neveu *m*.

nerve [nə:v] *n* nerf *m*; *(fig)* sang-froid *m*, courage *m*; aplomb *m*, toupet *m*; **to have a fit of** ~**s** avoir le trac; **~-racking** *a* angoissant(e).

nervous ['nə:vəs] *a* nerveux(euse); inquiet(ète), plein(e) d'appréhension; ~ **breakdown** *n* dépression nerveuse.

nest [nest] *n* nid *m* // *vi* (se) nicher, faire son nid; ~ **egg** *n* *(fig)* bas *m* de laine, magot *m*.

nestle ['nesl] *vi* se blottir.

net [net] *n* filet *m* // *a* net(te) // *vt* *(fish etc)* prendre au filet; *(profit)* rapporter; **~ball** *n* netball *m*; ~ **curtains** *npl* voilages *mpl*.

Netherlands ['neðələndz] *npl*: **the** ~ les Pays-Bas *mpl*.

nett [net] *a* = **net**.

netting ['netiŋ] *n* *(for fence etc)* treillis *m*, grillage *m*.

nettle ['netl] *n* ortie *f*.

network ['netwə:k] *n* réseau *m*.

neurotic [njuə'rɔtik] *a, n* névrosé(e).

neuter ['nju:tə*] *a, n* neutre *(m)* // *vt* *(cat etc)* châtrer, couper.

neutral ['nju:trəl] *a* neutre // *n* *(AUT)* point mort; **~ize** *vt* neutraliser.

never ['nevə*] *ad* (ne ...) jamais; ~ **again** plus jamais; ~ **in my life** jamais de ma vie; *see also* **mind**; **~-ending** *a* interminable; **~theless** [nevəðə'les] *ad* néanmoins, malgré tout.

new [nju:] *a* nouveau(nouvelle); *(brand new)* neuf(neuve); **~born** *a* nouveau-né(e); **~comer** ['nju:kʌmə*] *n* nouveau venu/nouvelle venue; **~-fangled** ['nju:fæŋgld] *a* *(pej)* ultramoderne (et farfelu(e)); **~-found** *a* de fraîche date; *(friend)* nouveau(nouvelle); **~ly** *ad* nouvellement, récemment; **~ly-weds** *npl* jeunes mariés *mpl*.

news [nju:z] *n* nouvelle(s) *f(pl)*; *(RADIO, TV)* informations *fpl*, actualités *fpl*; **a piece of** ~ une nouvelle; ~ **agency** *n* agence *f* de presse; **~agent** *n* *(Brit)* marchand *m* de journaux; **~caster** *n* présentateur/trice; **~dealer** *n* *(US)* = **~agent**; ~ **flash** *n* flash *m* d'information; **~letter** *n* bulletin *m*; **~paper** *n* journal *m*; **~print** *n* papier *m* (de) journal; **~reader** *n* = **~caster**; **~reel** *n* actualités (filmées); ~ **stand** *n* kiosque *m* à journaux.

newt [nju:t] *n* triton *m*.

New Year ['nju:'jiə*] *n* Nouvel An; ~**'s Day** *n* le jour de l'An; ~**'s Eve** *n* la Saint-Sylvestre.

New Zealand [nju:'zi:lənd] *n* la Nouvelle-Zélande; **~er** *n* Néo-zélandais/e.

next [nekst] *a* *(seat, room)* voisin(e), d'à côté; *(meeting, bus stop)* suivant(e); prochain(e) // *ad* la fois suivante; la prochaine fois; *(afterwards)* ensuite; **the** ~ **day** le lendemain, le jour suivant *or* d'après; ~ **year** l'année prochaine; **when do we meet** ~? quand nous revoyons-nous?; ~ **door** *ad* à côté; ~-**of-kin** *n* parent *m* le plus proche; ~ **to** *prep* à côté de; ~ **to nothing** presque rien.

NHS *n abbr of* **National Health Service**.

nib [nɪb] *n (of pen)* (bec *m* de) plume *f*.

nibble ['nɪbl] *vt* grignoter.

nice [naɪs] *a (holiday, trip)* agréable; *(flat, picture)* joli(e); *(person)* gentil(le); *(distinction, point)* subtil(e); ~-**looking** *a* joli(e); ~**ly** *ad* agréablement; joliment; gentiment; subtilement.

niceties ['naɪsɪtɪz] *npl* subtilités *fpl*.

nick [nɪk] *n* encoche *f* // *vt (col)* faucher, piquer; **in the** ~ **of time** juste à temps.

nickel ['nɪkl] *n* nickel *m*; *(US)* pièce *f* de 5 cents.

nickname ['nɪkneɪm] *n* surnom *m* // *vt* surnommer.

niece [niːs] *n* nièce *f*.

Nigeria [naɪ'dʒɪərɪə] *n* Nigéria *m or f*.

nigger ['nɪgə*] *n (col!: highly offensive)* nègre *m*, négresse *f*.

niggling ['nɪglɪŋ] *a* tatillon(ne).

night [naɪt] *n* nuit *f*; *(evening)* soir *m*; **at** ~ **la nuit; by** ~ de nuit; **the** ~ **before last** avant-hier soir; ~**cap** *n* boisson prise avant le coucher; ~ **club** *n* boîte *f* de nuit; ~**dress** *n* chemise *f* de nuit; ~**fall** *n* tombée *f* de la nuit; ~**gown** *n*, ~**ie** ['naɪtɪ] *n* chemise *f* de nuit.

nightingale ['naɪtɪŋgeɪl] *n* rossignol *m*.

night life *n* vie *f* nocturne.

nightly ['naɪtlɪ] *a* de chaque nuit *or* soir; *(by night)* nocturne // *ad* chaque nuit *or* soir; nuitamment.

nightmare ['naɪtmɛə*] *n* cauchemar *m*.

night: ~ **porter** *n* gardien *m* de nuit, concierge *m* de service la nuit; ~ **school** *n* cours *mpl* du soir; ~ **shift** *n* équipe *f* de nuit; ~**time** *n* nuit *f*.

nil [nɪl] *n* rien *m*; *(Brit SPORT)* zéro *m*.

Nile [naɪl] *n*: **the** ~ le Nil.

nimble ['nɪmbl] *a* agile.

nine [naɪn] *num* neuf; ~**teen** *num* dix-neuf; ~**ty** *num* quatre-vingt-dix.

ninth [naɪnθ] *num* neuvième.

nip [nɪp] *vt* pincer.

nipple ['nɪpl] *n (ANAT)* mamelon *m*, bout *m* du sein.

nitrogen ['naɪtrədʒən] *n* azote *m*.

no [nəu] ♦ *ad (opposite of 'yes')* non; **are you coming?** - ~ **(I'm not)** est-ce que vous venez? - non; **would you like some more?** - ~ **thank you** vous en voulez encore? - non merci ♦ *a (not any)* pas de, aucun(e) *(used with 'ne')*; **I have** ~ **money/books** je n'ai pas d'argent/de livres; ~ **student would have done it** aucun étudiant ne l'aurait fait; '~ **smoking**' 'défense de fumer'; '~ **dogs**' 'les chiens ne sont pas admis'

♦ *n (pl* ~**es)** non *m*.

nobility [nəu'bɪlɪtɪ] *n* noblesse *f*.

noble ['nəubl] *a* noble.

nobody ['nəubədɪ] *pronoun* personne *(with negative)*.

nod [nɔd] *vi* faire un signe de (la) tête *(affirmatif ou amical)*; *(sleep)* somnoler // *vt*: **to** ~ **one's head** faire un signe de (la) tête; *(in agreement)* faire signe que oui // *n* signe de (la) tête; **to** ~ **off** *vi* s'assoupir.

noise [nɔɪz] *n* bruit *m*; **noisy** *a* bruyant(e).

nominal ['nɔmɪnl] *a (rent, fee)* symbolique; *(value)* nominal(e).

nominate ['nɔmɪneɪt] *vt (propose)* proposer; *(elect)* nommer.

nominee [nɔmɪ'niː] *n* candidat agréé; personne nommée.

non... [nɔn] *prefix* non-; ~-**alcoholic** *a* non-alcoolisé(e); ~-**committal** ['nɔnkə'mɪtl] *a* évasif(ive).

nondescript ['nɔndɪskrɪpt] *a* quelconque, indéfinissable.

none [nʌn] *pronoun* aucun/e; ~ **of you** aucun d'entre vous, personne parmi vous; **I've** ~ **left** je n'en ai plus; **he's the worse for it** il ne s'en porte pas plus mal.

nonentity [nɔ'nentɪtɪ] *n* personne insignifiante.

nonetheless [nʌnðə'lɛs] *ad* néanmoins.

non: ~-**existent** *a* inexistant(e); ~-**fiction** *n* littérature *f* non-romanesque.

nonplussed [nɔn'plʌst] *a* perplexe.

nonsense ['nɔnsəns] *n* absurdités *fpl*, idioties *fpl*; ~! ne dites pas d'idioties!

non: ~-**smoker** *n* non-fumeur *m*; ~-**stick** *a* qui n'attache pas; ~-**stop** *a* direct(e), sans arrêt *(or* escale) // *ad* sans arrêt.

noodles ['nuːdlz] *npl* nouilles *fpl*.

nook [nuk] *n*: ~**s and crannies** recoins *mpl*.

noon [nuːn] *n* midi *m*.

no one ['nəuwʌn] *pronoun* = **nobody**.

noose [nuːs] *n* nœud coulant; *(hangman's)* corde *f*.

nor [nɔː*] *cj* = **neither** // *ad see* **neither**.

norm [nɔːm] *n* norme *f*.

normal ['nɔːml] *a* normal(e); ~**ly** *ad* normalement.

Normandy ['nɔːməndɪ] *n* Normandie *f*.

north [nɔːθ] *n* nord *m* // *a* du nord, nord *inv* // *ad* au *or* vers le nord; **N~ America** *n* Amérique *f* du Nord; ~-**east** *n* nord-est *m*; ~**erly** [nɔː'ðəlɪ] *a* du nord; ~**ern** ['nɔːðən] *a* du nord, septentrional(e); **N~ern Ireland** *n* Irlande *f* du Nord; **N~ Pole** *n* pôle *m* Nord; **N~ Sea** *n* mer *f* du Nord; ~**ward(s)** ['nɔːθwəd(z)] *ad* vers le nord; ~-**west** *n* nord-ouest *m*.

Norway ['nɔːweɪ] *n* Norvège *f*.

Norwegian [nɔː'wiːdʒən] *a* norvégien(ne) // *n* Norvégien/ne; (*LING*) norvégien *m*.

nose [nəuz] *n* nez *m*; (*fig*) flair *m* // *vi*: to ~ about fouiner *or* fureter (partout); **~-dive** *n* (descente *f* en) piqué *m*; **~y** *a* = **nosy**.

nostalgia [nɔs'tældʒɪə] *n* nostalgie *f*.

nostril ['nɔstrɪl] *n* narine *f*; (*of horse*) naseau *m*.

nosy ['nəuzɪ] *a* curieux(euse).

not [nɔt] *ad* (ne ...) pas; he is ~ *or* isn't here il n'est pas ici; you must ~ *or* you mustn't do that tu ne dois pas faire ça; it's too late, isn't it *or* is it ~? c'est trop tard, n'est-ce pas?; ~ yet/now pas encore/maintenant; ~ at all pas du tout; *see also* all, only.

notably ['nəutəblɪ] *ad* en particulier; (*markedly*) spécialement.

notary ['nəutərɪ] *n* (*also*: ~ public) notaire *m*.

notch [nɔtʃ] *n* encoche *f*.

note [nəut] *n* note *f*; (*letter*) mot *m*; (*banknote*) billet *m* // *vt* (*also*: ~ down) noter; (*notice*) constater; **~book** *n* carnet *m*; **~d** ['nəutɪd] *a* réputé(e); **~pad** *n* bloc-notes *m*; **~paper** *n* papier *m* à lettres.

nothing ['nʌθɪŋ] *n* rien *m*; he does ~ il ne fait rien; ~ new rien de nouveau; for ~ (*free*) pour rien, gratuitement.

notice ['nəutɪs] *n* avis *m*; (*of leaving*) congé *m* // *vt* remarquer, s'apercevoir de; to take ~ of prêter attention à; to bring sth to sb's ~ porter qch à la connaissance de qn; at short ~ dans un délai très court; until further ~ jusqu'à nouvel ordre; to hand in one's ~ donner sa démission, démissionner; **~able** *a* visible; ~ **board** *n* (*Brit*) panneau *m* d'affichage.

notify ['nəutɪfaɪ] *vt*: to ~ sth to sb notifier qch à qn; to ~ sb of sth avertir qn de qch.

notion ['nəuʃən] *n* idée *f*; (*concept*) notion *f*.

notorious [nəu'tɔ:rɪəs] *a* notoire (*souvent en mal*).

notwithstanding [nɔtwɪθ'stændɪŋ] *ad* néanmoins // *prep* en dépit de.

nought [nɔ:t] *n* zéro *m*.

noun [naun] *n* nom *m*.

nourish ['nʌrɪʃ] *vt* nourrir; **~ing** *a* nourrissant(e); **~ment** *n* nourriture *f*.

novel ['nɔvl] *n* roman *m* // *a* nouveau(nouvelle), original(e); **~ist** *n* romancier *m*; **~ty** *n* nouveauté *f*.

November [nəu'vembə*] *n* novembre *m*.

now [nau] *ad* maintenant // *cj*: ~ (that) maintenant que; right ~ tout de suite; by ~ à l'heure qu'il est; just ~: I saw her just ~ je viens de la voir, je l'ai vue à l'instant; I'll read it just ~ je vais le lire à l'instant *or* dès maintenant; ~ and then, ~ and again de temps en temps; from ~ on dorénavant; **~adays** ['nauədeɪz] *ad* de nos jours.

nowhere ['nəuwɛə*] *ad* nulle part.

nozzle ['nɔzl] *n* (*of hose*) jet *m*, lance *f*.

nuclear ['nju:klɪə*] *a* nucléaire.

nucleus, *pl* nuclei ['nju:klɪəs, 'nju:klɪaɪ] *n* noyau *m*.

nude [nju:d] *a* nu(e) // *n* (*ART*) nu *m*; in the ~ (tout(e)) nu(e).

nudge [nʌdʒ] *vt* donner un (petit) coup de coude à.

nudist ['nju:dɪst] *n* nudiste *m/f*.

nuisance ['nju:sns] *n*: it's a ~ c'est (très) ennuyeux *or* gênant; he's a ~ il est assommant *or* casse-pieds; what a ~! quelle barbe!

null [nʌl] *a*: ~ **and void** nul(le) et non avenu(e).

numb [nʌm] *a* engourdi(e).

number ['nʌmbə*] *n* nombre *m*; (*numeral*) chiffre *m*; (*of house, car, telephone, newspaper*) numéro *m* // *vt* numéroter; (*include*) compter; **a** ~ **of** un certain nombre de; **to be ~ed among** compter parmi; **they were seven in** ~ ils étaient (au nombre de) sept; ~ **plate** *n* (*Brit AUT*) plaque *f* minéralogique *or* d'immatriculation.

numeral ['nju:mərəl] *n* chiffre *m*.

numerate ['nju:mərɪt] *a*: to be ~ avoir des notions d'arithmétique.

numerical [nju:'merɪkl] *a* numérique.

numerous ['nju:mərəs] *a* nombreux(euse).

nun [nʌn] *n* religieuse *f*, sœur *f*.

nurse [nə:s] *n* infirmière *f* // *vt* (*patient, cold*) soigner; (*baby: Brit*) bercer (dans ses bras); (: *US*) allaiter, nourrir.

nursery ['nə:sərɪ] *n* (*room*) nursery *f*; (*institution*) pouponnière *f*; (*for plants*) pépinière *f*; ~ **rhyme** *n* comptine *f*, chansonnette *f* pour enfants; ~ **school** *n* école maternelle; ~ **slope** *n* (*Brit SKI*) piste *f* pour débutants.

nursing ['nə:sɪŋ] *n* (*profession*) profession *f* d'infirmière; ~ **home** *n* clinique *f*; maison *f* de convalescence.

nurture ['nə:tʃə*] *vt* élever.

nut [nʌt] *n* (*of metal*) écrou *m*; (*fruit*) noix *f*, noisette *f*, cacahuète *f* (*terme générique en anglais*); he's ~s (*col*) il est dingue; **~crackers** *npl* casse-noix *m inv*, casse-noisette(s) *m*.

nutmeg ['nʌtmeg] *n* (noix *f*) muscade *f*.

nutritious [nju:'trɪʃəs] *a* nutritif(ive), nourrissant(e).

nutshell ['nʌtʃel] *n* coquille *f* de noix; in a ~ en un mot.

nylon ['naɪlɔn] *n* nylon *m* // *a* de *or* en nylon.

O

oak [əuk] *n* chêne *m* // *a* de *or* en (bois de) chêne.

O.A.P. *abbr of* **old-age pensioner**.

oar [ɔ:*] *n* aviron *m*, rame *f*.

oasis, *pl* **oases** [əu'eɪsɪs] *n* oasis *f*.

oath [əuθ] *n* serment *m*; (*swear word*) juron *m*.

oatmeal ['əutmi:l] *n* flocons *mpl* d'avoine.

oats [əuts] *n* avoine *f*.

obedience [ə'bi:dɪəns] *n* obéissance *f*.

obedient [ə'bi:dɪənt] *a* obéissant(e).

obey [ə'beɪ] *vt* obéir à; (*instructions*) se conformer à // *vi* obéir.

obituary [ə'bɪtjuərɪ] *n* nécrologie *f*.

object *n* ['ɔbdʒɪkt] objet *m*; (*purpose*) but *m*, objet; (*LING*) complément *m* d'objet // *vi* [əb'dʒɛkt]: **to ~ to** (*attitude*) désapprouver; (*proposal*) protester contre; **expense is no ~** l'argent n'est pas un problème; **I ~!** je proteste!; **he ~ed that ...** il a fait valoir *or* a objecté que ...; **~ion** [əb'dʒɛkʃən] *n* objection *f*; (*drawback*) inconvénient *m*; **~ionable** [əb'dʒɛkʃənəbl] *a* très désagréable; choquant(e); **~ive** *n* objectif *m* // *a* objectif(ive).

obligation [ɔblɪ'geɪʃən] *n* obligation *f*, devoir *m*; (*debt*) dette *f* (de reconnaissance); **without ~** sans engagement.

oblige [ə'blaɪdʒ] *vt* (*force*): **to ~ sb to do** obliger *or* forcer qn à faire; (*do a favour*) rendre service à, obliger; **to be ~d to sb for sth** être obligé(e) à qn de qch; **obliging** *a* obligeant(e), serviable.

oblique [ə'bli:k] *a* oblique; (*allusion*) indirect(e).

obliterate [ə'blɪtəreɪt] *vt* effacer.

oblivion [ə'blɪvɪən] *n* oubli *m*.

oblivious [ə'blɪvɪəs] *a*: **~ of** oublieux(euse) de.

oblong ['ɔblɔŋ] *a* oblong(ue) // *n* rectangle *m*.

obnoxious [əb'nɔkʃəs] *a* odieux(euse); (*smell*) nauséabond(e).

oboe ['əubəu] *n* hautbois *m*.

obscene [əb'si:n] *a* obscène.

obscure [əb'skjuə*] *a* obscur(e) // *vt* obscurcir; (*hide: sun*) cacher.

observant [əb'zə:vnt] *a* observateur(trice).

observation [ɔbzə'veɪʃən] *n* observation *f*; (*by police etc*) surveillance *f*.

observatory [əb'zə:vətrɪ] *n* observatoire *m*.

observe [əb'zə:v] *vt* observer; (*remark*) faire observer *or* remarquer; **~r** *n* observateur/trice.

obsess [əb'sɛs] *vt* obséder; **~ive** *a* obsédant(e).

obsolescence [ɔbsə'lɛsns] *n* vieillissement *m*.

obsolete ['ɔbsəli:t] *a* dépassé(e); démodé(e).

obstacle ['ɔbstəkl] *n* obstacle *m*.

obstinate ['ɔbstɪnɪt] *a* obstiné(e); (*pain, cold*) persistant(e).

obstruct [əb'strʌkt] *vt* (*block*) boucher, obstruer; (*halt*) arrêter; (*hinder*) entraver.

obtain [əb'teɪn] *vt* obtenir // *vi* avoir cours; **~able** *a* qu'on peut obtenir.

obtrusive [əb'tru:sɪv] *a* (*person*) importun(e); (*smell*) pénétrant(e); (*building etc*) trop en évidence.

obvious ['ɔbvɪəs] *a* évident(e), manifeste; **~ly** *ad* manifestement; bien sûr.

occasion [ə'keɪʒən] *n* occasion *f*; (*event*) événement *m* // *vt* occasionner, causer; **~al** *a* pris(e) *or* fait(e) *etc* de temps en temps; occasionnel(le); **~ally** *ad* de temps en temps, quelquefois.

occupation [ɔkju'peɪʃən] *n* occupation *f*; (*job*) métier *m*, profession *f*; **~al hazard** *n* risque *m* du métier.

occupier ['ɔkjupaɪə*] *n* occupant/e.

occupy ['ɔkjupaɪ] *vt* occuper; **to ~ o.s. with** *or* **by doing** s'occuper à faire.

occur [ə'kə:*] *vi* se produire; (*difficulty, opportunity*) se présenter; (*phenomenon, error*) se rencontrer; **to ~ to sb** venir à l'esprit de qn; **~rence** *n* présence *f*, existence *f*; cas *m*, fait *m*.

ocean ['əuʃən] *n* océan *m*; **~-going** *a* de haute mer.

o'clock [ə'klɔk] *ad*: **it is 5 ~** il est 5 heures.

OCR *n abbr of* **optical character recognition/reader**.

October [ɔk'təubə*] *n* octobre *m*.

octopus ['ɔktəpəs] *n* pieuvre *f*.

odd [ɔd] *a* (*strange*) bizarre, curieux(euse); (*number*) impair(e); (*left over*) qui reste, en plus; (*not of a set*) dépareillé(e); **60~** 60 et quelques; **at ~ times** de temps en temps; **the ~ one out** l'exception *f*; **~s and ends** *npl* de petites choses; **~ity** *n* bizarrerie *f*; (*person*) excentrique *m/f*; **~ jobs** *npl* petits travaux divers; **~ly** *ad* bizarrement, curieusement; **~ments** *npl* (*COMM*) fins *fpl* de série; **~s** *npl* (*in betting*) cote *f*; **it makes no ~s** cela n'a pas d'importance; **at ~s** en désaccord.

odometer [ɔ'dɔmɪtə*] *n* odomètre *m*.

odour, (*US*) **odor** ['əudə*] *n* odeur *f*.

of [ɔv, əv] *prep* **1** (*gen*) de; **a friend ~ ours** un de nos amis; **a boy ~ 10** un garçon de 10 ans; **that was kind ~ you** c'était gentil de votre part
2 (*expressing quantity, amount, dates etc*) de; **a kilo ~ flour** un kilo de farine; **how much ~ this do you need?** combien vous en faut-il?; **there were 3 ~ them** (*people*) ils étaient 3; (*objects*) il y en

avait 3; **3 ~ us** went 3 d'entre nous sont allé(e)s; **the 5th ~ July** le 5 juillet
3 (*from, out of*) en, de; **a statue ~ marble** une statue de *or* en marbre; **made ~ wood** (fait) en bois.

off [ɔf] *a, ad* (*engine*) coupé(e); (*tap*) fermé(e); (*Brit: food: bad*) mauvais(e), avancé(e); (: *milk*) tourné(e); (*absent*) absent(e); (*cancelled*) annulé(e) // *prep* de; sur; **to be ~** (*to leave*) partir, s'en aller; **to be ~ sick** être absent pour cause de maladie; **a day ~** un jour de congé; **to have an ~ day** n'être pas en forme; **he had his coat ~** il avait enlevé son manteau; **10% ~** (*COMM*) 10% de rabais; **~ the coast** au large de la côte; **I'm ~ meat** je ne mange plus de viande; je n'aime plus la viande; **on the ~ chance** à tout hasard.

offal [ˈɔfl] *n* (*CULIN*) abats *mpl*.

offbeat [ˈɔfbiːt] *a* excentrique.

off-colour [ˈɔfˈkʌlə*] *a* (*Brit: ill*) malade, mal fiche(e).

offence, (US) offense [əˈfɛns] *n* (*crime*) délit *m*, infraction *f*; **to take ~ at** se vexer de, s'offenser de.

offend [əˈfɛnd] *vt* (*person*) offenser, blesser; **~er** *n* délinquant/e; (*against regulations*) contrevenant/e.

offensive [əˈfɛnsɪv] *a* offensant(e), choquant(e); (*smell etc*) très déplaisant(e); (*weapon*) offensif(ive) // *n* (*MIL*) offensive *f*.

offer [ˈɔfə*] *n* offre *f*, proposition *f* // *vt* offrir, proposer; **'on ~'** (*COMM*) 'en promotion'; **~ing** *n* offrande *f*.

offhand [ɔfˈhænd] *a* désinvolte // *ad* spontanément.

office [ˈɔfɪs] *n* (*place*) bureau *m*; (*position*) charge *f*, fonction *f*; (*US*) cabinet (*médical*); **to take ~** entrer en fonctions; **~ automation** *n* bureautique *f*; **~ block, (US) ~ building** *n* immeuble *m* de bureaux; **~ hours** *npl* heures *fpl* de bureau; (*US MED*) heures de consultation.

officer [ˈɔfɪsə*] *n* (*MIL etc*) officier *m*; (*of organization*) membre *m* du bureau directeur; (*also:* **police ~**) agent *m* (de police).

office worker *n* employé/e de bureau.

official [əˈfɪʃl] *a* (*authorized*) officiel(le) // *n* officiel *m*; (*civil servant*) fonctionnaire *m/f*; employé/e; **~dom** *n* administration *f*, bureaucratie *f*.

officiate [əˈfɪʃɪeɪt] *vi* (*REL*) officier; **to ~ at a marriage** célébrer un mariage.

officious [əˈfɪʃəs] *a* trop empressé(e).

offing [ˈɔfɪŋ] *n*: **in the ~** (*fig*) en perspective.

off: **~-licence** *n* (*Brit: shop*) débit *m* de vins et de spiritueux; **~-line** *a, ad* (*COMPUT*) (en mode) autonome; (: *switched off*) non connecté(e); **~-peak** *a* aux heures creuses; **~-putting** *a*

(*Brit*) rébarbatif(ive); rebutant(e), peu engageant(e); **~-season** *a, ad* hors-saison (*inv*).

offset [ˈɔfsɛt] *vt irg* (*counteract*) contrebalancer, compenser.

offshoot [ˈɔfʃuːt] *n* (*fig*) ramification *f*, antenne *f*; (: *of discussion etc*) conséquence *f*.

offshore [ɔfˈʃɔː*] *a* (*breeze*) de terre; (*island*) proche du littoral; (*fishing*) côtier(ère).

offside [ˈɔfˈsaɪd] *a* (*SPORT*) hors jeu // (*AUT: with right-hand drive*) côté droit.

offspring [ˈɔfsprɪŋ] *n* progéniture *f*.

off: **~-stage** *ad* dans les coulisses; **~-the-peg, (US) ~-the-rack** *ad* en prêt-à-porter; **~-white** *a* blanc cassé *inv*.

often [ˈɔfn] *ad* souvent; **how ~ do you go?** vous y allez tous les combien?; **how ~ have you gone there?** vous y êtes allé combien de fois?

ogle [ˈəʊgl] *vt* lorgner.

oh [əʊ] *excl* ô!, oh!, ah!

oil [ɔɪl] *n* huile *f*; (*petroleum*) pétrole *m*; (*for central heating*) mazout *m* // *vt* (*machine*) graisser; **~can** *n* burette *f* de graissage; (*for storing*) bidon *m* à huile; **~field** *n* gisement *m* de pétrole; **~ filter** *n* (*AUT*) filtre *m* à huile; **~-fired** *a* au mazout; **~ painting** *n* peinture *f* à l'huile; **~ rig** *n* derrick *m*; (*at sea*) plate-forme pétrolière; **~skins** *npl* ciré *m*; **~ tanker** *n* pétrolier *m*; **~ well** *n* puits *m* de pétrole; **~y** *a* huileux(euse); (*food*) gras(se).

ointment [ˈɔɪntmənt] *n* onguent *m*.

O.K., okay [ˈəʊˈkeɪ] *excl* d'accord! // *vt* approuver, donner son accord à; **is it ~?, are you ~?** ça va?

old [əʊld] *a* vieux(vieille); (*person*) vieux, âgé(e); (*former*) ancien(ne), vieux; **how ~ are you?** quel âge avez-vous?; **he's 10 years ~** il a 10 ans, il est âgé de 10 ans; **~er brother/sister** frère/sœur aîné(e); **~ age** *n* vieillesse *f*; **~-age pensioner (O.A.P.)** *n* (*Brit*) retraité/e; **~-fashioned** *a* démodé(e); (*person*) vieux jeu *inv*.

olive [ˈɔlɪv] *n* (*fruit*) olive *f*; (*tree*) olivier *m* // *a* (*also:* **~-green**) (vert) olive *inv*; **~ oil** *n* huile *f* d'olive.

Olympic [əʊˈlɪmpɪk] *a* olympique; **the ~ Games, the ~s** les Jeux *mpl* olympiques.

omelet(te) [ˈɔmlɪt] *n* omelette *f*.

omen [ˈəʊmən] *n* présage *m*.

ominous [ˈɔmɪnəs] *a* menaçant(e), inquiétant(e); (*event*) de mauvais augure.

omit [əʊˈmɪt] *vt* omettre.

on [ɔn] ♦ *prep* **1** (*indicating position*) sur; **~ the table** sur la table; **~ the wall** sur le *or* au mur; **~ the left** à gauche
2 (*indicating means, method, condition etc*): **~ foot** à pied; **~ the train/plane** (*be*) dans le train/l'avion; (*go*) en train/

avion; ~ **the telephone/radio/television** au téléphone/à la radio/à la télévision; **to be ~ drugs** se droguer; **~ holiday** en vacances

3 (*referring to time*): ~ **Friday** vendredi; ~ **Fridays** le vendredi; ~ **June 20th le** 20 juin; **a week ~ Friday** vendredi en huit; ~ **arrival** à l'arrivée; ~ **seeing this** en voyant cela

4 (*about, concerning*) sur, de; **a book ~ Balzac/physics** un livre sur Balzac/de physique

♦ *ad* **1** (*referring to dress, covering*): **to have one's coat ~** avoir (mis) son manteau; **to put one's coat ~** mettre son manteau; **what's she got ~?** qu'est-ce qu'elle porte?; **screw the lid ~ tightly** vissez bien le couvercle

2 (*further, continuously*): **to walk** *etc* ~ continuer à marcher *etc*; ~ **and off** de temps à autre

♦ *a* **1** (*in operation: machine*) en marche; (: *radio, TV, light*) allumé(e); (: *tap, gas*) ouvert(e); (: *brakes*) mis(e); **is the meeting still ~?** (*not cancelled*) est-ce que la réunion a bien lieu?; (*in progress*) la réunion dure-t-elle encore?; **when is this film ~?** quand passe ce film?

2 (*col*): **that's not ~!** (*not acceptable*) cela ne se fait pas!; (*not possible*) pas question!

once [wʌns] *ad* une fois; (*formerly*) autrefois // *cj* une fois que; ~ **he had left/it was done** une fois qu'il fut parti/que ce fut terminé; **at ~** tout de suite, immédiatement; (*simultaneously*) à la fois; ~ **more** encore une fois; ~ **and for all** une fois pour toutes; ~ **upon a time** il y avait une fois, il était une fois.

oncoming ['ɔnkʌmɪŋ] *a* (*traffic*) venant en sens inverse.

one [wʌn] ♦ *num* un(e); ~ **hundred and fifty cent** cinquante; ~ **day** un jour

♦ *a* **1** (*sole*) seul(e), unique; **the ~ book which** l'unique *or* le seul livre qui; **the ~ man who** le seul (homme) qui

2 (*same*) même; **they came in the ~ car** ils sont venus dans la même voiture

♦ *pronoun* **1**: **this ~** celui-ci/celle-ci; **that ~** celui-là/celle-là; **I've already got ~/a red ~** j'en ai déjà un(e)/un(e) rouge; ~ **by ~** un(e) à *or* par un(e)

2: ~ **another** l'un(e) l'autre; **to look at ~ another** se regarder

3 (*impersonal*) on; ~ **never knows** on ne sait jamais; **to cut ~'s finger** se couper le doigt.

one: **~-armed bandit** *n* machine *f* à sous; **~-day excursion** *n* (*US*) billet *m* d'aller-retour (valable pour la journée); **~-man** *a* (*business*) dirigé(e) *etc* par un seul homme; **~-man band** *n* homme-orchestre *m*; **~-off** *n* (*Brit col*) exemplaire *m* unique.

oneself [wʌn'sɛlf] *pronoun* (*reflexive*) se; (*after prep*) soi(-même); (*emphatic*) soi-même; **to hurt ~** se faire mal; **to keep sth for ~** garder qch pour soi; **to talk to ~** se parler à soi-même.

one: **~-sided** *a* (*argument*) unilatéral(e); **~-to-~** *a* (*relationship*) univoque; **~-upmanship** [-'ʌpmənʃɪp] *n* l'art de faire mieux que les autres; **~-way** *a* (*street, traffic*) à sens unique.

ongoing ['ɔngəʊɪŋ] *a* en cours; suivi(e).

onion ['ʌnjən] *n* oignon *m*.

on-line ['ɔn'laɪn] *a, ad* (*COMPUT*) en ligne; (: *switched on*) connecté(e).

onlooker ['ɔnlʊkə*] *n* spectateur/trice.

only ['əʊnlɪ] *ad* seulement // *a* seul(e), unique // *cj* seulement, mais; **an ~ child** un enfant unique; **not ~ ... but also** non seulement ... mais aussi; **I took ~ one** je n'en ai pris qu'un, j'en ai seulement pris un.

onset ['ɔnsɛt] *n* début *m*; (*of winter, old age*) approche *f*.

onshore ['ɔnʃɔ:*] *a* (*wind*) du large.

onslaught ['ɔnslɔ:t] *n* attaque *f*, assaut *m*.

onto ['ɔntu] *prep* = **on to**.

onus ['əʊnəs] *n* responsabilité *f*.

onward(s) ['ɔnwəd(z)] *ad* (*move*) en avant.

ooze [u:z] *vi* suinter.

opaque [əʊ'peɪk] *a* opaque.

OPEC ['əʊpɛk] *n abbr* (= *Organization of petroleum exporting countries*) O.P.E.P. *f* (= *Organisation des pays exportateurs de pétrole*).

open ['əʊpn] *a* ouvert(e); (*car*) découvert(e); (*road, view*) dégagé(e); (*meeting*) public(ique); (*admiration*) manifeste; (*question*) non résolu(e); (*enemy*) déclaré(e) // *vi* ouvrir // *vi* (*flower, eyes, door, debate*) s'ouvrir; (*shop, bank, museum*) ouvrir; (*book etc: commence*) commencer, débuter; **in the ~ (air)** en plein air; **to ~ on to** *vt fus* (*subj: room, door*) donner sur; **to ~ up** *vt* ouvrir; (*blocked road*) dégager // *vi* s'ouvrir; **~ing** *n* ouverture *f*; (*opportunity*) occasion *f*; débouché *m*; (*job*) poste vacant; **~ly** *ad* ouvertement; **~-minded** *a* à l'esprit ouvert; **~-plan** *a* sans cloisons.

opera ['ɔpərə] *n* opéra *m*; ~ **house** *n* opéra *m*.

operate ['ɔpəreɪt] *vt* (*machine*) faire marcher, faire fonctionner; (*system*) pratiquer // *vi* fonctionner; (*drug*) faire effet; **to ~ on sb (for)** (*MED*) opérer qn (de).

operatic [ɔpə'rætɪk] *a* d'opéra.

operating ['ɔpəreɪtɪŋ] *a*: ~ **table/theatre** table *f*/salle *f* d'opération.

operation [ɔpə'reɪʃən] *n* opération *f*; (*of machine*) fonctionnement *m*; **to be in ~** (*machine*) être en service; (*system*) être en vigueur; **to have an** ~ (*MED*) se faire opérer.

operative ['ɔpərətɪv] *a* (*measure*) en vigueur.

operator ['ɔpəreɪtə*] *n* (*of machine*) opérateur/trice; (*TEL*) téléphoniste *m/f.*

opinion [ə'pɪnɪən] *n* opinion *f*, avis *m*; **in my** ~ à mon avis; **~ated** *a* aux idées bien arrêtées; ~ **poll** *n* sondage *m* (d'opinion).

opponent [ə'pəunənt] *n* adversaire *m/f.*

opportunist [ɔpə'tjuːnɪst] *n* opportuniste *m/f.*

opportunity [ɔpə'tjuːnɪtɪ] *n* occasion *f*; **to take the** ~ **of doing** profiter de l'occasion pour faire; en profiter pour faire.

oppose [ə'pəuz] *vt* s'opposer à; **~d to** a opposé(e) à; **as ~d to** par opposition à; **opposing** *a* (*side*) opposé(e).

opposite ['ɔpəzɪt] *a* opposé(e); (*house etc*) d'en face // *ad* en face // *prep* en face de // *n* opposé *m*, contraire *m*; (*of word*) contraire.

opposition [ɔpə'zɪʃən] *n* opposition *f.*

oppress [ə'prɛs] *vt* opprimer.

opt [ɔpt] *vi*: **to** ~ **for** opter pour; **to** ~ **to do** choisir de faire; **to** ~ **out of** choisir de ne pas participer à *or* de ne pas faire.

optical ['ɔptɪkl] *a* optique; (*instrument*) d'optique; ~ **character recognition/reader (OCR)** *n* lecture *f*/lecteur *m* optique.

optician [ɔp'tɪʃən] *n* opticien/ne.

optimist ['ɔptɪmɪst] *n* optimiste *m/f*; **~ic** [-'mɪstɪk] *a* optimiste.

option ['ɔpʃən] *n* choix *m*, option *f*; (*SCOL*) matière *f* à option; (*COMM*) option; **~al** *a* facultatif(ive); (*COMM*) en option.

or [ɔː*] *cj* ou; (*with negative*): **he hasn't seen** ~ **heard anything** il n'a rien vu ni entendu; ~ **else** sinon; ou bien.

oral ['ɔːrəl] *a* oral(e) // *n* oral *m.*

orange ['ɔrɪndʒ] *n* (*fruit*) orange *f* // *a* orange *inv.*

orator ['ɔrətə*] *n* orateur/trice.

orbit ['ɔːbɪt] *n* orbite *f.*

orchard ['ɔːtʃəd] *n* verger *m.*

orchestra ['ɔːkɪstrə] *n* orchestre *m*; (*US: seating*) (fauteuils *mpl* d')orchestre; **orchestral** [-'kɛstrəl] *a* orchestral(e); (*concert*) symphonique.

orchid ['ɔːkɪd] *n* orchidée *f.*

ordain [ɔː'deɪn] *vt* (*REL*) ordonner; (*decide*) décréter.

ordeal [ɔː'diːl] *n* épreuve *f.*

order ['ɔːdə*] *n* ordre *m*; (*COMM*) commande *f* // *vt* ordonner; (*COMM*) commander; **in** ~ en ordre; (*of document*) en règle; **in (working)** ~ en état de marche; **in** ~ **of size** par ordre de grandeur; **in** ~ **to do/that** pour faire/que + *sub*; **on** ~ (*COMM*) en commande; **to** ~ **sb to do** ordonner à qn de faire; ~

form *n* bon *m* de commande; **~ly** (*MIL*) ordonnance *f* // *a* (*room*) en ordre; (*mind*) méthodique; (*person*) qui a de l'ordre.

ordinary ['ɔːdnrɪ] *a* ordinaire, normal(e); (*pej*) ordinaire, quelconque; **out of the** ~ exceptionnel(le).

ordnance ['ɔːdnəns] *n* (*MIL: unit*) service *m* du matériel.

ore [ɔː*] *n* minerai *m.*

organ ['ɔːgən] *n* organe *m*; (*MUS*) orgue *m*, orgues *fpl*; **~ic** [ɔː'gænɪk] *a* organique.

organization [ɔːgənaɪ'zeɪʃən] *n* organisation *f.*

organize ['ɔːgənaɪz] *vt* organiser; **~r** *n* organisateur/trice.

orgasm ['ɔːgæzəm] *n* orgasme *m.*

orgy ['ɔːdʒɪ] *n* orgie *f.*

Orient ['ɔːrɪənt] *n*: **the** ~ l'Orient *m*; **oriental** [-'ɛntl] *a* oriental(e).

origin ['ɔrɪdʒɪn] *n* origine *f.*

original [ə'rɪdʒɪnl] *a* original(e); (*earliest*) originel(le) // *n* original *m*; **~ly** *ad* (*at first*) à l'origine.

originate [ə'rɪdʒɪneɪt] *vi*: **to** ~ **from** être originaire de; (*suggestion*) provenir de; **to** ~ **in** prendre naissance dans; avoir son origine dans.

Orkneys ['ɔːknɪz] *npl*: **the** ~ (*also*: **the Orkney Islands**) les Orcades *fpl.*

ornament ['ɔːnəmənt] *n* ornement *m*; (*trinket*) bibelot *m*; **~al** [-'mɛntl] *a* décoratif(ive); (*garden*) d'agrément.

ornate [ɔː'neɪt] *a* très orné(e).

orphan ['ɔːfn] *n* orphelin/e // *vt*: **to be ~ed** devenir orphelin; **~age** *n* orphelinat *m.*

orthopaedic, (*US*) **orthopedic** [ɔːθə'piːdɪk] *a* orthopédique.

ostensibly [ɔs'tɛnsɪblɪ] *ad* en apparence.

ostentatious [ɔstɛn'teɪʃəs] *a* prétentieux(euse); ostentatoire.

ostracize ['ɔstrəsaɪz] *vt* frapper d'ostracisme.

ostrich ['ɔstrɪtʃ] *n* autruche *f.*

other ['ʌðə*] *a* autre // *pronoun*: **the** ~ (**one**) l'autre; **~s** (~ *people*) d'autres; ~ **than** autrement que; à part; **~wise** *ad*, *cj* autrement.

otter ['ɔtə*] *n* loutre *f.*

ouch [autʃ] *excl* aïe!

ought [ɔːt], *pt* **ought** [ɔːt] *auxiliary vb*: **I** ~ **to do it** je devrais le faire, il faudrait que je le fasse; **this** ~ **to have been corrected** cela aurait dû être corrigé; **he** ~ **to win** il devrait gagner.

ounce [auns] *n* once *f* (= 28.35g; 16 in a pound).

our ['auə*] *a* notre, nos *pl*; *see also* **my**; **~s** *pronoun* le(la) nôtre, les nôtres; *see also* **mine**; **~selves** *pronoun pl* (*reflexive, after preposition*) nous; (*emphatic*) nous-mêmes; *see also* **oneself**.

oust [aust] *vt* évincer.

out [aut] *ad* dehors; *(published, not at home etc)* sorti(e); *(light, fire)* éteint(e); ~ **here** ici; ~ **there** là-bas; **he's** ~ *(absent)* il est sorti; *(unconscious)* il est sans connaissance; **to be** ~ **in one's calculations** s'être trompé dans ses calculs; **to run/back** *etc* ~ sortir en courant/en reculant *etc*; ~ **loud** *ad* à haute voix; ~ **of** *(outside)* en dehors de; *(because of: anger etc)* par; *(from among)*: ~ **of 10** sur 10; *(without)*: ~ **of petrol** sans essence, à court d'essence; ~ **of order** *(machine)* en panne; *(TEL: line)* en dérangement; ~**-and**-~ *a (liar, thief etc)* véritable.

outback ['autbæk] *n* campagne isolée; *(in Australia)* intérieur *m*.

outboard ['autbɔ:d] *n*: ~ **(motor)** *(moteur m)* hors-bord *m*.

outbreak ['autbreɪk] *n* accès *m*; début *m*; éruption *f*.

outburst ['autbə:st] *n* explosion *f*, accès *m*.

outcast ['autkɑ:st] *n* exilé/e; *(socially)* paria *m*.

outcome ['autkʌm] *n* issue *f*, résultat *m*.

outcrop ['autkrɔp] *n (of rock)* affleurement *m*.

outcry ['autkraɪ] *n* tollé (général).

outdated [aut'deɪtɪd] *a* démodé(e).

outdo [aut'du:] *vt irg* surpasser.

outdoor [aut'dɔ:*] *a* de *or* en plein air; ~**s** *ad* dehors; au grand air.

outer ['autə*] *a* extérieur(e); ~ **space** *n* espace *m* cosmique.

outfit ['autfɪt] *n* équipement *m*; *(clothes)* tenue *f*; '~**ter's'** *(Brit)* 'confection pour hommes'.

outgoing ['autgəuɪŋ] *a (character)* ouvert(e), extraverti(e); ~**s** *npl (Brit: expenses)* dépenses *fpl*.

outgrow [aut'grəu] *vt irg (clothes)* devenir trop grand(e) pour.

outhouse ['authaus] *n* appentis *m*, remise *f*.

outing ['autɪŋ] *n* sortie *f*; excursion *f*.

outlandish [aut'lændɪʃ] *a* étrange.

outlaw ['autlɔ:] *n* hors-la-loi *m inv*.

outlay ['autleɪ] *n* dépenses *fpl*; *(investment)* mise *f* de fonds.

outlet ['autlet] *n (for liquid etc)* issue *f*, sortie *f*; *(US: ELEC)* prise *f* de courant; *(for emotion)* exutoire *m*; *(for goods)* débouché *m*; *(also: retail* ~) point *m* de vente.

outline ['autlaɪn] *n (shape)* contour *m*; *(summary)* esquisse *f*, grandes lignes.

outlive [aut'lɪv] *vt* survivre à.

outlook ['autluk] *n* perspective *f*.

outlying ['autlaɪɪŋ] *a* écarté(e).

outmoded [aut'məudɪd] *a* démodé(e); dépassé(e).

outnumber [aut'nʌmbə*] *vt* surpasser en nombre.

out-of-date ['autəv'deɪt] *a (passport)* périmé(e); *(theory etc)* dépassé(e); *(custom)* désuet(ète); *(clothes etc)* démodé(e).

out-of-the-way ['autəvðə'weɪ] *a (place)* loin de tout.

outpatient ['autpeɪʃənt] *n* malade *m/f* en consultation externe.

outpost ['autpəust] *n* avant-poste *m*.

output ['autput] *n* rendement *m*, production *f*; *(COMPUT)* sortie *f*.

outrage ['autreɪdʒ] *n* atrocité *f*, acte *m* de violence; scandale *m* // *vt* outrager; ~**ous** [-'reɪdʒəs] *a* atroce; scandaleux(euse).

outright *ad* [aut'raɪt] complètement; catégoriquement; carrément; sur le coup // *a* ['autraɪt] complet(ète); catégorique.

outset ['autset] *n* début *m*.

outside [aut'saɪd] *n* extérieur *m* // *a* extérieur(e) // *ad* (au) dehors, à l'extérieur // *prep* hors de, à l'extérieur de; **at the** ~ *(fig)* au plus *or* maximum; ~ **lane** *n (AUT: in Britain)* voie *f* de droite; ~**-left/-right** *n (FOOTBALL)* ailier gauche/droit; ~ **line** *n (TEL)* ligne extérieure; ~**r** *n (in race etc)* outsider *m*; *(stranger)* étranger/ère.

outsize ['autsaɪz] *a* énorme; *(clothes)* grande taille *inv*.

outskirts ['autskə:ts] *npl* faubourgs *mpl*.

outspoken [aut'spəukən] *a* très franc(franche).

outstanding [aut'stændɪŋ] *a* remarquable, exceptionnel(le); *(unfinished)* en suspens; en souffrance; non réglé(e).

outstay [aut'steɪ] *vt*: **to** ~ **one's welcome** abuser de l'hospitalité de son hôte.

outstretched [aut'stretʃt] *a (hand)* tendu(e); *(body)* étendu(e).

outstrip [aut'strɪp] *vt (competitors, demand)* dépasser.

out-tray ['auttreɪ] *n* courrier *m* 'départ'.

outward ['autwəd] *a (sign, appearances)* extérieur(e); *(journey)* (d')aller; ~**ly** *ad* extérieurement; en apparence.

outweigh [aut'weɪ] *vt* l'emporter sur.

outwit [aut'wɪt] *vt* se montrer plus malin que.

oval ['əuvl] *a, n* ovale *(m)*.

ovary ['əuvərɪ] *n* ovaire *m*.

oven ['ʌvn] *n* four *m*; ~**proof** *a* allant au four.

over ['əuvə*] *ad* (par-)dessus // *a (or ad) (finished)* fini(e), terminé(e); *(too much)* en plus // *prep* par-dessus; *(above)* au-dessus de; *(on the other side of)* de l'autre côté de; *(more than)* plus de; *(during)* pendant; ~ **here** ici; ~ **there** là-bas; **all** ~ *(everywhere)* partout; *(finished)* fini(e); ~ **and** ~ *(again)* à plusieurs reprises; ~ **and above** en plus de; **to ask sb** ~ inviter qn (à passer).

overall *a n*, ['ouvərɔːl] *a* (*length*) total(e); (*study*) d'ensemble // *n* (*Brit*) blouse *f* // *ad* [ouvər'ɔːl] dans l'ensemble, en général; ~**s** *npl* bleus *mpl* (de travail).

overawe [ouvər'ɔː] *vt* impressionner.

overbalance [ouvə'bæləns] *vi* basculer.

overbearing [ouvə'bɛərɪŋ] *a* impérieux(euse), autoritaire.

overboard ['ouvəbɔːd] *ad* (*NAUT*) par-dessus bord.

overbook [ouvə'buk] *vt* faire du surbooking.

overcast ['ouvəkɑːst] *a* couvert(e).

overcharge [ouvə'tʃɑːdʒ] *vt*: to ~ sb for sth faire payer qch trop cher à qn.

overcoat ['ouvəkəut] *n* pardessus *m*.

overcome [ouvə'kʌm] *vt irg* triompher de; surmonter; ~ **with grief** accablé(e) de douleur.

overcrowded [ouvə'kraudɪd] *a* bondé(e).

overdo [ouvə'duː] *vt irg* exagérer; (*overcook*) trop cuire.

overdose ['ouvədəus] *n* dose excessive.

overdraft ['ouvədrɑːft] *n* découvert *m*.

overdrawn [ouvə'drɔːn] *a* (*account*) à découvert.

overdue [ouvə'djuː] *a* en retard; (*recognition*) tardif(ive).

overflow [ouvə'fləu] *vi* déborder // *n* ['ouvəfləu] trop-plein *m*; (*also*: ~ **pipe**) tuyau *m* d'écoulement, trop-plein *m*.

overgrown [ouvə'grəun] *a* (*garden*) envahi(e) par la végétation.

overhaul *vt* [ouvə'hɔːl] réviser // *n* ['ouvəhɔːl] révision *f*.

overhead *ad* [ouvə'hɛd] au-dessus // *a, n* ['ouvəhɛd] *a* aérien(ne); (*lighting*) vertical(e) // *n* (*US*) = ~**s**; ~**s** *npl* frais généraux.

overhear [ouvə'hɪə*] *vt irg* entendre (par hasard).

overheat [ouvə'hiːt] *vi* (*engine*) chauffer.

overjoyed [ouvə'dʒɔɪd] *a* ravi(e), enchanté(e).

overkill ['ouvəkɪl] *n*: that would be ~ ce serait trop.

overlap [ouvə'læp] *vi* se chevaucher.

overleaf [ouvə'liːf] *ad* au verso.

overload [ouvə'ləud] *vt* surcharger.

overlook [ouvə'luk] *vt* (*have view of*) donner sur; (*miss*) oublier, négliger; (*forgive*) fermer les yeux sur.

overnight *ad* [ouvə'naɪt] (*happen*) durant la nuit; (*fig*) soudain // *a* ['ouvənaɪt] d'une (*or* de) nuit; soudain(e); **he stayed there** ~ il y a passé la nuit.

overpower [ouvə'pauə*] *vt* vaincre; (*fig*) accabler; ~**ing** *a* irrésistible; (*heat, stench*) suffocant(e).

overrate [ouvə'reɪt] *vt* surestimer.

override [ouvə'raɪd] *vt* (*irg: like* **ride**) (*order, objection*) passer outre à; (*decision*) annuler; **overriding** *a* prépondérant(e).

overrule [ouvə'ruːl] *vt* (*decision*) annuler; (*claim*) rejeter.

overrun [ouvə'rʌn] *vt* (*irg: like* **run**) (*country*) occuper; (*time limit*) dépasser.

overseas [ouvə'siːz] *ad* outre-mer; (*abroad*) à l'étranger // *a* (*trade*) extérieur(e); (*visitor*) étranger(ère).

overseer ['ouvəsɪə*] *n* (*in factory*) contremaître *m*.

overshadow [ouvə'ʃædəu] *vt* (*fig*) éclipser.

overshoot [ouvə'ʃuːt] *vt irg* dépasser.

oversight ['ouvəsaɪt] *n* omission *f*, oubli *m*.

oversleep [ouvə'sliːp] *vi irg* se réveiller (trop) tard.

overstep [ouvə'stɛp] *vt*: to ~ **the mark** dépasser la mesure.

overt [ou'vəːt] *a* non dissimulé(e).

overtake [ouvə'teɪk] *vt irg* dépasser; (*AUT*) dépasser, doubler.

overthrow [ouvə'θrəu] *vt irg* (*government*) renverser.

overtime ['ouvətaɪm] *n* heures *fpl* supplémentaires.

overtone ['ouvətəun] *n* (*also*: ~**s**) note *f*, sous-entendus *mpl*.

overture ['ouvətʃuə*] *n* (*MUS, fig*) ouverture *f*.

overturn [ouvə'təːn] *vt* renverser // *vi* se retourner.

overweight [ouvə'weɪt] *a* (*person*) trop gros(se); (*luggage*) trop lourd(e).

overwhelm [ouvə'wɛlm] *vt* accabler; submerger; écraser; ~**ing** *a* (*victory, defeat*) écrasant(e); (*desire*) irrésistible.

overwork [ouvə'wəːk] *n* surmenage *m*.

overwrought [ouvə'rɔːt] *a* excédé(e).

owe [ou] *vt* devoir; to ~ **sb sth, to** ~ **sth to sb** devoir qch à qn.

owing to ['ouɪŋtu:] *prep* à cause de, en raison de.

owl [aul] *n* hibou *m*.

own [oun] *vt* posséder // *a* propre; **a room of my** ~ une chambre à moi, ma propre chambre; **to get one's** ~ **back** prendre sa revanche; **on one's** ~ tout(e) seul(e); **to** ~ **up** *vi* avouer; ~**er** *n* propriétaire *m/f*; ~**ership** *n* possession *f*.

ox, *pl* **oxen** [ɔks, 'ɔksn] *n* bœuf *m*.

oxtail ['ɔksteɪl] *n*: ~ **soup** soupe *f* à la queue de bœuf.

oxygen ['ɔksɪdʒən] *n* oxygène *m*; ~ **mask** *n* masque *m* à oxygène.

oyster ['ɔɪstə*] *n* huître *f*.

oz. *abbr of* **ounce(s)**.

P

p [pi:] *abbr of* **penny, pence.**
pa [pɑ:] *n* (*col*) papa *m*.
P.A. *n abbr of* **personal assistant, public address system.**
p.a. *abbr of* **per annum.**
pace [peɪs] *n* pas *m*; (*speed*) allure *f*; vitesse *f* // *vi*: to ~ **up and down** faire les cent pas; **to keep** ~ **with** aller à la même vitesse que; (*events*) se tenir au courant de; ~**maker** *n* (*MED*) stimulateur *m* cardiaque.
pacific [pə'sɪfɪk] *a* pacifique // *n*: **the P~ (Ocean)** le Pacifique, l'océan *m* Pacifique.
pack [pæk] *n* paquet *m*; ballot *m*; (*of hounds*) meute *f*; (*of thieves etc*) bande *f*; (*of cards*) jeu *m* // *vt* (*goods*) empaqueter, emballer; (*in suitcase etc*) emballer; (*box*) remplir; (*cram*) entasser; (*press down*) tasser; damer; to ~ (**one's bags**) faire ses bagages; **to** ~ **off** *vt* (*person*) envoyer (promener), expédier.
package ['pækɪdʒ] *n* paquet *m*; ballot *m*; (*also:* ~ **deal**) marché global; forfait *m*; ~ **tour** *n* voyage organisé.
packed lunch *n* repas froid.
packet ['pækɪt] *n* paquet *m*.
packing ['pækɪŋ] *n* emballage *m*; ~ **case** *n* caisse *f* (d'emballage).
pact [pækt] *n* pacte *m*; traité *m*.
pad [pæd] *n* bloc(-notes) *m*; (*for inking*) tampon *m* encreur; (*col: flat*) piaule *f* // *vt* rembourrer; ~**ding** *n* rembourrage *m*.
paddle ['pædl] *n* (*oar*) pagaie *f*; (*US: for table tennis*) raquette *f* de ping-pong // *vi* barboter, faire trempette // *vt*: to ~ **a canoe** *etc* pagayer; ~ **steamer** *n* bateau *m* à aubes; **paddling pool** *n* (*Brit*) petit bassin.
paddy ['pædɪ]: ~ **field** *n* rizière *f*.
padlock ['pædlɔk] *n* cadenas *m*.
paediatrics, (*US*) **pediatrics** [pi:dɪ'ætrɪks] *n* pédiatrie *f*.
pagan ['peɪgən] *a, n* païen(ne).
page [peɪdʒ] *n* (*of book*) page *f*; (*also:* ~ **boy**) groom *m*, chasseur *m*; (*at wedding*) garçon *m* d'honneur // *vt* (*in hotel etc*) (faire) appeler.
pageant ['pædʒənt] *n* spectacle *m* historique; grande cérémonie; ~**ry** *n* apparat *m*, pompe *f*.
paid [peɪd] *pt, pp of* **pay** // *a* (*work, official*) rémunéré(e); **to put** ~ **to** (*Brit*) mettre fin à, régler.
pail [peɪl] *n* seau *m*.
pain [peɪn] *n* douleur *f*; **to be in** ~ souffrir, avoir mal; **to take** ~**s to do** se donner du mal pour faire; ~**ed** *a* peiné(e), chagrin(e); ~**ful** *a* doulou-

reux(euse); difficile, pénible; ~**fully** *ad* (*fig: very*) terriblement; ~**killer** *n* calmant *m*; ~**less** *a* indolore.
painstaking ['peɪnzteɪkɪŋ] *a* (*person*) soigneux(euse); (*work*) soigné(e).
paint [peɪnt] *n* peinture *f* // *vt* peindre; (*fig*) dépeindre; **to** ~ **the door blue** peindre la porte en bleu; ~**brush** *n* pinceau *m*; ~**er** *n* peintre *m*; ~**ing** *n* peinture *f*; (*picture*) tableau *m*; ~**work** *n* peintures *fpl*; (*of car*) peinture *f*.
pair [pɛə*] *n* (*of shoes, gloves etc*) paire *f*; (*of people*) couple *m*; duo *m*; paire; ~ **of scissors** (paire de) ciseaux *mpl*; ~ **of trousers** pantalon *m*.
pajamas [pɪ'dʒɑ:məz] *npl* (*US*) pyjama(s) *m(pl)*.
Pakistan [pɑ:kɪ'stɑ:n] *n* Pakistan *m*; ~**i** *a* pakistanais(e) // *n* Pakistanais/e.
pal [pæl] *n* (*col*) copain/copine.
palace ['pæləs] *n* palais *m*.
palatable ['pælɪtəbl] *a* bon(bonne), agréable au goût.
palate ['pælɪt] *n* palais *m* (*ANAT*).
palatial [pə'leɪʃəl] *a* grandiose, magnifique.
palaver [pə'lɑ:və*] *n* palabres *fpl or mpl*; histoire(s) *f(pl)*.
pale [peɪl] *a* pâle; **to grow** ~ pâlir // *n*: **beyond the** ~ au ban de la société.
Palestine ['pælɪstaɪn] *n* Palestine *f*; **Palestinian** [-'tɪnɪən] *a* palestinien(ne) // *n* Palestinien/ne.
palette ['pælɪt] *n* palette *f*.
paling ['peɪlɪŋ] *n* (*stake*) palis *m*; (*fence*) palissade *f*.
pall [pɔ:l] *n* (*of smoke*) voile *m* // *vi*: **to** ~ (**on**) devenir lassant (pour).
pallet ['pælɪt] *n* (*for goods*) palette *f*.
pallid ['pælɪd] *a* blême.
pallor ['pælə*] *n* pâleur *f*.
palm [pɑ:m] *n* (*ANAT*) paume *f*; (*also:* ~ **tree**) palmier *m*; (*leaf, symbol*) palme *f* // *vt*: **to** ~ **sth off on sb** (*col*) refiler qch à qn; **P~ Sunday** *n* le dimanche des Rameaux.
palpable ['pælpəbl] *a* évident(e), manifeste.
paltry ['pɔ:ltrɪ] *a* dérisoire; piètre.
pamper ['pæmpə*] *vt* gâter, dorloter.
pamphlet ['pæmflət] *n* brochure *f*.
pan [pæn] *n* (*also:* **sauce**~) casserole *f*; (*also:* **frying** ~) poêle *f*; (*of lavatory*) cuvette *f* // *vi* (*CINEMA*) faire un panoramique.
pancake ['pænkeɪk] *n* crêpe *f*.
panda ['pændə] *n* panda *m*; ~ **car** *n* (*Brit*) ≈ voiture *f* pie *inv*.
pandemonium [pændɪ'məunɪəm] *n* tohu-bohu *m*.
pander ['pændə*] *vi*: **to** ~ **to** flatter bassement; obéir servilement à.
pane [peɪn] *n* carreau *m* (de fenêtre).
panel ['pænl] *n* (*of wood, cloth etc*) panneau *m*; (*RADIO, TV*) panel *m*;

invités *mpl*, experts *mpl*; ~**ling**, (*US*) ~**ing** *n* boiseries *fpl*.

pang [pæŋ] *n*: ~s **of remorse** pincements *mpl* de remords; ~s **of hunger/ conscience** tiraillements *mpl* d'estomac/de la conscience.

panic ['pænɪk] *n* panique *f*, affolement *m* // *vi* s'affoler, paniquer; ~**ky** *a* (*person*) qui panique *or* s'affole facilement; ~**stricken** *a* affolé(e).

pansy ['pænzɪ] *n* (*BOT*) pensée *f*; (*col*) tapette *f*, pédé *m*.

pant [pænt] *vi* haleter.

panther ['pænθə*] *n* panthère *f*.

panties ['pæntɪz] *npl* slip *m*, culotte *f*.

pantihose ['pæntɪhəuz] *n* (*US*) collant *m*.

pantomime ['pæntəmaɪm] *n* (*Brit*) spectacle *m* de Noël.

pantry ['pæntrɪ] *n* garde-manger *m inv*; (*room*) office *f or m*.

pants [pænts] *n* (*Brit: woman's*) culotte *f*, slip *m*; (: *man's*) slip, caleçon *m*; (*US: trousers*) pantalon *m*.

paper ['peɪpə*] *n* papier *m*; (*also: wall~*) papier peint; (*also: news~*) journal *m*; (*study, article*) article *m*; (*exam*) épreuve écrite // *a* en *or* de papier // *vt* tapisser (de papier peint); ~s *npl* (*also:* **identity** ~s) papiers (d'identité); ~**back** *n* livre *m* de poche; livre broché *or* non relié; ~ **clip** *n* trombone *m*; ~ **hankie** *n* mouchoir *m* en papier; ~**weight** *n* presse-papiers *m inv*; ~**work** *n* paperasserie *f*.

par [pɑ:*] *n* pair *m*; (*GOLF*) normale *f* du parcours; **on a ~ with** à égalité avec, au même niveau que.

parable ['pærəbl] *n* parabole *f* (*REL*).

parachute ['pærəʃu:t] *n* parachute *m*.

parade [pə'reɪd] *n* défilé *m*; (*inspection*) revue *f*; (*street*) boulevard *m* // *vt* (*fig*) faire étalage de // *vi* défiler.

paradise ['pærədaɪs] *n* paradis *m*.

paradox ['pærədɔks] *n* paradoxe *m*; ~**ically** [-'dɔksɪklɪ] *ad* paradoxalement.

paraffin ['pærəfɪn] *n* (*Brit*): ~ (**oil**) pétrole (lampant).

paragraph ['pærəgrɑ:f] *n* paragraphe *m*.

parallel ['pærəlɛl] *a* parallèle; (*fig*) analogue // *n* (*line*) parallèle *f*; (*fig, GEO*) parallèle *m*.

paralysis [pə'rælɪsɪs] *n* paralysie *f*.

paralyze ['pærəlaɪz] *vt* paralyser.

paramount ['pærəmaunt] *a*: **of** ~ **importance** de la plus haute *or* grande importance.

paranoid ['pærənɔɪd] *a* (*PSYCH*) paranoïaque; (*neurotic*) paranoïde.

paraphernalia [pærəfə'neɪlɪə] *n* attirail *m*, affaires *fpl*.

parasol [pærə'sɔl] *n* ombrelle *f*; parasol *m*.

paratrooper ['pærətru:pə*] *n* parachutiste *m* (*soldat*).

parcel ['pɑ:sl] *n* paquet *m*, colis *m* // *vt* (*also:* ~ **up**) empaqueter.

parch [pɑ:tʃ] *vt* dessécher; ~**ed** *a* (*person*) assoiffé(e).

parchment ['pɑ:tʃmənt] *n* parchemin *m*.

pardon ['pɑ:dn] *n* pardon *m*; grâce *f* // *vt* pardonner à; (*LAW*) gracier; ~ **me!** excusez-moi!; **I beg your** ~! pardon!, je suis désolé!; (**I beg your**) ~?, (*US*) ~ **me?** pardon?

parent ['pɛərənt] *n* père *m or* mère *f*; ~s *npl* parents *mpl*.

Paris ['pærɪs] *n* Paris.

parish ['pærɪʃ] *n* paroisse *f*; (*civil*) ≈ commune *f* // *a* paroissial(e).

Parisian [pə'rɪzɪən] *a* parisien(ne) // *n* Parisien/ne.

park [pɑ:k] *n* parc *m*, jardin public // *vt* garer // *vi* se garer.

parking ['pɑ:kɪŋ] *n* stationnement *m*; '**no** ~' 'stationnement interdit'; ~ **lot** *n* (*US*) parking *m*, parc *m* de stationnement; ~ **meter** *n* parcomètre *m*; ~ **ticket** *n* P.V. *m*.

parlance ['pɑ:lns] *n* langage *m*.

parliament ['pɑ:ləmənt] *n* parlement *m*; ~**ary** [-'mɛntərɪ] parlementaire.

parlour, (*US*) **parlor** ['pɑ:lə*] *n* salon *m*.

parochial [pə'rəukɪəl] *a* paroissial(e); (*pej*) à l'esprit de clocher.

parody ['pærədɪ] *n* parodie *f*.

parole [pə'rəul] *n*: **on** ~ en liberté conditionnelle.

parrot ['pærət] *n* perroquet *m*.

parry ['pærɪ] *vt* esquiver, parer à.

parsley ['pɑ:slɪ] *n* persil *m*.

parsnip ['pɑ:snɪp] *n* panais *m*.

parson ['pɑ:sn] *n* ecclésiastique *m*; (*Church of England*) pasteur *m*.

part [pɑ:t] *n* partie *f*; (*of machine*) pièce *f*; (*THEATRE etc*) rôle *m*; (*MUS*) voix *f*; partie; (*US: in hair*) raie *f* // *a* partiel(le) // *ad* = **partly** // *vt* séparer // *vi* (*people*) se séparer; (*roads*) se diviser; **to take** ~ **in** participer à, prendre part à; **for my** ~ en ce qui me concerne; **to take sth in good** ~ prendre qch du bon côté; **to take sb's** ~ prendre le parti de qn, prendre parti pour qn; **for the most** ~ en grande partie; dans la plupart des cas; **to** ~ **with** *vt fus* se séparer de; se défaire de; ~ **exchange** *n* (*Brit*): **in** ~ **exchange** en reprise.

partial ['pɑ:ʃl] *a* partiel(le); (*unjust*) partial(e); **to be** ~ **to** aimer, avoir un faible pour.

participate [pɑ:'tɪsɪpeɪt] *vi*: **to** ~ (**in**) participer (à), prendre part (à); **participation** [-'peɪʃən] *n* participation *f*.

participle ['pɑ:tɪsɪpl] *n* participe *m*.

particle ['pɑ:tɪkl] *n* particule *f*.

particular [pə'tɪkjulə*] *a* particulier(ère); spécial(e); (*detailed*) détaillé(e); *(fussy)* difficile; méticuleux(euse); **~s** npl détails mpl; *(information)* renseignements mpl; **in ~** ad surtout, en particulier; **~ly** ad particulièrement; en particulier.

parting ['pɑ:tɪŋ] n séparation f; *(Brit: in hair)* raie f // a d'adieu.

partisan [pɑ:tɪ'zæn] n partisan/e // a partisan(e); de parti.

partition [pɑ:'tɪʃən] n *(POL)* partition f, division f; *(wall)* cloison f.

partly ['pɑ:tlɪ] ad en partie, partiellement.

partner ['pɑ:tnə*] n *(COMM)* associé/e; *(SPORT)* partenaire m/f; *(at dance)* cavalier/ère; **~ship** n association f.

partridge ['pɑ:trɪdʒ] n perdrix f.

part-time ['pɑ:t'taɪm] a, ad à mi-temps, à temps partiel.

party ['pɑ:tɪ] n *(POL)* parti m; *(team)* équipe f; groupe m; *(LAW)* partie f; *(celebration)* réception f; soirée f; fête f // a *(POL)* de or du parti; de partis; **~ dress** n robe habillée; **~ line** n *(TEL)* ligne partagée.

pass [pɑ:s] vt *(time, object)* passer; *(place)* passer devant; *(car, friend)* croiser; *(exam)* être reçu(e) à, réussir; *(candidate)* admettre; *(overtake, surpass)* dépasser; *(approve)* approuver, accepter // vi passer; *(SCOL)* être reçu(e) or admis(e), réussir // n *(permit)* laissez-passer m inv; carte f d'accès or d'abonnement; *(in mountains)* col m; *(SPORT)* passe f; *(SCOL: also: ~ mark)*: **to get a ~** être reçu(e) (sans mention); **to ~ sth through a ring** etc (faire) passer qch dans un anneau etc; **to make a ~ at sb** *(col)* faire des avances à qn; **to ~ away** vi mourir; **to ~ by** vi passer // vt négliger; **to ~ on** vt *(news, object)* transmettre; *(illness)* passer; **to ~ out** vi s'évanouir; **to ~ up** vt *(opportunity)* laisser passer; **~able** a *(road)* praticable; *(work)* acceptable.

passage ['pæsɪdʒ] n *(also: ~way)* couloir m; *(gen, in book)* passage m; *(by boat)* traversée f.

passbook ['pɑ:sbuk] n livret m.

passenger ['pæsɪndʒə*] n passager/ère.

passer-by [pɑ:sə'baɪ] n passant/e.

passing ['pɑ:sɪŋ] a *(fig)* passager(ère); **in ~** en passant; **~ place** n *(AUT)* aire f de croisement.

passion ['pæʃən] n passion f; amour m; **~ate** a passionné(e).

passive ['pæsɪv] a *(also LING)* passif(ive).

Passover ['pɑ:səuvə*] n Pâque *(juive)*.

passport ['pɑ:spɔ:t] n passeport m; **~ control** n contrôle m des passeports.

password ['pɑ:swə:d] n mot m de passe.

past [pɑ:st] prep *(further than)* au delà

de, plus loin que; après; *(later than)* après // a passé(e); *(president etc)* ancien(ne) // n passé m; **he's ~ forty** il a dépassé la quarantaine, il a plus de or passé quarante ans; **for the ~ few/3 days** depuis quelques/3 jours; ces derniers/3 derniers jours; **he ran ~ me** il m'a dépassé en courant; il a passé devant moi en courant.

pasta ['pæstə] n pâtes fpl.

paste [peɪst] n *(glue)* colle f *(de pâte)*; *(jewellery)* strass m; *(CULIN)* pâté m *(à tartiner)*; pâte f // vt coller.

pasteurized ['pæstəraɪzd] a pasteurisé(e).

pastille ['pæstl] n pastille f.

pastime ['pɑ:staɪm] n passe-temps m inv, distraction f.

pastor ['pɑ:stə*] n pasteur m.

pastry ['peɪstrɪ] n pâte f; *(cake)* pâtisserie f.

pasture ['pɑ:stʃə*] n pâturage m.

pasty n ['pæstɪ] petit pâté *(en croûte)* // a ['peɪstɪ] pâteux(euse); *(complexion)* terreux(euse).

pat [pæt] vt donner une petite tape à.

patch [pætʃ] n *(of material)* pièce f; *(spot)* tache f; *(of land)* parcelle f // vt *(clothes)* rapiécer; **(to go through) a bad ~** *(passer par)* une période difficile; **to ~ up** vt réparer; **~y** a inégal(e).

pâté ['pæteɪ] n pâté m, terrine f.

patent ['peɪtnt] n brevet m *(d'invention)* // vt faire breveter // a patent(e), manifeste; **~ leather** n cuir verni.

paternal [pə'tə:nl] a paternel(le).

path [pɑ:θ] n chemin m, sentier m; allée f; *(of planet)* course f; *(of missile)* trajectoire f.

pathetic [pə'θetɪk] a *(pitiful)* pitoyable; *(very bad)* lamentable, minable; *(moving)* pathétique.

pathological [pæθə'lɔdʒɪkl] a pathologique.

pathos ['peɪθɔs] n pathétique m.

patience ['peɪʃns] n patience f; *(Brit: CARDS)* réussite f.

patient ['peɪʃnt] n patient/e; malade m/f // a patient(e).

patriotic [pætrɪ'ɔtɪk] a patriotique; *(person)* patriote.

patrol [pə'trəul] n patrouille f // vt patrouiller dans; **~ car** n voiture f de police; **~man** n *(US)* agent m de police.

patron ['peɪtrən] n *(in shop)* client/e; *(of charity)* patron/ne; **~ of the arts** mécène m; **~ize** ['pætrənaɪz] vt être *(un)* client or un habitué de; *(fig)* traiter avec condescendance.

patter ['pætə*] n crépitement m, tapotement m; *(sales talk)* boniment m.

pattern ['pætən] n modèle m; *(SEWING)* patron m; *(design)* motif m; *(sample)* échantillon m.

paunch [pɔ:ntʃ] n gros ventre, bedaine

f.

pauper ['pɔ:pə*] n indigent/e.
pause [pɔ:z] n pause f, arrêt m; (MUS) silence m // vi faire une pause, s'arrêter.
pave [peɪv] vt paver, daller; **to ~ the way for** ouvrir la voie à.
pavement ['peɪvmənt] n (Brit) trottoir m.
pavilion [pə'vɪlɪən] n pavillon m; tente f.
paving ['peɪvɪŋ] n pavage m, dallage m; **~ stone** n pavé m.
paw [pɔ:] n patte f.
pawn [pɔ:n] n gage m; (CHESS, also fig) pion m // vt mettre en gage; **~broker** n prêteur m sur gages; **~shop** n mont-de-piété m.
pay [peɪ] n salaire m; paie f // vb (pt, pp paid) vt payer // vi payer; (be profitable) être rentable; **to ~ attention (to)** prêter attention (à); **to ~ back** vt rembourser; **to ~ for** vt payer; **to ~ in** vt verser; **to ~ off** vt régler, acquitter; rembourser // vi (scheme, decision) se révéler payant(e); **to ~ up** vt régler; **~able** a: **~able to sb** à l'ordre de qn; **~ee** n bénéficiaire m/f; **~ envelope** n (US) = **~ packet**; **~ment** n paiement m; règlement m; versement m; **advance ~ment** acompte m; paiement anticipé; **monthly ~ment** mensualité f; **~ packet** n (Brit) paie f; **~phone** n cabine f téléphonique, téléphone public; **~roll** n registre m du personnel; **~ slip** n bulletin m de paie.
PC n abbr of **personal computer**.
p.c. abbr of **per cent**.
pea [pi:] n (petit) pois.
peace [pi:s] n paix f; (calm) calme m, tranquillité f; **~able** a paisible; **~ful** a paisible, calme.
peach [pi:tʃ] n pêche f.
peacock ['pi:kɔk] n paon m.
peak [pi:k] n (mountain) pic m, cime f; (fig: highest level) maximum m; (: of career, fame) apogée m; **~ hours** npl heures fpl d'affluence.
peal [pi:l] n (of bells) carillon m; **~s of laughter** éclats mpl de rire.
peanut ['pi:nʌt] n arachide f, cacahuète f.
pear [pɛə*] n poire f.
pearl [pə:l] n perle f.
peasant ['pɛznt] n paysan/ne.
peat [pi:t] n tourbe f.
pebble ['pɛbl] n galet m, caillou m.
peck [pɛk] vt (also: ~ at) donner un coup de bec à; (food) picorer // n coup de bec; (kiss) bécot m; **~ing order** n ordre m des préséances; **~ish** a (Brit col): **I feel ~ish** je mangerais bien quelque chose.
peculiar [pɪ'kju:lɪə*] a étrange, bizarre, curieux(euse); particulier(ère); **~ to**

particulier à.
pedal ['pɛdl] n pédale f // vi pédaler.
pedantic [pɪ'dæntɪk] a pédant(e).
peddler ['pɛdlə*] n marchand ambulant.
pedestal ['pɛdəstl] n piédestal m.
pedestrian [pɪ'dɛstrɪən] n piéton m; **~ crossing** n (Brit) passage clouté.
pediatrics [pi:dɪ'ætrɪks] n (US) = **paediatrics**.
pedigree ['pɛdɪgri:] n ascendance f; (of animal) pedigree m // cpd (animal) de race.
pedlar ['pɛdlə*] n = **peddler**.
pee [pi:] vi (col) faire pipi, pisser.
peek [pi:k] vi jeter un coup d'œil (furtif).
peel [pi:l] n pelure f, épluchure f; (of orange, lemon) écorce f // vt peler, éplucher // vi (paint etc) s'écailler, (wallpaper) se décoller.
peep [pi:p] n (Brit: look) coup d'œil furtif; (sound) pépiement m // vi (Brit) jeter un coup d'œil (furtif); **to ~ out** vi se montrer (furtivement); **~hole** n judas m.
peer [pɪə*] vi: **to ~ at** regarder attentivement, scruter // n (noble) pair m; (equal) pair, égal/e; **~age** n pairie f.
peeved [pi:vd] a irrité(e), ennuyé(e).
peevish ['pi:vɪʃ] a grincheux(euse), maussade.
peg [pɛg] n cheville f; (for coat etc) patère f; (Brit: also: **clothes ~**) pince f à linge // vt (prices) contrôler, stabiliser.
Peking [pi:'kɪŋ] n Pékin.
pelican crossing ['pɛlɪkən-] n (Brit AUT) feu m à commande manuelle.
pellet ['pɛlɪt] n boulette f; (of lead) plomb m.
pelmet ['pɛlmɪt] n cantonnière f; lambrequin m.
pelt [pɛlt] vt: **to ~ sb (with)** bombarder qn (de) // vi (rain) tomber à seaux // n peau f.
pelvis ['pɛlvɪs] n bassin m.
pen [pɛn] n (for writing) stylo m; (for sheep) parc m.
penal ['pi:nl] a pénal(e); **~ize** vt pénaliser; (fig) désavantager.
penalty ['pɛnltɪ] n pénalité f; sanction f; (fine) amende f; (SPORT) pénalisation f; **~ (kick)** n (FOOTBALL) penalty m.
penance ['pɛnəns] n pénitence f.
pence [pɛns] npl of **penny**.
pencil ['pɛnsl] n crayon m; **~ case** n trousse f (d'écolier); **~ sharpener** n taille-crayon(s) m inv.
pendant ['pɛndnt] n pendentif m.
pending ['pɛndɪŋ] prep en attendant // a en suspens.
pendulum ['pɛndjuləm] n pendule m; (of clock) balancier m.
penetrate ['pɛnɪtreɪt] vt pénétrer dans; pénétrer.

penfriend ['pɛnfrɛnd] *n* (*Brit*) correspondant/e.

penguin ['pɛŋgwɪn] *n* pingouin *m*.

penicillin [pɛnɪ'sɪlɪn] *n* pénicilline *f*.

peninsula [pə'nɪnsjulə] *n* péninsule *f*.

penis ['piːnɪs] *n* pénis *m*, verge *f*.

penitent ['pɛnɪtnt] *a* repentant(e).

penitentiary [pɛnɪ'tɛnʃərɪ] *n* (*US*) prison *f*.

penknife ['pɛnnaɪf] *n* canif *m*.

pen name *n* nom *m* de plume, pseudonyme *m*.

penniless ['pɛnɪlɪs] *a* sans le sou.

penny, pl pennies or (*Brit*) **pence** ['pɛnɪ, 'pɛnɪz, pɛns] *n* penny *m* (*pl* pennies); (*US*) = cent.

penpal ['pɛnpæl] *n* correspondant/e.

pension ['pɛnʃən] *n* retraite *f*; (*MIL*) pension *f*; **~er** *n* (*Brit*) retraité/e.

penthouse ['pɛnthaus] *n* appartement *m* (de luxe) en attique.

pent-up ['pɛntʌp] *a* (*feelings*) refoulé(e).

people ['piːpl] *npl* gens *mpl*; personnes *fpl*; (*citizens*) peuple *m* // *n* (*nation, race*) peuple *m* // *vt* peupler; **several ~ came** plusieurs personnes sont venues; **the room was full of ~** la salle était pleine de monde *or* de gens.

pep [pɛp] *n* (*col*) entrain *m*, dynamisme *m*; **to ~ up** *vt* remonter.

pepper ['pɛpə*] *n* poivre *m*; (*vegetable*) poivron *m* // *vt* poivrer; **~mint** *n* (*plant*) menthe poivrée; (*sweet*) pastille *f* de menthe.

peptalk ['pɛptɔːk] *n* (*col*) (petit) discours d'encouragement.

per [pəː*] *prep* par; **~ hour** (*miles etc*) à l'heure; (*fee*) (de) l'heure; **~ kilo** *etc* le kilo *etc*; **~ day/person** par jour/personne; **~ annum** *ad* par an; **~ capita** *a*, *ad* par personne, par habitant.

perceive [pə'siːv] *vt* percevoir; (*notice*) remarquer, s'apercevoir de.

per cent [pəː'sɛnt] *ad* pour cent.

percentage [pə'sɛntɪdʒ] *n* pourcentage *m*.

perception [pə'sɛpʃən] *n* perception *f*; sensibilité *f*; perspicacité *f*.

perceptive [pə'sɛptɪv] *a* pénétrant(e); perspicace.

perch [pəːtʃ] *n* (*fish*) perche *f*; (*for bird*) perchoir *m* // *vi* (se) percher.

percolator ['pəːkəleɪtə*] *n* percolateur *m*; cafetière *f* électrique.

perennial [pə'rɛnɪəl] *a* perpétuel(le); (*BOT*) vivace // *n* plante *f* vivace.

perfect *a n*, ['pəːfɪkt] *a* parfait(e) // *n* (*also*: **~ tense**) parfait *m* // *vt* [pə'fɛkt] parfaire; mettre au point; **~ly** *ad* parfaitement.

perforate ['pəːfəreɪt] *vt* perforer, percer; **perforation** [-'reɪʃən] *n* perforation *f*; (*line of holes*) pointillé *m*.

perform [pə'fɔːm] *vt* (*carry out*) exé-

cuter, remplir; (*concert etc*) jouer, donner // *vi* jouer; **~ance** *n* représentation *f*, spectacle *m*; (*of an artist*) interprétation *f*; (*of player etc*) prestation *f*; (*of car, engine*) performance *f*; **~er** *n* artiste *m/f*; **~ing** *a* (*animal*) savant(e).

perfume ['pəːfjuːm] *n* parfum *m*.

perfunctory [pə'fʌŋktərɪ] *a* négligent(e), pour la forme.

perhaps [pə'hæps] *ad* peut-être.

peril ['pɛrɪl] *n* péril *m*.

perimeter [pə'rɪmɪtə*] *n* périmètre *m*; **~ wall** *n* mur *m* d'enceinte.

period ['pɪərɪəd] *n* période *f*; (*HISTORY*) époque *f*; (*SCOL*) cours *m*; (*full stop*) point *m*; (*MED*) règles *fpl* // *a* (*costume, furniture*) d'époque; **~ic** [-'ɔdɪk] *a* périodique; **~ical** [-'ɔdɪkl] *a* périodique // *n* périodique *m*.

peripheral [pə'rɪfərəl] *a* périphérique // *n* (*COMPUT*) périphérique *m*.

perish ['pɛrɪʃ] *vi* périr, mourir; (*decay*) se détériorer; **~able** *a* périssable.

perjury ['pəːdʒərɪ] *n* (*LAW: in court*) faux témoignage; (*breach of oath*) parjure *m*.

perk [pəːk] *n* avantage *m*, à-côté *m*; **to ~ up** *vi* (*cheer up*) se ragaillardir; **~y** *a* (*cheerful*) guilleret(te), gai(e).

perm [pəːm] *n* (*for hair*) permanente *f*.

permanent ['pəːmənənt] *a* permanent(e).

permeate ['pəːmɪeɪt] *vi* s'infiltrer // *vt* s'infiltrer dans; pénétrer.

permissible [pə'mɪsɪbl] *a* permis(e), acceptable.

permission [pə'mɪʃən] *n* permission *f*, autorisation *f*.

permissive [pə'mɪsɪv] *a* tolérant(e); **the ~ society** la société de tolérance.

permit *n* ['pəːmɪt] permis *m* // *vt* [pə'mɪt] permettre; **to ~ sb to do** autoriser qn à faire, permettre à qn de faire.

perpendicular [pəːpən'dɪkjulə*] *a*, *n* perpendiculaire (*f*).

perplex [pə'plɛks] *vt* rendre perplexe; (*complicate*) embrouiller.

persecute ['pəːsɪkjuːt] *vt* persécuter.

persevere [pəːsɪ'vɪə*] *vi* persévérer.

Persian ['pəːʃən] *a* persan(e) // *n* (*LING*) persan *m*; **the (~) Gulf** le golfe Persique.

persist [pə'sɪst] *vi*: **to ~ (in doing)** persister (à faire), s'obstiner (à faire); **~ent** *a* persistant(e), tenace.

person ['pəːsn] *n* personne *f*; **in ~** en personne; **~able** *a* de belle prestance, au physique attrayant; **~al** *a* personnel(le); individuel(le); **~al assistant (P.A.)** *n* secrétaire privé/e; **~al computer (PC)** *n* ordinateur individuel; **~ality** [-'nælɪtɪ] *n* personnalité *f*; **~ally** *ad* personnellement.

personnel [pə:səˈnɛl] n personnel m.

perspective [pəˈspɛktɪv] n perspective f.

perspiration [pə:spɪˈreɪʃən] n transpiration f.

persuade [pəˈsweɪd] vt: to ~ sb to do sth persuader qn de faire qch, amener or décider qn à faire qch.

pert [pə:t] a (bold) effronté(e), impertinent(e).

pertaining [pə:ˈteɪnɪŋ]: ~ to prep relatif(ive) à.

peruse [pəˈru:z] vt lire (attentivement).

pervade [pəˈveɪd] vt se répandre dans, envahir.

perverse [pəˈvə:s] a pervers(e); (stubborn) entêté(e), contrariant(e).

pervert n [ˈpə:və:t] perverti/e // vt [pəˈvə:t] pervertir.

pessimist [ˈpɛsɪmɪst] n pessimiste m/f; ~ic [-ˈmɪstɪk] a pessimiste.

pest [pɛst] n animal m (or insecte m) nuisible; (fig) fléau m.

pester [ˈpɛstə*] vt importuner, harceler.

pet [pɛt] n animal familier; (favourite) chouchou m // vt choyer // vi (col) se peloter.

petal [ˈpɛtl] n pétale m.

peter [ˈpi:tə*]: to ~ out vi s'épuiser; s'affaiblir.

petite [pəˈti:t] a menu(e).

petition [pəˈtɪʃən] n pétition f.

petrified [ˈpɛtrɪfaɪd] a (fig) mort(e) de peur.

petrol [ˈpɛtrəl] n (Brit) essence f; twostar ~ essence f ordinaire; four- star ~ super m; ~ can n bidon m à essence.

petroleum [pəˈtrəulɪəm] n pétrole m.

petrol: ~ pump n (Brit) pompe f à essence; ~ **station** n (Brit) stationservice f; ~ **tank** n (Brit) réservoir m d'essence.

petticoat [ˈpɛtɪkəut] n jupon m.

petty [ˈpɛtɪ] a (mean) mesquin(e); (unimportant) insignifiant(e), sans importance; ~ **cash** n menue monnaie; ~ **officer** n second-maître m.

petulant [ˈpɛtjulənt] a irritable.

pew [pju:] n banc m d'église).

pewter [ˈpju:tə*] n étain m.

phantom [ˈfæntəm] n fantôme m; (vision) fantasme m.

pharmacy [ˈfɑ:məsɪ] n pharmacie f.

phase [feɪz] n phase f, période f // vt: to ~ sth in/out introduire/supprimer qch progressivement.

Ph.D. abbr (= Doctor of Philosophy) title ≈ Docteur m en Droit or Lettres etc // n ≈ doctorat m; titulaire m d'un doctorat.

pheasant [ˈfɛznt] n faisan m.

phenomenon [fəˈnɔmɪnən] pl **phenomena** [fəˈnɔmɪnən, -nə] n phénomène m.

philosophical [fɪləˈsɔfɪkl] a philosophique.

philosophy [fɪˈlɔsəfɪ] n philosophie f.

phobia [ˈfəubjə] n phobie f.

phone [fəun] n téléphone m // vt téléphoner; to be on the ~ avoir le téléphone; (be calling) être au téléphone; to ~ **back** vt, vi rappeler; to ~ **up** vt téléphoner à // vi téléphoner; ~ **book** n annuaire m; ~ **box** or **booth** n cabine f téléphonique; ~ **call** n coup m de fil or de téléphone; ~-**in** n (Brit RADIO, TV) programme m à ligne ouverte.

phonetics [fəˈnɛtɪks] n phonétique f.

phoney [ˈfəunɪ] a faux(fausse), factice.

phonograph [ˈfəunəgrɑ:f] n (US) électrophone m.

phony [ˈfəunɪ] a = phoney.

photo [ˈfəutəu] n photo f.

photo... [ˈfəutəu] prefix: ~**copier** n machine f à photocopier; ~**copy** n photocopie f // vt photocopier; ~**graph** n photographie f // vt photographier; ~**grapher** [fəˈtɔgrəfə*] n photographe m/f; ~**graphy** [fəˈtɔgrəfɪ] n photographie f.

phrase [freɪz] n expression f; (LING) locution f // vt exprimer; ~ **book** n recueil m d'expressions (pour touristes).

physical [ˈfɪzɪkl] a physique; ~ **education** n éducation f physique; ~**ly** ad physiquement.

physician [fɪˈzɪʃən] n médecin m.

physicist [ˈfɪzɪsɪst] n physicien/ne.

physics [ˈfɪzɪks] n physique f.

physiotherapy [fɪzɪəuˈθɛrəpɪ] n kinésithérapie f.

physique [fɪˈzi:k] n physique m; constitution f.

pianist [ˈpi:ənɪst] n pianiste m/f.

piano [pɪˈænəu] n piano m.

pick [pɪk] n (tool: also: ~-axe) pic m, pioche f // vt choisir; (gather) cueillir; take your ~ faites votre choix; the ~ of le(la) meilleur(e) de; to ~ **off** vt (kill) (viser soigneusement et) abattre; to ~ **on** vt fus (person) harceler; to ~ **out** vt choisir; (distinguish) distinguer; to ~ **up** vi (improve) reprendre, s'améliorer // vt ramasser; (telephone) décrocher; (collect) passer prendre; (AUT: give lift to) prendre; (learn) apprendre; to ~ **up** speed prendre de la vitesse; to ~ **o.s. up** se relever.

picket [ˈpɪkɪt] n (in strike) gréviste m/f participant à un piquet de grève; piquet m de grève // vt mettre un piquet de grève devant.

pickle [ˈpɪkl] n (also: ~s: as condiment) pickles mpl // vt conserver dans du vinaigre or dans de la saumure.

pickpocket [ˈpɪkpɔkɪt] n pickpocket m.

pickup [ˈpɪkʌp] n (Brit: on record player) bras m pick-up; (small truck) pick-up m inv.

picnic [ˈpɪknɪk] n pique-nique m.

pictorial [pɪkˈtɔ:rɪəl] a illustré(e).

picture [ˈpɪktʃə*] n image f; (painting)

peinture *f*, tableau *m*; (*photograph*) photo(graphie) *f*; (*drawing*) dessin *m*; (*film*) film *m* // *vt* se représenter; (*describe*) dépeindre, représenter; **the ~s** (*Brit*) le cinéma; **~ book** *n* livre *m* d'images.

picturesque [pɪktʃə'resk] *a* pittoresque.

pie [paɪ] *n* tourte *f*; (*of meat*) pâté *m* en croûte.

piece [piːs] *n* morceau *m*; (*of land*) parcelle *f*; (*item*): **a ~ of furniture/ advice** un meuble/conseil // *vt*: **to ~ together** rassembler; **to take to ~s** démonter; **~meal** *ad* par bouts; **~work** *n* travail *m* aux pièces.

pie chart *n* graphique *m* à secteurs, camembert *m*.

pier [pɪə*] *n* jetée *f*; (*of bridge etc*) pile *f*.

pierce [pɪəs] *vt* percer, transpercer.

pig [pɪg] *n* cochon *m*, porc *m*.

pigeon ['pɪdʒən] *n* pigeon *m*; **~hole** *n* casier *m*.

piggy bank ['pɪgɪbæŋk] *n* tirelire *f*.

pigheaded ['pɪg'hedɪd] *a* entêté(e), têtu(e).

pigskin ['pɪgskɪn] *n* (peau *m* de) porc *m*.

pigsty ['pɪgstaɪ] *n* porcherie *f*.

pigtail ['pɪgteɪl] *n* natte *f*, tresse *f*.

pike [paɪk] *n* (*spear*) pique *f*; (*fish*) brochet *m*.

pilchard ['pɪltʃəd] *n* pilchard *m* (*sorte de sardine*).

pile [paɪl] *n* (*pillar, of books*) pile *f*; (*heap*) tas *m*; (*of carpet*) épaisseur *f* // *vb* (*also:* **~ up**) *vt* empiler, entasser // *vi* s'entasser; **~ into** (*car*) s'entasser dans.

piles [paɪlz] *npl* hémorroïdes *fpl*.

pileup ['paɪlʌp] *n* (*AUT*) télescopage *m*, collision *f* en série.

pilfering ['pɪlfərɪŋ] *n* chapardage *m*.

pilgrim ['pɪlgrɪm] *n* pèlerin *m*.

pill [pɪl] *n* pilule *f*; **the ~** la pilule.

pillage ['pɪlɪdʒ] *vt* piller.

pillar ['pɪlə*] *n* pilier *m*; **~ box** *n* (*Brit*) boîte *f* aux lettres.

pillion ['pɪljən] *n* (*of motor cycle*) siège *m* arrière.

pillow ['pɪləu] *n* oreiller *m*; **~case** *n* taie *f* d'oreiller.

pilot ['paɪlət] *n* pilote *m* // *cpd* (*scheme etc*) pilote, expérimental(e) // *vt* piloter; **~ light** *n* veilleuse *f*.

pimp [pɪmp] *n* souteneur *m*, maquereau *m*.

pimple ['pɪmpl] *n* bouton *m*.

pin [pɪn] *n* épingle *f*; (*TECH*) cheville *f* // *vt* épingler; **~s and needles** fourmis *fpl*; **to ~ sb down** (*fig*) obliger qn à répondre; **to ~ sth on sb** (*fig*) mettre qch sur le dos de qn.

pinafore ['pɪnəfɔː*] *n* tablier *m*.

pinball ['pɪnbɔːl] *n* (*also:* **~ machine**)

flipper *m*.

pincers ['pɪnsəz] *npl* tenailles *fpl*.

pinch [pɪntʃ] *n* pincement *m*; (*of salt etc*) pincée *f* // *vt* pincer; (*col: steal*) piquer, chiper // *vi* (*shoe*) serrer; **at a ~** à la rigueur.

pincushion ['pɪnkuʃən] *n* pelote *f* à épingles.

pine [paɪn] *n* (*also:* **~ tree**) pin *m* // *vi*: **to ~ for** aspirer à, désirer ardemment; **to ~ away** *vi* dépérir.

pineapple ['paɪnæpl] *n* ananas *m*.

ping [pɪŋ] *n* (*noise*) tintement *m*; **~-pong** *n* ® ping-pong *m* ®.

pink [pɪŋk] *n* rose *f* // *a* (*colour*) rose *m*; (*BOT*) œillet *m*, mignardise *f*.

pinpoint ['pɪnpɔɪnt] *vt* indiquer (avec précision).

pint [paɪnt] *n* pinte *f* (*Brit = 0.57 l; US = 0.47 l*); (*Brit col*) ≈ demi *m*, ≈ pot *m*.

pioneer [paɪə'nɪə*] *n* explorateur/trice; (*early settler, fig*) pionnier *m*.

pious ['paɪəs] *a* pieux(euse).

pip [pɪp] *n* (*seed*) pépin *m*; (*Brit: time signal on radio*) top *m*.

pipe [paɪp] *n* tuyau *m*, conduite *f*; (*for smoking*) pipe *f*; (*MUS*) pipeau *m* // *vt* amener par tuyau; **~s** *npl* (*also:* **bag~s**) cornemuse *f*; **to ~ down** *vi* (*col: be taire*; **~ cleaner** *n* cure-pipe *m*; **~ dream** *n* chimère *f*, utopie *f*; **~line** *n* pipe-line *m*; **~r** *n* joueur/euse de pipeau (*or de cornemuse*).

piping ['paɪpɪŋ] *ad*: **~ hot** très chaud(e).

pique ['piːk] *n* dépit *m*.

pirate ['paɪərət] *n* pirate *m*.

Pisces ['paɪsiːz] *n* les Poissons *mpl*.

piss [pɪs] *vi* (*col*) pisser; **~ed** *a* (*col: drunk*) bourré(e).

pistol ['pɪstl] *n* pistolet *m*.

piston ['pɪstən] *n* piston *m*.

pit [pɪt] *n* trou *m*, fosse *f*; (*also:* **coal ~**) puits *m* de mine; (*also:* **orchestra ~**) fosse *f* d'orchestre // *vt*: **to ~ sb against sb** opposer qn à qn; **~s** *npl* (*AUT*) aire *f* de service.

pitch [pɪtʃ] *n* (*throw*) lancement *m*; (*MUS*) ton *m*; (*of voice*) hauteur *f*; (*Brit SPORT*) terrain *m*; (*NAUT*) tangage *m*; (*tar*) poix *f* // *vt* (*throw*) lancer // *vi* (*fall*) tomber; (*NAUT*) tanguer; **to ~ a tent** dresser une tente; **~ed battle** *n* bataille rangée.

pitcher ['pɪtʃə*] *n* cruche *f*.

pitchfork ['pɪtʃfɔːk] *n* fourche *f*.

piteous ['pɪtɪəs] *a* pitoyable.

pitfall ['pɪtfɔːl] *n* trappe *f*, piège *m*.

pith [pɪθ] *n* (*of plant*) moelle *f*; (*of orange*) intérieur *m* de l'écorce; (*fig*) essence *f*; vigueur *f*.

pithy ['pɪθɪ] *a* piquant(e); vigoureux(euse).

pitiful ['pɪtɪful] *a* (*touching*) pitoyable; (*contemptible*) lamentable.

pitiless ['pɪtɪlɪs] *a* impitoyable.

pittance ['pɪtns] n salaire m de misère.
pity ['pɪtɪ] n pitié f // vt plaindre; **what a ~!** quel dommage!
pivot ['pɪvət] n pivot m.
pizza ['piːtsə] n pizza f.
placard ['plækɑːd] n affiche f.
placate [plə'keɪt] vt apaiser, calmer.
place [pleɪs] n endroit m, lieu m; (proper position, rank, seat) place f; (house) maison f, logement m; (home) at/to his ~ chez lui // vt (object) placer, mettre; (identify) situer; reconnaître; **to take ~** avoir lieu; se passer; **to change ~s with sb** changer de place avec qn; **to ~ an order** passer une commande; **out of ~** (not suitable) déplacé(e), inopportun(e); **in the first ~** d'abord, en premier.
plague [pleɪg] n fléau m; (MED) peste f // vt (fig) tourmenter.
plaice [pleɪs] n (pl inv) carrelet m.
plaid [plæd] n tissu écossais.
plain [pleɪn] a (clear) clair(e), évident(e); (simple) simple, ordinaire; (frank) franc(franche); (not handsome) quelconque, ordinaire; (cigarette) sans filtre; (without seasoning etc) nature inv; (in one colour) uni(e) // ad franchement, carrément // n plaine f; ~ **chocolate** n chocolat m à croquer; ~ **clothes**: **in ~ clothes** (police) en civil; ~**ly** ad clairement; (frankly) carrément, sans détours.
plaintiff ['pleɪntɪf] n plaignant/e.
plait [plæt] n tresse f, natte f.
plan [plæn] n plan m; (scheme) projet m// vt (think in advance) projeter; (prepare) organiser // vi faire des projets.
plane [pleɪn] n (AVIAT) avion m; (tree) platane m; (tool) rabot m; (ART, MATH etc) plan m // a plan(e), plat(e) // vt (with tool) raboter.
planet ['plænɪt] n planète f.
plank [plæŋk] n planche f.
planning ['plænɪŋ] n planification f; **family ~** planning familial; ~ **permission** n permis m de construire.
plant [plɑːnt] n plante f; (machinery) matériel m; (factory) usine f // vt planter; (colony) établir; (bomb) déposer, poser.
plaster ['plɑːstə*] n plâtre m; (also: ~ **of Paris**) plâtre à mouler; (Brit: also: **sticking ~**) pansement adhésif // vt plâtrer; (cover): **to ~ with** couvrir de; **in ~** (leg etc) dans le plâtre; ~**ed** a (col) soûl(e).
plastic ['plæstɪk] n plastique m // a (made of plastic) en plastique; (flexible) plastique, malléable; (art) plastique; ~ **bag** n sac m en plastique.
plasticine ['plæstɪsiːn] n ® pâte f à modeler.
plastic surgery n chirurgie f esthétique.
plate [pleɪt] n (dish) assiette f; (sheet of metal, PHOT) plaque f; (in book) gravure f.
plateau, ~s or **~x** ['plætəu, -z] n plateau m.
plate glass n verre m (de vitrine).
platform ['plætfɔːm] n (at meeting) tribune f; (Brit: of bus) plate-forme f; (stage) estrade f; (RAIL) quai m; ~ **ticket** n (Brit) billet m de quai.
platinum ['plætɪnəm] n platine m.
platoon [plə'tuːn] n peloton m.
platter ['plætə*] n plat m.
plausible ['plɔːzɪbl] a plausible; (person) convaincant(e).
play [pleɪ] n jeu m; (THEATRE) pièce f (de théâtre) // vt (game) jouer à; (team, opponent) jouer contre; (instrument) jouer de; (play, part, piece of music, note) jouer // vi jouer; **to ~ safe** ne prendre aucun risque; **to ~ down** vt minimiser; **to ~ up** vi (cause trouble) faire des siennes; ~**boy** n playboy m; ~**er** n joueur/euse; (THEATRE) acteur/trice; (MUS) musicien/ne; ~**ful** a enjoué(e); ~**ground** n cour f de récréation; ~**group** n garderie f; ~**ing card** n carte f à jouer; ~**ing field** n terrain m de sport; ~**mate** n camarade m/f, copain/copine; ~**-off** n (SPORT) belle f; ~**pen** n parc m (pour bébé); ~**school** n = ~**group**; ~**thing** n jouet m; ~**wright** n dramaturge m.
plc abbr (= public limited company) SARL f.
plea [pliː] n (request) appel m; (excuse) excuse f; (LAW) défense f.
plead [pliːd] vt plaider; (give as excuse) invoquer // vi (LAW) plaider; (beg): **to ~ with sb** implorer qn.
pleasant ['plɛznt] a agréable; ~**ries** npl (polite remarks) civilités fpl.
please [pliːz] vt plaire à // vi (think fit): **do as you ~** faites comme il vous plaira; ~**!** s'il te (or vous) plaît; ~ **yourself!** à ta (or votre) guise!; ~**d** a: ~**d** (with) content(e) (de); ~**d to meet you** enchanté (de faire votre connaissance); **pleasing** a plaisant(e), qui fait plaisir.
pleasure ['plɛʒə*] n plaisir m; 'it's a ~' 'je vous en prie'.
pleat [pliːt] n pli m.
pledge [plɛdʒ] n gage m; (promise) promesse f // vt engager; promettre.
plentiful ['plɛntɪful] a abondant(e), copieux(euse).
plenty ['plɛntɪ] n abondance f; ~ **of** beaucoup de; (bien) assez de.
pliable ['plaɪəbl] a flexible; (person) malléable.
pliers ['plaɪəz] npl pinces fpl.
plight [plaɪt] n situation f critique.
plimsolls ['plɪmsəlz] npl (Brit) (chaussures fpl de) tennis fpl.
plinth [plɪnθ] n socle m.
plod [plɔd] vi avancer péniblement; (fig)

peiner; ~**der** n bûcheur/euse.

plonk [plɔŋk] (col) n (Brit: wine) pinard m, piquette f // vt: **to ~ sth down** poser brusquement qch.

plot [plɔt] n complot m, conspiration f; (of story, play) intrigue f; (of land) lot m de terrain, lopin m // vt (mark out) pointer; relever; (conspire) comploter // vi comploter; ~**ter** n (instrument) table traçante, traceur m.

plough, (US) **plow** [plau] n charrue f // vt (earth) labourer; **to ~ back** vt (COMM) réinvestir; **to ~ through** vt fus (snow etc) avancer péniblement dans.

ploy [plɔɪ] n stratagème m.

pluck [plʌk] vt (fruit) cueillir; (musical instrument) pincer; (bird) plumer // n courage m, cran m; **to ~ up courage** prendre son courage à deux mains; ~**y** a courageux(euse).

plug [plʌg] n bouchon m, bonde f; (ELEC) prise f de courant; (AUT: also: **spark(ing)** ~) bougie f // vt (hole) boucher; (col: advertise) faire du battage pour, matraquer; **to ~ in** vt (ELEC) brancher.

plum [plʌm] n (fruit) prune f // a: ~ **job** (col) travail m en or.

plumb [plʌm] a vertical(e) // n plomb m // ad (exactly) en plein // vt sonder.

plumber ['plʌmə*] n plombier m.

plumbing ['plʌmɪŋ] n (trade) plomberie f; (piping) tuyauterie f.

plummet ['plʌmɪt] vi plonger, dégringoler.

plump [plʌmp] a rondelet(te), dodu(e), bien en chair // vt: **to ~ sth (down)** on laisser tomber qch lourdement sur; **to ~ for** vt fus (col: choose) se décider pour.

plunder ['plʌndə*] n pillage m // vt piller.

plunge [plʌndʒ] n plongeon m // vt plonger // vi (fall) tomber, dégringoler; **to take the ~** se jeter à l'eau; ~**r** n piston m; (débouchoir m à) ventouse f.

pluperfect [plu:'pə:fɪkt] n plus-que-parfait m.

plural ['pluərl] a pluriel(le) // n pluriel m.

plus [plʌs] n (also: ~ **sign**) signe m plus // prep plus; **ten/twenty ~** plus de dix/ vingt.

plush [plʌʃ] a somptueux(euse).

ply [plaɪ] n (of wool) fil m; (of wood) feuille f, épaisseur f // vt (tool) manier; (a trade) exercer // vi (ship) faire la navette; **to ~ sb with drink** donner continuellement à boire à qn; ~**wood** n contre-plaqué m.

P.M. abbr of **Prime Minister**.

p.m. ad abbr (= post meridiem) de l'après-midi.

pneumatic drill [nju:'mætɪk-] n marteau-piqueur m.

pneumonia [nju:'məunɪə] n pneumonie f.

poach [pəutʃ] vt (cook) pocher; (steal) pêcher (or chasser) sans permis // vi braconner; ~**er** n braconnier m.

P.O. Box n abbr of **Post Office Box**.

pocket ['pɔkɪt] n poche f // vt empocher; **to be out of ~** (Brit) en être de sa poche; ~**book** n (wallet) portefeuille m; (notebook) carnet m; ~ **knife** n canif m; ~ **money** n argent m de poche.

pod [pɔd] n cosse f.

podgy ['pɔdʒɪ] a rondelet(te).

podiatrist [pɔ'di:ətrɪst] n (US) pédicure m/f, podologue m/f.

poem ['pəuɪm] n poème m.

poet ['pəuɪt] n poète m; ~**ic** [-'ɛtɪk] a poétique; ~ **laureate** n poète lauréat (nommé et appointé par la Cour royale); ~**ry** n poésie f.

poignant ['pɔɪnjənt] a poignant(e); (sharp) vif(vive).

point [pɔɪnt] n (tip) pointe f; (in time) moment m; (in space) endroit m; (GEOM, SCOL, SPORT, on scale) point m; (subject, idea) point, sujet m; (also: **decimal** ~): **2 ~ 3 (2.3)** 2 virgule 3 (2,3) // vt (show) indiquer; (wall, window) jointoyer; (gun etc): **to ~** at braquer or diriger qch sur // vi montrer du doigt; ~**s** npl (AUT) vis platinées; (RAIL) aiguillage m; **to be on the ~ of doing sth** être sur le point de faire qch; **to make a ~** faire une remarque; **to get the ~** comprendre, saisir; **to come to the ~** en venir au fait; **there's no ~ (in doing)** cela ne sert à rien (de faire); **to ~ out** vt faire remarquer, souligner; **to ~ to** vt fus montrer du doigt; (fig) signaler; ~-**blank** ad (also: **at ~-blank range**) à bout portant; (fig) catégorique; ~**ed** a (shape) pointu(e); (remark) plein(e) de sous-entendus; ~**edly** ad d'une manière significative; ~**er** n (stick) baguette f; (needle) aiguille f; (dog) chien m d'arrêt; ~**less** a inutile, vain(e); ~ **of view** n point m de vue.

poise [pɔɪz] n (balance) équilibre m; (of head, body) port m; (calmness) calme m // vt placer en équilibre.

poison ['pɔɪzn] n poison m // vt empoisonner; ~**ing** n empoisonnement m; ~**ous** a (snake) venimeux(euse); (substance etc) vénéneux(euse).

poke [pəuk] vt (fire) tisonner; (jab with finger, stick etc) piquer; pousser du doigt; (put): **to ~ sth in(to)** fourrer or enfoncer qch dans; **to ~ about** vi fureter.

poker ['pəukə*] n tisonnier m; (CARDS) poker m; ~-**faced** a au visage impassible.

poky ['pəukɪ] a exigu(ë).

Poland ['pəulənd] n Pologne f.

polar ['pəulə*] a polaire; ~ **bear** n ours

blanc.

Pole [pəul] *n* Polonais/e.

pole [pəul] *n* (*of wood*) mât *m*, perche *f*; (*ELEC*) poteau *m*; (*GEO*) pôle *m*; ~ **bean** *n* (*US*) haricot *m* (à rames); ~ **vault** *n* saut *m* à la perche.

police [pə'li:s] *npl* police *f* // *vt* maintenir l'ordre dans; ~ **car** *n* voiture *f* de police; ~**man** *n* agent *m* de police, policier *m*; ~ **station** *n* commissariat *m* de police; ~**woman** *n* femme-agent *f*.

policy ['pɔlɪsɪ] *n* politique *f*; (*also:* **insurance** ~) police *f* (d'assurance).

polio ['pəulɪəu] *n* polio *f*.

Polish ['pəulɪʃ] *a* polonais(e) // *n* (*LING*) polonais *m*.

polish ['pɔlɪʃ] *n* (*for shoes*) cirage *m*; (*for floor*) cire *f*, encaustique *f*; (*for nails*) vernis *m*; (*shine*) éclat *m*, poli *m*; (*fig: refinement*) raffinement *m* // *vt* (*put polish on shoes, wood*) cirer; (*make shiny*) astiquer, faire briller; (*fig: improve*) perfectionner; **to ~ off** *vt* (*work*) expédier; (*food*) liquider; ~**ed** *a* (*fig*) raffiné(e).

polite [pə'laɪt] *a* poli(e); ~**ness** *n* politesse *f*.

politic ['pɔlɪtɪk] *a* diplomatique; ~**al** [pə'lɪtɪkl] *a* politique; ~**ally** *ad* politiquement; ~**ian** [-'tɪʃən] *n* homme *m* politique, politicien *m*; ~**s** *npl* politique *f*.

polka ['pɔlkə] *n* polka *f*; ~ **dot** *n* pois *m*.

poll [pəul] *n* scrutin *m*, vote *m*; (*also:* **opinion** ~) sondage *m* (d'opinion) // *vt* obtenir.

pollen ['pɔlən] *n* pollen *m*.

polling ['pəulɪŋ] (*Brit*): ~ **booth** *n* isoloir *m*; ~ **day** *n* jour *m* des élections; ~ **station** *n* bureau *m* de vote.

pollution [pə'lu:ʃən] *n* pollution *f*.

polo ['pəuləu] *n* polo *m*; ~-**neck** *a* à col roulé.

polytechnic [pɔlɪ'tɛknɪk] *n* (*college*) I.U.T. *m*, Institut *m* Universitaire de Technologie.

polythene ['pɔlɪθi:n] *n* polyéthylène *m*; ~ **bag** *n* sac *m* en plastique.

pomegranate ['pɔmɪgrænɪt] *n* grenade *f*.

pomp [pɔmp] *n* pompe *f*, faste *f*, apparat *m*.

pompous ['pɔmpəs] *a* pompeux(euse).

pond [pɔnd] *n* étang *m*; mare *f*.

ponder ['pɔndə*] *vt* considérer, peser; ~**ous** *a* pesant(e), lourd(e).

pong [pɔŋ] *n* (*Brit col*) puanteur *f*.

pony ['pəunɪ] *n* poney *m*; ~**tail** *n* queue *f* de cheval; ~ **trekking** *n* (*Brit*) randonnée *f* à cheval.

poodle ['pu:dl] *n* caniche *m*.

pool [pu:l] *n* (*of rain*) flaque *f*; (*pond*) mare *f*; (*artificial*) bassin *m*; (*also:*

swimming ~) piscine *f*; (*sth shared*) fonds commun; (*money at cards*) cagnotte *f*; (*billiards*) poule *f* // *vt* mettre en commun; **typing** ~ pool *m* dactylographique; (*football*) ~s *npl* ≈ loto sportif.

poor [puə*] *a* pauvre; (*mediocre*) médiocre, faible, mauvais(e) // *npl:* **the** ~ les pauvres *mpl*; ~**ly** *ad* pauvrement; médiocrement // *a* souffrant(e), malade.

pop [pɔp] *n* (*noise*) bruit sec; (*MUS*) musique *f* pop; (*US col: father*) papa *m* // *vt* (*put*) fourrer, mettre (rapidement) // *vi* éclater; (*cork*) sauter; **to ~ in** *vi* entrer en passant; **to ~ out** *vi* sortir; **to ~ up** *vi* apparaître, surgir; ~ **concert** *n* concert *m* pop.

pope [pəup] *n* pape *m*.

poplar ['pɔplə*] *n* peuplier *m*.

poppy ['pɔpɪ] *n* coquelicot *m*; pavot *m*.

popsicle ['pɔpsɪkl] *n* (*US*) esquimau *m*.

popular ['pɔpjulə*] *a* populaire; (*fashionable*) à la mode; ~**ize** *vt* populariser; (*science*) vulgariser.

population [pɔpju'leɪʃən] *n* population *f*.

porcelain ['pɔ:slɪn] *n* porcelaine *f*.

porch [pɔ:tʃ] *n* porche *m*.

porcupine ['pɔ:kjupaɪn] *n* porc-épic *m*.

pore [pɔ:*] *n* pore *m* // *vi:* **to ~ over** s'absorber dans, être plongé(e) dans.

pork [pɔ:k] *n* porc *m*.

pornography [pɔ:'nɔgrəfɪ] *n* pornographie *f*.

porpoise ['pɔ:pəs] *n* marsouin *m*.

porridge ['pɔrɪdʒ] *n* porridge *m*.

port [pɔ:t] *n* (*harbour*) port *m*; (*opening in ship*) sabord *m*; (*NAUT: left side*) bâbord *m*; (*wine*) porto *m*; ~ **of call** escale *f*.

portable ['pɔ:təbl] *a* portatif(ive).

portent ['pɔ:tɛnt] *n* présage *m*.

porter ['pɔ:tə*] *n* (*for luggage*) porteur *m*; (*doorkeeper*) gardien/ne; portier *m*.

portfolio [pɔ:t'fəulɪəu] *n* portefeuille *m*; (*of artist*) portfolio *m*.

porthole ['pɔ:thəul] *n* hublot *m*.

portion ['pɔ:ʃən] *n* portion *f*, part *f*.

portly ['pɔ:tlɪ] *a* corpulent(e).

portrait ['pɔ:treɪt] *n* portrait *m*.

portray [pɔ:'treɪ] *vt* faire le portrait de; (*in writing*) dépeindre, représenter.

Portugal ['pɔ:tjugl] *n* Portugal *m*.

Portuguese [pɔ:tju'gi:z] *a* portugais(e) // *n* (*pl inv*) Portugais/e; (*LING*) portugais *m*.

pose [pəuz] *n* pose *f*; (*pej*) affectation *f* // *vi* poser; (*pretend*): **to ~ as** se poser en // *vt* poser, créer.

posh [pɔʃ] *a* (*col*) chic *inv*.

position [pə'zɪʃən] *n* position *f*; (*job*) situation *f*.

positive ['pɔzɪtɪv] *a* positif(ive); (*certain*) sûr(e), certain(e); (*definite*) formel(le), catégorique; indéniable, réel(le).

posse ['pɒsɪ] n (US) détachement m.
possess [pə'zɛs] vt posséder; **~ion**
[pə'zɛʃən] n possession f.
possibility [pɒsɪ'bɪlɪtɪ] n possibilité f;
éventualité f.
possible ['pɒsɪbl] a possible; **as big as ~**
aussi gros que possible.
possibly ['pɒsɪblɪ] ad (perhaps) peut-
être; **if you ~ can** si cela vous est possible; **I cannot ~ come** il m'est impossible
de venir.
post [pəust] n poste f; (Brit: collection)
levée f; (: letters, delivery) courrier m;
(job, situation) poste m; (pole) poteau m
// (Brit: send by post, MIL): to ~
(Brit: appoint): **to ~ to** affecter à;
(notice) afficher; **~age** n affranchissement m; **~al order** n mandat(-
poste) m; **~box** n (Brit) boîte f aux lettres; **~card** n carte postale; **~code** n
(Brit) code postal.
poster ['pəustə*] n affiche f.
poste restante [pəust'rɛstɑ̃:nt] n poste
restante.
postgraduate ['pəust'grædjuət] n ≈
étudiant/e de troisième cycle.
posthumous ['pɒstjuməs] a posthume.
postman ['pəustmən] n facteur m.
postmark ['pəustmɑ:k] n cachet m (de
la poste).
postmaster ['pəustmɑ:stə*] n receveur
m des postes.
post-mortem [pəust'mɔ:təm] n autopsie f.
post office ['pəustɒfɪs] n (building)
poste f; (organization): **the Post Office**
les Postes; **Post Office Box (P.O. Box)**
n boîte postale (B.P.).
postpone [pəs'pəun] vt remettre (à plus
tard), reculer.
posture ['pɒstʃə*] n posture f, attitude f.
postwar [pəust'wɔ:*] a d'après-guerre.
posy ['pəuzɪ] n petit bouquet.
pot [pɒt] n (for cooking) marmite f;
casserole f; (for plants, jam) pot m;
(col: marijuana) herbe f // vt (plant)
mettre en pot; **to go to ~** (col: work,
performance) aller à vau-l'eau.
potato, **~es** [pə'teɪtəu] n pomme f de
terre; **~ peeler** n épluche-légumes m.
potent ['pəutnt] a puissant(e); (drink)
fort(e), très alcoolisé(e).
potential [pə'tɛnʃl] a potentiel(le) // n
potentiel m; **~ly** ad en puissance.
pothole ['pɒthəul] n (in road) nid m de
poule; (Brit: underground) gouffre m,
caverne f; **~ing** n (Brit): **to go**
potholing faire de la spéléologie.
potluck [pɒt'lʌk] n: **to take ~** tenter sa
chance.
potshot ['pɒtʃɒt] n: **to take ~s or a ~ at**
canarder.
potted ['pɒtɪd] a (food) en conserve;
(plant) en pot.
potter ['pɒtə*] n potier m // vi: **to ~**

around, **~ about** bricoler; **~y** n poterie
f.
potty ['pɒtɪ] a (col: mad) dingue // n
(child's) pot m.
pouch [pautʃ] n (ZOOL) poche f; (for
tobacco) blague f.
poultry ['pəultrɪ] n volaille f.
pounce [pauns] vi: **to ~ (on)** bondir
(sur), fondre sur.
pound [paund] n livre f (weight = 453g,
16 ounces; money = 100 pence); (for
dogs, cars) fourrière f // vt (beat)
bourrer de coups, marteler; (crush)
piler, pulvériser // vi (beat) battre
violemment, taper.
pour [pɔ:*] vt verser // vi couler à flots;
(rain) pleuvoir à verse; **to ~ away** or
off vt vider; **to ~ in** vi (people) affluer,
se précipiter; **to ~ out** vi (people)
sortir en masse // vt vider; déverser;
(serve: a drink) verser; **~ing** a: **~ing**
rain pluie torrentielle.
pout [paut] vi faire la moue.
poverty ['pɒvətɪ] n pauvreté f, misère f;
~-stricken a pauvre, déshérité(e).
powder ['paudə*] n poudre f // vt poudrer; **to ~ one's face** or **nose** se poudrer;
~ compact n poudrier m; **~ed milk** n
lait m en poudre; **~ puff** n houppette f;
~ room n toilettes fpl (pour dames).
power ['pauə*] n (strength) puissance f,
force f; (ability, POL: of party, leader)
pouvoir m; (MATH) puissance; (of
speech, thought) faculté f; (ELEC)
courant m // vt faire marcher; **to be in**
~ (POL etc) être au pouvoir; **~ cut** n
(Brit) coupure f de courant; **~ failure** n
panne f de courant; **~ful** a puissant(e);
~less a impuissant(e); **~ point** n
(Brit) prise f de courant; **~ station** n
centrale f électrique.
p.p. abbr (= per procurationem): **~ J.**
Smith pour M. J. Smith.
PR n abbr of **public relations**.
practicable ['præktɪkəbl] a (scheme)
réalisable.
practical ['præktɪkl] a pratique; **~ity**
[-'kælɪtɪ] n (no pl) (of situation etc)
aspect m pratique; **~ joke** n farce f;
~ly ad (almost) pratiquement.
practice ['præktɪs] n pratique f; (of
profession) exercice m; (at football etc)
entraînement m; (business) cabinet m;
clientèle f // vt, vi (US) = **practise**; **in ~**
(in reality) en pratique; **out of ~**
rouillé(e).
practise, (US) **practice** ['præktɪs] vt
(work at: piano, one's backhand etc)
s'exercer à, travailler; (train for: skiing,
running etc) s'entraîner à; (a sport, religion, method) pratiquer; (profession)
exercer // vi s'exercer, travailler; (train)
s'entraîner; **practising** a (Christian etc)
pratiquant(e); (lawyer) en exercice.
practitioner [præk'tɪʃənə*] n praticien/

ne.

prairie ['prɛərɪ] *n* savane *f*; (*US*): the ~s la Prairie.

praise [preɪz] *n* éloge(s) *m(pl)*, louange(s) *f(pl)* // *vt* louer, faire l'éloge de.

pram [præm] *n* (*Brit*) landau *m*, voiture *f* d'enfant.

prance [prɑːns] *vi* (*horse*) caracoler.

prank [præŋk] *n* farce *f*.

prawn [prɔːn] *n* crevette *f* (rose).

pray [preɪ] *vi* prier.

prayer [prɛə*] *n* prière *f*.

preach [priːtʃ] *vt, vi* prêcher.

precaution [prɪ'kɔːʃən] *n* précaution *f*.

precede [prɪ'siːd] *vt, vi* précéder.

precedence ['presɪdəns] *n* préséance *f*.

precedent ['presɪdənt] *n* précédent *m*.

precinct ['priːsɪŋkt] *n* (*round cathedral*) pourtour *m*, enceinte *f*; ~s *npl* (*neighbourhood*) alentours *mpl*, environs *mpl*; **pedestrian** ~ (*Brit*) zone piétonnière.

precious ['preʃəs] *a* précieux(euse).

precipitate *a* [prɪ'sɪpɪtɪt] (*hasty*) précipité(e) // *vt* [prɪ'sɪpɪteɪt] précipiter.

precise [prɪ'saɪs] *a* précis(e); ~**ly** *ad* précisément.

preclude [prɪ'kluːd] *vt* exclure.

precocious [prɪ'kəʊʃəs] *a* précoce.

precondition [priːkən'dɪʃən] *n* condition *f* nécessaire.

predecessor ['priːdɪsesə*] *n* prédécesseur *m*.

predicament [prɪ'dɪkəmənt] *n* situation *f* difficile.

predict [prɪ'dɪkt] *vt* prédire; ~**able** *a* prévisible.

predominantly [prɪ'dɒmɪnəntlɪ] *ad* en majeure partie; surtout.

preen [priːn] *vt*: to ~ itself (*bird*) se lisser les plumes; to ~ o.s. s'admirer.

prefab ['priːfæb] *n* bâtiment préfabriqué.

preface ['prefəs] *n* préface *f*.

prefect ['priːfekt] *n* (*Brit: in school*) élève *chargé*(e) *de certaines fonctions de discipline*; (*in France*) préfet *m*.

prefer [prɪ'fəː*] *vt* préférer; ~**ably** ['prefrəblɪ] *ad* de préférence; ~**ence** ['prefrəns] *n* préférence *f*; ~**ential** [prefə'renʃəl] *a* préférentiel(le); ~**ential treatment** traitement *m* de faveur.

prefix ['priːfɪks] *n* préfixe *m*.

pregnancy ['pregnənsɪ] *n* grossesse *f*.

pregnant ['pregnənt] *a* enceinte *af*.

prehistoric ['priːhɪs'tɔrɪk] *a* préhistorique.

prejudice ['predʒudɪs] *n* préjugé *m*; (*harm*) tort *m*, préjudice *m* // *vt* porter préjudice à; ~**d** *a* (*person*) plein(e) de préjugés; (*view*) préconçu(e), partial(e).

premarital ['priː'mærɪtl] *a* avant le mariage.

premature ['premətʃuə*] *a* prématuré(e).

premier ['premɪə*] *a* premier(ère),

capital(e), primordial(e) // *n* (*POL*) premier ministre.

première ['premɪɛə*] *n* première *f*.

premise ['premɪs] *n* prémisse *f*; ~**s** *npl* locaux *mpl*; **on the** ~**s** sur les lieux; sur place.

premium ['priːmɪəm] *n* prime *f*; **to be at a** ~ faire prime; ~ **bond** *n* (*Brit*) bon *m* à lot, obligation *f* à prime.

premonition [premə'nɪʃən] *n* prémonition *f*.

preoccupied [priː'ɔkjupaɪd] *a* préoccupé(e).

prep [prep] *n* (*SCOL: study*) étude *f*; ~ **school** *n* = **preparatory school**.

prepaid [priː'peɪd] *a* payé(e) d'avance.

preparation [prepə'reɪʃən] *n* préparation *f*; ~**s** *npl* (*for trip, war*) préparatifs *mpl*.

preparatory [prɪ'pærətərɪ]: ~ **school** *n* école primaire privée.

prepare [prɪ'pɛə*] *vt* préparer // *vi*: to ~ **for** se préparer à; ~**d to** prêt(e) à.

preposition [prepə'zɪʃən] *n* préposition *f*.

preposterous [prɪ'pɔstərəs] *a* absurde.

prerequisite [priː'rekwɪzɪt] *n* condition *f* préalable.

prescribe [prɪ'skraɪb] *vt* prescrire.

prescription [prɪ'skrɪpʃən] *n* prescription *f*; (*MED*) ordonnance *f*.

presence ['prezns] *n* présence *f*; ~ **of mind** présence d'esprit.

present ['preznt] *a* présent(e) // *n* cadeau *m*; (*also*: ~ **tense**) présent *m* // *vt* [prɪ'zent] présenter; (*give*): to ~ **sb with sth** offrir qch à qn; to give sb a ~ offrir un cadeau à qn; at ~ en ce moment; ~**ation** [-'teɪʃən] *n* présentation *f*; (*gift*) cadeau *m*, présent *m*; (*ceremony*) remise *f* du cadeau; ~-**day** *a* contemporain(e), actuel(le); ~**er** [-'zentə*] *n* (*RADIO, TV*) présentateur/trice; ~**ly** *ad* (*soon*) tout à l'heure, bientôt; (*at present*) en ce moment.

preservative [prɪ'zəː'vətɪv] *n* agent *m* de conservation.

preserve [prɪ'zəː'v] *vt* (*keep safe*) préserver, protéger; (*maintain*) conserver, garder; (*food*) mettre en conserve // *n* (*for game, fish*) réserve *f*; (*often pl: jam*) confiture *f*; (: *fruit*) fruits *mpl* en conserve.

president ['prezɪdənt] *n* président/e; ~**ial** [-'denʃl] *a* présidentiel(le).

press [pres] *n* (*tool, machine, newspapers*) presse *f*; (*for wine*) pressoir *m*; (*crowd*) cohue *f*, foule *f* // *vt* (*push*) appuyer sur; (*squeeze*) presser, serrer; (*clothes: iron*) repasser; (*pursue*) talonner; (*insist*): to ~ **sth on sb** presser qn d'accepter qch // *vi* appuyer, peser; se presser; **we are** ~**ed for time** le temps nous manque; to ~ **for sth** faire pression pour obtenir qch; **to** ~ **on** *vi* continuer;

~ conference n conférence f de presse; **~ing** a urgent(e), pressant(e) // n repassage m; **~ stud** n (Brit) bouton-pression m; **~-up** n (Brit) traction f.

pressure ['prɛʃə*] n pression f; (stress) tension f; **~ cooker** n cocotte-minute f; **~ gauge** n manomètre m; **~ group** n groupe m de pression.

prestige [prɛs'ti:ʒ] n prestige m.

presumably [prɪ'zju:məblɪ] ad vraisemblablement.

presume [prɪ'zju:m] vt présumer, supposer; to ~ to do (dare) se permettre de faire.

presumption [prɪ'zʌmpʃən] n supposition f, présomption f; (boldness) audace f.

pretence, (US) **pretense** [prɪ'tɛns] n (claim) prétention f; to make a ~ of doing faire semblant de faire.

pretend [prɪ'tɛnd] vt (feign) feindre, simuler // vi (feign) faire semblant; (claim): to ~ to sth prétendre à qch; to ~ to do faire semblant de faire.

pretense [prɪ'tɛns] n (US) = **pretence**.

pretension [prɪ'tɛnʃən] n prétention f.

pretext ['pri:tɛkst] n prétexte m.

pretty ['prɪtɪ] a joli(e) // ad assez.

prevail [prɪ'veɪl] vi (win) l'emporter, prévaloir; (be usual) avoir cours; (persuade): to ~ (up)on sb to do persuader qn de faire; **~ing** a dominant(e).

prevalent ['prɛvələnt] a répandu(e), courant(e); (fashion) en vogue.

prevent [prɪ'vɛnt] vt: to ~ (from doing) empêcher (de faire); **~ive** a préventif(ive).

preview ['pri:vju:] n (of film) avant-première f; (fig) aperçu m.

previous ['pri:vɪəs] a précédent(e); antérieur(e); **~ly** ad précédemment, auparavant.

prewar [pri:'wɔ:*] a d'avant-guerre.

prey [preɪ] n proie f // vi: to ~ on s'attaquer à.

price [praɪs] n prix m // vt (goods) fixer le prix de; tarifer; **~less** a sans prix, inestimable; **~ list** n liste f des prix, tarif m.

prick [prɪk] n piqûre f // vt piquer; to ~ up one's ears dresser or tendre l'oreille.

prickle ['prɪkl] n (of plant) épine f; (sensation) picotement m.

prickly ['prɪklɪ] a piquant(e), épineux(euse); (fig: person) irritable; **~ heat** n fièvre f miliaire.

pride [praɪd] n orgueil m; fierté f // vt: to ~ o.s. on se flatter de; s'enorgueillir de.

priest [pri:st] n prêtre m; **~hood** n prêtrise f, sacerdoce m.

prig [prɪg] n poseur/euse, fat m.

prim [prɪm] a collet monté inv, guindé(e).

primarily ['praɪmərɪlɪ] ad principalement, essentiellement.

primary ['praɪmərɪ] a primaire; (first in importance) premier(ère), primordial(e); **~ school** n (Brit) école primaire f.

prime [praɪm] a primordial(e), fondamental(e); (excellent) excellent(e) // vt (gun, pump) amorcer; (fig) mettre au courant; in the ~ of life dans la fleur de l'âge; **P~ Minister (P.M.)** n Premier ministre m.

primer ['praɪmə*] n (book) manuel m élémentaire; (paint) apprêt m.

primeval [praɪ'mi:vl] a primitif(ive); (forest) vierge.

primitive ['prɪmɪtɪv] a primitif(ive).

primrose ['prɪmrəuz] n primevère f.

primus (stove) ['praɪməs(stəuv)] n ® (Brit) réchaud m de camping.

prince [prɪns] n prince m.

princess [prɪn'sɛs] n princesse f.

principal ['prɪnsɪpl] a principal(e) // n (headmaster) directeur m, principal m.

principle ['prɪnsɪpl] n principe m; in/on ~ en/par principe.

print [prɪnt] n (mark) empreinte f; (letters) caractères mpl; (fabric) imprimé m; (ART) gravure f, estampe f; (PHOT) épreuve f // vt imprimer; (publish) publier; (write in capitals) écrire en majuscules; out of ~ épuisé(e); **~ed matter** n imprimés mpl; **~er** n imprimeur m; (machine) imprimante f; **~ing** n impression f; **~-out** n listage m.

prior ['praɪə*] a antérieur(e), précédent(e) // n prieur m; ~ to doing avant de faire.

priority [praɪ'ɔrɪtɪ] n priorité f.

prise [praɪz] vt: to ~ open forcer.

prison ['prɪzn] n prison f // cpd pénitentiaire; **~er** n prisonnier/ère.

pristine ['prɪsti:n] a virginal(e).

privacy ['prɪvəsɪ] n intimité f, solitude f.

private ['praɪvɪt] a privé(e); personnel(le); (house, car, lesson) particulier(ère) // n soldat m de deuxième classe; '~' (on envelope) 'personnelle'; in ~ en privé; **~ enterprise** n l'entreprise privée; **~ eye** n détective privé; **~ly** ad en privé; (within oneself) intérieurement; **~ property** n propriété privée; **privatize** vt privatiser.

privet ['prɪvɪt] n troène m.

privilege ['prɪvɪlɪdʒ] n privilège m.

privy ['prɪvɪ] a: to be ~ to être au courant de; **~ council** n conseil privé.

prize [praɪz] n prix m // a (example, idiot) parfait(e); (bull, novel) primé(e) // vt priser, faire grand cas de; **~ giving** n distribution f des prix; **~winner** n gagnant/e.

pro [prəu] n (SPORT) professionnel/le; the **~s and cons** le pour et le contre.

probability [prɔbə'bɪlɪtɪ] *n* probabilité *f*.
probable ['prɔbəbl] *a* probable; **probably** *ad* probablement.
probation [prə'beɪʃən] *n* (*in employment*) essai *m*; (*LAW*) liberté surveillée; **on ~** (*employee*) à l'essai; (*LAW*) en liberté surveillée.
probe [prəub] *n* (*MED, SPACE*) sonde *f*; (*enquiry*) enquête *f*, investigation *f* // *vt* sonder, explorer.
problem ['prɔbləm] *n* problème *m*.
procedure [prə'si:dʒə*] *n* (*ADMIN, LAW*) procédure *f*; (*method*) marche *f* à suivre, façon *f* de procéder.
proceed [prə'si:d] *vi* (*go forward*) avancer; (*go about it*) procéder; (*continue*): **to ~ (with)** continuer, poursuivre; **to ~ to** aller à; passer à; **~ to do** se mettre à faire; **~ings** *npl* mesures *fpl*; (*LAW*) poursuites *fpl*; (*meeting*) réunion *f*, séance *f*; (*records*) compte rendu; actes *mpl*; **~s** ['prəusi:dz] *npl* produit *m*, recette *f*.
process ['prəuses] *n* processus *m*; (*method*) procédé *m* // *vt* traiter; **~ing** *n* traitement *m*.
procession [prə'seʃən] *n* défilé *m*, cortège *m*; **funeral ~** cortège *m* funèbre; convoi *m* mortuaire.
proclaim [prə'kleɪm] *vt* déclarer, proclamer.
procrastinate [prəu'kræstɪneɪt] *vi* faire traîner les choses, vouloir tout remettre au lendemain.
prod [prɔd] *vt* pousser.
prodigal ['prɔdɪgl] *a* prodigue.
prodigy ['prɔdɪdʒɪ] *n* prodige *m*.
produce *n* ['prɔdju:s] (*AGR*) produits *mpl* // *vt* [prə'dju:s] produire; (*to show*) présenter; (*cause*) provoquer, causer; (*THEATRE*) monter, mettre en scène; **~r** *n* (*THEATRE*) metteur *m* en scène; (*AGR, CINEMA*) producteur *m*.
product ['prɔdʌkt] *n* produit *m*.
production [prə'dʌkʃən] *n* production *f*; (*THEATRE*) mise *f* en scène; **~ line** *n* chaîne *f* (de fabrication).
productivity [prɔdʌk'tɪvɪtɪ] *n* productivité *f*.
profane [prə'feɪn] *a* sacrilège; (*lay*) profane.
profession [prə'feʃən] *n* profession *f*; **~al** *n* (*SPORT*) professionnel/le // *a* professionnel(le); (*work*) de professionnel.
professor [prə'fesə*] *n* professeur *m* (*titulaire d'une chaire*).
proficiency [prə'fɪʃənsɪ] *n* compétence *f*, aptitude *f*.
profile ['prəufaɪl] *n* profil *m*.
profit ['prɔfɪt] *n* bénéfice *m*; profit *m* // *vi*: **to ~ (by or from)** profiter (de); **~able** *a* lucratif(ive), rentable.
profiteering [prɔfɪ'tɪərɪŋ] *n* (*pej*) mercantilisme *m*.

profound [prə'faund] *a* profond(e).
profusely [prə'fju:slɪ] *ad* abondamment; avec effusion.
progeny ['prɔdʒɪnɪ] *n* progéniture *f*; descendants *mpl*.
programme, (*US*) **program** ['prəugræm] *n* programme *m*; (*RADIO, TV*) émission *f* // *vt* programmer; **~r,** (*US*) **programer** *n* programmeur/euse.
progress *n* ['prəugres] progrès *m* // *vi* [prə'gres] progresser, avancer; **in ~** en cours; **to make ~** progresser, faire des progrès, être en progrès; **~ive** [-'gresɪv] *a* progressif(ive); (*person*) progressiste.
prohibit [prə'hɪbɪt] *vt* interdire, défendre.
project *n* ['prɔdʒekt] (*plan*) projet *m*, plan *m*; (*venture*) opération *f*, entreprise *f*; (*gen, SCOL: research*) étude *f*, dossier *m* // *vb* [prə'dʒekt] *vt* projeter // *vi* (*stick out*) faire saillie, s'avancer.
projection [prə'dʒekʃən] *n* projection *f*; saillie *f*.
projector [prə'dʒektə*] *n* projecteur *m*.
prolong [prə'lɔŋ] *vt* prolonger.
prom [prɔm] *n abbr of* **promenade**; (*US: ball*) bal *m* d'étudiants.
promenade [prɔmə'na:d] *n* (*by sea*) esplanade *f*, promenade *f*; **~ concert** *n* concert *m* (de musique classique).
prominent ['prɔmɪnənt] *a* (*standing out*) proéminent(e); (*important*) important(e).
promiscuous [prə'mɪskjuəs] *a* (*sexually*) de mœurs légères.
promise ['prɔmɪs] *n* promesse *f* // *vt, vi* promettre; **promising** *a* prometteur(euse).
promote [prə'məut] *vt* promouvoir; (*venture, event*) organiser, mettre sur pied; (*new product*) lancer; **~r** *n* (*of sporting event*) organisateur/trice; **promotion** [-'məuʃən] *n* promotion *f*.
prompt [prɔmpt] *a* rapide // *ad* (*punctually*) à l'heure // *n* (*COMPUT*) message *m* (de guidage) // *vt* inciter; provoquer; (*THEATRE*) souffler (son rôle or ses répliques à); **~ly** *ad* rapidement, sans délai; ponctuellement.
prone [prəun] *a* (*lying*) couché(e) (face contre terre); **~ to** enclin(e) à.
prong [prɔŋ] *n* pointe *f*; (*of fork*) dent *f*.
pronoun ['prəunaun] *n* pronom *m*.
pronounce [prə'nauns] *vt* prononcer // *vi*: **to ~ (up)on** se prononcer sur.
pronunciation [prənʌnsɪ'eɪʃən] *n* prononciation *f*.
proof [pru:f] *n* preuve *f*; (*test, of book, PHOT*) épreuve *f*; (*of alcohol*) degré *m* // *a*: **~ against** à l'épreuve de.
prop [prɔp] *n* support *m*, étai *m* // *vt* (*also*: **~ up**) étayer, soutenir; (*lean*): **to ~ sth against** appuyer qch contre or à.
propaganda [prɔpə'gændə] *n* propagande *f*.

propel [prə'pel] *vt* propulser, faire avancer; **~ler** *n* hélice *f*; **~ling pencil** *n* (*Brit*) porte-mine *m inv*.

propensity [prə'pensıtı] *n* propension *f*.

proper ['prɒpə*] *a* (*suited, right*) approprié(e), bon(bonne); (*seemly*) correct(e), convenable; (*authentic*) vrai(e), véritable; (*col: real*) *n* + fini(e), vrai(e); **~ly** *ad* correctement, convenablement; bel et bien; **he doesn't eat/study ~ly** il mange/étudie mal; **~ noun** *n* nom *m* propre.

property ['prɒpətı] *n* (*things owned*) biens *mpl*; propriété(s) *f(pl)*; immeuble *m*; terres *fpl*, domaine *m*; (*CHEM etc*: *quality*) propriété *f*; **~ owner** *n* propriétaire *m*.

prophecy ['prɒfısı] *n* prophétie *f*.

prophesy ['prɒfısaı] *vt* prédire.

prophet ['prɒfıt] *n* prophète *m*.

proportion [prə'pɔ:ʃən] *n* proportion *f*; (*share*) part *f*; partie *f*; **~al, ~ate** *a* proportionnel(le).

proposal [prə'pəuzl] *n* proposition *f*, offre *f*; (*plan*) projet *m*; (*of marriage*) demande *f* en mariage.

propose [prə'pəuz] *vt* proposer, suggérer // *vi* faire sa demande en mariage; **to ~ to do** avoir l'intention de faire.

proposition [prɒpə'zıʃən] *n* proposition *f*.

propriety [prə'praıtı] *n* (*seemliness*) bienséance *f*, convenance *f*.

prose [prəuz] *n* prose *f*; (*SCOL*: *translation*) thème *m*.

prosecute ['prɒsıkju:t] *vt* poursuivre; **prosecution** [-'kju:ʃən] *n* poursuites *fpl* judiciaires; (*accusing side*) accusation *f*; **prosecutor** *n* procureur *m*; (*also*: **public prosecutor**) ministère public.

prospect *n* ['prɒspekt] perspective *f*; (*hope*) espoir *m*, chances *fpl* // *vt*, *vi* [prə'spekt] prospecter; **~s** *npl* (*for work etc*) possibilités *fpl* d'avenir, débouchés *mpl*; **prospective** [-'spektıv] *a* (*possible*) éventuel(le); (*future*) futur(e).

prospectus [prə'spektəs] *n* prospectus *m*.

prosperity [prɒ'sperıtı] *n* prospérité *f*.

prostitute ['prɒstıtju:t] *n* prostituée *f*.

protect [prə'tekt] *vt* protéger; **~ion** *n* protection *f*; **~ive** *a* protecteur(trice).

protein ['prəuti:n] *n* protéine *f*.

protest *n* ['prəutest] protestation *f* // *vb* [prə'test] *vi* protester // *vt* protester de.

Protestant ['prɒtıstənt] *a, n* protestant(e).

protester [prə'testə*] *n* manifestant/e.

protracted [prə'træktıd] *a* prolongé(e).

protrude [prə'tru:d] *vi* avancer, dépasser.

proud [praud] *a* fier(ère); (*pej*) orgueilleux(euse).

prove [pru:v] *vt* prouver, démontrer // *vi*: **to ~ correct** *etc* s'avérer juste *etc*; **to ~ o.s.** montrer ce dont on est capable.

proverb ['prɒvə:b] *n* proverbe *m*.

provide [prə'vaıd] *vt* fournir; **to ~ sb with sth** fournir qch à qn; **to ~ for** *vt fus* (*person*) subvenir aux besoins de; (*emergency*) prévoir; **~d (that)** *cj* à condition que + *sub*.

providing [prə'vaıdıŋ] *cj* à condition que + *sub*.

province ['prɒvıns] *n* province *f*; **provincial** [prə'vınʃəl] *a* provincial(e).

provision [prə'vıʒən] *n* (*supply*) provision *f*; (*supplying*) fourniture *f*; approvisionnement *m*; (*stipulation*) disposition *f*; **~s** *npl* (*food*) provisions *fpl*; **~al** *a* provisoire.

proviso [prə'vaızəu] *n* condition *f*.

provocative [prə'vɒkətıv] *a* provocateur(trice), provocant(e).

provoke [prə'vəuk] *vt* provoquer; inciter.

prow [prau] *n* proue *f*.

prowess ['prauıs] *n* prouesse *f*.

prowl [praul] *vi* (*also*: **~ about**, **~ around**) rôder // *n*: **on the ~** à l'affût; **~er** *n* rôdeur/euse.

proxy ['prɒksı] *n* procuration *f*.

prudent ['pru:dnt] *a* prudent(e).

prudish ['pru:dıʃ] *a* prude, pudibond(e).

prune [pru:n] *n* pruneau *m* // *vt* élaguer.

pry [praı] *vi*: **to ~ into** fourrer son nez dans.

PS *n abbr* (= *postscript*) p.s.

psalm [sɑ:m] *n* psaume *m*.

pseudo- ['sju:dəu] *prefix* pseudo-; **pseudonym** *n* pseudonyme *m*.

psyche ['saıkı] *n* psychisme *m*.

psychiatric [saıkı'ætrık] *a* psychiatrique.

psychiatrist [saı'kaıətrıst] *n* psychiatre *m/f*.

psychic ['saıkık] *a* (*also*: **~al**) (*méta*)psychique; (*person*) doué(e) de télépathie *or* d'un sixième sens.

psychoanalyst [saıkəu'ænəlıst] *n* psychanalyste *m/f*.

psychological [saıkə'lɒdʒıkl] *a* psychologique.

psychologist [saı'kɒlədʒıst] *n* psychologue *m/f*.

psychology [saı'kɒlədʒı] *n* psychologie *f*.

P.T.O. *abbr* (= *please turn over*) T.S.V.P.

pub [pʌb] *n abbr* (= *public house*) pub *m*.

pubic ['pju:bık] *a* pubien(ne), du pubis.

public ['pʌblık] *a* public(que) *or* publique *m*; **in ~** en public; **~ address system (P.A.)** *n* (système *m* de) sonorisation *f*; hauts-parleurs *mpl*.

publican ['pʌblıkən] *n* patron *m* de pub.

public: ~ company *n* société *f*

anonyme (*cotée en bourse*); ~ **convenience** *n* (*Brit*) toilettes *fpl*; ~ **holiday** *n* jour férié; ~ **house** *n* (*Brit*) pub *m*.

publicity [pʌbˈlɪsɪtɪ] *n* publicité *f*.

publicize [ˈpʌblɪsaɪz] *vt* faire connaître, rendre public(ique).

publicly [ˈpʌblɪklɪ] *ad* publiquement.

public: ~ **opinion** *n* opinion publique; ~ **relations (PR)** *n* relations publiques; ~ **school** *n* (*Brit*) école privée; (*US*) école publique; ~-**spirited** *a* qui fait preuve de civisme; ~ **transport** *n* transports *mpl* en commun.

publish [ˈpʌblɪʃ] *vt* publier; ~**er** *n* éditeur *m*; ~**ing** *n* (*industry*) édition *f*.

puck [pʌk] *n* (*ICE HOCKEY*) palet *m*.

pucker [ˈpʌkə*] *vt* plisser.

pudding [ˈpudɪŋ] *n* (*Brit: sweet*) dessert *m*, entremets *m*; (*sausage*) boudin *m*; black ~ boudin (noir).

puddle [ˈpʌdl] *n* flaque d'eau.

puff [pʌf] *n* bouffée *f* // *vt*: to ~ one's pipe tirer sur sa pipe // vi sortir par bouffées; (*pant*) haleter; to ~ out smoke envoyer des bouffées de fumée; ~ed *a* (*col: out of breath*) tout(e) essoufflé(e); ~ **pastry** *n* pâte feuilletée; ~**y** *a* bouffi(e), boursouflé(e).

pull [pul] *n* (*tug*): to give sth a ~ tirer sur qch; (*fig*) influence *f* // *vt* tirer; (*muscle*) se claquer // *vi* tirer; to ~ to pieces mettre en morceaux; to ~ one's punches ménager son adversaire; to ~ one's weight y mettre du sien; to ~ o.s. together se ressaisir; to ~ apart *vt* séparer; (*break*) mettre en pièces, démantibuler; to ~ **down** *vt* baisser, abaisser; (*house*) démolir; (*tree*) abattre; to ~ in vi (*AUT*) se ranger; (*RAIL*) entrer en gare; to ~ **off** *vt* enlever, ôter; (*deal etc*) conclure; to ~ **out** vi (*AUT*) démarrer, partir; (*withdraw*) se retirer; (*AUT: come out of line*) déboîter // *vt* sortir; arracher; (*withdraw*) retirer; to ~ **over** vi (*AUT*) se ranger; to ~ **through** vi s'en sortir; to ~ **up** vi (*stop*) s'arrêter // *vt* remonter; (*uproot*) déraciner, arracher; (*stop*) arrêter.

pulley [ˈpulɪ] *n* poulie *f*.

pullover [ˈpuləuvə*] *n* pull-over *m*, tricot *m*.

pulp [pʌlp] *n* (*of fruit*) pulpe *f*; (*for paper*) pâte *f* à papier.

pulpit [ˈpulpɪt] *n* chaire *f*.

pulsate [pʌlˈseɪt] vi battre, palpiter; (*music*) vibrer.

pulse [pʌls] *n* (*of blood*) pouls *m*; (*of heart*) battement *m*; (*of music, engine*) vibrations *fpl*.

pummel [ˈpʌml] *vt* rouer de coups.

pump [pʌmp] *n* pompe *f*; (*shoe*) escarpin *m* // *vt* pomper; (*fig: col*) faire parler; to ~ **up** *vt* gonfler.

pumpkin [ˈpʌmpkɪn] *n* potiron *m*, citrouille *f*.

pun [pʌn] *n* jeu *m* de mots, calembour *m*.

punch [pʌntʃ] *n* (*blow*) coup *m* de poing; (*fig: force*) vivacité *f*, mordant *m*; (*tool*) poinçon *m*; (*drink*) punch *m* // *vt* (*hit*): to ~ sb/sth donner un coup de poing à qn/sur qch; (*make a hole*) poinçonner, perforer; ~ **line** *n* (*of joke*) conclusion *f*; ~-**up** *n* (*Brit col*) bagarre *f*.

punctual [ˈpʌŋktjuəl] *a* ponctuel(le).

punctuation [pʌŋktjuˈeɪʃən] *n* ponctuation *f*.

puncture [ˈpʌŋktʃə*] *n* crevaison *f*.

pundit [ˈpʌndɪt] *n* individu *m* qui pontifie, pontife *m*.

pungent [ˈpʌndʒənt] *a* piquant(e); (*fig*) mordant(e), caustique.

punish [ˈpʌnɪʃ] *vt* punir; ~**ment** *n* punition *f*, châtiment *m*.

punk [pʌŋk] *n* (*also:* ~ **rocker**) punk *m*/ *f*; (*also:* ~ **rock**) le punk; (*US col: hoodlum*) voyou *m*.

punt [pʌnt] *n* (*boat*) bachot *m*.

punter [ˈpʌntə*] *n* (*Brit: gambler*) parieur/euse.

puny [ˈpjuːnɪ] *a* chétif(ive).

pup [pʌp] *n* chiot *m*.

pupil [ˈpjuːpl] *n* élève *m*/*f*.

puppet [ˈpʌpɪt] *n* marionnette *f*, pantin *m*.

puppy [ˈpʌpɪ] *n* chiot *m*, petit chien.

purchase [ˈpɜːtʃɪs] *n* achat *m* // *vt* acheter; ~**r** *n* acheteur/euse.

pure [pjuə*] *a* pur(e).

purely [ˈpjuəlɪ] *ad* purement.

purge [pɜːdʒ] *n* (*MED*) purge *f*; (*POL*) épuration *f*, purge // *vt* purger.

purl [pɜːl] *n* maille *f* à l'envers.

purple [ˈpɜːpl] *a* violet(te); cramoisi(e).

purport [pɜːˈpɔːt] vi: to ~ to be/do prétendre être/faire.

purpose [ˈpɜːpəs] *n* intention *f*, but *m*; on ~ exprès; ~**ful** *a* déterminé(e), résolu(e).

purr [pɜː*] vi ronronner.

purse [pɜːs] *n* porte-monnaie *m* inv, bourse *f* // *vt* serrer, pincer.

purser [ˈpɜːsə*] *n* (*NAUT*) commissaire *m* du bord.

pursue [pəˈsjuː] *vt* poursuivre.

pursuit [pəˈsjuːt] *n* poursuite *f*; (*occupation*) occupation *f*, activité *f*.

purveyor [pəˈveɪə*] *n* fournisseur *m*.

push [puʃ] *n* poussée *f*; (*effort*) gros effort; (*drive*) énergie *f* // *vt* pousser; (*button*) appuyer sur; (*thrust*): to ~ sth (**into**) enfoncer qch (dans); (*fig*) mettre en avant, faire de la publicité pour // *vi* pousser; appuyer; to ~ **aside** *vt* écarter; to ~ **off** vi (*col*) filer, ficher le camp; to ~ **on** vi (*continue*) continuer; to ~ **through** *vt* (*measure*) faire voter;

to ~ up vt (total, prices) faire monter; **~chair** n (Brit) poussette f; **~er** n (drug ~er) revendeur/euse (de drogue), ravitailleur/euse (en drogue); **~over** n (col): it's a ~over c'est un jeu d'enfant; **~-up** n (US) traction f; **~y** a (pej) arriviste.

puss, pussy(-cat) [pus, 'pusɪ(kæt)] n minet m.

put, pt, pp **put** [put] vt mettre, poser, placer; (say) dire, exprimer; (a question) poser; (estimate) estimer; **to ~ about** vi (NAUT) virer de bord // vt (rumour) faire courir; **to ~ across** vt (ideas etc) communiquer; **to ~ away** vt (store) ranger; **to ~ back** vt (replace) remettre, replacer; (postpone) remettre; (delay) retarder; **to ~ by** vt (money) mettre de côté, économiser; **to ~ down** vt (parcel etc) poser, déposer; (pay) verser; (in writing) mettre par écrit, inscrire; (suppress: revolt etc) réprimer, faire cesser; (attribute) attribuer; **to ~ forward** vt (ideas) avancer, proposer; (date) avancer; **to ~ in** vt (gas, electricity) installer; (application, complaint) soumettre; **to ~ off** vt (light etc) éteindre; (postpone) remettre à plus tard, ajourner; (discourage) dissuader; **to ~ on** vt (clothes, lipstick etc) mettre; (light etc) allumer; (play etc) monter; (food, meal) servir; (: cook) mettre à cuire or à chauffer; (airs, weight) prendre; (brake) mettre; **to ~ out** vt mettre dehors; (one's hand) tendre; (news, rumour) faire courir, répandre; (light etc) éteindre; (person: inconvenience) déranger, gêner; **to ~ up** vt (raise) lever, relever, remonter; (pin up) afficher; (hang) accrocher; (build) construire, ériger; (a tent) monter; (increase) augmenter; (accommodate) loger; **to ~ up with** vt fus supporter.

putt [pʌt] vt poter (la balle) // n coup roulé; **~ing green** n green m.

putty ['pʌtɪ] n mastic m.

puzzle ['pʌzl] n énigme f, mystère m; (jigsaw) puzzle m; (also: crossword ~) problème m de mots croisés // vt intriguer, rendre perplexe // vi se creuser la tête.

pyjamas [pɪ'dʒɑ:məz] npl (Brit) pyjama m.

pyramid ['pɪrəmɪd] n pyramide f.

Pyrenees [pɪrɪ'ni:z] npl: the ~ les Pyrénées fpl.

Q

quack [kwæk] n (of duck) coin-coin m inv; (pej: doctor) charlatan m.

quad [kwɔd] abbr of **quadrangle**, **quadruplet**.

quadrangle ['kwɔdræŋgl] n (MATH) quadrilatère m; (courtyard: abbr: quad) cour f.

quadruple [kwɔ'drupl] vt, vi quadrupler.

quadruplet [kwɔ'dru:plɪt] n quadruplé/e.

quagmire ['kwægmaɪə*] n bourbier m.

quail [kweɪl] n (ZOOL) caille f // vi (person) perdre courage.

quaint [kweɪnt] a bizarre; (old-fashioned) désuet(ète); au charme vieillot, pittoresque.

quake [kweɪk] vi trembler // n abbr of earthquake.

qualification [kwɔlɪfɪ'keɪʃən] n (degree etc) diplôme m; (ability) compétence f, qualification f; (limitation) réserve f, restriction f.

qualified ['kwɔlɪfaɪd] a diplômé(e); (able) compétent(e), qualifié(e); (limited) conditionnel(le).

qualify ['kwɔlɪfaɪ] vt qualifier; (limit: statement) apporter des réserves à // vi: **to ~ (as)** obtenir son diplôme (de); **to ~ (for)** remplir les conditions requises (pour); (SPORT) se qualifier (pour).

quality ['kwɔlɪtɪ] n qualité f.

qualm [kwɑ:m] n doute m; scrupule m.

quandary ['kwɔndrɪ] n: **in a ~** devant un dilemme, dans l'embarras.

quantity ['kwɔntɪtɪ] n quantité f; **~ surveyor** n métreur m vérificateur.

quarantine ['kwɔrnti:n] n quarantaine f.

quarrel ['kwɔrl] n querelle f, dispute f // vi se disputer, se quereller; **~some** a querelleur(euse).

quarry ['kwɔrɪ] n (for stone) carrière f; (animal) proie f, gibier m // vt (marble etc) extraire.

quart [kwɔ:t] n ≈ litre m.

quarter ['kwɔ:tə*] n quart m; (of year) trimestre m; (district) quartier m // vt partager en quartiers or en quatre; (MIL) caserner, cantonner; **~s** npl logement m; (MIL) quartiers mpl, cantonnement m; **a ~ of an hour** un quart d'heure; **~ final** n quart m de finale; **~ly** a trimestriel(le) // ad tous les trois mois; **~master** n (MIL) intendant m militaire de troisième classe; (NAUT) maître m de manœuvre.

quartet(te) [kwɔ:'tɛt] n quatuor m; (jazz players) quartette m.

quartz [kwɔ:ts] n quartz m.

quash [kwɔʃ] vt (verdict) annuler.

quaver ['kweɪvə*] vi trembler.

quay [ki:] n (also: ~side) quai m.

queasy ['kwi:zɪ] a (stomach) délicat(e); **to feel ~** avoir mal au cœur.

queen [kwi:n] n (gen) reine f; (CARDS etc) dame f; **~ mother** n reine mère f.

queer [kwɪə*] a étrange, curieux(euse); (suspicious) louche // n (col) homosexuel

m.

quell [kwɛl] *vt* réprimer, étouffer.

quench [kwɛntʃ] *vt* (*flames*) éteindre; **to ~ one's thirst** se désaltérer.

querulous ['kwɛruləs] *a* (*person*) récriminateur(trice); (*voice*) plaintif(ive).

query ['kwɪərɪ] *n* question *f*; (*doubt*) doute *m*; (*question mark*) point *m* d'interrogation // *vt* mettre en question *or* en doute.

quest [kwɛst] *n* recherche *f*, quête *f*.

question ['kwɛstʃən] *n* question *f* // *vt* (*person*) interroger; (*plan, idea*) mettre en question *or* en doute; **it's a ~ of doing** il s'agit de faire; **beyond ~** sans aucun doute; **out of the ~** hors de question; **~able** *a* discutable; **~ mark** *n* point *m* d'interrogation.

questionnaire [kwɛstʃə'nɛə*] *n* questionnaire *m*.

queue [kju:] (*Brit*) *n* queue *f*, file *f* // *vi* faire la queue.

quibble ['kwɪbl] *vi* ergoter, chicaner.

quick [kwɪk] *a* rapide; (*reply*) prompt(e), rapide; (*mind*) vif(vive) // *ad* vite, rapidement // *n*: **cut to the ~** (*fig*) touché(e) au vif; **be ~!** dépêche-toi!; **~en** *vt* accélérer, presser; (*rouse*) stimuler // *vi* s'accélérer, devenir plus rapide; **~ly** *ad* vite, rapidement; **~sand** *n* sables mouvants; **~-witted** *a* à l'esprit vif.

quid [kwɪd] *n* (*pl inv*) (*Brit col*) livre *f*.

quiet ['kwaɪət] *a* tranquille, calme; (*ceremony, colour*) discret(ète) // *n* tranquillité *f*, calme *m* // *vt, vi* (*US*) = **~en**; **keep ~!** tais-toi!; **~en** (*also*: **~en down**) *vi* se calmer, s'apaiser // *vt* calmer, apaiser; **~ly** *ad* tranquillement, calmement; discrètement.

quilt [kwɪlt] *n* édredon *m*; (*continental ~*) couette *f*.

quin [kwɪn] *n abbr of* **quintuplet**.

quintuplet [kwɪn'tju:plɪt] *n* quintuplé/e.

quip [kwɪp] *n* remarque piquante *or* spirituelle, pointe *f*.

quirk [kwə:k] *n* bizarrerie *f*.

quit, *pt, pp* **quit** *or* **quitted** [kwɪt] *vt* quitter // *vi* (*give up*) abandonner, renoncer; (*resign*) démissionner.

quite [kwaɪt] *ad* (*rather*) assez, plutôt; (*entirely*) complètement, tout à fait; **I ~ understand** je comprends très bien; **~ a few of them** un assez grand nombre d'entre eux; **~ (so)!** exactement!

quits [kwɪts] *a*: **~ (with)** quitte (envers); **let's call it ~** restons-en là.

quiver ['kwɪvə*] *vi* trembler, frémir.

quiz [kwɪz] *n* (*game*) jeu-concours *m*; test *m* de connaissances // *vt* interroger; **~zical** *a* narquois(e).

quota ['kwəutə] *n* quota *m*.

quotation [kwəu'teɪʃən] *n* citation *f*; (*of shares etc*) cote *f*, cours *m*; (*estimate*) devis *m*; **~ marks** *npl* guillemets *mpl*.

quote [kwəut] *n* citation *f* // *vt* (*sentence*) citer; (*price*) donner, fixer; (*shares*) coter // *vi*: **to ~ from** citer.

R

rabbi ['ræbaɪ] *n* rabbin *m*.

rabbit ['ræbɪt] *n* lapin *m*; **~ hutch** *n* clapier *m*.

rabble ['ræbl] *n* (*pej*) populace *f*.

rabies ['reɪbi:z] *n* rage *f*.

RAC *n abbr* (*Brit*) = **Royal Automobile Club**.

race [reɪs] *n* race *f*; (*competition, rush*) course *f* // *vt* (*person*) faire la course avec; (*horse*) faire courir; (*engine*) emballer // *vi* courir; (*engine*) s'emballer; **~ car** *n* (*US*) = **racing car**; **~ car driver** *n* (*US*) = **racing driver**; **~course** *n* champ *m* de courses; **~horse** *n* cheval *m* de course; **~track** *n* piste *f*.

racial ['reɪʃl] *a* racial(e); **~ist** *a, n* raciste (*m/f*).

racing ['reɪsɪŋ] *n* courses *fpl*; **~ car** *n* (*Brit*) voiture *f* de course; **~ driver** *n* (*Brit*) pilote *m* de course.

racism ['reɪsɪzəm] *n* racisme *m*; **racist** *a, n* raciste (*m/f*).

rack [ræk] *n* (*also*: **luggage ~**) filet *m* à bagages; (*also*: **roof ~**) galerie *f* // *vt* tourmenter; **to ~ one's brains** se creuser la cervelle.

racket ['rækɪt] *n* (*for tennis*) raquette *f*; (*noise*) tapage *m*; vacarme *m*; (*swindle*) escroquerie *f*; (*organized crime*) racket *m*.

racquet ['rækɪt] *n* raquette *f*.

racy ['reɪsɪ] *a* plein(e) de verve; osé(e).

radar ['reɪdɑ:*] *n* radar *m*.

radial ['reɪdɪəl] *a* (*also*: **~-ply**) à carcasse radiale.

radiant ['reɪdɪənt] *a* rayonnant(e).

radiate ['reɪdɪeɪt] *vt* (*heat*) émettre, dégager // *vi* (*lines*) rayonner.

radiation [reɪdɪ'eɪʃən] *n* rayonnement *m*; (*radioactive*) radiation *f*.

radiator ['reɪdɪeɪtə*] *n* radiateur *m*.

radical ['rædɪkl] *a* radical(e).

radii ['reɪdɪaɪ] *npl of* **radius**.

radio ['reɪdɪəu] *n* radio *f*; **on the ~** à la radio.

radioactive [reɪdɪəu'æktɪv] *a* radioactif(ive).

radio station *n* station *f* de radio.

radish ['rædɪʃ] *n* radis *m*.

radius ['reɪdɪəs], *pl* **radii** *n* rayon *m*.

RAF *n abbr of* **Royal Air Force**.

raffle ['ræfl] *n* tombola *f*.

raft [rɑ:ft] *n* (*craft*; *also*: **life ~**) radeau *m*.

rafter ['rɑ:ftə*] *n* chevron *m*.

rag [ræg] *n* chiffon *m*; (*pej*: *newspaper*) feuille *f*, torchon *m*; (*for charity*) attrac-

tions organisées par les étudiants au profit d'œuvres de charité // (*Brit*) chahuter, mettre en boîte; **~s** *npl* haillons *mpl*; **~-and-bone man** *n* (*Brit*) = **~man**; **~ doll** *n* poupée *f* de chiffon.

rage [reɪdʒ] *n* (*fury*) rage *f*, fureur *f* // *vi* (*person*) être fou(folle) de rage; (*storm*) faire rage, être déchaîné(e); it's all the ~ cela fait fureur.

ragged ['rægɪd] *a* (*edge*) inégal(e), qui accroche; (*cuff*) effiloché(e); (*appearance*) déguenillé(e).

ragman ['rægmæn] *n* chiffonnier *m*.

raid [reɪd] *n* (*MIL*) raid *m*; (*criminal*) hold-up *m inv*; (*by police*) descente *f*, rafle *f* // *vt* faire un raid sur *or* un hold-up dans *or* une descente dans.

rail [reɪl] *n* (*on stair*) rampe *f*; (*on bridge, balcony*) balustrade *f*; (*of ship*) bastingage *m*; (*for train*) rail *m*; **~s** *npl* rails *mpl*, voie ferrée; **by ~** par chemin de fer; **~ing(s)** *n(pl)* grille *f*; **~way**, (*US*) **~road** *n* chemin *m* de fer; **~way line** *n* ligne *f* de chemin de fer; **~wayman** *n* cheminot *m*; **~way station** *n* gare *f*.

rain [reɪn] *n* pluie *f* // *vi* pleuvoir; in the ~ sous la pluie; it's ~ing il pleut; **~bow** *n* arc-en-ciel *m*; **~coat** *n* imperméable *m*; **~drop** *n* goutte *f* de pluie; **~fall** *n* chute *f* de pluie; (*measurement*) hauteur *f* des précipitations; **~y** *a* pluvieux(euse).

raise [reɪz] *n* augmentation *f* // *vt* (*lift*) lever, hausser; (*build*) ériger; (*increase*) augmenter; (*a protest, doubt*) provoquer, causer; (*a question*) soulever; (*cattle, family*) élever; (*crop*) faire pousser; (*army, funds*) rassembler; (*loan*) obtenir; to ~ one's voice élever la voix.

raisin ['reɪzn] *n* raisin sec.

rake [reɪk] *n* (*tool*) râteau *m*; (*person*) débauché *m* // *vt* (*garden*) ratisser; (*with machine gun*) balayer.

rally ['rælɪ] *n* (*POL etc*) meeting *m*, rassemblement *m*; (*AUT*) rallye *m*; (*TENNIS*) échange *m* // *vt* rassembler, rallier // *vi* se rallier; (*sick person*) aller mieux; (*Stock Exchange*) reprendre; **to ~ round** *vt fus* se rallier à; venir en aide à.

RAM [ræm] *n abbr* (= *random access memory*) mémoire vive.

ram [ræm] *n* bélier *m* // *vt* enfoncer; (*soil*) tasser; (*crash into*) emboutir; percuter; éperonner.

ramble ['ræmbl] *n* randonnée *f* // *vi* (*pej: also: ~ on*) discourir, pérorer; **~r** *n* promeneur/euse, randonneur/euse; (*BOT*) rosier grimpant; **rambling** *a* (*speech*) décousu(e); (*BOT*) grimpant(e).

ramp [ræmp] *n* (*incline*) rampe *f*; dénivellation *f*; (*in garage*) pont *m*; on

~, **off ~** (*US AUT*) bretelle *f* d'accès.

rampage [ræm'peɪdʒ] *n*: to be on the ~ se déchaîner.

rampant ['ræmpənt] *a* (*disease etc*) qui sévit.

ramshackle ['ræmʃækl] *a* (*house*) délabré(e); (*car etc*) déglingué(e).

ran [ræn] *pt of* **run**.

ranch [rɑːntʃ] *n* ranch *m*; **~er** *n* propriétaire *m* de ranch; cowboy *m*.

rancid ['rænsɪd] *a* rance.

rancour, (*US*) **rancor** ['ræŋkə*] *n* rancune *f*.

random ['rændəm] *a* fait(e) *or* établi(e) au hasard; (*COMPUT, MATH*) aléatoire // *n*: at ~ au hasard.

randy ['rændɪ] *a* (*Brit col*) excité(e); lubrique.

rang [ræŋ] *pt of* **ring**.

range [reɪndʒ] *n* (*of mountains*) chaîne *f*; (*of missile, voice*) portée *f*; (*of products*) choix *m*, gamme *f*; (*MIL: also:* **shooting ~**) champ *m* de tir; (*indoor*) stand *m* de tir; (*also:* **kitchen ~**) fourneau *m* (de cuisine) // *vt* (*place*) mettre en rang, placer; (*roam*) parcourir // *vi*: to ~ over couvrir; to ~ from ... to aller de ... à.

ranger ['reɪndʒə*] *n* garde forestier.

rank [ræŋk] *n* rang *m*; (*MIL*) grade *m*; (*Brit: also:* **taxi ~**) station *f* de taxis // *vi*: to ~ among compter *or* se classer parmi // *a* (qui sent) fort(e); extrême; the ~s (*MIL*) la troupe; the ~ and file (*fig*) la masse, la base.

rankle ['ræŋkl] *vi* (*insult*) rester sur le cœur.

ransack ['rænsæk] *vt* fouiller (à fond); (*plunder*) piller.

ransom ['rænsəm] *n* rançon *f*; to hold sb to ~ (*fig*) exercer un chantage sur qn.

rant [rænt] *vi* fulminer.

rap [ræp] *vt* frapper sur *or* à; taper sur.

rape [reɪp] *n* viol *m*; (*BOT*) colza *m* // *vt* violer; **~(seed) oil** *n* huile *f* de colza.

rapid ['ræpɪd] *a* rapide; **~s** *npl* (*GEO*) rapides *mpl*; **~ly** *ad* rapidement.

rapist ['reɪpɪst] *n* auteur *m* d'un viol.

rapport [ræ'pɔː*] *n* entente *f*.

rapture ['ræptʃə*] *n* extase *f*, ravissement *m*.

rare [rɛə*] *a* rare; (*CULIN: steak*) saignant(e).

rarely ['rɛəlɪ] *ad* rarement.

raring ['rɛərɪŋ] *a*: to be ~ to go (*col*) être très impatient(e) de commencer.

rascal ['rɑːskl] *n* vaurien *m*.

rash [ræʃ] *a* imprudent(e), irréfléchi(e) // *n* (*MED*) rougeur *f*, éruption *f*.

rasher ['ræʃə*] *n* fine tranche (de lard).

raspberry ['rɑːzbərɪ] *n* framboise *f*.

rasping ['rɑːspɪŋ] *a*: ~ noise grincement *m*.

rat [ræt] *n* rat *m*.

rate [reɪt] *n* (*ratio*) taux *m*, pourcentage

m; (*speed*) vitesse *f*, rythme *m*; (*price*) tarif *m* // *vt* classer; évaluer; **to ~ sb/ sth as** considérer qn/qch comme; **~s** *npl* (*Brit*) impôts locaux; (*fees*) tarifs *mpl*; **~able value** *n* (*Brit*) valeur locative imposable; **~payer** *n* (*Brit*) contribuable *m/f* (payant les impôts locaux).

rather ['rɑːðə*] *ad* plutôt; it's ~ expensive c'est assez cher; (*too much*) c'est un peu cher; **there's ~ a lot** il y en a beaucoup; **I would** *or* **I'd ~ go** j'aimerais mieux *or* je préférerais partir.

rating ['reɪtɪŋ] *n* classement *m*; cote *f*; (*NAUT*: *category*) classe *f*; (: *Brit* : *sailor*) matelot *m*.

ratio ['reɪʃɪəu] *n* proportion *f*.

ration ['ræʃən] *n* (*gen pl*) ration(s) *f(pl)*.

rational ['ræʃənl] *a* raisonnable, sensé(e); (*solution, reasoning*) logique; (*MED*) lucide; **~e** [-'nɑːl] *n* raisonnement *m*; justification *f*; **~ize** *vt* rationaliser; (*conduct*) essayer d'expliquer *or* de motiver.

rat race *n* foire *f* d'empoigne.

rattle ['rætl] *n* cliquetis *m*; (*louder*) bruit *m* de ferraille; (*object: of baby*) hochet *m*; (: *of sports fan*) crécelle *f* // *vi* cliqueter; faire un bruit de ferraille *or* du bruit // *vt* agiter (bruyamment); **~snake** *n* serpent *m* à sonnettes.

raucous ['rɔːkəs] *a* rauque.

rave [reɪv] *vi* (*in anger*) s'emporter; (*with enthusiasm*) s'extasier; (*MED*) délirer.

raven ['reɪvən] *n* corbeau *m*.

ravenous ['rævənəs] *a* affamé(e).

ravine [rə'viːn] *n* ravin *m*.

raving ['reɪvɪŋ] *a*: **~ lunatic** *n* fou furieux/folle furieuse.

ravishing ['rævɪʃɪŋ] *a* enchanteur(eresse).

raw [rɔː] *a* (*uncooked*) cru(e); (*not processed*) brut(e); (*sore*) à vif, irrité(e); (*inexperienced*) inexpérimenté(e); **~ deal** *n* (*col*) sale coup *m*; **~ material** *n* matière première.

ray [reɪ] *n* rayon *m*; **~ of hope** *n* lueur *f* d'espoir.

raze [reɪz] *vt* raser, détruire.

razor ['reɪzə*] *n* rasoir *m*; **~ blade** *n* lame *f* de rasoir.

Rd *abbr of* **road**.

re [riː] *prep* concernant.

reach [riːtʃ] *n* portée *f*, atteinte *f*; (*of river etc*) étendue *f* // *vt* atteindre; parvenir à // *vi* s'étendre; **out of/within ~** hors de/à portée; **to ~ out** *vi*: **to ~ out for** allonger le bras pour prendre.

react [riː'ækt] *vi* réagir; **~ion** [-'ækʃən] *n* réaction *f*.

reactor [riː'æktə*] *n* réacteur *m*.

read, *pt*, *pp* **read** [riːd, rɛd] *vi* lire // *vt* lire; (*understand*) comprendre, interpréter; (*study*) étudier; (*subj: instrument etc*) indiquer, marquer; **to ~ out**

vt lire à haute voix; **~able** *a* facile *or* agréable à lire; **~er** *n* lecteur/trice; (*book*) livre *m* de lecture; (*Brit*: *at university*) maître *m* de conférences; **~ership** *n* (*of paper etc*) (nombre *m* de) lecteurs *mpl*.

readily ['rɛdɪlɪ] *ad* volontiers, avec empressement; (*easily*) facilement.

readiness ['rɛdɪnɪs] *n* empressement *m*; **in ~** (*prepared*) prêt(e).

reading ['riːdɪŋ] *n* lecture *f*; (*understanding*) interprétation *f*; (*on instrument*) indications *fpl*.

ready ['rɛdɪ] *a* prêt(e); (*willing*) prêt, disposé(e); (*quick*) prompt(e); (*available*) disponible // *ad*: **~-cooked** tout(e) cuit(e) (d'avance) // *n*: **at the ~** (*MIL*) prêt à faire feu; (*fig*) tout(e) prêt(e); **to get ~** *vi* se préparer // *vt* préparer; **~-made** *a* tout(e) fait(e); **~ money** *n* (argent *m*) liquide *m*; **~ reckoner** *n* barème *m*; **~-to-wear** *a* en prêt-à-porter.

real [rɪəl] *a* réel(le); véritable; **in ~ terms** dans la réalité; **~ estate** *n* biens fonciers *or* immobiliers; **~istic** [-'lɪstɪk] *a* réaliste.

reality [riː'ælɪtɪ] *n* réalité *f*.

realization [rɪəlaɪ'zeɪʃən] *n* prise *f* de conscience; réalisation *f*.

realize ['rɪəlaɪz] *vt* (*understand*) se rendre compte de; (*a project, COMM: asset*) réaliser.

really ['rɪəlɪ] *ad* vraiment; **~?** c'est vrai?

realm [rɛlm] *n* royaume *m*.

realtor ['rɪəltə*] *n* (*US*) agent immobilier.

reap [riːp] *vt* moissonner; (*fig*) récolter.

reappear [riːə'pɪə*] *vi* réapparaître, reparaître.

rear [rɪə*] *a* de derrière, arrière *inv*; (*AUT: wheel etc*) arrière // *n* arrière *m*, derrière *m* // *vt* (*cattle, family*) élever // *vi* (*also*: **~ up**: *animal*) se cabrer.

rear-view ['rɪəvjuː]: **~ mirror** *n* (*AUT*) rétroviseur *m*.

reason ['riːzn] *n* raison *f* // *vi*: **to ~ with sb** raisonner qn, faire entendre raison à qn; **to have ~ to think** avoir lieu de penser; **it stands to ~ that** il va sans dire que; **~able** *a* raisonnable; (*not bad*) acceptable; **~ably** *ad* raisonnablement; **~ing** *n* raisonnement *m*.

reassurance [riːə'ʃuərəns] *n* réconfort *m*; assurance *f*, garantie *f*.

reassure [riːə'ʃuə*] *vt* rassurer; **to ~ sb of** donner à qn l'assurance répétée de.

rebate ['riːbeɪt] *n* (*on product*) rabais *m*; (*on tax etc*) dégrèvement *m*; (*repayment*) remboursement *m*.

rebel *n* ['rɛbl] rebelle *m/f* // *vi* [rɪ'bɛl] se rebeller, se révolter; **~lious** *a* rebelle.

rebound *vi* [rɪ'baund] (*ball*) rebondir // *n* ['riːbaund] rebond *m*.

rebuff [rɪ'bʌf] *n* rebuffade *f*.
rebuke [rɪ'bjuːk] *vt* réprimander.
rebut [rɪ'bʌt] *vt* réfuter.
recall [rɪ'kɔːl] *vt* rappeler; (*remember*) se rappeler, se souvenir de // *n* rappel *m*.
recant [rɪ'kænt] *vi* se rétracter; (*REL*) abjurer.
recap ['riːkæp] *vt*, *vi* récapituler.
recapitulate [riːkə'pɪtjuleɪt] *vt*, *vi* = **recap.**
rec'd *abbr* = *received.*
recede [rɪ'siːd] *vi* s'éloigner; reculer; redescendre; **receding** *a* (*forehead*, *chin*) fuyant(e); **receding hairline** front dégarni.
receipt [rɪ'siːt] *n* (*document*) reçu *m*; (*for parcel etc*) accusé *m* de réception; (*act of receiving*) réception *f*; **~s** *npl* (*COMM*) recettes *fpl*.
receive [rɪ'siːv] *vt* recevoir.
receiver [rɪ'siːvə*] *n* (*TEL*) récepteur *m*, combiné *m*; (*of stolen goods*) receleur *m*; (*LAW*) administrateur *m* judiciaire.
recent ['riːsnt] *a* récent(e); **~ly** *ad* récemment.
receptacle [rɪ'sɛptɪkl] *n* récipient *m*.
reception [rɪ'sɛpʃən] *n* réception *f*; (*welcome*) accueil *m*, réception; **~ desk** *n* réception *f*; **~ist** *n* réceptionniste *m/f*.
recess [rɪ'sɛs] *n* (*in room*) renfoncement *m*; (*for bed*) alcôve *f*; (*secret place*) recoin *m*; (*POL etc: holiday*) vacances *fpl*; **~ion** [-'sɛʃən] *n* récession *f*.
recipe ['rɛsɪpɪ] *n* recette *f*.
recipient [rɪ'sɪpɪənt] *n* bénéficiaire *m/f*; (*of letter*) destinataire *m/f*.
recital [rɪ'saɪtl] *n* récital *m*.
recite [rɪ'saɪt] *vt* (*poem*) réciter.
reckless ['rɛkləs] *a* (*driver etc*) imprudent(e).
reckon ['rɛkən] *vt* (*count*) calculer, compter; (*consider*) considérer, estimer; (*think*): **I ~ that** ... je pense que ...; **to ~ on** *vt fus* compter sur, s'attendre à; **~ing** *n* compte *m*, calcul *m*; estimation *f*.
reclaim [rɪ'kleɪm] *vt* (*land*) amender; (: *from sea*) assécher; (: *from forest*) défricher; (*demand back*) réclamer (le remboursement *or* la restitution de).
recline [rɪ'klaɪn] *vi* être allongé(e) *or* étendu(e); **reclining** *a* (*seat*) à dossier réglable.
recluse [rɪ'kluːs] *n* reclus/e, ermite *m*.
recognition [rɛkəg'nɪʃən] *n* reconnaissance *f*; **to gain ~** être reconnu(e); **transformed beyond ~** méconnaissable.
recognize ['rɛkəgnaɪz] *vt*: **to ~ (by/as)** reconnaître (à/comme étant).
recoil [rɪ'kɔɪl] *vi* (*person*): **to ~ (from)** reculer (devant) // *n* (*of gun*) recul *m*.
recollect [rɛkə'lɛkt] *vt* se rappeler, se souvenir de; **~ion** [-'lɛkʃən] *n* souvenir *m*.

recommend [rɛkə'mɛnd] *vt* recommander.
reconcile ['rɛkənsaɪl] *vt* (*two people*) réconcilier; (*two facts*) concilier, accorder; **to ~ o.s. to** se résigner à.
recondition [riːkən'dɪʃən] *vt* remettre à neuf; réviser entièrement.
reconnoitre, (*US*) **reconnoiter** [rɛkə'nɔɪtə*] (*MIL*) *vt* reconnaître // *vi* faire une reconnaissance.
reconstruct [riːkən'strʌkt] *vt* (*building*) reconstruire; (*crime*) reconstituer.
record *n* ['rɛkɔːd] rapport *m*, récit *m*; (*of meeting etc*) procès-verbal *m*; (*register*) registre *m*; (*file*) dossier *m*; (*also*: **police ~**) casier *m* judiciaire; (*MUS: disc*) disque *m*; (*SPORT*) record *m* // *vt* [rɪ'kɔːd] (*set down*) noter; (*relate*) rapporter; (*MUS: song etc*) enregistrer; **in ~ time** dans un temps record *inv*; **to keep a ~ of** noter; **off the ~** *a* officieux(euse) // *ad* officieusement; **~ card** *n* (*in file*) fiche *f*; **~ed delivery** *n* (*Brit POST*): **~ed delivery letter** *etc* lettre *etc* recommandée; **~er** *n* (*LAW*) avocat nommé à la fonction de juge; (*MUS*) flûte *f* à bec; **~ holder** *n* (*SPORT*) détenteur/trice du record; **~ing** *n* (*MUS*) enregistrement *m*; **~ player** *n* électrophone *m*.
recount [rɪ'kaunt] *vt* raconter.
re-count *n* ['riːkaunt] (*POL: of votes*) pointage *m* // *vt* [riː'kaunt] recompter.
recoup [rɪ'kuːp] *vt*: **to ~ one's losses** récupérer ce qu'on a perdu, se refaire.
recourse [rɪ'kɔːs] *n* recours *m*; expédient *m*.
recover [rɪ'kʌvə*] *vt* récupérer // *vi* (*from illness*) se rétablir; (*from shock*) se remettre; (*country*) se redresser.
recovery [rɪ'kʌvərɪ] *n* récupération *f*; rétablissement *m*; redressement *m*.
recreation [rɛkrɪ'eɪʃən] *n* récréation *f*, détente *f*; **~al** *a* pour la détente, récréatif(ive).
recruit [rɪ'kruːt] *n* recrue *f* // *vt* recruter.
rectangle ['rɛktæŋgl] *n* rectangle *m*; **rectangular** [-'tæŋgjulə*] *a* rectangulaire.
rectify ['rɛktɪfaɪ] *vt* (*error*) rectifier, corriger; (*omission*) réparer.
rector ['rɛktə*] *n* (*REL*) pasteur *m*; **rectory** *n* presbytère *m*.
recuperate [rɪ'kjuːpəreɪt] *vi* récupérer; (*from illness*) se rétablir.
recur [rɪ'kɔː*] *vi* se reproduire; (*idea*, *opportunity*) se retrouver; (*symptoms*) réapparaître; **~rent** *a* périodique, fréquent(e).
red [rɛd] *n* rouge *m*; (*POL: pej*) rouge *m/f* // *a* rouge; **in the ~** (*account*) à découvert; (*business*) en déficit; **~ carpet treatment** *n* réception *f* en grande pompe; **R~ Cross** *n* Croix-Rouge *f*; **~ currant** *n* groseille *f* (rouge); **~den** *vt*,

vi rougir; ~**dish** *a* rougeâtre; (*hair*) plutôt roux(rousse).

redeem [rɪ'diːm] *vt* (*debt*) rembourser; (*sth in pawn*) dégager; (*fig, also REL*) racheter; ~**ing** *a* (*feature*) qui sauve, qui rachète (le reste).

redeploy [riːdɪ'plɔɪ] *vt* (*resources*) réorganiser.

red-haired [rɛd'hɛəd] *a* roux(rousse).

red-handed [rɛd'hændɪd] *a*: to be caught ~ être pris(e) en flagrant délit *or* la main dans le sac.

redhead ['rɛdhɛd] *n* roux/rousse.

red herring *n* (*fig*) diversion *f*, fausse piste.

red-hot [rɛd'hɔt] *a* chauffé(e) au rouge, brûlant(e).

redirect [riːdaɪ'rɛkt] *vt* (*mail*) faire suivre.

red light *n*: to go through a ~ (*AUT*) brûler un feu rouge; **red-light district** *n* quartier réservé.

redo [riː'duː] *vt irg* refaire.

redolent ['rɛdələnt] *a*: ~ of qui sent; (*fig*) qui évoque.

redress [rɪ'drɛs] *n* réparation *f* // *vt* redresser.

Red Sea *n* la mer Rouge.

redskin ['rɛdskɪn] *n* Peau-Rouge *m/f*.

red tape *n* (*fig*) paperasserie (administrative).

reduce [rɪ'djuːs] *vt* réduire; (*lower*) abaisser; '~ **speed now**' (*AUT*) 'ralentir'; **reduction** [rɪ'dʌkʃən] *n* réduction *f*; (*of price*) baisse *f*; (*discount*) rabais *m*; réduction.

redundancy [rɪ'dʌndənsɪ] *n* licenciement *m*, mise *f* au chômage.

redundant [rɪ'dʌndnt] *a* (*worker*) mis(e) au chômage, licencié(e); (*detail, object*) superflu(e); to be made ~ être licencié(e), être mis(e) au chômage.

reed [riːd] *n* (*BOT*) roseau *m*.

reef [riːf] *n* (*at sea*) récif *m*, écueil *m*.

reek [riːk] *vi*: to ~ (of) puer, empester.

reel [riːl] *n* bobine *f*; (*TECH*) dévidoir *m*; (*FISHING*) moulinet *m*; (*CINEMA*) bande *f* // *vt* (*TECH*) bobiner; (*also:* ~ **up**) enrouler // *vi* (*sway*) chanceler.

ref [rɛf] *n abbr* (*col:* = *referee*) arbitre *m*.

refectory [rɪ'fɛktərɪ] *n* réfectoire *m*.

refer [rɪ'fəː*] *vt*: to ~ sth to (*dispute, decision*) soumettre qch à; to ~ sb to (*inquirer: for information*) adresser *or* envoyer qn à; (*reader: to text*) renvoyer qn à; to ~ to *vt fus* (*allude to*) parler de, faire allusion à; (*apply to*) s'appliquer à; (*consult*) se reporter à.

referee [rɛfə'riː] *n* arbitre *m*; (*Brit: for job application*) répondant/e.

reference ['rɛfrəns] *n* référence *f*, renvoi *m*; (*mention*) allusion *f*, mention *f*; (*for job application: letter*) références; lettre *f* de recommandation; (*: person*)

répondant/e; **with** ~ **to** en ce qui concerne; (*COMM: in letter*) me référant à; ~ **book** *n* ouvrage *m* de référence.

refill *vt* [riː'fɪl] remplir à nouveau; (*pen, lighter etc*) recharger // *n* ['riːfɪl] (*for pen etc*) recharge *f*.

refine [rɪ'faɪn] *vt* (*sugar, oil*) raffiner; (*taste*) affiner; ~**d** *a* (*person, taste*) raffiné(e).

reflect [rɪ'flɛkt] *vt* (*light, image*) réfléchir, refléter; (*fig*) refléter // *vi* (*think*) réfléchir, méditer; **to** ~ **on** *vt fus* (*discredit*) porter atteinte à, faire tort à; ~**ion** [-'flɛkʃən] *n* réflexion *f*; (*image*) reflet *m*; (*criticism*): ~ **on** critique *f* de; atteinte *f* à; **on** ~**ion** réflexion faite.

reflex ['riːflɛks] *a, n* réflexe (*m*); ~**ive** [rɪ'flɛksɪv] *a* (*LING*) réfléchi(e).

reform [rɪ'fɔːm] *n* réforme *f* // *vt* réformer; **the R~ation** [rɛfə'meɪʃən] *n* la Réforme; ~**atory** *n* (*US*) ≈ centre *m* d'éducation surveillée.

refrain [rɪ'freɪn] *vi*: to ~ **from doing** s'abstenir de faire // *n* refrain *m*.

refresh [rɪ'frɛʃ] *vt* rafraîchir; (*subj: food*) redonner des forces à; (*: sleep*) reposer; ~**er course** *n* (*Brit*) cours *m* de recyclage; ~**ing** *a* (*drink*) rafraîchissant(e); (*sleep*) réparateur(trice); ~**ments** *npl* rafraîchissements *mpl*.

refrigerator [rɪ'frɪdʒəreɪtə*] *n* réfrigérateur *m*, frigidaire *m*.

refuel [riː'fjuəl] *vi* se ravitailler en carburant.

refuge ['rɛfjuːdʒ] *n* refuge *m*; **to take** ~ **in** se réfugier dans.

refugee [rɛfju'dʒiː] *n* réfugié/e.

refund *n* [rɪ'fʌnd] remboursement *m* // *vt* [rɪ'fʌnd] rembourser.

refurbish [riː'fəːbɪʃ] *vt* remettre à neuf.

refusal [rɪ'fjuːzəl] *n* refus *m*; **to have first** ~ **on** avoir droit de préemption sur.

refuse *n* ['rɛfjuːs] ordures *fpl*, détritus *mpl* // *vt, vi* [rɪ'fjuːz] refuser; ~ **collection** *n* ramassage *m* d'ordures.

regain [rɪ'geɪn] *vt* regagner; retrouver.

regal ['riːgl] *a* royal(e); ~**ia** [rɪ'geɪlɪə] *n* insignes *mpl* de la royauté.

regard [rɪ'gɑːd] *n* respect *m*, estime *f*, considération *f* // *vt* considérer; **to give one's** ~**s to** faire ses amitiés à; 'with kindest ~s' 'bien amicalement'; ~**ing**, **as** ~**s, with** ~ **to** *prep* en ce qui concerne; ~**less** *ad* quand même; ~**less of** sans se soucier de.

régime [reɪ'ʒiːm] *n* régime *m*.

regiment *n* ['rɛdʒɪmənt] *n* régiment *m* // *vt* ['rɛdʒɪmɛnt] imposer une discipline trop stricte à; ~**al** [-'mɛntl] *a* d'un *or* du régiment.

region ['riːdʒən] *n* région *f*; **in the** ~ **of** (*fig*) aux alentours de; ~**al** *a* régional(e).

register ['rɛdʒɪstə*] *n* registre *m*; (*also:* **electoral** ~) liste électorale // *vt* enregistrer, inscrire; (*birth*) déclarer; (*vehicle*) immatriculer; (*luggage*) enregistrer; (*letter*) envoyer en recommandé; (*subj: instrument*) marquer // *vi* se faire inscrire; (*at hotel*) signer le registre; (*make impression*) être (bien) compris(e); ~**ed** *a* (*design*) déposé(e); (*Brit: letter*) recommandé(e); ~**ed trademark** *n* marque déposée.

registrar ['rɛdʒɪstra:*] *n* officier *m* de l'état civil; secrétaire (général).

registration [rɛdʒɪs'treɪʃən] *n* (*act*) enregistrement *m*; inscription *f*; (*AUT: also:* ~ **number**) numéro *m* d'immatriculation.

registry ['rɛdʒɪstrɪ] *n* bureau *m* de l'enregistrement; ~ **office** *n* (*Brit*) bureau *m* de l'état civil; **to get married in a** ~ office ≈ se marier à la mairie.

regret [rɪ'grɛt] *n* regret *m* // *vt* regretter; ~**fully** *ad* à *or* avec regret.

regular ['rɛgjulə*] *a* régulier(ère); (*usual*) habituel(le), normal(e); (*soldier*) de métier; (*COMM: size*) ordinaire // *n* (*client etc*) habitué/e; ~**ly** *ad* régulièrement.

regulate ['rɛgjuleɪt] *vt* régler; **regulation** [-'leɪʃən] *n* (*rule*) règlement *m*; (*adjustment*) réglage *m*.

rehabilitation ['ri:həbɪlɪ'teɪʃən] *n* (*of offender*) réhabilitation *f*; (*of disabled*) rééducation *f*, réadaptation *f*.

rehearsal [rɪ'hə:səl] *n* répétition *f*.

rehearse [rɪ'hə:s] *vt* répéter.

reign [reɪn] *n* règne *m* // *vi* régner.

reimburse [ri:ɪm'bə:s] *vt* rembourser.

rein [reɪn] *n* (*for horse*) rêne *f*.

reindeer ['reɪndɪə*] *n* (*pl inv*) renne *m*.

reinforce [ri:ɪn'fɔ:s] *vt* renforcer; ~**d concrete** *n* béton armé; ~**ments** *npl* (*MIL*) renfort(s) *m(pl)*.

reinstate [ri:ɪn'steɪt] *vt* rétablir, réintégrer.

reject *n* ['ri:dʒɛkt] (*COMM*) article *m* de rebut // *vt* [rɪ'dʒɛkt] refuser; (*COMM: goods*) mettre au rebut; (*idea*) rejeter; ~**ion** [rɪ'dʒɛkʃən] *n* rejet *m*, refus *m*.

rejoice [rɪ'dʒɔɪs] *vi*: **to** ~ (**at** *or* **over**) se réjouir (de).

rejuvenate [rɪ'dʒu:vəneɪt] *vt* rajeunir.

relapse [rɪ'læps] *n* (*MED*) rechute *f*.

relate [rɪ'leɪt] *vt* (*tell*) raconter; (*connect*) établir un rapport entre // *vi*: **to** ~ **to** se rapporter à; ~**d** *a* apparenté(e); **relating to** *prep* concernant.

relation [rɪ'leɪʃən] *n* (*person*) parent/e; (*link*) rapport *m*, lien *m*; ~**ship** *n* rapport *m*, lien *m*; (*personal ties*) relations *fpl*, rapports; (*also:* family ~**ship**) lien de parenté; (*affair*) liaison *f*.

relative ['rɛlətɪv] *n* parent/e // *a* relatif(ive); (*respective*) respectif(ive); **all her** ~**s** toute sa famille.

relax [rɪ'læks] *vi* se relâcher; (*person:*

unwind) se détendre // *vt* relâcher; (*mind, person*) détendre; ~**ation** [ri:læk'seɪʃən] *n* relâchement *m*; détente *f*; (*entertainment*) distraction *f*; ~**ed** *a* relâché(e); détendu(e); ~**ing** *a* délassant(e).

relay ['ri:leɪ] *n* (*SPORT*) course *f* de relais // *vt* (*message*) retransmettre, relayer.

release [rɪ'li:s] *n* (*from prison, obligation*) libération *f*; (*of gas etc*) émission *f*; (*of film etc*) sortie *f*; (*record*) disque *m*; (*device*) déclencheur *m* // *vt* (*prisoner*) libérer; (*book, film*) sortir; (*report, news*) rendre public, publier; (*gas etc*) émettre, dégager; (*free: from wreckage etc*) dégager; (*TECH: catch, spring etc*) déclencher; (*let go*) relâcher; lâcher; desserrer.

relegate ['rɛləgeɪt] *vt* reléguer; (*SPORT*): **to be** ~**d** descendre dans une division inférieure.

relent [rɪ'lɛnt] *vi* se laisser fléchir; ~**less** *a* implacable.

relevant ['rɛləvənt] *a* approprié(e); (*fact*) significatif(ive); (*information*) utile, pertinent(e); ~ **to** ayant rapport à, approprié à.

reliable [rɪ'laɪəbl] *a* (*person, firm*) sérieux(euse), fiable; (*method, machine*) fiable; **reliably** *ad*: **to be reliably informed** savoir de source sûre.

reliance [rɪ'laɪəns] *n*: ~ (**on**) confiance *f* (en); besoin *m* (de), dépendance *f* (de).

relic ['rɛlɪk] *n* (*REL*) relique *f*; (*of the past*) vestige *m*.

relief [rɪ'li:f] *n* (*from pain, anxiety*) soulagement *m*; (*help, supplies*) secours *m(pl)*; (*of guard*) relève *f*; (*ART, GEO*) relief *m*.

relieve [rɪ'li:v] *vt* (*pain, patient*) soulager; (*bring help*) secourir; (*take over from: gen*) relayer; (: *guard*) relever; **to** ~ **sb of sth** débarrasser qn de qch; **to** ~ **o.s.** se soulager, faire ses besoins.

religion [rɪ'lɪdʒən] *n* religion *f*; **religious** *a* religieux(euse); (*book*) de piété.

relinquish [rɪ'lɪŋkwɪʃ] *vt* abandonner; (*plan, habit*) renoncer à.

relish ['rɛlɪʃ] *n* (*CULIN*) condiment *m*; (*enjoyment*) délectation *f* // *vt* (*food etc*) savourer; **to** ~ **doing** se délecter à faire.

relocate [ri:ləu'keɪt] *vt* installer ailleurs // *vi* déménager, s'installer ailleurs.

reluctance [rɪ'lʌktəns] *n* répugnance *f*.

reluctant [rɪ'lʌktənt] *a* peu disposé(e), qui hésite; ~**ly** *ad* à contrecœur, sans enthousiasme.

rely [rɪ'laɪ]: **to** ~ **on** *vt fus* compter sur; (*be dependent*) dépendre de.

remain [rɪ'meɪn] *vi* rester; ~**der** *n* reste *m*; (*COMM*) fin *f* de série; ~**ing** *a* qui reste; ~**s** *npl* restes *mpl*.

remand [rɪ'mɑ:nd] *n*: **on** ~ en détention

préventive // vt: **to ~ in custody** écrouer; renvoyer en détention provisoire; **~ home** n (Brit) maison f d'arrêt.

remark [rɪ'mɑːk] n remarque f, observation f // vt (faire) remarquer, dire; (notice) remarquer; **~able** a remarquable.

remedial [rɪ'miːdɪəl] a (tuition, classes) de rattrapage.

remedy ['rɛmədɪ] n: ~ **(for)** remède m (contre or à) // vt remédier à.

remember [rɪ'mɛmbə*] vt se rappeler, se souvenir de; **remembrance** n souvenir m; mémoire f.

remind [rɪ'maɪnd] vt: **to ~ sb of sth** rappeler qch à qn; **to ~ sb to do** faire penser à qn à faire, rappeler à qn qu'il doit faire; **~er** n rappel m; (note etc) pense-bête m.

reminisce [rɛmɪ'nɪs] vi: **to ~ (about)** évoquer ses souvenirs (de).

reminiscent [rɛmɪ'nɪsnt] a: ~ **of** qui rappelle, qui fait penser à.

remiss [rɪ'mɪs] a négligent(e).

remission [rɪ'mɪʃən] n rémission f; (of debt, sentence) remise f; (of fee) exemption f.

remit [rɪ'mɪt] vt (send: money) envoyer; **~tance** n envoi m, paiement m.

remnant ['rɛmnənt] n reste m, restant m; **~s** npl (COMM) coupons mpl; fins fpl de série.

remorse [rɪ'mɔːs] n remords m; **~ful** a plein(e) de remords; **~less** a (fig) impitoyable.

remote [rɪ'məut] a éloigné(e), lointain(e); (person) distant(e); **~ control** n télécommande f; **~ly** ad au loin; (slightly) très vaguement.

remould ['riːməuld] n (Brit: tyre) pneu rechapé.

removable [rɪ'muːvəbl] a (detachable) amovible.

removal [rɪ'muːvəl] n (taking away) enlèvement m; suppression f; (Brit: from house) déménagement m; (from office: dismissal) renvoi m; (MED) ablation f; ~ **van** n (Brit) camion m de déménagement.

remove [rɪ'muːv] vt enlever, retirer; (employee) renvoyer; (stain) faire partir; (doubt, abuse) supprimer; **~rs** npl (Brit: company) entreprise f de déménagement.

render ['rɛndə*] vt rendre; **~ing** n (MUS etc) interprétation f.

rendez-vous ['rɔndɪvuː] n rendez-vous m inv // vi opérer une jonction, se rejoindre.

renew [rɪ'njuː] vt renouveler; (negotiations) reprendre; (acquaintance) renouer; **~al** n renouvellement m; reprise f.

renounce [rɪ'nauns] vt renoncer à; (disown) renier.

renovate ['rɛnəveɪt] vt rénover; (art work) restaurer.

renown [rɪ'naun] n renommée f; **~ed** a renommé(e).

rent [rɛnt] n loyer m // vt louer; **~al** n (for television, car) (prix m de) location f.

rep [rɛp] n abbr (COMM: = representative) représentant m (de commerce); (THEATRE: = repertory) théâtre m de répertoire.

repair [rɪ'pɛə*] n réparation f // vt réparer; **in good/bad ~** en bon/mauvais état; ~ **kit** n trousse f de réparations.

repartee [rɛpɑː'tiː] n repartie f.

repatriate [riː'pætrɪeɪt] vt rapatrier.

repay [riː'peɪ] vt irg (money, creditor) rembourser; (sb's efforts) récompenser; **~ment** n remboursement m; récompense f.

repeal [rɪ'piːl] n (of law) abrogation f; (of sentence) annulation f // vt abroger; annuler.

repeat [rɪ'piːt] n (RADIO, TV) reprise f // vt répéter; (pattern) reproduire; (promise, attack, also COMM: order) renouveler; (SCOL: a class) redoubler // vi répéter; **~edly** ad souvent, à plusieurs reprises.

repel [rɪ'pɛl] vt (lit, fig) repousser; **~lent** a repoussant(e) // n: **insect ~lent** insectifuge m.

repent [rɪ'pɛnt] vi: **to ~ (of)** se repentir (de); **~ance** n repentir m.

repertory ['rɛpətərɪ] n (also: ~ **theatre**) théâtre m de répertoire.

repetition [rɛpɪ'tɪʃən] n répétition f.

repetitive [rɪ'pɛtɪtɪv] a (movement, work) répétitif(ive); (speech) plein(e) de redites.

replace [rɪ'pleɪs] vt (put back) remettre, replacer; (take the place of) remplacer; **~ment** n replacement m, remplacement m; (person) remplaçant/e.

replay ['riːpleɪ] n (of match) match rejoué; (of tape, film) répétition f.

replenish [rɪ'plɛnɪʃ] vt (glass) remplir (de nouveau); (stock etc) réapprovisionner.

replete [rɪ'pliːt] a rempli(e); (well-fed) rassasié(e).

replica ['rɛplɪkə] n réplique f, copie exacte.

reply [rɪ'plaɪ] n réponse f // vi répondre; ~ **coupon** n coupon-réponse m.

report [rɪ'pɔːt] n rapport m; (PRESS etc) reportage m; (Brit: also: **school ~**) bulletin m (scolaire); (of gun) détonation f // vt rapporter, faire un compte rendu de; (PRESS etc) faire un reportage sur; (bring to notice: occurrence) signaler; (: person) dénoncer // vi (make a report) faire un rapport (or un reportage); (present o.s.): **to ~ (to sb)** se présenter (chez qn); ~ **card** n (US, Scottish) bulletin m scolaire; ~**edly** ad: she is ~edly living in ... elle habiterait ...; he ~edly told them to ... il leur aurait ordonné de ...; ~**er** n reporter m.

repose [rɪ'pəuz] n: in ~ en or au repos.

represent [reprɪ'zent] vt représenter; ~**ation** [-'teɪʃən] n représentation f; ~**ations** npl (protest) démarche f; ~**ative** n représentant/e; (US POL) député m // a représentatif(ive), caractéristique.

repress [rɪ'pres] vt réprimer; ~**ion** [-'preʃən] n répression f.

reprieve [rɪ'priːv] n (LAW) grâce f; (fig) sursis m, délai m.

reprisal [rɪ'praɪzl] n représailles fpl.

reproach [rɪ'prəutʃ] vt: to ~ sb with sth reprocher qch à qn; ~**ful** a de reproche.

reproduce [riːprə'djuːs] vt reproduire // vi se reproduire; **reproduction** [-'dʌkʃən] n reproduction f.

reproof [rɪ'pruːf] n reproche m.

reptile ['reptaɪl] n reptile m.

republic [rɪ'pʌblɪk] n république f; ~**an** a, n républicain(e).

repulsive [rɪ'pʌlsɪv] a repoussant(e), répulsif(ive).

reputable ['repjutəbl] a de bonne réputation; (occupation) honorable.

reputation [repju'teɪʃən] n réputation f.

repute [rɪ'pjuːt] n (bonne) réputation; ~**d** a réputé(e); ~**dly** ad d'après ce qu'on dit.

request [rɪ'kwest] n demande f; (formal) requête f // vt: to ~ (of or from sb) demander (à qn); ~ **stop** n (Brit: for bus) arrêt facultatif.

require [rɪ'kwaɪə*] vt (need: subj: person) avoir besoin de; (: thing, situation) demander; (want) vouloir; exiger; (order) obliger; ~**ment** n exigence f; besoin m; condition requise.

requisite ['rekwɪzɪt] n chose f nécessaire // a requis(e), nécessaire.

requisition [rekwɪ'zɪʃən] n: ~ (for) demande f (de) // vt (MIL) réquisitionner.

rescue ['reskjuː] n sauvetage m; (help) secours mpl // vt sauver; ~ **party** n équipe f de sauvetage; ~**r** n sauveteur m.

research [rɪ'səːtʃ] n recherche(s) f(pl) // vt faire des recherches sur.

resemblance [rɪ'zembləns] n ressemblance f.

resemble [rɪ'zembl] vt ressembler à.

resent [rɪ'zent] vt éprouver du ressentiment de, être contrarié(e) par; ~**ful** a irrité(e), plein(e) de ressentiment; ~**ment** n ressentiment m.

reservation [rezə'veɪʃən] n (booking) réservation f; (doubt) réserve f; (protected area) réserve; (Brit: on road: also: central ~) bande f médiane; to

make a ~ (in an hotel/a restaurant/on a plane) réserver or retenir une chambre/une table/une place.

reserve [rɪ'zəːv] n réserve f; (SPORT) remplaçant/e // vt (seats etc) réserver, retenir; ~**s** npl (MIL) réservistes mpl; in ~ en réserve; ~**d** a réservé(e).

reshuffle [riː'ʃʌfl] n: Cabinet ~ (POL) remaniement ministériel.

residence ['rezɪdəns] n résidence f; ~ **permit** n (Brit) permis m de séjour.

resident ['rezɪdənt] n résident/e // a résidant(e); ~**ial** [-'denʃəl] a de résidence; (area) résidentiel(le).

residue ['rezɪdjuː] n reste m; (CHEM, PHYSICS) résidu m.

resign [rɪ'zaɪn] vt (one's post) se démettre de // vi démissionner; to ~ o.s. to (endure) se résigner à; ~**ation** [rezɪg'neɪʃən] n démission f; résignation f; ~**ed** a résigné(e).

resilience [rɪ'zɪlɪəns] n (of material) élasticité f; (of person) ressort m.

resilient [rɪ'zɪlɪənt] a (person) qui réagit, qui a du ressort.

resist [rɪ'zɪst] vt résister à; ~**ance** n résistance f.

resolution [rezə'luːʃən] n résolution f.

resolve [rɪ'zɔlv] n résolution f // vi (decide): to ~ to do résoudre or décider de faire // vt (problem) résoudre.

resort [rɪ'zɔːt] n (town) station f; (recourse) recours m // vi: to ~ to avoir recours à; in the last ~ en dernier ressort.

resounding [rɪ'zaundɪŋ] a retentissant(e).

resource [rɪ'sɔːs] n ressource f; ~**s** npl ressources.

respect [rɪs'pekt] n respect m // vt respecter; ~**s** npl respects, hommages mpl; with ~ to en ce qui concerne; in this ~ sous ce rapport, à cet égard; ~**able** a respectable; ~**ful** a respectueux(euse).

respite ['respaɪt] n répit m.

resplendent [rɪs'plendənt] a resplendissant(e).

respond [rɪs'pɔnd] vi répondre; (to treatment) réagir.

response [rɪs'pɔns] n réponse f; (to treatment) réaction f.

responsibility [rɪspɔnsɪ'bɪlɪtɪ] n responsabilité f.

responsible [rɪs'pɔnsɪbl] a (liable): ~ (for) responsable (de); (person) digne de confiance; (job) qui comporte des responsabilités; **responsibly** ad avec sérieux.

responsive [rɪs'pɔnsɪv] a qui n'est pas réservé(e) or indifférent(e).

rest [rest] n repos m; (stop) arrêt m, pause f; (MUS) silence m; (support) support m, appui m; (remainder) reste m, restant m // vi se reposer; (be *supported*): to ~ on appuyer *or* reposer sur; (*remain*) rester // *vt* (*lean*): to ~ sth on/against appuyer qch sur/contre; the ~ of them les autres; it ~s with him to c'est à lui de.

restaurant ['rɛstərɔŋ] *n* restaurant *m*; ~ **car** *n* (*Brit*) wagon-restaurant *m*.

restful ['rɛstful] *a* reposant(e).

restitution [rɛstɪ'tjuːʃən] *n* (*act*) restitution *f*; (*reparation*) réparation *f*.

restive ['rɛstɪv] *a* agité(e), impatient(e); (*horse*) rétif(ive).

restless ['rɛstlɪs] *a* agité(e).

restoration [rɛstə'reɪʃən] *n* restauration *f*; restitution *f*.

restore [rɪ'stɔː*] *vt* (*building*) restaurer; (*sth stolen*) restituer; (*peace, health*) rétablir.

restrain [rɪs'treɪn] *vt* (*feeling*) contenir; (*person*): to ~ (*from doing*) retenir (de faire); ~ed *a* (*style*) sobre; (*manner*) mesuré(e); ~t *n* (*restriction*) contrainte *f*; (*moderation*) retenue *f*.

restrict [rɪs'trɪkt] *vt* restreindre, limiter; ~ion [-kʃən] *n* restriction *f*, limitation *f*.

rest room *n* (*US*) toilettes *fpl*.

result [rɪ'zʌlt] *n* résultat *m* // *vi*: to ~ in aboutir à, se terminer par; **as a** ~ **of** à la suite de.

resume [rɪ'zjuːm] *vt, vi* (*work, journey*) reprendre.

résumé ['reɪzjumeɪ] *n* résumé *m*; (*US*) curriculum vitae *m*.

resumption [rɪ'zʌmpʃən] *n* reprise *f*.

resurgence [rɪ'sə:dʒəns] *n* réapparition *f*.

resurrection [rɛzə'rɛkʃən] *n* résurrection *f*.

resuscitate [rɪ'sʌsɪteɪt] *vt* (*MED*) réanimer.

rev [rɛv] *n abbr* (= *revolution*: *AUT*) tour *m* // *vb* (*also*: ~ **up**) *vt* emballer // *vi* s'emballer.

revamp ['riː'væmp] *vt* (*house*) retaper; (*firm*) réorganiser.

retail ['riːteɪl] *n* (vente *f* au) détail *m* // *cpd* de *or* au détail // *vt* vendre au détail; ~**er** *n* détaillant/e; ~ **price** *n* prix *m* de détail.

retain [rɪ'teɪn] *vt* (*keep*) garder, conserver; (*employ*) engager; ~**er** *n* (*servant*) serviteur *m*; (*fee*) acompte *m*, provision *f*.

retaliate [rɪ'tælɪeɪt] *vi*: to ~ (**against**) se venger (de); **retaliation** [-'eɪʃən] *n* représailles *fpl*, vengeance *f*.

retarded [rɪ'tɑːdɪd] *a* retardé(e).

retch [rɛtʃ] *vi* avoir des haut-le-cœur.

retentive [rɪ'tɛntɪv] *a*: ~ **memory** excellente mémoire.

retina ['rɛtɪnə] *n* rétine *f*.

retinue ['rɛtɪnjuː] *n* suite *f*, cortège *m*.

retire [rɪ'taɪə*] *vi* (*give up work*) prendre sa retraite; (*withdraw*) se retirer, partir; (*go to bed*) (aller) se coucher; ~**d** *a* (*person*) retraité(e); ~**ment** *n* retraite *f*; **retiring** *a* (*person*) réservé(e).

retort [rɪ'tɔːt] *vi* riposter.

retrace [riː'treɪs] *vt* reconstituer; to ~ one's steps revenir sur ses pas.

retract [rɪ'trækt] *vt* (*statement, claws*) rétracter; (*undercarriage, aerial*) rentrer, escamoter // *vi* se rétracter; rentrer.

retrain [riː'treɪn] *vt* (*worker*) recycler.

retread ['riː'trɛd] *n* (*tyre*) pneu rechapé.

retreat [rɪ'triːt] *n* retraite *f* // *vi* battre en retraite; (*flood*) reculer.

retribution [rɛtrɪ'bjuːʃən] *n* châtiment *m*.

retrieval [rɪ'triːvəl] *n* (*see vb*) récupération *f*; réparation *f*; recherche *f* et extraction *f*.

retrieve [rɪ'triːv] *vt* (*sth lost*) récupérer; (*situation, honour*) sauver; (*error, loss*) réparer; (*COMPUT*) rechercher; ~**r** *n* chien *m* d'arrêt.

retrospect ['rɛtrəspɛkt] *n*: **in** ~ rétrospectivement, après coup; ~**ive** [-'spɛktɪv] *a* (*law*) rétroactif(ive).

return [rɪ'təːn] *n* (*going or coming back*) retour *m*; (*of sth stolen etc*) restitution *f*; (*recompense*) récompense *f*; (*FINANCE: from land, shares*) rapport *m*; (*report*) relevé *m*, rapport // *cpd* (*journey*) de retour; (*Brit: ticket*) aller et retour; (*match*) retour // *vi* (*person etc: come back*) revenir; (: *go back*) retourner // *vt* rendre; (*bring back*) rapporter; (*send back*) renvoyer; (*put back*) remettre; (*POL: candidate*) élire; ~**s** *npl* (*COMM*) recettes *fpl*; bénéfices *mpl*; **in** ~ (**for**) en échange (de); **by** ~ (**of post**) par retour (du courrier); **many happy** ~**s** (**of the day**)! bon anniversaire!

reunion [riː'juːnɪən] *n* réunion *f*.

reunite [riːjuː'naɪt] *vt* réunir.

reveal [rɪ'viːl] *vt* (*make known*) révéler; (*display*) laisser voir; ~**ing** *a* révélateur(trice); (*dress*) au décolleté généreux *or* suggestif.

revel ['rɛvl] *vi*: to ~ **in sth/in doing** se délecter de qch/à faire.

revelry ['rɛvlrɪ] *n* festivités *fpl*.

revenge [rɪ'vɛndʒ] *n* vengeance *f*; (*in game etc*) revanche *f* // *vt* venger; **to take** ~ se venger.

revenue ['rɛvənjuː] *n* revenu *m*.

reverberate [rɪ'və:bəreɪt] *vi* (*sound*) retentir, se répercuter; (*light*) se réverbérer.

reverence ['rɛvərəns] *n* vénération *f*, révérence *f*.

Reverend ['rɛvərənd] *a* (*in titles*): **the** ~ **John Smith** (*Anglican*) le révérend John Smith; (*Catholic*) l'abbé (John) Smith; (*Protestant*) le pasteur (John) Smith.

reversal [rɪ'və:sl] *n* (*of opinion*) revirement *m*.

reverse [rɪ'vɜːs] n contraire m, opposé m; (back) dos m, envers m; (AUT: also: ~ **gear**) marche f arrière // a (order, direction) opposé(e), inverse // vt (turn) renverser, retourner; (change) renverser, changer complètement; (LAW: judgment) réformer // vi (Brit AUT) faire marche arrière; ~**d charge call** n (Brit TEL) communication f en PCV; **reversing lights** npl (Brit AUT) feux mpl de marche arrière or de recul.

revert [rɪ'vɜːt] vi: to ~ to revenir à, retourner à.

review [rɪ'vjuː] n revue f; (of book, film) critique f // vt passer en revue; faire la critique de; ~**er** n critique m.

revile [rɪ'vaɪl] vt injurier.

revise [rɪ'vaɪz] vt (manuscript) revoir, corriger; (opinion) réviser, modifier; (study: subject, notes) réviser; **revision** [rɪ'vɪʒən] n révision f.

revival [rɪ'vaɪvəl] n reprise f; rétablissement m; (of faith) renouveau m.

revive [rɪ'vaɪv] vt (person) ranimer; (custom) rétablir; (hope, courage) redonner; (play, fashion) reprendre // vi (person) reprendre connaissance; (hope) renaître; (activity) reprendre.

revolt [rɪ'vəʊlt] n révolte f // vi se révolter, se rebeller // vt révolter, dégoûter; ~**ing** a dégoûtant(e).

revolution [rɛvə'luːʃən] n révolution f; (of wheel etc) tour m, révolution; ~**ary** a, n révolutionnaire (m/f).

revolve [rɪ'vɒlv] vi tourner.

revolver [rɪ'vɒlvə*] n revolver m.

revolving [rɪ'vɒlvɪŋ] a (chair) pivotant(e); (light) tournant(e); ~ **door** n (porte f à) tambour m.

revulsion [rɪ'vʌlʃən] n dégoût m, répugnance f.

reward [rɪ'wɔːd] n récompense f // vt: to ~ (for) récompenser (de); ~**ing** a (fig) qui (en) vaut la peine, gratifiant(e).

rewire [riː'waɪə*] vt (house) refaire l'installation électrique de.

reword [riː'wɜːd] vt formuler or exprimer différemment.

rheumatism ['ruːmətɪzəm] n rhumatisme m.

Rhine [raɪn] n: the ~ le Rhin.

rhinoceros [raɪ'nɒsərəs] n rhinocéros m.

Rhone [rəʊn] n: the ~ le Rhône.

rhubarb ['ruːbɑːb] n rhubarbe f.

rhyme [raɪm] n rime f; (verse) vers mpl.

rhythm ['rɪðm] n rythme m.

rib [rɪb] n (ANAT) côte f // vt (mock) taquiner.

ribald ['rɪbəld] a paillard(e).

ribbon ['rɪbən] n ruban m; in ~s (torn) en lambeaux.

rice [raɪs] n riz m.

rich [rɪtʃ] a riche; (gift, clothes) somptueux(euse); the ~ npl les riches

mpl; ~**es** npl richesses fpl; ~**ly** ad richement; (deserved, earned) largement, grandement; ~**ness** n richesse f.

rickets ['rɪkɪts] n rachitisme m.

rickety ['rɪkɪtɪ] a branlant(e).

rickshaw ['rɪkʃɔː] n pousse(-pousse) m inv.

rid, pt, pp **rid** [rɪd] vt: to ~ sb of débarrasser qn de; to get ~ of se débarrasser de.

ridden ['rɪdn] pp of **ride**.

riddle ['rɪdl] n (puzzle) énigme f // vt: to be ~d with être criblé(e) de.

ride [raɪd] n promenade f, tour m; (distance covered) trajet m // vb (pt **rode**, pp **ridden** [rəʊd, 'rɪdn]) vi (as sport) monter (à cheval), faire du cheval; (go somewhere: on horse, bicycle) aller (à cheval or bicyclette etc); (journey: on bicycle, motor-cycle, bus) rouler // vt (a certain horse) monter; (distance) parcourir, faire; to ~ a horse/bicycle/ camel monter à cheval/à bicyclette/à dos de chameau; to ~ at **anchor** (NAUT) être à l'ancre; to **take sb for a** ~ (fig) faire marcher qn; rouler qn; ~**r** n cavalier/ ère; (in race) jockey m; (on bicycle) cycliste m/f; (on motorcycle) motocycliste m/f; (in document) annexe f, clause additionnelle.

ridge [rɪdʒ] n (of hill) faîte m; (of roof, mountain) arête f; (on object) strie f.

ridicule ['rɪdɪkjuːl] n ridicule m; dérision f.

ridiculous [rɪ'dɪkjuləs] a ridicule.

riding ['raɪdɪŋ] n équitation f; ~ **school** n manège m, école f d'équitation.

rife [raɪf] a répandu(e); ~ **with** abondant(e) en.

riffraff ['rɪfræf] n racaille f.

rifle ['raɪfl] n fusil m (à canon rayé) // vt vider, dévaliser; ~ **range** n champ m de tir; (indoor) stand m de tir.

rift [rɪft] n fente f, fissure f; (fig: disagreement) désaccord m.

rig [rɪg] n (also: **oil** ~: on land) derrick m; (: at sea) plate-forme pétrolière f // vt (election etc) truquer; to ~ **out** vt (Brit) habiller; (: pej) fringuer, attifer; to ~ **up** vt arranger, faire avec des moyens de fortune; ~**ging** n (NAUT) gréement m.

right [raɪt] a (true) juste, exact(e); (correctly chosen: answer, road etc) bon(bonne); (suitable) approprié(e), convenable; (just) juste, équitable; (morally good) bien inv; (not left) droit(e) n (in title, claim) droit m; (not left) droite f // ad (answer) correctement; (not on the left) à droite // vt redresser // excl bon!; to be ~ (person) avoir raison; (answer) être juste or correct(e); by ~ en toute justice; on the ~ à droite; to be in the ~ avoir raison; ~ **now** en ce moment même; tout de suite; ~ **against the wall** tout contre le mur; ~ **ahead** tout droit; droit devant; ~ **in the middle** en plein milieu; ~ **away** immédiatement; ~ **angle** n angle droit; ~**eous** ['raɪtʃəs] a droit(e), vertueux(euse); (*anger*) justifié(e); ~**ful** a (*heir*) légitime; ~**handed** a (*person*) droitier(ère); ~**hand man** n bras droit (*fig*); ~**hand side** n côté droit; ~**ly** ad bien, correctement; (*with reason*) à juste titre; ~ **of way** n droit m de passage; (*AUT*) priorité f; ~**wing** a (*POL*) de droite.

rigid ['rɪdʒɪd] a rigide; (*principle*) strict(e).

rigmarole ['rɪgmərəul] n galimatias m, comédie f.

rigorous ['rɪgərəs] a rigoureux(euse).

rile [raɪl] vt agacer.

rim [rɪm] n bord m; (*of spectacles*) monture f; (*of wheel*) jante f.

rind [raɪnd] n (*of bacon*) couenne f; (*of lemon etc*) écorce f.

ring [rɪŋ] n anneau m; (*on finger*) bague f; (*also:* **wedding** ~) alliance f; (*for napkin*) rond m; (*of people, objects*) cercle m; (*of spies*) réseau m; (*of smoke etc*) rond; (*arena*) piste f, arène f (*for boxing*) ring m; (*sound of bell*) sonnerie f; (*telephone call*) coup m de téléphone // vb (pt **rang**, pp **rung**) vi (*person, bell*) sonner; (*also:* ~ **out:** *voice, words*) retentir; (*TEL*) téléphoner // vt (*Brit TEL:* also: ~ **up**) téléphoner à; **to** ~ **the bell** sonner; **to** ~ **back** vt, vi (*TEL*) rappeler; **to** ~ **off** vi (*Brit TEL*) raccrocher; ~**ing** n tintement m; sonnerie f; (*in ears*) bourdonnement m; ~**ing tone** n (*Brit TEL*) sonnerie f; ~**leader** n (*of gang*) chef m, meneur m.

ringlets ['rɪŋlɪts] npl anglaises fpl.

ring road n (*Brit*) route f de ceinture.

rink [rɪŋk] n (*also:* **ice** ~) patinoire f.

rinse [rɪns] vt rincer.

riot ['raɪət] n émeute f, bagarres fpl // vi faire une émeute, manifester avec violence; **to run** ~ se déchaîner; ~**ous** a tapageur(euse); tordant(e).

rip [rɪp] n déchirure f // vt déchirer // vi se déchirer; ~**cord** n poignée f d'ouverture.

ripe [raɪp] a (*fruit*) mûr(e); (*cheese*) fait(e); ~**n** vt mûrir // vi mûrir; se faire.

rip-off ['rɪpɔf] n (*col*): **it's a** ~! c'est du vol manifeste!

ripple ['rɪpl] n ride f, ondulation f; égrènement m, cascade f // vi se rider, onduler // vt rider, faire onduler.

rise [raɪz] n (*slope*) côte f, pente f; (*hill*) élévation f; (*increase: in wages: Brit*) augmentation f; (: *in prices, temperature*) hausse f, augmentation; (*fig: to power etc*) essor m, ascension f // vi (pt

rose, pp **risen** ['rəuz, rɪzn]) s'élever, monter; (*prices*) augmenter, monter; (*waters, river*) monter; (*sun, wind, person: from chair, bed*) se lever; (*also:* ~ **up:** *rebel*) se révolter; se rebeller; **to give** ~ **to** donner lieu à; **to** ~ **to the occasion** se montrer à la hauteur; **rising** a (*increasing: number, prices*) en hausse; (*tide*) montant(e); (*sun, moon*) levant(e) // n (*uprising*) soulèvement m, insurrection f.

risk [rɪsk] n risque m; danger m // vt risquer; **at** ~ en danger; **at one's own** ~ à ses risques et périls; ~**y** a risqué(e).

rissole ['rɪsəul] n croquette f.

rite [raɪt] n rite m; **last** ~s derniers sacrements.

ritual ['rɪtjuəl] a rituel(le) // n rituel m.

rival ['raɪvl] n rival/e; (*in business*) concurrent/e // a rival(e); qui fait concurrence // vt être en concurrence avec; **to** ~ **sb/sth** in rivaliser avec qn/qch de; ~**ry** n rivalité f, concurrence f.

river ['rɪvə*] n rivière f; (*major, also fig*) fleuve m // cpd (*port, traffic*) fluvial(e); **up/down** ~ en amont/aval; ~**bank** n rive f, berge f.

rivet ['rɪvɪt] n rivet m // vt riveter; (*fig*) river, fixer.

Riviera [rɪvɪ'ɛərə] n: **the (French)** ~ la Côte d'Azur; **the Italian** ~ la Riviera (italienne).

road [rəud] n route f; (*small*) chemin m; (*in town*) rue f; (*fig*) chemin, voie f; **major/minor** ~ route principale or à priorité/voie secondaire; ~**block** n barrage routier; ~**hog** n chauffard m; ~ **map** n carte routière; ~ **safety** n sécurité routière; ~**side** n bord m de la route, bas-côté m; ~**sign** n panneau m de signalisation; ~**way** n chaussée f; ~**works** npl travaux mpl (de réfection des routes); ~**worthy** a en bon état de marche.

roam [rəum] vi errer, vagabonder // vt parcourir, errer par.

roar [rɔ:*] n rugissement m; (*of crowd*) hurlements mpl; (*of vehicle, thunder, storm*) grondement m // vi rugir; hurler; gronder; **to** ~ **with laughter** éclater de rire; **to do a** ~**ing trade** faire des affaires d'or.

roast [rəust] n rôti m // vt (*meat*) (faire) rôtir; ~ **beef** n rôti m de bœuf, rosbif m.

rob [rɔb] vt (*person*) voler; (*bank*) dévaliser; **to** ~ **sb of sth** voler or dérober qch à qn; (*fig: deprive*) priver qn de qch; ~**ber** n bandit m, voleur m; ~**bery** n vol m.

robe [rəub] n (*for ceremony etc*) robe f; (*also:* **bath** ~) peignoir m; (*US*) couverture f // vt revêtir (d'une robe).

robin ['rɔbɪn] n rouge-gorge m.

robot ['rəubɔt] n robot m.

robust [rəu'bʌst] *a* robuste; (*material, appetite*) solide.

rock [rɔk] *n* (*substance*) roche *f*, roc *m*; (*boulder*) rocher *m*; roche; (*Brit: sweet*) ≈ sucre *m* d'orge // *vt* (*swing gently: cradle*) balancer; (*: child*) bercer; (*shake*) ébranler, secouer // *vi* (*se*) balancer; être ébranlé(e) *or* secoué(e); **on the ~s** (*drink*) avec des glaçons; (*ship*) sur les écueils; (*marriage etc*) en train de craquer; **~ and roll** *n* rock (and roll) *m*, rock'n'roll *m*; **~-bottom** *n* (*fig*) niveau le plus bas // *a* (*fig: prices*) sacrifié(e); **~ery** *n* (jardin *m* de) rocaille *f*.

rocket ['rɔkɪt] *n* fusée *f*; (*MIL*) fusée, roquette *f*.

rocking ['rɔkɪŋ]: **~ chair** *n* fauteuil *m* à bascule; **~ horse** *n* cheval *m* à bascule.

rocky ['rɔkɪ] *a* (*hill*) rocheux(euse); (*path*) rocailleux(euse); (*unsteady: table*) branlant(e).

rod [rɔd] *n* (*metallic*) tringle *f*; (*TECH*) tige *f*; (*wooden*) baguette *f*; (*also: fishing ~*) canne *f* à pêche.

rode [rəud] *pt of* **ride.**

rodent ['rəudnt] *n* rongeur *m*.

rodeo ['rəudɪəu] *n* rodéo *m*.

roe [rəu] *n* (*species: also:* **~ deer**) chevreuil *m*; (*of fish, also:* **hard ~**) œufs *mpl* de poisson; **soft ~** laitance *f*.

rogue [rəug] *n* coquin/e.

role [rəul] *n* rôle *m*.

roll [rəul] *n* rouleau *m*; (*of banknotes*) liasse *f*; (*also:* **bread ~**) petit pain; (*register*) liste *f*; (*sound: of drums etc*) roulement *m*; (*movement: of ship*) roulis *m* // *vt* rouler; (*also:* **~ up:** *string*) enrouler; (*also:* **~ out:** *pastry*) étendre au rouleau // *vi* rouler; (*wheel*) tourner; **to ~ about** *or* **around** *vi* rouler ça et là; (*person*) se rouler par terre; **to ~ by** *vi* (*time*) s'écouler, passer; **to ~ in** *vi* (*mail, cash*) affluer; **to ~ over** *vi* se retourner; **to ~ up** *vi* (*col: arrive*) arriver, s'amener // *vt* (*carpet*) rouler; **~ call** *n* appel *m*; **~er** *n* rouleau *m*; (*wheel*) roulette *f*; **~er coaster** *n* montagnes *fpl* russes; **~er skates** *npl* patins *mpl* à roulettes.

rolling ['rəulɪŋ] *a* (*landscape*) onduleux(euse); **~ pin** *n* rouleau *m* à pâtisserie; **~ stock** *n* (*RAIL*) matériel roulant.

ROM [rɔm] *n abbr* (= *read only memory*) mémoire morte.

Roman ['rəumən] *a* romain(e) // *n* Romain/e; **~ Catholic** *a, n* catholique (*m/f*).

romance [rə'mæns] *n* histoire *f* (*or* film *m or* aventure *f*) romanesque; (*charm*) poésie *f*; (*love affair*) idylle *f*.

Romania [rəu'meɪnɪə] *n* = **Rumania.**

Roman numeral *n* chiffre romain.

romantic [rə'mæntɪk] *a* romantique;

sentimental(e).

Rome [rəum] *n* Rome.

romp [rɔmp] *n* jeux bruyants // *vi* (*also:* **~ about**) s'ébattre, jouer bruyamment.

rompers ['rɔmpəz] *npl* barboteuse *f*.

roof, *pl* **~s** [ru:f] *n* toit *m*; (*of tunnel, cave*) plafond *m* // *vt* couvrir (d'un toit); **the ~ of the mouth** la voûte du palais; **~ing** *n* toiture *f*; **~ rack** *n* (*AUT*) galerie *f*.

rook [ruk] *n* (*bird*) freux *m*; (*CHESS*) tour *f*.

room [ru:m] *n* (*in house*) pièce *f*; (*also:* **bed~**) chambre *f* (à coucher); (*in school etc*) salle *f*; (*space*) place *f*; **~s** *npl* (*lodging*) meublé *m*; **'~s to let'**, (*US*) **'~s for rent'** 'chambres à louer'; **~ing house** *n* (*US*) maison *f or* immeuble *m* de rapport; **~mate** *n* camarade *m/f* de chambre; **~ service** *n* service *m* des chambres (*dans un hôtel*); **~y** *a* spacieux(euse); (*garment*) ample.

roost [ru:st] *n* juchoir *m* // *vi* se jucher.

rooster ['ru:stə*] *n* coq *m*.

root [ru:t] *n* (*BOT, MATH*) racine *f*; (*fig: of problem*) origine *f*, fond *m* // *vi* (*plant*) s'enraciner; **to ~ about** *vi* (*fig*) fouiller; **to ~ for** *vt fus* applaudir; **to ~ out** *vt* extirper.

rope [rəup] *n* corde *f*; (*NAUT*) cordage *m* // *vt* (*box*) corder; (*climbers*) encorder; **to ~ sb in** (*fig*) embringuer qn; **to know the ~s** (*fig*) être au courant, connaître les ficelles.

rosary ['rəuzərɪ] *n* chapelet *m*.

rose [rəuz] *pt of* **rise** // *n* rose *f*; (*also:* **~bush**) rosier *m*; (*on watering can*) pomme *f* // *a* rose.

rosé ['rəuzeɪ] *n* rosé *m*.

rose: **~bud** *n* bouton *m* de rose; **~bush** *n* rosier *m*.

rosemary ['rəuzmərɪ] *n* romarin *m*.

roster ['rɔstə*] *n*: **duty ~** tableau *m* de service.

rostrum ['rɔstrəm] *n* tribune *f* (*pour un orateur etc*).

rosy ['rəuzɪ] *a* rose; **a ~ future** un bel avenir.

rot [rɔt] *n* (*decay*) pourriture *f*; (*fig: pej*) idioties *fpl*, balivernes *fpl* // *vt, vi* pourrir.

rota ['rəutə] *n* liste *f*, tableau *m* de service; **on a ~ basis** par roulement.

rotary ['rəutərɪ] *a* rotatif(ive).

rotate [rəu'teɪt] *vt* (*revolve*) faire tourner; (*change round: crops*) alterner; (*: jobs*) faire à tour de rôle // *vi* (*revolve*) tourner; **rotating** *a* (*movement*) tournant(e).

rote [rəut] *n*: **by ~** machinalement, par cœur.

rotten ['rɔtn] *a* (*decayed*) pourri(e); (*dishonest*) corrompu(e); (*col: bad*) mauvais(e), moche; **to feel ~** (*ill*) être mal fichu(e).

rough [rʌf] a (cloth, skin) rêche, rugueux(euse); (terrain) accidenté(e); (path) rocailleux(euse); (voice) rauque, rude; (person, manner: coarse) rude, fruste; (: violent) brutal(e); (district, weather) mauvais(e); (plan) ébauché(e); (guess) approximatif(ive) // n (GOLF) rough m; **to** ~ **it** vivre à la dure; **to sleep** ~ (Brit) coucher à la dure; **~age** n fibres fpl diététiques; **~-and-ready** a rudimentaire; **~cast** n crépi m; ~ **copy**, ~ **draft** n brouillon m; **~ly** ad (handle) rudement, brutalement; (make) grossièrement; (approximately) à peu près, en gros.

roulette [ru:ˈlɛt] n roulette f.

Roumania [ruːˈmeɪnɪə] n = **Rumania**.

round [raund] a rond(e) // n rond m, cercle m; (Brit: of toast) tranche f; (duty: of policeman, milkman etc) tournée f; (: of doctor) visites fpl; (game: of cards, in competition) partie f; (BOXING) round m; (of talks) série f // vt (corner) tourner; (bend) prendre; (cape) doubler // prep autour de // ad: **all** ~ tout autour; **the long way** ~ (par) le chemin le plus long; **all the year** ~ toute l'année; **it's just** ~ **the corner** c'est juste après le coin; (fig) c'est tout près; ~ **the clock** ad 24 heures sur 24; **to go** ~ faire le tour ou un détour; **to go** ~ **to sb's** (**house**) aller chez qn; **to go** ~ **the back** passez par derrière; **to go** ~ **a house** visiter une maison, faire le tour d'une maison; **enough to go** ~ assez pour tout le monde; **to go the** ~s (disease, story) circuler; ~ **of ammunition** n cartouche f; ~ **of applause** n ban m, applaudissements mpl; ~ **of drinks** n tournée f; ~ **of sandwiches** n sandwich m; **to** ~ **off** vt (speech etc) terminer; **to** ~ **up** vt rassembler; (criminals) effectuer une rafle de; (prices) arrondir (au chiffre supérieur); **~about** n (Brit AUT) rond-point m (à sens giratoire); (: at fair) manège m (de chevaux de bois) // a (route, means) détourné(e); **~ers** npl (game) ≈ balle f au camp; **~ly** ad (fig) tout net, carrément; **~-shouldered** a au dos rond; ~ **trip** n (voyage m) aller et retour m; **~up** n rassemblement m; (of criminals) rafle f.

rouse [rauz] vt (wake up) réveiller; (stir up) susciter; provoquer; éveiller; **rousing** a (welcome) enthousiaste.

rout [raut] n (MIL) déroute f.

route [ruːt] n itinéraire m; (of bus) parcours m; (of trade, shipping) route f; ~ **map** n (Brit: for journey) croquis m d'itinéraire.

routine [ruːˈtiːn] a (work) ordinaire, courant(e); (procedure) d'usage // n (pej) routine f; (THEATRE) numéro m; **daily** ~ occupations journalières.

roving [ˈrəʊvɪŋ] a (life) vagabond(e).

row [rəu] n (line) rangée f; (of people, seats, KNITTING) rang m; (behind one another: of cars, people) file f; [rau] (noise) vacarme m; (dispute) dispute f, querelle f; (scolding) réprimande f, savon m // vi (in boat) ramer; (as sport) faire de l'aviron; [rau] se disputer, se quereller // vt (boat) faire aller à la rame ou à l'aviron; **in a** ~ (fig) d'affilée; **~boat** n (US) canot m (à rames).

rowdy [ˈraudɪ] a chahuteur(euse); bagarreur(euse) // n voyou m.

rowing [ˈrəuɪŋ] n canotage m; (as sport) aviron m; ~ **boat** n (Brit) canot m (à rames).

royal [ˈrɔɪəl] a royal(e); **R~ Air Force (RAF)** n armée de l'air britannique.

royalty [ˈrɔɪəltɪ] n (royal persons) (membres mpl de la) famille royale; (payment: to author) droits mpl d'auteur; (: to inventor) royalties fpl.

r.p.m. abbr (AUT: = revs per minute) tr/mn (= tours/minute).

R.S.V.P. abbr (= répondez s'il vous plaît) R.S.V.P.

Rt Hon. abbr (Brit: = Right Honourable) titre donné aux députés de la Chambre des communes.

rub [rʌb] n (with cloth) coup m de chiffon ou de torchon; (on person) friction f // vt frotter; frictionner; **to** ~ **sb up** or (US) ~ **sb the wrong way** prendre qn à rebrousse-poil; **to** ~ **off** vi partir; **to** ~ **off on** vt fus déteindre sur; **to** ~ **out** vt effacer.

rubber [ˈrʌbə*] n caoutchouc m; (Brit: eraser) gomme f (à effacer); ~ **band** n élastique m; ~ **plant** n caoutchouc m (plante verte).

rubbish [ˈrʌbɪʃ] n (from household) ordures fpl; (fig: pej) choses fpl sans valeur; camelote f; bêtises fpl, idioties fpl; ~ **bin** n (Brit) boîte f à ordures, poubelle f; ~ **dump** n (in town) décharge publique, dépotoir m.

rubble [ˈrʌbl] n décombres mpl; (smaller) gravats mpl.

ruby [ˈruːbɪ] n rubis m.

rucksack [ˈrʌksæk] n sac m à dos.

ructions [ˈrʌkʃənz] npl grabuge m.

rudder [ˈrʌdə*] n gouvernail m.

ruddy [ˈrʌdɪ] a (face) coloré(e); (col: damned) sacré(e), fichu(e).

rude [ruːd] a (impolite: person) impoli(e); (: word, manners) grossier(ère); (shocking) indécent(e), inconvenant(e).

rueful [ˈruːful] a triste.

ruffian [ˈrʌfɪən] n brute f, voyou m.

ruffle [ˈrʌfl] vt (hair) ébouriffer; (clothes) chiffonner; (water) agiter; (fig: person) émouvoir, faire perdre son flegme à.

rug [rʌg] n petit tapis; (Brit: for knees) couverture f.

rugby [ˈrʌgbɪ] n (also: ~ **football**) rugby

m.

rugged ['rʌgɪd] *a (landscape)* accidenté(e); *(features, kindness, character)* rude; *(determination)* farouche.

rugger ['rʌgə*] *n (Brit col)* rugby *m.*

ruin ['ru:ɪn] *n* ruine *f // vt* ruiner; *(spoil: clothes)* abîmer; **~s** *npl* ruine(s).

rule [ru:l] *n* règle *f*; *(regulation)* règlement *m*; *(government)* autorité *f*, gouvernement *m // vt (country)* gouverner; *(person)* dominer; *(decide)* décider *// vi* commander; décider; *(LAW)* statuer; **as a ~** normalement, en règle générale; **to ~ out** *vt* exclure; **~d** *a (paper)* réglé(e); **~r** *n (sovereign)* souverain/e; *(leader)* chef *m* (d'État); *(for measuring)* règle *f*; **ruling** *a (party)* au pouvoir; *(class)* dirigeant(e) *// n (LAW)* décision *f.*

rum [rʌm] *n* rhum *m // a (col)* bizarre.

Rumania [ru:'meɪnɪə] *n* Roumanie *f.*

rumble ['rʌmbl] *vi* gronder; *(stomach, pipe)* gargouiller.

rummage ['rʌmɪdʒ] *vi* fouiller.

rumour, *(US)* **rumor** ['ru:mə*] *n* rumeur *f*, bruit *m* (qui court) *// vt*: **it is ~ed that** le bruit court que.

rump [rʌmp] *n (of animal)* croupe *f*; **~ steak** *n* rumsteck *m.*

rumpus ['rʌmpəs] *n (col)* tapage *m*, chahut *m*; *(quarrel)* prise *f* de bec.

run [rʌn] *n (pas m de)* course *f*; *(outing)* tour *m or* promenade *f* (en voiture); parcours *m*, trajet *m*; *(series)* suite *f*, série *f*; *(THEATRE)* série de représentations; *(SKI)* piste *f*; *(in tights, stockings)* maille filée, échelle *f // vb (pt* ran, *pp* run) *vt (operate: business)* diriger; *(: competition, course)* organiser; *(: hotel, house)* tenir; *(COMPUT)* exécuter; *(force through: rope, pipe)*: **to ~ sth through** faire passer qch à travers; *(to pass: hand, finger)*: **to ~ sth over** promener *or* passer qch sur; *(water, bath)* faire couler *// vi* courir; *(pass: road etc)* passer; *(work: machine, factory)* marcher; *(bus, train: operate)* être en service; *(: travel)* circuler; *(continue: play)* se jouer; *(: contract)* être valide; *(slide: drawer etc)* glisser; *(flow: river, bath)* couler; *(colours, washing)* déteindre; *(in election)* être candidat, se présenter; **there was a ~ on** *(meat, tickets)* les gens se sont rués sur; **in the long ~** à longue échéance; à la longue; en fin de compte; **on the ~** en fuite; **I'll ~ you to the station** je vais vous emmener *or* conduire à la gare; **to ~ a risk** courir un risque; **to ~ about** *or* **around** *vi (children)* courir çà et là; **to ~ across** *vt fus (find)* trouver par hasard; **to ~ away** *vi* s'enfuir; **to ~ down** *vt (production)* réduire progressivement; *(factory)* réduire progressivement la production de; *(AUT)* renverser; *(criticize)* critiquer, dénigrer; **to be ~ down** *(person: tired)* être fatigué(e) *or* à plat; **to ~ in** *vt (Brit: car)* roder; **to ~ into** *vt fus (meet: person)* rencontrer par hasard; *(: trouble)* se heurter à; *(collide with)* heurter; **to ~ off** *vi* s'enfuir *// vt (water)* laisser s'écouler; **to ~ out** *vi (person)* sortir en courant; *(liquid)* couler; *(lease)* expirer; *(money)* être épuisé(e); **to ~ out of** *vt fus* se trouver à court de; **to ~ over** *vt (AUT)* écraser *// vt fus (revise)* revoir, reprendre; **to ~ through** *vt fus (instructions)* reprendre, revoir; **to ~ up** *vt (debt)* laisser accumuler; **to ~ up against** *(difficulties)* se heurter à; **~away** *a (horse)* emballé(e); *(truck)* fou(folle); *(inflation)* galopant(e).

rung [rʌŋ] *pp of* **ring** *// n (of ladder)* barreau *m.*

runner ['rʌnə*] *n (in race: person)* coureur/euse; *(: horse)* partant *m*; *(on sledge)* patin *m*; *(for drawer etc)* coulisseau *m*; *(carpet: in hall etc)* chemin *m*; **~ bean** *n (Brit)* haricot *m* (à rames); **~-up** *n* second/e.

running ['rʌnɪŋ] *n* course *f*; direction *f*; organisation *f*; marche *f*, fonctionnement *m // a (water)* courant(e); *(costs)* de gestion; *(commentary)* suivi(e); **to be in/out of the ~ for sth** être/ne pas être sur les rangs pour qch; **6 days ~** 6 jours de suite.

runny ['rʌnɪ] *a* qui coule.

run-of-the-mill ['rʌnəvðə'mɪl] *a* ordinaire, banal(e).

runt [rʌnt] *n (also pej)* avorton *m.*

run-up ['rʌnʌp] *n*: **~ to sth** *(election etc)* période *f* précédant qch.

runway ['rʌnweɪ] *n (AVIAT)* piste *f* (d'envol *or* d'atterrissage).

rupee [ru:'pi:] *n* roupie *f.*

rupture ['rʌptʃə*] *n (MED)* hernie *f.*

rural ['ruərl] *a* rural(e).

rush [rʌʃ] *n* course précipitée; *(of crowd)* ruée *f*, bousculade *f*; *(hurry)* hâte *f*, bousculade; *(current)* flot *m*; *(BOT)* jonc *m // vt* transporter *or* envoyer d'urgence; *(attack: town etc)* prendre d'assaut *// vi* se précipiter; **~ hour** *n* heures *fpl* de pointe *or* d'affluence.

rusk [rʌsk] *n* biscotte *f.*

Russia ['rʌʃə] *n* Russie *f*; **~n** *a* russe *// n* Russe *m/f*; *(LING)* russe *m.*

rust [rʌst] *n* rouille *f // vi* rouiller.

rustic ['rʌstɪk] *a* rustique.

rustle ['rʌsl] *vi* bruire, produire un bruissement *// vt (paper)* froisser; *(US: cattle)* voler.

rustproof ['rʌstpru:f] *a* inoxydable.

rusty ['rʌstɪ] *a* rouillé(e).

rut [rʌt] *n* ornière *f*; *(ZOOL)* rut *m*; **to be in a ~** suivre l'ornière, s'encroûter.

ruthless ['ru:θlɪs] *a* sans pitié, impitoyable.

rye [raɪ] *n* seigle *m*.

S

Sabbath ['sæbəθ] *n* (*Jewish*) sabbat *m*; (*Christian*) dimanche *m*.

sabotage ['sæbətɑ:ʒ] *n* sabotage *m* // *vt* saboter.

saccharin(e) ['sækərɪn] *n* saccharine *f*.

sachet ['sæʃeɪ] *n* sachet *m*.

sack [sæk] *n* (*bag*) sac *m* // *vt* (*dismiss*) renvoyer, mettre à la porte; (*plunder*) piller, mettre à sac; **to get the ~** être renvoyé(e) *or* mis(e) à la porte; **~ing** *n* toile *f* à sac; renvoi *m*.

sacrament ['sækrəmənt] *n* sacrement *m*.

sacred ['seɪkrɪd] *a* sacré(e).

sacrifice ['sækrɪfaɪs] *n* sacrifice *m* // *vt* sacrifier.

sad [sæd] *a* (*unhappy*) triste; (*deplorable*) triste, fâcheux(euse).

saddle ['sædl] *n* selle *f* // *vt* (*horse*) seller; **to be ~d with sth** (*col*) avoir qch sur les bras; **~bag** *n* sacoche *f*.

sadistic [sə'dɪstɪk] *a* sadique.

sadness ['sædnɪs] *n* tristesse *f*.

s.a.e. *n abbr* = *stamped addressed envelope*.

safe [seɪf] *a* (*out of danger*) hors de danger, en sécurité; (*not dangerous*) sans danger; (*cautious*) prudent(e); (*sure: bet etc*) assuré(e) // *n* coffre-fort *m*; **~ from** à l'abri de; **~ and sound** sain(e) et sauf(sauve); (*just*) **to be on the ~ side** pour plus de sûreté, par précaution; **~-conduct** *n* sauf-conduit *m*; **~-deposit** *n* (*vault*) dépôt *m* de coffres-forts; (*box*) coffre-fort *m*; **~guard** *n* sauvegarde *f*, protection *f* // *vt* sauvegarder, protéger; **~keeping** *n* bonne garde; **~ly** *ad* sans danger, sans risque; (*without mishap*) sans accident.

safety ['seɪftɪ] *n* sécurité *f*; **~ belt** *n* ceinture *f* de sécurité; **~ pin** *n* épingle *f* de sûreté *or* de nourrice; **~ valve** *n* soupape *f* de sûreté.

sag [sæg] *vi* s'affaisser, fléchir; pendre.

sage [seɪdʒ] *n* (*herb*) sauge *f*; (*man*) sage *m*.

Sagittarius [sædʒɪ'tɛərɪəs] *n* le Sagittaire.

Sahara [sə'hɑːrə] *n*: **the ~ (Desert)** le (désert du) Sahara.

said [sɛd] *pt, pp of* **say**.

sail [seɪl] *n* (*on boat*) voile *f*; (*trip*): **to go for a ~** faire un tour en bateau // *vt* (*boat*) manœuvrer, piloter // *vi* (*travel: ship*) avancer, naviguer; (*: passenger*) aller *or* se rendre (en bateau); (*set off*) partir, prendre la mer; (*SPORT*) faire de la voile; **they ~ed into Le Havre** ils sont entrés dans le port du Havre; **to ~ through** *vi, vt fus* (*fig*) réussir haut la main; **~boat** *n* (*US*) bateau *m* à voiles, voilier *m*; **~ing** *n* (*SPORT*) voile *f*; **to go ~ing** faire de la voile; **~ing ship** *n* grand voilier; **~or** *n* marin *m*, matelot *m*.

saint [seɪnt] *n* saint/e.

sake [seɪk] *n*: **for the ~ of** pour (l'amour de), dans l'intérêt de; par égard pour.

salad ['sæləd] *n* salade *f*; **~ bowl** *n* saladier *m*; **~ cream** *n* (*Brit*) (sorte *f* de) mayonnaise *f*; **~ dressing** *n* vinaigrette *f*.

salary ['sælərɪ] *n* salaire *m*, traitement *m*.

sale [seɪl] *n* vente *f*; (*at reduced prices*) soldes *mpl*; **'for ~'** 'à vendre'; **on ~** en vente; **on ~ or return** vendu(e) avec faculté de retour; **~room** *n* salle *f* des ventes; **~s assistant**, (*US*) **~s clerk** *n* vendeur/euse; **~sman** *n* vendeur *m*; (*representative*) représentant *m* de commerce; **~swoman** *n* vendeuse *f*.

salient ['seɪlɪənt] *a* saillant(e).

sallow ['sæləʊ] *a* cireux(euse).

salmon ['sæmən] *n* (*pl inv*) saumon *m*.

saloon [sə'lu:n] *n* (*US*) bar *m*; (*Brit AUT*) berline *f*; (*ship's lounge*) salon *m*.

salt [sɔlt] *n* sel *m* // *vt* saler // *cpd* de sel; (*CULIN*) salé(e); **to ~ away** *vt* (*col: money*) mettre de côté; **~ cellar** *n* salière *f*; **~-water** *a* (d'eau) de mer; **~y** *a* salé(e).

salute [sə'lu:t] *n* salut *m* // *vt* saluer.

salvage ['sælvɪdʒ] *n* (*saving*) sauvetage *m*; (*things saved*) biens sauvés *or* récupérés // *vt* sauver, récupérer.

salvation [sæl'veɪʃən] *n* salut *m*; **S~ Army** *n* Armée *f* du Salut.

same [seɪm] *a* même // *pronoun*: **the ~** le(la) même, les mêmes; **the ~ book as** le même livre que; **at the ~ time** en même temps; **all** *or* **just the ~** tout de même, quand même; **to do the ~** faire de même; **to do the ~ as** sb faire comme qn; **the ~ to you!** et à vous de même!; (*after insult*) toi-même!

sample ['sɑːmpl] *n* échantillon *m*; (*MED*) prélèvement *m* // *vt* (*food, wine*) goûter.

sanctimonious [sæŋktɪ'məʊnɪəs] *a* moralisateur(trice).

sanction ['sæŋkʃən] *n* sanction *f*.

sanctity ['sæŋktɪtɪ] *n* sainteté *f*, caractère sacré.

sanctuary ['sæŋktjuərɪ] *n* (*holy place*) sanctuaire *m*; (*refuge*) asile *m*; (*for wild life*) réserve *f*.

sand [sænd] *n* sable *m* // *vt* sabler.

sandal ['sændl] *n* sandale *f*.

sandbox ['sændbɒks] *n* (*US*) = **sandpit**.

sandcastle ['sændkɑːsl] *n* château *m* de sable.

sandpaper ['sændpeɪpə*] n papier m de verre.

sandpit ['sændpɪt] n (for children) tas m de sable.

sandstone ['sændstəun] n grès m.

sandwich ['sændwɪtʃ] n sandwich m // vt (also: ~ in) intercaler; **cheese/ham ~** sandwich au fromage/jambon; ~ **board** n panneau publicitaire (porté par un homme-sandwich); ~ **course** n (Brit) cours m de formation professionnelle.

sandy ['sændɪ] a sablonneux(euse); couvert(e) de sable; (colour) sable inv, blond roux inv.

sane [seɪn] a (person) sain(e) d'esprit; (outlook) sensé(e), sain(e).

sang [sæŋ] pt of **sing**.

sanitary ['sænɪtərɪ] a (system, arrangements) sanitaire; (clean) hygiénique; ~ **towel**, (US) ~ **napkin** n serviette f hygiénique.

sanitation [sænɪ'teɪʃən] n (in house) installations fpl sanitaires; (in town) système m sanitaire; ~ **department** n (US) service m de voirie.

sanity ['sænɪtɪ] n santé mentale; (common sense) bon sens.

sank [sæŋk] pt of **sink**.

Santa Claus [sæntə'klɔːz] n le Père Noël.

sap [sæp] n (of plants) sève f // vt (strength) saper, miner.

sapling ['sæplɪŋ] n jeune arbre m.

sapphire ['sæfaɪə*] n saphir m.

sarcasm ['saːkæzm] n sarcasme m, raillerie f.

sardine [saː'diːn] n sardine f.

Sardinia [saː'dɪnɪə] n Sardaigne f.

sash [sæʃ] n écharpe f.

sat [sæt] pt, pp of **sit**.

satchel ['sætʃl] n cartable m.

sated ['seɪtɪd] a repu(e); blasé(e).

satellite ['sætəlaɪt] a, n satellite (m).

satin ['sætɪn] n satin m // a en or de satin, satiné(e).

satire ['sætaɪə*] n satire f.

satisfaction [sætɪs'fækʃən] n satisfaction f.

satisfactory [sætɪs'fæktərɪ] a satisfaisant(e).

satisfy ['sætɪsfaɪ] vt satisfaire, contenter; (convince) convaincre, persuader; ~ing a satisfaisant(e).

Saturday ['sætədɪ] n samedi m.

sauce [sɔːs] n sauce f; ~pan n casserole f.

saucer ['sɔːsə*] n soucoupe f.

saucy ['sɔːsɪ] a impertinent(e).

Saudi ['saudɪ]: ~ **Arabia** n Arabie Saoudite; ~ **(Arabian)** a saoudien(ne) // n Saoudien/ne.

sauna ['sɔːnə] n sauna m.

saunter ['sɔːntə*] vi: to ~ to aller en flânant or se balader jusqu'à.

sausage ['sɔsɪdʒ] n saucisse f; ~ **roll** n friand m.

savage ['sævɪdʒ] a (cruel, fierce) brutal(e), féroce; (primitive) primitif(ive), sauvage // n sauvage m/f // vt attaquer férocement.

save [seɪv] vt (person, belongings) sauver; (money) mettre de côté, économiser; (time) (faire) gagner; (food) garder; (COMPUT) sauvegarder; (avoid: trouble) éviter // vi (also: ~ up) mettre de l'argent de côté // n (SPORT) arrêt m (du ballon) // prep sauf, à l'exception de.

saving ['seɪvɪŋ] n économie f // a: the ~ **grace of** la seule rachète; ~s npl économies fpl; ~s **bank** n caisse f d'épargne.

saviour, (US) **savior** ['seɪvjə*] n sauveur m.

savour, (US) **savor** ['seɪvə*] vt savourer; ~y a savoureux(euse); (dish: not sweet) salé(e).

saw [sɔː] pt of **see** // n (tool) scie f // vt (pt sawed, pp sawed or sawn [sɔːn]) scier; ~**dust** n sciure f; ~**mill** n scierie f; ~**n-off shotgun** n carabine f à canon scié.

saxophone ['sæksəfəun] n saxophone m.

say [seɪ] n: to have one's ~ dire ce qu'on a à dire; to have a or some ~ in sth avoir son mot à dire dans qch // vt (pt, pp said) dire; could you ~ that again? pourriez-vous répéter ceci?; that goes without ~ing cela va sans dire, cela va de soi; ~ing n dicton m, proverbe m.

scab [skæb] n croûte f; (pej) jaune m.

scaffold ['skæfəuld] n échafaud m; ~ing n échafaudage m.

scald [skɔːld] n brûlure f // vt ébouillanter.

scale [skeɪl] n (of fish) écaille f; (MUS) gamme f; (of ruler, thermometer etc) graduation f, échelle (graduée); (of salaries, fees etc) barème m; (of map, also size, extent) échelle // vt (mountain) escalader; ~s npl balance f; (larger) bascule f; on a **large** ~ sur une grande échelle, en grand; ~ **of charges** tableau m des tarifs; (ECON) barème m des redevances; to ~ **down** vt réduire; ~ **model** n modèle m à l'échelle.

scallop ['skɔləp] n coquille f Saint-Jacques.

scalp [skælp] n cuir chevelu // vt scalper.

scamper ['skæmpə*] vi: to ~ away, ~ off détaler.

scampi ['skæmpɪ] npl langoustines (frites), scampi mpl.

scan [skæn] vt scruter, examiner; (glance at quickly) parcourir; (TV, RADAR) balayer.

scandal ['skændl] n scandale m; (gossip) ragots mpl.

Scandinavia [skændɪ'neɪvɪə] n Scandinavie f; **~n** a scandinave // n Scandinave m/f.

scant [skænt] a insuffisant(e); **~y** a peu abondant(e), insuffisant(e), maigre.

scapegoat ['skeɪpgəʊt] n bouc m émissaire.

scar [skɑ:] n cicatrice f.

scarce [skɛəs] a rare, peu abondant(e); **~ly** ad à peine, presque pas; **scarcity** n rareté f, manque m, pénurie f.

scare [skɛə*] n peur f, panique f // vt effrayer, faire peur à; **to ~ sb stiff** faire une peur bleue à qn; **bomb ~** alerte f à la bombe; **~crow** n épouvantail m; **~d** a: **to be ~d** avoir peur.

scarf, pl **scarves** [skɑ:f, skɑ:vz] n (long) écharpe f; (square) foulard m.

scarlet ['skɑ:lɪt] a écarlate.

scathing ['skeɪðɪŋ] a cinglant(e), acerbe.

scatter ['skætə*] vt éparpiller, répandre; (crowd) disperser // vi se disperser; **~brained** a écervelé(e), étourdi(e).

scavenger ['skævəndʒə*] n éboueur m.

scene [si:n] n (THEATRE, fig etc) scène f; (of crime, accident) lieu(x) m(pl), endroit m; (sight, view) spectacle m, vue f; **~ry** n (THEATRE) décor(s) m(pl); (landscape) paysage m; **scenic** a scénique; offrant de beaux paysages or panoramas.

scent [sɛnt] n parfum m, odeur f; (fig: track) piste f; (sense of smell) odorat m.

sceptical ['skɛptɪkəl] a sceptique.

schedule ['ʃɛdju:l, (US) 'skɛdju:l] n programme m, plan m; (of trains) horaire m; (of prices etc) barème m, tarif m // vt prévoir; **on ~** à l'heure (prévue); à la date prévue; **to be ahead of/behind ~** avoir de l'avance/du retard; **~d flight** n vol régulier.

scheme [ski:m] n plan m, projet m; (method) procédé m; (dishonest plan, plot) complot m, combine f; (arrangement) arrangement m, classification f; (pension ~ etc) régime m // vt, vi comploter, manigancer; **scheming** a rusé(e), intrigant(e) // n manigances fpl, intrigues fpl.

scholar ['skɒlə*] n érudit/e; **~ly** a érudit(e), savant(e); **~ship** n érudition f; (grant) bourse f (d'études).

school [sku:l] n (gen) école f; (in university) faculté f; (secondary school) collège m, lycée m // cpd scolaire // vt (animal) dresser; **~book** n livre m scolaire or de classe; **~boy** n écolier m; collégien m, lycéen m; **~children** npl écoliers mpl; collégiens mpl, lycéens mpl; **~days** npl années fpl de scolarité; **~girl** n écolière f; collégienne f, lycéenne f; **~ing** n instruction f, études fpl; **~master** n (primary) instituteur m; (secondary) professeur m;

~mistress n institutrice f; professeur m; **~teacher** n instituteur/trice; professeur m.

sciatica [saɪ'ætɪkə] n sciatique f.

science ['saɪəns] n science f; **~ fiction** n science-fiction f; **scientific** [-'tɪfɪk] a scientifique; **scientist** n scientifique m/f; (eminent) savant m.

scissors ['sɪzəz] npl ciseaux mpl.

scoff [skɒf] vt (Brit col: eat) avaler, bouffer // vi: **to ~ (at)** (mock) se moquer (de).

scold [skəʊld] vt gronder, attraper.

scone [skɒn] n sorte de petit pain rond au lait.

scoop [sku:p] n pelle f (à main); (for ice cream) boule f à glace; (PRESS) reportage exclusif or à sensation; **to ~ out** vt évider, creuser; **to ~ up** vt ramasser.

scooter ['sku:tə*] n (motor cycle) scooter m; (toy) trottinette f.

scope [skəʊp] n (capacity: of plan, undertaking) portée f, envergure f; (: of person) compétence f, capacités fpl; (opportunity) possibilités fpl; **within the ~ of** dans les limites de.

scorch [skɔ:tʃ] vt (clothes) brûler (légèrement), roussir; (earth, grass) dessécher, brûler.

score [skɔ:*] n score m, décompte m des points; (MUS) partition f; (twenty) vingt // vt (goal, point) marquer; (success) remporter // vi marquer des points; (FOOTBALL) marquer un but; (keep score) compter les points; **on that ~** sur ce chapitre, à cet égard; **to ~ 6 out of 10** obtenir 6 sur 10; **to ~ out** vt rayer, barrer, biffer; **~board** n tableau m.

scorn [skɔ:n] n mépris m, dédain m.

Scorpio ['skɔ:pɪəʊ] n le Scorpion.

Scot [skɒt] n Écossais/e.

scotch [skɒtʃ] vt faire échouer; enrayer; étouffer; **S~** n whisky m, scotch m.

scot-free ['skɒt'fri:] ad: **to get off ~** (unpunished) s'en tirer sans être puni.

Scotland ['skɒtlənd] n Écosse f.

Scots [skɒts] a écossais(e); **~man/woman** n Écossais/e.

Scottish ['skɒtɪʃ] a écossais(e).

scoundrel ['skaundrl] n vaurien m.

scour ['skaʊə*] vt (clean) récurer; frotter; décaper; (search) battre, parcourir.

scourge [skə:dʒ] n fléau m.

scout [skaʊt] n (MIL) éclaireur m; (also: boy ~) scout m; **to ~ around** vi explorer, chercher.

scowl [skaʊl] vi se renfrogner, avoir l'air maussade; **to ~ at** regarder de travers.

scrabble ['skræbl] vi (claw): **to ~ (at)** gratter; (also: ~ around): search) chercher à tâtons // n ® Scrabble m ®.

scraggy ['skrægɪ] a décharné(e).

scram [skræm] *vi* (*col*) ficher le camp.
scramble ['skræmbl] *n* bousculade *f*, ruée *f* // *vi* avancer tant bien que mal (à quatre pattes *or* en grimpant); **to ~ out** sortir *or* descendre à toute vitesse; **to ~ for** se bousculer *or* se disputer pour (avoir); **~d eggs** *npl* œufs brouillés.
scrap [skræp] *n* bout *m*, morceau *m*; (*fight*) bagarre *f*; (*also*: ~ **iron**) ferraille *f* // *vt* jeter, mettre au rebut; (*fig*) abandonner, laisser tomber // *vi* (*fight*) se bagarrer; **~s** *npl* (*waste*) déchets *mpl*; **~book** *n* album *m*; **~ dealer** *n* marchand *m* de ferraille.
scrape [skreɪp] *vt*, *vi* gratter, racler // *n*: **to get into a ~** s'attirer des ennuis; **to ~ through** réussir de justesse; **~r** *n* grattoir *m*, racloir *m*.
scrap: ~ **heap** *n* (*fig*): **on the ~ heap** au rancart *or* rebut; ~ **merchant** *n* (*Brit*) marchand *m* de ferraille; ~ **paper** *n* papier *m* brouillon.
scratch [skrætʃ] *n* égratignure *f*, rayure *f*; éraflure *f*; (*from claw*) coup *m* de griffe // *a*: ~ **team** équipe *f* de fortune *or* improvisée // *vt* (*record*) rayer; (*paint etc*) érafler; (*with claw, nail*) griffer // *vi* (se) gratter; **to start from ~** partir de zéro; **to be up to ~** être à la hauteur.
scrawl [skrɔ:l] *vi* gribouiller.
scrawny ['skrɔ:nɪ] *a* décharné(e).
scream [skri:m] *n* cri perçant, hurlement *m* // *vi* crier, hurler.
scree [skri:] *n* éboulis *m*.
screech [skri:tʃ] *vi* hurler; (*tyres, brakes*) crisser, grincer.
screen [skri:n] *n* écran *m*, paravent *m*; (*CINEMA, TV*) écran; (*fig*) écran, rideau *m* // *vt* masquer, cacher; (*from the wind etc*) abriter, protéger; (*film*) projeter; (*candidates etc*) filtrer; **~ing** *n* (*MED*) test *m* (*or* tests) de dépistage; **~play** *n* scénario *m*.
screw [skru:] *n* vis *f*; (*propeller*) hélice *f* // *vt* visser; **to ~ up** *vt* (*paper etc*) froisser; (*col: ruin*) bousiller; **~driver** *n* tournevis *m*.
scribble ['skrɪbl] *vt* gribouiller, griffonner.
script [skrɪpt] *n* (*CINEMA etc*) scénario *m*, texte *m*; (*in exam*) copie *f*.
Scripture ['skrɪptʃə*] *n* Ecriture Sainte.
scroll [skrəul] *n* rouleau *m*.
scrounge [skraundʒ] *vt* (*col*): **to ~ sth** (*off or from sb*) se faire payer qch (par qn), emprunter qch (à qn) // *vi*: **to ~ on sb** vivre aux crochets de qn.
scrub [skrʌb] *n* (*clean*) nettoyage *m* (à la brosse); (*land*) broussailles *fpl* // *vt* (*floor*) nettoyer à la brosse; (*pan*) récurer; (*washing*) frotter; (*reject*) annuler.
scruff [skrʌf] *n*: **by the ~ of the neck** par la peau du cou.
scruffy ['skrʌfɪ] *a* débraillé(e).

scrum(mage) ['skrʌm(ɪdʒ)] *n* (*RUGBY*) mêlée *f*.
scruple ['skru:pl] *n* scrupule *m*.
scrutiny ['skru:tɪnɪ] *n* examen minutieux.
scuff [skʌf] *vt* érafler.
scuffle ['skʌfl] *n* échauffourée *f*, rixe *f*.
scullery ['skʌlərɪ] *n* arrière-cuisine *f*.
sculptor ['skʌlptə*] *n* sculpteur *m*.
sculpture ['skʌlptʃə*] *n* sculpture *f*.
scum [skʌm] *n* écume *f*, mousse *f*; (*pej: people*) rebut *m*, lie *f*.
scupper ['skʌpə*] *vt* saborder.
scurrilous ['skʌrɪləs] *a* haineux(euse), virulent(e); calomnieux(euse).
scurry ['skʌrɪ] *vi* filer à toute allure; **to ~ off** détaler, se sauver.
scuttle ['skʌtl] *n* (*NAUT*) écoutille *f*; (*also*: **coal ~**) seau *m* (à charbon) // *vt* (*ship*) saborder // *vi* (*scamper*): **to ~ away, ~ off** détaler.
scythe [saɪð] *n* faux *f*.
SDP *n abbr* (*Brit*) = *Social Democratic Party*.
sea [si:] *n* mer *f* // *cpd* marin(e), de (la) mer, maritime; **by ~** (*travel*) par mer, en bateau; **on the ~** (*boat*) en mer; (*town*) au bord de la mer; **to be all at ~** (*fig*) nager complètement; **out to ~** au large; (*out*) **at ~** en mer; **~board** *n* côte *f*; **~food** *n* fruits *mpl* de mer; ~ **front** *n* bord *m* de mer; **~gull** *n* mouette *f*.
seal [si:l] *n* (*animal*) phoque *m*; (*stamp*) sceau *m*, cachet *m*; (*impression*) cachet, estampille *f* // *vt* sceller; (*envelope*) coller; (: *with seal*) cacheter; **to ~ off** *vt* (*close*) condamner; (*forbid entry to*) interdire l'accès de.
sea level *n* niveau *m* de la mer.
seam [si:m] *n* couture *f*; (*of coal*) veine *f*, filon *m*.
seaman ['si:mən] *n* marin *m*.
seamy ['si:mɪ] *a* louche, mal famé(e).
seance ['seɪɔns] *n* séance *f* de spiritisme.
seaplane ['si:pleɪn] *n* hydravion *m*.
search [sə:tʃ] *n* (*for person, thing*) recherche(s) *f(pl)*; (*of drawer, pockets*) fouille *f*; (*LAW: at sb's home*) perquisition *f* // *vt* fouiller; (*examine*) examiner minutieusement; scruter // *vi*: **to ~ for** chercher; **to ~ through** *vt fus* fouiller; **in ~ of** à la recherche de; **~ing** *a* pénétrant(e); minutieux(euse); **~light** *n* projecteur *m*; ~ **party** *n* expédition *f* de secours; ~ **warrant** *n* mandat *m* de perquisition.
seashore ['si:ʃɔ:*] *n* rivage *m*, plage *f*, bord *m* de (la) mer.
seasick ['si:sɪk] *a* qui a le mal de mer.
seaside ['si:saɪd] *n* bord *m* de la mer; ~ **resort** *n* station *f* balnéaire.
season ['si:zn] *n* saison *f* // *vt* assaisonner, relever; **~al** *a* saisonnier(ère); **~ed** *a* (*fig*) expérimenté(e);

~ **ticket** n carte f d'abonnement.

seat [si:t] n siège m; (in bus, train: place) place f; (PARLIAMENT) siège; (buttocks) postérieur m; (of trousers) fond m // vt faire asseoir, placer; (have room for) avoir des places assises pour, pouvoir accueillir; ~ **belt** n ceinture f de sécurité.

sea water n eau f de mer.

seaweed ['si:wi:d] n algues fpl.

seaworthy ['si:wə:ðɪ] a en état de naviguer.

sec. abbr of **second(s)**.

secluded [sɪ'klu:dɪd] a retiré(e), à l'écart.

seclusion [sɪ'klu:ʒən] n solitude f.

second ['sɛkənd] num deuxième, second(e) // ad (in race etc) en seconde position // n (unit of time) seconde f; (in series, position) deuxième m/f, second/e; (AUT: also: ~ **gear**) seconde f; (COMM: imperfect) article m de second choix // vt (motion) appuyer; ~**ary** a secondaire; ~**ary school** n collège m, lycée m; ~**class** a de deuxième classe // ad (RAIL) en seconde; ~**hand** a d'occasion; de seconde main; ~ **hand** n (on clock) trotteuse f; ~**ly** ad deuxièmement; ~**ment** [sɪ'kɔndmənt] n (Brit) détachement m; ~**rate** a de deuxième ordre, de qualité inférieure; ~ **thoughts** npl doutes mpl; on ~ **thoughts** or (US) **thought** à la réflexion.

secrecy ['si:krəsɪ] n secret m.

secret ['si:krɪt] a secret(ète) // n secret m; in ~ ad en secret, secrètement, en cachette.

secretary ['sɛkrətərɪ] n secrétaire m/f; (COMM) secrétaire général; S~ **of State (for)** (Brit POL) ministre m (de).

secretive ['si:krətɪv] a réservé(e); (pej) cachottier(ère), dissimulé(e).

sectarian [sɛk'tɛərɪən] a sectaire.

section ['sɛkʃən] n coupe f, section f; (department) section; (COMM) rayon m; (of document) section, article m, paragraphe m.

sector ['sɛktə*] n secteur m.

secular ['sɛkjulə*] a profane; laïque; séculier(ère).

secure [sɪ'kjuə*] a (free from anxiety) sans inquiétude, sécurisé(e); (firmly fixed) solide, bien attaché(e) (or fermé(e) etc); (in safe place) en lieu sûr, en sûreté // vt (fix) fixer, attacher; (get) obtenir, se procurer.

security [sɪ'kjuərɪtɪ] n sécurité f, mesures fpl de sécurité; (for loan) caution f, garantie f.

sedan [sɪ'dæn] n (US AUT) berline f.

sedate [sɪ'deɪt] a calme; posé(e) // vt donner des sédatifs à.

sedative ['sɛdɪtɪv] n calmant m, sédatif m.

seduce [sɪ'dju:s] vt (gen) séduire; **se-**

duction [-'dʌkʃən] n séduction f; **seductive** [-'dʌktɪv] a séduisant(e), séducteur(trice).

see [si:] vb (pt saw, pp seen) vt (gen) voir; (accompany): **to ~ sb to the door** reconduire or raccompagner qn jusqu'à la porte // vi voir // n évêché m, évêque m; **to ~ that** (ensure) veiller à ce que + sub, faire en sorte que + sub, s'assurer que; ~ **you soon!** à bientôt!; **to ~ about** vt fus s'occuper de; **to ~ off** vt accompagner (à la gare or à l'aéroport etc); **to ~ through** vt mener à bonne fin // vt fus voir clair dans; **to ~ to** vt fus s'occuper de, se charger de.

seed [si:d] n graine f; (fig) germe m; (TENNIS) tête f de série; **to go to ~** monter en graine; (fig) se laisser aller; ~**ling** n jeune plant m, semis m; ~**y** a (shabby) minable, miteux(euse).

seeing ['si:ɪŋ] cj: ~ **(that)** vu que, étant donné que.

seek [si:k], pt, pp **sought** vt chercher, rechercher.

seem [si:m] vi sembler, paraître; **there ~s to be ...** il semble qu'il y a ...; on dirait qu'il y a ...; ~**ingly** ad apparemment.

seen [si:n] pp of **see**.

seep [si:p] vi suinter, filtrer.

seesaw ['si:sɔ:] n (jeu m de) bascule f.

seethe [si:ð] vi être en effervescence; **to ~ with anger** bouillir de colère.

see-through ['si:θru:] a transparent(e).

segregate ['sɛgrɪgeɪt] vt séparer, isoler.

seize [si:z] vt (grasp) saisir, attraper; (take possession of) s'emparer de; (LAW) saisir; **to ~ (up)on** vt fus saisir, sauter sur; **to ~ up** vi (TECH) se gripper.

seizure ['si:ʒə*] n (MED) crise f, attaque f; (LAW) saisie f.

seldom ['sɛldəm] ad rarement.

select [sɪ'lɛkt] a choisi(e), d'élite; select inv // vt sélectionner, choisir; ~**ion** [-'lɛkʃən] n sélection f, choix m.

self [sɛlf] n (pl **selves**): **the ~** le moi inv // prefix auto-; ~**catering** a (Brit) avec cuisine, où l'on peut faire sa cuisine; ~**centred**, (US) ~**centered** a égocentrique; ~**coloured**, (US) ~**colored** a uni(e); ~**confidence** n confiance f en soi; ~**conscious** a timide, qui manque d'assurance; ~**contained** a (Brit: flat) avec entrée particulière, indépendant(e); ~**control** n maîtrise f de soi; ~**defence**, (US) ~**defense** n légitime défense f; ~**discipline** n discipline personnelle; ~**employed** a qui travaille à son compte; ~**evident** a évident(e), qui va de soi; ~**governing** a autonome; ~**indulgent** a qui ne se refuse rien; ~**interest** n intérêt personnel; ~**ish** a égoïste; ~**ishness** n égoïsme m; ~**less** a désintéressé(e);

~-**pity** *n* apitoiement *m* sur soi-même; ~-**possessed** *a* assuré(e); ~-**preservation** *n* instinct *m* de conservation; ~-**respect** *n* respect *m* de soi, amour-propre *m*; ~-**righteous** *a* satisfait(e) de soi, pharisaïque; ~-**sacrifice** *n* abnégation *f*; ~-**satisfied** *a* content(e) de soi, suffisant(e); ~-**service** *a, n* libre-service *(m)*, self-service *(m)*; ~-**sufficient** *a* indépendant(e); ~-**taught** *a* autodidacte.

sell [sɛl], *pt, pp* **sold** *vt* vendre // *vi* se vendre; **to ~ at** *or* **for 10 F** se vendre 10 F; **to ~ off** *vt* liquider; **to ~ out** *vi*: to ~ out (to sb/sth) (*COMM*) vendre son fonds *or* son affaire (à qn/qch) // *vt* vendre tout son stock de; **the tickets are all sold out** il ne reste plus de billets; ~-**by date** *n* date *f* limite de vente; ~**er** *n* vendeur/euse, marchand/e; ~**ing price** *n* prix *m* de vente.

sellotape ['sɛləuteip] *n* ® (*Brit*) papier collant, scotch *m* ®.

sellout ['sɛlaut] *n* trahison *f*, capitulation *f*; (*of tickets*): it was a ~ tous les billets ont été vendus.

selves [sɛlvz] *npl of* **self.**

semblance ['sɛmbləns] *n* semblant *m*.

semen ['si:mən] *n* sperme *m*.

semester [sɪ'mɛstə*] *n* (*US*) semestre *m*.

semi ['sɛmɪ] *prefix* semi-, demi-; à demi, à moitié; ~**circle** *n* demi-cercle *m*; ~**colon** *n* point-virgule *m*; ~**detached (house)** *n* (*Brit*) maison jumelée *or* jumelle; ~**final** *n* demi-finale *f*.

seminar ['sɛmɪna:*] *n* séminaire *m*.

seminary ['sɛmɪnərɪ] *n* (*REL*: *for priests*) séminaire *m*.

semiskilled ['sɛmɪ'skɪld] *a*: ~ **worker** *n* ouvrier/ère spécialisé(e).

senate ['sɛnɪt] *n* sénat *m*; **senator** *n* sénateur *m*.

send [sɛnd], *pt, pp* **sent** *vt* envoyer; **to ~ away** *vt* (*letter, goods*) envoyer, expédier; **to ~ away for** *vt fus* commander par correspondance, se faire envoyer; **to ~ back** *vt* renvoyer; **to ~ for** *vt fus* envoyer chercher; faire venir; **to ~ off** *vt* (*goods*) envoyer, expédier; (*Brit SPORT*: *player*) expulser *or* renvoyer du terrain; **to ~ out** *vt* (*invitation*) envoyer (par la poste); **to ~ up** *vt* (*person, price*) faire monter; (*Brit*: *parody*) mettre en boîte, parodier; ~**er** *n* expéditeur/trice; ~-**off** *n*: **a good ~-off** des adieux chaleureux.

senior ['si:nɪə*] *a* (*older*) aîné(e), plus âgé(e); (*of higher rank*) supérieur(e) // *n* aîné/e; (*in service*) personne *f* qui a plus d'ancienneté; ~ **citizen** *n* personne âgée; ~**ity** [-'ɔrɪtɪ] *n* priorité *f* d'âge, ancienneté *f*.

sensation [sɛn'seɪʃən] *n* sensation *f*; ~**al** *a* qui fait sensation; (*marvellous*) sensationnel(le).

sense [sɛns] *n* sens *m*; (*feeling*) sentiment *m*; (*meaning*) signification *f*; (*wisdom*) bon sens // *vt* sentir, pressentir; it makes ~ c'est logique; ~ *npl* raison *f*; ~**less** *a* insensé(e), stupide; (*unconscious*) sans connaissance.

sensibility [sɛnsɪ'bɪlɪtɪ] *n* sensibilité *f*; **sensibilities** *npl* susceptibilité *f*.

sensible ['sɛnsɪbl] *a* sensé(e), raisonnable; sage; pratique.

sensitive ['sɛnsɪtɪv] *a* sensible.

sensual ['sɛnsjuəl] *a* sensuel(le).

sensuous ['sɛnsjuəs] *a* voluptueux(euse), sensuel(le).

sent [sɛnt] *pt, pp of* **send.**

sentence ['sɛntns] *n* (*LING*) phrase *f*; (*LAW*: *judgment*) condamnation *f*, sentence *f*; (: *punishment*) peine *f* // *vt*: **to ~ sb to death/to 5 years** condamner qn à mort/à 5 ans.

sentiment ['sɛntɪmənt] *n* sentiment *m*; (*opinion*) opinion *f*, avis *m*; ~**al** [-'mɛntl] *a* sentimental(e).

sentry ['sɛntrɪ] *n* sentinelle *f*, factionnaire *m*.

separate *a* ['sɛprɪt] séparé(e), indépendant(e), différent(e) // *vb* ['sɛpəreɪt] *vt* séparer // *vi* se séparer; ~**s** *npl* (*clothes*) coordonnés *mpl*; ~**ly** *ad* séparément; **separation** [-'reɪʃən] *n* séparation *f*.

September [sɛp'tɛmbə*] *n* septembre *m*.

septic ['sɛptɪk] *a* septique; (*wound*) infecté(e); ~ **tank** *n* fosse *f* septique.

sequel ['si:kwl] *n* conséquence *f*; séquelles *fpl*; (*of story*) suite *f*.

sequence ['si:kwəns] *n* ordre *m*, suite *f*.

sequin ['si:kwɪn] *n* paillette *f*.

serene [sɪ'ri:n] *a* serein(e), calme, paisible.

sergeant ['sa:dʒənt] *n* sergent *m*; (*POLICE*) brigadier *m*.

serial ['sɪərɪəl] *n* feuilleton *m*; ~ **number** *n* numéro *m* de série.

series ['sɪərɪs] *n* (*pl inv*) série *f*; (*PUBLISHING*) collection *f*.

serious ['sɪərɪəs] *a* sérieux(euse), réfléchi(e); grave; ~**ly** *ad* sérieusement, gravement.

sermon ['sə:mən] *n* sermon *m*.

serrated [sɪ'reɪtɪd] *a* en dents de scie.

servant ['sə:vənt] *n* domestique *m/f*; (*fig*) serviteur/servante.

serve [sə:v] *vt* (*employer etc*) servir, être au service de; (*purpose*) servir à; (*customer, food, meal*) servir; (*apprenticeship*) faire, accomplir; (*prison term*) faire; purger // *vi* (*also TENNIS*) servir; (*be useful*): **to ~ as/for/ to do** servir de/à faire // *n* (*TENNIS*) service *m*; it ~s him right c'est bien fait pour lui; **to ~ out, ~ up** *vt* (*food*) servir.

service ['sə:vɪs] n (gen) service m; (AUT: maintenance) révision f // vt (car, washing machine) réviser; the S~s les forces armées; to be of ~ to sb rendre service à qn; dinner ~ service m de table; ~able a pratique, commode; ~ charge n (Brit) service m; ~man n militaire m; ~ station n station-service f.

serviette [sə:vɪ'ɛt] n (Brit) serviette f (de table).

session ['sɛʃən] n (sitting) séance f; (SCOL) année f scolaire (or universitaire).

set [sɛt] n série f, assortiment m; (of tools etc) jeu m; (RADIO, TV) poste m; (TENNIS) set m; (group of people) cercle m, milieu m; (CINEMA) plateau m; (THEATRE: stage) scène f; (: scenery) décor m; (MATH) ensemble m; (HAIRDRESSING) mise f en plis // a (fixed) fixe, déterminé(e); (ready) prêt(e) // vb (pt, pp set) vt (place) mettre, poser, placer; (fix, establish) fixer; (: record) établir; (adjust) régler; (decide: rules etc) fixer, choisir; (TYP) composer // vi (sun) se coucher; (jam, jelly, concrete) prendre; to be ~ on doing être résolu à faire; to ~ (to music) mettre en musique; to ~ on fire mettre le feu à; to ~ free libérer; to ~ sth going déclencher qch; to ~ sail partir, prendre la mer; to ~ about vt fus (task) entreprendre, se mettre à; to ~ aside vt mettre de côté; to ~ back vt (in time): to ~ back (by) retarder (de); to ~ off vi se mettre en route, partir // vt (bomb) faire exploser; (cause to start) déclencher; (show up well) mettre en valeur, faire valoir; to ~ out vi: to ~ out to do entreprendre de faire, avoir pour but or intention de faire // vt (arrange) disposer; (state) présenter, exposer; to ~ up vt (organization) fonder, constituer; ~back n (hitch) revers m, contretemps m; ~ menu n menu m.

settee [sɛ'ti:] n canapé m.

setting ['sɛtɪŋ] n cadre m; (of jewel) monture f.

settle ['sɛtl] vt (argument, matter) régler; (problem) résoudre; (MED: calm) calmer // vi (bird, dust etc) se poser; (sediment) se déposer; (also: ~ down) s'installer, se fixer; se calmer; se ranger; to ~ for sth accepter qch, se contenter de qch; to ~ in vi s'installer; to ~ on sth opter or se décider pour qch; to ~ up with sb régler (ce que l'on doit à) qn; ~ment n (payment) règlement m; (agreement) accord m; (colony) colonie f; (village etc) établissement m; hameau m; ~r n colon m.

setup ['sɛtʌp] n (arrangement) manière f dont les choses sont organisées; (situation) situation f, allure f des choses.

seven ['sɛvn] num sept; ~teen num dix-sept; ~th num septième; ~ty num soixante-dix.

sever ['sɛvə*] vt couper, trancher; (relations) rompre.

several ['sɛvərl] a, pronoun plusieurs m/ fpl; ~ of us plusieurs d'entre nous.

severance ['sɛvərəns] n (of relations) rupture f; ~ pay n indemnité f de licenciement.

severe [sɪ'vɪə*] a sévère, strict(e); (serious) grave, sérieux(euse); (hard) rigoureux(euse), dur(e); (plain) sévère, austère; **severity** [sɪ'vɛrɪtɪ] n sévérité f; gravité f; rigueur f.

sew [səu], pt sewed, pp sewn vt, vi coudre; to ~ up vt (re)coudre.

sewage ['su:ɪdʒ] n vidange(s) f(pl).

sewer ['su:ə*] n égout m.

sewing ['səuɪŋ] n couture f; ~ machine n machine f à coudre.

sewn [səun] pp of sew.

sex [sɛks] n sexe m; to have ~ with avoir des rapports (sexuels) avec; ~ist a, n sexiste (m/f).

sexual ['sɛksjuəl] a sexuel(le).

sexy ['sɛksɪ] a sexy inv.

shabby ['ʃæbɪ] a miteux(euse); (behaviour) mesquin(e), méprisable.

shack [ʃæk] n cabane f, hutte f.

shackles ['ʃæklz] npl chaînes fpl, entraves fpl.

shade [ʃeɪd] n ombre f; (for lamp) abat-jour m inv; (of colour) nuance f, ton m; (small quantity): a ~ of un soupçon de // vt abriter du soleil, ombrager; in the ~ à l'ombre; a ~ smaller un tout petit peu plus petit.

shadow ['ʃædəu] n ombre f // vt (follow) filer; ~ cabinet n (Brit POL) cabinet parallèle formé par le parti qui n'est pas au pouvoir; ~y a ombragé(e); (dim) vague, indistinct(e).

shady ['ʃeɪdɪ] a ombragé(e); (fig: dishonest) louche, véreux(euse).

shaft [ʃɑ:ft] n (of arrow, spear) hampe f; (AUT, TECH) arbre m; (of mine) puits m; (of lift) cage f; (of light) rayon m, trait m.

shaggy ['ʃægɪ] a hirsute; en broussaille.

shake [ʃeɪk] vb (pt shook, pp shaken [ʃuk, 'ʃeɪkn]) vt secouer; (bottle, cocktail) agiter; (house, confidence) ébranler // vi trembler // n secousse f; to ~ one's head (in refusal) dire or faire non de la tête; (in dismay) secouer la tête; to ~ hands with sb serrer la main à qn; to ~ off vt secouer; (fig) se débarrasser de; to ~ up vt secouer; **shaky** a (hand, voice) tremblant(e); (building) branlant(e), peu solide.

shall [ʃæl] auxiliary vb: I ~ go j'irai; ~ I open the door? j'ouvre la porte?; I'll get the coffee, ~ I? je vais chercher le café, d'accord?

shallow ['ʃæləu] a peu profond(e); (fig) superficiel(le).

sham [ʃæm] n frime f; (jewellery, furniture) imitation f.

shambles ['ʃæmblz] n confusion f, pagaïe f, fouillis m.

shame [ʃeɪm] n honte f // vt faire honte à; it is a ~ (that/to do) c'est dommage (que + sub/de faire); **what a ~!** quel dommage!; ~**faced** a honteux(euse), penaud(e); ~**ful** a honteux(euse), scandaleux(euse); ~**less** a éhonté(e), effronté(e); (immodest) impudique.

shampoo [ʃæm'puː] n shampooing m // vt faire un shampooing à; ~ **and set** n shampooing m et mise f en plis.

shamrock ['ʃæmrɔk] n trèfle m (emblème national de l'Irlande).

shandy ['ʃændɪ] n bière panachée.

shan't [ʃaːnt] = shall not.

shanty town ['ʃæntɪ-] n bidonville m.

shape [ʃeɪp] n forme f // vt façonner, modeler; (statement) formuler; (sb's ideas) former; (sb's life) déterminer // vi (also: ~ **up**: events) prendre tournure; (: person) faire des progrès, s'en sortir; **to take** ~ prendre forme or tournure; **-shaped** suffix: heart-shaped en forme de cœur; ~**less** a informe, sans forme; ~**ly** a bien proportionné(e), beau(belle).

share [ʃɛə*] n (thing received, contribution) part f; (COMM) action f // vt partager; (have in common) avoir en commun; **to** ~ **out** (among or between) partager (entre); ~**holder** n actionnaire m/f.

shark [ʃaːk] n requin m.

sharp [ʃaːp] a (razor, knife) tranchant(e), bien aiguisé(e); (point) aigu(guë); (nose, chin) pointu(e); (outline) net(te); (cold, pain) vif(vive); (MUS) dièse; (voice) coupant(e); (person: quick-witted) vif(vive), éveillé(e); (: unscrupulous) malhonnête // n (MUS) dièse m // ad: **at 2 o'clock** ~ à 2 heures pile or tapantes; ~**en** vt aiguiser; (pencil) tailler; (fig) aviver; ~**ener** n (also: **pencil** ~**ener**) taille-crayon(s) m inv; ~**eyed** a à qui rien n'échappe; ~**ly** ad (turn, stop) brusquement; (stand out) nettement; (criticize, retort) sèchement, vertement.

shatter ['ʃætə*] vt briser; (fig: upset) bouleverser; (: ruin) briser, ruiner // vi voler en éclats, se briser.

shave [ʃeɪv] vt raser // vi se raser // n: **to have a** ~ se raser; ~**r** n (also: **electric** ~**r**) rasoir m électrique.

shaving ['ʃeɪvɪŋ] n (action) rasage m; ~**s** npl (of wood etc) copeaux mpl; ~ **brush** n blaireau m; ~ **cream** n crème f à raser.

shawl [ʃɔːl] n châle m.

she [ʃiː] pronoun elle; ~**-cat** n chatte f;

~**-elephant** n éléphant m femelle; NB: for ships, countries follow the gender of your translation.

sheaf [ʃiːf], pl **sheaves** n gerbe f.

shear [ʃɪə*] vt (pt ~**ed**, pp ~**ed** or shorn) (sheep) tondre; **to** ~ **off** vi (branch) partir, se détacher; ~**s** npl (for hedge) cisaille(s) f(pl).

sheath [ʃiːθ] n gaine f, fourreau m, étui m; (contraceptive) préservatif m.

sheaves [ʃiːvz] npl of sheaf.

shed [ʃed] n remise f, resserre f // vt (pt, pp shed) (leaves, fur etc) perdre; (tears) verser, répandre.

she'd [ʃiːd] = she had, she would.

sheen [ʃiːn] n lustre m.

sheep [ʃiːp] n (pl inv) mouton m; ~**dog** n chien m de berger; ~**ish** a penaud(e), timide; ~**skin** n peau f de mouton.

sheer [ʃɪə*] a (utter) pur(e), pur et simple; (steep) à pic, abrupt(e); (almost transparent) extrêmement fin(e) // ad à pic, abruptement.

sheet [ʃiːt] n (on bed) drap m; (of paper) feuille f; (of glass, metal) feuille, plaque f.

sheik(h) [ʃeɪk] n cheik m.

shelf [ʃelf], pl **shelves** n étagère f, rayon m.

shell [ʃel] n (on beach) coquillage m; (of egg, nut etc) coquille f; (explosive) obus m; (of building) carcasse f // vt (crab, prawn etc) décortiquer; (peas) écosser; (MIL) bombarder (d'obus).

she'll [ʃiːl] = she will, she shall.

shellfish ['ʃelfɪʃ] n (pl inv) (crab etc) crustacé m; (scallop etc) coquillage m; (pl: as food) crustacés; coquillages.

shelter ['ʃeltə*] n abri m, refuge m // vt abriter, protéger; (give lodging to) donner asile à // vi s'abriter, se mettre à l'abri.

shelve [ʃelv] vt (fig) mettre en suspens or en sommeil; ~**s** npl of shelf.

shepherd ['ʃepəd] n berger m // vt (guide) guider, escorter; ~**'s pie** n ≈ hachis m Parmentier.

sheriff ['ʃerɪf] n shérif m.

sherry ['ʃerɪ] n xérès m, sherry m.

she's [ʃiːz] = she is, she has.

Shetland ['ʃetlənd] n (also: **the** ~**s**, **the** ~ **Isles**) les îles fpl Shetland.

shield [ʃiːld] n bouclier m // vt: **to** ~ (**from**) protéger (de or contre).

shift [ʃɪft] n (change) changement m; (of workers) équipe f, poste m // vt déplacer, changer de place; (remove) enlever // vi changer de place, bouger; ~**less** a (person) fainéant(e); ~ **work** n travail m en équipe or par relais m par roulement; ~**y** a sournois(e); (eyes) fuyant(e).

shilling ['ʃɪlɪŋ] n (Brit) shilling m (= 12 old pence; 20 in a pound).

shilly-shally ['ʃɪlɪʃælɪ] vi tergiverser,

atermoyer.

shimmer ['ʃɪmə*] vi miroiter, chatoyer.

shin [ʃɪn] n tibia m.

shine [ʃaɪn] n éclat m, brillant m // vb (pt, pp shone) vi briller // vt faire briller or reluire; (torch): **to ~ on** braquer sur.

shingle ['ʃɪŋgl] n (on beach) galets mpl; (on roof) bardeau m; **~s** n (MED) zona m.

shiny ['ʃaɪnɪ] a brillant(e).

ship [ʃɪp] n bateau m; (large) navire m // vt transporter (par mer); (send) expédier (par mer); (load) charger, embarquer; **~building** n construction navale; **~ment** n cargaison f; **~ping** n (ships) navires mpl; (traffic) navigation f; **~shape** a en ordre impeccable; **~wreck** n épave f; (event) naufrage m // vt: **to be ~wrecked** faire naufrage; **~yard** n chantier naval.

shire ['ʃaɪə*] n (Brit) comté m.

shirk [ʃəːk] vt esquiver, se dérober à.

shirt [ʃəːt] n (man's) chemise f; **in ~ sleeves** en bras de chemise.

shit [ʃɪt] excl (col!) merde! (!).

shiver ['ʃɪvə*] vi frissonner.

shoal [ʃəʊl] n (of fish) banc m.

shock [ʃɔk] n (impact) choc m, heurt m; (ELEC) secousse f; (emotional) choc, secousse; (MED) commotion f, choc // vt choquer, scandaliser; bouleverser; **~absorber** n amortisseur m; **~ing** a choquant(e), scandaleux(euse); épouvantable; révoltant(e).

shod [ʃɔd] pt, pp of **shoe**.

shoddy ['ʃɔdɪ] a de mauvaise qualité, mal fait(e).

shoe [ʃuː] n chaussure f, soulier m; (also: horse~) fer m à cheval // vt (pt, pp shod) (horse) ferrer; **~horn** n chausse-pied m; **~lace** n lacet m (de soulier); **~ polish** n cirage m; **~shop** n magasin m de chaussures; **~string** n (fig): **on a ~string** avec un budget dérisoire.

shone [ʃɔn] pt, pp of **shine**.

shoo [ʃuː] excl (allez,) ouste!

shook [ʃuk] pt of **shake**.

shoot [ʃuːt] n (on branch, seedling) pousse f // vb (pt, pp shot) vt (game) chasser; tirer; abattre; (person) blesser (or tuer) d'un coup de fusil (or de revolver); (execute) fusiller; (film) tourner // vi (with gun, bow): **to ~ (at)** tirer (sur); (FOOTBALL) shooter, tirer; **to ~ down** vt (plane) abattre; **to ~ in/out** vi entrer/sortir comme une flèche; **to ~ up** vi (fig) monter en flèche; **~ing** n (shots) coups mpl de feu, fusillade f; (HUNTING) chasse f; **~ing star** n étoile filante.

shop [ʃɔp] n magasin m; (workshop) atelier m // vi (also: go ~ping) faire ses courses or ses achats; **~ assistant** n

(Brit) vendeur/euse; **~ floor** n (Brit: fig) ouvriers mpl; **~keeper** n marchand/e, commerçant/e; **~lifting** n vol m à l'étalage; **~per** n personne f qui fait ses courses, acheteur/euse; **~ping** n (goods) achats mpl, provisions fpl; **~ping bag** n sac m (à provisions); **~ping centre**, (US) **~ping center** n centre commercial; **~-soiled** a défraîchi(e), qui a fait la vitrine; **~ steward** n (Brit INDUSTRY) délégué/e syndical(e); **~ window** n vitrine f.

shore [ʃɔː*] n (of sea, lake) rivage m, rive f // vt: **to ~ (up)** étayer.

shorn [ʃɔːn] pp of **shear**.

short [ʃɔːt] a (not long) court(e); (soon finished) court, bref(brève); (person, step) petit(e); (curt) brusque, sec(sèche); (insufficient) insuffisant(e) // n (also: ~ **film**) court métrage; (a pair of) **~s** un short; **to be ~ of sth** être à court de or manquer de qch; **in ~** bref; **en bref**; **~ of doing** à moins de faire; **everything ~ of** tout sauf; **it is ~ for** c'est l'abréviation or le diminutif de; **to cut ~** (speech, visit) abréger, écourter; (person) couper la parole à; **to fall ~ of** ne pas être à la hauteur de; **to stop ~** s'arrêter net; **to stop ~ of** ne pas aller jusqu'à; **~age** n manque m, pénurie f; **~bread** n ≈sablé m; **~-change** vt ne pas rendre assez à; **~-circuit** n court-circuit m; **~coming** n défaut m; **~(crust) pastry** n (Brit) pâte brisée; **~cut** n raccourci m; **~en** vt raccourcir; (text, visit) abréger; **~fall** n déficit m; **~hand** n (Brit) sténo(graphie) f; **~hand typist** n (Brit) sténodactylo m/f; **~ list** n (Brit: for job) liste f des candidats sélectionnés; **~ly** ad bientôt, sous peu; **~-sighted** a (Brit) myope; (fig) qui manque de clairvoyance; **~-staffed** a à court de personnel; **~ story** n nouvelle f; **~-tempered** a qui s'emporte facilement; **~-term** a (effect) à court terme; **~wave** n (RADIO) ondes courtes.

shot [ʃɔt] pt, pp of **shoot** // n coup m (de feu); (person) tireur m; (try) coup, essai m; (injection) piqûre f; (PHOT) photo f; **like a ~** comme une flèche; (very readily) sans hésiter; **~gun** n fusil m de chasse.

should [ʃud] auxiliary vb: **I ~ go now** je devrais partir maintenant; **he ~ be there now** il devrait être arrivé maintenant; **I ~ go if I were you** si j'étais vous j'irais; **I ~ like to** j'aimerais bien, volontiers.

shoulder ['ʃəʊldə*] n épaule f; (Brit: of road): **hard ~** accotement m // vt (fig) endosser, se charger de; **~ bag** n sac m à bandoulière; **~ blade** n omoplate f; **~ strap** n bretelle f.

shouldn't ['ʃudnt] = **should not**.

shout [ʃaut] n cri m // vt crier // vi crier,

pousser des cris; **to ~ down** *vt* huer;
~ing *n* cris *mpl*.

shove [ʃʌv] *vt* pousser; (*col: put*): **to ~**
sth in fourrer *or* ficher qch dans; **to ~**
off *vi* (*NAUT*) pousser au large; (*fig:*
col) ficher le camp.

shovel [ʃʌvl] *n* pelle *f*.

show [ʃəu] *n* (*of emotion*) manifestation
f, démonstration *f*; (*semblance*) semblant *m*, apparence *f*; (*exhibition*)
exposition *f*, salon *m*; (*THEATRE*) spectacle *m*, représentation *f*; (*CINEMA*)
séance *f* // *vb* (*pt* **~ed**, *pp* **shown**) *vt*
montrer; (*courage etc*) faire preuve de,
manifester; (*exhibit*) exposer // *vi* se
voir, être visible; **on ~** (*exhibits etc*)
exposé(e); **to ~ in** *vt* (*person*) faire entrer; **to ~ off** *vi* (*pej*) crâner // *vt* (*dis-*
play) faire valoir; (*pej*) faire étalage
de; **to ~ out** *vt* (*person*) reconduire
(jusqu'à la porte); **to ~ up** *vi* (*stand*
out) ressortir; (*col: turn up*) se montrer
// *vt* démontrer; (*unmask*) démasquer,
dénoncer; **~ business** le monde du
spectacle; **~down** *n* épreuve *f* de force.

shower [ʃauə*] *n* (*rain*) averse *f*; (*of*
stones etc) pluie *f*, grêle *f*; (*also: ~bath*)
douche *f* // *vi* prendre une douche, se
doucher // *vt*: **to ~ sb with** (*gifts etc*)
combler qn de; (*abuse etc*) accabler qn
de; (*missiles*) bombarder qn de;
~proof *a* imperméable.

showing [ʃəuɪŋ] *n* (*of film*) projection
f.

show jumping *n* concours *m* hippique.

shown [ʃəun] *pp of* **show**.

show-off [ʃəuɔf] *n* (*col: person*)
crâneur/euse, m'as-tu-vu/e.

showroom [ʃəurum] *n* magasin *m or*
salle *f* d'exposition.

shrank [ʃræŋk] *pt of* **shrink**.

shrapnel [ʃræpnl] *n* éclats *mpl* d'obus.

shred [ʃred] *n* (*gen pl*) lambeau *m*, petit
morceau *f* // *vt* mettre en lambeaux, déchirer; (*CULIN*) râper; couper en
lanières; **~der** *n* (*for vegetables*)
râpeur *m*; (*for documents*) destructeur
m de documents.

shrewd [ʃru:d] *a* astucieux(euse),
perspicace.

shriek [ʃri:k] *vt, vi* hurler, crier.

shrill [ʃril] *a* perçant(e), aigu(guë),
strident(e).

shrimp [ʃrɪmp] *n* crevette grise.

shrine [ʃraɪn] *n* châsse *f*; (*place*) lieu *m*
de pèlerinage.

shrink [ʃrɪŋk], *pt* **shrank**, *pp* **shrunk** *vi*
rétrécir; (*fig*) se réduire; se contracter //
vt (*wool*) (faire) rétrécir // *n* (*col: pej*)
psychanalyste *m/f*; **to ~ from** (*doing*) sth
reculer devant (la pensée de faire) qch;
~age *n* rétrécissement *m*; **~wrap** *vt*
emballer sous film plastique.

shrivel [ʃrɪvl] (*also: ~ up*) *vt* ratatiner,
flétrir // *vi* se ratatiner, se flétrir.

shroud [ʃraud] *n* linceul *m* // *vt*: **~ed in**
mystery enveloppé(e) de mystère.

Shrove Tuesday [ʃrəuv-] *n* (le) Mardi
gras.

shrub [ʃrʌb] *n* arbuste *m*; **~bery** *n*
massif *m* d'arbustes.

shrug [ʃrʌg] *vt, vi*: **to ~** (**one's shoul-**
ders) hausser les épaules; **to ~ off** *vt*
faire fi de.

shrunk [ʃrʌŋk] *pp of* **shrink**.

shudder [ʃʌdə*] *vi* frissonner, frémir.

shuffle [ʃʌfl] *vt* (*cards*) battre; **to ~**
(**one's feet**) traîner les pieds.

shun [ʃʌn] *vt* éviter, fuir.

shunt [ʃʌnt] *vt* (*RAIL: direct*) aiguiller;
(*: divert*) détourner.

shut, *pt, pp* **shut** [ʃʌt] *vt* fermer // *vi*
(se) fermer; **to ~ down** *vt, vi* fermer
définitivement; **to ~ off** *vt* couper,
arrêter; **to ~ up** *vi* (*col: keep quiet*) se
taire // *vt* (*close*) fermer; (*silence*) faire
taire; **~ter** *n* volet *m*; (*PHOT*)
obturateur *m*.

shuttle [ʃʌtl] *n* navette *f*; (*also: ~*
service) (service *m* de) navette *f*.

shuttlecock [ʃʌtlkɔk] *n* volant *m* (*de*
badminton).

shy [ʃaɪ] *a* timide.

siblings [sɪblɪŋz] *npl* enfants *mpl* d'un
même couple.

Sicily [sɪsɪlɪ] *n* Sicile *f*.

sick [sɪk] *a* (*ill*) malade; (*vomiting*): **to**
be ~ vomir; (*humour*) noir(e), maca-
bre; **to feel ~** avoir envie de vomir,
avoir mal au cœur; **to be ~ of** (*fig*) en
avoir assez de; **~ bay** *n* infirmerie *f*;
~en *vt* écœurer // *vi*: **to be ~ening for**
sth (*cold etc*) couver qch.

sickle [sɪkl] *n* faucille *f*.

sick: **~ leave** *n* congé *m* de maladie;
~ly *a* maladif(ive), souffreteux(euse);
(*causing nausea*) écœurant(e); **~ness** *n*
maladie *f*; (*vomiting*) vomissement(s)
m(pl); **~ pay** *n* indemnité *f* de maladie.

side [saɪd] *n* côté *m*; (*of lake, road*) bord
m // *cpd* (*door, entrance*) latéral(e) // *vi*:
to ~ with sb prendre le parti de qn, se
ranger du côté de qn; **by the ~ of** au
bord de; **~ by ~** côte à côte; **to take ~s**
(**with**) prendre parti (pour); **~board** *n*
buffet *m*; **~boards**, **~burns** *npl*
(*whiskers*) pattes *fpl*; **~ effect** *n* (*MED*)
effet *m* secondaire; **~light** *n* (*AUT*)
veilleuse *f*; **~line** *n* (*SPORT*) (ligne *f* de)
touche *f*; (*fig*) activité *f* secondaire;
~long *a* oblique, de coin; **~saddle** *ad*
en amazone; **~ show** *n* attraction *f*;
~step *vt* (*fig*) éluder; éviter; **~ street**
n rue transversale; **~track** *vt* (*fig*) faire
dévier de son sujet; **~walk** *n* (*US*)
trottoir *m*; **~ways** *ad* de côté.

siding [saɪdɪŋ] *n* (*RAIL*) voie *f* de
garage.

sidle [saɪdl] *vi*: **to ~ up** (**to**) s'approcher
furtivement (de).

siege [si:dʒ] *n* siège *m*.

sieve [sɪv] *n* tamis *m*, passoire *f*.

sift [sɪft] *vt* passer au tamis *or* au crible; *(fig)* passer au crible.

sigh [saɪ] *n* soupir *m* // *vi* soupirer, pousser un soupir.

sight [saɪt] *n* (faculty) vue *f*; (spectacle) spectacle *m*; (on gun) mire *f* // *vt* apercevoir; in ~ visible; *(fig)* en vue; out of ~ hors de vue; **~seeing** *n* tourisme *m*; to go **~seeing** faire du tourisme.

sign [saɪn] *n* (gen) signe *m*; (with hand etc) signe, geste *m*; (notice) panneau *m*, écriteau *m* // *vt* signer; **to ~ on** *vi* (MIL) s'engager; (as unemployed) s'inscrire au chômage // *vt* (MIL) engager; (employee) embaucher; **to ~ over** *vt*: to ~ sth over to sb céder qch par écrit à qn; **to ~ up** (MIL) *vt* engager // *vi* s'engager.

signal ['sɪgnl] *n* signal *m* // *vi* (AUT) mettre son clignotant // *vt* (person) faire signe à; (message) communiquer par signaux; **~man** *n* (RAIL) aiguilleur *m*.

signature ['sɪgnətʃə*] *n* signature *f*; **~ tune** *n* indicatif musical.

signet ring ['sɪgnət-] *n* chevalière *f*.

significance [sɪg'nɪfɪkəns] *n* signification *f*; importance *f*.

significant [sɪg'nɪfɪkənt] *a* significatif(ive); (important) important(e), considérable.

signpost ['saɪnpəust] *n* poteau indicateur.

silence ['saɪlns] *n* silence *m* // *vt* faire taire, réduire au silence; **~r** *n* (on gun, Brit AUT) silencieux *m*.

silent ['saɪlnt] *a* silencieux(euse); (film) muet(te); **to remain ~** garder le silence, ne rien dire; **~ partner** *n* (COMM) bailleur *m* de fonds, commanditaire *m*.

silhouette [sɪlu:'et] *n* silhouette *f*.

silicon chip ['sɪlɪkən-] *n* puce *f* électronique.

silk [sɪlk] *n* soie *f* // *cpd* de *or* en soie; **~y** *a* soyeux(euse).

silly ['sɪlɪ] *a* stupide, sot(te), bête.

silt [sɪlt] *n* vase *f*; limon *m*.

silver ['sɪlvə*] *n* argent *m*; (money) monnaie *f* (en pièces d'argent); (also: **~ware**) argenterie *f* // *cpd* d'argent, en argent; **~ paper** *n* (Brit) papier *m* d'argent *or* d'étain; **~-plated** *a* plaqué(e) argent; **~smith** *n* orfèvre *m/f*; **~y** *a* argenté(e).

similar ['sɪmɪlə*] *a*: ~ (to) semblable (à); **~ly** *ad* de la même façon, de même.

simile ['sɪmɪlɪ] *n* comparaison *f*.

simmer ['sɪmə*] *vi* cuire à feu doux, mijoter.

simpering ['sɪmpərɪŋ] *a* minaudier(ère), nunuche.

simple ['sɪmpl] *a* simple; **simplicity**

[-'plɪsɪtɪ] *n* simplicité *f*.

simultaneous [sɪməl'teɪnɪəs] *a* simultané(e).

sin [sɪn] *n* péché *m* // *vi* pécher.

since [sɪns] *ad*, *prep* depuis // *cj* (time) depuis que; (because) puisque, étant donné que, comme; ~ **then** depuis ce moment-là.

sincere [sɪn'sɪə*] *a* sincère; **sincerity** [-'serɪtɪ] *n* sincérité *f*.

sinew ['sɪnju:] *n* tendon *m*; **~s** *npl* muscles *mpl*.

sinful ['sɪnful] *a* coupable.

sing [sɪŋ], *pt* **sang**, *pp* **sung** *vt*, *vi* chanter.

singe [sɪndʒ] *vt* brûler légèrement; (clothes) roussir.

singer ['sɪŋə*] *n* chanteur/euse.

singing ['sɪŋɪŋ] *n* chant *m*.

single ['sɪŋgl] *a* seul(e), unique; (unmarried) célibataire; (not double) simple // *n* (Brit: also: ~ **ticket**) aller *m* (simple); (record) 45 tours *m*; **~s** *npl* (TENNIS) simple *m*; **to ~ out** *vt* choisir; distinguer; **~ bed** *n* lit *m* à une place *or* d'une personne; **~-breasted** *a* droit(e); **~ file** *n*: in ~ file en file indienne; **~-handed** *ad* tout(e) seul(e), sans (aucune) aide; **~-minded** *a* résolu(e), tenace; **~ room** *n* chambre *f* à un lit *or* pour une personne.

singlet ['sɪŋglɪt] *n* tricot *m* de corps.

singly ['sɪŋglɪ] *ad* séparément.

singular ['sɪŋgjulə*] *a* singulier(ère), étrange; (LING) (au) singulier, du singulier // *n* (LING) singulier *m*.

sinister ['sɪnɪstə*] *a* sinistre.

sink [sɪŋk] *n* évier *m* // *vb* (*pt* **sank**, *pp* **sunk**) *vt* (ship) (faire) couler, faire sombrer; (foundations) creuser; (piles etc): **to ~ sth into** enfoncer qch dans // *vi* couler, sombrer; (ground etc) s'affaisser; **to ~ in** *vi* s'enfoncer, pénétrer.

sinner ['sɪnə*] *n* pécheur/eresse.

sinus ['saɪnəs] *n* (ANAT) sinus *m inv*.

sip [sɪp] *vt* boire à petites gorgées.

siphon ['saɪfən] *n* siphon *m*; **to ~ off** *vt* siphonner.

sir [sə*] *n* monsieur *m*; S~ **John Smith** sir John Smith; yes ~ oui Monsieur.

siren ['saɪərn] *n* sirène *f*.

sirloin ['sə:lɔɪn] *n* aloyau *m*.

sissy ['sɪsɪ] *n* (col: coward) poule mouillée.

sister ['sɪstə*] *n* sœur *f*; (nun) religieuse *f*, (bonne) sœur; (Brit: nurse) infirmière *f* en chef; **~-in-law** *n* belle-sœur *f*.

sit [sɪt], *pt*, *pp* **sat** *vi* s'asseoir; (assembly) être en séance, siéger; (for painter) poser // *vt* (exam) passer, se présenter à; **to ~ down** *vi* s'asseoir; **to ~ in on** *vt fus* assister à; **to ~ up** *vi* s'asseoir; (not go to bed) rester debout, ne pas se coucher.

sitcom ['sɪtkɔm] *n abbr* (= situation

comedy) comédie *f* de situation.
site [saɪt] *n* emplacement *m*, site *m*; (*also*: **building ~**) chantier *m*.
sit-in ['sɪtɪn] *n* (*demonstration*) sit-in *m* *inv*, occupation *f* de locaux.
sitting ['sɪtɪŋ] *n* (*of assembly etc*) séance *f*; (*in canteen*) service *m*; **~ room** *n* salon *m*.
situated ['sɪtjueɪtɪd] *a* situé(e).
situation [sɪtju'eɪʃən] *n* situation *f*; '**~s vacant/wanted**' (*Brit*) 'offres/demandes d'emploi'.
six [sɪks] *num* six; **~teen** *num* seize; **~th** *a* sixième; **~ty** *num* soixante.
size [saɪz] *n* taille *f*; dimensions *fpl*; (*of clothing*) taille; (*of shoes*) pointure *f*; (*glue*) colle *f*; **to ~ up** *vt* juger, jauger; **~able** *a* assez grand(e) *or* gros(se), assez important(e).
sizzle ['sɪzl] *vi* grésiller.
skate [skeɪt] *n* patin *m*; (*fish: pl inv*) raie *f* // *vi* patiner; **~board** *n* skateboard *m*, planche *f* à roulettes; **~r** *n* patineur/euse; **skating** *n* patinage *m*; **skating rink** *n* patinoire *f*.
skeleton ['skelɪtn] *n* squelette *m*; (*outline*) schéma *m*; **~ key** *n* passe-partout *m*; **~ staff** *n* effectifs réduits.
skeptical ['skeptɪkl] *a* (*US*) = **sceptical**.
sketch [sketʃ] *n* (*drawing*) croquis *m*, esquisse *f*; (*THEATRE*) sketch *m*, saynète *f* // *vt* esquisser, faire un croquis *or* une esquisse de; **~ book** *n* carnet *m* à dessin; **~y** *a* incomplet(ète), fragmentaire.
skewer ['skjuːə*] *n* brochette *f*.
ski [skiː] *n* ski *m* // *vi* skier, faire du ski; **~ boot** *n* chaussure *f* de ski.
skid [skɪd] *vi* déraper.
skier ['skiːə*] *n* skieur/euse.
skiing ['skiːɪŋ] *n* ski *m*.
ski jump *n* saut *m* à skis.
skilful ['skɪlful] *a* habile, adroit(e).
ski lift *n* remonte-pente *m* *inv*.
skill [skɪl] *n* habileté *f*, adresse *f*, talent *m*; **~ed** *a* habile, adroit(e); (*worker*) qualifié(e).
skim [skɪm] *vt* (*milk*) écrémer; (*soup*) écumer; (*glide over*) raser, effleurer // *vi*: **to ~ through** (*fig*) parcourir; **~med milk** *n* lait écrémé.
skimp [skɪmp] *vt* (*work*) bâcler, faire à la va-vite; (*cloth etc*) lésiner sur; **~y** *a* étriqué(e); maigre.
skin [skɪn] *n* peau *f* // *vt* (*fruit etc*) éplucher; (*animal*) écorcher; **~-deep** *a* superficiel(le); **~ diving** *n* plongée sous-marine; **~ny** *a* maigre, maigrichon(ne); **~tight** *a* (*dress etc*) collant(e), ajusté(e).
skip [skɪp] *n* petit bond *or* saut; (*container*) benne *f* // *vi* gambader, sautiller; (*with rope*) sauter à la corde // *vt* (*pass over*) sauter.
ski: ~ pants *npl* fuseau *m* (de ski); **~**

pole *n* bâton *m* de ski.
skipper ['skɪpə*] *n* (*NAUT, SPORT*) capitaine *m*.
skipping rope ['skɪpɪŋ-] *n* (*Brit*) corde *f* à sauter.
skirmish ['skɜːmɪʃ] *n* escarmouche *f*, accrochage *m*.
skirt [skɜːt] *n* jupe *f* // *vt* longer, contourner.
ski suit *n* combinaison *f* (de ski).
skit [skɪt] *n* sketch *m* satirique.
skittle ['skɪtl] *n* quille *f*; **~s** *n* (*game*) (jeu *m* de) quilles *fpl*.
skive [skaɪv] *vi* (*Brit col*) tirer au flanc.
skulk [skʌlk] *vi* rôder furtivement.
skull [skʌl] *n* crâne *m*.
skunk [skʌŋk] *n* mouffette *f*.
sky [skaɪ] *n* ciel *m*; **~light** *n* lucarne *f*; **~scraper** *n* gratte-ciel *m* *inv*.
slab [slæb] *n* plaque *f*; dalle *f*.
slack [slæk] *a* (*loose*) lâche, desserré(e); (*slow*) stagnant(e); (*careless*) négligent(e), peu sérieux(euse) *or* consciencieux(euse) // *n* (*in rope etc*) mou *m*; **~s** *npl* pantalon *m*; **~en** (*also*: **~en off**) *vi* ralentir, diminuer // *vt* relâcher.
slag [slæg] *n* scories *fpl*; **~ heap** *n* crassier *m*.
slain [sleɪn] *pp of* **slay**.
slam [slæm] *vt* (*door*) (faire) claquer; (*throw*) jeter violemment, flanquer; (*criticize*) éreinter, démolir // *vi* claquer.
slander ['slɑːndə*] *n* calomnie *f*; diffamation *f*.
slang [slæŋ] *n* argot *m*.
slant [slɑːnt] *n* inclinaison *f*; (*fig*) angle *m*, point *m* de vue; **~ed** *a* tendancieux(euse); **~ing** *a* en pente, incliné(e); couché(e).
slap [slæp] *n* claque *f*, gifle *f*; tape *f* // *vt* donner une claque *or* une gifle *or* une tape à // *ad* (*directly*) tout droit, en plein; **~dash** *a* fait(e) sans soin *or* à la va-vite; (*person*) insouciant(e), négligent(e); **~stick** *n* (*comedy*) grosse farce, style *m* tarte à la crème; **~-up** *a*: a **~-up meal** (*Brit*) un repas extra *or* fameux.
slash [slæʃ] *vt* entailler, taillader; (*fig: prices*) casser.
slat [slæt] *n* latte *f*, lame *f*.
slate [sleɪt] *n* ardoise *f* // *vt* (*fig: criticize*) éreinter, démolir.
slaughter ['slɔːtə*] *n* carnage *m*, massacre *m* // *vt* (*animal*) abattre; (*people*) massacrer.
slave [sleɪv] *n* esclave *m/f* // *vi* (*also*: **~ away**) trimer, travailler comme un forçat; **~ry** *n* esclavage *m*.
slay [sleɪ], *pt* **slew**, *pp* **slain** *vt* (*formal*) tuer.
sleazy ['sliːzɪ] *a* miteux(euse), minable.
sledge [sledʒ] *n* luge *f*; **~hammer** *n* marteau *m* de forgeron.
sleek [sliːk] *a* (*hair, fur*) brillant(e),

luisant(e); (*car, boat*) aux lignes pures *or* élégantes.

sleep [sli:p] *n* sommeil *m* // *vi* (*pt, pp* slept [slɛpt]) dormir; (*spend night*) dormir, coucher; (*be going to go to* ~ s'endormir; **to** ~ **in** *vi* (*lie late*) faire la grasse matinée; (*oversleep*) se réveiller trop tard; **~er** *n* (*person*) dormeur/euse; (*Brit* RAIL: *on track*) traverse *f*; (: *train*) train *m* de voitures-lits; **~ing bag** *n* sac *m* de couchage; **~ing car** *n* wagon-lits *m*, voiture-lits *f*; **~ing pill** *n* somnifère *m*; **~less** *a*: **a ~less night** une nuit blanche; **~walker** *n* somnambule *m/f*; **~y** *a* qui a envie de dormir; (*fig*) endormi(e).

sleet [sli:t] *n* neige fondue.

sleeve [sli:v] *n* manche *f*.

sleigh [sleɪ] *n* traîneau *m*.

sleight [slaɪt] *n*: ~ **of hand** tour *m* de passe-passe.

slender ['slɛndə*] *a* svelte, mince; faible, ténu(e).

slept [slɛpt] *pt, pp* of **sleep**.

slew [slu:] *vi* virer, pivoter // *pt* of **slay**.

slice [slaɪs] *n* tranche *f*; (*round*) rondelle *f* // *vt* couper en tranches (*or* en rondelles).

slick [slɪk] *a* brillant(e) en apparence; mielleux(euse) // *n* (*also*: **oil ~**) nappe *f* de pétrole, marée noire.

slide [slaɪd] *n* (*in playground*) toboggan *m*; (*PHOT*) diapositive *f*; (*Brit*: *also*: **hair ~**) barrette *f*; (*in prices*) chute *f*, baisse *f* // *vb* (*pt, pp* **slid** [slɪd]) *vt* (faire) glisser // *vi* glisser; ~ **rule** *n* règle *f* à calcul; **sliding** *a* (*door*) coulissant(e); **sliding scale** *n* échelle *f* mobile.

slight [slaɪt] *a* (*slim*) mince, menu(e); (*frail*) frêle; (*trivial*) faible, insignifiant(e); (*small*) petit(e), léger(ère) (*before n*) // *n* offense *f*, affront *m* // *vt* (*offend*) blesser, offenser; **not in the ~est** pas le moins du monde, pas du tout; **~ly** *ad* légèrement, un peu.

slim [slɪm] *a* mince // *vi* maigrir, suivre un régime amaigrissant.

slime [slaɪm] *n* vase *f*; substance visqueuse.

slimming ['slɪmɪŋ] *n* amaigrissement *m*.

sling [slɪŋ] *n* (*MED*) écharpe *f* // *vt* (*pt, pp* **slung**) lancer, jeter.

slip [slɪp] *n* faux pas; (*mistake*) erreur *f*; étourderie *f*; bévue *f*; (*underskirt*) combinaison *f*; (*of paper*) petite feuille, fiche *f* // *vt* (*slide*) glisser // *vi* (*slide*) glisser; (*move smoothly*): **to ~ into/out of** se glisser *or* se faufiler dans/hors de; (*decline*) baisser; **to ~ sth on/off** enfiler/ enlever qch; **to give sb the ~** fausser compagnie à qn; **a ~ of the tongue** un lapsus; **to ~ away** *vi* s'esquiver; **~ped disc** *n* déplacement *m* de vertèbres.

slipper ['slɪpə*] *n* pantoufle *f*.

slippery ['slɪpərɪ] *a* glissant(e); insaisissable.

slip road *n* (*Brit*: *to motorway*) bretelle *f* d'accès.

slipshod ['slɪpʃɔd] *a* négligé(e), peu soigné(e).

slip-up ['slɪpʌp] *n* bévue *f*.

slipway ['slɪpweɪ] *n* cale *f* (de construction *or* de lancement).

slit [slɪt] *n* fente *f*; (*cut*) incision *f*; (*tear*) déchirure *f* // *vt* (*pt, pp* slit) fendre; couper; inciser; déchirer.

slither ['slɪðə*] *vi* glisser, déraper.

sliver ['slɪvə*] *n* (*of glass, wood*) éclat *m*; (*of cheese etc*) petit morceau, fine tranche.

slob [slɔb] *n* (*col*) rustaud/e.

slog [slog] *n* (*Brit*) *n* gros effort; tâche fastidieuse // *vi* travailler très dur.

slogan ['sləugən] *n* slogan *m*.

slop [slɔp] *vi* (*also*: ~ **over**) se renverser; déborder // *vt* répandre; renverser.

slope [sləup] *n* pente *f*, côte *f*; (*side of mountain*) versant *m*; (*slant*) inclinaison *f* // *vi*: **to ~ down** être *or* descendre en pente; **to ~ up** monter.

sloppy ['slɔpɪ] *a* (*work*) peu soigné(e), bâclé(e); (*appearance*) négligé(e), débraillé(e); (*film etc*) sentimental(e).

slot [slɔt] *n* fente *f* // *vt*: **to ~ sth into** encastrer *or* insérer qch dans // *vi*: **to ~ into** s'encastrer *or* s'insérer dans; ~ **machine** *n* (*Brit*: *vending machine*) distributeur *m* (automatique), machine *f* à sous; (*for gambling*) appareil *m or* machine à sous.

sloth [sləuθ] *n* (*laziness*) paresse *f*.

slouch [slautʃ] *vi* avoir le dos rond, être voûté(e); **to ~ about** *vi* (*laze*) traîner à ne rien faire.

slovenly ['slʌvənlɪ] *a* sale, débraillé(e).

slow [sləu] *a* lent(e); (*watch*): **to be ~** retarder // *ad* lentement // *vt, vi* (*also*: ~ **down**, ~ **up**) ralentir; ' ~ ' (*road sign*) 'ralentir'; **~ly** *ad* lentement; ~ **motion** *n*: **in ~ motion** au ralenti.

sludge [slʌdʒ] *n* boue *f*.

slug [slʌg] *n* limace *f*; (*bullet*) balle *f*; **~gish** *a* mou(molle), lent(e).

sluice [slu:s] *n* vanne *f*; écluse *f*.

slum [slʌm] *n* taudis *m*.

slumber ['slʌmbə*] *n* sommeil *m*.

slump [slʌmp] *n* baisse soudaine, effondrement *m*; crise *f* // *vi* s'effondrer, s'affaisser.

slung [slʌŋ] *pt, pp* of **sling**.

slur [slə:*] *n* bredouillement *m*; (*smear*): ~ **(on)** atteinte *f* (à); insinuation *f* (contre) // *vt* mal articuler.

slush [slʌʃ] *n* neige fondue; ~ **fund** *n* caisse noire, fonds secrets.

slut [slʌt] *n* souillon *f*.

sly [slaɪ] *a* rusée(e); sournois(e).

smack [smæk] *n* (*slap*) tape *f*; (*on face*)

gifle f // vt donner une tape à; gifler; (child) donner la fessée à // vi: to ~ of avoir des relents de, sentir.

small [smɔːl] a petit(e); ~ **ads** npl (Brit) petites annonces; ~ **change** n petite or menue monnaie; ~**holder** n (Brit) petit cultivateur; ~ **hours** npl: in the ~ hours au petit matin; ~**pox** n variole f; ~ **talk** n menus propos.

smart [smɑːt] a élégant(e), chic inv; (clever) intelligent(e), astucieux(euse), futé(e); (quick) rapide, vif(vive), prompt(e) // vi faire mal, brûler; to ~**en up** vi devenir plus élégant(e), se faire beau(belle) // vt rendre plus élégant(e).

smash [smæʃ] n (also: ~-up) collision f, accident m // vt casser, briser, fracasser; (opponent) écraser; (hopes) ruiner, détruire; (SPORT: record) pulvériser // vi se briser, se fracasser; s'écraser; ~**ing** a (col) formidable.

smattering ['smætərɪŋ] n: a ~ of quelques notions de.

smear [smɪə*] n tache f, salissure f; trace f; (MED) frottis m // vt enduire; (fig) porter atteinte à.

smell [smel] n odeur f; (sense) odorat m // vb (pt, pp smelt or smelled [smelt, smeld]) vt sentir // vi (food etc): to ~ (of) sentir; (pej) sentir mauvais: it ~s good/~s of garlic ça sent bon/sent l'ail; ~**y** a qui sent mauvais, malodorant(e).

smile [smaɪl] n sourire m // vi sourire.

smirk [smɜːk] n petit sourire suffisant or affecté.

smith [smɪθ] n maréchal-ferrant m; forgeron m; ~**y** ['smɪðɪ] n forge f.

smock [smɔk] n blouse f, sarrau m.

smog [smɔg] n brouillard mêlé de fumée.

smoke [sməuk] n fumée f // vt, vi fumer; ~**d** a (bacon, glass) fumé(e); ~**r** n (person) fumeur/euse; (RAIL) wagon m fumeurs; ~ **screen** n rideau m or écran m de fumée; (fig) paravent m; **smoking** n: 'no smoking' (sign) 'défense de fumer'; **smoky** a enfumé(e).

smolder ['sməuldə*] vi (US) = **smoulder**.

smooth [smuːð] a lisse; (sauce) onctueux(euse), (flavour, whisky) moelleux(euse); (movement) régulier(ère), sans à-coups or heurts; (person) douceureux(euse), mielleux(euse) // vt lisser, défroisser; (also: ~ out: creases, difficulties) faire disparaître.

smother ['smʌðə*] vt étouffer.

smoulder, (US) **smolder** ['sməuldə*] vi couver.

smudge [smʌdʒ] n tache f, bavure f // vt salir, maculer.

smug [smʌg] a suffisant(e), content(e) de soi.

smuggle ['smʌgl] vt passer en contrebande or en fraude; ~**r** n contrebandier/ère; **smuggling** n contrebande f.

smutty ['smʌtɪ] a (fig) grossier(ère), obscène.

snack [snæk] n casse-croûte m inv; ~ **bar** n snack(-bar) m.

snag [snæg] n inconvénient m, difficulté f.

snail [sneɪl] n escargot m.

snake [sneɪk] n serpent m.

snap [snæp] n (sound) claquement m, bruit sec; (photograph) photo f, instantané m; (game) sorte de jeu de bataille // a subit(e); fait(e) sans réfléchir // vt faire claquer; (break) casser net; (photograph) prendre un instantané de // vi se casser net or avec un bruit sec; to ~ **open/shut** s'ouvrir/se refermer brusquement; **to ~ at** vt fus (subj: dog) essayer de mordre; **to ~ off** vt (break) casser net; **to ~ up** vt sauter sur, saisir; ~**py** a prompt(e); (slogan) qui a du punch; ~**shot** n photo f, instantané m.

snare [snɛə*] n piège m.

snarl [snɑːl] vi gronder.

snatch [snætʃ] n (fig) vol m; (small amount): ~**es of** des fragments mpl or bribes fpl de // vt saisir (d'un geste vif); (steal) voler.

sneak [sniːk] vi: to ~ **in/out** entrer/sortir furtivement or à la dérobée; ~**ers** npl chaussures fpl de tennis or basket; ~**y** a sournois(e).

sneer [snɪə*] vi ricaner, sourire d'un air sarcastique.

sneeze [sniːz] vi éternuer.

sniff [snɪf] vi renifler // vt renifler, flairer.

snigger ['snɪgə*] vi ricaner; pouffer de rire.

snip [snɪp] n petit bout; (bargain) (bonne) occasion or affaire f // vt couper.

sniper ['snaɪpə*] n (marksman) tireur embusqué.

snippet ['snɪpɪt] n bribes fpl.

snivelling ['snɪvlɪŋ] a (whimpering) larmoyant(e), pleurnicheur(euse).

snob [snɔb] n snob m/f; ~**bish** a snob inv.

snooker ['snuːkə*] n sorte de jeu de billard.

snoop ['snuːp] vi: to ~ **on sb** espionner qn; to ~ **about** somewhere fourrer son nez quelque part.

snooty ['snuːtɪ] a snob inv, prétentieux(euse).

snooze [snuːz] n petit somme // vi faire un petit somme.

snore [snɔː*] vi ronfler; **snoring** n ronflement(s) m(pl).

snorkel ['snɔːkl] n (of swimmer) tuba m.

snort [snɔːt] vi grogner; (horse) renâcler.

snotty ['snɒtɪ] a morveux(euse).

snout [snaut] n museau m.

snow [snəu] n neige f // vi neiger; **~ball**
n boule f de neige; **~bound** a
enneigé(e), bloqué(e) par la neige;
~drift n congère f; **~drop** n perce-
neige m; **~fall** n chute f de neige;
~flake n flocon m de neige; **~man** n
bonhomme m de neige; **~plough**, (US)
~plow n chasse-neige m inv; **~shoe** n
raquette f (pour la neige); **~storm** n
tempête f de neige.

snub [snʌb] vt repousser, snober // n
rebuffade f; **~-nosed** a au nez re-
troussé.

snuff [snʌf] n tabac m à priser.

snug [snʌg] a douillet(te), confortable.

snuggle ['snʌgl] vi: to ~ up to sb se
serrer or se blottir contre qn.

so [səu] ♦ ad 1 (thus, likewise) ainsi; if
~ si oui; ~ do/have I moi aussi; it's 5
o'clock - ~ it is! il est 5 heures - en
effet! or c'est vrai!; I hope/think ~ je
l'espère/le crois; ~ far jusqu'ici, jusqu'à
maintenant; (in past) jusque-là
2 (in comparisons etc: to such a degree)
si, tellement; ~ big (that) si or tellement
grand (que); she's not ~ clever as her
brother n'est pas aussi intelligente
que son frère
3: ~ much a, ad tant (de); I've got ~
much work j'ai tant de travail; I love
you ~ much je vous aime tant; ~ many
tant (de)
4 (phrases): 10 or ~ à peu près or
environ 10; ~ long! (col: goodbye) au
revoir!, à un de ces jours!
♦ cj 1 (expressing purpose): ~ as to do
pour or afin de faire; ~ (that) pour que
or afin que + sub
2 (expressing result) donc, par
conséquent; ~ that si bien que, de (telle)
sorte que.

soak [səuk] vt faire tremper // vi
tremper; to ~ in vi être absorbé(e); to
~ up vt absorber.

so-and-so ['səuəndsəu] n (somebody)
un tel(une telle).

soap [səup] n savon m; **~flakes** npl
paillettes fpl de savon; **~ opera** n
feuilleton télévisé; **~ powder** n lessive
f; **~y** a savonneux(euse).

soar [sɔː*] vi monter (en flèche),
s'élancer.

sob [sɒb] n sanglot m // vi sangloter.

sober ['səubə*] a qui n'est pas (or plus)
ivre; (sedate) sérieux(euse), sensé(e);
(moderate) mesuré(e); (colour, style)
sobre, discret(ète); to ~ up vt dégriser
// vi se dégriser.

so-called ['səu'kɔːld] a soi-disant inv.

soccer ['sɒkə*] n football m.

social ['səuʃl] a social(e) // n (petite)
fête; ~ **club** n amicale f, foyer m;

~ism n socialisme m; **~ist** a,
socialiste (m/f); **~ize** vi: to **~ize** (with)
lier connaissance (avec); parler (avec);
~ **security** n aide sociale; ~ **work** n
assistance sociale; ~ **worker** n
assistant/e social(e).

society [sə'saɪətɪ] n société f; (club)
société, association f; (also: high ~)
(haute) société, grand monde.

sociology [səusɪ'ɒlədʒɪ] n sociologie f.

sock [sɒk] n chaussette f // vt (col: hit)
flanquer un coup à.

socket ['sɒkɪt] n cavité f; (ELEC: also:
wall ~) prise f de courant; (: for light
bulb) douille f.

sod [sɒd] n (of earth) motte f; (Brit
col!) con m (!); salaud m (!).

soda ['səudə] n (CHEM) soude f; (also:
~ water) eau f de Seltz; (US: also: ~
pop) soda m.

sodden ['sɒdn] a trempé(e); dé-
trempé(e).

sofa ['səufə] n sofa m, canapé m.

soft [sɒft] a (not rough) doux(douce);
(not hard) doux; mou(molle); (not loud)
doux, léger(ère); (kind) doux, gentil(le);
(weak) indulgent(e); (stupid) stupide,
débile; ~ **drink** n boisson non
alcoolisée; **~en** ['sɒfn] vt (r)amollir;
adoucir; atténuer // vi se ramollir;
s'adoucir; s'atténuer; **~ly** ad
doucement; gentiment; **~ness** n
douceur f.

software ['sɒftwɛə*] n (COMPUT)
logiciel m, software m.

soggy ['sɒgɪ] a trempé(e); détrempé(e).

soil [sɔɪl] n (earth) sol m, terre f // vt
salir; (fig) souiller.

solace ['sɒlɪs] n consolation f.

solar ['səulə*] a solaire.

sold [səuld] pt, pp of sell; ~ **out** n
(COMM) épuisé(e).

solder ['səuldə*] vt souder (au fil à
souder) // n soudure f.

soldier ['səuldʒə*] n soldat m, militaire
m.

sole [səul] n (of foot) plante f; (of shoe)
semelle f; (fish: pl inv) sole f // a
seul(e), unique.

solemn ['sɒləm] a solennel(le); sé-
rieux(euse), grave.

sole trader n (COMM) chef m d'entreprise individuelle.

solicit [sə'lɪsɪt] vt (request) solliciter // vi
(prostitute) racoler.

solicitor [sə'lɪsɪtə*] n (Brit: for wills
etc) ≈ notaire m; (: in court) ≈ avocat
m.

solid ['sɒlɪd] a (not hollow) plein(e),
compact(e), massif(ive); (strong, sound,
reliable, not liquid) solide; (meal)
consistant(e), substantiel(le) // n solide
m.

solidarity [sɒlɪ'dærɪtɪ] n solidarité f.

solitary ['sɒlɪtərɪ] a solitaire; ~ **con-**

finement n (*LAW*) isolement m.

solo ['səuləu] n solo m; **~ist** n soliste m/f.

soluble ['sɔljubl] a soluble.

solution [sə'lu:ʃən] n solution f.

solve [sɔlv] vt résoudre.

solvent ['sɔlvənt] a (*COMM*) solvable // n (*CHEM*) (dis)solvant m.

some [sʌm] ♦ a **1** (*a certain amount or number of*): ~ tea/water/ice cream du thé/de l'eau/de la glace; ~ children/apples des enfants/pommes **2** (*certain: in contrasts*): ~ people say that ... il y a des gens qui disent que ...; ~ films were excellent, but most were mediocre certains films étaient excellents, mais la plupart étaient médiocres **3** (*unspecified*): ~ woman was asking for you il y avait une dame qui vous demandait; he was asking for ~ book (or other) il demandait un livre quelconque; ~ day un de ces jours; ~ day next week un jour la semaine prochaine ♦ pronoun **1** (*a certain number*) quelques-un(e)s, certain(e)s; I've got ~ (*books etc*) j'en ai (quelques-uns); ~ (of them) have been sold certains ont été vendus **2** (*a certain amount*) un peu; I've got ~ (*money, milk*) j'en ai un peu ♦ ad: ~ 10 people quelque 10 personnes, 10 personnes environ.

somebody ['sʌmbədɪ] pronoun = **someone**.

somehow ['sʌmhau] ad d'une façon ou d'une autre; (*for some reason*) pour une raison ou une autre.

someone ['sʌmwʌn] pronoun quelqu'un.

someplace ['sʌmpleɪs] ad (*US*) = **somewhere**.

somersault ['sʌməsɔ:lt] n culbute f, saut périlleux // vi faire la culbute or un saut périlleux; (*car*) faire un tonneau.

something ['sʌmθɪŋ] pronoun quelque chose m; ~ interesting quelque chose d'intéressant.

sometime ['sʌmtaɪm] ad (*in future*) un de ces jours, un jour ou l'autre; (*in past*): ~ last month au cours du mois dernier.

sometimes ['sʌmtaɪmz] ad quelquefois, parfois.

somewhat ['sʌmwɔt] ad quelque peu, un peu.

somewhere ['sʌmwɛə*] ad quelque part.

son [sʌn] n fils m.

song [sɔŋ] n chanson f.

sonic ['sɔnɪk] a (*boom*) supersonique.

son-in-law ['sʌnɪnlɔ:] n gendre m, beau-fils m.

sonny ['sʌnɪ] n (*col*) fiston m.

soon [su:n] ad bientôt; (*early*) tôt; ~

afterwards peu après; *see also* as; **~er** ad (*time*) plus tôt; (*preference*): I would ~er do j'aimerais autant *or* je préférerais faire; **~er or later** tôt ou tard.

soot [sut] n suie f.

soothe [su:ð] vt calmer, apaiser.

sophisticated [sə'fɪstɪkeɪtɪd] a raffiné(e); sophistiqué(e); hautement perfectionné(e), très complexe.

sophomore ['sɔfəmɔ:*] n (*US*) étudiant/e de seconde année.

sopping ['sɔpɪŋ] a (*also*: ~ wet) tout(e) trempé(e).

soppy ['sɔpɪ] a (*pej*) sentimental(e).

soprano [sə'prɑ:nəu] n (*voice*) soprano m; (*singer*) soprano m/f.

sorcerer ['sɔ:sərə*] n sorcier m.

sore [sɔ:*] a (*painful*) douloureux(euse), sensible; (*offended*) contrarié(e), vexé(e) // n plaie f; **~ly** ad (*tempted*) fortement.

sorrow ['sɔrəu] n peine f, chagrin m.

sorry ['sɔrɪ] a désolé(e); (*condition, excuse*) triste, déplorable; ~! pardon!, excusez-moi!; to feel ~ for sb plaindre qn.

sort [sɔ:t] n genre m, espèce f, sorte f // vt (*also*: ~ out: *papers*) trier; classer; ranger; (: *letters etc*) trier; (: *problems*) résoudre, régler; **~ing office** n bureau m de tri.

SOS n abbr (= save our souls) S.O.S. m.

so-so ['səusəu] ad comme ci comme ça.

sought [sɔ:t] pt, pp of **seek**.

soul [səul] n âme f; **~-destroying** a démoralisant(e); **~ful** a plein(e) de sentiment.

sound [saund] a (*healthy*) en bonne santé, sain(e); (*safe, not damaged*) solide, en bon état; (*reliable, not superficial*) sérieux(euse), solide; (*sensible*) sensé(e) // ad: ~ asleep dormant d'un profond sommeil // n (*noise*) son m; bruit m; (*GEO*) détroit m, bras m de mer // vt (*alarm*) sonner; (*also*: ~ out: *opinions*) sonder // vi sonner, retentir; (*fig: seem*) sembler (être); to ~ like ressembler à; ~ barrier n mur m du son; ~ effects npl bruitage m; **~ly** ad (*sleep*) profondément; (*beat*) complètement, à plate couture; **~proof** a insonorisé(e); **~track** n (*of film*) bande f sonore.

soup [su:p] n soupe f, potage m; in the ~ (*fig*) dans le pétrin; ~ plate n assiette creuse *or* à soupe; **~spoon** n cuiller f à soupe.

sour ['sauə*] a aigre; it's ~ grapes (*fig*) c'est du dépit.

source [sɔ:s] n source f.

south [sauθ] n sud m // a du sud inv, du sud // ad au sud, vers le sud; S~ Africa n Afrique f du Sud; S~ African a sud-africain(e) // n Sud-Africain/e; S~

America *n* Amérique *f* du Sud; **S~ American** *a* sud-américain(e) // *n* Sud-Américain/e; **~-east** *n* sud-est *m*; **~erly** ['sʌðəlɪ] *a* du sud; au sud; **~ern** ['sʌðən] *a* (du) sud; méridional(e); exposé(e) au sud; **S~ Pole** *n* Pôle *m* Sud; **~ward(s)** *ad* vers le sud; **~-west** *n* sud-ouest *m*.

souvenir [su:və'nɪə*] *n* souvenir *m* (objet).

sovereign ['sɔvrɪn] *a*, *n* souverain(e).

soviet ['səʊvɪət] *a* soviétique; **the S~ Union** l'Union *f* soviétique.

sow *n* [sau] truie *f* // *vt* [səu] (*pt* **~ed**, *pp* **sown** [səun]) semer.

soya ['sɔɪə], (US) **soy** [sɔɪ] *n*: **~ bean** *n* graine *f* de soja; **~ sauce** *n* sauce *f* de soja.

spa [spa:] *n* (town) station thermale; (US: also: **health ~**) établissement *m* de cure de rajeunissement *etc*.

space [speɪs] *n* (gen) espace *m*; (room) place *f*; espace; (length of time) laps *m* de temps // *cpd* spatial(e) // *vt* (also: **~ out**) espacer; **~craft** *n* engin spatial; **~man/woman** *n* astronaute *m/f*, cosmonaute *m/f*; **~ship** *n* = **~craft**; **spacing** *n* espacement *m*.

spade [speɪd] *n* (tool) bêche *f*, pelle *f*; (child's) pelle; **~s** *npl* (CARDS) pique *m*.

Spain [speɪn] *n* Espagne *f*.

span [spæn] *pt* of **spin** // *n* (of bird, plane) envergure *f*; (of arch) portée *f*; (in time) espace *m* de temps, durée *f* // *vt* enjamber, franchir; (fig) couvrir, embrasser.

Spaniard ['spænjəd] *n* Espagnol/e.

spaniel ['spænjəl] *n* épagneul *m*.

Spanish ['spænɪʃ] *a* espagnol(e), d'Espagne // *n* (LING) espagnol *m*; **the ~** *npl* les Espagnols *mpl*.

spank [spæŋk] *vt* donner une fessée à.

spanner ['spænə*] *n* (Brit) clé *f* (de mécanicien).

spar [spa:*] *n* espar *m* // *vi* (BOXING) s'entraîner.

spare [spɛə*] *a* de réserve, de rechange; (surplus) en trop, de reste // *n* (part) pièce *f* de rechange, pièce détachée // *vt* (do without) se passer de; (afford to give) donner, accorder, passer; (refrain from hurting) épargner; (refrain from using) ménager; **to ~** (surplus) en surplus, de trop; **~ part** *n* pièce *f* de rechange, pièce détachée); **~ time** *n* moments *mpl* de loisir; **~ wheel** *n* (AUT) roue *f* de secours.

sparing ['spɛərɪŋ] *a*: **to be ~ with** ménager; **~ly** *ad* avec modération.

spark [spa:k] *n* étincelle *f*; **~(ing) plug** *n* bougie *f*.

sparkle ['spa:kl] *n* scintillement *m*, étincellement *m*, éclat *m* // *vi* étinceler, scintiller; (bubble) pétiller; **sparkling** *a* étincelant(e), scintillant(e); (wine)

mousseux(euse), pétillant(e).

sparrow ['spærəu] *n* moineau *m*.

sparse [spa:s] *a* clairsemé(e).

spartan ['spa:tən] *a* (fig) spartiate.

spasm ['spæzəm] *n* (MED) spasme *m*; (fig) accès *m*; **~odic** [-'mɔdɪk] *a* (fig) intermittent(e).

spastic ['spæstɪk] *n* handicapé/e moteur.

spat [spæt] *pt*, *pp* of **spit**.

spate [speɪt] *n* (fig): **~ of** avalanche *f* or torrent *m* de; **in ~** (river) en crue.

spatter ['spætə*] *vt* éclabousser // *vi* gicler.

spawn [spɔ:n] *vi* frayer // *n* frai *m*.

speak [spi:k], *pt* **spoke**, *pp* **spoken** *vt* (language) parler; (truth) dire // *vi* parler; (make a speech) prendre la parole; **to ~ to sb/of or about sth** parler à qn/de qch; **~ up!** parle plus fort!; **~er** *n* (in public) orateur *m*; (also: loud~er) haut-parleur *m*; (POL): **the S~er** le président de la chambre des Communes (Brit) or des Représentants (US).

spear [spɪə*] *n* lance *f*; **~head** *vt* (attack etc) mener.

spec [spɛk] *n* (col): **on ~** à tout hasard.

special ['spɛʃl] *a* spécial(e); **~ist** *n* spécialiste *m/f*; **~ity** [spɛʃɪ'ælɪtɪ] *n* spécialité *f*; **~ize** *vi*: **to ~ize (in)** se spécialiser (dans); **~ly** *ad* spécialement, particulièrement.

species ['spi:ʃi:z] *n* espèce *f*.

specific [spə'sɪfɪk] *a* précis(e); particulier(ère); (BOT, CHEM etc) spécifique; **~ally** *ad* expressément, explicitement.

specimen ['spɛsɪmən] *n* spécimen *m*, échantillon *m*; (MED) prélèvement *m*.

speck [spɛk] *n* petite tache, petit point; (particle) grain *m*.

speckled ['spɛkld] *a* tacheté(e), moucheté(e).

specs [spɛks] *npl* (col) lunettes *fpl*.

spectacle ['spɛktəkl] *n* spectacle *m*; **~s** *npl* lunettes *fpl*; **spectacular** [-'tækjulə*] *a* spectaculaire // *n* (CINEMA etc) superproduction *f*.

spectator [spɛk'teɪtə*] *n* spectateur/trice.

spectrum, *pl* **spectra** ['spɛktrəm, -rə] *n* spectre *m*; (fig) gamme *f*.

speculation [spɛkju'leɪʃən] *n* spéculation *f*; conjectures *fpl*.

speech [spi:tʃ] *n* (faculty) parole *f*; (talk) discours *m*, allocution *f*; (manner of speaking) façon *f* de parler, langage *m*; (enunciation) élocution *f*; **~less** *a* muet(te).

speed [spi:d] *n* vitesse *f*; (promptness) rapidité *f*; **at full** or **top ~** à toute vitesse or allure; **to ~ up** *vi* aller plus vite, accélérer // *vt* accélérer; **~boat** *n* vedette *f*, hors-bord *m inv*; **~ily** *ad* rapidement, promptement; **~ing** *n* (AUT) excès *m* de vitesse; **~ limit** *n* limitation *f* de vitesse, vitesse maximale permise; **~ometer** [spɪ'dɒmɪtə*] *n* compteur *m* (de vitesse); **~way** *n* (*SPORT*) piste *f* de vitesse pour motos; (*also:* **~way racing**) épreuve(s) *f(pl)* de vitesse de motos; **~y** *a* rapide, prompt(e).

spell [spɛl] *n* (*also:* **magic ~**) sortilège *m*, charme *m*; (*period of time*) (courte) période *f* // *vt* (*pt, pp* spelt (*Brit*) *or* **~ed** [spɛlt, spɛld]) (*in writing*) écrire, orthographier; (*aloud*) épeler; (*fig*) signifier; **to cast a ~ on sb** jeter un sort à qn; **he can't ~** il fait des fautes d'orthographe; **~bound** *a* envoûté(e), subjugué(e); **~ing** *n* orthographe *f*.

spend, *pt, pp* spent [spɛnd, spɛnt] *vt* (*money*) dépenser; (*time, life*) passer; consacrer; **~thrift** *n* dépensier/ère.

sperm [spə:m] *n* spermatozoïde *m*; (*semen*) sperme *m*.

spew [spju:] *vt* vomir.

sphere [sfɪə*] *n* sphère *f*.

spice [spaɪs] *n* épice *f*.

spick-and-span ['spɪkən'spæn] *a* impeccable.

spicy ['spaɪsɪ] *a* épicé(e), relevé(e); (*fig*) piquant(e).

spider ['spaɪdə*] *n* araignée *f*.

spike [spaɪk] *n* pointe *f*.

spill, *pt, pp* spilt *or* **~ed** [spɪl, -t, -d] *vt* renverser; répandre // *vi* se répandre; **to ~ over** *vi* déborder.

spin [spɪn] *n* (*revolution of wheel*) tour *m*; (*AVIAT*) (chute *f* en) vrille *f*; (*trip in car*) petit tour, balade *f* // *vb* (*pt* spun, span, *pp* spun) *vt* (*wool etc*) filer; (*wheel*) faire tourner // *vi* tourner, tournoyer; **to ~ out** *vt* faire durer.

spinach ['spɪnɪtʃ] *n* épinard *m*; (*as food*) épinards.

spinal ['spaɪnl] *a* vertébral(e), spinal(e); **~ cord** *n* moelle épinière.

spindly ['spɪndlɪ] *a* grêle, filiforme.

spin-dryer [spɪn'draɪə*] *n* (*Brit*) essoreuse *f*.

spine [spaɪn] *n* colonne vertébrale; (*thorn*) épine *f*, piquant *m*.

spinning ['spɪnɪŋ] *n* (*of thread*) filage *m*; (*by machine*) filature *f*; **~ top** *n* toupie *f*; **~ wheel** *n* rouet *m*.

spin-off ['spɪnɔf] *n* avantage inattendu; sous-produit *m*.

spinster ['spɪnstə*] *n* célibataire *f*; vieille fille.

spiral ['spaɪərl] *n* spirale *f* // *a* en spirale // *vi* (*fig*) monter en flèche; **~ staircase** *n* escalier *m* en colimaçon.

spire ['spaɪə*] *n* flèche *f*, aiguille *f*.

spirit ['spɪrɪt] *n* (*soul*) esprit *m*, âme *f*; (*ghost*) esprit, revenant *m*; (*mood*) esprit, état *m* d'esprit; (*courage*) courage *m*, énergie *f*; **~s** *npl* (*drink*) spiritueux *mpl*, alcool *m*; **in good ~s** de bonne humeur; **~ed** *a* vif(vive), fou-

gueux(euse), plein(e) d'allant; **~ level** *n* niveau *m* à bulle.

spiritual ['spɪrɪtjuəl] *a* spirituel(le); religieux(euse).

spit [spɪt] *n* (*for roasting*) broche *f* // *vi* (*pt, pp* spat) cracher; (*sound*) crépiter.

spite [spaɪt] *n* rancune *f*, dépit *m* // *vt* contrarier, vexer; **in ~ of** en dépit de, malgré; **~ful** *a* malveillant(e), rancunier(ère).

spittle ['spɪtl] *n* salive *f*; bave *f*; crachat *m*.

splash [splæʃ] *n* éclaboussement *m*; (*of colour*) tache *f* // *excl* (*sound*) plouf // *vt* éclabousser // *vi* (*also:* **~ about**) barboter, patauger.

spleen [spli:n] *n* (*ANAT*) rate *f*.

splendid ['splɛndɪd] *a* splendide, superbe, magnifique.

splint [splɪnt] *n* attelle *f*, éclisse *f*.

splinter ['splɪntə*] *n* (*wood*) écharde *f*; (*metal*) éclat *m* // *vi* se fragmenter.

split [splɪt] *n* fente *f*, déchirure *f*; (*fig: POL*) scission *f* // *vb* (*pt, pp* split) *vt* fendre, déchirer; (*party*) diviser; (*work, profits*) partager, répartir // *vi* (*divide*) se diviser; **to ~ up** *vi* (*couple*) se séparer, rompre; (*meeting*) se disperser.

splutter ['splʌtə*] *vi* bafouiller; postillonner.

spoil, *pt, pp* spoilt *or* **~ed** [spɔɪl, -t, -d] *vt* (*damage*) abîmer; (*mar*) gâcher; (*child*) gâter; **~s** *npl* butin *m*; **~sport** *n* trouble-fête *m*, rabat-joie *m*.

spoke [spəuk] *pt of* speak // *n* rayon *m*.

spoken ['spəukn] *pp of* speak.

spokesman ['spəuksmən], **spokeswoman** ['-wumən] *n* porte-parole *m inv*.

sponge [spʌndʒ] *n* éponge *f* // *vt* éponger // *vi*: **to ~ off** *or* **on** vivre aux crochets de; **~ bag** *n* (*Brit*) trousse *f* de toilette; **~ cake** *n* ≈ biscuit *m* de Savoie.

sponsor ['spɒnsə*] *n* (*RADIO, TV*) personne *f* (*or* organisme *m*) qui assure le patronage // *vt* patronner; parrainer; **~ship** *n* patronage *m*; parrainage *m*.

spontaneous [spɒn'teɪnɪəs] *a* spontané(e).

spooky ['spu:kɪ] *a* qui donne la chair de poule.

spool [spu:l] *n* bobine *f*.

spoon [spu:n] *n* cuiller *f*; **~-feed** *vt* nourrir à la cuiller; (*fig*) mâcher le travail à; **~ful** *n* cuillerée *f*.

sport [spɔ:t] *n* sport *m*; (*person*) chic type/chic fille *f* // *vt* arborer; **~ing** *a* sportif(ive); **to give sb a ~ing chance** donner sa chance à qn; **~ jacket** *n* (*US*) = **~s jacket**; **~s car** *n* voiture *f* de sport; **~s jacket** *n* veste *f* de sport; **~sman** *n* sportif *m*; **~smanship** *n* esprit sportif, sportivité *f*; **~swear** *n* vêtements *mpl* de sport; **~swoman** *n* sportive f; ~y a sportif(ive).

spot [spɔt] n tache f; (dot: on pattern) pois m; (pimple) bouton m; (place) endroit m, coin m; (small amount): **a ~ of** un peu de // vt (notice) apercevoir, repérer; **on the ~** sur place, sur les lieux; **~ check** n sondage m, vérification ponctuelle; **~less** a immaculé(e); **~light** n projecteur m; (AUT) phare m auxiliaire; **~ted** a tacheté(e), moucheté(e); à pois; **~ty** a (face) boutonneux(euse).

spouse [spauz] n époux/épouse.

spout [spaut] n (of jug) bec m; (of liquid) jet m // vi jaillir.

sprain [spreɪn] n entorse f, foulure f // vt: **to ~ one's ankle** se fouler or se tordre la cheville.

sprang [spræŋ] pt of spring.

sprawl [sprɔːl] vi s'étaler.

spray [spreɪ] n jet m (en fines gouttelettes); (container) vaporisateur m, bombe f; (of flowers) petit bouquet // vt vaporiser, pulvériser; (crops) traiter.

spread [spred] n propagation f; (distribution) répartition f; (CULIN) pâte f à tartiner // vb (pt, pp spread) vt étendre, étaler; répandre; propager // vi s'étendre; se répandre; se propager; **~-eagled** ['spredɪːgld] a étendu(e) bras et jambes écartés; **~sheet** n (COMPUT) tableur m.

spree [spriː] n: **to go on a ~** faire la fête.

sprightly ['spraɪtlɪ] a alerte.

spring [sprɪŋ] n (leap) bond m, saut m; (coiled metal) ressort m; (season) printemps m; (of water) source f // vi (pt sprang, pp sprung) bondir, sauter; **to ~ from** provenir de; **to ~ up** vi (problem) se présenter, surgir; **~board** n tremplin m; **~-clean** n (also: **~-cleaning**) grand nettoyage de printemps; **~time** n printemps m; **~y** a élastique, souple.

sprinkle ['sprɪŋkl] vt (pour) répandre; verser; **to ~ water** etc **on**, **~ with water** etc asperger d'eau etc; **to ~ sugar** etc **on**, **~ with sugar** etc saupoudrer de sucre etc; **~r** n (for lawn) arroseur m; (to put out fire) diffuseur m d'extincteur automatique d'incendie.

sprint [sprɪnt] n sprint m // vi sprinter.

sprout [spraut] vi germer, pousser; **~s** npl (also: **Brussels ~s**) choux mpl de Bruxelles.

spruce [spruːs] n épicéa m // a net(te), pimpant(e).

sprung [sprʌŋ] pp of spring.

spry [spraɪ] a alerte, vif(vive).

spun [spʌn] pt, pp of spin.

spur [spəː*] n éperon m; (fig) aiguillon m // vt (also: **~ on**) éperonner; aiguillonner; **on the ~ of the moment** sous l'impulsion du moment.

spurious ['spjuərɪəs] a faux(fausse).

spurn [spəːn] vt repousser avec mépris.

spurt [spəːt] vi jaillir, gicler.

spy [spaɪ] n espion/ne // vi: **to ~ on** espionner, épier // vt (see) àpercevoir; **~ing** n espionnage m.

sq. (MATH), **Sq.** (in address) abbr of **square**.

squabble ['skwɔbl] vi se chamailler.

squad [skwɔd] n (MIL, POLICE) escouade f, groupe m; (FOOTBALL) contingent m.

squadron ['skwɔdrn] n (MIL) escadron m; (AVIAT, NAUT) escadrille f.

squalid ['skwɔlɪd] a sordide, ignoble.

squall [skwɔːl] n rafale f, bourrasque f.

squalor ['skwɔlə*] n conditions fpl sordides.

squander ['skwɔndə*] vt gaspiller, dilapider.

square [skwɛə*] n carré m; (in town) place f; (instrument) équerre f // a carré(e); (honest) honnête, régulier(ère); (col: ideas, tastes) vieux jeu inv, qui retarde // vt (arrange) régler; arranger; (MATH) élever au carré // vi (agree) cadrer, s'accorder; **all ~** quitte; à égalité; **a ~ meal** un repas convenable; **2 metres ~** (de) 2 mètres sur 2; **1 ~ metre** 1 mètre carré.

squash [skwɔʃ] n (Brit: drink): **lemon/orange ~** citronnade f/orangeade f; (SPORT) squash m // vt écraser.

squat [skwɔt] a petit(e) et épais(se), ramassé(e) // vi s'accroupir; **~ter** n squatter m.

squawk [skwɔːk] vi pousser un or des gloussement(s).

squeak [skwiːk] vi grincer, crier.

squeal [skwiːl] vi pousser un or des cri(s) aigu(s) or perçant(s).

squeamish ['skwiːmɪʃ] a facilement dégoûté(e); facilement scandalisé(e).

squeeze [skwiːz] n pression f; restrictions fpl de crédit // vt presser; (hand, arm) serrer; **to ~ out** vt exprimer; (fig) soutirer.

squelch [skwɛltʃ] vi faire un bruit de succion; patauger.

squib [skwɪb] n pétard m.

squid [skwɪd] n calmar m.

squiggle ['skwɪgl] n gribouillis m.

squint [skwɪnt] vi loucher // n: **he has a ~** il louche, il souffre de strabisme; **to ~ at sth** regarder qch du coin de l'œil; (quickly) jeter un coup d'œil à qch.

squire ['skwaɪə*] n (Brit) propriétaire terrien.

squirm [skwəːm] vi se tortiller.

squirrel ['skwɪrəl] n écureuil m.

squirt [skwəːt] vi jaillir, gicler.

Sr abbr of **senior**.

St abbr of **saint**, **street**.

stab [stæb] n (with knife etc) coup m (de couteau etc); (col: try): **to have a ~ at (doing) sth** s'essayer à (faire) qch // vt poignarder.

stable ['steɪbl] n écurie f // a stable.
stack [stæk] n tas m, pile f // vt empiler, entasser.
stadium ['steɪdɪəm] n stade m.
staff [stɑ:f] n (work force) personnel m; (: Brit SCOL) professeurs mpl; (: servants) domestiques mpl; (MIL) état-major m; (stick) perche f, bâton m // vt pourvoir en personnel.
stag [stæg] n cerf m.
stage [steɪdʒ] n scène f; (profession): the ~ le théâtre; (point) étape f, stade m; (platform) estrade f // vt (play) monter, mettre en scène; (demonstration) organiser; (fig: perform: recovery etc) effectuer; in ~s par étapes, par degrés; ~**coach** n diligence f; ~ **door** n entrée f des artistes; ~ **manager** n régisseur m.
stagger ['stægə*] vi chanceler, tituber // vt (person) stupéfier; bouleverser; (hours, holidays) étaler, échelonner.
stagnate [stæg'neɪt] vi stagner, croupir.
stag party n enterrement m de vie de garçon.
staid [steɪd] a posé(e), rassis(e).
stain [steɪn] n tache f; (colouring) colorant m // vt tacher; (wood) teindre; ~**ed glass window** n vitrail m; ~**less** a (steel) inoxydable; ~ **remover** n détachant m.
stair [stɛə*] n (step) marche f; ~**s** npl escalier m; on the ~s dans l'escalier; ~**case**, ~**way** n escalier m.
stake [steɪk] n pieu m, poteau m; (BETTING) enjeu m // vt risquer, jouer; to be at ~ être en jeu.
stale [steɪl] a (bread) rassis(e); (beer) éventé(e); (smell) de renfermé.
stalemate ['steɪlmeɪt] n pat m; (fig) impasse f.
stalk [stɔ:k] n tige f // vt traquer // vi marcher avec raideur.
stall [stɔ:l] n éventaire m, étal m; (in stable) stalle f // vt (AUT) caler // vi (AUT) caler; (fig) essayer de gagner du temps; ~**s** npl (Brit: in cinema, theatre) orchestre m.
stallion ['stælɪən] n étalon m (cheval).
stalwart ['stɔ:lwət] n partisan m fidèle.
stamina ['stæmɪnə] n vigueur f, endurance f.
stammer ['stæmə*] n bégaiement m // vi bégayer.
stamp [stæmp] n timbre m; (mark, also fig) empreinte f; (on document) cachet m // vi (also: ~ one's foot) taper du pied // vt tamponner, estamper; (letter) timbrer; ~ **album** n album m de timbres(-poste); ~ **collecting** n philatélie f.
stampede [stæm'pi:d] n ruée f.
stance [stæns] n position f.
stand [stænd] n (position) position f; (MIL) résistance f; (structure) guéridon m; support m; (COMM) étalage m, stand

m; (SPORT) tribune f // vb (pt, pp stood) vi être or se tenir (debout); (rise) se lever, se mettre debout; (be placed) se trouver // vt (place) mettre, poser; (tolerate, withstand) supporter; to make a ~ prendre position; to ~ for parliament (Brit) se présenter aux élections (comme candidat à la députation); to ~ by vi (be ready) se tenir prêt(e) // vt fus (opinion) s'en tenir à; to ~ down vi (withdraw) se retirer; to ~ for vt fus (signify) représenter, signifier; (tolerate) supporter, tolérer; to ~ in for vt fus remplacer; to ~ out vi (be prominent) ressortir; to ~ up vi (rise) se lever, se mettre debout; to ~ up for vt fus défendre; to ~ up to vt fus tenir tête à, résister à.
standard ['stændəd] n niveau voulu; (flag) étendard m // a (size etc) ordinaire, normal(e); courant(e); ~**s** npl (morals) morale f, principes mpl; ~ **lamp** n (Brit) lampadaire m; ~ **of living** n niveau m de vie.
stand-by ['stændbaɪ] n remplaçant/e; to be on ~ se tenir prêt(e) (à intervenir); être de garde; ~ **ticket** n (AVIAT) billet m sans garantie.
stand-in ['stændɪn] n remplaçant/e; (CINEMA) doublure f.
standing ['stændɪŋ] a debout inv // n réputation f, rang m, standing m; of many years' ~ qui dure or existe depuis longtemps; ~ **order** n (Brit: at bank) virement m automatique, prélèvement m bancaire; ~ **orders** npl (MIL) règlement m; ~ **room** n places fpl debout.
stand-offish [stænd'ɔfɪʃ] a distant(e), froid(e).
standpoint ['stændpɔɪnt] n point m de vue.
standstill ['stændstɪl] n: at a ~ à l'arrêt; (fig) au point mort; to come to a ~ s'immobiliser, s'arrêter.
stank [stæŋk] pt of **stink**.
staple ['steɪpl] n (for papers) agrafe f // a (food etc) de base, principal(e) // vt agrafer; ~**r** n agrafeuse f.
star [stɑ:*] n étoile f; (celebrity) vedette f // vi: to ~ (in) être la vedette (de) // vt (CINEMA) avoir pour vedette.
starboard ['stɑ:bəd] n tribord m.
starch [stɑ:tʃ] n amidon m.
stardom ['stɑ:dəm] n célébrité f.
stare [stɛə*] n regard m fixe // vi: to ~ at regarder fixement.
starfish ['stɑ:fɪʃ] n étoile f de mer.
stark [stɑ:k] a (bleak) désolé(e), morne // ad: ~ **naked** complètement nu(e).
starling ['stɑ:lɪŋ] n étourneau m.
starry ['stɑ:rɪ] a étoilé(e); ~-**eyed** a (innocent) ingénu(e).
start [stɑ:t] n commencement m, début m; (of race) départ m; (sudden

movement) sursaut *m* // *vt* commencer // *vi* partir, se mettre en route; (*jump*) sursauter; **to ~ doing** *or* **to do sth** se mettre à faire qch; **to ~ off** *vi* commencer; (*leave*) partir; **to ~ up** *vi* commencer; (*car*) démarrer // *vt* déclencher; (*car*) mettre en marche; **~er** *n* (*AUT*) démarreur *m*; (: *runner, horse*) partant *m*; (*Brit CULIN*) entrée *f*; **~ing point** *n* point *m* de départ.

startle ['sta:tl] *vt* faire sursauter; donner un choc à.

starvation [sta:'veɪʃən] *n* faim *f*, famine *f*.

starve [sta:v] *vi* mourir de faim; être affamé(e) // *vt* affamer.

state [steɪt] *n* état *m* // *vt* déclarer, affirmer; formuler; **the S~s** les États-Unis *mpl*; **to be in a ~** être dans tous ses états; **~ly** *a* majestueux(euse), imposant(e); **~ment** *n* déclaration *f*; (*LAW*) déposition *f*; **~sman** *n* homme *m* d'État.

static ['stætɪk] *n* (*RADIO*) parasites *mpl* // *a* statique.

station ['steɪʃən] *n* gare *f*; poste *m* (militaire *or* de police *etc*); (*rank*) condition *f*, rang *m* // *vt* placer, poster.

stationary ['steɪʃnərɪ] *a* à l'arrêt, immobile.

stationer ['steɪʃənə*] *n* papetier/ère; **~'s (shop)** *n* papeterie *f*; **~y** *n* papier *m* à lettres, petit matériel de bureau.

station master *n* (*RAIL*) chef *m* de gare.

station wagon *n* (*US*) break *m*.

statistic [stə'tɪstɪk] *n* statistique *f*; **~s** *n* (*science*) statistique *f*.

statue ['stætju:] *n* statue *f*.

status ['steɪtəs] *n* position *f*, situation *f*; prestige *m*; statut *m*; **~ symbol** *n* marque *f* de standing.

statute ['stætju:t] *n* loi *f*; **~s** *npl* (*of club etc*) statuts *mpl*; **statutory** *a* statutaire, prévu(e) par un article de loi.

staunch [stɔ:ntʃ] *a* sûr(e), loyal(e).

stave [steɪv] *n* (*MUS*) portée *f* // *vt*: **to ~ off** (*attack*) parer; (*threat*) conjurer.

stay [steɪ] *n* (*period of time*) séjour *m* // *vi* rester; (*reside*) loger; (*spend some time*) séjourner; **to ~** put ne pas bouger; **to ~ with friends** loger chez des amis; **to ~ the night** passer la nuit; **to ~ behind** *vi* rester en arrière; **to ~ in** *vi* (*at home*) rester à la maison; **to ~ on** *vi* rester; **to ~ out** *vi* (*of house*) ne pas rentrer; **to ~ up** *vi* (*at night*) ne pas se coucher; **~ing power** *n* endurance *f*.

stead [stɛd] *n*: **in sb's ~** à la place de qn; **to stand sb in good ~** être très utile *or* servir beaucoup à qn.

steadfast ['stɛdfɑ:st] *a* ferme, résolu(e).

steadily ['stɛdɪlɪ] *ad* progressivement; sans arrêt; (*walk*) d'un pas ferme.

steady ['stɛdɪ] *a* stable, solide, ferme; (*regular*) constant(e), régulier(ère); (*person*) calme, pondéré(e) // *vt* stabiliser; assujettir; calmer; **to ~ o.s.** reprendre son aplomb.

steak [steɪk] *n* (*meat*) bifteck *m*, steak *m*; (*fish*) tranche *f*.

steal [sti:l], *pt* **stole**, *pp* **stolen** *vt*, *vi* voler.

stealth [stɛlθ] *n*: **by ~** furtivement; **~y** *a* furtif(ive).

steam [sti:m] *n* vapeur *f* // *vt* passer à la vapeur; (*CULIN*) cuire à la vapeur // *vi* fumer; (*ship*): **to ~ along** filer; **~ engine** *n* locomotive *f* à vapeur; **~er** *n* (bateau *m* à) vapeur *m*; **~roller** *n* rouleau compresseur; **~ship** *n* = **~er**; **~y** *a* embué(e), humide.

steel [sti:l] *n* acier *m* // *cpd* d'acier; **~works** *n* aciérie *f*.

steep [sti:p] *a* raide, escarpé(e); (*price*) très élevé(e), excessif(ive) // *vt* (faire) tremper.

steeple ['sti:pl] *n* clocher *m*.

steer [stɪə*] *n* bœuf *m* // *vt* diriger, gouverner; guider // *vi* tenir le gouvernail; **~ing** *n* (*AUT*) conduite *f*; **~ing wheel** *n* volant *m*.

stem [stɛm] *n* (*of plant*) tige *f*; (*of leaf, fruit*) queue *f*; (*of glass*) pied *m* // *vt* contenir, endiguer, juguler; **to ~ from** *vt fus* provenir de, découler de.

stench [stɛntʃ] *n* puanteur *f*.

stencil ['stɛnsl] *n* stencil *m*; pochoir *m* // *vt* polycopier.

stenographer [stə'nɔgrəfə*] *n* (*US*) sténographe *m/f*.

step [stɛp] *n* pas *m*; (*stair*) marche *f*; (*action*) mesure *f*, disposition *f* // *vi*: **to ~ forward** faire un pas en avant, avancer; **~s** *npl* (*Brit*) = **stepladder**; **to be in/out of ~ (with)** (*fig*) aller dans le sens (de)/être déphasé(e) (par rapport à); **to ~ down** *vi* (*fig*) se retirer, se désister; **to ~ off** *vt fus* descendre de; **to ~ up** *vt* augmenter; intensifier; **~brother** *n* demi-frère *m*; **~daughter** *n* belle-fille *f*; **~father** *n* beau-père *m*; **~ladder** *n* escabeau *m*; **~mother** *n* belle-mère *f*; **~ping stone** *n* pierre *f* de gué; (*fig*) tremplin *m*; **~sister** *n* demi-sœur *f*; **~son** *n* beau-fils *m*.

stereo ['stɛrɪəu] *n* (*system*) stéréo *f*; (*record player*) chaine *f* stéréo // *a* (*also*: **~phonic**) stéréophonique.

sterile ['stɛraɪl] *a* stérile; **sterilize** ['stɛrɪlaɪz] *vt* stériliser.

sterling ['stə:lɪŋ] *a* (*silver*) de bon aloi, fin(e); (*fig*) à toute épreuve, excellent(e) // *n* (*ECON*) livres *fpl* sterling *inv*; **a pound ~** une livre sterling.

stern [stə:n] *a* sévère // *n* (*NAUT*) arrière *m*, poupe *f*.

stew [stju:] *n* ragoût *m* // *vt*, *vi* cuire à la casserole.

steward ['stjuːəd] *n* (*AVIAT, NAUT, RAIL*) steward *m*; (*in club etc*) intendant *m*; **~ess** *n* hôtesse *f*.

stick [stɪk] *n* bâton *m*; morceau *m* // *vb* (*pt, pp* **stuck**) *vt* (*glue*) coller; (*thrust*): **to ~ sth into** piquer *or* planter *or* enfoncer qch dans; (*col: put*) mettre, fourrer; (*col: tolerate*) supporter // *vi* se planter; tenir; (*remain*) rester; **to ~ out, to ~ up** *vi* dépasser, sortir; **to ~ up for** *vt fus* défendre; **~er** *n* autocollant *m*; **~ing plaster** *n* sparadrap *m*, pansement adhésif.

stickler ['stɪklə*] *n*: **to be a ~ for** être pointilleux(euse) sur.

stick-up ['stɪkʌp] *n* braquage *m*, hold-up *m*.

sticky ['stɪkɪ] *a* poisseux(euse); (*label*) adhésif(ive).

stiff [stɪf] *a* raide; rigide; dur(e); (*difficult*) difficile; ardu(e); (*cold*) froid(e), distant(e); (*strong, high*) fort(e), élevé(e); **~en** *vt* raidir, renforcer // *vi* se raidir; se durcir; **~ neck** *n* torticolis *m*.

stifle ['staɪfl] *vt* étouffer, réprimer.

stigma, ** *pl* (*BOT, MED, REL*) **~ta, (*fig*) **~s** ['stɪgmə, stɪg'mɑːtə] *n* stigmate *m*.

stile [staɪl] *n* échalier *m*.

stiletto [stɪ'lɛtəʊ] *n* (*Brit: also: ~ heel*) talon *m* aiguille.

still [stɪl] *a* immobile; calme, tranquille // *ad* (*up to this time*) encore, toujours; (*even*) encore; (*nonetheless*) quand même, tout de même; **~born** *a* mort-né(e); **~ life** *n* nature morte.

stilt [stɪlt] *n* échasse *f*; (*pile*) pilotis *m*.

stilted ['stɪltɪd] *a* guindé(e), emprunté(e).

stimulate ['stɪmjʊleɪt] *vt* stimuler.

stimulus, ** *pl* **stimuli ['stɪmjʊləs, 'stɪmjʊlaɪ] *n* stimulant *m*; (*BIOL, PSYCH*) stimulus *m*.

sting [stɪŋ] *n* piqûre *f*; (*organ*) dard *m* // *vt, vi* (*pt, pp* **stung**) piquer.

stingy ['stɪndʒɪ] *a* avare, pingre.

stink [stɪŋk] *n* puanteur *f* // *vi* (*pt* **stank**, *pp* **stunk**) puer, empester; **~ing** *a* (*fig: col*) infect(e), vache; **a ~ing ... un(e)** foutu(e) ....

stint [stɪnt] *n* part *f* de travail // *vi*: **to ~ on** lésiner sur, être chiche de.

stir [stəː*] *n* agitation *f*, sensation *f* // *vt* remuer // *vi* remuer, bouger; **to ~ up** *vt* exciter.

stirrup ['stɪrəp] *n* étrier *m*.

stitch [stɪtʃ] *n* (*SEWING*) point *m*; (*KNITTING*) maille *f*; (*MED*) point de suture; (*pain*) point de côté // *vt* coudre, piquer; suturer.

stoat [stəʊt] *n* hermine *f* (*avec son pelage d'été*).

stock [stɔk] *n* réserve *f*, provision *f*; (*COMM*) stock *m*; (*AGR*) cheptel *m*, bétail *m*; (*CULIN*) bouillon *m*;

(*FINANCE*) valeurs *fpl*, titres *mpl* // *a* (*fig: reply etc*) courant(e); classique // *vt* (*have in stock*) avoir, vendre; **in/out of ~** en stock *or* en magasin/épuisé(e); **to take ~** (*fig*) faire le point; **~s and shares** valeurs (mobilières), titres; **to ~ up** *vi*: **to ~ up (with)** s'approvisionner (en).

stockbroker ['stɔkbrəʊkə*] *n* agent *m* de change.

stock cube *n* bouillon-cube *m*.

stock exchange *n* Bourse *f* (des valeurs).

stocking ['stɔkɪŋ] *n* bas *m*.

stock: ~ market *n* Bourse *f*, marché financier; **~ phrase** *n* cliché *m*; **~pile** *n* stock *m*, réserve *f* // *vt* stocker, accumuler; **~taking** *n* (*Brit COMM*) inventaire *m*.

stocky ['stɔkɪ] *a* trapu(e), râblé(e).

stodgy ['stɔdʒɪ] *a* bourratif(ive), lourd(e).

stoke [stəʊk] *vt* garnir, entretenir; chauffer.

stole [stəʊl] *pt of* **steal** // *n* étole *f*.

stolen ['stəʊln] *pp of* **steal**.

stolid ['stɔlɪd] *a* impassible, flegmatique.

stomach ['stʌmək] *n* estomac *m*; (*abdomen*) ventre *m* // *vt* supporter, digérer; **~ ache** *n* mal *m* à l'estomac *or* au ventre.

stone [stəʊn] *n* pierre *f*; (*pebble*) caillou *m*, galet *m*; (*in fruit*) noyau *m*; (*MED*) calcul *m*; (*Brit: weight*) = 6.348 *kg*; *14 pounds* // *cpd* de *or* en pierre // *vt* dénoyauter; **~-cold** *a* complètement froid(e); **~-deaf** *a* sourd(e) comme un pot; **~work** *n* maçonnerie *f*.

stood [stʊd] *pt, pp of* **stand**.

stool [stuːl] *n* tabouret *m*.

stoop [stuːp] *vi* (*also: have a ~*) être voûté(e); (*bend*) se baisser.

stop [stɔp] *n* arrêt *m*; halte *f*; (*in punctuation*) point *m* // *vt* arrêter; (*break off*) interrompre; (*also: put a ~ to*) mettre fin à // *vi* s'arrêter; (*rain, noise etc*) cesser, s'arrêter; **to ~ doing** sth cesser *or* arrêter de faire qch; **to ~ dead** *vi* s'arrêter net; **to ~ off** *vi* faire une courte halte; **to ~ up** *vt* (*hole*) boucher; **~gap** *n* (*person*) bouche-trou *m*; (*measure*) mesure *f* intérimaire; **~lights** *npl* (*AUT*) signaux *mpl* de stop, feux *mpl* arrière; **~over** *n* halte *f*; (*AVIAT*) escale *f*.

stoppage ['stɔpɪdʒ] *n* arrêt *m*; (*of pay*) retenue *f*; (*strike*) arrêt de travail.

stopper ['stɔpə*] *n* bouchon *m*.

stop press *n* nouvelles *fpl* de dernière heure.

stopwatch ['stɔpwɔtʃ] *n* chronomètre *m*.

storage ['stɔːrɪdʒ] *n* emmagasinage *m*; (*COMPUT*) mise *f* en mémoire *or* réserve; **~ heater** *n* radiateur *m* électrique par accumulation.

store [stɔː*] n provision f, réserve f; (depot) entrepôt m; (Brit: large shop) grand magasin; (US) magasin m // vt emmagasiner; ~s npl provisions; to ~ up vt mettre en réserve, emmagasiner; ~room n réserve f, magasin m.

storey, (US**) story** ['stɔːri] n étage m.

stork [stɔːk] n cigogne f.

storm [stɔːm] n orage m, tempête f; ouragan m // vi (fig) fulminer // vt prendre d'assaut; ~y a orageux(euse).

story ['stɔːri] n histoire f; récit m; (US) = storey; ~book n livre m d'histoires or de contes.

stout [staut] a solide; (brave) intrépide; (fat) gros(se), corpulent(e) // n bière brune.

stove [stəuv] n (for cooking) fourneau m; (: small) réchaud m; (for heating) poêle m.

stow [stəu] vt ranger; cacher; ~away n passager/ère clandestin(e).

straddle ['strædl] vt enjamber, être à cheval sur.

straggle ['strægl] vi être (or marcher) en désordre; ~r n traînard/e.

straight [streit] a droit(e); (frank) honnête, franc(franche) // ad (tout) droit; (drink) sec, sans eau; to put or get ~ mettre en ordre, mettre de l'ordre dans; ~ away, ~ off (at once) tout de suite; ~en vt (also: ~en out) redresser; ~-faced a impassible; ~forward a simple; honnête, direct(e).

strain [strein] n (TECH) tension f; pression f; (physical) effort m; (mental) tension (nerveuse); (MED) entorse f; (streak, trace) tendance f; élément m // vt tendre fortement; mettre à l'épreuve; (filter) passer, filtrer // vi peiner, fournir un gros effort; ~s npl (MUS) accords mpl, accents mpl; ~ed a (laugh etc) forcé(e), contraint(e); (relations) tendu(e); ~er n passoire f.

strait [streit] n (GEO) détroit m; ~jacket n camisole f de force; ~-laced a collet monté inv.

strand [strænd] n (of thread) fil m, brin m; ~ed a en rade, en plan.

strange [streindʒ] a (not known) inconnu(e); (odd) étrange, bizarre; ~r n inconnu/e; étranger/ère.

strangle ['stræŋgl] vt étrangler; ~hold n (fig) emprise totale, mainmise f.

strap [stræp] n lanière f, courroie f, sangle f; (of slip, dress) bretelle f // vt attacher (avec une courroie etc).

strategic [strə'tiːdʒɪk] a stratégique.

strategy ['strætidʒɪ] n stratégie f.

straw [strɔː] n paille f; that's the last ~! ça c'est le comble!

strawberry ['strɔːbərɪ] n fraise f.

stray [streɪ] a (animal) perdu(e), errant(e) // vi s'égarer; ~ bullet n balle

perdue.

streak [striːk] n raie f, bande f, filet m; (fig: of madness etc): a ~ of une or des tendance(s) à // vt zébrer, strier // vi: to ~ past passer à toute allure.

stream [striːm] n ruisseau m; courant m, flot m; (of people) défilé ininterrompu, flot // vt (SCOL) répartir par niveau // vi ruisseler; to ~ in/out entrer/sortir à flots.

streamer ['striːmə*] n serpentin m, banderole f.

streamlined ['striːmlaind] a (AVIAT) fuselé(e), profilé(e); (AUT) aérodynamique; (fig) rationalisé(e).

street [striːt] n rue f // cpd de la rue; des rues; ~car n (US) tramway m; ~ lamp n réverbère m; ~ plan n plan m des rues; ~wise a (col) futé(e), réaliste.

strength [strɛŋθ] n force f; (of girder, knot etc) solidité f; ~en vt fortifier; renforcer; consolider.

strenuous ['strɛnjuəs] a vigoureux(euse), énergique; (tiring) ardu(e), fatigant(e).

stress [strɛs] n (force, pressure) pression f; (mental strain) tension (nerveuse); (accent) accent m // vt insister sur, souligner.

stretch [strɛtʃ] n (of sand etc) étendue f // vi s'étirer; (extend): to ~ to or as far as s'étendre jusqu'à // vt tendre, étirer; (spread) étendre; (fig) pousser (au maximum); to ~ out vi s'étendre // vt (arm etc) allonger, tendre; (to spread) étendre.

stretcher ['strɛtʃə*] n brancard m, civière f.

strewn [struːn] a: ~ with jonché(e) de.

stricken ['strɪkən] a (person) très éprouvé(e); (city, industry etc) dévasté(e); ~ with (disease etc) frappé(e) or atteint(e) de.

strict [strɪkt] a strict(e).

stride [straid] n grand pas, enjambée f // vi (pt strode, pp stridden [strəud, 'strɪdn]) marcher à grands pas.

strife [straif] n conflit m, dissensions fpl.

strike [straik] n grève f; (of oil etc) découverte f; (attack) raid m // vb (pt, pp struck) vt frapper; (oil etc) trouver, découvrir // vi faire grève; (attack) attaquer; (clock) sonner // on ~ (workers) en grève; to ~ a match frotter une allumette; to ~ down vt (fig) terrasser; to ~ out vt rayer; to ~ up vt (MUS) se mettre à jouer; to ~ up a friendship with se lier d'amitié avec; ~r n gréviste m/f; (SPORT) buteur m; **striking** a frappant(e), saisissant(e).

string [strɪŋ] n ficelle f, fil m; (row) rang m; chapelet m; file f; (MUS) corde f // vt (pt, pp strung): to ~ out échelonner; to ~ together enchaîner; the

~s *npl* (*MUS*) les instruments *mpl* à cordes; **to pull ~s** (*fig*) faire jouer le piston; **~ bean** *n* haricot vert; **~(ed) instrument** *n* (*MUS*) instrument *m* à cordes.

stringent ['strɪndʒənt] *a* rigoureux(euse); (*need*) impérieux(euse).

strip [strɪp] *n* bande *f* // *vt* déshabiller; dégarnir, dépouiller; (*also: ~ down: machine*) démonter // *vi* se déshabiller; **~ cartoon** *n* bande dessinée.

stripe [straɪp] *n* raie *f*, rayure *f*; **~d** *a* rayé(e), à rayures.

strip lighting *n* éclairage *m* au néon or fluorescent.

stripper ['strɪpə*] *n* strip-teaseuse *f*.

strive [straɪv], *pt* **strove** [strəuv], *pp* **striven** ['strɪvn] *vi*: **to ~ to do** s'efforcer de faire.

strode [strəud] *pt of* **stride**.

stroke [strəuk] *n* coup *m*; (*MED*) attaque *f*; (*caress*) caresse *f* // *vt* caresser; **at a ~** d'un (seul) coup.

stroll [strəul] *n* petite promenade *m* // *vi* flâner, se promener nonchalamment; **~er** *n* (*US*) poussette *f*.

strong [strɔŋ] *a* fort(e); vigoureux(euse); solide; vif(vive); **they are 50 ~** ils sont au nombre de 50; **~box** *n* coffre-fort *m*; **~hold** *n* bastion *m*; **~ly** *ad* fortement, avec force; vigoureusement; solidement; **~room** *n* chambre forte.

strove [strəuv] *pt of* **strive**.

struck [strʌk] *pt, pp of* **strike**.

structural ['strʌktʃərəl] *a* structural(e); (*CONSTR*) de construction; affectant les parties portantes.

structure ['strʌktʃə*] *n* structure *f*; (*building*) construction *f*; édifice *m*.

struggle ['strʌgl] *n* lutte *f* // *vi* lutter, se battre.

strum [strʌm] *vt* (*guitar*) gratter de.

strung [strʌŋ] *pt, pp of* **string**.

strut [strʌt] *n* étai *m*, support *m* // *vi* se pavaner.

stub [stʌb] *n* bout *m*; (*of ticket etc*) talon *m* // *vt*: **to ~ one's toe** se heurter le doigt de pied; **to ~ out** *vt* écraser.

stubble ['stʌbl] *n* chaume *m*; (*on chin*) barbe *f* de plusieurs jours.

stubborn ['stʌbən] *a* têtu(e), obstiné(e), opiniâtre.

stucco ['stʌkəu] *n* stuc *m*.

stuck [stʌk] *pt, pp of* **stick** // *a* (*jammed*) bloqué(e), coincé(e); **~-up** *a* prétentieux(euse).

stud [stʌd] *n* clou *m* (à grosse tête); bouton *m* de col; (*of horses*) écurie *f*, haras *m*; (*also: ~ horse*) étalon *m* // *vt* (*fig*): **~ded with** parsemé(e) or criblé(e) de.

student ['stju:dənt] *n* étudiant/e // *cpd* estudiantin(e); universitaire; d'étudiant; **~ driver** *n* (*US*) (conducteur/trice)

débutant(e).

studio ['stju:dɪəu] *n* studio *m*, atelier *m*.

studious ['stju:dɪəs] *a* studieux(euse), appliqué(e); (*studied*) étudié(e); **~ly** *ad* (*carefully*) soigneusement.

study ['stʌdɪ] *n* étude *f*; (*room*) bureau *m* // *vt* étudier; examiner // *vi* étudier, faire ses études.

stuff [stʌf] *n* chose(s) *f(pl)*, truc *m*; affaires *fpl*, trucs; (*substance*) substance *f* // *vt* rembourrer; (*CULIN*) farcir; **~ing** *n* bourre *f*, rembourrage *m*; (*CULIN*) farce *f*; **~y** *a* (*room*) mal ventilé(e) or aéré(e); (*ideas*) vieux jeu *inv*.

stumble ['stʌmbl] *vi* trébucher; **to ~ across** (*fig*) tomber sur; **stumbling block** *n* pierre *f* d'achoppement.

stump [stʌmp] *n* souche *f*; (*of limb*) moignon *m* // *vt*: **to be ~ed** sécher, ne pas savoir que répondre.

stun [stʌn] *vt* étourdir; abasourdir.

stung [stʌŋ] *pt, pp of* **sting**.

stunk [stʌŋk] *pp of* **stink**.

stunt [stʌnt] *n* tour *m* de force; truc *m* publicitaire; (*AVIAT*) acrobatie *f* // *vt* retarder, arrêter; **~ed** *a* rabougri(e); **~man** *n* cascadeur *m*.

stupendous [stju:'pɛndəs] *a* prodigieux(euse), fantastique.

stupid ['stju:pɪd] *a* stupide, bête; **~ity** [-'pɪdɪtɪ] *n* stupidité *f*, bêtise *f*.

sturdy ['stə:dɪ] *a* robuste, vigoureux(euse); solide.

stutter ['stʌtə*] *vi* bégayer.

sty [staɪ] *n* (*of pigs*) porcherie *f*.

stye [staɪ] *n* (*MED*) orgelet *m*.

style [staɪl] *n* style *m*; (*distinction*) allure *f*, cachet *m*, style; **stylish** *a* élégant(e), chic *inv*; **stylist** *n* (*hair stylist*) coiffeur/euse.

stylus ['staɪləs] *n* (*of record player*) pointe *f* de lecture.

suave [swɑ:v] *a* doucereux(euse), onctueux(euse).

sub... [sʌb] *prefix* sub..., sous-; **~conscious** *a* subconscient(e) // *n* subconscient *m*; **~contract** *vt* soustraiter.

subdue [sʌb'dju:] *vt* subjuguer, soumettre; **~d** *a* contenu(e), atténué(e); (*light*) tamisé(e); (*person*) qui a perdu de son entrain.

subject *n* ['sʌbdʒɪkt] sujet *m*; (*SCOL*) matière *f* // *vt* [səb'dʒɛkt]: **to ~ to** soumettre à; exposer à; **to be ~ to** (*law*) être soumis(e) à; (*disease*) être sujet(te) à; **~ive** [səb'dʒɛktɪv] *a* subjectif(ive); **~ matter** *n* sujet *m*; contenu *m*.

subjunctive [səb'dʒʌŋktɪv] *n* subjonctif *m*.

sublet [sʌb'lɛt] *vt* sous-louer.

submachine gun ['sʌbmə'ʃi:n-] *n* fusil-mitrailleur *m*.

submarine [sʌbmə'ri:n] *n* sous-marin

m.

submerge [səb'mə:dʒ] *vt* submerger; immerger // *vi* plonger.

submission [səb'mɪʃən] *n* soumission *f*.

submissive [səb'mɪsɪv] *a* soumis(e).

submit [səb'mɪt] *vt* soumettre // *vi* se soumettre.

subnormal [sʌb'nɔ:məl] *a* au-dessous de la normale; (*backward*) arriéré(e).

subordinate [sə'bɔ:dɪnət] *a*, *n* subordonné(e).

subpoena [səb'pi:nə] *n* (LAW) citation *f*, assignation *f*.

subscribe [səb'skraɪb] *vi* cotiser; to ~ to (*opinion*, *fund*) souscrire à; (*newspaper*) s'abonner à; être abonné(e) à; ~**r** *n* (*to periodical*, *telephone*) abonné/e.

subscription [səb'skrɪpʃən] *n* souscription *f*; abonnement *m*.

subsequent ['sʌbsɪkwənt] *a* ultérieur(e), suivant(e); consécutif(ive); ~**ly** *ad* par la suite.

subside [səb'saɪd] *vi* s'affaisser; (*flood*) baisser; (*wind*) tomber; ~**nce** [-'saɪdns] *n* affaissement *m*.

subsidiary [səb'sɪdɪərɪ] *a* subsidiaire, accessoire // *n* filiale *f*.

subsidize ['sʌbsɪdaɪz] *vt* subventionner.

subsidy ['sʌbsɪdɪ] *n* subvention *f*.

substance ['sʌbstəns] *n* substance *f*; (*fig*) essentiel *m*.

substantial [səb'stænʃl] *a* substantiel(le); (*fig*) important(e).

substantiate [səb'stænʃɪeɪt] *vt* étayer, fournir des preuves à l'appui de.

substitute ['sʌbstɪtju:t] *n* (*person*) remplaçant/e; (*thing*) succédané *m* // *vt*: to ~ sth/sb for substituer qch/qn à, remplacer par qch/qn.

subterranean [sʌbtə'reɪnɪən] *a* souterrain(e).

subtitle ['sʌbtaɪtl] *n* (CINEMA) sous-titre *m*.

subtle ['sʌtl] *a* subtil(e).

subtotal [sʌb'təutl] *n* total partiel.

subtract [səb'trækt] *vt* soustraire, retrancher; ~**ion** [-'trækʃən] *n* soustraction *f*.

suburb ['sʌbə:b] *n* faubourg *m*; the ~**s** la banlieue; ~**an** [sə'bə:bən] *a* de banlieue, suburbain(e); ~**ia** [sə'bə:bɪə] *n* la banlieue.

subway ['sʌbweɪ] *n* (US) métro *m*; (*Brit*) passage souterrain.

succeed [sək'si:d] *vi* réussir; avoir du succès // *vt* succéder à; to ~ in doing réussir à faire; ~**ing** *a* (*following*) suivant(e).

success [sək'sɛs] *n* succès *m*; réussite *f*; ~**ful** *a* (*venture*) couronné(e) de succès; to be ~**ful** (in doing) réussir (à faire); ~**fully** *ad* avec succès.

succession [sək'sɛʃən] *n* succession *f*.

successive [sək'sɛsɪv] *a* successif(ive);

consécutif(ive).

such [sʌtʃ] *a* tel(telle); (*of that kind*): ~ a book un livre de ce genre or pareil, un tel livre; ~ books des livres de ce genre or pareils, de tels livres; (*so much*): ~ courage un tel courage // *ad* si; ~ a long trip un si long voyage; ~ good books de si bons livres; ~ a lot of tellement or tant de; ~ as (*like*) tel(telle) que, comme; a noise ~ as to un bruit de nature à; as ~ *ad* en tant que tel(telle), à proprement parler; ~**-and-**~ *a* tel(telle) ou tel(telle).

suck [sʌk] *vt* sucer; (*breast*, *bottle*) téter; ~**er** *n* (BOT, ZOOL, TECH) ventouse *f*; (*col*) naï/ive, poire *f*.

suction ['sʌkʃən] *n* succion *f*.

sudden ['sʌdn] *a* soudain(e), subit(e); all of a ~ soudain, tout à coup; ~**ly** *ad* brusquement, tout à coup, soudain.

suds [sʌdz] *npl* eau savonneuse.

sue [su:] *vt* poursuivre en justice, intenter un procès à.

suede [sweɪd] *n* daim *m*, cuir suédé // *cpd* de daim.

suet ['suɪt] *n* graisse *f* de rognon or de bœuf.

suffer ['sʌfə*] *vt* souffrir, subir; (*bear*) tolérer, supporter // *vi* souffrir; ~**er** *n* malade *m/f*; victime *m/f*; ~**ing** *n* souffrance(s) *f(pl)*.

sufficient [sə'fɪʃənt] *a* suffisant(e); ~ money suffisamment d'argent; ~**ly** *ad* suffisamment, assez.

suffocate ['sʌfəkeɪt] *vi* suffoquer; étouffer.

suffused [sə'fju:zd] *a*: to be ~ with baigner dans, être imprégné(e) de.

sugar ['ʃugə*] *n* sucre *m* // *vt* sucrer; ~ beet *n* betterave sucrière; ~ cane *n* canne *f* à sucre; ~**y** *a* sucré(e).

suggest [sə'dʒɛst] *vt* suggérer, proposer; dénoter; ~**ion** [-'dʒɛstʃən] *n* suggestion *f*.

suicide ['suɪsaɪd] *n* suicide *m*.

suit [su:t] *n* (*man's*) costume *m*, complet *m*; (*woman's*) tailleur *m*, ensemble *m*; (CARDS) couleur *f* // *vt* aller à; convenir à; (*adapt*): to ~ sth to adapter or approprier qch à; ~**able** *a* qui convient; approprié(e); ~**ably** *ad* comme il se doit (*or se devait etc*), convenablement.

suitcase ['su:tkeɪs] *n* valise *f*.

suite [swi:t] *n* (*of rooms*, *also* MUS) suite *f*; (*furniture*): bedroom/dining room ~ (ensemble *m* de) chambre *f* à coucher/salle *f* à manger.

suitor ['su:tə*] *n* soupirant *m*, prétendant *m*.

sulfur ['sʌlfə*] *n* (US) = **sulphur**.

sulk [sʌlk] *vi* bouder; ~**y** *a* boudeur(euse), maussade.

sullen ['sʌlən] *a* renfrogné(e), maussade; morne.

sulphur, (US**) sulfur** ['sʌlfə*] *n* soufre

m.

sultana [sʌl'tɑ:nə] *n* (*fruit*) raisin (sec) de Smyrne.

sultry ['sʌltrɪ] *a* étouffant(e).

sum [sʌm] *n* somme *f*; (*SCOL etc*) calcul *m*; **to ~ up** *vt*, *vi* résumer.

summarize ['sʌmɜraɪz] *vt* résumer.

summary ['sʌmɜrɪ] *n* résumé *m* // *a* (*justice*) sommaire.

summer ['sʌmə*] *n* été *m* // *cpd* d'été, estival(e); **~house** *n* (*in garden*) pavillon *m*; **~time** *n* (*season*) été *m*; **~ time** *n* (*by clock*) heure *f* d'été.

summit ['sʌmɪt] *n* sommet *m*.

summon ['sʌmən] *vt* appeler, convoquer; **to ~ up** *vt* rassembler, faire appel à; **~s** *n* citation *f*, assignation *f*.

sump [sʌmp] *n* (*Brit AUT*) carter *m*.

sun [sʌn] *n* soleil *m*; **in the ~** au soleil; **~bathe** *vi* prendre un bain de soleil; **~burn** *n* coup *m* de soleil; (*tan*) bronzage *m*.

Sunday ['sʌndɪ] *n* dimanche *m*; **~ school** *n* ≈ catéchisme *m*.

sundial ['sʌndaɪəl] *n* cadran *m* solaire.

sundown ['sʌndaun] *n* coucher *m* du soleil.

sundry ['sʌndrɪ] *a* divers(e), différent(e); **all and ~** tout le monde, n'importe qui; **sundries** *npl* articles divers.

sunflower ['sʌnflauə*] *n* tournesol *m*.

sung [sʌŋ] *pp of* **sing**.

sunglasses ['sʌnglɑ:sɪz] *npl* lunettes *fpl* de soleil.

sunk [sʌŋk] *pp of* **sink**.

sun: ~light *n* (lumière *f* du) soleil *m*; **~ny** *a* ensoleillé(e); (*fig*) épanoui(e), radieux(euse); **~rise** *n* lever *m* du soleil; **~ roof** (*AUT*) toit ouvrant; **~set** *n* coucher *m* du soleil; **~shade** *n* (*over table*) parasol *m*; **~shine** *n* (lumière *f* du) soleil *m*; **~stroke** *n* insolation *f*, coup *m* de soleil; **~tan** *n* bronzage *m*; **~tan oil** *n* huile *f* solaire.

super ['su:pə*] *a* (*col*) formidable.

superannuation [su:pərænju'eɪʃən] *n* cotisations *fpl* pour la pension.

superb [su:'pə:b] *a* superbe, magnifique.

supercilious [su:pə'sɪlɪəs] *a* hautain(e), dédaigneux(euse).

superficial [su:pə'fɪʃəl] *a* superficiel(le).

superintendent [su:pərɪn'tendənt] *n* directeur/trice; (*POLICE*) ≈ commissaire *m*.

superior [su'pɪərɪə*] *a*, *n* supérieur(e); **~ity** [-'ɔrɪtɪ] *n* supériorité *f*.

superlative [su'pə:lətɪv] *a* sans pareil(le), suprême // *n* (*LING*) superlatif *m*.

superman ['su:pəmæn] *n* surhomme *m*.

supermarket ['su:pəmɑ:kɪt] *n* supermarché *m*.

supernatural [su:pə'nætʃərəl] *a*

surnaturel(le).

superpower ['su:pəpauə*] *n* (*POL*) superpuissance *f*.

supersede [su:pə'si:d] *vt* remplacer, supplanter.

superstitious [su:pə'stɪʃəs] *a* superstitieux(euse).

supervise ['su:pəvaɪz] *vt* surveiller; diriger; **supervision** [-'vɪʒən] *n* surveillance *f*; contrôle *m*; **supervisor** *n* surveillant/e; (*in shop*) chef *m* de rayon.

supine ['su:paɪn] *a* couché(e) *or* étendu(e) sur le dos.

supper ['sʌpə*] *n* dîner *m*; (*late*) souper *m*.

supple ['sʌpl] *a* souple.

supplement *n* ['sʌplɪmənt] supplément *m* // *vt* [sʌplɪ'mɛnt] ajouter à, compléter; **~ary** [-'mɛntərɪ] *a* supplémentaire.

supplier [sə'plaɪə*] *n* fournisseur *m*.

supply [sə'plaɪ] *vt* (*provide*) fournir; (*equip*): **to ~ (with)** approvisionner *or* ravitailler (en); fournir (en); alimenter (en) // *n* provision *f*, réserve *f*; (*supplying*) approvisionnement *m*; (*TECH*) alimentation *f* // *cpd* (*teacher etc*) suppléant(e); **supplies** *npl* (*food*) vivres *mpl*; (*MIL*) subsistances *fpl*.

support [sə'pɔ:t] *n* (*moral, financial etc*) soutien *m*, appui *m*; (*TECH*) support *m*, soutien // *vt* soutenir, supporter; (*financially*) subvenir aux besoins de; (*uphold*) être pour, être partisan de, appuyer; **~er** *n* (*POL etc*) partisan/e; (*SPORT*) supporter *m*.

suppose [sə'pəuz] *vt*, *vi* supposer; imaginer; **to be ~d to do** être censé(e) faire; **~dly** [sə'pəuzɪdlɪ] *ad* soi-disant; **supposing** *cj* si, à supposer que + *sub*.

suppress [sə'pres] *vt* réprimer; supprimer; étouffer; refouler.

supreme [su'pri:m] *a* suprême.

surcharge ['sə:tʃɑ:dʒ] *n* surcharge *f*; (*extra tax*) surtaxe *f*.

sure [ʃuə*] *a* (*gen*) sûr(e); (*definite, convinced*) sûr, certain(e); **~!** (*of course*) bien sûr!; **~ enough** effectivement; **to make ~ of** sth s'assurer de *or* vérifier qch; **to make ~ that** s'assurer *or* vérifier que; **~ly** *ad* sûrement; certainement.

surety ['ʃuərətɪ] *n* caution *f*.

surf [sə:f] *n* ressac *m*.

surface ['sə:fɪs] *n* surface *f* // *vt* (*road*) poser le revêtement de // *vi* remonter à la surface; faire surface; **~ mail** *n* courrier *m* par voie de terre (*or* maritime).

surfboard ['sə:fbɔ:d] *n* planche *f* de surf.

surfeit ['sə:fɪt] *n*: **a ~ of** un excès de; une indigestion de.

surfing ['sə:fɪŋ] *n* surf *m*.

surge [sə:dʒ] *n* vague *f*, montée *f* // *vi*

déferler.

surgeon ['sə:dʒən] n chirurgien m.

surgery ['sə:dʒərɪ] n chirurgie f; (Brit: room) cabinet m (de consultation); to undergo ~ être opéré(e); ~ hours npl (Brit) heures fpl de consultation.

surgical ['sə:dʒɪkl] a chirurgical(e); ~ spirit n (Brit) alcool m à 90°.

surly ['sə:lɪ] a revêche, maussade.

surname ['sə:neɪm] n nom m de famille.

surplus ['sə:pləs] n surplus m, excédent m // a en surplus, de trop.

surprise [sə'praɪz] n (gen) surprise f; (astonishment) étonnement m // vt surprendre; étonner; **surprising** a surprenant(e), étonnant(e); **surprisingly** ad (easy, helpful) étonnamment, étrangement.

surrender [sə'rɛndə*] n reddition f, capitulation f // vi se rendre, capituler.

surreptitious [sʌrəp'tɪʃəs] a subreptice, furtif(ive).

surrogate ['sʌrəgɪt] n substitut m; ~ mother n mère porteuse or de substitution.

surround [sə'raund] vt entourer; (MIL etc) encercler; ~ing a environnant(e); ~ings npl environs mpl, alentours mpl.

surveillance [sə:'veɪləns] n surveillance f.

survey n ['sə:veɪ] enquête f, étude f; (in housebuying etc) inspection f, (rapport m d')expertise f; (of land) levé m // vt [sə:'veɪ] passer en revue; enquêter sur; inspecter; ~or n expert m; (arpenteur m) géomètre m.

survival [sə'vaɪvl] n survie f; (relic) vestige m.

survive [sə'vaɪv] vi survivre; (custom etc) subsister // vt survivre à; **survivor** n survivant/e.

susceptible [sə'sɛptəbl] a: ~ (to) sensible (à); (disease) prédisposé(e) (à).

suspect a n, ['sʌspɛkt] suspect(e) // vt [sə'spɛkt] soupçonner, suspecter.

suspend [sə'spɛnd] vt suspendre; ~ed sentence n condamnation f avec sursis; ~er belt n porte-jarretelles m inv; ~ers npl (Brit) jarretelles fpl; (US) bretelles fpl.

suspense [sə'spɛns] n attente f; (in film etc) suspense m.

suspension [sə'spɛnʃən] n (gen, AUT) suspension f; (of driving licence) retrait m provisoire; ~ bridge n pont suspendu.

suspicion [sə'spɪʃən] n soupçon(s) m(pl).

suspicious [sə'spɪʃəs] a (suspecting) soupçonneux(euse), méfiant(e); (causing suspicion) suspect(e).

sustain [sə'steɪn] vt supporter; soutenir; corroborer; (suffer) subir; recevoir; ~ed a (effort) soutenu(e), prolongé(e).

sustenance ['sʌstɪnəns] n nourriture f;

moyens mpl de subsistance.

swab [swɔb] n (MED) tampon m; prélèvement m.

swagger ['swægə*] vi plastronner.

swallow ['swɔləu] n (bird) hirondelle f // vt avaler; (fig) gober; to ~ up vt engloutir.

swam [swæm] pt of **swim**.

swamp [swɔmp] n marais m, marécage m // vt submerger.

swan [swɔn] n cygne m.

swap [swɔp] vt: to ~ (for) échanger (contre), troquer (contre).

swarm [swɔ:m] n essaim m // vi fourmiller, grouiller.

swarthy ['swɔ:ðɪ] a basané(e), bistré(e).

swastika ['swɔstɪkə] n croix gammée.

swat [swɔt] vt écraser.

sway [sweɪ] vi se balancer, osciller; tanguer // vt (influence) influencer.

swear [swɛə*], pt **swore**, pp **sworn** vi jurer; to ~ to sth jurer de qch; ~word n gros mot, juron m.

sweat [swɛt] n sueur f, transpiration f // vi suer.

sweater ['swɛtə*] n tricot m, pull m.

sweaty ['swɛtɪ] a en sueur, moite or mouillé(e) de sueur.

Swede [swi:d] n Suédois/e.

swede [swi:d] n (Brit) rutabaga m.

Sweden ['swi:dn] n Suède f.

Swedish ['swi:dɪʃ] a suédois(e) // n (LING) suédois m.

sweep [swi:p] n coup m de balai; (curve) grande courbe; (range) champ m; (also: chimney ~) ramoneur m // vb (pt, pp **swept**) vt balayer // vi avancer majestueusement or rapidement; s'élancer; s'étendre; to ~ away vt balayer; entraîner; emporter; to ~ past vi passer majestueusement or rapidement; to ~ up vt, vi balayer; ~ing a (gesture) large; circulaire; a ~ing statement une généralisation hâtive.

sweet [swi:t] n (Brit: pudding) dessert m; (candy) bonbon m // a doux(douce); (not savoury) sucré(e); (fresh) frais(fraîche), pur(e); (fig) agréable, doux; gentil(le); mignon(ne); ~corn n maïs doux; ~en vt sucrer; adoucir; ~heart n amoureux/euse; ~ness n goût sucré; douceur f; ~ pea n pois m de senteur.

swell [swɛl] n (of sea) houle f // a (col: excellent) chouette // vb (pt ~ed, pp **swollen** or ~ed) vt augmenter; grossir // vi grossir, augmenter; (sound) s'enfler; (MED) enfler; ~ing n (MED) enflure f; grosseur f.

sweltering ['swɛltərɪŋ] a étouffant(e), oppressant(e).

swept [swɛpt] pt, pp of **sweep**.

swerve [swə:v] vi faire une embardée or

un écart; dévier.

swift [swɪft] n (bird) martinet m // a rapide, prompt(e).

swig [swɪg] n (col: drink) lampée f.

swill [swɪl] n pâtée f // vt (also: ~ out, ~ down) laver à grande eau.

swim [swɪm] n: to go for a ~ aller nager or se baigner // vb (pt swam, pp swum) vi nager; (SPORT) faire de la natation; (head, room) tourner // vt traverser (à la nage); faire (à la nage); ~**mer** n nageur/euse; ~**ming** n nage f, natation f; ~**ming cap** n bonnet m de bain; ~**ming costume** n (Brit) maillot m (de bain); ~**ming pool** n piscine f; ~**suit** n maillot m (de bain).

swindle ['swɪndl] n escroquerie f.

swine [swaɪn] n (pl inv) pourceau m, porc m; (col!) salaud m (!).

swing [swɪŋ] n balançoire f; (movement) balancement m, oscillations fpl; (MUS) swing m; rythme m // vb (pt, pp swung) vt balancer, faire osciller; (also: ~ round) tourner, faire virer // vi se balancer, osciller; (also: ~ round) virer, tourner; to be in full ~ battre son plein; ~ **door**, (US) ~**ing door** n porte battante.

swingeing ['swɪndʒɪŋ] a (Brit) écrasant(e); considérable.

swipe [swaɪp] vt (hit) frapper à toute volée; gifler; (col: steal) piquer.

swirl [swə:l] vi tourbillonner, tournoyer.

swish [swɪʃ] a (col: smart) rupin(e) // vi siffler.

Swiss [swɪs] a suisse // n (pl inv) Suisse/ esse.

switch [swɪtʃ] n (for light, radio etc) bouton m; (change) changement m, revirement m // vt (change) changer; intervertir; to ~ **off** vt éteindre; (engine) arrêter; to ~ **on** vt allumer; (engine, machine) mettre en marche; ~**board** n (TEL) standard m.

Switzerland ['swɪtsələnd] n Suisse f.

swivel ['swɪvl] vi (also: ~ round) pivoter, tourner.

swollen ['swəulən] pp of swell.

swoon [swu:n] vi se pâmer.

swoop [swu:p] vi (also: ~ down) descendre en piqué, piquer.

swop [swɔp] vt = swap.

sword [sɔ:d] n épée f; ~**fish** n espadon m.

swore [swɔ:*] pt of swear.

sworn [swɔ:n] pp of swear.

swot [swɔt] vt, vi bûcher, potasser.

swum [swʌm] pp of swim.

swung [swʌŋ] pt, pp of swing.

syllable ['sɪləbl] n syllabe f.

syllabus ['sɪləbəs] n programme m.

symbol ['sɪmbl] n symbole m.

symmetry ['sɪmɪtrɪ] n symétrie f.

sympathetic [sɪmpə'θɛtɪk] a compatissant(e); bienveillant(e), compré-

hensif(ive); ~ **towards** bien disposé(e) envers.

sympathize ['sɪmpəθaɪz] vi: to ~ **with** sb plaindre qn; s'associer à la douleur de qn; ~**r** n (POL) sympathisant/e.

sympathy ['sɪmpəθɪ] n compassion f; in ~ **with** en accord avec; (strike) en or par solidarité avec; **with our deepest** ~ en vous priant d'accepter nos sincères condoléances.

symphony ['sɪmfənɪ] n symphonie f.

symptom ['sɪmptəm] n symptôme m; indice m.

synagogue ['sɪnəgɔg] n synagogue f.

syndicate ['sɪndɪkɪt] n syndicat m, coopérative f.

synonym ['sɪnənɪm] n synonyme m.

syntax ['sɪntæks] n syntaxe f.

synthetic [sɪn'θɛtɪk] a synthétique.

syphon ['saɪfən] n, vb = siphon.

Syria ['sɪrɪə] n Syrie f.

syringe [sɪ'rɪndʒ] n seringue f.

syrup ['sɪrəp] n sirop m; (also: golden ~) mélasse raffinée.

system ['sɪstəm] n système m; (order) méthode f; (ANAT) organisme m; ~**atic** [-'mætɪk] a systématique; méthodique; ~ **disk** n (COMPUT) disque m système; ~**s analyst** n analyste-programmeur m/f.

T

ta [tɑ:] excl (Brit col) merci!

tab [tæb] n (loop on coat etc) attache f; (label) étiquette f; to keep ~s on (fig) surveiller.

tabby ['tæbɪ] n (also: ~ cat) chat/te tigré(e).

table ['teɪbl] n table f // vt (Brit: motion etc) présenter; to lay or set the ~ mettre le couvert or la table; ~ **of contents** n table f des matières; ~**cloth** n nappe f; ~ **d'hôte** [tɑ:bl'dəut] a (meal) à prix fixe; ~ **lamp** n lampe décorative; ~**mat** n (for plate) napperon m, set m; (for hot dish) dessous-de-plat m inv; ~**spoon** n cuiller f de service; (also: ~**spoonful**: as measurement) cuillerée f à soupe.

tablet ['tæblɪt] n (MED) comprimé m; (: for sucking) pastille f; (for writing) bloc m; (of stone) plaque f.

table: ~ **tennis** n ping-pong m, tennis m de table; ~ **wine** n vin m de table.

tabulate ['tæbjuleɪt] vt (data, figures) mettre sous forme de table(s).

tacit ['tæsɪt] a tacite.

tack [tæk] n (nail) petit clou; (stitch) point m de bâti; (NAUT) bord m, bordée f // vt clouer; bâtir // vi tirer un or des bord(s).

tackle ['tækl] n matériel m, équipement m; (for lifting) appareil m de levage;

(*RUGBY*) plaquage *m* // *vt* (*difficulty*) s'attaquer à; (*RUGBY*) plaquer.

tacky ['tækɪ] *a* collant(e); pas sec(sèche).

tact [tækt] *n* tact *m*; **~ful** *a* plein(e) de tact.

tactical ['tæktɪkl] *a* tactique.

tactics ['tæktɪks] *n*, *npl* tactique *f*.

tactless ['tæktlɪs] *a* qui manque de tact.

tadpole ['tædpəul] *n* têtard *m*.

taffy ['tæfɪ] *n* (*US*) (bonbon *m* au) caramel *m*.

tag [tæg] *n* étiquette *f*; **to ~ along** *vi* suivre.

tail [teɪl] *n* queue *f*; (*of shirt*) pan *m* // *vt* (*follow*) suivre, filer; **to ~ away, ~ off** *vi* (*in size, quality etc*) baisser peu à peu; **~back** *n* (*Brit AUT*) bouchon *m*; **~ coat** *n* habit *m*; **~ end** *n* bout *m*, fin *f*; **~gate** *n* (*AUT*) hayon *m* arrière.

tailor ['teɪlə*] *n* tailleur *m* (*artisan*); **~ing** *n* (*cut*) coupe *f*; **~-made** *a* fait(e) sur mesure; (*fig*) conçu(e) spécialement.

tailwind ['teɪlwɪnd] *n* vent *m* arrière *inv*.

tainted ['teɪntɪd] *a* (*food*) gâté(e); (*water, air*) infecté(e); (*fig*) souillé(e).

take, *pt* **took**, *pp* **taken** [teɪk, tuk, 'teɪkn] *vt* prendre; (*gain: prize*) remporter; (*require: effort, courage*) demander; (*tolerate*) accepter, supporter; (*hold: passengers etc*) contenir; (*accompany*) emmener, accompagner; (*bring, carry*) apporter, emporter; (*exam*) passer, se présenter à; **to ~ sth from** (*drawer etc*) prendre qch dans; **I ~ it that** je suppose que; **to ~ for a walk** (*child, dog*) emmener promener; **to ~ after** *vt fus* ressembler à; **to ~ apart** *vt* démonter; **to ~ away** *vt* emporter; enlever; **to ~ back** *vt* (*return*) rendre, rapporter; (*one's words*) retirer; **to ~ down** *vt* (*building*) démolir; (*letter etc*) prendre, écrire; **to ~ in** *vt* (*deceive*) tromper, rouler; (*understand*) comprendre, saisir; (*include*) couvrir, inclure; (*lodger*) prendre; **to ~ off** *vi* (*AVIAT*) décoller // *vt* (*remove*) enlever; (*imitate*) imiter, pasticher; **to ~ on** *vt* (*work*) accepter, se charger de; (*employee*) prendre, embaucher; (*opponent*) accepter de se battre contre; **to ~ out** *vt* sortir; (*remove*) enlever; (*licence*) prendre, se procurer; **to ~ sth out of sth** enlever qch de; (*drawer, pocket etc*) prendre qch dans qch; **to ~ over** *vt* (*business*) reprendre // *vi*: **to ~ over from sb** prendre la relève de qn; **to ~ to** *vt fus* (*person*) se prendre d'amitié pour; (*activity*) prendre goût à; **to ~ up** *vt* (*one's story, a dress*) reprendre; (*occupy: time, space*) prendre, occuper; (*engage in: hobby etc*) se mettre à; **~away** *a* (*food*) à emporter; **~-home**

pay *n* salaire net; **~off** *n* (*AVIAT*) décollage *m*; **~out** *a* (*US*) = **~away**; **~over** *n* (*COMM*) rachat *m*.

takings ['teɪkɪŋz] *npl* (*COMM*) recette *f*.

talc [tælk] *n* (*also*: **~um powder**) talc *m*.

tale [teɪl] *n* (*story*) conte *m*, histoire *f*; (*account*) récit *m*; (*pej*) histoire; **to tell ~s** (*fig*) rapporter.

talent ['tælnt] *n* talent *m*, don *m*; **~ed** *a* doué(e), plein(e) de talent.

talk [tɔːk] *n* propos *mpl*; (*gossip*) racontars *mpl* (*pej*); (*conversation*) discussion *f*; (*interview*) entretien *m*; (*a speech*) causerie *f*, exposé *m* // *vi* (*chatter*) bavarder; **~s** *npl* (*POL etc*) entretiens *mpl*; conférence *f*; **to ~ about** parler de; (*converse*) s'entretenir *or* parler de; **to ~ sb out of/into doing** persuader qn de ne pas faire/de faire; **to ~ shop** parler métier *or* affaires; **to ~ over** *vt* discuter (de); **~ative** *a* bavard(e); **~ show** *n* causerie (télévisée *or* radiodiffusée).

tall [tɔːl] *a* (*person*) grand(e); (*building, tree*) haut(e); **to be 6 feet ~** ≈ mesurer 1 mètre 80; **~boy** *n* (*Brit*) grande commode; **~ story** *n* histoire *f* invraisemblable.

tally ['tælɪ] *n* compte *m* // *vi*: **to ~ (with)** correspondre (à).

talon ['tælən] *n* griffe *f*; (*eagle*) serre *f*.

tame [teɪm] *a* apprivoisé(e); (*fig: story, style*) insipide.

tamper ['tæmpə*] *vi*: **to ~ with** toucher à (*en cachette ou sans permission*).

tampon ['tæmpɔn] *n* tampon *m* hygiénique *or* périodique.

tan [tæn] *n* (*also*: **sun~**) bronzage *m* // *vt*, *vi* bronzer, brunir // *a* (*colour*) brun roux *inv*.

tang [tæŋ] *n* odeur (*or* saveur) piquante.

tangent ['tændʒənt] *n* (*MATH*) tangente *f*; **to go off at a ~** (*fig*) changer complètement de direction.

tangerine [tændʒə'riːn] *n* mandarine *f*.

tangle ['tæŋgl] *n* enchevêtrement *m* // *vt* enchevêtrer.

tank [tæŋk] *n* réservoir *m*; (*for processing*) cuve *f*; (*for fish*) aquarium *m*; (*MIL*) char *m* d'assaut, tank *m*.

tanker ['tæŋkə*] *n* (*ship*) pétrolier *m*, tanker *m*; (*truck*) camion-citerne *m*.

tantalizing ['tæntəlaɪzɪŋ] *a* (*smell*) extrêmement appétissant(e); (*offer*) terriblement tentant(e).

tantamount ['tæntəmaunt] *a*: **~ to** qui équivaut à.

tantrum ['tæntrəm] *n* accès *m* de colère.

tap [tæp] *n* (*on sink etc*) robinet *m*; (*gentle blow*) petite tape // *vt* frapper *or* taper légèrement; (*resources*) exploiter, utiliser; (*telephone*) mettre sur écoute; **on ~** (*fig: resources*) disponible; **~-dancing** *n* claquettes *fpl*.

tape [teɪp] *n* ruban *m*; (*also*: **magnetic**

~) bande *f* (magnétique) // *vt* (*record*) enregistrer (sur bande); ~ **measure** *n* mètre *m* à ruban.

taper ['teɪpə*] *n* cierge *m* // *vi* s'effiler.

tape recorder *n* magnétophone *m*.

tapestry ['tæpɪstrɪ] *n* tapisserie *f*.

tar [tɑ:] *n* goudron *m*.

target ['tɑ:gɪt] *n* cible *f*; (*fig: objective*) objectif *m*.

tariff ['tærɪf] *n* (*COMM*) tarif *m*; (*taxes*) tarif douanier.

tarmac ['tɑ:mæk] *n* (*Brit: on road*) macadam *m*; (*AVIAT*) aire *f* d'envol.

tarnish ['tɑ:nɪʃ] *vt* ternir.

tarpaulin [tɑ:'pɔ:lɪn] *n* bâche goudronnée.

tarragon ['tærəgən] *n* estragon *m*.

tart [tɑ:t] *n* (*CULIN*) tarte *f*; (*Brit col: pej: woman*) poule *f* // *a* (*flavour*) âpre, aigrelet(te); **to ~ o.s. up** (*col*) se faire beau(belle); (: *pej*) s'attifer.

tartan ['tɑ:tn] *n* tartan *m* // *a* écossais(e).

tartar ['tɑ:tə*] *n* (*on teeth*) tartre *m*; ~ **sauce** *n* sauce *f* tartare.

task [tɑ:sk] *n* tâche *f*; **to take to ~** prendre à partie; ~ **force** *n* (*MIL, POLICE*) détachement spécial.

tassel ['tæsl] *n* gland *m*; pompon *m*.

taste [teɪst] *n* goût *m*; (*fig: glimpse, idea*) idée *f*, aperçu *m* // *vt* goûter // *vi*: **to ~ of** (*fish etc*) avoir le *or* un goût de; **it ~s like fish** ça a un *or* le goût de poisson, on dirait du poisson; **you can ~ the garlic (in it)** on sent bien l'ail; **can I have a ~ of this wine?** puis-je goûter un peu de ce vin?; **to have a ~ for sth** aimer qch, avoir un penchant pour qch; **in good/bad ~** de bon/mauvais goût; ~**ful** *a* de bon goût; ~**less** *a* (*food*) qui n'a aucun goût; (*remark*) de mauvais goût; **tasty** *a* savoureux(euse), délicieux(euse).

tatters ['tætəz] *npl*: **in ~** (*also:* tattered) en lambeaux.

tattoo [tə'tu:] *n* tatouage *m*; (*spectacle*) parade *f* militaire // *vt* tatouer.

taught [tɔ:t] *pt, pp of* **teach**.

taunt [tɔ:nt] *n* raillerie *f* // *vt* railler.

Taurus ['tɔ:rəs] *n* le Taureau.

taut [tɔ:t] *a* tendu(e).

tawdry ['tɔ:drɪ] *a* (d'un mauvais goût) criard.

tax [tæks] *n* (*on goods etc*) taxe *f*; (*on income*) impôts *mpl*, contributions *fpl* // *vt* taxer; imposer; (*fig: strain: patience etc*) mettre à l'épreuve; ~**able** *a* (*income*) imposable; ~**ation** [-'seɪʃən] *n* taxation *f*; impôts *mpl*, contributions *fpl*; ~ **avoidance** *n* évasion fiscale; ~ **collector** *n* percepteur *m*; ~ **disc** *n* (*Brit AUT*) vignette *f* (automobile); ~ **evasion** *n* fraude fiscale; ~**-free** *a* exempt(e) d'impôts.

taxi ['tæksɪ] *n* taxi *m* // *vi* (*AVIAT*) rouler (lentement) au sol; ~ **driver** *n* chauffeur *m* de taxi; ~ **rank** (*Brit*), ~ **stand** *n* station *f* de taxis.

tax: ~ **payer** *n* contribuable *m/f*; ~ **relief** *n* dégrèvement *or* allègement fiscal; ~ **return** *n* déclaration *f* d'impôts *or* de revenus.

TB *n abbr* = tuberculosis.

tea [ti:] *n* thé *m*; (*Brit: snack: for children*) goûter *m*; (*Brit*) collation combinant goûter et dîner; ~ **bag** *n* sachet *m* de thé; ~ **break** *n* (*Brit*) pausethé *f*.

teach [ti:tʃ] , *pt, pp* taught *vt*: **to ~ sb sth**, ~ **sth to sb** apprendre qch à qn; (*in school etc*) enseigner qch à qn // *vi* enseigner; ~**er** *n* (*in secondary school*) professeur *m*; (*in primary school*) instituteur/trice; ~**ing** *n* enseignement *m*.

tea cosy *n* couvre-théière *m*.

teacup ['ti:kʌp] *n* tasse *f* à thé.

teak [ti:k] *n* teck *m*.

team [ti:m] *n* équipe *f*; (*of animals*) attelage *m*; ~**work** *n* travail *m* d'équipe.

teapot ['ti:pɔt] *n* théière *f*.

tear *n* [tɛə*] déchirure *f*; [tɪə*] larme *f* // *vb* [tɛə*] (*pt* tore, *pp* torn) *vt* déchirer // *vi* se déchirer; **in ~s** en larmes; **to ~ along** *vi* (*rush*) aller à toute vitesse; **to ~ up** *vt* (*sheet of paper etc*) déchirer, mettre en pièces *or* pièces; ~**ful** *a* larmoyant(e); ~ **gas** *n* gaz *m* lacrymogène.

tearoom ['ti:ru:m] *n* salon *m* de thé.

tease [ti:z] *vt* taquiner; (*unkindly*) tourmenter.

tea set *n* service *m* à thé.

teaspoon ['ti:spu:n] *n* petite cuiller; (*also:* ~**ful:** *as measurement*) ≈ cuillerée *f* à café.

teat [ti:t] *n* tétine *f*.

teatime ['ti:taɪm] *n* l'heure *f* du thé.

tea towel *n* (*Brit*) torchon *m* (à vaisselle).

technical ['tɛknɪkl] *a* technique; ~**ity** [-'kælɪtɪ] *n* technicité *f*; (*detail*) détail *m* technique.

technician [tɛk'nɪʃən] *n* technicien/ne.

technique [tɛk'ni:k] *n* technique *f*.

technological [tɛknə'lɔdʒɪkl] *a* technologique.

technology [tɛk'nɔlədʒɪ] *n* technologie *f*.

teddy (bear) ['tɛdɪ(bɛə*)] *n* ours *m* (en peluche).

tedious ['ti:dɪəs] *a* fastidieux(euse).

tee [ti:] *n* (*GOLF*) tee *m*.

teem [ti:m] *vi*: **to ~ (with)** grouiller (de); **it is ~ing (with rain)** il pleut à torrents.

teenage ['ti:neɪdʒ] *a* (*fashions etc*) pour jeunes, pour adolescents; ~**r** *n* jeune *m/f*, adolescent/e.

teens [ti:nz] *npl*: to be in one's ~ être adolescent(e).

tee-shirt ['ti:ʃə:t] *n* = **T-shirt**.

teeter ['ti:tə*] *vi* chanceler, vaciller.

teeth [ti:θ] *npl of* **tooth**.

teethe [ti:ð] *vi* percer ses dents.

teething ['ti:ðɪŋ]: ~ **ring** *n* anneau *m* (*pour bébé qui perce ses dents*); ~ **troubles** *npl* (*fig*) difficultés initiales.

teetotal ['ti:'təutl] *a* (*person*) qui ne boit jamais d'alcool.

telegram ['tɛlɪɡræm] *n* télégramme *m*.

telegraph ['tɛlɪɡrɑ:f] *n* télégraphe *m*.

telephone ['tɛlɪfəun] *n* téléphone *m* // *vt* (*person*) téléphoner à; (*message*) téléphoner; ~ **booth**, (*Brit*) ~ **box** *n* cabine *f* téléphonique; ~ **call** *n* coup *m* de téléphone, appel *m* téléphonique, communication *f* téléphonique; ~ **directory** *n* annuaire *m* (du téléphone); ~ **number** *n* numéro *m* de téléphone; ~ **operator** téléphoniste *m/f*, standardiste *m/f*; **telephonist** [tə'lɛfənɪst] *n* (*Brit*) téléphoniste *m/f*.

telephoto ['tɛlɪ'fəutəu] *a*: ~ **lens** *n* téléobjectif *m*.

telescope ['tɛlɪskəup] *n* télescope *m*.

televise ['tɛlɪvaɪz] *vt* téléviser.

television ['tɛlɪvɪʒən] *n* télévision *f*; ~ **set** *n* poste *m* de télévision.

telex ['tɛlɛks] *n* télex *m*.

tell [tɛl], *pt*, *pp* **told** *vt* dire; (*relate: story*) raconter; (*distinguish*): to ~ **sth from** distinguer qch de // *vi* (*talk*): to ~ (**of**) parler (de); (*have effect*) se faire sentir, se voir; to ~ **sb to do** dire à qn de faire; **to** ~ **off** *vt* réprimander, gronder; ~**er** *n* (*in bank*) caissier/ère; ~**ing** *a* (*remark, detail*) révélateur(trice); ~**tale** *a* (*sign*) éloquent(e), révélateur(trice).

telly ['tɛlɪ] *n abbr* (*Brit col*: = **television**) télé *f*.

temp [tɛmp] *n abbr* (= *temporary*) (secrétaire *f*) intérimaire *f*.

temper ['tɛmpə*] *n* (*nature*) caractère *m*; (*mood*) humeur *f*; (*fit of anger*) colère *f* // *vt* (*moderate*) tempérer, adoucir; to **be in a** ~ être en colère; to **lose one's** ~ se mettre en colère.

temperament ['tɛmprəmənt] *n* (*nature*) tempérament *m*; ~**al** [-'mɛntl] *a* capricieux(euse).

temperate ['tɛmprət] *a* modéré(e); (*climate*) tempéré(e).

temperature ['tɛmprətʃə*] *n* température *f*; to **have** *or* **run a** ~ avoir de la fièvre.

tempest ['tɛmpɪst] *n* tempête *f*.

template ['tɛmplət] *n* patron *m*.

temple ['tɛmpl] *n* (*building*) temple *m*; (*ANAT*) tempe *f*.

temporary ['tɛmpərəri] *a* temporaire, provisoire; (*job, worker*) temporaire; ~ **secretary** *n* (secrétaire *f*) intérimaire *f*.

tempt [tɛmpt] *vt* tenter; to ~ **sb into doing** induire qn à faire; ~**ation** [-'teɪʃən] *n* tentation *f*.

ten [tɛn] *num* dix.

tenable ['tɛnəbl] *a* défendable.

tenacity [tə'næsɪti] *n* ténacité *f*.

tenancy ['tɛnənsɪ] *n* location *f*; état *m* de locataire.

tenant ['tɛnənt] *n* locataire *m/f*.

tend [tɛnd] *vt* s'occuper de // *vi*: to ~ **to do** avoir tendance à faire.

tendency ['tɛndənsɪ] *n* tendance *f*.

tender ['tɛndə*] *a* tendre; (*delicate*) délicat(e); (*sore*) sensible; (*affectionate*) tendre, doux(douce) // *n* (*COMM*: *offer*) soumission *f* // *vt* offrir.

tenement ['tɛnəmənt] *n* immeuble *m* (de rapport).

tenet ['tɛnət] *n* principe *m*.

tennis ['tɛnɪs] *n* tennis *m*; ~ **ball** *n* balle *f* de tennis; ~ **court** *n* (court *m* de) tennis; ~ **player** *n* joueur/euse de tennis; ~ **racket** *n* raquette *f* de tennis; ~ **shoes** *npl* (chaussures *fpl* de) tennis *mpl*.

tenor ['tɛnə*] *n* (*MUS*) ténor *m*; (*of speech etc*) sens général.

tense [tɛns] *a* tendu(e) // *n* (*LING*) temps *m*.

tension ['tɛnʃən] *n* tension *f*.

tent [tɛnt] *n* tente *f*.

tentative ['tɛntətɪv] *a* timide, hésitant(e); (*conclusion*) provisoire.

tenterhooks ['tɛntəhuks] *npl*: **on** ~ sur des charbons ardents.

tenth [tɛnθ] *num* dixième.

tent: ~ **peg** *n* piquet *m* de tente; ~ **pole** *n* montant *m* de tente.

tenuous ['tɛnjuəs] *a* ténu(e).

tenure ['tɛnjuə*] *n* (*of property*) bail *m*; (*of job*) période *f* de jouissance; statut *m* de titulaire.

tepid ['tɛpɪd] *a* tiède.

term [tə:m] *n* (*limit*) terme *m*; (*word*) terme, mot *m*; (*SCOL*) trimestre *m*; (*LAW*) session *f* // *vt* appeler; ~**s** *npl* (*conditions*) conditions *fpl*; (*COMM*) tarif *m*; ~ **of imprisonment** peine *f* de prison; **in the short/long** ~ à court/long terme; to **come to** ~**s with** (*problem*) faire face à.

terminal ['tə:mɪnl] *a* terminal(e); (*disease*) dans sa phase terminale // *n* (*ELEC*) borne *f*; (*for oil, ore etc*, *COMPUT*) terminal *m*; (*also*: **air** ~) aérogare *f*; (*Brit*: *also*: **coach** ~) gare routière.

terminate ['tə:mɪneɪt] *vt* mettre fin à // *vi*: to ~ **in** finir en or par.

terminus, *pl* **termini** ['tə:mɪnəs, 'tə:mɪnaɪ] *n* terminus *m inv*.

terrace ['tɛrəs] *n* terrasse *f*; (*Brit*: *row of houses*) rangée *f* de maisons (*attenantes les unes aux autres*); **the** ~**s** (*Brit SPORT*) les gradins *mpl*; ~**d** *a* (*garden*) en terrasses.

terracotta [ˈtɛrəˈkɔtə] *n* terre cuite.

terrain [tɛˈreɪn] *n* terrain *m* (*sol*).

terrible [ˈtɛrɪbl] *a* terrible, atroce; (*weather*, *work*) affreux(euse), épouvantable; **terribly** *ad* terriblement; (*very badly*) affreusement mal.

terrier [ˈtɛrɪə*] *n* terrier *m* (*chien*).

terrific [təˈrɪfɪk] *a* fantastique, incroyable, terrible; (*wonderful*) formidable, sensationnel(le).

terrify [ˈtɛrɪfaɪ] *vt* terrifier.

territory [ˈtɛrɪtərɪ] *n* territoire *m*.

terror [ˈtɛrə*] *n* terreur *f*; **~ism** *n* terrorisme *m*; **~ist** *n* terroriste *m*/*f*.

terse [təːs] *a* (*style*) concis(e); (*reply*) laconique.

Terylene [ˈtɛrɪliːn] *n* ® tergal *m* ®.

test [tɛst] *n* (*trial*, *check*) essai *m*; (: *of goods in factory*) contrôle *m*; (*of courage etc*) épreuve *f*; (*MED*) examens *mpl*; (*CHEM*) analyses *fpl*; (*exam: of intelligence etc*) test *m* (d'aptitude); (: *in school*) interrogation *f* de contrôle; (*also*: **driving ~**) (examen du) permis *m* de conduire // *vt* essayer; contrôler; mettre à l'épreuve; examiner; analyser; tester; faire subir une interrogation (de contrôle) à.

testament [ˈtɛstəmənt] *n* testament *m*; **the Old/New T~** l'Ancien/le Nouveau Testament.

testicle [ˈtɛstɪkl] *n* testicule *m*.

testify [ˈtɛstɪfaɪ] *vi* (*LAW*) témoigner, déposer; **to ~ to sth** (*LAW*) attester qch; (*gen*) témoigner de qch.

testimony [ˈtɛstɪmənɪ] *n* (*LAW*) témoignage *m*, déposition *f*.

test: **~ match** *n* (*CRICKET*, *RUGBY*) match international; **~ pilot** *n* pilote *m* d'essai; **~ tube** *n* éprouvette *f*.

tetanus [ˈtɛtənəs] *n* tétanos *m*.

tether [ˈtɛðə*] *vt* attacher // *n*: **at the end of one's ~** à bout (de patience).

text [tɛkst] *n* texte *m*; **~book** *n* manuel *m*.

textile [ˈtɛkstaɪl] *n* textile *m*.

texture [ˈtɛkstʃə*] *n* texture *f*; (*of skin*, *paper etc*) grain *m*.

Thames [tɛmz] *n*: **the ~** la Tamise.

than [ðæn, ðən] *cj* que; (*with numerals*): **more ~ 10/once** plus de 10/ d'une fois; **I have more/less ~ you** j'en ai plus/moins que toi; **she has more apples ~ pears** elle a plus de pommes que de poires.

thank [θæŋk] *vt* remercier, dire merci à; **~ you** (**very much**) merci (beaucoup); **~s** *npl* remerciements *mpl* // *excl* merci!; **~s to** *prep* grâce à; **~ful** *a*: **~ful** (**for**) reconnaissant(e) (de); **~less** *a* ingrat(e); **T~sgiving** (**Day**) *n* jour *m* d'action de grâce.

that [ðæt] ♦ *a* (*demonstrative*: *pl* **those**) ce, cet + *vowel or h mute*, *f* cette; **~ man/woman/book** cet homme/cette femme/ce livre; (*not 'this'*) cet homme-là/cette femme-là/ce livre-là; **~ one** celui-là (celle-là)

♦ *pronoun* **1** (*demonstrative*: *pl* **those**) ce; (*not 'this one'*) cela, ça; **who's ~?** qui est-ce?; **what's ~?** qu'est-ce que c'est?; **is ~ you?** c'est toi?; **I prefer this to ~** je préfère ceci à cela *or* ça; **~'s what he said** c'est *or* voilà ce qu'il a dit; **~ is (to say)** c'est-à-dire, à savoir

2 (*relative: subject*) qui; (: *object*) que; (: *indirect*) lequel(laquelle), *pl* lesquels(lesquelles); **the book ~ I read** le livre que j'ai lu; **the books ~ are in the library** les livres qui sont dans la bibliothèque; **all ~ I have** tout ce que j'ai; **the box ~ I put it in** la boîte dans laquelle je l'ai mis; **the people ~ I spoke to** les gens auxquels *or* à qui j'ai parlé

3 (*relative: of time*) où; **the day ~ he came** le jour où il est venu

♦ *cj* que; **he thought ~ I was ill** il pensait que j'étais malade

♦ *ad* (*demonstrative*): **I can't work ~ much** je ne peux pas travailler autant que cela; **I didn't know it was ~ bad** je ne savais pas que c'était si *or* aussi mauvais; **it's about ~ high** c'est à peu près de cette hauteur.

thatched [θætʃt] *a* (*roof*) de chaume; **~ cottage** chaumière *f*.

thaw [θɔː] *n* dégel *m* // *vi* (*ice*) fondre; (*food*) dégeler // *vt* (*food*) (faire) dégeler; **it's ~ing** (*weather*) il dégèle.

the [ðiː, ðə] *definite article* **1** (*gen*) le, *f* la, l' + *vowel or h mute*, *pl* les (NB: à + **le**(*s*) = au(x); de + **le** = du; de + **les** = des); **~ boy/girl/ink** le garçon/la fille/ l'encre; **~ children** les enfants; **~ history of ~ world** l'histoire du monde; **give it to ~ postman** donne-le au facteur; **to play ~ piano/flute** jouer du piano/de la flûte; **~ rich and ~ poor** les riches et les pauvres

2 (*in titles*): **Elizabeth ~ First** Élisabeth première; **Peter ~ Great** Pierre le Grand

3 (*in comparisons*): **~ more he works, ~ more he earns** plus il travaille, plus il gagne de l'argent.

theatre, (*US*) **theater** [ˈθɪətə*] *n* théâtre *m*; **~-goer** *n* habitué/e du théâtre.

theatrical [θɪˈætrɪkl] *a* théâtral(e).

theft [θɛft] *n* vol *m* (*larcin*).

their [ðɛə*] *a* leur, *pl* leurs; **~s** *pronoun* le(la) leur, les leurs; *see also* **my**, **mine**.

them [ðɛm, ðəm] *pronoun* (*direct*) les; (*indirect*) leur; (*stressed*, *after prep*) eux(elles); *see also* **me**.

theme [θiːm] *n* thème *m*; **~ song** *n* chanson principale.

themselves [ðəmˈsɛlvz] *pl pronoun* (*reflexive*) se; (*emphatic*) eux-mêmes(elles-mêmes); *see also* **oneself**.

then [ðɛn] *ad* (*at that time*) alors, à ce

moment-là; (next) puis, ensuite; (and also) et puis // cj (therefore) alors, dans ce cas // a: the ~ president le président d'alors or de l'époque; by ~ (past) à ce moment-là; (future) d'ici là; from ~ on dès lors.

theology [θɪˈɔlədʒɪ] n théologie f.
theoretical [θɪəˈretɪkl] a théorique.
theory [ˈθɪərɪ] n théorie f.
therapy [ˈθerəpɪ] n thérapie f.
there [ðeə*] ad 1: ~ is, ~ are il y a; ~ are 3 of them (people, things) il y en a 3; ~ has been an accident il y a eu un accident

2 (referring to place) là, là-bas; it's ~ c'est là(-bas); in/on/up/down ~ là-dedans/là-dessus/là-haut/en bas; he went ~ on Friday il y est allé vendredi; I want that book ~ je veux ce livre-là; ~ he is! le voilà!

3: ~, ~ (esp to child) allons, allons!
thereabouts [ðeərəˈbauts] ad (place) par là, près de là; (amount) environ, à peu près.
thereafter [ðeərˈɑːftə*] ad par la suite.
thereby [ðeəˈbaɪ] ad ainsi.
therefore [ˈðeəfɔː*] ad donc, par conséquent.
there's [ðeəz] = there is, there has.
thermal [ˈθəːml] a thermique.
thermometer [θəˈmɔmɪtə*] n thermomètre m.
Thermos [ˈθəːməs] n ® (also: ~ flask) thermos m or f inv ®.
thermostat [ˈθəːməustæt] n thermostat m.
thesaurus [θɪˈsɔːrəs] n dictionnaire m synonymique.
these [ðiːz] pl pronoun ceux-ci(celles-ci) // il a ces; (not 'those'): ~ books ces livres-ci.
thesis, pl **theses** [ˈθiːsɪs, ˈθiːsiːz] n thèse f.
they [ðeɪ] pl pronoun ils(elles); (stressed) eux(elles); ~ say that ... (it is said that) on dit que ...; ~'d = they had, they would; ~'ll = they shall, they will; ~'re = they are; ~'ve = they have.
thick [θɪk] a épais(se); (crowd) dense; (stupid) bête, borné(e) // n: in the ~ of au beau milieu de, en plein cœur de; it's 20 cm ~ ça a 20 cm d'épaisseur; ~en vi s'épaissir // vt (sauce etc) épaissir; ~ness n épaisseur f; ~set a trapu(e), costaud(e); ~skinned a (fig) peu sensible.
thief, pl **thieves** [θiːf, θiːvz] n voleur/euse.
thigh [θaɪ] n cuisse f.
thimble [ˈθɪmbl] n dé m (à coudre).
thin [θɪn] a mince; (person) maigre; (soup) peu épais(se); (hair, crowd) clairsemé(e); (fog) léger(ère) // vt (hair) éclaircir; to ~ (down) (sauce, paint) délayer.

thing [θɪŋ] n chose f; (object) objet m; (contraption) truc m; ~s npl (belongings) affaires fpl; the best ~ would be to le mieux serait de; how are ~s? comment ça va?

think [θɪŋk] vi penser, réfléchir // vt penser, croire; (imagine) s'imaginer; to ~ of penser à; what did you ~ of them? qu'avez-vous pensé d'eux?; to ~ about sth/sb penser à qch/qn; I'll ~ about it je vais y réfléchir; to ~ of doing avoir l'idée de faire; I ~ so/not je crois or pense que oui/non; to ~ well of avoir une haute opinion de; to ~ over vt bien réfléchir à; to ~ up vt inventer, trouver; ~ tank n groupe m de réflexion.
third [θəːd] num troisième // n troisième m/f, (fraction) tiers m; (Brit SCOL: degree) ≈ licence f avec mention passable; ~ly ad troisièmement; ~ party insurance n (Brit) assurance f au tiers; ~rate a de qualité médiocre; the T~ World n le Tiers-Monde.
thirst [θəːst] n soif f; ~y a (person) qui a soif, assoiffé(e).
thirteen [ˈθəːˈtiːn] num treize.
thirty [ˈθəːtɪ] num trente.
this [ðɪs] ♦ a (demonstrative: pl these) ce, cet + vowel or h mute, f cette; ~ man/woman/book cet homme/cette femme/ce livre; (not 'that') cet homme-ci/cette femme-ci/ce livre-ci; ~ one celui-ci(celle-ci)
♦ pronoun (demonstrative: pl these) ce; (not 'that one') celui-ci(celle-ci), ceci; who's ~? qui est-ce?; what's ~? qu'est-ce que c'est?; I prefer ~ to that je préfère ceci à cela; ~ is what he said voici ce qu'il a dit; ~ is Mr Brown (in introductions) je vous présente Mr Brown; (in photo) c'est Mr Brown; (on telephone) ici Mr Brown
♦ ad (demonstrative): it was about ~ big c'était à peu près de cette grandeur or grand comme ça; I didn't know it was ~ bad je ne savais pas que c'était si or aussi mauvais.
thistle [ˈθɪsl] n chardon m.
thong [θɔŋ] n lanière f.
thorn [θɔːn] n épine f.
thorough [ˈθʌrə] a (search) minutieux(euse); (knowledge, research) approfondi(e); (work) consciencieux(euse); (cleaning) à fond; ~bred n (horse) pur-sang m inv; ~fare n rue f; 'no ~fare' 'passage interdit'; ~ly ad minutieusement; en profondeur; à fond; he ~ly agreed il était tout à fait d'accord.
those [ðəuz] pl pronoun ceux-là(celles-là) // pl a ces; (not 'these'): ~ books ces livres-là.

though [ðəu] cj bien que + sub, quoique

+ *sub* // *ad* pourtant.

thought [θɔ:t] *pt, pp of* think // *n* pensée *f*; (*opinion*) avis *m*; (*intention*) intention *f*; ~**ful** *a* pensif(ive); réfléchi(e); (*considerate*) prévenant(e); ~**less** *a* étourdi(e); qui manque de considération.

thousand ['θauzənd] *num* mille; one ~ mille; ~**s of** des milliers de; ~**th** *num* millième.

thrash [θræʃ] *vt* rouer de coups; donner une correction à; (*defeat*) battre à plate couture; **to** ~ **about** *vi* se débattre; **to** ~ **out** *vt* débattre de.

thread [θrɛd] *n* fil *m*; (*of screw*) pas *m*, filetage *m* // *vt* (*needle*) enfiler; ~**bare** *a* râpé(e), élimé(e).

threat [θrɛt] *n* menace *f*; ~**en** *vi* (*storm*) menacer // *vt*: **to** ~**en sb with sth/to do** menacer qn de qch/de faire.

three [θri:] *num* trois; ~**-dimensional** *a* à trois dimensions; (*film*) en relief; ~-**piece suit** *n* complet *m* (avec gilet); ~-**piece suite** *n* salon *m* comprenant un canapé et deux fauteuils assortis; ~-**ply** *a* (*wood*) à trois épaisseurs; (*wool*) trois fils *inv*.

thresh [θrɛʃ] *vt* (*AGR*) battre.

threshold ['θrɛʃhəuld] *n* seuil *m*.

threw [θru:] *pt of* throw.

thrifty ['θrɪftɪ] *a* économe.

thrill [θrɪl] *n* frisson *m*, émotion *f* // *vi* tressaillir, frissonner // *vt* (*audience*) électriser; **to be** ~**ed** (*with gift etc*) être ravi; ~**er** *n* film *m* (*or* roman *m or* pièce *f*) à suspense; ~**ing** *a* saisissant(e), excitant(e).

thrive, *pt* **thrived, throve,** *pp* **thrived, thriven** [θraɪv, θrəuv, 'θrɪvn] *vi* pousser *or* se développer bien; (*business*) prospérer; **he** ~**s on it** cela lui réussit; **thriving** *a* vigoureux(euse); prospère.

throat [θrəut] *n* gorge *f*; **to have a sore** ~ avoir mal à la gorge.

throb [θrɔb] *vi* (*heart*) palpiter; (*engine*) vibrer; (*with pain*) lanciner; (*wound*) causer des élancements.

throes [θrəuz] *npl*: **in the** ~ **of** au beau milieu de; en proie à.

throne [θrəun] *n* trône *m*.

throng [θrɔŋ] *n* foule *f* // *vt* se presser dans.

throttle ['θrɔtl] *n* (*AUT*) accélérateur *m* // *vt* étrangler.

through [θru:] *prep* à travers; (*time*) pendant, durant; (*by means of*) par, par l'intermédiaire de; (*owing to*) à cause de // *a* (*ticket, train, passage*) direct(e) // *ad* à travers; **to put sb** ~ **to sb** (*TEL*) passer qn à qn; **to be** ~ (*TEL*) avoir la communication; (*have finished*) avoir fini; '**no** ~ **way**' (*Brit*) 'impasse'; ~**out** *prep* (*place*) partout dans; (*time*) durant tout(e) le(la) // *ad* partout.

throve [θrəuv] *pt of* thrive.

throw [θrəu] *n* jet *m*; (*SPORT*) lancer *m*

// *vt* (*pt* **threw,** *pp* **thrown** [θru:, θrəun]) lancer, jeter; (*SPORT*) lancer; (*rider*) désarçonner; (*fig*) décontenancer; (*pottery*) tourner; **to** ~ **a party** donner une réception; **to** ~ **away** *vt* jeter; **to** ~ **off** *vt* se débarrasser de; **to** ~ **out** *vt* jeter dehors; (*reject*) rejeter; **to** ~ **up** *vi* vomir; ~**away** *a* à jeter; ~-**in** *n* (*SPORT*) remise *f* en jeu.

thru [θru:] *prep, a, ad* (*US*) = **through**.

thrush [θrʌʃ] *n* grive *f*.

thrust [θrʌst] *n* (*TECH*) poussée *f* // *vt* (*pt, pp* **thrust**) pousser brusquement; (*push in*) enfoncer.

thud [θʌd] *n* bruit sourd.

thug [θʌg] *n* voyou *m*.

thumb [θʌm] *n* (*ANAT*) pouce *m* // *vt* (*book*) feuilleter; **to** ~ **a lift** faire de l'auto-stop, arrêter une voiture; ~**tack** *n* (*US*) punaise *f* (*clou*).

thump [θʌmp] *n* grand coup; (*sound*) bruit sourd // *vt* cogner sur // *vi* cogner, frapper.

thunder ['θʌndə*] *n* tonnerre *m* // *vi* tonner; (*train etc*): **to** ~ **past** passer dans un grondement *or* un bruit de tonnerre; ~**bolt** *n* foudre *f*; ~**clap** *n* coup *m* de tonnerre; ~**storm** *n* orage *m*; ~**y** *a* orageux(euse).

Thursday ['θə:zdɪ] *n* jeudi *m*.

thus [ðʌs] *ad* ainsi.

thwart [θwɔ:t] *vt* contrecarrer.

thyme [taɪm] *n* thym *m*.

tiara [tɪ'ɑ:rə] *n* (*woman's*) diadème *m*.

tick [tɪk] *n* (*sound: of clock*) tic-tac *m*; (*mark*) coche *f*; (*ZOOL*) tique *f*; (*Brit col*): **in a** ~ dans un instant // *vi* faire tic-tac // *vt* cocher; **to** ~ **off** *vt* cocher; (*person*) réprimander, attraper; **to** ~ **over** *vi* (*engine*) tourner au ralenti; (*fig*) aller *or* marcher doucettement.

ticket ['tɪkɪt] *n* billet *m*; (*for bus, tube*) ticket *m*; (*in shop: on goods*) étiquette *f*; (*: from cash register*) reçu *m*, ticket; (*for library*) carte *f*; ~ **collector** *n* contrôleur/euse; ~ **office** *n* guichet *m*, bureau *m* de vente des billets.

tickle ['tɪkl] *n* chatouillement *m* // *vt* chatouiller; (*fig*) plaire à; faire rire.

tidal ['taɪdl] *a* à marée; ~ **wave** *n* raz-de-marée *m inv*.

tidbit ['tɪdbɪt] *n* (*US*) = **titbit**.

tiddlywinks ['tɪdlɪwɪŋks] *n* jeu *m* de puce.

tide [taɪd] *n* marée *f*; (*fig: of events*) cours *m* // *vt*: **to** ~ **sb over** dépanner qn; **high/low** ~ marée haute/basse.

tidy ['taɪdɪ] *a* (*room*) bien rangé(e); (*dress, work*) net(nette), soigné(e); (*person*) ordonné(e), qui a le sens de l'ordre // *vt* (*also:* ~ **up**) ranger; **to** ~ **o.s. up** s'arranger.

tie [taɪ] *n* (*string etc*) cordon *m*; (*Brit: also:* **neck**~) cravate *f*; (*fig: link*) lien *m*; (*SPORT: draw*) égalité *f* de points;

match nul // vt (parcel) attacher; (ribbon) nouer // vi (SPORT) faire match nul; finir à égalité de points; to ~ sth in a bow faire un nœud à or avec qch; to ~ a knot in sth faire un nœud à qch; **to ~ down** vt attacher; (fig): to ~ sb down to contraindre qn à accepter; **to ~ up** vt (parcel) ficeler; (dog, boat) attacher; (arrangements) conclure; to be ~d up (busy) être pris or occupé.

tier [tɪə*] n gradin m; (of cake) étage m.

tiff [tɪf] n petite querelle.

tiger ['taɪgə*] n tigre m.

tight [taɪt] a (rope) tendu(e), raide; (clothes) étroit(e), très juste; (budget, programme, bend) serré(e); (control) strict(e), sévère; (col: drunk) ivre, rond(e) // ad (squeeze) très fort; (shut) à bloc, hermétiquement; ~s npl (Brit) collant m; ~**en** vt (rope) tendre; (screw) resserrer; (control) renforcer // vi se tendre, se resserrer; ~**-fisted** a avare; ~**ly** ad (grasp) bien, très fort; ~**rope** n corde f raide.

tile [taɪl] n (on roof) tuile f; (on wall or floor) carreau m.

till [tɪl] n caisse (enregistreuse) // vt (land) cultiver // prep, cj = until.

tiller ['tɪlə*] n (NAUT) barre f (du gouvernail).

tilt [tɪlt] vt pencher, incliner // vi pencher, être incliné(e).

timber ['tɪmbə*] n (material) bois m de construction; (trees) arbres mpl.

time [taɪm] n temps m; (epoch: often pl) époque f, temps; (by clock) heure f; (moment) moment m; (occasion, also MATH) fois f; (MUS) mesure f // vt (race) chronométrer; (programme) minuter; (remark etc) choisir le moment de; a long ~ un long moment, longtemps; for the ~ being pour le moment; 4 at a ~ 4 à la fois; from ~ to ~ de temps en temps; in ~ (soon enough) à temps; (after some time) avec le temps, à la longue; (MUS) en mesure; in a week's ~ dans une semaine; in no ~ en un rien de temps; any ~ n'importe quand; on ~ à l'heure; 5 ~s 5 5 fois 5; what ~ is it? quelle heure est-il?; to have a good ~ bien s'amuser; ~'s up! c'est l'heure!; ~ **bomb** n bombe f à retardement; ~ **lag** n décalage m; (in travel) décalage horaire; ~**less** a éternel(le); ~**ly** a opportun(e); ~ **off** n temps m libre; ~**r** n (~ switch) minuteur m; (in kitchen) compte-minutes m inv; ~ **scale** n délais mpl; ~ **switch** n (Brit) minuteur m; (for lighting) minuterie f; ~**table** n (RAIL) (indicateur m) horaire m, (SCOL) emploi m du temps; ~ **zone** n fuseau m horaire.

timid ['tɪmɪd] a timide; (easily scared) peureux(euse).

timing ['taɪmɪŋ] n minutage m; chronométrage m; the ~ of his resignation le moment choisi pour sa démission.

timpani ['tɪmpənɪ] npl timbales fpl.

tin [tɪn] n étain m; (also: ~ plate) fer-blanc m; (Brit: can) boîte f (de conserve); (for baking) moule m (à gâteau); ~**foil** n papier m d'étain.

tinge [tɪndʒ] n nuance f // vt: ~d with teinté(e) de.

tingle ['tɪŋgl] vi picoter.

tinker ['tɪŋkə*] n rétameur ambulant; (gipsy) romanichel m; **to ~ with** vt fus bricoler, rafistoler.

tinkle ['tɪŋkl] vi tinter.

tinned [tɪnd] a (Brit: food) en boîte, en conserve.

tin opener ['-əupnə*] n (Brit) ouvre-boîte(s) m.

tinsel ['tɪnsl] n guirlandes fpl de Noël (argentées).

tint [tɪnt] n teinte f; (for hair) shampooing colorant; ~**ed** a (hair) teint(e); (spectacles, glass) teinté(e).

tiny ['taɪnɪ] a minuscule.

tip [tɪp] n (end) bout m; (protective: on umbrella etc) embout m; (gratuity) pourboire m; (for coal) terril m; (Brit: for rubbish) décharge f; (advice) tuyau m // vt (waiter) donner un pourboire à; (tilt) incliner; (overturn: also: ~ over) renverser; (empty: also: ~ out) déverser; ~**-off** n (hint) tuyau m; ~**ped** a (Brit: cigarette) (à bout) filtre inv.

tipsy ['tɪpsɪ] a un peu ivre, éméché(e).

tiptoe ['tɪptəu] n: on ~ sur la pointe des pieds.

tiptop ['tɪp'tɔp] a: in ~ condition en excellent état.

tire ['taɪə*] n (US) = tyre // vt fatiguer // vi se fatiguer; ~**d** a fatigué(e); to be ~d of en avoir assez de, être las(lasse) de; ~**some** a ennuyeux(euse); **tiring** a fatigant(e).

tissue ['tɪʃuː] n tissu m; (paper handkerchief) mouchoir m en papier, kleenex m ®; ~ **paper** n papier m de soie.

tit [tɪt] n (bird) mésange f; to give ~ for tat rendre coup pour coup.

titbit ['tɪtbɪt], (US) **tidbit** ['tɪdbɪt] n (food) friandise f; (news) potin m.

titivate ['tɪtɪveɪt] vt pomponner.

title ['taɪtl] n titre m; ~ **deed** n (LAW) titre (constitutif) de propriété; ~ **role** n rôle principal.

titter ['tɪtə*] vi rire (bêtement).

titular ['tɪtjulə*] a (in name only) nominal(e).

TM abbr of **trademark**.

to [tuː, tə] ♦ prep **1** (direction) à; to go ~ France/Portugal/London/school aller en France/au Portugal/à Londres/à l'école; to go ~ Claude's/the doctor's aller chez Claude/le docteur; the road ~

Edinburgh la route d'Édimbourg
2 (*as far as*) (jusqu')à; **to count** ~ **10**
compter jusqu'à 10; **from 40** ~ **50 people**
de 40 à 50 personnes
3 (*with expressions of time*): **a quarter**
~ **5** 5 heures moins le quart; **it's twenty**
~ **3** il est 3 heures moins vingt
4 (*for, of*) de; **the key** ~ **the front door**
la clé de la porte d'entrée; **a letter** ~ **his**
wife une lettre (adressée) à sa femme
5 (*expressing indirect object*) à; **to give**
sth ~ **sb** donner qch à qn; **to talk** ~ **sb**
parler à qn
6 (*in relation to*) à; **3 goals** ~ **2** 3 (buts)
à 2; **30 miles** ~ **the gallon** ≈ 9,4 litres
aux cent (km)
7 (*purpose, result*): **to come** ~ **sb's aid**
venir au secours de qn, porter secours à
qn; **to sentence sb** ~ **death** condamner
qn à mort; ~ **my surprise** à ma grande
surprise
♦ *with vb* **1** (*simple infinitive*): ~ **go/eat**
aller/manger
2 (*following another vb*): **to want/try/**
start ~ **do** vouloir/essayer de/
commencer à faire; *see also relevant*
verb
3 (*with vb omitted*): **I don't want** ~ je
ne veux pas
4 (*purpose, result*) pour; **I did it** ~ **help**
you je l'ai fait pour vous aider
5 (*equivalent to relative clause*): **I have**
things ~ **do** j'ai des choses à faire; **the**
main thing is ~ **try** l'important est
d'essayer
6 (*after adjective etc*): **ready** ~ **go**
prêt(e) à partir; **too old/young** ~ **...** trop
vieux/jeune pour ...; *see also*
relevant adjective etc
♦ *ad*: **push/pull the door** ~ tirez/poussez
la porte.

toad [təud] *n* crapaud *m*; ~**stool** *n*
champignon (vénéneux).

toast [təust] *n* (*CULIN*) pain grillé, toast
m; (*drink, speech*) toast // *vt* (*CULIN*)
faire griller; (*drink to*) porter un toast
à; **a piece** *or* **slice of** ~ un toast; ~**er** *n*
grille-pain *m inv*.

tobacco [tə'bækəu] *n* tabac *m*; ~**nist** *n*
marchand/e de tabac; ~**nist's (shop)** *n*
(bureau *m* de) tabac *m*.

toboggan [tə'bɔgən] *n* toboggan *m*;
(*child's*) luge *f*.

today [tə'deɪ] *ad*, *n* (*also fig*)
aujourd'hui *(m)*.

toddler ['tɔdlə*] *n* enfant *m/f* qui
commence à marcher, bambin *m*.

toddy ['tɔdɪ] *n* grog *m*.

to-do [tə'du:] *n* (*fuss*) histoire *f*, affaire
f.

toe [təu] *n* doigt *m* de pied, orteil *m*; (*of*
shoe) bout *m*; **to** ~ **the line** (*fig*) obéir,
se conformer.

toffee ['tɔfɪ] *n* caramel *m*.

toga ['təugə] *n* toge *f*.

together [tə'geðə*] *ad* ensemble; (*at*
same time) en même temps; ~ **with**
prep avec.

toil [tɔɪl] *n* dur travail, labeur *m*.

toilet ['tɔɪlət] *n* (*Brit: lavatory*) toilettes
fpl, cabinets *mpl* // *cpd* (*bag, soap etc*)
de toilette; ~ **bowl** *n* cuvette *f* des
w.-c.; ~ **paper** *n* papier *m* hygiénique;
~**ries** *npl* articles *mpl* de toilette; ~
roll *n* rouleau *m* de papier hygiénique;
~ **water** *n* eau *f* de toilette.

token ['təukən] *n* (*sign*) marque *f*, témoignage *m*; (*voucher*) bon *m*, coupon
m; **book/record** ~ *n* (*Brit*) chèque-
livre/-disque *m*.

told [təuld] *pt, pp of* **tell**.

tolerable ['tɔlərəbl] *a* (*bearable*) tolérable; (*fairly good*) passable.

tolerant ['tɔlərnt] *a*: ~ (**of**) tolérant(e)
(à l'égard de).

tolerate ['tɔləreɪt] *vt* supporter; (*MED,*
TECH) tolérer.

toll [təul] *n* (*tax, charge*) péage *m* // *vi*
(*bell*) sonner; **the accident** ~ **on the**
roads le nombre des victimes de la
route.

tomato, ~**es** [tə'mɑ:təu] *n* tomate *f*.

tomb [tu:m] *n* tombe *f*.

tomboy ['tɔmbɔɪ] *n* garçon manqué.

tombstone ['tu:mstəun] *n* pierre
tombale.

tomcat ['tɔmkæt] *n* matou *m*.

tomorrow [tə'mɔrəu] *ad*, *n* (*also fig*)
demain *(m)*; **the day after** ~ après-
demain; **a week** ~ demain en huit; ~
morning demain matin.

ton [tʌn] *n* tonne *f* (*Brit* = 1016 kg; *US* =
907 kg; *metric* = 1000 kg); (*NAUT: also:*
register ~) tonneau *m* (= 2.83 cu.m); ~**s**
of (*col*) des tas de.

tone [təun] *n* ton *m*; (*of radio*) tonalité *f*
// *vi* s'harmoniser; **to** ~ **down** *vt*
(*colour, criticism*) adoucir; (*sound*)
baisser; **to** ~ **up** *vt* (*muscles*) tonifier;
~-**deaf** *a* qui n'a pas d'oreille.

tongs [tɔŋz] *npl* pinces *fpl*; (*for coal*)
pincettes *fpl*; (*for hair*) fer *m* à friser.

tongue [tʌŋ] *n* langue *f*; ~ **in cheek** *ad*
ironiquement; ~-**tied** *a* (*fig*) muet(te);
~-**twister** *n* phrase *f* très difficile à
prononcer.

tonic ['tɔnɪk] *n* (*MED*) tonique *m*; (*also:*
~ **water**) tonic *m*.

tonight [tə'naɪt] *ad*, *n* cette nuit; (*this*
evening) ce soir.

tonsil ['tɔnsl] *n* amygdale *f*; ~**litis**
[-'laɪtɪs] *n* amygdalite *f*.

too [tu:] *ad* (*excessively*) trop; (*also*)
aussi; ~ **much** *ad* trop // *a* trop de; ~
many *a* trop de; ~ **bad!** tant pis!

took [tuk] *pt of* **take**.

tool [tu:l] *n* outil *m* // *vt* travailler,
ouvrager; ~ **box** *n* boîte *f* à outils.

toot [tu:t] *vi* siffler; (*with car-horn*)
klaxonner.

tooth [tu:θ], *pl* **teeth** *n* (*ANAT TECH*), dent *f*; ~**ache** *n* mal *m* de dents; ~**brush** *n* brosse *f* à dents; ~**paste** *n* (pâte *f*) dentifrice *m*; ~**pick** *n* cure-dent *m*.

top [tɔp] *n* (*of mountain, head*) sommet *m*; (*of page, ladder*) haut *m*; (*of box, cupboard, table*) dessus *m*; (*lid: of box, jar*) couvercle *m*; (*: of bottle*) bouchon *m*; (*toy*) toupie *f* // *a* du haut; (*in rank*) premier(ère); (*best*) meilleur(e) // *vt* (*exceed*) dépasser; (*be first in*) être en tête de; **on ~ of** sur; (*in addition to*) en plus de; **from ~ to bottom** de fond en comble; **to ~ up**, (*US*) **to ~ off** *vt* remplir; ~ **floor** *n* dernier étage; ~ **hat** *n* haut-de-forme *m*; ~-**heavy** *a* (*object*) trop lourd(e) du haut.

topic ['tɔpɪk] *n* sujet *m*, thème *m*; ~**al** *a* d'actualité.

top: ~**less** *a* (*bather etc*) aux seins nus; ~-**level** *a* (*talks*) à l'échelon le plus élevé.

topple ['tɔpl] *vt* renverser, faire tomber // *vi* basculer; tomber.

top-secret ['tɔp'si:krɪt] *a* ultra-secret(ète).

topsy-turvy ['tɔpsi'tə:vɪ] *a*, *ad* sens dessus-dessous.

torch [tɔ:tʃ] *n* torche *f*; (*Brit: electric*) lampe *f* de poche.

tore [tɔ:*] *pt of* **tear**.

torment *n* ['tɔ:mɛnt] tourment *m* // *vt* [tɔ:'mɛnt] tourmenter; (*fig: annoy*) agacer.

torn [tɔ:n] *pp of* **tear**.

tornado, ~**es** [tɔ:'neɪdəu] *n* tornade *f*.

torpedo, ~**es** [tɔ:'pi:dəu] *n* torpille *f*.

torrent ['tɔrnt] *n* torrent *m*.

tortoise ['tɔ:təs] *n* tortue *f*; ~**shell** ['tɔ:təʃɛl] *a* en écaille.

torture ['tɔ:tʃə*] *n* torture *f* // *vt* torturer.

Tory ['tɔ:rɪ] (*Brit POL*) *a* tory (*pl* tories), conservateur(trice) // *n* tory *m/f*, conservateur/trice.

toss [tɔs] *vt* lancer, jeter; (*pancake*) faire sauter; (*head*) rejeter en arrière; **to ~ a coin** jouer à pile ou face; **to ~ up for sth** jouer qch à pile ou face; **to ~ and turn** (*in bed*) se tourner et se retourner.

tot [tɔt] *n* (*Brit: drink*) petit verre; (*child*) bambin *m*.

total ['təutl] *a* total(e) // *n* total *m* // *vt* (*add up*) faire le total de, totaliser; (*amount to*) s'élever à.

totally ['təutəlɪ] *ad* totalement.

totter ['tɔtə*] *vi* chanceler.

touch [tʌtʃ] *n* contact *m*, toucher *m*; (*sense, also skill: of pianist etc*) toucher; (*fig: note, also FOOTBALL*) touche *f* // *vt* (*gen*) toucher; (*tamper with*) toucher à; **a ~ of** (*fig*) un petit peu de; **in ~ with** en contact *or* rapport avec; **to get in ~ with** prendre contact

avec; **to lose ~** (*friends*) se perdre de vue; **to ~ on** *vt fus* (*topic*) effleurer, toucher; **to ~ up** *vt* (*paint*) retoucher; ~-**and-go** *a* incertain(e); ~**down** *n* atterrissage *m*; (*on sea*) amerrissage *m*; (*US FOOTBALL*) but *m*; ~**ed** *a* touché(e); (*col*) cinglé(e); ~**ing** *a* touchant(e), attendrissant(e); ~**line** *n* (*SPORT*) (ligne *f* de) touche *f*; ~**y** *a* (*person*) susceptible.

tough [tʌf] *a* dur(e); (*resistant*) résistant(e), solide; (*meat*) dur, coriace.

toupee ['tu:peɪ] *n* postiche *m*.

tour ['tuə*] *n* voyage *m*; (*also:* **package** ~) voyage organisé; (*of town, museum*) tour *m*, visite *f*; (*by artist*) tournée *f* // *vt* visiter; ~**ing** *n* voyages *mpl* touristiques, tourisme *m*.

tourism ['tuərɪzm] *n* tourisme *m*.

tourist ['tuərɪst] *n* touriste *m/f* // *ad* (*travel*) en classe touriste // *cpd* touristique; ~ **office** *n* syndicat *m* d'initiative.

tournament ['tuənəmənt] *n* tournoi *m*.

tousled ['tauzld] *a* (*hair*) ébouriffé(e).

tout [taut] *vi*: **to ~ for** essayer de raccrocher, racoler // *n* (*also:* **ticket** ~) revendeur *m* de billets.

tow [təu] *vt* remorquer; **'on ~'**, (*US*) **'in ~'** (*AUT*) 'véhicule en remorque'.

toward(s) [tə'wɔ:d(z)] *prep* vers; (*of attitude*) envers, à l'égard de; (*of purpose*) pour.

towel ['tauəl] *n* serviette *f* (de toilette); (*also:* **tea** ~) torchon *m*; ~**ling** *n* (*fabric*) tissu-éponge *m*; ~ **rail**, (*US*) ~ **rack** *n* porte-serviettes *m inv*.

tower ['tauə*] *n* tour *f*; ~ **block** *n* (*Brit*) tour *f* (d'habitation); ~**ing** *a* très haut(e), imposant(e).

town [taun] *n* ville *f*; **to go to ~** aller en ville; (*fig*) y mettre le paquet; ~ **centre** *n* centre *m* de la ville, centre-ville *m*; ~ **clerk** *n* ≈ secrétaire *m/f* de mairie; ~ **council** *n* conseil municipal; ~ **hall** *n* ≈ mairie *f*; ~ **plan** *n* plan *m* de ville; ~ **planning** *n* urbanisme *m*.

towrope ['təurəup] *n* (câble *m* de) remorque *f*.

tow truck *n* (*US*) dépanneuse *f*.

toy [tɔɪ] *n* jouet *m*; **to ~ with** *vt fus* jouer avec; (*idea*) caresser.

trace [treɪs] *n* trace *f* // *vt* (*draw*) tracer, dessiner; (*follow*) suivre la trace de; (*locate*) retrouver; **tracing paper** *n* papier-calque *m*.

track [træk] *n* (*mark*) trace *f*; (*path: gen*) chemin *m*, piste *f*; (*: of bullet etc*) trajectoire *f*; (*: of suspect, animal*) piste; (*RAIL*) voie ferrée, rails *mpl*; (*on tape, SPORT*) piste; (*on record*) plage *f* // *vt* suivre la trace *or* la piste de; **to keep ~ of** suivre; **to ~ down** *vt* (*prey*) trouver et capturer; (*sth lost*) finir par retrouver; ~**suit** *n* survêtement *m*.

tract [trækt] n (GEO) étendue f, zone f; (pamphlet) tract m.

tractor ['træktə*] n tracteur m.

trade [treɪd] n commerce m; (skill, job) métier m // vi faire du commerce; **to ~ with/in** faire du commerce avec/le commerce de; **to ~ in** vt (old car etc) faire reprendre; **~ fair** n foire (-exposition) commerciale; **~-in price** n prix m à la reprise; **~mark** n marque f de fabrique; **~name** n marque déposée; **~r** n commerçant/e, négociant/e; **~sman** (shopkeeper) commerçant; **~ union** n syndicat m; **~ unionist** n syndicaliste m/f; **trading** n affaires fpl, commerce m; **trading estate** n (Brit) zone industrielle.

tradition [trə'dɪʃən] n tradition f; **~al** a traditionnel(le).

traffic ['træfɪk] n trafic m; (cars) circulation f // vi: **to ~ in** (pej: liquor, drugs) faire le trafic de; **~ circle** n (US) rond-point m; **~ jam** n embouteillage m; **~ lights** npl feux mpl (de signalisation); **~ warden** n contractuel/le.

tragedy ['trædʒədɪ] n tragédie f.

tragic ['trædʒɪk] a tragique.

trail [treɪl] n (tracks) trace f, piste f; (path) chemin m, piste; (of smoke etc) traînée f // vt traîner, tirer; (follow) suivre // vi traîner; **to ~ behind** vi traîner, être à la traîne; **~er** n (AUT) remorque f; (US) caravane f; (CINEMA) bande-annonce f; **~er truck** n (US) (camion m) semi-remorque m.

train [treɪn] n train m; (in underground) rame f; (of dress) traîne f // vt (apprentice, doctor etc) former; (sportsman) entraîner; (dog) dresser; (memory) exercer; (point: gun etc): **to ~ sth on** braquer qch sur // vi recevoir sa formation; s'entraîner; **one's ~ of thought** le fil de sa pensée; **~ed** a qualifié(e), qui a reçu une formation; dressé(e); **~ee** [treɪ'niː] n stagiaire m/f; (in trade) apprenti/e; **~er** n (SPORT) entraîneur/euse; (of dogs etc) dresseur/euse; **~ing** n formation f; entraînement m; dressage m; **in ~ing** (SPORT) à l'entraînement; (fit) en forme; **~ing college** n école professionnelle; (for teachers) ≈ école normale; **~ing shoes** npl chaussures fpl de sport.

traipse [treɪps] vi (se) traîner, déambuler.

trait [treɪt] n trait m (de caractère).

traitor ['treɪtə*] n traître m.

tram [træm] n (Brit: also: **~car**) tram(way) m.

tramp [træmp] n (person) vagabond/e, clochard/e; (col: pej: woman): **to be a ~** être coureuse // vi marcher d'un pas lourd // vt (walk through: town, streets) parcourir à pied.

trample ['træmpl] vt: **to ~ (underfoot)** piétiner; (fig) bafouer.

trampoline ['træmpəliːn] n trampolino m.

tranquil ['træŋkwɪl] a tranquille; **~lizer** n (MED) tranquillisant m.

transact [træn'zækt] vt (business) traiter; **~ion** [-'zækʃən] n transaction f; **~ions** npl (minutes) actes mpl.

transatlantic ['trænzət'læntɪk] a transatlantique.

transfer n ['trænsfə*] (gen, also SPORT) transfert m; (POL: of power) passation f; (picture, design) décalcomanie f; (: stick-on) autocollant m // vt [træns'fə:*] transférer; passer; décalquer.

transform [træns'fɔːm] vt transformer.

transfusion [træns'fjuːʒən] n transfusion f.

transient ['trænzɪənt] a transitoire, éphémère.

transistor [træn'zɪstə*] n (ELEC; also: **~ radio**) transistor m.

transit ['trænzɪt] n: **in ~** en transit.

transitive ['trænzɪtɪv] a (LING) transitif(ive).

translate [trænz'leɪt] vt traduire; **translation** [-'leɪʃən] n traduction f; (SCOL: as opposed to prose) version f; **translator** n traducteur/trice.

transmission [trænz'mɪʃən] n transmission f.

transmit [trænz'mɪt] vt transmettre; (RADIO, TV) émettre; **~ter** n émetteur m.

transparency [træns'pɛərnsɪ] n (Brit PHOT) diapositive f.

transparent [træns'pærnt] a transparent(e).

transpire [træn'spaɪə*] vi (turn out): **it ~d that ...** on a appris que ...; (happen) arriver.

transplant vt [træns'plɑːnt] transplanter; (seedlings) repiquer // n ['trænsplɑːnt] (MED) transplantation f.

transport n ['trænspɔːt] transport m // vt [træns'pɔːt] transporter; **~ation** [-'teɪʃən] n (moyen m de) transport m; (of prisoners) transportation f; **~ café** n (Brit) ≈ restaurant m de routiers.

trap [træp] n (snare, trick) piège m; (carriage) cabriolet m // vt prendre au piège; (immobilize) bloquer; (jam) coincer; **~ door** n trappe f.

trapeze [trə'piːz] n trapèze m.

trappings ['træpɪŋz] npl ornements mpl; attributs mpl.

trash [træʃ] n (pej: goods) camelote f; (: nonsense) sottises fpl; **~ can** n (US) boîte f à ordures.

trauma ['trɔːmə] n traumatisme m; **~tic** [-'mætɪk] a traumatisant(e).

travel ['trævl] n voyage m, voyage(s) m(pl) // vi voyager; (move) aller, se déplacer // vt (distance) parcourir; **~ agency** n agence *f* de voyages; ~ **agent** *n* agent *m* de voyages; ~**ler**, *(US)* ~**er** *n* voyageur/euse; ~**ler's cheque** *n* chèque *m* de voyage; ~**ling**, *(US)* ~**ing** *n* voyage(s) *m(pl)* // *cpd (bag, clock)* de voyage; *(expenses)* de déplacement; ~ **sickness** *n* mal *m* de la route *(or* de mer *or* de l'air).

travesty ['trævəstɪ] *n* parodie *f*.

trawler ['trɔːlə*] *n* chalutier *m*.

tray [treɪ] *n (for carrying)* plateau *m*; *(on desk)* corbeille *f*.

treachery ['tretʃərɪ] *n* traîtrise *f*.

treacle ['triːkl] *n* mélasse *f*.

tread [trɛd] *n* pas *m*; *(sound)* bruit *m* de pas; *(of tyre)* chape *f*, bande *f* de roulement // *vi (pt* trod, *pp* trodden) marcher; **to ~ on** *vi fus* marcher sur.

treason ['triːzn] *n* trahison *f*.

treasure ['trɛʒə*] *n* trésor *m* // *vt (value)* tenir beaucoup à; *(store)* conserver précieusement.

treasurer ['trɛʒərə*] *n* trésorier/ère.

treasury ['trɛʒərɪ] *n* trésorerie *f*; the T~, *(US)* the T~ **Department** le ministère des Finances.

treat [triːt] *n* petit cadeau, petite surprise // *vt* traiter; **to ~ sb to sth** offrir qch à qn.

treatise ['triːtɪz] *n* traité *m (ouvrage)*.

treatment ['triːtmənt] *n* traitement *m*.

treaty ['triːtɪ] *n* traité *m*.

treble ['trɛbl] *a* triple // *vt, vi* tripler; ~ **clef** *n* clé *f* de sol.

tree [triː] *n* arbre *m*.

trek [trɛk] *n* voyage *m*; randonnée *f*; *(tiring walk)* tirée *f* // *vi (as holiday)* faire de la randonnée.

tremble ['trɛmbl] *vi* trembler.

tremendous [trɪ'mɛndəs] *a (enormous)* énorme, fantastique; *(excellent)* formidable.

tremor ['trɛmə*] *n* tremblement *m*; *(also:* **earth** ~) secousse *f* sismique.

trench [trɛntʃ] *n* tranchée *f*.

trend [trɛnd] *n (tendency)* tendance *f*; *(of events)* cours *m*; *(fashion)* mode *f*; ~**y** *a (idea)* dans le vent; *(clothes)* dernier cri *inv*.

trepidation [trɛpɪ'deɪʃən] *n* vive agitation.

trespass ['trɛspəs] *vi:* **to ~ on** s'introduire sans permission dans; *(fig)* empiéter sur; **'no** ~**ing'** 'propriété privée', 'défense d'entrer'.

tress [trɛs] *n* boucle *f* de cheveux.

trestle ['trɛsl] *n* tréteau *m*; ~ **table** *n* table *f* à tréteaux.

trial ['traɪəl] *n (LAW)* procès *m*, jugement *m*; *(test: of machine etc)* essai *m*; *(hardship)* épreuve *f*; *(worry)* souci *m*; **by ~ and error** par tâtonnements.

triangle ['traɪæŋgl] *n (MATH, MUS)* triangle *m*.

tribe [traɪb] *n* tribu *f*.

tribunal [traɪ'bjuːnl] *n* tribunal *m*.

tributary ['trɪbjuːtərɪ] *n (river)* affluent *m*.

tribute ['trɪbjuːt] *n* tribut *m*, hommage *m*; **to pay ~** rendre hommage à.

trice [traɪs] *n:* **in a ~** en un clin d'œil.

trick [trɪk] *n (clever act)* astuce *f*; *(joke)* tour *m*; *(CARDS)* levée *f* // *vt* attraper, rouler; **to play a ~ on sb** jouer un tour à qn; **that should do the ~** ça devrait faire l'affaire; ~**ery** *n* ruse *f*.

trickle ['trɪkl] *n (of water etc)* filet *m* // *vi* couler en un filet *or* goutte à goutte.

tricky ['trɪkɪ] *a* difficile, délicat(e).

tricycle ['traɪsɪkl] *n* tricycle *m*.

trifle ['traɪfl] *n* bagatelle *f*; *(CULIN)* ≈ diplomate *m* // *ad:* **a ~ long** un peu long; **trifling** *a* insignifiant(e).

trigger ['trɪgə*] *n (of gun)* gâchette *f*; **to ~ off** *vt* déclencher.

trim [trɪm] *a (house, garden)* bien tenu(e); *(figure)* svelte // *n (haircut etc)* légère coupe; *(embellishment)* finitions *fpl*; *(on car)* garnitures *fpl* // *vt* couper légèrement; *(decorate):* **to ~ (with)** décorer (de); *(NAUT: a sail)* gréer; ~**mings** *npl* décorations *fpl*; *(extras: gen CULIN)* garniture *f*.

trinket ['trɪŋkɪt] *n* bibelot *m*; *(piece of jewellery)* colifichet *m*.

trip [trɪp] *n* voyage *m*; *(excursion)* excursion *f*; *(stumble)* faux pas // *vi (stumble)* faire un faux pas, trébucher; *(go lightly)* marcher d'un pas léger; **on a ~** en voyage; **to ~ up** *vi* trébucher // *vt* faire un croc-en-jambe à.

tripe [traɪp] *n (CULIN)* tripes *fpl*; *(pej: rubbish)* idioties *fpl*.

triple ['trɪpl] *a* triple.

triplets ['trɪplɪts] *npl* triplés/ées.

tripod ['traɪpɔd] *n* trépied *m*.

trite [traɪt] *a* banal(e).

triumph ['traɪʌmf] *n* triomphe *m* // *vi:* **to ~ (over)** triompher (de).

trivia ['trɪvɪə] *npl* futilités *fpl*.

trivial ['trɪvɪəl] *a* insignifiant(e); *(commonplace)* banal(e).

trod [trɔd] *pt of* **tread**; ~**den** *pp of* **tread**.

trolley ['trɔlɪ] *n* chariot *m*.

trombone [trɔm'bəun] *n* trombone *m*.

troop [truːp] *n* bande *f*, groupe *m*; ~**s** *npl (MIL)* troupes *fpl*; (: *men)* hommes *mpl*, soldats *mpl*; **to ~ in/out** *vi* entrer/sortir en groupe; ~**er** *n (MIL)* soldat *m* de cavalerie; ~**ing the colour** *n (ceremony)* le salut au drapeau.

trophy ['trəufɪ] *n* trophée *m*.

tropic ['trɔpɪk] *n* tropique *m*; ~**al** *a* tropical(e).

trot [trɔt] *n* trot *m* // *vi* trotter; **on the ~** *(Brit fig)* d'affilée.

trouble ['trʌbl] *n* difficulté(s) *f(pl)*, problème(s) *m(pl)*; *(worry)* ennuis *mpl*, soucis *mpl*; *(bother, effort)* peine *f*;

(POL) conflits mpl, troubles mpl; (MED): **stomach** etc ~ troubles gastriques etc // vt déranger, gêner; (worry) inquiéter // vi: to ~ to do prendre la peine de faire; ~s npl (POL etc) troubles mpl; to be in ~ avoir des ennuis; (ship, climber etc) être en difficulté; it's no ~! je vous en prie!; what's the ~? qu'est-ce qui ne va pas?; ~d a (person) inquiet(ète); (epoch, life) agité(e); **~maker** n élément perturbateur, fauteur m de troubles; **~shooter** n (in conflict) conciliateur m; **~some** a ennuyeux(euse), gênant(e).

trough [trɔf] n (also: **drinking ~**) abreuvoir m; (also: **feeding ~**) auge f; (channel) chenal m.

trousers ['trauzəz] npl pantalon m; **short ~** culottes courtes.

trout [traut] n (pl inv) truite f.

trowel ['trauəl] n truelle f.

truant ['truənt] n: to play ~ (Brit) faire l'école buissonnière.

truce [tru:s] n trêve f.

truck [trʌk] n camion m; (RAIL) wagon m à plate-forme; (for luggage) chariot m (à bagages); ~ **driver** n camionneur m; ~ **farm** n (US) jardin maraîcher.

truculent ['trʌkjulənt] a agressif(ive).

trudge [trʌdʒ] vi marcher lourdement, se traîner.

true [tru:] a vrai(e); (accurate) exact(e); (genuine) vrai, véritable; (faithful) fidèle.

truffle ['trʌfl] n truffe f.

truly ['tru:lɪ] ad vraiment, réellement; (truthfully) sans mentir; (faithfully) fidèlement.

trump [trʌmp] n atout m; ~**ed-up** a inventé(e) (de toutes pièces).

trumpet ['trʌmpɪt] n trompette f.

truncheon ['trʌntʃən] n bâton m (d'agent de police); matraque f.

trundle ['trʌndl] vt, vi: to ~ along rouler bruyamment.

trunk [trʌŋk] n (of tree, person) tronc m; (of elephant) trompe f; (case) malle f; (US AUT) coffre m; ~s npl (also: **swimming ~s**) maillot m or slip m de bain.

truss [trʌs] n (MED) bandage m herniaire; to ~ (up) vt (CULIN) brider.

trust [trʌst] n confiance f; (LAW) fidéicommis m; (COMM) trust m // vt (rely on) avoir confiance en; (entrust): to ~ sth to sb confier qch à qn; ~**ed** a en qui l'on a confiance; ~**ee** [trʌs'ti:] n (LAW) fidéicommissaire m/f; (of school etc) administrateur/trice; ~**ful**, ~**ing** a confiant(e); ~**worthy** a digne de confiance.

truth, ~**s** [tru:θ, tru:ðz] n vérité f; ~**ful** a (person) qui dit la vérité; (description) exact(e), vrai(e).

try [traɪ] n essai m, tentative f; (RUGBY)

essai // vt (LAW) juger; (test: sth new) essayer, tester; (strain) éprouver // vi essayer; to ~ to do essayer de faire; (seek) chercher à faire; to ~ on vt (clothes) essayer; **to ~ out** vt essayer, mettre à l'essai; ~**ing** a pénible.

T-shirt ['ti:ʃə:t] n tee-shirt m.

T-square ['ti:skweə*] n équerre f en T.

tub [tʌb] n cuve f; baquet m; (bath) baignoire f.

tuba ['tju:bə] n tuba m.

tubby ['tʌbɪ] a rondelet(te).

tube [tju:b] n tube m; (Brit: underground) métro m; (for tyre) chambre f à air.

tubing ['tju:bɪŋ] n tubes mpl; **a piece of ~** un tube.

TUC n abbr (Brit: = Trades Union Congress) confédération f des syndicats britanniques.

tuck [tʌk] n (SEWING) pli m, rempli m // vt (put) mettre; **to ~ away** vt cacher, ranger; **to ~ in** vt rentrer; (child) border // (eat) manger de bon appétit; attaquer le repas; **to ~ up** vt (child) border; ~ **shop** n boutique f à provisions (dans une école).

Tuesday ['tju:zdɪ] n mardi m.

tuft [tʌft] n touffe f.

tug [tʌg] n (ship) remorqueur m // vt tirer (sur); ~-**of-war** n lutte f à la corde.

tuition [tju:'ɪʃən] n (Brit) leçons fpl; (: private ~) cours particuliers; (US: school fees) frais mpl de scolarité.

tulip ['tju:lɪp] n tulipe f.

tumble ['tʌmbl] n (fall) chute f, culbute f // vi tomber, dégringoler; (with somersault) faire une or des culbute(s); to ~ to sth (col) réaliser qch; ~**down** a délabré(e); ~ **dryer** n (Brit) séchoir m (à linge) à air chaud.

tumbler ['tʌmblə*] n verre (droit), gobelet m.

tummy ['tʌmɪ] n (col) ventre m.

tumour, (US) **tumor** ['tju:mə*] n tumeur f.

tuna ['tju:nə] n (pl inv) (also: ~ **fish**) thon m.

tune [tju:n] n (melody) air m // vt (MUS) accorder; (RADIO, TV, AUT) régler, mettre au point; to be in/out of ~ (instrument) être accordé/désaccordé; (singer) chanter juste/faux; **to ~ in (to)** (RADIO, TV) se mettre à l'écoute (de); **to ~ up** vi (musician) accorder son instrument; ~**ful** a mélodieux(euse).

tunic ['tju:nɪk] n tunique f.

tuning ['tju:nɪŋ] n réglage m; ~ **fork** n diapason m.

Tunisia [tju:'nɪzɪə] n Tunisie f.

tunnel ['tʌnl] n tunnel m; (in mine) galerie f.

turbulence ['tə:bjuləns] n (AVIAT) turbulence f.

tureen [tə'ri:n] *n* soupière *f*.

turf [tə:f] *n* gazon *m*; (*clod*) motte *f* (de gazon) // *vt* gazonner; **to ~ out** *vt* (*col*) jeter; jeter dehors.

turgid ['tə:dʒɪd] *a* (*speech*) pompeux(euse).

Turk [tə:k] *n* Turc/Turque.

Turkey ['tə:kɪ] *n* Turquie *f*.

turkey ['tə:kɪ] *n* dindon *m*, dinde *f*.

Turkish ['tə:kɪʃ] *a* turc(turque) // (*LING*) turc *m*.

turmoil ['tə:mɔɪl] *n* trouble *m*, bouleversement *m*.

turn [tə:n] *n* tour *m*; (*in road*) tournant *m*; (*tendency: of mind, events*) tournure *f*; (*performance*) numéro *m*; (*MED*) crise *f*, attaque *f* // *vt* tourner; (*collar, steak*) retourner; (*milk*) faire tourner; (*change*): **to ~ sth into** changer qch en // *vi* tourner; (*person: look back*) se (re)tourner; (*reverse direction*) faire demi-tour; (*change*) changer; (*become*) devenir; **to ~ into** se changer en; **a good ~** un service; **it gave me quite a ~** ça m'a fait un coup; '**no left ~**' (*AUT*) 'défense de tourner à gauche'; **it's your ~** c'est (à) votre tour; **in ~** à son tour; **à tour de rôle**; **to take ~s** se relayer; **to take ~s at** faire à tour de rôle; **to ~ away** *vi* se détourner, tourner la tête; **to ~ back** *vi* revenir, faire demi-tour; **to ~ down** *vt* (*refuse*) rejeter, refuser; (*reduce*) baisser; (*fold*) rabattre; **to ~ in** *vi* (*col: go to bed*) aller se coucher // *vt* (*fold*) rentrer; **to ~ off** *vi* (*from road*) tourner // *vt* (*light, radio etc*) éteindre; (*engine*) arrêter; **to ~ on** *vt* (*light, radio etc*) allumer; (*engine*) mettre en marche; **to ~ out** *vt* (*light, gas*) éteindre // *vi*: **to ~ out to be ...** s'avérer ..., se révéler ...; **to ~ over** *vi* (*person*) se retourner // *vt* (*object*) retourner; (*page*) tourner; **to ~ round** *vi* faire demi-tour; (*rotate*) tourner; **to ~ up** (*person*) arriver, se pointer; (*lost object*) être retrouvé(e) // *vt* (*collar*) remonter; (*increase: sound, volume etc*) mettre plus fort; **~ing** *n* (*in road*) tournant *m*; **~ing point** *n* (*fig*) tournant *m*, moment décisif.

turnip ['tə:nɪp] *n* navet *m*.

turnout ['tə:naut] *n* (nombre *m* de personnes dans l')assistance *f*.

turnover ['tə:nəuvə*] *n* (*COMM: amount of money*) chiffre *m* d'affaires; (: *of goods*) roulement *m*; (*CULIN*) sorte de chausson.

turnpike ['tə:npaɪk] *n* (*US*) autoroute *f* à péage.

turnstile ['tə:nstaɪl] *n* tourniquet *m* (d'entrée).

turntable ['tə:nteɪbl] *n* (*on record player*) platine *f*.

turn-up ['tə:nʌp] *n* (*Brit: on trousers*) revers *m*.

turpentine ['tə:pəntaɪn] *n* (*also*: **turps**) (essence *f* de) térébenthine *f*.

turquoise ['tə:kwɔɪz] *n* (*stone*) turquoise *f* // *a* turquoise *inv*.

turret ['tʌrɪt] *n* tourelle *f*.

turtle ['tə:tl] *n* tortue marine; **~neck (sweater)** *n* pullover *m* à col montant.

tusk [tʌsk] *n* défense *f*.

tussle ['tʌsl] *n* bagarre *f*, mêlée *f*.

tutor ['tju:tə*] *n* (*in college*) directeur/trice d'études; (*private teacher*) précepteur/trice; **~ial** [-'tɔ:rɪəl] *n* (*SCOL*) (séance *f* de) travaux *mpl* pratiques.

tuxedo [tʌk'si:dəu] *n* (*US*) smoking *m*.

TV [ti:'vi:] *n abbr* (= *television*) télé *f*.

twang [twæŋ] *n* (*of instrument*) son vibrant; (*of voice*) ton nasillard.

tweed [twi:d] *n* tweed *m*.

tweezers ['twi:zəz] *npl* pince *f* à épiler.

twelfth [twelfθ] *num* douzième.

twelve [twelv] *num* douze; **at ~** (*o'clock*) à midi; (*midnight*) à minuit.

twentieth ['twentɪɪθ] *num* vingtième.

twenty ['twentɪ] *num* vingt.

twice [twaɪs] *ad* deux fois; **~ as much** deux fois plus.

twiddle ['twɪdl] *vt, vi*: **to ~ (with) sth** tripoter qch; **to ~ one's thumbs** (*fig*) se tourner les pouces.

twig [twɪg] *n* brindille *f* // *vt, vi* (*col*) piger.

twilight ['twaɪlaɪt] *n* crépuscule *m*.

twin [twɪn] *a, n* jumeau(elle) // *vt* jumeler; **~(-bedded) room** *n* chambre *f* à deux lits.

twine [twaɪn] *n* ficelle *f* // *vi* (*plant*) s'enrouler.

twinge [twɪndʒ] *n* (*of pain*) élancement *m*; (*of conscience*) remords *m*.

twinkle ['twɪŋkl] *vi* scintiller; (*eyes*) pétiller.

twirl [twə:l] *vt* faire tournoyer // *vi* tournoyer.

twist [twɪst] *n* torsion *f*, tour *m*; (*in wire, flex*) tortillon *m*; (*in story*) coup *m* de théâtre // *vt* tordre; (*weave*) entortiller; (*roll around*) enrouler; (*fig*) déformer // *vi* s'entortiller; s'enrouler; (*road*) serpenter.

twit [twɪt] *n* (*col*) crétin/e.

twitch [twɪtʃ] *vi* se convulser; avoir un tic.

two [tu:] *num* deux; **to put ~ and ~ together** (*fig*) faire le rapport; **~-door** *a* (*AUT*) à deux portes; **~-faced** *a* (*pej: person*) faux(fausse); **~fold** *ad*: **to increase ~fold** doubler; **~-piece (suit)** *n* (*costume m*) deux-pièces *m inv*; **~-piece (swimsuit)** *n* (maillot *m* de bain) deux-pièces *m inv*; **~-seater** *n* (*plane*) (avion *m*) biplace *m*; (*car*) voiture *f* à deux places; **~some** *n* (*people*) couple *m*; **~-way** *a* (*traffic*) dans les deux sens.

tycoon [taɪ'ku:n] *n*: (*business*) ~ gros homme d'affaires.

type [taɪp] *n* (*category*) genre *m*, espèce *f*; (*model*) modèle *m*; (*example*) type *m*; (*TYP*) type, caractère *m* // *vt* (*letter etc*) taper (à la machine); **~-cast** *a* (*actor*) condamné(e) à toujours jouer le même rôle; **~face** *n* (*TYP*) police *f* (de caractères); **~script** *n* texte dactylographié; **~writer** *n* machine *f* à écrire; **~written** *a* dactylographié(e).

typhoid ['taɪfɔɪd] *n* typhoïde *f*.

typical ['tɪpɪkl] *a* typique, caractéristique.

typing ['taɪpɪŋ] *n* dactylo(graphie) *f*.

typist ['taɪpɪst] *n* dactylo *m/f*.

tyrant ['taɪərnt] *n* tyran *m*.

tyre, (*US*) **tire** ['taɪə*] *n* pneu *m*; **~ pressure** *n* pression *f* (de gonflage).

U

U-bend ['ju:'bɛnd] *n* (*AUT, in pipe*) coude *m*.

udder ['ʌdə*] *n* pis *m*, mamelle *f*.

UFO ['ju:fəu] *n abbr* (= *unidentified flying object*) ovni *m*.

Uganda [ju:'gændə] *n* Ouganda *m*.

ugh [ə:h] *excl* pouah!

ugly ['ʌglɪ] *a* laid(e), vilain(e); (*fig*) répugnant(e).

UK *n abbr see* **united**.

ulcer ['ʌlsə*] *n* ulcère *m*; (*also*: mouth ~) aphte *f*.

Ulster ['ʌlstə*] *n* Ulster *m*.

ulterior [ʌl'tɪərɪə*] *a* ultérieur(e); **~ motive** *n* arrière-pensée *f*.

ultimate ['ʌltɪmət] *a* ultime, final(e); (*authority*) suprême; **~ly** *ad* en fin de compte; finalement; par la suite.

ultrasound ['ʌltrəsaund] *n* (*MED*) ultrason *m*.

umbilical cord [ʌmbɪ'laɪkl-] *n* cordon ombilical.

umbrella [ʌm'brɛlə] *n* parapluie *m*.

umpire ['ʌmpaɪə*] *n* arbitre *m*.

umpteen [ʌmp'ti:n] *a* je ne sais combien de; **for the ~th time** pour la nième fois.

UN, UNO *n abbr of* **United Nations (Organization)**.

unable [ʌn'eɪbl] *a*: **to be ~ to** ne (pas) pouvoir, être dans l'impossibilité de; être incapable de.

unaccompanied [ʌnə'kʌmpənɪd] *a* (*child, lady*) non accompagné(e).

unaccountably [ʌnə'kauntəblɪ] *ad* inexplicablement.

unaccustomed [ʌnə'kʌstəmd] *a* inaccoutumé(e), inhabituel(le); **to be ~ to sth** ne pas avoir l'habitude de qch.

unanimous [ju:'nænɪməs] *a* unanime; **~ly** *ad* à l'unanimité.

unarmed [ʌn'ɑ:md] *a* (*without a*

weapon) non armé(e); (*combat*) sans armes.

unassuming [ʌnə'sju:mɪŋ] *a* modeste, sans prétentions.

unattached [ʌnə'tætʃt] *a* libre, sans attaches.

unattended [ʌnə'tɛndɪd] *a* (*car, child, luggage*) sans surveillance.

unauthorized [ʌn'ɔ:θəraɪzd] *a* non autorisé(e), sans autorisation.

unavoidable [ʌnə'vɔɪdəbl] *a* inévitable.

unaware [ʌnə'wɛə*] *a*: **to be ~ of** ignorer, ne pas savoir, être inconscient(e) de; **~s** *ad* à l'improviste, au dépourvu.

unbalanced [ʌn'bælənst] *a* déséquilibré(e).

unbearable [ʌn'bɛərəbl] *a* insupportable.

unbeknown(st) [ʌnbɪ'nəun(st)] *ad*: **~ to** à l'insu de.

unbelievable [ʌnbɪ'li:vəbl] *a* incroyable.

unbend [ʌn'bɛnd] *vb* (*irg*) *vi* se détendre // *vt* (*wire*) redresser, détordre.

unbias(s)ed [ʌn'baɪəst] *a* impartial(e).

unborn [ʌn'bɔ:n] *a* à naître.

unbreakable [ʌn'breɪkəbl] *a* incassable.

unbroken [ʌn'brəukən] *a* intact(e); continu(e).

unbutton [ʌn'bʌtn] *vt* déboutonner.

uncalled-for [ʌn'kɔ:ldfɔ:*] *a* déplacé(e), injustifié(e).

uncanny [ʌn'kænɪ] *a* étrange, troublant(e).

unceasing [ʌn'si:sɪŋ] *a* incessant(e), continu(e).

unceremonious [ʌnsɛrɪ'məunɪəs] *a* (*abrupt, rude*) brusque.

uncertain [ʌn'sə:tn] *a* incertain(e); mal assuré(e); **~ty** *n* incertitude *f*, doutes *mpl*.

unchecked [ʌn'tʃɛkt] *a* non réprimé(e).

uncivilized [ʌn'sɪvɪlaɪzd] *a* (*gen*) non civilisé(e); (*fig: behaviour etc*) barbare.

uncle ['ʌŋkl] *n* oncle *m*.

uncomfortable [ʌn'kʌmfətəbl] *a* inconfortable; (*uneasy*) mal à l'aise, gêné(e); désagréable.

uncommon [ʌn'kɔmən] *a* rare, singulier(ère), peu commun(e).

uncompromising [ʌn'kɔmprəmaɪzɪŋ] *a* intransigeant(e), inflexible.

unconcerned [ʌnkən'sə:nd] *a*: **to be ~** (*about*) ne pas s'inquiéter (de).

unconditional [ʌnkən'dɪʃənl] *a* sans conditions.

unconscious [ʌn'kɔnʃəs] *a* sans connaissance, évanoui(e); (*unaware*) inconscient(e) // *n*: **the ~** l'inconscient *m*; **~ly** *ad* inconsciemment, sans s'en rendre compte.

uncontrollable [ʌnkən'trəuləbl] *a* irrépressible; indiscipliné(e).

unconventional [ʌnkən'vɛnʃənl] *a*

non conventionnel (le).

uncouth [ʌn'ku:θ] *a* grossier(ère), fruste.

uncover [ʌn'kʌvə*] *vt* découvrir.

undecided [ʌndɪ'saɪdɪd] *a* indécis(e), irrésolu(e).

under ['ʌndə*] *prep* sous; *(less than)* (de) moins de; au-dessous de; *(according to)* selon, en vertu de // *ad* au-dessous; en dessous; from ~ sth de sous *or* de sous qch; ~ there là-dessous; ~ repair en (cours de) réparation.

under... ['ʌndə*] *prefix* sous-; ~-age *a* qui n'a pas l'âge réglementaire; ~carriage *n* (*Brit AVIAT*) train *m* d'atterrissage; ~charge *vt* ne pas faire payer assez à; ~coat *n* (*paint*) couche *f* de fond; ~cover *a* secret(ète), clandestin(e); ~current *n* courant sous-jacent; ~cut *vt irg* vendre moins cher que; ~developed *a* sous-développé(e); ~done *a* (*CULIN*) saignant(e); (*pej*) pas assez cuit(e); ~estimate *vt* sous-estimer, mésestimer; ~fed *a* sous-alimenté(e); ~foot *ad* sous les pieds; ~go *vt irg* subir; (*treatment*) suivre; ~graduate *n* étudiant/e (qui prépare la licence); ~ground *n* (*Brit: railway*) métro *m*; (*POL*) clandestinité *f* // *a* souterrain(e); (*fig*) clandestin(e); ~growth *n* broussailles *fpl*, sous-bois *m*; ~hand(ed) *a* (*fig*) sournois(e), en dessous; ~lie *vt irg* être à la base de; ~line *vt* souligner; ~ling ['ʌndəlɪŋ] *n* (*pej*) sous-fifre *m*, subalterne *m*; ~mine *vt* saper, miner; ~neath [ʌndə'ni:θ] *ad* (en) dessous // *prep* sous, au-dessous de; ~paid *a* sous-payé(e); ~pants *npl* caleçon *m*, slip *m*; ~pass *n* (*Brit*) passage souterrain; (: *on motorway*) passage inférieur; ~privileged *a* dé-favorisé(e), économiquement faible; ~rate *vt* sous-estimer, mésestimer; ~shirt *n* (*US*) tricot *m* de corps; ~shorts *npl* (*US*) caleçon *m*, slip *m*; ~side *n* dessous *m*; ~skirt *n* (*Brit*) jupon *m*.

understand [ʌndə'stænd] *vb* (*irg: like* stand) *vt*, *vi* comprendre; I ~ that ... je me suis laissé dire que ...; je crois comprendre que ...; ~able *a* compréhensible; ~ing *a* compréhen-sif(ive) // *n* compréhension *f*; (*agreement*) accord *m*.

understatement ['ʌndəsteɪtmənt] *n*: that's an ~ c'est (bien) peu dire, le terme est faible.

understood [ʌndə'stud] *pt*, *pp* of understand *a* entendu(e); (*implied*) sous-entendu(e).

understudy ['ʌndəstʌdɪ] *n* doublure *f*.

undertake [ʌndə'teɪk] *vt irg* entrepren-dre; se charger de; to ~ to do sth s'engager à faire qch.

undertaker ['ʌndəteɪkə*] *n* entre-preneur *m* des pompes funèbres, croque-mort *m*.

undertaking ['ʌndəteɪkɪŋ] *n* entreprise *f*; (*promise*) promesse *f*.

undertone ['ʌndətəun] *n*: in an ~ à mi-voix.

underwater [ʌndə'wɔ:tə*] *ad* sous l'eau // *a* sous-marin(e).

underwear ['ʌndəwɛə*] *n* sous-vêtements *mpl*; (*women's only*) dessous *mpl*.

underworld ['ʌndəwə:ld] *n* (*of crime*) milieu *m*, pègre *f*.

underwriter ['ʌndəraɪtə*] *n* (*INSURANCE*) souscripteur *m*.

undies ['ʌndɪz] *npl* (*col*) dessous *mpl*, lingerie *f*.

undo [ʌn'du:] *vt irg* défaire; ~ing *n* ruine *f*, perte *f*.

undoubted [ʌn'dautɪd] *a* indubitable, certain(e); ~ly *ad* sans aucun doute.

undress [ʌn'dres] *vi* se déshabiller.

undue [ʌn'dju:] *a* indu(e), excessif(ive).

undulating ['ʌndjuleɪtɪŋ] *a* ondoyant(e), onduleux(euse).

unduly [ʌn'dju:lɪ] *ad* trop, excessive-ment.

unearth [ʌn'ə:θ] *vt* déterrer; (*fig*) dé-nicher.

unearthly [ʌn'ə:θlɪ] *a* surnaturel(le); (*hour*) indu(e), impossible.

uneasy [ʌn'i:zɪ] *a* mal à l'aise, gêné(e); (*worried*) inquiet(ète).

unemployed [ʌnɪm'plɔɪd] *a* sans travail, au chômage // *n*: the ~ les chômeurs *mpl*.

unemployment [ʌnɪm'plɔɪmənt] *n* chômage *m*.

unending [ʌn'endɪŋ] *a* interminable.

unerring [ʌn'ə:rɪŋ] *a* infaillible, sûr(e).

uneven [ʌn'i:vn] *a* inégal(e); irrégu-lier(ère).

unexpected [ʌnɪk'spektɪd] *a* inattendu(e), imprévu(e); ~ly *ad* à l'im-proviste.

unfailing [ʌn'feɪlɪŋ] *a* inépuisable; infaillible.

unfair [ʌn'fɛə*] *a*: ~ (to) injuste (envers).

unfaithful [ʌn'feɪθful] *a* infidèle.

unfamiliar [ʌnfə'mɪlɪə*] *a* étrange, inconnu(e).

unfashionable [ʌn'fæʃnəbl] *a* (*clothes*) démodé(e); (*district*) dés-hérité(e), pas à la mode.

unfasten [ʌn'fɑ:sn] *vt* défaire; détacher.

unfavourable, (*US*) **unfavorable** [ʌn'feɪvərəbl] *a* défavorable.

unfeeling [ʌn'fi:lɪŋ] *a* insensible, dur(e).

unfit [ʌn'fɪt] *a* en mauvaise santé; pas en forme; (*incompetent*): ~ (for) impro-pre (à); (*work, service*) inapte (à).

unfold [ʌn'fəuld] *vt* déplier; (*fig*) révéler, exposer // *vi* se dérouler.

unforeseen [ˈʌnfɔːˈsiːn] *a* imprévu(e).

unforgettable [ʌnfəˈgetəbl] *a* inoubliable.

unfortunate [ʌnˈfɔːtʃnət] *a* malheureux(euse); (*event, remark*) malencontreux(euse); **~ly** *ad* malheureusement.

unfounded [ʌnˈfaundɪd] *a* sans fondement.

unfriendly [ʌnˈfrɛndlɪ] *a* froid(e), inamical(e).

ungainly [ʌnˈgeɪnlɪ] *a* gauche, dégingandé(e).

ungodly [ʌnˈgɒdlɪ] *a*: **at an ~ hour** à une heure indue.

ungrateful [ʌnˈgreɪtful] *a* ingrat(e).

unhappiness [ʌnˈhæpɪnɪs] *n* tristesse *f*, peine *f*.

unhappy [ʌnˈhæpɪ] *a* triste, malheureux(euse); **~ with** (*arrangements etc*) mécontent(e) de, peu satisfait(e) de.

unharmed [ʌnˈhɑːmd] *a* indemne, sain(e) et sauf(sauve).

unhealthy [ʌnˈhɛlθɪ] *a* (*gen*) malsain(e); (*person*) maladif(ive).

unheard-of [ʌnˈhɜːdɒv] *a* inouï(e), sans précédent.

uniform [ˈjuːnɪfɔːm] *n* uniforme *m* // *a* uniforme.

uninhabited [ʌnɪnˈhæbɪtɪd] *a* inhabité(e).

union [ˈjuːnjən] *n* union *f*; (*also:* **trade ~**) syndicat *m* // *cpd* du syndicat, syndical(e); **U~ Jack** *n* drapeau du Royaume-Uni.

unique [juːˈniːk] *a* unique.

unit [ˈjuːnɪt] *n* unité *f*; (*section: of furniture etc*) élément *m*, bloc *m*; (*team, squad*) groupe *m*, service *m*.

unite [juːˈnaɪt] *vt* unir // *vi* s'unir; **~d** *a* uni(e); unifié(e); (*efforts*) conjugué(e); **U~d Kingdom (UK)** *n* Royaume-Uni *m*; **U~d Nations (Organization) (UN, UNO)** *n* (Organisation *f* des) Nations Unies (O.N.U.); **U~d States (of America) (US, USA)** *n* États-Unis *mpl*.

unit trust *n* (*Brit*) société *f* d'investissement, ≈ SICAV *f*.

unity [ˈjuːnɪtɪ] *n* unité *f*.

universal [juːnɪˈvɜːsl] *a* universel(le).

universe [ˈjuːnɪvɜːs] *n* univers *m*.

university [juːnɪˈvɜːsɪtɪ] *n* université *f*.

unjust [ʌnˈdʒʌst] *a* injuste.

unkempt [ʌnˈkɛmpt] *a* mal tenu(e), débraillé(e); mal peigné(e).

unkind [ʌnˈkaɪnd] *a* peu gentil(le), méchant(e).

unknown [ʌnˈnəun] *a* inconnu(e).

unlawful [ʌnˈlɔːful] *a* illégal(e).

unleash [ʌnˈliːʃ] *vt* détacher; (*fig*) déchaîner, déclencher.

unless [ʌnˈlɛs] *cj*: **~ he leaves** à moins qu'il (ne) parte; **~ we leave** à moins de partir, à moins que nous (ne) partions; **~ otherwise stated** sauf indication contraire.

unlike [ʌnˈlaɪk] *a* dissemblable, différent(e) // *prep* à la différence de, contrairement à.

unlikely [ʌnˈlaɪklɪ] *a* improbable; invraisemblable.

unlisted [ʌnˈlɪstɪd] *a* (*US TEL*) sur la liste rouge.

unload [ʌnˈləud] *vt* décharger.

unlock [ʌnˈlɒk] *vt* ouvrir.

unlucky [ʌnˈlʌkɪ] *a* malchanceux(euse); (*object, number*) qui porte malheur; **to be ~** ne pas avoir de chance.

unmarried [ʌnˈmærɪd] *a* célibataire.

unmistakable [ʌnmɪsˈteɪkəbl] *a* indubitable; qu'on ne peut pas ne pas reconnaître.

unmitigated [ʌnˈmɪtɪgeɪtɪd] *a* non mitigé(e), absolu(e), pur(e).

unnatural [ʌnˈnætʃrəl] *a* non naturel(le); contre nature.

unnecessary [ʌnˈnɛsəsərɪ] *a* inutile, superflu(e).

unnoticed [ʌnˈnəutɪst] *a*: **(to go) ~** (passer) inaperçu(e).

UNO [ˈjuːnəu] *n abbr of* **United Nations Organization**.

unobtainable [ʌnəbˈteɪnəbl] *a* (*TEL*) impossible à obtenir.

unobtrusive [ʌnəbˈtruːsɪv] *a* discret(ète).

unofficial [ʌnəˈfɪʃl] *a* non officiel(le); (*strike*) ≈ non sanctionné(e) par la centrale.

unpack [ʌnˈpæk] *vi* défaire sa valise.

unpalatable [ʌnˈpælətəbl] *a* (*truth*) désagréable (à entendre).

unparalleled [ʌnˈpærəleld] *a* incomparable, sans égal.

unpleasant [ʌnˈplɛznt] *a* déplaisant(e), désagréable.

unplug [ʌnˈplʌg] *vt* débrancher.

unpopular [ʌnˈpɒpjulə*] *a* impopulaire.

unprecedented [ʌnˈprɛsɪdəntɪd] *a* sans précédent.

unpredictable [ʌnprɪˈdɪktəbl] *a* imprévisible.

unprofessional [ʌnprəˈfɛʃənl] *a* (*conduct*) contraire à la déontologie.

unqualified [ʌnˈkwɒlɪfaɪd] *a* (*teacher*) non diplômé(e), sans titres; (*success*) sans réserve, total(e).

unquestionably [ʌnˈkwɛstʃənəblɪ] *ad* incontestablement.

unravel [ʌnˈrævl] *vt* démêler.

unreal [ʌnˈrɪəl] *a* irréel(le).

unrealistic [ʌnrɪəˈlɪstɪk] *a* irréaliste; peu réaliste.

unreasonable [ʌnˈriːznəbl] *a* qui n'est pas raisonnable.

unrelated [ʌnrɪˈleɪtɪd] *a* sans rapport; sans lien de parenté.

unreliable [ʌnrɪˈlaɪəbl] *a* sur qui (or

quoi) on ne peut pas compter, peu fiable.

unremitting [ʌnrɪ'mɪtɪŋ] *a* inlassable, infatigable, acharné(e).

unreservedly [ʌnrɪ'zɜːvɪdlɪ] *ad* sans réserve.

unrest [ʌn'rɛst] *n* agitation *f*, troubles *mpl*.

unroll [ʌn'rəul] *vt* dérouler.

unruly [ʌn'ruːlɪ] *a* indiscipliné(e).

unsafe [ʌn'seɪf] *a* dangereux(euse), hasardeux(euse).

unsaid [ʌn'sɛd] *a*: **to leave sth ~** passer qch sous silence.

unsatisfactory ['ʌnsætɪs'fæktərɪ] *a* qui laisse à désirer.

unsavoury, (US) **unsavory** [ʌn'seɪvərɪ] *a* (*fig*) peu recommandable, répugnant(e).

unscathed [ʌn'skeɪðd] *a* indemne.

unscrew [ʌn'skruː] *vt* dévisser.

unscrupulous [ʌn'skruːpjuləs] *a* sans scrupules.

unsettled [ʌn'sɛtld] *a* perturbé(e); instable; incertain(e).

unshaven [ʌn'ʃeɪvn] *a* non *or* mal rasé(e).

unsightly [ʌn'saɪtlɪ] *a* disgracieux(euse), laid(e).

unskilled [ʌn'skɪld] *a*: **~ worker** manœuvre *m*.

unspeakable [ʌn'spiːkəbl] *a* indicible; (*awful*) innommable.

unstable [ʌn'steɪbl] *a* instable.

unsteady [ʌn'stɛdɪ] *a* mal assuré(e), chancelant(e), instable.

unstuck [ʌn'stʌk] *a*: **to come ~** se décoller; (*fig*) faire fiasco.

unsuccessful [ʌnsək'sɛsful] *a* (*attempt*) infructueux(euse); (*writer, proposal*) qui n'a pas de succès; (*marriage*) malheureux(euse), qui ne réussit pas; **to be ~** (*in attempting sth*) ne pas réussir; ne pas avoir de succès; (*application*) ne pas être retenu(e).

unsuitable [ʌn'suːtəbl] *a* qui ne convient pas, peu approprié(e); inopportun(e).

unsure [ʌn'ʃuə*] *a* pas sûr(e); **to be ~ of o.s.** manquer de confiance en soi.

unsympathetic [ʌnsɪmpə'θɛtɪk] *a* (*person*) antipathique; (*attitude*) hostile.

untapped [ʌn'tæpt] *a* (*resources*) inexploité(e).

unthinkable [ʌn'θɪŋkəbl] *a* impensable, inconcevable.

untidy [ʌn'taɪdɪ] *a* (*room*) en désordre; (*appearance*) désordonné(e), débraillé(e); (*person*) sans ordre, désordonné; débraillé; (*work*) peu soigné(e).

untie [ʌn'taɪ] *vt* (*knot, parcel*) défaire; (*prisoner, dog*) détacher.

until [ən'tɪl] *prep* jusqu'à; (*after negative*) avant // *cj* jusqu'à ce que + *sub*, en attendant que + *sub*; (*in past*,

after negative) avant que + *sub*; **~ now** jusqu'à présent, jusqu'ici; **~ then** jusque-là.

untimely [ʌn'taɪmlɪ] *a* inopportun(e); (*death*) prématuré(e).

untold [ʌn'təuld] *a* incalculable; indescriptible.

untoward [ʌntə'wɔːd] *a* fâcheux(euse), malencontreux(euse).

untranslatable [ʌntrænz'leɪtəbl] *a* intraduisible.

unused [ʌn'juːzd] *a* neuf(neuve).

unusual [ʌn'juːʒuəl] *a* insolite, exceptionnel(le), rare.

unveil [ʌn'veɪl] *vt* dévoiler.

unwavering [ʌn'weɪvərɪŋ] *a* inébranlable.

unwelcome [ʌn'wɛlkəm] *a* importun(e); de trop.

unwell [ʌn'wɛl] *a* indisposé(e), souffrant(e); **to feel ~** ne pas se sentir bien.

unwieldy [ʌn'wiːldɪ] *a* difficile à manier.

unwilling [ʌn'wɪlɪŋ] *a*: **to be ~ to do** ne pas vouloir faire; **~ly** *ad* à contrecœur, contre son gré.

unwind [ʌn'waɪnd] *vb* (*irg*) *vt* dérouler // *vi* (*relax*) se détendre.

unwise [ʌn'waɪz] *a* déraisonnable.

unwitting [ʌn'wɪtɪŋ] *a* involontaire.

unworkable [ʌn'wɔːkəbl] *a* (*plan*) inexploitable.

unworthy [ʌn'wɜːðɪ] *a* indigne.

unwrap [ʌn'ræp] *vt* défaire; ouvrir.

unwritten [ʌn'rɪtn] *a* (*agreement*) tacite.

up [ʌp] ♦ *prep*: **he went ~ the stairs/the hill** il a monté l'escalier/la colline; **the cat was ~ a tree** le chat était dans un arbre; **they live further ~ the street** ils habitent plus haut dans la rue
♦ *ad* **1** (*upwards, higher*): **~ in the sky/ the mountains** (là-haut) dans le ciel/les montagnes; **put it a bit higher ~** mettez-le un peu plus haut; **~ there** là-haut; **~ above** au-dessus
2: **to be ~** (*out of bed*) être levé(e); (*prices etc*) avoir augmenté *or* monté
3: **~ to** (*as far as*) jusqu'à; **~ to now** jusqu'à présent
4: **to be ~ to** (*depending on*): **it's ~ to you** c'est à vous de décider; (*equal to*): **he's not ~ to it** (*job, task etc*) il n'en est pas capable; (*col: be doing*): **what is he ~ to?** qu'est-ce qu'il peut bien faire?
♦ *n*: **~s and downs** hauts et bas *mpl*.

up-and-coming [ʌpənd'kʌmɪŋ] *a* plein(e) d'avenir *or* de promesses.

upbringing ['ʌpbrɪŋɪŋ] *n* éducation *f*.

update [ʌp'deɪt] *vt* mettre à jour.

upheaval [ʌp'hiːvl] *n* bouleversement *m*; branle-bas *m*; crise *f*.

uphill [ʌp'hɪl] *a* qui monte; (*fig: task*) difficile, pénible // *ad*: **to go ~** monter.

uphold [ʌp'həuld] *vt irg* maintenir;

soutenir.

upholstery [ʌp'həʊlstəri] *n* rembourrage *m*; (*of car*) garniture *f*.

upkeep ['ʌpki:p] *n* entretien *m*.

upon [ə'pɒn] *prep* sur.

upper ['ʌpə*] *a* supérieur(e); du dessus // *n* (*of shoe*) empeigne *f*; ~**class** *a* ≈ bourgeois(e); ~ **hand** *n*: to have the ~ hand avoir le dessus; ~**most** *a* le(la) plus haut(e).

upright ['ʌpraɪt] *a* droit(e); vertical(e); (*fig*) droit, honnête // *n* montant *m*.

uprising ['ʌpraɪzɪŋ] *n* soulèvement *m*, insurrection *f*.

uproar ['ʌprɔ:*] *n* tumulte *m*, vacarme *m*.

uproot [ʌp'ru:t] *vt* déraciner.

upset *n* ['ʌpset] dérangement *m* // *vt* [ʌp'set] (*irg: like* set) (*glass etc*) renverser; (*plan*) déranger; (*person: offend*) contrarier; (: *grieve*) faire de la peine à; bouleverser // *a* [ʌp'set] contrarié(e); peiné(e); (*stomach*) détraqué(e), dérangé(e).

upshot ['ʌpʃɔt] *n* résultat *m*.

upside-down ['ʌpsaɪd'daʊn] *ad* à l'envers.

upstairs [ʌp'stɛəz] *ad* en haut // *a* (*room*) du dessus, d'en haut.

upstart [ʌp'stɑ:t] *n* parvenu/e.

upstream [ʌp'stri:m] *ad* en amont.

uptake ['ʌpteɪk] *n*: he is quick/slow on the ~ il comprend vite/est lent à comprendre.

uptight [ʌp'taɪt] *a* (*col*) très tendu(e), crispé(e).

up-to-date ['ʌptə'deɪt] *a* moderne; très récent(e).

upturn ['ʌptə:n] *n* (*in luck*) retournement *m*; (*COMM: in market*) hausse *f*.

upward ['ʌpwəd] *a* ascendant(e); vers le haut; ~(**s**) *ad* vers le haut.

urban ['ə:bən] *a* urbain(e).

urbane [ə:'beɪn] *a* urbain(e), courtois(e).

urchin ['ə:tʃɪn] *n* gosse *m*, garnement *m*.

urge [ə:dʒ] *n* besoin *m*; envie *f*; forte envie, désir *m* // *vt*: to ~ sb to do to exhorter qn à faire, pousser qn à faire; recommander vivement à qn de faire.

urgency ['ə:dʒənsɪ] *n* urgence *f*; (*of tone*) insistance *f*.

urgent ['ə:dʒənt] *a* urgent(e).

urine ['juərɪn] *n* urine *f*.

urn [ə:n] *n* urne *f*; (*also*: tea ~) fontaine *f* à thé.

US, USA *n abbr of* **United States (of America)**.

us [ʌs] *pronoun* nous; *see also* me.

use *n* [ju:s] emploi *m*, utilisation *f*; usage *m* // *vt* [ju:z] se servir de, utiliser, employer; she ~d to do it elle le faisait (autrefois), elle avait coutume de le faire; in ~ en usage; out of ~ hors d'usage; to be of ~ servir, être utile; it's no ~ ça ne sert à rien; to be ~d to to avoir l'habitude de, être habitué(e) à; to ~ up *vt* finir, épuiser; consommer; ~**d** *a* (*car*) d'occasion; ~**ful** *a* utile; ~**fulness** *n* utilité *f*; ~**less** *a* inutile; ~**r** *n* utilisateur/trice, usager *m*; ~**r-friendly** *a* (*computer*) convivial(e), facile d'emploi.

usher ['ʌʃə*] *n* placeur *m*; ~**ette** [-'rɛt] *n* (*in cinema*) ouvreuse *f*.

USSR *n*: the ~ l'URSS *f*.

usual ['ju:ʒuəl] *a* habituel(le); as ~ comme d'habitude; ~**ly** *ad* d'habitude, d'ordinaire.

utensil [ju:'tensl] *n* ustensile *m*; **kitchen** ~**s** batterie *f* de cuisine.

uterus ['ju:tərəs] *n* utérus *m*.

utility [ju:'tɪlɪtɪ] *n* utilité *f*; (*also*: **public** ~) service public; ~ **room** *n* buanderie *f*.

utmost ['ʌtməʊst] *a* extrême, le(la) plus grand(e) // *n*: to do one's ~ faire tout son possible.

utter ['ʌtə*] *a* total(e), complet(ète) // *vt* prononcer, proférer; émettre; ~**ance** *n* paroles *fpl*; ~**ly** *ad* complètement, totalement.

U-turn ['ju:'tə:n] *n* demi-tour *m*.

V

v. *abbr of* **verse, versus, volt**; (= *vide*) voir.

vacancy ['veɪkənsɪ] *n* (*Brit: job*) poste vacant; (*room*) chambre *f* disponible.

vacant ['veɪkənt] *a* (*post*) vacant(e); (*seat etc*) libre, disponible; (*expression*) distrait(e); ~ **lot** *n* (*US*) terrain inoccupé; (*for sale*) terrain à vendre.

vacate [və'keɪt] *vt* quitter.

vacation [və'keɪʃən] *n* vacances *fpl*.

vaccinate ['væksɪneɪt] *vt* vacciner.

vacuum ['vækjum] *n* vide *m*; ~ **bottle** *n* (*US*) = ~ **flask**; ~ **cleaner** *n* aspirateur *m*; ~ **flask** *n* (*Brit*) bouteille *f* thermos ®; ~**-packed** *a* emballé(e) sous vide.

vagina [və'dʒaɪnə] *n* vagin *m*.

vagrant ['veɪgrnt] *n* vagabond/e, mendiant/e.

vague [veɪg] *a* vague, imprécis(e); (*blurred: photo, memory*) flou(e); ~**ly** *ad* vaguement.

vain [veɪn] *a* (*useless*) vain(e); (*conceited*) vaniteux(euse); in ~ en vain.

valentine ['væləntaɪn] *n* (*also*: ~ **card**) carte *f* de la Saint-Valentin.

valiant ['vælɪənt] *a* vaillant(e).

valid ['vælɪd] *a* valide, valable; (*excuse*) valable.

valley ['vælɪ] *n* vallée *f*.

valour, (*US*) **valor** ['vælə*] *n* courage *m*.

valuable ['væljuəbl] a (*jewel*) de grande valeur; (*time*) précieux(euse); ~s npl objets mpl de valeur.

valuation [vælju'eɪʃən] n évaluation f, expertise f.

value ['vælju:] n valeur f // vt (*fix price*) évaluer, expertiser; (*cherish*) tenir à; ~ **added tax (VAT)** n (*Brit*) taxe f à la valeur ajoutée (T.V.A.); ~**d** a (*appreciated*) estimé(e).

valve [vælv] n (*in machine*) soupape f; (*on tyre*) valve f; (*in radio*) lampe f.

van [væn] n (*AUT*) camionnette f; (*Brit RAIL*) fourgon m.

vandal ['vændl] n vandale m/f; ~**ism** n vandalisme m; ~**ize** vt saccager.

vanilla [və'nilə] n vanille f.

vanish ['vænɪʃ] vi disparaître.

vanity ['vænɪtɪ] n vanité f; ~ **case** n sac m de toilette.

vantage ['va:ntɪdʒ] n: ~ **point** bonne position.

vapour, (*US*) **vapor** ['veɪpə*] n vapeur f; (*on window*) buée f.

variable ['vɛərɪəbl] a variable; (*mood*) changeant(e).

variance ['vɛərɪəns] n: to be at ~ (*with*) être en désaccord (avec); (*facts*) être en contradiction (avec).

varicose ['værɪkəus] a: ~ **veins** varices fpl.

varied ['vɛərɪd] a varié(e), divers(e).

variety [və'raɪətɪ] n variété f; (*quantity*) nombre m, quantité f; ~ **show** n (spectacle m de) variétés fpl.

various ['vɛərɪəs] a divers(e), différent(e); (*several*) divers, plusieurs.

varnish ['va:nɪʃ] n vernis m // vt vernir.

vary ['vɛərɪ] vt, vi varier, changer.

vase [va:z] n vase m.

vaseline ['væsɪli:n] n ® vaseline f.

vast [va:st] a vaste, immense; (*amount, success*) énorme; ~**ly** ad infiniment, extrêmement.

VAT [væt] n abbr of **value added tax**.

vat [væt] n cuve f.

vault [vɔ:lt] n (*of roof*) voûte f; (*tomb*) caveau m; (*in bank*) salle f des coffres; chambre forte; (*jump*) saut m // vt (*also:* ~ **over**) sauter (d'un bond).

vaunted ['vɔ:ntɪd] a: much-~ tant célébré(e).

VCR n abbr of **video cassette recorder**.

VD n abbr of **venereal disease**.

VDU n abbr of **visual display unit**.

veal [vi:l] n veau m.

veer [vɪə*] vi tourner, virer.

vegetable ['vedʒtəbl] n légume m // a végétal(e).

vegetarian [vedʒɪ'tɛərɪən] a, n végétarien(ne).

vehement ['vi:ɪmənt] a violent(e), impétueux(euse); (*impassioned*) ardent(e).

vehicle ['vi:ɪkl] n véhicule m.

veil [veɪl] n voile m // vt voiler.

vein [veɪn] n veine f; (*on leaf*) nervure f; (*fig: mood*) esprit m.

velvet ['velvɪt] n velours m.

vending machine ['vendɪŋ-] n distributeur m automatique.

veneer [və'nɪə*] n placage m de bois; (*fig*) vernis m.

venereal [vɪ'nɪərɪəl] a: ~ **disease (VD)** n maladie vénérienne.

Venetian [vɪ'ni:ʃən] a: ~ **blind** store vénitien.

vengeance ['vendʒəns] n vengeance f; with a ~ (*fig*) vraiment, pour de bon.

venison ['venɪsn] n venaison f.

venom ['venəm] n venin m.

vent [vent] n conduit m d'aération; (*in dress, jacket*) fente f // vt (*fig: one's feelings*) donner libre cours à.

ventilate ['ventɪleɪt] vt (*room*) ventiler, aérer; **ventilator** n ventilateur m.

ventriloquist [ven'trɪləkwɪst] n ventriloque m/f.

venture ['ventʃə*] n entreprise f // vt risquer, hasarder // vi s'aventurer, se risquer.

venue ['venju:] n lieu m de rendez-vous or rencontre.

verb [və:b] n verbe m; ~**al** a verbal(e); (*translation*) littéral(e).

verbatim [və:'beɪtɪm] a, ad mot pour mot.

verdict ['və:dɪkt] n verdict m.

verge [və:dʒ] n (*Brit*) bord m; on the ~ of doing sur le point de faire; **to** ~ **on** vt fus approcher de.

vermin ['və:mɪn] npl animaux mpl nuisibles; (*insects*) vermine f.

vermouth ['və:məθ] n vermouth m.

versatile ['və:sətaɪl] a polyvalent(e).

verse [və:s] n vers mpl; (*stanza*) strophe f; (*in bible*) verset m.

version ['və:ʃən] n version f.

versus ['və:səs] prep contre.

vertical ['və:tɪkl] a vertical(e) // n verticale f; ~**ly** ad verticalement.

vertigo ['və:tɪgəu] n vertige m.

verve [və:v] n brio m; enthousiasme m.

very ['verɪ] ad très // a: the ~ **book** which le livre même que; at the ~ **end** tout à la fin; the ~ **last** le tout dernier; at the ~ **least** au moins; ~ **much** beaucoup.

vessel ['vesl] n (*ANAT, NAUT*) vaisseau m; (*container*) récipient m.

vest [vest] n (*Brit*) tricot m de corps; (*US: waistcoat*) gilet m; ~**ed interests** npl (*COMM*) droits acquis.

vestry ['vestrɪ] n sacristie f.

vet [vet] n abbr (= **veterinary surgeon**) vétérinaire m/f // vt examiner minutieusement; (*text*) revoir.

veteran ['vetərn] n vétéran m; (*also:* **war** ~) ancien combattant.

veterinary ['vetrɪnərɪ] a vétérinaire; ~

surgeon, (*US*) **veterinarian** [vɛtrə-'nɛərɪən] *n* vétérinaire *m/f*.

veto ['vi:təu] *n* (*pl* ~es) veto *m* // *vt* opposer son veto à.

vex [vɛks] *vt* fâcher, contrarier; ~ed *a* (*question*) controversé(e).

VHF *abbr* (= *very high frequency*) VHF *f*.

via ['vaɪə] *prep* par, via.

viable ['vaɪəbl] *a* viable.

vibrate [vaɪ'breɪt] *vi*: to ~ (with) vibrer (de); (*resound*) retentir (de).

vicar ['vɪkə*] *n* pasteur *m* (*de l'Église anglicane*); ~age *n* presbytère *m*.

vicarious [vɪ'kɛərɪəs] *a* indirect(e).

vice [vaɪs] *n* (*evil*) vice *m*; (*TECH*) étau *m*.

vice- [vaɪs] *prefix* vice-.

vice squad *n* ≈ brigade mondaine.

vice versa ['vaɪsɪ'və:sə] *ad* vice versa.

vicinity [vɪ'sɪnɪtɪ] *n* environs *mpl*, alentours *mpl*.

vicious ['vɪʃəs] *a* (*remark*) cruel(le), méchant(e); (*blow*) brutal(e); ~ **circle** *n* cercle vicieux.

victim ['vɪktɪm] *n* victime *f*.

victor ['vɪktə*] *n* vainqueur *m*.

Victorian [vɪk'tɔːrɪən] *a* victorien(ne).

victory ['vɪktərɪ] *n* victoire *f*.

video ['vɪdɪəu] *cpd* vidéo *inv* // *n* (~ *film*) vidéo *f*; (*also*: ~ **cassette**) vidéocassette *f*; (*also*: ~ **cassette recorder**) magnétoscope *m*; ~ **tape** *n* bande *f* vidéo *inv*; (*cassette*) vidéocassette *f*.

vie [vaɪ] *vi*: to ~ with rivaliser avec.

Vienna [vɪ'ɛnə] *n* Vienne.

Vietnam [vjɛt'næm] *n* Viet-Nam *m*, Vietnam *m*; ~ese [-nə'miːz] *a* vietnamien(ne) // *n* (*pl inv*) Vietnamien-ne.

view [vju:] *n* vue *f*; (*opinion*) avis *m*, vue // *vt* (*situation*) considérer; (*house*) visiter; **on** ~ (*in museum etc*) exposé(e); **in full** ~ **of** sous les yeux de; (*building etc*) devant; **in** ~ **of the fact that** étant donné que; ~er *n* (*viewfinder*) viseur *m*; (*small projector*) visionneuse *f*; (*TV*) téléspectateur/trice; ~finder *n* viseur *m*; ~point *n* point *m* de vue.

vigil ['vɪdʒɪl] *n* veille *f*.

vigorous ['vɪgərəs] *a* vigoureux(euse).

vile [vaɪl] *a* (*action*) vil(e); (*smell*) abominable; (*temper*) massacrant(e).

villa ['vɪlə] *n* villa *f*.

village ['vɪlɪdʒ] *n* village *m*; ~r *n* villageois/e.

villain ['vɪlən] *n* (*scoundrel*) scélérat *m*; (*criminal*) bandit *m*; (*in novel etc*) traître *m*.

vindicate ['vɪndɪkeɪt] *vt* défendre avec succès; justifier.

vindictive [vɪn'dɪktɪv] *a* vindicatif(ive), rancunier(ère).

vine [vaɪn] *n* vigne *f*; (*climbing plant*) plante grimpante.

vinegar ['vɪnɪgə*] *n* vinaigre *m*.

vineyard ['vɪnjaːd] *n* vignoble *m*.

vintage ['vɪntɪdʒ] *n* (*year*) année *f*, millésime *m*; ~ **wine** *n* vin *m* de grand cru.

violate ['vaɪəleɪt] *vt* violer.

violence ['vaɪələns] *n* violence *f*; (*POL etc*) incidents violents.

violent ['vaɪələnt] *a* violent(e).

violet ['vaɪələt] *a* (*colour*) violet(te) // *n* (*plant*) violette *f*.

violin [vaɪə'lɪn] *n* violon *m*; ~ist *n* violoniste *m/f*.

VIP *n abbr* (= *very important person*) V.I.P. *m*.

virgin ['və:dʒɪn] *n* vierge *f* // *a* vierge.

Virgo ['və:gəu] *n* la Vierge.

virile ['vɪraɪl] *a* viril(e).

virtually ['və:tjuəlɪ] *ad* (*almost*) pratiquement.

virtue ['və:tju:] *n* vertu *f*; (*advantage*) mérite *m*, avantage *m*; **by** ~ **of** par le fait de.

virtuous ['və:tjuəs] *a* vertueux(euse).

virus ['vaɪərəs] *n* virus *m*.

visa ['viːzə] *n* visa *m*.

visibility [vɪzɪ'bɪlɪtɪ] *n* visibilité *f*.

visible ['vɪzəbl] *a* visible.

vision ['vɪʒən] *n* (*sight*) vue *f*, vision *f*; (*foresight*, *in dream*) vision.

visit ['vɪzɪt] *n* visite *f*; (*stay*) séjour *m* // *vt* (*person*) rendre visite à; (*place*) visiter; ~ing hours *npl* (*in hospital etc*) heures *fpl* de visite; ~or *n* visiteur/euse; (*in hotel*) client/e; ~ors' **book** *n* livre *m* d'or; (*in hotel*) registre *m*.

visor ['vaɪzə*] *n* visière *f*.

vista ['vɪstə] *n* vue *f*, perspective *f*.

visual ['vɪzjuəl] *a* visuel(le); ~ **aid** *n* support visuel (pour l'enseignement); ~ **display unit** (**VDU**) *n* console *f* de visualisation, visuel *m*.

visualize ['vɪzjuəlaɪz] *vt* se représenter; (*foresee*) prévoir.

vital ['vaɪtl] *a* vital(e); ~ly *ad* extrêmement; ~ **statistics** *npl* (*fig*) mensurations *fpl*.

vitamin ['vɪtəmɪn] *n* vitamine *f*.

vivacious [vɪ'veɪʃəs] *a* animé(e), qui a de la vivacité.

vivid ['vɪvɪd] *a* (*account*) frappant(e); (*light*, *imagination*) vif(vive); ~ly *ad* (*describe*) d'une manière vivante; (*remember*) de façon précise.

V-neck ['viːnɛk] *n* décolleté *m* en V.

vocabulary [vəu'kæbjulərɪ] *n* vocabulaire *m*.

vocal ['vəukl] *a* vocal(e); (*articulate*) qui sait s'exprimer; ~ **chords** *npl* cordes vocales.

vocation [vəu'keɪʃən] *n* vocation *f*; ~al *a* professionnel(le).

vociferous [və'sɪfərəs] *a* bruyant(e).

vodka ['vɔdkə] n vodka f.

vogue [vəug] n mode f; (popularity) vogue f.

voice [vɔɪs] n voix f; (opinion) avis m // vt (opinion) exprimer, formuler.

void [vɔɪd] n vide m // a nul(le); ~ of vide de, dépourvu(e) de.

volatile ['vɔlətaɪl] a volatil(e); (fig) versatile.

volcano, ~es [vɔl'keɪnəu] n volcan m.

volition [və'lɪʃən] n: of one's own ~ de son propre gré.

volley ['vɔlɪ] n (of gunfire) salve f; (of stones etc) pluie f, volée f; (TENNIS etc) volée f; ~**ball** n volley(-ball) m.

volt [vəult] n volt m; ~**age** n tension f, voltage m.

volume ['vɔljuːm] n volume m.

voluntarily ['vɔləntrɪlɪ] ad volontairement; bénévolement.

voluntary ['vɔləntərɪ] a volontaire; (unpaid) bénévole.

volunteer [vɔlən'tɪə*] n volontaire m/f // vi (MIL) s'engager comme volontaire; to ~ to do se proposer pour faire.

vomit ['vɔmɪt] vt, vi vomir.

vote [vəut] n vote m, suffrage m; (cast) voix f, vote; (franchise) droit m de vote // vt (chairman) élire // vi voter; ~ of censure motion f de censure; ~ of thanks discours m de remerciement; ~**r** n électeur/trice; **voting** n scrutin m.

vouch [vautʃ]: to ~ for vt fus se porter garant de.

voucher ['vautʃə*] n (for meal, petrol) bon m; (receipt) reçu m.

vow [vau] n vœu m, serment m // vi jurer.

vowel ['vauəl] n voyelle f.

voyage ['vɔɪdʒ] n voyage m par mer, traversée f.

vulgar ['vʌlgə*] a vulgaire.

vulnerable ['vʌlnərəbl] a vulnérable.

vulture ['vʌltʃə*] n vautour m.

W

wad [wɔd] n (of cotton wool, paper) tampon m; (of banknotes etc) liasse f.

waddle ['wɔdl] vi se dandiner.

wade [weɪd] vi: to ~ through marcher dans, patauger dans // vt passer à gué.

wafer ['weɪfə*] n (CULIN) gaufrette f.

waffle ['wɔfl] n (CULIN) gaufre f; (col) rabâchage m; remplissage m.

waft [wɔft] vt porter // vi flotter.

wag [wæg] vt agiter, remuer // vi remuer.

wage [weɪdʒ] n (also: ~s) salaire m, paye f // vt: to ~ war faire la guerre; ~ **packet** n (enveloppe f de) paye f.

wager ['weɪdʒə*] n pari m.

waggle ['wægl] vt, vi remuer.

wag(g)on ['wægən] n (horse-drawn) chariot m; (Brit RAIL) wagon m (de marchandises).

wail [weɪl] vi gémir; (siren) hurler.

waist [weɪst] n taille f, ceinture f; ~**coat** n (Brit) gilet m; ~**line** n (tour m de) taille f.

wait [weɪt] n attente f // vi attendre; to lie in ~ for guetter; to ~ for attendre; I can't ~ to (fig) je meurs d'envie de; to ~ **behind** vi rester (à attendre); **to ~ on** vt fus servir; ~**er** n garçon m (de café), serveur m; ~**ing** n: 'no ~**ing**' (Brit AUT) 'stationnement interdit'; ~**ing list** n liste f d'attente; ~**ing room** n salle f d'attente; ~**ress** n serveuse f.

waive [weɪv] vt renoncer à, abandonner.

wake [weɪk] vb (pt woke, ~d, pp woken, ~d) vt (also: ~ up) réveiller // vi (also: ~ up) se réveiller // n (for dead person) veillée f mortuaire; (NAUT) sillage m; ~**n** vt, vi = **wake**.

Wales [weɪlz] n pays m de Galles.

walk [wɔːk] n promenade f; (short) petit tour; (gait) démarche f; (path) chemin m; (in park etc) allée f // vi marcher; (for pleasure, exercise) se promener // vt (distance) faire à pied; (dog) promener; 10 minutes' ~ from à 10 minutes de marche de; from all ~s of life de toutes conditions sociales; **to ~ out on** vt fus (col) quitter, plaquer; ~**er** n (person) marcheur/euse; ~**ie-talkie** ['wɔːkɪ'tɔːkɪ] n talkie-walkie m; ~**ing** n marche f à pied; ~**ing stick** n canne f; ~**out** n (of workers) grève-surprise f; ~**over** n (col) victoire f or examen m etc facile; ~**way** n promenade f.

wall [wɔːl] n mur m; (of tunnel, cave) paroi m; ~**ed** a (city) fortifié(e).

wallet ['wɔlɪt] n portefeuille m.

wallflower ['wɔːlflauə*] n giroflée f; to be a ~ (fig) faire tapisserie.

wallop ['wɔləp] vt (col) taper sur.

wallow ['wɔləu] vi se vautrer.

wallpaper ['wɔːlpeɪpə*] n papier peint.

wally ['wɔlɪ] n (col) imbécile m/f.

walnut ['wɔːlnʌt] n noix f; (tree) noyer m.

walrus, pl ~ or ~**es** ['wɔːlrəs] n morse m.

waltz [wɔːlts] n valse f // vi valser.

wan [wɔn] a pâle; triste.

wand [wɔnd] n (also: magic ~) baguette f (magique).

wander ['wɔndə*] vi (person) errer, aller sans but; (thoughts) vagabonder; (river) serpenter // vt errer dans.

wane [weɪn] vi (moon) décroître; (reputation) décliner.

wangle ['wæŋgl] vt (Brit col) se débrouiller pour avoir; carotter.

want [wɔnt] vt vouloir; (need) avoir besoin de; (lack) manquer de // n: for ~ of par manque de, faute de; ~**s** npl (*needs*) besoins *mpl*; **to ~ to do** vouloir faire; **to ~ sb to do** vouloir que qn fasse; **~ing** *a*: **to be found ~ing** ne pas être à la hauteur.

wanton ['wɔntn] *a* capricieux(euse); dévergondé(e).

war [wɔː*] *n* guerre *f*; **to make ~ (on)** faire la guerre (à).

ward [wɔːd] *n* (*in hospital*) salle *f*; (*POL*) section électorale; (*LAW: child*) pupille *m/f*; **to ~ off** *vt* parer, éviter.

warden ['wɔːdn] *n* (*Brit: of institution*) directeur/trice; (*of park, game reserve*) gardien/ne; (*Brit: also:* **traffic ~**) contractuel/le.

warder ['wɔːdə*] *n* (*Brit*) gardien *m* de prison.

wardrobe ['wɔːdrəub] *n* (*cupboard*) armoire *f*; (*clothes*) garde-robe *f*; (*THEATRE*) costumes *mpl*.

warehouse ['wɛəhaus] *n* entrepôt *m*.

wares [wɛəz] *npl* marchandises *fpl*.

warfare ['wɔːfɛə*] *n* guerre *f*.

warhead ['wɔːhed] *n* (*MIL*) ogive *f*.

warily ['wɛərɪlɪ] *ad* avec prudence.

warm [wɔːm] *a* chaud(e); (*thanks, welcome, applause*) chaleureux(euse); **it's ~** il fait chaud; **I'm ~** j'ai chaud; **to ~ up** *vi* (*person, room*) se réchauffer; (*water*) chauffer; (*athlete, discussion*) s'échauffer // *vt* réchauffer; chauffer; (*engine*) faire chauffer; **~-hearted** *a* affectueux(euse); **~ly** *ad* chaudement; vivement; chaleureusement; **~th** *n* chaleur *f*.

warn [wɔːn] *vt* avertir, prévenir; **~ing** *n* avertissement *m*; (*notice*) avis *m*; **~ing light** *n* avertisseur lumineux; **~ing triangle** *n* (*AUT*) triangle *m* de présignalisation.

warp [wɔːp] *vi* travailler, se voiler // *vt* voiler; (*fig*) pervertir.

warrant ['wɔrnt] *n* (*guarantee*) garantie *f*; (*LAW: to arrest*) mandat *m* d'arrêt; (*: to search*) mandat de perquisition.

warranty ['wɔrəntɪ] *n* garantie *f*.

warren ['wɔrən] *n* (*of rabbits*) terriers *mpl*, garenne *f*.

warrior ['wɔrɪə*] *n* guerrier/ère.

Warsaw ['wɔːsɔː] *n* Varsovie.

warship ['wɔːʃɪp] *n* navire *m* de guerre.

wart [wɔːt] *n* verrue *f*.

wartime ['wɔːtaɪm] *n*: **in ~** en temps de guerre.

wary ['wɛərɪ] *a* prudent(e).

was [wɔz] *pt of* **be**.

wash [wɔʃ] *vt* laver // *vi* se laver // *n* (*paint*) badigeon *m*; (*washing programme*) lavage *m*; (*of ship*) sillage *m*; **to have a ~** se laver, faire sa toilette; **to ~ away** *vt* (*stain*) enlever au lavage; (*subj: river etc*) emporter; **to ~ off** *vi* partir au lavage; **to ~ up** *vi* (*Brit*) faire la vaisselle; (*US*) se débarbouiller; **~able** *a* lavable; **~basin**, (*US*) **~bowl**

n lavabo *m*; **~cloth** *n* (*US*) gant *m* de toilette; **~er** *n* (*TECH*) rondelle *f*, joint *m*; **~ing** *n* (*linen etc*) lessive *f*; **~ing machine** *n* machine *f* à laver; **~ing powder** *n* (*Brit*) lessive *f* (en poudre); **~ing-up** *n* vaisselle *f*; **~ing-up liquid** *n* produit *m* pour la vaisselle; **~-out** *n* (*col*) désastre *m*; **~room** *n* toilettes *fpl*.

wasn't ['wɔznt] = **was not**.

wasp [wɔsp] *n* guêpe *f*.

wastage ['weɪstɪdʒ] *n* gaspillage *m*; (*in manufacturing, transport etc*) déchet *m*; **natural ~** départs naturels.

waste [weɪst] *n* gaspillage *m*; (*of time*) perte *f*; (*rubbish*) déchets *mpl*; (*also:* **household ~**) ordures *fpl* // *a* (*material*) de rebut; (*land*) inculte // *vt* gaspiller; (*time, opportunity*) perdre; **~s** *npl* étendue *f* désertique; **to lay ~** (*destroy*) dévaster; **to ~ away** *vi* dépérir; **~ disposal unit** *n* (*Brit*) broyeur *m* d'ordures; **~ful** *a* gaspilleur(euse); (*process*) peu économique; **~ ground** *n* (*Brit*) terrain *m* vague; **~paper basket** *n* corbeille *f* à papier; **~ pipe** *n* (tuyau *m* de) vidange *f*.

watch [wɔtʃ] *n* montre *f*; (*act of watching*) surveillance *f*; guet *m*; (*guard: MIL*) sentinelle *f*; (: *NAUT*) homme *m* de quart; (*NAUT: spell of duty*) quart *m* // *vt* (*look at*) observer; (: *match, programme*) regarder; (*spy on, guard*) surveiller; (*be careful of*) faire attention à // *vi* regarder; (*keep guard*) monter la garde; **to ~ out** *vi* faire attention; **~dog** *n* chien *m* de garde; **~ful** *a* attentif(ive), vigilant(e); **~maker** *n* horloger/ère; **~man** *n* gardien *m*; (*also:* **night ~man**) veilleur *m* de nuit; **~ strap** *n* bracelet *m* de montre.

water ['wɔːtə*] *n* eau *f* // *vt* (*plant*) arroser // *vi* (*eyes*) larmoyer; **in British ~s** dans les eaux territoriales Britanniques; **to ~ down** *vt* (*milk*) couper d'eau; (*fig: story*) édulcorer; **~colour** *n* aquarelle *f*; **~colours** *npl* couleurs *fpl* pour aquarelle; **~cress** *n* cresson *m* (de fontaine); **~fall** *n* chute *f* d'eau; **~ heater** *n* chauffe-eau *m*; **~ ice** *n* sorbet *m*; **~ing can** *n* arrosoir *m*; **~ lily** *n* nénuphar *m*; **~logged** *a* détrempé(e); imbibé(e) d'eau; **~line** *n* (*NAUT*) ligne *f* de flottaison; **~ main** *n* canalisation *f* d'eau; **~mark** *n* (*on paper*) filigrane *m*; **~melon** *n* pastèque *f*; **~proof** *a* imperméable; **~shed** *n* (*GEO*) ligne *f* de partage des eaux; (*fig*) moment *m* critique, point décisif; **~-skiing** *n* ski *m* nautique; **~tight** *a* étanche; **~way** *n* cours *m* d'eau navigable; **~works** *npl* station *f* hydraulique; **~y** *a* (*colour*) délavé(e); (*coffee*) trop faible.

watt [wɔt] *n* watt *m*.

wave [weɪv] *n* vague *f*; (*of hand*) geste *m*, signe *m*; (*RADIO*) onde *f*; (*in hair*) ondulation f // vi faire signe de la main; (flag) flotter au vent // vt (handkerchief) agiter; (stick) brandir; **~length** n longueur f d'ondes.

waver ['weɪvə*] vi vaciller; (voice) trembler; (person) hésiter.

wavy ['weɪvɪ] a ondulé(e); onduleux(euse).

wax [wæks] n cire f; (for skis) fart m // vt cirer; (car) lustrer // vi (moon) croître; **~works** npl personnages mpl de cire; musée m de cire.

way [weɪ] n chemin m, voie f; (path, access) passage m; (distance) distance f; (direction) chemin, direction f; (manner) façon f, manière f; (habit) habitude f, façon; (condition) état m; which ~? — this ~ par où or de quel côté? — par ici; on the ~ (en route) en route; to be on one's ~ être en route; to be in the ~ bloquer le passage; (fig) gêner; to go out of one's ~ to do (fig) se donner du mal pour faire; to lose one's ~ perdre son chemin; in a ~ d'un côté; in some ~s à certains égards; by the ~ ... à propos ...; '~ in' (Brit) 'entrée'; '~ out' (Brit) 'sortie'.

waylay ['weɪleɪ] vt irg attaquer; (fig): I got waylaid quelqu'un m'a accroché.

wayward ['weɪwəd] a capricieux(euse), entêté(e).

W.C. ['dʌblju:'si:] n (Brit) w.-c. mpl, waters mpl.

we [wi:] pl pronoun nous.

weak [wi:k] a faible; (health) fragile; (beam etc) peu solide; **~en** vi faiblir // vt affaiblir; **~ling** n gringalet m; faible m/f; **~ness** n faiblesse f; (fault) point m faible.

wealth [wɛlθ] n (money, resources) richesse(s) f(pl); (of details) profusion f; **~y** a riche.

wean [wi:n] vt sevrer.

weapon ['wɛpən] n arme f.

wear [wɛə*] n (use) usage m; (deterioration through use) usure f; (clothing): sports/baby~ vêtements mpl de sport/pour bébés // vb (pt wore, pp worn) vt (clothes) porter; mettre; (damage: through use) user // vi (last) faire de l'usage; (rub etc through) s'user; evening ~ tenue f de soirée; **to ~ away** vt user, ronger // vi s'user, être rongé(e); **to ~ down** vt user; (strength) épuiser; **to ~ off** vi disparaître; **to ~ on** vi se poursuivre; passer; **to ~ out** vt user; (person, strength) épuiser; **~ and tear** n usure f.

weary ['wɪərɪ] a (tired) épuisé(e); (dispirited) las(lasse); abattu(e).

weasel ['wi:zl] n (ZOOL) belette f.

weather ['wɛðə*] n temps m // vt (wood) faire mûrir; (tempest, crisis) essuyer, être pris(e) dans; survivre à, tenir le coup durant; **under the ~** (fig:

ill) mal fichu(e); **~-beaten** a (person) hâlé(e); (building) dégradé(e) par les intempéries; **~cock** n girouette f; **~forecast** n prévisions fpl météorologiques, météo f; **~ vane** n = ~cock.

weave, pt wove, pp woven [wi:v, wəuv, 'wəuvn] vt (cloth) tisser; (basket) tresser; **~r** n tisserand(e).

web [wɛb] n (of spider) toile f; (on foot) palmure f; (fabric, also fig) tissu m.

wed [wɛd], pt, pp wedded vt épouser // vi se marier.

we'd [wi:d] = we had, we would.

wedding ['wɛdɪŋ] n mariage m; silver/golden ~ anniversary noces fpl d'argent/d'or; **~ day** n jour m du mariage; **~ dress** n robe f de mariage; **~ ring** n alliance f.

wedge [wɛdʒ] n (of wood etc) coin m; (under door etc) cale f; (of cake) part f // vt (fix) caler; (push) enfoncer, coincer.

wedlock ['wɛdlɔk] n (union f du) mariage m.

Wednesday ['wɛdnzdɪ] n mercredi m.

wee [wi:] a (Scottish) petit(e); tout(e) petit(e).

weed [wi:d] n mauvaise herbe // vt désherber; **~killer** n désherbant m; **~y** a (man) gringalet.

week [wi:k] n semaine f; a ~ today/on Friday aujourd'hui/vendredi en huit; **~day** n jour m de semaine; (COMM) jour ouvrable; **~end** n week-end m; **~ly** ad une fois par semaine, chaque semaine // a, n hebdomadaire (m).

weep [wi:p], pt, pp wept vi (person) pleurer; **~ing willow** n saule pleureur.

weigh [weɪ] vt, vi peser; **to ~ down** vt (branch) faire plier; (fig: with worry) accabler; **to ~ up** vt examiner.

weight [weɪt] n poids m; to lose/put on ~ maigrir/grossir; **~ing** n (allowance) indemnité f, allocation f; **~ lifter** n haltérophile m; **~y** a lourd(e).

weir [wɪə*] n barrage m.

weird [wɪəd] a bizarre; (eerie) surnaturel(le).

welcome ['wɛlkəm] a bienvenu(e) // n accueil m // vt accueillir; (also: bid ~) souhaiter la bienvenue à; (be glad of) se réjouir de; **to be ~** être le(la) bienvenu(e); **thank you — you're ~!** merci — de rien or il n'y a pas de quoi.

weld [wɛld] n soudure f // vt souder.

welfare ['wɛlfɛə*] n bien-être m; **~ state** n État-providence m.

well [wɛl] n puits m // ad bien // a: to be ~ aller bien // excl eh bien!; bon!; enfin!; as ~ aussi, également; as ~ as aussi bien que or de; en plus de; ~ done! bravo! // get ~ soon remets-toi vite!; to do ~ in sth bien réussir en or dans qch; **to ~ up** vi monter.

we'll [wi:l] = **we will, we shall.**

well: **~-behaved** a sage obéissant(e); **~-being** n bien-être m; **~-built** a (person) bien bâti(e); **~-dressed** a bien habillé(e), bien vêtu(e); **~-heeled** a (col: wealthy) fortuné(e), riche.

wellingtons ['welɪŋtənz] npl (also: **wellington boots**) bottes fpl de caout-chouc.

well: **~-known** a (person) bien connu(e); **~-mannered** a bien éle-vé(e); **~-meaning** a bien intention-né(e); **~-off** a aisé(e), assez riche; **~-read** a cultivé(e); **~-to-do** a aisé(e), assez riche; **~-wisher** n: scores of **~-wishers had gathered** de nombreux amis et admirateurs s'étaient rassemblés.

Welsh [welʃ] a gallois(e) // n (LING) gallois m; **the ~** npl les Gallois mpl; **~man/woman** n Gallois/e; **~ rarebit** n croûte f au fromage.

went [went] pt of **go.**

wept [wept] pt, pp of **weep.**

were [wə:*] pt of **be.**

we're [wɪə*] = **we are.**

weren't [wə:nt] = **were not.**

west [west] a ouest m // a ouest inv, de or à l'ouest // ad à or vers l'ouest; **the W~** n l'Occident m, l'Ouest; **the W~ Country** n (Brit) le sud-ouest de l'An-gleterre; **~erly** a (wind) d'ouest; **~ern** a occidental(e), de or à l'ouest // n (CINEMA) western m; **W~ Germany** n Allemagne f de l'Ouest; **W~ Indian** a antillais(e) // n Antillais/e; **W~ Indies** npl Antilles fpl; **~ward(s)** ad vers l'ouest.

wet [wet] a mouillé(e); (damp) humide; (soaked) trempé(e); (rainy) pluvieux (euse); **to get ~** se mouiller; **'~ paint'** 'attention peinture fraîche'; **~ blanket** n (fig) rabat-joie m inv; **~ suit** n combinaison f de plongée.

we've [wi:v] = **we have.**

whack [wæk] vt donner un grand coup à.

whale [weɪl] n (ZOOL) baleine f.

wharf, pl **wharves** [wɔ:f, wɔ:vz] n quai m.

what [wɒt] ♦ a quel(le), pl quels(quelles); **~ size is he?** quelle taille fait-il?; **~ colour is it?** de quelle couleur est-ce?; **~ books do you need?** quels li-vres vous faut-il?; **~ a mess!** quel désor-dre!

♦ pronoun **1** (interrogative) que, prep + quoi; **~ are you doing?** que faites-vous?, qu'est-ce que vous faites?; **~ is happen-ing?** qu'est-ce qui se passe?, que se passe-t-il?; **~ are you talking about?** de quoi parlez-vous?; **~ is it called?** comment est-ce que ça s'appelle?; **~ about me?** et moi?; **~ about doing ...?** et si on faisait ...?

2 (relative: subject) ce qui; (: direct object) ce que; (: indirect object) ce +

prep + quoi, ce dont; **I saw ~ you did/ was on the table** j'ai vu ce que vous avez fait/ce qui était sur la table; **tell me ~ you remember** dites-moi ce dont vous vous souvenez

♦ excl (disbelieving) quoi!, comment!

whatever [wɒt'evə*] a: **~ book** quel que soit le livre que (or qui) + sub; n'importe quel livre // pronoun: **do ~ is necessary** faites (tout) ce qui est nécessaire; **~ happens** quoi qu'il arrive; **no reason ~** or **whatsoever** pas la moin-dre raison; **nothing ~** rien du tout.

wheat [wi:t] n blé m, froment m.

wheedle [wi:dl] vt: **to ~ sb into doing sth** cajoler or enjôler qn pour qu'il fasse qch; **to ~ sth out of sb** obtenir qch de qn par des cajoleries.

wheel [wi:l] n roue f; (AUT: also: steer-ing ~) volant m; (NAUT) gouvernail m // vt pousser, rouler // vi (also: ~ round) tourner; **~barrow** n brouette f; **~chair** n fauteuil roulant; **~ clamp** n (AUT) sabot m (de Denver).

wheeze [wi:z] vi respirer bruyamment.

when [wen] ♦ ad quand; **~ did it hap-pen?** c'est arrivé quand?

♦ cj **1** (at, during, after the time that) quand, lorsque; **she was reading ~ I came in** elle lisait quand or lorsque je suis entré

2 (on, at which): **on the day ~ I met him** le jour où je l'ai rencontré

3 (whereas) alors que; **you said I was wrong ~ in fact I was right** vous avez dit que j'avais tort alors qu'en fait j'avais raison.

whenever [wen'evə*] ad quand donc // cj quand; (every time that) chaque fois que; **you may leave ~ you like** vous pouvez partir quand vous voudrez.

where [weə*] ad, cj où; **this is ~** c'est là que; **~abouts** ad où donc // n: sb's **~abouts** l'endroit où se trouve qn; **~as** cj alors que; **~by** pronoun par lequel (or laquelle etc); **~upon** cj sur quoi, et sur ce; **wherever** [-'evə*] ad où donc // cj où que + sub; **~withal** n moyens mpl.

whet [wet] vt aiguiser.

whether ['weðə*] cj si; **I don't know ~ to accept or not** je ne sais pas si je dois accepter ou non; **it's doubtful ~** il est peu probable que; **~ you go or not que** vous y alliez ou non.

which [wɪtʃ] ♦ a **1** (interrogative: di-rect, indirect) quel(le), pl quels(quel-les); **~ picture do you want?** quel tableau voulez-vous?; **~ one?** lequel (la-quelle)?

2: in ~ case auquel cas

♦ pronoun **1** (interrogative) lequel (la-quelle), pl lesquels(lesquelles); **I don't mind ~** peu importe lequel; **~ (of these) are yours?** lesquels sont à vous?; **here**

are the books — tell me ~ you want
voici les livres — dites-moi lesquels *or*
ceux que vous voulez

2 *(relative: subject)* qui; (: *object)* que,
prep + lequel(laquelle) (NB: *à* + *lequel*
= auquel; *de* + *lequel* = duquel); the
apple ~ you ate/~ is on the table la
pomme que vous avez mangée/qui est
sur la table; the chair on ~ you are sitting la chaise sur laquelle vous êtes
assis; the book of ~ you spoke le livre
dont vous avez parlé; he said he knew,
~ is true/I feared il a dit qu'il le savait,
ce qui est vrai/ce que je craignais; after
~ après quoi.

whichever [wɪtʃˈɛvə*] *a*: take ~ book
you prefer prenez le livre que vous
préférez, n'importe lequel; ~ way you
de quelque façon que vous + *sub*.

whiff [wɪf] *n* bouffée *f*.

while [waɪl] *n* moment *m* // *cj* pendant
que; *(as long as)* tant que; *(whereas)*
alors que; bien que + *sub*; for a ~
pendant quelque temps; **to ~ away** *vt*
(time) (faire) passer.

whim [wɪm] *n* caprice *m*.

whimper [ˈwɪmpə*] *vi* geindre.

whimsical [ˈwɪmzɪkl] *a* *(person)* ca-
pricieux(euse); *(look)* étrange.

whine [waɪn] *vi* gémir, geindre; pleurnicher.

whip [wɪp] *n* fouet *m*; *(for riding)*
cravache *f*; *(POL: person)* chef *m* de file
*(assurant la discipline dans son groupe
parlementaire)* // *vt* fouetter; *(snatch)*
enlever *(or* sortir) brusquement; **~ped
cream** *n* crème fouettée; **~-round** *n*
(Brit) collecte *f*.

whirl [wə:l] *vt* faire tourbillonner; faire
tournoyer // *vi* tourbillonner; **~pool** *n*
tourbillon *m*; **~wind** *n* tornade *f*.

whirr [wə:*] *vi* bruire; ronronner;
vrombir.

whisk [wɪsk] *n* *(CULIN)* fouet *m* // *vt*
fouetter, battre; **to ~ sb away** *or* **off**
emmener qn rapidement.

whisker [ˈwɪskə*] *n*: **~s** *(of animal)*
moustaches *fpl*; *(of man)* favoris *mpl*.

whisky, *(Irish, US)* **whiskey** [ˈwɪskɪ] *n*
whisky *m*.

whisper [ˈwɪspə*] *vt*, *vi* chuchoter.

whistle [ˈwɪsl] *n* *(sound)* sifflement *m*;
(object) sifflet *m* // *vi* siffler.

white [waɪt] *a* blanc(blanche); *(with
fear)* blême // *n* blanc *m*; *(person)*
blanc/blanche; **~ coffee** *n* *(Brit)* café *m*
au lait, *(café)* crème *m*; **~-collar
worker** *n* employé/e de bureau; **~ elephant** *n* *(fig)* objet dispendieux *et*
superflu; **~ lie** *n* pieux mensonge; **~
paper** *n* *(POL)* livre blanc; **~wash** *vt*
blanchir à la chaux; *(fig)* blanchir.

whiting [ˈwaɪtɪŋ] *n* *(pl inv)* *(fish)*
merlan *m*.

Whitsun [ˈwɪtsn] *n* la Pentecôte.

whittle [ˈwɪtl] *vt*: to ~ away, ~ down
(costs) réduire, rogner.

whizz [wɪz] *vi* aller *(or* passer) à toute
vitesse; ~ **kid** *n* *(col)* petit prodige.

who [hu:] *pronoun* qui.

whodunit [hu:ˈdʌnɪt] *n* *(col)* roman
policier.

whoever [hu:ˈevə*] *pronoun*: ~ finds it
celui(celle) qui le trouve, (qui que ce
soit), quiconque le trouve; ask ~ you
like demandez à qui vous voulez; ~ he
marries qui que ce soit *or* quelle que soit
la personne qu'il épouse; ~ told you
that? qui a bien pu vous dire ça?

whole [həʊl] *a* *(complete)* entier(ère),
tout(e); *(not broken)* intact(e),
complet(ète) // *n* *(total)* totalité *f*; *(sth
not broken)* tout *m*; the ~ of the town la
ville tout entière; on the ~, as a ~ dans
l'ensemble; **~hearted** *a* sans
réserve(s), sincère; **~meal** *a* *(bread,
flour)* complet(ète); **~sale** *n* *(vente f
en)* gros *m* // *a* de gros; *(destruction)*
systématique; **~saler** *n* grossiste *m/f*;
~some *a* sain(e); *(advice)* salutaire;
~wheat *a* = **~meal**; **wholly** *ad*
entièrement, tout à fait.

whom [hu:m] *pronoun* **1** *(interrogative)*
qui; ~ did you see? qui avez-vous vu?;
to ~ did you give it? à qui l'avez-vous
donné?

2 *(relative)* que, *prep* + qui *(check syntax of French verb used)*; the man ~ I
saw/to ~ I spoke l'homme que j'ai vu/à
qui j'ai parlé.

whooping cough [ˈhu:pɪŋkɔf] *n*
coqueluche *f*.

whore [hɔ:*] *n* *(col: pej)* putain *f*.

whose [hu:z] ♦ *a* **1** *(possessive:
interrogative)*: ~ book is this? à qui est
ce livre?; ~ pencil have you taken? à
qui est le crayon que vous avez pris?,
c'est le crayon de qui que vous avez
pris?; ~ daughter are you? de qui êtes-
vous la fille?

2 *(possessive: relative)*: the man ~ son
you rescued l'homme dont *or* de qui vous
avez sauvé le fils; the girl ~ sister you
were speaking to la fille à la sœur de qui
or de laquelle vous parliez; the woman
~ car was stolen la femme dont la
voiture a été volée

♦ *pronoun* à qui; ~ is this? à qui est
ceci?; I know ~ it is je sais à qui c'est.

why [waɪ] *ad* pourquoi // *excl* eh bien!,
tiens!; the reason ~ la raison pour
laquelle; tell me ~ dites-moi pourquoi; ~
not? pourquoi pas?; **~ever** *ad* pourquoi
donc, mais pourquoi.

wick [wɪk] *n* mèche *f* *(de bougie)*.

wicked [ˈwɪkɪd] *a* mauvais(e), mé-
chant(e); inique; cruel(le); *(mischievous)* malicieux(euse).

wicker [ˈwɪkə*] *n* osier *m*; *(also:
~work)* vannerie *f*.

wicket |'wɪkɪt| n (CRICKET) guichet m; espace compris entre les deux guichets.

wide |waɪd| a large; (area, knowledge) vaste, très étendu(e); (choice) grand(e) // ad: **to open ~** ouvrir tout grand; **to shoot ~** tirer à côté; **~-angle lens** n objectif m grand-angulaire; **~-awake** a bien éveillé(e); **~ly** ad (differing) radicalement; (spaced) sur une grande étendue; (believed) généralement; **~n** vt élargir; **~ open** a grand(e) ouvert(e); **~spread** a (belief etc) très répandu(e).

widow |'wɪdəu| n veuve f; **~er** n veuf m.

width |wɪdθ| n largeur f.

wield |wi:ld| vt (sword) manier; (power) exercer.

wife, wives |waɪf, waɪvz| n femme (mariée), épouse f.

wig |wɪg| n perruque f.

wiggle |'wɪgl| vt agiter, remuer.

wild |waɪld| a sauvage; (sea) déchaîné(e); (idea, life) fou(folle); extravagant(e); **~s** npl régions fpl sauvages; **~erness** n |'wɪldənɪs| n désert m, région f sauvage; **~-goose chase** n (fig) fausse piste; **~life** n faune f (et flore f) sauvage(s); **~ly** ad (applaud) frénétiquement; (hit, guess) au hasard; (happy) follement.

wilful |'wɪlful| a (person) obstiné(e); (action) délibéré(e); (crime) prémédité(e).

will |wɪl| ♦ auxiliary vb **1** (forming future tense): I **~** finish it tomorrow je le finirai demain; I **~** have finished it by tomorrow je l'aurai fini d'ici demain; **~** you do it? — yes I **~/no** I won't le ferez-vous? — oui/non **2** (in conjectures, predictions): he **~** or he'll be there by now il doit être arrivé à l'heure qu'il est; that **~** be the postman ça doit être le facteur **3** (in commands, requests, offers): **~** you be quiet! voulez-vous bien vous taire!; **~** you help me? est-ce que vous pouvez m'aider?; **~** you have a cup of tea? voulez-vous une tasse de thé?; I won't put up with it! je ne le tolérerai pas!

♦ vt (pt, pp **~ed**): **to ~** sb to do souhaiter ardemment que qn fasse; he **~ed** himself to go on par un suprême effort de volonté, il continua

♦ n volonté f; testament m.

willing |'wɪlɪŋ| a de bonne volonté, serviable; he's **~** to do it il est disposé à le faire, il veut bien le faire; **~ly** ad volontiers; **~ness** n bonne volonté.

willow |'wɪləu| n saule m.

will power n volonté f.

willy-nilly |'wɪlɪ'nɪlɪ| ad bon gré mal gré.

wilt |wɪlt| vi dépérir.

wily |'waɪlɪ| a rusé(e).

win |wɪn| n (in sports etc) victoire f // vb (pt, pp **won** |wʌn|) vt (battle, money) gagner; (prize) remporter; (popularity) acquérir // vi gagner; **to ~ over**, (Brit) **~ round** vt gagner, se concilier.

wince |wɪns| vi tressaillir.

winch |wɪntʃ| n treuil m.

wind n |wɪnd| (also MED) vent m // vb |waɪnd| (pt, pp **wound** |waund|) vt enrouler; (wrap) envelopper; (clock, toy) remonter; (take breath away: |wɪnd|) couper le souffle à // vi (road, river) serpenter; **to ~ up** vt (clock) remonter; (debate) terminer, clôturer; **~fall** n coup m de chance; **~ing** a (road) sinueux(euse); (staircase) tournant(e); **~ instrument** n (MUS) instrument m à vent; **~mill** n moulin m à vent.

window |'wɪndəu| n fenêtre f; (in car, train, also: **~pane**) vitre f; (in shop etc) vitrine f; **~ box** n jardinière f; **~ cleaner** n (person) laveur/euse de vitres; **~ ledge** n rebord m de la fenêtre; **~ pane** n vitre f, carreau m; **~sill** n (inside) appui m de la fenêtre; (outside) rebord m de la fenêtre.

windpipe |'wɪndpaɪp| n gosier m.

windscreen, (US) windshield |'wɪndskri:n, 'wɪndʃi:ld| n pare-brise m inv; **~ washer** n lave-glace m inv; **~ wiper** n essuie-glace m inv.

windswept |'wɪndswept| a balayé(e) par le vent.

windy |'wɪndɪ| a venté(e), venteux(euse); it's **~** il y a du vent.

wine |waɪn| n vin m; **~ cellar** n cave f à vins; **~ glass** n verre m à vin; **~ list** n carte f des vins; **~ tasting** n dégustation f (de vins); **~ waiter** n sommelier m.

wing |wɪŋ| n aile f; **~s** npl (THEATRE) coulisses fpl; **~er** n (SPORT) ailier m.

wink |wɪŋk| n clin m d'œil // vi faire un clin d'œil; (blink) cligner des yeux.

winner |'wɪnə*| n gagnant/e.

winning |'wɪnɪŋ| a (team) gagnant(e); (goal) décisif(ive); **~s** npl gains mpl; **~ post** n poteau m d'arrivée.

winter |'wɪntə*| n hiver m // vi hiverner; **~ sports** npl sports mpl d'hiver.

wintry |'wɪntrɪ| a hivernal(e).

wipe |waɪp| n coup m de torchon (or de chiffon or d'éponge); **to ~ off** vt essuyer; **to ~ out** vt (debt) régler; (memory) oublier; (destroy) anéantir; **to ~ up** vt essuyer.

wire |'waɪə*| n fil m (de fer); (ELEC) fil électrique; (TEL) télégramme m // vt (house) faire l'installation électrique de; (also: **~ up**) brancher.

wireless |'waɪəlɪs| n (Brit) télégraphie f sans fil; (set) T.S.F. f.

wiring |'waɪərɪŋ| n installation f électrique.

wiry ['waɪərɪ] a noueux(euse), nerveux(euse).

wisdom ['wɪzdəm] n sagesse f; (of action) prudence f; ~ **tooth** n dent f de sagesse.

wise [waɪz] a sage, prudent(e), judicieux(euse).

...wise [waɪz] suffix: time~ en ce qui concerne le temps, question temps.

wish [wɪʃ] n (desire) désir m; (specific desire) souhait m, vœu m // vt souhaiter, désirer, vouloir; best ~es (on birthday etc) meilleurs vœux; with best ~es (in letter) bien amicalement; to ~ sb good-bye dire au revoir à qn; he ~ed me well il me souhaitait de réussir; to ~ to do/sb to do désirer or vouloir faire/que qn fasse; to ~ for souhaiter; it's ~ful thinking c'est prendre ses désirs pour des réalités.

wishy-washy ['wɪʃɪ'wɔʃɪ] a (col: colour) délavé(e); (: ideas, argument) faiblard(e).

wisp [wɪsp] n fine mèche (de cheveux); (of smoke) mince volute f.

wistful ['wɪstful] a mélancolique.

wit [wɪt] n (gen pl) intelligence f, esprit m; présence f d'esprit; (wittiness) esprit; (person) homme/femme d'esprit.

witch [wɪtʃ] n sorcière f.

with [wɪð, wɪθ] prep **1** (in the company of) avec; (at the home of) chez; we stayed ~ friends nous avons logé chez des amis; I'll be ~ you in a minute je suis à vous dans un instant **2** (descriptive): a room ~ a view une chambre avec vue; the man ~ the grey hat/blue eyes l'homme au chapeau gris/aux yeux bleus **3** (indicating manner, means, cause): tears in her eyes les larmes aux yeux; to walk ~ a stick marcher avec une canne; red ~ anger rouge de colère; to shake ~ fear trembler de peur; to fill sth ~ water remplir qch d'eau **4**: I'm ~ you (I understand) je vous suis; to be ~ it (col: up-to-date) être dans le vent.

withdraw [wɪθ'drɔ:] vb (irg) vt retirer // vi se retirer; (go back on promise) se rétracter; ~al n retrait m; (MED) état m de manque; ~n a (person) renfermé(e).

wither ['wɪðə*] vi se faner.

withhold [wɪθ'həuld] vt irg (money) retenir; (decision) remettre; (permission): to ~ (from) refuser (à); (information): to ~ (from) cacher (à).

within [wɪð'ɪn] prep à l'intérieur de // ad à l'intérieur; ~ sight of en vue de; ~ a mile of à moins d'un mille de; ~ the week avant la fin de la semaine.

without [wɪð'aut] prep sans.

withstand [wɪθ'stænd] vt irg résister à.

witness ['wɪtnɪs] n (person) témoin m; (evidence) témoignage m // vt (event) être témoin de; (document) attester l'authenticité de; ~ **box**, (US) ~ **stand** n barre f des témoins.

witticism ['wɪtɪsɪzm] n mot m d'esprit.

witty ['wɪtɪ] a spirituel(le), plein(e) d'esprit.

wives [waɪvz] npl of **wife**.

wizard ['wɪzəd] n magicien m.

wk abbr of **week**.

wobble ['wɔbl] vi trembler; (chair) branler.

woe [wəu] n malheur m.

woke [wəuk] pt of **wake**; ~n pp of **wake**.

wolf, pl **wolves** [wulf, wulvz] n loup m.

woman, pl **women** ['wumən, 'wɪmɪn] n femme f; ~ **doctor** n femme f médecin; **women's lib** n (col) MLF m.

womb [wu:m] n (ANAT) utérus m.

women ['wɪmɪn] npl of **woman**.

won [wʌn] pt, pp of **win**.

wonder ['wʌndə*] n merveille f, miracle m; (feeling) émerveillement m // vi: to ~ whether se demander si; to ~ at s'étonner de; s'émerveiller de; to ~ about songer à; it's no ~ that il n'est pas étonnant que + sub; ~ful a merveilleux(euse).

won't [wəunt] = will not.

woo [wu:] vt (woman) faire la cour à.

wood [wud] n (timber, forest) bois m; ~ **carving** n sculpture f en or sur bois; ~ed a boisé(e); ~en a en bois; (fig) raide; inexpressif(ive); ~pecker n pic m (oiseau); ~wind n (MUS) bois m; the ~wind (MUS) les bois; ~work n menuiserie f; ~worm n ver m du bois.

wool [wul] n laine f; to pull the ~ over sb's eyes (fig) en faire accroire à qn; ~len, (US) ~en a de laine; (industry) lainier(ère); ~lens npl lainages mpl; ~ly, (US) ~y a laineux(euse); (fig: ideas) confus(e).

word [wə:d] n mot m; (spoken) mot, parole f; (promise) parole; (news) nouvelles fpl // vt rédiger, formuler; in other ~s en d'autres termes; to break/ keep one's ~ manquer à/tenir sa parole; ~ing n termes mpl, langage m; libellé m; ~ processing n traitement m de texte; ~ processor n machine f de traitement de texte.

wore [wɔ:*] pt of **wear**.

work [wə:k] n travail m; (ART, LITERATURE) œuvre f // vi travailler; (mechanism) marcher, fonctionner; (plan etc) marcher; (medicine) agir // vt (clay, wood etc) travailler; (mine etc) exploiter; (machine) faire marcher or fonctionner; to be out of ~ être au chômage; ~s n (Brit: factory) usine f // npl (of clock, machine) mécanisme m; to ~ loose vi se défaire, se desserrer; to

~ **on** vt fus travailler à; (principle) se baser sur; **to ~ out** vi (plans etc) marcher // vt (problem) résoudre; (plan) élaborer; it ~s out at £100 ça fait 100 livres; **to get ~ed up** se mettre dans tous ses états; **~able** a (solution) réalisable; **~aholic** n bourreau m de travail; **~er** n travailleur/euse, ouvrier/ère; **~force** n main-d'œuvre f; **~ing class** n classe ouvrière; **~ing-class** a ouvrier(ère); **~ing man** n travailleur m; **~ing order** n: **in ~ing order** en état de marche; **~man** n ouvrier m; **~manship** n métier m, habileté f; facture f; **~sheet** n feuille f de programmation; **~shop** n atelier m; ~ **station** n poste m de travail; **~-to-rule** n (Brit) grève f du zèle.

world [wə:ld] n monde m // cpd (champion) du monde; (power, war) mondial(e); **to think the ~ of sb** (fig) ne jurer que par qn; **~ly** a de ce monde; **~-wide** a universel(le).

worm [wə:m] n ver m.

worn [wɔ:n] pp of **wear** // a usé(e); **~ out** a (object) complètement usé(e); (person) épuisé(e).

worried ['wʌrɪd] a inquiet(ète).

worry ['wʌrɪ] n souci m // vt inquiéter // vi s'inquiéter, se faire du souci.

worse [wə:s] a pire, plus mauvais(e) // ad plus mal // n pire m; **a change for the ~** une détérioration; **~n** vt, vi empirer; **~ off** a moins à l'aise financièrement; (fig): **you'll be ~ off this way** ça ira moins bien de cette façon.

worship ['wə:ʃɪp] n culte m // vt (God) rendre un culte à; (person) adorer; **Your W~** (Brit: to mayor) Monsieur le Maire; (: to judge) Monsieur le Juge.

worst [wə:st] a le(la) pire, le(la) plus mauvais(e) // ad le plus mal // n pire m; **at ~** au pis aller.

worsted ['wustɪd] n: (wool) ~ laine peignée.

worth [wə:θ] n valeur f // a: **to be ~** valoir; **it's ~ it** cela en vaut la peine; **it is ~ one's while** (to do) on gagne (à faire); **~less** a qui ne vaut rien; **~while** a (activity) qui en vaut la peine; (cause) louable.

worthy [wə:ðɪ] a (person) digne; (motive) louable; **~ of** digne de.

would [wud] auxiliary vb **1** (conditional tense): **if you asked him he ~ do it** si vous le lui demandiez, il le ferait; **if you had asked him he ~ have done it** si vous le lui aviez demandé, il l'aurait fait **2** (in offers, invitations, requests): **~ you like a biscuit?** voulez-vous or voudriez-vous un biscuit?; **~ you close the door please?** voulez-vous fermer la porte, s'il vous plaît **3** (in indirect speech): **I said I ~ do it** j'ai dit que je le ferais

4 (emphatic): **it WOULD have to snow today!** naturellement il neige or il fallait qu'il neige aujourd'hui! **5** (insistence): **she ~n't do it** elle n'a pas voulu or elle a refusé de le faire **6** (conjecture): **it ~ have been midnight** il devait être minuit **7** (indicating habit): **he ~ go there on Mondays** il y allait le lundi.

would-be ['wudbi] a (pej) soi-disant.

wouldn't ['wudnt] = **would not**.

wound vb [waund] pt, pp of **wind** // n, vt [wu:nd] n blessure f // vt blesser.

wove [wəuv] pt of **weave**; **~n** pp of **weave**.

wrangle ['ræŋgl] n dispute f.

wrap [ræp] n (stole) écharpe f; (cape) pèlerine f // vt (also: ~ **up**) envelopper; **~per** n (Brit: of book) couverture f; **~ping paper** n papier m d'emballage; (for gift) papier cadeau.

wrath [rɔθ] n courroux m.

wreak [ri:k] vt: **to ~ havoc on** avoir un effet désastreux sur; **to ~ vengeance (on)** se venger (de).

wreath, ~s [ri:θ, ri:ðz] n couronne f.

wreck [rɛk] n (sea disaster) naufrage m; (ship) épave f; (pej: person) loque humaine // vt démolir; (ship) provoquer le naufrage de; (fig) briser, ruiner; **~age** n débris mpl; (of building) décombres mpl; (of ship) épave f.

wren [rɛn] n (ZOOL) roitelet m.

wrench [rɛntʃ] n (TECH) clé f (à écrous); (tug) violent mouvement de torsion; (fig) arrachement m // vt tirer violemment sur, tordre; **to ~ sth from** arracher qch (violemment) à or de.

wrestle ['rɛsl] vi: **to ~ (with sb)** lutter (avec qn); **to ~ with** (fig) se débattre avec, lutter contre; **~r** n lutteur/euse; **wrestling** n lutte f; (also: **all-in wrestling**) catch m.

wretched ['rɛtʃɪd] a misérable; (col) maudit(e).

wriggle ['rɪgl] vi se tortiller.

wring [rɪŋ], pt, pp **wrung** vt tordre; (wet clothes) essorer; (fig): **to ~ sth out of** arracher qch à.

wrinkle ['rɪŋkl] n (on skin) ride f; (on paper etc) pli m // vt rider, plisser // vi se plisser.

wrist [rɪst] n poignet m; **~watch** n montre-bracelet f.

writ [rɪt] n acte m judiciaire.

write [raɪt], pt **wrote**, pp **written** vt, vi écrire; **to ~ down** vt noter; (put in writing) mettre par écrit; **to ~ off** vt (debt) passer aux profits et pertes; (depreciate) amortir; **to ~ out** vt écrire; (copy) recopier; **to ~ up** vt rédiger; **~-off** n perte totale; **~r** n auteur m, écrivain m.

writhe [raɪð] vi se tordre.

writing ['raɪtɪŋ] n écriture f; (of

author) œuvres *fpl*; **in ~** par écrit; **~ paper** *n* papier *m* à lettres.

written ['rɪtn] *pp of* **write**.

wrong [rɒŋ] *a* faux(fausse); (*incorrectly chosen: number, road etc*) mauvais(e); (*not suitable*) qui ne convient pas; (*wicked*) mal; (*unfair*) injuste // *ad* // *n* tort *m* // *vt* faire du tort à, léser; **you are ~** to do it tu as tort de le faire; **you are ~ about that**, you've got it **~** tu te trompes; **to be in the ~** avoir tort; **what's ~?** qu'est-ce qui ne va pas?; **to go ~** (*person*) se tromper; (*plan*) mal tourner; (*machine*) tomber en panne; **~ful** *a* injustifié(e); **~ly** *ad* à tort.

wrote [rəut] *pt of* **write**.

wrought [rɔːt] *a*: **~ iron** fer forgé.

wrung [rʌŋ] *pt, pp of* **wring**.

wry [raɪ] *a* désabusé(e).

wt. *abbr of* **weight**.

X Y Z

Xmas ['ɛksməs] *n abbr of* **Christmas**.

X-ray ['ɛks'reɪ] *n* rayon *m* X; (*photograph*) radio(graphie) *f*.

xylophone ['zaɪləfəun] *n* xylophone *m*.

yacht [jɒt] *n* yacht *m*; voilier *m*; **~ing** *n* yachting *m*, navigation *f* de plaisance.

Yank [jæŋk], **Yankee** ['jæŋkɪ] *n* (*pej*) Amerloque *m/f*.

yap [jæp] *vi* (*dog*) japper.

yard [jɑːd] *n* (*of house etc*) cour *f*; (*measure*) yard *m* (= 914 mm; 3 feet); **~stick** *n* (*fig*) mesure *f*, critère *m*.

yarn [jɑːn] *n* fil *m*; (*tale*) longue histoire.

yawn [jɔːn] *n* bâillement *m* // *vi* bâiller; **~ing** *a* (*gap*) béant(e).

yd. *abbr of* **yard(s)**.

yeah [jɛə] *ad* (*col*) ouais.

year [jɪə*] *n* an *m*, année *f*; **to be 8 ~s old** avoir 8 ans; **an eight-~-old child** un enfant de huit ans; **~ly** *a* annuel(le) // *ad* annuellement.

yearn [jə:n] *vi*: **to ~ for sth** aspirer à qch, languir après qch; **to ~ to do** aspirer à faire; **~ing** *n* désir ardent, envie *f*.

yeast [jiːst] *n* levure *f*.

yell [jɛl] *vi* hurler.

yellow ['jɛləu] *a, n* jaune (*m*).

yelp [jɛlp] *vi* japper; glapir.

yeoman ['jəumən] *n*: **Y~ of the Guard** hallebardier *m* de la garde royale.

yes [jɛs] *ad* oui; (*answering negative question*) si // *n* oui *m*; **to say/answer ~** dire/répondre oui.

yesterday ['jɛstədɪ] *ad, n* hier (*m*); **~ morning/evening** hier matin/soir; **all day ~** toute la journée d'hier.

yet [jɛt] *ad* encore; déjà // *cj* pourtant, néanmoins; **it is not finished ~** ce n'est pas encore fini *or* toujours pas fini; **the best ~** le meilleur jusqu'ici *or* jusque-là;

as ~ jusqu'ici, encore.

yew [juː] *n* if *m*.

yield [jiːld] *n* production *f*, rendement *m*; rapport *m* // *vt* produire, rendre, rapporter; (*surrender*) céder // *vi* céder; (*US AUT*) céder la priorité.

YMCA *n abbr* (= *Young Men's Christian Association*) YMCA *m*.

yoga ['jəugə] *n* yoga *m*.

yog(h)ourt, yog(h)urt ['jəugət] *n* yaourt *m*.

yoke [jəuk] *n* joug *m*.

yolk [jəuk] *n* jaune *m* (d'œuf).

yonder ['jɒndə*] *ad* là(-bas).

you [juː] *pronoun* **1** (*subject*) tu; (*polite form*) vous; (*pl*) vous; **~ French enjoy your food** vous autres Français, vous aimez bien manger; **~ and I will go** toi et moi *or* vous et moi, nous irons

2 (*object: direct, indirect*) te, t' + *vowel*; vous; **I know ~** je te *or* vous connais; **I gave it to ~** je te l'ai donné, je vous l'ai donné

3 (*stressed*) toi; vous; **I told YOU to do it** c'est à toi *or* vous que j'ai dit de le faire

4 (*after prep, in comparisons*) toi; vous; **it's for ~** c'est pour toi *or* vous; **she's younger than ~** elle est plus jeune que toi *or* vous

5 (*impersonal: one*) on; **fresh air does ~ good** l'air frais fait du bien; **~ never know** on ne sait jamais.

you'd [juːd] = **you had**, **you would**.

you'll [juːl] = **you will**, **you shall**.

young [jʌŋ] *a* jeune // *npl* (*of animal*) petits *mpl*; (*people*): **the ~** les jeunes, la jeunesse; **~er** *a* (*brother etc*) cadet(te); **~ster** *n* jeune *m* (garçon *m*); (*child*) enfant *m/f*.

your [jɔː*] *a* ton(ta), tes *pl*; (*polite form, pl*) votre, vos *pl*; *see also* **my**.

you're [juə*] = **you are**.

yours [jɔːz] *pronoun* le(la) tien(ne), les tiens(tiennes); (*polite form, pl*) le(la) vôtre, les vôtres; **yours sincerely/faithfully** je vous prie d'agréer l'expression de mes sentiments les meilleurs/mes sentiments respectueux *or* dévoués; *see also* **mine**.

yourself [jɔː'sɛlf] *pronoun* (*reflexive*) te; (: *polite form*) vous; (*after prep*) toi; vous; (*emphatic*) toi-même; vous-même; **yourselves** *pl pronoun* vous; (*emphatic*) vous-mêmes; *see also* **oneself**.

youth [juːθ] *n* jeunesse *f*; (*young man*) (*pl* **~s** [juːðz]) jeune homme *m*; **~ club** *n* centre *m* de jeunes; **~ful** *a* jeune de jeunesse; juvénile; **~ hostel** *n* auberge *f* de jeunesse.

you've [juːv] = **you have**.

YTS *n abbr* (*Brit*: = *Youth Training Scheme*) ≈ TUC *m*.

Yugoslav ['juːgəuslɑːv] *a* yougoslave // *n* Yougoslave *m/f*.

Yugoslavia [ˈjuːgəʊˈslɑːvɪə] n
Yougoslavie f.

yuppie [ˈjʌpɪ] n yuppie m/f.

YWCA n abbr (= Young Women's Christian Association) YWCA m.

zany [ˈzeɪnɪ] a farfelu(e), loufoque.

zap [zæp] vt (COMPUT) effacer.

zeal [ziːl] n zèle m, ferveur f; empressement m.

zebra [ˈziːbrə] n zèbre m; ~ **crossing** n (Brit) passage m pour piétons.

zero [ˈzɪərəʊ] n zéro m.

zest [zɛst] n entrain m, élan m; zeste m.

zigzag [ˈzɪgzæg] n zigzag m.

Zimbabwe [zɪmˈbɑːbwɪ] n Zimbabwe m.

zinc [zɪŋk] n zinc m.

zip [zɪp] n (also: ~ **fastener**, (US) ~**per**) fermeture f éclair ® // vt (also: ~ **up**) fermer avec une fermeture éclair ®; ~ **code** n (US) code postal.

zodiac [ˈzəʊdɪæk] n zodiaque m.

zone [zəʊn] n zone f; (subdivision of town) secteur m.

zoo [zuː] n zoo m.

zoology [zuːˈɔlədʒɪ] n zoologie f.

zoom [zuːm] vi: to ~ **past** passer en trombe; ~ **lens** n zoom m.

zucchini [tsuːˈkiːnɪ] n(pl) (US) courgette(s) f(pl).

FRENCH VERB FORMS

1 Participe présent *2* Participe passé *3* Présent *4* Imparfait *5* Futur *6* Conditionnel *7* Subjonctif présent

acquérir *1* acquérant *2* acquis *3* acquiers, acquérons, acquièrent *4* acquérais *5* acquerrai *7* acquière

ALLER *1* allant *2* allé *3* vais, vas, va, allons, allez, vont *4* allais *5* irai *6* irais *7* aille

asseoir *1* asseyant *2* assis *3* assieds, asseyons, asseyez, asseyent *4* asseyais *5* assiérai *7* asseye

atteindre *1* atteignant *2* atteint *3* atteins, atteignons *4* atteignais *7* atteigne

AVOIR *1* ayant *2* eu *3* ai, as, a, avons, avez, ont *4* avais *5* aurai *6* aurais *7* aie, aies, ait, ayons, ayez, aient

battre *1* battant *2* battu *3* bats, bat, battons *4* battais *7* batte

boire *1* buvant *2* bu *3* bois, buvons, boivent *4* buvais *7* boive

bouillir *1* bouillant *2* bouilli *3* bous, bouillons *4* bouillais *7* bouille

conclure *1* concluant *2* conclu *3* conclus, concluons *4* concluais *7* conclue

conduire *1* conduisant *2* conduit *3* conduis, conduisons *4* conduisais *7* conduise

connaître *1* connaissant *2* connu *3* connais, connaît, connaissons *4* connaissais *7* connaisse

coudre *1* cousant *2* cousu *3* couds, cousons, cousez, cousent *4* cousais *7* couse

courir *1* courant *2* couru *3* cours, courons *4* courais *5* courrai *7* coure

couvrir *1* couvrant *2* couvert *3* couvre, couvrons *4* couvrais *7* couvre

craindre *1* craignant *2* craint *3* crains, craignons *4* craignais *7* craigne

croire *1* croyant *2* cru *3* crois, croyons, croient *4* croyais *7* croie

croître *1* croissant *2* crû, crue, crus, crues *3* croîs, croissons *4* croissais *7* croisse

cueillir *1* cueillant *2* cueilli *3* cueille, cueillons *4* cueillais *5* cueillerai *7* cueille

devoir *1* devant *2* dû, due, dus, dues *3* dois, devons, doivent *4* devais *5* devrai *7* doive

dire *1* disant *2* dit *3* dis, disons, dites, disent *4* disais *7* dise

dormir *1* dormant *2* dormi *3* dors, dormons *4* dormais *7* dorme

écrire *1* écrivant *2* écrit *3* écris, écrivons *4* écrivais *7* écrive

ÊTRE *1* étant *2* été *3* suis, es, est, sommes, êtes, sont *4* étais *5* serai *6* serais *7* sois, sois, soit, soyons, soyez, soient

FAIRE *1* faisant *2* fait *3* fais, fais, fait, faisons, faites, font *4* faisais *5* ferai *6* ferais *7* fasse

falloir *2* fallu *3* faut *4* fallait *5* faudra *7* faille

FINIR *1* finissant *2* fini *3* finis, finis, finit, finissons, finissez, finissent *4* finissais *5* finirai *6* finirais *7* finisse

fuir *1* fuyant *2* fui *3* fuis, fuyons, fuient *4* fuyais *7* fuie

joindre *1* joignant *2* joint *3* joins, joignons *4* joignais *7* joigne

lire *1* lisant *2* lu *3* lis, lisons *4* lisais *7* lise

luire *1* luisant *2* lui *3* luis, luisons *4* luisais *7* luise

maudire *1* maudissant *2* maudit *3* maudis, maudissons *4* maudissait *7* maudisse

mentir *1* mentant *2* menti *3* mens, mentons *4* mentais *7* mente

mettre *1* mettant *2* mis *3* mets, mettons *4* mettais *7* mette

mourir *1* mourant *2* mort *3* meurs, mourons, meurent *4* mourais *5* mourrai *7* meure

naître *1* naissant *2* né *3* nais, naît, naissons *4* naissais *7* naisse

offrir *1* offrant *2* offert *3* offre, offrons *4* offrais *7* offre

PARLER *1* parlant *2* parlé *3* parle, parles, parle, parlons, parlez, parlent *4* parlais, parlais, parlait, parlions, parliez, parlaient *5* parlerai, parleras, parlera, parlerons, parlerez, parleront *6* parlerais, parlerais, parlerait, parlerions, parleriez, parleraient *7* parle, parles, parle, parlions, parliez, parlent *impératif* parle! parlez!

partir *1* partant *2* parti *3* pars, partons *4* partais *7* parte

plaire *1* plaisant *2* plu *3* plais, plaît, plaisons *4* plaisais *7* plaise

pleuvoir *1* pleuvant *2* plu *3* pleut, pleuvent *4* pleuvait *5* pleuvra *7* pleuve

pourvoir *1* pourvoyant *2* pourvu *3* pourvois, pourvoyons, pourvoient *4* pourvoyais *7* pourvoie

pouvoir *1* pouvant *2* pu *3* peux, peut, pouvons, peuvent *4* pouvais *5* pourrai *7* puisse

prendre *1* prenant *2* pris *3* prends, prenons, prennent *4* prenais *7* prenne

prévoir like **voir** *5* prévoirai

RECEVOIR *1* recevant *2* reçu *3* reçois, reçois, reçoit, recevons, recevez, reçoivent *4* recevais *5* recevrai *6* recevrais *7* reçoive

RENDRE *1* rendant *2* rendu *3* rends, rends, rend, rendons, rendez, rendent *4* rendais *5* rendrai *6* rendrais *7* rende

résoudre *1* résolvant *2* résolu *3* résous, résolvons *4* résolvais *7* résolve

rire *1* riant *2* ri *3* ris, rions *4* riais *7* rie

savoir *1* sachant *2* su *3* sais, savons, savent *4* savais *5* saurai *7* sache *impératif* sache, sachons, sachez

servir *1* servant *2* servi *3* sers, servons *4* servais *7* serve

sortir *1* sortant *2* sorti *3* sors, sortons *4* sortais *7* sorte

souffrir *1* souffrant *2* souffert *3* souffre, souffrons *4* souffrais *7* souffre

suffire *1* suffisant *2* suffi *3* suffis, suffisons *4* suffisais *7* suffise

suivre *1* suivant *2* suivi *3* suis, suivons *4* suivais *7* suive

taire *1* taisant *2* tu *3* tais, taisons *4* taisais *7* taise

tenir *1* tenant *2* tenu *3* tiens, tenons, tiennent *4*

tenais 5 tiendrai 7 tienne
vaincre 1 vainquant 2 vaincu 3 vaincs, vainc, vainquons 4 vainquais 7 vainque
valoir 1 valant 2 valu 3 vaux, vaut, valons 4 valais 5 vaudrai 7 vaille
venir 1 venant 2 venu 3 viens, venons, viennent 4 venais 5 viendrai 7 vienne

vivre 1 vivant 2 vécu 3 vis, vivons 4 vivais 7 vive
voir 1 voyant 2 vu 3 vois, voyons, voient 4 voyais 5 verrai 7 voie
vouloir 1 voulant 2 voulu 3 veux, veut, voulons, veulent 4 voulais 5 voudrai 7 veuille
impératif veuillez

LE VERBE ANGLAIS

present	pt	pp	present	pt	pp
arise	arose	arisen	**dwell**	dwelt	dwelt
awake	awoke	awaked	**eat**	ate	eaten
be (am, is, are; being)	was, were	been	**fall**	fell	fallen
			feed	fed	fed
			feel	felt	felt
bear	bore	born(e)	**fight**	fought	fought
beat	beat	beaten	**find**	found	found
become	became	become	**flee**	fled	fled
begin	began	begun	**fling**	flung	flung
behold	beheld	beheld	**fly (flies)**	flew	flown
bend	bent	bent	**forbid**	forbade	forbidden
beseech	besought	besought	**forecast**	forecast	forecast
beset	beset	beset	**forego**	forewent	foregone
bet	bet, betted	bet, betted	**foresee**	foresaw	foreseen
bid	bid, bade	bid, bidden	**foretell**	foretold	foretold
bind	bound	bound	**forget**	forgot	forgotten
bite	bit	bitten	**forgive**	forgave	forgiven
bleed	bled	bled	**forsake**	forsook	forsaken
blow	blew	blown	**freeze**	froze	frozen
break	broke	broken	**get**	got	got, (US) gotten
breed	bred	bred			
bring	brought	brought	**give**	gave	given
build	built	built	**go (goes)**	went	gone
burn	burnt, burned	burnt, burned	**grind**	ground	ground
			grow	grew	grown
burst	burst	burst	**hang**	hung, hanged	hung, hanged
buy	bought	bought			
can	could	(been able)	**have (has; having)**	had	had
cast	cast	cast			
catch	caught	caught	**hear**	heard	heard
choose	chose	chosen	**hide**	hid	hidden
cling	clung	clung	**hit**	hit	hit
come	came	come	**hold**	held	held
cost	cost	cost	**hurt**	hurt	hurt
creep	crept	crept	**keep**	kept	kept
cut	cut	cut	**kneel**	knelt, kneeled	knelt, kneeled
deal	dealt	dealt			
dig	dug	dug	**know**	knew	known
do(3rd person; he/she/it/does)	did	done	**lay**	laid	laid
			lead	led	led
			lean	leant, leaned	leant, leaned
draw	drew	drawn	**leap**	leapt, leaped	leapt, leaped
dream	dreamed, dreamt	dreamed, dreamt	**learn**	learnt, learned	learnt, learned
drink	drank	drunk			
drive	drove	driven	**leave**	left	left

221

present	pt	pp	present	pt	pp
lend	lent	lent	speak	spoke	spoken
let	let	let	speed	sped,	sped,
lie	lay	lain		speeded	speeded
(lying)			spell	spelt,	spelt,
light	lit,	lit,		spelled	spelled
	lighted	lighted	spend	spent	spent
lose	lost	lost	spill	spilt,	spilt,
make	made	made		spilled	spilled
may	might	—	spin	spun	spun
mean	meant	meant	spit	spat	spat
meet	met	met	split	split	split
mistake	mistook	mistaken	spoil	spoiled,	spoiled,
mow	mowed	mown,		spoilt	spoilt
		mowed	spread	spread	spread
must	(had to)	(had to)	spring	sprang	sprung
pay	paid	paid	stand	stood	stood
put	put	put	steal	stole	stolen
quit	quit,	quit,	stick	stuck	stuck
	quitted	quitted	sting	stung	stung
read	read	read	stink	stank	stunk
rid	rid	rid	stride	strode	stridden
ride	rode	ridden	strike	struck	struck,
ring	rang	rung			stricken
rise	rose	risen	strive	strove	striven
run	ran	run	swear	swore	sworn
saw	sawed	sawn	sweep	swept	swept
say	said	said	swell	swelled	swollen,
see	saw	seen			swelled
seek	sought	sought	swim	swam	swum
sell	sold	sold	swing	swung	swung
send	sent	sent	take	took	taken
set	set	set	teach	taught	taught
shake	shook	shaken	tear	tore	torn
shall	should	—	tell	told	told
shear	sheared	shorn,	think	thought	thought
		sheared	throw	threw	thrown
shed	shed	shed	thrust	thrust	thrust
shine	shone	shone	tread	trod	trodden
shoot	shot	shot	wake	woke,	woken,
show	showed	shown		waked	waked
shrink	shrank	shrunk	waylay	waylaid	waylaid
shut	shut	shut	wear	wore	worn
sing	sang	sung	weave	wove,	woven,
sink	sank	sunk		weaved	weaved
sit	sat	sat	wed	wedded,	wedded,
slay	slew	slain		wed	wed
sleep	slept	slept	weep	wept	wept
slide	slid	slid	win	won	won
sling	slung	slung	wind	wound	wound
slit	slit	slit	withdraw	withdrew	withdrawn
smell	smelt,	smelt,	withhold	withheld	withheld
	smelled	smelled	withstand	withstood	withstood
sow	sowed	sown,	wring	wrung	wrung
		sowed	write	wrote	written